History of the Arabic Written Tradition

Volume 1

Handbook of Oriental Studies

Handbuch der Orientalistik

SECTION ONE

The Near and Middle East

Edited by

VOLUME 117/1

The titles published in this series are listed at *brill.com/ho1*

History of the Arabic Written Tradition

VOLUME 1

By

Carl Brockelmann

Translated by

Joep Lameer

with a Preface by

Jan Just Witkam

BRILL

LEIDEN | BOSTON

Originally published as *Geschichte der Arabischen Litteratur* in 1898 and 1902.
Subsequent editions by Brill between 1937 and 1943, and in 1996.

Library of Congress Cataloging-in-Publication Data

Names: Brockelmann, Carl, 1868-1956, author. | Lameer, Joep, translator. |
Witkam, J. J., writer of preface.
Title: History of the Arabic written tradition / by Carl Brockelmann ;
translated by Joep Lameer ; with a preface by Jan Just Witkam.
Other titles: Geschichte der arabischen Litteratur. English | Handbook of
Oriental studies. Section one, Near and Middle East (2014) ; vol. 117.
Description: Leiden ; Boston : Brill, 2016. | Series: Handbook of Oriental
studies. Section one, The Near and Middle East ; volume 117 | Originally
published as Geschichte der Arabischen Litteratur in 1898 and 1902 —
Title page verso of volume 1. | Includes bibliographical references.
Identifiers: LCCN 2016032425 (print) | LCCN 2016041105 (ebook) | ISBN
9789004323308 (hardback : alk. paper) | ISBN 9789004326262 (E-book) | ISBN
9789004323308 (hardback) | ISBN 9789004326316 (hardback) | ISBN
9789004334618 (hardback) | ISBN 9789004335806 (hardback) | ISBN
9789004335813 (hardback)
Subjects: LCSH: Arabic literature—History and criticism.
Classification: LCC PJ7510 .B713 2016 (print) | LCC PJ7510 (ebook) | DDC
892.7/09—dc23
LC record available at https://lccn.loc.gov/2016032425

Typeface for the Latin, Greek, and Cyrillic scripts: "Brill". See and download: brill.com/brill-typeface.

ISSN 0169-9423
ISBN 978-90-04-32330-8 (hardback)
ISBN 978-90-04-32626-2 (e-book)

This book is printed on acid-free paper and produced in a sustainable manner.

Printed by Printforce, the Netherlands

Brockelmann's *Geschichte* Revisited Once More

By Jan Just Witkam

Brockelmann's GAL

In 1898 and 1902, the publishing house of E. Felber produced two volumes entitled *Geschichte der Arabischen Litteratur* (GAL). The author Carl Brockelmann (1868–1956) was a young German university teacher from Breslau (now Wroczlaw in Poland). His objective was to outline the external history of Arabic literature, excluding all internal developments. He had estimated then that it would take at least a further century of hard philological work before even the most important landmarks of Arabic literature would be known and accessible (I, p. iii). It is a sobering thought that a century has indeed passed without Brockelmann's expectations being realized. Brockelmann restricted his *Geschichte* to the surviving works of authors. Had he added the titles of those works that are only known from references and quotations, the size of his GAL would easily have doubled.

The basic idea of GAL was to provide a framework which divided Arabic literature into periods and subjects and then to add to this structure using information extracted from manuscript catalogues and bibliographies concerning extant texts, and subsequently to add supplementary information on the authors from the biographical dictionaries.

The first volume of GAL treated the classical period up to 1258 (the fall of Baghdad to the Mongol armies), while the second volume contained an account of Arabic literature produced in what Brockelmann styled as the age of decline. This age Brockelmann divided into three periods, firstly up to the Ottoman conquest of Egypt (1517), then up to the Napoleonic conquest (1798) and, finally, up to the present day (then 1902). Within each section there is usually a geographical division first, which is then subdivided according to subject. This division was used for the second edition, published forty years later, as well.

In using the term '*Litteratur*' Brockelmann understood literature in the broadest sense, that is, all verbal utterances of the human mind, and refused to limit the scope of this subject to just '*belles lettres*' His main justification was that Arabic has been the vehicle of thought over a long period of time and has covered an enormous territory, all of which he wished to include in his GAL. The German language has another word for literature in that broad sense,

Schrifttum, meaning anything that is recorded in writing. There were two fields, however, which Brockelmann mainly excluded from his survey, namely, the Christian and Jewish Arabic literatures, as these did not address the wider Islamic audience, but only addressed their own limited denominational circles.

GAL is very much the work of a confident youth. Nowadays no individual would dare to start such a project since the number of sources to be surveyed is simply too large for one lifetime. But a hundred years ago the number of sources was limited. Then there were a mere thirty-four manuscript catalogues which Brockelmann had to peruse and make extracts from. These catalogues described the major collections in Europe, North-Africa and Istanbul. The European catalogues in particular offered a wealth of information both on the contents of the texts and on their authors. The best of these catalogues—which remains unsurpassed—was just being completed by a compatriot of Brockelmann. It is the ten-volume monumental catalogue of the Berlin collection by Wilhelm Ahlwardt. When one sees the detail of information on texts and authors in Ahlwardt's work, one understands why this work was the perfect basis for Brockelmann to found his GAL. But the Berlin catalogue was by no means an isolated effort. The detailed catalogues of such vast collections as the British Museum and the Bibliothèque Nationale, and the medium-sized collections of the Escorial, Oxford, Cambridge, Gotha, Leiden, Algiers, etc., together provided the material for Brockelmann to use in his GAL.

A Word about the Author

Carl Brockelmann was born into a middle-class commercial milieu in Rostock, Germany, on 17 September 1868 as the fourth child in a family of six. At secondary school he was keen to devote himself to foreign studies. It was the period of the great discoveries and the carving-up of the world by the colonial powers, with which the newly-founded German empire had joined ranks. The geographical journals and accounts of discoveries in far-away regions of Asia and Africa were the source of young Brockelmann's romantic fantasies of the Orient. The German language has one compact word for this, *Fernweh*, the longing for distant places. The fact that quite a number of Rostockians, including his family's friends and acquaintances, had spread over the world only served to widen the youngster's cultural horizon. The young Carl must have been quite a prodigy. As a pupil of the secondary school he devised grammars for the Bantu language of Angola and the biblical Aramaic language. As a youth he hesitated between the careers of missionary, medical doctor and dragoman professions which had the common advantage of bringing him into direct contact with exotic peoples. But they proved to be daydreams, nor were his grammars ever published, of course, and Brockelmann was later grateful that he never pursued these options.

Brockelmann's university career, first as student and later as a professor, was unimpressive. It was rather his wide scholarly interests, his incredible memory and the enormous energy with which he pursued his goals, that have made him an outstanding figure even today. In 1886 he enrolled as a student of Oriental studies and classical philology and history at the University of Rostock. In spring 1887 he moved to the University of Breslau, and a year later he moved again, this time to Strasbourg in order to complete his studies with the most famous German Orientalist of his time, Theodor Nöldeke (1836–1930). In the course of these scholarly wanderings, young Brockelmann vigorously studied classical philology (Latin and Greek), Akkadian, Arabic, Ethiopian, Hebrew, Turkish, Persian, Sanskrit, Armenian, Egyptian and Indo-Germanic studies—and the list is probably far from complete. He engaged in classical philology as a sort of life insurance, should he be unable to find a job in Oriental studies. But apart from a short period (1890–1892) as an assistant-teacher in the Protestant Gymnasium in Strasbourg, Brockelmann was always employed in academic positions. In 1890 he had defended his inaugural doctoral thesis in Strasbourg on the relationship between Ibn al-Athīr's *Kāmil* and al-Tabarī's *Tȧrīkh*. In the German university system it was, and is, normal to write two doctoral theses, the inaugural thesis, completing a course of study, and the habilitation thesis, which opens the road to a professorship. In 1892 he returned to Breslau as a private university teacher. This was basically an unpaid position, but Brockelmann's participation in projects such as E. Sachau's edition of Ibn Saʿd's *Tabaqāt*, and other activities, mainly teaching, earned him a living. In 1893 he defended his habilitation thesis which contained a study on Ibn al-Jawzi's *Talqīh fuhūm ahl al-Āthār fī Mukhtasar al-siyar wa-al-akhbār*.

In 1895–1896 he made a journey to Istanbul, stopping in London and Paris. In 1900 he was appointed to the Institute of Oriental Languages in Berlin, but not for long. From 1900-1903 he occupied the extra-ordinariate chair in Breslau, and in 1903 he was appointed as ordinarius in Königsberg, now Kaliningrad in Russia, where he stayed until 1910. Next, he was appointed in Halle an der Saale where he stayed until 1922. It was there, as rector of the university, that he experienced the chaotic aftermath of the Great War and saw the German empire disintegrate and change into an unstable republic with the seeds of disaster already visible. It was also the pinnacle of his scholarly activities. In at least four specialized fields, Syriac studies, Arabic studies, Semitic linguistics and Turkish studies, his name had become famous throughout the world. But as author of GAL he was to earn eternal fame. From 1922–1923 he took an appointment in Berlin, but this proved to be a bad move. He came into conflict with the minister of culture, the Islamologist C.H. Becker, who was to take the Berlin professorship to provide himself with an emergency exit from politics. Brockelmann never forgave him, and called him in the preface of his *GAL*, among other things, the minister *against* German culture. Brockelmann was lucky to be able to return to the university of Breslau, where he stayed until his retirement in 1935. In 1932 he had become rector of the university, but he was obliged to step down because of the vehement attacks on his views on academic liberty by the Nazi press. In 1937 he moved back to Halle, where he was able to use the library of the German Oriental Society (DMG) for the completion of the new edition he wished to publish of his *GAL*. Between 1937–1942 the three supplementary volumes came out, and these were followed in 1943–1949 by the publication of an updated version of the original two volumes. In 1945 he was destitute and he took up the librarianship of the DMG. In this job he was able to return most of the 'evacuated' books to their rightful place. In 1947 he was appointed honorary professor for Turkish studies in Halle (which was now in the Russian zone, later the German Democratic Republic), and in 1953 he retired once more, at the age of 85. He died in his sleep on 6 May 1956 in Halle.

Brockelmann has left us an autobiographical account, which he wrote in the course of 1947 for his son Carl, after the latter was reported to have survived Soviet captivity at Stalingrad in 1943. Johann Fück has used this account for his two *In Memoriams*, and large parts of it have been published by Rudolf Sellheim—but the text, valuable as it is, was for private use only and clearly not intended for publication. When one first reads Brockelmann's invariably disgusted remarks on the Jewish scholars he had met and experienced, it is as if a hard-core Nazi is speaking. But Brockelmann was far too intelligent to indulge in simple anti-Semitic bragging. Being primarily an academic, he would have defended academic liberties against attack from any quarter, fascist and communist alike. However, when the Nazis took power in Germany in 1933, he was in the comfortable position of being already 65 years old and was soon to retire. He survived the war as a private scholar, and was never compromised in any official capacity before, during or after the war.

The Aims of Arabic Bibliography

Arabic literature by its very nature presents a problem of bibliographical control. It is as yet impossible to make even a rough estimate of how many works were written in Arabic by so many prolific authors over a period of some fourteen centuries in an area ranging from China to deepest Africa and from Morocco to the Philippines, let alone to fully establish the links between those works. The vast scope of Islamic manuscript literature was only recently bibliographically defined for the first time ever. The *World Survey of Islamic Manuscripts* (Leiden 1992–1994) has provided us with an insight into the enormous potential of Islamic literatures, of which Arabic is the major component. The development of our learning is also clearly visible. By the middle of the seventeenth century the Turkish bibliographer Ḥājjī Khalīfa (d. 1657) gave an account of his knowledge of Arabic literature. His *Kashf al-Ẓunūn* contains some 15,000 titles by about 9,500 authors. This is approximately the same proportion that one encounters in Brockelmann's GAL: the index in the third supplementary volume, which was published in 1942, contains some 25,000 titles and 18,000 authors. If the data contained in the bibliographical sources mentioned in *World Survey* were to be added to GAL, there would be an increase of many times the original number of titles and authors and there would be many additions of manuscripts to the references already known. Unique manuscripts would prove to be not so unique after all, and texts which fifty years ago were thought to be preserved in relatively few manuscripts would prove to exist in abundance. But the most considerable result of reviewing the data of *World Survey* would be our increased knowledge of Arabic literature as produced on the periphery of the Arab world and, even more important, that from Islamic countries outside the Arab world.

In the third supplementary volume to GAL, Brockelmann made a quite successful attempt to describe the modern literatures of the Arab world. An update of this covering the past fifty years would result in a reference work of unheard of dimensions. In fact, such an endeavor has not been attempted for any of the larger literatures of the modern age.

When Brockelmann compiled the final version of GAL, the manuscript treasures of peripheral areas such as Mauritania, Morocco and the Yemen, had barely been explored. The extent of Arabic literature in Sub-Saharan Africa, East Turkestan, the rest of China, South-East Asia's mainland and Indonesia is, even today, almost a closed book. The Indian subcontinent has had its own contribution to Arabic literature, but that branch of Arabic literature too is relatively little known. An additional complication is that the Arabic literature of these areas can only be put into true perspective if their complementary indigenous literary tradition is taken into account as well. For the bibliographer this poses additional, linguistic, problems.

Arabic traditional literature is probably the largest body of literature in the world. Incorporating all new bio-bibliographical information in one large database would be of prime importance. It has been tried, but so far it has failed. It could never be the work of one man, but at best a dedicated institution with large and long-term funds might be able to perform that task.

Brockelmann's *GAL*, now more than half a century old, still stands out as the only successful comprehensive attempt at bibliographical control of the vast body of Arabic literature. Arabic bibliography must move forward, and this is happening, as can be witnessed by the numerous bibliographical surveys on specific subjects and areas and by the veritable boom of manuscript catalogues. *GAL* is still a safe point of departure for most of the bibliographical work that lies ahead.

One recent instance of creative use of *GAL* should be mentioned here. Some 1690 titles taken from the title-index of the third supplementary volume of *GAL* were the source material for A.A. Ambros for an enlightening analysis of the composition and function of rhyming titles in classical Arabic literature. It shows that *GAL*, apart from its obvious use as a bibliographical reference work, has more in store than probably even the author himself was aware of.

In many libraries all over the world copies of *GAL* are in use that contain numerous handwritten additions of generations of learned librarians and other users. Brockelmann's own interleaved copy, which he constantly updated until shortly before his death, lies in the library of the DMG in Halle. This is certainly not the only copy with extensive glosses; there must be at least a hundred copies of similar importance. It would be interesting to make a survey of those copies including the remarks and corrections of learned librarians, and to make an attempt to incorporate that cumulated bibliographical knowledge into a modern database.

Updating and Reprinting *GAL*

Carl Brockelmann had always wanted to publish an updated reprint of the first edition of *GAL*. Alongside his numerous other activities he had recorded additions and corrections in his interleaved copy of the edition of 1898–1902. That first edition was published by E. Felber, a small publisher in Weimar and later in Berlin. He had agreed to publish Brockelmann's edition of Ibn Qutayba's *ʿUyūn al-Akhbār* on the condition that he would have the right to publish another work by Brockelmann which would yield him more profit than Ibn Qutayba. Brockelmann agreed and offered him his *GAL*, a project about which he had already been thinking for quite a while. This decision would have far-reaching consequences for generations of students of Arabic literature. Felber proved to be a crook and Brockelmann was not his first and only victim. When the typesetting and printing of half of the first volume of Ibn Qutayba's text had been completed, the work was stopped and Felber disappeared. Sometime later he re-emerged and fulfilled his engagements albeit in a reduced form, restricting the publication to four volumes, whereas Brockelmann had had ten volumes in mind. Brockelmann was forced to pay if he wanted the work to proceed, a classic trick. To appease Brockelmann's anger for a while Felber gave him a typewriter, his first. Brockelmann grudgingly accepted it. *GAL*, which in the contract with Felber was Brockelmann's subsidy to finance the Ibn Qutayba edition, was printed more or less simultaneously with the Ibn Qutayba edition, but instead of the one thousand copies which he was allowed to produce, Felber had three thousand copies printed, thereby cashing in for himself on a possible second and third edition. Three thousand copies is quite exceptional for any Orientalist publication where print runs usually do not exceed a few hundred copies. But there was more mishap to come. During several involuntary peregrinations, Felber (who was always on the run from his creditors and authors) had lost part of his stock, the printed sheets of about half of the second volume of *GAL*. Complete copies of *GAL* became a rare item and it took a long time before Felber made a photographic reprint of those lost sheets. *GAL* thereby became a work that, for many years, one could only procure through the antiquarian book trade, if at all. Later on, it was also Felber who hindered the publication of a new edition, since he had so much old stock left. Recourse to juridical action by Brockelmann was to no avail. The German copyright law apparently could not be applied. The book was considered a commodity that, once sold, transferred ownership. The author, who in such a situation was considered to be the former owner, could never again exercise a right to his work. The only way to regain the rights on the book was if someone was to buy the entire remaining stock. During Felber's lifetime this proved to be impossible, and also after Felber's death the successors to his estate asked such an extravagant price for the remaining copies of *GAL* that this possibility proved to be impractical.

Brockelmann then found the director of Brill's of Leiden, Mr. Th. Folkers, ready to publish the additional data in three supplementary volumes, which appeared between 1937–1942. In order to maintain the connection between the original two volumes and the three supplements, the page-numbers of the original edition were constantly referred to. At the end of each supplementary volume, additions and corrections to the original edition were included. The indexes in the third supplement had references to both the original two volumes of 1898–1902 and the three newly published supplements.

It was only after the publication of the third supplementary volume that it became possible for Brill to acquire the rights to the original work. Then nothing stood in the way of an updated second edition of the two original volumes. With ample reference to the supplementary volumes these were published in 1943–1949.

The pagination of the first edition of *GAL* had been the source of reference for the supplementary volumes and they had been included in the indexes of the supplements. Now, in the new edition of the two original volumes, it was to be that same, old, pagination that would be used. This is why the new edition of the two original volumes has the page-numbers of the first edition retained in the margins. And it is to those marginal page numbers that the indexes of the entire new set refer. It is all perfectly logical if one takes the printing history of the book into account, but for the newly initiated bibliographer it is a source of bewilderment and confusion. The use of the marginal page-numbers is, therefore, not just an innocent peculiarity in which Carl Brockelmann indulged, but a complication imposed upon each and every user of the book, now and in the future. With the English edition, which also retains references to the old page numbers, this problem does not exist anymore.

Whereas Brockelmann dared to undertake the compilation of his *GAL* single-handedly a hundred years ago, it is out of the question that anyone would do this now, not even Brockelmann himself. This is proven by the very fact that no one has indeed dared to make even an updated version. Attempts of a more limited nature have been made, of course. The most notable of these is Fuat Sezgin's *Geschichte des Arabischen Schrifttums* (*GAS*), which is still in progress (nine volumes published between 1967–1984, plus an index volume published in 1995). But although Sezgin treats all subjects and sciences, he has limited his work for the time being to the early history of Arabic literature, up to approximately the year 430 of the hegira, that is, mainly texts from the first millennium (plus later commentaries on these). If the literature of the second millennium were to be treated in the same way, the size of such a survey would amount to a great number of volumes.

Another attempt to further bibliographic control which deserves to be mentioned is the serial publication *Arabic Literature of Africa*, edited by J.O. Hunwick and R.S. O'Fahey. The first volume came out in 1994, and in the meantime volume 5, by Charles C. Steward, was published in 2015. The entire series is projected in six volumes. Here the regional element is the selective factor, and although Islam in Africa has a long history, the bulk of its literature dates from a relatively recent time. Even this limited approach required a team of authors, rather than relying on a soloist like Brockelmann.

Has Arabic bibliography come to a standstill? On the contrary, it is precisely because of the fast-growing and ever increasing output of manuscript catalogues over the past fifty years that the production of a new *GAL* has been hampered. The paradox is rather that the success of Arabic bibliography hinders the creation of a *GAL*-like synthesis. This has gone beyond the capabilities of a single scholar, but no project based on teamwork has ever yet been organized to address the problem in its entirety. New techniques of presentation, production and distribution will have to be decided upon if ever such a project for an updated 'History of Arabic Literature' should come into being. Perhaps the present English translation, which will make Brockelmann's still invaluable work more accessible world-wide, will stimulate the start of a project to create a new reference work which aims to comprehensively describe the Arabic manuscript culture.

Literature Quoted in the Introduction

A.A. Ambros, 'Beobachtungen zu Aufbau und Funktionen der gereimten klassisch-arabischen Buchtitel', in: *WZKM* 80 (1990), 13–57.

Arabic Literature of Africa, edited by J.O. Hunwick and R.S. O'Fahey.

Vol. 1. *The Writings of Eastern Sudanic Africa to c. 1900*, compiled by R.S. O'Fahey, Leiden 1994.

Vol. 2. *The Writings of Central Sudanic Africa*, compiled by John O. Hunwick with the assistance of Razaq Abubakre, Hamidu Bobboyi, Roman Loimeier, Stefan Reichmuth and Muhammad Sani Umar, Leiden 1995.

Vol. 3a. *The Writings of the Peoples of Northeastern Africa*, compiled by R.S. O'Fahey with the assistance of Hussein Ahmed, Lidwien Kapteijns, Mohamed M. Kassim, Jonathan Miran, Scott S. Reese and Ewald Wagner, Leiden 2003.

Vol. 4. *The Writings of Western Sudanic Africa*, compiled by John O. Hunwick with the assistance of Ousmane Kane, Bernard Salvaing, Rüdiger Seesemann, Mark Sey and Ivor Wilks, Leiden 2003.

Vol. 5. *The Writings of Mauritania and the Western Sahara* (2 vols.), compiled by Charles C. Stewart with Sidi Ahmed ould Ahmed Salim and the assistance of Mohamed Nouhi, Babacar Mbengue, Abdel Wedoud ould Cheikh and Bruce S. Hall, Leiden 2015.

A.F.L. Beeston, *Arabic Nomenclature. A Summary Guide for Beginners*, Oxford 1971.

Carl Brockelmann, *Geschichte der Arabischen Litteratur*. I (Weimar 1898) xii, 528 pp; II (Berlin 1902) xi, 714 pp.

Johann Fück, 'Carl Brockelmann als Orientalist', *Wissenschaftliche Zeitschrift der Martin-Luther-Universitat Halle-Wittenberg* VII/4 (July 1958), pp. 857–875 (with portrait), (pp. 863–875: 'Verzeichnis der Schriften Carl Brockelmanns').

Johann Fück, 'Carl Brockelmann (1868–1956)', in: ZDMG 108 (1958), 1–13.

Geoffrey Roper (ed.), *World Survey of Islamic Manuscripts*, 4 volumes, London (Al-Furqan Foundation), 1992–1994.

Rudolf Sellheim, 'Autobiographische Aufzeichnungen und Erinnerungen von Carl Brockelmann, als Manuskript herausgegeben' (with portrait), *Oriens* 27–28 (1981), 1–65.

Fuat Sezgin, *Geschichte des Arabischen Schrifttums*, Vols. 1–9, Leiden 1967–1984; vols. 10–15. Frankfurt am Main, 2000–2010.

Translator's Note

The present translation reproduces the original German of Carl Brockelmann's *Geschichte der Arabischen Litteratur* (GAL) as accurately as possible. Nevertheless, some minor changes were made:

Perhaps the most important change is the unabbreviated reproduction of all Arabic names, with the exception of 'b.' for 'ibn', 'Ibn' only being written in full at the beginning of a name, e.g. 'Ibn Rushd.' As an example, one may cite 'Abu 'l-Ḥasan 'Alī b. Aḥmad b. Muḥammad b. 'Alī b. Mattūya al-Wāḥidī al-Nīsābūrī,' which renders Brockelmann's 'Abu 'l-Ḥ. 'A. b. A. b. M. b. 'A. b. Mattūya al-Wāḥidī al-Nīsābūrī' (GAL I 524, no. 3). In connection with the names of Ottoman sultans, Turkish spelling has been used.

Brockelmann's transliteration of Arabic and Persian words was adapted to comply with the system of transliteration of Brill's *Encyclopaedia Islamica*, the changes being: 'j' for ج (Br. 'ǧ'), 'ch' for چ (Br. č), 'kh' for خ (Br. 'ḫ'), 'th' for ث (Br. 'ṯ'), 'dh' for ذ (Br. 'ḏ'), 'zh' for ژ (Br. 'ž'), 'sh' for ش (Br. 'š'), and 'gh' for غ (Br. 'ġ'); no sun letters (e.g. *al-salām* instead of *as-salām*). The following table lists all the characters with their transliterations as used in this work.

In transliterations of names, GAL's 'o' and 'ō' were changed to 'u' and 'ū' (e.g. 'Ṭaybughā' for 'Ṭayboġā,' and 'Rūzbihān' for 'Rōzbihān'), but 'Mollā' was left unchanged; 'ē' becomes 'ī' (e.g. 'Jamshīd' for 'Ǧamšēd'), while 'e' becomes 'a' (e.g. 'Zangī' for 'Zengī', 'al-Kardarī' for 'al-Kerderī'); when 'i' refers to an unvocalized consonant, it is changed to 'y' (e.g. 'Taymūr' instead of 'Taimūr', and '*shi'riyya*' instead of '*ši'rīya*'); sometimes 'i' is changed to 'a', as in 'Tabrīzī' instead of 'Tibrīzī'; finally, transliterations of the names of manuscript collections in Turkish libraries and Hebrew booktitles were left unchanged.

Whenever the name of a place or region has a modern spelling in English that is commonly known, this spelling will be used rather than GAL's transliterations (with the exception of occurrences in people's names or booktitles or for reasons of emphasis), examples: 'Damascus' (Br. 'Dimašq'), 'Kairouan' (Br. 'Qayrawān'), 'Maghreb' (Br. 'Maġrib').

The article 'al-' is written as follows: 1) 'Al-' : a) at the beginning of a sentence, and b) whenever the name of an author mentioned at the beginning of a lemma dedicated to him/her starts with the article; 2) 'al-' : in all other cases, also in listings, whether these start with: '1. al-', or with 'I. al-', or something similar, e.g. 'a. al-', and all items following starting with 'al-'; 3) ''l': in all cases where the article is read in conjunction with a vowel preceding it: u, i, a (e.g. Abu 'l-ʿAbbās, Muḥyi 'l-Dīn, *Dhakhīrat man jarradahu 'l-ḥubb ʿani 'l-khawf*), but when connected to the conjunction '*wa*' and the prepositions '*li*' and '*bi*' the article is rendered as 'l' and joined directly to '*wa*', '*bi*', or '*li*' preceding it (e.g. *Kitāb al-ashbāh wal-naẓāʾir, al-Wāfī bil-wafayāt*, and *al-Shāfiya lil-amrāḍ al-fāshiya*).

Against modern usage, Brockelmann's 'al-Ghazzālī' has been retained throughout. In *GAL* I, 535, note 1, and especially in *GAL* Supplement I, 744, note 1, the author explains this reading at length and, at the same time, he also rejects the other, now common, reading of 'al-Ghazālī' with a series of concrete arguments.

GAL often uses Arabic terms where English equivalents could have been used instead, such as '*qāḍī*' instead of 'judge' or '*wazīr*' instead of 'vizier' or 'minister'; Arabic terms like these have been retained while the term 'Tradition' was often translated with the contextually less ambiguous '*ḥadīth*'.

Page numbers in blue in the margins of volumes 1 and 2 refer to GAL's first edition. In GAL's second edition, the placement of these numbers is often approximate, but sufficient to find one's way; in this translation, this situation has not changed. Page numbers in red in the margins of volumes 1 through 5 refer to GAL's second, enlarged and supplemented edition.

Finally, the present work being a translation, no effort has been made to re-edit or revise any part of the text.

Joep Lameer
Rozendaal, May 2016

Transliteration Table of Arabic and Persian Characters

Consonants						Short vowels	
ء	ʾ	ز	z	ك	k	ـَ	a
ب	b	ژ	zh	گ	g	ـُ	u
پ	p	س	s	ل	l	ـِ	i
ت	t	ش	sh	م	m		
ث	th	ص	ṣ	ن	n	Long vowels	
ج	j	ض	ḍ	ه	h	ای	ā
چ	ch	ط	ṭ	و	w	و	ū
ح	ḥ	ظ	ẓ	ی	y	ي	ī
خ	kh	ع	ʿ				
د	d	غ	gh			Diphtongs	
ذ	dh	ف	t			ـَوْ	aw
ر	r	ق	q			ـَيْ	ay
ة	-a (pausa) / -at (construct state)						
ال	al- (article)						

Contents

Brockelmann's *Geschichte* Revisited Once More v
Translator's Note xv

Introduction 1
- I The Task of Literary History 1
- II Sources and Early Accounts of the Literary History of the Arabs 3
- III Division of the History of Arabic Literature 7

FIRST BOOK
The National Literature of the Arabs

First Section. From the Beginnings until the Appearance of Muḥammad 11
- *For Chapters 1-6, see Supplement Volume I*
- Chapter 7. The Six Poets 13
- Chapter 8. Other Poets of Pre-Islamic Times 15
- Chapter 9. Jewish and Christian Poets before Islam 18
- Chapter 10. The Beginnings of Arabic Prose 21

Second Section. Muḥammad and His Time 23
- Chapter 1. Muḥammad the Prophet 23
- Chapter 2. The Qur'ān 25
- Chapter 3. Labīd and al-Aʿshā 27
- Chapter 4. Ḥassān b. Thābit 29
- Chapter 5. Kaʿb b. Zuhayr 30
- Chapter 6. Mutammin b. Nuwayra 31
- Chapter 7. Al-Khansā' 32
- Chapter 8. Abū Miḥjan and al-Ḥuṭay'a 33
- Chapter 9. Minor Poets 34
- Chapter 10. Two Forgeries 36

Third Section. The Period of the Umayyads 38
- Chapter 1. General Characteristics 38
- Chapter 2. ʿUmar b. Abī Rabīʿa 39
- Chapter 3. Other Poets in Arabia 41
- Chapter 4. Al-Akhṭal 43

Chapter 5. Al-Farazdaq 46
Chapter 6. Jarīr 49
Chapter 7. Dhu 'l-Rumma 51
Chapter 8. The *Rajaz* Poets 52
Chapter 9. Minor Poets 53
Chapter 10. Prose Writing at the Time of the Umayyads 58

SECOND BOOK
Islamic Literature in the Arabic Language

First Section. The Classical Period from ca. 750 until ca. 1000 63
Chapter 1. Introduction 63
Chapter 2. Poetry 64
A *The Poets of Baghdad* 64
B *Poets of Iraq and the Jazīra* 73
C *Poets from Arabia and Syria* 73
D *The Circle of Sayf al-Dawla* 76
E *Egyptian and North African Poets* 79
Chapter 3. Rhymed Prose 81
Chapter 4. Philology 85
I *The School of Basra* 85
II *The School of Kufa* 102
III *The School of Baghdad* 108
IV *Linguistics in Persia and the East* 115
V *Linguistics in Egypt and Spain* 120
Chapter 4. Historiography 122
1 *The Life of Muḥammad* 122
2 *Urban History* 124
3 *The History of the Pre-Islamic Arabs* 125
4 *Imperial and World History* 126
5 *Cultural and Literary History* 131
6 *The History of Egypt and North Africa* 132
7 *The History of Spain* 134
Chapter 5. Belles Lettres in Prose 136
Chapter 6. *Ḥadīth* 141
Chapter 7. *Fiqh* 153
1 *The Ḥanafīs* 153
2 *The Mālikīs* 160
3 *The Shāfiʿīs* 163

4 *The Lesser Schools* 167
5 *The Shīʿa* 169
1 The Zaydīs 170
2 The Imāmīs 172
Chapter 8. Sciences of the Qurʾān 176
1 *The Reading of the Qurʾān* 176
2 *Qurʾānic Exegesis* 176
Chapter 9. Dogmatics 179
Chapter 10. Mysticism 184
Chapter 11. The Translators 191
Chapter 12. Philosophy 200
Chapter 13. Mathematics 208
Chapter 14. Astronomy and Astrology 216
Chapter 15. Geography 224
Chapter 16. Medicine 231
Chapter 17. Natural and Occult Sciences 242
Chapter 18. Encyclopaedias 246

Second Section. The Post-Classical Period of Islamic Literature from ca. 400/1000 until ca. 656/1258 247
Chapter 1. Poetry 249
A *Poets of Baghdad, Iraq, and the Jazīra* 249
B *Persian Poets* 253
C *Syrian Poets* 256
D *Arabian Poets* 262
E *Egyptian Poets* 263
F *North African and Sicilian Poets* 273
G *Spanish Poets* 276
Chapter 2. Rhymed Prose and Stylistics 282
Chapter 3. Philology 288
1 *Philology in Iraq* 288
2 *Philology in Persia and Neighbouring Countries* 293
3 *Philology in Syria* 311
4 *Philology in South Arabia* 316
5 *Philology in Egypt* 317
6 *Philology in North Africa and Sicily* 325
7 *Philology in Spain* 327
Chapter 4. Historiography 333
1 *Individual Biographies* 333
2 *Histories of Dynasties* 340

3 *Histories of Individuals and Genealogy* 342
4 *Local History* 348
  A Baghdad 348
  B Damascus 350
  C Jerusalem 351
  D Aleppo 351
  E Dunaysir 352
  F South Arabia 353
  G Jurjān 354
  H Egypt 354
  I The Maghreb 355
  J Spain 357
5 *Histories of the Caliphs and World History* 362
6 *Histories of Prophets* 371
Chapter 5. Belles Lettres in Prose 373
Chapter 6. *Ḥadīth* 377
1 *Iraq, the Jazīra, Syria, and Arabia* 377
2 *Persia* 387
3 *Egypt and North Africa* 393
4 *Spain* 394
Chapter 7. *Fiqh* 400
1 *The Ḥanafīs* 400
2 *The Mālikīs* 417
3 *The Shāfiʿīs* 420
4 *The Ḥanbalīs* 437
5 *The Ẓāhirīs and Almohads* 440
6 *The Shīʿa* 441
  A The Zaydīs 441
  B The Imāmīs 444
Chapter 8. Sciences of the Qurʾān 450
1 *The Art of Reading the Qurʾān* 450
2 *Qurʾānic Exegesis* 456
Chapter 9. Dogmatics 467
Chapter 10. Mysticism 486
Chapter 11. Philosophy and Politics 516
Chapter 12. Mathematics 540
Chapter 13. Astronomy 545
Chapter 14. Travelogues and Geographies 549

Chapter 15. Medicine 556
Chapter 16. 571
A *Natural Sciences and Technology* 571
B *Games, Sports, and War* 572
C *Music* 573
Chapter 17. Occult Sciences 574
Chapter 18. Encyclopaedias and Polyhistories 578

Introduction 1

I The Task of Literary History

In its widest sense, one may call "literature" everything that has been written, 1
or spoken and then written down, for the purpose of having it remembered. For this reason, A. Boeckh suggested including inscriptions as part of a people's literature. In cases where the history of a dead language is written using a limited number of monuments one can also employ charters, letters, and the like. But when a language has such a rich abundance of examples as does Arabic, then one will, from among these, only regard those that address themselves from the outset to a larger audience, with the aim of affecting its mood or enriching its knowledge, as literature. Among the "civilised" nations these manifestations have accumulated to such a degree that the literary historian is compelled to limit himself purely to poetry. However, Arabic poetry did not have the same significance for the development of human culture and knowledge as a whole compared to the achievements of scholars writing in Arabic for the development of the sciences. This is because the Arabic language was not limited to a single nation, but was the bearer of all culture and education in the vast area where Islam penetrated as a religion, from the banks of the Pontus to Zanzibar, from Fez and Timbuktu to Kashgar and the Sunda islands, ceding this role only
belatedly to various national languages, and then only in part. | This is why the 2
historian of Arabic literature must draw all these manifestations into his orbit; it is only for the outputs of the modern era, in which the world of Islam has
become | more and more aligned with European culture, that one can limit 2
oneself to poetry alone.

Given that Arabic literature will only be considered here insofar as it is a manifestation of Islamic culture, all works by Christians and Jews that were only directed at their co-religionists will be excluded. Furthermore, the amount of material, which is in any case enormous, forces us to focus mainly on those works that do survive, and, from the vast multitude of works that are no longer extant but known to us through later citations, to only draw attention to those that had an important impact and influence on the later development of literature.

The study of literature in the elevated sense of the word[1] is a means by which modern scholars try to understand both the literary heritage of a people

1 B. Ten Brink, *Über die Aufgabe der Litteraturgeschichte* (rectorial address), Strasburg 1891. E. Elster, *Die Aufgaben der Litteraturgeschichte* (academic acceptance speech), Halle 1894, the

 | DOI 10.1163/9789004326262_002

in terms of it being part of its culture as a whole, and how the circumstances of its composition and personalities of authors are reflected in individual works. This is why, at present, it is only possible to deal with individual areas of Arabic literature, employing the same methodology that was used by Goldziher in
3 the field of *ḥadīth*. | Anyone hoping to give an account of the field as a whole will have to limit themselves, at least for the time being, to the outward phenomena of any literature as reflected in the lives and times of its authors and their works, thereby preparing the ground for future study of its origins and development.

works mentioned in Supp. I, 3, n. 1 and 934, and Horst Oppel, *Die Literaturwissenschaft in der Gegenwart, Methodologie und Wissenschaftslehre*, Stuttgart 1939.

II Sources and Early Accounts of the Literary History of the Arabs

With the exception of those monographs that will be mentioned in their proper places throughout these volumes, the most important biographical and bibliographical sources for the field as a whole are as follows:

1. Biographical works 3

Ibn Khall. = Ibn Khallikān (p. 326), *Wafayāt al-aʿyān*, Būlāq 1299[1]; *Vitae illustrium virorum*, ed. F. Wüstenfeld, Göttingen 1835–40; *Ibn Khallikan's biographical dictionary translated from the Arabic*, by MacGuckin de Slane, 4 vols., Paris-London 1843–71.

Fawāt = Muḥammad b. Shākir al-Kutubī (II, 48), *Fawāt al-wafayāt*, 2 vols., Būlāq 1299.

2. Bibliographical works

Fihr. = *Kitāb al-Fihrist, hsgb. von* G. Flügel, *nach dessen Tode besorgt von* J. Rödiger *und* A. Müller, 2 vols., Leipzig 1871/2.

ḤKh = *Lexicon bibliographicum et encyclopaedicum a Mustapha ben Abdallah Katib Jelebi dicto et nomine Haji Khalfa celebrato compositum, ed. latine vertit et commentario indicibusque instruxit* G. Flügel, 7 vols, Leipzig-London 1835–58; *Keşf el-Zunun, Birinci Cilt, Katib Çelebi elde mevcut yazma ve basma nüshalari ve zeyilleri gözden geçirilerek, müellifin elyazisiyle olan nüshaya göre fazlalari çikarilmak, eksikleri tamamlanmak suretiyle Maarif Vekilliğin karari üzerine Istanbul Universitesinde Ord. Prof.* Şerefettin Yaltkaya *ile Lektör Kilisli Rifat Bilge tarafindan hazirlanmiştir*, Maarif Matbaasi 1941.

Ellis, A.G., *Catalogue of Arabic books in the British Museum*, London I 1894, II 1901, III (indices by A.S. Fulton) 1938.

---

1 Since this edition is by preference cited according to the numbering of the vitae, the following short concordance with Wüstenfeld may be helpful: W 1–75 = K 1–75. Missing in K: W 76, 78, 133, 147, 149, 150, 154, 186–199, 201, 202 (= *Fawāt* I, 145), 213, 214 (= *Fawāt* I, 149), 217, 277, 278 (= *Fawāt* I, 171), 288, 291, 292, 293, 294, 303, 317, 318, 337–347, 364, 380, 381, 528; mostly just captions, but here and there they also have the date of death. On the other hand, 297 K is missing in W; 357 was misnumbered in W; 405 W as an appendix to 404 = 367 K is not counted separately. In the following vitae K is more elaborate than W: 220 K = 233 W; 223 K = 236 W; 230 K = 243 W; 233 K = 246 W; 248 K = 261 W; on the other hand, only 242 W is more elaborate than 229 K. As a result of a transposition, 181 K = 186 W. Because the order hāʾ-wāw of K is reversed in W, the correspondence is now W 778–90 = K 745–57 and W 791–96 = K 739–44.

4 Euting, J., *Katalog der Kaiserlichen Universitäts- und* | *Landesbibliothek in Strassburg, Arabische Literatur*, Strasburg 1877.

BO = J. Th. Zenker, *Bibliotheca orientalis, Manuel de bibliographie orientale*, 2 vols., Leipzig 1846, 1861.

Herrm. = Herrmann C.H., *Bibliotheca orientalis et linguistica, Verzeichnis der vom Jahre 1850 bis incl. 1868 in Deutschland erschienenen Bücher, Schriften und Abhandlungen orientalischer und sprachvergleichender Literatur*, Halle a. S 1870.

Fried. = Friederici K., *Bibliotheca orientalis oder vollständige Liste aller 1876–83 in Deutschland, Frankreich, England und den Kolonien erschienenen Bücher usw*, Leipzig 1877–84.

L. Bl. = *Literaturblatt für orientalische Philologie, hsgb. von* E. Kuhn, Leipzig 1883/8.

4 | *OB.* = *Orientalische Bibliographie, begründet von* A. Müller, *hsgb. von* L. Scherman, Berlin 1887ff.

Manuscript catalogues represent the most important source of information and are mentioned here according to the alphabetical order of their sigla:

Algiers: *Catalogue général des mss. des bibliothèques publiques de France, Départements, Tome XVIII, Alger par* E. Fagnan, Paris 1893.

AS: *Defteri Kütübḫāne'ī Aya Sofia*, Istanbul 1304.

Berl.: W. Ahlwardt, *Verzeichnis der arabischen Hdss. der Königl. Bibliothek zu Berlin*, vols. I–X, Berlin 1887ff.[2]

Bodl.: *Bibliothecae Bodleianae codd. mss. or. Catalogus, pars I a* J. Uri, Oxford 1787. *Pars II, vol. I, ab* Alex. Nicoll, Oxford 1821, *vol. II ab* E.B. Pusey, Oxford 1835.

Br. Mus.: *Catalogus codd. mss. qui in Musaeo Britannico asservantur, Pars II, codd. arab. amplectens*, 3 vols., London 1846–79.

Br. Mus. Suppl.: Ch. Rieu, *Supplement to the Catalogue of the Arabic Manuscripts in the British Museum*, London 1894.

Brill-H.: Houtsma M. Th., *Catalogue d'une collection de mss. arabes et turcs appartenant à la maison E.J. Brill à Leide*, Leiden 1886, 1889[2] (now in Princeton, Garrett Collection).

5 | Cairo, *Fihrist al-kutub al-ʿarabiyya al-maḥfūẓa bil-kutubkhāne al-Khidīwiyya al-Miṣriyya*, vols. I–VII, Cairo 1306/9.

2 In the listings at the end of each entry the reference is: Ahlw. no. New acquisitions that have not yet been catalogued are cited according to the number of the manuscript.

Cambr.: Palmer, E., *Descriptive Catalogue of the Arabic, Persian and Turkish Manuscripts in the Library of Trinity College*, Cambridge 1870.

Copenhagen: *Codices arabici Bibliothecae Regiae Hafniensis, enumer. et descr. a* F. Mehren, Copenhagen 1851.

Daḥdāḥ M—y Bīṭār: Daḥdāḥ Rocheid, *Catalogue d'une collection de mss. ar. précieux et de livres rares*, Paris 1912, now in Berlin, cited here as Berl. Brill M.

Dresd.: Fleischer, H.L., *Catalogus codd. mss. or. Bibl. Reg. Dresdensis*, Leipzig 1831.

Escur.:[1] *Bibliotheca Arabico-Hispana Escurialensis opera*, M. Casiri, 2 vols., Madrid 1760–70.

Escur.:[2] Derenbourg, H., *Les manuscrits arabes de l'Escurial*, I, Paris 1884; II, *fs.* I. *Morale et Politique*, Paris 1903.

Gotha: Pertsch, W., *Die arabischen Hdss. der Herzoglichen Bibliothek zu Gotha*, vols. I–V, Gotha 1877–92.

Ind. Off.: Loth, O., *Catalogue of the Ar. Mss. in the Library of the India Office*, London 1877.

Jong: P. de Jong, *Catalogus codd. or. bibl. acad. scient.*, Leiden 1862.

| Köpr.: *Köprülüzāde Meḥmed Pāšā Kütübḫānesinde maḥfūẓ kütübi* 5
mevǧūdenin defteri, Istanbul n.d.

Krafft H.: *Die arab. pers. und türk. Hdss. der k.k. Orientalischen Akademie zu Wien*, Vienna 1842.

Leid.: *Catalogus codd. or. bibl. acad. Lugd. Bat. ed.* Dozy, de Jong, de Goeje *et* Houtsma, vols. I–VI, Leiden 1851–77. *Catalogus codd. arab. ed. II auctoribus* M.J. de Goeje *et* M. Th. Houtsma, vol. I, Leiden. 1888, vol. II *pars I, auct.* M.J. de Goeje *et* W. Th. Juynboll, Leiden 1907.

Leipz.: *Catalogus librorum mss. bibl. senatus Lipsiensis ed.* A.G.R. Neumann. *Cod. or. ling. descr.* H.O. Fleischer *et* F. Delitzsch, Grimma 1838.

Madr.: (Robles, F.G.) *Catálogo de los manuscritos árabes exist. en la Biblioteca Nacional de Madrid*, Madrid 1889.

Med.: *Bibliothecae Mediceae Laurentianae et Palatinae codd. mss. or. catalogus*, St. Evodius Assemani *recensuit*, Florence 1742.

Munich: Aumer J., *Die arab. und pers. Hdss. der Hof-und Staatsbibliothek in München*, Munich 1866.

Nan.: *Catalogo dei Codd. Mss. or. della Bibliotheca Naniana comp. dall' Ab.* S. Assemani. p. I, II, Padua 1792.

| NO: *Nūru Osmānīye kütübḫānesinde maḥfūẓ kütübi mevǧūdenin defteri*, 6
Istanbul n.d.

Paris: *Bibliothèque Nationale, Département des manuscrits. Catalogue des mss. arabes par* de Slane, Paris 1883–95.

Patna: *Fihrist-i dastī-i kutub-i qalamī Library-i mawqūfa-i Khān Bahādur Khudābakhsh musammā bi-Miftāḥ al-khafiyya murattaba-i Maulawī ʿAbdalḥamīd*, 2 vols., Patna 1918, 1922 (=Bank.).

Pet.: *Catologue des mss. et xylographes orientaux de la Bibliothèque Impériale publique de St. Pétersbourg* 1852.

Pet. A.M.: = Rosen, V., *Notices sommaires des mss. arab. du Musée Asiatique* I, St. Petersburg 1881.

Pet. Ros.: *Collection scientifique de l'Institut des langues orientales du Ministère des affaires étrangères. I. Les mss. arabes par* V. Rosen, St. Pétersbourg 1877. *VI Les mss. arabes (non compris dans le no. I) Karchounis etc. de l'Inst. d. l. or. décrits par* D. Günzburg, V. Rosen, B. Dorn, K. Patkanoff, J. Tchoubinof, 1st fs. St. Petersburg 1891.

Rāġib: *Defteri kütübkhāneʾi Rāġib Pāshā*, Istanbul 1310 AH.

Ref.: *Die Refāʿīja*, Fleischer, Kl. Schr. III, 366ff.

Upps.: Tornberg, C.J., *Codices arab. pers. et turc. bibl. regiae univ. Upsal.*, Lund 1849.

Vat.: *Bibliothecae apost. Vaticanae codd. mss. or. cat.* p. I, vol. I, Rome 1766.

Vienna: Flügel, G., *Die arab. pers. und türk. Hdss. der K.K. Hofbibliothek.* 3 vols., Vienna 1863–7.

Yeni = *Yeni Ǧāmiʿ kütübḫānesinde maḥfūẓ kütübi mevǧūdenin defteri dir*, Istanbul n.d.

2. The first attempt to provide a comprehensive account of the history of Arabic literature was made by J. von Hammer-Purgstall.[3] The shortcomings
6 of this work are so well-known | that we may ignore it in what follows. The same goes for the study by Arbuthnot.[4] On the other hand, the brief sketch by A. von Kremer is masterly,[5] and to him this study is indebted.

3 *Literaturgeschichte der Araber, von ihrem Beginne bis zu Ende des zwölften Jahrhunderts der Hidschret*, 7 vols., Vienna 1850–56.

4 *Arabic authors. A manual of Arabian history and literature*, London 1890.

5 *Kulturgeschichte des Orients unter den Chalifen*, vol. II, Vienna 1877, 341–484.

III. Division of the History of Arabic Literature 7

When Arab philologists separated the history of the poetry of their people into the two periods of the *jāhiliyya*[1] (pre-Islamic time) and Islam, this was not to disparage the former in an act of religious self-conceit. Quite the opposite, in fact, for its pre-Islamic exponents were regarded as unsurpassable models, and pedantecism often went so far that a poet whose achievement was highly regarded was nevertheless belittled merely because he was born after Muḥammad.[2] For this reason they created the intermediary class of the *mukhaḍramūn*, those who had spent their youth, at least, as pagans. In reality, Islam was not the decisive turning-point for Arabic literature that these critics would have us believe, and during the reign of the Umayyads poets continued to unconcernedly follow the paths of their heathen predecessors. It was only during the period of the ʿAbbāsids that the spirit of Islam took full control, turning not only against the religious indifference of the Arabs but also against their national identity. After all, the ʿAbbāsids had only come to power thanks to the backing of non-Arab, especially Persian, supporters of Islam. The consequence of this was that an Islamic literature in the Arabic language came to 7
be developed among them.[3] As such, Arabic literature will be divided into two main periods:

I. The national literature of the Arabs from its beginnings until the ʿAbbāsid revolution in the year 132/750.

1. Before the appearance of Muḥammad.
2. Muḥammad and his lifetime.
3. The period of the Umayyads.

II. Islamic literature in the Arabic language 8

The flourishing of Arabic literature lasted less than three centuries. By the mid-fourth/tenth century, material prosperity and intellectual life were in rapid decline within the ʿAbbāsid empire, reflecting its political disunity. Admittedly, it was to experience a second blooming that lasted another three centuries, before it was put to a definite end by the Mongol onslaught of the seventh/thirteenth century. While these problems did not completely destroy Arabic literature, in subsequent times it ossified into a rigid kind of schematism, with

1 See Goldziher, *Muhammed. Studien* I, 219/29.
2 Idem, *Abh. zur arab. Philologie* I, 136.
3 See A. Müller, *Der Islam* I, 470.

only poetry and historiography bearing some small pieces of fruit. It was only at the turn of the twentieth century that a new efflorescence appeared.

What Arabic literature lacked in originality in this period it made up by its civilising influence on the many peoples that were won over to Islam. The most important political event of this period was the conquest of Egypt by the Ottoman sultan Selīm I in the year 1517, by which the Sunnī people on the eastern shores of the Mediterranean were united into a single state once more.

As such, the history of Islamic literature shall be divided into four periods:

1. The golden age under the ʿAbbāsids, from ca. 750 until ca. 1000

8 | 2. The second blooming, from ca. 1000 until the destruction of Baghdad by Hūlāgū in 1258

3. From the Mongol domination until the conquest of Egypt by Selīm in the year 1517

4. From 1517 until the present day.

FIRST BOOK

The National Literature of the Arabs

FIRST SECTION

From the Beginnings until the Appearance of Muḥammad

Supplement I

1. The oldest preserved anthology is the *Muʿallaqāt*, i.e. those poems that,
by | their brilliance, had been elevated to a place of honour. As recognised by 18
Nöldeke (*Beitr.* XVIIff., *Enc. Brit.* XVI, 536), a literal interpretation of this term
gave rise to the belief that these poems had been recognised as masterpieces
in pre-Islamic times, and as such had been suspended on the Kaʿba. In reality,
however, this collection originated with Ḥammād al-Rāwiya. It is not unanimously agreed which poems belong to the *Muʿallaqāt*. Five are included by
all, those written by Imraʾ al-Qays, Ṭarafa, Zuhayr, Labīd, and ʿAmr b. Kulthūm.
ʿAntara and al-Ḥārith b. Ḥilliza usually appear sixth and seventh, although
al-Mufaḍḍal replaced them with al-Nābigha and al-Aʿshā. These are the | poets 12
who are usually also considered to have been the most famous. The only exception to this is al-Ḥārith b. Ḥasan. The reason for Ḥammād's including him in
his collection was discovered by Nöldeke: Ḥammād was a client of the tribe of
Bakr b. Wāʾil. In ancient times, this tribe was engaged in constant warfare with
the Taghlib tribe. The poem written by ʿAmr b. Kulthūm, included in Ḥammād's
collection, was devoted to the glorification of this latter tribe, and due to the
universal presence of the Taghlib this poem was held in high regard. Since
there was no way for Ḥammād to avoid including this song in his collection, he
was forced to counter it with another one that would glorify his own lord and
master, Bakr b. Wāʾil. Thus, he chose a song by one of their common tribesmen,
the otherwise little-known Ḥārith. Later compilers, who did not have the same
tribal interests, replaced him with poets of greater fame. Furthermore, other
compilers counted nine *Muʿallaqāt*, a figure they came to by adding the two
selected by al-Mufaḍḍal to those chosen by al-Ḥammād.

Septem Moallakat, ed. F. Arnold, Leipzig 1850; L. Abel, *Wörterverzeichnisse zur altarabischen Poesie* I, Berlin 1891, on which see G. Jacob, *Dr. Abels Muʿallaqāt-Ausgabe nachgeprüft, Studien in arabischen Dichter* I, Berlin 1893/4. On the commentaries, see Supplement.

 | DOI 10.1163/9789004326262_003

2. *Al-Mufaḍḍaliyyāt.* See Supplement I.

Commentary by al-Tabrīzi, d. 502/1108, p. 279, also Berl. Brill M 295, Fātiḥ 3963 (*MFO* V, 502).

4. The *Ḥamāsa* of Abū Tammām, commentary 2. *al-Tanbīh fī sharḥ mushkil abyāt al-Ḥamāsa*, also Patna I, $200,_{789}$.

21 | 7. Al-Sukkārī also compiled a work in which he collected the poems of famous Bedouin robbers. Among these was the *dīwān* of Ṭahmān b. ʿAmr al-Kilābī, who flourished under ʿAbd al-Malik. This *dīwān* was published by W. Wright
13 in *Opuscula Arabica*, Leiden, London, and Edinburgh | 1859, pp. 76–95, on the basis of MS Leiden 582.

Ibn Ḥazm (*Ṭawq al-ḥamāma*, $65,_{17}$) studied the commentary by Abū Jaʿfar al-Naḥḥās (no. 3) under Saʿīd al-Fata ʾl-Jaʿfarī in a mosque in Cordova.

Other poems by Ṭahmān are found in Bodl. Nic. $315,_{1}$ Esc.^{2} $363,_{1}$ 466.[1] Further fragments of the *Akhbār al-luṣūṣ* are found in Yāqūt's geographical dictionary, in Tabrīzī's commentary on the *Ḥamāsa*, etc.

---

1 But not in Berl. Ahlw. 496/8, as noted in connection with Leid. 582.

Chapter 7. The Six Poets 22

For Chapters 1-6, see Supplement Volume I.

1. Al-Nābigha al-Dhubyānī Ziyād b. Muʿāwiya lived in the latter half of the century before Muḥammad, mostly in al-Ḥīra, under the kings al-Mundhir III and IV and al-Nuʿmān Abū Qābūs. He fell into disgrace with the latter, the story goes, because he had praised the beauty of the queen too openly in one of his poems. However, it is more likely to have been because he had developed friendly relations with the Ghassānids of Damascus, who were the enemies of the Lakhmid rulers of al-Ḥīra. He also found refuge in that city, at the court of ʿAmr b. al-Ḥārith. It was only when the latter's son al-Nuʿmān, who had showered him with honours, as his father had, passed away, that he decided to return to al-Ḥīra, where he succeeded in regaining the favour of Abū Qābūs. However, he did not enjoy this for long, as the latter was soon imprisoned by his overlord, the Sasanid ruler Khusraw II, where he died. Following these events al-Nābigha returned to his tribe, the Dhubyān, whose interests he had already represented to his various patrons, and remained with them until his death.

2. ʿAntara b. Shaddād (or ʿAmr b. Muʿāwiya) al-ʿAbsī was the son of a black female slave by the name of Zabība, | which is why he is reckoned among the 14
aghribat al-ʿarab. However, he obliterated this birth defect by the courage that he displayed in the War of Dāḥis and Ghabrāʾ.[1] He died in battle against the Ṭayyiʾ tribe. His place as the most popular Arab hero continues today in the romance of ʿAntar, as well as in numerous geographical place-names. Even though his art, which we know mainly through his *Muʿallaqa*, is that of a typical Bedouin poet, it does have some modern features, as, for example, it depicts a love scene in almost the same manner as ʿUmar b. Abī Rabīʿa, while also connecting it, in the *nasīb*, like elsewhere in the poem (Ahlw. no. 20), with other themes.

Agh. [1]VII 149/53, [2]141/6, [3]VIII 237/45. W. Ahlwardt, *Bemerkungen über die Echtheit der alten Arabischen Gedichte*, Greifswald 1872, 50/7, H. Thorbecke, *Antarah, ein vorislamischer Dichter*, Leipzig 1867, I. Goldziher, Der arabische Held Antar in der geographischen Nomenklatur, *Globus* LXIV, 65/7.

1 A. Müller, *Der Islam* I, 5ff.

23 | 3. Ṭarafa b. ʿAmr b. al-ʿAbd al-Bakrī lived at the court of al-Ḥīra as the boon-companion of Qābūs, the brother of king ʿAmr b. Hind, who reigned until 568 or 569 CE.[2] Arab critics greatly admire his verbal prowess, which is most clearly displayed in his description of the camel in his *Muʿallaqa*, while some even call him the greatest poet of the Jāhiliyya.

Khiz. I, 414/8, A. Perron, *JA* s. III, v. 9. pp. 46, 215. Fr. Rückert, *Sieben Bücher morgenländischer Sagen und Geschichten*, books 1–4, Stuttgart 1837, p. 136, Ahlwardt,
15 *Bemerkungen*, pp. 57/61, B. Vandenhoff, *Nonnulla Tarafae* | *poetae carmina ex arabico in latinum sermonem versa notisque adumbrata*, Diss. Berlin 1895.

4. Legend has it that Zuhayr b. Abī Sulmā Rabīʿa b. Rabāḥ al-Muzanī met the Prophet when he was himself a hundred years old. It is, however, more likely that at the time of the latter's appearance the former had already been dead for a considerable period of time.

Ahlwardt, *Bemerkungen*, 61/5.

24 | 5. ʿAlqama b. ʿAbada al-Tamīmī al-Faḥl was a regular visitor at the courts of both the Ghassānid al-Ḥārith and the Lakhmid Nuʿmān III Abū Qābūs, although he did not permanently associate himself with either one of these. A real desert poet, he is especially famous for his depiction of the ostrich. The contest he is said to have had with Imraʾ al-Qays is a myth.

Agh. ^{1}XXI, 172/5, ^{2}III/3, Ahlwardt, op. cit., 65/71, *Die Gedichte des ʿAlḳama elfaḥl mit Anmm. hsg. von* A. Socin, Leipzig 1867, on which see Ahlwardt, pp. 146/68, *Sharḥ dīwān ʿAlqama* by al-Aʿlam (see p. 309) Cairo^{2} III, 205.

6. Imraʾ al-Qays b. Ḥunduj b. Ḥujr b. al-Ḥārith al-Kindī.

Ahlwardt, op. cit., 72–84, *Le diwan d'Amro'lkais par le baron* de Slane, Paris 1837. It was al-Riyāshī who confirmed that a large part of the poems attributed to him were not actually written by him but by *fityān* in his company, such as ʿAmr b. Qamīʿa and al-Marzubānī, *al-Muwashshaḥ*, 34_{10}.

---

2 Th. Nöldeke, *Geschichte der Perser und Araber zur Zeit der Sasaniden*, p. 170ff.

Chapter 8. Other Poets of Pre-Islamic Times

The below list is limited to the most famous poets, as well as those whose independent collections have been preserved.

| 1. Ta'abbaṭa Sharran Thābit b. Jābir al-Fahmī. The son of a black female slave, 25
he is counted | among the *aghribat al-ʿArab*, just like ʿAntara. Others, however, 16
contend that his mother was the Fahmī woman Amīna. Fending for himself, he led an unsteady life. The descriptions of his adventures bear all the hallmarks of popular fiction, while most of the reports on the life of the ancient poets were teased out of their poems by literary scholars in later times. From among his works, which have only been preserved scattered through anthologies, there is an elegy for a relative, which is contained in *Ḥamāsa* 382/6.[1]

Baur, ZDMG X, 71ff., G.W. Freytag, *Carmen arabicum perpetuo comment. et versione jambica Germanica illustravit,* Göttingen 1814. Goethe, *Noten zum westöstl. Diwan, Werke,* Weimar 1888, vol. 7, p. 12, Jubil.–Ausg. V, 152. *Carmen quod cecinit Taabbata Sharran vel Chaleph Elahmar in vindictae sanguinis et fortitudinis laudem, Arabice et Suethice exhibet* Haquinus Hellmann, Lund 1834.

2. Al-Shanfarā was Ta'abbaṭa Sharran's companion in many of his exploits. Slightly older, he died before the latter and was commemorated by him in a song of mourning. On his *Lāmiyyat al-ʿArab,* see Supplement I.

S. de Sacy, *Chrest. Arabe,* ed. I. v. I, 309ff., ed. II v. II, 134ff. Shanfara, *Lamijat ul Arab. A preislamic Arabian Qasida,* transl. into English verses by G. Hughes, 1896. Also, a commentary by Muḥammad b. Ḥusayn al-Turkī and Muḥammad b. Qāsim b. Zākūr, *Tafrīj al-karab ʿan qulūb ahl al-ʿarab* (Alex. Adab 135$_5$), B. M. Daḥdaḥ 233, Berl. Brill M 111. *Shiʿr al-Shanfara al-Azdī,* ed. ʿAbd al-ʿAzīz al-Maymanī (based on Khusraw P., Ayyūb no. 149) in *al-Ṭarāʾif al-adabiyya,* C. 1937, 26/42.

| 3. Less celebrated than these two real representatives of ancient Arab life, 26
albeit better known because of the much greater volume of his output, is ʿUrwa
b. al-Ward | b. Ḥābis of the tribe of ʿAbs, who must have lived shortly before the 17
rise of Islam. His father, extolled by ʿAntara as a brave man, played a role in the

1 Brilliant Arab critics have questioned its authenticity, attributing it to Khalaf al-Aḥmar instead. Their reasoning is, however, not conclusive, as pointed out by Rückert in his annotations to the *Ḥamāsa.*

War of Dāḥis. His mother came from the little-esteemed tribe of Najd, which cast a shadow over him. While the more famous ʿAntara was more appreciated because of his status as a hero, his tribe recognised Ibn Ḥābis as the greater poet. His songs are known to us through the recension of Ibn al-Sikkīt (d. 243/857, see p. 117).

Agh. [1]II, 190/7, [2]II, 184/90, [3]III 73/8, *Die Gedichte des ʿUrwa b. al-Ward hsg., übers. und erläutert von* Th. Nöldeke, Göttingen 1863, *Abh. der Kgl. Ges. d. Wiss.*, vol. 11. R. Boucher, Notice sur Orwa b. al-Ward, *JA* s. VI, v. 9, p. 97.

4. Quṭba b. Aws al-Ḥādira, of the tribe of the Banū Thaʿlaba b. Saʿd, a subdivision of the Ghaṭafān, was involved in a bitter and prolonged quarrel with Zabbān b. Sayyār al-Fazārī and exchanged satirical verses with him. Only a few of his poems have been preserved, in the collection of Abū ʿAbdallāh al-Yazīdī, who died in 310/922.

Agh. [1]III, 82/4, [2]III, 79/81, [3]III 270/4. *Specimen litt. exhibens Al-Hadirae Diwanum, cum al-Yezidii scholiis, e cod. ms. ar. ed. versione lat. et annotatione illustravit* Dr. G. H. Engelmann, Leiden 1858; other MSS Br. Mus. 1525 and Suppl. I, 54 (where al-Fazārī should be excised).

5. ʿAbīd b. al-Abraṣ, of the Asad tribe, lived at the court of al-Ḥīra, where he enjoyed social relations with al-Nābigha al-Dhubyānī. It seems he was killed in his old age by King Mundhir b. Māʾ al-Samāʾ (d. 554), symbolically at the grave of two of his friends whom the king, in a fit of anger, had once ordered to be buried alive. His *dīwān* includes genuine Bedouin poetry, full of bold energy in its *fakhr*, combined with a sincere attitude to life and magnificent descriptive
18 passages. | *Agh.* [1]XIX, 84/90, [2]84/9, *Khiz.* I, 322/4. Ibn Sallām, *Ṭabaqāt al-shuʿarāʾ*, 30. *Dīwān* in Hibatallāh al-Shajarī's (d. 542/1147) *Mukhtārāt al-shuʿarāʾ*, Cairo 1306, pp. 87/108, see F. Hommel, *Aufsätze u. Abh.*, Munich 1890, pp. 52/92; a *qaṣīda* Berl. 7475,$_1$ Ind. Off. 801, iia. A. Fischer, Ein angeblicher Vers des ʿAbīd b. al-Abraṣ, *MIFAO* LXVIII, 361/75, Fr. Gabrieli, La Poesia di ʿAbīd b. al-Abraṣ, *Reale Ac. d'Italia Rend. della Cl. di sc. mor. e stor.* s. VII, vol. I, 1940, XVIII 1/12.

27 | 6. Ḥātim b. ʿAbdallāh b. Saʿd al-Ṭāʾī, famous as a paragon of largesse, had social relations with ʿAbīd and al-Nābigha. At the time of the Prophet, his son and daughter fell into the hands of the Muslims. Some of the poems that bear his name have certainly been misattributed to him.

Agh. [1]XVI, 96/110, [2]93/106. *Shiʿr Ḥātim wa-akhbāruhu* after Hishām b. Muḥammad al-Kalbī and Yaḥyā b. Mudrik al-Ṭāʾī, Br. Mus. 566,$_2$. *Hatim Tai, diss. praeside* J. Bolmeer *exhib.* P.E. Oseen, Lond. Goth. 1832. *Dīwān Ḥātim al-Ṭāʾī wa-akhbāruhu*, London (R. Hassoun) 1872, on which marginal notes by Fayḍ al-Ḥasan, Lahore 1878. *Der Diwan des arabischen Dichters Ḥātim Ṭej*, ed. Fr. Schulthess, Leipzig 1897.—On Persian, Turkish, and Hindustani stories about Ḥātim al-Ṭāʾī, see C. van Arendonk, *EI* II, 308.

7. Laqīṭ b. Yaʿmar (Maʿmar) al-Iyādī belonged to the Arabs of Iraq and is particularly famous for a *qaṣīda* in which he warned his fellow tribesmen against Kisrā.

Agh. [1]XXI, 23/5, *Mukhtārāt al-shuʿarāʾ*, p. 2/7. Th. Nöldeke, *Orient u. Occident* I, p. 689ff. Two poems, Berl. 7479/80.

8. Aws b. Ḥajar, of the tribe of Tamīm, was a contemporary of King ʿAmr b. Hind of al-Ḥīra whose father had fallen in the Battle of al-Ḥijār, around 554 CE. He was a native of al-Baḥrayn and roamed as a travelling minstrel through all of northern Arabia and Iraq, spending most of his time at the court of al-Ḥīra.
His adopted son and *rāwī* was the famous | Zuhayr (see p. 15). His poems were 19
especially famous because of their hunting scenes. Collected by Ibn al-Sikkīt, they have nonetheless only been preserved fragmentarily.

Agh. [1]X, 6/8, [2]5/8. R. Geyer, *Gedichte und Fragmente des Aws b. Ḥajar. SB Wien. Ak. phil.-hist. Cl.* vol. 126, Vienna 1892, on which see A. Fischer, *GGA* 1895, no. 5, *ZDMG* 49, pp. 85/144, 673/80, S. Fraenkel, ibid. 297, R. Basset *ZA* 26, 295/304. *al-Qaṣīda al-lāmiyya* Patna II, 425, $2598_{,1}$.

9. Umayya b. Abi ʾl-Ṣalt al-Thaqafī; see Supplement I.

| 10. Qays b. al-Khaṭīm of the Aws tribe, who played a prominent part in its 28
ongoing conflict with the Khazraj, composed his poetry in Yathrib, the original name of Medina. He is particularly famous for the blood vengeance that he took against his father's and grandfather's Khazrajī murderers. In folklore, his story is adorned with familiar motifs of the wanderer. Although he lived to see the appearance of the Prophet, he died before the Hijra after being hit by an arrow as he rode past a Khazrajī stronghold.

Agh. [1]II, 159/70, [2]154/64, [3]III, 1/26, *Ḥamāsa* I, 94, III, 104. *Dīwān* MS Top Kapu Sarāi, dated 419 AH, copy Cairo [1]IV, 251, [2]III, 144.

Chapter 9. Jewish and Christian Poets before Islam

1. The Jewish colonies in the northern Hijaz were most probably founded by refugees from Palestine after the crushing of their revolt by the Roman emperors Titus and Hadrian. Even though they had been completely Arabised and had also adopted members of authentic Arab tribes into their midst they remained connected to their country of origin not only by their written laws, but also through the further development of these in Halakha and Haggada.
20 | Notwithstanding the fact that they were indispensable to the Arabs as farmers and craftsmen, notably goldsmiths, they were generally held in low esteem.

The most important of their poets was Samaw'al b. ʿĀdiyāʾ. However, some sources regard him as a true Arab while, according to others, his mother at least was from the tribe of Ghassān. Be that as it may, there is no doubt that he was committed to Judaism. He lived in the castle of al-Ablaq, in or near Taymāʾ. He did not owe his fame as much to his talents as a poet as to his loyalty to Imraʾ al-Qays, a loyalty that he upheld by sacrificing his own son, an act that was praised by al-Aʿshā, *Dīwān*, 25_5ff. Apart from a number of fragments, we also find a beautiful, proud song in his name in the *Ḥamāsa*, pp. 49ff., a song that is, however, more justifiably attributed to ʿAbd al-Malik b. ʿAbd al-Raḥmān al-Ḥārithī. His son Gharīḍ, his nephew Saʿīd b. Gharīḍ (Ibn ʿAsākir, *Taʾrīkh Dimashq* VI, 157), and his grandson Shuʿba were also known as poets. It should also be mentioned here that at the time of the Prophet the Jewish tribe of Qurayẓa in Medina could boast of several poets, fragments of whose works have been preserved in the biographies of Muḥammad.

29 | *Agh.* [1]VI, 87/8, XIX, 94/102, XXI, 91/3. Th. Nöldeke, *Beiträge*, pp. 52/86. Franz Delitzsch, *Jüdisch-arabische Poesien aus vormuhammedanischer Zeit*, Leipzig 1874. A commentary on the *qaṣīda* of Samaw'al from the *Ḥamāsa* by Aḥmad al-Sijāʿī (d. 1190/1776) is contained in Berl. 7465.

2. On the borders of the Syrian desert the Arabs were in constant touch with Christianity, which, in Syria, they encountered in the form of a state religion, and in Mesopotamia as the religion of the—culturally superior—Aramaic rural
21 population. | Because of this, the Ghassānids of Damascus had converted to Christianity at an early stage, while the Lakhmids of al-Ḥīra later also converted. In Muḥammad's time Christianity was widespread among the tribes of Quḍāʿa, Rabīʿa, Tamīm, and Ṭayyiʾ, while in the Hijaz and Najd most people had at least heard about this new religion. The Christian hermit or *rāhib* is a popular figure in poetry.

It may well be that the Christians, and in particular the ʿIbādīs of al-Ḥīra, should be given the credit for having been the first to use the Arabic script. They had also developed their own literature, with ʿAdī b. Zayd as its main representative. He belonged to a family of good standing that had been living in al-Ḥīra from time immemorial. His father had been brought up and educated at the Persian court and, after the death of the first Nuʿmān, he had temporarily been in charge of the government in al-Ḥīra, before the appointment of al-Mundhir. When the latter made himself loathed because of his greed, the former again assumed the civil administration in his stead. Together with the son of a *marzbān*, ʿAdī was brought up in the tradition of the Persian aristocracy, living at the court of al-Madāʾin where he was held in high esteem by King Kisrā b. Hurmuz (Khusraw II Parvīz). Apparently, the latter once even sent him on a diplomatic mission to Byzantium. This trip included a stop in Damascus, where his first poem is said to have seen the light of day. When he returned to his homeland his father and the *marzbān* who had educated him had both passed away. He could have taken the place of his father, but instead he preferred to live according to his fancy, wandering between al-Ḥīra,
al-Madāʾin, and the hunting-grounds of Jafīr. When al-Mundhir | was on his 30
deathbed, ʿAdī was the one who recommended to him his son al-Nuʿmān, whom he is said to have brought to the throne by deception, thus earning him the hatred of the Banū Marīna, who had taken the side of al-Mundhir's other
sons. | Once, when he was again in al-Madāʾin, his enemies succeeded in rais- 22
ing al-Nuʿmān's suspicion by the accusation that he had scornfully referred to al-Nuʿmān as "his creation." Using a fake invitation, al-Nuʿmān enjoined him to come to his territory and then threw him in prison. When the king of the Persians received news of this he sent an emissary to al-Ḥīra to obtain his release but, when the latter arrived, ʿAdī had already been murdered in prison.

Initially, ʿAdī's genre was the drinking song (*Agh.* [1]VI, 123). Even after 150 years, his poems were still popular among his countrymen. One of them, the ʿIbādī al-Qāsim b. al-Ṭufayl, introduced the caliph Walīd II, whose boon-companion he was, to ʿAdī's songs. This induced the ruler to come up with his own songs, which formed the basis for Islamic wine poetry. Often, however, ʿAdī also struck a more serious note, and it is in the surviving fragments of his poems that notions of death and the transient nature of existence predominate.

Agh. [1]II, 18/43, [2]17/40, [3]II, 97/154, *Khiz.* I, 184/6, *Jamhara* 103. His *dīwān* is also mentioned in *Khiz.* II, 20, 5.

A fair number of Christian ideas are also found in al-Nābigha and Zuhayr, and, especially, in Labīd and al-Aʿshā, who both lived some time after them, which suggests that Christianity played a silent role in the spiritual formation embodied in poetry. However, to be familiar with a religion does not imply that one adheres to it, and for this reason it was wrong for Cheikho to claim that almost all major poets of pagan times were Christians.

J. Wellhausen, *Skizzen und vorarb.* III, 197ff., L. Cheikho, Les poètes arabes
chrétiens. Poètes ante-islamiques. Qouss évêque de Najrān, *Études relig. phil.
et lit.* 1888, pp. 592/611; idem, *Shuʿarāʾ al-Naṣrāniyya. Les poètes arab. chré-
23 *tiens,* | fs. 1/6, Beirut 1890/1. Baumgartner, Die altarabische Dichtung und das
Christentum, *Stimmen aus Maria Laach* XLIV, pp. 325/46.

Chapter 10. The Beginnings of Arabic Prose 31

Besides poets, storytellers also played an important role in the nighly conversations or *samar* of pagan times, be it in the encampments of the wandering tribes or in the gatherings of the townsfolk. Of course, we do not possess any contemporary account of their stories, but reports in ancient works of literature, the *Kitāb al-aghānī* in particular, provide an authentic image of their spirit.

Storytellers drew their material in part from the fairytales and fables of international folklore, while also relying on the historical and legendary traditions of their own people and their neighbours. With his stories taken from heroic Persian sagas, al-Naḍr b. al-Ḥārith of Mecca is said to have competed successfully against the Prophet when the latter wanted to edify and convince his fellow citizens with legends. In the aftermath of the Battle of Badr, he paid for this with his life.

Of all the stories, it was the accounts of the great battles of old, the *Ayyām al-ʿarab*, that were the most popular. These stories were collected numerous times by later generations, especially by Abū ʿUbayda (see p. 102), and these have been preserved in great abundance in the *Kitāb al-aghānī* and in the commentaries on *Naqāʾid Jarīr wa-Farazdaq*. Here, too, the storytellers were more interested in suspense and glorifying their own tribe than in historical facts. A comparison between the Roman and Arab accounts of the story of Zenobia
is indicative of this. Here (*Agh.* ²xvi, p. 70ff.), Zenobia (Zaynab) is turned 24
into a minor character. Her Syrian general Zabday, whose name was probably more feared by the inhabitants of the border zone than that of the sovereign herself, has turned into her sister and now plays the leading part. The story is moved from Palmyra-Tadmur, which only receives a mention in passing, to two
unnamed cities along the Euphrates. The underground tunnel that connects 32
the two symbolises the hole in the wall through which Zenobia tried to escape from Aurelian. Odenatus's death at the banquet is replaced by the death of the enemy of the Zabbāʾ. As such, in the same way in which all the essential features were altered in this story, the facts in other tales may have been altered as well.

Redhouse, Were Zenobia and Zebbā identical?, *JRAS* XIX, 583/97, A. Müller, *Der Islam* I, 11ff.

Proverbs, many of which may very well date back to pagan times, may also be included amongst the traces of the earliest prose. These often allude to events that have long since been forgotten. Nevertheless, the learned compilers never failed to explain them, although they are not to be believed any more than the accounts that they tease out of many a recondite, ancient verse.

It is possible that collections of proverbs by individual tribes were already in existence at an early date; at least, there is a verse—ascribed to the pagan poet Bishr b. Abī Khāzim (Ibn Qutayba, *Poes.*, 145), but which Abū ʿUbayda declared must be by al-Ṭirimmāḥ (Suppl. I, 97)—which cites a proverb with an introductory "*wajadnā fī kitābi banī Tamīmin*" (Maydānī I, 137_{12}). Abū Hilāl al-ʿAskarī (d. 395/1005, see p. 126), *Jamharat al-amthāl*, Bombay 1306/7, and in the margin of al-Maydānī (d. 518/1124, see p. 289), *Majmaʿ al-amthāl* C. 1310; see Goldziher, ZDMG XXXII 355, *MSt* II, 205. On possible foreign borrowings see S. Fraenkel, ZDMG 46, 737ff; R. Pischel, ibid. 47, 86ff.

25 | It can also be assumed that the art of affecting the opinions or decisions of one's fellow men by means of well-chosen words flourished in ancient Arabia, an art that also bore the seeds of later literary growth.

I. Goldziher, Der Chaṭīb bei den Arabern, WZKM VI, 97/102.

SECOND SECTION

Muḥammad and His Time

Chapter 1. Muḥammad the Prophet

Arab paganism, with its primitive worship of power and raw animism, had left deeper spirits dissatisfied for a long time, especially those who had become acquainted with "higher" forms of religion such as Judaism and Christianity. | There are reports about a number of such *ḥanīfs*[1] who, turning away from 33
paganism, had nevertheless not gone so far as to join either of the monotheistic religions. Driven by a stronger kind of religious need, it was only Muḥammad, a Meccan trader, who succeeded in clarifying his relationship with the Allāh that was already known to his contemporaries as a universal god, over and above the deities,[2] and who urged his compatriots to worship no other god but Him. As such, he employed the practices of the *kāhin* or soothsayer that the people were familiar with and, just like him, he attributed his ecstatic states and ramblings to a companion spirit. Later, he identified this spirit as the angel Gabriel, whom he regarded as his intermediary with | God. Here, we need not 26
go into the history of his preaching that he had, while still in Mecca, adapted to match the style of Christian sermons, a style that Nestorian missionaries must have made him familiar with. His preaching brought him into conflict with his compatriots, for whom his struggle against idolatry represented a threat against the flourishing state of their business, dependent as it was on the festivals of the Meccan cult. He found a refuge, away from them, in neighbouring Yathrib, which had been torn apart by decades of internal strife, and where he was taken on as an arbitrator. From there he did not only conquer his hometown but, before his early death, his belief, Islam, was to win over or subjugate the greater part of northern Arabia and almost all of the East.

1 Fr. Buhl in *EI* II, 274/5.

2 Brockelmann, *Arch. f. Rel.* XXI, 1922, 99/121.

Th. Nöldeke, *Das Leben Muhammeds*, Hannover 1863. A. Sprenger, *Das Leben und die Lehre des Mohammed*, second edition, Berlin 1869. W. Muir, *The Life of Mahomet and history of Islam*, 4 vols., London 1858/61. L. Krehl, *Das Leben und die Lehre des Muhammed*, Part I, *Das Leben des Muhammed*, Leipzig 1884. H. Grimme, *Mohammed* (*Darst. a. d. Gebiete der nichtchristl. Religionsgesch. 7*), Münster 1892, 1895, on which Snouck Hurgronje, *Revue de l'hist. des rel.* XXX (1893), 48/70, 149/78, *Verspr. Geschr.* I, 321ff. Harris Birkeland, *Muhammed Allahs Sendebud*, Oslo 1942.

Chapter 2. The Qur'ān

| In the earliest period of his religious activity, the Prophet emptied his soul 34
in true ecstasy; in passionately emotional, and, for the most part, short and incoherent phrases in *saj*ʿ, i.e. the rhyming prose of the *kāhin*. Later, when he transformed himself more and more from an ecstatic into a preacher, reciting his admonitions in long phrases that were often adorned with stories from the Old Testament and the Haggada, he continued to employ this form. Traditions
about Muḥammad's life in Mecca do not provide us with any firm | indications 27
on which to base a chronology, which is why the Meccan suras can only be classified, on the basis of stylistic features, roughly into three groups; suras that are characterised by the frequent use of the divine name al-Raḥmān are placed in the middle, between the earliest and the latest ones. This classification is complicated by the fact that many suras were apparently only put together by later compilers, joining various elements that were initially independent. In contrast, other suras, especially the narratives, leave the definite impression of homogeneous compositions.

| In Medina, on the other hand, where the Prophet assumes the role of a 35
supreme ruler and acts as a legislator, his sermons and commandments, though preserving a rhyme that is badly maintained, became an unadulterated prose whose style he had to invent from scratch, even though he did not have any proper linguistic skills or schooling. The Medinan suras mostly involve events with which we are more or less familiar, so that it is possible to place the majority of these in chronological order. His observations and admonitions often indulged in violent polemics against the Jews and sceptics within his own community. In addition, he issued decrees on all ritual matters, on civil and penal law, in accordance with the needs of the moment. Similarly, he took also care of the business of his harem, which he also traced back to divine inspiration.

Even though some of the revelations may have been committed to writing during the Prophet's lifetime, it is certain that they were principally transmitted orally. However, when the source of these revelations, which were all-important for the continuance of the flock, ran dry upon the Prophet's death,
| it was decided that all of the parts and pieces that were still available should 28
be written down for posterity. It is, however, doubtful that the decisive battle against Musaylima in the year 12/633, and in which many of those who had first-hand knowledge of the Qur'ān had perished, was the cause of this, as maintained by tradition, as a number of suras had apparently been joined together into groups at an earlier stage. At the top of the text, each of these groups was marked by a letter from the alphabet, by which they were also held together in

later times. It seems that the Ḥ-M group must have been particularly old and important, so much so that even Ibn Masʿūd, who had separated and arranged all the others on the basis of their length, kept these together and called them the *Dībāj al-Qurʾān*. Yet it was not until the time of the caliph ʿUmar that the young Medinan Zayd b. Thābit, who had previously served the Prophet on several occasions as a scribe, received the order to collect all these records. His work remained in his possession and was bequeathed to his daughter Ḥafṣa. While this collection appears to have been composed of loose leaves only, Zayd probably created a second one as well, in which he arranged the suras according to their length, starting with the longest one, with the exception of the Fātiḥa, which was placed at the beginning. Others, too, collected the suras on the basis of the same principle: Ubayy b. Kaʿb, Miqdād b. ʿAmr, ʿAbdallāh b. Masʿūd, and ʿAbdallāh al-Ashʿarī. The latter two individuals distributed their texts in Kufa and Basra where they worked, while the people of Damascus followed Ubayy and those of Homs Miqdād.

However, disparities between the texts in circulation frequently gave rise to disputes. This is why Ḥudhayfa, the conqueror of Nihāwand, much annoyed by such disputes during his military campaigns in Armenia, asked the caliph ʿUthmān to ensure the official recognition of a standard edition. Again it was Zayd who was entrusted with the task, in which he was assisted by three
29 prominent | members of the Quraysh. Falling back on the leaves that were in Ḥafṣa's possession, they must have based themselves on Zayd's collection, copies of which were then sent to Basra, Kufa, and Damascus, where they were duplicated. Without there being any need to revert to more violent means, this text soon acquired canonical status; only in Kufa were the people said to have continued to use the text of Ibn Masʿūd for a time. The imperfect script nevertheless gave ample opportunity for variant readings, the more so as its vocalisa-
36 tion | had not yet been specified in any way. This was the job of the reciters of the Qurʾān, about whom we shall learn in the second book.

For the literature, see Suppl. I, 64, 937, with H. Speyer, *Die biblischen Erzählungen im Qorʾān*, Gräfenhainichen n.d. [1939].

Chapter 3. Labīd and al-Aʿshā

In the period of transition from paganism to Islam there were two eminent poets, both of whom had touched upon religious themes even before the coming of Muḥammad, one of whom was to adopt the latter's teachings.

1. Abū ʿAqīl Labīd b. Rabīʿa came from a distinguished family of the Banū Jaʿfar, a branch of the Kilāb, which belonged to the Banū ʿĀmir, a subdivision of the Hawāzin tribe. Since he died of old age in the year 40/660 or soon after, with his age something to which he refers from time to time in his poetry, he may have been born around 560. In his younger days he played an active role in the feuds of his tribe, while later he prided himself on having rendered much good service through his verbal prowess. Thus, even while a famous poet he
remained faithful to his kinsmen and rejected the calling of a | minstrel. When 30
the Prophet rose to power in Medina, Labīd was part of a delegation of his tribe that went there, and which put its affiliation with the new state into effect. This happened in the wake of a private mission to the Prophet on behalf of his uncle Arbad that had taken place the previous year, and which had left him full of enthusiasm about the Prophet's teachings. He then stayed on in Medina before moving to Kufa during the caliphate of ʿUmar, where he died.

| His works, one of which is included among the *Muʿallaqāt*, are usually 37
counted among the best that Bedouin poetry has produced, and whose traditional themes he ably presents in an attractive fashion. Occasional religious overtones give his poems additional force. The myth that he did not compose any more poetry after his conversion to Islam is disproved by various passages from his *dīwān* that were apparently inspired by the Qurʾān, even if these do contain some interpolations. From among the editions of his *dīwān*, which were prepared by the very best philologists, only that by ʿAlī b. ʿAbdallāh al-Ṭūsī, a student of Ibn al-ʿArabī, d. 231/844 (see p. 116)[1], has survived, with a commentary on the first 20 poems.

Dīwān Labīd al-ʿĀmirī riwāyat al-Ṭūṣī. Al-Ṭabʿa al-ūlā bi-ḥasab al-nuskha al-mawjūda ʿinda tābiʿihi al-Shaykh Yūsuf Ḍiyāʾ al-Dīn al-Khālidī al-Maqdisī, Vienna 1297/1880. A. v. Kremer, Über die Gedichte des Labyd, *SBWA, phil.-hist. Cl.* XCVIII, ii, 565/605. *Die Gedichte des Lebīd, nach der Wiener Ausg. übers. und mit Anmm. versehn, aus dem Nachlass des Dr. A. Huber, hsg. von* C. Brockelmann, Leiden 1891. Dīwān *des Lebīd, nach den Hdss. zu Strassburg und Leiden mit den Fragmenten, Übersetzung und Biographie des Dichters aus*

1 *Fihrist* 71, Ibn al-Anbārī, *Nuzhat al-alibbāʾ*, 241, Flügel, *Die grammat. Schulen*, 256.

dem Nachlasse des Dr. A. Huber, hsg. von C. Brockelmann, Leiden 1891. There are two thusfar unused MSS, one from Mecca dated 1287, and another one from the Maghreb dated 1293, Cairo ^{2}III, 144.

31 | 2. Al-Aʿshā Maymūn b. Qays of the Qays b. Thaʿlaba tribe was born in Manfūḥa in al-Yamāma, which is where his grave was also said to be in later times. Like his sovereign and patron Ḥawdha b. ʿAlī al-Ḥanafī he was Christian, and he also paid frequent visits to the bishop of Najrān; his *rāwī* Yaḥyā b. Mattā was an ʿIbādī from al-Ḥīra. However, al-Aʿshā's Christian belief was not deep, and even though he spoke at times of one God, the last judgment, and resurrection, he stood firmly in the poetical tradition of his time. As a travelling minstrel he traversed the whole of Arabia, from Hadramawt to al-Ḥīra, honoured and richly rewarded as a panegyrist, and feared for the sting of his mocking poems. What people particularly admired in his writings, apart from the music of his language and its smart versification, were his descriptions of wine and the wild ass, the refinement of his praise, and the sharpness of his wit. However, his song in praise of the Prophet, which was appreciated the most by posterity and which was therefore also transmitted outside of his *dīwān*, has been proven to be spurious.

Agh. ^{1}VIII, 77/87, ^{2}74/84. *Dīwān*, collected by Thaʿlab, d. 291/904, Esc. 303 (photograph from Thorbecke's estate in the library of the DMG). *Carmen Ashae arab. et sueth. propos.* M.F. Brag *et* T. Thorelius, Lund 1842. H. Thorbecke, Al Aʿshās Lobgedicht auf Muhammed, in *Morgenl. Forsch.* (Festschrift for Fleischer), Leipzig 1875.

Chapter 4. Ḥassān b. Thābit

was born in Yathrib, later Medina, and belonged to the tribe of Khazraj. In his youth he had tried his luck as a wandering poet, in both al-Ḥīra and Damascus.
| When the Messenger of God settled in his own hometown as a ruler, Ḥassān 38
b. Thābit soon made himself indispensable as a court poet. Even though, at
heart, Muḥammad had a strong aversion to poets and their art, | because they 32
often were a part of the delegations to Medina by which individual Arab tribes displayed their conversion and submission, he needed someone who could answer them. The fact that Ḥassān did not hold a particularly honourable station within the community was a result of his weak character, which manifested itself most glaringly in his extramarital affair with ʿĀʾisha. He cannot have been very old at that time, since during the campaigns following the murder of ʿUthmān he was still intervening with various fiery stanzas. He died in 54/674. On the whole his poems, with their simple and sometimes even common language, are not of a very high calibre, and if they remained popular for such a long time, this was solely due to the fact that praise of the Prophet was their central theme.

Agh. IV[1,2] 2/17, [3]134/70, XIV[1,2] 2/9. *Dīwān* Tunis 1281, based on dictations by Muḥammad b. Ḥabīb, d. 245/859, Berl. 7507; other collections Paris 3004, Br. Mus. 1065, Pet. AM 258, AS 3916, Köpr. 1256, Top Kapu 2613 (*RSO* IV, 721), Cairo[1] IV, 244, [2]III, 126; individual poems Berl. 7518. H. Hirschfeld, Prolegomena to an edition of the *dīwān* of Hassan b. Thabit, *Transact. Congr. Or.* London 1892, II, 99/103.

Chapter 5. Kaʿb b. Zuhayr

had inherited his talent as a poet from his father (see p. 15). He flourished during the time Islam conquered the whole of Arabia in its unstoppable, victorious
march. Both his tribe, Muzayna, and his brother Bujayr adopted the new faith,
and as such the poet made fun of this in mocking verse. When Muḥammad
learned of this he pronounced the death sentence on him. In order not to fall
victim to a random fanatic, Kaʿb now had to obtain the Prophet's pardon at any
33 39 price. || Through a daring gambit, he succeeded in doing so. Out of gratitude,
he composed a song in praise of the Prophet, for which the latter rewarded him
by giving him his personal cloak. Called *Bānat Suʿād*, after the poem's opening
words, or *Qaṣīdat al-burda*, after the cloak by which he was rewarded, this one
poem earned him eternal fame.

Agh. XV, [1]147/51, [2]140/4. *Kaab ben Zohair, carmen panegyricum in laudem Muhammedis etc.* ed. G.J. Lette, Leiden 1748, *C. b. Z. carmen in laudem Muhammedis dictum etc.* ed. G.G. Freytag, Bonn 1822. Commentaries: 1. Ibn Durayd, d. 321/933, Berl. 7489.—2. al-Tabrīzī, d. 502/1108, Berl. 7490/1, abstract Ind. Off. 802.—3. ʿĪsā b. ʿAbd al-ʿAzīz al-Jazūlī, d. 607/1201 (p. 308), Algiers 1830,$_{2}$.—4. ʿAbdallāh b. Yūsuf b. Hishām, d. 761/1360 (II, 23), also Berl. Brill M. 198, ed. I. Guidi, Leipzig 1871/4, with glosses by Ibrāhīm al-Bājūrī in the margin, Cairo see Suppl.—5. Bakr b. Ḥijja, d. 834/1433 (II, 17), Berl. 7493.—6. al-Suyūṭī, d. 911/1505, Berl. 7495, Brill M. 214,$_{2}$, Copenhagen 249.—7. Aḥmad b. Muḥammad al-Haytamī, d. 973/1565, see Suppl., also Berl. Brill M. 167.—8. Ṣāliḥ b. Ṣiddīq al-Khazrajī, ca. 975/1567 (Suppl. II, 555), Esc.[2] 304,$_{1}$.—9. al-Qāriʾ al-Harawī, d. 1014/1606, Berl. 7498/9, Munich 886, fol. 209b.—10. ʿAbdallāh al-Hītī, Berl. 7596.—11. *al-Isʿād* by Ibrāhīm b. Abi ʾl-Qāsim b. Aḥmad b. Ibrāhīm b. Muḥammad b. ʿĪsā, Patna II, 445,$_{2621,7}$.—12. Luṭf ʿAlī, Berl. 7500.—13. Muḥammad b. Aḥmad Suʿūdī, Munich 542.—14. ʿAbdallāh al-Mawṣilī, Paris 3078,$_{1}$.—15. Muḥammad b. Ḥumayd al-Kaffawī, 12th cent. (Ahlw. IV, 544), ibid., 2.—16. Abū Bakr b. ʿUmar b. ʿAbd al-ʿAzīz, Berl. Brill M. 298, 2, who also has a work on music, ibid. 1 (= Suppl. I, 37 z. 7?).—17. Anon., Berl. 7942, 7501/2. *Takhmīs*: 1. Maḥmūd al-Najjār, ca. 1088/1677, Berl. 7503.—2. Ṣadaqatallāh al-Qāhirī, d. 1115/1703, Berl. 7502.—3. Shaʿbān b. Muḥammad al-Qurashī, d. 828/1452 (II, 180), Algiers 1830,$_{3}$.—4. al-Saktānī, ibid. 4.—5. Shams al-Dīn al-Badamāṣī, Paris 3080,$_{1}$.—6. Anon., Goth. 2227, Paris 3248,$_{4,5}$, Ind. Off. 1044/6.—*Tashṭīr* ʿAlī Āghā al-Jalīlī, d. ca. 1180/1766, and ʿAbd al-Razzāq b. al-Jundī, d. 1189/1775, Berl. 7505.

| Chapter 6. Mutammin b. Nuwayra 34

Mālik b. Nuwayra, chieftain of the tribe of Yarbūʿ, a subdivision of the Tamīm, adopted Islam and was appointed by Muḥammad as a tax collector. But after Muḥammad's death he was one of the first to join the uprising through which most of the tribes tried to break away from Muslim domination. When Khālid b. al-Walīd invaded his territory Mālik surrendered after a brief fight. But even though Mālik adopted Islam, the general broke his word and had him executed. His brother Mutammim bewailed his death in deeply emotional elegies, several of which have been wholly or partially preserved.

Agh. XIV, [1]66/76, [2]63/64, *Khiz.* I, 234/8, *Mufaḍḍ.* no. 8 (9), *Jamhara* p. 141. Nöldeke, *Beitr.* 87/151.

40 | Chapter 7. Al-Khansāʾ

The poetic genre of the *marthiya* seems to have first developed out of the inchoate wailings of women, which is also why its cultivation remained primarily in the hands of women. Among these, al-Khansāʾ attained the highest fame. Her real name was Tumāḍir (as in Abū Tamāḍir or Tamāḍur, *Khiz.* III, 403, 22ff.) and she belonged to the tribe of Sulaym, a branch of the Qays, which pitched its tents from the northern Hijaz all the way to Najd. When she was a girl, Durayd b. al-Ṣimma, the most eminent man of her tribe and himself a poet (*Agh.* IX, [1]1/20, [2]2/19, Ibn Qutayba, *Poes.*, 470, *Aṣmaʿiyyāt* no. 8, 15, see Suppl. I, p. 938 ad 70), asked for her hand in marriage but was turned down. Later, she married Mirdās b. Abī ʿĀmir—whose son ʿAbbās (*Agh.* XIII, 164/72, 262/70,
35 Ibn Qutayba, *Poes.*, 467) was also | a poet—and, when he died, ʿAbdallāh b. ʿAbd al-ʿUzzā. Both of her brothers, Muʿāwiya and Ṣakhr, had been killed in pagan times, and as a poetess she owes her fame primarily to her elegies on them. Shortly after the Battle of Badr she settled in Mecca. When, later in life, she went to visit ʿUmar and ʿĀʾisha in Medina, she had already reached the age of 50. The year of her death is uncertain. Her poetical talent was inherited by her daughter ʿAmra, several of whose poems have been preserved in her mother's *dīwān*.

Agh. XIII, [1]136/47, [2]29/44, Nöldeke, *Beitr.* 152/82. *Anīs al-julasāʾ fī dīwān al-Khansāʾ*, Beirut 1888, ed. L. Cheikho, Beirut 1895, ed. and French tr. by P.V. de Coppier, Beirut 1889. *Riyāḍ al-adab fī marāthī shawāʿir al-ʿArab*, ed. Cheikho, Beirut 1896. Idem, *Diwan de trois poétesses arabes, Ḫirniq, sœur de Tarafa, Amrah fille d'al-Ḫansāʿ et Laila l'Aḫialite*, Beirut 1897.

Chapter 8. Abū Miḥjan and al-Ḥuṭay'a

A younger contemporary of Muḥammad was Abū Miḥjan—whose real name is sometimes given as ʿAmr, though at other times as Mālik or ʿAbdallāh b. Ḥabīb—of the tribe of Thaqīf in the Hijaz. When the Prophet, after his capture of Mecca, also wanted to conquer this tribe, Abū Miḥjan took part in the defence of al-Ṭāʾif, the capital. However, when his tribe surrendered he converted to Islam, on 9 Ramaḍān/December 630. Under ʿUmar he participated in the war against the Persians, in which he distinguished himself in the Battle of Qādisiyya.[1] His love for wine, for which he had incurred a prison sentence earlier in his life, sealed his fate once more: because of his constant relapses he was banished by ʿUmar to Bāṣiʿ, i.e. Maṣṣawa on the Ethiopian coast,[2] where he died not long after.

| From among his otherwise quite conventional poems, his winesongs— 36
which have been only partially preserved and in which he defiantly opposes the prohibition—are the most famous of all.

Agh. XXI, ^{1}210/20, ^{2}137/42, *Dīwān* by Ibn al-Aʿrābī, d. 231/846, Krafft 176; by Abū Hilāl al-ʿAskarī, d. 395/1005, AS 388, Cairo III, 200, Leid. 672, ed. C. Landberg, *Primeurs arabes*, fs. I, Leiden 1886, L. Abel, ibid. 1887.

2. Al-Ḥuṭay'a, "the midget," was the nickname of Jarwal b. Aws. He actually belonged to the Banū ʿAbs, though he only counted himself as a member of that tribe when it suited him and did likewise for other tribes. As a freeloading, wandering bard he blackmailed the elite of his time into paying for his upkeep—through flattering eulogies and, even more so, out of fear of his caustic wit. He caused so much harm with this that ʿUmar eventually threw him in jail. He is said to have died in the year 30/650. Among the ancient poets, he owed his fame primarily to his mastery of the *hijāʾ*, which also ensured the preservation of his poems.

1. Goldziher, Der Dīwān des Garwal b. Aus al-Hutej'a, ZDMG XLVI, 1/53, XLVII, 43/85, 163/201, also as offprint.

---

1 A. Müller, *Der Islam* I, 240.

2 L. Caetani, *Annali del Islam*, anno 16, III, § 348n.

Chapter 9. Minor Poets

1. Abū Dhu'ayb Khuwaylid b. Khālid al-Qaṭīl was the most important poet of the Hudhayl tribe (see Suppl. I, 42). He took part in the wars of conquest, went with ʿAbdallāh b. Saʿd to Africa in the year 26/646, and died some years later
42 in Egypt while he and | ʿAbdallāh b. al-Zubayr were on their way to the caliph ʿUthmān to inform him of the conquest of Carthage. His five sons had died one year before him in Egypt of the plague and are bewailed by him in a song of mourning.

37 | *Agh.* VI, [1]58/69,[2] 56/62, [3]I 264/79. *Khiz.* I, 203; on cod. Landberg of his *Dīwān* see Goldziher in Fischer, ZDMG XLIX, 679, recension by al-Sukkarī, Berl. Brill M. 129. *Marthiya* for his sons *Jamh.* 128, Ref. 221 = Leipz. 510.

2. Al-Shammākh b. Ḍirār of the Dhubyān tribe was a contemporary of al-Ḥuṭay'a, who supposedly called him the greatest poet of the Ghaṭafān. He had taken part in the Battle of Qādisiyya and in the campaign to Azerbaijan. Muḥammad b. Sallām al-Jumaḥī (d. 232/847) ranked him in his *Kitāb ṭabaqāt al-shuʿarā'* (ed. Hell, 26, 29) in the third class, together with Abū Dhu'ayb, al-Nābigha, and Labīd. His main strength lay in the description of the wild ass and the bow, as well as in improvisation and *rajaz*.

Agh. VIII, [1]109/9, [2]97/107, *Dīwān* Leid. 575, Cairo[1] IV, 247, [2]III, 134.

3. Suḥaym was a black Nubian slave of the Banu'l-Ḥasḥās who died in the year 40/660.

Agh. XX, [1,2]2/9, *Fawāt* I, 166, *Khiz.* I, 273, *Dīwān* Leipz. 505, ʿUm. 118,$_2$, 5756, ʿĀṭif 2777 (*MFO* V, 496), Yeni 1187.

4. Abu 'l-Aswad al-Du'alī is particularly famous for his connections with ʿAlī. In Basra he was respected as a traditionist and a jurisconsult. This is why, when his governor ʿAbdallāh b. ʿAbbās went to the Hijaz, ʿAlī appointed him the former's substitute, and, when ʿAlī finally came to Iraq himself, Abu 'l-Aswad accompanied him in the Battle of Ṣiffīn, although later he made his own peace with Muʿāwiya. His death is placed by some in the year of the plague, 69/688, while according to others he died under ʿUmar II in 99/101–717/20. In Arabic literary history he is the legendary inventor of grammar (see al-Jumaḥī, *Ṭabaqāt al-shuʿarā'* 5, 15ff., Ibn ʿAsākir VII, 111,$_{17}$ff.), which is why the famous philologist
38 Ibn al-Jinnī (d. 392/ | 1002, p. 125) personally copied his poems. A copy of this

copy, made by one of his students when he was still alive, is extant. Apart from this, these poems are not of a very high calibre and do not provide us with any noteworthy historical pickings.

Agh. [1]XI, 105/24, [2]101/19, *Khiz.* I, 136/8; *Dīwān* Leipz. 505, and a *qaṣīda* Berl. 7519,3.

43 | Chapter 10. Two Forgeries

1. The manuscript Ref. 33 (Leipz. 505) contains, in addition to the two *dīwāns* just mentioned, another, supposedly by Abū Ṭālib, the uncle of Muḥammad, and the poems contained within it deal with relations between the Prophet and the Quraysh. Although some of the songs, whose tone is in accordance with the real situation in which Abū Ṭālib found himself, may actually be authentic, most of them were invented in later times. People did this because they wanted to embellish the earliest episodes in Muḥammad's biography with verses of the kind that were in abundant supply for the Medinan period. On top of this was the fact that the ʿAlids had an interest in presenting the relationship between their forebear and the Prophet in as favourable a light as possible. The fact that they still represent the Banū Hāshim as being unified instead of having split into the ʿAbbāsids and the ʿAlids is an argument in favour of the advanced age of these songs. This is also why Ibn Isḥāq incorporated most of them into his biography of the Prophet.

Th. Nöldeke, *ZDMG* XVIII, 220ff.

2. The poems and sayings ascribed to the caliph ʿAlī are more recent still. Nevertheless, ʿAlī's poetical talent is well documented. However, it is doubtful that his *dīwān* contains any authentic pieces. In the majority of them Shīʿī fabrications are so conspicuous that they were easily spotted by Sunnī critics.

39 | ʿAlī's *dīwān* was quoted as early as Ibn Qutayba, d. 276/889, *ʿUyūn* III, $5_{,7}$ff. The Turkish commentator Mustaqīmzāde Saʿdaddīn Sulaymān (d. 1202/1788) ascribes the poems to al-Murtaḍā (d. 436/1044, see p. 404), see *JA* s. IV, v. 13, p. 7.—*Ali ben abi Taleb carmina arabice et lat. ed. et notis illustr.* G. Kuypers, Leiden 1745. *Dīwān* Būlāq 1251, Cairo 1276, 1311, Bombay 1883, under the title *Anwār al-ʿuqūl min ashʿār waṣiyy al-rasūl*, collected by Saʿdī b. Tājī in the year 897/1492, Vienna 448, Br. Mus. 577/8 (cf. Ewald, *WZKM* II, 192), Bodl. I, 1204, Copenhagen $242_{,10}$ Kazan 167, AS 3937/42, Patna I, $195_{,749}$, selection, ibid. 204, Persian comm. by Ḥusayn al-Maybudhī, composed in 890/1485, Leid. 579, Br. Mus. 579, 1665, introduction only Gotha 2228, Turkish comm. (translated from Maybudhī?)
44 by Saʿd al-Dīn b. Sulaymān, Būlāq 1255 (*JA* 1845, ii, 654, 186). | Individual poems Berl. 7513/5. *Al-Qaṣīda al-Zaynabiyya*, presumedly by Ṣāliḥ b. ʿAbd al-Quddūs (Suppl. I, 110), Berl. 7511/8, with comm. by ʿAbd al-Muʿṭī al-Simillāwī (Suppl. II, 444), *al-Tuffāḥa al-wardiyya*, in Berl. Brill M. 114, Alex. Adab 26/40 (see Suppl.), Brill, Cat. pér. no. 412, Cairo 1306, different from Cairo ^{1}IV, 219, ^{2}III, 391, see *Transact. IXth Congr. Or.*, London 1893, II, 155, Goldziher, *Abh.* I,

126.—*Alis 100 Sprüche, arab. u. persisch paraphrasiert von Rešīdeddīn Waṭwāṭ* (d. after 578/1182, see p. 275), *nebst einem doppelten Anhang arab. Sprüche, hsg. übers. und mit Anmm. begleitet von* H.L. Fleischer, Leipzig 1837. Persian comm. by Maybudhī, Br. Mus. 1665, by Muḥammad al-ʿUmarī, Paris $3954_{,1}$.—*Ghurar al-ḥikam wa-durar al-kalim*, in alphabetical order by ʿAbd al-Wāḥid al-Āmidī al-Tamīmī (d. 436/1144, *Rawḍāt al-jannāt* 464), Berl. 8861/2, Paris $2502_{,14}$, Brit. Mus. 721, Ind. Off. 162 (see Suppl.).—Collection of sayings by Ibn Durayd (see p. 111), Paris 3971.—*Sharḥ al-khuṭba al-Ṭaṭajiyya* by Muḥammad Kāẓim b. Muḥammad Qāsim, Patna I, 201.—*Kitāb jafr*, a prophecy about things to come until the end of the world, Krafft 363, *Bayān mamālik Ifranj*, a prophecy in verse, ibid. 364.—*ʿAqīda*, Paris 667.—*Ḥijāb ʿaẓīm*, amulet, ibid. 1072, *al-Ṣaḥīfa al-kāmila*, a prayer book (also attributed to Zayn al-ʿĀbidīn, Suppl. I, 76), ibid. 1174/5, Patna I, $155_{,1471/8}$. *Urjūza* about the phases of the moon, Paris $2292_{,6}$.

The Period of the Umayyads

Chapter 1. General Characteristics

The first days of Umayyad rule, with their seemingly endless state of war, left no room for poetry to develop. However, when the heavy storms that had shaken the state founded by ʿUmar to its very core had finally died down, the life of the Arabs entered calmer waters. With his talents as a ruler and strong-arm tactics, ʿAbd al-Malik succeeded in unifying the tottering Islamic empire once again and overcoming the dissenting powers that would seal the fate of the ʿAbbāsid empire later on. While preserving the Arab national character, he allowed the different tribes their independence on minor points, which were then all the more vigorously maintained. So, despite the fact that conditions had changed in many ways, Arab features of life were strongly maintained and had room to develop once again.[1]

45 | Under these circumstances poetry, too, went through a second blossoming of some importance. But the energy and boldness of the works of the pre-Islamic poets was gone. Although their descendants still followed the old format of the *qaṣīda*, they gave up any pretence at originality. The uniform technique of the ancient poets leaving little room for innovation any-
41 way, | from the time that it froze into mannerism, all liberty to experiment had vanished. However, for most of the poets from the time of the Umayyads, the *qaṣīda* merely and inevitably formed the basis for poems composed in celebration of an event, poems that take a stand on contemporary issues, ones they often depict in a lively manner.

We know much more about this second blooming than about the intrinsically more appealing and important poetry of pre-Islamic times. Information about the conditions in which the poets lived had been gathered and recorded within a century, by scholars from the time of the ʿAbbāsids. These were also able to produce editions of a much greater reliability than that which was possible for earlier poems.

1 Cf. the apt description of the time of the Umayyads in al-Jāḥiẓ, *al-Bayān* ii, 154, 16.

 | DOI 10.1163/9789004326262_005

Chapter 2. ʿUmar b. Abī Rabīʿa

Up to this time, the tribe of Quraysh in Mecca had played hardly any role in poetry. However, in the first century of the Hijra there arose in their midst a poet whose skill was already—and deservedly—recognised by his contemporaries, | and which the modern Arab world has learned to appreciate once 46
again after a long period of relative neglect.

ʿUmar b. Abī Rabīʿa came from the famous house of Makhzūm. His father ʿAbdallāh, who was one of the richest traders of Mecca, had been appointed the governor of Janad in Southern Arabia, where he remained in office until ʿUmar's death, and, according to some, also under ʿUthmān. A female prisoner of war from Hadramawt bore him his son ʿUmar, supposedly on the same day that the caliph ʿUmar was murdered. This intrinsically dubious synchronism is proven completely false by the assertion of Ḥasan al-Baṣrī (see p. 66) that is linked with it. Nevertheless, he may still have been born around the year 23/643. ʿUmar seems to have spent his youth in Medina but | moved to Mecca at an 42
early age, remaining in the city of his forebears until the end of his life. As a son of his father he had no material worries, and the sense of honour that drew his relatives into the wars raging during this period had no attraction for him. As a free man he enjoyed life to the full, pouring the emotions of his intense lovelife into songs. These are so lively and full of expression that they must have come from personal experiences, even though legend may have added various aspects, such as the presentation of his brother as a grumpy puritan, or the caliphs ʿAbd al-Malik and Sulaymān treating him disdainfully, or even banishing him, because he supposedly had the temerity to assault one of the female members of their household during the hustle and bustle of the celebrations concluding the pilgrimage.[1] There may, however, be some credence in the report that the pious ʿUmar II summoned him and his comrade in such arts, al-Aḥwaṣ, both in shackles, to his court in Damascus in order to demand they halt their activities. While al-Aḥwaṣ was banished to the Dahlak Islands in the Red Sea, ʿUmar was released on the solemn promise that he would forever foreswear his art. Since he must have been over 70 years old at the time, it will not have been too hard for him to abide by his word. He must have died soon after, around the year 101/712.

| ʿUmar's poems are devoted purely to love. We do not know if he was 47
the first to turn this theme—in the ancient *qaṣīda* only allowed in the *nasīb*—into an independent art-form. What is certain, however, was that he is

1 Apparently Sulaymān sent him to al-Ṭāʾif for the duration of his pilgrimage following his composition of a frivolous verse. Al-Marzubānī, *al-Muwashshaḥ*, 203, 14ff.

the first to have brought it fully to life, the reason being that it was the only
43 artform that | was suitable for him. He usually sketches small, attractive genre scenes without a background of deeper passion. The full metre employed by the Bedouin poets did not suit his art as well as did the more pliable *khafīf* or *ramal*. They lent his poems that pleasant melody that would soon carry them on the wings of songs throughout the Arab world.

Agh. I, ^{1}30/97, ^{2}28/94, ^{3}61/247, Ibn Khall. 463, *Khiz.* I, 240. *Dīwān* (MSS also Patna I, $197_{,775}$) Cairo 1311. P. Schwarz, *ʿUmar ibn abī Rebīʿa, ein arabischer Dichter der Umajjadenzeit*, Diss. Leipzig 1893.

Chapter 3. Other Poets in Arabia

1. ʿUbaydallāh b. Qays al-Ruqayyāt, who apparently acquired that sobriquet because of his love for three women all called Ruqayya, mostly used his art in the service of politics, despite often being mentioned in the same breath as ʿUmar as a composer of love poems. See Suppl. I, 78.

Agh. IV, ^{1}155/67, ^{2}154/66, ^{3}V, 73/100. *Dīwān* Cairo ^{1}IV, 235, ^{2}III, 111, ʿĀšir Ef. 746, comm. by al-Sukkarī (see p. 108), Cairo ^{1}IV, 271.

| 2. Qays b. Dharīḥ (see Suppl. I, 81), of the tribe of Bakr b. ʿAbd Manāt, was the 48
foster brother of Ḥusayn b. ʿAlī. He lived in Medina and died in 68/687.

Agh. VIII ^{1}112/37, ^{2}107/32, *Fawāt* II, 135. A *qaṣīda* with a commentary by Abū ʿAbdallāh Muḥammad al-Rashīdī al-Umawī (9th cent.), Esc.^{2} 132 (continuation of 409), different from Berl. $7519_{,1}$, see P. Schwarz, *Escurialstudien zur arab. Lit. und Sprach*, Stuttgart 1922, 17ff., al-Qālī *Amālī* II, 318/21. According to al-Jāḥiẓ, *Agh.* ^{1}I, $169_{,20}$, all love songs of unknown origin in which there was mention of a Lubnā were ascribed to him, in the same way in which all songs dedicated to Laylā were ascribed to Majnūn b. ʿĀmir.

3. Qays b. Mulawwaḥ, Majnūn b. ʿĀmir apparently died around 70/689; see Suppl. I, 81.

Agh. I, ^{1}167/89, ^{2}161/82, ^{3}II, 1/96, II, ^{1}2/18, ^{2}2/17, *Fawāt* II, 136. *Dīwān*, collected and explained by Abū Bakr al-Wālibī | (not al-Wālī), Berl. 7520, Copenhagen 44
285, Pet. AM 260/1, Ind. Off. 804, Paris 3672, Algiers 1818/9, Cairo^{1} IV, 252, ^{2}III, 147, AS 3788, Köpr. 1265 (Rescher, *MSOS* XIV, 9), print. Beirut 1882, C., 1300, 1309 etc.

4. Jamīl b. ʿAbdallāh al-ʿUdhrī, see Suppl. I, 78, III, 1193.

Agh. VII ^{1}77/110, ^{2}72/104, ^{3}VIII 90/154. Poems in Berl. $7523_{,2}$. *Dīwān* ed. Bashīr Yamūt, Beirut 1934.

5. Kuthayyiru ʿAzzata, see Suppl. I, 79.

Agh. VIII ^{1}27/44, ^{2}25/42, XI, ^{1}46/52, ^{2}43/55. *Khiz.* II, 381/3, Shahrastānī I, 111, Ibn Khall. 519. A poem with a commentary by ʿAbdallāh Muḥammad b. Ḥasan b. Makhlūf al-Rashīdī al-Umawī (9th cent., see above) Esc. 409. Individual *qaṣīda*s Berl. 7574,.—Fr. Gabrieli, Rapporti tra poeta e rāwī: echi di Gamīl in Kuṯayyir ʿAzzah, *ZDMG* 93, 161/8.

6. Medina was also the hometown of al-Aḥwaṣ ʿAbdallāh b. Muḥammad al-Anṣārī. Because of his amorous escapades with the wives of prominent Medinans under Sulaymān b. ʿAbd al-Malik he was captured and publicly made an example of by the latter's governor, Abū Bakr b. Muḥammad b. ʿAmr. Together with ʿUmar b. Abī Rabīʿa he was summoned to Damascus during the
49 reign of | ʿUmar II and banished to the Dahlak Islands. He was pardoned by Yazīd II and returned to Damascus, where he died around the year 110/728.

Agh. IV, [1,2]40/59, [3]IV, 224/68, VI, 254/59, VI, [1]52/6, [2]51/6, *Khiz.* I, 232/4; *qaṣīda* Berl. 7528.

7. Yūnus al-Kātib was a composer of poems of Persian descent who was on the payroll of the *dīwān* in Medina and who had learned music from Surayj b. Muḥriz and al-Gharīḍ. During a business trip to Syria he made the acquaintance of the then-prince Walīd b. Yazīd (see p. 62), who called him to his court
45 | when he ascended the throne in 125/742. It is not known what happened to him when the latter died suddenly in the following year.

Agh. IV [1]114/8, [2]113/7 [3]398/404. He was the first to write a *Kitāb al-aghānī*, which is often cited in *Agh.*

8. The Umayyad ʿAbdallāh b. ʿUmar, nicknamed al-ʿArjī after an estate near al-Ṭāʾif, and the great-grandson of the caliph ʿUthmān on his mother's side, was an emulator of ʿUmar b. Abī Rabīʿa. He sang the praises of Jaydāʾ, the mother of Muḥammad b. Hishām al-Makhzūmī. Apparently he did this not out of love for her, but rather to hurt her son. When the latter became a governor under ʿAbd al-Malik he arrested the former and, taking his revenge, made a public example of him by keeping him in jail for nine years until his death. According to other sources he incurred this punishment because of the brutal rape of one of Muḥammad's clients.

Agh. I, [1]153/87, [2]147/61, [3]I, 382/417.

Chapter 4. Al-Akhṭal

While the offspring of the Islamic aristocracy that had stayed behind in Mecca and Medina pursued amorous adventures in inglorious passivity, jangling their languishing songs on the fashionable lute, the war against the infidels was raging along the borders. Furthermore, there was also civil war in Mesopotamia and Iraq as well as the never-ending strife between the various Arab tribes. The songs of the poets who rallied around the court in Damascus, singing the praises of the Umayyads and the leaders of the warring tribes, are therefore of an entirely different nature. Ghiyāth b. Ghawth, famous under the *laqab* of al-Akhṭal ("the windbag"), | was born in al-Ḥīra and 50
belonged to the | Taghlib tribe, which had a large presence in Mesopotamia. 46
Like most of his fellow-tribesmen he was a committed Christian who stuck to his religion, despite how often he may have been tempted to convert to Islam in his later years. However, his commitment to Christianity was, at times, extremely useful for his Umayyad patrons because, as a Christian, he could both openly praise their deeds, even if these would be offensive to any good Muslim, while also being free to lavish his mockery on the pious gentlemen of Mecca, who were often a real nuisance to the rulers. However, in general, one should not think too highly of his Christian leanings. It is true that he bowed to the clerics in whom power (*baraka*) was invested[1] and that, fearing death, he abased himself to the performance of penitential exercises in his old age. But for most of his life he must have used the freedom that his religion granted him—particularly compared to Islam—more often than let himself be curbed by its moral codes.

As a young man he had tried his luck as a wandering poet in his home province before going to Damascus, where his fellow-tribesman Kaʿb b. Juʿayl was a respected poet at the court of Muʿāwiya. In those days, even a man like ʿAbd al-Raḥmān b. al-Ḥakam, from the Anṣār, could risk enflaming the Umayyads and their relatives; when he openly and publicly celebrated an amorous affair with the daughter of the caliph himself, the anger of her brother, Prince Yazīd, was aroused. Because his father did not want to provoke the Anṣār by punishing this poet, he turned to Kaʿb | b. Juʿayl with the 47
request that he chastise him with a satirical poem. The latter recommended his fellow tribesman al-Akhṭal for the job instead, and his criticism turned out to be so biting that he only narrowly escaped the revenge of the Anṣār.

1 This is the implication of the anecdote in *Agh.* VII, $^{1}183_{,7}$, $^{2}174_{,4}$ (Lammens 17, Rescher, *Abr.* I, 245), according to which it made no difference to him whether his pregnant wife could touch a passing bishop with her hand or just his donkey's tail.

When Yazīd came to power in the year 60/679 he invited the poet to his court. His successors too, ʿAbd al-Malik in particular, held him in high esteem, and only the miser Hishām failed to reward him as generously as the others had done before. As a real Bedouin, al-Akhṭal could not resist the call of the wild from time to time. In those days he would live with his tribe in
51 Mesopotamia, where he also married. | At the time, it was just as easy for Christians to divorce as it was for Muslims, and al-Akhṭal exercised his right to repudiate his wife several times. Like a true Bedouin, he also actively participated in the feuds in which his tribe was engaged. The Taghlib had fought for some time against the Southern Arabians on the side of the Qays, who had entrenched themselves at Circesium under their leader Zufar b. al-Ḥārith al-Kilābī. A series of small iritations between the allies led to a long and bloody war that only ended in the year 73/692. ʿAbd al-Malik had invited the leaders of both tribes to Damascus to bring about their reconciliation where, in his presence, the disputes flared up again, at first verbally. But when al-Akhṭal recited a biting satire against the Qays, one of the latter felt so offended that he took it upon himself to seek revenge for his tribe. He organised a night raid on al-Akhṭal's encampment after the latter had returned to his tribe. While his son was butchered, al-Akhṭal himself escaped death only because, wearing the dress of a slave, he was not recognised. Despite this, the leader of the Qays once more received a friendly reception from ʿAbd al-Malik. When al-Akhṭal learned
48 of this, he enraged the caliph | so much against the leader that the latter only escaped death by appealing to his right to safe conduct.

When the conflict between Jarīr and al-Farazdaq broke out in Iraq, al-Akhṭal was at the peak of his fame. According to a report by his son Mālik, at first he took the side of Jarīr. Yet when he went to visit the brother of the caliph and governor of Kufa, Bishr b. Marwān, al-Farazdaq's relatives purportedly pursuaded
52 him, by the use of presents, to turn his sarcasm on Jarīr. | A poetic rivalry that lasted for many years was thus ignited between them, even if they had never met each other in the flesh before then. This encounter only occurred when Jarīr made a courtesy call to the caliph in Damascus, but by that time they were already so embittered that it was only with great effort that the caliph could prevent them from coming to blows.

This conflict kept al-Akhṭal busy until the very end of his life. Before dying at an old age around the year 92/710 he supposedly admonished al-Farazdaq—using his relatives as intermediaries—to grant no peace to Jarīr.

Arab critics have never been able to agree on which of the three quarreling poets should have precedence, although many were inclined to grant it to al-Akhṭal. Abū ʿAmr b. al-ʿAlāʾ even thought he would have been elevated above all the other poets, if only he had lived just one day in pagan times. Al-Akhṭal

took pride in never having descended to using the offensive language of his adversaries, although this claim is not entirely justified.[2] Pairing the humourous dexterity of satire with brilliant poetical technique, he nevertheless follows the ancients so slavishly that the Arab | philologists were even able to 49
identify the prototypes of many of his poems.

Agh. VII, [1]169/88, [2]161/79, [3]VIII, 280/320, X, [1]2/6, [2]2/5, *Khiz.* I, 220/1. Caussin de Perceval, Notice sur les poètes arabes, Akhtal, Férazdaq et Djérir, *JA* s. 2, v. XIII, p. 289, 570, v. XIV, p. 5ff. B. Dorn, *Muhammed. Quellen zur Geschichte der südl. Küstenländer des Kasp. Meeres* IV, St. Petersburg 1858, pp. 64/70. H. Lammens, Le chantre des Omiades, *JA* s. 9, v. IV, p. 94/176, 193/241, 381/459. Akhtal, *Encomium Omayadarum*, ed. M. Th. Houtsma, Leiden 1878. *Le dīwan d'al-Aḫṭal*, ed. P.A. Salhani S.J., Beirut 1891/2, see Th. Nöldeke, *WZKM* V, 160ff., VI, 340ff., an additional MS Berl. Brill M. 302. *Naqāʾiḍ Jarīr wal-Akhṭal taʾlīf al-imām Abū Tammām*, Istanbul ʿUm. 5471.

2 See *Agh.* VII, [1]172,8, cf. Goldziher, *Abh.* I, 135.

Chapter 5. Al-Farazdaq

Hammām b. Ghālib b. Ṣaʿṣaʿa Abu ʾl-Firās, nicknamed al-Farazdaq (the flatbread), from the Dārim tribe, a subdivision of the Tamīm, was born towards the end of the reign of ʿUmar, in the year 20/641. His father, and especially his grandfather, were famous for their generosity, which for Ṣaʿṣaʿa was a means to eradicate the barbarous custom of disposing of newborn girls.[1] Soon after the Battle of the Camel in the year 36/656[2] his father was able to present him to ʿAlī as one of the poets of the Muḍar. Upon the advice of the caliph that it would be better for him to study the Qurʾān instead, al-Farazdaq supposedly chained his ankles together, swearing that he would not untie them until he knew the entire Qurʾān by heart. Soon after, at the beginning of the reign of Muʿāwiya, he lost his father, whose death he mourned in a *marthiya*. About ten years later he had to leave his hometown because he had angered the Banū
50 Nahshal | with his satires and risked being punished by the governor of Iraq, Ziyād b. Abī Sufyān, with whom the Banū Nahshal were held in high esteem. Since he did not feel safe in Kufa either, as it also lay in the sphere of influence of Ziyād, he went to Medina, where he was amiably received by the governor there, Saʿīd b. al-ʿĀṣī. However, this patron was soon replaced by Marwān b. al-Ḥakam, whom he had ridiculed in a poem. Since, in one of his poems, al-Farazdaq had boasted how, on one of his amorous adventures, he had scaled the walls of a harem with a rope ladder, Marwān could now take his revenge
54 by banishing him, in the best of pious traditions, | from the city of the Prophet. Yet, while making his way to Mecca, al-Farazdaq learned of the death of Ziyād and so he returned to his homeland, where he was even amiably received by Ziyād's son and successor ʿUbaydallāh.

His later life, such as it is reflected in his poems, was especially affected by his relationship with his wife Niwār and by Jarīr. Through a contemptible artifice he had forced his cousin Niwār, whose legal guardian he was, to marry him. When she wanted to divorce him in Basra there was no one who dared to confront the dangerous satirist. When she then sought refuge with different tribes, the verses with which al-Farazdaq disparaged her protectors drove her from one sanctuary to another. It was only in Mecca that she gained the protection of the wife of ʿAbdallāh b. al-Zubayr, the caliphal opponent of ʿAbd al-Malik. But al-Farazdaq came after her and gained access to his sons and, initially, was also listened to by ʿAbdallāh b. al-Zubayr himself. However, when the latter let himself be brought around by his wife, al-Farazdaq did not shrink from verbally

1 See the anthology to my *Arab. Gramm.*, p. 50.

2 See A. Müller, *Der Islām* I, 316.

assaulting him with his scorn. For this, he received a dishonorable punishment; indeed, the caliph offered to Niwār that he be banished or even killed, should
she so | desire. However, because she did not consent to this, al-Farazdaq again 51
tried to win over ʿAbdallāh through his sons, while at the same time seeking to persuade Niwār to recognise their marriage after all. In the end she agreed to do so, and it was ʿAbdallāh himself who confirmed their marriage. However, as early as their trip home, the two broke up once again. Because Niwār confronted al-Farazdaq with his promiscuous lifestyle, he took his revenge on her by marrying a Christian woman from the tribe of Qays while they were still on
their journey. | Niwār was all the more upset because she, the distinguished 55
lady, could not recognise this insignificant, plain Bedouin woman as a worthy rival. Since her own objections made no impression on her husband, she induced Jarīr to ridicule her rival. When the Bedouin woman died soon after, al-Farazdaq married someone else. As a result, his relationship with his wife became more and more intolerable until, in the end, he capitulated and was divorced from her by al-Ḥasan al-Baṣrī. All these different episodes from his marital life are mentioned in his poems while Jarīr, too, often refers to them.

Al-Farazdaq probably died in the year 110/728 from pleurisy while on a journey in the desert.

The literary tradition has a very negative view of his character, and his poems do indeed not only bear witness to his recklessness, but also to his rather disgraceful actions. The only thing that contrasts with this was his loyalty to the house of ʿAlī, which he managed to maintain even in the most adverse of circumstances. When Ḥusayn was planning his move to Iraq, al-Farazdaq, who had just gone from Basra to Mecca on pilgrimage, supposedly warned him in vain of the disloyalty of the people of Iraq. When, at the age of 70, during the
pilgrimage to Mecca, he ran into Prince Hishām b. ʿAbd al-Malik, | he did not 52
hesitate to recite a poem in praise of Zayn al-ʿĀbidīn, ʿAlī's grandson to him, a boldness for which he was punished with imprisonment.

Al-Farazdaq's strength lay in the *hijāʾ*, and many anecdotes refer to his caustic wit. In later times people particularly praised the richness of expres-
sion in his poems. | The grammarian Yūnus b. Ḥabīb (see p. 97) used to say: 56
"If al-Farazdaq's poems had not have been preserved, one-third of the Arabic vocabulary would have perished." However, al-Aṣmaʿī accused him, not without reason, of plagiarism. Even the verses by which he, in the mosque of Medina, once convinced a sceptic of his greatness as a poet were partly taken from Jamīl.[3] He even supposedly once forced Dhu 'l-Rumma to hand over four verses to him that were so beautiful that he thought he should have composed

3 Cf. also *Agh.* [1]VII, 80.

them himself.[4] When Ibn Mayyāda[5] recited a verse in praise of his own lineage al-Farazdaq misappropriated it without further ado by replacing the name Ẓālim by that of his own ancestor Dārim, instructing his *rāwī* to spread it under his own (al-Farazdaq's) name.

Agh. VIII, [1]186/97, [2]180/90, XIX, [1,2]2/52, Ibn Khall. 755, *Khiz.* I, 105/8. *Dīwān*, compiled by Muḥammad b. Ḥabīb, d. 245/959, AS 3884, Cairo [1]IV, 271, [2]III, 206. *Divan de Férazdak, récits de M. b. H. d'après Ibn al-Aʿrābī, publié sur le ms. de St. Sophie de Cple avec une traduction franç. par* R. Boucher, Paris 1870 (incomplete), edition by al-Sukkarī (see p. 108), Bodl. II, 306, part III, Br. Mus. 1066 (?). *Dīwān*, together with al-Nābigha, ʿUrwa, Ḥātim, ʿAlqama, Cairo 1239. Poem on Zayn al-ʿĀbidīn, Gotha, $14_{,26}$, Leid. 590. Individual poems, Berl. 7525.

4 *Dīwān* $313_{,9/11}$. *Agh.* XVI, [1]116, Goldziher, *Abh.* I, 137, n. 1.

5 I.e. al-Rammāḥ b. Abrad al-Murrī, see *Agh.* II, [1]88/120, [2]85/116, Yāqūt, *Irshād* IV, 212/4, *Khiz.* I, 77/8.

Chapter 6. Jarīr 53

Abū Ḥazra Jarīr b. ʿAṭiyya b. al-Khaṭafā, of the tribe of Kulayb, a subdivision of the Tamīm, was born in Iraq during the reign of ʿAlī. The story goes that in his early childhood he wrote a poem in which he criticised his father for his meanness, and which was then appropriated by the crown prince Yazīd to use it against his own father. When he came to power Yazīd is said to have rewarded the poet sumptuously for this. However, it was not long before Jarīr got involved in *hijāʾ* disputes with various poets from Iraq. He first tried his luck as a panegyrist with al-Ḥakam b. Ayyūb, an official working for the celebrated governor al-Ḥajjāj. The former recommended him to his master, who summoned him to al-Wāsiṭ, deciding that he would be useful for his political ends.
In the meantime, Jarīr's fame steadily increased because of his feuds with 57
al-Farazdaq and al-Akhṭal, and the only thing that he still lacked was recognition at the Damascus court, so when his patron's son Muḥammad went there on a political mission he went along with him. Having been set against him by his favourite al-Akhṭal, ʿAbd al-Malik at first refused to receive him. It was only when it was suggested to him that his faithful proconsul would take offence at such treatment of his court poet that he received him in audience without, however, granting him any special recognition. His successor al-Walīd did not wish him well either because he had to defend his own court poet, ʿAdī b. al-Riqāʿ,[1] against him on several occasions. When al-Walīd was once staying in Medina he heard about a dispute between Jarīr and ʿUmar b. Lajaʾ. Because both had mentioned ladies of the court in the *nasīb* of their poems he had
them exposed to public scorn, being chained up together. But when the pious 54
ʿUmar II ascended to the throne, it was, from among all the poets vying for his favour, only Jarīr who found this in his eyes,[2] apparently because of his chastity.

The feuds that Jarīr had started as a young man were to occupy the whole 58
of his life. No less than 43 poets supposedly pitched their skills against his, but even to be defeated by him was still considered an honour. A single satire that he wrote sufficed to make remaining in Basra impossible for Rāʿi ʾl-Ibil,[3] an

---

1 *Agh.* VIII, ^{1}179/84, ^{2}172/7, al-Jumaḥī, *Ṭab. al-shuʿarāʾ* 142.

2 *ʿIqd* I, 114, 116, cod. Goth. 1553, fol. 133r, 1589, fol. 70, cod. Landberg, Berl. 833, f. 48,$_{2}$ff., Suyūṭī, *Mughnī* in Weil, *Gesch. der Chal.* I, 591.

3 I.e. ʿUbayd b. Ḥuṣayn al-Numayrī, who was known under this name because, following ancient custom, it was mostly the camel that he described in his poems; see al-Jumaḥī, *Ṭab. al-Sh.*, 103/5,$_{2}$, *Agh.* XX, ^{1}168/74, Ibn Qutayba, *Poes.*, 246ff.; a fragment from an *urjūza*, al-ʿAynī III, 457.

old and respected poet who had angered him with a negative judgment of his poetic achievements, although this did cause that poet's entire tribe to range itself against him, as he had also insulted their honour. His feud with al-Baʿīth,[4] who was seconded by al-Farazdaq, is supposed to have lasted for forty years. But most famous of all was his dispute with his great opponent, who was the only one who could measure up to him, a dispute which had started during the caliphate of ʿAbdallāh b. al-Zubayr 65–67/684–6 and in which al-Akhṭal also confronted him. The whole nation took part in this dispute. When ʿAbd al-Malik's general al-Muhallab was fighting the Azraqīs in Persia a quarrel broke out among his troops over the pre-eminence of the two poets. Very wisely al-Muhallab declined to render a judgment, so as not to arouse the anger of one of the camps. He relegated the matter to his enemies, who were
55 bi-partisan and surely well-informed about poetry; | their leader was al-Qaṭarī (see p. 58), himself a respected poet. One of the latter's confidants decided in favour of Jarīr.

Towards the end of his life Jarīr retired to his estate in the Yamāma. He passed away there, probably in 110/728.

Agh. VII, [1]38/77, [2]35/72, [3]VIII, 3/89, *Khiz.* I, 36/7, al-Jumaḥī, *Ṭab.* 86/108. *Dīwān*, compiled by Muḥammad b. Ḥabīb, d. 245/859, Leid. 589, Pet. AM 262, Beirut, *JA* s. 9, v. IV, 108, n. 1. *Naqāʾiḍ Jarīr wal-Farazdaq*, compiled by Muḥammad b. Ḥabīb, with a commentary by Muḥammad b. al-ʿAbbās al-Yazīdī (p. 109), Bodl. I, 1224$_{,1}$.

---

4 I.e. Abū Yazīd Khidāsh b. Bishr b. Khālid al-Tamīmī, d. 134/751 in Basra, see al-Jumaḥī, *Ṭab.* 121, Ibn Qutayba, *al-Shiʿr*, 312, Yāqūt, *Irshād* IV, 173.

Chapter 7. Dhu 'l-Rumma

Ghaylān b. ʿUqba, nicknamed Dhu 'l-Rumma, belonged to the tribe of the Banū ʿAdī. Although he generally led a nomadic existence as a Bedouin, he also came to Basra and Kufa from time to time, which is why he was considered to have been half-urbanised. From his life we know little more than the fact that he was in love with Mayya—which must have lasted for 20 years—and al-Kharqāʾ, that he was friends with Bilāl b. Abī Burda al-Ashʿarī, to whom he dedicated some of his poems, and the details of a number of minor events that occurred during his visits to the Damascus court. He died in the year 101/719 (or, according to others, later, in 117/735) and is said to have been buried in the desert. | 59

Dhu 'l-Rumma was the last exponent of the old Bedouin poetry, which had been transmitted to him by Rāʿi 'l-ibil (see p. 54), whose *rāwī* he was, but which caused his style to ossify into a state of rigidity. Apparently he was aware of this one-dimensional style himself; as he once said, after starting a comparison with *ka-annahu*, there was no way for him to stop. According to al-Farazdaq, Dhu 'l-Rumma could have been one of the greatest poets were it not for this shortcoming. Being the last exponent of ancient poetry he was held in high regard by philologists. Apparently, Abū ʿAmr b. al-ʿAlāʾ | had called Imraʾ al- 56
Qays the first, and him the last, poet. Scholars were especially captivated by his preference for rare and remote expressions, which gave them an opportunity to shine with their knowledge and sharpness of wit. His *dīwān*, which comprises eighty, mostly rather long, *qaṣīda*s, was compiled and commented upon by al-Aṣmaʿī (see p. 104), the most famous of the ancient philologists.

Agh. XVI, ^{1}110/28, ^{2}106/23, al-Jumaḥī, *Ṭab.* 125/8. *Dīwān* Br. Mus. 580, Leid. 586, more inclusive ibid. 587, Cairo ^{1}IV, 245, ^{2}III, 129; individual poems Berl. 7528,$_{2}$, Br. Mus. 561,$_{5}$, Leid. 588, de Jong 211. Commentary by al-Aṣmaʿī, Berl. Brill M. 278. The most famous *qaṣīda* has the beginning *mā bālu ʿaynika*, on which R. Smend, *De Dsurrumma poeta arabico et carmine ejus*, Bonn 1874.

Chapter 8. The *Rajaz* Poets

While in pagan times the *rajaz* (Suppl. I, 22) had only been used in improvisations, under the Umayyads it received special attention from some poets, particularly as a way of honing their *qaṣīda* technique. They sought to compensate for the simplicity of the *rajaz* metre by embellishing it with rather
60 obscure expressions. | Indeed, the two most important representatives of this movement are rightly seen as having enriched the Arabic lexicon as a result of their daring coinages. The first poet who wrote longer *urjūza*s that will be mentioned is al-Aghlab b. Jusham b. Saʿd b. ʿUmar (ʿAmr) b. ʿUbayda al-ʿIjlī,[1] who perished in 21/641 at the Battle of Nihāwand. But this art form was only made to flourish by his fellow-tribesmen Abu ʾl-Najm, his rival al-ʿAjjāj, and the latter's son Ruʾba. Al-ʿAjjāj ʿAbdallāh b. Ruʾba, of the clan Mālik, was a panegyrist who was mostly active under ʿAbd al-Malik, and who died during the reign of al-Walīd, in the year 97/715. Abu ʾl-Najm al-Faḍl b. Qudāma al-ʿIjlī was highly regarded by the caliph Hishām (105–25/723–42) and only died towards the end of the Umayyad dynasty; a *dīwān* by him has not come down to us. On Ruʾba (d. 145/762 or 147/764) and a number of other *rajaz* poets, see Suppl. I, 90/1.

Dīwān al-ʿAjjāj NO, see D.H. Müller, SBWA 1878, 335/42, with commentary Cairo [1]IV, 271, [2]III, 138, 205. *Das erste Gedicht aus dem Diwan des arabischen Dichters al-ʿAjjāj, nach den Handschriften von Constantinopel, Cairo und Leiden, hsg. v.* M. Bittner, Vienna 1896, see Th. Nöldeke, ZDMG 50, 523/8. This poem of 180 verses, known as *al-Gharrāʾ* (Wright, *op. ar.* 55), celebrates the victory of ʿUmar b. ʿUbaydallāh b. Maʿmar, d. 82/701, over the leader of the Khārijites, Fudayk (see Ṭabarī II, 852).

Ruʾba, *Agh.* XXI, [1]84/91, [2]57/61, *Khiz.* I, 43/5. *Dīwān* with commentary by Muḥammad b. Ḥabīb, Berl. 8155, Cairo [1]IV, 270, [2]III, 203, cod. Spitta, Strasburg, ZDMG 40, 313.

Abu ʾl-Najm, *Lāmiyya*, ed. ʿAbd al-ʿAzīz al-Maymanī in *al-Ṭarāʾif al-adabiyya*, C. 1937, 57/71.

1 *Agh.* XVIII, [1,2]164/7, al-Jumaḥī, *Ṭab.* 148/9 (with the *rajaz* on the prophetess Sajāḥ adopted from the *Agh.*, *Khiz.* I, 33, after Ibn Qutayba, *Poes.* 389, and al-Āmidī, *al-Muʾtalif* 22).

Chapter 9. Minor Poets

1. Ziyād b. Salmā (according to some sources, Salīm or Sulaymān) al-Aʿjam, a client of the ʿAbd al-Qays from the tribe ʿĀmir b. al-Ḥārith, see Suppl. I, 92.

Agh. XIV, [1]102/9, [2]98/105, panegyric on ʿUmar b. ʿUbaydallāh, *Ḥamāsa* IV, 148, *Marthiya* on Muhallab b. Abī Ṣufra, d. 82/701, which was regarded as the best of its time, Berl. $7519_{,5}$.

1a. Yazīd b. Ziyād b. Rabīʿa b. Mufarrij al-Ḥimyarī, see Suppl., loc. cit. (read al-Jumaḥī, *Ṭab.* 143).

2. Khālid b. Ṣafwān al-Qannāṣ was a friend of Yazīd b. al-Muhallab, d. 102/720, who died in the year 90/709.

| *Qaṣīdat al-ʿarūs*, a panegyric devoted to a young girl, with commentary, Berl. 61
7523, Leid. 585, Br. Mus. $565_{,2}$, Ind. Off. | $1043_{,14}$, Vat. V, $364_{,9}$, Cairo [1]IV, 272, ed. 58
ʿAbd al-ʿAzīz al-Maymanī in *al-Ṭarāʾif al-adabiyya*, C. 1937, 102/11ff.

3. Qaṭarī b. al-Fujāʾa, the leader of the Khārijites in Persia who perished in 78/697 in combat against Sufyān al-Kalbī, is almost more famous as an historical figure than as a poet. His works are distinguished by their belligerent vigour and the liveliness of their language.

Ibn Khall. 517, ʿAbd al-Qāhir al-Baghdādī, *al-Farq bayna ʾl-firaq*, ed. M. Badr, 65/6 (transl. C. Seelye, New York 1919, p. 80), al-Shahrastānī 90 (Haarbr. 134), *Ḥamāsa* I, 49, 68, II, 111. J. Wellhausen, *Oppositionsparteien* 36.

4. In the same way in which, before Islam, women occupied an important place in the matter of *marāthī*, so it was under the Umayyads. Laylā al-Akhyaliyya was the daughter of ʿAbdallāh b. al-Raḥḥāl of the Banū ʿĀmir b. Ṣaʿṣaʿa tribe. She was courted by her fellow tribesman Tawba b. al-Ḥumayyir,[1] but her father gave her to a man from outside the tribe. Tawba remained faithful to her until, in the year 85/704, he was killed on a *ghazwa* by the Banū ʿAwf b. ʿUqayl. She then mourned his death in countless songs. Once she had become famous on account of this, she seems to have devoted herself entirely to the arts and to have frequented the royal courts in much the same way as did her male colleagues. This is how she came to ʿAbd al-Malik, who appears to

1 Ibn Qutayba, *Poes.* 269ff., *Fawāt* I, 95.

have been especially impressed by her witty repartees, but she was also much admired by al-Ḥajjāj. She died while on the way to visit her cousin Qutayba b. Muslim, who was a commanding officer in Khurasān, allegedly while on the trail of a *hijā'* opponent of her husband, Sawwār b. Awfā al-Qushayrī (for other versions, see Suppl. I, 94).

Agh. X, [1]68/84, [2]63/80, *Hijā'* with al-Nābigha al-Ja'dī, ibid. IV, [1]133/4, 129/30, *Fawāt* II, 141. Poems, Berl. $7523_{,1}$, see p. 35.

59 | 5. Nābighat Banī Shaybān ʿAbdallāh b. al-Mukhāriq was, for the ancient philologists, a Christian because he swore by the Gospels and other things holy to the Christians. However, his *dīwān* shows him to have been a good Muslim. From the desert he often went to Damascus and composed songs in praise of ʿAbd al-Malik and al-Walīd.

Agh. VI, [1]151/4, [2]146/9, [3]VII, 106/13; *Dīwān* Cairo [1]IV, 254, [2]III, 150, ʿĀšir Ef. 981, print. C. 1932.

6. ʿUmayr b. Shuyaym al-Taghlibī, who had the nicknames al-Quṭāmī and Ṣarīʿ al-Ghawānī, was also a Christian at first, and converted to Islam only at a rela-
62 tively late point in his life. | He died in 110/728. He was actively involved in the battles between Qays and Kalb, and occasionally also tried his luck as a panegyrist of the Umayyads and their emirs.

Agh. XX, [1,2]118/32, *Khiz.* I, 392/3, al-Jumaḥī, *Ṭab.* 131/2, *Dīwān* with anonymous commentary, copy dated 364/974, collated by the famous philologist al-Marzūqī, d. 421/1030, Berl. 7327, Cairo [1]IV, 250, [2]III, 143; on the edition by Barth see also Th. Nöldeke, *WZKM* XVI, 275/85.

7. Aʿshā Hamdān ʿAbd al-Raḥmān b. ʿAbdallāh b. al-Ḥārith, of the southern Arabian tribe of the Banū Jusham and the brother-in-law of the famous traditionist and poet Abū ʿAmr ʿĀmir b. Sharāḥil al-Shaʿbī (d. 104, 105, or 110/728),[2] lived in Kufa and started as a traditionist and reciter of the Qurʾān. He related the events in Iraq under Muṣʿab b. al-Zubayr through his poems. During a campaign against the Daylamīs he was taken prisoner, but was liberated by a young Daylamī woman because of her love for him. In the year 83/702 he joined the

---

2 He prided himself on having given literary form to traditions without changing their sense; al-ʿAskarī, *Kitāb al-ṣināʿatayn*, $172_{,5}$ from below.

rebellion of ʿAbd al-Raḥmān b. al-Ashʿath,[3] fell into the hands of al-Ḥajjāj, and was | executed. As early as during his lifetime, his poems were put to music by 60
Aḥmad al-Naṣībī.

Agh. V, [1]146/61, [2]138/53, [3]VI, 33/62, al-Balādhurī, *Ansāb al-Ashrāf*, vol. V, index; some *qaṣīda*s in Berl. 7524,$_1$.

8. Muḥammad b. ʿAbdallāh al-Numayrī of al-Ṭāʾif had fallen in love with Zaynab, the sister of his celebrated fellow-countryman al-Ḥajjāj b. Yūsuf, and he even seems to have followed the latter to Iraq. Because the governor would not tolerate his sister's name being mentioned in al-Numayrī's poems the latter fled first to Yemen, and then by ship, via Aden, to ʿAbd al-Malik.

Agh. VI, [1]24/32, [2]23/30, *Dīwān*, compiled by Muḥammad b. Ḥabīb, AS 3978.

9. Ismāʿīl b. Yasār, from Azerbaijan, was a client of the Banū Murra Taym Quraysh and a supporter of the Zubayrids, and he accompanied ʿUrwa b. al-Zubayr on his journey to al-Walīd and composed an elegy for his son Muḥammad, who died on the journey. Later he visited the caliph Hishām in al-Ruṣāfa, but forfeited his favour because, as usual, he prided himself too much on his Persian roots.

Agh. IV, [1]119/28, [2]118/27, [3]408/29, A. v. Kremer, *Streifzüge* 29, Goldziher, *MSt.* I, 100.

10. Al-Walīd, the son of the Umayyad caliph Yazīd b. ʿAbd al-Malik, lost his father early, in the year 105/723, when he was only 15 years old. From him he had inherited his artistic talent, his love for wine, and his cheerful enjoyment of life. | His uncle Hishām, who had at first taken the place of his father on the 63
throne, wanted to change Walīd's right of inheritance in favour of his own son Maslama; for this reason Hishām once sent Walīd as the leader of the pilgrimage to Mecca, hoping that he would make himself impossible there because of his wine-drinking. Walīd spent his youth in a desert fortress in Palestine. But after | Hishām's death in 125/742, the caliphate was handed over to him and the 61
people of Damascus cheered him in the hope that they would be freed from the oppressive rule of his predecessor. However, he soon retreated to his desert fortress again, in order to live a life dedicated to artistic expression and exercise. Because he did not demand less money than Hishām, he became estranged

3 See A. Müller, *Der Islām* I, 390, Wellhausen, *Das arab. Reich*, 146ff.

from the people, and because he appointed his two underage sons as his successors his relatives became ranged against him. For this reason, after two just years, a counter-caliph was installed: Yazīd b. al-Walīd b. ʿAbd al-Malik. On 17 April 744, in his stronghold of al-Bakhrāʾ, just south of Palmyra, after putting up a brave resistance during which he read the Qurʾān just as ʿUthmān had done in earlier times, al-Walīd was butchered by the troops that had been sent against him. His contemporary, the Ibāḍī al-Qāsim b. al-Ṭufayl, had acquainted him with the songs of ʿAdī b. Zayd (see p. 21), and he adopted the latter's style for his own wine songs that were later imitated by Abū Nuwās.

Agh. VI, [1]101/41, [2]98/137, [3]VII, 1/84, on his person as a singer and composer, ibid. VIII, [1]161/2, [2]155/6.

11. Born in 60/679, al-Kumayt b. Zayd al-Asadī of the tribe of Saʿd b. Thaʿlaba was an adversary of the southern Arabians and an ardent admirer of the Fāṭimids, who for him were the only rightful representatives of the house of Hāshim. Because of a song praising them, the caliph Hishām condemned him to death and had him incarcerated in Kufa by Khālid al-Qasrī. However, a woman helped him to escape and Maslama, the caliph's son, obtained for him his father's pardon. In the year 126/743 he perished, nevertheless, in al-Jaʿfariyya, during a revolt against Khālid.

Agh. XV, [1]113/30, [2]108/25, *Jamhara* 187, *Khiz.* I, 69/70, 86/7. *Al-Hāshimiyyāt*, Leid. 518, Br. Mus. 1063, Suppl. 1034, excerpts Ambr. AF 429 v. A *Kitāb sariqāt al-kumayt min al-Qurʾān wa-ghayrihi*, by Ibn Kunāsa, d. 207/822, is mentioned in *Fihrist*, 71.

62 | 12. Abū ʿAṭāʾ Aflaḥ (or Marzūq) b. Yasār al-Sindī was born in Kufa, the son of a man from Sind, and lived there as a client of the Banū Asad. His poor pronunciation betrayed his origin. He composed songs praising of the Umayyads and ridiculed the ʿAbbāsids. He only died towards the end of the reign of al-Manṣūr in 158/774.

Agh. XVI, [1]81/7, [2]78/84, *Ḥamāsa* II, 150.

13. Hammād b. Ṣābūr (or Hurmuz or Maysara) al-Rāwiya should be mentioned here more as a transmitter and high-handed multiplier of ancient poetry than as a poet in his own right. He was born in Kufa in 75/694 and was of Daylamī stock, something that was often highlighted in later times by the many mis-
64 takes in his Arabic. | He had sought the favour of Yazīd and thereby aroused

the displeasure of Hishām. When the latter came to power in 105/723, Hammād apparently did not leave his house for an entire year. Then, however, the caliph personally summoned him to Damascus and loaded him with presents. Under the ʿAbbāsids it was only during the reign of al-Mahdī that he gained favour, and it was during his reign that he died, in 155/771 (or, according to others, in 158/774).

Agh. v, [1]164/75, [2]156/66, [3]vi, 70/96, Ibn Khall. 197, Wüstenf., *Gesch.* 31. He is the one who collected the *Muʿallaqāt*, see p. 11. A book, the *dīwān* of ʿĀmir b. al-Ṭufayl, is mentioned by him, schol. *Mufaḍḍ.* $33_{,14}$.

14.–18., see Suppl. I, 98/9 (p. 99, line 1, better: "His daughter Ḥumayda").

19. Another poet must be mentioned here, whose lifetime cannot be determined with any precision. The only thing that we know about al-Sarī ʿAbdallāh b. ʿUbaydallāh b. Aḥmad b. al-Dumayna is that he killed a man who had committed adultery with his wife—a certain Muzāḥim b. ʿAmr from the Khathʿamī tribe Salūl—and | that he was incarcerated because of this by Aḥmad b. Ismāʿīl. 63
If—with Van Arendonk, EI II, 397—this person is identical with the governor of Mecca mentioned in Ṭab. III, 740, then he would belong to the era of Hārūn al-Rashīd.

Agh. xv, [1]145/50, [2]144/51, Ibn Qutayba, *Poes.* 458/9, the *Akhbār b. al-Dumayna* was composed by al-Zubayr b. Bakkār (see p. 141) and Ibn Abī Ṭāhir Ṭayfūr (p. 138), *Fihr.* $11_{,12}$, $147_{,1}$. *Dīwān* ʿĀšir Ef. 950 (MSOS XIV, 12, MFO V, 515), Cairo [2]III, 107, ed. by ʿAbdallāh al-Hāshimī (Suppl. III, 490), Cairo 1918. Individual poems *Ḥamāsa* 541, p. 598f., 604/6, 620, after Thaʿlab al-Zajjājī, *Amālī* 80, 101, 110, Berl. $7476_{,1}$, $8255_{,1}$.

Chapter 10. Prose Writing at the Time of the Umayyads

Venerated as coming from God, the example of religious prose that Muḥammad had set out in the Qur'ān could not be imitated. Public statements were still couched in a traditional metric form, while recordings of religious and historical traditions were at first few and far between, and mostly directed at some inner circle. As such, direct traces of these have not generally come down to us.

1a. It is doubtful if Ziyād, half-brother and proconsul of Muʿāwiya, composed a work on suspicious family histories that was meant as a weapon for his sons against jibes about their lineage.

Wüstenfeld, *Geschichtenschreiber*, no. 2.

1b. ʿAbīd b. Sharya al-Jumhurī, see Suppl. I, 100.

According to al-Hamdānī, d. 334/945 (see p. 229), the various recensions of his book circulating during his life were so different that two identical copies could hardly be found. His younger contemporay al-Masʿūdī,
65 | d. 346/957 (see p. 143), calls it a well-known and widely available book; *Murūj*
64 IV, 89, Goldziher, *MSt.* I, 182. | M. Lidzbarski, *De propheticis qu. d. legendis arabicis*, Leipzig $1893_{,1/2}$, Wüst., *Gesch.* no. 5.

1c. Wahb b. Munabbih, see Suppl. I, 101.

1d. Abū Mikhnaf Lūṭ b. Yaḥyā al-Azdī was, for the most part, active during the reign of the ʿAbbāsids. *Fihrist* 93 lists the titles of 32 tracts dealing with individuals and events.

Yāqūt, *Irshād* VI, 220/2 (places his death in the year 157/774), al-Yaʿqūbī, *Hist.* II, $486_{,15}$ (mentions him among the men of learning of the time of al-Mahdī 158–69/775–85), *Fawāt* II, 140, Wüst., *Gesch.* 19. Wellhausen, *Das arab. Reich* 111ff., Bartold, *Zap.* VOIRAO XVII, 147/9. The spurious *Dhikr maqtal sayyidinā wa-mawlānā al-Ḥusayn b. ʿAlī* or *al-Maṣraʿ al-shayn fī qatl al-Ḥusayn*, ed. by ʿAbdallāh b. Mūsā b. Jaʿfar b. Muḥammad b. Ṭāwūs al-Ḥusaynī, Goth. 1828, Leid. $909_{,2}$, Pet. AM 78, Ros. 151, and the *Akhbār al-Mukhtār b. Abī ʿUbayd* or *Akhdh al-tha'r ʿalā yad al-sāda al-akhyār Ibrāhīm al-Thaqafī al-Mukhtār* Berl. $9039_{,}$. Gotha $1838_{,2}$, Leid. $909_{,3}$, Bombay 1311, are very late concoctions. See Wüstenfeld, *Der Tod Ḥusains und die Rache*, *Abh. G.G.W.* 1883, XXX.

2. Born between 50–8/670–7, even Muḥammad b. Muslim al-Zuhrī, the court theologian of the Marwānids, was still open to worldly interests, having a special interest in poetry. As a young man he had been a driven collector of traditions in Medina, where he had not let himself be influenced by the opposition of the pious against the Umayyads. From Medina he went to Damascus, where he accepted the office of *qāḍī* from Yazīd II, before being entrusted with the education of the caliph Hishām's sons. In his old age he retired to his estate at Adāmā, on the road from Damascus to Medina, where he died on 17 Ramaḍān 124/25 July 742.

Ibn Khall. 535, Wüst., *Gesch.* 18, Goldziher, *MSt.* II, 38/39, Horovitz, *Isl. Cult.* II, 33. *Kitāb al-maghāzī*, ḤKh 10513, 12464. Traditions stemming from him, Leipz. 320,$_2$.

| His student Muḥammad b. ʿAbd al-Raḥmān al-ʿĀmirī, d. 120/737, was appar- 65
ently the first to have collected traditions in book form as the basis of *fiqh*.

| His *Kitāb al-muwaṭṭaʾ* is cited by al-Zurqānī, *Sharḥ al-muwaṭṭaʾ*, C. 1279, I, 16,$_{10}$. 66
People valued this work more highly than the later one by Mālik (p. 176), but criticised its author for not being strict enough about his sources.

A work about dream interpretation with the title *Kitāb al-jawāmiʿ* is attributed to the famous traditionist Muḥammad b. Sīrīn, d. 110/728 (Ibn Khall. 576), Paris 2742/3, no. 3751, print. C. 1310 (on Greek and Latin translations and adaptations see Schöll, *Griech. Lit.-Gesch. transl. Pinder*, III, 487), abstract Gotha 842, see Steinschneider, ZDMG XVII, 227; on *Kitāb al-ishāra fī ʿilm al-ʿibāra*, Paris 2744, Copenhagen 295, see Suppl.

3. During the reign of the Umayyads, the Muslims of Syria were often in such close contact with Christians—who were indispensable for the purposes of administration and many of whom enjoyed high positions at the court—that the exchange of religious ideas became inevitable. The last great dogmatist of the Greek church, John of Damascus (b. 676), whose father was held in high esteem by the later Umayyads, wrote a defence of the Christian religion against Islam in the form of a dialogue between a Christian and a Saracen. It is therefore hardly a coincidence if the teachings of precisely this John with regard to God's mercy, directed at the salvation of all human beings, and with regard to the free will, were adopted by the schools of the Murjiʿa and the Qadariyya in Syrian Islam. In Iraq, on the other hand, people clung rigidly to the fundamental

teachings of the Qur'ān. The head of the theologians there, Ḥasan al-Baṣrī, d. 110/728 in Basra, dodged dogmatic issues wherever possible. This notwith-
66 standing, his ascetic devotion provided the basis for | the mystical movement
67 in later theology. | Important literary works from this oldest period of Islamic
theology have not been preserved.

A. v. Kremer, *Kulturgesch. Streifzüge* 5/6, M. Th. Houtsma, *De strijd over het dogma in den Islam tot op el Ash'arī*, Leiden 1875. A commentary on the Qur'ān attributed to al-Ḥasan al-Baṣrī, in the transmission of 'Amr b. 'Ubayd, was still used by al-Tha'labī, d. 427/1035 (see p. 350), see Br. Mus. 821. Attributed to him is, amongst others, the *Risāla fī faḍl ḥaram Makka al-musharrafa,* which is a letter to a friend who wants to leave Mecca, Gotha $23_{,3}$, Berl. 6064, Paris $2250_{,1}$, AS 1849.

4. The recording of proverbs and maxims had already started under the Umayyads.

Goldziher, *MSt.* II, 204. 'Ilāqa b. Karīm al-Kilābī composed a *Kitāb al-amthāl* under Yazīd b. Mu'āwiya (60–4/679–83), *Fihr.* 90, Wüst., *Gesch.* 11.

4b. Ja'far al-Ṣādiq (see Suppl. I, 104). 2. *Tafsīr* also Patna I, $25_{,284/5}$.

5. The Umayyad prince Khālid b. Yazīd, d. 85/704, occupied himself with the study of alchemy, in which the monk Marianus (?) was his teacher. There are three *rasā'il* that are attributed to him, one of which is about his teacher and his teaching, as well as poems on alchemy.

Agh. XVI, ^{1}88/93, ^{2}84/90, Ibn Khall. 201, unjustly questioned by Ibn Khaldūn, *Proleg. trad. de Slane*, p. 207. *Dīwān al-nujūm* Köpr. 924, Ğārullāh 1641 (Ritter in *Rescher*, Abr. I, 330), *Dīwān firdaws al-ḥikma* ḤKh IV, 413, no. 9060, Beirut 255. *Liber de compositione alchemiae, quem edidit Morienus Romanus Calid regi Aegyptiorum*, transl. 1182 by Robert Castrensis, Leclerc I, 64, Berthelot, *La chimie au moyen âge* III, 2.

SECOND BOOK

Islamic Literature in the Arabic Language

FIRST SECTION

The Classical Period from ca. 750 until ca. 1000

Chapter 1. Introduction

The thoroughly Arab and, to a certain degree, traditional rule of the Umayyads had already long been weakened by discord amongst the various tribes before it collapsed completely following the influx of the Persians, who, oppressed until then, had been shaken into renewed self-awareness by the successive upheavals of the ʿAlids and ʿAbbāsids. At the court of Baghdad, too, the Persians soon gained much influence, and the Iranian House of the Barmakids asserted itself in the highest public offices for almost half a century. In literature, too, it was not long before Persian influence made itself felt. Nevertheless, there was no independent literature in New Persian yet, which would only develop two centuries later, when Persia gradually regained its political independence. Arabic still remained the only literary language, and thus had to be used by Persians as well. Although they could not yet boast of their own representatives in poetry, their elegance and exquisite taste did permeate Bedouin poetry ever more until, within the space of three generations, Bedouin poetry was no more. Light prose was supplied with new material through translations from Pahlavī. Persian influence in various scientific fields, which now unexpectedly blossomed, was, however, no less important. | | Even if philology was originally invented by the 70 72
Arabs, some of its most important representatives were Persian. Historiography received an enormous impetus from Middle Persian annalists, and in theology and jurisprudence the Persians soon turned from the Arabs' students into their masters. The cultivation of the secular sciences, on the other hand, was mainly carried out by the Arameans, who transmitted their knowledge of Hellenistic culture to the Arabs. As such, in what follows the origin of every author must be determined.

The golden age of the arts and sciences under the ʿAbbāsids of Iraq lasted hardly two hundred years. As early as the fifth century of the Hijra, the vast Islamic empire was in a state of total collapse. In the provinces, increasingly autonomous states came into existence, which strived to establish their own culture, independent from Baghdad. So even if it is true that cultural life was manifested in a great many ways, with the rapid onset of a decline in material conditions, original ideas and independent thinking soon disappeared as well.

 | DOI 10.1163/9789004326262_006

Chapter 2. Poetry

As early as the latter years of Umayyad rule, the *qaṣīda* had disappeared as a poetic art form. Considering that its limited, traditional subject matter was entirely linked to the life of the desert, it was no longer suitable for the entirely different conditions of the creolised, Arabo-Persian population of the big cities, which now formed the centre of intellectual life. The different elements of the old *qaṣīda*, to the extent to which these had retained their viability,
71 now developed with the great poets into the separate genres of wine-, | love-,
73 and hunting-poems, among many others. | However, philology, which developed at the same time, established the dogma of the inimitable superiority of old Bedouin poetry, thereby forcing poets of lesser talent time and again back into the ways of the ancients. Even in the fourth century, al-Ḥātimī,[1] himself a poet of some renown, wanted to impose the *qaṣīda* onto his contemporaries as the true artistic ideal—on condition that they first ennoble it by lending it an inner cohesion.[2] Yet it seems unlikely that the great poets allowed themselves to be constantly influenced by such prejudices. Before the end of the fourth century AH these prejudices were also overcome from a theoretical point of view, so that this new poetry came to be accepted by learned critics as a legitimate art form.

I. Goldziher, Alte und neue Poesie im Urteile der arabischen Kritiker, *Abh.* I, 112/74.

A The Poets of Baghdad

At the beginning of this period Baghdad, the capital of the ʿAbbāsid empire that al-Manṣūr had constructed from scratch, attracted all the great poets, for it was at the caliph's court that they could find full recognition of their talents.

1. The first representative of the new movement was Muṭīʿ b. Iyās. His father came from Palestine and was one of the troops that had been dispatched by ʿAbd al-Malik to assist in the war against Ibn al-Zubayr and Ibn al-Ashʿath. He
72 himself was born and raised in Kufa. During Umayyad rule he was | highly

1 Muḥammad b. al-Ḥasan b. al-Muẓaffar al-Ḥasan, a student of Ghulām Thaʿlab (p. 123), d. 388/998, author of numerous works on literary criticism, see al-Thaʿālibī, *Yatīmat al-dahr* II, 273, 293, Yāqūt, *Irshād* VI, 501/18, Ibn al-Khaṭīb, *Ta'r. Baghdād* II, 214, Ibn Khall. no. 621, Suyūṭī, *Bughyat al-wuʿāt* 35, see Suppl. I, 136, 140 (also II, 1006,$_{98}$?); his *Ḥilyat al-muḥāḍara* is still quoted in the *Dīwān Jarir* [1]II, 88,$_{3}$.

2 See al-Ḥuṣrī, *Zahr al-ādāb*, in the margin of the *ʿIqd*, C. 1305, II, 202/3.

regarded at the court of al-Walīd b. Yazīd, and after their downfall he went to al-Manṣūr who, in spite of a number of incidents, bestowed his favours upon him time after time. He died in Rajab 170/January 787. His poetry bears the full imprint of the new culture: softness, intimacy and sensitivity, combined with a cynical frivolousness.

Agh. XII, [1]81/111, [2]75/105, A. v. Kremer, *Culturgesch.*, II, 368ff.

2. Bashshār b. Burd al-ʿUqaylī al-Muraʿʿath Abū Muʿādh was born blind in Basra, the son of an Iranian slave from Khurāsān or Ṭukhāristān and who took pride in his royal descent. After he had been set free by his mistress, who was a distinguished Arab lady, he remained in his hometown, although every now and then he also travelled to the caliphal court in Baghdad. In his youth he apparently spent time with Wāṣil b. al-ʿAṭāʾ (Suppl. I, 337), the founder of Muʿtazilī
dogma, and other freethinkers. | Yet he did not want to sacrifice the Mazdaic 74
belief of his ancestors to Islam. So long as he dedicated laudatory poems to the caliph al-Mahdī, though, he was left in peace, although his *hijāʾ* earned him many enemies. When he had the audacity to attack the caliph and his vizier Yaʿqūb b. Dāʾūd in the year 167/783, he paid for it with his life.

Agh. III, [1]19/72, [2]20/70, [3]135/250, VI, [1]47/52, [2]45/51, Ibn Khall. 110, A. v. Kremer, *Culturgesch. Streifz.* 57ff., Goldziher, *MSt.* I, 162, individual poems, Berl. 7530,$_2$, Leid. 591. For the *qaṣīda* by Ṣafwān al-Anṣārī in praise of the earth, in answer to Bashshār's fire worship, see al-Jāḥiẓ, *Bayān* I, 16/9.

3. Abū Dulāma Zand b. al-Jawn, a negro and client of the Banū Asad in Kufa, was more of a joker and court jester than a poet. Having participated in the
wars of the ʿAbbāsids against the Umayyads, | he was as a poet a frequent visi- 73
tor to al-Manṣūr and al-Mahdī. He was, too, a bad Muslim, not out of conviction, but laziness. He was extremely funny, as well as a shameless beggar. He died in the year 161/777, although some claim he died only after Hārūn's ascent to the throne.

Agh. IX, [1]120/40, [2]115/39, Ibn Khall. 230, al-Ḥuṣrī, *Dhayl Zahr al-ādāb*, C. 1927, 81/93.

4. Marwān b. Sulaymān b. Yaḥyā b. Abī Ḥafṣa was born in the year 103/721, the great-grandson of a Jew from Khurāsān who, after he had been enfranchised by Marwān b. al-Ḥakam when the latter was the governor of Medina, had made his way up the social ladder as a tax-collector in al-Yamāma, marrying a free

Arab woman. His father before him had also been a poet. He himself attained honours as the court poet of al-Mahdī. Having pronounced himself an opponent of the ʿAlids in some of his verses (see Suppl. I, 113), he was killed in revenge in 182/798.

Agh. IX, ^{1}36/48, ^{2}34/46, Ibn Khall. 687: his famous *marthiya* on Maʿn b. Zāʾida, Berl. 7530.

5. ʿAbbās b. al-Aḥnaf was famous almost exclusively as a writer of love poems. His ancestors had been Arabs who had settled in Khurāsān and who must have
75 been greatly mixed with Persian stock.[1] | He had grown up in Baghdad and was a regular visitor to the court of Hārūn al-Rashīd, whom he also accompanied on his campaigns to Azerbaijan and Armenia. He died in the year 191/806 (according to others, in 188/803,[2] and to yet others in 198/813) in Baghdad (or in Basra, or in the desert).

Agh. VIII, ^{1}15/25, ^{2}14/21, ^{3}252/72. *Dīwān* Köpr. 1259/60 (see Rescher, *MSOS* XIV, 9), print. Istanbul 1298.

74 | 6. Abū Nuwās al-Ḥasan b. Hāniʾ al-Ḥakamī was the greatest poet of this period and one of the greatest ever figures in Arabic literature. He was born in the year 139/756 (or, according to some sources, in 130/747 or 145/762) in Ahwaz, the son of an Arab who had been part of the army of the last Umayyad caliph, Marwān, and a Persian wool laundress by the name of Jullubān.[3] He spent his childhood in Basra where he may have enjoyed the teaching of the philologists Abū Zayd and Abū ʿUbayda. As an adolescent he went with his teacher and lover, the poet Abū Usāma Wāliba b. al-Ḥubāb al-Asadī, first to Ahwaz and then to Kufa, where he heard Khalaf al-Aḥmar speak. On the latter's advice he supposedly also spent one year in the desert to perfect his Arabic. He then went to Baghdad where he met Hārūn, following the recommendation of Isḥāq al-Mawṣilī. After the fall of the Barmakids in 187/803 he went for a time to Egypt where he tried to win the favour of the Head of the Exchequer, Ibn ʿAbd al-Ḥamīd al-ʿAjamī. However, he soon returned to Baghdad where he experienced a new period of courtly splendour under the successor of Hārūn. He did not only sing the praise of wine and pederasty, but also was enthusiastic about these subjects

---

1 See Th. Nöldeke, *Orient. Skizzen*, p. 117.

2 Suspect because of its synchronism with Ibrāhīm al-Mawṣilī and al-Kisāʾī, see *Agh.* ^{2}V, $43_{,20}$, Ibn Ṭaghr. II, 130.

3 That he did not feel like an Arab is shown by the verse in *Ahlw.* $26_{,4}$.

in his own life. It is reported that a female slave by the name of al-Janān once captured his heart, though only for a limited period of time. However, in his old age he seems to have repented of his earlier ways. In revenge for a satirical poem he wrote against the Banū Nawbakht (see *Dīwān* 171/2) he is said to have been so severely beaten by a member of this distinguished family that he died of his injuries. According to others, he died in prison, where he had been thrown because of a blasphemous poem; this seems to have happened between 195/806 and 198/813.

| In his wine songs, which were his central theme, he followed | the example 76 75
of Walīd b. Yazīd (see p. 60), and thus of ʿAdī b. Zayd. In this field he was a competitor of his contemporary Ḥusayn b. al-Ḍaḥḥāk al-Khalīʿ (Ibn Khall. 183, Suppl. I, 112), whose poems were partially attributed to him in later times. The attraction of his melodious language must all too often compensate for the shallowness of his ideas and imagery. "Less valuable from a poetical point of view are his laudatory poems, in which a certain artificiality makes itself felt rather strongly, while in the elegies deep emotions and a moving elegiac tonality make good for many shortcomings, notably the artificial language and oriental exaggeration. The love poems contain just as much tender feelings and things truly poetical as they do cynical and cruel elements. The satirical poems are crude and coarse at times, bitingly funny, but often malicious. This latter observation also applies to his buffoonery (*mujūn*) and his jokes, while his censuring poems (*ʿitāb*) again, show a more serious attitude."[4] The hunting poems developed out of the descriptions of the animals of the desert that had been very popular in ancient poetry. It seems, however, that Abū Nuwās found a definite precedent for his style of these, even though we have no further information on his predecessors.[5] The ascetic pieces (*zuhdiyyāt*) that conclude his *dīwān* should apparently not merely be understood as nice words, but as the expression of true and easily explainable moods.

Agh. XVI, [1]148/51, [2]142/6, XVIII [1,2]2/8 (in greater detail in the so-called "small *Aghānī*" of Gotha used by Ahlwardt), Ibn al-Anbārī, *Nuzhat al-alibbāʾ* 99/113, Ibn Khall. 163. Th. Nöldeke, in *Orient und Occident* I, 367ff., | A. v. Kremer, 77
Culturgesch. II, 369ff., A. Wünsche in *Nord und Süd*, Febr. 1891, 182/97, | A. v. 76
Kremer, *Dīwān des A. N. des grössten lyrischen Dichters der Araber*, Vienna 1855. *Dīwān des Abu nowas, hsg. v.* W. Ahlwardt, I, *Die Weinlieder*, Greifswald 1861. *Dīwān* lith. C. 1277, print. Beirut 1301, ed. Iskandar Āṣāf, C. 1898. Recension of al-Ṣūlī, d. 335/946 (see p. 143), in 10 chapters, Berl. 7531, Vienna 2016, Leid. 592,

4 See A. v. Kremer, *Culturgesch.* II, 371.

5 Ibid. 372, n. I.

Bodl. I, 1217, by Ḥamza b. al-Ḥasan al-Iṣfahānī,[6] much larger, but with many falsely attributed or at least questionable poems, cod. Landberg (Goldziher, *ZDMG* 50, 128, n. 1.), Vat. V, 456, Pet. Am 263, Istanbul Un. R. 843 (*ZS* III, 253), Cairo^{1} IV, 239, ^{2}III, 116, other recensions Leid. 593, Br. Mus. 1067, 1408 (see ḤKh III, 259), Paris $3251_{,7,10}$, 4829/30, Esc.^{2} 311, Pet. AM $263_{,2}$ (perhaps the recension by Ibrāhīm b. Aḥmad al-Ṭabarī Tūzūn, see Suppl. I, 117, bottom page), Köpr. 1250/1 (*MSOS* XIV, 19, 1), AS 3880.

7. Abu 'l-Walīd Muslim b. al-Walīd al-Anṣārī, nicknamed Ṣarīʿ al-Ghawānī,[7] born between 130/747 and 140/757, lived at the court of Hārūn in Baghdad as a professional panegyrist and writer of celebratory poems, in particular of the Barmakids and, afterwards, of Faḍl b. Sahl, the vizier of al-Maʾmūn. Al-Maʾmūn appointed him as a postmaster in Jurjān, where he died in 208/823. In his laudatory poems he surpassed the style of the ancients through his excessive employment of metaphors. In a long-lasting feud with the poet Qanbar,[8] in which he defended the Anṣār against the Quraysh, he brought the style of the Umayyad period back to life again. Of his wine-songs that were much praised by the Arabs at the time, and of his love songs, too, very little has remained.

Dīwān poetae Abu'l-Walid Muslim ibno'l-Walid al-Ançari, ed. (after Leid. 595) M.J. de Goeje, Leiden 1875, see Nöldeke, *GGA* 1875, 705ff., A. v. Kremer, *Culturgesch.* II, 377.

8. Abu 'l-ʿAtāhiya Ismāʿīl b. al-Qāsim, a *mawlā* of the ʿAnaza, was born in 130/748
77 in ʿAyn al-Tamar in the Hijaz | (or, according to others, near al-Anbār) and died on 8 Jumādā II 211/16 September 826 (or in 210 or 213). See Suppl. I, 119.

Agh. III, ^{1}126/82, ^{2}122/72, ^{3}IV, 1/112, Ibn Khall. 91, Ahlwardt, *Abu nowas*, 21. A. v. Kremer, *Culturgesch.* II, 372/6, *Dīwān Abu 'l-ʿAtāhiya* Beirut 1887/8, Pet. AM 264.

9. ʿAlī b. Jabala, nicknamed al-ʿAkawwak,[9] whose family originated in Khurāsān, was born in 160/776 in al-Ḥarbiyya on the western side of Baghdad, and was blind at birth or, at least, from early childhood. In his laudatory poems on the generals Abū Dulaf al-Qāsim b. ʿĪsā al-ʿIjlī and Abū Ghānim Ḥumayd b. ʿAbd al-Ḥamīd al-Ṭūsī he went so far that he actually aroused the envy and the wrath

6 *Khiz.* I, 168, incorrectly ʿAlī b. Ḥamza al-Iṣfahānī, see no. 15.

7 Already carried before him by al-Quṭāmī, see p. 59.

8 *Agh.* XIII, ^{1}9/12, ^{2}8/11.

9 Apparently given to him by al-Aṣmaʿī; al-Bakrī, *Simṭ al-laʾālī* I, 330.

of al-Maʾmūn, who supposedly had his tongue torn out. According to others, he had to live in hiding from the caliph until his death in the year 213/828.

Agh. XVIII, $^{1,\,2}$100/14, Ibn Khall. 434. A *qaṣīda* with *takhmīs* Berl. $7535_{,4}$, ibid. 5, attributed to al-Ḥasan b. Wahb al-Manbijī.

| 10. Diʿbil b. ʿAlī, see Suppl. I, 121. 79

Agh. XVIII, $^{1,\,2}$29/61, Ibn Khall. 213, Wüstenfeld, *Gesch.* 60. *Dīwān* and *Ṭabaqāt al-shuʿarāʾ*, Fihr. 161, cited as *Akhbār al-shuʿarāʾ* by al-Akhfash on Mubarrad's *Kāmil* $122_{,17}$; a long *qaṣīda* Berl. $7539_{,3}$, see ḤKh III, 5420.

11. ʿUmāra b. ʿAqīl b. Bilāl b. Jarīr, see Suppl. I, 122.

Ḍādiyyat ʿUmāra b. ʿAqīl (in praise of Khālid b. Yazīd) *riwāyat Thaʿlab ʿan b. al-Aʿrābī*, ed. ʿAbd al-ʿAzīz al-Maymanī in *al-Ṭarāʾif al-adabiyya*, C. 1937, 6/54.

11a. Abū Isḥāq Ibrāhīm b. al-ʿAbbās b. Muḥammad al-Ṣūlī, the son of the sister of ʿAbbās b. al-Aḥnaf, was born in 176/792 or 167/783, served the vizier al-Faḍl b. Sahl as | his secretary, managed the finances of Ahwaz under al-Wāthiq, 78 and was, during the reign of al-Mutawakkil, in charge of the *dīwān al-nafaqāt wal-ḍiyāʾ* in Samarra, where he died on 15 Shaʿbān 243/8 December 857.

Fihr. 126, *Agh.* ^{2}IX, 20/32, Ibn al-Khaṭīb, *Taʾr. Baghdād* VI, 117, Yāqūt, *Irshād* I, 260/77, Ibn Khall., 10, Goldziher, *MSt.* I, 112, Bartold, *Turkest.* 15. *Dīwān*, compiled by his nephew Abū Bakr (p. 143), MS Wehbi Ef. 1744, ed. by ʿAbd al-ʿAzīz al-Maymanī, *al-Ṭarāʾif al-adabiyya*, 118/88.

12. Al-Sāmī ʿAlī b. Jahm, from Khurāsān, lived in Baghdad at the court of al-Mutawakkil where he eventually made himself *persona non grata* because of his libellous works. Owing to a satirical poem about the caliph (or his personal physician Bukhtīshūʿ) he was thrown into prison and subsequently deported to his native country. There the proconsul Ṭāhir had him arrested and tied to a cross for an entire day. He then went to Syria where he was ambushed by a group of horsemen from the Banū Kalb on his way back from Aleppo to Baghdad, dying in battle in the year 249/863.

Agh. IX, ^{1}104/20, ^{2}99/115, Ibn Khall. 435, ḤKh III, 5576; songs in praise of the ʿAbbāsids, Esc. $^{2}369_{,3}$, another one on al-Mutawakkil, Berl. $7539_{,4}$.

13. While social life in Baghdad became more and more dominated by female slaves who had been educated as singers, there appeared in their midst a poetess of some repute, Faḍl of Basra, whose mother hailed from Yamāma. Later she would become part of al-Mutawakkil's court, dying in Baghdad in 260/873. Her poems are mostly addressed to the poet Saʿd b. Ḥumayd,[10] and illustrate her changing love-life.

Agh. XXI, [1]176/85, [2]114/20, *Fawāt* II, 126, Cl. Huart, La poétesse Fadl, *JA* s. VII, v. 17, p. 5ff.

79 | 14. Ibn al-Rūmī ʿAlī b. al-ʿAbbās b. Jurayj, born 27 Jumādā I 221/19
80 May 836, | was poisoned at the instigation of Abu ʾl-Ḥasan al-Qāsim b. ʿUbaydallāh, the vizier of al-Muʿtaḍid, out of fear of his *hijāʾ*, in the year 283/896 (though, according to others, this occurred in 284 or 276/889) (see Suppl. I, 123).

Ibn Khall. 436, *Dīwān*, alphabetically ordered by al-Ṣūlī, d. 335/946, Leid. 610, Esc. [2]277, NO 3859/60, Cairo[1] IV, 223, [2]III, 107.

15. Al-Buḥturī al-Walīd b. ʿUbayd Abū ʿUbāda al-Ṭāʾī was born in 206/821 in Manbij or a small settlement in its vicinity. As a young man he went to his fellow tribesman Abū Tammām, in those days highly regarded as a poet, who was staying in Homs at that time. Having convinced himself of his talent, the latter recommended him to the notables of Maʿarrat al-Nuʿmān, who paid him well for his panegyrics.[11] He later went to Baghdad where he lived for a long time as a panegyrist for al-Mutawakkil and his entourage. He died around 284/897 in Manbij or Aleppo (see Suppl. I, 125).

Agh. XVIII, [1,2]167/75, Ibn Khall. 741, cod. Goth. 26, fol. 156a. His *Dīwān* was organised alphabetically by al-Ṣūlī, and according to subject by ʿAlī b. Ḥamza al-Iṣfahānī, Berl. Brill M. 126, Munich 508, Vienna 450, Leid. 611/3, Pet. AM 267, Paris 3086, Köpr. 1252/3, Yeni 946, Cairo [1]IV, 241, [2]III, 120, print. Istanbul 1300, excerpts Berl. 7540, Paris 3300. *Ḥamāsa* see Suppl. I, 39.—al-Ḥasan b. Bishr al-Āmidī, *al-Muwāzana bayna ʾl-Ṭāʾiyyayn Abī Tammām wal-Buḥturī fi ʾl-shiʿr*, Istanbul 1287.

10 Of Persian origin, *Agh.* XVII[1, 2], 1/9.

11 Al-Ṣūlī, *Akhbār Abī Tammām*, 66.

16. Abu 'l-ʿAbbās ʿAbdallāh b. al-Muʿtazz (as caliph 252–5/866–9) was born 23 Shaʿbān 247/2 November 861. Under al-Muʿtaḍid he led the free life of a poet and scholar, but by the time of al-Muktafī's rule he became implicated in the
intrigues of the court. When his nephew al-Muqtadir came to | power and left 80
the administration entirely in the hands of his mother and her following of women and eunuchs, the disgruntled rallied around al-Muʿtazz as the most
important representative of their clan. | On 12 Rabīʿ I 296/10 December 998 81
he was proclaimed caliph with the honorific name of al-Murtaḍā. However, al-Muqtadir's guards went after him on that very same day; he was forced to take refuge in the house of a jeweller, but was soon discovered, and strangled on 1 Rabīʿ II/28 December (see Suppl. I, 128).

Agh. IX, ^{1}140/6, ^{2}135/9, al-Ṣūlī, *Ashʿār awlād al-khulafāʾ*, ed. Heyworth-Dunne, London 1936, 107/296 (almost exclusively poems and examples of prose styles), Ibn al-Anbārī 299/301, Ibn Khall. 314, *Fawāt* I, 241, Wüstenfeld, *Gesch.* 84, A. v. Kremer, *Culturgesch.* II, 379. O. Loth, *Über Leben und Werke des ʿAbdallāh b. al-Muʿtazz*, Leipzig 1882.—1. *Dīwān*, compiled by al-Ṣūlī, d. 335/946, Berl. 7542, Paris 3087, Copenhagen 251/2, Cairo ^{1}IV, 235, ^{2}III, 111, print. 2 vols., C. 1891; individual poems, Berl. 7543,$_{1-3}$, Gotha 26; Al-Muʿtaḍid als Prinz und Regent, ein historisches Heldengedicht, ed. C. Lang, ZDMG XL, 563ff, XLI 232ff.—2. *Kitāb al-ādāb*, moral sayings, Br. Mus. 1530,$_{3}$.—3. *Fuṣūl al-tamāthīl*, about drinking and its etiquette, a natural history of wine, and similes for wine as prevalent in poetry, Berl. 8316,$_{1-38}$, Leipz. 512, Copenhagen 298,$_{2}$, Paris 3239, cod. Landberg in Goldziher, *Abh.* I, 166, Cairo ^{1}VII, 653.—4. *Ṭabaqāt al-shuʿarāʾ al-muḥdathīn*, reproduced in facsimile from a manuscript dated 1285/1869, with an introduction, notes, and variants, by A. Eghbal, *Gibb Mem.* N.S. XIII, 1939, anonymous abstract Esc. ^{2}279, excerpts in Ḥamza al-Iṣfahānī's edition of Abū Nuwās, Berl. 7532, *Bāb* XV, see Goldziher, *Abh.* I, 166n.—5. *Ashʿār al-mulūk* Ahlw. 7434,$_{38}$.—6. *Sariqāt al-shuʿarāʾ, Khiz.* I, 3087.—7. *Kitāb al-badīʿ*, the first work about poetics, Esc. ^{2} 328.—Six other works are mentioned in *Fihrist* 116,$_{11-17}$.

17. His friend and, like him, one of the companions of the caliph al-Muʿtaḍid, was Ibn al-ʿAllāf al-Ḥasan b. ʿAlī, who d. 318/930 or 319.

His elegy for a cat, which served as a metaphor for Ibn al-Muʿtazz, al-Muḥsin
b. | al-Furāt, or a female slave, was famous. Ibn Khall. 164, al-Damīrī, *Ḥayāt* 81
al-ḥayawān II, 336.

18. Ibn al-Ḥajjāj Abū ʿAbdallāh al-Ḥusayn b. Aḥmad, see Suppl. I, 130.

82 | Ibn Khall. 184, al-Thaʿālibī, *Yatīmat al-dahr*, II, 211/7c, Abu ʾl-Fidāʾ, *Ann. Mosl.* II, 604, Istanbul 1287, II, 142. *Dīwān* in 10 vols., ḤKh II, 244, no. 5174, ^{2}I, 765, from which vol. II, Br. Mus. 584. Abstract by Jamāl al-Dīn b. al-Nubāta, d. 768/1366 (see II, 10), entitled *Talṭīf al-mizāj min shiʿr Ibn al-Ḥallāj*, ḤKh II, 415, no. 3554, ^{2}I, 480, Copenhagen 260, from which in turn *Laṭāʾif al-talṭīf* by Ibn Ḥijja al-Ḥamawī, d. 837/1433 (II, 15), Gotha 2235.

19. Al-Sharīf al-Raḍī Muḥammad b. al-Ṭāhir al-Ḥusayn al-Mūsawī was born in 359/970 in Baghdad, the son of a high official of ʿAlid stock. Under the mentorship of Ibn al-Jinnī (p. 125) and al-Sīrāfī (p. 115) he devoted himself to the study of philology and composed two works on Qurʾānic exegesis, which, however, fell short of his achievements as a poet. He died in his hometown on 6 Muḥarram 406/26 June 1016.

Al-Thaʿālibī, *Yatīma* II, 297ff., Ibn Khall. 639. *Dīwān*, in 4 vols., arranged alphabetically, ḤKh II, 5483, ^{2}I, 794, Berl. 7599/600, Br. Mus. 1072 (vol. III, arranged by ʿAbdallāh b. Ibrāhīm al-Khabrī, d. 476/1083, see p. 388), 1526, Cairo ^{1}IV, 246, ^{2}III, 133, the *Bāb al-ghazal* Esc. ^{2}349, *al-Ḥijāziyyāt* Dam. Z. 85$_{,5,2}$, selection Berl. 7601/2, Leid. 637 (incomplete), under the title *Insirāḥ al-ṣadr* Cairo ^{1}IV, 208, ^{2}III, 28, 339; individual poems Berl. 7603, Br. Mus. 630$_{,2}$, elegy for Abū Isḥāq al-Ṣābiʾ Gotha 26, f. 151a.

20. Abu ʾl-Ḥasan Mihyār b. Marzūya was a student of Sharīf. A Daylamī by birth, he professed Zoroastrianism until he was converted to Islam by Sharīf in 394/1003.[12] Following that, he seems to have lived in Baghdad. He died on 5 Jumādā II 428/27 March 1037.

82 | Ibn Khall. 726, Abu ʾl-Fidāʾ, *Ann.* II, 92, Ist. II. 168. *Dīwān* Ḥkh ^{1}III, 316, ^{2}I, 816, *qaṣīdas, ghazals*, and riddles, Munich 516, Gotha 2235$_{,2}$ (incomplete?), Köpr. 1243; individual poems, Berl. 7609$_{,3,4}$, 8157, Gotha 26, Br. Mus. 630$_{,2}$, Esc. ^{2}467$_{,1}$, cf. 524$_{,1}$.

21. Abu ʾl-Ḥasan ʿAlī b. al-Zurayq lived around 420/1029 and was a secretary in Baghdad.

---

12 See T.W. Arnold, *The Preaching of Islam*, Westminster 1896, p. 180. Brockelmann, *GAL* I.

| *Qaṣīda ʿayniyya*, in 40 verses, Berl. 7606/7, comm. by ʿAlī b. ʿAbdallāh al-ʿAlawī, 83
d. 1199/1785, ibid. $7607_{,3}$, *Takhmīs* by Aḥmad b. Nāṣir al-Bāʿūnī, d. 816/1413, ibid. 2.

B *Poets of Iraq and the Jazīra*

In the heyday of the ʿAbbāsids there were only few poets in Mesopotamia who, for political or personal reasons, stayed away from the capital in order to bestow a certain literary splendour upon local governors' courts.

1. Al-Sayyid al-Ḥimyarī Ismāʿīl b. Muḥammad Yazīd b. Mufarrij was born in Basra in 105/723. While his parents adhered to the Khārijī Ibāḍiyya sect, he himself joined the Shīʿī Qaysāniyya movement in his youth, and had to flee to Kufa because of this. Even though he embraced their most radical views, such as the belief in reincarnation, he still paid homage to al-Saffāḥ on his entry to Kufa, in the same way he did later to al-Manṣūr and a number of local governors. He died in Wāsiṭ in the year 173/789. Like those of Abu 'l-ʿAtāhiya and Bashshār, his poems are distinguished by their simple language, but were never particularly popular due to his religious and political views.

Agh. VII, [1]1/31, [2]11/29, [3]229/78, *Fawāt* I, 19, al-Shahrastānī III, Barbier de Meynard, *JA* s. VII, v. 4, p. 159ff., Brockelmann, *EI* IV, 81. For his *Qaṣīda mudhahhaba*, in praise of the Prophet and his family, Br. Mus. $886_{,1}$, Ind. Off. $371_{,12}$, see Suppl. I, 133.

| 2. Abu 'l-Shīṣ Muḥammad b. ʿAbdallāh b. Razīn b. Sulaymān, of the tribe of 83
ʿĀmir b. Thaʿlaba, was a nephew (or, according to others, an uncle) of Diʿbil (p. 77). Because he was no match for the great poets of his days in Baghdad he joined the emir ʿUqba b. al-Ashʿath al-Khuzāʿī in al-Raqqa as his panegyrist. However, he also composed wine songs and, when he became blind in his old age, songs of mourning for his eyes. In the year 196/811 he was killed by a drunken slave.

Agh. XV, [1]108/13, [2]104/8, *Fawāt* II, 225.

C *Poets from Arabia and Syria*

1. Ibn Harma Abū Isḥāq Ibrāhīm b. ʿAlī, born in 90/709, lived for most of his life in Medina and died after 150/767. Although he was a supporter of the ʿAlids, he nevertheless recited a laudatory *qaṣīda* to al-Manṣūr.

Agh. IV, [1]102/14, [2]101/13, [3]367/97, *Khiz.* I, 204; *Akhbār b. Harma* by Isḥāq al-Mawṣilī (Suppl. I, 223), *Fihrist* 142,$_4$. Two *qaṣīdas*, Berl. 7529,$_2$. He is credited with a *qaṣīda* consisting only of undotted letters, *Agh.* [1]IV, 106/7, an artificiality whose invention is usually attributed to the metrician Razīn al-ʿArūḍī, whose laudatory poem on al-Ḥasan b. Sahl, d. 236/850, is mentioned in Yāqūt, *Irshād* VI, 16/7, Abu 'l-ʿAlāʾ al-Maʿarrī, *Letters*, ed. Margoliouth, 75.

2. Abū Tammām Ḥabīb b. Aws al-Ṭāʾī was born in the year 192/807 (according to others, 172, 182, or 190) in Jasīm in the district of Jaydūr, north-east of Lake Tiberias, apparently the son of a Christian by the name of Tadūs (Thaddeus). Possibly he only claimed membership of the Ṭayyiʾ when, still a young man, he seconded the Ṭayyiʾī ʿAbd al-Karīm in Homs in an affair of *hijāʾ*. In Egypt he did not gain the success he had been hoping for, and so he went to Damascus, where he vainly attempted to gain access to the caliph al-Maʾmūn when the
84 latter was touring Syria. | He settled in Mosul for two years because al-Ḥasan
b. Wahb had appointed him as a postmaster there.[1] It was probably from there that he went to Armenia, where the governor Khālid b. Yazīd, famous for his wars against the Byzantines, showered him with gifts. After al-Maʾmūn's death in 218/833 he went to Baghdad, where he won the favour of al-Muʿtaṣim and his entourage.[2] Later he went to ʿAbdallāh b. Ṭāhir, who had made himself almost completely independent as the governor of Khurāsān. On the way back to Iraq he was surprised by a huge snowstorm in Hamadan, forcing him into
85 a long stay. | Abu 'l-Wafāʾ b. Salama put his library of belles lettres there at his
disposal, out of which he compiled four large anthologies, among them the *Ḥamāsa*. These were the major reasons for his fame, so that his commentator al-Tabrīzī could say of him: *Abū Tammām fī Ḥamāsatihi ashʿaru minhu fī shiʿrihi* (see Suppl. I, 134/7). He died in 231/846 (or, according to al-Khaṭīb, in 228, and according to others 229 or 236).

Agh. XV, [1]100/8, [2]96/104, Ibn al-Anbārī, 213/6, Yāqūt, GW II, 8, Abū Bakr Muḥammad b. Yaḥyā al-Ṣūlī, d. 243/851, see p. 143, *Akhbār Abī Tammām wa-bi-awwalihi Risālat al-Ṣūlī ilā Muzāḥim b. Fātik fī taʾlīf Akhbār Abī Tammām wa-shiʿrihi*, ed. by Khalīl Maḥmūd ʿAsākir, Muḥammad ʿAbduh Gharām, Naẓīr al-Islām al-Hindī, C. 1937/1356, Ibn Khall. 143. *Dīwān*, arranged by al-Ṣūlī according to the alphabet and by ʿAlī b. Ḥamza al-Iṣfahānī according to subject

1 Others place this episode towards the end of his life, something which was rejected by Ibn Khallikān, and rightly so.

2 His first vist to al-Muʿtaṣim in al-Maṣṣīṣa had been fruitless because the caliph disliked his hoarse voice. He was only successful when he let a well-voiced *rāwī* recite his famous *qaṣīda* on the conquest of ʿAmmūriyya; al-Ṣūlī, *Akhbār Abī Tammām*, 143/4.

(*Khiz.* I, 172), Berl. 7536, Leid. 596, Br. Mus. 581/2, Ind. Off. 806, Bodl. I, 1255, Pet
AM 265/6, Paris 3085, Esc. ^{2}290/1 (by al-Ṣūlī), 415 (by Abū ʿAlī Ismāʿīl al-Qālī,
p. 132), *As. Soc. Calcutta*, p. 32, | Cairo ^{1}IV, 237, ^{2}III, 113, print. C. 1292,[3] com- 85
mentary by al-Tabrīzī, d. 502/1108 (p. 279), Leid. 597/8, 5 other commentaries in
Ahlw. 7537. *Ḥamāsa* see Suppl. I, 39. *Kitāb al-Intiṣār min ẓalamat Abī Tammām*
by al-Marzūqī, d. 421/1030, Ahlw. 7539.

3. Dīk al-Jinn ʿAbd al-Salām b. Raghbān, a descendant of Ḥabīb b. ʿAbdallāh b. Raghbān, the secretary of al-Manṣūr (al-Jahshiyārī, *Wuzarāʾ*, 108,$_{6}$), was born in 161/778 in Homs. He represented the patriotism of the Syrian people against the Arabs in the spirit of the Shuʿūbiyya, which is why he could not bring himself to leave his native country. As a moderate Shīʿī he composed elegies on al-Ḥusayn. He died in 235/849.

Agh. XII, ^{1}142/9, ^{2}136/43, Ibn Khall. 357, Goldziher, *M.St.* I, 156.

4. Kushājim Abu ʾl-Fatḥ Maḥmūd b. al-Ḥusayn b. Shahāq was the grandson of an Indian, whence al-Sindī, and lived for a time in Ramla, whence al-Ramlī. He entered into the service of Sayf al-Dawla as an astrologer and kitchen-master and died in 350/961 or 360/971.

Dīwān, arranged alphabetically, Leid. 625, Garr. 23, Br. Mus. 1071, Pet. AM 269,$_{2}$, Köpr. 1261, Cairo ^{2}III, 144, selection Berl. 7584. *Adab al-nadīm*, a collection of anecdotes and verses, Berl. Oct. 1094, Paris 3301, Cairo ^{1}IV, 20, ^{2}III, 9, Būlāq 1298. *Kitāb al-bazyara* Gotha 2091,$_{2}$ (fragm.). *Al-Ṭardiyyāt*, ḤKh IV, 158, no. 4954, *Kitāb al-maṣāyid wal-maṭārid*, quoted by Ibn Khall. I, 130,$_{23}$, 151,$_{25}$, al-Juzūlī, *Maṭāliʿ al-budūr* I, 217,$_{11}$, see Suppl.

| 5. Al-Waʾwāʾ Muḥammad b. Aḥmad al-Ghassānī al-Dimashqī, see Suppl. I, 138. 86

6. Manṣūr b. Kaiġylyġ (?),[4] the son of a Syrian emir of Turkish stock of the fourth century, was famous, like his brother Aḥmad, because of his invention of unique similes.

86 | Al-Thaʿālibī, *Yatīma* I, 65/7, a love poem Esc. ^{2}470,$_{15}$, at the beginning of an
anonymous anthology.

---

3 As the place of publication of the edition by Muḥyi ʾl-Dīn al-Khayyāṭ (see Suppl.) Sarkis gives Beirut, while *Akhbār*, 336, gives Cairo.

4 Probably for Kaiqylyq, 'of good character', with a change of 'q' to 'ġ', which often occurs in Turkish dialects.

7. Abu 'l-Ḥasan ʿAlī b. Muḥammad al-Tihāmī seems to have lived for most of his life in Syria. In the year 416/1025, while on a secret mission to Cairo on behalf of the emir al-Ḥassān b. al-Mufarrij al-Badawī, who revolted four years later against al-Ẓāhir, he was caught, and was killed in prison on 9 Jumādā I/8 July of that year.

Ibn Khall. 444, see Suppl. I, 147$_{,7}$. *Dīwān* also Patna I, 197$_{,1769}$.

D *The Circle of Sayf al-Dawla*

When the lustre of the caliphate in Baghdad had long since died out and control over Iraq had become something tossed about amongst various generals and proconsuls of mostly Persian and Turkish stock, the ʿAlid-minded Ḥamdānid Sayf al-Dawla succeeded—in the midst of the general confusion—to once more construct an imposing Arab state in northern Syria, with Aleppo as its capital. Even though he had to defend his empire in endless battles against external enemies, especially the Byzantines, his state nevertheless gave rise to a short flourishing of intellectual life among a number of distinguished men at his residence, from among whom only the poets shall be mentioned.

Al-Thaʿālibī, *Yatīma* I, 8/22, A. Müller, *Der Islam* I, 570/8.

1. Al-Mutanabbī Abu 'l-Ṭayyib Aḥmad b. al-Ḥusayn al-Juʿfī was born in 303/905 in the Kinda quarter of Kufa but spent his youth in Syria. In tandem with the Qarmaṭian movements of his time he was active as a politico-religious agitator amongst the Bedouins of the Samāwa desert there, but he and his followers were soon put down by Lu'lu', the Ikhshīdid emir of Homs, and thrown into
87 prison for a time. From this period stems the nickname | by which he became famous. In prison he seems to have become aware of his real calling as a poet.
87 | In the year 337/948 he came to the court of Sayf al-Dawla, to whose glory his talent unfolded so brilliantly that their names became inseparable. However, his stay in Aleppo only lasted nine years. For reasons unknown he fell out with Sayf al-Dawla,[1] and in 346/957 he went over to his enemy in Egypt, the Ikhshīdid Kāfūr. Because the latter fell short of his expectations, he ridiculed him and had to flee to Baghdad in 350/961. Here, the vizier al-Muhallabī wanted to draw him into his service, but when he refused to accept this, the former incited the poets who were dependent on him to an *hijā'* against him. Thus, he turned to

1 According to Ibn Khallikān it was as a result of a dispute with the philologist Khālawayh (p. 125), who had been against him all along.

the Būyid ʿAḍud al-Dawla in Persia. On the way back, near al-Ṣāfiya, not far from al-Nuʿmāniyya in the vicinity of Nahrawān, he was ambushed by robbers and killed, on 24 Ramaḍān 254/23 September 965 (see Suppl. I, 139/40).

Al-Thaʿālibī *Yatīma* I, 78/162, Ibn al-Anbārī 366/74, Ibn Khall. 49, *Khiz.* I, 382/9. P. v. Bohlen, *Commentatio de Motanebbio*, Bonn 1824, F. Dieterici, *Mutanabbi und Seifuddaula*, Leipzig 1847, A. v. Kremer, *Culturgesch.* II, 380. *Dīwān*, now alphabetically, then chronologically arranged, available in almost any library, print. Calcutta 1230, Beirut 1860, Bombay 1310 (with marginal commentary)—Commentaries: 1. Ibn Jinnī, d. 392/1001, in three volumes, ḤKh II, 307, Pet. AM, 275, II, Esc. ^{2}309, Istanbul Un. R 615 (*ZS* III, 253), not Leid. 630 (contrary to Juynboll, *Orient.* I, 231ff.); against this work Abū ʿAlī b. Fūrraja (see Suppl.) wrote, ca. 437/1045, his *al-Tajannī ʿalā Ibn Jinnī*, ḤKh ^{1}III, 308, ^{2}I, 810, Esc. ^{2}307.—2. Abu ʾl-Qāsim Ibrāhīm b. Muḥammad al-Iflīlī, d. 441/1049, Berl. 7569 (?anon.).—3. Abu ʾl-ʿAlāʾ al-Maʿarrī, d. 449/1057, Munich 514, Br. Mus. 592/5, Pet. AM 276, NO 3980/1.—4. See Suppl.—5. ʿAlī b. Aḥmad | al-Wāḥidī, d. 468/1075 88
(see p. 411), also Berl. Brill M. 201, *Mutanabbii carmina cum cmtario al-W.* ed. Fr. Dieterici, Berlin 1861.—6. al-Tabrīzī, d. 502/1108, see p. 279, Paris 3101/4.—7. al-ʿUkbarī, d. 616/1219, see p. 282, Būlāq 1860, 1287, C. 1308.—8. Anon., Berl. 7573/4, Paris 3105/6, Esc. ^{2}272.—9. Nāṣif al-Yāzījī (II, 494), *al-ʿArf al-ṭayyib fī sharḥ dīwān Abi ʾl-Ṭayyib*, ed. by his son Ibrāhīm, Beirut 1888, 1325. Ahlwardt 7579 mentions 15 commentaries.—*al-Mukhtār min dīwān al-Mutanabbī* by Abu ʾl-Sanāʾ Maḥmūd b. Salmān, d. 725/1325, Berl. 7575.—Ismāʿīl al-Ṭālqānī, d. 385/995 (see p. 380), who also wrote a supplement to the commentary by al-Jinnī (see *Khiz.* I, 382,$_{5}$), *al-Amthāl al-sāʾira min shiʿr al-Mutanabbī*, Cairo ^{1}IV, 207, ^{2}III, 23.—Muḥammad b. al-Ḥasan al-Ḥātimī al-Baghdādī, d. 388/998, *al-Risāla al-Ḥātimiyya*, sayings by Aristotle used by Mutanabbī and al-Riyāḍī, Gotha 2234, Algiers 566,$_{4}$ (without the passages from al-Riyāḍī, Gotha 1 f. 3b), print. in *al-Tuḥfa al-bahiyya wal-ṭurfa al-shahiyya*, Constantinople 1302, p. 144/59 (idem. Gotha 29, f. 174b).—al-Ḥasan b. ʿAlī al-Tinnīsī al-Wakīʿ, d. 393/1003 (see p. 91), *al-Munṣif lil-sāriq wal-masrūq minhu*, against the overestimation of al-Mutanabbī's originality, Berl. 7577.—Yūsuf al-Badīʿī, d. 1073/1663 (II, 286), *al-Subḥ al-munabbiʾ ʿan ḥaythiyyat al-Mutanabbī*, on the life, work, genius, precursors, and emulators of al-Mutanabbī, cf. de Sacy, *Anth. gramm.* 476, de Slane, *Ibn Khall.* transl. I, 110, Berl. 7516, Leipz. 873, Gotha 2233, Paris 3107, Br. Mus. 597, | Cairo ^{1}IV, 279, ^{2}III, 239.—Abū Saʿīd Muḥammad b. Aḥmad 89
al-ʿAmīdī, *al-Ibāna ʿan sariqāt al-Mutanabbī lafẓan wa-maʿnan*, Pet. Ros. 83, Bodl. I, 108.—*Risālat al-ṣāḥib kāfi ʾl-kufāt Abi ʾl-Ḥusayn Ḥamza b. Muḥammad al-Iṣbahānī* (when?) *fī kashf ʿuyūb al-Mutanabbī* Esc. ^{2}470,$_{1}$.

2. Abū Firās al-Ḥārith b. Saʿīd b. Ḥamdān al-Ḥamdānī, born in 320/932, was the cousin of Sayf al-Dawla and governor for him in Manbij. He was taken prisoner in the struggle against the Byzantines in 348/959 and kept in a dungeon by the sea—which probably means near Constantinople—for two years. According to others, he had first been transported to Kharshana on the Euphrates in 348, whence he had escaped by a daring jump, only to be taken prisoner again in 351/962, on which occasion he was shipped off to Constantinople where he remained for four years. During his captivity he addressed several moving
89 | elegies to his loved ones, among them the famous song for his mother.[2] When Sayf al-Dawla died in in 356/967 he tried to seize power in Homs, and in 357/968 he perished in combat near Mount Sanīr fighting the troops of Qarghūya, the legal guardian of his sister's son Abu ʾl-Maʿālī (see Suppl. I, 143/4).

Al-Thaʿālibī, *Yatīma* I, 22/62, A. v. Kremer, *Culturgesch.* II, 381/6. R. Dvořak, *Abū Firās, ein arabischer Dichter und Held mit Ṯaʿālibīs Auswahl aus seiner Poesie in Text und Übersetzung mitgeteilt*, Leiden 1895, see J. Wellhausen, GGA 1896, 173/6, Dvořak, A.F. und seine Poesie, *Actes du Xème congr. des or. sect.* III, 69/83. *Dīwān*, ed. by Ibn Khālawayh, d. 370/980, Berl. 7580/1, Strasburg, Spitta 30, Leipz. 863, ii, Tüb. $139_{,1}$ frgm. ibid. $137_{,3}$, Br. Mus. Suppl. 1044/5, Bodl. I, $1298_{,5}$, Cambr. 375, 429, Palat. 507, Pet. Am 270/2, Patna I, $197_{,1765}$, print. Beirut 1873, 1910; individual poems Berl. 7582/3, Gotha 26, f. 204b, Leid. 631, Esc. $^2408_{,2}$; German by Fr. Rückert in Lagarde, *Symmicta* 206/8.

90 | 3. Al-Zāhī ʿAlī b. Isḥāq, born in 318/930, mostly lived in Baghdad, and occasionally in Aleppo, where he sang the praise of the ʿAbbāsids and their vizier al-Muhallabī. He died in the year 352/963.

Yatīma I, 171/3 (did not know of any *dīwān* by him), Ibn Khall. 440.

4. In the beginning, al-Raffāʾ al-Sarī b. Aḥmad al-Kindī had been a tailor in Mosul, which is how he got his nickname. As a poet, he lived at the court of Sayf al-Dawla in Aleppo and, after the latter's death,[3] in Baghdad, with the vizier al-Muhallabī. Statements about his year of death place it variously as

---

2 Ahlwardt, *Poesie und Poetik der Araber*, p. 44, v. Kremer, op. cit., 383/4.

3 According to Ibn Khallikān. According to al-Samʿanī he had been forced to leave Aleppo before this time because the al-Khālidiyyān brothers (p. $146_{,2}$) had brought him into bad repute with Sayf al-Dawla.

shortly after 360 (al-Khaṭīb), in 362 (Yāqūt), and in 366/976 (Ibn Khall. based on Ibn al-Athīr, not in the *Taʾrīkh*).[4]

| *Yatīma* I, 450/507, al-Samʿānī, *Ansāb* 255v, Ibn Khall. 243. *Dīwān*, mostly lauda- 90
tory poems, Berl. 7587, Paris 3098,$_{21}$, Cairo [1]IV, 246, [2]III, 132, print. C. 1355 (288 pp.). *Kitāb al-muḥibb wal-maḥbūb wal-mashmūm wal-mashrūb*, in 4 books: 1. Descriptions of the appearance of the beloved, 2. Poems about love, 3. Perfume and flowers, 4. Wine and its names, Vienna 359, Leid. 448, *Scheidii Cat.*, p. 92. no. 28.

5. Abu ʾl-Faraj ʿAbd al-Wāḥid (ʿAbd al-Malik) b. Naṣr b. Muḥammad al-Makhzūmī al-Naṣībīnī, also called al-Babbaghā because of a speech defect, lived at the court of Sayf al-Dawla and, after the latter's death, in Mosul and Baghdad. He died on 27 Shaʿbān 398/8 May 1008.

Yatīma I, 173/205, al-Samʿānī, *Ansāb* 64sv. Ph. Wolff, *Abulfaragii Babbaghae carminum specimen ex cod. Gothano primum ed., lat. vert. adnot. illustr.; accedunt aliquot carmina Abu Ishaci* (see p. 95,$_{d}$), Leipzig 1834. E.G. Schultz, *Variae lectiones e cod. ms. Parisino collectae ad A.B. carmina a. Ph. Wolffio edita*, diss. Konigsberg 1838.

6. After al-Mutanabbī's departure, al-Nāmī Aḥmad b. Muḥammad al-Dārimī took over his role as court poet for Sayf al-Dawla, before dying in Aleppo in 399/1009 (or, according to other sources, in 370/980 or 371). He also composed dictates in the field of belles lettres (*Amālī*).

Yatīma I, 164/71, Ibn Khall. 50.

| E *Egyptian and North African Poets* 91

In spite of the splendour of the material culture that blossomed under the Ṭūlūnids (254–92/869–904) in Egypt, neither this dynasty nor its successors the Ikhshīdids (321–58/933–69) and the first Fāṭimids could provide intellectual life with the kind of stimulus that would have allowed them to attract and retain foreign poets. Thus, we can only relate the works of a few mediocre talents.

---

4 According to cod. Pet. 579, f. 54b his *dīwān* also contains an elegy for Abū Iṣhāq Ibrāhīm al-Ṣābiʾ, d. 384/944, which would mean that his death would have to be placed even later; Ahlw. 7587.

1. Ibn Ṭabāṭabā Aḥmad b. Muḥammad b. Ismāʿīl al-Rassī, *naqīb* of the ʿAlids in Egypt who died on 25 Shaʿbān 345/1 December 956.

91 | *Yatīma* I, 328/30, Ibn Khall. 52 (see Suppl.).

2. Abu ʾl-Qāsim Muḥammad b. Ibrāhīm b. Hāniʾ al-Andalusī al-Azdī was born in Seville, where his father had emigrated from a village near al-Mahdiyya in Africa. As a poet he had gained the favour of the sovereign of his native country, but he then ridiculed him in verses in the style of al-Maʿarrī, which exposed him as a freethinker. At the age of 27 he was thus banished, whereupon he went to Jawhar, the general of the Fāṭimids in Africa, and thence to Jaʿfar b. ʿAlī b. Rūmān in Masīla, in the Zāb. After his ascension to the throne in 341/953 al-Manṣūr's son al-Muʿizz gave him a position at his court. In 358/969 he took part in the conquest of Egypt. Once the situation had stabilised somewhat he returned to the Maghreb to fetch his family, but was murdered on the way in 362/973.

Ibn Khall. 640, A. v. Kremer, ZDMG XXIV, 481/94. *Dīwān*, for the most part panegyrics on al-Muʿizz, arranged alphabetically, Berl. 7385/6, Paris 3108, Bodl. I, $129,_{1}$, see II, 618, Esc.[2] 443 Pet. AM, 80/1, Patna I, $197,_{1763}$, print. C. 1276.

3. Tamīm, the second son of the Fāṭimid al-Muʿizz, born in 337/948, composed love poems, mostly about his brother al-ʿAzīz (365–86/975–96). He died in Egypt in 374/984.

Yatīma I, 347/55, Ibn Khall. 122. *Dīwān* Leid. 632.

92 | 4. Ibn Wakīʿ al-Ḥasan b. ʿAlī b. Aḥmad was born in Tinnīs near Damietta, where he died in 393/1003.

Yatīma I, 281/305, Ibn Khall. 163. A *qaṣīda*, Berl. 7589; for his work on al-Mutanabbī, see p. 88.

5. Abu ʾl-Raqaʿmaq Aḥmad b. Muḥammad of Antioch composed laudatory poems for the upper classes of Egypt, dying in 399/1008.

Yatīma I, 238/61, Ibn Khall. no. 53.

| Chapter 3. Rhymed Prose 92

As it had become quasi-sanctified by the Qur'ān, the profane use of rhymed prose, or *saj*ʿ (see Suppl. I, 22), disappeared almost entirely in the first two centuries of Islam. It was only in the middle of the third century that it emerged again in the *khuṭba*, which in those days was left more and more in the hands of professional preachers, who developed it artistically. From there, *saj*ʿ also penetrated into literature in the form of epistles (*rasāʾil*) and in the newly emerging genre of the *maqāma*.[1]

1. Ibn Nubāta ʿAbd al-Raḥīm b. Muḥammad b. Ismāʿīl al-Ḥudhāqī al-Fāriqī, who was born in 335/946 in Mayyāfāriqīn, lived as a preacher at the court of Sayf al-Dawla in Aleppo and died in his native town in 374/984.

Ibn Khall. 346, de Slane, *JA* s. III, vol. 9, p. 66ff. *Khuṭab*, on death and resurrection, the death of the Prophet, contempt for the world, changing times, the months of Rajab, Shaʿbān, Ramaḍān, festivals, Hell, war against the infidels etc., at times drawing on dated events, further *Fuṣūl*, short orations held on important occasions, Berl. 3944 (compiled around 629/1223, also containing sermons by his son Abū Ṭāhir Muḥammad b. ʿAbd al-Raḥīm, | ca. 390/999, cf. Paris 1289,2 93 and his grandson Abu 'l-Faraj Ṭāhir ca. 420/1029), Brill M. 269, Munich 153, Bodl. I, 96, Leid. 2138, Copenhagen 71, Paris 1289,1 Esc. ²522, print. C. 1282, 1286, 1292, 1302, 1304, 1309, Beirut 1311.—Comm. by al-ʿUkbarī, d. 616/1219, Leid. 2138 and ʿAbd al-Raḥīm b. Ibrāhīm al-Bārizī, d. 683/1294 (see p. 349), Bodl. I, 139, see II, 570, excerpts by his son in Gotha 827, anonymous Paris 1290,3; other commentaries in ḤKh III, no. 4727, ²I, 714, Ahlw. 3344.

2. Abū Bakr Muḥammad b. al-ʿAbbās al-Khwārazmī or al-Ṭabarkhazī[2]—his father being from Khwārazm | and his mother, the sister of the famous his- 93 torian al-Ṭabarī, from Ṭabaristān—was born in 323/935. When he was young he lived for a time at the court of Sayf al-Dawla in Aleppo, then went to the vizier of the Sāmānids, Abū ʿAlī al-Balʿamī (see p. 143), in Bukhārā, whom he soon left, continuing on towards Nishapur and Sijistān, where he was incarcerated for a long period of time because of a satirical poem he had written about the proconsul Ṭāhir b. Muḥammad. After succesful tours of Isfahan

---

1 See Goldziher, *Abh.* I, 62/8.

2 Thus in al-Samʿānī, *Ansāb*, 366v, and subsequently Ibn Khall., cf. *Lubb* 167a, *Yatīma* IV, 123 al-Ṭabarkhazmī.

and Shiraz he settled down in Nishapur. But because he had the temerity to ridicule the vizier al-ʿUtbī the local proconsul punished him by confiscating all his possessions and putting him in jail. However, he succeeded in escaping to Jurjān and, after the assassination of al-ʿUtbī, the latter's successor Abu 'l-Ḥasan al-Muzanī called him back to Nishapur and compensated him for his losses. Towards the end of his life his younger rival al-Hamadhānī had thoroughly shaken his reputation. He died in 382/993 or, according to Ibn al-Athīr, in 393/1002. From his poems, only samples have survived, in the *Yatīma*; however, his epistles in rhymed prose on a wide variety of fields of belles lettres have immortalised his name.

Yatīma IV, 114/54, Ibn Khall. 636. *Rasāʾil* Berl. 8626/7, Tüb. $71_{,1}$, Vienna 279, Leid. 343/4, Köpr. 1274, Būlāq 1279, Istanbul 1297, Bombay 1301, 1891.

3. Badīʿ al-Zamān Aḥmad b. al-Ḥusayn b. Yaḥyā b. Saʿīd Abu 'l-Faḍl al-Hamadhānī was born on 13 Jumādā II 358/5 May 969 in Hamadan, where he
94 was educated by the philologist Abu 'l-Ḥusayn b. Fāris. In the year 380/990 | he went to Jurjān, and then in 384 to Nishapur as the favourite of the *dihqān* Abū Saʿīd Muḥammad b. Manṣūr. As he writes in one of his letters, he once badly harrassed al-Khwārazmī, who was then at the height of his fame, in a verbal
94 duel there.[3] | Later he travelled through the whole of Khurāsān and Sijistān, where he enjoyed the favours of the prince Khalaf b. Aḥmad. In the end he seems to have settled in Ghazna. He died in 398/1007 in Herat, after he had been buried seemingly dead of a stroke (see Suppl. I, 150/2).

95 | *Yatīma* IV, 167/204, Ibn Khall. 81, *Khiz.* IV, 71, 175, de Sacy, *Mag. enc.* 1814, I, 195, v. Kremer, *Culturgesch.* II, 470/6, J. Kubat, Bedi el-Hamadani, ein arab. Dichterprofil, *Mag. für die Lit. des In-u. Auslandes* 1884, 91/2, 98/100. *Dīwān* Paris $2147_{,2}$, poem in praise of Muḥammad b. ʿĪsā al-Dāmaghānī, Berl. $7589_{,3}$.—*Rasāʾil* Istanbul 1298, *commentées par le cheikh Ibr. al-Ahdab*, Beirut 1890, *Risāla fī 'l-ʿilm* Patna II, $427_{,2600,5}$.—*Maqāmāt* Paris 3923, Copenhagen 224, Cambr. 118, Berl. 8535 (cf. ZDMG 45, 478, no. 103), NO 4270, Būlāq 1291, Istanbul 1298, C. 1304, *commentées par le cheikh M. ʿAbdo* (Suppl. III, 315), Beirut 1889. *Consessus Hamadanensis vulgo dicti Bedialzaman e cod. ms. fratris sui ejusdemque typis arab.* ed. J. Scheidius, n.p., n.d. (Euting 1572), de Sacy, *Chrest. ar.* III, 78/83, cf. 261, Grangeret de la Grange, *Anthol. ar.* 153/60, German by E. Amthor, *Klänge aus dem Osten* 1843.

---

3 See v. Kremer, *Culturgesch.* II, 471ff.

4. Abū Naṣr ʿAbd al-ʿAzīz b. ʿUmar b. Nubāta al-Saʿdī, born in 327/939 in Baghdad, lived as a court poet with Sayf al-Dawla and with Muḥammad b. ʿAbd al-Ḥamīd in Rayy. He died in 405/1014 in Baghdad.

Ibn Khall. 359. A *maqāma*, Berl. 8536.

5. Collections of sample letters in rhymed prose that are still extant:

a. Abu ʾl-Husayn al-Ahwāzī, ca. 330/941.

| *Kitāb al-durar wal-ghurar*, letters to the emirs Abu ʾl-Ḥārith Muḥammad 96
b. Farīghūn,[4] Abu ʾl-Asad al-Ḥārith b. Muḥammad, Abū Aḥmad al-Ḥusayn b. Ṭāhir, Abu ʾl-Qāsim ʿAlī b. Muḥammad al-Kāshānī, and Abū Manṣūr Naṣr b. Aḥmad (d. 331/943), arranged by subject, Leid. 346/7.—2. *Kitāb al-farāʾid wal-qalāʾid fi ʾl-istiʿāna ʿala ʾl-afʿāl* | *al-maḥmūda*, an *adab* work, Leid. 451, Paris 95
2419,$_2$, wrongly attributed to Qābūs b. Washmgīr, d. 403/1012 (see Suppl. I, 154), in Vienna 1838 attributed to al-Thaʿālibī, who partially summarised it in his *Siḥr al-balāgha* (see *Anth. sent.* 128), Krafft 479, Paris 3956.

b. Abū Aḥmad Manṣūr b. Muḥammad al-Azdī al-Harawī, *qāḍī* of Herat and panegyrist for the caliph al-Qādir billāh, d. 440/1048.

Munyat al-rāḍī bi-rasāʾil al-qāḍī, collected by al-Maydānī (p. 289), Berl. 8647 (see Suppl. I, 155).

c. ʿAbd al-ʿAzīz b. Yūsuf al-Shīrāzī, secretary and vizier to the Būyid ʿAḍud al-Dawla (338–72/949–82) and his sons.

Rasāʾil to various high-ranking people with interesting stories surrounding the reign of the Būyids, dating from the period 335–80/946–90, Berl. 8825.

d. Abū Isḥāq Ibrāhīm b. Hilāl b. Ibrāhīm al-Ḥarrānī al-Ṣābiʾ (see Suppl. I, 153), d. 384/994.

Yatīma II, 23/86, *Fihr.* 134, Ibn Khall. 12, Wüstenf., *Gesch.* 149.—1. *Rasāʾil* a. *Fi ʾl-muʿātabāt*, b. *Fi ʾl-shafāʿāt*, c. *Mā nafadha ila ʾl-ʿummāl wal-muṣarrifīn wal-nawāḥī*, important for the history of the Būyids, Leid. 345, part II Paris

4 See Ibn Ḥawqal 208, 322/3, al-Iṣṭakhrī 148, 272, Ibn al-Athīr IX, 103, Mirchond, *Sāmān.* 67, Munajjim Bāshī II, 270.

3314,3.—2. Some poems, ed. by Ph. Wolff in *Carminum Abu 'l-Faragii Babbaghae specimen*, Leipzig 1834 and *WZKM* III, 64/76.—3. He composed his lost history of the Būyids, the *Kitāb al-tājī fī akhbār al-dawla al-Daylamiyya* (ḤKh II, 94, no. 2061, [2]I, 370, Ibn Ḥassūl, *Tafḍīl al-atrāk*, ed. ʿAbbās ʿAzzāwī, 27ff.), at the request of ʿAḍud al-Dawla Fannā Khusraw, as a means of being released from prison. He had angered the latter with his chronicles, and was to be trampled to death by elephants at the conquest of Baghdad in 367/977. He was, however, pardoned and imprisoned instead, where he stayed until 371/981. Because he had labelled the book that he had been forced to write as a fraud in later times he had to hide from the wrath of the sovereign until the latter's death in 372/982.

Chapter 4. Philology

On the beginnings of Arabic linguistics see Suppl. I, 155/8.

| G. Flügel, *Die grammatischen Schulen der Araber, Abh. f. d. C. d. Morg.* II, 4, 96
Leipzig 1862, Muḥammad As'ad Ṭalas, Ta'rīkh al-naḥw, RAAD XIV 67/73, 227/31, 271/6.—On its dependence on Aristotelian logic see also Renan, *Hist. gén. des langues sém.*, ^{4}377ff., G. Hoffmann, *de herm.*, 128 (cf. F. Praetorius, *Zum Verständnis Sibawaihis*, Halle 1895, 30), I. Guidi, *Bollet. ital. degli studii or.* of 25 May 1877 (cf. Nuova serie, 1878, no. 6, 104/8), A. Merx, *Hist. artis gramm. apud Syros* 137/53.

| I *The School of Basra* 98

In Basra, the capital of Iraq that had been founded by 'Utba b. Ghazwān under 'Umar I in 15/636, Arabs from many different tribes lived in close contact with the local Arameans and Persians. Differences between the tribal dialects, the language of the Qur'ān and ancient poetry on the one hand and, on the other, the need for the non-Arabs who had converted to Islam to learn the language of the Holy Scripture and administration, must together have been what prompted the Muslims to undertake their first linguistic investigations. In a similar manner, differences between the Veda and the popular dialects of India, between the language of Homer, Attic and Koinē in Greece, between Sumeric and Akkadian in Babylonia, and between Ge'ez and Amharic in Ethiopia, had all led to the development of linguistics. It remains, however, unclear who first inspired the Arabs in this; that which is reported about the supposed students of Abu 'l-Aswad al-Du'alī (see Flügel 27/9) is just as uncertain as the latter's own connections with these studies.

1. It is only from the immediate predecessors of al-Khalīl and Sībawayhi onward
that the history of Arabic linguistics is documented. | Their teacher seems to 99
have been 'Īsā b. 'Umar al-Thaqafī, d. 149/766, who also had a reputation as a
reciter of the Qur'ān.[1] | He was credited with two works, *al-Jāmi'* and *al-Ikmāl* 97
(or *al-Mukammal*), of which al-Mubarrad (Yāqūt, *Irshād* VI, 101,$_{3}$, followed by Suyūṭī, *Muzhir* ^{2} II, 248,$_{5}$) claims to have seen some folia, but of which the author of the *Fihrist* knew no more than their names. Apparently Sībawayhi used the first work as the basis for his *Kitāb*.

1 See Nöldeke, *Gesch. des Qorans* 288, ^{2}III, 120.

Ibn al-Anbārī, *Nuzhat al-alibbāʾ* 25/31, Flügel 29/32.

2. The tradition around his friend Abū ʿAmr Zabbān b. ʿAmmār b. ʿUryān b. al-ʿAlāʾ al-Māzinī offers a somewhat clearer picture, even though none of his works are extant. He was born in Mecca around the year 70/689 and lived in Basra, where he was already a scholar of some renown during al-Farazdaq's time, having social relations with al-Ḥasan al-Baṣrī. Returning from Damascus where he had tried to gain the favour of the governor ʿAbd al-Wahhāb, he died around 154/770 (or, according to others, in 159) in Kufa. Throughout his life he had collected ancient Arabic poems, especially those from pre-Islamic times, and supplied them with linguistic observations. While early in his life he never cited a single verse in Ramaḍān, in old age he supposedly even burned his entire collection out of religious misgivings in order to devote himself exclusively to the reading of the Qurʾān from then on. He is counted among the seven canonical readers.

Ibn al-Anbārī 29/38, al-Jazarī, *Ṭabaqāt al-qurrāʾ* I, 288/92, Flügel, 32/4, Nöldeke, *Gesch. d. Qor.* 290, ^{2}III pass. (see Index), Goldziher, *Abh.* I, 138.

3. His student, and also of the older al-Akhfash (see p. 102, Suppl. I, 162), was
Yūnus b. Ḥabīb Abū ʿAbd al-Raḥmān al-Ḍabbī, *mawlā* of Bilāl b. Harmī of the
tribe Ḍubayʿa b. Bajāla (comm. Naq. I, $323_{,2}$). He came from Jabbul, a small
98 town on the Tigris between | Wāsiṭ and Baghad. The author of the *Mafākhir
al-ʿajam* counted him as one of the Persians, perhaps because he confused his
birthplace with al-Jabal = al-Jibāl, Media, but he may also have been of Aramaic
100 stock. Like his teachers, he mainly collected interesting items: | *nawādir*
(Suyūṭī, *Muzhir*^{1} II, 143, $_{16,22}$), *lughāt*, and *amthāl*, but a *Kitāb al-qiyās fi ʾl-naḥw*
is also attributed to him. He died at the age of 88 (see al-Jāḥiẓ, *Ḥay.* V, 171) in the
year 182/798 (though, according to others, in 152/769).

Ibn al-Anbārī 59/64, Ibn Khall. 823, Flügel 34/7, works in *Fihrist* $42_{,6-18}$.

4. New ground in Arabic linguistics was broken by Abū ʿAmr's student al-Khalīl b. Aḥmad b. ʿUmar b. Tamīm al-Farāhīdī Abū ʿAbd al-Raḥmān, who belonged to the Azd ʿUmān, and he is unanimously credited with the invention of metrics. In his *Kitāb*, Sībawayhi invokes his authority for almost each and every chapter on grammar. Following the example of the Syrians, he also seems to have been the first to introduce vocalisation and other diacritics. He was also the first to engage in collecting the entire Arabic lexicon in a single

work. He died at the age of 74 in the year 175/791 (or, according to others, in 170 or 160).

Ibn al-Anbārī 54/9, Flügel 37/42. The following works are attributed to him: 1. *Kitāb fī maʿna ʾl-ḥurūf,* on the connotations of the names of the letters of the alphabet, Berl. 7015/6, Leid. 140.—2. *Sharḥ ṣarf al-Khalīl,* frgm. Berl. 6909.—3. *Kitāb fīhi jumlat ālāt al-iʿrāb* AS 4456 (after ZDMG 64, 508, *Kitāb al-jumal fi ʾl-naḥw*).—4. Inquiry into the question of why the root *f-ʿ-l* is used as a paradigm.—5. *Kitāb al-ʿayn,* a large dictionary, arranged on the basis of phonetic rather than alphabetical considerations, starting with *ʿayn* and ending with *yāʾ*. He supposedly started working on it in Khurāsān, and after his death it was completed by al-Layth b. al-Muẓaffar b. Naṣr b. Sayyār, a grandson of the governor there (Ibn Durayd, *Gen.-et. Handb.* 107, Yāqūt, *Irsh.* VII, 222/7, al-Nawawī, *Biogr. Dict.* 231). It was only in 248/862 that the book went from the library of the Ṭāhirids | to Baghdad where it was revised several times, as 99
has been inferred from the verses of later poets that are quoted as *shawāhid* (Goldziher, *Abhh.* I, 140), *Fihrist* I, 43, Zamakhsharī, *al-Mufaṣṣal* 191, Suyūṭī, *Muzhir* I, ^{1}38, ^{2}47ff., II ^{2}232,$_{14}$ (where he is blamed for making many mistakes, which were corrected by a student of Thaʿlab Abū Ṭālib al-Mufaḍḍal b. Salama b. ʿĀṣim al-Kūfī in a work called *Kitāb al-istidrāk ʿala ʾl-ʿayn,* al-Anbārī 265, Yāqūt, *Irsh.* VII, 170, *Muzhir* ^{2}I, 53/4), Flügel 39/42. The original was, in the fourteenth century, apparently still known to the Jews of Provence (Steinschneider, ZDMG VI, 414). Excerpt by Muḥammad b. Ḥasan al-Zubaydī, d. 379/989, Berl. 6950/2, Esc. ^{2}569/71, Köpr. 1574. 7, other revisions and supplements *Ahlw.* 6953. I. Kračkovsky, K istorii slovara al Xalila, *Izv. AC. Nauk SSR* 1926. On his lost musicological *Kitāb al-īqāʿ* see Farmer, *JRAS* 1925, p. 72. The work on the different readings of the Qurʾān that has been attributed to him was written by al-Layth, see al-Azharī in *TA* II, 411,$_{9}$.—Titles of 8 other works in see Flügel, 38.

5. Al-Khalīl's most important student, and the composer of the first work that summarised the results of his own as well as of previous research, was the Persian Sībawayhi[2] Abū Bishr (or Abu ʾl-Ḥasan) ʿAmr b. ʿUthmān b. Qanbar,[3] who was born in Bayḍāʾ near Shiraz. As a *mawlā* of the Banū Ḥārith he had gone to Basra early in his life. After he completed his studies he tried his luck

2 In reality Sībūi, i.e. an affectionate form of, probably, Sēbokht, see Nöldeke, *SBWA* 116, 404; in popular etymology associated with *sīb* 'apple' and *būy* 'smell'.

3 This form is confirmed by a verse by al-Zamakhsharī, in which it rhymes with *minbar* (see *Bughya* 366), Ibn al-Anbārī: Qunbura.

at the caliphal court in Baghdad, but came off worst in a conflict with the Kufan grammarian al-Kisāʾī, the tutor of Amīn, the son of Hārūn al-Rashīd. Exasperated, he returned to his native country and died there, aged only 40 (or, according to others, just 33) years old, in the year 177/793 (according to others 180/796, 188, or 194/809).[4] His *Kitāb* is the oldest coherent representation
100 of Arabic grammar | whose assertions, though often rephrased along clearer and sharper lines, were never increased by new observations. Even though one can often see—by the clumsiness, indeed, obscureness of his expressions—that the author is struggling with the language—which even in daily life he seems never to have fully mastered—rather than with the difficulty of the subject matter, in the East his work has always been regarded as the most perfect example of its type (see *Khiz.* I, 179). It remains to be ascertained to what extent his text was revised by later authors.[5]

Ibn al-Anbārī 71/81, Ibn Khall. 477, Flügel 42/5. *Le livre de Sibawaihi, traité de grammaire arabe par Sibouya dit Sibawaihi, texte ar. publié d'après les mss. du Caire, de l'Escurial, d'Oxford, de Paris et de St. Pétersbourg et de Vienne par* H. Derenbourg, 2 vols., Paris 1881/89 (MSS also Mosul 163$_{,252}$, Patna I, 172$_{,1596}$). *Sībawaihi's Buch über die Grammatik, nach der Ausgabe von H. Derenbourg und dem Cmt. des Sīrāfī (d. 368/978), übers. und erklärt und mit Auszügen aus Sīrāfī*
102 *u. a. Cmtaren versehn von* G. Jahn, Berlin 1895/1900 | (see F. Praetorius, GGA 1894, no. 9). A. Schaade, *Zur Lautlehre des S.*, Leiden 1911. Comm. see Suppl. I, 160; *Sharḥ ʿuyūn K.S.* by Abū Naṣr Hārūn b. Mūsā, d. 401/1010 in Cordova, *Br. Mus. Quart.* X, 31; anon. *shawāhid*—Comm. *Sharḥ alghāz S. wa-ghayrihi min al-nuḥāt* Bank. XX, 2139; others mentioned in Ahlw. 6460.

6. Abū Fayḍ Muʾarrij b. ʿAmr al-Sadūsī al-ʿIjlī was also one of the students of al-Khalīl and Abū Zayd al-Anṣārī (p. 103). Born in the desert and familiar with the subtleties of his native language, he studied the methods of linguistics in Basra and devoted himself to the compilation of linguistic and geneological notes, as well as to Qurʾānic exegesis. If it is true that he visited the caliph al-Maʾmūn in Khurāsān then he cannot have died in 195/810 because al-Maʾmūn
101 did not become caliph until 198. | In those days he was apparently teaching in Marw and Nishapur, and possibly also in Jurjān. According to al-Khaṭīb (*Taʾr.*

---

4 According to Ibn al-Jawzī he died in Sāwa, and according to ʿAbd al-Qādir b. Abi ʾl-Wafāʾ, *Jawāhir* I, 254, in Sinjār.

5 According to *Khiz.* I, 178, ʿUmar al-Jarmī (Flügel, p. 62) provided the names of the poets for all the verses that had been quoted anonymously by Sībawayhi.

Baghdād XIII, 258) he went with al-Ma'mūn to Baghdad—which must have been in Ṣafar 204/August 819—and then died in Basra.

Ibn Qutaiba, *Maʿārif* 169, Ibn al-Anb. 179/84, Ibn Khall. 716, Flügel 52; 5 works are mentioned in *Fihrist* 48$_{,8,9}$.

7. Likewise, Abu 'l-Ḥasan al-Naḍr b. Shumayl al-Māzinī al-Tamīmī was a student of al-Khalīl. Born in Marw, he had mastered the Arabic language after a long sojourn in the desert. He completed his studies in Basra and became a respected scholar. Nevertheless, he was unable to make a living and so returned to his homeland. There, al-Ma'mūn entrusted him with a judicial office, and he was the first person in Khurāsān to openly represent the doctrines of the Sunna. He died in 203/818.

Ibn al-Anb. 110/7, Ibn Khall. 735, Flügel 58/61. His works, of which the *Kitāb al-ṣifāt*—a comprehensive encyclopaedia of Bedouin life that was later imitated by the *Gharīb al-muṣannaf* of Ibn ʿUbayd (p. 105)—was the most famous, are listed in *Fihrist* 52$_{,3-16}$. Al-Thaʿālibī, d. 427/1035, still used his *Gharīb al-Qur'ān*, Br. Mus. 821, while Ibn al-Athīr, d. 606/1209, used his *Gharīb al-ḥadīth* in his *Nihāya*.

8. Abū Muḥammad b. al-Mustanīr was a student of Sībawayhi who gave him the nickname Quṭrub. Born in Basra and enfranchised by Sālim b. Ziyād, he studied under Sībawayhi and al-Thaqafī. He was then appointed to oversee the education of the prince al-Amīn, but due to rumours concerning his alleged homosexual inclinations he was soon supplanted by Ḥammād ʿAjrad, although this did not stop Abū Dulaf al-ʿIjlī from entrusting him with the same responsibility for his own children. When al-ʿIjlī died in 206/821 he became the tutor of the children of his son al-Ḥusayn. Quṭrub's fame rests on his lexical | collection 102
which has been studied and revised right up to the present day.

| Ibn al-Anb. 119, Ibn Khall. 607, Flügel 65. Of the 28 works listed in *Fihrist* 52/3, 103
the following have been preserved: 1. *Kitāb al-aḍdād*, on words with opposite meanings, ḤKh I, 342, no. 871, ^{2}I, 115, Berl. 7091.—2. *Mā khālafa fīhi insān al-bahīma* Vienna 355$_{,4}$, ed. R. Geyer, SBWA, 1888, 380ff.—3. *Kitāb al-azmina* Br. Mus. 536.—4. *Kitāb al-muthallath*, about *faʿl-*, *fiʿl-* and *fuʿl* forms of the same root with different connotations which, according to Vilmar's preface, was, however, revised in later times, Berl. 7071/3, Leid. 42/3, Paris 825$_{,4}$, 1206$_{,6}$, 4067$_{,2}$, 4230$_{,1}$, Esc. ^{2}30$_{,3}$, 143$_{,4}$.—Versifications: *a.* ʿAbd al-Wahhāb al-Muhallabī al-Bahnasī, d. 685/1286, see I. Guidi, RSO I, 326, Berl. 7074, Gotha 36$_{,2}$, 61, 410/3, Leid. 44, ed. E. Vilmar, *Carmen de vocibus tergeminis ad Qutrubum auctorem*

relatum, Marburg 1857. Commentaries by Ibrāhīm b. Hibatallāh al-Maḥallī al-Lakhmī, d. 721/1321, Berl. 7075/6, Leid. 45, by Muḥammad b. ʿAlī b. Zurayq, d. 803/1400 (Suppl. II, 157), Berl. 7079/80, Vienna 76,$_{1}$, by al-Ramlī (d. 844/1440) or Zakariyyāʾ al-Anṣārī (d. 926/1520), Vienna 76,$_{2}$, by Saʿd al-Dīn al-Bārizī, ibid. 5, by ʿAbd al-Raḥmān b. Nuʿaym al-Maghribī, Algiers 1836,$_{8}$, by Ibn ʿAbd al-Salām, Krafft 30, by Shihāb al-Dīn al-Qalyūbī, Paris 4230,$_{2}$.—*b.* Ibrāhīm al-Azharī (II, 315), Berl. 7086/7, Gotha 43,$_{2}$, Munich 558.—*c.* ʿAbd al-ʿAzīz al-Dīrīnī, d. 694/1295 (S. 451), Bodl. II, 237,$_{5}$ prosified Berl. 7081, Gotha 408,$_{3}$, Dresd. 254,$_{3}$, Munich 558, comm. (on which version?) Berl. 7078, Br. Mus. 513, ed. by Cheikho, *al-Mashriq* 1909, 685/94.—*d.* Anonymous, Berl. 7082/4, Gotha 61,$_{2}$, 408,$_{1}$, 409, Vienna 76,$_{3}$, Cairo ^{2}II, 41.—*e.* Shams al-Dīn Abu ʾl-Qāsim ʿAbd al-Wahhāb b. al-Ḥasan b. Barakāt, Brill-H. ^{1}126, ^{2}288 (not in Garr.).—Imitations in verse with commentary by: *a.* ʿAbd al-Raḥmān al-Sakhāwī, d. 1025/1616, ḤKh V, 557 no. 9520, Vienna 76,$_{4}$.—*b.* Jabrāʾīl b. Farḥāt, d. 1732 (Suppl. II, 389), *Boll. ital.* I 255, no. 13, Pet. Ros. 156, excerpt Vienna I, 490.—Ibn al-Athīr mentions his *Gharīb al-ḥadīth* in the preface to the *Nihāya*.

9. A contemporary of al-Khalīl and his school, but not directly influenced by him, was Abū ʿUbayda Maʿmar b. al-Muthannā. Born in 110/728 in Basra as a slave, he was the son of Jewish-Persian parents who hailed from Bājarwān.
103 A *mawlā* of the | Taym Quraysh, he received his primary education from Abū ʿAmr b. al-ʿAlāʾ and Yūnus b. Ḥabīb. He tried to compensate for the blemish of his non-Arab origin by joining the Khārijī Ṣufriyya sect and by writing tracts in the spirit of the Arab-loathing Shuʿūbiyya movement. At the instigation of al-Faḍl b. al-Rabīʿ, in 188/803 Hārūn b. al-Rashīd invited him to recite his work to him. However, the harsh rhetoric contained within his *Kitāb al-mathālib* (ḤKh no. 11362, quoted by Yāqūt, *Irshād* VII 218,$_{8}$) apparently made him so despised that when he died in 210/825 (according to others 207/9, 211, or 213) there was no one in Basra who would follow his corpse.

104 | Ibn Qutayba, *Maʿārif* 268, Ibn al-Anb. 137/50, Ibn Khall. 702, Flügel 68/70, Wüstenf., *Gesch.* 45, Goldziher, *MSt.* I, 194/206. From among the nearly 200 historical and philological works he is said to have written, *Fihrist* 53 lists the titles of 105 works. Apart from the works mentioned in Suppl. I, 162 (on work 2., see Suppl. III, 1194) there also remain a *Tafsīr gharīb al-Qurʾān*, Cairo I^{2}, 40 and a *qaṣīda* rhyming on *lām*, Berl. 7535,$_{3,2}$. Apart from the works mentioned there, the following are also quoted: 1. *Kitāb ayyām al-ʿArab*, by al-Suyūṭī, *Muzhir* I^{1}, 84,$_{3}$ and elsewhere, the main source of similar reports in the *Aghānī* and in the *Kāmil* of Ibn al-Athīr.—2. *Gharīb al-ḥadīth*, by Ibn al-Athīr in the preface

to the *Nihāya*.—3. *Kitāb al-dībāj*, by al-Masʿūdī, *Tanbīh* 243,$_3$ = *Kitāb al-dībāj fī alwān al-khayl*, in al-Bakrī, *Simṭ al-laʾālī* I, 157,$_8$ = *Kitāb al-dībāja*, Suppl. 10 (?) *Kitāb al-khayl* ibid. 3 (?)—4. *Kitāb al-dirʿ wal-bayḍa*, by Suyūṭī, *Muzhir* II^1, 105 penultimate, ^{2}130,$_4$.—5. *Kitāb al-tamthīl*, ibid. 138 bottom.

10. Another student of Abū ʿAmr b. al-ʿAlāʾ, but also of the Kufan scholar al-Mufaḍḍal, was Abū Zayd Saʿīd b. Aws b. Thābit al-Anṣārī of the Khazraj tribe, who devoted himself almost entirely to collecting lexical material. When al-Mahdī ascended the throne in 158/774, he called him, along with many other scholars, to Baghdad. He died in his late nineties in 214 or 215/830.

Ibn Qutayba 270, Ibn al-Anb. 173/9, Ibn Khall. 249, Flügel 70/2. From his works (*Fihrist* 55,$_{1-7}$) the following survive: 1. *Kitāb al-nawādir fī 'l-lugha*, in the recension of Abu 'l-Ḥasan | al-Akhfash, d. 315–6/927–8, which is why in *Khiz.* III, 199, 104
403 it is called a commentary by him, ed. by Saʿīd al-Khūrī al-Shartūnī, Beirut 1894 (without using Köpr. 1406), see Fleischer, *Kl. Schr.* III, 471ff, Nöldeke, ZDMG 49, 318ff.—2. *Kitāb al-maṭar*, transcribed from a manuscript in the Bibliothèque Nationale (no. 4231,$_1$) by R. Gottheil, JAOS XVI, 282/312. Also quoted: *Kitāb al-ibil*, in al-Jawharī *Ṣaḥāḥ*, s.v. *ʿmthl* (see Suppl.).

11. Abū Saʿīd ʿAbd al-Malik b. Qurayb al-Aṣmaʿī al-Bāhilī, who was a student of Abu 'l-ʿAlāʾ and Khalaf al-Aḥmar, see Suppl. I, 163.

| Ibn al-Anb. 150/72, Ibn Khall. 352, Flügel 72/80. From his numerous works 105
listed in *Fihr.* 55 the following have been preserved: 1. *Kitāb al-farq*, ed. D.H. Müller, SBWA 82, 1876, 235/88.—2. *Kitāb al-wuḥūsh*, ed. R. Geyer, ibid. 1888, 353/420 (without using Paris 3939,$_2$).—3. *Kitāb al-khayl*, ed. A. Haffner, ibid. 1895, 132, X (Köpr. 1360).—4. *Kitāb al-shāʾ*, ed. Haffner, ibid. 1895, 133, VI (Esc. ^{2}1705,$_4$, Cairo^2 II, 28).—5. *Kitāb al-ibil* Vienna 355,$_5$, ed. by Haffner, *Texte zur arab. Lexikographie*, Leipzig 1905, 66/157.—6. *Kitāb al-aḍdād* ibid. 6, ed. by Ṣālḥānī in Haffner, *Drei arab. Quellenwerke*, Beirut 1913, 5/70.—7. *al-Ikhtiyār* see ad p. 116,$_4$. Also cited: 1. *Gharīb al-ḥadīth*, by Ibn al-Athīr, in the preface to the *Nihāya*.—2. *Kitāb al-ajnās*, in Suyūṭī, *Muzhir* I, ^{1}179,$_8$.—3. *Kitāb al-abwāb*, in *Khiz.* IV, 200,$_4$.—4. *Kitāb al-amthāl*, by al-Bakrī, *Simṭ al-laʾālī* I, 426f. (al-Qālī, *Amālī* I, 250, Gotha 423?).

12. A student of Sībawayhi, even if he was older than him, was al-Akhfash al-Awsaṭ Abu 'l-Ḥasan Saʿīd b. Masʿada of Balkh (thus probably of Iranian origin), a *mawlā* of the Banū Mujāshiʿ b. Dārim. His chief merit lies in his

preservation of the *Kitāb* of his master, even though he often disagreed with the latter's opinions.[6] He died in 221/835 (or, according to others, in 215/830).

Fihrist 52, Ibn Qutayba 271, Ibn Khall. 250, Ibn al-Anb. 184/8, Flügel 61. Of his
105 works, *Fihr.* $52_{,17-28}$, | only two have been preserved (see Suppl.). Al-Thaʿālibī, d. 427/1035, used his *Gharīb al-Qurʾān*, Br. Mus. 821.

106 | 13. One student of Quṭrub was Abū Jaʿfar Muḥammad b. Ḥabīb, called thus after his mother, a freedwoman of Muḥammad b. ʿAbbās al-Hāshimī. His unusual fecundity in the areas of philology and history caused al-Marzūbānī to accuse him of plagiarism, an accusation that we cannot verify. He died in Samarra on 23 Dhu 'l-Ḥijja 245/21 March 860.

Fihrist 106, Flügel p. 67, Wüstenf., *Gesch.* 59. A fragment of his magnum opus, the *Kitāb al-qabāʾil wal-ayyām al-kabīr*, which the *Fihrist* estimated at 40 *juzʾ* of 200 folios each, is probably the *Mukhtalif al-qabāʾil* cited by al-Āmidī, *al-Muʾtalif* $115_{,20}$, and edited by F. Wüstenfeld, *Muhammed Ben Habib über die Gleichheit und Verschiedenheit der arabischen Stammesnamen*, Göttingen 1850. For works other than the *dīwān* of Farazdaq (p. 52) and the *Naqāʾiḍ Jarīr wal-Farazdaq* see Suppl. (broad overview in *Khiz.* I, $274_{,4}$, $324_{,9}$, II, $262_{,24}$, IV, $231_{,3}$). Also mentioned: 1. *Kitāb khalq al-insān*, by al-Suyūṭī in Berl. 7038.—2. *Sharḥ dīwān Dhi 'l-Rumma, Khiz.* I, $312_{,14}$.—3. *Sharḥ Dīwān Jirān* (Suppl. 56), ibid. II, $160_{,14}$.

14. From among the students of al-Aṣmaʿī, ʿUbayd al-Qāsim b. Sallām al-Harawī was the most significant. He was born in 154/770 in Herat as the son of a Greek slave. Apart from attending the lectures of al-Aṣmaʿī, he also took the classes of Abū ʿUbayda and Abū Zayd in Basra, as well as those of Ibn al-Aʿrābī and al-Kisāʾī in Kufa. In addition, he studied *fiqh*, following al-Shāfiʿī.[7] He then became tutor to the children of the Harāthima,[8] and later to those of the proconsul of Tarsus, Thābit b. Naṣr b. Mālik. The latter appointed him to a judicial office, which

6 It was apparently out of greed that he wrote his works in a language that was difficult to understand, so that people would pay for his lessons. See Kremer, *Culturg. Streifzüge* 26.

7 Ibn Abī Yaʿlā, *Ṭab. al-Ḥanābila* 190/2 on the other hand, claims that he was a Ḥanbalī.

8 I.e. of the family of Harthama, who became governor of Khurāsān under Hārūn al-Rashīd.

he held for 18 years. | He also lived for some time[9] with ʿAbdallāh b. Ṭāhir, the 106
governor of Khurāsān, who allegedly offered him a monthly pension of 10,000 dirhams for his *Gharīb al-ḥadīth*. He then went to Baghdad, before moving to Mecca in 214/829, where he resided as a *mujāwir*, passing away in 223/837 or 224 (although, according to some, he died in Medina). | 107

Ibn al-Anb. 188/98, Ibn Khall. 507, al-Subkī, *Ṭab. al-Shāf.* I, 270/4, Flügel 86, Wüstenf., *Schafiiten* no. 2. Of his works (*Fihr.* 71) the following have survived: 1. *Gharīb al-ḥadīth*, based on a work by Abū ʿUbayda, Leid. 1725, see de Goeje, ZDMG XVIII, 781/817, Köpr. 378, II, 64, selection ibid. 455 (Weisweiler, *Istanb. Hdssstudien* 135), Qawāla I, 138, *Lughat al-ʿarab* VI, 33ff.—*Mukhtaṣar gharīb al-ḥadīth* by Abū ʿAlī Ḥusayn b. Aḥmad al-Astarābādhī, Berl. Oct. 3162.—his own excerpt *Kitāb al-ajnās*, ed. by ʿAlī ʿArshī, Rampur State Libr. Publ. Ser. 2. Bombay 1938.—2. *al-Gharīb al-muṣannaf*, in 1000 chapters with 1200 *Shawāhid*, his magnum opus, which he supposedly worked on for 40 years, AS 4706, Cairo ^{1}IV, 176.[10]—3. *Kitāb al-amthāl* (after *Khiz.* II, $11,_{2}$; on the title *al-Majalla* see Goldziher, *MSt.* II, 204, n. 4), Paris 3969, Köpr. 1219, Mosul 206, arranged alphabetically in *al-Tuḥfa al-bahiyya*, Istanbul 1302, 2/16; E. Bertheau, *Libri proverbiorum Abu Obaid Elqasimi f. Salami Elchuzzami lectiones duo, octava et septima decima, arab. ed. lat. vertit, annot. instr. diss.* Göttingen 1836, is a later work, see Freytag, *Ar. Prov.* III, viii–ix.—Comm. *Faṣl al-maqāl* by ʿAbdallāh al-Bakrī, d. 487/1094 (see p. 476), Esc, ^{2}526.—4. *Faḍāʾil al-Qurʾān wa-ādābuhu*, on the excellence of the Qurʾān in general and of particular suras especially, in addition to all kinds of matters related to the script, the reading, and the interpretation thereof, edited by an unknown student of the Qurʾān reciter Muḥammad b. al-Ḥajjāj, ca 320/932, Berl. 451, Tüb. 95, see Bergstr.-Pretzl, *Gesch. d. Q.* III, Index.—5.–11. see Suppl.—12. *Kitāb al-amwāl*, an exposition of financial and fiscal law on the basis of *ḥadīth* material. Its relation to the *Kitāb al-kharāj*
(see pp. 171, 181, 228), a work that had emerged from administrative | practice 107
(see Suppl. I, 284) and other schools of *fiqh*, still needs to be investigated. Edition on the basis of the manuscripts in Damascus (Berl. sim. 31/2) and one from Cairo by Muḥammad Ḥāmid al-Fiqī, Cairo 1353.—13. *Risāla fī-mā ishtabaha al-lafẓ waikhtalafa al-maʿnā* Rāmpūr I, $510,_{31b}$.—Being a devout man, he tried to avoid causing umbrage as much as possible, and as such he went so

9 According to Ibn Abī Yaʿlā and al-Subkī he went from Tarsus straight to Mecca. In that case, his sojourn with ʿAbdallāh b. Ṭāhir must have taken place earlier.

10 Other MSS that cannot be checked in al-Nadwī, *Tadhk. al-nawādir* 107 (partly after Krenkow).

far as to replace all personal names in the *hijāʾ* verses that he would quote as witnesses in his linguistic collections with fictitious words, adapted to fit the metre. See Qāḍī ʿIyāḍ, *Shifāʾ* II, 237, Goldziher, *MSt* I, 193, n. 4.

15. The second most important student of al-Aṣmaʿī was Abu ʾl-Ḥātim Sahl b. Muḥammad b. ʿUthmān al-Sijistānī, who had also studied with Abū ʿUbayda and Abū Zayd, and who had read Sībawayhī's *Kitāb* twice under al-Akhfash. Because of some unpleasant experiences during a stay in Baghdad he spent most of his life in Basra, but turned more to the booktrade in later times. He died around 250/864 (according to Ibn Durayd in Yāqūt, 255).

Ibn al-Anb. 251/4, Ibn Khall. 266, de Sacy, *Anth. gramm.* 143 (162), Flügel, 87. Apart from his works (*Fihr.* 58/9) as mentioned in Suppl. I, 167, there also remains a *Kitāb al-nakhl*, see S. Cusa, Sopra il codice arabo sulle palme, *Estratto del Arch. stor. Siciliano*, I, i, Palermo 1873, C.B. Lagumina, Il libro delle palme di al-Ḥ. al-S., *Atti della R. Acc. dei Lincei*, ser. IV, vol. VIII, i, 6/41.—Also cited is a *Kitāb al-layl wal-nahār*, by al-Suyūṭī, *Muzhir* [1] II, $169_{,19}$, $263_{,23}$, [2]$160_{,13}$, $317_{,16}$.

16. Other students of al-Aṣmaʿī, of whom no works have remained, will be briefly mentioned here (see Flügel, 80/5):

a. Abū Naṣr b. Ḥātim al-Bāhilī, d. 235/845.

Fihr. $56_{,7-11}$, *ZDMG* 12, 595, Ibn al-Khaṭīb, *Taʾrīkh Baghdād* IV, 114, Yāqūt, *Irshād* I, 405, Suyūṭī, *Bughya*, 130, al-Yāfiʿī, *Mirʾāt al-jānān* II, $46_{,2}$; his *Kitāb al-maʿānī* is quoted in al-Jurjānī, *Kināyāt* $93_{,13}$.

108 | *b.* Abu ʾl-Ḥasan ʿAlī b. al-Mughīra al-Athram, d. 231/844.

Fihrist $56_{,12-28}$, Ibn al-Anb. 218/21, Yāqūt, *Irshād* V, 451, Suyūṭī, *Bughya* 355.

108 | *c.* Abū ʿUmar Ṣāliḥ b. Isḥāq al-Jarmī, d. 225/839.

Fihrist 56/7, Ibn al-Anb. 198/203, Yāqūt, *Irshād* IV, 267/8, Ibn Khall. 278, Ibn Durayd, *Handb.* 302, 314, 318, Suyūṭī, *Bughya* 216, see above p. 100, note 1.

d. Abū Muḥammad ʿAbdallāh b. Muḥammad b. Hārūn al-Tawwazī, d. 233/847.[11]

11 He was believed to have been two people by Flügel: al-Tawwazī, p. 82, and al-Thawrī, p. 84.

Fihrist 57/8, Suyūṭī, *Bughya* 290. Apparently by him, *Kitāb al-taṣrīf*, with a comm. by Ibn Jinnī, d. 392/1001, Petersb. 211, identified by Dorn by the incipit rather than the title, see Suppl.

e. Abū ʿUthmān Bakr b. Muḥammad b. ʿUthmān al-Māzinī, d. 249/863 or 236 (Ibn Khall. 115), see Suppl.

f. Abū Isḥāq Ibrāhīm b. Sufyān al-Ziyādī, d. 249/863.

Ibn al-Anb. 269, Yāqūt, *Irshād* I, 162/3, Suyūṭī, *Bughya* 181.

g. Abu ʾl-Faḍl al-ʿAbbās b. Faraj al-Riyāshī, d. 257/870.

Fihrist 58,$_{8-17}$, Ibn Durayd 218, Ibn al-Anb. 262/5, Ibn Khall. 296, Suyūṭī, *Bughya* 275, de Sacy, *Anth. gramm.* 316 (112), *ZDMG* XII, 59.

17. One of the youngest students of al-Aṣmaʿī, who also attended the classes of his student al-Riyāshī, was Abū Saʿīd al-Ḥasan b. al-Ḥusayn al-Sukkarī, b. 212/827, d. 275/888. He rendered outstanding service as a collector and recensionist of ancient Arabic poems.

Fihrist 78,$_{20-27}$, Ibn al-Anb. 274, Flügel 89. 1. *Kitāb akhbār al-luṣūṣ*, see above, p. 12, quoted with *isnād* by al-Tabrīzī in connection with | *Ḥamāsa* 103, top of 109
page, excerpts *Khiz.* I, 297/9.—2. *Sharḥ ashʿār al-Hudhaliyyīn*, see Suppl. 42.—3. *Sharḥ Dīwān Imra al-Qays*, see Suppl. 50. 4—*Sharḥ dīwān al-Quṭāmī*, quoted in *Khiz.* I, 81,$_{10}$.—5. *Ashʿār Taghlib*, quoted ibid. I, 304,$_{11}$.—6. *Jāmiʿ shiʿr Nuʿmān b. Bashīr*, quoted in *Agh.* ^{1}XIV, 119,$_{9}$, p. 124,$_{9}$ from below.—7. *Man qāla baytan fa-luqqiba bihi*, ibid. XVII, 107/8.

18. Al-Mubarrad[12] Abu ʾl-ʿAbbās Muḥammad b. Yazīd al-Azdī al-Thumālī, born in Basra around 210/825 (according to others in 220), was a student of al-Māzinī and Abū Ḥātim. He was the most important representative of the Basran school of his time, in the same way in which Thaʿlab was the undeclared head of the Kufans, and the rivalry between the two schools also determined their personal relations. As a grammarian he followed his own path and did not even shy away from deviating from such an authority as Sībawayhi, whose *Kitāb* he

12 On this *laqab* see Suppl. I, 168.

sought to refute in a separate treatise.[13] He spent his final days in Baghdad and died there in Shawwāl 285/November 898 (according to others in 286).

109 | *Fihrist* 59, Ibn al-Anbārī 279/93, Ibn Khall. 608, Flügel 93, Wüstenf., *Gesch.* 80. From his numerous works, the following remain: 1. *The Kamil of el Mubarrad*, ed. by W. Wright, Leipzig 1864ff., Istanbul 1286, Cairo 1308, 1313, 1339.—2. *al-Fāḍil*, its counterpart, mainly chronicles from Umayyad times with grammatical explanations, Asʿad 3598.—3. *al-Muqtaḍab*, with comm. by Saʿīd b. Saʿīd al-Fāriqī, d. 391/1000, Esc. ^{2}111.—4. *Kitāb al-taʿāzī* ibid. 534$_{,1}$.—5. Aḥmad b. Wāthiq's letter to al-Mubarrad concerning the question of whether poetry or prose is preferable, with Mubarrad's answer, Munich 791, Berl. 7177 frgm.—6. *Nasab ʿAdnān wa-Qaḥṭān* (see Suppl. no. 3) print. C. 1936.—Also cited: 1. *Gharīb al-ḥadīth*, cited by Ibn al-Athīr in the preface to *al-Nihāya*.—2. *Kitāb al-rawḍa*, whence a typology of the poet al-ʿAbbās b. al-Aḥnaf, *Agh.* VIII, 15$_{,20}$.—3. *Kitāb al-iʿtinān, Khiz.* I. 305$_{,21}$.—4. *al-Sharḥ* (i.e. *Sharḥ kalām*
110 *al-ʿArab ?*) | ibid. II, 193^{u}.—5. *al-Fitan wal-miḥan*, cited by al-Ṣūlī, *Akhbār Abī Tammām* 158$_{,6}$.

19. A student of al-Tawwazī (15, d) and the teacher of Ibn Durayd was Abū ʿUthmān Saʿīd b. Hārūn al-Ushnāndānī, about whom nothing is known other than that he died in 288/901.

Fihrist 60, 83, Ibn al-Anb. 266, Ibn Khall. transl. Slane III, 39, Flügel 96. *Kitāb maʿāni al-shiʿr* in the recension of Abū Saʿīd al-Sīrāfī, d. 368/978, after Ibn Durayd, d. 321/933, Esc.^{2} 406$_{,2}$, print. Damascus 1340/1922, C. 1932.

20. The house of the Yazīdiyyūn supplied students for the older school of Abū ʿAmr b. al-ʿAlāʾ, as well as for the younger school of al-Aṣmaʿī.

Fihrist 50/1, Flügel 89/92.

a. The founder of this house, Abū Muḥammad Yaḥyā b. al-Mubārak al-ʿAdawī, a student of Abū ʿAmr and Yūnus b. Ḥabīb, had taken part in the uprising of Ibrāhīm b. ʿAbdallāh b. al-Ḥasan in Basra and because of this he had to spend time in hiding. His teacher recommended him to Yazīd b. al-Manṣūr

13 His *Masāʾil al-ghalaṭ*, too, though later repudiated by him as an immature and juvenile work, was a critique of the *Kitāb*; Suyūṭī, *Muzhir*^{1} II, 188.

al-Ḥimyarī, the uncle of al-Mahdī, to be tutor to his sons, and it was after him that he took on the *nisba* of al-Yazīdī. He died at the age of 74 in 202/817 in Khurāsān.

Agh. XVIII[1,2] 72/83, al-Samʿānī, *Ansāb* 599/600, Ibn al-Anb. 103/10, Ibn Khall. 770. His *Jāmiʿ shiʿr wa-adab* contained laudatory poems on the Basran grammarians and satirical ones on the Kufans. His *Nawādir* is quoted in Suyūṭī, *Muzhir* II, [1]144,$_{13}$, [2]176,$_{15}$.

b. Of his sons, Ibrāhīm was active as a writer. He went to Asia Minor as part of the retinue of al-Ma'mūn, and to Damascus with al-Muʿtaṣim. He died in 225/839.

Agh. XVIII, [1,2]87/91.

c. His eldest grandson, Abū Jaʿfar Aḥmad b. Muḥammad b. Abī Muḥammad Yaḥyā, was held in high regard by al-Ma'mūn and al-Muʿtaṣim.

| *Agh.* XVIII, [2]91/4, al-Khaṭīb, *Ta'r. Baghdād* V, 117, Ibn ʿAsākir, *Ta'r. Dimashq* II, 79/80, which contains the quite impossible statement that he died long before 160. 111

d. His great-grandson Muḥammad b. al-ʿAbbās b. Muḥammad b. Yaḥyā was, in his later years, the tutor of the caliph al-Muqtaḍir's children. He died in 310/922.

Ibn al-Anb. 308, Ibn Khall. 612, Wüstenf., *Gesch.* 97. *Sharḥ dīwān al-Ḥādira* p. 17; *Kitāb al-naqā'iḍ*, quoted in *Agh.* X, [1]31,$_{5}$ from below, *Kitāb al-jawābāt* ibid. XV, 3,$_{6}$. Other members of the house *Agh.*, *Fihrist*, and al-Samʿāni, loc. cit., see Suppl.

21. A student of Mubarrad, but at the same time also of Thaʿlab, was Abu 'l-Ḥasan Muḥammad b. Aḥmad b. Kaysān, who died in the year 299/911 (according to others 320/932, see Suppl.) after a succesful teaching career.

Ibn al-Anb. 301, Flügel 98. Of his works, there remain extant: 1. *Kitāb talqīb al-qawāfī wa-talqīb ḥarakātihā* Leid. 264, ed. by W. Wright, *Opuscula arab.* 47/74.—2. *Sharḥ al-muʿallaqāt* see Suppl. I, 35, on Imra' al-Qays, ed. by F.L. Bernstein, *ZA* XXIX, 1/77.

22. Even more important was Mubarrad's student Abū Isḥāq Ibrāhīm b. al-Sarī b. Sahl al-Zajjāj, who started his studies with him when he still was a glass-cutter, and who committed himself to paying him a daily fee of 1 dirham until the end of his life. He upheld his word even when, on al-Mubarrad's recommendation, he became a private tutor with the Banū Māriqa in al-Ṣarāt, and later also when he held the same position under ʿUbaydallāh b. Sulaymān, the vizier of the caliph al-Muʿtaḍid. When his pupil al-Qāsim, the vizier's son, became vizier himself, he entered his service as a secretary, and remained with him until he died, at about 80 years of age, on 9 Jumādā II 311/25 September 923 (or, according to others, in 310 or 316).

Ibn al-Anb. 308/12, Ibn Khall. 12, Flügel 98. Of his works, there remain (see *Fihrist* 61): 1. see Suppl.—2. *al-Ibāna wal-tafhīm ʿan maʿānī bismillāh al-raḥmān al-raḥīm* Gotha 727.—3. *Maʿāni 'l-Qurʾān* or *Iʿrāb al-Qurʾān wa-maʿānīhi* NO 115, 320, ʿUm. 247 with continuation Ğārullāh 44, of the year
112 | 368/978, Cairo^2 I, 32 s. App. 3.—4, 5 see Suppl.—6. *Ḥurūf al-maʿānī* Lālelī $3740,_7$, according to Rescher, *Abriss* 155, while in *MO* VII, 107 (after which Suppl. I, 171) he ascribed it to al-Zajjājī.—7. *Kitāb al-shajara al-musammā bi-Kiṭab al-taqrīb* Kairouan, *Bull. de Corr. Afr.* 1884, $186._{50}$.

23. His student Abu 'l-Qāsim ʿAbd al-Raḥmān b. Isḥāq, called al-Zajjājī after him, was born in Nihāwand. He followed his master's lectures in Baghdad and later taught in Damascus, Ayla, and Ṭabariyya, where he died in 377/949 (or, according to others, in 339 or 340).

Akhbār al-Z. ʿĀšir I, 879, Ibn al-Anb. 379, Ibn Khall. 340, Flügel 98. Of his works, *Fihrist* 80, there remain: 1. *Kitāb al-jumal fi 'l-naḥw*, his magnum opus that he is said to have written in Mecca, Berl. 6461, Esc. ^{2}30, $108,_1$, Algiers 38/9, Köpr. 1462, Bāyezīd 3026, Ḥamīd. 1277ff.—Commentaries (see Suppl. I, 171).—4. *b. Iṣlāḥ al-khalal al-wāqiʿ fi 'l-J.* by al-Baṭalyawsī, d. 521/1127 (see p. 427), Berl. 6463, Leid. 142.—7. ʿAlī b. Muḥammad b. ʿUṣfūr al-Ishbīlī, d. 669/1270, Leid. 43, Ambros. 154.—21 commentaries are mentioned in Ahlw. 6464.—II–X, see Suppl.

111 | 24. Likewise a student of al-Zajjāj and Ibn Durayd was Abu 'l-Qāsim al-Ḥasan b. Bishr al-Āmidī who, being a poet himself, devoted himself to the critical study of poetry. In Baghdad he worked as a secretary for Jaʿfar Hārūn b. Muḥammad, the political adviser to the ruler of Oman, Abū b. Hilāl, and later in the administration of the *awqāf* in his hometown of Basra, where he died in 371/987 (see Suppl. I, 171/2).

Al-Muwāzana etc. also Berl. Brill M. 260.

25. The school of Basra was given a very special lustre by Muḥammad b. al-Ḥasan b. Durayd al-Azdī. Born in the city in 223/837, he excelled as both a poet and a scholar. In Basra he studied under Abū Ḥātim al-Sijistānī, al-Riyāshī, al-Ushnāndānī, and others. When the Zanj perpetrated a terrible bloodbath in Basra in 257/871[14] he fled with his uncle | al-Ḥusayn to the homeland of his 113 tribe, Oman, and stayed there for 12 years. He then went to Khurāsān where he gained the favour of the governor ʿAbdallāh b. Muḥammad b. Mīkāl and his son Ismāʿīl in Nishapur. He composed his famous *al-Qaṣīda al-maqṣūra* in praise of them, and his magnum opus *al-Jamhara* was also written for them. After Ismāʿīl had been removed from office in 308/920 Ibn Durayd went to Baghdad. There, the caliph al-Muqtaḍir granted him a pension so that he could devote himself entirely to scholarship and teaching. He died there on 18 Shaʿbān 321/ 12 August 933.

Ibn al-Anb. 322/6, Ibn Khall. 609, al-Subkī, *Ṭab. al-shāfiʿiyya* II, 145/9, *Khiz.* I, 490, Flügel 101, Wüstenf., *Schaf.* 192. I. *al-Maqṣūra, Poemation Ibn Doreidi cum scholiis arabicis excerptis e codd. mss. ed. lat. convers. et observat. miscellis illustr. cura et ed.* A. Haitsma, Franeker 1773. *Abu Becri Mohammedis ebn Hoseini ebn Doreidi Azdiensis Katsijda 'l-Mektsoura sive Idyllium arabicum lat. redd. et brev. schol. illustr. ed.* E. Scheidius, Harderwijk 1786. *Carmen Maksura dictum Abu Becri Muhammedis ibn Hoseini ibn Doreidi Azdiensis cum scholiis integris nunc primum editis Abu Abdallah ibn Haschami ed. interpret. lat. proleg. et not. instr.* Nannestad Boysen, Copenhagen 1828.—Commentaries: 1. By his student Ibn Khālawayh, d. 370/980, Berl. 7574/5, Leid. 618, de Jong 86, Paris 4231$_{,4}$, together with the commentary by al-Sīrāfī, d. 368/978, Leid. 619.—6. Muḥammad b. Aḥmad b. Hishām al-Lakhmī, d. 570/1174, Leid. 620, Paris 792$_{,2}$, | Bodl. 1257$_{,3}$, 112 Munich 564, Esc. ^{2}476, Algiers 1831/2, fragments from this Berl. 7418.—16. Anon., Berl. 7550/3, Leid. 621, Munich 565, Paris 3088/9, Köpr. 1325.—Other commentaries Ahlw. 7558, Suppl. I, 172/3.—*Takhmīs a.* Saʿd b. ʿAlī al-Irbilī Leid. 623, *b.* ʿAbdallāh b. ʿUmar al-Anṣārī al-Wazīr, d. 777/1375, Berl. 7554/5, *c.* al-Ḥasan b. al-Ḥusayn b. ʿAlī, ibid. 7556, *d.* al-Muṭahhar Fakhr al-Dīn, ibid. 7557.—II. Satirical poem on the philologist al-Bāhilī (p. 107$_{,16,1}$), Leid. 624.—III. *Qaṣīda*s Berl. 7561.—IV. *Qaṣīda* rhyming in *ṭāʾ*, Bodl. II, 380$_{,7,2}$—V. Poem in praise of Yaḥyā b. ʿAbd al-Wahhāb al-Baṣrī al-Kātib, ibid. 3.—VI. *al-Maqṣūra al-kubrā* or *Kitāb al-maqṣūr wal-mamdūd naẓman*, 55 verses, each of which contains two identical words that only differ by an *alif maqṣūra* or *mamdūda*

14 Cf. Th. Nöldeke, *Orientalische Skizzen*, 168.

114 and in part also in meaning, | in 7 chapters with headings, according to the vocalisation of the first two radicals and in part according to the meaning, Berl. 7559/60, Gotha 207,$_2$, Munich 564, f. 123, Vienna 146, 1805,$_2$, Leid. 615/7, de Jong 28/9, Paris 792,$_4$, Pet. AM 268.—VII. 13 verses on the parts of the human body that are masculine or feminine, Paris 792,$_3$.—VIII. *al-Jamhara fi 'l-lugha*, a large but impractical dictionary, circulating in different recensions, Leid. 52, Paris 4231,$_5$, 4233, Köpr. 1541/2, Yeni 1124, Welīeddīn 3100, Dāmād Ibr. 1117, Fātiḥ 5187, NO 4745/6, AS 4672, Cairo ^{1}IV, 171, ^{2}II, 11.—IX. *Kitāb al-sarj wal-lithām* Leid. 53, ed. W. Wright, *Op. ar.* 1/14.—X. *Kitāb ṣifāt al-saḥāb wal-ghayth wa-akhbār al-ruwwād wa-mā ḥamidū min al-kala'*, Leid. 54, *Op. ar.* 15/46 = (?) *Kitāb al-maṭar* Berl. 7050.—XI. *Kitāb al-malāḥin* (linguistic tricks in swearing, MSS in Suppl. with Bešīr Āġā Ayyūb 193, *MFO* V, 535), ed. H. Thorbecke, *Festschr. der or. Section d. 36. Vers. deutscher Philolog. u. Schulm.*, Heidelberg 1882, C. 1347.—XII. *Kitāb al-ishtiqāq* (in refutation of the allegation—in disparagement of the Arabic language—that the names of the tribes have no etymology in it, see Goldziher, *MSt.* I, 209), *Genealogisch-etymologisches Handbuch aus der Hds. der Un.-bibl. zu Leyden hsg. v.* F. Wüstenfeld, Göttingen 1854 (only 100 copies and an anastatic reprint).—XIII. *Kitāb al-mujtanā*, sayings by the Prophet and his successors up to the time of al-Ḥasan, by sages and philosophers, ḤKh V, 146, Br. Mus. 723, Bodl. II, 381, Hyderabad 1342.—His *Amālī* is quoted in al-Suyūṭī, *Muzhir* I, ^{1}62,$_{19}$, 80,$_3$, ^{2}76,$_{10}$, 99,$_6$ and elsewhere.

26. From among al-Mubarrad's students the following also need to be mentioned:

a. Muḥammad b. al-Sarī b. al-Sarrāj, d. 316/928.

Fihrist 62, Ibn al-Anb. 313/4, Ibn Khall. 613, Flügel 103. His *Kitāb al-uṣūl* is quoted in *Khiz.* III, 61, penult. 95,$_{10}$.

b. Abū Muḥammad ʿAbdallāh b. Jaʿfar b. Durustawayh al-Fasawī was born in 258/871 in the Persian province of Fasā and died on 24 Ṣafar 347/18 May 958 in Baghdad.

113 *Fihrist* 63, Ibn al-Anb. 356/8, Ibn Khall. 305, Flügel 105, | Wüst., *Gesch.* 122. His *Kitāb al-alfāẓ lil-kuttāb*, Bodl. II, 354, is a handbook on phonetics and typography for secretaries.

115 | 27. Likewise of Persian origin was Abū Saʿīd al-Ḥasan b. ʿAbdallāh b. al-Marzubān al-Sīrāfī, who was born in 280/893. His father, whose real name

was Behzād, had still professed Zoroastrianism. Al-Sīrāfī began his studies in his hometown. He then studied jurisprudence in Oman and, in ʿAskar Mukram, under Muḥammad b. ʿUmar al-Ṣaymarī, dogmatics, astronomy, and mathematics. He eventually went to Baghdad where he followed the philology classes of Ibn Durayd. Because of his knowledge of *fiqh*, the *qāḍī* Abū Muḥammad b. Maʿrūf appointed him as his representative, first on the eastern bank of the Tigris, then on both banks and finally again on the eastern bank. There, in the mosque of the Ruṣāfa fortress, he issued Ḥanafī fatwas for almost 50 years. At the same time he was also a teacher of philology. He died on 2 Rajab 368/3 February 979.

Fihrist 62, Ibn al-Anb. 379/82, Ibn Khall. 153, Flügel 107, Wüst., *Gesch.* 142. Comm. on Sībawayhi's *Kitāb*, see p. 100 and also Suppl. I, 175. *Akhbār al-naḥwiyyīn* Shahīd ʿAlī Pāshā 1842 (Rescher, *Abr.* 163).

His son Yūsuf, d. Rabīʿ I 385/April 995 at the age of 55, continued his father's works and completed some of them.

Yāqūt, *Irshād* VII, 307, Ibn Khall. 809, Flügel 242. 1. *Sharḥ shawāhid Sībawayhi*, NO 4576, p. 120 n.—2. *Sharḥ abyāt Iṣlāḥ al-manṭiq*, p. 120.

28. A student of Ibn al-Sarrāj and Ibn Durayd was Abu 'l-Ḥasan ʿAlī b. ʿĪsā al-Rummānī al-Ikhshīdī al-Warrāq, born in 276/889 in Baghdad, where he died on 11 Jumādā I 384/24 June 994. His contemporaries criticised him for allowing logical speculation to have too much of an influence on his linguistics.

Fihrist 63, Ibn al-Anb. 389/92, Ibn Khall. 446, Flügel 108. 1. *Tawjīh iʿrāb abyāt mulghazāt al-iʿrāb* Paris 3303.—2. *Kitāb al-nukat fī majāz al-Qurʾān* (Wehbī Efendi 62), ed. Dr. Abalalim, Delhi 1934 (*Isl. Cult.* 1933, 374), see Suppl. I, 175.

| 29. Another student of Ibn al-Sarrāj and Zajjāj was the Iranian Abū ʿAlī 116
al-Ḥasan b. ʿAlī b. Aḥmad (Muḥammad) b. ʿAbd al-Ghaffār al-Fasawī al-Fārisī. Born in 288/900 in Fasā, the son of an Arab woman, he went to Baghdad in 307/919. After finishing his studies he went to the Aleppan court of Sayf al-
Dawla in 341/952, and later to the Būyid ʿAḍud al-Dawla in Persia, | for whom 114
he composed his major works *al-Īḍāḥ* and *al-Takmila*. He died in Baghdad on 17 Rabīʿ I 377/17 July 987.

Fihrist 64, Ibn al-Anb. 387/9, Ibn Khall. 155, Flügel 110. I. *al-Īḍāḥ* (*wal-takmila*) *fī 'l-naḥw* Esc. ^{2}42/3, 125, 194, AS 4451, Köpr. 1456/7, Patna I, 161,$_{522}$ (see Suppl.).

Comm.: *b.* ʿAbd al-Qāhir al-Jurjānī, d. 471/1078 (see p. 287), Esc. ^{2}44.—II. *Kitāb al-shiʿr* or *al-ʿAḍudī*, ed. by his student Ibn Jinnī, d. 391/1001, grammatical comments on poetical fragments, Berl. 6465.[1]—III. *Kitāb al-ḥujja etc.* (Suppl.) Patna I, 13, 114/5, see Pretzl, *Islca* VI, 17.—V. *al-Masāʾil al-Shīrāziyyāt* Rāġib 1379.—VII. *Kitāb al-tadhkira*, grammatical comments on difficult verses, ḤKh II^{1}, 2788, I, ^{2}384, quoted *Khiz.* IV, $390_{,7}$, $392_{,9}$, 421 bottom and elsewhere.[2]

30. Abu ʾl-Qāsim ʿAlī b. Ḥamza al-Baṣrī, who attended the lectures of al-Mutanabbī in Baghdad and died in Sicily in 375/985.

Kitāb al-tanbīhāt ʿalā aghlāṭ al-ruwāt Br. Mus. Suppl. 841, Strasburg, *ZDMG* 1886, 313; Excerpts: against Ibn al-Sikkīt's *Iṣlāḥ al-manṭiq*, Leid. 46, against al-Mubarrad's *Kāmil*, ibid. 445.

Many of the men who have been mentioned towards the end could also be counted as representatives of the school of Baghdad. In this school, which dates from the fourth century A.H., the antagonisms of the two previous schools balanced one another. But before we turn to this new development in linguistics we must first consider the school of Kufa, which was the rival of that of Basra.

117 | II *The School of Kufa*

The beginnings of linguistic studies in Kufa, the second capital of Iraq, are just as murky as they are for Basra. It seems that they started somewhat later than in the latter and that, at their inception, they may even have been influenced by them. Unfortunately, we are very ill-informed on this school, which is mainly due to the fact that almost none of its works have survived. Reports on the rivalries between the two schools in later authors are not very positive for the Kufans. This is because the prevailing precisionist school of thought was not able to deal with other's more practice-oriented studies.

Cf. *Kitāb al-inṣāf fī masāʾil al-khilāf bayna ʾl-naḥwiyyīn al-Baṣriyyīn wal-Kūfiyyīn* by ʿAbd al-Raḥmān b. Muḥammad b. al-Anbārī, d. 577/1181, Leid. 169, Esc. ^{2}119, Yeni 1060, ʿAlī Šehīd, P. 2340 (*MFO* V, 520), after which Koshut, *Fünf Streitfragen der Basrenser und Kufenser*, Vienna 1878.

1 Contrary to Ahlwardt's misgivings, the quotation at *Khiz.* IV, $372_{,14}$ = Cap. 11 in Rödiger, *ZDMG* XXIII, 304 confirms the title of the Berlin MS. See also *Khiz.* IV, $425_{,12}$, $427_{,23}$, $437_{,21}$.

2 Against it, Abū Muḥammad al-Aswad al-ʿArabī (see p. 120, n. 1) wrote his *Kitāb nuzhat al-adīb*, Khiz. I, 21.

1. Regarded as the founder of the school of Kufa is Abū Jaʿfar Muḥammad b. Abī Sāra al-Ḥasan (Yāqūt ʿAlī) al-Ruʾāsī, a contemporary of Khalīl, who supposedly used one of the latter's works. It was he that Sībawayhi referred to in his *Kitāb* through the simple title al-Kūfī (al-Suyūṭī, *Muzhir* ^{2}II, $248,_{20}$).

Flügel 118.

2. ʿAlī b. Ḥamza b. ʿAbdallāh b. Bahman b. Fayrūz al-Kisāʾī, who hailed from a small Iranian family, was a student of al-Ruʾāsī and his uncle Abū Muslim Muʿādh b. Muslim al-Harrāʾ. He also attended the lectures of al-Khalīl in Basra, and it was at the latter's advice that he went for a time to the desert to learn the unadulterated language of the Bedouins.[3] His teacher in the art of reciting the Qurʾān was | Ḥamza al-Zayyāt, d. 156/773. Later he developed his 118
own way of reading, so that he is counted as one of the seven canonical readers. Hārūn al-Rashīd, who was himself one of his students, entrusted him with the education of his sons al-Amīn and al-Maʾmūn. As mentioned earlier, Sībawayhi made a failed attempt to unsettle his reputation. He died in Ranbūya near Rayy in 189/865 (Fihr. 179) (or, according to others, in 179, 182, 183, or 192).

Fihrist 29, 30, 65, Ibn Qutayba, *Maʿārif* 279, Ibn al-Anbārī 83/94, Ibn Khall. 406, Flügel 121/6, Nöldeke, *Gesch. des Qor.* 291, Bergstr., *Pretzl* III, Index. On his works see Suppl. I, 178; in addition, *Kitāb mā tashābaha min alfāẓ al-Qurʾān wa-tanāẓara min kalimāt al-furqān* Qawala I, 28, $q15,_{2}$.

| 3. The most important of al-Kisāʾī's students, who had nevertheless also 116
attended the lectures of the Basran Yūnus b. Ḥabīb, was Abū Zakariyyāʾ Yaḥyā b. Ziyād b. ʿAbdallāh b. Manẓūr al-Daylamī al-Farrāʾ, like his teacher of Iranian stock. Al-Maʾmūn appointed him as the tutor to his sons. In Baghdad he also developed a very succesful public lectureship, mainly on the interpretation of the Qurʾān. He died on his way to Mecca in the year 207/822, aged 67.

Flügel 129/36 (ibid. 134, table of contents of his lost grammatical magnum opus, the *Kitāb al-ḥudūd*). Other works Suppl. I, 178/9. His *Ḥurūf al-muʿjam* is quoted by Ibn Rashīq, *al-ʿUmda* I, 100.

3 In the same way, for Abyssinian scholars it is the tribe of the Habab that is regarded as an authority on obscure words in Geʿez (see Praetorius, *Gramm. der Tigriñaspr.* 4, n. 1), while there are also comparable reports from India.

4. Abū ʿAbd al-Raḥmān (or Abu ʾl-ʿAbbās) al-Mufaḍḍal b. Muḥammad b. Yaḥyā al-Ḍabbī was born in Kufa and took part in the uprising of the ʿAlid Ibrāhīm b. ʿAbdallāh b. al-Ḥasan al-Nafs al-Zakiyya[4] against the caliph al-Manṣūr. He was taken hostage, then pardoned and enrolled in the retinue of the crown
119 prince al-Mahdī. It was for the latter that he compiled his famous | collections of poems *al-Mufaḍḍaliyyāt* and *al-Ikhtiyār*. He died around the year 170/786.

Fihrist 68f, Ibn al-Anb. 67/9, Flügel 142/5. *Nukhaba min Kitāb al-ikhtiyārayn, ikhtiyār al-Mufaḍḍal al-Ḍabbī wa-ʿAbd al-Malik b. Qurayb al-Aṣmaʿī min ashʿār fuṣaḥāʾ al-ʿarab fi ʾl-jāhiliyya wal-islām mimmā ruwiya min mashāyikh ahl al-lugha al-mawthūq bi-riwāyatihim*, ed. and transl. by Dr. Syed Muazzam Hussain (based on the unique MS Ind. Off. Libr.), Univ. of Dacca, 1938. Of his other works there only remains the *Kitāb al-amthāl*, print. Constantinople, Jawāʾib 1300, C. 1327/1909.

5. His student was Abū ʿAmr Isḥāq b. Mirār al-Shaybānī al-Aḥmar, who occasionally also lived in Baghdad. Like his teacher he devoted himself primarily to ancient poetry and also to Tradition, for which he was considered so trustworthy that Aḥmad b. Ḥanbal took much material from him. He is believed to have collected the poems of more than 80 tribes, which he deposited in the mosque of Kufa. He died of old age in the year 206/821.

Fihrist 68, Ibn al-Anb. 120/5, Ibn Khall. 83, Flügel 139/42. 1. *Kitāb al-jīm fi ʾl-lugha*, a large lexical compilation on Arabic dialects, Esc. ^{2}572.—2. *Ashʿār Banī Jaʿda* quoted in *Agh.* XIX, ^{1}82 penult., $83_{,4}$.—3. *al-Nawādir*, Suyūṭī, *Muzhir* ^{1}$261_{,23}$, II, $105_{,4}$ from below.

6. Abū ʿAbdallāh Muḥammad b. Ziyād b. al-Aʿrābī was born in 150/767 in Kufa, the son of a slave from Sind. He was enfranchised by the Hāshimī ʿAbbās b. Muḥammad. Later his mother married al-Mufaḍḍal, and he became the lat-
117 ter's most assiduous student. After a very successful | teaching career he died in Samarra, at 81 years of age, in 231/844 (or, according to others, in 230 or 232).

Fihrist 69, Ibn al-Anb. 207/12, Ibn Khall. 605, Flügel 145/9, Wüst., *Gesch.* 54. On his works see Suppl. I, 179/80; to no. 4, *al-Nawādir*, transmitted by Thaʿlab, allegedly in the Khālidiyya Library in Jerusalem, quoted in Suyūṭī, *Muzhir* I, ^{1}$251_{,17}$,
120 *Khiz.* III, 59 bottom page, | Abū Muḥammad al-Ḥasan b. Aḥmad al-Aswad

4 See C. van Arendonk, *De opkomst van het Zaidietische imamaat*, p. 52.

al-Aʿrābī al-Ghandajānī[5] wrote addenda under the title *Ḍāllat al-adīb*, *Khiz.* I, 516,$_{14}$, II, 364,$_{3}$, III, 83,$_{9}$, 84,$_{5}$, 166,$_{7}$, 263,$_{19}$.

7. Abū Yūsuf Yaʿqūb b. Isḥāq b. al-Sikkīt was the son of a schoolteacher from Dawraq in Khūzistān, probably of Aramaic origin, who had studied philology under al-Kisāʾī and al-Farrāʾ. Abū Yūsuf, too, attended the lectures of the latter, and those of Abū ʿAmr al-Shaybānī and of the Basrans al-Aṣmaʿī and Abū ʿUbayda, while further increasing his knowledge through interactions with Bedouins. When he had made a name for himself as an author the caliph al-Mutawakkil entrusted him with the education of his son al-Muʿtazz. But because he made no secret of his preference for the ʿAlids the caliph had him trampled to death by his Turkish guards on 25 Rajab 243/18 November 857 (or, according to others, in 244 or 246).

Fihrist 72/3, Ibn al-Anb. 238/41, Ibn Khall. 798, Flügel 158/61. 1. *Kitāb iṣlāḥ al-manṭiq* Berl. Brill M. 187, Leid. 46 (in the recension of al-Tabrīzī), Bodl. II, 213,$_{1}$, Br. Mus. Suppl. 831, Esc. ^{2}29 (recension of Abū ʿAlī Ismāʿīl b. Abi ʾl-Qāsim al-Baghdādī al-Qālī, d. 356/966, p. 130), 112 (based on a copy that was made in the author's lifetime), Köpr. 1207/9, 256,$_{3}$, NO 4692, Cairo ^{1}IV, 202, ^{2}II, 2, old MS Alex. Lugha 3, Āṣaf. II, 1428,$_{152}$.—Commentary on the verses by Abū Muḥammad Yūsuf b. al-Ḥasan b. al-Sīrāfī, d. 385/995 (p. 115), Köpr. 1296, 1300, see Rescher, *MSOS* XIV, 13, in the defter wrongly attributed to Ibrāhīm b. Yūsuf al-Marzubānī, see *Khiz.* I, 405,$_{1}$, ḤKh I, ^{1}328,^{2}108).—Excerpts: *a. Jawāmiʿ Iṣlāḥ al-manṭiq* by Zayd b. Rifāʿa (see p. 213), Berl. 6929, see A. Ahmedali, *ZDMG* 90, 201/8, print. Hyderabad 1354/1935.—*b.* under the title *al-Munakhkhal* by Abu ʾl-Qāsim al-Ḥusayn b. ʿAlī b. al-Ḥusayn al-Wazīr al-Maghribī, d. 418/1027 (see 353), Esc. ^{2}605 (MS d. 486/1093), one folio ibid. 378 (wrongly attributed to Abu ʾl-Qāsim Ismāʿīl b. ʿAlī b. al-Ḥusayn).—2. *Kitāb al-alfāẓ* Paris 4232, *Tahdhīb al-a.* by al-Tabrīzī, | d. 502/1108, Leid. 44, *Kanz al-ḥuffāẓ fī kitāb T. al-a.*, *La Critique du langage par Ibn al-S. avec les cmt. du Cheikh Abū Yaḥyā Zakariyyāʾ al-Tabrīzī*, ed. L. Cheikho, Beirut 1896/8.—3. *Sharḥ dīwān al-Khansāʾ*, see p. 35. 3a.—12. Suppl. I, 180/1.—Cited are also: 1. *Kitāb al-amthāl*, *Agh.* XXI, ^{1}189,$_{15}$, 203,$_{8}$.—2. *Kitāb al-mudhakkar wal-muʾannath*, *Khiz.* I, 377,$_{22}$, II, 310,$_{17}$.—3. *Kitāb abyāt al-maʿānī*, ibid. I, 487,$_{4}$ from below, II, 301,$_{20}$.—4. *Kitāb al-aḍdād*, ibid. II 147,$_{9}$, IV 200,$_{10}$.—5. *Kitāb al-farq*, Jawālīqī, *Muʿarrab* 134 penult.—6. 121

5 A protégé of Abū Manṣūr Bahrām, d. 433/1041, and of the Būyid vizier Abū Kalījār b. Sulṭān al-Dawla of Shiraz, and the author of a number of polemical tracts in philology; Yāqūt, *Irshād* III, 22/4, after which *Khiz.* I, 21. His *Kitāb farḥat al-adīb* against Yūsuf al-Sīrāfī's *Sharḥ shaw. Sībawayhi* (p. 115), *Khiz.* II, 141,$_{1}$; see p. 116 n. 2.

Sharḥ dīwān Ṭarafa, Khiz. I, $505_{,13}$, IV, $139_{,21}$.—7. *Sharḥ dīwān Ṭufayl,* ibid. IV, $246_{,4}$ from below.—8. *Kitāb al-maqṣūr wal-mamdūd,* Ibn Sīda, *al-Mukhaṣṣaṣ* I, $12_{,4}$ from below, Suyūṭī, *Muzhir* ^{1}I, $212_{,4}$, II, 37 penult., ^{2}II, $160_{,17}$.—9. *Kitāb al-muthannā wal-mukannā wal-mubannā wal-muʾākhā wa-mā ḍumma ilayhi, Muzhir* I, $^{1}244_{,5}$, $245_{,6}$, $^{2}299_{,19}$, $301_{,3}$, II, 72, 93/7, 100, 102/3, 129, 168, see Seybold,
118 ZDMG XLIX, 232.— | 10. *Kitāb al-aṣwāt,* Ibn Sīda I, $12_{,4}$ from below, *Muzhir* I, $^{1}266_{,18}$, $^{2}327_{,14}$, $331_{,18}$, II, $148_{,9}$, $^{2}59_{,9}$, $114_{,8}$, $134_{,5}$, $168_{,9}$.

8. A student of his, and also of Ibn al-Aʿrābī, was Abū Ṭālib al-Mufaḍḍal b. Salama b. ʿĀṣim al-Ḍabbī, who was part of the entourage of two of al-Mutawakkil's viziers, Fatḥ b. Khāqān and Ismāʿīl b. Bulbul. He died after 290/903.

Fihrist 73, Ibn al-Anb. 263, Ibn Khall. 551, Flügel 162/4. Of his numerous works there remain only: 1. *Kitāb al-fākhir,* see Suppl. I, 181.—2. *Kitāb al-malāhī, Ancient Arabic musical instruments in the handwriting of Yāqūt al-Mustaʿṣimī, AD 1298, Text in facs. and transl. with notes by* James Robson, *including notes on the instruments by* H.G. Farmer, Glasgow 1938 (Collection of Or. Writers on Music IV).

9. The most important representative of the Kufan school was Abu 'l-ʿAbbās Aḥmad b. Yaḥyā Thaʿlab, a student of al-Farrāʾ and Ibn al-Aʿrābī and a *mawlā* of the Shaybān tribe. Even though he had also been to the lectures of Basran scholars he kept strictly to the Kufan school when it came to grammatical methodology. His rivalry with al-Mubarrad has already been mentioned. He was born in the year 200/815 and died in an accident on 17 Jumādā I 291/8 April 904.

122 | Ibn al-Anb. 293/9, Ibn Khall. 42, Flügel 165/7. Of his works there remain: I. *al-Faṣīḥ,* on the form and meaning of obscure words, ed. J. Barth, Leipzig 1876 (see Lane, ZDMG III, 94). On this, Abu 'l-Qāsim ʿAlī b. Ḥamza al-Baṣrī, d. 375/985, see p. 116, wrote *al-Tanbīh ʿalā mā fi 'l-Faṣīḥ min al-ghalaṭ,* Esc. ^{2}188; because he had criticised al-Farrāʾ at some points, an anonymous contemporary proved him wrong in ten cases, Berl. 6933.—*Dhayl al-Faṣīḥ* by ʿAbd al-Laṭīf b. Yūsuf al-Baghdādī, d. 629/1231 (see p. 481), Cairo ^{1}IV, 267, ^{2}II, 14, print. in *al-Ṭuraf al-adabiyya* by Muḥammad Amin al-Khānjī, C. 1325.—Commentaries see Suppl. I. 81/2, and additionally Abu 'l-Qāsim ʿAbdallāh b. ʿAbd al-Raḥīm b. Thaʿlab al-Iṣfahānī, Rāmpūr I, $510_{,38}$.—Versifications: *a.* ʿAbd al-Ḥamīd b. Abi 'l-Ḥadīd, d. 655/1257, see p. 249, Esc. ^{2}188, *b.* Muḥammad b. Aḥmad b. Ghābir al-Hawwārī, d. 780/1378, see II, 13, cf. Suppl. Paris $4452_{,6}$. Other recensions in Ahlw. 6934.—II. *Kitāb qawāʿid al-Shiʿr* Vat. 357, Th. L'arte poetica secondo la

tradizione di a. ʿUbaidallāh M. b. ʿImrān al-Marzubānī (d. 384/993, Suppl. I, 190/1), publ. da C. Schiaparelli, *Actes du 8ème congr. intern. des or.* Leiden 1890, 42 pp.—III. *Dīwān Zuhayr* see Suppl. 48.—IV. *Dīwān al-Aʿshā* p. 31.—V.–X. see Suppl.—Also quoted: XI. *Gharīb al-ḥadīth*, by Ibn al-Athīr in the preface to the *Nihāya*.—XII. *Kitāb majāz al-kalām wa-taṣārīfihi*, Suyūṭī, *Muzhir* ^{1}I, $190,_{5}$.

| 10. Thaʿlab's most important student was Abū Bakr Muḥammad b. al-Qāsim 119
b. Muḥammad b. Bashshār b. al-Anbārī, whose father, d. 304/916, had already established a reputation as a traditionist and philologist, and who educated his son himself. Born on 11 Rajab 231/3 January 885, al-Anbārī lived a completely ascetic existence, devoting himself purely to scholarship, and extending his learned activities beyond philology to the science of Tradition, Qurʾānic exegesis, and history. It was only at the beginning of the reign of al-Rāḍī in 322/934, when the latter entrusted him with the education of the prince ʿAbd al-Wāḥid b. al-Muqtadir,[6] that he became associated with the court in Baghdad. He died in Dhu 'l-Ḥijja 328/October 940.

Fihrist 75, Ibn al-Anb. 330/42, Ibn Khall. 614, Flügel 168/72.—Of his writings
the following are extant: 1. *Kitāb al-aḍdād,* | *sive liber de vocabulis arabicis* 123
quae plures habent significationes inter se oppositas,[7] *ex unico qui superest cod. Lugd.* (*no. 55*), ed. M. Th. Houtsma, Leiden 1881, repr. C. 1325.—2.–4. see Suppl.—5. On passages from the Qurʾān where a *tāʾ* is written instead of a *hāʾ*, Paris $651,_{2}$ (probably from the *Kitāb al-hāʾāt fī kitāb Allāh*).—6. *Gharīb al-ḥadīth* is mentioned by Ibn al-Athīr in the preface to the *Nihāya*.—7.–9. see Suppl. (in connection with 9. read Bergsträsser, *Gesch. d. Qorʾāntextes* [III] p. 2, n. 2).

11. His student was Abū Bakr Muḥammad b. ʿUmar b. Aḥmad b. ʿUzayr al-ʿUzayrī al-Sijistānī, d. 330/941.

Ibn al-Anb. 386, Flügel 173. *Nuzhat al-qulūb fī gharīb al-Qurʾān*, arranged not by root but alphabetically by word form, Berl. 684/94, Gotha 522/3, Leid. 1652, Br. Mus. 1188, Bodl. I, 27, Upps. 388, Paris 590/1 (see Derenbourg, *Rev. crit.* 1882, I, 206, n. 1), AS 426/8 (other MSS cf. Suppl. I, 183, 943, with Garr. 1189/90, Qawāla I, 85, Mosul $126,_{32}$, Patna I 34_{345}), print. C. 1325, 1355, arranged in the usual order

6 See al-Ṣūlī, *Akhbār al-rāḍī* $9,_{6}$, ed. Heyworth-Dunne, who confuses master and pupil in his Index.

7 See W.C.F. Giese, *Untersuchungen über die Aḍdād aufgrund von Stellen in altar. Dichtern*, Diss. Berlin 1894, but especially Th. Nöldeke, *Neue Beitr. z. sem. Sprachw*, 67/108.

and provided with some additions by al-Suyūṭī (?), Berl. 695, cf. J. Feilchenfeld, *Ein einleitender Beitrag zum gharīb al-qur'ān mit einer Probe aus dem Lexikon des Sijistānī*, Diss. Jena (Vienna), 1892.

12. The most faithful student of Thaʿlab, which is why he was also known as *ghulām* Thaʿlab, was Abū ʿUmar Muḥammad b. ʿAbd al-Waḥīd al-Zāhid al-Muṭarriz al-Warrāq al-Bāwardī, who was born in 261/874. His exceptional memory aroused the envy of his rivals, who vainly tried to cast doubts on his trustworthiness a number of times. If he excessively venerated the Umayyads at a time when the power of the ʿAbbāsids had already sunk to an all-time low, this must have been due to his preference for the Arabs. Thus, he expected his students in philology to first take his class on *Fī faḍā'il Muʿāwiya*, a work that he had written himself. He died on 13 Dhu 'l-Qaʿda 345/17 February 957 in Baghdad.

124 | Ibn al-Anb. 345/54, Flügel 174/8, al-Rājkūtī, RAAD IX, 601/16. From among his numerous writings (*Fihrist* 76) there only remain: 1. *Kitāb al-ʿasharāt*, explanations of ten words each that have the same ending, edited by his student Ibn Khālawayh, d. 370/980, Berl. 7014, see I. Kračkovsky, *Islca* III, 333. 2.—4. Suppl.; ad 4. RAAD IX, 532/44.

120 | III *The School of Baghdad*

From the third/ninth century onward the rival schools of Basra and Kufa became more and more integrated. Baghdad, the magnificent new capital of the caliphate, soon became the centre of all intellectual life and overshadowed the towns of the provinces. Nevertheless, even in the capital many scholars held fast to the traditions of the schools from which they had originated. But the younger generation, which had the opportunity of listening to representatives from both schools, was no longer interested in the old antagonisms and tried to unite the advantages of both schools using a new, eclectic method. Of course, this method developed only gradually at first, and with regard to some of those men whom we have already discussed, or who are still to be mentioned, one cannot be sure as to which school they were part of, the more so since it is only with great difficulty that we can have some sense of their actual grammatical ideas. In general, we shall have to be content to rely on the authority of the *Fihrist*.

1. The first representative mentioned here—as in the *Fihrist*—was a man whose importance spread far beyond the field of linguistics, but who himself wanted

his philological works to be regarded as the essence of his literary achievement. Abū Muḥammad ʿAbdallāh b. Muslim b. Qutayba (al-Qutaybī or al-Qutabī[1]) | 125
was born in 213/828 in Baghdad (or, according to others, in Kufa). His father hailed from Marw—which is also why he had the *nisba* al-Marwazī—and he was thus of Iranian or Turkish stock. After extensive studies in philology and the science of Tradition, he held the office of *qāḍi* in Dīnawar, in the province of al-Jabal (Jibāl, i.e. Media), for some time, which explains his second *nisba*, al-Dīnawarī. Later he was a teacher in Baghdad, which is where he died on 1 Rajab 276/30 October 889 (according to others in Dhu ʾl-Qaʿda 270/May 884). The principal aim of his writing was to provide the (at the time) highly respected and influential class of secretaries, the *kuttāb*, the predecessors of the later *munshiʾ*, | with the tools of a belletristic and historical education nec- 121
essary for their profession. But in two of his writings he also intervened in the theological disputes of his time,[2] as he defended the Qurʾān and *ḥadīth* against attacks by philosophically educated sceptics.

Ibn al-Anb. 272/4, Ibn Khall. 304, al-Nawawī 771, Flügel 178/92, Wüstenf., *Gesch.* 73. His extant works are: 1. *ʿUyūn al-akhbār*, which examines, in 10 books, sovereignty, war, aristocracy, learning and eloquence, asceticism, friendship, appeals, food, and women, while documenting individual themes by means of sayings from the *ḥadīth*, examples from history, and verses from ancient poetry, Pet. AM 691 (see V. v. Rosen, *Bull. de l'Ac. d. Sc. de. St. Pétersbourg* XXVII, 62ff, *Mélanges Asiatiques de St. P.* VIII, 1880, 777), Köpr. 1344, see Suppl. Going by the preface, we are to regard as an addenda to the aforementioned work: 2. *Kitāb al-maʿārif, Handbuch der Geschichte, hsg. v.* F. Wüstenfeld, Göttingen 1850 (on the | MSS, see Suppl. and on those in Istanbul, Cahen, *REI* 1936 SA 126
2). The book begins with the Creation and the Fall of Man, using passages that were taken straight from the Bible.[3] There then follows the history of the patriarchs, using biblical and Arab legends, and of the Arabs who had

---

1 Thus Abū Nuwās calls himself once al-Nuwāsī, *Dīwān* ed. Āṣaf, 196,$_2$ and Ibn Ḥazm, *Faṣl* I, 19,$_{19}$, cf. 9, mentions a certain Ibn Shunayf al-Shunayfī.

2 According to al-Dhahabī's *Mīzān al-iʿtidāl*, in al-Yāfiʿī, *Mirʾāt al-janān* II, 191 (cf. Grünert, *Adab al-C.* VII, n. 1), and al-Bayhaqī (adopted in Flügel, 188), he had leanings towards the Karrāmiyya or the Mushabbiha. Following al-Dāraquṭnī in Suyūṭī's *Bughya*, 291, he wrote the *Kitāb al-radd ʿala ʾl-Mushabbiha* (*Fihrist* 78,$_7$ Suppl. I, 186,$_6$) precisely to defend himself against accusations of this kind.

3 His knowledge of the Bible also shows itself in a hitherto unknown work in which he correlates passages that were given a messianic interpretation by the Christians with the person of Muḥammad, and which was incorporated by Ibn al-Jawzī (p. 503) in his *Kitāb al-wafāʾ* and

abandoned paganism before the time of the Prophet. A detailed geneology of the Arab tribes is followed by the life of Muḥammad and his Companions, ending with the lives of the caliphs up to his own lifetime. Next follow brief notes on *fuqahāʾ*, traditionists, reciters of the Qurʾān, historians, and philologists, then on the *awāʾil, futūḥ*, and the *ayyām al-ʿarab*. The work is completed with a
122 chronicle on the | pre-Islamic dynasties of South and North Arabia, and the kings of the Persians. Cf. v. Kremer, *Culturgesch.* II, 419.—2. *Kitāb al-sharāb* or *al-ashriba wakhtilāf al-nās fīhā* Copenhagen 291, or *Kitāb ikhtilāf al-ʿulamāʾ fī-mā yaḥullu min al-ashriba wa-yaḥrumu wa-ḥujjat kulli farīq minhum* Br. Mus. $864,_{3}$, Cairo ^{1}VII, 653, see Suppl. (cf. Goldziher, *Ẓāhir.* 67, n. 1).—3.–5. *Kitāb al-shiʿr wal-shuʿarāʾ*, see Suppl. Introduction, transl. by Nöldeke, *Beitr.* 1ff., ed. H.W. Chr. Rittershausen, *Verhandelingen over de poezie, Feestgave*, Leiden 1875; reprint by Muḥammad al-Saqqāʾ, C. 1350/1932.—6. *Maʿānī al-shiʿr* in 12 books, whose titles are mentioned in the *Fihrist*, part I *Abyāt al-maʿānī fi 'l-khayl*, AS 4050, see Suppl.—7. *Adab al-kātib*, composed before the *ʿUyūn*, on the MSS and printed editions see Suppl., with Berl. Brill M. 104, Mosul $172,_{1}$, Bank. XX, 1962, C. 1355/1936, cf. W.O. Sproull, *An Extract from Ibn Kutaiba's Adab al-Kātib or the Writers Guide with Transl. and Notes*, Leipzig 1877.—Commentaries by: *a.* al-Zajjājī (see p. 112), Br. Mus. $426,_{8}$.—*b.* al-Jawālīqī, d. 539/1144 (see p. 280), Pet. AM 203, Esc. ^{2}222, print. C. 1350.—*c.* al-Baṭalyawsī, d. 521/1127 (p. 309), Esc. ^{2}222, 503, Köpr. 1297/9.—8. *Kitāb al-anwāʾ* Bodl. I, 1000, 1033, cf. II, 605 (quoted in Suyūṭī, *Muzhir* ^{1}II, $36,_{2}$).—9. see Suppl. I, 185/6.—10. *Kitāb (taʾwīl) mukhtalif al-ḥadīth* Berl. 1262, Leid. 1730 = *Sharḥ al-aḥādīth al-nabawiyya* Rāġib 1261. While trying to refute all the objections of the philosophers against the tradi-
127 tions from the | standpoint of orthodoxy, he is sometimes obliged to make use of rather desperate methods of interpretation in order to justify the preposterous, and to invoke parallels from the Old and the New Testament. In the end, he nevertheless has to set some limits to the credibility and the authority of the *ḥadīth*; see Goldziher, *MSt.* II, 136, Houtsma, *De Strijd* p. 13. Excerpts under the title *al-Mughīth min mukhtalif al-ḥadīth* by Maḥmūd b. Ṭāhir b. al-Muẓaffar al-Sanjārī, Ind. Off. 196, Āṣaf. I, $674,_{135}$.—11. *Kitāb mushkil(āt) al-Qurʾān*, Leid. 1650, Köpr. 211, Asʿad 101, Fātiḥ 232, Rāmpūr I, $58,_{4}$, print. C. 1935, tries to solve the same problem for the Qurʾān.—12. *Kitāb al-masāʾil wal-jawābāt*, mostly from the *ḥadīth*, Gotha 636.—13.–19. see Suppl.—20. *Kitāb fī manāqib al-khulafāʾ al-rāshidīn* Āṣaf. III, $658,_{121}$.—Falsely attributed to Ibn Qutayba is

---

edited by Brockelmann in *BASS* III, 46/55, see Brockelmann, *ZATW* XV, 138/42, 312, Bacher, ibid. 309, Goldziher, *REJ*, 1895, 1ff., M. Schreiner in *Kohut Semitic Studies* 496ff.

the *Kitāb al-imāma wal-siyāsa*, Berl. 9412, Brill M. 221, 268, Paris 1566, Br. Mus 1272, 1649, Lund XV, Patna I 275,$_{2291}$, cf. *Ex libro Ibn Kutaibae excerpta p. I. Expositio de quattuor primis khalifis*, ed. Petersson, p. II, ed. Andersson, Lund 1856, partly translated by Gayangos in *The Muhamm. Dynasties in Spain by Makkari*, vol. I, App. E, vol. II, App. A. Part of the book was derived from a work of history that has been falsely attributed to Ibn Ḥabīb, d. 239/853, | see Dozy, 123
Recherches, 2nd ed. vol. I, p. 23, 3rd ed. vol. I, 9, Nöldeke, ZDMG 1886, p. 316, see Suppl.

2. Just as wide-ranging in terms of subjects as Ibn Qutayba was his contemporary Abū Ḥanīfa Aḥmad b. Dā'ūd b. Wanand al-Dīnawarī. He was certainly of Iranian stock as is shown by his grandfather's name. Besides philology, in which the Kufan Ibn al-Sikkīt (see p. 120) was his teacher, he also added mathematics, astronomy, geography, and history to the range of his studies and literary works. However, his great work on plants seems to have arisen from the study of philology rather than natural history. If the numerous quotations in the *Khizānat al-adab* are to be trusted, it was especially concerned with plants mentioned by the ancient poets. Nevertheless, it also offered a number of observations that are independent from those made by the Greeks. He died on 26 Jumādā I 282/4 July 895.

| S. de Sacy, *Relation de l'Égypte*, 64, 78, Steinschneider, ZDMG XXIV, 373, 128
Leclerc, *Hist. de la méd. ar.* I, Paris 1876, p. 298, Flügel 190, Wüstenf., *Gesch.* 79, Suter, *Math.* no. 60. 1. *Kitāb al-akhbār al-ṭiwāl* Leid. 822, 1122, Pet. Ros. 29, *Bibl. Italinsky*, see Hammer, *Lettere*, IV, 205, ed. W. Guirgass, Leiden 1888. After a brief overview of ancient history in which only Alexander and the Persians stand out, the history of the Sasanids is narrated in detail. This is immediately followed by the Muslim conquest of Iraq, with a lively description of the Battle of Qādisiyya. The battles between ʿAlī and Muʿāwiya and the Khārijis are reported in great detail, while from the time of the Umayyads there is only a description of the death of Ḥusayn and the uprisings of the Azraqīs and Mukhtār. At the end there is a brief history of the caliphs from ʿAbd al-Malik to al-Muʿtaṣim, in which only the fall of the Umayyads and activities of the ʿAlids—especially in Khurāsān—are treated in greater detail.—2. *Kitāb al-nabāt* (see Suppl.), abridged in the *Mufradāt* of Ibn al-Bayṭār (see p. 492), quoted in the *Amālī* of al-Zajjājī, cod. Berl. Pet 111, 218/9 (not in the printed edition), LA XVI, 135,$_{19}$, *Khiz.* III 39,$_{15}$, 41u, 71,$_{5vu}$, 93,$_{5vu}$, 194,$_{9}$, 244,$_{2,17}$, IV, 22,$_{9}$, 46,$_{25}$, 175,$_{4}$, 268, penult., 291,$_{17}$, 504,$_{23}$, 570,$_{14}$. The work was criticised by ʿAlī b. Ḥamza al-Baṣrī (p. 116) in a chapter of his *Kitāb al-tanbīhāt ʿalā aghlāṭ al-ruwāt*, see *Khiz.* I, 12,$_{1}$, III,

344,$_{5}$vu.—3.–4. see Suppl.—5. *al-Durra al-farīda fī 'l-durūs al-mufīda*, in 9 volumes, Āṣaf. II, 15,$_{10}$, 126/34.

3. Abu 'l-ʿAbbās ʿAbdallāh b. Muḥammad al-Anbārī al-Nāshiʾ al-Akbar b.
124 Shirshīr was both a philologist and a poet. | Born in Anbār, he lived for a time in Baghdad, dying in Egypt in the year 293/906. Apart from grammar, which he liked to approach from a philosophical perspective, he was particularly interested in metrics and logic. As a poet, he gave a special attention to hunting scenes, *ṭardiyyāt*.

Ibn Khall. 318. A *qaṣīda* of 77 verses on Muḥammad, his merits over the rest of humanity, and on each and every one of his ancestors, Berl. 7540, Br. Mus. 1054, Algiers 613,$_{14}$. His *Risāla fī tafḍīl al-sūdān ʿala 'l-bīḍ* and *Mufākhara bayna al-dhahab wal-zujāj* are criticised by Suyūṭī in Berl. 8413.

129 | 4. Ibrāhīm b. Isḥāq b. Bashīr (Bishr) b. ʿAbdallāh al-Ḥarbī, Shaykh al-Islām, born in 198/813, one of the teachers of Ibn al-Anbārī and Aḥmad b. Ḥanbal, was a philologist dedicated to theology and *fiqh*. He died in Baghdad in Dhu 'l-Ḥijja 285/January 899.

Fawāt I, 3, Flügel 197. His enormous *Gharīb al-ḥadīth*, in 5 volumes, is mentioned by Ibn al-Athīr in the preface to the *Nihāya*, vol. V. Dam Z. 63,$_{42}$.—A tract mentioned by Flügel is not devoted to the pigeon, *al-ḥamām*, but the bath, *al-ḥammām*, as indicated by the addition *wa-ādābihi*.

5. Abu 'l-Ṭayyib Muḥammad b. Aḥmad b. Isḥāq b. Yaḥyā al-Washshāʾ was a student of both Mubarrad and Thaʿlab. Even though he made a living as a school teacher, as an author he represented the elegant *adīb* of the old school. He died in 325/936 in Baghdad.

Flügel 212, Wüstenf., *Gesch.* 87. Of his works (*Fihrist* 85) the following are extant: 1. *Kitāb al-muwashshā*, which, in 56 chapters, deals with upper-class lifestyles and is, therefore, a rich source for the culture of the time, Leid. 446, ed. by R. Brünnow, Leiden 1887, reprint Cairo, al-Maṭbaʿa al-Ḥusayniyya, 1324, Maṭbaʿat al-Taqaddum 1342/5.—2. *Tafrīj al-muhaj wa-sabab al-wuṣūl ila 'l-faraj* or *Surūr al-muhaj wal-albāb fī rasāʾil al-aḥbāb*, a manual for writing letters, Berl. 8638.—3. See Suppl.—4. *al-Fāḍil min al-adab al-shāmil*, Berl. 3351, Alex. (not in catalogue.), see *Lughat al-ʿarab* IX, 193, 674 (where the reference is to Ibrāhīm b. Aḥmad al-Washshāʾ).

6. Abu 'l-Faḍl Muḥammad b. Abī Jaʿfar al-Mundhirī al-Marwazī al-Harawī, an Iranian by birth, was also a student of Mubarrad and Thaʿlab.[4] He died in 329/940.

Suyūṭī, *Bughya* 29, Flügel 216, see Suppl.

|| 7. To the same school belonged Abu 'l-Ḥasan ʿAlī b. Sulaymān b. al-Mufaḍḍal 130 125
al-Akhfash al-Aṣghar. In 287/900 he went to Egypt, from where he returned to Baghdad by way of Aleppo in 306/918. He died there, at almost 80 years old, in 315/920.

Suyūṭī, *Bughya* 338, Flügel 63, 224. He published the *Kāmil* of al-Mubarrad and commented on the *Nawādir* of Abū Zayd (p. 103) and the *Kitāb* of Sībawayhi (*Khiz.* II, 251_{6}).

8. Abū Bakr Muḥammad b. Khalaf al-Baghdādī b. al-Marzubān lived in the Bāb al-Muḥawwal quarter of Baghdad and died in 309/921.

Flügel 238. 1. *Tafḍīl al-kilāb ʿalā kathīr man labisa 'l-thiyāb*, on the baseness of man, Berl. 5425, Lening. Un. 911, Cairo ^{2}I, 338 (see Suppl.), attributed by ḤKh IV, $454_{,91,65}$ s.v. *faḍl* to ʿAlī b. Aḥmad b. al-Marzubān, d. 366/976.—2. *Kitāb al-hadāyā* Cairo ^{2}III, 388, excerpts Landb.-Brill 100.

9. Abū ʿAbdallāh al-Ḥasan b. Aḥmad b. Khālawayh of Hamadan came to Baghdad in 314/926 and attended the lectures of Ibn Durayd and Ibn al-Anbārī. He also studied *ḥadīth*. He worked for some time as a teacher of *ḥadīth* in the central mosque of Medina. Later, he joined the retinue of Sayf al-Dawla in Aleppo, where he took part in many a controversy with al-Mutanabbī, dying there in the year 370/980.

Al-Thaʿālibī, *Yatīma* I, 76, Ibn al-Anb. 383/5, Ibn Khall. 186, Flügel 230, Wüstenf., *Schaf.* 184. Of his works (*Fihrist* $84_{,3-11}$) the following remain: 1. *Risāla fī iʿrāb thalāthīna sūra min al-Qurʾān (al-mufaṣṣal)* Br. Mus. 83, AS 69, Cairo ^{2}I, 32.—1b. see Jeffery, *Islca* (AKM XXXIII, 6) 130/55.—1c. *al-Ḥujja fī qirāʾāt al-aʾimma*, MS d. 496, Egypt. Nat. Libr. Collection Ṭalʿat Bey.—2. *Kitāb al-shajar* Berl. 7051, see Suppl.—3. *Kitāb laysa*, le Livre intitulé Laisa sur les exceptions de la langue

4 Flügel's assumption that al-Azharī, d. 370/980 (p. 134), was his teacher rather than his student is based on a misreading (*ʿan* instead of *ʿanhu*) in the text of al-Suyūṭī.

arabe par Ibn Khalouya, dit Ibn Khalawaihi, texte ar. publié d'après le ms. unique du Br. Mus. (536,$_{2}$) par H. Derenbourg, *Hebr.* x, 88/105 (only a part, after
131 Suyūṭī, *Muzhir* ^{1}II, 2,$_{3}$ in three hefty volumes, exerpts ibid. | ^{2}II, 50/8).—4.–7. see Suppl.—8. *Ishtiqāq al-shuhūr wal-ayyām*, of which 93 pages of the first volume ed. by v. Dyck, *Iktifāʾ al-qunūʿ* (? *Dharīʿa* II, 101,$_{395}$).

10. The son of a Greek slave (Γενναῖοζ?), Abu 'l-Fatḥ ʿUthmān b. Jinnī al-Mawṣilī was born in Mosul sometime before 300/912. While he was working as teacher of philology, Abū ʿAlī al-Fārisī, passing through his hometown one day, made him feel like an absolute beginner. So he joined the latter, staying with him for the next 40 years, and eventually becoming his successor in Baghdad. He also lived for some time in Aleppo where he engaged in disputes with al-Mutanabbī. He died on 28 or 29 Ṣafar 392/15 or 16 January 1002 (see Suppl.).

126 | Al-Thaʿālibī, *Yatīma* I, 77, Ibn al-Anb. 406/9, Ibn Khall. 385. 1. *Kitāb sirr al-ṣināʿa*, on phonetics, Berl. 6469, Leid. 144, Paris 3988, Pal. Med. 360, Köpr. 1469, Rāġib 1315, ʿĀšir 817 (*MFO* V, 508), Dāmād Ibr. 1058 (ibid. 528), ʿĀṭif 2476 (ibid. 492 bottom), Šehīd ʿA.P. (ibid. 520), Āṣaf. III, 66, 317.—2. *Kitāb al-khaṣāʾiṣ fi 'l-naḥw* ḤKh ^{1}III, 141,$_{1721}$, ^{2}I, 706, Berl. Fol. 3054/5, III and IV, Gotha 186/7, Rāġib 1316, NO 4545/7, Br. Mus. Or. I 1353, Rāmpūr I, 539,$_{103/4}$, Āṣaf. III, 696,$_{267}$, Bank. XX, 2015, Patna I, 166,$_{1550}$.—3. *al-Munṣif sharḥ* (*tafsīr*) *Taṣrīf al-Māzinī* (d. 249/863) Rāġib 1391, Köpr. 150.—4. *Kitāb al-ʿarūḍ*, a brief overview of metrics, Berl. 7108, Vienna 222, Br. Mus. Or. 8498.—5. *Mukhtaṣar al-qawāfī* Esc. ^{2}442,$_{4}$.—6. *Kitāb al-lumaʿ fi 'l-naḥw* Berl. 6466, AS 4578/9, Bank. XX, 2016, Patna I, 172,$_{1577}$.—Comm. (see Suppl.) by ʿAbdallāh b. Ḥusayn al-ʿUkbarī (p. 282), Pet. AM Buch. 913, Alex. Naḥw 33, Bank. XX, 2017.—17 other commentaries are mentioned in Ahlw. 6468.—7. *al-Muḥtasab fī iʿrāb al-shawādhdh*, grammatical analysis of uncanonical readings of the Qurʾān, Rāġib 13, Patna I, 16,$_{142}$.—8. *Sharḥ dīwān al-Mutanabbī* p. 88.—9. *Jumal uṣūl al-Taṣrīf* or *Mukhtaṣar Taṣrīf al-Mulūkī* ḤKh II, 304, ^{2}I, 412, Leid. 146, *Ibn Ginnii de flexione libellus, ar. num primum ed. in lat. sermonem transt. not. illustr.* G. Hoberg, Leipzig 1885, C. 1331/1913.—10. *ʿIlal al-tathniya*, on the duals, Leid. 145.—see Suppl.

11. Abū Aḥmad b. al-Ḥasan b. ʿAbdallāh b. Saʿīd al-ʿAskarī, born on 20 Shawwāl
132 293/15 August 906, died on 23 Dhu 'l-Ḥijja | 382/20 February 933, and his sister's son and student, Abū Hilāl al-Ḥasan b. ʿAbdallāh b. Sahl al-ʿAskarī, died after 395/1005.

Flügel 254, Wüstenf., *Gesch.* 157, Suppl. I, 193/4. Additionally I. 1. *Taṣḥīfāt al-muḥaddithīn* C. 1326, vol. I.—2. *al-Zawājir wal-mawāʿiẓ* Köpr. 730, according to Rescher, *MSOS* 1911, 197 a work by Ibn Ḥajar al-Haytamī (II, 388,$_{5}$) instead.—11. *Jamharat al-amthāl* also Alex. Adab 32, in *Majmūʿat rasāʾil* Dāmād Ibr. 1464.—5. *al-Muʿjam fī baqiyyat al-ashyāʾ* C. 1934.—8. *Kitāb al-awāʾil,* BDMG 56, Aligarh 136, Rāmpūr I, 645,$_{202}$, abridged by al-Suyūṭī in *Kitāb al-wasāʾil,* edited in part by R. Gosche in the *Kitāb al-awāʾil, eine literarhist. Studie, Festgabe zur 25. Vers. Deutscher Phil.* Halle 1867.[1]—Excerpt by Kamāl al-Dīn ʿAbd al-Raḥmān b. Muḥammad b. Ibrāhīm b. al-ʿAtāʾiqī al-Ḥillī, autograph in al-Khizāna al-Gharawiyya, together with *al-Shuhda fī sharḥ al-Muʿarrab* and *al-Zuhdiyya,* composed in 788/1386, *Dharīʿa* II, 481,$_{1889}$.—9. *al-Furūq fī ʾl-lugha* Alex. Lugha 16, Āṣaf. II, 1440,$_{172}$.—12. *Kitāb al-kuramāʾ* under the title *Faḍl al-ʿaṭāʾ ʿala ʾl-ʿusr* C. 1353.—20. *Maḥāsin al-nathr wal-naẓm min al-kitāba wal-shiʿr,* undated 170 pp.

| 12. Abū Naṣr al-Ḥasan b. Asad b. al-Hasan al-Fāriqī, d. 467/1074, see Suppl. 194/5. 127

Kitāb al-ifṣāḥ fi ʾl-ʿawīṣ (*sharḥ al-abyāt al-mushkila al-ṣiḥāḥ*) Leid. 635, Esc. ^{2}386, see Nöldeke, *ZDMG* 16, 742/9; there he quotes his *Kitāb al-ḥurūf.*

IV *Linguistics in Persia and the East*

In the preceding sections, we met some scholars who had gone to Iraq for their studies, returning to their homelands after that. From among those who wrote on Arabic philology in regions where Persian and Turkish were spoken, a few more must be mentioned here.

| 1. ʿAbd al-Raḥmān b. ʿĪsā al-Hamadhānī was a secretary of Abū Bakr ʿAbd 133
al-ʿAzīz b. Abī Dulaf and died in the year 320/932.

Fihrist 137. *Kitāb al-alfāẓ al-kitābiyya* (on synonymy), ed. P. L. Cheikho, Beirut 1885 (based on Leid. 51, Br. Mus. 1384, other MSS see Suppl. and AS 4865,$_{2}$ probably identical with *Adab al-rasāʾil,* Āṣaf. III, 52,$_{318}$).

2. Abū Ibrāhīm Isḥāq b. Ibrāhīm al-Fārābī, from Fārāb in East Turkistan, apparently lived for a time in Zabīd in Yemen. However long that may have been, later he taught in | his hometown, dying there in 350/961. 128

1 On similar works in classical literatures cf. W. Kremmer, *de catalogis heurematum.* Diss. 1890 (J. Ruska, *Das Quadrivium aus Severus bar Šakkūs Buch der Dialoge,* Leipzig 1896, p. 43, n. 1).

Flügel 225. *Dīwān al-adab*, in 6 books: 1. *al-sālim*, 2. *al-muḍāʿaf*, 3. *al-mithāl*, 4. *dhawāt al-thalātha*, 5. *dhawāt al-arbaʿa*, 6. *al-hamz*; each book is divided into two parts, for nouns and verbs, Leid. 56/7, Bodl. I, 1087, 1118, 1123, 1156, AS 4677/8, Cairo [1]IV, 170, [2]II, 13, see Suppl.

3. His nephew and student Abū Naṣr Ismāʿīl b. Ḥammād al-Jawharī began his studies in his native Fārāb and then continued them in Baghdad under al-Fārisī and al-Sīrafī. He strengthened his knowledge of Arabic by living with the Rabīʿa and Muḍar tribes in Iraq and Syria, before he returned to the East. From Dāmaghān he soon moved to Nishapur, the capital of Khurāsān, where he worked as a teacher and author. In an attempt to fly from the roof of the central mosque or his house he jumped, crashed, and died in 393/1003 (according to others in 398 or 400).

Ibn al-Anbārī 418/21, Flügel 253. A. Zeki, *L'aviation chez les musulmans*, Cairo 1912, 4ff. 1. *Tāj al-lugha wa-ṣiḥāḥ* (*ṣaḥāḥ*) *al-ʿarabiyya*, a dictionary arranged alphabetically according to the last radical, of which his own fair copy only ran up to the letter *ḍād*, and which was completed, though not entirely without mistakes, by his student Abū Isḥāq Ibrāhīm b. Ṣāliḥ al-Warrāq; see Suyūṭī, *Muzhir* I, [1]49ff., 260ff. Manuscripts of this can be found in almost any library; lith. with vocals Tabriz (Tehran ?) 1270, print. Būlāq 1282, 1292.—Revised editions see
134 Suppl. | and also b. *al-Tanqīḥ* Berl. 6943, Paris 4246, Garr. 261.—c. *al-Ṣurāḥ* (on the author see W. Barthold, *12 Vorlesungen über die Geschichte der Türken Mittelasiens, deutsch v.* Th. Menzel, Berlin 1935, 194/8) Berl. 6947, Br. Mus. 1007/8, Stewart 133, Ind. Off. 1015/22, AS 4699, Āṣaf, *JRASB* CXIC, 1917, 92, print. Calcutta 1812/5, 1832.—d. *al-Mukhtār* Berl. 6944/5, Brill M. 242, Leipz. 455, Munich 779, Uppsala 9, Br. Mus. 468, 470, 1378, Bodl. I, 1080, 1125, Köpr. II, 325, Qawala II, 8, Garr. 262/4, print. C. 1287/9, Būlāq 1302, C. 1305.—e. Abu 'l-Karam ʿAbd al-Raḥīm b. ʿAbdallāh b. Shākir b. Ḥāmid al-Maʿdānī, Ind. Off. 1027 iv, Paris 192 (not in de Slane, see Flügel, *Wien. Jahrb.* 92, Anz. Bl. p. 34).—f. Muḥammad b. Aḥmad b. Najm al-Dīn b. Jamāl al-Dīn al-Ḥanafī, Bodl. I, 1055, 1126.—g. ʿAlī al-ʿAlīʾābādī, Esc. [2]586.—h. Anon., Berl. 6946, compilation of the *Shawāhid* ibid.
129 6148.—Reviews: a. *Qayd al-awābid min al-fawāʾid* by al-Maydānī, d. 518/1124 | (p. 289), juxtaposition of the lemmata of the letter Ṣ with the diverging explanations in the *Tahdhīb al-lugha* by al-Azharī (no. 4), Berl. 6942.—b. *al-Tanbīh wal-īḍāḥ ʿalā mā waqaʿa fī Kitāb al-Ṣaḥāḥ* by Abū Muḥammad ʿAbdallāh b. Barrī, d. 582/1186 (p. 302), ḤKh [1]IV, 93, Berl. Qu. 1954, Esc. [2]585$_{,1}$, Köpr. 1521 (*Taʿlīqāt ʿala 'l-Ṣ.* or another work?)—c. *al-Takmila wal-dhayl wal-ṣila* by al-Ḥasan b. Muḥammad b. al-Ḥasan al-Ṣaghānī, d. 650/1252, ḤKh IV, 94, Berl. 6939$_{,49}$,

Br. Mus. 468, Köpr. 1522/5.—d. *Ghawāmiḍ al-Ṣ.* by Khalīl b. Aybak al-Ṣafadī, d. 764/1362 (II, 31), ḤKh IV, 96, Esc. ^{2}192 (autograph d. 757). Of the same author *Khiz.* IV, $42,_{9}$ records *Nufūdh al-sahm fī-mā waqaʿa lil-Jawharī min al-wahm.*—Further literature in Ahlw. 6949.—II. Some poems, Berl. 7589, 2.

4. Abū Manṣūr Muḥammad b. Aḥmad b. al-Azhar b. Ṭalḥa al-Azharī al-Harawī was born in 282/895 in Herat, where he studied under al-Mundhirī (p. 129). As a young man he went to Baghdad, where Ibn al-Sarrāj and Niftawayh were his teachers. On the way back from the pilgrimage, which had set out in 311/923, his caravan was raided by the Qarmaṭians on the Medina-to-Kufa road, an incident that took place on 18 Muḥarram 312/26 April 924.[2] This is how | he 135 came to live as a prisoner with a Bedouin tribe that would spend its winters in al-Dahnāʾ, wander in the spring to al-Ṣammān, and move in the summer to the springs of al-Sitār. Here he had the opportunity to get to know the Arabic language in its purest and most unadulterated form. Released from captivity, he returned to his hometown, where he died, after a long career as a teacher, in Rabīʿ II 370/Oct.–Nov. 980.

Ibn Khall. 611, Yāqūt, GW IV, 951, Flügel 217/9, Wüstenf., *Gesch.* 143, Schaf. 188. 1. *Tahdhīb al-lugha*, actually a work by his teacher al-Mundhirī, a dictionary which ordered the sounds in accordance with the placement of the organs, like the *Kitāb al-ʿayn* of al-Khalīl (p. 98), AS 4671, NO 4686/7, Köpr. 1526/39, Cairo ^{1}IV, 169, ^{2}II, 100, Bank. XX, 1964/5.—2. *al-Zāhir fī gharīb alfāẓ al-Shāfiʿī* based on a work by Ismāʿīl b. Yaḥyā al-Muzanī Abū Ibrāhīm, d. 264/878 (p. $190,_{2}$), ḤKh IV, $330,_{8616}$, perhaps part of the *Gharīb al-alfāẓ allatī yastamiʿluhu ʾl-fuqahāʾ* mentioned by Ibn Khallikān (? Or is that just an imprecise title?), Berl. 4852, Köpr. 568.

130 | 5. Abu ʾl-Ḥusayn Aḥmad b. Fāris b. Zakariyyāʾ b. al-Ḥabīb al-Qazwīnī al-Hamadhānī al-Rāzī was born in Qazvin and grew up in Hamadan. When he started teaching there Badīʿ al-Zamān was one of his students. Then the Būyid Fakhr al-Dawla appointed him as tutor to his son Abū Ṭālib in Rayy. Even though he was most likely of Iranian origin himself, he was so enthusiastic about Arabic that he defended it energetically against the attacks of the Shuʿūbiyya.[3] He also knew how to manipulate the language in elegant verses,

2 Cf. M.J. de Goeje, *Mémoire sur les Carmathes*, Leiden 1886, p. 84/5.

3 See Goldziher, SBWA, *phil.-hist. Kl.* 73, 1873, p. 530ff.

as is shown by samples of his poems (*Yatīma* III, 214/20).[4] He died in Rayy in 395/1005 (though according to others, it was in 396).

136 | Ibn Khall. 48, Flügel 247. 1. *Kitāb al-mujmal*[56] *fi 'l-lugha*, a dictionary of classical Arabic arranged by the first radical (see Weijers, *Orientalia* I, 357), Berl. 6954/7, Qu. 1129, Gotha 377, Leid. 58/60, Paris 4347/50, Br. Mus. 1683, Suppl. 843, Ind. Off. 991, Bodl. I, 1065, Ambros. 99, Pal. 356, 421, Yeni 1163, Köpr. 1572, NO 4855, Alex. Lugha 25.—2. *Fiqh al-lugha al-musammā bil-Ṣāḥibī*, dedicated to al-Ṣāḥib (no. 6), an introduction to Arabic lexicology based on philosophical considerations, see Goldziher, *SBWA* 1873, vol. 73, p. 511ff., detailed table of contents *ZDMG* XXVIII, 163, 200, AS 4715.—3. *Kitāb al-thalātha*, synonyms with three identical consonants (cf. the *Muthallath* of Quṭrub, p. 102), Esc. ^{2}363$_{,3}$.—4. *Dhamm al-khaṭa' fi 'l-shiʿr*, evidence that poetic licences are reprehensible mistakes, ḤKh ^{1}III, 335$_{,5,817}$, I, ^{2}817 Berl. 7181, the same as the *Kitāb naqd al-shiʿr* in Suyūṭī, *Muzhir* II, ^{1}250(?), see Goldziher, *SBWA* 1873, vol. 73, p. 515.—6. (see Suppl.) *Mukhtaṣar siyar rasūl Allāh*, additionally Bāyezīd 1256, 1286, 1828, under the title *Akhṣar sīrat sayyid al-bashar* Hamb. Or. Sem. 14$_{,10}$.—12. *Maqāyīs al-lugha* see al-Maghribī, *RAAD* XI, 650/71, excerpts ibid. 352/5.

6. Abu 'l-Qāsim Ismāʿīl b. ʿAbbād b. al-ʿAbbās Kāfi 'l-Kufāt al-Ṣāḥib al-Ṭālqānī was born on 16 Dhu 'l-Qaʿda 324/5 October 936 (or, according to others, in 326) in Iṣṭakhr (according to others in Ṭālqān). He was the son of a secretary of the Būyids Rukn al-Dawla and ʿAḍud al-Dawla who himself engaged in literary pursuits, who had leanings towards the moderate Shīʿa and the Muʿtazila, and who only died in the same year as his son. Apart from receiving the education he was given by his father, whose politico-religious views he adopted as his own, Abu 'l-Qāsim also took the classes of Ibn Fāris in Rayy and com-
131 pleted his studies in Baghdad. | Upon his return to his native country he started his career in the office of the vizier Abu 'l-Faḍl b. al-ʿAmīd. When the Būyid Mu'ayyad al-Dawla became ruler of Rayy and Isfahan after the death of his father in 366/976, removing Ibn al-ʿAmīd from office, he appointed
137 Abu 'l-Qāsim as the vizier in the latter's place, bestowing upon him the | honorific titles of al-Ṣāḥib and Kāfi 'l-Kufāt. His position of power, which he extended even further by conquering some 50 new strongholds for the Būyids, he also managed to consolidate after Mu'ayyad al-Dawla's death in 373/983 with his brother and successor Fakhr al-Dawla, who had fled from Mu'ayyad

4 While al-Bākharzī, *Dumyat al-qaṣr* 297, knew only three verses by him, see Goldziher, op. cit., 526.

5 *Sic*, and not *Mujmil*, as in Goldziher, op. cit., 552 and Rieu, Suppl. 574b.

to the Sāmānids[6] but whom he had called back to the country again. His job, which he held for 18 years and one month, enabled him to promote the arts and the sciences. Among his dependants were, apart from his teacher Ibn Fāris, the author of the *Kitāb al-aghānī*, Badīʿ al-Zamān, and others. In addition, he was also an author and poet in his own right. He died in Rayy on 24 Ṣafar 385/31 May 995.

Yatīma III, 31ff., Ibn al-Anb. 397/401, Ibn Khall. 93, Flügel 240, Khalīl Mardam Bek, *al-Ṣāḥib ʿAbbād*, Damascus 1932 (365pp). 1. *Kitāb al-muḥīṭ*, an Arabic dictionary, rich in material but poor in evidence, vol. III, Cairo ^{1}III, 185, ^{2}II, 35.—2. Abstract of his collection of letters, Paris 3314,$_{2}$.—3. Two *qaṣīdas*, Berl. 7588.—4. *Dīwān* ḤKh ^{1}III, 289,$_{5500}$, ^{2}I, 796, AS 3953/4, Āṣaf. I, 702,$_{111}$.—5.–10. see Suppl.—11. *al-Ibāna ʿan madhhab ahl al-ʿadl bi-ḥujaj min al-Qurʾān wal-ʿaql*, libraries of Muḥammad al-Ṭihrānī in Samarra, of Abu ʾl-Qāsim al-Iṣfahānī in Najaf, and of Shaykh Hādī Kāshif al-Ghiṭāʾ, *Dharīʿa* I, 56/7,$_{288}$.

7. We know nothing more about the circumstances of the life of Abū ʿUbayd Aḥmad b. Muḥammad b. Muḥammad b. ʿAbd al-Raḥmān al-Harawī al-Bāshānī other than that he was a student of al-Azharī (p. 134) and al-Khaṭṭābī (p. 165) and that he died in Rajab 401/February 1011.

Ibn Khall. 35. *Kitāb al-gharībayn fi ʾl-Qurʾān wal-ḥadīth* or *Gharībay al-Q. wal-ḥ.* or *Kitāb al-gharībayn fī lughat kalām Allāh wa-āḥādīth rasūlihi* Berl. 696/7, Leipz. 457 (part II), Leid. 65, Ind. Off. 992, Köpr. 265, 375/7 379 (other MSS in Istanbul in Weisweiler no. 138), Garr. 1445/6, Alex. Lugha 15, | Bank. 138
XX, 1968, Patna I, 522,$_{2805}$, Lucknow Shāh Ḥabīb Ḥaydar Libr. *JRASB* 1917, CXXXIII, 131.

8. Abu ʾl-Qāsim Yūsuf b. ʿAbdallāh al-Zujājī of Hamadan lived in Jurjān and died in 415/1024 in Astarābād.

Yāqūt, *Irshād* VII, 308, Suyūṭī, *Bughya* 422. 1. *Kitāb al-bayān fī ma ʾshtamala ʿalayhi khalq al-insān*, on the names of the limbs in alphabetical order ḤKh ^{1}III, 173,$_{4791}$, ^{2}I, 722, Berl. 7037 (anon.).—2. *ʿUmdat al-kātib* (*kuttāb*), recension based on Qudāma b. Jaʿfar (p. 228), Cairo ^{2}III, 258.

---

6 Rescher's (Abr. II, 223) conjecture with regard to the text of *Irshād* II, 275,$_{10}$ is mistaken: after all, Qābūs was not a Sāmānid, see Suppl. I, 154.

V *Linguistics in Egypt and Spain*

Reports on the history of science in the western lands are, for this period, very sketchy. Nevertheless, it is sufficiently clear that the schools that existed there were entirely based on those of Iraq.

1. Aḥmad b. Muḥammad b. Wallād b. Muḥammad Abu 'l-ʿAbbās al-Tamīmī was a student of al-Zajjāj, who held him in high esteem, as well as of Mubarrad and Thaʿlab. He died in Cairo in 332/943.

Suyūṭī, *Bughya* 112, Flügel 100. *Kitāb al-maqṣūr wal-mamdūd*, in alphabetical order, ḤKh V, 10518, Berl. 7028, Paris 4234, Murād Mollā 1793 (or 1795, *MFO* V, 532), Br. Mus. Suppl. 838 (see Sprenger, *ZDMG* XXXI, 751/7).

132 | 2. Abū Jaʿfar Aḥmad b. Muḥammad b. Ismāʿīl al-Naḥḥās (al-Ṣaffār) was also a student of al-Zajjāj, who did not, however, hold him in very high esteem. In addition, he attended the lectures of al-Akhfash the Younger, Ibn al-Anbārī, and others. He lived as a teacher in Cairo. When, on 5 Dhu 'l-Ḥijja 338/26 May 950 (according to others 337), he sat near the Nilometer chanting verses, a passer-by, who was under the false impression that he wanted to put a spell on the Nile so that its waters would not rise, pushed him into the river, whereupon he drowned.

Ibn Khall. 39, Flügel 64, Wüstenf., *Gesch.* 116. *Sharḥ al-muʿallaqāt* Suppl. p. 35. Ad 3. *al-Nāsikh wal-mansūkh fi 'l-Qūr'ān al-karīm*, Berl. Fol. 3095, C. 1938.

139 3. Under the Fāṭimid caliph Muʿizz al-Dīn, d. 341/942, Bariyya b. Abi 'l-Yusr al-Riyāḍī wrote a collection of proverbs with the title *Talqīḥ al-ʿuqūl* (ḤKh [1]II, 417, [2]I, 481, anon.), in 157 very short chapters.

4. In Spain, linguistics was only introduced in the fourth/tenth century by Abū ʿAlī Ismāʿīl b. al-Qāsim b. ʿAydhūn b. Hārūn b. ʿĪsā b. Muḥammad b. Sulaymān al-Qālī. He was born in 288/901 in Manāzjird in Armenia, but when he came to Baghdad in 303/915 he called himself al-Qālī because Qālīqalā = Erzerum, being the base of operations of religious warriors, was better known in the capital. He studied there under al-Zajjāj, al-Akhfash al-Aṣghar, Ibn Durayd, and others. After spending some time in Mosul, where he studied *ḥadīth* under Abū Yaʿlā al-Mawṣilī, he returned in the year 305/917 to his teachers in Baghdad. When, after 25 years, his studies still had not bore any fruit, he set out for the west, in the year 328/939. In Shaʿbān 330/942 he arrived in Cordova and, being

the first teacher of linguistics ever in that place, soon became very popular. He died there in Rabīʿ II (or, according to others, in Jumādā I or II) 356/April or May 965.

Al-Ḍabbī (*Bibl. Ar. hisp.* III), p. 216, no. 547, Ibn Khall. 92, al-Maqqarī II, 48/52, Flügel 112. 1. *al-Amālī*, with the supplement *al-Nawādir*, an anthology like the *Kāmil* of al-Mubarrad, which he had dictated in the mosque of the suburb of Cordova, al-Zahrāʾ, Berl. 6935, Paris 4236, 1, II, Esc. ^{2}359, see Suppl. with *Fahāris Simṭ al-laʾālīʾ* by ʿAbd al-ʿAzīz al-Maymanī, C. 1937/1356.

5. His most important student was Abū Bakr Muḥammad b. al-Ḥasan al-Zubaydī al-Ishbīlī, whose ancestors were from Homs. He was born in 316/918 in Seville and studied in Cordova. There, the caliph al-Ḥākim al-Mustanṣir billāh entrusted him with the education of his son. | When the latter | came 133 140
to power he appointed him *qāḍī* of Seville, where he died on 1 Jumādā I 379/6 September 989.

Al-Thaʿālibī, *Yatīma* I, 409, Ibn Khall. 623, Wüstenf., *Gesch.* 147. 1. *Kitāb al-wāḍiḥ fī ʾl-naḥw* Esc. ^{2}197.—2. *Kitāb al-istidrāk* (also Garr. 245), ed. I. Guidi, *Mem. Acc. Lincei* IV, vi, Rome 1890, p. 414/57, excerpt by ʿUmar b. Aḥmad b. Khalīfa al-Ḥalabī al-Saʿdī in Br. Mus. Suppl. 128.—3. Excerpt from Khalīl's *Kitāb al-ʿayn*, see p. 99.—4. see Suppl.—5. *Laḥn al-ʿawāmm* ʿĀšir I, 1121, see Suppl. I, 541$_{3,1}$.

6a. Among the students of Ibn al-Qūṭiyya (p. 157) there was also al-Ḥusayn b. al-Walīd b. Naṣr Abu ʾl-Qāsim b. al-ʿArīf, who studied with him in Cordova and then resided for a number of years in Egypt. Back in his home country al-Manṣūr Muḥammad b. Abī ʿĀmir charged him with the education of his children. He died in Toledo in Rajab 390/June 1000.

Suyūṭī, *Bughya* 237, Flügel 265. 1. *Risāla fī iʿrāb qawlihim inna al-ḍāriba al-shātima wālidahu kāna Zaydan*, in which he discusses some 58 different views, Cairo ^{2}II, 112.—2. *Sharḥ al-Jumal* see Suppl. I, 171.

Chapter 4. Historiography

Cf. Suppl. I, 203/4

F. Wüstenfeld, *Die Geschichtschreiber der Araber und ihre Werke, Abh. d. Kgl. Ges. d. Wiss zu Göttingen*, vols. 28 and 29, 1882/3 (quoted as Wüst.). E. Sachau, Studien zur ältesten Geschichtsüberlieferung der Araber, *MSOS* VII *Westas. St.* 154/96.

1 *The Life of Muḥammad*

1. The lifetime of Mūsā b. ʿUqba b. Abi ʾl-ʿAyyāsh al-Asadī, who had the honorific title Imām al-Maghāzī, coincided mostly with the reign of the Umayyads. He was a freedman of the House of Zubayr b. al-ʿAwwām in Medina and died in the year 141/758.

141 | Wüst. no. 21. *Kitāb al-maghāzī*, compiled by Yūsuf b. Muḥammad b. ʿUmar b. Qāḍī Shuhba, d. 789/1387, ḤKh V, 647$_{,12464}$, Berl. 1554.

2. Abū ʿAbdallāh Muḥammad b. Isḥāq b. Yasār, see Suppl. I, 205.

135 | Ad 1. *Kitāb al-mubtadaʾ* (*mabdaʾ*), see al-Maqrīzī, *Khiṭaṭ* II, 79, penult. (Solomon as the inventor of the baths).

3. The work by Ibn Isḥāq is only preserved in the recension of Abū Muḥammad ʿAbd al-Malik b. Hishām b. Ayyūb al-Ḥimyarī al-Baṣrī, who had read it in Kufa with Ziyād b. ʿAbdallāh. He later lived in Fusṭāṭ, and died on 13 Rabīʿ II 218/8 May 834 (or, according to others, in 213).

Wüst. 48. 1. *Das Leben Muhammeds nach M. b. I. bearbeitet von A. b. H. hsg. v.* F. Wüstenfeld, Göttingen 1858/60, translated by G. Weil, Stuttgart 1864. On the MSS see Suppl. I, 206, 944, BDMG 11, Āṣaf. I, 870$_{,317/8}$, reprint by Muḥammad al-Saqqāʾ, al-Abyārī and Aḥmad Shabbī, C. 1936, by Muḥammad Muḥyi ʾl-Dīn ʿAbd al-Ḥamīd, C. 1937, 4 vols. Abstracts: a. ʿImād al-Dīn Aḥmad b. Ibrāhīm al-Wāsiṭī, d. 711/1311 (II, 162), see Suppl. and Berl. 9506/7, Šehīd ʿAlī 1894.—b. Anonymous, Br. Mus. 1489, Pers. transl. *Bull. de St. Pétersbourg* I, 361, no. 44. S.P. Brönnle, *Die Commentatoren des Ibn Isḥāq und ihre Scholien*, Diss. Halle 1895.—2. *Kitāb al-Tījān*, biblical and South Arabian legends, see M. Lidzbarski, *De propheticis, quae dicuntur, legendis arabicis*, diss. Leipzig 1893, p. 5ff. *ZA* VIII, 271ff.

4. Abū ʿAbdallāh Muḥammad b. ʿUmar al-Wāqidī, born in 130/747 in Medina, operated a trading house in cereals there, but because of poor management he fell so deeply in debt that he had to leave the city. In Baghdad, where he went in 180/796, the vizier Yaḥyā b. Khālid al-Barmakī supplied him with the means to settle his affairs and then entrusted him with the office of *qāḍī* in the eastern part of town. | Al-Ma'mūn transferred him subsequently, in this same capacity, 136
to the ʿAskar al-Mahdī quarter, the later Ruṣāfa, where he died four years later, on 11 Dhu 'l-Ḥijja 207/28 April 823.

| Yāqūt, *Irshād* VII 55/8,[1] Wüst. 43. 1. *Kitāb al-maghāzī, History of Muhammeds Campaigns by Aboo Abdollah Mohammed bin Omar al-Wakidy, ed. by* A. Kremer (Bibl. Ind.), Calcutta 185 (incomplete), *Muhammed in Medina, das ist Vakidis Kitab al Maghazi in verkürzter deutscher Wiedergabe hsg. v.* J. Wellhausen, Berlin 1882.—2. *Tafsīr al-Qur'ān*, used by al-Thaʿālibī, d. 428/1037, Br. Mus. 832.—Falsely attribted to al-Wāqidī, and disseminated in particular during the Crusades with the purpose of galvanizing the religious warriors, are numerous *futūḥ* works: a. *The Conquest of Syria, commonly adscribed to Abū ʿAbdallāh Muḥammad b. ʿUmar al-Wāqidī*, ed. with notes by W. Nassau Lees, I–III (Bibl. Ind.), Calcutta 1854/62, *Futūḥ al-Sha'm* C. 1278, 1282, 1296, 1302, 1304, 1309, 1315, 1348, cf. D.B. Haneberg, Erörterungen über Pseudo-W.'s Gesch. der Eroberung Syriens, *Abh. d. Akad. zu München, philos. philolog. Cl.* IX (1860) 1863 p. 127ff., de Goeje, *Mém. sur la conquête de la Syrie*, Leiden 1864.—b. *Auctoris incerti liber de expugnatione Memphidis et Alexandriae vulgo adscriptus Wakidaeo*, ed. H.A. Hamaker, Leiden 1825, *Futūḥ Miṣr*, Calcutta 1277 (Euting 3261).—c. *Libri Wakedii de Mesopotamiae expugnatae hist.*, p. I, ed. G.H.A. Ewald, Göttingen 1827. *Geschichte der Eroberung von Mesopotamien und Armenien von M.b.ʿO. el W. aus dem Arab. übers. v.* B.G. Niebuhr, *hsg. v.* A.D. Mordtmann, Hamburg 1847.—d. *Futūḥ al-Bahnasā* Berl. Brill M. 188, C. 1278, 1280, 1290, 1305, attributed to Abū ʿAbdallāh Muḥammad b. Muḥammad al-Maqqarī (al-Muʿizz? v. Dyck 293), Br. Mus. 293, Copenhagen 138.—e. *Futūḥ al-Ifrīqiyya*, see Suppl., see R. Basset, *Le livre des conquêtes de l'Afrique et du Maghreb, Mél. Ch. de Harlez*, 26/34. Finally, there is also a biography of the Prophet falsely attributed to him, of which there are 35 fragments covering his background and the time from before his appearance as a prophet, Berl. 9548, see Horovitz, MSOS, West-as. St II, 254. 142

1 According to al-Ṭūsī, *Fihrist* [2]3, some Shīʿīs contend that the real author of these works was Ibrāhīm b. Muḥammad b. Abī Yaḥyā Abū Isḥāq al-Madanī, d. 184/800 or 191/806, and that al-Wāqidī claimed them as his own.

5. A student and assistant of al-Wāqidī was Abū ʿAbdallāh Muḥammad b. Saʿd b. Manīʿ al-Zuhrī, mostly referred to as Kātib al-Wāqidī. He died in Baghdad on 4 Jumādā II 230/17 February 845.

143 | Wüst. 53. *Kitāb al-ṭabaqāṭ al-kabīr*, a detailed biography of the Prophet, which also circulated as a separate work (*Fihrist* 99), and the biographies of his companions and successors, organised by class; see O. Loth, *Das Klassenbuch des*
137 *Ibn Saʿd*, Leipzig 1869, idem, Ursprung und | Bedeutung der Ṭabaqāt, vornehmlich des Ibn Saʿd, ZDMG XXIII, 539/614, see J. Wellhausen, *Die Schreiben Muhammeds und die Gesandtschaften an ihn, Skizz. u. Vorarb.* 4, Berlin 1889. On the lacunae in vol. V, see H. Ritter, *Isl.* XVIII, 196/9.

2 *Urban History*

The history of the two holy cities of Mecca and Medina is closely related to the biography of the Prophet.

1. The first one to collect the traditions on the legendary background of Mecca and the fortunes of the city in the days of the Prophet and his successors was Abu ʾl-Walīd Aḥmad b. Muḥammad b. al-Walīd b. ʿUqba b. al-Azraq, a descendant of the Ghassānid dynasty from the House of Jafna who died in 219/834 (or, according to others, in 212 or 222). His accounts were recorded by his grandson Abu ʾl-Walīd Muḥammad b. ʿAbdallāh al-Azraqī, d. soon after 244/858, then newly edited by Abū Muḥammad Isḥāq al-Khuzāʿī, d. 308/920, and revised by the latter's nephew Abu ʾl-Ḥasan Muḥammad al-Khuzāʿī, who was alive in 350/961.

Wüst. 49, 58, 93, 127. *Die Chroniken der Stadt Mekka, hsg. v.* F. Wüstenfeld, vol. I, *Die Geschichte und Beschreibung der Stadt Mekka von el-Azraqī*, Leipzig 1858.

2. Abū ʿAbdallāh Muḥammad b. Isḥāq b. al-ʿAbbās al-Fākihī wrote, in 272/885 in Mecca:

(Wüst. 69) *Taʾrīkh Mekka, Fihr.* 109, ḤKh ^{1}II, 151,$_{2317}$, ^{2}I, 306, Leid. 924. *Die Chroniken*, vol. II, *Auszüge aus al-Fākihī*, Leipzig 1859.

3. Not preserved is the oldest history of Medina, written by Muḥammad b.
144 al-Ḥasan b. Zabāla, a student | of Mālik b. Anas, in Ṣafar of the year 199/Sept.–Oct. 814.

Fihr. 108, ḤKh ^{1}I, 190,$_{228}$, 144,$_{2302}$, ^{2}I, 29, 302, see Wüstenfeld, *Geschichte der Stadt Medina, im Auszug aus dem Arab. des Samhūdī*, Göttingen, *Abh.GW* IX, 1864, p. 6.

4. See Suppl. I, 209/10. Ad f., the abstract by Yaḥyā b. Ibrāhīm b. ʿAlī al-Mālikī, Br. Mus. 1621, Medina, *ZDMG* 90, 118.

5. Only one at least partly preserved urban history also examined political history, which is the history of Baghdad by Abu 'l-Faḍl Aḥmad b. Abī Ṭāhir Ṭayfūr. Born in Baghdad in 204/819, he originated from a royal family in Khurāsān, attended the lectures of ʿUmar b. Shabba, and was active as a modestly talented poet. He died in 280/893.

Wüst. 78, *Fihrist* 146 sums up 48 titles of his works, see Suppl.

3 *The History of the Pre-Islamic Arabs*

In the matter of the preservation of reports about Arab antiquity, for which there was a renewed interest as a result of the revival of ancient poetry, the greatest merit goes to the two al-Kalbī's, Muḥammad b. al-Sā'ib and his son Abu 'l-Mundhir Hishām. Even though he also wrote a commentary on the Qurʾān,[1] the father—who in 82/701 had participated in the Battle of Dayr al-Jamājim[2] along side the rebel Ibn al-Ashʿath, and who died in 146/763—had a particular predilection for the collection of reports on the genealogy and the history of the ancient Arabs. The son was born in Kufa, lived for some time in Baghdad, and died in 204/819 or 206. | He continued the studies of his father, trying to 145
supplement the reports collected by him by means of research into relics of the history of the Lakhmids in the churches of al-Ḥīra, and condensed it into literary form. In his own cultural environment such an unusual way of doing things sometimes aroused suspicion. Although he was not lacking supporters,[3] others associated him with a complete lack of critical sense, indeed, even branding him as a forger.[4] However, modern research has confirmed many of the assertions for which he was heavily criticised by his co-religionists.[5]

---

1 Used by al-Thaʿlabī, d. 427/1036, Br. Mus. 821; from which (?) the history of Abraham in Ibn al-ʿAsākir, *Taʾrīkh Dimashq* II, 138ff., cf. Suppl. I, 331.

2 See A. Müller, *Der Islam* I, 391, J. Wellhausen, *Das arabische Reich* 153.

3 Yāqūt, *Geogr. Wb* II, 158.

4 *Agh.* ^{1}IX, 19, XVIII, 161, ^{2}X, 148, 17, Goldziher, *MSt.* I, 686.

5 See Th. Nöldeke, *Gesch. der Perser und Araber* XXVII.

Ibn al-Anb. 116/8, Wüst. 26, 42. Of the 140 works listed in *Fihrist* 95/8 remain: 1. *Kitāb al-nasab al-kabīr* or *al-Jamhara fi 'l-nasab*, the geneologies of the Arabs,[6] Esc. ^{2}1698, frgm. Paris 2047 (?), see Suppl. *Mukhtaṣar* Rāġib 999, which goes back to a copy in Yāqūt's own hand.—2. *Nasab fuḥūl al-khayl fi 'l-jāhiliyya wal-islām* Gotha 2078, Esc. $^2 1705_{,2}$, Bāyezīd 3178, ʿĀṭif 2003 (*MFO* 1912, 491)
140 see Suppl.—3. *Kitāb al-aṣnām* or *Tankīs al-aṣnām*, | on the basis of numerous excerpts in Yāqūt, translated by J. Wellhausen, *Reste arab. Heidentums* 10/61 (cf. ibid. 243) MS in Medina, *ZDMG* 90, 120, see S. Nyberg in *Dragma: Martino P. Nilsson … dedicatum*, 1939, p. 346/66, R. Klinke-Rosenberger, *Das Götzenbuch K. al-Aṣnām des b. al-K.*, Leipzig 1941.—see Suppl.

2. It was, however, not only a love for the memory of their ancestors, but also a hatred towards their enemies that contributed to the resuscitation of the history of Arab antiquity. Mutual jealousy among the Arab tribes had led to the preservation of many a defamatory account of their past, and the Arabs
146 themselves, such as the disreputable Haytham b. ʿAdī (d. 207/821 or | 206 or 208, Wüst. 44, Suppl. I, 213), had laid down such accounts in *mathālib* works. This material was taken up with particular zeal by the Shuʿūbiyya, that group of non-Arab scholars and writers who opposed the dogma of the absolute unsurpassability of Arabhood by referring to the merits of ancient nations and to the backwardness of the Jāhiliyya (see Goldziher, *MSt.* I, 147/208). ʿAllān b. al-Ḥasan al-Shuʿūbī, who openly prided himself on his Iranian origins and who was a copyist in the scientific library of Hārūn and al-Maʾmūn, assembled in his *Ḥalbat al-mathālib* (quoted in *Agh.* ^{1}XII, 156) everything blameworthy about the history of the Arab tribes.

4 *Imperial and World History*

1. Located on the borderline between personal and imperial history are the many—sadly lost—works by Abu 'l-Ḥasan ʿAlī b. Muḥammad al-Madāʾinī, a freedman of a family of the Quraysh who was born in 135/753 and who died in 215/830 (or, according to others, in 225/840 or 231/845) in Baghdad.

Wüst. 47. *Fihrist* 101 mentions 239 works and/or tracts on the history of the Prophet in general or more specific aspects, on the history of the Quraysh
141 and individual families and persons, the history | of the caliphs, battles and heroes. Balādhurī, Ṭabarī, *Agh.*, Yāqūt, and others have preserved numerous excerpts from the *Kitāb al-maghāzī* and *Taʾrīkh al-khulafāʾ*. Also quoted are: 1. *Kitāb al-nisāʾ al-fawārik*, *Khiz.* I, $408_{,11}$.—2. *Kitāb al-nisāʾ al-nāshizāt*, ibid.

---

6 Quoted very often in *Agh.* (IV, 74, VII, $42_{,4,vu}$, XIX, $58_{,10,vu}$, XX, 170) and elsewhere.

$366_{,5}$, $479_{,15}$.—3. *Kitāb al-mugharribīn*, ibid. II, $109_{,1}$.—4. *Kitāb al-jawābāt*, *Agh.* X, $^{1}86_{,12}$, $^{2}81_{,17}$. See Suppl.

2. His student Abū ʿAbdallāh al-Zubayr b. Abī Bakr Bakkār al-Qurashī was active in the same domain. He was a member of the | noble Zubayrid family 147
in Medina, where he came into conflict with the ʿAlids. In Baghdad he did not receive the support against his rivals that he had hoped for, but was appointed *qāḍī* in Mecca upon his return. However, he seems to have been more attracted to the bustling intellectual life of the capital than to a life in the Holy City. He went to Baghdad several more times to recite from his works, the last of which was in 253/867. He also lived for a time with Muḥammad b. ʿAbdallāh b. Ṭāhir, as he was the tutor of his son. He died at the age of 84, after an unfortunate fall from the roof of his house in Mecca, on 23 Dhu ʾl-Qaʿda 256/22 October 870.

Wüst. 61. Of the more than 30 works listed in *Fihr.* 111 the following remain: 1. *Nasab Quraysh wa-akhbārihim* (see Suppl.), see Ahmedali, *JRAS* 1936, 55/63.—2. *al-Muwaffaqiyyāt*, historical tales as a reading book for Prince al-Muwaffaq, the son of caliph al-Mutawakkil, in 5 volumes or 19 parts, of which part 16/9 Gött. ar. 17, 1, from which "der Tod des Muṣʿab b. az-Zubair" in Wüstenfeld, *Die Familie el Zubair, Abh. GGW*. 1876, cf. F. Schulthess, *der Dīwān des Ḥātim Ṭej.* p. 1.

3. Abu ʾl-ʿAbbās (Abū Bakr, Abu ʾl-Ḥasan, Abū Jaʿfar) Aḥmad b. Yaḥyā b. Jābir al-Balādhurī,[1] of Iranian stock, lived in the entourage of the caliphs al-Mutawakkil and al-Mustaʿīn and was in charge of the education of ʿAbdallāh b. al-Muʿtazz (see p. 80). He died in 270/892.

| Wüst. 74. 1. *Kitāb futūḥ al-buldān (al-ṣaghīr)*, *Liber de expugnatione regionum*, 142
ed. M.J. de Goeje, Leiden 1870. The larger, unfinished and lost version of this work was apparently used by Ibn Khallikān (ed. Wüst. 127).—2. *Kitāb ansāb al-ashrāf* ḤKh I[1] no. 1346, [2]179, or *al-Akhbār wal-ansāb*, *Fihr.*, complete ʿĀšir 597/8, vol. I, Paris 6068, see de Goeje, *ZDMG* 38, 382/406, vol. XI, *Anonyme arab. Chronik Bd. XI, vermutlich das Buch der Verwandtschaft der Adligen von elbelāḏorī, autogr. u. hsg. v.* W. Ahlwardt, Greifswald 1883, see Th. Nöldeke, *GGA* 1883, p. 1096ff., vol. IV B ed. by M. Schloessinger, Jerusalem | 1938, V ed. S.D.F. 148
Goitein, Jerusalem 1936, *Il Califfo Moawiya I secondo il* Kitāb Ansāb al-ashrāf *tradotto e annotato da* O. Pinto *e* G. Levi della Vida, Rome 1938.—3. Excerpt from a certain *al-Radd ʿala ʾl-Shuʿūbiyya*, Masʿūdī, *Murūj*, III, 109/13, probably not an independent work but an excursus in a geneological book, see Goldziher,

1 On this *nisba*, which had been carried by his grandfather, see Suppl. I, 216.

MSt I, 166.—4. Of his translations from the Persian (see ḤKh III, 98), among which was a metrical *ʿAhd Ardashīr, Fihr.* 113, nothing has remained.

4. It was an Iranian who wrote the first comprehensive world history in the Arabic language. Abū Jaʿfar Muḥammad b. Jarīr al-Ṭabarī was born around New Year 224–5/Autumn 839 in Āmul, in Ṭabaristān. After a study trip to Egypt, Syria, and Iraq, he settled down in Baghdad as a teacher of *ḥadīth* and *fiqh*, declining the offer of a judgeship by the vizier Khāqānī so he could devote himself entirely to scholarship. In *fiqh* he was at first a follower of al-Shāfiʿī but later he founded his own *madhhab*, not without success. This earned him the bitter enmity of the fanatical Ḥanbalīs of Baghdad. As a writer he was unusually productive, not only in the fields of history and Tradition, but also in Qurʾānic exegesis and jurisprudence. Even though it is true that he was not independent-minded, we owe the preservation of much important information to his diligence as a collector.

Wüst., *Gesch.* 94, *Schaf.* 80, de Goeje, *Enc. Brit.* ^{9}XXIII 1/5, Goldziher, Die literarische Tätigkeit des Ṭ. nach Ibn ʿAsākir, *WZKM* IX, 358/71. Of his many works remain: 1. *Kitāb akhbār al-rusul wal-mulūk*, a world history from the Creation up to his own time, from the Hijra onwards in annalistic form: *Annales quos scripsit Abū Djafar M. b. Djarīr al-Ṭ. cum aliis* ed. M.J. de Goeje, 3 Series, Leiden 1879/98, Annex *al-Muntakhab min Kitāb Dhayl al-mudhayyal min taʾrīkh al-ṣaḥāba wal-tābiʿīn* ser. III 1295/2561, vol. 14, 15. Introduction etc. Indices 1901.
149 | *Geschichte der Perser und Araber zur Zeit der Sasaniden, aus der arab. Chronik des T. übers. von* Th. Nöldeke, Leiden 1879. Sommario degli Annali di al-Ṭ. per gli anni dell' eg. 65–99/684–710, I. Guidi, *Rend. Lincei* VI, 1925, 352/407. The *Mukhtaṣar*, containing many improvements and augmented with a history of
143 Africa and Spain, was written between | 363–6/973–6 by ʿArīb b. Saʿd al-Kātib al-Qurṭubī, Gotha 1554, and of which a part, namely the sections on Africa and Spain that Ibn al-ʿIdhārī (see p. 337) had taken for his *al-Bayān al-mughrib*, is included in the edition of this latter work by Dozy; the rest, which comprises the history of years 291/320 in Iraq, is contained in *Ṣilat taʾrīkh al-Ṭ. Tabari continuatus*, ed. de Goeje, Leiden 1897.—For other continuations, see Suppl. A Persian abstract, made at the order of the vizier of the Sāmānids, Abū ʿAbdallāh Muḥammad al-Balʿamī, d. 363/972 (see Z. Validi Togan, *KCs.A.* III, 54), *Chronique d'Abou Djafer M. b. Djarir T. trad. sur la vers. pers. par* H. Zotenberg, vols. 1–4, Paris 1867/74, Turkish transl. Istanbul 1260, Chagatai transl., made in 927/1521 by Wāḥidī Balkhī for ʿAbd al-Laṭīf, the youngest son of the Shaybānid Köčkünǧī, 916–37/1510–30, Pet. Öff. Bibl., see Beresine, *Chrest. Turque*, Kazan 1857, 104/13.—2. *Tahdhīb al-āthār*, an exhaustive work on Tradition,

unfinished, Köpr. 269/70, see M. Weisweiler, *Istanb. Hdsstudien* no. 142 (other MSS Suppl.).—3. *Jāmiʿ al-bayān fī tafsīr* (*taʾwīl*) *al-Qurʾān*, extremely thorough and very comprehensive, see O. Loth, ZDMG 35, 588/628, individual MSS Berl 733, AS 100/12, NO 149/56, Cairo ²I, 1, 58, see Suppl. Turkish transl. Dresd. 22, AS 87.—4. *Ikhtilāf al-fuqahāʾ*, 4 vols., Berl. Fol. 4155.—5.–7. see Suppl.—8. A treatise on archery, Br. Mus. Or. 9265 (cf. 9454), Krenkow.—Also quoted is *Jāmiʿ al-qirāʾāt min al-mashhūr wal-shawādhdh wa-ʿilal dhālika wa-sharḥuhu*, see Bergstr.-Pretzl, *Gesch. des Qorʾānt.* 208.

5. Abū Bakr Muḥammad b. Yaḥyā al-Ṣūlī, the grand-nephew of the poet, was a descendant of a Turkish prince by the name of Ṣol-Tigin of Jurjān who had been conquered, dethroned, and converted to Islam by Yazīd b. al-Muhallab, and who had perished with him in the uprising against the Umayyads. He was part of the entourage of the caliphs al-Muktafī and al-Muqtadir, the latter of whom particularly appreciated him because of his brilliance at chess, which is why he was also called al-Shiṭranjī. He had been the teacher of the later Caliph | al-Rāḍī and of his brother Hārūn,[2] and so he enjoyed the highest favour. But 150
when, after al-Rāḍī's death in 329/940, al-Muttaqī ascended the throne, the latter dissolved his predecessor's court. Consequently, al-Ṣūlī went to the governor Bajkam in Wāsiṭ, who received him with all honours.[3] After Muttaqī's death in 333/944 he returned to Baghdad. However, due to the fact that he had shown his ʿAlid leanings too openly, he had to leave the capital once again and go into hiding in Basra, where he died in 336/916.

Wüst., 115. For his works, see Suppl. I, 218/9, with: *Ashʿār awlād al-khulafāʾ wa-akhbāruhum*, from the *Kitāb al-awrāq* of Abū B. M. b. Ya. al-Ṣ., ed. by J. Heyworth-Dunne, London 1936—*Akhbār Abī Tammām wa-yalīhi Risālat al-Ṣūlī ilā Muzāḥim b. Fātik fī taʾlīf akhbār Abī Tammām wa-ashʿārihi*, ed. Khalīl Maḥmūd ʿAsākir, Muḥammad ʿAbduh Gharam, Naẓīrulislām al-Hindī, C. 1937 (translated by Naẓīrulislām, Diss. Breslau 1940).

5c. Muḥammad b. ʿAlī b. Aʿtham al-Kūfī, d. ca. 314/926.

Suppl. I, 220. The original of the *Kitāb al-futūḥ* is preserved in Sarāi no. 2956, see Z.V. Togan, *KCs A.* III, 47.

---

2 See *Akhbār al-Rāḍī* 25.

3 Ibid. 193/4.

6. The most important and muli-faceted author of this whole period is prob-
144 ably Abu 'l-Ḥasan ʿAlī b. al-Ḥusayn al-Masʿūdī. | Born in Baghdad from a family
that traced its origin to Masʿūd, one of the companions of the Prophet, he did
not content himself with the usual educational programme of the traditionalists of his time, which required a study trip through the most important lands
of Islam, but let his thirst for knowledge lead him beyond the Islamic world.
Having roamed through Persia and Kirmān and after a sojourn in Iṣṭakhr in
151 303/915, he went to India in 304, where he first visited Multān | and al-Manṣūra.
Passing through Kanbāya and Ṣaymūr he reached Ceylon. From there he travelled with traders by sea to China, and then back via Zanzibar and Oman. After
a side trip to the regions of the Caspian we find him, in 314/926, in Tiberias in
Palestine. In 332/943 he was in Antioch and the Syrian border towns, then in
Basra and in Damascus in 334. In 336/947 he was in Fusṭāṭ, but visited Syria
from Egypt another couple of times. He died in Fusṭāṭ, where he had been living since 344/955, in Jumādā II 345/956 or 346.

The restlessness of his life is reflected in his works. His range of interest reaches much further than the usual erudition of a traditionalist to encompass, in addition to linguistics, natural philosophy, ethics and politics, and also and especially the transmitted accounts of people of other creeds: of the Jews, the Christians, and the wisdom of the Indians. But throughout he is merely content with superficial inquiries, and does not examine anything in depth. Nevertheless, we owe him many valuable reports from cultural and political history as well as geography. His accounts are not wedded to a particular ideal but show a preference for switching from one theme to another.

Fihrist 154 (which takes him to be from the Maghreb), al-Najjāshī, *Rijāl* 178/9
(which claims he was an Imāmite), Quatremère, *JA* s. 3, v. VII, 1ff., Wüst. 119.
From his works, listed by de Goeje in his foreword to the edition of the *Kitāb*
al-tanbīh, p. VI, the following are extant: 1. *Kitāb akhbār al-zamān wa-man*
abādahu 'l-ḥadathān min al-umam al-māḍiya wal-ajyāl al-khāliya wal-mamālik
al-dāthira, see Suppl., vol. I, C. 1938.—2. *Kitāb al-awsaṭ*, from which an excerpt,
145 AS $2938_{,4}$ | (from a MS d.d. 332), perhaps Bodl. I, 666.—3. *Murūj al-dhahab*
wa-maʿādin al-jawāhir, see Suppl., Patna I, $228_{,2229}$, partial Esc. $^{2}280_{,2}$ (see
Antuña, *al-Andalus* III, 1935, 447/9, contra Derenb. I, 171), on the Istanbul MSS
152 see Cahen, *REI* 1938 (1936) SA, 4, *Macoudi, les prairies d'or, texte et* | *traduc-*
tion par C. Barbier de Meynard *et* Pavet de Courteille, vols. 1–9. Paris 1861/77,
Būlāq 1283, C. 1303, in the margin of Ibn al-Athīr, Būlāq 1303, in the margin
of Maqqarī, C. 1302, vols. 1–3.—4. *Kitāb al-tanbīh wal-ishrāf*, his last work, in
which he makes up the balance, so to speak, of his whole literary production,

composed in 345/956, ed. by de Goeje, *Bibl. Geogr. ar.* VIII, Leiden 1894, reprint by ʿAbdallāh Ismāʿīl al-Ṣāwī, C. 1357/1938.—5. *Risāla fī ithbāt al-waṣiyya li-ʿAlī b. Abī Ṭālib*, libr. Najafābādī VII, 115, print. Tehran 1320.—6. *Fī aḥwāl al-imāma* ibid.—On the anonymous abstract from his magnum opus *Akhbār al-zamān wa-ʿajāʾib al-buldān* or *al-Jumān fī mukhtaṣar akhbār al-zamān*, translated by Carra de Vaux, *L'Abrégé des merveilles, trad. de l'Ar. d'après les mss. de la Bibl. Nat.* Paris 1898, see also M. Kurd ʿAlī, RAAD III, 239/42.

7. Abu 'l-Ḥasan Hamza b. al-Ḥasan (Ḥusayn) al-Iṣfahānī, see Suppl. I, 221/2.

In addition: 1. *Hamzae Ispahanensis annalium libri X*, ed. J.M.P. Gottwaldt, I, text. ar. Leipzig 1844, v. I, Lat. transl. ibid. 1848, completed in Jumādā 350/June–July 961, Transl. by Daudpota, Bombay 1932.—6. *al-Amthāl al-ṣādira ʿan buyūt al-shiʿr* ḤKh [1]I, 437, [2]I, 168, Berl. Qu. 1215.—7. *Kitāb al-afʿāl* Qawala II, 210.

5 *Cultural and Literary History*

1. Abu 'l-Faraj ʿAlī b. al-Ḥusayn b. Muḥammad b. Aḥmad al-Qurashī al-Iṣfahānī was born in 284/897 in Isfahan and studied in Baghdad. Later he appears to have led the life of a wandering litterateur. We find him with both Sayf al-Dawla and the Būyid viziers Ismāʿīl b. ʿAbbād (see p. 136) and al-Muhallabī. Being a descendant of the Umayyads, he supposedly also entertained secret liaisons with the Spanish branch of his house, even though he professed Shīʿism. His origin probably also explains his particular interest in the history of the ancient Arabs, on which we owe him for some extremely important information. In old age his mental capacities | had greatly diminished. He died on 14 Dhu 'l-Ḥijja 153
356/21 November 967.

Wüst. 132. 1. *Kitāb al-aghānī*, see Suppl. 43, J. Wellhausen, ZDMG L, 146ff. On the MSS see Suppl. and Berl. Brill M. $250,_{1-11}$, Garr. 179 (vol. I), Faiẓ. 1561/9 (see ZDMG 68, 377 and Holter, *Jahrb. des Kunsthist. Inst. Wien*, N.F. VI, 1937, S. 38), Fātiḥ 3669/70. 3. Print. C. [1]Būlāq 1285, 20 vols., [2]C. 1323 (with *fihrist*), *The XXI vol. of the K. al-Agh.* ed. by R.E. Brünnow, Leiden 1883. *Tables alphabétiques du K. al-Agh. réd. par* I. Guidi, Leiden 1895/1900. Dār al-kutub, vols. I–IX, 1927/36. Abstracts see Suppl., anonymous Algiers 1795/9, *Ḥadāʾiq al-funūn fi 'khtiṣār al-Aghānī*, Tunis, Zayt. see *Bull. de Corr. Afr.* 1884, 8.—2. (3) *Maqātil al-Ṭālibiyyīn*, with Berl. Oct. 2909, print. Najaf 1353.

2. The two brothers Abū ʿUthmān Saʿīd, d. ca. 350/961, and Abū Bakr Muḥammad b. Hāshim, d. 380/990, al-Khālidiyyān, lived at the court of Sayf al-Dawla. Both

were poets and, apart from a history of Mosul, they jointly wrote monographs on Abū Tammām and Ibn al-Rūmī, as well as an anthology of contemporary poets entitled *al-Ḥamāsa*.

Al-Thaʿālibī, *Yatīma* I, 507/30, *Fawāt* II, 281, Wüst. 148. *Ḥamāsat al-Khālidiyyayn* or *Kitāb al-ashbāh wal-naẓāʾir* Cairo [1]IV, 202, [2]III, 126.—*Qaṣīdas* by Saʿīd, Berl. $7567_{,3,4}$, see Suppl.

3. Abu ʾl-Faraj Muḥammad b. Isḥāq b. Abī Yaʿqūb b. al-Nadīm al-Warrāq al-Baghdādī, see Suppl. I, 226/7.

Kitāb al-Fihrist mit Anmm. hsg. von G. Flügel, *nach dessen Tode besorgt von* J. Rödiger *und* A. Müller 2 vols., Leipzig 1871/2, see Flügel, *ZDMG* XIII, 559/650. On the MSS see also Fück, *ZDMG* 90, 302ff., Kraus, *Orientalia* VI, 286. M.Th. Houtsma, Zum Kitāb al-Fihrist, *WZKM* IV, 217ff. (completion of a lacuna in Flügel's edition, on the history of *kalām*). S. Fraenkel, Zum Fihrist, *ZDMG* 46, 741/3. H. Suter, Das Mathematikerverzeichnis im Fihrist des I.a.I. an-N. zum ersten Mal Vollständig ins Deutsche übersetzt und mit Anmm. versehn, *Abh. z.*
148 *Gesch. d. Math.* VI | (Suppl. z. Z. f. Math. u. Phys.), 371/87. Addendum Z. f. Math. u. Phys. 38, hist.-lit. Abt. 126ff.—J. Lippert, Ibn al-Kūfī ein Vorgänger Nadīms, *WZKM* XI, 147ff.

154 | 6 ***The History of Egypt and North Africa***

1. Abu ʾl-Qāsim ʿAbd al-Raḥmān b. ʿAbdallāh b. ʿAbd al-Ḥakam, a son of the *qāḍī* and the head of the Mālikīs in Egypt who died in 214/829, wrote a large work on the conquest of Egypt and the Maghreb. He died in Fusṭāṭ in the year 257/871.

Wüst. 63. *Futūḥ Miṣr wal-Maghrib* ḤKh 8930, Paris 1686/7, Leid. 962, Br. Mus. S. 520 (Torrey, *JAOS* XX, 209/16), from which: *Ibn Abdolhakami libellus de historia Aegypti antiqua*, ed. J. Karle, Göttingen 1856. *Ibn Abdalhakems History of the Conquest of Spain* ed. and transl. by John Harris Jones, Göttingen and London 1858, Spanish transl. in *La Fuente y Alcantara*, Ajbar Machmua, App. II, 6, p. 208/19, Traditions anciennes relatives à l'établissement des Musulmans en l'Afrique septentrionale in *Hist. des Berbères* par Ibn Khaldūn, transl. B. de Slane, v. I, App.

2. Eutychius, Saʿīd b. al-Biṭrīq, was born in 263/876 in Fusṭāṭ. As a Coptic Christian he immersed himself entirely in the literary culture of the Arabs and excelled as a physician and historian. Elevated to the rank of patriarch of Alexandria in 321/933, he died in 328/939.

Wüst. 108, Leclerc, *Hist. de la méd. ar.* I, 405. 1. *Naẓm al-jawhar* Paris 288/93, Fir. Ricc. II, Asʿad 2093, see Cahen, *REI* 1936, SA 3, *Contextio gemmarum s. Eutychii Annales, interprete E. Pocockio*, Oxford 1658/9. Continuation *Taʾrīkh al-Dhayl* by Yaḥyā b. Saʿīd al-Anṭākī, who went to Antioch in 403/1012, where he found the documents that he needed to conclude his work. His account covers the Byzantine empire, the ʿAbbāsids and the Fāṭimids, as well as the patriarchates of Alexandria, Antioch and Constantinople, Paris 291 and Moscow, Pet. AM p. 130 n. 2. From which: *J. b. S. b. B. Kaiser Basilios Bulgaroktonos, Auszüge aus der Chronik Jahjas von Antiochia, im Originaltext mit russ. Übers. u. ausführl. Cmt. Einleitung und Namensregister hsg. v.* V. Rosen (*Zap. Imp. Ak. Nauk*, vol. 44. part 1), cf. *Archiv für slav. Philologie* VII, 3, 515/6.—2. *Eutychii epistola* Paris 1642.—3. *Kitāb al-burhān* or *Kamāl al-burhān ʿalā ḥaqīqat al-īmān*, a theological work, Cairo, Coptic | Patriarchate 356, 155
see G. Graf, Ein bisher unbekanntes Werk des Patriarchen Eutychios von Alexandrien in *Or. Chr.* N.S. I, 1911, 227/44, *Cat. des mss. ar chrét. conservés au Caire* p. 134, partially edited by Mānassā Yūḥannā, C. 1928.—Appended to the codex in Cambridge and therefore falsely attributed to Eutychius is the work of a later and unidentified Sicilian: *Chronicon Siculum ab anno Chr. 827 ad annum 965, ex. cod. ar. Cantabr. ar. et lat. in Bibl. hist. regn. Sic. op. et studio J.B. Carusii*, Palermo 1723. *Chron. Sic. e ms. cod. bibl. Cantabr. a.J.B. Carusio ar. et lat. antea ed., nunc vero ad fidem textus ar. castigatius recusum in: Rerum ar. quae ad hist. Sic. spectant, ampla collectio, op. et st. R. Gregorio*, Palermo 1790. G. Cozza Luzi, *La cronaca sicula saracena di Cambridge con doppio testo greco | scoperto in codd. contemporanei delle Biblioteche Vaticana* 149
e Parigiana con accompagnamento del testo ar. pel C.B. Lagumina (Docum. p. servire alla stor. di Sic.) Palermo 1890. C. Cipolla, I testi greci della cronaca arabico-sicula di Cambridge, publ. da G. Cozza Luzi in *Atti della R. Ac. delle scienzie di Torino* XXVII, 1882, 830/7. G. Cozza Luzi, *Sulla scoperta di due cronache greche Siculo-saraceniche e lora correlazione coll'ar. de Cambridge*, Rome 1893.

3. Abū Jaʿfar Aḥmad b. Yūsuf b. al-Dāya al-Miṣrī Kātib Āl Ṭūlūn, d. 340/951.

Wüst. 111, Suter, *Math.* 78, Becker, *Beitr. z. Gesch. Äg.* II, 151/3. 1. *Sīrat Aḥmad b. Ṭūlūn wabnihi Khumārawayh*, for the most part included in the work by Ibn Saʿīd, d. 685/1286 (p. 336), cf. Fragmente aus dem *Mughrib* des b. Saʿīd, hsg. von C. Vollers in *Semit. Stud.* (*Beihefte zur ZA*) I, Berl. 1894.—2.–5. see Suppl., ad 5. *Sharḥ al-thamara* also Taymūr Akhlāq 290,$_{13}$, Patna I, 238,$_{2064}$.—6. *Fi 'l-nisba wal-tanāsub* Algiers 1446,$_{2}$, Cairo I V, 198.—7. *de arcubus similibus* Bodl. I, 941.—8. On the *Ṣaḥīfa* in all its forms, ibid.

4. Muḥammad b. Yūsuf b. Yaʿqūb al-Kindī al-Tujībī was born on 10 Dhu ʾl-Ḥijja 283/30 January 895 and died in 350/961, and for his son ʿUmar, see Suppl. I, 229/30.

1. On the father's *Umarāʾ Miṣr* see also Torrey, *Islca* II, 55. Excerpts from it, under the title *Akhbār Miṣr* in the Nūraḥmadiyya in Acre, *RAAD* X, 577$_{,5}$.—2. For the son's *Faḍāʾil Miṣr*, see also Berl. Qu. 1080, Copenhagen 147$_{,1}$, Qilič ʿA. 756,
156 | Bank. XV, 1070, Garr. 759 (with the same author as Būhār), Cairo ^{1}V, ^{2}290, *ʿU. b. M. al-K. Beskrivelse af Ägypten, udgivet og oversatt af* J. Oestrup, *Verh. d. Ak. d. Wiss. zu Kopenhagen* 1896, no. 4, see de Goeje, *ZDMG* L, 736.

5. Abū Muḥammmad al-Ḥasan b. Ibrāhīm b. Zūlāq al-Laythī was born in Shaʿbān 306/January 919 and died on 25 Dhu ʾl-Ḥijja 387/30 November 998 (or, according to others, in 386).

Wüst. 151, see Suppl. I, 230. Ad 5. *Akhbār Sībawayh Miṣr* i.e. Muḥammad b. Mūsā b. ʿAbd al-ʿAzīz al-Kindī al-Ṣayrafī, d. 358/967, also Berl. Qu. 1079$_{,1}$, Cairo V, ^{1}6, ^{2}14.

7 *The History of Spain*

1. The supposedly oldest preserved work on the history of Spain is attributed to Abū Marwān ʿAbd al-Malik b. Ḥabīb al-Sulamī al-Mirdāsī al-Ilbīrī al-Qurṭubī, who was born after 180/796 in Ḥiṣn Wāṭ (Hutor Vega) near Granada. While on the pilgrimage in Medina he became acquainted with the doctrine of Mālik b. Anas, and after his return he was influential in its dissemination throughout Spain. In addition, he also distinguished himself as a linguist and a poet. He died in Cordova on 4 Ramadan 238/18 February 853 (or, according to others, on 12 Dhu ʾl-Ḥijja 239/5 April 854).

Wüst. 56, Flügel, *Gramm.* 256/7. From among his theologico-juridical works, of which Abū Bakr b. Khayr, *Index libr.* 290 also mentions a *Kitāb makārim al-akhlāq*, only the beginning of the *Kitāb uṣūl al-farāʾiḍ* (on the law of inheritance), Berl. 4687, has survived. The *Taʾrīkh* circulating under his name, which comprises a history of Creation, the Prophet, the caliphs up to Walīd I, and a history of Spain until the year 275/888, Bodl. II, 127, 258, and which is of no historical value, may be the work of his student Ibn Abi ʾl-Riqāʿ; see Dozy, *Recherches* ^{2}I, 33, ^{3}I, 28.

2. The first Spanish historian whose works have at least been preserved in a revised form is Abū Bakr Aḥmad b. Muḥammad b. Mūsā al-Rāzī, d. 325/937.

Wüst. 105 a. His description of the main roads, ports, major cities and the six provinces, and also his | history of the Spanish kings, form the basis of the 157
Spanish *Cronica del Moro Rasis*, see Casiri II, 329; P. de Gayangos, *Memoria sobre la autenticidad de la Cronica denominada del Moro Rasis* in *Memorias de la R. Ac. de la Historia*, vol. VIII, Madrid 1852.—The chronicle by his son ʿĪsā, which concludes with the reign of al-Ḥakam, underpins—until the year 361—Ibn Ḥayyān's *al-Muqtabis* (p. 338), see ed. Antuña XVII.

3. Abū ʿAbdallāh Muḥammad b. al-Ḥārith b. Asad al-Ḥushanī, d. 371/981, see Suppl. I, 232.

4. Abū Bakr Muḥammad b. ʿUmar ʿAbd al-ʿAzīz b. al-Qūṭiyya was just as excellent a philologist as he was an historian. He carried the surname "descendant of the female Goth" because his ancestor ʿĪsā b. Muzāḥim had married a Gothic princess from Spain, Sara, the daughter of Oppa, king of the Goths, when she came to Caliph Hishām b. ʿAbd al-Malik in Damascus to complain about her uncle Ardabast. ʿĪsā moved with his wife to Spain and his descendants lived in Seville. Abū Bakr was born in Cordova | and studied there and in Seville. 151
Al-Qālī (p. 139) is said to have described him to Caliph al-Ḥakam II as one of the most important scholars of Spain. He died on 27 Rabīʿ I 367/3 November 977 in Cordova.

Wüst 141. Of his works remain: 1. *Taʾrīkh iftitāḥ al-Andalus*, from the Islamic conquest until the year 280/893, Paris 1867 (see Suppl.), cf. Dozy, *Ibn Adhari*, Introd. 28ff., *Recherch.* [2]I, app. 85, [3]78. Cherbonneau, Histoire du règne d'Elhakam fils de Hicham, *JA* s. 5, v. I, p. 458. Ibn al-Qoutiya, *Histoire de la conquête de l'Andalousie*, ed. O. Houdas in *Recueil de textes et de traductions publié par les professeurs de l'École des lang. or. viv.* v. I, Paris 1889, 219ff.—*Kitāb al-afʿāl, Il libro dei verbi di Abu Bekr ibn al-Qutiya, pubblicato da* I. Guidi, Leid. 1894 (MS also Murād Mollā 1790).

158 ## | Chapter 5. Belles Lettres in Prose

Zakī Mubārak, *al-Nathr al-fannī fi 'l-qarn al-rābi'*, C. 1934/1352; *La Prose arabe au IVe siècle de l'Hégire (Xe s.)*, Paris 1931.
Anīs Khūrī al-Muqaddasī, *Taṣawwur al-asālīb al-nathriyya* I, Beirut 1935.
M. Kurd ʿAlī, *Umarāʾ al-bayān*, C. 1937.
M. Sprengling, From Persian to Arabic, *AJSL* LVI, 175/224, 325/36.

1. ʿAbdallāh b. al-Muqaffaʿ, see Suppl. 233/7.

Khiz. III, 459/60, Kraus, *RSO* XIV, 1/20. 1. Kalīla wa-Dimna, *the fables of Bidpai from the Pahlavi translation of the Indian mirror for princes Pančatantra*, ed. de Sacy, Paris 1816, on which I. Guidi, *Studii sul testo arabo del libro Calila e Dimna*, Roma 1873. *Morgenländische Erzählungen, verdeutscht von* Ph. Wolff, *Calila und*
152 *Dimna oder die Fabeln* | *Bidpais aus dem Arab.* I, II, Stuttgart 1837. *Das Buch des Weisen in lust- und lehrreichen Erzählungen des indischen Philosophen Bidpai, aus dem Arab. von* Ph. Wolff, 2. Aufl. I, II, Stuttgart 1839.—MSS also AS 4213/4.—Print. Beirut 1878, 1882, 1890, Būlāq 1285, C. 1305, Mosul 1869, 1883, Bombay 1887, Kazan 1889 and see ed. A. Ṭabbāra, Beirut 1937 (the translations of Aristotle's *Categories and Analytics* as well as of Porphyry's *Eisagoge*, Āṣaf. III, 668, are the work of his son Aḥmad; see Kraus, *RSO*, XIV, 1934, 1/30).—2. ff. see Suppl. (the authenticity of the *Muʿāraḍa lil-Qurʾān* is also questioned by G. Vajda, *JA* 228, 349/52).

1a. There is also a *Kitāb al-ḥanīn ila 'l-awṭān* by the translator Mūsā b. ʿĪsā al-Kisrawī, AS 2052, f. 77b/84b, see F. Meier, *Isl.* XXIV, 20, n. 1.

1b. There is a longer fragment of the *Kitāb Bilawhar wa-Būdāsaf* in Taymūr, Akhlāq 290,$_{17}$. Quotations in *Rasāʾil ikhwān al-ṣafāʾ*, Bombay 1305, 135, 215, C. 1347, IV, 120,$_{19}$, 223,$_{23}$, see Goldziher, *Isl.* I, 24, n. b.

2. The son of a negro, ʿAmr b. Baḥr al-Jāḥiẓ was born in Basra around 150/767.
153 He had close | ties with Ibn al-Zayyāt, vizier of al-Wāthiq, and when the latter
159 was killed by al-Mutawakkil he | almost shared his fate. When this caliph summoned him to Baghdad to oversee the education of his son, he was apparently so intimidated by the former's ugliness that he immediately sent him away again, with a generous compensation. He died in 255/868. See Suppl. 239/47.

Ibn al-Anb. 254/9, Ibn Khall. 479, Shahrast. 52/3, Flügel, *Gr.* 187, Houtsma, *De Strijd* 113/5, G. van Vloten, in *Tweemaandelijksch Tijdschr.* 1897, May, al-Bustānī

Rawāʾiʿ no. 18/20, Beirut 1928.—Collective manuscripts *Mukhtār min rasāʾil al-J.* Berl. Oct. 1499, Dāmād Ibr. 949, *Majmūʿat rasāʾil al-J.* C. 1324.

1. *Kitāb al-bayān wal-tabyīn* (cf. V. v. Rosen, ZDMG 28, 169) Pet. Rosen 158, Leningr. Un. 724, AS 3814, Köpr. 1222/4, NO 3688, 3696/7, Halet 765, Asʿad 3883, ʿĀšir 762, Cairo ^{1}IV, 216, ^{2}III, 40, C. 1313, ed. by ʿAbd al-Salām Muḥammad Hārūn, vol. I, C. 1938. On the section on rhetoric see Kračkovsky, *Vost. Zap. Leningrad* 1927, p. 26ff.—2. *Kitāb al-ḥayawān* Vienna 1433, Köpr. 992/7, NO 3031. Excerpts in G. van Vloten, Dämonen, Geister und Zauber bei den alten Arabern, *WZKM* VIII, 167/87, 233/47, VII, 59/73, 290/2, idem., Worgers in ʿIrāq in *Feestbundel Veth*, 57/63, 315, on alchemy in G.E. Wiedemann, *Journal für prakt. Chemie*, N.S. 76 (1907), 73/8, *Beitr.* XLVI, *SBPhMS Erl.* 47, 130/1, excerpts Esc. ^{2}897, 901.—3. *Kitāb al-bukhalāʾ*, emendations by W. Marçais in *Mél. H. Basset*, Paris 1925, 1/31, reprint with comm. by al-ʿAwāmirī Bek and Muṣṭafā al-Jārim Bek, C. 1938 (Maṭb. Wizārat al-maʿārif).—Vol. I, theology: 14. *Khalq al-Qurʾān.*—15. *Fi ʾl-radd ʿala ʾl-Mushabbiha.*—16. *al-Radd ʿalā b. Isḥāq al-Naẓẓām wa-aṣḥābihi* Br. Mus. Suppl. 1129 (not mentioned by Rieu, see *Or. Stud.* Browne 200, 9).

IV. 46a. *Risāla ila ʾl-Muʿtaṣim (wa-qīla ila ʾl-Mutawakkil) fi ʾl-ḥaḍḍ ʿalā taʿlīm awlādihī ḍurūb al-ʿulūm wa-anwāʿ al-adab*, in al-Ḥuṣrī, *Dhayl Zahr al-ādāb* 116/21.

V. 47a. *al-Tabaṣṣur fi ʾl-tijāra* ed. Ḥ. Ḥusnī ʿAbd al-Wāhhāb, Damascus, Maṭb. al-Majmaʿ al-ʿilmī, see *RAAD* XII, 321/55.—XI. 90. From the *Kitāb al-buldān* the description of the Umayyad Mosque in Yāqūt, *GW* II, 593, 7ff.—Fragments of his *Kitāb al-akhbār* are in the *Kitāb al-munya wal-amal* of al-Mahdī li-Dīn Allāh Aḥmad b. Yaḥyā (II, 187). *Lughat al-ʿArab* IX, 174/81, see Mosul 100, 24.—D. 5. *Kitāb al-dalāʾil wal-iʿtibār.* Krenkow, *RAAD* IX, 558/62, is perhaps a work by a | 160
Christian, see H. Baneth, *Magnes Anniversary Vol.*, Jerusalem 1938, 24ff.

2a. Aḥmad b. Abī al-Sarḥ al-Kātib, whom *Fihrist* 128 credits with *Rasāʾil* and a *Kitāb al-ʿilm wa-mā jāʾa fīhi*, wrote, in 274/887, a *Kitāb rumūz*, Rāġib 1463, f. 100/6, ed. by S.M. Ḥusein, *RAAD* XI, 642/55.

3. The works of Abū Bakr ʿAbdallāh (ʿUbaydallāh) b. Muḥammad b. Abī Dunyā al-Qurashī aim at being entertainment and edification at the same time. Born in Baghdad in the year 208/823 and a client of the Umayyads, he nevertheless entered into relations with the ʿAbbāsids and was the teacher of the later Caliph al-Muktafī (289–95/902–8). He died on 14 Jumādā II 281/22 August 894.

Fawāt I, 236. 1. *Kitāb al-faraj baʿd al-shidda*, an imitation of a lost work by al-Madāʾinī that had the same title, Berl. 8731, Brill M. 173, criticised by

154 al-Tanūkhī in the preface to his own work by the same | title, Cat. Leid. ^{2}I, 255; an abstract, augmented from other sources and entitled *al-Araj fi 'ntiẓār al-faraj* by al-Suyūṭī d. 911/1505, Berl. 8732/3, Gotha 622/3, Paris 659,$_4$.—2. *Makārim al-akhlāq*, an account of the good qualities essential for man, based on sayings of the Prophet, ḤKh VI no. 12823, Berl. 5388, see Bishr Fāris, *Mabāḥith ʿarabiyya*, C. 1939, p. 32; therefrom especially *Kitāb mudārāt al-nās* Berl. 5436,$_2$.—3. *Kitāb dhamm al-malāhī*, on the censure of musical instruments, Berl. 5504, together Majd al-Dīn al-Ṭūsī al-Ghazzālī's (p. 426) *Bawāriq al-ilmāʿ*, ed. with introd. and transl. by J. Robson, London 1938 (Or. Transl. Fund, N.S. XXXIV).—4. *Fī faḍā'il ʿashr Dhi 'l-Ḥijja* Leid. 1732, Landb.-Br. 55.—5. *Kitāb al-ʿaẓama*, on the wonders of creation, Krafft 423, Garr. 764, Ğārullāh 400.—6. *Kitāb man ʿāsha baʿd al-mawt*, short stories, Munich 885,$_3$.—7. *Kitāb al-yaqīn* Köpr. 388.—8. *Kitāb al-shukr* NO 1208, Garr. 1420, Cairo ^{2}I, 129.—10. *Kitāb qira 'l-ḍayf* Landb. Br. 54.—11.–44. see Suppl. I, 247/8, 946/7.—45. *Kitāb al-humūl wal-tawāḍuʿ*, quoted in al-Damīrī I, 324,$_{24}$.—*Majmūʿat al-rasā'il li-Ibn Abi 'l-Dunyā* (*al-Tawakkul ʿala 'llāh, al-Ḥilm, Ḥusn al-ẓann billāh, Qaḍā' al-ḥawā'ij, Kitāb al-awliyā'*), C. 1935.

4. Abū Bakr Aḥmad b. Marwān al-Dīnawarī al-Mālikī, d. 310/922.

161 | *Kitāb al-mujālasa*, a collection of traditions, anecdotes, and *maqāmas* in 47 chapters, the last 15 of which are contained in Paris 3481, see Suppl. I, 249, 947.

5.–7. see Suppl. I, 250.

8. Abū ʿUmar (ʿAmr) Aḥmad b. Muḥammad b. ʿAbd Rabbih, born on 10 Ramadan 246/860 in Cordova, was a freedman of the ruling Umayyads. He was an active poet of great productivity until he was paralysed by a stroke. He died some years later, on 18 Jumādā II 328/3 March 940.

Al-Thaʿālibī, *Yatīma* I, 412/36, Ibn Khall. 45, Wüst., *Gesch.* 107, Hartmann, *Muwashshaḥ* 23. *Kitāb al-ʿiqd* (*al-farīd* was only added later), a very rich anthology of stories and poems, in style similar to Ibn Qutayba's *ʿUyūn al-akhbār*, Berl. 8318/9, BDMG 115, Gotha 2121/3, Vienna 357, Munich 594, Paris 3287/91, Br. Mus. 1091/3, Bodl. I, 334, 350, 400, 743, Milan, Bibl. Ital. LVI, 297, AS 4139/44, NO 4119/20, Rāġib 1174, Köpr. 1339/41 (see Cahen, *REI* 1936, SA 3), print. Būlāq 1293, C. 1302, 1305, 1314, 1321, 1913, 1928, 1935, ed. by Aḥmad Amīn Abu 'l-Zayn, Ibrāhīm al-Abyārī I C. 1940. The work is divided into 25 books, each named after a precious stone; the 13th book is formed by the central stone, *al-wāsiṭa*, of the necklace, with which the other books are connected from both sides, in such a way that similar gems (though after the 13th, with the addition *al-thāniya*) face each other, equidistant from the central stone.

9. Abū Isḥāq Ibrāhīm b. al-Qāsim al-Kātib al-Qayrawānī al-Raqīq al-Nadīm went, in 388/998, as an envoy of Bādīs b. Zīrī to al-Ḥākim in Cairo. He died sometime after 417/1026.

Kitāb quṭb al-surūr fī waṣf al-anbidha wal-khumūr, anecdotes and samples of poetry, for and against the enjoyment of wine, ḤKh IV, 9531, Berl. 8324, Gotha 2124/5, Vienna 358, Leipz. 517, Lund 4, Esc. ^{2}558, anon. *Mukhtār* Halet 105, see de Slane, *Hist. des Berbères* I, 292, n. 3.

10. Abū ʿAlī al-Muḥassin b. ʿAlī al-Tanūkhī was born on 26 Rabīʿ I 329/20 December 940 in Basra, the son of the *qāḍī* and poet ʿAlī b. Muḥammad. After | completing his studies with al-Ṣūlī and Abu ʾl-Faraj al-Iṣfahānī he went to 162
Baghdad. In the year 349/960 he was appointed *qāḍī* for Qaṣr, Bābil, and their surroundings. After occupying similar offices in ʿAskar Mukarram, Īdhaj, Rāmhurmuz and some other places, he died in Baghdad on 25 Muḥarram 384/2 March 994.

Al-Thaʿālibī, *Yatīma* II, 115/6, Ibn Khall. 529, Ibn Quṭlūbughā 229. 1. *Kitāb al-faraj baʿd al-shidda*, a collection of stories based on the example of the works by al-Madāʾinī (p. 146) and Ibn Abi ʾl-Dunyā (p. 160), Berl. 8737/8, Gotha 2687, Leid. 449, Paris 3483/4, Bodl. I, 326, Vat V, 777, Esc. ^{2}714, Köpr. 1349/50, Dam. ʿUm. 87,$_{34}$, Alex. Mawāʿiẓ 29, Patna I, 150,$_{1432}$, C. 1903/4, 1938, see F. Gabrieli, Il valore letterario-historico del *F. b. al-sh.* di T., RSO XIX, 16/44; according to Gotha 1596 and Ibn Taghr. C. III, 310,$_{15}$ this is in fact a work by his father.—Abstract, *Najāt al-muhaj*, by ʿAlī b. Abī Ṭālib b. ʿAlī al-Khashshāb al-Ḥalabī, Paris 3485, anon. ibid. 3486,$_{1,2}$, Berl. 8739.—2. *Kitāb al-mustajād min faʿalāt al-ajwād*, a collection of anecdotes and character traits, mostly taken from the lives of the ʿAbbāsid caliphs, Berl. Brill M. 128, Gotha 1596/7, Leipz. 590, AS 4263 (WZKM XXVI, 88, excerpt), Āṣaf. III, 520,$_{185}$, Esc. ^{2}1727 (folios 9/264 identical with vol. 1 of Ibn ʿAbd Rabbih's *ʿIqd*, see Antuña, *al-Andalus* I, 191/2). *T. s. al-K. M. min f. al-a.* ed. (i.e. photolith. of MS Aligarh) and analysis by L. Pauly, Stuttgart 1939 (Bonner Or. St. 23). The MSS Berl. 8433, Bodl. I, 834 (see Amedroz, RSO III, 558), Leningr. As. Mus. 757, and Algiers 1883 contain later imitations. 3.–5., see Suppl. (on 3 see Ritter, *Isl.* XIV, 1924, 148/51).

156 | 11. The story of Abu 'l-Muṭahhar Muḥammad b. Aḥmad al-Azdī probably also dates from the fifth century.

Ḥikāyat Abi 'l-Qāsim al-Baghdādī al-Tamīmī which, through the words of an authentic inhabitant of Baghdad, describes a saucy, good-for-nothing but eloquent elderly man and his adventures over the course of 24 hours, Br. Mus. 1127, s. Suppl.

12. See Suppl. I, 254 (Patna I, 203$_{181,1}$).

Chapter 6. Ḥadīth 163

Al-Suyūṭī, *Ṭabaqāt al-ḥuffāẓ* (hereafter *Ḥuff.*). *Liber classium virorum qui Korani et Traditionum cognitione excelluerunt auctore Dahabio*, ed. F. Wüstenfeld, Göttingen 1833/4.

I. Goldziher, Über die Entwicklung des Ḥadīth, *MSt.* II, 1/274.

1. Apart from the works by Mālik b. Anas and Aḥmad b. Ḥanbal, which will be discussed in the chapter on *fiqh*, little remains of the oldest period in *ḥadīth* literature, as documented in Suppl. I, 255/9.

Ad p. 257 β. Abū Muḥammad ʿAbdallāh b. Wahb b. Muslim al-Qurashī al-Fihrī, d. 197/812, *Kitāb al-jāmiʿ fī ʾl-ḥadīth*, also Cairo ^{2}I, 13 (MS d.d. 270, see Suppl. I, 948, contra al-Dhahabī's statement in *Mīzān* II, 86, that the year of death is 177, see also ḤKh II 380, VI 264), edit. prepared by J. David-Weill (Textes ar. de l'Inst. F.A.O.C. III, IV, 1942). His *Tafsīr* ḤKh II, 350,$_{3194}$.

Ad p. 257 ε. Abstract by Naṣr b. ʿAbd al-Munʿim al-Tamīmī al-Ḥanafī, Dam. Z. 82,$_{62}$, p. 259.—ρ al-Rabīʿ b. Ḥabīb b. ʿUmar al-Azdī al-Baṣrī al-Ibāḍī, d. 170/786, see *Bull. de Corr. Afr.* 1885, p. 71/5, see p. 691.

2. The *muṣannaf* works, in which traditions are arranged according to their 157
significance for juridical and ritual, as well as historical, ascetic and ethical questions, represent a higher stage of literary development. These works provided the *aṣḥāb al-ḥadīth* with conveniently formatted tradition material, necessary in their struggle against the *aṣḥāb al-raʾy* in matters relating to *fiqh*. Earlier attempts of this kind were eclipsed by Bukhārī's *Ṣaḥīḥ*. Abū ʿAbdallāh Muḥammad b. Ismāʿīl b. Ibrāhīm b. Mughīra b. Bardizbah al-Bukhārī al-Juʿfī, who was born into an Iranian family on 13 Shawwāl 194/21 July 810 in Bukhārā, made the pilgrimage when he was sixteen years old. In Egypt he continued 158
his study of Tradition which he had started in Mecca and Medina, and for the same purpose he then travelled all over Asia. After an absence of 16 years, five 164
of which he spent in Basra, he returned to his hometown where he wrote his *Ṣaḥīḥ*. He died in Khartanak on 30 Ramaḍān 256/31 August 870.

His work is based on a grid of chapter-headings taken from *fiqh*, for which he could not supply the necessary *ḥadīth* material in every case. This is because he was very demanding as regards witnesses, in the same way in which he was in the matter of the transmission of the text. Nevertheless, he did not shrink from elucidating the traditions by brief remarks now and then, which were, however, sharply delineated from the text. Even though the text of the *Ṣaḥīḥ* has been very carefully transmitted, the emergence of variant readings could not altogether be prevented, and it is thanks to the commentators that we know about these. The text as we have it was prepared by Sharaf al-Dīn ʿAlī b. Muḥammad al-Yunīnī, d. 701/1302 (*Ḥuff.* XXI), with philological backing from Ibn Mālik, d. 672/1273 (p. 298).

Wüst. *Gesch.* 62, *Schaf.* 44, Krehl, *ZDMG* IV, 1ff., Goldziher, *MSt.* I, 234/45,
J. Fück, Beiträge zur Überlieferungsgeschichte von B.'s Traditionssammlung,
ZDMG 92, 60/87. I. *al-Jāmiʿ al-ṣaḥīḥ* see Suppl. I, 261/4. Commentaries: 1. *Iʿlām*
al-muḥaddith etc. Garr. 1349, Patna I, $39_{,401}$.—4. *a. al-Tawḍīḥ* Alex. Ḥad. 34.—5.
al-Kawākib al-darārī fī sharḥ al-B. by Muḥammad b. Yūsuf b. ʿAlī al-Kirmānī,
d. 786/1384, Berl. 1194 (?), Gotha 592/4, Bodl. I, 90/1, Garr. 1351, Esc. ^{2}1461, Algiers
4452/5, Rāġib 295/6, Yeni 217/22, AS 654/70, Patna I, $575_{,581,5}$.—6. *al-Tanqīḥ fī alfāẓ*
al-Jāmiʿ al-ṣaḥīḥ by Muḥammad b. Bahādur b. ʿAbdallāh al-Miṣrī al-Zarkashī,
159 d. 794/1392 (II, 91), Berl. 1195/8, Paris 696, Br. Mus. 181, AS 682/4, | Alex. Ḥad. 12,
Patna I, $42_{,426}$.—7. *al-Tawḍīḥ* by ʿUmar b. ʿAlī b. al-Mulaqqin, d. 805/1402 (II, 92),
Br. Mus. 1561/2, fragm. Berl. 1199.—8. *al-Ifhām* by ʿAbd al-Raḥmān al-Bulqīnī,
d. 824/1421 (II, 112), AS 479.—9. *Maṣābīḥ al-Jāmiʿ al-ṣaḥīḥ* by Muḥammad b.
Abī Bakr al-Damāmīnī, d. 827/1424 (II, 26), Garr. 1352, NO 849/50.—10. *al-Kawkab*
al-sārī fī sharḥ al-B. by Muḥammad b. Aḥmad b. Mūsā (b. Yūsuf) al-Kafīrī,
165 d. 831/1428 (al-Sakhāwī, *al-Ḍawʾ* | *al-l.* VII, 111/2), Berl. 1200.—11. *al-Lāmiʿ al-ṣabīḥ*
by Muḥammad b. ʿAbd al-Dāʾim al-Birmāwī, d. 831/1428 (II, 95), NO 845/6,
AS 804.—12. *Fatḥ al-bārī fī sharḥ al-B.* by Ibn Ḥajar al-ʿAsqalānī, d. 852/1448
(II, 67), Berl. 1203/5, Leipz. 309, Paris 697, Yeni 210/2, AS 626/32, 634/53, Köpr.
316/21, on which a *muqaddima*, Berl. 1201/2, Ind. Off. 125, Br. Mus. $181_{,2}$, 1599,
Algiers 446/7, Yeni 211, AS 625, 633, Patna I, $55_{,553}$.—13. *ʿUmdat al-qāriʾ fī sharḥ*
al-B. by Maḥmūd b. Aḥmad b. Mūsā al-ʿAynī, d. 855/1451 (II, 51), Berl. 1206/9,
Paris 698/700, Algiers 448/58, Rāġib 300/5, Yeni 213/6, NO 854/61, AS 671/8, Patna
I, $52_{,522/4}$, II, $502_{,2691/8}$, print. C. 1308, Istanbul 1309/10.—13a. *al-Durr* by Aḥmad
b. Ibrāhīm al-Ḥalabī, d. 884/1479 (II, 70), Cairo ^{2}I, 125.—14. *al-Kawthar al-jārī*
fī sharḥ al-B. by Aḥmad b. Ismāʿīl al-Kūrānī, d. 893/1488 (II, 228), AS 686, Rāġib
297, Qawala I, 146.—15. *al-Tawshīḥ ʿala 'l-Jāmiʿ al-ṣaḥīḥ* by al-Suyūṭī, d. 911/1505,
Qawala I, 108, Patna I, $42_{,429}$, *Dībāja* Gotha 253, glosses Berl. 1216.—16. *Irshād*
al-sārī fī sharḥ al-B. by Ibn Muḥammad b. Abī Bakr al-Qasṭallānī, d. 923/1517
(II, 63), Berl. 1210/1, Paris 701/3, Ind. Off. 127/8, Algiers 460/73, Köpr. 322/5, Rāġib
291/4, NO 862/84, AS 603/24, Patna I, $38_{,384,93}$, print. Lucknow 1876, Nawalkishor
1284, Būlāq 1304/5, C. 1276, 1307 (bad reprint *OB* IV, 1474), Delhi 1891.—17.
Tuḥfat al-bārī by Zakariyyāʾ al-Anṣārī, d. 926/1520 (II, 88), NO 847/8.—18. *Sharḥ*
ʿiddat aḥādīth Ṣaḥīḥ al-B. by Muḥammad b. ʿUmar b. Aḥmad al-Safīrī al-Ḥalabī,
d. 956/1549 (II, 99), Berl. 1212, Alex. Ḥad. 31.—18a. *Bidāyat al-qāriʾ fī khatm Saḥīḥ*
al-B. by Muḥammad b. Sālim b. ʿAlī al-Ṭablāwī, d. 969/1549 (Suppl. II, 443), Garr.

1353, Cairo ^{1}I, 275.—19. *Iʿrāb al-qāriʾ ʿalā awwal bāb al-B.* by al-Qāriʾ al-Harawī, d. 1014/1605 (II, 314), Berl. 1213, Patna II, 388,$_{2568,50}$, glosses by Muḥammad b. Muḥammad al-Bakhshī, d. 1096/1685, ibid. 1214.—20. *Tazyīn al-ʿibāra* by the same, ibid. 1217.—21. On the last tradition, by Tāj al-ʿĀrifīn b. Muwaffaq al-Dīn, ca. 1160/1747, Berl. 1218, and by Sulaymān al-ʿUjaylī, d. 1204/1789, ibid. 1219.—22. *Najāḥ al-qāriʾ* by ʿAbdallāh Yūsuf Effendīzāde al-Ḥilmī, d. 1167/1753 (Suppl. II, 653), AS 685, NO 894/932.—23. *al-ʿIqd al-ghālī fī ḥall ishkāl al-Ṣ. al-B.* by Aḥmad al-Kurdī, Paris 2677,$_7$.—24. *Zād al-mujidd al-sārī* by Abū ʿAbdallāh Muḥammad al-Tāwudī b. Sūda al-Murrī, d. 1209/1795, Br. Mus. 1482/4, Algiers 474.—25. Maḥmūd b. Ibrāhīm b. Muḥammad al-Salāmī, AS 688/9.—26. *Ghāyat al-tawḍīḥ* by ʿUthmān b. Ibrāhīm al-Ṣiddīqī al-Ḥanafī, tenth cent., Ind. Off. 129/30, see Suppl. II, 994,$_{53}$, with Patna II, 445,$_{2621,5}$.—27. Introduction and comment. to the first two books | by ʿUmar b. Muḥammad ʿArīf al-Nahrawālī, Ind. Off. 131.— 166
28.–41. see Suppl. (40 = 26).—42. *al-Iʿlām bi-sharḥ aḥādīth sayyid al-anām* by Ismāʿīl al-Jarrāḥī, d. 1162/1749 (II, 308), Garr. 1355.—43. *Taʿlīqāt ʿalā abwāb al-B.* by Shāh ʿUbaydallāh b. Shāh ʿAbd al-Raḥīm al-Dihlawī, Patna I, 41,$_{425}$. 60 commentaries are mentioned in Ahlw. 1215.—Abstracts: 1. *Jamʿ al-nihāya fī badʾ al-khayr wal-ghāya* by ʿAbdallāh b. Saʿd b. Abī Jamra, d. 699/1300 (p. 372), Algiers 476/86, Rāmpūr II, 117,$_{438}$ (see Suppl.), Patna I, 48,$_{483/5}$, on which the author's own comm. *Bahjat al-nufūs* Berl. 1221, Brill M. 229, Munich 117, Paris 695, 5351, Algiers 478,$_2$/87, NO 845/6, Alex. Ḥad. 49,$_4$, and by Muḥammad ʿAbbās ʿAlī Khān *al-Taʿlīq al-Fakhrī* Cairo ^{2}I, 97.—2. *ʿIqd al-jumān al-lāmiʿ al-muntaqā min qaʿr al-baḥr al-jāmiʿ*, the traditionalists in alphabetical order by Muḥammad b. Muḥammad b. ʿAlī Qūjilī, Algiers 488.—3. *Mukhtaṣar* by Ibn Abī Ḥamza, Rāġib 351.—*Tajrīd al-Ṣ.* (see Suppl.) Qawala I, 103, Patna I, 40,$_{413}$. 4 other abstracts are mentioned in Ahlw. 1225,$_{61-64}$.—Other reworkings, see Suppl. I, 264, with: 6. *Ishārāt Ṣaḥīḥ al-B. wa-asānīdihi* by Muḥammad ʿAfīf al-Dīn ʿAbdallāh b. Sālim al-Baṣrī al-Shāfiʿī, d. 1134/1721, Garr. 1354.—9. *Asāmī ruwāt Ṣ. al-B.* by Ḥasan b. Ḥasan Ṣāfīzāde, d. 1279/1864, Istanbul 1282.—10. *Taḥrīr ʿalā Kitāb al-ʿilm min Ṣ. al-imām al-B.* by ʿAbd al-Sayyid Muḥammad al-Najjār, Mufti ʾl-Diyār al-Tūnisiyya, Tunis 1325.—11. *Miftāḥ al-B.* by Muḥammad Shukrī b. Ḥasan, Istanbul 1313.

II. *al-Thalāthiyyāt*, three-tier traditions, ḤKh ^{1}II, 3827, ^{2}I, 522, Berl. 1620/1, Patna I, 42,$_{435}$, on which commentaries by: a. Aḥmad b. Muḥammad al-ʿAjamī al-Wafāʾī, d. 1086/1675 (II, 308), Köpr. 298.—b. al-Qāriʾ al-Harawī, d. 1014/1605 (II, 394), Šehīd ʿA. 1841,$_2$.—Abstract *al-Fawāʾid al-marwiyyāt fī fawāʾid al-thalāthiyyāt* by Muḥammad b. Ibrāhīm al-Ḥadramī, d. 777/1375, Algiers 475.

III. a. *al-Taʾrīkh al-kabīr*, on the transmitters, AS 3069/71, library of Yāsīn Bāshayān al-ʿAbbāsī in Basra (following a letter by Ritter, see Krenkow, *Isl. Culture* VIII, 1934, 643/8).—b. *al-Taʾrīkh al-awsaṭ*, chronologically arranged, bought in 1937 in Hyderabad (communication by Krenkow).—c. *al-Taʾrīkh al-ṣaghīr* Patna II, $304_{,2411}$, $371_{,2557,1}$.—*Kitāb al-ḍuʿafāʾ al-kabīr* ibid. $557_{,2932,7}$, *Kitāb al-ḍuʿafāʾ al-ṣaghīr* ibid. $538_{,2897}$.

IV. *Tafsīr al-Qurʾān* (Esc. ^{1}1255 after ^{2}1260, rather a part of an anonymous
160 Qurʾān commentary, while Paris 242/5 in | Wüst. rather contains the *Ṣaḥīḥ*, see de Slane 688, 690/1, 694), commentary on sura 21, 48, Algiers 1688, 3.

V–IX. see Suppl. (IX Patna II, $438_{,2614,1}$).

3. Abu ʾl-Ḥusayn Muslim b. al-Ḥajjāj al-Qushayrī al-Nīshābūrī was born in
167 202/817 or 206. He went to Baghdad several times, | the last of which was in 259/873, and died on 25 Rajab 261/6 May 875 in Naṣrābād, a suburb of Nishapur. His collection of traditions *al-Ṣaḥīḥ* contains basically the same material as the one by al-Būkhārī, taken from other sources. His work is likewise arranged according to the chapters of *fiqh*, but without headings so as not to forestall the user. Also, he did not intend to document the entire framework of *fiqh* with traditions, which is why he assembled traditions with different *isnād*s rather than using them as evidence in different places as his predecessor had done. The author discusses the science of Tradition at length in an introduction.

Wüst, *Gesch.* 65, Goldziher 245/6. I. *al-Ṣaḥīḥ* in MSS almost just as numerous as the one of Bukhārī, print. Calcutta 1265, with a short comm. C. 1348/9.—Commentaries: 1. *Ikmāl al-muʿlim* by Qāḍī ʿIyāḍ al-Yaḥṣabī, d. 544/1149 (p. 369), Rāġib 310, NO 1035, Qawala I, 101.—2. *al-Minhāj fī sharḥ M. b. al-Ḥ.* or *Minhāj al-muḥaddithīn wa-sabīl talbiyat al-muḥaqqiqīn* by al-Nawawī, d. 676/1277 (p. 394), Berl. 1234/9, AS 690/704, Yeni 244, Rāġib 308/9, Patna I, $53_{,525,32}$, print. in 5 vols. C. 1283, Delhi 1304.—3. *Ghurar al-fawāʾid al-majmūʿa fī bayān mā waqaʿa fī Ṣaḥīḥ M. min al-aḥādīth al-maqṭūʿa* by Yaḥyā b. ʿAlī al-Qurashī al-ʿAṭṭār al-Mālikī, d. 662/1264, Berl. 1232/3.–4. *Ikmāl al-ikmāl* by Muḥammad b. Khalīfa b. ʿUmar al-Washtātī al-Ubbī al-Mālikī al-Tūnisī, d. 827/1424 or 828 (M. b. Cheneb, *Idjāza* § 262), Munich 120, Algiers 490/1, Rāġib 306/7, Köpr. 329, Patna I, $39_{,402/3}$.—5. *Khatm Ṣ. M.* by ʿAbd al-Qādir al-Nādimī, d. 927/1521, Berl. 1240.—6. by Ibrāhīm b. Muḥammad b. al-ʿAjamī al-Ḥalabī, Bodl. I, $150_{,1}$.—7. *ʿInāyat al-malik al-munʿim* by ʿAbdallāh Yūsufeffendīzāde Ḥilmī, d. 1167/1754
161 (Suppl. II, 652), NO 1042/3.—| Abstracts: 1. *al-Musnad al-mukhraj ʿalā kitāb M. b. al-Ḥ.* by Abū ʿAwāha Yaʿqūb b. Isḥāq al-Nīsābūrī al-Shāfiʿī, d. 310/922 (Ibn Khall. 797), Köpr. 401/6, Patna II, $503_{,2701}$.—2. *Mukhtaṣar* (*Mulakhkhaṣ*) by ʿAbd al-ʿAẓīm b. ʿAbd al-Qawī b. ʿAbdallāh al-Mundhirī, d. 656/1258 (p. 367), Berl. 1241, Munich 119, Yeni 275.—3. by Shams al-Dīn, Patna I, $53_{,533}$.—Index *Rijāl*

Ṣaḥīḥ al-imām Muslim by Abū Bakr Aḥmad b. ʿAlī b. Manjawayh al-Iṣfahānī, d. 428/1036, Alex. Taʾr. 70, Muṣṭ. al-Ḥ. 10 (MS d. 664).—On both *Ṣaḥīḥ*s: 1. *Sharḥ mushkilāt al-ṣaḥīḥayn* by al-Qāḍī al-Yaḥṣabī, d. 544/ | 1149, Köpr. 334.—2. 168
al-Jamʿ bayna ʾl-Ṣaḥīḥayn see Suppl. I, 578, 3, 3.–27 commentaries and abstracts are mentioned in Ahlw. 1244.—II. *al-Kunā wal-asmāʾ* Patna II, 538,$_{2898}$.

4. Apart from the two *Ṣaḥīḥ*s, which acquired a canonical status in the Islamic world that has never been challenged, there are four other works that originated in the third century, works that, even though they never attained the authority of the two *Ṣaḥīḥ*s, were nevertheless often conflated with these to form a "canonical six". Common to them all is the somewhat looser criterion of the *shurūṭ* which they applied to the credibility of the traditions. These four works are:

a. The *Sunan* of Abū Dāʾūd Sulaymān b. al-Jārūd b. al-Ashʿath al-Azdī al-Sijistānī, born in 202/817. After extensive study tours during which he went to Baghdad several times, he settled in Basra at the instigation of al-Muwaffaq, who hoped to enrich the city through him and his students after it had been ravaged by the Zanj. He died there on 16 Shawwāl 275/22 February 889. His work is called *Sunan* because it contains traditions that have juridical and ritual significance while excluding everything to do with history, ethics, and dogmatics. Any source that was not unanimously rejected sufficed him as a witness toward the inclusion of a tradition. In the beginning, his book seems to have been a serious competitor for the two *Ṣaḥīḥ*s, and even in the fourth century it was enthusiastically praised by some, but finally it receded into the background more and more.

Ibn Khall. 285, Goldziher 250/1, 255/6, Wüst., *Schaf.* 47. I. *Kitāb al-sunan* Berl. 1246/8, Brill M. 301, Munich 121, Paris 707/8, Bodl. I, 207, Algiers 494, Yeni 208, AS 545/6, NO 822/4, Köpr. 124, Qawala I, 123, print. C. 1280, Lucknow 1888, with glosses Delhi 1890. Commentaries: 1. *Maʿālim al-sunan* by Ḥamd b. Muḥammad b. Ibrāhīm al-Khaṭṭābī, d. 388/998 (p. 174), Ind. Off. 1038,$_5$, Algiers 1274,$_2$, Yeni 293/4, AS 582/3.—2. Maḥmūd b. Aḥmad al-ʿAynī, d. 855/1457 (II, | 52), Cairo, ^{2}I, 169
127.—3. *Mirqāt al-ṣuʿūd* by al-Suyūṭī, d. 911/1505, Köpr. 417.—4. *Fatḥ al-wuʿūd* (*wadūd*) by Abu ʾl-Ḥasan Muḥammad b. ʿAbd al-Ḥamīd al-Sindī al-Ḥanafī, Cairo ^{2}I, 134, 149, Qawala I, 141.—Abstract *al-Mujtabā* by ʿAbd al-ʿAẓīm al-Mundhirī, d. 656/1258 (p. 367), Br. Mus. 1865/8, Garr. 1366, Alex. Ḥad. 58, fragm. Gotha 600.—10 commentaries are mentioned in Ahlw. 1249.—II. *Marāsīl*, indirect traditions, Cairo ^{2}I, 146, print. C. 1310.—III. *Suʾālāt Abī ʿUbayd Muḥammad*

b. ʿAlī b. ʿUthmān al-Ghurrī ʿan Abī Dāʾūd, on the credibility of a number of traditions, revised by Aḥmad b. Muḥammad al-Silafī, d. 576/1180, Paris 2085, Köpr. 292.

b. The *Jāmiʿ* of Abū ʿĪsā Muḥammad b. ʿĪsā b. Sahl al-Tirmidhī. He originated from Būgh near Tirmidh on the Jayḥūn river and was a student of al-Bukhārī.
162 | Having wandered through Khurāsān, Iraq and the Hijaz in a further search for traditions he died in his homeland on 13 Rajab 279/892. In his work he included any tradition that had ever served a *faqīh* as an argument for a decision. Because he records in every case which *madhhab* bases itself on a particular tradition and what the others bring against it, his book is one of the most important sources for the differences between the schools of *fiqh*.

Wüst., *Gesch.* 75, Goldziher 250, 254, ZDMG 38, 671ff. I. *al-Jāmiʿ al-ṣaḥīḥ* Paris 709, Bodl. I, 187, Leid. 1731, Esc. ^{2}1695, Algiers 495, NO 825/8, 1166, AS 547/9, Köpr. 295, Qawala I, 109, Patna I, 46,$_{463/7}$, print. Būlāq 1292.—Commentaries: 1. *ʿAriḍat al-aḥwadhī fī sharḥ al-T.* by Abū Bakr Muḥammad b. al-ʿArabī, d. 543/1148 (suppl. I, 532), C. 1350–2/1933–4.—2. Ibn Sayyid al-Nās, d. 734/1333 (II, 71), in 10 vols., ḤKh. ^{1}II, 3910, 2^{I}, 559, book 5 Berl. 1250, *Dībāja* Gotha 2, 67.—3. *Takmila* on it by al-ʿIrāqī, d. 816/1403 (II 65), Esc. ^{2}1464, Makram 12, Medina ZDMG 90, 109, *Dībāja* Gotha 2, 68, an abstract by Muḥammad b. ʿAqīl al-Bālisī, d. 729/1329 (al-Subkī, *Ṭab. al-Shāf.* II 231), Paris 710/1.—For further commentaries and abstracts see Suppl. I, 268, 948.

II. *Kitāb al-shamāʾil*, on the looks of the prophet, see Nöldeke, *Gesch. d. Qorans* ^{1}XX, MSS see Suppl. I, 268, with Garr. 628/30, Qawala I, 135/6, Makram
170 45, Patna I, 272,$_{2262/3}$, II, 534,$_{2876}$, print. Calcutta 1262, C. 1273, Mirtah | 1282, Fez 1310 and in other places. Commentaries: 1. Aḥmad al-Qasṭallānī, d. 923/1517 (II, 73), Ind. Off 137 (?)—2. Ibrāhīm b. Muḥammad al-Isfarāʾinī, d. 943/1536 (II, 410), Köpr. 315, Rāġib 280, Alex. Ḥad. 6, Patna I, 272,$_{2253}$.—3. *Ashraf al-wasāʾil* by Aḥmad b. Ḥajar al-Haytamī, d. 973/1565 (II, 387), Br. Mus. 149, Ind. Off. 136, Paris 714/5, Algiers 662/4, Köpr. 314, Garr. 631, Alex. Ḥad, 54,$_{1}$, Qawala I, 101.—4. Muḥammad b. Jalāl al-Lārī, d. 979/1571 (II, 420), NO 1033.—5. *Jamʿ al-wasāʾil* by al-Qāriʾ al-Harawī, d. 1014/1605 (II, 394), BDMG 14, AS 597/9, NO 1030/2, Rāġib 282/3, Garr. 632, Qawala I, 113.—6. (based on 5) *al-Fawāʾid al-jalīla al-bahiyya* by Muḥammad b. Qāsim Jassūs, d. 1182/1768 (see Suppl.), Būlāq 1296, C. 1306.—7. ʿAbd al-Raʾūf al-Munāwī, d. 1031/1621 (II, 306), Algiers 1666, Yeni 241/2, Rāġib 281, AS 601, NO 1034, Patna I, 271,$_{254/5}$.—8. *Bahjat al-maḥāfil* by al-Lāqānī, d. 1041/1631 (II, 317), Berl. 9959, Paris 2092, Algiers 1667,$_{3}$, Alex. Had. 9.—9. Bakkār al-Mālikī, Gotha 1829.—10. *al-Mawāhib al-laduniyya* by Ibrāhīm al-Bājūrī,

d. 1277/1861 (II, 486), print. Būlāq 1280, 1309, C. 1290, 1319.—11.–19. See Suppl. (12. Garr. 639, Cairo ^{2}I, 154, Patna II, 534,$_{2878}$).—Abstract *al-Shiyam* by Ismāʿīl b. Ghunaym al-Jawharī, ca. 1160/1747, Paris 716.—with comm. *Ḥulal al-iṣṭifāʾ* Alex. Ḥad. 21.—anon. comm. Paris 4540.—*Ṣalāt al-shamāʾil wa-kanz al-ḥaṣāʾil* by Muḥammad b. Khalīl al-Ḥākim, Alex. *Fawāʾid* 12.

III. see Suppl.—IV. *Nawādir al-uṣūl* Berl. Qu. 1958.

c. The *Sunan* of Abū ʿAbd al-Raḥmān Aḥmad b. ʿAlī b. Shuʿayb al-Nasāʾī. Born in 215/830 in Nasāʾ in Khurāsān, he lived until 302/914 in Egypt and was beaten to death in Ramla on 13 Ṣafar 303/19 August 915, apparently for refusing to recognise the merits of Muʿāwiya. His collection of traditions takes even the minutest details of ritual life into consideration. Thus, he documents all the *duʿā*'s that have to be pronounced between *rakʿas* | with texts that trace their authority back to the Prophet. 163 Popular expressions of piety, such as the *istiʿādhāt*, too, he documents with numerous traditions. In the juridical chapters he includes a mention of templates for all kinds of legal transactions.

| Ibn Khall. 28, Wüst., *Schaf.* 70, Goldziher 232. 1. *Kitāb al-sunan*, MSS see Suppl. 171
with Garr. 1367, Qawala I, 123, Yeni 207, NO 830, AS 552/5, Patna I, 509/12, print. 2 vols. C. 1312, with comm. by al-Suyūṭī and glosses by al-Sindī, C. 1932, 4 vols.—Abstract by the author *al-Mujtabā*, excluding the weak traditions, Delhi 1850, with comm. *Zahr al-rubā* by al-Suyūṭī, d. 911/1505, Patna I, 51,$_{499}$, 2 vols. C. 1213, Kanpur 1882.—2. *Kitāb al-khaṣāʾiṣ fī faḍl ʿAlī b. Abī Ṭālib*, a collection of traditions about ʿAlī and his family, composed in Damascus, Cairo ^{2}I, 114, Bank. XV, 1048/9 (Patna I, 276,$_{2295/6}$), Rāmpūr I, 81, 128, print. C. 1308, see Goldziher, *ZDMG* L, 112.—3. *Kitāb al-ḍuʿafāʾ wal-matrūkīn*, on untrustworthy transmitters, Br. Mus. 864,$_4$, Bodl. II, 378, Patna I, 276,$_{2295/6}$.

d. The *Sunan* of Abū ʿAbdallāh Muḥammad b. Yūsuf b. Māja al-Qazwīnī. Born in 209/824, he made study tours through Khurāsān, Iraq, Egypt, and Syria, and died in 273/886. His work initially found little recognition because he had included many weak traditions. It was only towards the end of the sixth century that it was included among the canonical works.

Wüst., *Gesch.* 71, Goldziher 262/3. *Kitāb al-sunan* Paris 706, Br. Mus. 1564, Algiers 492/3, Rāġib 259/60, NO 811/20, AS 542/4, Köpr. 293, Qawala I, 122, Patna I, 51,$_{506}$, lith. Delhi 1283, with comm. by Fakhr al-Ḥasan, ibid. 1889, by Mughulṭāy al-Ḥikrī, d. 762/1361 (II, 48), Cairo ^{1}I, 269, ^{2}I, 90, 269, Qawala I, 122, Patna I, 52,$_{513}$, *Miṣbāḥ al-zajāja* by al-Suyūṭī (see Suppl.) also Patna I, 62,$_{636}$.

5. Apart from these six works that attained canonical status, some of the other collections that were put together around the same time failed to make a mark. Those which are extant include the *Kitāb al-sunan* by ʿAbdallāh b. ʿAbd al-Raḥmān al-Dārimī al-Samarqandī, a teacher of Muslim, Abū Dāʾūd, and al-Tirmidhī. He was born in 181/797, held the office of *qāḍī* in Samarqand for a short period of time, and died in 255/869. Although his work also includes the non-legal chapters of the traditions, it hardly reaches a third of the size of the other Sunan works. Just like Bukhārī, he wanted to render a service
172 to the *faqīh*, and thus he offers | instructions for the practical application of
164 each tradition, | instructions which are, however, inconsistent. In addition, he discusses the credibility of the *isnād* in every case. It would seem that its subjective character and modest size stood in the way of its recognition as a canonical code of law.

Goldziher 258/9. *Kitāb al-musnad al-jāmiʿ* Leid. 1726, Patna I, 60,$_{616/7}$, lith. Kanpur 1293.

6. A work on Tradition that is lost was by Baqī b. Makhlad al-Qurṭubī, a Spaniard of Christian origin who had studied for fourteen, and then for another twenty, years in the East, and who rendered great service to the spread of the science of Tradition in Spain. He died on 29 Jumādā II 276/30 October 889. Even though his work was still ordered by *isnād*s, within these groups he divided the traditions, like the *muṣannaf* works, by juridical category.

Ibn Bashkuwāl no. 77, al-Ḍabbī p. 229, no. 584, Maqqarī I, 491, 812, Dozy, *ZDMG* XX, 598, Goldziher 260.

7. The last original work on *ḥadīth*, which admittedly only distinguished itself by its artificial character, was written by Muḥammad b. Aḥmad b. Ḥibbān al-Bustī. Born in Būst in Sijistān between Herat and Ghazna, and thus probably of Afghan descent, after lengthy journeys to study he assumed the office of *qāḍī* in Samarqand. His understanding of prophethood as a combination of *ʿilm* and *ʿamal* led to his being accused of heresy, so that he had to escape to Nasā and in 334/945 to Nishapur. When tempers had calmed down in Samarqand he returned there as a teacher of Tradition, dying there, at 80 years old, on 22 Shawwāl 354/21 October 965.

Wüst. *Gesch.* 130, *Schaf.*, 152. 1. *Kitāb al-taqāsīm wal-anwāʿ* ḤKh IV, 9916 ^{2}I, 463, Cairo ^{2}I, 97, *Dībāja* Berl. 1286, revised by ʿAlī b. Balabān al-Fārisī, d. 739/1338,
173 with glosses by Ibn Ḥajar, Br. Mus. 1570, cf. Goldziher | 269, n. 5. Other works

see Suppl. 273, where ad 6. *Kitāb al-ʿaẓama*, Dam. Ẓāh. Majmūʿa 42, 1.—9. *Tafsīr* Medina, *ZDMG* 90, 104.

8. Abū Bakr Muḥammad b. al-Ḥusayn b. ʿAbdallāh al-Ājurrī lived in Ājurr, an area on the western side of Baghdad, where he was a Shāfiʿī jurisconsult and where he wrote monographs on the science of Tradition. In the year 330/942 he made the pilgrimage, following which he stayed in Mecca, where he died in Muḥarram 360/November 970.

| Wüst., *Gesch.* 134. 1. *Kitāb al-arbaʿīn*, a collection of 40 traditions, such as they 165
were compiled from time to time, comprising the minimum amount of knowledge that every believer should have, Berl. 1456, Br. Mus. Suppl. 155.—2. *Kitāb farḍ ṭalab al-ʿilm*, on the question of the amount of knowledge that a believer has to acquire, Berl. 101.—3. *Kitāb akhlāq ḥamalat al-Qurʾān*, on the necessary qualities of experts on the Qurʾān, Berl. 576.—4.–10. see Suppl.—11. *Mā warada fī laylat al-niṣf min Shaʿbān* Cairo ^{2}I, 142.

9. Al-Ḥasan b. ʿAbd al-Raḥman b. Khallād al-Rāmhurmuzī, d. 360/971, wrote

1. *Kitāb al-muḥaddith al-fāṣil bayna ʾl-rāwī wal-wāʿī*, an introduction to the science of Tradition, Berl. 1141, 2 cod. sim. 68 (= Köpr. 397), 71 (= Šehīd ʿA.P. 531); see *Ḥuff.* XII, 22.

10. Aḥmad b. Muḥammad b. Isḥāq al-Dīnawarī b. al-Sunnī was a student of al-Nasāʾī who died in 364/974.

Kitāb ʿamal al-yawm wal-layla, on prayers, ḤKh IV, 8367, ed. by Muḥammad b. Abī ʿAbdallāh b. Abi ʾl-Fatḥ al-Nahrawānī, ca. 540/1145, Berl. 3505, Patna I, 55,5520, see Suppl.

11. Abu ʾl-Ḥasan ʿAlī b. ʿUmar al-Dāraquṭnī al-Shāfiʿī was born in 306/918 in Dāraquṭn, a neighbourhood of Baghdad, and studied under Ibn Abī Dāʾūd and Ibn Durayd. Because of his veneration for al-Sayyid al-Ḥimyarī (p. 82), whose *dīwān* he knew by heart, he was regarded as a closet Shīʿī. Having assisted the vizier of the Ikhshīdid Kāfūr in the composition of a *Musnad*, he became *Imām al-qurrāʾ* in Baghdad, where he died on 5 Dhu ʾl-Qaʿda 385/2 December 995.

| Ibn Khall. 407, *Ḥuff.* XII, 70, Wüst., *Schaf.* 235. *Kitāb al-sunan* AS 550, on which 174
Takhrīj al-aḥādīth al-ḍiʿāf min (Deft. *wa*) *sunan al-Dāraquṭnī* by Abū ʿAbdallāh

b. Yaḥyā al-Ghālī, ibid. 464.—2.–13. see Suppl. I, 275, 949 (6. Patna I, $55_{549/51}$, 8 ibid. I, 39_{398}),—In his *Kitāb al-istidrākāt wal-tatabbuʿ* he showed the weaknesses of 200 traditions in the two *Ṣaḥīḥ*s; see Goldziher, 257.

12. Abū Sulaymān Ḥamd (usually distorted to Aḥmad) b. Muḥammad b. Ibrāhīm al-Khaṭṭābī al-Bustī was both a poet and a specialist of Tradition. He was born in 319/931 and wrote critical and expository works on the canonical collections. Towards the end of his life he inclined to mysticism and joined a Sufi convent (*ribāṭ*) on the banks of the Hilmand in Būst, in Sijistān. He died there on 16 Rabīʿ II 386/9 May 996 (or, according to others, in 388/998).

Al-Thaʿālibī, *Yatīma* IV, 231/3, Ibn Khall. 196, *Ḥuff.* XIII, 20, *Khiz.* I, 282. 1. *Kitāb iṣlāḥ ghalaṭ al-muḥaddithīn* AS 457, print. C. 1936.—2. Commentary on Bukhārī, Suppl. p. 261, on Abū Dāʾūd p. 168.—3. *Gharīb al-ḥadīth*, see Weisweiler *Ist. Hdssstudien* 137.—4. *Kitāb al-ʿUzla* Garr. 1421, print. C. 1936.—5.–8. see Suppl. (6. Cairo ^{2}I, 149, Patna II, 504_{2706}).—9. *Risāla fi 'l-ghunya ʿani 'l-kalām wa-ahlihi* is quoted by Ibn Taymiyya, *Majmūʿat al-rasāʾil al-kubrā* I, 439, penult.

13. Abū Ḥafṣ ʿUmar b. Aḥmad b. ʿUthmān b. Shāhīn, whose family hailed from Marwarrūdh, was born in Ṣafar 297/November 909. He started his studies of Tradition as early as 308/920, and then became a specialist of Tradition and a preacher in Baghdad. He supposedly authored 330 works, and died on 12 Dhu 'l-Ḥijja 385/8 January 995.

Wüst., 150. *Kitāb nāsikh al-ḥadīth wa-mansūkhuhu* Paris 718.

14. Abū Bakr Muḥammad b. ʿUmar b. ʿAlī b. Muḥammad b. Zunbūr al-Warrāq was regarded as a weak traditionalist and died in 390/1000 or 396/1005.

Ibn al-Khaṭīb, *Taʾr. Baghdād* III, 35/6, al-Samʿānī, *Ansāb* 580r. *Kitāb al-ʿālim*
175 *wal-mutaʿallim*, transmitted by Abū Naṣr | b. Abi 'l-Ḥusayn Muḥammad b. Muḥammad b. Ḥāmid b. Abī Bakr al-Srmnjī in Muḥarram 396/October 1005, Alex. Fun. $144_{,1}$.

166 | 15. Abu 'l-Ḥusayn Muḥammad al-Ghassānī, d. 402/1011, wrote a

Musnad with an alphabetical ordering of the sources, Landberg, Cat. Brill p. 12, no. 37, see Goldziher 229.

16. Muḥammad b. ʿAbdallāh b. Muḥammad al-Ḥākim al-Nīsābūrī b. al-Bayyiʿ, d. 3 Ṣafar 405/3 August 1014, see Suppl. I, 276.

Wüst., 167. 1. *Kitāb al-mustadrak ʿala ʾl-ṣaḥīḥayn*, in which he defended the credibility of several traditions that had been omitted from the *Ṣaḥīḥ*s and in which he proved that the two *Ṣaḥīḥ*s suppressed many *ḥadīth*s that, according to their own *shurūṭ*, should be regarded as entirely sound, cf. Goldziher 273, MSS see Suppl., Cairo ^{2}I, 146, Medina, *ZDMG* 90, 111, Patna I, $60,_{606}$. *Mukhtaṣar* with refuting glosses by al-Dhahabī, d. 748/1347 (II, 46), ḤKh V, 521, Cairo ^{1}I, 417, Berl. Qu. 1127, *Dībāja* Gotha $2,_{21}$.—2. *al-Madkhal ilā maʿrifat al-ṣaḥīḥ wal-saqīm min al-akhbār al-marwiyya* or *al-Madkhal ila ʾl-iklīl*, Halet Efendi see *Dharīʿa* II, $280,_{1138}$; on this work, ʿAbd al-Ghanī b. Saʿīd b. ʿAlī al-Azdī al-Ḥajrī, d. 409/1008 (Suppl. I, 281), wrote *Kitāb al-awhām allatī fi ʾl-M.*, a correction of mistakes and oversights that he did not hold so much against the author himself as against the copyists and the disseminators; he offered his work to the author who thanked him for this, ḤKh V, 11677, Berl. 1033, Leipz. 892.—3. *Maʿrifat uṣūl ʿulūm al-ḥadīth*, on 52 classes of traditionalists, AS 449, Berl. sim. 69, under the title *Maʿrifat ʿulūm al-ḥadīth wa-anwāʿihi* Alex. Ḥad. 63.—4. *Taʾrīkh Nīshābūr* ḤKh ^{1}II, 155/6, ^{2}I, 308, Bartold, *Turkestan*, 16, Pers. table of contents in Bursa, Ḥü. Čelebī Taʾr. 12, see Hamdani, *JRAS* 1938, 561.

17. Abū Bakr Muḥammad b. al-Ḥasan b. Fūrak al-Anṣārī al-Iṣfahānī was a philosopher, philologist, and preacher. Having studied in Baghdad he went to Rayy, and from there to Nishapur, where he had a successful career as a teacher and author. Later he accepted an invitation by Maḥmūd to come to Ghazna where, being an Ashʿarī, he had a dispute with the Karrāmiyya. It was on his way back from there that he was allegedly poisoned in 406/1015. See Suppl.

| Wüst., *Gesch.* 170. 1. *Kitāb al-ḥudūd fi ʾl-uṣūl*, definitions regarding the foun- 176
dations of Ḥanafī law, Br. Mus. $421,_{7}$, Ibn Quṭlūbughā 185.—2. His main work, under various titles (see Suppl.), also as *Sharḥ mushkil al-ḥadīth*, Alex. Ḥad. 32, Patna I, $61,_{628}$, as *Bayān mushkil al-ḥadīth*, selection after MSS in Leipzig, Leiden, London and the Vatican by R.A. Köbert, *Analecta or.* 22, Rome (Pont. Inst. Bibl.) 1941.—3. *Kitāb asmāʾ al-rijāl* (author?) Berl. 9918.—4. *al-Niẓāmī fī uṣūl al-dīn*, a refutation of dogmatic sects, AS 2378.

18. Abu ʾl-Qāsim Tammām b. Muḥammad b. ʿAbdallāh b. Jaʿfar b. al-Junayd al-Rāzī, who was born in 330/941 in Damascus and died on 3 Muḥarram 414/29 March 1023.

Fawāʾid al-ḥadīth Leid. 1733, Dam. ʿUm. $25_{,339}$.

167 | 19. The critical study of the sources developed into the separate science of *ʿIlm al-rijāl* that, prepared by the *Ṭabaqāt* of Ibn Saʿd and *Taʾrīkh*-works by al-Bukhārī, soon gave rise to a rich literature; see Suppl. I, 278/81 (with Dam. ʿUm. $25_{,362}$, h. 3, Patna I, $62_{,639/40}$).

Chapter 7. *Fiqh* 168

See Suppl. I, 282/3

Older literature: A. v. Kremer, *Culturgeschichte des Islāms* I, 470/500, E. Sachau, Zur ältesten Geschichte des muhammedanischen Rechts, *SBWA* 65 (1875), 669/723, A. Sprenger, Eine Skizze der Entwicklungsgeschichte des muslimischen Gesetzes, *Z. f. vergl. Rechtswiss.* X, 1/31, Goldziher, *Die Ẓāhiriten* 3/19, *MSt.* II, 73/8.

1 *The Ḥanafīs*

Die Krone der Lebensbeschreibungen, enthaltend die Klassen der Ḥanefiten von Zayn al-Dīn Qāsim b. Qutlūbughā (II, 82), zum erstenmale hsg. und mit Anm. u. einem Index begleitet v. G. Flügel, Leipzig 1862 (*Abh. f. d. K. d. M.* I, no. 3). G. Flügel, *die Klassen der Ḥanefitischen Rechtsgelehrten, Abh. d. Kgl. Säch. Ges. d. Wiss.* VIII, *ph.-hist.* CLIII, Leipzig 1863.

1. Abū Ḥanīfa al-Nuʿmān b. Thābit b. Zūṭa (according to others ʿAtīk b. Zawṭara), who died 150/767 or 151, see Suppl. 284/7.

Ad I, *al-Fiqh al-akbar*, commentaries: 5. Abu ʾl-Muntahā Aḥmad b. Muḥammad al-Maghnīsāwī, completed in 939/1532, also Berl. Brill M. 177, BDMG 32, Garr. 1666/8, Alex. Tawḥīd 23, Mawāʿiẓ $35_{,3}$, Fun. $76_{,1}$, $156_{,2}$, $194_{,9}$, Qawala I, 192.—6. *al-Manḥ al-azhar*, BDMG 30b, 31a, Garr. $2091_{,4}$, Patna I, $122_{,1223/6}$.—17. anon. *Mukhtaṣar al-ḥikam al-nabawiyya* Alex. Tawḥīd 43.—V. *Musnad Abī Ḥ., riwāyat al-Khwārizmī* also Alex. Ḥad. $16_{,2}$, Qilič ʿAlī 273/4, Patna I, $47_{,481}$, II, $502_{,2688}$, *riwāyat Ḥusām al-Dīn al-Rāzī*, Serāi 364, commentaries: al-Qāriʾ al-Harawī, Patna I, $53_{,537}$, ʿAbīd al-Sindī, ibid. $54_{,538}$.—VI. *Waṣiyya* Garr. 1769, Qawala I, 213, 270.—VII. *Waṣiyya* to his son Ḥammād, Alex. Fun. $156_{,7}$.—IX. *Waṣiyya* to his students, Heid. *ZDMG* 91, 397.—IXa. *Waṣiyya* to the *qāḍī* Abū Yūsuf, Alex. Fun. $156_{,7}$.—X. *Waṣāyā*, Patna II, $429_{,2603,2}$.—XI. *Kitāb al-ʿālim wal-mutaʿallim*, Garr. $2021_{,1}$, $2122_{,1}$, Rāmpūr I, $318_{,270}$.—XII. *al-Qaṣīda al-Nuʿmāniyya*, Heid. ZDMG 91, $386_{,327}$.—XV. *Maʿrifat al-madhāhib*, Rāmpūr I, $322_{,305b}$, $716_{,11}$.—XVI. *Naṣāʾiḥ* with comm. *Zubdat al-N.* by ʿUthmān b. Muṣṭafā, completed 1039/1629, Alex. Mawāʿiẓ 36, Fun. $102_{,5}$.—XVII. *Ḍawābiṭ al-thalātha*, comm. *al-Wuṣūl ila ʾl-kanz al-akbar wa-ilā mā huwa ʾl-anfaʿ min al-kibrīt al-aḥmar* by Abū Ḥasan Garr. $2120_{,3}$.—XVIII. *Risāla fi ʾl-farāʾiḍ* Patna II, $362_{,2545,3}$.—XIX. *al-Duʿāʾ al-maʾthūr ʿan Abī Ḥanīfa* ibid. $423_{,2593/6}$. 177

171 | 2. Abū Ḥanīfa's most important student was Abū Yūsuf Yaʿqūb b. Ibrāhīm b. Ḥabīb al-Kūfī al-Anṣārī, who was born in 113/731 in Kufa, and who had an old Arabian background. He was appointed as a *qāḍī* in Baghdad by al-Hādī and also kept his post under Hārūn until his death on 5 Rabīʿ I 182/21 April 798. He was the first *qāḍi 'l-quḍāt* in Islam to occupy all the magistracies, and this is how he rendered his master's doctrine dominant. But, contrary to him, he is believed to have given more weight to oral transmission than to *raʾy*.

Flügel 282, Goldziher, *MSt* II, 77. *Kitāb al-kharāj*, on land tax according to the Qurʾān and Tradition, with an admonishing foreword addressed to Hārūn, ed. by his student Muḥammad b. al-Ḥasan al-Shaybānī, Berl. 5605/6, Paris 2452/3, Ind. Off. 1511, AS 1145, NO 1516/7, Köpr. 559/60, Rāmpūr I, 239, 465/6. Comm. *Fiqh al-mulūk* (see Suppl. I 950) also Medina, *ZDMG* 90, 115.

178 | 3. His student Muḥammad b. al-Ḥasan al-Shaybānī was born in Wāsiṭ between 131–5/748–52 and grew up in Kufa. Even though he had heard the lectures of Abū Ḥanīfa, he owed his education mainly to Abū Yūsuf. In order to deepen his knowledge of Tradition he also went to Mālik b. Anas in Medina. Having completed his studies, he became a *qāḍī* in Raqqa, but was removed from this office in 187/803. He then lived in Baghdad, accompanied the caliph Hārūn to Rayy in 189/804, and died in neighbouring Rambūya (Ṭab. III, 2521).

172 | Ibn Quṭlūb. no. 159, Flügel 283, Goldziher, loc. cit., Cherbonneau, *JA* s. IV, v. XX, 406/19. I. *Kitāb al-mabsūṭ* or *Kitāb al-aṣl fi 'l-furūʿ*, whose first redaction may have had its origins with Abū Yūsuf (ḤKh [1]I, 318, no. 818, [2]107), AS 1026, NO 1377, Cairo [1]III, 6, Qawala I, 306, abstract by Muḥammad b. Ibrāhīm, written in 705/1305, Cairo [1]III, 216, 225.—Part of an anonymous comm. Ind. Off. 1422.

II. *al-Ziyādāt*, and additions to it, with *taʿlīq* by the author, Cairo [1]III, 27.—Commentaries: 1. Aḥmad b. Muḥammad al-Bukhārī, d. 586/1190, Cairo [1]III, 73.—2. Fakr al-Dīn Qāḍīkhān, d. 592/1196 (p. 376), Cairo [1]III, 74, Alex. Fiqh Ḥan. 13, Bank. XIX, 1594, abstract by Ṣadr al-Dīn Sulaymān, fragm. Berl. 4441.

III. *al-Jāmiʿ al-kabīr*, on the *furūʿ*, the derived laws, Yeni 392, Cairo [1]III, 34, print. C. 1356.—Commentaries: 1. Aḥmad b. ʿAlī al-Jaṣṣāṣ (p. 191), d. 370/980, Cairo [1]III, 69.—2. Aḥmad b. Muḥammad al-Sarakhsī, d. 483/1090, ibid. 70.—2a. ʿUmar b. ʿAbd al-ʿAzīz b. Māza al-Ṣadr al-Shahīd, d. 536/1141 (p. 374), Welīeddīn 1157, Alex. Fiqh. Ḥan. 17.—3. Muḥammad b. Aḥmad al-Ḥaṣīrī al-Bukhārī, d. 636/1238 (p. 380), a. *al-Taḥrīr* (see Suppl.), Garr. 1685, Alex. Fiqh Ḥan. 11, Cairo [1]III, 17, Rāmpūr I, 174,76/9.—b. *al-Wajīz* also Bank. XIX, 1592.—4. ʿAbd

al-Muṭṭalib b. al-Faḍl al-Hāshimī al-Ḥalabī, d. 616/1219, Cairo [1]III, 67.—5. *Kashf al-Jāmiʿ al-kabīr* by al-Nasafī, d. 537/1142 (p. 427), Berl. Qu. 1343.—6. ʿUthmān b. Muṣṭafā, completed 1159/1746, Br. Mus. Suppl. 252.—7. Anon., *al-Taysīr*, Cairo [1]III, 68.—Abstracts: 1. *al-Talkhīṣ* by Muḥammad b. ʿAbbād al-Khilāṭī, d. 652/1254 (p. 381), Berl. 4508, Qawala I, 314. Commentaries: a. ʿAlī b. Balabān al-Fārisī, d. 739/1338, Yeni 426/7, Cairo [1]III, 19, abridged by Sirāj al-Dīn ʿUmar b. Isḥāq al-Shiblī, d. 773/1371 (II, 80), Berl. 4509.—b. al-Bābartī, d. 827/1424 | (II, 225), 179
Cairo [1]III, 68.—c. Muḥammad b. Sihāb al-Kardarī al-Fārisī, d. 739/1338, Yeni 426/7, Cairo [1]III, 19.—d. Masʿūd b. Muḥammad al-Ghujduwānī, Yeni 428/9, Cairo [1]III, 74.—e. Abstract thereof by ʿUmar al-Taftāzānī, d. 792/1390 (II, 215), Yeni 428, Dāmādzāde 848.—2. Versified and commented upon by Aḥmad b. Abi 'l-Mu'ayyad al-Maḥmūdī al-Nasafī, d. 519/1125, written in 515/1121, Paris 820, Pet. AM 104, Cairo[1]III 143. Comm. by Maḥmūd b. Ṣāʿid al-Ḥārithī, d. 606/1209, Cairo [1]III, 28.

IV. *al-Jāmiʿ al-ṣaghīr*, possibly composed together with Abū Yūsuf, NO 1438/9, Cairo [1]III, 32, Garr. 1672/3, Alex. Fiqh Ḥan. 17, printed in the margin of the *Kitāb al-kharāj*, Būlāq 1302. Commentaries: ʿAlī b. Muḥammad al-Pazdawī, d. 482/1089 (p. 373), Rāmpūr I, 207,$_{262}$, revised and explicated by ʿUmar b. ʿAbd al-ʿAzīz b. Māza al-Ṣadr al-Shahīd, d. 536/1141, Berl. 4437, Yeni 434, Cairo [1]III, 32, Ind. Off. 1512, Bank. XIX, 1593, Alex. Fiqh Ḥan. 32, Rāmpūr I, 207,$_{260}$.—Aḥmad b. Muḥammad b. ʿUmar al-Bukhārī, d. 586/1190, Gotha 998, Munich 261/3, Dresd. 105, Leid. 1774, Paris 821/2, Yeni 435, Cairo [1]III, 73.—Ḥasan b. Manṣūr Qāḍīkhān, d. 592/1196 (p. 376), Yeni 436, Cairo [1]III, 74, Alex. Fiqh Ḥan. 32, Rāmpūr I, 206,$_{289}$.—Maḥmūd b. Aḥmad al-Ḥaṣīrī, d. 636/1238 (p. 380), Patna I 91,$_{928}$.—Versifications: a. al-Nasafī, d. 537/1142, Cairo [1]III, 123, 143.—b. Badr al-Dīn Abū Naṣr Maḥmūd b. Abī Bakr al-Farāhī, d. 617/1220, Paris 823, Cairo [1]III, 107.—20 other revisions are mentioned in Ahlw. 4439.

V. *Kitāb al-āthār*, the traditional foundations of the doctrine of Abū Ḥanīfa, Cairo [1]III, 2, Bank. XIX, 1595, see Goldziher, *MSt.* II, 77.

VI. *Kitāb al-siyar al-kabīr*, on the laws of war, his last work, which he wrote after leaving Iraq, comm. by Muḥammad b. Aḥmad b. Abi 'l-Sarakhsī, d. 495/1101, Berl. 4975, Vienna 1778, Leid. 1775, Paris 784/5, 837/8, Yeni 440/1, Cairo [1]III, 70, Qawala I 361.

VII. A work on *uṣūl al-fiqh*, Paris 784, comm. by al-Sarakhsī, d. 483/1090, however, allegedly composed in 499, ibid. 785, probably identical with the *Kitāb al-aṣl*, Cairo [1]III, 102 (Suppl. I, 292).

VIII. *ʿAqīda* in 79 verses, of doubtful authenticity because the custom for every scholar to compose such an *ʿaqīda* only developed later, and also because we know of no ancient commentary, Berl. 1933/34, Goth. 659/60, Paris 4585,

Bodl. I, $811_{,3}$, $127_{,3}$, II, 596, Pet. Chanykow $161_{,2}$. Commentaries by Muḥammad b. ʿAlī b. Qāḍī ʿAjlūn al-Zaraʿī, d. 876/1471, Gotha 661, $1299_{,13}$, Paris $3024_{,6}$, Garr.
180 1563, $2003_{,18}$, Rāmpūr I, $315_{,252}$, and ʿAlawān | b. ʿAlī b. ʿAṭiyya al-Ḥamawī, d. 936/1539 (II, 333), Berl. 1935, Dam. ʿUm. $62_{,42}$, Alex. Fun. 115, 2, attributed to Najm al-Dīn Abū ʿAlī Muḥammad al-ʿAjlūnī, Garr. $2003_{,8}$, Rāmpūr I, $284_{,21}$ (*Badīʿ al-maʿānī*).

X. *al-Iktisāb fi 'l-rizq al-mustaṭāb* see Suppl., print. C. 1938.

XI. *Kitāb al-ḥujaj* see Suppl., Patna I, $68_{,869}$.

XII. *Qaṣīda* ibid. $377_{,6561,5}$.

173 | 4. A student of al-Shaybānī was Abū Sulaymān Mūsā b. Sulaymān al-Jūzajānī, who rejected the magistracy offered to him by al-Maʾmūn, and who died sometime after 280/893.

Flügel 286. *Kitāb al-shurūṭ al-kabīr* Cairo ^{2}I, 455. An untitled work, which is actually al-Shaybānī's *Kitāb al-aṣl,* is mistakenly attributed to him in Cairo ^{1}III, 102.

4a. Another student of al-Shaybānī was ʿĪsā b. Abān.

Al-Ḥujja al-ṣaghīra Bank. XIX, 1596, s. ḤKh III, $16_{,4403}$, ^{2}I, 631.

5. Hilāl b. Yaḥyā b. Muslim al-Baṣrī received the nickname Hilāl al-Raʾy because he allowed *raʾy* to have a greater influence in legal matters again. He died in 245/859.

Ibn Quṭlūbughā, no. 246. *Kitāb aḥkām al-waqf,* on the law concerning pious endowments, Leid. 1776, Cairo ^{1}III 116, Alex. Fiqh Ḥan. 4, Rāmpūr I, $240_{,477}$ (see Suppl.), print. Hyderabad 1355.

5a. Yaḥyā b. Bakr al-Ḥanafī.

Fihrist 208, Ibn Quṭlūbughā no. 257, see Suppl. with 2. *Fī bayān al-iʿtiqād* also Alex. Fiqh Ḥan. 54, Qawala I, 186.—3. *Asīr al-malāḥida fi 'l-alfāẓ al-mukaffira* Alex. Fiqh Ḥan. 6, Fun. I, $194_{,10}$.

6. At the forefront of the third generation of Ḥanafī scholars stands Abū Bakr Aḥmad b. ʿUmar (ʿAmr) al-Shaybānī al-Khaṣṣāf, who belonged to the retinue of Prince Muḥammad b. Wāthiq, who would later be the caliph al-Muhtadī. When

the latter was killed after barely a year in power in 256/870 Turkish soldiers plundered the former's house, too, and he lost his library. He died in 261/874.

| *Fihrist* 206, Ibn Quṭlūbughā no. 15, Flügel 291. 1. *Kitāb aḥkām al-waqf* (*wuqūf,* 181
awqāf) Berl. 4761, Qu. 1803, Goth. 1127, Leid. 1778, AS 1012, NO 1891, Yeni 349/50, Cairo ^{1}III, 3, 116, 124, see Goldziher, *MSt.* II, 68.—2. *Kitāb adab al-qāḍī* see Suppl. Qawala I, 304, a handbook for the judge, with a commentary: a. Aḥmad b. ʿAlī al-Jaṣṣāṣ al-Rāzī, d. 370/980 (p. 191), Leid. 1777, Patna I, 92,$_{933}$.—b. ʿUmar b. ʿAbd al-ʿAzīz b. Māza al-Ṣadr al-Shahīd, d. 536/1141 (p. 374), Yeni 356/7, 423, Köpr. 531/2, Cairo ^{1}III, 72, Alex. Fiqh Ḥan. 31, Ind. Off. 1514, Āṣaf. 1088.—c. Muḥammad b. ʿAlī al-Qāʿidī al-Khujandī, Yeni 424.—3. *Kitāb al-ḥiyal wal-makhārij,* directives on how to behave in social situations and in one's doings and dealings so as to profit from one's situation, Berl. 4972/3, AS 1143, Cairo ^{1}III, 42, Alex. Fiqh Ḥan. 23, abstract Ind. Off. 1696.

7. Abū Jaʿfar Aḥmad b. Muḥammad b. Salāma al-Ḥajrī al-Ṭaḥāwī was born in Ṭaḥā in Egypt in 229/843 (or, according to others, in 228 or 238). Having fallen out with his uncle and first teacher, the Shāfiʿī al-Muzanī (see p. 190), he went to Syria where he joined the Ḥanafī Abū Ḥāzim. He then became one of the most important Ḥanafī scholars. He died in 321/933.

| Ibn Khall. 27, Flügel, p. 296, Wüst., *Gesch.* 102. 1. *Kitāb al-sunan* AS 551, Cairo 174
^{1}I, 424, comm. by al-ʿAynī, d. 855/1451 (II, 52), ibid. 396, 442, Garr. 1394.—2. (*Sharḥ*) *Maʿāni ʾl-āthār* Berl. 1263/5, Yeni 571, Qawala I, 153, Patna I, 54,$_{542/4}$, print. Lucknow 1300/2, 2 vols.—3. *Kitāb mushkil al-āthār* Berl. 1266/7, abstract by Sulaymān b. Khalaf al-Bājī, d. 474/1081 (p. 419), Br. Mus. 1569.—4. *Kitāb al-jāmiʿ al-kabīr fi ʾl-shurūṭ* Berl. sim. 41/2, Cairo ^{1}III, 102.—5. *Kitāb ikhtilāf al-fuqahāʾ* Cairo ^{1}III, 3.—6. *al-Mukhtaṣar fi ʾl-fiqh,* commentaries: a. Aḥmad b. ʿAlī al-Jaṣṣāṣ, d. 370/980, Cairo ^{1}III, 69.—b. Bahāʾ al-Dīn al-Samarqandī, d. 535/1140, Yeni 457/8.—c. Aḥmad b. Manṣūr al-Isbījābī, d. ca. 480/1087 (see Suppl.), also Bombay no. 48.—7. *Risāla* (or *Muqaddima*) *fī uṣūl al-dīn* or *ʿAqīdat ahl al-sunna wal-jamāʿa* Berl. 1938/9, Gotha 663, Cairo ^{1}II, 50, Köpr. 348, print. Kazan 1893 (with the title *Bayān al-sunna*).—Commentaries: a. Najm al-Dīn Mankubars al-Qubrusī al-Turkī, d. 652/1254, Yeni 760, AS 2311, Köpr. 861, Garr. 2127, 1, Alex. Tawḥīd 25, Rāmpūr I, 315,$_{253}$.—b. ʿUmar b. Isḥāq al-Hindī,
| d. 773/1371, Cairo ^{1}II, 30.—c. *Nūr al-yaqīn fī uṣūl al-dīn* by Kāfī al-Āqḥiṣārī, 182
d. 1025/1616 (II, 443), Leipz. 1902.—d. Sirāj al-Dīn Hibatallāh b. Aḥmad b. al-Muʿallā al-Turkistānī, d. 733/1333, Garr. 1543.—e. Maḥmūd b. Aḥmad b. Masʿūd al-Qūnawī, d. 770/1368 (or, according to others, in 797/1395) (II, 81),

Alex. Tawḥīd 30 (which has "Muḥammad", see Esc.²1563,3).—f. Anonymous, Berl. 1940, anonymous version on the order of Sayf al-Dīn al-Nāṣirī (d. 758/1357, Weil, *Gesch d. Chal.* IV, 501), ḤKh ¹IV, 216, Gotha 665, Ind. Off. 4569 (*JRAS* 1939, 359).—8. *Ṣaḥīḥ al-āthār* Patna I, 54,548.

8. Isḥāq b. Ibrāhīm al-Shāshī al-Samarqandī worked in various regions of Egypt as a *qāḍī* and died in 325/937.

The *Kitāb al-uṣūl*, attributed to him in various Indian printings and manuscripts (see Suppl.), see also Qawala I, 274, Cairo ²I, 378, Rāmpūr I, 267,11, Patna I, 66,684, is the work of a later scholar, called Niẓām al-Dīn al-Shāshī in *Ḥad. Ḥan.* 270, which moves it to the seventh century (Bank. XIX 12), while Pesh. 592 calls him Badr al-Dīn al-Shirwānī and fixes him tentatively around 752 or 852. The oldest commentary mentioned in ḤKh V, 81, was written by Muḥammad b. Ḥasan al-Farāhī in 781, later than the one by Mawlawī ʿAynallāh, *Fuṣūl al-ḥawādith fī uṣūl al-Shāshī*, Pet. AM Buch. 402, print. Delhi 1302.

9. Muḥammad b. Muḥammad b. Aḥmad al-Marwazī al-Ḥākim was a judge in Bukhārā and was later appointed vizier by the Sāmānid Ḥamīd, the ruler of Khurāsān. After a battle in Rabīʿ II 334/November 945 he fell into the hands of the Turks and was tied to two treetops, whose flinging apart then precipitated his death. This is why he was revered as *al-Shahīd*, "The Martyr."

Flügel 296. His *al-Kāfī fi 'l-fiqh* Berl. Qu. 1662, AS 1362/3, Cairo ¹III, 101, I, 455, is based on the *Jāmiʿ* and *Ziyādāt* of al-Shaybānī.

10. Abu 'l-Qāsim Isḥāq b. Muḥammad b. al-Ḥakīm al-Samarqandī al-Māturīdī was a judge in Samarqand for a considerable period of time, and died on 10 Muḥarram 342/28 May 953. He was more interested in questions of dogmatics than in *fiqh*.

183 | 1. *Kitāb al-sawād al-aʿẓam* (see Suppl.), with Garr. 2127,2, Rāmpūr I, 304,74, print. Būlāq 1253. Commentaries by Sulaymān b. Khalaf al-Bājī, d. 474/1081, Cairo I, 430, al-Harawī ibid. 362, and Muḥammad b. ʿAbd al-Bāqī al-Zuqānī, d. 1122/1710, ibid. 363.—2. *Risāla fī bayān anna 'l-īmān juzʾ min al-ʿamal*, print. in *Majmūʿa*, Istanbul 1288 (Qawala I, 186).

11. Abu 'l-Qāsim Ismāʿīl b. al-Ḥasan (Ḥusayn) b. ʿAlī al-Bayhaqī, d. 402/1011, wrote:

Al-Shāmil, legal issues in fatwas based on the *Mabsūṭ* and *Ziyādāt*, Cairo [1]III, 65.

12. Abu 'l-Ḥusayn Aḥmad b. Muḥammad al-Qudūrī al-Baghdādī, b. 362/972, d. 5 Rajab 428/24 April 1037, wrote a much commented-upon handbook on Ḥanafī *furūʿ* that is still often used today.

| Ibn Khall. 29, Ibn Quṭlūbughā no. 13, Flügel, p. 305. I. *Mukhtaṣar al-Qudūrī*, 175
Berl. 4451/2, Gotha 994/5 (where other MSS are listed, additionally), BDMG 33/4, Paris 827/33, Algiers 978/80, Br. Mus. 267, Garr. 1674/6, Flor. Naz. 7, AS 1424/31, Yeni 527, Alex. Fiqh Ḥan. 62, Qawala I, 392/3, Teh. Sip. I, 509, Aligarh $102_{,13}$, Bank. XIX, 1600/1, Ind. Off. 1516/9, print. Delhi 1847, Istanbul 1291, 1309, Kazan 1880, with comm. Lucknow 1338, whence the section on Islamic marital law, translated by G. Helmsdörfer, Frankfurt 1832.—The *Kitāb al-siyar* in *Analecta Arabica*, ed. Rosenmüller, vol. I, Leipzig 1825.—Commentaries: a. Aḥmad b. Muḥammad b. al-Aqṭaʿ al-Baghdādī, d. 474/1081, Paris 834, Cairo [1]III, 76.—b. (5) see Suppl.—c. (4) Khwāharzāde Muḥammad b. al-Ḥusayn Abū Bakr al-Bukhārī, d. 482/1089, Yeni 404, Köpr. 589, Alex. Fiqh Ḥan. 21.—d. (6) *Khulāṣat al-dalāʾil fī tanqīḥ al-masāʾil* by ʿAlī b. Aḥmad b. Makkī al-Rāzī, d. 598/1201, Gotha 996, Munich 258, Pet. AM 107, AS 1261, Yeni 461, NO 1263, Alex. Fiqh Ḥan. 24.—e. *al-Fawāʾid al-badriyya* by Ḥamīd al-Dīn ʿAlī b. Muḥammad b. ʿAlī al-Ḍarīr al-Rāshī al-Bukhārī, d. 667/1268, Qawala I, 381.—f. (8) *al-Jawhara al-nayyira* by Abū Bakr b. ʿAlī al-Ḥaddād al-ʿAbbādī, d. 880/1397 (II, 189), Berl. 4453, Paris 835, AS 1264/6, Cairo [1]III, 37, Qawala I, 319, Rāmpūr I, $184_{,137}$, Aligarh 106, 67/8, Bank. XIX, 1604, print. Lahore 1328.—g. *al-Sirāj al-wahhāj* by the same author, Yeni 462/5, Köpr. 590/4, Cairo [1]III, 63, Bank. XIX, 1603.—h. *Jāmiʿ al-muḍmarāt wal-mushkilāt* by Yūsuf b. ʿUmar b. Yūsuf al-Ṣūfī al-Kādūzī,
ca. 800/1397, Ind. Off. | 1521/2, Rāmpūr I, $183_{,127}$.—i. *al-Yanābīʿ fī maʿrifat al-uṣūl* 184
wal-tafārīʿ by Rashid al-Dīn Abū ʿAbdallāh Muḥammad b. Ramaḍān al-Rūmī al-Shiblī, ca. 723/1323, ḤKh V, 453, VI, 53, Berl. Qu. 1848, Alex. Fiqh Ḥan. 73, Dam. ʿUm. $57_{,21}$.—k. (7) *al-Mujtabā* by Mukhtār b. Maḥmūd al-Zāhidī, d. 658/1260 (p. 382), AS 1262, Yeni 469, Bank. XIX, 1602.—l. (12) by ʿAbd al-Ghanī al-Maydānī, written in 1268/1851, Istanbul 1275, Qawala I, 386.—m. anon., Munich 257, Br. Mus. 1600, Algiers 983/4, Ind. Off. 1520 (*Fātiḥ al-Q.*).—16 commentaries, 6 abstracts, two supplements, and two versifications in Ahlw. 4454.—*Taṣḥīḥ al-Q.* by Qāsim b. ʿAlī b. Quṭlūbughā, d. 879/1474 (II, 82), Alex. Fiqh Ḥan. 13.—IIa. *Takmilat al-mukhtaṣar* Munich 259 (see Suppl.).—IIb. *Mushkilāt al-Q.* by the author (?), Alex. Fun. $87_{,1}$.—III. *al-Tajrīd*, a defence of Abū Ḥanīfa against al-Shāfiʿī, Br. Mus. 1194, Cairo [1]III, 17 with comm. (part II), Berl. 4455.

13. Abū Zayd ʿAbdallāh (ʿUbaydallāh) b. ʿUmar b. ʿĪsā al-Dabūsi is regarded as the founder of *ʿilm al-khilāf*, the science of the doctrines that distinguish the different *madhhabs*.[1] He died in Bukhārā in 430/1039.

Ibn Khall. 309, Ibn Quṭlūbughā, no. 107, 266, Flügel 274. 1. *al-Amad al-aqṣā*, moral and dogmatic admonitions, Berl. Oct. 1495, Esc.^{2}559.—2. *Taqwīm al-adilla fī uṣūl al-fiqh* or *Taqwīm uṣūl al-fiqh wa-taḥdīd adillat al-sharʿ* Yeni 310, Cairo ^{2}I, 381, anon. abstract Gotha 929.—3. *Taʾsīs al-naẓar*, on controversial legal issues, Cairo ^{1}III, 15, 124, ^{2}I, 379.—4. *Asrār al-uṣūl wal-furūʿ* (see Suppl.) Rāmpūr I, 164,$_{19}$.

2 *The Mālikīs*

1. Abū ʿAbdallāh Mālik b. Anas b. Abī ʿĀmir b. ʿAmr al-Aṣbaḥī was born in Medina in 97/715 (or, according to others, in 93/711), the descendant of a Ḥimyarite prince. As a young man, he supposedly spent time with the singers of the city, until his mother suggested to him that he study *fiqh*. He then went to the classes of the traditionist al-Zuhrī (p. 64) and of the Qurʾān reciter Nāfiʿ. In politics he was on the side of the ʿAlids. When Muḥammad b. ʿAbdallāh rose
185 176 up against the ʿAbbāsids in Medina in 145/762, || he pronounced a fatwa to the effect that any oath of allegiance to him was made under duress and thus null and void (Ṭab. III, 200, Nöldeke, *Or. Skizzen*, 129). Later he apparently reconciled with their government. When the caliph Hārūn visited Medina on the pilgrimage shortly before Mālik's death in 179/795, he is said to have gone to his lectures (*Fragm. hist. ar.* I, 298).

Ibn Khall. 522, *Manāqib al-imām Mālik* by Abu ʾl-Rūḥ ʿĪsā b. Abī Masʿūd b. Manṣūr al-Naklātī al-Ḥimyarī al-Zawāwī, d. 774/1372, Alex. Taʾr. 133, Cairo ^{2}V, 366, printed in the margin of al-Suyūṭī's *Tazyīn al-mamālik*, C. 1325.

I. The *Kitāb al-muwaṭṭaʾ* is not a work on Tradition, but a *corpus iuris* which aims to define statute and law, the rites and praxis of religious worship according to the *ijmāʿ* and the dominant Sunna in Medina, and to settle any outstanding issues from that point of view. In many sections he does not invoke any tradition, just fatwas by recognised authorities, and concludes by outlining the Medinan *ijmāʿ*. While his work was not the only one of its kind, it did outlive all its rivals. Apparently Mālik was not very concerned about accuracy in the transmission of his work, casually declaring any copy presented to him to be authentic. This is why his work was available in a number of

1 But the fact that there had been earlier attempts at such a science has been demonstrated by Goldziher, *Ẓāh.* 37, n. 1.

often significantly different recensions, two of which have been preserved: I. The *vulgata* in the recension of Yaḥyā b. Yaḥyā b. Kathīr b. Waslān b. Manqāyā al-Laythī al-Maṣmūdī, d. 234/848, a Spaniard who had become acquainted with the *madhhab* of Mālik in Medina and who worked for its dissemination in Spain, Berl. 1143, Paris 675/8, 4538, Br. Mus. 1590, Algiers 421/4, Garr. 1338, lith. with marginal glosses Delhi 1216, Lahore 1889.—Commentaries: 1.–3. see Suppl.—3a. Muḥammad b. Khalaf al-Qurṭubī, d. 557/1162, Br. Mus. 191.—5. *Tanwīr al-ḥawālik* by al-Suyūṭī, additionally Alex. Ḥad. 12, Qawala I, 107.—6. Muḥammad b. ʿAbd al-Bāqī al-Zurqānī, d. 1122/1710 (II, 318), additionally Qawala I, 132, print. 4 vols. C. 1279/80.—10. anon. *Khulāṣat al-dalāʾil fī tanqīḥ al-masāʾil*, Berl. Fol. 3524.—11. Islāmallāh b. Shaykh al-Islām al-Dihlawī, Patna I, 54,$_{546}$.—Restructured *al-Musawwā* (see Suppl.), ibid. I, 61,$_{619/20}$.—II. The | recension by Muḥammad b. al-Ḥasan al-Shaybānī (p. 177), Berl. 1144, Br. 186
Mus. 1590, Cairo ^{1}I, 328, print. Ludiana 1291/2, Lucknow 1297, Kazan 1909, with comm. *al-Taʿlīq al-munajjad* by Muḥammad b. ʿAbd al-Ḥayy al-Laknawī (Suppl. II, 857), Hyderabad 1291, in the margin of the print from Lucknow 1325. Comm. by al-Qāriʾ al-Harawī, d. 1014/1605 (II, 394), Rāġib 328, with the title *Sharḥ mushkilāt al-M.*, Cairo ^{2}I, 128. For other commentaries and recensions, see Ahlw. 1145, Suppl. I, 298, cf. Goldziher, *MSt.* II, 213/26.—II. *Risālat waʿẓ* to the caliph Hārūn al-Rashīd and to Yaḥyā al-Barmakī, Esc.^{2}556,$_{3}$, print. Būlāq 1311.—III. *Kitāb al-masāʾil*, edited and furnished with answers and explanations by his student ʿAbdallāh b. ʿAbd al-Ḥakam al-Miṣrī, d. 214/829 (p. 154), Gotha 1143.

2. Mālik's most important student was Abū ʿAbdallāh ʿAbd al-Raḥmān b. al-Qāsim al-ʿUtāqī, who was born in 128/746 (or 132/749) in Ramla, in Palestine. He has the merit of having introduced Mālik's doctrine to the Maghreb, where it still dominates today. He died in Cairo in 191/806.

| Ibn Khall. 335. On him and his student Saḥnūn, d. 6 or 7 Rajab 280/1 or 2 177
December 854, see Suppl. I, 299, and also parts of a parchment manuscript of the *Mudawwana* in Louvain, on which see Heffening, *Muséon* L, 86ff.; other ancient MSS Alex. Fiqh Māl. 18, Garr. 1894.

3. Muḥammad b. Aḥmad al-ʿUtbī, the most important representative of the Mālikī school in Spain (on its introduction there, see Suppl. I, 300), died in Rabīʿ I 255/March 869.

Maqq. I, 603, López Ortiz, *La recepción de la escuela malegui* 143/52. 1. *al-Mustakhraja al-ʿUtbiyya*, on particularly, difficult issues in Mālikī *fiqh*, Paris 1055 (complete ?), see Vincent, *Études sur le droit musulman* 41.—2. *Kitāb kirāʾ*

al-dūr wal-araḍīn wa-kirāʾ al-rawāḥil wal-dawābb min al-Mustakhraja mimma ʾstaḥalla (?) jumiʿa mimmā laysa fi ʾl-Mudawwana Esc.[2]612,[1].

4. Abu ʾl-Qāsim ʿUbaydallāh b. al-Ḥasan b. al-Ḥusayn b. al-Jallāb al-Baṣrī, whose year of death is given as 306/918, 378/988, or 398/1007.

Kitāb al-tafrīʿ fi ʾl-fiqh Br. Mus. 228,[1], Algiers 1036, a fragment of the *Kitāb al-ṣalāt*
187 Alex. Fiqh Māl. 15, abstract *al-Sahl al-badīʿ* | ḤKh [1]III, 7924, II, 3151, [2]I, 427, a fragment from it Berl. 3943, anon. comm. Cairo [1]III, 157.

5. The most famous Mālikī teacher of law of the fourth century was Abū Muḥammad ʿAbdallāh (ʿUbaydallāh) b. Abī Zayd ʿAbd al-Raḥmān al-Qayrawānī al-Nafzāwī, who was born in 316/928 in Nafzāwa, in Ifrīqiya. He lived for most of his life in Kairouan and died in 386/996 in Fez (or, according to others, in 388, 390, or 396).

Maqq. I, 553, Vincent, *Études*, p. 45. 1. *al-Risāla*, a compendium of Mālikī law,
178 Berl. 4446/7, Gotha 1045 (where other MSS are mentioned, additionally:) | Paris 1057/61, Algiers 768,[5], 1037/46, Cambr. 77, Cairo [1]III, 165.—Commentaries: 1. Dāʾūd al-Mālikī, before 731/1330, Cairo [1]III, 155.—1a. Yūsuf b. ʿUmar al-Anfāsī, d. 761/1360 (see Suppl.), also Alex. Fiqh Māl. 6, 10 (*taqyīd*).—2. ʿAbdallāh b. Yūsuf al-Balawī al-Shabībī, d. 782/1380 (see Suppl.), also Alex. Fiqh Māl. 10.—3. Qāsim b. ʿĪsā b. al-Nājī, d. 837/1433 (II, 239), Esc.[1]1123, Algiers 1049/50.—4. Aḥmad b. Muḥammad b. ʿAbdallāh al-Qalshānī, d. 863/1459, Esc.[1]1060, Algiers 1047/8.—5. *Murshid al-mubtadiʾīn* by Saʿīd b. al-Ḥusayn b. Muḥammad al-Ḥumaydī, completed in 864/1460, Alex. Fiqh Māl. 18.—6. Aḥmad Zarrūq, d. 899/1493 (II, 253), also Alex. Fiqh Māl. 6, 10.—7. See Suppl.—8. Abu ʾl-Ḥasan ʿAlī b. Muḥammad al-Manūfī al-Shādhilī, d. 939/1532: a. *al-Fatḥ al-rabbānī*, Leid. 1780.—b. see Suppl.—c. *Kifāyat al-ṭālib*, completed in 925/1519, Br. Mus. Suppl. 302, Algiers 1051/9, 1950/1, Cairo [2]I, 490, Rāmpūr I, 242, 486. Selection from c. (with c's title but labelled as commentary 4) Gotha 1046/7, Leid. 1781, Krafft 460, Paris 1062, 1, Esc. [1]1221.—Glosses on c. by ʿAlī b. Aḥmad b. Makram al-ʿAdawī al-Ṣaʿīdī al-Manāfīsī, d. 1189/1775 (II, 319), also Makram 23.—9. *Tafassur* (*Tanwīr*) *al-maqāla bi-ḥall alfāẓ al-R.* by Muḥammad b. Ibrāhīm al-Tatāʾī, d. 942/1535 (II, 316), Paris 4548, Algiers 1062, Cairo [1]III, 158, Alex. Fiqh Māl. 9.—10.–11. see Suppl.—12. Aḥmad b. Ghunaym b. Sālim b. Muhannā al-Nafzāwī, d. 1125/1713, also Alex. Fiqh Māl. 13.—13. ʿAlī b. Muḥammad al-Ujhūrī, d. 1066/1655 (II, 317), Cairo [1]III, 167.—14. Glosses by Abū Zayd ʿAbd al-Raḥmān b. ʿAffān al-Jazūlī, collected by al-Yaʿlānī before 890/1485, Munich 343, Br. Mus. 164, Algiers 1061.—15. ʿAbdallāh b. Aḥmad al-Fākihī, d. 972/1564 (II, 380), Rāmpūr I, 207,[268].—

| 16. Anon., Berl. 3548, Br. Mus 852/3, Paris 1070, Munich 344, Algiers 1065/70, 188
Madr. 114, Fez Qar. 965.—Versification *Naẓm al-R.* by Muḥammad b. Aḥmad b. al-Ghāzī al-ʿUthmānī al-Miknāsī, d. 919/1513 (II, 240), composed in 867/1462, with comm. by Muḥammad b. Muḥammad b. al-Ḥaṭṭāb, d. 953/1546 (II, 387), Algiers 1059,$_{2}$, 1063/4, Br. Mus. Suppl. 302, ii.

II. *Sunan*, a collection of traditions, Br. Mus. 888,$_{8}$.

IIa. *ʿAqīda*, a creed, with comm., by Aḥmad b. ʿĪsā al-Burnusī, Yeni 744.

IIb. Poems in praise of the Prophet, Br. Mus. 1617, 9.–11.

5a. Abū Muḥammad b. Abī Zayd al-Qayrawānī, probably his son, wrote:

Al-Madkhal ilā ʿilm al-dīn wal-diyāna Esc.^{1}1241, identified as being written by the father by Casiri.

6. A student of Abū Zayd was Khalaf b. Abi ʾl-Qāsim Abū Saʿīd al-Azdī al-Barādhiʿī, who composed, in 372/982 in Kairouan:

Tahdhīb masāʾil al-Mudawwana wal-Mukhtaliṭa Paris 1051/4, 3, on which glosses, possibly by Muḥammad b. Abi ʾl-Qāsim al-Bijāʾī al-Mashdālī, Algiers 1071.

3 *The Shāfiʿīs*

F. Wüstenfeld, *Der Imām el Schāfiʿī, seine Schüler und Anhänger bis zum J. 300, Abh. d. Kgl. Ges. d. Wiss. zu Göttingen*, vol. 36, 1890.

Idem, *Die gelehrten Schāfiʿiten des IV. Jahrhs.*, ibid., vol. 37, 1891.

1. Muḥammad b. Idrīs al-Shāfiʿī was born in 150/767 in Ghazza (or, according to others, in Ashkelon or Mina or Yemen). His father belonged to the Quraysh and his mother to the Azd. In early childhood he moved to Mecca where began to study Tradition. He then lived with the Banū Hudhayl in the desert until he was about 20 years of age, acquiring a thorough knowledge of classical Arabic. | In later times, the famous philologist al-Aṣmaʿī studied | the 179 189
poetry of the Hudhayl and Shanfarā with him in Mecca. Around 170/786 he went to Mālik b. Anas in Medina. After the latter's death he accompanied his uncle Abū Muṣʿab to Yemen, as he had been appointed a *qāḍī* there. When the imām of the Zaydiyya, Yaḥyā b. ʿAlī,[1] made his appearance there he paid him homage, but together with other followers of his he fell into captivity and was brought before Hārūn in Raqqa. Thanks to the intercession of Faḍl b. Rabīʿ he

1 See C. van Arendonk, *De opkomst van het Zaidietische imamaat*, 60, 290.

was pardoned, but he was not allowed to leave the town. It was here that he became acquainted with the works of the Ḥanafī scholar al-Shaybānī, whom he soon felt he had surpassed, although he did not dare confront this influential man. Thus, he first went to Egypt, where, as a student of Mālik, he was initially well received by the governor, until his new doctrinal ideas became widely known. When he had developed this further, he went once more to Baghdad, where he worked successfully as a teacher. However, just three years later he returned to Egypt with ʿAbdallāh,[2] the son and representative of the new governor ʿAbbās b. Mūsā, arriving in Cairo on 28 Shawwāl 198/21 June 814. But since his patron lasted only a few months in office, he next went to Mecca and only returned to Egypt at the end of 199 or the beginning of 200. He died in Fusṭāṭ on a Friday, which was the last day of Rajab 204/20 January 820, and was buried at the foot of the Muqaṭṭam in the crypt of the Banū ʿAbd al-Ḥakam. At his grave Ṣalāh al-Dīn founded a madrasa which the Ayyūbid ruler al-Malik al-Kāmil adorned with a cupola in 608/1211, and which still stands today.

190 | His *madhhab* tried to mediate between Mālik's adherence to the traditions and Abū Ḥanīfa's principle of *raʾy*. He is regarded as the founder of the science of *uṣūl al-fiqh*, which gave a methodical structure to legal practice.

Manāqib al-imām al-Sh. by Abū ʿAbdallāh b. ʿUmar al-Rāzī, Cairo n.d., others see Suppl. De Goeje, ZDMG 46, 106/7, Goldziher, *Ẓāh.* 20/6. L.J. Graf, *Al-Sh. 's verhandelingen over de wortelen van den fiqh*, Diss. Leiden, Amsterdam 1935, based on the *Risāla*. On his works (*Fihrist* 109) see Suppl. I, 304/5; additionally *Kitāb al-umm*, also Berl. Qu. 1339, Rāmpūr I, 356,$_{659}$, Ğārullāh 591/2, 594.—1. *al-Sunan al-maʾthūra* Köpr. 296.—2. *al-Musnad*, on which *al-Shāfī al-ʿayn* (or *al-ʿiyy*) *ʿalā Musnad al-Sh.* by al-Suyūṭī, d. 911/1505, Rāmpūr I, 89,$_{186}$.—3. *Ikhtilāf al-ḥadīth* add. Rāmpūr II, 225.—4.–6. see Suppl.—7. *Risāla fī uṣūl al-fiqh*, Berl. Oct. 1827, Goldziher, *MSt.* II, 83, print. C. 1321.—8. *al-Tamhīd fī uṣūl al-fiqh* Ind. Off. 1428.—9. *Munāẓara* Āṣaf. II, 1326,$_{584}$.—10. *Munājāt* Heid. ZDMG 91, 387,$_{6}$.—10. Some poems, according to information kindly provided by J. Hell, related to the poetry of Abu ʾl-ʿAtāhiya, Berl. 7534, Leid. 594, 770, al-Masʿūdī, *Murūj* VIII, 66, Ibn Khall. I, 448, al-ʿAsqalānī, *Tawāli ʾl-taʾsīs bi-maʿālī Ibn Idrīs fī manāqib al-Sh.*, 73ff., see Shihāb al-Dīn Aḥmad b. Aḥmad b. ʿAbd al-Raḥmān b. al-ʿAjamī, ca. 1029/1620 (Suppl. II, 410), *Natījat al-afkār fīmā yuʿzā ila ʾl-imām al-Sh. min al-ashʿār* Cairo ^{2}III, 402.[3]—11. Attributed to him is a *ḥijāb*, a prayer that he had learned from the Prophet and that had saved him when

2 According to al-Kindī, ed. Guest 154, contra Yāqūt, *Irshād* VI, 394,9.

3 Wrongly attributed to the younger Ibn al-ʿAjamī in Suppl. II, 420.

the caliph wanted to kill him, Berl. 392.—12. *Waṣāyā* Patna II, 426,$_{2399,1}$.—13. *Kitāb al-sabq wal-ramy*, ibid. 342,$_{2527,2}$.

2. Al-Shāfiʿī's most important student and supporter of his *madhhab* in Egypt was Abū Ibrāhīm Ismāʿīl b. Yaḥyā al-Muzanī, who was born in 175/794 and who died on 24 Ramadan 264/21 May 878 in Cairo.

Wüst., no. 30. 1. *Mukhtaṣar min ʿilm al-imām al-nafīs M. b. Idrīs*, whose study is recommended by al-Ghazzālī in the *Iḥyāʾ*, C. 1316, I, 35,$_{1}$, and from which he extracted the *Khulāṣat al-Mukhtaṣar* (see Suppl. I, 754,$_{53a}$), in fragments Gotha 938, Cairo ^{1}III, 273, ^{2}I, 537, Niẓām, Hyderabad, *JRASB* 1917, Proc. CVI, 50.—Commentary by Abu 'l-Ṭayyib Ṭāhir b. ʿAbdallāh b. Ṭāhir | al-Ṭabasī, d. 450/1058, 191
Cairo ^{1}III, 239, ^{2}I, 337 (*Mukhtaṣar qism al-ṣadaqāt*).—2. *Risāla* Āṣaf. II, 1722,$_{3,13}$.

3. Abū Bakr Muḥammad b. Ibrāhīm b. al-Mundhir al-Mundhirī al-Nīsābūrī had studied under Muḥammad b. ʿAbdallāh b. ʿAbd al-Ḥakam and al-Rabīʿ b. Sulaymān, both immediate students of al-Shāfiʿī, but wanted to be considered as an independent *mujtahid*. He took up residence in Mecca and probably died in 318/930, or 324.

Wüst. 90. 1. *Kitāb al-ijmāʿ* (*wal-ishrāf*) AS 1011, probably identical with the *Kitāb al-ikhtilāf* (see Suppl.).—2. *Kitāb al-awsaṭ fi 'l-sunan wal-ijmāʿ wal-ikhtilāf* AS 1034 (fragm.) probably identical with *al-Ishrāf ʿalā madhāhib ahl al-ʿilm*, Cairo ^{2}I, 497.—3. *Tafsīr al-Qurʾān* Gotha 521 (only sura 2,$_{27}$—4,$_{94}$).

4. Abū ʿAbdallāh al-Zubayr b. Aḥmad b. Sulaymān b. ʿAbdallāh b. ʿĀṣim al-Zubayrī, a descendant of the famous companion of the Prophet al-Zubayr b. al-ʿAwwām, was the most important jurisconsult of his time. He first lived in Basra, then in Baghdad. He died sometime before 320/932.

Wüst. 89. *Sharḥ al-īmān wal-islām* Munich 893,$_{17}$.

5. Abu 'l-ʿAbbās Aḥmad b. Abī Aḥmad al-Ṭabarī al-Qāṣṣ, who was thus called because he had worked as a preacher in Āmul in Ṭabaristān, was a student of Aḥmad b. ʿUmar b. Surayj, d. 305/917, who was branded the *mujaddid* of his time. He died in the year 335/946 on a trip to Tarsus; according to others, he had been a *qāḍī* there.

Wüst. 112. 1. *al-Talkhīṣ fi 'l-furūʿ*, one of the most thorough law books, which also takes the deviant views of the Ḥanafīs into consideration, AS 1074.—2. *Dalāʾil al-qibla*, Beirut, see Cheikho, *al-Mashriq* XVII, 1913, 439/42.

181 | 6. One of the youngest students of Ibn Surayj was Abu 'l-Ḥasan Aḥmad b. Muḥammad b. al-Qaṭṭān, who died as a respected jurisconsult in Baghdad in 359/970.

Wüst. 161. *Kitāb al-aḥkām li-siyāq āyāt al-nabī ʿalayhi 'l-salām* Rāġib 971.

192 | 6a. Al-Ḥasan b. Ḥarb al-Ḥassānī wrote, around 400/1010 at the order of the vizier Abu 'l-Ḥasan Aḥmad b. Muḥammad al-Suhaylī:

Al-Suhayl fi 'l-madhhab al-Shāfiʿī wal-Ḥanafī (ḤKh III, 637,$_{7300}$ *fi 'l-furūʿ al-Shāfiʿiyya*) Alex. Fiqh Shāf. 24.

7. Abu 'l-Ḥasan Aḥmad b. Muḥammad b. al-Maḥāmilī al-Ḍabbī was born in 368/978 in Baghdad, where he studied and taught. He died on 20 Rabīʿ I 415/1 July 1024.

Wüst. 109c. *Kitāb al-lubāb fi 'l-fiqh*, abstract *Tanqīḥ al-L.* by Abū Zurʿa al-ʿIrāqī, d. 826/1423 (II, 66). Shortened again, with the title *Taḥrīr Tanqīḥ al-L.* with comm. *Tuḥfat al-ṭullāb* by Zakariyyāʾ al-Anṣārī, d. 926/1520 (II, 99), Gotha 984/5, Paris 1038/40, on which glosses by Muḥammad b. Aḥmad al-Shawbarī, d. 1069/1659 (II, 330), Gotha 986, by Muḥammad b. Dāʾūd al-ʿInānī, d. 1098/1687, Berl. 4499, by ʿAbd al-Barr b. ʿAbdallāh al-Ujhūrī, died ca. 1070/1659, Alex. Fiqh Shāf. 42, by al-Qalyūbī, ibid. 19, by Ḥasan al-Madābighī, d. 1070/1659 (II, 328), ibid. 20.—10 other glosses are mentioned in Ahlw., 4450.—Commentary on the original work by ʿAbd al-Raʾūf al-Munāwī, d. 1031/1622 (II, 306), Paris 1046, 1 (fragm.).—2. *al-Mughnī bi-madhhab al-Shāfiʿī*, copied in 488/1095, Berl. Oct. 1409, Cairo ^{2}I, 503, Alex. Fiqh Shāf. 18.

8. Abu 'l-Qāsim Hibatallāh b. al-Ḥasan b. Manṣūr al-Ṭabarī al-Lālakāʾī ("the sandal-maker") lived as a traditionalist and *faqīh* in Baghdad, before going to Dīnawar, where he died at a ripe old age on 6 Ramaḍān 418/11 October 1027.

Ḥuff. XIII, 56, Wüst., *Gesch.* 177. *Ḥujaj uṣūl ahl al-sunna wal-jamāʿa* Leipz. 318 (see Suppl.).

4 *The Lesser Schools*

1. Among the third-century scholars of Tradition who were primarily concerned with legal issues but did not adhere to any particular school was Yaḥyā b. Ādam b. Sulaymān, who died in 203/818.

Fihrist 227, Naw. 620, Ibn Quṭlūbughā 258, *Ḥuff.* VII, 34. Kitāb al-kharāj, *Le Livre de l'impôt foncier, publié d'après* | *le ms. unique appartenant à Charles Schefer* 193
(*Paris 6030*) *par* Th. W. Juynboll, Leiden 1896, C. 1347.

2. Abū ʿAbdallāh Aḥmad b. Muḥammad b. Ḥanbal, d. 241/855. See Suppl. I, 309.

| *Manāqib al-imām A. b. Ḥ.* by Shaykh al-Islām Muḥammad b. Muḥammad b. 182
Abī Bakr, Rāmpūr I, 671, 37, Wüst. *Schaf.* 13. 1. *Musnad*, transmitted and edited by his son ʿAbdallāh with additions by Abū Bakr al-Qāṭiʿī, Berl. 1257, Garr. 1365, AS 890/3, Dāmād Ibr. 389/93, Köpr. 411, Patna I, $60_{608/12}$, II, $503_{2702/4}$, print. C. 1311, 6 vols.; see Goldziher, *ZDMG* 50, 465/506. Individual parts *Musnad al-shaʾmiyyīn*, Berl. 1259, Köpr. 412/6 (after Abū Zurʿa, d. 276/889, *Ḥuff.* IX, 78, or an independent work by this student of his), *Musnad ʿAbdallāh b. ʿUmar* Berl. 1260, *Musnad al-Kūfiyyīn* Gotha 589, *Musnad Abī Saʿīd al-Khudrī* Köpr. 424/5.—*Khaṣāʾiṣ Musnad A. b. Ḥ.* by Abū Mūsā Muḥammad b. ʿUmar b. Aḥmad al-Madīnī, d. 581/1185 (al-Subkī, *Ṭab.* IV, 90), Berl. 1258, print. C. 1342, 1347 (*wa-yalīhi al-Musʿad al-aḥmad fī khatm Musnad al-imām A. li-Ibn al-Jazarī*).—*Tartīb Musnad A. b. Ḥ. ʿalā ḥurūf al-muʿjam* by Abū Bakr Muḥammad b. Abī Muḥammad ʿAbdallāh al-Maqdisī al-Ḥanbalī, Cairo ^{2}I, 96.—*Ghāyat al-maqṣad fī zawāʾid al-Musnad* by Nūr al-Dīn Abu ʾl-Ḥasan ʿAlī b. Abī Bakr b. Sulaymān al-Haythamī, d. 807/1404 (II, 76), Alex. Ḥad. 37—Linguistic commentary *ʿUqūd al-zabarjad* by al-Suyūṭī, d. 911/1505, Br. Mus. 189, Cairo Ḥad. 612.—2. *Kitāb al-sunna mūṣil al-muʿtaqid ila ʾl-janna*, profession of faith in the form of an *ʿaqīda*, Berl. 1937, Patna II, 503_{2700}.—3. *Kitāb fi ʾl-zuhd*, character traits and sayings of pious men, abstract without *isnād*s Berl. 3156, cf. *Kitāb zawāʾid al-zuhd, Khiz.* I, 341_{15}.—4. *Risāla* or *Kitāb al-ṣalāt wa-mā yalzam fīhā*, against the nuisance in the mosque of many people bending over, prostrating themselves, or raising their voices during prayer without paying due attention to the imām, Berl. 3567, Br. Mus. 900_{3}, with the title *Risāla saniyya fi ʾl-ṣalāt* Rāmpūr II, 176.—5. Poem on death and the hereafter, Berl. 7539_{1}, on humility before God, although not, however, before man, ibid. 2.—6.–12. See Suppl. (on 7. Qawala I, 184, on 10. Berl. cod. sim. 35).

3. Only a few of the works of the Ḥanbalīs of the third and fourth centuries (see Suppl.) are extant, among which are:

a. ʿUmar b. al-Ḥusayn b. ʿAbdallāh al-Khiraqī, d. 334/945 in Damascus, where he had fled from the popular rage of the people of Baghdad against the Ḥanbalīs.

194 | Ibn Khall. 465 (503). After his departure from Baghdad his works were, to a large extent, lost in a fire. What remained was his *Mukhtaṣar fi ʾl-fiqh*, which is much used by Ḥanbalīs, Berl. $4663_{,9}$, Cairo ^{1}III, 298.

b. Abū ʿAbdallāh al-Ḥasan b. Ḥumayd b. ʿAlī al-Baghdādī, d. 403/1012.

Tahdhīb al-ajwiba, answers to legal issues, Berl. 4784.

f. ʿUbaydallāh b. Muḥammad b. Muḥammad b. Ḥamdān al-ʿUkbarī b. Baṭṭa, d. 387/997.

1. *al-Ibāna bi-uṣūl al-diyāna* Rāmpūr I, $59_{,1}$.—2. *al-Khalʿ wa-ibṭāl al-ḥīla*, ed. M. Ḥāmid al-Faqqī in *Min dafāʾin al-kunūz*, C. 1349, no. I (which has Abū ʿAbdallāh b. Baṭṭa).

4. Abū Sulaymān Dāʾūd b. ʿAlī b. Khalaf al-Iṣfahānī al-Ẓāhirī, who was born around 200/815 in Kufa, studied in Baghdad under the most famous theologians and specialists of Tradition of his time and completed his formative period in Nishapur with Isḥāq b. Rāhwayhi, d. 238/847. He then settled in Baghdad, where he became famous as a teacher, dying in Ramaḍān 270/March 884. He had started out from Shāfiʿī dogma, but soon countered it with his own *madhhab al-ẓāhir*. Where al-Shāfiʿī had opposed the principle of *raʾy* of Abū Ḥanīfa in an attempt to trace *fiqh* back to the foundations of Tradition, Dāʾūd did not only reject *qiyās*, but also *taqlīd*, which is the invocation of the authority of an imam. Only the outer sense (*ẓāhir*) of the wording of the Qurʾān and
184 the *ḥadīth* should determine the Sunna. | In the fourth century, his doctrine found many adherents in Iraq, Persia, Sind, and Oman. It had a special attraction for the Sufis, to whom it seemed to offer the freedom from ritualistic constraint. However, in the Orient his doctrine could not maintain itself for very long. Consequently, not much is left of his and his immediate students' works
195 (see Suppl.). However, | from the fourth century onwards, his doctrine found its most devoted literary exponents in the Maghreb and in Spain in particular, and an account of this will duly follow in the next section.

I. Goldziher, *Die Ẓāhiriten, ihr Lehrsystem und ihre Geschichte, Beitrag zur Geschichte der muhammedanischen Theologie*, Leipzig 1884.

5. Alongside the dominant doctrinal systems the *madhhab* founded by Muḥammad b. Jarīr al-Ṭabarī (see p. 148) was not able to hold its ground for very long either. In the fourth century it was mainly represented by Abu ʾl-Faraj al-Muʿāfā b. Zakariyyāʾ b. Yaḥyā b. Ṭarrāra al-Jarīrī al-Nahrawānī. Born on 7 Rajab 305/25 December 917 (or, according to others, in 303/915), he not only devoted himself to *fiqh* but, as a student of Nifṭawayh, also gained detailed knowledge of grammar and poetry. Having worked for some time as an assistant judge in the Bāb al-Ṭāq district on the eastern side of Baghdad, he died on 12 Dhu ʾl-Ḥijja 380/14 November 1000 in Nahrawān.

Ibn Khall. 697, Ibn al-Anbārī 403/6, Flügel, *Gr. Sch.* 245/6. *Kitāb al-jalīs al-ṣāliḥ al-kāfī wal-anīs al-nāṣiḥ al-ṣāfī* in 100 *majālis*, which usually start with an anecdote about or a saying by the Prophet or his dependants which it then elucidates linguistically and materially by bringing in verses from the Qurʾān, ḤKh [1]II, 4144, [2]I, 593, Berl. 8325, Paris 3847/9, Garr. 1369, Camber. Preston 50, Dāmād Ibr. 282 (ZDMG XIII, 621), abstract Gotha 864,$_2$.

5 The Shīʿa[1]

Ṭūsys (see p. 405) *List of Shyʿah Books and ʿAlam al-hodās* (Muḥammad b. al-Fayḍ al-Kashānī, d. after 1112/1700, see Suppl. II 584), *Notes on Shyah Biography*, ed. by Dr. A. Sprenger and Mawlawy Abdalhaqq, Bibl. Ind. no. 60, 71, 91, 107, 1853/5.

| New edition: *al-Fihris taʾlīf Shaykh al-Ṭāʾifa Abū Jaʿfar Muḥammad b.* 196
al-Ḥasan al-Ṭūsī al-mutawaffā sanat 460, ṣaḥḥaḥahu wa-ʿallaqa ʿalayhi ʾl-ʿallāma al-sayyid Muḥammad Ṣādiq Āl Baḥr al-ʿUlūm, Najaf 1937/1356.

M. Muḥsin nazīl Sāmarrāʾ al-shahīr bil-Shaykh Āghā Buzurg al-Ṭihrānī, *al-Dharīʿa ilā taṣānīf al-Shīʿa*, I, II, Najaf 1355/6.

| The Shīʿa dissociated themselves relatively late from the main body of Islam. 185
During the first centuries, ʿAlid tendencies were widespread throughout the Islamic world, and as long as they did not degenerate, they did not endanger the orthodoxy of those who professed them. Like the adherents of the Sunna, they based themselves on the Qurʾān and Tradition, but had a preference for *ḥadīth*

1 Here, dogmatic literature is already discussed, while Qurʾān interpretation has been excluded.

from the family of the Prophet, and in the fabrication thereof they accomplished even more than the others. It was only the idea of suffering, which since the martyrdom of ʿAlī and Ḥusayn had repeated itself so often with the leaders of their dynasty, which brought their adherents a new and fertile motive, by which they were separated from the religious attitude of the community as a whole. Connected with this was the idea of *parousia*, the expectation of the return (*rajʿa*) of an Imam who had been miraculously transported from the temporal world, thus turning him into the Mahdī. While the moderate sect of the Zaydīs, which stands closest to the Sunnīs, claims for its Imam no more than God's guidance, this idea escalated among the extremists (the *ghulāt*) to the belief in the indwelling (*ḥulūl*) of the divine spirit in the Imam. In Persia, where Shīʿism and its national pendant of Iranism linked up early against Arab domination, there soon evolved an independent Shīʿī literature under the encouragement of the Sāmānids and the Būyids. But of the numerous works whose titles were listed by al-Ṭūsī very little remains. In Sunnī Asia Minor, from
197 | where most of our manuscript collections originate, people have extirpated the works of heretics, while in those countries that are still Shīʿī, the material conditions for the preservation of literary monuments were far from favorable.

A. v. Kremer, *Geschichte der herrschenden Ideen des Islams*, Leipzig 1868, p. 272ff. I. Goldziher, *Beiträge zur Litteraturgeschichte der Schīʿa und der sunnitischen Polemik*, SBWA 1874, vol. 781 p. 439ff. R. Strothmann, Die Shīʿa, *EI* IV, 377/85.

1 The Zaydīs

In Yemen the Zaydīs came to power as early as the second century, and amidst quite a few vicissitudes they have stood their ground until this very day. Here a rich literature soon developed, whose monuments first came to Berlin and other libraries through Glaser, and then, through Caprotti, among other places, in particular the Ambrosiana library in Milan.

1. On Zayd b. ʿAlī, see Suppl. I, 313.

Kitāb al-majmūʿ also Hamb. Or. Sem. 12, Rāmpūr I, 246,$_{5/8}$, see Kračkovsky, *Zap. Koll. Vost.* I, 1925, 531/5. *Musnad* Patna I, 60,$_{615}$. On his reading of the Qurʾān, Jeffery, *RSO* XVI (1937), 249/89.

1a. The Imam Tarjumān al-Dīn al-Qāsim b. Ibrāhīm al-Ḥasanī Ṭabāṭabāʾ al-Rassī, d. 246/860.

| See Suppl. 314/5. Of his smaller works, Berl. 4876 contains: 1. Dogmatics: a. 186
al-Dalīl ʿala ʾllāh al-kabīr.—b. *al-Maknūn*.—c. *Uṣūl al-ʿadl wal-tawḥīd nafy*
al-jabr wal-tashbīh.—d. *Ṣifat al-ʿarsh wal-kursī wa-tafsīruhumā*.—e. *al-Hijra*.—
f. *al-ʿAdl wal-tawḥīd wa-nafy al-jabr wal-tashbīh*.—g. *al-Dalīl al-ṣaghīr*.—2. *Fiqh*
and ethics: a. *Masʾalat al-Ṭabariyyīn*.—b. *al-Imāma*.—c. *al-Mustarshid*.—
d. *Siyāsat al-nafs*.—e. *al-Qatl wal-qitāl*.—3. Science of the Qurʾān: a.
al-Madīḥ al-kabīr lil-Qurʾān al-mubīn.—b. *al-Madḥ al-ṣaghīr*.—c. *al-Nāsikh*
wal-mansūkh.—Polemics: a. *al-Radd ʿala ʾl-zindīq al-laʿīn b. al-Muqaffaʿ*
(see p. 158).—b. *al-Radd ʿala ʾl-mulḥid*.—c. *al-Radd ʿala ʾl-Rawāfiḍ min* | *aṣḥāb* 198
al-ghuluww.—d. *al-Radd ʿala ʾl-Rāfiḍa*.—11 more titles are mentioned in Ahlw.
4950$_{,1}$.

2. His grandson Abu ʾl-Ḥusayn Yaḥyā b. al-Ḥusayn b. al-Qāsim b. Ibrāhīm al-Ḥasanī al-Hādī ila ʾl-Ḥaqq, d. 245/859, founded the Zaydī imamate in Yemen, and died on 19 Dhu ʾl-Ḥijja 298/18 July 910.

See Suppl. I, 315/6. Ad III, 10. *Kitāb al-diyāna* also Hamb. Or. Sem. 132$_{,2}$.—17. *Kitāb al-bāligh wal-mudrik* ibid. 132$_{,1}$.

3. A descendant of the same al-Qāsim, in the fifth degree, was Imam al-Mahdī li-Dīn Allāh al-Ḥusayn b. al-Qāsim b. ʿAlī b. ʿAbdallāh b. Muḥammad b. al-Qāsim b. Ibrāhīm, d. 404/1013.

1. *Kitāb al-akfāʾ*, on those who are equal for marriage, by religion and origin, Berlin 4976.—2. *Kitāb al-sabīlayn al-ʿaql wal-nafs* ibid. 5340.—3. *Tafsīr al-gharīb min kitāb Allāh*, book 3, Berl. 10238.—4. *al-Taḥaddī lil-ʿulamāʾ wal-juhhāl wal-radd ʿala ʾl-zanīm wa-ghayrihi min al-ḍullāl* ibid. 10266.—5. *al-Radd ʿalā ahl al-taqlīd wal-nifāq* ibid. 10267.—6. *al-Radd ʿalā man ankara ʾl-waḥy baʿd khātam al-nabiyyīn* ibid. 10268.—7. *Mawʿiẓa* ibid. 10269.—8. *al-Radd ʿala ʾl-mulḥidīn wa-ghayrihim* ibid. 10279, Šehīd ʿA. Pāshā, 6.–9. *al-Tawḥīd wal-tanāhī wal-taḥdīd*, part I, Berl. 10271, Šehīd ʿA. Pāshā, 1.–10. *Bināʾ al-ḥikma* Berl. 10272.—11. *al-Radd ʿalā man ankara qatl ʿaduww Allāh Ḥātim* ibid. 10273.—12. *al-Farq bayna ʾl-afʿāl wal-radd ʿala ʾl-kafara wal-juhhāl* ibid. 10274.—13. *al-Imāma* ibid. 10275.—14. *al-Adilla ʿala ʾllāh* ibid. 10314.—15. *Mukhtaṣar min al-tawḥīd* ibid. 10315.—16. *al-Tawakkul ʿala ʾllāh dhi ʾl-jalāl wal-radd ʿala ʾl-mushabbiha al-ḍullāl* ibid. 10316, Šehīd ʿA. Pāshā, 2.–17. *al-Raḥma wabtidāʾ Allāh subḥānahu li-ʿibādihi bil-niʿma* Berl. 10317.—18. *al-Dalīl ʿalā ḥadath al-ajsām* Šehīd ʿA. Pāshā, 3.–19. *al-Ṭabāʾiʿ* ibid. 4.–20. *Shawāhid al-ṣunʿ* ibid. 5. Other titles in Ahlw. 4950, V.

4. Al-Imām al-Muʾayyad billāh Aḥmad b. al-Ḥusayn b. Hārūn al-Buṭḥānī al-Hārūnī Abu 'l-Ḥusayn, d. 411/1020.

See Suppl. I, 317/8, with: 6. *Amālī*, print. Ṣanʿāʾ 1355 (E. Rossi, *Or. Mod* XVIII, 572).

199 | 2 The Imāmīs

Muḥsin al-Amīn al-Ḥusaynī al-ʿĀmilī, *Aʿyān al-Shīʿa*, I–V, Damascus 1936.

1. The oldest book of the Shīʿa was, according to *Fihrist* $219,_{14}$, the *Kitāb al-aṣl* of Sulaym b. Qays al-Hilālī, who fled from al-Ḥajjāj to Abān b. Abī ʿAyyāsh, and to whom he passed it on.

Al-Ṭūsī, *Fihrist* ^{2}81, *Dharīʿa* II, 152/9, 590.

2. Mūsā al-Kāẓim and ʿAlī al-Riḍā, see Suppl. I, 318.

Ad 5, *Ṣaḥīfat al-Riḍā* also Teh. Sip. I, 272/5, 491/4.

2a. ʿAlī al-Riḍā's student, Abū Muḥammad al-Faḍl b. Sādhān b. Khalīl al-Nīshābūrī, d. 260/874.

Al-Ṭūsī, *Fihrist* ^{2}124, *Manhaj al-maqāl* 260. *Kitāb al-īḍāḥ* (*āt*) *fī 'l-radd ʿalā sāʾir al-firaq* Mashh. I, 20, 38, and in several libraries in Iraq, *Dharīʿa* II, 490, 1946 (with a mistaken quotation from the *Tadhkirat al-nawādir*).

3. The real founder of Imāmī *fiqh* in Persia was Muḥammad b. al-Ḥasan b. al-Farrūḥ al-Ṣaffār al-Aʿraj Abū Jaʿfar al-Qummī, who died after 307/919.

187 | Al-Ṭūsī^2, no. 611, *Kitāb baṣāʾir al-darajāt fī ʿulūm āl Muḥammad wa-mā khaṣṣahumu 'llāh bihi*, Shīʿī collection of traditions, perhaps an augmented edition of the *Kitāb baṣāʾir al-darajāt fī faḍāʾil āl M.* by Saʿd b. ʿAbdallāh al-Qummī Abu 'l-Qāsim, d. 300/913 (or, according to others, in 299 or 301, al-Ṭūsī, *Fihr.*^{2} no. 306), print. 1285 n.p. (= *Taṣdīr al-darajāt*, Fihrist $223,_{2}$), Ind. Off. 143 (see Suppl.).

3a. Regarded as an innovator of Imāmī *fiqh* at the beginning of the fourth century is Jaʿfar Muḥammad b. Yaʿqūb b. Isḥāq al-Kulīnī al-Rāzī, who died in 328/939 in Baghdad.

Al-Ṭūsī, no. 709, ^{2}no. 591, Ibn al-Athīr (ed. Tornberg) VIII, 283, C. 1303, VIII, 118, Sprenger, *Life of M.* 68, *Rawḍāt al-jannāt* 550/4, Yūsuf al-Baḥrānī, *Luʾluʾat*

al-Baḥrayn 314/21. 1. *al-Kāfī fī ʿilm al-dīn*, on Imāmī theology, one of the four
canonical books of the Shīʿa, Berl. 1855, Garr. 1608/9, Alex. Firaq 10, Teh. Sip. I,
| 288/97, Patna I, $57_{570/4}$, Aligarh 99_{29}, $100_{35,38}$ (see Suppl.), abstracts Ind. 200
Off. 144, Br. Mus. 980, Trinity College Dublin.—Commentaries: see Suppl. and
also: b. Teh. Sip. I, 258/60.—c. ibid. 265/8.—d. ibid. 269/70.—g. Glosses by
Mīrzā Rafīʿa Muḥammad b. Sayyid Ḥaydar Ḥusaynī Ṭabāṭabāʾī Nāʾīnī, d. 1080 or
1082/1671, ibid. 245/7.—h. *Huda ʾl-ʿuqūl fī sharḥ aḥādīth al-uṣūl* by Muḥammad
b. ʿAbdʿalī b. Muḥammad b. Aḥmad b. ʿAlī b. ʿAbd al-Jabbār, composed in
1218/1803, Teh. Sip. I, 260/1.

4. The most important literary exponent of the Imāmis in the fourth century, Abū Jaʿfar Muḥammad b. ʿAlī b. al-Ḥusayn b. Mūsā b. Bābūya al-Qummī al-Ṣadūq, whose father had been a shaykh of the Shīʿa in Qum and who wrote a *Risāla fī ʾl-sharāʾiʿ* that was used in no. 4, below, went from Khurāsān to Baghdad in 355/966, where he approached the Būyid Rukn al-Dawla, who could use his doctrine of the imāmate to his political advantage. He died in 381/991 in Rayy (or, according to others, in 391).

Al-Ṭūsī, no. 661, [2]695, Yūsuf al-Baḥrānī, *Luʾluʾat al-Baḥrayn* 300/9. Of his many,
supposedly around 300, works, the following remain: 1. *Maʿāni ʾl-akhbār*,[1] a
collection of traditions, Ind. Off. 145, Aligarh 98_{13}.—2. *Majālis al-mawāʿiẓ fī
ʾl-aḥādīth* Berl. 1269, see *Dharīʿa* II, 315_{1251}.—3. *ʿUyūn* (ḤKh IV, 270 *ʿUnwān*)
akhbār al-Riḍā, the life and sayings of ʿAlī Riḍā, Berl. 9663, Munich 456, Paris
2018_{1}, Br. Mus. 1619, Ind. Off. 146, Pet. AM Nov. 39, Āṣaf. III, 270_{951}, Rāmpūr II,
137_{461}, Patna I, 277_{2300}, Teh. Sip. I, 282/3, lith. Tehran 1287.—4. *Kitāb man lā
yaḥḍuruhu ʾl-faqīh*, a handbook of legal practice, one of the four foundational
works of the Shīʿa, Berl. 4782/3, Pet. 250, Paris 1108, Br. Mus. 905, Ind. Off. 289,
Bodl. II, $84/6_{1}$, Teh. Sip. I, 325/30, Rāmpūr I, 254_{583}, Aligarh 101_{3}, Patna I,
$64_{663/5}$, II, 504_{2707}, the commentary *Rawḍat al-muttaqīn* by Muḥammad Taqī
b. Maqṣūd ʿAlī al-Majlisī, d. 1070/1659, also Teh. Sip. I, 254/7, in addition *Nawādir
man lā yaḥḍuruhu ʾl-faqīh*, probably by Walīallāh Ḥusaynī, the author of the
Tuḥfat al-mulūk, Teh. Sip. I, 334.—5. *al-ʿIlal* or *ʿIlal al-sharāʾiʿ* (*wal-aḥkām*),
examines in a series of brief, | numberless chapters the reasons for this or that 201
to be such, why it happened or is called thus, in the process touching upon
many areas of life, including nature, history, and learning, Berl. 1196, Br. Mus.
1196, Teh. Sip. I, 278/9, Rāmpūr I, 96, 231/2.–7. *Iʿtiqādāt al-Imāmiyya*, Br. Mus.

1 The *Jāmiʿ al-akhbār* that is attributed to him is probably the work of a certain Muḥammad b. Muḥammad al-Shaʿīrī, though according to others it was by a certain ʿAlī b. Saʿd al-Khayyāṭ; see al-Majlisī, *Biḥār al-anwār*, Preface, *Rawḍāt al-jannāt* 558, Kentūrī, *Kashf al-ḥujub* 150, Mashh. I, 30, Teh. Sip. I, 242/3 (printed several times).

851, Pet. AM 61, Āṣaf. II, $1296,_{102}$.—8. *al-Nuṣūṣ ʿala ʾl-aʾimma al-ithnay ʿashra* (author?) Paris $2018,_{2}$.—9. *Munāẓarat al-malik Rukn al-Dawla maʿa ʾl-Ṣadūq Bābūya*, on the caliphs after ʿAlī, Br. Mus. $886,_{31}$.—10. *Kitāb al-khiṣāl*, praise- or blameworthy attributes, additionally Āṣaf. III, 262, 308, Patna I, $147,_{1416}$, print. Tehran n.d., selection *Nukhaba* Teh. Sip. I, 332.—11. *Thawāb al-aʿmāl* and 12. *ʿIqāb al-aʿmāl*, printed together Tehran 1299.—13. see Suppl.—14. *al-Hidāya* additionally Berl. Qu. 1779, Ind. Off. 4632 (*JRAS* 1939, 395).—15. *Ikmāl* (*kamāl*) *al-dīn wa-itmām* (*tamām*) *al-niʿma fī ithbāt al-ghayba wa-kashf al-ḥayra*, also Teh. Sip. I, 204, Patna I, $114,_{1151}$, lith. Tehran 1301 (*RSO* XIV, 353).—16. *Kitāb ṣifāt al-shīʿa, see Lughat al-ʿArab* VII (1920), 223.—17. see Suppl.—18. *Kitāb al-tawḥīd* also Berl. Oct. 3269, Teh. Sip. I, 229/30, print. Bombay 1321.—19. *Kitāb al-ikhtiṣāṣ*, library of Amīn al-Wāʿiẓīn Ibrāhīm b. Muḥammad ʿAlī al-Iṣfahānī, *Dharīʿa* I, $358,_{1889}$.—20. *Ghanāʾim al-anām fī masʾalat al-ḥalāl wal-ḥarām* Tehran 1319.

5. Al-Nuʿmān Muḥammad b. Manṣūr b. Aḥmad b. Ḥayyān al-Tamīmī al-Qāḍī Abū Ḥanīfat al-Shīʿa was first a Mālikī, then joined the Ithnā ʿAshariyya and crossed over to the Fāṭimids. Together with al-Muʿizz li-Dīn Allāh, d. 365/975,
188 he went from Ifrīqiya to Egypt, | became a *qāḍī* there, and died at the end of Jumādā II 363/March 974.

Ibn Khall. 737, see Suppl. I, 324/5, with: 4. *Daʿāʾim al-islām etc.*, see *BSOS* VII, 34, A. A. Fyzee, An ancient Copy of the D., *Journ. of the Un. of Bombay*, vol. II, part. VI, May 1936, 127/33.—6. *Sharḥ al-akhbār etc.* see *BSOS* VII, 34, *Dharīʿa* I, $310,_{1609}$.—9. *al-Majālis etc.*, see *BSOS* VII, 34.—12. *al-Tawḥīd billāh* Berl. Oct. 2958.—13. *Asās al-taʾwīl al-bāṭin*, written before 400, *BSOS* VII, 33.

6. The head of the Imāmis during his lifetime was Abū ʿAbdallāh Muḥammad b. Muḥammad b. al-Nuʿmān b. ʿAbd al-Salām al-ʿUkbarī al-ʿArabī al-Ḥārithī al-Baghdādī al-Mufīd b. al-Muʿallim, who was born in 336/947 and who died on 3 Ramadan 413/1 December 1022.

202 | See Suppl. I, 322. Yūsuf al-Baḥrānī, *Luʾluʾat al-Baḥrayn* 281/301. 1. *al-Risāla al-muqniʿa*, on the principles of law with a factual commentary by his student Abū Jaʿfar Muḥammad al-Ṭūsī, d. 460/1067 (p. 405), part I, Berl. 4785/6, Manch. 186, Teh. Sip. I, 530.—2. (12) *Kitāb al-majālis* and 3. *Kitāb al-ʿuyūn wal-majālis*, from which *Talkhīṣ al-ʿuyūn wal-majālis*, a collection of aphorisms, perhaps collected by al-Ṭūsī, Ind. Off. $471,_{9}$.—4. Treatise on slaughter among the Jews and the Christians, Berl. 10276.—5. *al-Irshād etc.*, Alex. Taʾr. 10, with the title *al-Irshād fī ʾl-ansāb*, Rāmpūr $625,_{11}$ print. also Tehran 1308.—13. *al-Ikhtiṣāṣ*, a summary of the work with the same title by Abū ʿAlī b. ʿAlī b. al-Ḥusayn b.

Aḥmad b. ʿImrān, a contemporary of al-Ṣadūq (Kentūrī 125), Mashh. (not in the catalogue), Teh. Sip. I, 197/8, *Dharīʿa* I, 358,$_{1889/90}$.—14. *Awāʾil al-maqālāt fi ʾl-madhāhib al-mukhtārāt,* manuscripts *Dharīʿa* II, 472,$_{1844}$.—15. *al-Iʿlām fī-ma ʾttafaqat al-Imāmiyya ʿalayhi min al-aḥkām,* written as a supplement to it, at the request of al-Sharīf al-Murtaḍā, of which many copies were circulating, ibid. II, 237,$_{944}$.—16. *al-Ishrāf fī farāʾid al-islām,* many copies, ibid. II, 106,$_{901}$.—17. *Uṣūl al-fiqh,* included by al-Karājakī (p. 354) in his *Kanz al-fawāʾid,* print. ibid. II, 209,$_{814}$.—18. *Fiqh al-Riḍā* Tabriz 1274.—19. *Aḥkām al-nisāʾ*, library of ʿAbd al-Ḥusayn al-Ḥillī al-Najafī, ibid. I, 302,$_{1578}$.—20. *al-Ifṣāḥ fi ʾl-imāma,* many copies Iraq, ibid. II, 258/9,$_{1051}$.—21. *al-Asʾila al-Sarawiyya,* questions asked by al-Sayyid al-Fāḍil al-Sharīf in Sāriya, in the libraries of Hādī āl Kāshif al-Ghiṭāʾ in Najaf and Rājā Muḥammad Mahdī in Fayḍābād, ibid. II, 83,$_{330}$. 22. *Radd al-ṣūfiyyīn* Āṣaf. II, 404,$_{130}$.

Chapter 8. Sciences of the Qur'ān

1 *The Reading of the Qur'ān*

With its imperfect script, the text of the Qur'ān as determined by ʿUthmān
189 still gave rise to countless variant readings. | This is why, in different capitals
of the Muslim empire, especially in Mecca, Medina, Basra and Kufa, different
schools arose, which transmitted styles of performance as regards readings
and pronunciation that were based on the authority of a master. The masters
of linguistics, Abū ʿAmr b. al-ʿAlā' and al-Kisā'ī, in Basra and Kufa respectively,
203 also belonged to these older readers of the Qur'ān. | With the passing of time,
the intially rigidly maintained principle of oral transmission turned out to be
impracticable, due to the amount of detail that had to be remembered. From
among the older works describing the art of Qur'ānic recitation, that by Abū
ʿUbayd al-Qāsim b. Sallām (d. 224/839, see p. 105) received special acclaim. On
the others, see Suppl. I, 328/92.

1c. Abū Bakr b. Mujāhid al-Tamīmī al-Baṣrī, d. 324/936.

Kitāb al-sabʿa also Fātiḥ Waqf Ibr. 69 (Ritter).

2. From the fourth century there remain:

b. by Mūsā b. ʿUbaydallāh b. Khāqān Abū Muzāḥim, d. 325/937.

Qaṣīda fi 'l-tajwīd, see Suppl. La Q. fi 'l-t. attribuita a. M. b. ʿU. b. Kh., nota da P. Boneschi, *Rend. Acc. Lincei cl. sc. mor. stor. e fil.* s. VI, v. XIV, fs. 1/2, 1938, *RSO* XVIII, 258/67.

d. by Abū Bakr Aḥmad b. al-Ḥusayn b. Mihrān al-Nīsābūrī, who died at the age of 86 in Shawwāl 381/December 991. See Suppl., with *Tuḥfat al-anām fi 'l-tajwīd*, Āṣaf I, 296,$_{57}$.

2 *Qur'ānic Exegesis*

Sojutii liber de interpretibus Korani, ar. ed. et annot. illustravit A. Meursinge, Leiden 1839.

On the beginnings of Qur'ān interpretation see Suppl. I, 330/3.

On 1. *Tafsīr ʿAbdallāh b. al-ʿAbbās* also Qawala I, 45 (*Riwāyat al-Kalbī ʿan Abī Ṣāliḥ ʿan b. ʿAbbās*).

2e. *Tafsīr al-ʿAskarī*, which al-Majlisī and Mīr Dāmād branded as spurious, also Teh. Sip. I, 81/2. *Tanqīʿ fī uṣūl al-dīn wal-furūʿ* ibid. I, 230/1.

3. From the third century, the works by al-Farrā' (p. 118), Ibn Qutayba (p. 125), al-Zajjāj (p. 111), and al-Ṭabarī (p. 148) have already been mentioned.

| *a*. Sahl b. ʿAbdallāh al-Tustarī was a student of the mystic Dhu 'l-Nūn (p. 214), 204
whom he had met in Mecca. He lived in Basra and was regarded as a saint who was credited with miracles. His death is placed in 273/886 or 283.

| Ibn Khall. 265, Jāmī, *Nafaḥāt*, ed. Lees 73, see Suppl. 191

b. Abū Muḥammad ʿAbdallāh b. Muḥammad b. Wahb b. Mubārak al-Dīnawarī, who died in 308/920.

Al-Wāḍiḥ fī tafsīr al-Qur'ān, mostly based on Ibn ʿAbbās, Leid. 1651, AS 221/2.

c. The Zaydī ʿAbdallāh b. al-Ḥusayn b. al-Qāsim al-Ḥasanī Ṣāḥib al-Zaʿfarān went to Yemen in 284/897, together with his brother Yaḥyā al-Hādī ila 'l-Ḥaqq (p. 198).

Kitāb al-nāsikh wal-mansūkh Berl. 10226.

d. The Ḥanafī Abū Bakr b. ʿAlī al-Jaṣṣāṣ al-Rāzī (b. 305/917) can be mentioned here because of his first work only, as otherwise he belongs entirely to the *fuqahā'*. He started studying in Baghdad in 325/937 and worked as a teacher of *fiqh* there. He died on 7 Dhu 'l-Ḥijja 370/14 June 981 in Nishapur, where he had been living.

Flügel, *Hanaf.* 274, 299. 1. *Kitāb aḥkām al-Qur'ān* Köpr. 35, NO 107, Rāmpūr I, $162,_{5}$, print. C. 1347, 3 vols.—2. *Kitāb al-uṣūl* Cairo ^{1}II, 237, ^{2}I, 378.—3. Commentary on *al-Jāmiʿ al-kabīr* by Shaybānī, see p. 178, on the *Mukhtaṣar* by Ṭaḥāwī, p. 181.

e. Muḥammad b. Aḥmad al-Zuhrāwī, d. 370/980 (?).

Kitāb al-nāsikh wal-mansūkh, the abrogating and abrogated passages in the Qur'ān, NO 606 (not in ḤKh).

f. ʿAbdallāh b. ʿAṭiyya al-Dimashqī, who died in Shawwāl 383/November–December 903, rendered great service to Qur'ānic exegesis, especially by his thorough knowledge of *shawāhid* from ancient poetry.

Suyūṭī, no. 43. *Tafsīr* AS 119/21, Köpr. 185/6.

205 | *g*. Abū ʿAbdallāh Muḥammad b. ʿAlī b. Abī Zamanīn al-Marʿī al-Ilbīrī, a distinguished specialist in Mālikī *fiqh*, was born in 324/936 and died in 399/1008 in Spain.

Ibn Farḥūn, *Dībāj*, Fez 246, C. 370, Nallino, *Rend. Lincei* ser. VI, vol. VII, 324, Suyūṭī no. 102. *Tafsīr al-Qurʾān*, concise, Br. Mus. 820.

h. Muḥammad b. ʿAlī b. Aḥmad Abū Bakr al-Adfuwī al-Miṣrī al-Muqriʾ al-Naḥwī, who was a student of al-Naḥḥās (p. 138). He died aged 88 in Cairo, on 22 Rabīʿ I 388/24 April 998.

Suyūṭī no. 113, *Bughya* 81 (where: 7 Rabīʿ I). *Al-Istiftāʾ fī ʿulūm al-dīn*, in 120 volumes, ḤKh [1]I, 273,$_{616}$, II, 353,$_{2216}$ (ḤKh [2]I, 79, where *al-Istighnāʾ*, as in the *Bughya*, against ibid. 442 *al-Istiftāʾ*), Selīm Āġā 63, 146.

192 | *i*. Abu ʾl-Qāsim Hibatallāh b. Salāma (Sallām) b. Naṣr b. ʿAlī al-Baghdādī taught in the mosque of al-Manṣūr in Baghdad and died in Rajab 410/November 1019.

Suyūṭī 132. *Kitāb al-nāsikh wal-mansūkh fi ʾl-Qurʾān*, edited by his son ʿAbd al-Khāliq, discusses 201 passages on the basis of 95 commentaries, ḤKh VI, 13516, Berl. 4757, Leid. 1635, Leipz. 110,$_{6}$, Köpr. 211 (Ritter, *Isl.* XVIII, 37), 215, AS 65,$_{2}$, Garr. 1335/6, Alex. Fun. 186,$_{2}$, see Nöldeke, *Gesch. des Qorans* [1]41, [2]53.

k. The Shīʿī interpreter of the Qurʾān Abu ʾl-Ḥasan ʿAlī b. Ibrāhīm b. Hāshim al-Qummī also belongs to the fourth century.

Ṭūsī[1] no. 451, [2]370. *Tafsīr al-Qurʾān*, concise, on the basis of the authority of the Ahl al-bayt, Berl. Spr. 406, Ind. Off. 50, Teh. Sip. I, 138/9.—2. *Qurb al-isnād* (Kentūrī 2267), library Najafābādī 161.

Chapter 9. Dogmatics

Book of religious and philosophical sects by M. al-Shahrastani (d. 528/1153, p. 428), now first ed. by W. Cureton, 2 vols., London 1846.—*Schahrastanis Religionspartheien* | *und Philosophenschulen, aus dem Arab. übersetzt mit* 206
Anmm. von Th. Haarbrücker, 2 vols., Halle 1850/1.

H.S. Nyberg, al-Muʿtazila, *EI* III, 850/6.

H. Ritter, Muhammedanische Haeresiographien, *Isl.* XVIII, 34/55.

1. On the beginnings of dogmatic discussions in Islam, see Suppl. I, 336/45.

Ad p. 339, *Υ* 1. Kračkovsky, *Izv. Rossk. Ak. Nauk* 1919, 441/50.—p. 340, *ε Kitāb al-ḥayda wal-iʿtidhār*, also Tüb. 94, Br. Mus. Or. 9575, print. Mecca 1339.—*ζ* 1. Ḥushaysh, *Kitāb al-tanbīh ʿalā ahl al-ahwāʾ wal-bidaʿ*, ed. S. Dedering, *Bibl. Isl.* IX, 1936.—*ι* The opponent of al-Rāzī cited in *Fihrist* $301_{1,8}$ was Abū Bakr al-Ḥusayn b. al-Tammār, see al-Bīrūnī, *al-Āthār al-bāqiya* $253_{,18}$, Épître de Beruni 12, Kraus, *Or.* NS V, $54_{,25/7}$.—*κ* His *Kitāb naqd ʿUthmān Saʿīd ʿala ʾl-kādhib al-ʿanīd fī-ma ʾftarā ʿala ʾllāh fi ʾl-tawḥīd* is quoted by Ibn Taymiyya in *al-ʿAqīda al-Ḥamawiyya al-kubrā*, in *Majmūʿat al-rasāʾil al-kubrā*, C. 1323, I, $426_{,12}$.—p. 343 *ο* 1. al-Asadābādī, Ritter, *Isl.* XVIII, 42, n. 18, Borisov, *Bibliografia Vostoka*, 8/9, 1936, 63/95. 1. *Tanzīh al-Qurʾān ʿani ʾl-maṭāʿin*, also Āṣaf. III, $224_{,499}$.—p. 345, *ρ* MS Berl. Brill M. 259, Leonhardt Rost, Die Risāla al-Kindis, eine missionsapologetische Schrift in *Allgem. Missionsztzchr.* L (1923), 134/44, new edition announced by Rabbath, *Mél. U.J.* Beirut XIV, fs. 3, 43/5. Abu ʾl-Barakāt Nuʿmān Khayr al-Dīn Efendi, *al-Qawl al-faṣīḥ ʿalā ʿAbd al-Masīḥ*, Lahore 1304.

| 2. Against the Muʿtazila Abū Bakr Muḥammad b. Isḥāq b. Khuzayma 193
al-Nīsābūrī wrote from the standpoint of orthodoxy. He was born in Ṣafar 223/January 838 and died in 311/923 as one of the most distinguished theologians of Khurāsān.

Ḥuff. X, 79, Wüst. *Schaf.* 83. *Kitāb al-tawḥīd wa-ithbāt ṣifāt al-rabb*, against the Jahmiyya and the Muʿtazila, written because of dubious talk heard from his students, ḤKh V, 9999, Berl. 2394, Alex. Fun. $144_{,2}$, print. C. 1937, a teaching certificate for this text, issued by Yūsuf b. ʿAbd al-Raḥmān al-Mizzī, d. 742/1341 (II, 94), dated 692/1293, Berl. $153_{,3}$.

| 3. The Muʿtazila, who have often falsely been branded as freethinkers or 194
liberals, were in fact the ones who founded | scholastic theology (*kalām*) in 207
the first place. Their point of departure had been their struggle against the

extremist Shīʿis, the Rāfiḍa, in the face of whom they defended the claims of the ʿAbbāsids, against the Jahmiyya, who denied God all anthropomorphic attributes and who advocated the strictest doctrine of predestination, and against the Manichean dualists and the natural philosophy of late Hellenism they represented. In their struggle against them, they adopted the tool of speculative philosophy, which they also used against the *Aṣḥāb al-ḥadīth*. As opposed to the latter, they developed—or adopted from the Jahmiyya—the dogma of the createdness of the Qurʾān, which for them, too, was the sole foundation of their creed. Through the favour of al-Maʾmūn they succeeded, in 827, in elevating this dogma to a state doctrine, whose recognition was enforced by a public inquisition. But under the influence of the Shāfiʿīs, this monopoly of the Muʿtazila was abolished by al-Maʾmūn's third successor al-Mutawakkil (847/61), and, less than a lifetime later, the man who was to put the philosophical tool of the Muʿtazila into the service of traditionalism came onto the scene. Abu 'l-Ḥasan ʿAlī b. Ismāʿīl al-Ashʿarī was born in 260/873 in Basra into one of the oldest families of noble Arabian stock. Before the age of forty he belonged to the circle of students around the Muʿtazilī al-Jubbāʾī (Suppl. I, 342). Apparently he only confronted his teacher in Ramaḍān 299/912. Those who had shared his views until then tried to explain this breakup as being the result of personal motives. In truth, however, it was probably the tradition of his house (his ancestor Abū Burda, d. 103/722, had been a respected transmitter), combined with the political realities of time, which had motivated him to
208 join the Shāfiʿīs. He then moved to Baghdad and | began an extremely productive literary career. The titles of 99 of his works are known, although many of these are short treatises. His understanding and foundation of dogma received general recognition in those countries where the *madhhab*s of al-Shāfiʿī and al-Mālikī were dominant, even though there was no lack of setbacks until al-Ghazzālī secured its definitive triumph. However, the Ḥanafīs preferred the system of someone from their own ranks, al-Māturīdī, which rested on the same foundation. Only the Ḥanbalīs and the Ẓāhirīs confronted him in open confrontation. For these rigid traditionalists, even his moderate *kalām* seemed a *bidʿa*.

W. Spitta, *Zur Geschichte Abu 'l-Ḥasan al-Ashʿarīs*, Leipzig 1876, M.A.F. Mehren, Exposé de la réforme de l'islamisme commencée au IVème siècle de l'hégire par Abou l-Hasan Ali el-Ashʿarī et continuée par son école in *Travaux de la IVème session du Congr. intern. des orient.* St. Petersbourg 1876, vol. II, Leiden 1879, p. 169/331 (both based on Ibn ʿAsākir, d. 571/1175, p. 331, *Tabyīn kadhib al-muftarī*
195 *fī-mā nasaba ila 'l-imām Abi 'l-Ḥasan al-Ashʿarī*, see Suppl. with | Köpr. 856, defter mistaken).—Schreiner, Zur Geschichte des Ashʿaritentums, in *Actes du VIIIème*

Congr. intern. des Or. Sect. I, fs. 1, Leiden 1891, p. 79/117. Of his works remain: 1. *Maqālāt al-islāmiyyīn*, AS 2363/6, ed. H. Ritter, *Bibl. Isl.* 12, 1929/30.—2. See Suppl.—3. *Kitāb al-luma'*, on God, the Qur'ān, divine will, the beholding of God with one's own (physical) eyes, predestination, faith, and the imamate, Br. Mus. Suppl. 172, see Spitta, p. 25.—4.–6. See Suppl.—7. *al-Ibāna fī uṣūl al-diyāna*, see Suppl. *The Elucidation of Islam's Foundation, a Transl. with Introduction and Notes by* Walter C. Klein, Am. Or. Series, vol. XIX, New Haven 1940.—A fragment in which he investigates the claim that all inquiry into religious and philosophical questions is an innovation and a heresy and that all one needs to know has already been taken care of by the Prophet and his Companions, Berl. 2162.

| 4. At the same time as al-Ash'arī, among the Ḥanafīs Abū Manṣūr Muḥammad 209
b. Muḥammad b. Maḥmūd al-Māturīdī, from Māturīd near Samarqand, undertook a philosophical reform of orthodox dogmatics. His doctrine was accepted in countries that were dominated by Ḥanafīs, notably in Transoxania, but also in India and Turkey. In keeping with the tenets of Abū Ḥanīfa, al-Māturīdī's doctrine distinguishes itself from al-Ash'arī in the appreciation of free will which he, like Abū Ḥanīfa, acknowledges. Punishment and reward are therefore validated from a moral point of view, while al-Ash'arī derives all human action from God's will alone. However, on this point al-Māturīdī's doctrine later also found recognition among the Ash'arīs. Al-Māturīdī died in 333/944 in Samarqand.

Ibn Quṭlūbughā 173, Flügel, *Ḥanef.* 295, Spitta op. cit. 112, al-Sayyid al-Murtaḍā, *Sharḥ al-Iḥyā'* II, 5/14, Goldziher, *Vorl.* 110ff., Horten, *Philosophische Systeme* 531, D.B. Macdonald, *EI* III, 475/7. 1. *Kitāb ta'wīlāt al-Qur'ān*, Berl. Fol. 4156, Rāġib 35/7, Köpr. 47/8, NO 122/5, Qawala I, 43.—2. *Kitāb al-tawḥīd* or *al-Maqālāt*,[1] Cambr. 398, Add. 3632, Köpr. 856, Āṣaf. III, $532_{,1049}$.—3. *'Aqīda*, see Suppl.—4. Excerpts from a paraenetic work in translation, Fātiḥ $5426_{,235a/240a}$.—Also mentioned: *Kitāb radd awā'il al-adilla lil-Ka'bī* (this is Abu 'l-Qāsim 'Abdallāh b. Aḥmad b. Maḥmūd al-Balkhī, al-Sam'ānī, *Ansāb*, 485a); *Kitāb bayān wahm al-Mu'tazila, Kitāb al-jadal, Kitāb ma'khadh al-sharā'i'*, ḤKh II, 333, ^{2}I, 111, V, $70_{,10014}$, $351_{,11263}$.—Falsely attributed to him is the *Kitāb al-uṣūl* or *Uṣūl al-dīn*, Berl. Oct. 3566, Gotha $100_{,1}$ (see Suppl.).

5. Abū Muḥammad 'Abdallāh b. Muḥammad b. Ja'far b. Ḥayyān b. al-Shaykh al-Iṣfahānī, who was born in 274/887 and died in 369/979.

1 Which are, however, also distinguished in the listings of Ibn Quṭlūbughā and al-Murtaḍā.

Ḥuff. XII, 43 (wrong 329). *Kitāb fī ʿaẓamat Allāh wa-makhlūqātihi,* which like his other works (see Suppl.) belongs more to the field of Tradition. In the introduction he invokes ʿAbdallāh b. al-Sallām and the writings by Daniel used by
210 him | which he supposedly copied from the tablets of Adam kept in Serendīb (Ceylon), Berl. 6159, Alex. Mawāʿiẓ 31, Cairo[1] VI, 178.

6. Another writer should be mentioned here, one whose activity ranged over the whole domain of theology, and, as well as dogma, included *fiqh,* Qurʾān
196 interpretation and paraenesis; | Abu ʾl-Layth Naṣr b. Muḥammad b. Aḥmad b. Ibrāhīm al-Samarqandī al-Ḥanafī, who died in 373/983 (or, according to others, in 375, 383, or 393).

Ibn Quṭlūbughā 242, Flügel, *Hanef.* p. 302. 1. *Tafsīr al-Qurʾān,* ḤKh [1]II, 3209, [2]I, 441, vol. II, Berl. 734/5, fragm. ibid. 736, Munich 78, Leid. 1653, Esc. [2]1434, AS 148/9, Köpr. 72, NO 228/32, Qawala I, 47, q, 4.—2. *Khizānat al-fiqh* on the *furūʿ,* ḤKh [1]III, 135$_{,4698}$, [2]I, 703, Gotha 991/3 (where other MSS are mentioned), in addition: Berl. 4444/5, Oct. 2025, Pet. AM 105, Paris 826, AS 1148, Yeni 416, Garr. 1670/1, Alex. Fiqh Ḥan. 23, Cairo [1]III, 43, Rāmpūr I, 190$_{,1731}$.—3. *Fatāwī,* Yeni 677 = *al-Nawāzil min al-fatāwī,* Cairo III, 144 (?). Abstract *al-Multaqaṭ min al-masāʾil al-wāqiʿāt* by Masʿūd b. Shujāʿ al-Ḥanafī al-Dimashqī al-Umawī, d. 16. Jum. II 599/4 March 1203, Munich 249.—4. *Mukhtalif al-riwāya,* on the deviations from Abū Ḥanīfa by Ḥanafī teachers, in three recensions (see Suppl.), the vulgata Paris 825$_{,1}$, Br. Mus. 193, Köpr. 650.—Commentaries: a. Abū Ḥafṣ ʿUmar al-Nasafī, d. 537/1142 (p. 427), *Br. Mus. Quart,* IV, 8.—b. *Multaqa ʾl-biḥār* by Muḥammad al-Zawzanī al-Sharīdī al-Ḥanafī, Yeni 471 (or an independent work? ḤKh [1]VI, 106$_{,12850}$).—5. *al-Muqaddima fi ʾl-ṣalāh,* on the obligation of prayer for believers, ḤKh VI, 71$_{,12756}$, Gotha 762 (where other MSS are mentioned, in addition:), Berl. 3506/7, Paris 1121/3, 1141$_{,2}$, 1142$_{,2}$, Algiers 764, AS 1442/3, Alex. Fiqh Ḥan. 66, Cairo [1]III, 134, Qawala I, 396/7, Rāmpūr I, 253$_{,567}$, with Turkish translation in Berl. 3512.—Commentaries: a. on selected passages, *al-Taqdima* by Jabrāʾīl b. Ḥasan b. ʿUthmān al-Ganjāʾī al-Maʿkalī, ca. 750/1349, Berl. 3508, Munich 151, Alex. Fiqh Ḥan. 13.—b. *al-Tawḍīḥ,* more detailed, by Muṣṭafā b. Zakariyyāʾ b. Aidoğmiš al-Qaramānī Muṣliḥ al-Dīn, d. 809/1406, completed in 792/1349, Berl. 3509, Paris 1124/7, Garr. 1944, Alex. Fiqh Ḥan. 15, 55, [1]III, 30, 74, Qawala I, 314$_{,15}$, Rāmpūr I, 210$_{,289}$, Bank. IX, 1598.—
211 c. Ḥasan b. Ḥusayn al-Ṭūlūnī, d. 830/1427, Alex. Fiqh Ḥan. 34.—| d. Ibrāhīm b. Muḥammad al-Ḥalabī, d. 956/1549 (II, 432), Makram 34, Munich 160 (where Muḥammad b. Ibrāhīm b. Muḥammad).—e., f. see Suppl.—g. anon. Berl. 3510, Paris 1128$_{,2}$, Garr. 1890.—6. *Bayān ʿaqīdat al-uṣūl,* creed, Br. Mus. 871$_{,2}$, with anon. comm. *Bahjat al-ʿulūm,* Berl. 1945.—7. A catechism, see Suppl., also

Garr. 920, $2133_{,1}$.—8. *Bustān al-ʿārifīn* examines, on the basis of many books, a number of subjects, including *fiqh*, theology, philosophy etc. and advises in particular on good morals and appropriate conduct, Berl. 8322/3, Brill M. 142, Vienna 1837, Pet. AM 55, AS 1683/6, NO 2283/4, Fātiḥ 2563, Cairo ^{1}II, 70, 147, Aligarh $103_{,30}$, Bombay $244_{,166}$, print. Calcutta 1868, Būlāq 1289, Bombay 1304 (with no. 9 in the margin).—9. *Tanbīh al-ghāfilīn*, reflections on morality and piety, aphorisms and admonitions, drawing on sayings by Muḥammad, in 94 chapters, Berl. 8735/6, Vienna 1837, Leipz. 159/60, Ind. Off. 147, Algiers 872/5, Garr. 1889, AS 1741/2, Fātiḥ 2597, Alex. Mawāʿiẓ 11, Cairo ^{1}II, 151, print. Bombay 1884, Cairo 1305, ʾ6 (with no. 8 in the margin), ʾ7, ʾ8—10. *Asrār al-wajh* (Berl. *waḥy*), conversations between God and Muḥammad on the night of the *miʿrāj*, on religious precepts, Berl. 2600/1 with a personal commentary by Burhān al-Dīn and Bakhtiyār Bukhārī, AS 2016.—11. *Qurrat al-ʿuyūn wa-mufarriḥ al-qalb al-maḥzūn*, on the punishment of grave sins, Būlāq 1300 (in the margin of al-Shaʿrānī's *Mukhtaṣar al-tadhkira al-Qurṭubiyya*).—12.–14. see Suppl.—15. *ʿUyūn al-masāʾil fī ʾl-furūʿ al-Ḥanafiyya*, see Suppl. Comm. by Muḥammad b. ʿAbd al-Ḥamīd al-Usmandī al-Samarqandī al-ʿAlāʾ al-ʿĀlim, d. 552/1157 (Suppl. I, 641), Rāmpūr I, $208_{,274}$.—16. *Taʾsīs al-fiqh*, Alex. Fiqh Ḥan. 10.—17. *Sarʿ al-islām*, Patna II, $445_{,2621,6}$.

| 7. One of the most important second-generation students of al-Ashʿarī was 197
Abū Bakr Muḥammad b. (ʿAbd) al-Ṭayyib al-Baṣrī al-Bāqillānī, founder of the sceptical school of dogmatics and an outstanding polemicist, who died in Baghdad on 23 Dhu ʾl-Qaʿda 402/6 June 1013.

Ibn Khall. 580, Mehren, op. cit., 228, Schreiner, op. cit., 108. 1. *Kitāb al-iʿjāz fī ʾl-Qurʾān*, Berl. Oct. 1436, Köpr. 40, Cairo ^{1}I, 54, no. 15, print. C. 1349 and in the margin of al-Suyūṭī's *al-Itqān* C. 1935.—2.–8. see Suppl.—9. *al-Ibāna* is cited in Ibn Taymiyya, *Majmūʿat al-rasāʾil al-kubrā* I, $452_{,9}$.

8. Abū ʿAbdallāh al-Ḥusayn b. al-Ḥasan b. Muḥammad al-Ḥalīmī | al-Shāfiʿī, 212
who was born in 338/949 in Jurjān, was regarded as the greatest theologian of Transoxania of his time. He died in 403/1012.

Ibn Khall. (Wüst.) 185. *Kitāb suʿab al-īmān*, on religious ethics, Cairo ^{1}II, 53, see Suppl.

Chapter 10. Mysticism

A. Merx, *Idee und Grundlinien einer allgemeinen Geschichte der Mystik*, Inaugural address, Heidelberg 1893.

L. Massignon, Taṣawwuf, *EI* IV, 737/42.

Alongside the traditional ritualistic piety of the oldest version of Islam and under the pressure of the political and social crises of the first two centuries there developed at an early stage a spiritual movement that, based on a deeper study of the Qur'ān, strove for a personal relationship with God[1] that wanted to regard everything in this world in that light. In Islam, this mystical-ascetic movement developed according to the same laws as in other religions, and the similarities conditioned thereby led earlier researchers to conclude there was a direct dependence upon other cultures. Thus Dozy and A. v. Kremer wanted to derive Islamic mysticism mainly from Buddhism, while Merx wanted to trace it to the Syriac church. Against them, it was R.A. Nicholson in particular who demonstrated the purely Islamic origin of the Sufi.[2] The oldest ascetics called themselves thus, probably at first in Kufa, because they gave evidence of their unworldliness by wearing a white woollen mantle. Ḥasan al-Baṣrī (p. 65) was one of them, and two generations after him ʿAbd al-Wāhid b. Zayd
213 (d. 177/793 | al-Shaʿrānī, *Ṭab.* I, 38) assembled his students in a settlement in ʿAbbadān in order to live a communal life. Because culture, whatever its form or aspect, always converged on Baghdad, it was not long before Sufis moved there too. Abu 'l-ʿAtāhiya, who went there from Kufa, could be regarded as one of them. When a contemporary and friend of Aḥmad b. Ḥanbal, Abū Ḥamza Muḥammad b. Ibrāhīm[3] (d. 269/882), came from Mecca to Baghdad, he was greeted by a band of Sufi shaykhs. He then held lectures, first in al-Ruṣāfa, later in the main mosque of Baghdad, and was soon regarded as the head of the Sufis. By 250/864, separate halls for *ḥalqa*-sessions, with sermons and music, had apparently already started to operate.

On this soil saturated with Greek culture, mysticism was nevertheless not able to escape a foreign influence altogether. The Syriac church transmitted its Neoplatonic outlook, which it even appropriated in part under its Syriac name.

---

1 *Ṣafāʾ al-dhikr wa-jamʿ al-himma wal-maḥabba wal-shawq wal-qurb wal-uns*, Ibn al-Khaṭīb, *Taʾrīkh Baghdād* I, 390,$_{9}$.

2 Nöldeke, *ZDMG* 48, 45/8, has proven the word's derivation from *ṣūf*, 'wool', such against Merx who wanted to trace it to σοφός.

3 Ibn al-Khaṭīb, *Taʾr. Baghdād* I, 390/4.

In the East, in Khurāsān, where the special movement of the Malāmatiyya[4] developed, its asceticism adopted some of the methods of the Indian yogis, although they did not acquire wider significance until later times.

1. On the oldest Sufi writers, see Suppl. I, 350/1.

ʿAbdallāh b. al-Mubārak, who was born in 118/736 and died in 181/797 in Hīt on the Euphrates while returning from a military campaign, having lived for a time in Khurāsān (al-Shaʿrānī, *Ṭab.* I, 51/2), is credited with *al-Raqāʾiq*, Alex. Mawāʿiẓ 18.

1d. Bishr b. al-Ḥārith al-Ḥāfī, *Kitāb al-taṣawwuf*, Patna I, 141,$_{1374}$.

1e. Al-Muḥāsibī: Ibn Khall. 145, v. Kremer, *Ideen* 67. *Abdalhalim, Mahmoud, al-Mohasibi: un mystique musulman religieux et moraliste*, Paris 1940.

| 1. *Kitāb al-riʿāya etc.* also Cairo ²I, 313, ed. Margaret Smith, Gibb Mem. NS XV, 1940.—2. *al-Naṣāʾiḥ etc.* also Berl. Oct. 1435, Ind. Off. 4598 (copy of Cairo ²I, 370, *JRAS* 1939, 378), see H. Ritter, *Die Schrift des al-Ḥ. b. A. al-M.* (see ad 7) p. 7—3. *Kitāb al-tawahhum*, ed. A.J. Arberry, C. 1937.—4. *Risālat al-makāsib wal-waraʿ wal-shubha.*—5. *Risālat ādāb al-nufūs.*—7. *Risālat badʾ man anāba ila ʾllāh* ed. H. Ritter, *Die Schrift des al-Ḥ. b. A. al-M. über den Anfang der Umkehr zu Gott* (for the 19th Congress of Orientalists, Rome), Glückstadt 1935.—14. *Sharḥ al-maʿrifa*, abbreviated excerpts Köpr. 1601, 98b/100b.—19. *Kitāb al-mustarshid*, Alex. Fun. 100,$_{13}$.—21. *Risāla fi ʾl-taṣawwuf*, Alex. Taṣ. 35,$_{11}$. 214

2. Mystico-ascetic ideals seem to have become commingled with alchemistic fantasies as early as the Egyptian Dhu ʾl-Nūn Abu ʾl-Fayḍ Thawbān b. Ibrāhīm b. Aḥmad al-Miṣrī, although the authenticity of the works attributed to him does not seem to have been confirmed. He died on 2 Dhu ʾl-Qaʿda 246/19 January 861 in Giza.

| 1. *Mujarrabāt*, recipes for medicine, chemistry, magic, talismans, spells etc. Paris 2608.—2. Poems on the philosopher's stone, ibid. 2609,$_{4}$, Br. Mus. 601, IV, 2 (see Suppl.), comm. by Aḥmad b. ʿĀmir b. ʿAlī al-Hamdānī al-Ḥāshīdī, written in 855/1451, also Āṣaf. III, 146.—4. The *Kitāb al-ʿajāʾib* was falsely attributed to him, Cairo ¹V, 58 photographs, *Qu. u. St.* VII, 85,$_{VI,13}$.—6. *Duʿāʾ*, Rāmpūr I, 337. 198

4 See Abdülbâki, *Melâmîlik ve Melâmîler*, Istanbul 1931.

2a. Abū Yazīd al-Bisṭāmī, see Suppl. I, 353.

Anon. *Manāqib* and *Waṣāyā*, Alex. Ta'r. 116.—Legend of his ascension to heaven, based on the *Manāqib Abī Y. al-B.* of ʿAlī b. ʿAbd al-Raḥīm al-Qannād, d. ca. 340/951 (Massignon, *Essai* 244), from chapter 9 of the *Kitāb al-qaṣd* by al-Qāsim al-ʿĀrif (9a), see Nicholson, *Islca* II, 402/15. Regarding the late apocryphon *Kitāb masāʾil al-ruhbān* (addenda, 954), additionally Ind. Off. 4585 (*JRAS* 1939, 373), see Arberry, *JRAS* 1938, 89/91.

2b. Abū Saʿīd Aḥmad b. ʿĪsā al-Kharrāz, see Suppl. I, 354.

1. *Kitāb al-ṣidq*.—2. *Kitāb al-masāʾil*, Berl. cod. sim. 65, ed. and transl. from the Istanbul unicum by A.J. Arberry, London 1937, Isl. Research Assoc. Series 6.

3. Al-Junayd b. Muḥammad b. Junayd al-Qawārīrī al-Kharrāz Abu 'l-Qāsim al-Nihāwandī, cf. Suppl.

215 | Ibn Khall. 140, Arberry, *JRAS* 1935, 499/507. Of the *Kitāb maʿālim al-himam* that was falsely attributed to him—attributed to al-Junayd al-Baghdādī (Suppl. II, $214_{,3a}$) in Berl. Oct. 1801 (with the title *Maʿāni 'l-himma*, Rāmpūr I, $366_{,313}$)—there is a copy in Ind. Off. 4597 (*JRAS* 1939, 375), ed. H.K. Ghazanfar, *Allahabad Un. Studies* XI, 1935, 263/97, XIII, 1937, 226/54, see Nicholson, *Islca* II, 402.

4. Al-Junayd's most important student was al-Ḥusayn b. Manṣūr al-Ḥallāj, the only son of a benefactor. In Tustar he had belonged to the circle around Sahl al-Tustarī, who had further developed al-Muḥāsibī's doctrine of a return to God to the point of remorse and who had adopted from the Shīʿa the gnostic doctrine of the column of light, which at the beginning of time had united all souls so that these might feel one with God. Thus prepared, he came to al-Junayd and, having stayed with him for six years, felt superior to him because he considered that he had already reached this stage of perfection, this ideal which the former vainly sought to attain. After his split with him he roamed through the Islamic world as a wandering preacher, going all the way to India. He let himself be introduced to Greek philosophy by the great physician al-Rāzī (p. 266), and he also established contact with the Qarmaṭians. After a pilgrimage to Mecca he returned to Baghdad in 295/908. With his doctrine that, in his resignation to suffering and to the will of God, the ascetic places himself on the same level as Truth, he attracted a great circle of students, which soon aroused the suspicion of the dominant theologians. Suspected by the authorities, he spent eight years in prison. Because the mother of the caliph al-Muqtadir and her *ḥājib* al-Naṣr wanted to save him, the vizier Ḥāmid put him through a

summary trial in which he was found guilty and sentenced to death by senior judges from all four schools of law. On 12 Dhu 'l-Qaʿda 921/26 March 922 he was hanged in the courtyard of the new prison | on the right bank of the Tigris, 216
his corpse decapitated, and subsequently burnt. His students fled to Khurāsān where they cherished the memory of his martyrdom, which continued to live on in the mystical poetry of the Persians and the Turks.

Ibn Khall. (Wüst.) 186, Ibn al-Athīr VIII, 93 v. Kremer, *Ideen* 70, see Suppl. Listing of some of his writings Berl. 15.—*Kitāb al-sayhūr fī naqd al-duhūr* according to Kračkovsky in MS Leningrad Firkowitsch 4885 (Akhbar 52, n. b).—*Nūr al-muqal fī 'l-aʿmāl al-rūḥāniyya wal-dakk wal-ḥiyal*, apocryphal, Rāmpūr I, 690,$_{21}$.

5. Muḥammad b. ʿAlī b. al-Ḥusayn al-Ḥakīm al-Tirmidhī, d. 320/932, see Suppl. I, 335/6.

1. *Khatm al-awliyāʾ*, anon. comm. on *al-Masāʾil al-rūḥāniyya*, Alex. Taṣ. 40,$_{3}$.—b. *al-Masāʾil al-maknūna*, ibid. Fun. 145,$_{1}$.—c. *al-Masāʾil al-muʿaṭṭila*, ibid. 2.—11. Leipz. 212 contains, though with the wrong title, *al-Durra al-maknūna etc.* individual treatises, among which nos. 5 and 8, see Arberry *RSO*, XVIII, 1940, p. 315/27.—12. *Nawādir al-uṣūl etc.*, Istanbul MSS in Weisweiler, *Trad.* 193, n. 1, Qawala I, 158, comm. *Mirqāt al-wuṣūl* by Muṣṭafā al-Dimashqī, completed in 1313, in *Majmūʿa*, Istanbul 1313.—13. *Kitāb al-furūq etc.*, on seemingly similar actions that are different from a spiritual point of view (Ritter), Esʿad 1479,$_{5}$, now in the Awqāf museum, with *Ḥaqīqat al-ādamiyyīn* and *al-ʿAql wal-hudā*, Alex. Fiqh Shāf. 33.—20. *Ghawr al-umūr*, Berl. 3130 = (?) *Fī bayān al-farq bayna 'l-ṣadr wal-qalb wal-fuʾād wal-lubb*, Cairo ^{2}I, 345.—20a. The *Kitāb fī 'l-adʿiya wal-ṭilasmāt wal-ʿazāʾim*, AS 1814, is Persian (Ritter).

5a. Abū Bakr Muḥammad b. Mūsā al-Wāsiṭī of Farghāna, who died in 331/942 in Marw.

Suppl. I, 357, Hujwīrī, Nich. 154/5, ʿAṭṭār, *Tadhkirat al-awliyāʾ*, II, 265/81. *Kitāb al-kabāʾir wal-ṣaghāʾir*, Köpr. 1603,$_{7}$.

| 6. Abū Bakr Dulaf b. Jaḥdar al-Shiblī, d. 334/946. 200

Suppl. I, 357, Ibn Khall. 215. Conversation with a friend while on the pilgrimage, Br. Mus. 136,$_{2}$.

6b. Al-Nasafī, see Suppl. I, 293. 6a. 2. Under the title *Kitāb al-luʾaylīʾa*, Esʿad 437 f. 59a/69b, abstract, Cairo ^{2}I, 356.

217 | 7. Muḥammad b. ʿAbd al-Jabbār b. al-Ḥasan al-Baṣrī wrote in 352/963:

Kitāb al-mawāqif samiʿahu min kalām shaykhihi Abī ʿAbdallāh Muḥammad b. ʿAbdallāh al-Niffarī (as such in AS 2121), on the 77 stages of the Sufi, the first of which is the *mawqif al-ʿizz*, and the last the *mawqif al-kayf*, ḤKh VI, 235,$_{13355}$, Gotha 880, Köpr. 875, with comm. by ʿAfīf al-Dīn al-Tilimsānī (p. 258), Bodl. I, 106, 110, Köpr. 785 (dating from 695 AH), Bursa Ulu Jāmiʿ Taṣ. 5, Šehīd ʿA. P. 1433,$_{1}$, Uskudār Nūr Bānū 107 with another comm. Bodl. I, 352, cf. II, 579, ed. Arberry (see Suppl.), not used AS 2121, Bursa Ulu Jāmiʿ Taṣ. 4.

7a. Ibn al-Khafīf 2. *Al-ʿAqīda al-ṣaḥīḥa*, Fātiḥ 5391.

7c. Ibn al-Sarrāj, *Kitāb al-lumaʿ*, oldest MS dates from 483 AH, Bank. XIII, 825.

8. Abū Ṭālib Muḥammad b. ʿAlī b. ʿAṭiyya al-Ḥārithī al-Wāʿiẓ al-Makkī lived as an ascetic and preacher in Mecca, Basra, and Baghdad, and died in 386/996.

Ibn Khall. 602, Jāmī, *Nafaḥāt* p. 135, no. 125. *Qūt al-qulūb fī muʿāmalat al-maḥbūb wa-waṣf ṭarīq al-murīd ilā maqām al-tawḥīd*, ḤKh IV, 580,$_{9636}$, Leipz. 215, Gotha 881 (fragm.), Esc. ^{2}729, Algiers 907, Constantine *JA* 1860, I, 438, Cairo ^{1}II, 103, Garr. 1570/1, ʿĀšir I, 481, Nāfiz 436, AS 2001, Köpr. 865, Yeni 723, Fātiḥ 2766/7 (revised ibid. 2765, from 575 AH), Calcutta p. 48, no. 39, Tippu 113, print. C. 1310, 2 vols., excerpts Berl. 2816/7, Paris 2016,$_{2}$, Esc. ^{2}739,$_{1}$, by Ḥusayn b. Maʿn, Fātiḥ 2768. Explanation of difficult passages from this text and from the lost *al-Bayān al-shāfī* by Muḥammad b. Ibrāhīm b. ʿAbbād al-Nafzī al-Rundī, d. 791/1390 (II, 118), Esc. ^{2}740,$_{2}$.

9. Muḥammad b. Isḥāq b. Ibrāhīm al-Kalābadhī al-Ḥanafī Abū Bakr, d. 380/990 or 390.

1. *Kitāb al-taʿarruf li-madhhab ahl al-taṣawwuf*, ḤKh ^{1}II, 116, ^{2}I, 419, Algiers 906, Bodl. I, 253, Garr. 2117,$_{1}$, Rāmpūr I, 359,$_{268}$, printed in the margin of al-Ghazzālī's *al-Iḥyāʾ*, Istanbul 1321 (see Suppl.), abstract Ind. Off. 657,$_{6}$.—Commentaries: a. *Ḥusn al-taṣarruf* by ʿAlī b. Ismāʿīl al-Qūnawī, d. 729/1329 (II, 86), Vienna 1888, Berl. Qu. 1202, Bāyezīd 1709; all kinds of notes from this by ʿAlī b. Aḥmad b. Muḥammad b. Aḥmad al-Manūfī, ca. 880/1475, Berl. 3087.—c. *Nūr al-murīdīn etc.* also Bursa, Haraccizade Taṣ. 32.—2. *Baḥr al-fawāʾid al-musammā bi-maʿāni ʾl-akhbār*, Garr. 1368, Yeni 274, Alex. Ḥad. 8, Cairo ^{2}I, 92.

| 9a. Al-Qāsim al-ʿĀrif, who died on 14 Shaʿbān 395/26 May 1005. 218

Kitāb al-qaṣd, a manual for attaining mystical union (attributed by ḤKh VI, $90,_{2792}$ to al-Junayd al-Baghdādī, Suppl. II, $214,_{3}$a , under the title *al-Maqṣad ila ʾllāh*), MSS from Lucknow and Hyderabad, R. Nicholson, *Islca* II, 402.

10. Abū Saʿīd ʿAbd al-Malik b. ʿUthmān al-Wāʿiẓ al-Kharkūshī, d. 406/1015 or 407.

Suppl. I, 361. 1. *Tahdhīb al-asrār*, an account of Sufism in 70 chapters, published by one of his students, Berl. 2819, abstract ibid. 2820, see A.J. Arberry, Khargushi's Manual of Sufism, *BSOS* IX, 345/9.—2. *Kitāb al-bishāra etc.*, Leid. 1213.—3. see Suppl.

11. Abū ʿAbd al-Raḥmān Muḥammad b. al-Ḥusayn b. Mūsā al-Sulamī al-Azdī al-Nīsābūrī, born in 330/941, was an extremely productive author in the fields of | Qurʾān interpretation and history. Nevetheless, he was regarded as being 201
not very trustworthy because he did not shrink from inventing traditions with a Sufi slant. He died in Shaʿbān of the year 412/1021.

Ibn al-Athīr IX, 230, *Ḥuff.* XIII, 33, Wüst. *Gesch.* 136. 1. *Ḥaqāʾiq al-tafsīr*, Qurʾān commentary, NO 319, Riḍā P. 737, Khāliṣ 69, Üsküdār, Hüdāʾī, Tefs. 20, Cairo ^{1}I, 170, anon. abstract, ibid. 209.—2. *Ṭabaqāt al-ṣūfiyyīn*, a continuation of his *Kitāb al-zuhd*, in which he had treated the classes of the *Ṣaḥāba*, the *Tābiʿūn* and *Tābiʿu ʾl-tābiʿīn* (Preface 5), ḤKh 3168, Berl. 9972, Br. Mus. 961, Faiẕ. 280, ʿĀšir 677, ʿUm. 5064, Asʿad 2313, Qawala II, 239, excerpts Köpr. 1603, ff. 219b/252a, *Texte ar. publié par* Johs. Pedersen, fs. 1 (Collection de textes inédits relatifs à la mystique musulmane, III), Paris 1938.—3. *Manāhij al-ʿārifīn*, a short exposition of Sufism (different from ḤKh VI, 13063), Berl. 2821, Munich 264, ff. 60b/73.—4. (*Jawāmiʿ*) *ādāb al-ṣūfiyya*, ḤKh ^{1}I, 213, 309, ^{2}I, 42, Berl. 3001, Köpr. 701 (lost), Lālelī 516, (with the title *Bayān aḥwāl al-ṣūfiyyīn*).—5. *Kitāb ʿuyūb al-nafs wa-dawāʾihā*, on the errors of the soul, ḤKh IV, 8448, Berl. 3131, Br. Mus. Suppl. 228, Pertew P. 616, Köpr. 1603, ff. 208a/218b, Bursa, Ulu Ǧāmiʿ Taṣ. 8, Taymūr $74,_{1}$.—A metrical adaptation entitled *al-Uns fī sharḥ ʿuyūb al-nafs* or *Rajaz al-maʿyūb* by Abu ʾl-ʿAbbās Aḥmad b. Muḥammad al-Burnusī b. Zarrūq, d. 899/1493 (II, 250), with comm. by Muḥammad b. ʿAlī | al-Kharrūbī, d. 963/1556 (Suppl. II, 701), Br. Mus. 629 (see 219
Suppl.).—6. *Risālat al-Malāmatiyya*, Berl. 3380, Spr. 851, ff. 47v/58r, Cairo ^{1}VII, 238, ff. 67r/73v, see R. Hartmann, *Isl.* VIII, 157/204.—7. *Darajāt al-muʿāmalāt*, an explanation of Sufi technical terms, Berl. 3453.—8. *Ādāb al-ṣuḥba wa-ḥusn*

al-ʿushra, Leipz. 881,$_1$ (see Suppl.), Šehīd ʿA. P. 1114, 8, Alex. Mawāʿiẓ 3.—9. *Ādāb al-faqr wa-sharāʾiṭuhu*, Fātiḥ 2553, ff. 60v/62v.—10. *al-Farq bayna ʿilm al-sharīʿa wal-ḥaqīqa*, AS 4218,$_2$.—11. *Masʾalat darajāt al-ṣādiqīn* (not identical with Berl. 3435), Fātiḥ 2653, ff. 59r/68v.—12. *Ghalaṭāt al-ṣūfiyya*, Cairo ¹VI, 228, ff. 68v/79v, another recension in al-Sarrāj, *al-Lumaʿ*, 409ff.—13. *Bayān zalal al-fuqarāʾ wa-manāqib ādābihim*, Fātiḥ 2650, ff. 77r/99v.—14. *Kitāb al-futuwwa*, AS 2049,$_4$, see Taeschner, *Islca* V, 314.—15. *Sulūk al-ʿārifīn*, Taymūr Taṣ. 74,$_2$.—16. *Uṣūl al-Malāmatiyya* (= 8?) ibid. 237.—17. *Muqaddima fi ʾl-taṣawwuf*, Alex. Taṣ. 46.

Chapter 11. The Translators

M. Steinschneider, *Die arabischen Übersetzungen aus dem Griechischen*, Einleitung 1–24, Centralblatt für Bibliothekswesen Beiheft 5 Jahrg. VI, 1889, I *Abschnitt Philosophie* (25–84), Beiheift 12, Jahrg. X 1893, III *Die griechischer Ärzte* § 1–34, *Virchows Archiv* 124 (1891), 115/36, 268/96, 455/87, II *Mathematik*, § 85–139, §140, *Alchemie*, Index, ZDMG 50, 161/219, 357/417.[1]

W. Kutsch, Zur Geschichte der syrisch-arab. Übersetzungsliteratur, *Orientalia*, NS VI, 1/2, 1937.

P. Kraus, Plotin chez les Arabes, *Bull. de l'Inst. Egypt.* 23, 1941, 263/95.

Hellenistic education, which had gained a foothold in Syria and Mesopotamia under Alexander and the Diadochi, profited greatly from the spread of Christianity. In Syria particularly, which was part of the Byzantine empire, monasteries were religious institutions and, at the same time, places of Greek education, which their residents adopted through numerous translations,
even though they were unable to develop or enhance it any further. | Although 202
| the study of theology predominated, philosophy and medicine were not 220
overlooked.

In the empire of the Sasanids, Greek medicine in particular was highly regarded. In the year 531 CE Khusraw Anūshirwān founded an academy in Jundīshāpūr, in Khūzistān, for its development, a place where philosophy also found a home, and which continued to flourish into ʿAbbāsid times.[2]

Greek science found a third home in the Mesopotamian city of Ḥarrān. In spite of its entirely Christian surroundings, its inhabitants had kept their old Semitic paganism, which was strongly influenced by Hermeticism. Here, mathematical and astronomical studies flourished and these, having been cultivated in Akkadian culture, were also promoted in Hellenistic times.

Each of these three sources supplied the Muslims with Greek science in translation. If we ignore the ancient, possibly pre-Islamic translations of the Bible, then the translations of a Hermetic book of astrology called the *Miftāḥ asrār al-nujūm*, which may have been a translation of the *Παρανατέλλοντα* of Teukros—named by the Arabs, from a distorted Pahlavi form, Tankalūshā[3]—and perhaps also the translation of the *Geoponika* from the Persian *Varznāmeh* (see Suppl.), started in Umayyad times. As early as the time of al-Manṣūr there

---

1 Quoted by section number, just like Steinschneider, *Die hebr. Übersetzungen des Mittelalters*, 2 vols., Berlin 1893.

2 Cf. Schulz, *Disputatio de Gundisapora*, Commentaria Soc. scient. Petropol. vol. XII.

3 See A. Borissov, *JA* 226, 300/5.

was a physician from Jundīshāpūr working at the court who is believed to have translated medical works into Arabic. However, these studies saw their greatest upsurge under the caliph al-Maʾmūn, who had a keen interest in them. In 221 Baghdad he founded the Bayt al-Ḥikma with a library | and an observatory which, under the leadership of Salm, who was himself active as a translator from Persian (*Fihrist* 120, Ibn Abī Uṣaybiʿa I, 162), became the focal point of energetic academic pursuits. The translations that were made under al-Maʾmūn and his immediate successors superseded those of the older schools, and are the only ones that have survived.[4]

Here, the latter are arranged by translator and not by their Greek authors 203 as with Steinschneider. | For anonymous translations, the reader is referred entirely to him.

1. Al-Ḥajjāj b. Yūsuf b. Maṭar (Maṭarān) al-Ḥāsib.

See Suppl. I, 363. *Euclidis Elementa*, vol. II ed. Junge, Raeder and Thompson, Copenhagen 1932; Latin version of the commentary by Nayrīzī ed. M. Curtze, Leipzig 1899. On his translations of Euclid, see M. Klamroth, *ZDMG* 35, 265/81; Fātiḥ 3439 f. 45r/61v, Books 11–13 only.

2. Yuḥannā or Yaḥyā b. Biṭrīq, ca. 200/815.

Steinschneider, *Virchows Archiv* vol. 52, p. 364, *Übers.* 368. *Kitāb al-siyāsa fī tadbīr al-riyāsa taṣnīf al-ḥakīm al-fāḍil Arisṭāṭālīs* ḤKh V, 10202, a concoction pieced together from different sources by an Arab of the tenth or eleventh century (see R. Förster, de *Aristotelis Secretis secretorum commentatio*, Kiel 1888, *Script. physiogn.* I, p. CLXXIX, Steinschneider, *Centralbl. für Bibliothekswesen*, supplement XII, 79/80), Berl. 5603, more detailed ibid. ʾ4, Munich 650 = *Sirr al-asrār li-taʾsīs al-siyāsa wa-tartīb aḥwāl al-riyāsa* Vienna 1827/8, Bodl. I, 341/2, Paris 2417/21, another recension ibid. 22, Garr. 779/81, ʿĀšir 1002 (Ritter, *RSO* XVI, 212) Sulaim. 872, Mosul 55,134, translated into Latin by Philippus in Antioch on the order of Guido Vera de Valentia, Bishop of Tripoli, *Secreta secretorum Aristotelis*, Leiden 1528, *Epistola Aristotilis ad Alexandrum cum prologo Johannis Hispaliensis* ed. H. Suchier, Denkm. prov. Lit., Halle 1883, 473/80, Engl. by Fulton in *Rogeri Baconis Opera hactenus inedita*, V, 1920 (AS 2890 is, contra 222 *Tadhk. al-Nawādir* | 207, not an independent translation but identical with the

4 Traces of older translations are found in al-Yaʿqūbī's (p. 258) *Tarʾīkh*, see M. Klamroth *ZDMG* 40, 189ff.

text of the Berlin MS).—2.–3. see Suppl.—4. Aristotle's *Meteorology* also Yeni 1179 (R. Walzer, *Gnomon* 1934, 278, Bouyges, *MFO* IX, 1924, 43ff.).

3. ʿAbd al-Masīḥ b. ʿAbdallāh b. Nāʿima al-Ḥimṣī translated around the year 220/835 for the caliph al-Muʿtaṣim (218–27/833–42):

Ibn Abī Uṣaybiʿa I, 204, Baumstark, *Syr. Lit.* 230. *Kitāb Arisṭāṭālīs al-faylasūf al-musammā bil-Yūnāniyya Ūthūlūjiyya aw Rubūbiyya* (see Suppl.), also AS 2457$_{,11}$ (*Islca* IV, 528), Patna I, 208$_{,1855/6}$, 476$_{,2641,17}$, Fr. Dieterici, *Die sogenannte Theologie des Aristoteles*, Leipzig 1882, see Merx, *Mystik* p. 35, Nallino, *RSO* VIII, 95, *Or. Mod.* X, 49/50. Fragments of the Arabic original that was the basis for the Latin translation by Faventius, and which still contained all kinds of Christian ideas that were eradicated in the recension of al-Kindī that was published by Dieterici, were found by A. Borrissov in the Firkovitch Collection of the Library of Leningrad, see *Zap. Koll. Vost.* V (1930), 83/98. A complete translation of Plotinus' *Enneads* IVff. was used by al-Ghazzālī in *Mishkāt al-anwār*, see Wensinck, *Semietische Studien*, Leiden 1941, 192ff.—Recension by Taqī al-Dīn Abu 'l-Khayr al-Fārisī, Mashh. I, 14$_{,14}$, Library of Akbar al-Khwānsārī *Dharīʿa* I, 120$_{,577}$.

4. Qusṭā b. Lūqā al-Baʿlabakkī, d. ca. 300/912.

Suppl. I, 305/6. Wüst. *Ärzte* no. 100, inventory of his writings in Ibn Abī Uṣaybiʿa I, 244/5.

I. Works, as author: a. *Risāla fi 'khtilāf al-nās fī siyarihim wa-akhlāqihim wa-shahawātihim wakhtiyārātihim ʿan Abī ʿAlī al-Ḥārithī* Berl. 5387, a *faṣl* thereof Gotha 2096$_{,3}$.—b. *Risāla fi 'l-sahar*, on the causes of sleeplessness and its cures, for Abu 'l-Ghiṭrīf, Berl. 6357.—c. *Fī tadbīr al-abdān fi 'l-safar lil-salāma min al-maraḍ wal-khaṭar*, for Abū Muḥammad al-Ḥasan b. al-Makhlad, Br. Mus. 424$_{,2}$, Āṣaf. II, 934$_{,201}$, included as chapter 16 in the *Kitāb al-amān min akhṭār al-asfār wal-azmān* by al-Ṭāʾūsī, second half of the seventh cent., Ind. Off. 341.—d. *Kitāb fi 'l-balgham wa-ʿilalihi*, the first *maqāla* of a work in six *maqālāt* for Abu 'l-Ghiṭrīf, Munich 805.—e. *Kitāb fī ʿilal al-shaʿr* for Ḥasan b. Makhlad, Br. Mus. 434$_{,3}$.—f. *Risāla fi 'l-ʿamal bil-kura dhāt al-kursī*, on an astronomical instrument, Berl. 5836, Br. Mus. 1615$_{,7}$, Suppl. 753$_{,6}$ (where Afanṭā b. Lūqā), | Paris 2544$_{,10}$ anon.).—g. *Kitāb al-ʿamal bil-asṭurlāb al-kurī* Leid. 1053, 223 Serāi 3505$_{,3}$.—h. *Risāla fi 'l-kura 'l-falakiyya* Berl. 5836, Br. Mus. 407$_{,10}$, AS 2633, under the title *Kurat al-falak Zāwiyat Sīdī Ḥamza*, Renaud, *Hespéris* XVIII, 93.—i. *Kitāb al-ʿamal bil-kura 'l-falakiyya (fi 'l-nujūm)* Bodl. II, 297, Garr. 2096$_{,22}$ another treatise with the same title for Abu 'l-Ṣaqr b. Ismāʿīl b. Bulbul, vizier of al-Muʿtamid, Serāi $3505_{,5}$, AS 2635, 2637, Asʿad $2015_{,1,3}$, Āṣaf. I, $796_{,120}$, Hebr. Steinschneider 342.—k. see Suppl. i.–l. *Kitāb hayʾat al-aflāk* Bodl. I, $879_{,2}$.—m. *Kitāb al-faṣl bayn a ʾl-rūḥ wal-nafs* Gotha 1158 (according to Pertsch by Ibn Sīnā) Berl. Qu. 1075, see Suppl. *De differentia animi et spiritus, lat. versa a Baroch, Bibl. philos. medii aevi*, Innsbruck 1878.—n.–x. see Suppl. (n. also Šehīd ʿA. P. 2103). An uncertain *Kitāb qusṭā* Rāmpūr I, $493_{,201}$.

II. Translations: a. Plato's outlines of geometry in Steinschneider § 37.—b. Alexander's and Johannes Philoponos' commentaries on Aristotle's *Physics* ibid. 52.—c. Aristotle on sleep, dreams and the length of life ibid. 57.—d. Theophrastus, *Questions* ibid. 70.—e. Plutarch, *Opinions of the philosophers on physics and the practice of virtue* ibid. $77_{,1,2}$ (see Suppl.).—f. Euclid's *Elementa* Upps. 321, Fātiḥ $3439_{,10}$ (Books XIV, XV).—g. Hypsicles's *Kitāb al-maṭāliʿ*, revised by al-Kindī around 250/864, Berl. 5652, other MSS Steinschneider $101_{,2}$, ed. by Naṣīr al-Dīn al-Ṭūsī (see Suppl.) Sulaimān Qaṣīdağī Sirrī, $452_{,2}$.—h. Hypsicles's Supplement to Euclid's *Elementa*, Book XV, Copenhagen 81 (not in Steinschn. 107).—i. Theodosius' *Sphaerica* at the instigation of Aḥmad b. al-Muʿtaṣim, translated up to the fifth section of the third *maqāla*, the rest by someone else, the whole edited by Thābit b. Qurra, d. 288/901 (p. 217), Berl. 5933, other MSS Steinschn. $130_{,1}$ (see Suppl.), Pet. Am K. 922, Serāi $346_{,4}$, Bursa, Haraccizade Heyet 7, print. Tehran n.d.—k. idem, *Kitāb al-masākin*, Berl. 5649/50, Steinschn. $130_{,2}$ (Suppl.), Qaṣīdağī Sulaimān Sirrī $452_{,1}$, Serāi $3464_{,7}$.—l. idem, *Kitāb al-ayyām wal-layālī*, Berl. 5648, Steinschn. $130_{,3}$, Serāi $3464_{,7}$, ibid. 8 still before the revision by al-Ṭūsī (Krause 444).—m. Hero of Alexandria, Barulcus, *Kitāb sayl athqāl* Leid. 983, Cairo ^{1}V, 199 under the title *Fī rafʿ al-ashyāʾ al-thaqīla*, Serāi 3466, AS 2755, ed. Carra de Vaux, Les Mécaniques ou l'Elevateur de Heron d'Alexandria publiées pour la première fois sur la version arabe de Q. b. L. et
205 trad. en franç, *JA* s. IX, vol. 1, 385/472, v. 2. 152/269, 420/514, by | L. Nix and W. Schmidt in *Heronis Alex. opera quae supersunt omnia*, II, 1, Leipzig 1901, on
224 which A. | Favoro, Intorno delle Mechaniche di Erone Alessandrino edite par la prima volta sulla vers. ar. dal C. d. V. *Atti del. R. Ist. Veneto di Sc.* s. VII, v. 5. disp. 7.—o. Autolykus *Kitāb al-ṭulūʿ wal-ghurūb*, Leid. 1042, Steinschn. $152_{,2}$.—p. Inventory of the writings of Galen, Esc. ^{1}795, Steinschn. 13, p. 273, AS 3509, Meyerhof, *SBBA* 1928, p. 545.

5. The most famous translator of this whole period was Abū Zayd Ḥunayn (among Latin scholars Johannitius) b. Isḥāq al-ʿIbādī. Born in 194/809 (?) in Ḥīra where his father was a pharmacist, he remained true to the Christian religion of his fellow tribesmen, the ʿIbād, until the end of his life. He had studied in Basra with al-Khalīl, whose *Kitāb al-ʿayn* he was the first to bring to Baghdad.

There he attended the classes of the famous physician Yaḥyā b. Māsawayh (p. 265). He is believed to have completed his education with a trip to Asia Minor, where he learned Greek. He then became a teacher of medicine in Baghdad and was appointed by al-Mutawakkil as his personal physician, and he composed numerous medical and philosophical works. His fame is, however, chiefly based on his translation of Greek works, in which his son Isḥāq, his nephew Ḥubaysh, Stefan b. Basīl, Mūsā b. Khālid, and Yaḥyā b. Hārūn all participated. Due to the iconoclastic controversy that was raging in the oriental churches at the time he fell out with bishop Theodosius and was excommunicated. In a state of grief over this he then took poison and died on 6 Ṣafar 260/30 November 873.

Ibn Abī Uṣaybiʿa I, 184/206, Ibn Khall. 198, Michael Syrus 263, Barhebraeus, *Chron. eccl.* III, 199, *Mukhtaṣar* 250/3, Wüst., *Ärzte* no. 6, Leclerc I, 139/52, Suter, *Mathem.* 44.

I. Works, as author: 1. *Kitāb al-mudkhal fī ʾl-ṭibb*, an introduction to medicine, Esc. ^{1}848, Lat. *Isagoge Johannitii in Tegni Galeni*, n.p. & n.d., and Venice 1487, Leipzig 1497. *Joannitii isagoge in artem parvam Galeni*, Strasbourg 1534.—2. *Masāʾil fī ʾl-ṭibb lil-mutaʿallimīn* (*ʿalā* | *ṭarīq al-taqsīm wal-tashjīr*) Berlin 6258, 225
Bodl. II, 333,$_3$, in the augmented edition of his nephew Ḥubaysh, Gotha 1933, 2023, 2028, 2036,$_3$, Bodl. II, 195,$_2$, Serāi 2131 (see Suppl.), supplement by Ibn al-Tilmīdh, d. 560/1165 (p. 487) Bodl. I, 636,$_2$, under the title *al-Asās*, Rāmpūr I, 492.—Commentaries: a. Abu ʾl-Qāsim ʿAbd al-Raḥmān b. ʿAlī b. Aḥmad b. Abī Ṣādiq al-Nīsābūrī, | a student of Ibn Sīnā, d. 428/1037 (p. 484), with a divi- 206
sion into 10 chapters introduced by him and a text whose relation to other witnesses has not yet been sufficiently clarified, not even by Bergsträsser (*Ḥunayn Ibn Isḥāq und seine Schule* 5/6), Berl. Qu. 1040, Gotha 1932, Munich 804, Leid. 1303, Utrecht—Leid. 2689, Paris 2861/2, 6654, Sbath 1098 (see Suppl.), Garr. 1097.—b. Ibn al-Nafīs, d. 687/1288 (p. 493), Berl. Qu. 1040, Leid. 1304.—2a. *Kitāb al-ʿayn* (see Suppl. 4, Patna I, 251,$_{2142}$) *Le livre des questions sur l'œil de Ḥ. b. I., publié par* P. Sbath et M. Meyerhof, *Mém. de l'Inst. d'Égypte*, Cairo 1938.—3. *Kitāb fī awjāʿ al-maʿida*, Esc. ^{2}852,$_3$, AS 3555, f. 149v/156r—4. *Pharmacopoee*, Bodl. Hebr. 428.—5. *Compendium historiae Hermetum* Nan. I, 35.—6. Excerpts from a work on comets, Bodl. II, 285,$_7$.—7. On opposite virtues and vices, ibid. II, 349,$_5$.—8. *Ijtimāʿāt al-falāsifa fī buyūt al-ḥikma fī ʾl-aʿyād wa-tafāwuḍ al-ḥikma baynahum* Munich 651,$_2$, Br. Mus. Or. 8681.—9. *Honain b. Isḥaḳ Sefer Musre ha-filosofim* (*Sinnsprüche der Philosophen*) *aus dem Ar. ins Hebr. übers. v. Jehuda ben Salomo Alcharizi, nach Hdss. hsg. v.* A. Löwenthal, Frankfurt a. M. 1896, *H. b. I. Sinnsprüche der Philosophen nach der hebr. Übers. v. Charizi*

ins Deutsche übertr. v. A. Löwenthal, Berlin 1896, *Maṣḥafa falāsfā ṭabībān, das Buch der weisen Philosophen nach dem Äthiop. untersucht v.* C. H. Cornill, Leipzig 1875, cf. A. Müller, ZDMG 31, 506, 508, 526, Steinschneider, *Jahrb. f. roman. u. engl. Lit.* XII, 354, *Revue des Et. Juiv.* III, 242, supplement V, 26, *hebr. Übers.* 197 (cf. Suppl.).—10. *al-Mudkhal al-kabīr ilā ʿilm al-rūḥāniyyāt* Alex. Ḥurūf 16. 11—18. see Suppl. (on 14, p. 956).—19. *Jawāmiʿ al-Iskandarāniyyīn* Rāmpūr I, 473$_{,56}$.

II. Translations: 1. Old Testament after the Septuagint, al-Masʿūdī, *Tanbīh* 112, Ibn al-Qifṭī 99$_{,7}$.—2. Plato: a. *Republic*, Steinschn. § 33.—b. *Laws, Kitāb al-nawāmīs*, ibid. 34.—c. *Timaeus*, maybe just an improvement of a translation by Ibn al-Biṭrīq, ibid.—d. Information on synopses of Platonic dialogues by Galen, ibid.—e. Treatise on what one should read of Plato, ibid. 35.—3.
226 Aristotle: | a. *Syllogism* (after the translation by Theodorus), ibid. 46.—b. Alexander's commentary on *Physics* II, ibid. 52.—c. *De coelo et mundo* (after Ibn al-Biṭrīq) with explanations (*Masāʾil*), ibid. 55.—d. *De anima*, ibid. 56.—e. *Metaphysics* with the commentary by Alexander, ibid. 59.—f. Porphyry's commentary on the *Ethics*, ibid. 60.—g. *Problemata*, ibid. 62.—h. *Physiognomy*, ibid. 64, Serāi 3207$_{,1}$.—i. Pseudo-Aristotle on magic *Istamatis* etc., ibid. 68$_{,21}$, *Kitāb jawāmiʿ li-Kitāb A. fi ʾl-āthār al-ʿulwiyya*, Mosul 34$_{,154/5}$.—4. Alexander of Aphrodisias, on seeing and on the difference between matter and genus, ibid. 72$_{,2,17}$.—5. Porphyry, prolegomena to the *Eisagoge*, ibid. 73.—6. Artemidorus' *Oneirocritica*, ibid. 80.—7. Ptolemy's *Quadripartitum*, ibid. 116.—8. Euclid (see Suppl. p. 368$_{,2}$ no. 6).—9. Theodosios.—10. Menelaus' *Sphaerica*, ibid.—11. Autolykos *Fi ʾl-kura al-mutaḥarrika*, Steinschn. 125, Serāi 3462$_{,3}$ (Krause 440).—12. Apollonios, Steinschn. ZDMG XLV, 439ff., *Risāla Bālīnūs fī taʾthīr al-rūḥāniyyāt, fi ʾl-murakkabāt wa-aʿmāl al-ṣuwar wa-dafʿ al-amrāḍ wa-ḥulūlihā*, Wehbi Ef. 892, Alex. *Ḥurūf* 16$_{,2}$, Āṣaf II, 1688.—13. Hippocrates Esc. ^{2}857$_{,2-5}$: a. Aphorisms, *Fuṣūl*, Steinschn. 4 (see Suppl.), Rāmpūr I, 498$_{,172}$.—b. see Suppl.—c. Prognostica, *Taqdimat al-maʿrifa*, Steinschn. 7 (see Suppl.), Alex. Ṭibb 12, ed. M. Klamroth ZDMG 40, 204/33.—d. *περὶ τοῦ ὀκταμήνου, Kitāb al-mawlūdīn li-thamāniyat ashhur*, revised with a commentary Munich 805$_{,6}$, by Galen, Paris 2837, Esc. ^{2}789/91, see Bergstr., loc. cit., 7.–14. Galen, see Steinschn. 1–9, 10(?), 11/5, 21(?), 26, 28(?), 29, 32, 35, 36(?), 37/8, 40/1, 43/9, 50/3, 59, 60, 62, 68/9, 70(?), 71, 85/6, 99, 106/8, see Suppl. 368/9 (h. not by Ḥunayn, see Bergstr., loc.cit., 54/9).—i. *Firaq al-ṭibb*, also Garr. 1075$_{,6}$.—k. *Kitāb al-ṣināʿa al-ṣaghīra* also ibid. 1075$_{,1}$.—l. *al-Nabḍ lil-mutaʿallimīn*, ibid. 1075$_{,7}$ (*ilā Ṭaṭārūn* i.e. Teuthras).—m. *Kitāb ilā Glaukōn fi ʾl-taʾattī li-shifāʾ al-amrāḍ*, ibid. 1075$_{,8}$, Rāmpūr I, 468$_{,11}$.—n. *Fi ʾl-usṭuqisāt ʿalā raʾy Ibbuqrāṭ*, Garr. 1075$_{,9}$.—q. *Fi ʾl-quwa ʾl-ṭabīʿiyya*, Berl. Oct. 1122.—r. *Tashrīḥ al-ʿilal wal-aʿrāḍ*, ibid.—s. *al-Mawāḍiʿ*

al-ālima, ibid.—t. *Kitāb al-buḥrān* with *Ayyām al-buḥrān*, Garr. 1075,$_2$.—u. *Aṣnāf al-ḥummayāt* ibid. 3.—v. *Ḥīlat al-bur'* ibid. 4.—w. *Tadbīr al-aṣiḥḥā'* ibid. 5.—x. *περὶ τῶν ἑπταμήνων βρέφων*, ed. Walzer, RSO XV (1935), 323/87, XVI (1936), 22ff.—y. *De simplicium medicamentorum temperamentis et facultatibus libri IX*, Esc. ^{2}793, abbreviation ibid. 802,$_2$.—z. *Fī tarkīb al-adwiya bi-ḥasb ajnāsihā al-mawṣūf bi κατα γένος*, Berl. 6231, Esc. ^{2}796 (see also Esc. ^{2}797,$_4$, | 798,$_4$, 227
846/51, 853, 860,$_4$, 879/80).—15. Dioscorides *περὶ τέχνης ἰατρικης*, translated by Stephanus b. Basīl, revised by Ḥunayn, Paris 2849/50, Bodl. I, 373, Leclerc, *JA*, 1867, Jan. (see Suppl.).

6. His son Isḥāq b. Ḥunayn was in close contact with al-Qāsim b. ʿUbaydallāh, vizier to the caliph al-Muʿtaḍid. | He had assisted his father in his translations, 207
but in his own work showed a preference for philosophy. Towards the end of his life he was paralysed following a stroke. He died in Rabīʿ I 298/November 910 or 911.

Fihrist 285, Ibn Khall. 85, Ibn Abī Uṣaybiʿa I, 200, Wüst., *Ärzte* 71, *Gesch.* 88, Leclerc I, 139, Steinschneider, *ZDMG* L, 393, Suter, *Math.* 39. 1. *Aristotelis Categoriae* (*περὶ ἑρμηνείας*) *cum versione arab. Is. Honeini f. et variis lectionibus textus graeci e vers. arab. ductis a* J. Th. Zenker, Leipzig 1846. *Hermeneutik*, ed. J. Pollak, *AKM* XIII, 1 (according to *Fihrist* 248,$_{20}$, Ibn al-Qifṭī 35,$_2$ by Ḥunayn).—2.–5. see Suppl.—6. Euclid's *Elementa Uṣūl*, revised by Thābit b. Qurra, Upps. Tornb. 321 (d. 443 AH), Copenhagen 81, Fātiḥ 3439,$_1$ (Books IV–IX), Teh. II, 200, Rāmpūr I, 412, (see Suppl. I, 956 ad 370).—7. idem *Kitāb al-manāẓir*, revised by Thābit b. Qurra, Leid. 976, abstract maybe by Naṣīr al-Dīn al-Ṭūsī, ibid. 977.—8. Theodosius' *Sphaerica*, Leid. 984, see p. 474.—9. Ptolemy's *Almagest*, augmented by Thābit b. Qurra, Paris 2487, Esc. ^{1}915, see O.J. Tallgren, *Rev. d. fil. esp.* XV (1928), 57.—10. *Jawāmiʿ kutub Jālīnūs*, Qawala II, 287.

7. Ḥunayn's nephew and student Ḥubaysh b. al-Ḥasan al-Aʿsam al-Dimashqī lived at the court of al-Mutawakkil and the latter's successors until roughly the end of the third century. It is not always easy to definitively distinguish his works from those of his uncle, whom he assisted on various occasions, the more so because the similarity between their names gave rise to confusion in the manuscripts.

Ibn Abī Uṣaybiʿa I, 202. Translations: a. Hippocrates' oath, Steinschn. 31.—b. idem, *Book on waters*, ibid. | 9,$_{10}$.—c. Dioscorides' *Book of herbs*, ibid. 30.—d. 228
Galen, ibid. 9/11, 15/23, 28, 30/2, 34, 36, 40, 50, 53, 57/8, 61, 66, 69, 70, 86.

7a. Abū ʿUthmān Saʿīd b. Yaʿqūb al-Dimashqī, see Suppl. I, 369, III, 1204.

Esc, ^{2}799$_{,11,2,9,10}$, translation of Maghnīs al-Ḥimṣī's *Fī 'l-bawl*, AS 3563$_{,78v/100}$.

8. ʿĪsā b. Yaḥyā b. Ibrāhīm was also a student of Ḥunayn.

Ibn Abī Uṣaybiʿa I, 204, Steinschneider, *ZDMG* 50, 393, see Suppl. Dioscorides' *al-Ḥashāʾish*, Patna I, 251$_{,2189}$.

9. Abū Bishr Mattā b. Yūnus (Yūnān) al-Qunnāʾī of the monastery of Dayr Qunnā or of the apostle Mār Mārī (17 parasangs south of Baghdad), in whose famous school he received his scientific education, was regarded as the foremost logician of his time. He died in Baghdad on 19 Ramaḍān 328/29 May 940.

Ibn Abī Uṣaybiʿa I, 235, see Suppl. Translation of Aristotle's *Poetics*, see *Analecta orientalia ad poeticam Aristotelis*, ed. D.S. Margoliouth, London 1887, idem *The Poetics of Aristotle, transl. from Greek into English and from Arabic into Latin, with a revised Text, Introd. etc.* London 1911, H. Diels, Über die arab. Übers. der aristot. Poetik, *BBA* 1888, 49/54, A. Gudemann, Die syr.-arab. Übers. der aristotel. Poetik, *Philologus* LXXXVI (1920) 239/65, J. Tkatsch, *Die ar. Übers. der Poetik des A. und die Grundlage der Kritik des griechischen Textes, Abh. d. Wiener AC.* 1928, F. Gabrieli, Intorno alla vers. ar. della P. di A., *Rend. Lincei Sc. Mor.* etc. ser. VI, v. V, (1929) 224/35, see also Esc. ^{2}798$_{,11,7}$.

10. Abū Zakariyyāʾ Yaḥyā b. ʿAdī al-Manṭiqī al-Takrītī was a Jacobite Christian and a student of Abū Bishr and al-Fārābī. He died at the age of 81 in the year 363/973 or 364.

Fihrist 264$_{,5-14}$, Ibn Abī Uṣaybiʿa I, 235, see Suppl. I, 370, 956.—7. *Tafsīr al-alif al-ṣughrā* Patna II, 372$_{,2557,1}$.—9. *Maqāla fī 'l-mawjūdāt* ibid. 2.–10. *Risāla fī 'l-kull wal-juzʾ* ibid. 8.

229 | 11. In 380/999, al-Ḥusayn b. Ibrāhīm b. al-Ḥasan b. Khurshīd al-Ṭabarī al-Nātilī dedicated to Prince Abū ʿAlī al-Sāmjūrī[5] an improved translation of Dioscorides' *Kitāb al-ḥashāʾish*, Leid. 1301, Br. Mus. Suppl. 785, Bat. III, 227, Bank. IV, 91.

---

5 See al-Samʿānī, *Ansāb* 323a, Ibn Isfandiyār, *History of Tabaristan*, transl. Browne 208, Barthold, *Turkestan down to the Mongol Invasion* 253.

| 12. Abū ʿAlī b. Isḥāq b. Zurʿa, a Jacobite Christian and physician of Baghdad, 208
translated medical and philosophical works and died on 23 Shaʿbān 398/4 May 1008.

Fihrist 264,$_{26/7}$, Ibn Abī Uṣaybiʿa I, 235, Wüst., *Ärzte* 121, Leclerc I, 374, Steinschneider, *ZDMG* L, 412, see Suppl.

Chapter 12. Philosophy

S. Munk, Des principaux philosophes arabes et leurs doctrines, in: *Mélanges de philosophie juive et arabe*, Paris 1859.

Goffredo Quadri, *La filosofia degli Arabi nel suo fiore, I. dalle origini fino ad Averroe, II. Il Pensiero di Averroe*, Florence 1939.

Apart from major medical works, these translators also supplied the Islamic world with important works in philosophy. Aristotelian logic had already stimulated grammatical theorising and, together with Christian dogmatics, produced the foundations of *kalām*. In addition, the *mutakallimūn* paid special attention to metaphysics, in which they were often influenced by Neoplatonism. Ethics remained the privileged territory of the *fuqahā'*. Scholars who employed Greek thought outside of these circles had to contend themselves therefore mostly with the further development of psychology or logic. Whether and to what extent Indian thought contributed to this has not yet been ascertained. Only in politics, which had developed at an early stage in the
230 form of the "Mirrors for Princes" texts, did Indian influence | make its mark.[1] The study of philosophy remained, however, restricted to a small circle. Once it had adopted some of its basic ideas through al-Ashʿarī, orthodoxy remained mostly hostile to any further development. This is why we are mostly dependent upon Jewish sources for its history. It is, of course, not possible to discuss the progression of the movement of its ideas; only its literary characteristics shall be recorded here.

1. Son of the local governor, Abū Yūsuf Yaʿqūb b. Isḥāq al-Kindī Faylasūf al-ʿArab was born in Kufa into a prominent South Arabian family. He studied in Basra and Baghdad, where he worked under al-Ma'mūn and al-Muʿtaṣim as a translator and revisor of Greek works, as an astrologer, and as the tutor of the son of al-Muʿtaṣim. Because he was close to the Muʿtazila, he was also affected by their prosecution, initiated under al-Mutawakkil. His library was confiscated and only returned to him shortly before the caliph's death. Despite an unfavorable conjunction of the stars in 256/870, he still confidently predicted that the empire, threatened as it was by the Qarmaṭians, would have a lifespan of another 450 years. He probably died soon after.

---

1 The allegedly oldest work of this kind, the *Kitāb sulūk al-mālik fī tadbīr al-mamālik*, Paris 2448, lith. C. 1286 (see Goldziher, Abh. I, 66) by Shihāb al-Dīn Aḥmad b. Muḥammad b. Abi 'l-Rabīʿ, supposedly for the caliph al-Muʿtaṣim (218–27/835–42), is a much later work; see Suppl. I, 372.

Ibn Abī Uṣaybiʿa I, 206, Wüst., *Ärzte* 57, G. Flügel, *Al Kindi, genannt der Philosoph der Araber, ein Vorbild seiner Zeit und seines Volkes, AKM* I, Leipzig 1857, Steinschneider, *ZDMG* XXIV, 349. Of his many (around 200), mostly very short, treatises[2] remain: 1. A revision | of the *Theology* of Aristotle (p. 222) for 231
his student Aḥmad b. al-Muʿtaṣim, Berl. 5121 (see Suppl. I, 2), Persian transl. Bodl. Pers. 870.—III. Psychology (see L. Gauthier, *Antecédents gréco-arabes de la psychophysique*, Beirut 1939). 1a. *Risāla fi ʾl-qawl fi ʾl-nafs al-mukhtaṣar min kutub Arisṭāṭālīs wa-Aflāṭūn wa-sāʾir al-falāsifa*, Taymūr, Ḥikma 55 f. 63/76, Br. Mus. Or. 8069, f. 9b/12a, Patna II, $373_{,2558,13}$, see R. Walzer, Un frammento nuovo di Aristotele, *Stud. Ital. di Fil. class.* NS XIV, 1937, 125/37.—3. *Risāla fi ʾl-ḥīla li-dafʿ al-aḥzān* AS $4832_{,15}$, ed. H. Ritter and R. Walzer, *Studi sul Kindi II, Uno scritto morale inedito di al-K.* (*Themistios περὶ ἀλυπίας*), *Mem. R. Acc. Lincei*, ser. VI, vol. VIII, I, Rome 1938.

II. Philosophy I. *Risāla fī kammiyyat kutub Arisṭūṭālīs wa-mā yuḥtāju ilayhi fi ʾl-falsafa*, ed. M. Guidi and R. Walzer, *Studi sul Kindi*, I, Rome 1938.—3. *Kitāb al-ḥurūf*, ed. Guidi, ibid. III.—IV. Physics. 9. *Alkindus de pluviis, imbribus et ventis ac aëris mutatione*, Venice 1507, see Steinschneider, *ZDMG* XVIII, 181, Hebr. Steinschn. $351_{,2}$.—10. *Risāla fi ʾl-ibāna ʿani ʾl-ʿilla etc.*, also Patna II, $372_{,2258,7}$.—10a. *Fi ʾl-ʿilla allatī lahā qīla anna ʾl-nār wal-hawāʾ wal-māʾ wal-arḍ ʿanāṣir li-jamīʿ al-kāʾina al-fāsida wa-khuṣṣat bi-dhālika dūna ghayrihā min al-kāʾina* Lālelī $2487_{,4}$ (Ritter).—V. Astronomy and astrology: 5a. *De planetarum conjunctionibus* Esc. $^{1}913_{,3}$.—b. *De judiciis ex ecclipsibus* ibid. 4.–7. see E. Wiedemann, Über einen astrologischen Traktat von al-K., *Arch. f. Gesch. d. Nat. u. Technik* III, 224/6.—VII. Music. 1. Berl. 5539, see Farmer, *JRAS* 1926, 92.—3. *Mukhtaṣar al-mūsīqī fī taʾlīf al-naghm wa-ṣināʿat al-ʿūd*, Bodl. $553_{,1}$, see Farmer, *Sources* 20.—4. *Kitāb al-ʿiẓam fī taʾlīf al-luḥūn* Br. Mus. Or. 2361, f. 165v, ibid.—5. *Risāla fī tarkīb al-naghm al-dālla ʿalā ṭabāʾiʿ al-ashkhāṣ*, maybe Berl. 5503, ibid.—XI. 1a. *al-Taraffuq fi ʾl-ʿitr* Br. Mus. Or. 9678, Taymūr, Ṣināʿa 46 (Kraus).—3. Scapulomancy, Bursa Ḥü. Čelebi 36.—7. *De somniorum visione*, Latin by Gerard of Cremona (see Jourdain, *Recherches critiques sur l'âge et l'origine des traductions latines d'Aristote*, p. 123).

| 3. Abu ʾl-ʿAbbās Aḥmad b. Muḥammad b. al-Ṭayyib (Marwān) b. al-Farāʾiqī 210
al-Sarakhsī Tilmīdh al-Kindī al-Ṭabīb, his most important student, was part of the retinue of the caliph al-Muʿtaḍid. Appointed as *muḥtasib* and curator of the estate in Rajab 282/September 895, he was soon after arrested as a heretic

2 8 on music, 23 on astronomy, 26 on geometry, 23 on medicine, 9 on astrology, 17 polemical, 5 on psychology, 12 on politics, 14 on meteorology, 10 on distances, 5 on lexicology, 35 on varia.

232 on 5 Jumādā I 283/21 June 896 | and died in prison in Ṣafar 286/February–March 899.

Fihrist 261, Ibn Abī Uṣaybiʿa I, 214/5, Wüst., *Ärzte* 80, Leclerc 294, Suter, *Math.* 63. Of his numerous works, nothing remains. A *Kitāb adab al-nafs min kalām sayyid al-ʿarab wal-ʿajam* for al-Muʿtaḍid, ḤKh ^{1}I, 224$_{,34}$, ^{2}I, 49, may be preserved in the anonymous Alex. Mawāʿiẓ 4.

4. Abū Naṣr Muḥammad b. Muḥammad b. Ṭarkhān b. Ūzlāgh (not Ibn Ūzlāgh b. Ṭarkhān) al-Fārābī hailed from a Turkish family in Wasīj on the left bank of the Syr-Daryā, less than two parasangs from Kadar, the old centre of Fārāb.[3] After initially studying in Khurāsān where the Christian Yuḥannā b. Ḥaylān had been his teacher he went to Baghdad where, as well as medicine and mathematics, he became particularly interested in philosophy, under the tutelage of Muḥammad b. Jallād and Abū Bishr Mattā b. Yūnus (p. 228). In Aleppo, where he then moved, the surroundings and contemplative leisure of the court of the Ḥamdānid ruler Sayf al-Dawla proved eminently suitable to academic work. In 339/950, while on a trip in which he accompanied Sayf al-Dawla, he was supposedly murdered by robbers between Damascus and Ashkelon (see Suppl.).

211 | Ibn Abī Uṣaybiʿa II, 134/45, Ibn Khall. 677, Wüst. no. 716, Wüst. *Ärzte* 105, Leclerc I, 389, M. Steinschneider, *Al-Fārābī, des arabischen Philosophen, Leben und Schriften*, St. Petersburg 1869, *Mém. de l'Ac. Imp. des sciences de St. Pét.*, s. VII, v. XIII, no. 4, Carra de Vaux, *EI* II, 55/7, Nallino, *Enc. Ital.* XIV, 797/9, Mieli, *La science ar.* 94, Ilyās Faraḥ, *al-F.* Jounieh (Lebanon) 1937, Muʿtazid Walī al-Raḥmān, al-F. and his theory of dreams, *Isl. Cult.* IX (1937), The Psychology of al-F., ibid. XI, 228/47, *al-F.s philosophische Abhandlungen, hsg. v.* Fr. Dieterici, Leiden 1890. List of his works, Esc. ^{2}884$_{,10}$ (50 works), *Majmūʿat rasāʾil* (E 2, D 16$_{,3}$), Garr. 794, Rāmpūr I, 403 (28 works *Journ. Proc. As. Soc. Bengal* XIC, ccxiv), II, 837$_{,220}$ (15 works).

A. Logic: 1. Introduction to logic, Hebrew transl. Munich 307, Steinschn. p. 13, n. 2.—2. *Fuṣūl yuḥtāju ilayhā fī ṣināʿat al-manṭiq*, Paris Hebr. anc. fonds
233 303, Hebr. | transl. Steinschn. 13$_{,3}$.—3. Compendium of logic Hebr. Paris a.f. 333, Orel 107.—4. *Kitāb taʿlīq Isāghūjī ʿalā Furfūriyūs*, Bodl. I, 457 on which *Taʿlīq* by Abū Bakr Muḥammad b. Yaḥyā b. al-Ṣāʾigh b. Bājja, d. 525/1131 (p. 460), Esc. ^{2}612$_{,2}$.—5. *Categories* Esc. ^{2}612$_{,13}$, Hebr. Munich 307$_{,2}$.—6. Commentary on Aristotle's *περὶ ερμηνείας*, ḤKh ^{1}II, 5$_{,1606}$, ^{2}I, 217, on which glosses by Ibn Bājja (?) Esc. ^{2}612$_{,3}$, extract ibid. 4.—7. *Kitāb fī 'l-qiyās*, on the *Prior Analytics*, Esc. ^{2}612$_{,5}$.

3 See Barthold, *Turkestan* 176/7.

Hebrew transl. in Steinschn. p. 30, on which maybe a commentary by Ibn Bājja, *Irtiyāḍ fī Kitāb al-taḥlīl*, Esc. $^{2}612_{,6}$ (see Suppl.).—8. *al-Qawl fī sharāʾiṭ al-yaqīn*, on the *Posterior Analytics*, in Hebrew script Paris Hebr. a.f. 303, Hebr. transl. ibid. 383, comment. by Ibn Bājja Esc. $^{2}612_{,7}$, *Kalām ʿalā awwal Kitāb al-burhān, qawl fī Kitāb al-burhān*, ibid. 8, *Kitāb al-burhān*, Manch. 374 B, Teh. I, $7_{,5}$.—9. *Topics*, Hebr. transl. Steinschn. p. 54.—10. Compendium of the *Sophistical Refutations*, Hebr. transl. Steinschn. 56.—11. *Declaratio compendiosa supra libris rhetoricorum Aristotillis* (*sici*) Venice 1484, *Rhetorica Aristotelis cum fundatissimi artium et theologiae doctoris Egidij de Roma loculentissimis commentariis nunc primum in lucem editis: nec non Alpharabij compendiosa declaratione, addita ejusdem Aristotelis Poetica cum magni Averroys in eamdem summa: novissime recognita cunctisque erroribus castigata*, Venice 1515, cf. A. Nagy, Notizie intorno alla retorica d'Al Farabi, *Rend. Linc.* 1893, II, 684/91.

B. Ethics and politics. 1. *Kitāb al-alfāẓ al-Aflāṭūniyya wa-taqwīm al-siyāsa al-mulūkiyya wal-akhlāq* (not in Steinschn.) AS 2820/2 (see Suppl.).—2. *Talkhīṣ nawāmīs aflāṭūn* Leid. 1429.—3. *al-Tanbīh ʿalā sabīl al-saʿāda* or simply *Risālat al-saʿāda* Berl. 5034, Br. Mus. $425_{,10}$, Steinschn. 158, print. Hyderabad 1346.—3a. *Kitāb taḥṣīl al-saʿāda* Hyderabad 1345, summary translated by Falquera in the third part of the *Rēšīṯ haḥoḵmā* (see L. Strauss, MGWJ 80, 1936, 104ff.).—4. *Kitāb siyāsat al-madīna* | Leid. 1930, Br. Mus. $425_{,11}$, AS $4839_{,6}$, = *Kitāb mabādiʾ* 212
al-mawjūdāt, de Jong 113, Hebr. transl. *Sefer Tehillōṯ hannimṣāʾōṯ* in the almanac *Sefer hāʾāsīf*, London 5610, 1850, Steinschn. $158_{,2}$, a longer excerpt in Miskawayh, *Jāwīdān khirad*, Paris $3957_{,134a/144a}$ (Kraus).—5. *Kitāb fī mabādiʾ ārāʾ ahl al-madīna al-fāḍila*, commenced in Baghdad and completed in 334 in Damascus, revised in 337 in Cairo and divided into *fuṣūl* (Boustany, al-Fārābī and Thomas Morus, *al-Mashriq* XXVI, 126/34), Br. Mus. $725_{,3}$, Bodl. I, $102_{,3}$, *Alf.'s Abh. über den Musterstaat nach Lond. u. Oxf. Hdss. hsg. v.* Fr. Dieterici, Leiden 1895.—6. *Kitāb al-milla al-fāḍīla* | Leid. 1931 (without title, wrongly identified 234
in the catalogue, see Steinschn. p. 70), partly Taymūr, Akhlāq $290_{,19}$.—7. *Fuṣūl*, aphorisms, *Collectio sententiarum variarum ad regimen politicum spectantium* Bodl. I, $102_{,4}$, Hebr. Steinschn. 158.—8. *Jawāmiʿ al-siyar al-marḍiyya fi ʾqtināʾ al-faḍāʾil al-insiyya* Leid. 1932.

C. Mathematics, astrology, alchemy, divination, music. 1. Commentary on Euclid, introductions to Books I and V, Hebr. Munich 36, 290.—2. *Risālat tadhākīr fī-mā yaṣiḥḥu wa-mā lam yaṣiḥḥi min aḥkām al-nujūm* Rāmpūr I, 400, II, 840, Āṣaf. III, $756_{,731,1}$, ed. Dieterici, p. 104/14.—3. *Fī wujūb ṣināʿat al-kīmiyyāʾ* (*al-ṣināʿa*) Berl. 4178, Leid. 1270, see E. Wiedemann, *Journ. für prakt. Chemie* N.F. 76 (1907), 115/23.—4. *Kitāb fī ʿilm al-mizāj* Landberg-Brill 1484 (wrongly *Tadhk. al-Naw.* 184).—5. *al-Maqālāt al-rafīʿa fī uṣūl ʿilm al-ṭabīʿa* ibid. 570.—6. *Bughyat al-amal fī ṣināʿat al-raml wa-taqwīm al-ashkāl* Bodl. I, 956 = *Kitāb al-ḥiyal al-rūḥāniyya wal-asrār al-ṭabīʿiyya fī daqāʾiq al-ashkāl al-handasiyya* Upps. 324, divination, not likely to be authentic because it is not mentioned by any biographer.—7. *Kitāb ustuqiṣāt ʿilm al-mūsīqī* Madr. 602, J.P.N. Land, Recherches sur la gamme arabe, *Act. du VI Congr. intern d. or.* Leiden 1903, I, 44, n. 1. Excerpt ibid. 133/68.—8. *Kitāb al-mūsīqī al-kabīr* Leid. 1423 (= Ambr. 289 ?), photograph of a manuscript from Istanbul *Nashra* 22, from which, especially:—9. *al-Mudkhal fi 'l-mūsīqī* Rāġib 876, Köpr. 953, ḤKh VII, 318$_{,736}$, 453$_{,873}$, 510$_{,946}$.—10–13. see Suppl.—14. *Risāla fī qawānīn ṣināʿat al-shiʿr* Alf. canon of poetry, see Arberry, *RSO* XVII, 266 ff.—15. *Muntakhab min Kitāb al-mudkhal fi 'l-ḥisāb* Rāmpūr I, 418$_{,68}$.—16. *Ibṭāl aḥkām al-nujūm* in a *majmūʿa* in the hand of Maḥmūd al-Nayrīzī, a student of Ṣadr al-Dīn al-Dashtakī (II, 414) library of Naṣrallāh al-Taqawī in Tehran, *Dharīʿa* I, 66, 326 (= 2?).—17. *Sharḥ al-mijisṭī* Br. Mus. Or. 7368 (628 AH Kraus).

D. Varia. 1. *Kitāb iḥṣāʾ al-ʿulūm*, enumeration of the sciences, Esc. ^{1}646$_{,3}$ (page 2 lost), Köpr. (not Rāġib) 1604$_{,1}$, Lat. transl. by Gerard of Cremona in Palencia, Madrid 1932, Hebr. Steinschn. 159$_{,4}$, in Falqueras *Rēšīṯ ha-ḥokmā*, see I. Efros, *JQRNS* XXV, 227, L. Strauss, *MGWJ* 80 (1936) 96ff.—2. *De ortu scientiarum*, Lat. Paris 6298, Bodl. (Cat. Mss. Angl. I, 173) no. 5623$_{,29}$, f. 173/87(?), Steinschn. 89, ed. Baeumker, Alfārābī, über den Ursprung der Wissenschaften, *Beitr. z. Gesch. d. Phil. des MA* XIX, 3.—3. *Kitāb ʿuyūn al-masāʾil* also Köpr. (not Rāġib) 1604$_{,3}$,
235 Rāmpūr | I, 402, Āṣaf. III, 756$_{,736}$, ed. Schmoelders, *Documenta philosophiae Arabum*, Bonn 1836, 24/34, ed. Dieterici, p. 56/60, Hebr. Steinschn. 160$_{,5}$.—4. *Maqāla* (*Risāla*) *fi* (*maʿāni*) *'l-ʿaql* Teh. II, 634$_{,2}$, Āṣaf. II, 1210, III, 488$_{,399}$, Rāmpūr I, 402$_{,145}$, 405, Aligarh 79, ed. Dieterici, p. 39/48, Hebr. Steinschn. 161$_{,7}$, see L. Massignon, Notes sur le texte original arabe du "De intellectu" d'Alf. in *Arch. d'hist. doct. et litt. du MA* IV, 151/8, *Texte ar. intégral en partie inédit* (*Ms. de Stamboul*) ed. M. Bouyges (*Bibl. Ar. Schol. VIII, 1*), Beirut 1938.—5. *Risāla fi 'l-nafs* Bodl. I, 980 (see II, 605), Hebr. transl. Steinschn. 162$_{,8}$.—6. *Taʿlīqāt*, notes, Br. Mus. 421$_{,4}$, Rāmpūr I, 401, Patna II, 475$_{,2641,5}$ (see Suppl.)—7. *Risālat al-fuṣūṣ fi 'l-ḥikma* (*Fuṣūṣ al-ḥikma*), ed. Dieterici, 66/82, Āṣaf. III, 756$_{,73,7}$, Rāmpūr I, 400$_{,130}$, 401, II, 843, Patna II, 410$_{,2579,21}$, commentary by Maḥmūd b. Masʿūd al-Shīrāzī, d. 710/1312 (II, 212), Rāmpūr I, 396$_{,102/3}$ (see Suppl.)—8. *Risāla fī jawāb masāʾil suʾila ʿanhā*, ed. Dieterici, 83/103.[4]—9. *Alfarabius de tempore* Cat. Mss. Angl. II, 202, no. 6605.—10. *Risāla fī faḍīlat al-ʿulūm* Br. Mus. Or. 8069$_{,13}$, Āṣaf. II, 1718$_{,28}$, Hyderabad 1345.—11. *Rasāʾil fī masāʾil mutafarriqa* Rāmpūr I, 393, Āṣaf. III, 756$_{,73,8}$, Hyderabad 1344.—12. *al-Daʿwa 'l-qalbiyya* Rāmpūr I, 387, see Suppl.—13. *Risāla fī ithbāt al-mufāraqāt* (*mutafāriqāt*) see Suppl. Aligarh 81$_{,46}$, Patna II, 474$_{,2641,3}$.—14.–16. see Suppl.—17. *Risāla fī ḥudūth al-ʿālam* Rāmpūr I,

4 On Steinschneider, p. 112, no. 15, see here p. 458, 32 (Steinschn. 37, no. 44), Dieterici XII.

$302_{,1576}$.—18. *Risāla fī taʿrīf al-falsafa* Āṣaf. II, $1716_{,11}$.—19. *Risāla fi 'l-taṣawwuf* ibid. 12.–20. *Risāla fi 'l-akhlāq* ibid. 13.–21. *Kayfa yastawi 'lladhīna yaʿlamūna walladhīna lā yaʿlamūna* Hyderabad 1341.—22. *Maqālat al-Iskandar al-Afrūdīsī* Patna II, $475_{,2641,6}$.—23. *ʿUlūm al-masāʾil wa-natāʾij al-ʿulūm* ibid. 4.

E. Works about Aristotle: a. Introduction. 1. *Risāla fī-mā yanbaghī an yuqaddama qabla taʿallum al-falsafa*, ed. Schmoelders, 3/10, Dieterici, 49/55, Hebr. Steinschn. $160_{,6}$.—2. *Kitāb al-jamʿ bayna raʾyay al-ḥakīm Aflāṭūn al-ilāhī wa-Arisṭūṭālīs*, ed. Dieterici 1/33, Āṣaf. III, $756_{,73,3}$, Rāmpūr I, 401, Bank. XXI, 2336, Aligarh $79_{,18}$, $81_{,49}$, Persian Bodl. 1422, xix.—| b. Individual works: 1. *Risāla* 213
fī aghrāḍ Mā baʿd al-ṭabīʿa (*fī aghrāḍ al-ḥakīm fī kulli maqāla min al-kitāb al-mawsūm bil-Ḥurūf*) ed. Dieterici 34/8.—2. *Risāla fi 'l-ʿālam al-aʿlā*, a commentary (not a translation as indicated by Ahlw.) on a work by Zenon the Elder, | a student of Aristotle, Berl. 5123, see Suppl. under the title *Sharḥ Zenon* Āṣaf. 236
III, $756_{,73,9}$, Rāmpūr I, $404_{,159b}$, Br. Mus. Or. $8069_{,3}$, Cairo Ḥikma 453, excerpt in al-Lāhijī, *Maḥbūb al-qulūb*, Tehran 1317, 134ff., see Rosenthal, *Orientalia* NS VI, 64.—3. *Sharḥ Risālat al-nafs li-Arisṭūṭālīs* Rāmpūr I, 395, $710_{,73,3}$.—4. (spurious) *Risāla fi 'l-ʿilm al-ilāhī* Taymūr Ḥikma 117, 1/15 (Kraus).

F. Works on Plato: 1. *al-Multaqaṭāt li-Aflāṭūn* Rāmpūr II, 841.—2. *Risālat Aflāṭūn fī radd man qāla bi-talāshi 'l-insān* ibid.

4a. Abū Sulaymān Muḥammad b. Ṭāhir b. Bahrām al-Sijazī, see Suppl. I, 377.

1. *Mukhtaṣar ṣiwān al-ḥikma* Bešīr Āġā 494, Murād Mollā 1408, Köpr. 903 (*Islca* IV, 534/8).—5. *Īḍāḥ maḥajjat al-ʿilāj* Rāmpūr I, $469_{,21b}$.—6. A longer philosophical fragment, Taymūr, Akhlāq $290_{,14}$ (Kraus).

4b. Abu 'l-Khayr al-Ḥasan b. Siwār b. Bābā b. Bahmān b. al-Khammār al-Baghdādī, see Suppl.

Bayhaqī, *Tatimma* 13, Rosenthal, *Orient.* NS VI, 39, n. 2. *Risāla fi 'l-āthār al-mutakhayyala etc.* also Rāmpūr II, 815.

4bb. Abu 'l-Ḥasan Muḥammad b. Yūsuf al-ʿĀmirī, d. 381/991.

Risālat al-ibṣār wal-mubṣar, Taymūr, Ḥikma 98 (Kraus).

5. Following a long oppression of free thinking by the orthodox reaction of al-Mutawakkil, which had particularly stifled the pursuit of philosophy, the ascent to power of the Būyid Muʿizz al-Dawla Aḥmad in Baghdad in 334/945 brought at least some relief from this since, being a Shīʿī, he had no interest

in siding with Sunnī orthodoxy. Soon after, the aspirations of the Bāṭiniyya also became manifest, mingling with various ideas of Manicheism that were prevalent among the learned. In its wake, Neoplatonic philosophy also gained in influence, pushing back the Aristotelianism of al-Kindī and his school. 237 Some philosophically trained men, | who found themselves together in Basra around the middle of the fourth century, wanted to ensure victory for this new movement. After all, there had already been such conventicles there, for example at the time of the poet Bashshār b. al-Burd (p. 72). They called themselves *Ikhwān al-Ṣafāʾ*, "the brethen of purity." Among their members are mentioned: Abū Sulaymān b. Musʿir al-Bustī al-Maqdisī, Abu ʾl-Ḥasan b. ʿAlī b. Zahrūn al-Rayḥānī (corrupted to Zanjānī), Muḥammad b. Aḥmad al-Nahrajūrī (Mihrajānī), al-ʿAwfī, and perhaps also Zayd b. Rifāʿa (see Suppl. I, 380, n.), whom we met earlier as a philologist (p. 120, *Kitāb al-amthāl*, Hyderabad 1352). It is highly doubtful if this association was ever able to bring the permanent organisation that is mentioned in their 45th letter into effect. It is even more doubtful that it ever spread beyond Basra. While Zayd b. Rifāʿa was indeed in Baghdad in 373/983, there are no reports of him having been active there 214 on behalf of the organisation, | which lacked, most of all, a leading mind that could have asserted its principles in the face of the general aversion of the time. But their *Rasāʾil* did not remain without literary success. These are 52 in all, of which 14 deal with mathematics and logical propaedeutics, 17 with the natural sciences and psychology, 10 with metaphysics, and the last ten with mysticism, astrology, and divination. They thus offer a kind of encyclopaedia of the wordly sciences, written in a very accessible, verbose, and often uplifting style. Returning from a study trip to the east the mathematician Abu ʾl-Qāsim Maslama b. Aḥmad al-Majrīṭī, d. 395/1004 (p. 243), brought them to Spain; as such, he is even mistakenly designated as their author in some manuscripts, while others attribute the authorship to his student ʿUmar b. ʿAbd al-Raḥmān al-Kirmānī, d. 458/1066 (Ibn al-Qifṭī 243), instead.

K. Nauwerck, *Notiz über das arab. Buch* Tuḥfat Ikhwān aṣ-ṣafāʾ *d. h. Gabe der* 238 *aufrichtigen Freunde nebst Probe* | *desselben arabisch und deutsch*, Berlin 1837, G. Flügel, *ZDMG* XIII, 1ff., R. Gosche, *Abh. Berl. AC.* 1858, p. 240ff., Leclerc I, 393, Dieterici, *ZDMG* XVIII, 691, M. Cantor, *Vorl. über die Gesch. d. Math.* I, 633/6, A. Müller, in *Ersch. u. Grubers Enc. Sect.* II, vol. 42, p. 272/7, E. Hungerford, The Arabian Brothers of Purity, *Andover Review* Nov. 1888, p. 281/93, (see Suppl. I, 380), T. de Boer, *Gesch. d. Phil. im Islam* 76/89, A. Mieli, *La science Ar.* § 24, Sayyid ʿAbd al-Laṭīf Ṭībawī, Jamāʿat Ikhwān al-ṣafāʾ, *Journ. Americ. Un. Beyrouth* 1933/4, ʿAbd al-Muḥyī al-Ḥuwayzī al-ʿArabī, *al-Risāla al-musammāt bil-ʿasal al-muṣaffā fī taḥqīq ism muṣannif rasāʾil Ikhwān al-ṣafāʾ*, Bombay 1929 (al-imām al-mastūr Aḥmad b. ʿAlī, following the thesis of the Ismāʿīlī Bohra community). On the MSS Pertsch, Gotha 157, with Berl. 5035/42, Ind. Off. 474, Pet. Ros. 194, see Suppl., with Garr. 1129, ʿĀṭif 1681 (578 AH), Bank. XXI, 2222, *Mukhtaṣar rasāʾil Ikhwān al-ṣafāʾ* by Maslama b. Aḥmad al-Majrīṭī, Esc. ²300, by Dāʾūd al-Ṭabīb, Lālelī 3639. Editions *BO* I, 1344/6, II, 1011/2, 4668/70 (see Suppl.). Complete in 4 vols., Bombay 1303/6, vol. I, C. 1306, *Ikhwān al-ṣafāʾ*, ed. Mawlawi Wilayat Husayn, Calcutta 1888 (struggle between man and beast, *OB* IV, 3633). *Die Abhh. der Ikhwān al-Ṣafāʾ in Auswahl. ar. hsg. v.* Fr. Dieterici, Leipzig 1883 (see A. Müller, *GGA* 1804, 953/70), idem, *Der Streit zwischen Tier und Mensch, ein arab. Märchen aus den Schriften der lauteren Brüder übers. und mit einer Abh. über diesen Orden, sowie mit Anmm. versehn*, Berlin 1858, idem, *Die Propädeutik der Araber*, Leipzig 1865, *Logik und Psychologie der A.*, 1868 *Naturwissenschaft der A.*, 2nd ed. 1878, *Anthropologie der A.* 1871, *die Lehre von der Weltseele bei den A.* 1873, *Die Philosophie der Araber im X. Jahrh.* a. *Makrokosmus*, Leipzig 1876, b. *Mikrokosmus* 1879, *Darwinismus im X. und XIX. Jahrh.* 1878.—Turkish transl. by Lāmiʿī, d. 940/1533, *Kitāb sharaf al-insān*, Paris turc. 157, SGerm. 342, 546, Vienna 436 (R. 22 Man and beast), Upps. 480, Ambr. 192, *Ikhwān al-ṣafāʾ, transl. from the Ar. into Hindustani by Maulwi Ali, a new edition revised and corr. by* Duncan Forbes *and* Ch. Rieu, London 1861.

215 ## | Chapter 13. Mathematics

L.P.E.A. Sédillot, *Matériaux pour servir à l'histoire comparée des sciences mathématiques chez les Grecs et les Orientaux*, 2 vols., Paris 1845/9.

239 | M. Cantor, *Vorlesungen über Geschichte der Mathematik*, vol. I, Leipzig 1880, 593/700.

H.P.J. Renaud, Additions et corrections à Suter, *Isis* XVIII, 1932, 166/88.

Aldo Mieli, *La Science Arabe et son rôle dans l'évolution scientifique mondiale, avec quelques additions de H.P.J. Renaud, M. Meyerhof, J. Ruska*, Leiden 1938.

In the Islamic world, mathematics was, just like philosophy, first developed by the Greeks. In geometry the work of Euclid remained the basis, but this was revised over and over again. In arithmetic too, the initial leaders were the Greeks, and from their works, in chanceries in Syria and Egypt, the Arabs adopted the use of Greek letters as labels for numbers, but, like the Greeks with their use of the abacus, they limited these to the first column of nine signs which thereby received place-value. Among Moroccan notaries, these older signs have survived as the so-called *ghubārī* or *Fās* numbers, which they adopted from Spain. It was only in the ninth century that al-Khwārizmī adopted Indian computing methods and, with these, Indian numbers, which themselves may have evolved out of the first nine letters of the Greek alphabet. But it was only the invention of zero by the Indians that gave these number-signs their full value for arithmetic.[1]

240 1. The oldest[2] writer whose | mathematical work is still extant is Abū ʿAbdallāh
216 Muḥammad b. Mūsā | al-Khwārizmī,[3] who worked under the caliph al-Maʾmūn in the Bayt al-Ḥikma, and who died sometime after 232/846. For al-Maʾmūn

1 Woepcke, Mémoire sur la propagation des chiffres indiens, *JA* 1863, s. 6, v. 1, 27/79, 442/529, G.S. Colin, De l'origine grecque des "chiffres de Fes" et de nos "chiffres arabes", *JA* CCXXII, 193/215. On the oldest documented evidence of Indian numbers from the year 260/873 and 275/888 cf. Karabacek, *Führer* 216ff, *WZKM* XI, 13.

2 In the Index to ḤKh Flügel identified the otherwise unknown al-Ahwāzī, who commented on the 10th *maqāla* of Euclid (ḤKh [1]I, 382, [2]I, 138, Berl. 5293, Leid. 967/70, Paris $2467_{,18}$), without explanation with ʿAbdallāh b. Hilāl al-Ahwāzī, who translated *Kalīla wa-Dimna* for Yaḥyā b. Khālid al-Barmakī in 165/781, ḤKh [1]V, 238, and Ahlwardt followed him in this; see Steinschneider, *ZDMG* L, 167, Suter no. 123, Suppl. I, 387.

3 His name, which appears in a Latin translation in the *Trattati d'aritmetica*, ed. Boncompagni, Book I as Algoritmi, lives on in 'algorithm', a term for a particular computation procedure that has turned into a rule (see Renaud, *Mém. sur l'Inde*, p. 303, who did not know the Latin translation yet).

he composed a digest of Indian astronomy, the *Sindhind* (see chapter 14), and a revision of the tables of Ptolemy. However, he acquired particular fame through his two works on algebra—whose name he invented—and arithmetic which, soon translated into Latin, remained authoritative in the subject in Europe into Renaissance times.

Ibn al-Qifṭī 289, Cantor 611/29, Mieli § 15. 1. *Mukhtaṣar min ḥisāb al-jabr wal-muqābala*[4] *nach einer Hds. hsg. von* Fr. Rosen, *The Algebra of Muḥammad b. Mūsā*, ed. and transl., London 1831, good Latin transl. by Gerard of Cremona, ed. Gugl. Libri, *Histoire des sciences math. en Italie* I, Paris 1838, 253/97, more freely by Robert of Chester (see Suppl.). Wieleitner, Die Erbteilungaufgaben bei Muḥammad b. Mūsā, *Mitt. z. Math. u. Nat.* 53 (1922), 57/67, S. Gandz, Sources of al-Khowārizmis Algebra, *Isis* 1936, 272/4.—The first part, *Bāb al-misāḥa*, on geometry, cf. A. Marre, Partie géometrique de l'Algèbre par Abū ʿAbdallāh Muḥammad b. Mūsā, *Nouvelles Annales des Mathématiques* V (1846), 557/70 and in *Annali di matematica pura ed applicata* VII, Roma 1866, goes, according to S. Gandz (see Suppl.), back to a Jewish work (see Ruska, OLZ 37, 613/6).—2. *Kitāb al-jamʿ wal-tafrīq*, *Algoritmi de numero Indorum* (from a manuscript in Cambridge) in *Trattati d'aritmetica*, ed. Bald. Boncompagni, Book I.—3. The astronomical | tables, translated into Latin by Adelard of Bath around 1120, 241
cf. M. Cantor, *Mathematische Beiträge zum Culturleben der Völker*, Halle 1863, 268/9, see Suppl.[5]

2. In Baghdad, the three sons of Mūsā b. Shākir who had already served al-Maʾmūn as an astronomer, i.e. Aḥmad, al-Ḥasan, and Muḥammad, d. Rabīʿ I 259/January 873, together composed numerous mathematical, astronomical, and technical works, and stimulated translation activity by having their agents buy up books in Asia Minor.

Fihrist 271,9–23, Ibn Khall. 679, Ibn al-Qifṭī 315, 441, M. Steinschneider, Die Söhne des Mūsā b. Schākir (bibliography of works attributed to them), *Bibl. Math.* 1887, 44ff., 71ff., Mieli § 12, n. 9. Şerefeddin, *Meşahiri Mühendisini Arabden Banu Musa*, Istanbul 1321. 1. Liber trium fratrium de geometria, Lat. ed. M. Curtze in

4 Construction and settlement of equations; *jabr* is medical in origin for the setting of a fracture; unlikely is the hypothesis of S. Gandz, The Origin of the Term Algebra, *Am. Math. Monthly* 33, 1926, 437/40, that the Babylonian *gabru* "mutually corresponding" would be the underlying term because a transmission to the Arabs cannot be proven.

5 Against Ahlwardt's identification of Khwārizmī with Abū Jaʿfar Muḥammad b. Mūsā al-Khāzin (Suppl. I, 387, 6g) see Steinschneider, Euklid bei den Arabern, 89, ZDMG L, 166.

Nova Acta der Kais. Leopold. Akademie der Naturforscher, vol. 49, Halle 1885, p. 105/67.—2. *Maʿrifat misāḥat al-ashkāl al-basīṭa wal-kuriyya*, extension of plane and circular figures, ḤKh v, 12414, 10481, Berl. 5938, Paris $2467_{,3}$ (see Suppl.).—3. *Kitāb al-ḥiyal*, tricks, e.g. constructing a beaker in such a way that when it is full and one more drop is added, all the water runs away, or
217 the construction of a water basin near a river | that is always full of water and that shows decrease nor increase, Berl. 5562 (see Suppl.), see E. Wiedemann, *SBErl.* 38 (1906) 341/8, XII (1907) 200/5, *Mitt. der Wetterauischen Ges.* 1908, 29/36 (Die Konstruktion von Springbrunnen durch muslimische Gelehrte), Über Musikautomaten bei den Arabern, *Centenario della Nascita di Michele Amari*, II, 1909, 164/85.—4.–5. see Suppl.—6. *Kitāb al-darajāt fī ṭabāʾiʿ al-burūj* Pet. Inst. $119_{,3}$ NO 2800, iia.—7. *Aḥkām al-daraj lil-mawālīd* Garr. 968.

3. The most important mathematician of this period was Abu ʾl-Ḥasan Thābit b. Qurra al-Ṣābiʾ. He was born around 219/834 in Ḥarrān and belonged to the
242 town's indigenous sect of the Ṣābiʾa. After first | working as a money-changer he went to Baghdad where he studied philosophy and mathematics. The ideas that he picked up during this period drew him, after his return to his hometown, into dogmatic conflict with his fellow believers, leading to his exclusion from the community. In Kafartūthā, where he went afterwards, he got to know Muḥammad b. Mūsā, who took him along with him to Baghdad, where he introduced him to al-Muʿtaḍid. The latter's favour provided the leisure-time for unlimited academic pursuits. He revised the translations of numerous Greek works and composed books on medicine and mathematics himself. In particular, his research promoted the theory of amicable numbers. He died on 6 Ṣafar 288/18 February 901.

Fihrist 272, Ibn Khall. 125, Ibn Abī Uṣaybiʿa I, 215, Wüst., *Ärzte*, no. 81, D. Chwolsohn, *Die Sabier* I, 546/67, Woepcke, Notice sur une théorie ajoutée par Th. b. K. à l'arithmétique spéculative des Grecs, *JA* 1852, II, 420/6, Mieli § 15, n. 4.

I. Translations and revisions of Greek works, see Steinschneider, Index, *ZDMG*, L 409 (see Suppl).—1. Archimedes. a. *Kitāb al-kura wal-usṭuwāna* Bursa, Haraccizade, Heyet 22.—b. *al-Maʾkhūdhāt* also Bank. 28/2519, *Tadhk. al-nawādir* 152, see Suppl. I, 384, wrongly attributed to Ibrāhīm b. Sinān according to a communcation by Masʿūd Alam Nadwi to P. Luckey (not in Cat. XXII).—2. a. *al-Muʿṭayāt*, the original version NO $2958_{,1}$, the revision by al-Ṭūsī Fātiḥ $3441_{,2}$, see Krause, *QSB* III, 499/500.—b. *Elementa* after Ḥunayn b. Isḥāq, revised, edition planned by Claire Boudoux, see *Archeion* XIX, $1937_{,70}$.—c. *ʿAmal al-dāʾira al-marsūma bi-sabʿat aqsām mutasāwiya* Cairo ¹V 203 (photo *QSt.* VII. 12, E, 16).—3. Autolykos. a. *al-Kura al-mutaḥarrika*, in the original

version AS 2671,$_{6}$.—b. *Fi 'l-ṭulūʿāt wal-ghurūbāt* AS 4832,$_{11}$, Serāi 3464,$_{10}$.—6. Apollonius of Perga, *Das 5. Buch der Conica des A. v. P. in der arab. Übers. des Th. b. K. hsg. ins Deutsche übertragen mit einer Einl. v.* L. Nix, Leipzig 1889.—7. | Ptolemy. a. *Tashīl al-Mijisṭī* AS 4832,$_{10}$.—b. *Fi 'qtiṣāṣ jumal ḥālāt al-kawākib* 243
al-mutaḥayyira also Br. Mus. 426,$_{11}$ (Book 2 only preserved in Arabic, translation in Heiberg's *Ptolemaios*).—8. Aristotle. a. *περὶ φυτῶν* in the revision by Nicolaus Damascenus, see P. M. Bouyges, Sur le "De Plantis" d'Aristote-Nicolas à propos d'un ms. arabe de Constantinople (Yeni) in *Notes sur les philosophes ar. connus des Latins au Moyen Âge*, no. 7 (*MFO* 1922/4).

II. Independent works. A. Medicine: 1. *Kitāb al-rawḍa fi 'l-ṭibb*, on the pulse and the causes, symptoms, and cures for individual diseases, Bodl. I, 574.—2. *Jawāmiʿ min Kitāb Jālīnūs fi 'l-dubūl* ibid. I, 579,$_{3}$.—3. *Risāla fī tawallud al-ḥaṣāt*, on the bladder and kidney stones, Berl. 6359.[6]

B. Mathematics and astronomy. 4. *de Horometria* Esc. ^{1}955.—5. *de Descriptione trianguli rectilinei* ibid. 955,$_{8}$.—6. *al-Qawl* (*Kitāb*) *fi 'l-shakl* (*al-mulaqqab bi*) *al-qaṭṭāʿ wal-nisba al-muʾallafa*, on secants, de ratione composita, i.e. Menelaus' theorem, Berl. 5940 (fragm.), Bodl. II, 279,$_{5}$, Paris 2457, Esc. ^{1}967,$_{2}$, Algiers 1446,$_{4}$, the first section only AS 4832,$_{33}$, Serāi 3464,$_{13}$, the second by itself Paris 2457,$_{15}$, Serāi 3464,$_{1}$, Hebr. Steinschn. 368.—7. *Kitāb al-mafrūḍāt, Liber datorum sive determinatorum*, revised by al-Ṭūsī, d. 672/1273, p. 508, Berl. 5939, Paris 2467,$_{4}$, Bodl. I, 875,$_{14}$, 895,$_{10}$, 960,$_{6}$, Flor. Med. 273, Ind. Off. 743, Cairo ^{1}V, 200, Leid. 1029, see Steinschneider, *ZDMG* L, 171.—| 8. *de Cylindris* 218
et conis Bodl. Hebr. 433.—9. *Fi 'l-qarasṭūn*, theory of the gold balance, Berl. 6023, Ind. Off. 767,$_{7}$, see Steinschneider 172 (see Suppl.).—10. *Fī sanat al-shams bil-arṣād* Ind. Off. 734, see Esc. ^{1}I, 390,$_{21}$.—11. *Kitāb fī ibṭāʾ al-ḥaraka fī falak al-burūj wa-surʿatihā bi-ḥisāb al-mawāḍiʿ al-khārija min al-markaz* Paris 2457,$_{13}$, see O. Schirmer, Studien zur Astronomie der Araber *SBPhMG Erl.* 58/9, 33/88.—12. *Fī tāʾlīf al-nasab* = 6, b.—13. *Fī misāḥat al-mujassamāt al-mukāfiya* Paris 2457,$_{24}$.—14. *Fī misāḥat qaṭʿ al-makhrūṭ alladhī yusamma 'l-mukāfī*, ibid 25.—15.–16. see Suppl.—17. *Risāla ilā Ibn Wahb fi 'l-taʾattī listikhrāj ʿamal al-masāʾil al-handasiyya* Paris 2457,$_{43}$.—18. *Qismat al-zāwiya al-mustaqīma bi-thalāth aqsām mutasāwiya* ibid. 45.—19. *al-Masāʾil* | *allatī saʾala ʿanhā Abū Mūsā* 244
ʿAlī b. Asad Br. Mus. 426,$_{3}$.—20. *Fī ḥisāb ruʾyat al-ahilla* ibid. 13.–21. *Risāla fī kayfa yanbaghī an yuslaka ilā nayl al-maṭlūb min al-maʿāni 'l-handasiyya*, Cairo ^{1}V, 196, 200, AS 4832,$_{1}$ (Ritter, *Arch. Orientálny* IV, 1932, 303/72).—22. *Kitāb al-rawābiʿ li-Aflāṭūn* with a commentary by Abu 'l-ʿAbbās Aḥmad b. al-Ḥusayn

---

6 The attribution to him of a tract on the diseases of horses translated from the Persian can hardly be correct, Paris 2710,$_{2}$, Wüst. no. 2. The *Kitāb al-dhakhīra*, also falsely attributed to him, additionally Bursa Haraccizade Tip 13, Rāmpūr, I, 476,$_{79/81}$.

b. Jihān Bukhtār, which Thābit b. Qurra recorded after conversations with him. "Now Abu 'l-ʿAbbās and Thābit are quoted in conversation, then again Plato is speaking and commented upon by Aḥmad. It treats in 4 chapters of the 4 substances: compound, separated, individual, and simple substance. One of its main parts consists of reflections on the intellectual powers of man, on the nature of reason, and also on the functions of the soul and on sensation. There is a lot of talk about the system of the universe, the workings of causes and powers, and about the earth and the things that it contains. In addition, alchemical questions are also raised, but answering these is not the primary objective," Munich 649, Leid. 1431, Steinschn. *Übers.* 13, Latin translation *Liber quartorum cum cmt. im Theatrum chym.* 1602, I, 23–37, see Suppl.—26. *Fī taṣḥīḥ masāʾil al-jabr etc.*, see P. Luckey, Thābit. b. Qurra über den geometrischen Richtigkeitsnachweis der Auflösung der quadratischen Gleichungen, *Berichte der Math. phys. Kl. der Sächs. Ak. d. Wiss.* XCIII (1941) 93/114.—29. *Kitāb fī ālāt al-sāʿāt etc.*, Garbers, Ein Werk Thābit. b. Qurra's über ebene Sonnenuhren, *Quellen u. Stud. z. Gesch. der Math. u. Nat.* IV, Berlin 1936, P. Luckey, Thābit b. Qurra's Buch über die eb. S., ibid. IV (1937), 95/148.—30. *Kitāb fī īḍāḥ al-wajh etc.*, introduction in Bessel-Hagen and O. Spies, *QSt.* II, 187/9, edition in preparation by Garbers.—38. *Min kalām Thābit. b. Qurra fi 'l-hayʾa* AS $4832_{,1}$ (Krause, *Hdss.* 16).—39. *Risāla mushawwiqa* Rāmpūr II, 808.—40. *Risāla* ibid. 819.—His works in Syriac are mentioned in Barhebraeus, *Chron. syr.*, ed. Bedjan 168_{11} (Assemani, *BO* II, 317), a work on the religion of the Ṣābians in Ibn al-Qifṭī $128_{,14}$ff.

4. His son Abū Saʿīd Sinān b. Thābit b. Qurra was the personal physician of the caliphs al-Muqtadir and al-Qāhir, who used threats to force him to adopt Islam. But since the latter continued to mistreat him anyway, he fled to Khurāsān. Later he returned to Baghdad where he died on 1 Dhu 'l-Qaʿda 331/12 July 943.

245 | Ibn Abī Uṣaybiʿa I, 220, *Fihr.* 272, 302, al-Ṣūlī, *Akhbār al-Rāḍī wal-Muttaqī*, 245, Chwolsohn I, 569/77, Wüst., *Ärzte* 83, *Gesch.* 109, Leclerc I, 365. Of his historical and mathematical works nothing is known.

5. His son Abū Isḥāq Ibrāhīm b. Sinān, d. 335/946, is known to have written on mathematics.

Ibn Abī Uṣaybiʿa I, 260, Suter 113, Krause, *Handschriften* 113, Chwolsohn I, 577 (but who seems to mistakenly associate the article by Ibn Khall., Wüst. I, no. 127, de Slane I, 288/9, with him). 1. *Fī misāḥat qaṭʿ al-makhrūṭ al-mukāfī* (or *fī*

m. al-q. al-m.), | on the measuring of parabolas, Paris $2457_{,26}$, Ind. Off. $767_{,6}$, 219
Br. Mus. II, 444, Cairo ^{1}V, 199, 208, H. Suter, Abh. über die Ausmessung der Parabel, *Vierteljahrsschr. der Naturforsch. Ges. in Zürich* LXIII (1918), 214.—2. *Maqāla fī ṭarīq al-taḥlīl wal-tarkīb fi 'l-masā'il al-handasiyya* Paris 2457, Cairo ^{1}V, 200, cf. Woepcke, *Mém. présentés par divers savants à l'acad. des sciences*, vol. XIV, A. Taymūr, *RAAD* III, 304.—3. *Maqāla fī rasm al-quṭūʿ al-thalātha* Br. Mus. $975_{,8}$ (Suppl. 8. delete: see 3, I. 1, b).—For his nephew Hilāl see p. 323.

5a. His contemporary Najm al-Dīn Abu 'l-Futūḥ Aḥmad b. Muḥammad b. al-Sarī discusses two geometrical problems in Leid. 1006.

6. The circumstances of the life of Abū Saʿīd Jābir b. Ibrāhīm al-Ṣābiʾ are unknown, but he did live in the fourth/tenth century.

Kitāb īḍāḥ al-burhān ʿalā ḥisāb al-khaṭaʾayn Leid. 1004, Bodl. I, 913, glosses thereon Leid. 1005.

6a.—g. see Suppl. I, 387.—6b. al-Nayrīzī, 2. *Risāla fi 'l-muṣādara etc.*, Berl. 5927.—6. On the spherical astrolabe, Esc. $^{1}956_{,3}$, $^{2}961_{,6}$ (Renaud 171). 7. Commentary on the first 10 books of Euclid in the translation of Gerard of Cremona (1114/87) *Anaritii in decem libros priores elementorum Euclidis commentarii*, ed. M. Curtze, Leipzig 1899.—6e. Naẓīf b. Yumn, a contemporary of al-Bīrūnī, who mentions an observation by him about the year 378 (*Taḥdīd nihāyat amākin* 9), and who calls him Abū ʿAlī in *al-Qānūn al-Masʿūdī* VII, 6 (Welīeddin 173a) (Krause).—6f. Yaʿqūb al-Sijistānī cites al-Bīrūnī's *al-Qānūn al-Masʿūdī* III, 4, see Schoy, *Die trigonometrischen Lehren* | *der Araber* 30.— 246
6g. Abū Jaʿfar Muḥammad b. al-Ḥusayn al-Khāzin (according to *Jāmiʿ qawānīn ʿilm al-hayʾa*, *QS* III, 811, f. 42a), a further unidentified treatise Paris 4821.

7. Of the works of Saʿīd Aḥmad b. Muḥammad b. ʿAbdallāh al-Sijāzī a significant number remain. All we know of him as a person is that al-Bīrūnī, *Chron.*, $42_{,17}$, refers to him as a contemporary. Evidence for when he lived is provided by MS Paris 2457, which goes back to an exemplar that he wrote in 358/969,[7] and by treatise no. 3, which he composed in 389/999.

G. Junge and W. Thomson, *The Commentary of Pappus on Book X of Euclids Elements*, Cambridge, Harvard Press, 1930, p. 47/51.

---

7 See Bergsträsser, *Islam* XXI, 198.

1. *Risāla fī waṣf al-quṭūʿ al-makhrūṭiyyāt* Leid. 995.—2. *Risāla fī qismat al-zāwiya al-mustaqīmat al-khaṭṭayn bi-thalāthat aqsām mutasāwiya* Leid. 996, cf. Woepcke, *L'Algèbre d'Omar al-Khayyami* p. 117ff.—3. *Fī taḥṣīl īqāʿ al-nisba al-muʾallafa al-ithnay ʿashara fi 'l-shakl al-qaṭṭāʿ al-musaṭṭaḥ bi-tarjama wāḥida wa-kayfiyyat al-aṣl alladhī tatawallad minhu hādhihi 'l-awjuh*, written in 389/999, Leid. 997. *Risāla fi 'l-shakl al-qaṭṭāʿ* Patna II, 335,$_{2519,38}$.—4. On the relation of the hyperbola to its asymptote from the 5th book of the *Conica*, perhaps just a part of 1, Leid. 998 (see Suppl.).—5. *Risāla fī ṣanʿat āla tuʿraf biha 'l-abʿād wa-ʿamal hādhihi 'l-āla* Leid. 999.—6. *Thabt barāhīn baʿḍ ashkāl kitāb Uqlīdis* Ind. Off. 734,$_{14}$.—7. *Dalāʾil fī ʿilm aḥkām al-nujūm*, on astrology, Br. Mus. 415,$_{8}$ (Suppl.).—8. *al-Qawānīn allatī yastaʿmiluha 'l-munajjim fi 'stinbāṭ al-qaḍāʾ min al-nujūm* ibid.—9. *al-Asʿār* an astrological treatise on the method of calculating the prices of crops, ibid. 10.—10.–31. see Suppl.—22. = 27. (J. Th. 17,$_{8}$) also AS 2672,$_{3}$ (ʿĀšir etc. should be excised in 10).—29. J. Th. 17,$_{2}$, also Ḥamīd. 873,$_{2}$, ʿĀšir 570,$_{2}$, Asʿad 998,$_{2}$.—30. *Kitāb fī ʿamal al-asṭurlāb* Serāi 3342,$_{9}$, Krause 185,$_{1}$, J. Th. 16.–31. *Kitāb Zarādusht fī ṣuwar darajāt al-falak*, the second part of the *Pentateuch* attributed to Zoroaster, Ḥamīd. 837,$_{15}$, ʿĀšir 570,$_{12}$, Asʿad 1998,$_{14}$,
247 part 5 NO 2800, II, 7.–32. A further unidentified | mathematical treatise in Paris 4821.—33. *ʿAmal al-musabbaʿ fi 'l-dāʾira wa-qismat al-zāwiya al-mustaqīma al-khaṭṭayn bi-thalātha aqsām mutasāwiya* Cairo ^{1}V, 203, photograph *QSt.* VII, 13, I, 18, translation by Schoy, *Isis* VIII, 1926, 21/31.—34. Astronomical explanation for the miraculous splitting asunder of the moon, AS 2052,$_{208b/214a}$.

7a. Abū Saʿīd al-Ḍarīr al-Jurjānī.

Suter 27,$_{48}$ (who, without explanation, identifies him as the student of Ibn al-ʿArābī, Abū Sulayman the Blind, mentioned without source reference by Flügel, *Gr. Schulen* 147).—1. *Masāʾil handasiyya* Cairo ^{1}V, 205, photograph *QSt.* VII, 14, I, 23.—2. *Kitāb istikhrāj khaṭṭ niṣf al-nahār min Kitāb analīmā* (Analemma) *wal-burhān ʿalayhi* Cairo, photograph *QSt.* VII, 36, II, 30, translation by Schoy, *Ann. d. Hydrogr.* 50, 1922, 265/71.

8. Abū Bakr Muḥammad b. al-Ḥusayn al-Karajī[8] dedicated a compendium on arithmetic to Fakhr al-Mulk (d. 407/1016, Ibn Khall. Wüst. no. 710), vizier of the Būyid Bahāʾ al-Dawla.

8 Corrupted to al-Karkhī, see Levi della Vida, *RSO* XIV, 264.

1. *al-Kāfī fī ʿilm al-ḥisāb* Gotha 1474, Köpr. 950, Sbath 111 (see Suppl.), commentary by ʿAbdallāh Ḥusayn b. Aḥmad al-Shaqqāq, Serāi 3155,2 (QS III, 516). *al-K. fi ʾl-Ḥ. des A.B.M. b. al-Ḥ. al-K. nach der auf der Herz. Gothaischen Schlossbibl. befindl. Hds. übers. v.* A. Hochheim, Halle a. S. I, 1878, II, 1879, III, 1880.—2. *al-Fakhrī*, algebra, as a continuation of the first, Paris 2459, Cairo [1]V, 212, Asʿad 3157, Bursa, Haraccizade, Heyet 17,2 (see Suppl.), cf. *Extrait du Fakhri, traité d'algèbre par Abou Bekr M. b. al-Ḥ. al-Karkhi, précédé d'un mémoire sur l'algèbre indéterminée chez les Arabes par* F. Woepcke, Paris 1853.—3.–4. see Suppl. (3. Patna II, 335,2519,1).—5. *ʿIlal ḥisāb al-jabr wal-muqābala* Bodl. I, 986,3, see RSO XIV, 249/64.—6. *Mukhtaṣar fi ʾl-ḥisāb wal-misāḥa* Alex. Fun. 82,4.

8a.—12. see Suppl. 8a. *Sharḥ ṣudūr maqālāt Uqlīdis* Patna I, 232,2034.—11.3. Translation by Schirmer, *Studien zur Astronomie der Araber*.—12.2. (= 3?), translation by Kohl, Zur Geschichte der Dreiteilung des Winkels, SB *Erl.* 54/5, 1925, 186/9.—4. Proof that the sum of two square numbers cannot be a square number, Paris 2457,49.

248 220 || Chapter 14. Astronomy and Astrology

J.B.J. Delambre, *Histoire de l'astronomie au moyen âge*, Paris 1819.

The study of astronomy, which was closely linked to that of mathematics and for the most part pursued by the same scholars, was from its beginnings likewise just as much indebted to the Indians as it was to the Greeks. The translation of the *Μεγάλη σύνταξις* of Ptolemy is mentioned in Suppl. I, 363. As reported by Ḥusayn b. Muḥammad al-Ādamī[1] (*Fihrist* $280,_{21}$, Casiri I, 429, Steinschneider, ZDMG 24, 372, n. 44, Suter no. 5), an Indian is said to have brought a work on astronomy with the title *Sindhind* to the court of al-Manṣūr as early as 152/773, describing it as an abridgement of the *Kardaja*, which had been written under King Figar. Woepcke, *Recherches* I, 58, discovered an Indian work therein, the *Siddhānta*, i.e. the *Brāhma-spuṭa-siddhānta*, which Brāhmagupta composed on the basis of the *Kramagyā* during the reign of King Vyâghramuka in 628.[2] Al-Manṣūr then ordered Ibrāhīm b. Ḥabīb al-Fazārī (see Yāqūt, *Irsh.* VI, 268, Suter 4, Suppl. I, 391) to translate the work into Arabic, and of this translation Muḥammad b. Mūsā al-Khwārizmī (p. 239) produced an abridgement during the reign of al-Ma'mūn.

This same caliph initiated a revision of Ptolemy's astronomical tables by means of simultaneous observations in Baghdad and Damascus, as well as the measuring of one degree of the meridian (see Ṣā'id al-Andalusī, *Ṭab.* 79u,
249 transl. Blachère 103, Sprenger, *Ausland* | 1867, no. 50). In this way Muslims were soon able to surpass their Greek and Indian masters on the basis of independent research. However, a purely scientific interest in astronomy went at the same time invariably hand in hand with a superstitious belief in astrology which, because of its practical application, secured for it the favour of the rulers. Objections by theologians only came later; as such al-Nuwayrī, I, $40,_{18}$, for example, rejected it as heretical.

1. Astrological works are mentioned first:

a. Those of the Jew Māshā' Allāh (Manasse) b. Atharī al-Baṣrī, who died around 200/815.

---

1 His son Muḥammad b. Ḥusayn b. Ḥamīd al-Ādamī wrote a set of tables, the *Naẓm al-ʿiqd*, which were published by his student al-Qāsim b. Muḥammad b. Hishām al-ʿAlawī in 308/920; *Ibn al-Qifṭī* ed. Lippert 282, C. 185, *Not. et Extr.* VII, 126, 128, Suter p. 44.

2 See G. Thibaut, *Grundriss der Indo-Iran. Philologie* III, 9, *Astronomie* 58.

See Suppl. I, 391, lx. 8. On an astrological work, known as “The Key” in its Latin translation, see M. Šangin, Latinskaya parafraza iz utrčennogo socineniya Mašallaha “Semi kliučei”, *Zap. Koll. Vost.* V, 235/42, *Izv. Ak. Nauk* 1929, 707/13, S.R.F. Gunther, *Chaucer and Meshallaha on the Astrolab*, Oxford 1922.

b. Those of Abū Yūsuf Yaʿqūb b. ʿAlī al-Qarṣī al-Qaṣrānī, whose dates cannot be fixed with precision.

See Suppl. I, p. 392, 1d.

c. His contemporary ʿUmar b. Farrukhān al-Ṭabarī, who must have died around 200/815.

See Suppl. I, 1.e., 959. *The book of Dorotheus*, translation in Yeni 784, fragm. Berl. Oct. 2603.—*al-Ikhtiyārāt*, Alex. Ḥurūf 12.

2. At the same time, or a little later, Aḥmad b. Muḥammad b. Kathīr al-Farghānī flourished, about whose life nothing further is known.

Ibn Abī Uṣaybiʿa I, 207, Mieli § $15_{,7}$. 1. *Kitāb fi ʾl-ḥarakāt al-samāwiyya wa-jawāmiʿ ʿilm al-nujūm*, Bodl. I, 879, de Jong, 110, under the title *ʿIlal al-aflāk* (see Suppl.), also Garr. 967, under the title *Risālat al-fuṣūl mudkhal fī Mijisṭī wa-huwa thalāthūna faṣlan* or *Kitāb al-hayʾa, al-fuṣūl al-thalāthīn*, Paris $2504_{,3}$, see Woepcke, JA s. V, v. 19, p. 114ff., esp. 120, *Hespéris* XVIII, $88_{,5b}$, | *Muhammedis* (*sic*) *Ketiri Ferga-* 250
nensis, qui vulgo Alfraganus dicitur, Elementa astronomica, arabice et latine, cum notis ad res exoticas sive orientales, quae in iis occurunt, opera Jacobi Golii, Amsterdam 1609, Steinschneider, ZDMG XVIII, 148, Hebr. Steinschn. 343.—2. *al-Kāmil fi ʾl-asṭurlāb* Berl. 5790/2.–3. *Fī ṣanʿat al-asṭurlāb* ibid. 5793, Paris $2546_{,5}$, under the title *Kitāb ʿamal al-asṭurlāb* Rāmpūr I, $428_{,64b}$.—4. *ʿIlm al-hayʾa*, Zāwiyat Sidi Ḥamza, *Hesp.* XVIII, $88_{,5b}$.—5. *Jadwal al-Farghānī* Patna II, $336_{,2520,8}$.

2a. Yaḥyā b. (Abū) Manṣūr, the author of *al-Zīj al-Maʾmūnī al-mujarrab* or *al-mumtaḥan* (Suppl. I, 393, with E. Honigmann, *Die sieben Klimate*, Heidelberg 1929, 143 ff.) was supposedly first called Bizīst b. Fīrūzān, receiving his Muslim name from al-Maʾmūn.

Ibn Isfandiyār, *Hist. of Ṭabaristān*, transl. Browne, 87.

3. (4) Aḥmad b. ʿAbdallāh al-Ḥāsib Ḥabash al-Marwazī flourished around the year 220/835.

Steinschneider, *Zeitsch. f. Math.* X, 478, ZDMG XXIV, 334, Mieli § 15,$_8$, ḤKh III, 6943 (imprecise), *al-Zīj al-ṣaghīr* or *al-Shāh*, Berl. 5750, Yeni 704,$_2$, see Nallino in Suter, 208/9.

3. (4) a. Abū Bakr al-Ḥasan b. al-Khaṣīb al-Fārisī al-Kūfī.

Suppl. I, 394. *al-Muqniʿ fī ʾl-mawālīd* Esc. ^{1}935, 973, ^{2}940, 978 (incomplete), *Kitāb al-mawālīd* Ḥamīd. 856,$_1$.

3. (4) b. ʿAlī b. ʿĪsā al-Asṭurlābī al-Ḥarrānī.

Suppl. I, 394. *Risāla fī ʿilm al-asṭurlāb* Esc. ^{1}972, ^{2}976,$_3$ (Renaud 170), Dam. Z. 89,$_1$, from which Alex. Ḥisāb 52.

4. (5) Abū ʿAlī Yaḥyā b. Ghālib (according to others Ismāʿīl b. Muḥammad) al-Khayyāṭ, ca. 240/854.

1. *Sirr al-ʿamal*, on astrology, ḤKh V, 11907, Berl. 5876.—2. *Aḥkām al-mawālīd* (see Suppl.) Alex. Ḥurūf 12,$_1$.—3. see Suppl.—4. *al-Masāʾil fī aḥkām al-nujūm* Alex. Ḥisāb 52.

5. (6) Abū Maʿshar Jaʿfar b. Muḥammad b. ʿUmar al-Balkhī, one of the greatest
251 est astronomers and astrologers of his | time, was originally a *ḥadīth* scholar, and was already 47 when al-Kindī won him over to science. According to al-Tanūkhīs's *Nishwār* (in Yāqūt), al-Balkhī started out on the pilgrimage from Khurāsān, but when he visited the library of ʿAlī b. Yaḥyā al-Munajjim in Karkar—near al-Qufs, not far from Baghdad—he was apparently taken by such a passion for astronomy that he gave up his earlier plan. He died, at over a hundred years old, in Wāsiṭ on 28 Ramaḍān 272/8 March 886.

Fihrist 277, Ibn Khall. no. 132, Yāqūt, *Irshād* V, 467,$_{4-11}$. 1. *Kitāb al-ulūf fī buyūt al-ʿibādāt*, a corpus monumentorum arranged chronologically in 8 books based on the 8 civilizations, see Lippert, WZKM IX, 351/8.—2. a. *al-Mudkhal al-kabīr ilā ʿilm aḥkām al-nujūm*, introduction to astrology in 8 chapters, Leid. 1051, Br. Mus. Or. 7964, Bodl. II, 272, 294, Esc. ^{1}912, Patna I, 239,$_{2068}$, 550,$_{29231}$, Hebr. Steinschn. 353,$_1$.—b. *Mukhtaṣar* or *al-Mudkhal al-ṣaghīr* Paris 2696,$_2$, Br. Mus. 425,$_4$, Yeni 1193,$_6$ (QS III, 450ff.).—3. *Kitāb mawālīd al-rijāl wal-nisāʾ*, astrology in 12 sections each, Berl. 5801/2 (see Suppl.), Cat. Boustany 1930, 100, under the title *Kitāb ʿala (fī) ʾl-tamām wal-kamāl* Vienna 1419, under the title *Aḥkām al-mawālīd* with Persian translation Br. Mus. Or. 9604.—4. *Traité des nativités*
222 (genuine?) Paris 2586/7 = | *al-Qawl fī ʾl-numūdhārāt* Br. Mus. 426/7 (?) = Bodl.

I, 112,$_{3}$ (? see Suppl.).—5. *Kitāb al-ṭawāliʿ wal-nujūm* Bodl. I, 114,$_{1}$.—6. = 3.–7. *Kitāb qirānāt al-kawākib* Paris 2580,$_{3}$ Bodl. II, 284,$_{1}$, Fātiḥ 3426,$_{3}$ (see Suppl. 19), Halet 541, Ǧārullāh 1539 (parchment 352 AH, Ritter), Āṣaf. II, 1702,$_{81}$, *Muqāranāt al-kawākib* ʿUm. 4658, *Aḥkām al-qirānāt* in Pers. transl. library of Muḥammad ʿAlī al-Khwānsārī al-Najafī, *Dharīʿa* I, 301,$_{570}$.—8. *Aḥkām taḥwīl sini ʾl-mawālīd* Paris 2588, Bodl. I, 878, Esc. ^{1}912, ^{2}917, 977 (incomplete, Renaud 170).—9. *Kitāb ikhtiyārāt al-sāʿāt* Br. Mus. 445,$_{12}$, Hebr. Steinschn. 355.—10. *Kitāb al-nukat wal-asrār* Br. Mus. Or. 11214 (Kraus), excerpts Bodl. II, 286,$_{3,1}$.—11. *Kitāb al-sirr* Esc. ^{1}933, ^{2}938, excerpts Bodl. II, 286,$_{2}$, different from *Asrār al-nujūm*, Esc. ^{1}913, ^{2}916,$_{6}$, Asʿad 1907, Cairo ^{1}V, 309, Rāmpūr I, 681,$_{1}$.—12. Twelve astrological dicta, Bodl. I, 332,$_{4}$.—13.–27. (see Suppl. 15, cites *Rasāʾil Ikhwān al-ṣafāʾ*, Bombay IV, 292, Kraus).—28. Persian translation of an untitled treatise, Köpr. 1624,$_{1}$.—29. Persian translation of an untitled astrological treatise, Fātiḥ 1362,$_{3}$, 2144,$_{2}$ (Krause, *Hdss.* 11).

| 5. (6) a. Abu ʾl-ʿAnbas Muḥammad b. Isḥāq al-Ṣaymarī, d. 275/888. 252

Supp. I, 396.

5. (6) b. Abū ʿUthmān Sahl b. Bishr b. Hāniʾ al-Isrāʾīlī.

Suppl. I, 396, Suter 26, Krause 26. 1. *al-Majmūʿ fi ʾl-aḥkām* Esc. ^{1}914, ^{2}919,$_{1}$, Cairo ^{1}V, 268 (*fi ʾl-Aḥkām fī ʿilm al-mīqāt*, Renaud 170).—6. *Risāla fi ʾl-khusūf* Asʿad 1967 (towards the end) = *Kitāb al-nujūm* Beirut 199 (*MFO* VII, 275).—7. Under the title *al-Aḥkām fī taḥwīl al-nujūm* Alex. Ḥurūf 16.—10. *al-Qirānāt wal-ittiṣālāt fi ʾl-burūj al-ithnay ʿashar* Alex. Ḥurūf 16.

6. (7) Jamāl al-Dīn Abu ʾl-Qāsim b. Maḥfūẓ al-Baghdādī wrote around the year 310/922.

Suter, 490. 1. *Zīj*, astronomical tables, Paris 2486.—2. Treatise on the use of the astrolabe, Br. Mus. 1002,$_{4}$, Or. 5734 (DL 39).

7. (8) Muḥammad b. Jābir b. Sinān al-Battānī, d. 317/929 (see Suppl. I, 397). Al-Masʿūdī counts him as one of the most famous astronomers of Islam, and the introduction of trigonometrical functions into the Western world is connected with his name, transcribed as Albategnius.

Fihrist 279, Ibn Khall. 680. Chwolsohn, *Ssabier* I, 611f., Cantor 632, Mieli § 15,$_{9}$. 1. *Iṣlāḥ al-Mijisṭī* Berl. 5653, ascribed to Jābir b. Aflaḥ, ḤKh V, 11413.—2. *al-Maqālāt al-arbaʿ fi ʾl-qaḍāʾ bil-nujūm*, adaptation of the astrological *τετράβιβλος* of Ptolemy, ḤKh VI, 12878, Berl. 5875, Esc. ^{2}1829$_{,1}$, are wrongly attributed to him, see Suppl.

8. (3) Ibn Hibintā al-Munajjim al-Naṣrānī wrote, after 330/941:

Al-Mughnī, on astronomy, ḤKh V, 654, no. 12943 (where mistakenly Hnbtā), part 2 Munich 852, cf. Nallino in Suter, *Nachr.* 160.

9. Kushyār b. Labbān al-Jīlī, who flourished around the year 350/966.

253 | Al-Bayhaqī, *Tatimma* 83, Suter 192, Lelewel, *Géographie du Moyen Âge* I, XLVIII,
III, Reinaud, *Géographie d'Aboulfeda* I, p. CI (mistaken 459), Steinschneider,
ZDMG XXIV, 375, Mieli § 21$_{,12}$ (who places him around 971–1029).—1. *al-Zīj*
al-jāmiʿ, astronomical tables, Berl. 5751, Leid. 1054, Alex. Ḥisāb 50, excerpt Leid.
1055, cf. Ideler, *Handbuch der mathematischen und technischen Chronologie*,
Berlin 1825/6, II, 547, 624/33, the tables of longitude and latitude in Lelewel,
I, 178ff., Persian translation by ʿUmar b. Abī Ṭālib al-Munajjim al-Tabrīzī,
made in 483/1090, Leid. 1056.—2. *Kitāb al-mudkhal (mujmal) fī ṣināʿat aḥkām*
al-nujūm ḤKh V, 11695, 11475, Berl. 5884, Esc. ^{1}972, Br. Mus. 415, Stewart I, 105,
223 no. XVI, Garr. 969, Asʿad 2004, Serāi 3498 | (Krause 192$_{,2}$, Suppl.), Qawala II,
281, Rāmpūr I, 429$_{,67}$.—under the title *Aṣl ṣināʿat al-aḥkām al-falakiyya* Alex.
Ḥurūf 7.—3. *Maqāla fi 'l-ḥisāb* ḤKh VI, 12961, *al-Maqāla al-ūlā fī ḥisāb al-abwāb*
min al-maqālāt al-arbaʿ Cairo ^{1}V, 317, Hebr. under the title *ʿĪyūn hā-ʿiqqārīm*
by Shalom Ben Yosef Anabi, Oppenheim 272, see Steinschneider, *Z. f. Math.*
XII, 33, cf. 58, *ZDMG* XXIV, 332, Hebr. transl. 352.—4. *Kitāb al-asṭurlāb wa-kay-*
fiyyat ʿamalihi waʿtibārihi ʿala 'l-tamām wal-kamāl Paris 3487$_{,1}$, 4731 Cairo ^{1}V,
298 (photograph *QSt.* VII, 40, II, 35).—5. *Risālat al-abʿād wal-ajrām* Patna II,
331$_{,2519,5}$ (see Suppl.).

10. Abū Naṣr al-Ḥasan b. ʿAlī al-Munajjim al-Qummī wrote, in 357/968:

Kitāb al-bāriʿ (al-mudkhal) ilā (ʿilm) aḥkām al-nujūm (wal-ṭawāliʿ), an introduction to astrology in 5 *maqālāt* and 64 *fuṣūl*, dedicated to Shaykh Abū ʿAmr b. Saʿīd b. Marzubān, ḤKh II, 1602, V, 11680, Berl. 5601, Paris 2582, Pet. Rosen 186, (see Suppl.), abstract Berl. 5662, Ind. Off. 769$_{,4}$, Persian translation Berl. 5603, see Steinschneider, *ZDMG* XVIII, 140, XXV, 396, Suter 174.

11. Abu 'l-Ḥusayn b. ʿUmar al-Ṣūfī, born in Rayy on 14 Muḥarram 291/8 December 903, was an astronomer in the service of the Būyid ʿAḍud al-Dawla Abū Shujāʿ. He died in Muḥarram 376/986.

Steinschneider, ZDMG XVIII, 140, XXV, 349, Suter 138. 1. *Kitāb al-kawākib al-thābita* or *Ṣuwar al-kawākib*, dedicated to the Būyid ʿAḍud al-Dawla Fannā Khusraw (338–72/949–82), Berl. 5658/60, Paris 2488/92, 6528, Ind. Off. 731/2, Copenhagen 83, Pet. Rosen 185, Serāi 2493 (525 AH), Rāmpūr I, $428,_{63}$, | cf. 254
Caussin de Perceval, *Not. et extr.* XII, 236ff. Delambre, 204, *Description des étoiles fixes par ʿAbd al-Raḥmān al-Ṣūfī trad. par* H.C.F.C. Schelljerup, St. Petersburg 1874 (see Suppl.), J. Upton, *Metropolitan Museum Studies* IV (1933), 179/99, Holter, *Jahrb. d. Kunsthist. Instituts Vienna*, N.F. XI, 1937, 36f. (ad Fātiḥ 3422).—2. *Kitāb al-mudkhal fi ʾl-aḥkām*, on astrology, Book V, Ind. Off. 733 = Esc. $^{1}915$ (?)—3. *Kitāb al-ʿamal bil-asṭurlāb* Paris 2493 (?), $2498,_{2}$, Pet. Rosen $190,_{4}$, Bodl. I, 899, see B. Dorn, *Drei astronom. Instrumente*, St. Petersburg 1865, p. 77/9.—4. Excerpt from a lost work on the astrolabe in 1760 capita, Serāi $2642/_{2}$ (Krause, see Suppl.).—On the star catalogue apparently attributed to his son Abū ʿAlī see Suppl. I, $863,_{4a}$.

11a. ʿAbd al-ʿAzīz b. ʿUthmān b. ʿAlī al-Ṣaqr al-Qabīṣī (known as Alcabitius among the Latins), d. 356/967, see Suppl.

1. *al-Mudkhal ilā ṣināʿat aḥkām al-nujūm* (*ʿilm al-falak*) Ḥamīd. $856,_{2}$, Alex. Ḥurūf 17, Patna I, $239,_{2070,1}$.

12. Abū Sahl Wayjan b. Rustam al-Kūhī (see Suppl.) wrote around the year 380/990:

(Cantor 642ff.). 1. Notes on Euclid's *Elements*: a. on Book 1 and 2, Cairo ^{1}V, 203, b. on Book 3, Berl. 5922.—2. Addenda to Archimedes's *On Conoids and Spheroids*, Paris 952, $2467,_{2}$, Leid. 1001, cf. Woepcke, *L'algèbre d'Omar al-Khayyami* p. 55.—3. On the manufacture of astrolabes, with a commentary by Abū Saʿd al-ʿAlāʾ Sahl, Leid. 1058.—4. *Fi ʾl-barkār al-tāmm wal-ʿamal bihi* Leid. 1059, Rāġib $569,_{5}$, Cairo ^{1}V, 203.—5. *Risāla fī ʿamal ḍilʿ al-musabbaʿ al-mutasāwi ʾl-aḍlāʿ fi ʾl-dāʾira* Ind. Off. $767,_{4}$ (see Suppl.) AS $4832,_{27}$.—6. *Ṭarīq fi ʾstikhrāj khaṭṭayn bayna khaṭṭayn fa-tatawālā ʿalā nisba* Ind. Off. $767,_{5}$, AS $4832,_{27}$ (see Suppl.).—7., 8., 9. (Patna II, $335,_{2519,33}$) see Suppl.—10. *Masʾalatāni handasiyyatān* AS $4832,_{22}$, $4830,_{9d}$.—11. An otherwise unidentified mathematical and astronomical treatise, Paris 4821.—12.–16. see Suppl.—17. *Ziyādāt li-kitāb Uqlīdis fi ʾl-muʿṭayāt* AS $4830,_{9e}$, $4832,_{26}$.—19. *Risāla fī miqdār* (*maʿrifat*) *mā yurā min al-samāʾ* (*wal-baḥr*) AS $2587,_{2}$, $4832,_{22}$ (Ritter, *Arch. Or.* IV, 368, Krause $175,_{8}$), *Mashh.* XVII, $69,_{186}$.—20. *al-Mafrūḍāt* AS $4830,_{6}$ (Kr. 11).—21. Correspondence with Abū Isḥāq al-Ṣābiʾ AS $4832,_{24,25}$.—22. *Risāla fī tathlīth al-zāwiya wa-ʿamal al-musabbaʿ al-musāwi ʾl-aḍlāʿ fi ʾl-dāʾira* Berl. 9408, photograph *QSt.* VII, 9, I, 7.

255 | 13. Abu 'l-Wafāʾ Muḥammad b. Muḥammad b. Yaḥyā al-Būzajānī was born in Būzajān near Nishapur on 1 Ramaḍān 328/10 June 940, went to Iraq in 348/959, and died in 387/997 or in Rajab 388/988.

224 | *Fihrist* 283, Ibn Khall. 681, Cantor p. 697. 1. *Kitāb al-Mijisṭī*, an imitation of the work by Ptolemy, Paris 2494, see Sédillot, *Matériaux*, p. 42ff., Carra de Vaux, *JA* s. VIII, v. 19, p. 408/71. On the question of whether Tycho Brahe's discovery of the variation was contained in it, see R. Wolf, *Geschichte der Astronomie*, p. 53, 204.—2. *Risāla fī-mā yaḥtāj ilayhi al-ṣāniʿ min aʿmāl al-handasa*, a work on geometrical designs, Ambr. Hammer, Cat. 44, no. 68, AS 2753. Commentary *Sharḥ al-aʿmāl al-handasiyya* by Kamāl al-Dīn Abu 'l-Fatḥ Mūsā b. Yūnus b. Muḥammad b. Manʿa al-Shāfiʿī, d. 639/1241 (p. 472), Mashh. XVII, 42$_{,30}$, see Woepcke, *JA* s. V, v. 5 (1855), p. 246/51, Suter, *Abh. z. Gesch. der Math. u. Nat.*, Erlangen 1922.—3. *Kitāb fī-mā yaḥtāj ilayhi 'l-kuttāb wal-ʿummāl min ʿilm al-ḥisāb* Leid. 993, Cairo [1]V, 185 = *Kitāb al-manāzil fi 'l-ḥisāb* Esc. [1]933, see Woepcke, loc. cit., 243ff. = *al-Mudkhal al-ḥifẓī ilā ṣināʿat al-arithmāṭīqī, Risāla fi 'l-ḥisāb* Rāmpūr I, 414.—4. Method for the calculation of sine tables, Woepcke, *JA* 1860, I, 298/9.—5., 6., 7. see Suppl. (on 6. *Risāla fī iqāmat al-burhān ʿala 'l-daraja min al-falak min qaws al-nahār wartifāʿ niṣf al-nahār wartifāʿ al-waqt* Patna II, 331$_{,2519,6}$; 7 Ğārullāh 1479, Krause 167).—7. *Qānūn juzʾ al-taʾlīf li-Uqlīdis* Rāmpūr I, 417$_{,576}$.

14. Abu 'l-Ḥasan ʿAlī b. Abī Saʿīd ʿAbd al-Raḥmān b. Aḥmad b. Yūnus b. ʿAbd al-Aʿlā al-Ṣadafī, who, besides al-Battānī, was probably the greatest astronomer of the Arabs, served the Fāṭimid caliph al-Ḥākim (387–411/996–1020) and died on 3 Shawwāl 399/3 May 1009.

Ibn Khall. 461, Delambre 76ff., Jourdain, *Biogr. Univ.* XXI, 159, F. Mehren in *Annaler for Nord. Oldkynd.* 1857, p. 25. 1. *al-Zīj al-Ḥākimī*, very thorough astronomical tables, whose second edition was dedicated to al-Ḥākim (see Suppl.), Leid. 1057, Paris 2495/6, Bodl. II, 298, Esc. [1]919$_{,5}$ (photograph *QSt.* VII, 42, II, 39, 59, II, 39, see Delambre 125ff., Caussin de Perceval, *Not. et extr.* VII, 16/240, see Schoy, *Isis* V, 1923, 364/6, *Annalen der Hydrogr.* 49, 1921, 124/33, 50, 1922, 3/20;
256 | Clarifications to chapters 1 and 3 Gotha 1401.—2. *Kitāb bulūgh al-umniyya fī-mā yataʿallaq bi-ṭulūʿ al-shiʿrā al-yamāniyya*, astrological reflections on the signs of the zodiac involving the moon and the rising of Sirius, Gotha 1459.—3. *al-Jayb*, astronomical tables, Berl. 5752.—4. *Kitāb fīhi 'l-samt*, azimuth tables, ibid. 5753, Esc. [1]1129$_{,5}$ (photograph *QSt.* VII, 56, II, 55) (see Suppl.).—5. *Risāla fī ṭarīq istikhrāj khaṭṭay al-qusṭās* Ambr. 289b (photograph *QSt.* VII, 31), see Schoy, *Gnomonik der Araber*, Berl.-Lpz. 1923, 35/6.

15. Abu 'l-Ḥasan ʿAlī b. Abi 'l-Rijāl (the Abenragel of the Latins) al-Shaybānī al-Kātib al-Maghribī al-Qayrawānī, who may have taken part in al-Kūhī's observations in Baghdad. He sporadically lived at the court of the Zīrid Muʿizz b. Bādis al-Manṣūr (406–54/1016–62) in Tunis, and died sometime after 432/1040.

Sanchez Pérez 58, Mieli § 37. 1. *Kitāb al-bāriʿ fī aḥkām al-nujūm*, on astrology, ḤKh [1]II, 4, [2]I, 217, Br. Mus. 1347, Ind. Off. 735, Paris 2590, Stewart 104, Ḥamīd. 826/7, Zāwiyat Sīdī Ḥamza, *Hesp.* XVIII, $88,_{5a}$, Alex. Ḥisāb 43, Rāmpūr I, $682,_{10}$ (see Suppl.), *Praeclarissimus liber completus in judiciis astrorum, quem edidit Albohazen Haly f. Abenragel*, Venice 1485, Basle 1551, Hebr. Steinschn. 361, see Steinschneider, *Zur pseudepigr. Literatur* p. 83, ZDMG XVIII, 155ff., V. Stegemann, *Beiträge zur Geschichte der Astrologie* (*Studien zur Gesch. u. Kultur der Antike und des MA, hsg. v. Bilabel und A. Grohmann, Reihe A, Heft* 2), Heidelberg 1935, p. 98ff., Astrologische Zarathushtrafragmente bei Ibn Abi 'l-Rijāl *Orientalia* VI, 317/36.—2. *Urjūza* (*Naẓm*) *fi 'l-aḥkām*, see Suppl., Esc. [1]911, [2]916, (Renaud, *Isis* XVIII, 174), *Qst.* VII, 64, II, 13, Garr. 972, under the title *al-Dalāla al-kulliyya ʿani 'l-ḥarakāt al-falakiyya*. Commentaries: a. Aḥmad b. Ḥasan al-Qunfudhī al-Qusṭanṭīnī, d. 810/1407 (II, 241), written in 774/1372, Br. Mus. $977,_{29}$.—b. Kamāl al-Tūrakānī, written in 755/1354 in Gulistān, Garr. $2104,_{3}$.—3. See Suppl.

16. Abu 'l-Qāsim Aḥmad b. ʿAbdallāh b. ʿUmar b. al-Ṣaffār al-Ghāfiqī al-Andalusī, a student of Maslama al-Majrīṭī (p. 280), went from Cordova to Denia during the civil war, where he died in 426/1035.

Ibn Bashkuwāl 83. *Risālat al-asṭurlāb wal-asmāʾ al-wāqiʿa ʿalayhā* Br. Mus. $408,_{8}$, 976 (but where the author is called Muḥammad b. Aḥmad b. ʿAbdallāh etc.), composed in 413/1022, see Suppl., also Esc. [2]946, | Rabāṭ $455,_{iv}$ (which has 257
al-Qāsim b. Aḥmad b. ʿAbdallāh), $502,_{iii}$ (Renaud, *Isis* XVIII, 171), Alex. Ḥisāb $60,_{1}$ (with wrong date) probably different from the anonymous Bodl. I, 453, Hebrew translation in Steinschneider 363, ZDMG XVIII, 123, XLVII, 363.

17. Muḥammad b. Raḥīq b. ʿAbd al-Karīm wrote an astronomical work around the year 411/1020, Berl. 5664.

225 | Chapter 15. Geography

F. Wüstenfeld, *Die Literatur der Erdbeschreibung bei den Arabern, Zeitschr. f. vergl. Erdkunde* I, Magdeburg 1842.

M. Reinaud, Introduction générale à la géographie des orientaux, in *Géographie d'Aboulfeda* I, Paris 1848.

J. Lelewel, *Géographie du moyen âge*, 4 vols., Bruxelles 1850/7, *Géographie des Arabes*, Paris 1851 (see Günther, *Geschichte der Erdkunde*, 1904, p. 40 n.).

M.J. de Goeje, Eenige mededeelingen van de Arabische geographen, in *Tijdschrift van het Aardrijkskundig Genootschap* 1876, p. 190ff.

Idem, *Bibliotheca geographorum Arabicorum* I–VIII, Leid. 1870ff. (hereafter BG).

J.H. Kramers, *Bibliotheca geographorum Arabicorum, nova editio*, Leiden 1938ff.

P. Schwarz, Die ältere geographische Literatur der Araber in Hettner's *Geograph. Zeitschr.* III (1897), fascicle 3.

A. Mieli, *La science arabe*, § 14, 22, 32, 44.

I. Kračkovsky, Arabskie geografy putešestvenniki, *Izv. Gos. Geogr. Občestva* 1937, no. 5, 738/65.

1. Incentives from various sides for the study of geography (see Suppl. I, 402/3) were only taken to a scientific level when the Arabs became acquainted with Ptolemy's *Γεωγραφικὴ ὑφήγησις*. From the various adaptations, the oldest of which goes back to Ibn Khurradādhbeh (see Kramers, EI Suppl. 64), only the one by Muḥammad b. Mūsā al-Khwārizmī (see Suppl. I, 381) has been preserved, which turned its source, in imitation of the astronomical *zīj*, into tabular form, while adding information regarding the Muslim world.

258 | 2. Abu 'l-Qāsim 'Ubaydallāh b. 'Abdallāh b. Khurradādhbeh, whose grandfather had converted to Islam and whose father was the governor of Ṭabaristān in 201/816 (Ṭabarī III, 104ff.), grew up in Baghdad where he was trained in music and belles lettres by Isḥāq al-Mawṣilī, d. 235/849 (see Suppl. I, 223). Later he became a postmaster in Jabal (Media) and wrote, between 230–4/844–8, probably in Samarra while serving in the central post office, the following:

226 | 1. *Kitāb al-masālik wal-mamālik*, BG VI, 1889, an official road book with precise indication of waystations, relay points, and the amount of taxes for every province, see Barbier de Meynard, JA s. VI, v. V, p. 227 ff.—2. *Kitāb al-lahw wal-malāhī* in the possession of Ḥabīb Efendi Zayyāt in Alexandria, see *Hilāl*

XXVIII, 214, Farmer, *Sources*, 33.—3. A speech on the origin of music, singing, and rhythm which he delivered to the caliph al-Muʿtamid, in al-Masʿūdī, *Murūj* VIII, 80/100 see Farmer, *JRAS* 1924, 94 (see Suppl.).

2a. Muḥammad b. Abī Muslim al-Jarmī, see Suppl. I, 404.

2b. Isḥāq b. al-Ḥusayn al-Munajjim, ibid. 405.

1. *Ākām al-marjān etc.* see Angela Codazzi, Compendio geografico Arabo di Ishaq b. al-Hu., *Rend. della R. Accad. Naz. dei Lincei, Cl. di scienze mor.* etc., serie VI, vol. V, Roma 1929, 373/463. V. Minorsky, The Khazars and the Turks in the *Ā. al-m. BSOAS* 1938, 141/50.—2. Cosmography, Paris 2186, excerpts in Seippel, *Rerum Normannicarum fontes arabici*, p. 28, no. XXIV.

3. Aḥmad b. Abī Yaʿqūb b. Jaʿfar b. Wahb b. Wāḍiḥ al-Kātib al-Yaʿqūbī al-ʿAbbāsī was a descendant of Wāḍiḥ, the freedman of al-Manṣūr, who, in spite of his close ties with the ʿAbbāsids and its high officials, and his earlier governorships in Armenia, Azerbaijan, and Egypt, secretly sympathised with the Shīʿa. He paid for this with his life when, after the Battle of al-Fakhkh, | he helped the 259
ʿAlid Idrīs escape to the Maghreb. This attachment to the Shīʿa was hereditary in his family, and thus Aḥmad, too, acknowledged the Mūsawiyya, a group of moderate Imāmīs. He had spent his youth in Armenia and in the service of the Ṭāhirids in Khurāsān, whose deeds he glorified in a separate work. It appears to have been here that he also wrote his world history, which he continued up to the year 259/872. After the fall of the Ṭāhirids he went to Egypt, where he wrote his geography in 278/891. He died in 284/897.

EI IV, 1247, Suppl. I, 405. 1. *Kitāb al-buldān*, *BG* VII, 1892 (earlier M.J. de Goeje, *Specimen e literis or. exhibens, descriptionem al-Maghribi sumtam e libro regionum al-J.*, Leiden 1860), reprint Baghdad 1938, *Les Pays, trad. par* G. Wiet (*Textes et traductions d'auteurs Or. I*), Cairo 1937. The book is based on literary research and the questioning of travellers and, as well as topography, in particular that of larger cities, it also includes economic geography and tax statistics.—2. *Ibn Wadhih qui dicitur al-Jaʿqūbī Historiae* ed. M. Th. Houtsma, 2 vols., Leiden 1883. The first book, whose introduction is lost, starts in the middle of the history of Adam, continuing with the patriarchs of Israel (mostly following the *Cave of Treasures*), the Messiah and the Apostles, the rulers of Syria, Assur, and Babel, the Indians, the Greeks and the Romans, the Persians, the peoples of the north as far as the Turks, the Chinese, the Egyptians, the Berbers, the Abyssinians,

the Beja and the negroes, before finally coming to the pre-Islamic Arabs. The second volume, almost double the size of the first, is devoted to the history of Islam, which is not adversely influenced by his Shīʿī leaning, but which refrains from mentioning the sources used and which limits itself to sparse notes for contemporary history, despite the account often being bloated by speeches and letters in other places, while still preserving a lot of valuable information from reliable old sources. See M.J. de Goeje, Über die Geschichte der ʿAbbāsiden von al-Jaʿḳūbī, *Travaux de la 3ème session du Congr. Intern. des Or.*,
227 St. Petersburg and Leiden 1879, II, 153/166, | M. Klamroth, Der Auszug aus den
260 Evanglien bei dem arab. Historiker al-Jaʿqūbī, | *Festschrift zur Einweihung des Wilhelm-Gymnasiums in Hamburg 1885*, idem, Über die Auszüge aus griech. Schriftstellern bei al-Jaʿqūbī, *ZDMG* XL, 189/233, 612/838, XLI, 415/42.

4. Abū Bakr Aḥmad b. Muḥammad b. Isḥāq b. al-Faqīh al-Hamadhānī was born in the Persian city of Hamadan and wrote, soon after the death of Caliph al-Muʿtaḍid in 289/902:

Kitāb al-buldān, whose original has been preserved in Mashhad (see Suppl.). The summary by ʿAlī b. Jaʿfar b. Aḥmad al-Shayzarī ca. 413/1022, *BG* V, 1885, starts with the formation of the earth and the seas, compares the Chinese and the Indians, then describes Arabia, Egypt, the Maghreb, Syria, Palestine, Mesopotamia, the Byzantine empire and Iraq (Kufa and Basra in particular), although Baghdad does not even receive a mention. Among his sources he also mentions works by al-Jāḥiẓ (p. 158).

5. Abū ʿAlī Aḥmad b. ʿUmar b. Rusta wrote in Isfahan, sometime after 310/922, an encyclopaedia named *al-Aʿlāq al-nafīsa*, whose seventh volume deals with geography, and which has been preserved in the manuscript Br. Mus. 1310.

BG VII, 1892. The work starts with a chapter on the wonders of the heavens, in whose centre there is the earth in the form of a globe, then explains the movement of the heavens and the size and distances of the stars. After some observations on the size of the earth, geography proper starts with Mecca and Medina. There then follows a description of the seas, rivers, and climates, with a detailed description of Iran and its surrounding countries (see Suppl.). On the dating, see Harkavy, *Skazanie musulmanskich pisatelei o slavjanach i russkich* (St. Petersburg 1870), 200ff., Westberg, Analizi vostočnich istočnikov o Vostočnoj Evrope, *Žurn. Min. Narodn. Prosv.*, NS XIV (1908), 7ff.

5a. Around the year 300/912 an Arab by the name of Hārūn b. Yaḥyā went as a prisoner of war to Constantinople and from there to Rome, of which he gave a description that Ibn Rusta included in his book (119/28).

| J. Marquart, *Osteurop. und ostas. Streifzüge*, Leipz. 1903, 200ff., A. Vasiliev, 261
Hārūn b. Yaḥyā and his description of Constantinople in *Seminarium Kondakovianum, Recueil d'Études* V, 1932, 149/63, G. Ostrogorsky, Zum Reisebericht des H.b.Y. ibid. 251/7 (who fixes the year of his visit in 912).

6. After the death of al-Muʿtaḍid in 289/902 and before the seizure of power by the Būyids in Baghdad in 334/945, a certain Suhrāb (alias?) wrote a revised edition of al-Khwārizmī's *Ṣūrat al-arḍ*, which he attributed to an otherwise unknown Ibn Sarābiyūn.

See Suppl. 406. Ibn Serapion, Description of Mesopotamia and Baghdad, ed. G. Le Strange, *JRAS* 1895, 1/76, 255/315.

7. In Ṣafar 309/June 921, Aḥmad b. Faḍlān b. ʿAbbās b. Rashīd b. Ḥammād was sent by the caliph al-Muqtadir as an envoy to the ruler of the Volga Bulgarians, where he arrived on 13 Muḥarram 310/11 May 922. | Back in Baghdad, he 228
described his trip in a *risāla* that is characterised by keen powers of observation and an objectivity that is only rarely tarnished by exaggerated rumours, and which provided the first dependable account of the countries visited by him.

The original, discovered in Mashhad (see Suppl.), was included by Yāqūt in his geographical dictionary in the form of an extensive abstract. *Ibn Foszlans und anderer Araber Berichte über die Russen älterer Zeit, Text, Übers. unsw. v.* C.M. Frähn, St. Petersburg 1823, Die ältesten Nachrichten über die Wolgabulgharen aus Ibn Foszlans Reiseberichte, *Mém. de l'Ac. Imp. des Sciences de St.-P. VIè s. Sc. pol. hist. et phil.*, v. 1, 527/77, Veteres Memoriae Chasarorum ex Iben Foszlano[1] etc. De Baschkiris quae memoriae prodita sunt ab I.F. etc., ibid. VIII, V. v. Rosen, Prolegomena k novomu izdaniu Ibn Fadlana, *Zapiski VOI RAO* XV, 1904, 39/74, A. Zeki Validi Togan, *Ibn F.'s Reisebericht, hsg. und übers. etc. AKM* XXIV, 1940. Putešestvike Ibn Fadlana Volgu, Perevod i Kommentarii pad redakzei akademika N.I. Kračkovskogo (author Kovalevskij), | *Izdateljstvo Ak. Nauk SSSR*, 262
Moscow, Leningrad 1939, see H. Ritter, Zum Text von I.F.s Reisebericht, *ZDMG* 96, 98/126.

1 This report in Yāqūt was inserted by him into that by Ibn Faḍlān.

8. Abu 'l-Faraj Qudāma b. Jaʿfar al-Kātib al-Baghdādī, who had converted from Christianity to Islam during the reign of al-Muktafī (289–95/902–8), composed several belletristic works, as well as his book on landtaxes. He died probably in 310/922, although according to others it was in 327/948, or as late as 337/958.

Fihrist $130,_{20-7}$, M. de Slane, Notice sur Codama et ses écrits, *JA* s. V, v. 20, p. 185 ff. 1. *Kitāb al-Kharāj*, in the form of an extract in *BG* VI. After an overview of the organisation of the postal service, there follows a general description of the world, which gives special consideration to the lands of Islam and their tax revenues. From an initial description of neighbouring foreign peoples and their countries it moves to finance, the tax system, and administrative law. A short history of conquests was copied straight from Balādhurī, see v. Kremer, *Culturgesch.* II, 427.—2. *Naqd al-shiʿr*, a poetic work, Esc. $^{2}242,_{2}$, Köpr. $1445,_{2}$ (*MSOS* IV, 17), print. Istanbul 1302.—3. *Kitāb naqd al-nathr al-maʿrūf bi-Kitāb al-bayān*, see Suppl. Ṭāhā Ḥusayn, *Min ḥadīth al-shiʿr wal-nathr*, 125ff. holds on to its authenticity and believes it to be an imitation of Aristotle's *Rhetoric*.—4. See Suppl. (revised edition AS $4194,_{1}$, Ritter).

9. Between 279–95/892–907 Aḥmad b. Muḥammad b. Naṣr al-Jayhānī, the vizier of the Sāmānid ruler Naṣr b. Aḥmad b. Naṣr (261–79/874–92), wrote in Bukhārā, on the basis of the *Kitāb al-kharāj* of Qudāma, a much more elaborate work whose original has been lost. It is, however, possible that it formed the basis for al-Idrīsī's description of Asia.

Fihrist, $138,_{1-4}$, al-Muqaddasī, 3, 19ff., Yāqūt, *Irshād* II, 59, Sprenger, Post- und Reiserouten *AKM*, III, 3, p. XVII, J. Marquart, *Osteuropäische und ostas. Streifzüge*, 206, 466/73 (see Suppl.).

10. Abū Dulaf Misʿar b. al-Muhalhil al-Khazrajī al-Yanbūʿī, *ʿAjāʾib al-buldān*, see Suppl. I, 407.

263 227 || Al-Thaʿālibī, *Yatīma* III, 174/94. *Des a. D. M. Bericht über die türk. Horden, übers. v.* F. Wüstenfeld, *Zeitschr. f. vergl. Erdkunde, I, Jahrg. Bd. II, Heft* 9, Magdeburg 1842, *Abu Dolaf Misaris ben Mohalhal de itinere suo asiatico commentarius*, ed. C. Schlözer, Berlin 1845. Translation in G. Ferrand, *Relations de voyages et textes géogr. arabes, pers. et turcs* I, Paris 1913, 208/29, see G. Jacob, *Berichterstatter*, 71/2, against his overly-severe judgement see J. Ruska, *Geogr. Ztschr.* III, 591, J. Marquart, *Osteurop. u. ostas. Streifzüge*, 74/95. A. v. Rohr-Sauer, *Des a. D. Bericht über seine Reise nach Turkistan, China*

und Indien, neu übers. und erklärt, Stuttgart 1939. On the Mashhad manuscript, see Togan, *Ibn Faḍlāns Reisebericht*, VII.

11. Abū Zayd Aḥmad b. Sahl al-Balkhī, d. 322/934, see Suppl. I, 408.

W. Barthold in V. Minorsky, *Ḥudūd al-ʿālam* transl. (Gibb Mem. NS VI, 1937), 15ff. *Opus geographicum auctore Ibn Ḥawqal secundum textum et imagines codicis Constantinopolitani conservati in Bibl. Antiqui Palatii no. 3346, cui titulus est Liber Imaginis terrae*, ed. J.H. Kramers, *BG* I, 1, Leiden 1938.

12. Abū Muḥammad al-Ḥasan b. Aḥmad b. Yaʿqūb al-Ḥamdānī b. al-Ḥāʾik, who died in 334/945 in Ṣanʿāʾ (see Suppl.). Enthralled by the splendour of ancient South Arabia, he did his utmost to explore its history and archaeology, but as a poet and astronomer he also produced significant works.

Flügel, *Gramm. Schulen* 220, Wüst., *Gesch.* 110, cf. Suppl. 409. 1. *Kitāb al-iklīl*, vol. 8 also in MS al-Bārūdī, now Garr. 748, see al-Ḥ. *The 8th Book of the Antiquities of South Arabia, Records of al-Ḳarmaṭis* (*P. Anastase Marie Ed. and a Ms. in the Garrett Coll. Princeton Un.*) *transl. from the Arabic with linguistic, geographical and hist. notes by* N.A. Faris, London 1938 (Princ. Or. Texts III). *Al-Iklīl al-juzʾ al-thāmin ed. with linguistic geographic and hist. notes by N.A. Faris*, Princeton NJ 1940. Alleged excerpt from vol. 8, *Risāla fī maʿrifat al-ghālib wal-maghlūb wal-ṭālib wal-maṭlūb* written by Aristotle to Alexander, Alex. Ḥurūf 4 (not in ed. Anastase Marie de St. Elie). A volume on the Arab tribes Patna I, 280,$_{2312}$. D.H. Muller, Die Burgen und Schlösser Südarabiens, *SBWA* vol. 94 (1879), 335ff., vol. 97 (1880), 955ff., see C. Landberg, *Arabica* III, 1895, 116/22.—2. *Ṣifat* | 264
jazīrat al-ʿArab, composed after 1., Paris 5822, Köpr. 1067, ʿA. Emiri Ef. 2687/8. *al-Ḥamdānīs Geographie der Arab. Halbinsel, nach den Hdss. hsg. v.* D.H. Müller, Leiden 1884, A. Sprenger, Versuch einer Kritik von H.s. Beschreibung der arab. Halbinsel, *ZDMG* XLV, 361/90.—3. see Suppl.

| 13. The last and most famous geographer of this period was Abū ʿAbdallāh 230
Muḥammad b. Aḥmad b. Abī Bakr al-Bannāʾ al-Bashshārī al-Muqaddasī. Of his life, we only know what he tells us himself. Born in Jerusalem as the grandson of the architect who built the gates of Acre for Ibn Ṭūlūn, he journeyed through most Muslim lands. The only places he did not go appear to have been Sind, Sijistān, and Spain. On these trips not only did he exploit all available literary sources but, in order to acquire a comprehensive and thorough understanding of life, he also exercised various professions. On the basis of his own

experiences and the findings of his predecessors, he was thus able to draw a lively and rich picture of the Muslim world, which he often judges against the backdrop of the circumstances of life back home. Even though his style is not entirely free from the kind of artificiality that was to spread ever more from the offices of the secretaries of the state into the literary world, nowhere does he sacrifice substance for form. He wrote his book in 375/985, putting the Sāmānids at the centre. After a second journey, during which he had become better acquainted with the empire of the Fāṭimids, he prepared a new, augmented edition that was based on their point of view.

Aḥsan al-taqāsīm fī maʿrifat al-aqālīm, BG III, *Descriptio imperii Moslemici*, ed. IIa, 1906, see A. v. Kremer, *Kulturgesch.* II, 429/33, E. Wiedemann, Schilderung der einzelnen Klimata durch M., *Arch. f. Gesch. der Nat. u. d. Technik* V, 61/4.

Chapter 16. Medicine 265

Ibn Abū Uṣaybiʿa (d. 668/1270, p. 325/6), *Kitāb ʿuyūn al-anbāʾ fī ṭabaqāt al-aṭibbāʾ*, ed. A. Müller, Königsberg 1884 (hereafter Uṣ.).

F. Wüstenfeld, *Geschichte der arabischen Ärzte und Naturforscher*, Göttingen 1840 (quoted by number).

L. Leclerc, *Histoire de la médecine arabe*, 2 vols., Paris 1876.

M. Neuburger, *Geschichte der Medizin* I, Stuttgart 1908, 142/228.

Mieli, § 16, 23, 33, 38, 45, 50.

On the beginnings of Arabic medicine, see Suppl. I, 412/14.

Even though the book on poisons attributed to Shānāq (Çanakya)—additionally Asʿad 2491—goes back to an Indian source in which parts of the *Kautiliya Arthashastra* attributed to Çanakya were mixed with elements from medical literature, it was nonetheless augmented with data of Greek origin. See Strauss, *Quellen u. Studien zur Gesch. der Nat. u. Med.* IV, 2, Berlin 1935.

1. Abu ʾl-Ḥasan ʿAlī b. Sahl Rabban al-Ṭabarī, d. after 240/855, see Suppl. I, 414/5.

Uṣ. I, 309, Wüst. 55, Leclerc I, 292. 1. *al-Kunnāsh* or *Firdaws al-ḥikma* Berl. 6257, Br. Mus. 445, Rāmpūr I, 489$_{171}$, excerpts Gotha 1910. Gynäkologie, Embryologie und Frauenhygiene aus dem "Paradies der Weisheit über die Medizin" des a. ʾl-Ḥ. ʿA. b. S. R. al-Ṭ. übers. v. A. Siggel, *Qu. u. St. z. Gesch. der Nat. u. Med.* VIII, 1941, part 1/2.—2. *Kitāb ḥifẓ al-ṣiḥḥa*, from Greek and Indian sources, Bodl. I, 578 (where the author is wrongly identified as Abū ʿAlī b. Rayyān).

2. Even though Abu ʾl-ʿAbbās Aḥmad b. Muḥammad b. ʿAlī al-Kātib al-Yamanī b. Qulayta (Fulayta), d. 231/845, was apparently not a physician by profession, he composed the oldest preserved work on copulation, a theme that medical 232
doctors were keen on discussing in later times.

Kitāb rushd al-labīb ilā muʿāsharat al-ḥabīb ḤKh ^{1}III, 463$_{6454}$, ^{2}I, 904, Gotha 2038, Paris 3051/2, Algiers 1782, Esc. ^{2}563, Alex. Adab 158 (*Murshid*).

3. Abū Zakariyyāʾ Yaḥyā (Yuḥannā) b. Māsawayh (the Māsuya, or Mesuë, of 266
the Latins) was the son of a pharmacist in Jundīshāpūr. Having studied in Baghdad under Jibrīl b. Bukhtīshūʿ, the personal physician of Hārūn, he became a hospital director there, and later the personal physician of the caliphs from al-Maʾmūn to al-Wāthiq. On the basis of various translations from Greek works he wrote a series of independent medical books. He died in 243/857 in Samarra.

Uṣ. I, 175/83, Wüst. 59, Leclerc I, 103. 1. *Nawādir al-ṭibb*, dedicated to Ḥunayn b. Isḥāq, Leid. 1302, Garr. 2154$_{,2}$ (see Suppl.). *Amphorismi Johannis Damasceni*, Bonn 1489, *J.D. Aphorismi* in the apparatus to *Aph. Maimonidis*, Basle 528/42, Hebr. Steinschn. 463.—2. *Kitāb al-ḥummayāt* (see Suppl.), *De Febribus*, Hebrew, from a Latin translation with commentary by Petrus Hispanus, Steinschn. 464.—3. *Perfectum de medicina* Paris Hebr. 379, 408.—4. *Kitāb jawāhir al-ṭīb al-mufrada* (*Mukhtaṣar fī maʿrifat ajnās al-ṭīb etc.*, Suppl.), Traité sur les substances simples aromatiques par J. b. M., publié par P. Sbath, *Bull. de l'Inst. d'Égypte* XIX, 1936/7.—5. *Kitāb mā' al-shaʿīr* Algiers 1746$_{,2}$.—6.–11. see Suppl. (9. *Kitāb al-azmina* additionally Bursa, Ḥü. Čelebi Heyet 1 [Ritter], Alex. Ḥikma 16, G. 3328, Kraus, not in the catalogue).—Some other works in Hebrew translation in Steinschn. 464$_{,3}$.

4. Sābūr b. Sahl, director of the hospital in Jundīshāpūr, who died on 24 Dhu 'l-Ḥijja 255/2 December 869.

Uṣ. I, 161, Wüst. 64, Leclerc I, 112, Ben Milad, *L'École médicale de Cairouan*, Paris 1933.—*Aqrābādhīn*, Antidotarium after the copy of the ʿAḍudī hospital in Baghdad, Munich 808$_{,2}$.

5. Isḥāq b. ʿImrān was a native of Baghdad and was appointed in Kairouan by the Aghlabid Ziyādatallāh (r. 290–6/903–07). Having fallen out with the prince, who suffered from melancholia, accusations against him by a Jewish rival led to his brutal death by torture.

Uṣ. II, 35, Wüst. 77. 1. *Maqāla fi 'l-mālīkhūliyya* Munich 805, 2 (see Suppl.).—2. Fragment of a pharmacopoeia, Esc. $^{2}887_{,6}$.

267 | 6. ʿĪsā b. Māssa, a Christian, was a physician in the hospital in Marw during the third century.

Uṣ. I, 184, Wüst. 75, Leclerc 296. *Kitāb al-jimāʿ*, on copulation, Esc. $^{1}883_{,9}$.

233 | 7. Yaḥyā (Yūḥannā) b. Sarābiyūn, the son of a physician of Bājarmā, also lived in the third century. He wrote in Syriac, but his book was soon absorbed into the Arabic literary corpus.

Fihrist 296, Uṣ. I, 109, Wüst. 89, Leclerc I, 113. *Al-Kunnāsh*, a work in Syriac, which existed in both a large edition of twelve books and a smaller one of seven, was translated into Arabic by Mūsā b. Ibrāhīm al-Ḥadīthī and Ibn Bahlūl, Esc. ^{2}818,$_{4}$, frgm. Paris 2918,$_{7}$, Hebr. Steinschneider 474 (see Suppl.). The smaller edition, translated into Latin under the title *Breviarium* or *Practica Therapeuticae Methodus*, was printed several times. The publisher of the edition Basle 1543, Albanus Torinus, called him Janus Damascenus, which gave rise to a confusion with the famous theologian (Mieli § 16, n. 3).—On his younger namesake who is often confused with him see p. 485.

8. ʿAlī b. ʿĪsā b. ʿAlī was a student of Isḥāq b. Ḥunayn and the personal physician of the caliph al-Muʿtamid (256–79/870–92).

Fihrist 284, Uṣ. I, 203, Wüst. 97 (who lumps him together with the ophtalmologist ʿĪsā b. ʿAlī, 236,$_{12}$), Leclerc I, 303. 1. *Kitāb manāfiʿ al-ḥayawān* Gotha 67,$_{2}$, similar Vienna 1481,$_{2}$, Esc. ^{1}893 (not ^{2}838), Bodl. I, Karshuni 112,$_{3}$.—2.,3. see Suppl.—4. *Kitāb al-ʿamal bil-asṭurlāb* in a Bārūdī MS (not in Garr.) and Dam. Ẓāh. Falak 1 (Cat. 99), ed. L. Cheikho, *al-Mashriq* XVI, 1913, 29/46, *RAAD*, XII, 634, where the author is believed to have been Ibrāhīm b. Ḥabīb al-Fazārī (Suppl. 391) because in MS Damascus the author's name ʿAlī b. ʿĪsā is written on an erasure.

9. The most important physician of this period, and maybe the most creative genius of medieval medicine as a whole,[1] was Abū Bakr Muḥammad b. Zakariyyāʾ al-Rāzī (the Rhazes of the Latins). He was apparently born in 251/865 in Rayy, and before | the age of thirty he had only been engaged in 268
music and chemistry. It seems that it was not until he attempted to find a cure for his eyes, which had been weakened as a result of his chemical experiments, that he turned to medicine in Baghdad, under the mentorship of Ibn Rabban al-Ṭabarī. According to some he had already studied medicine in Rayy, but this seems impossible, even if one is to follow Ruska in fixing his date of birth much earlier than al-Bīrūnī. After the completion of his studies he directed the hospital in his hometown, and was later called to Baghdad to take on a similar role there. Having become famous through his works, he visited several courts to cash in on his fame, as was the custom of the time. In this manner he also visited the court of the Sāmānid Abū Ṣāliḥ Manṣūr b. Isḥāq,[2] the ruler of

1 A. Müller, *Der Islam* I, 513.

2 Who revolted in 302/924 against Naṣr b. Aḥmad (Ibn al-Athīr, Būlāq VIII, 28, Barthold, *Turkestan* 241), according to the second statement in Ibn Khallikān which is based on a copy of *al-Manṣūrī* itself. His first statement, to the effect that one must understand Manṣūr b. Nūḥ, is impossible, for the latter only reigned in 350–66/961–76, while Ibn Khallikān's

Kirmān and Khurāsān, to whom he dedicated his famous work *al-Manṣūrī*. It is not likely that he lost his eyesight after being physically abused by Manṣūr when he could not carry out some of the experiments described in his *Kitāb ithbāt al-kīmiyāʾ*, because his eyes had presumably weakened some time before then. He died in Baghdad or Rayy in 311/923 (or 320/932).

Ibn Khall. 678, Uṣ. I, 309/21, Wüst. 98, Leclerc I, 337, H.P.J. Renaud, A propos du millénaire de Razes, *Bull. de la Soc. franç. d'histoire de la médecine* 1931, March–April, 203ff., A. Eisen, Kīmiyāʾ al-Rāzī *RAAD*, XIV, 62/4, J. Ruska, Über den gegenwärtigen Stand der Raziforschung, *Archeion* V, 1924, 335/47, Mieli, § $16_{,4}$.—1. *al-Ḥāwī*, according to al-Bīrūnī left behind unfinished and compiled
269 out of his papers after his death at the order of Muḥammad b. al-ʿAmīd, | the vizier of the Būyid sultan Rukn al-Dawla, Munich 806 (vol. 12), Br. Mus. 446, Bodl. I, 565, 607, II, 179, Esc. ^{2}806/16, 854/56 (see M. Antuña, Medicina, *Revista Mensual de Ciencias Medicas* 1935, 20ff.), Garr. $2160_{,1}$, Pet. $12_{,1}$, Book 2 and 8, Br. Mus. Or. $9790_{,1}$, incomplete ibid. Or. 9799 (see Suppl.), M. Meyerhof, Thirty three clinical observations of R., *Isis* 1935, 320/72, *Liber Elhavi* (translated by Sālim b. Faraj in Sicily in 1279, Mieli § 54, n. 9), Brescia 1486, *Continens Rasis*, Venice 1542, other editions *BO* I, 145.—Abstract by ʿAlī b. Dāʾūd ca. 530/1135, Med. 227, by Ibn al-Tilmīdh, d. 560/1164 (p. 487), Berl. 6260, anon. Med. 290.—2. *Kitāb al-ṭibb al-Manṣūrī* (see Suppl.), an overview of medicine in 10 books, Paris 2866, 6203, Bodl. I, $529_{,4,5}$, 577, 592 (Hebr. $419_{,3}$), Dresd. 140, Esc. ^{2}819/21, 858/60_{1} (see Suppl.), AS 3751, Alex. Ṭibb 48, Aligarh $124_{,28}$, on which glosses by Ibn al-Ḥashshāʾ in Leid. $331_{,5}$ (cat. III, 256), Rabat, Renaud, *Hesp.* XX, 7, *Ibn al-Hachcha XIII s. d. J.-C. Glossaire sur le Mansouri de Razes, Texte ar. publ. avec introduction par* G. Colin *et* H.P.J. Renaud, Rabat 1941 (Coll. de textes ar. publ. par l'Inst. des Hautes Ét. Maroc. XI), Hebr. transl. Steinschn. $469_{,2}$, *Ad Almansorem libri X*, Milan 1487, and see W. Brunner, *Die Augenheilkunde des Rhazes*, diss. Berl. 1900.—3. *Kitāb al-jadarī wal-ḥaṣba* Leid. 1312, Nan. II, 239, *ar. et lat. cura* J. Channing, London 1766, ed. van Dyck, Beirut 1872, Lat. transl. by G. Valla, Venice 1498 (see Suppl.), Greek by Jacques Goupyl, Paris 1548, French by J. Paulet, Paris 1763, by Leclerc and Lenoir ibid. 1866, English by Greenhill, *A Treatise on the Smallpox and Meesles*, London 1848.—4. *Aqrābādhīn*, antidotarium, Bodl. I, $611_{,3}$, Nan. II, 238, Hebr. Steinschn. $470_{,9}$.—5. *Taqsīm al-ʿilal* Nan. II, 238 = *Kitāb al-taqsīm wal-tashjīr* Br. Mus. 447, Hebr. Steinschn. $470_{,8}$.—6. *Kitāb al-mudkhal ila 'l-ṭibb* (*al-ṣaghīr*) Paris $2865_{,1}$, Bodl. Pers. $92_{,5}$ (see Suppl.).—7. *al-Fuṣūl fi 'l-ṭibb* or *al-Murshid* Garr. 1076 (see Suppl.), Hebr. *Pᵉrāqīm*, Leid. Scal. 2, *Amphorismi Rasis*

---

assumption that the work was dedicated to him as a child is absurd. I do not know who Uṣ. I, $313_{,20}$, intends to refer to by Manṣūr b. Ismāʿīl b. Khāqān, prince of Khurāsān and Mā warāʾ al-nahr.

in Aphor., R. Moysis, Bonn 1489.[3]—8. *Kitāb al-kāfī*, a medical compendium, Bodl. hebr. 427.—9. *Kitāb bur' al-sā'a*, on diseases that can be cured within the
hour, composed at the order of Vizier Abu 'l-Qāsim b. ʿAbdallāh, Berl. 6343, | 270
| Munich 808, 843 f., 148v., Copenhagen 108, Leid. 1313, Paris $2776_{,9}$, Bodl. I, 235
Pers. $92_{,9}$, apparently in two recensions Qawala II, 287, Aligarh $122_{,11}$, $124_{,32}$, print. also C. 1936.—Abstracts Gotha 2033, Algiers $1322_{,3}$.—10. *Kitāb al-bāh wa-manāfiʿihi wa-maḍārrihi wa-mudāwātihi* Leid. 1308, Nan. 107.—11. *Kitāb khawāṣṣ al-ashyā'*, alphabetical Nan. II, 234, Steinschn. *Virchows Archiv* 86, p. 122.—12. *Fī abdāl al-adwiya, de permutatione medicamentorum* Nan. II, 237.—13. *Kitāb sirr al-ṣināʿa* Esc. $^{2}833_{,3}$ (see Suppl.), *Razi's Buch Geheimnis der Geheimnisse* (*Kitāb sirr al-asrār* Gött. 95, photograph *QSt.* VII, 100, VI, 33) *mit Einl. Übers. u. Erläut. v.* J. Ruska (*QSt. Gesch. d. Nat. u. Med.* 6) Berlin 1937, idem, Das chemische Hauptwerk des Arztes Razi, *Umschau* 1937, 852/3.—14. *Kitāb al-fākhir*, a comprehensive work on therapy, ḤKh IV, 8679, part II, Berl. 6259, Leid. 1306/7, Paris 2687, Pet. 120, Alex. Ṭibb 32.—Excerpts on kidney stones in P. de Koning, *Traité sur le calcul dans les reins et dans la vessie* (35) 56—124.—15. *Kitāb al-qūlanj* Leid. 1310.—16. *As'ila min al-ṭibb* Leid. 1314.—17. *Kitāb al-ṭibb al-mulūkī* Leid. 1311.—18. *Fī maṣāliḥ al-aghdhiya* Esc. $^{2}833_{,4}$. $871_{,2}$.—19. *de arte medendi commentarii X* Esc. $^{1}797_{,1}$ = (?) *Maqālāt fī ṣināʿat al-ṭibb* Upps. 341.—20. Commentary on Galen's *de medicamentorum compositione*, based on the translation by Ḥunayn, Esc. $^{1}797_{,2}$.—21. *Fi 'l-fasḍ* Esc. $^{2}857_{,1}$, Āṣaf. II, 934, Hebr. Steinschn. 470/1.—22. *de tumoribus* Esc. $^{1}856$.—23. *de viris frigidis et ad venerem ineptis eorumque curatione* ibid. $^{2}881_{,1}$ = (?) *Risāla fi 'l-bāh* Mosul D. $34_{,154,3}$ or 10.—24. *de immoderato calore* ibid. $881_{,2}$.—25. (27) *Fī tartīb al-fākiha* Esc. $^{2}870_{,3}$, $887_{,3}$.—26. *de seminibus ac de radicibus aromaticis* ibid. 4.—27. *de vini potu ejusque speciebus* ibid. 4, *Fi 'l-sharāb maqālatān* = Madr. $601_{,5}$.—28. *de medicamentis simplicibus* ibid. $810_{,2}$.—29. *Talkhīṣ Kitāb Jālīnūs fī ḥīlat al-bur'* Esc. $^{2}801_{,1}$.—30. *quod nimis thermarum usus noceat* Nan. II, 231.—31. *Sefer happᵉsūqōṯ*, Hebr., *Virchow Archiv* 52, no. $470_{,6}$.—32. *de vena*, Hebr. de Rossi 347.—33. *Rhazis praeparatio salis aromatici in theatrum chemicum*, ed. L. Zetzner, Oberursel-Strasbourg 1602, III, no. 64.—34. *de Febribus liber* in *Medici graeci et arabi, qui de f. scripserunt* Venice 1594.—35. *Maqāla fi 'l-ḥaṣā fi 'l-kulā wal-mathāna, Traité sur le calcul dans les reins et dans la vessie, traduction accompagnée du texte par* P. de Koning, Leiden 1896 (Leid. Warn. 585), Latin in *Opera parva Abubetri*, Leid. 1510, under the title *Tractatus de preservatione ab egretudine lapidis*.—36. *Man lā yaḥḍuruhu 'l-ṭabīb* (see Suppl.) Lucknow 1886.—37.,
38. *Kitāb* | *manāfiʿ al-aghdhiya wa-dafʿ maḍārrihā*, part II Munich 840, Paris 271
$2868_{,1}$, part I C. 1305.—39. (42.) *Kitāb al-fuqarā' wal-masākīn* Munich 807.—40. (43) *al-Majmūʿa fi 'l-ṭibb* AS 3725/6.—41. (45.) *de aegritudinibus juncturarum*,

3 Nos. 4–7 with several other small tracts in *Opera parva Abubetri*, Leiden 1510.

Hebr. Steinschn., loc. cit., 470,$_{3}$.—42. (46.) *de aegritudinibus puerorum* Hebr. ibid. 4.—43. (47.) 119 aphorisms, Hebr. ibid. 5.—44. (48.) *de proprietatibus membrorum* Hebr. ibid. 7.—45. (49.) *Apology of the honorable physician against quackery* Hebr. Steinschn. 470,$_{10}$, German *Virchows Archiv* 35, 571, cf. 37, 562, 39, 313.—46 (44) *Kitāb al-ṭibb al-rūḥānī*, on ethics, as a complement to the *Kitāb al-Manṣūrī* Br. Mus. 1530,$_{2}$, see Suppl.—48.–58. see Suppl. 51.–71. Ad 59. *al-Sīra al-falsafiyya* Br. Mus. 1530,$_{2}$, see Suppl. *Abu Bekr Muhammedis f. Zachariae Rhagensis (Rhazis) opera philosophica fragmentaque quae supersunt, collegit edidit* P. Kraus (Univ. Fouad I, Lit. Fac. Publ. fs. XXII, Cairo 1939).—Ps.-Razes, *Nuzhat al-mulūk*, on poisons, Fātiḥ 3644 (Ritter).

10. Isḥāq b. Sulaymān al-Isrāʾīlī originated from Egypt and moved to Kairouan during the reign of the Aghlabid Ziyādatallāh (290–6/903–9), where he studied under Isḥāq b. ʿImrān (p. 266). After the downfall of Ziyādatallāh he entered the service of the Fāṭimid ʿUbaydallāh al-Mahdī and died around the year 320/932 (or, according to others, after 341/953).

236 | Uṣ. II, 36/7, Wüst. 101, Leclerc I, 409, Steinschneider, *Der ar. Lit. der Juden*, p. 28, Guttmann, Die philosophischen Schriften des Isrāʾelī, *Beitr. z. Gesch. d. Phil. im MA* X, 4. 1. *Kitāb al-ḥummayāt* Leid. 1305, Bodl. hebr. 416, Hebr. Steinschn. 479,$_{3}$, cf. Choulant, *Handbuch der Bücherkunde für die ältere Medizin*, 348.—2. *Kitāb al-aghdhiya (wal-adwiya)*, vol. I, Munich 809, Hebr. transl. Steinschn. 479,$_{11a}$.—3. *Kitāb al-bawl* AS 3563 f. 63b/78a, *Ikhtiṣār*, Bodl. 611,$_{2}$, Hebr. Steinschn. 479,$_{2}$.—4. *Kitāb al-usṭūqisāt*, Hebr. Steinschn. 255, Leid. Warn. 13, de Rossi 207, 423, 771, Vat. 53,$_{9}$.—5. *Viaticum* = (?) no. 2, Hebr. de Rossi 1168.—6. *de diaetis universalibus et particularibus*, Patavia 1487, Basle 1570.—*Mūsar hārōf^{e}ʾīm*, Hebr. transl. of 50 aphorisms in *Ōṣar ṭōb*, 1884, Italian by Soave in *Giornale di scienze mediche* XVIII, 1861 (real ?), Steinschn. 479,$_{4}$.—*Omnia opera Isaaci*, Leid. 1515.

272 | 11. (13) Gharīb b. Saʿīd al-Qurṭubī, secretary of the Spanish caliphs ʿAbd al-Raḥmān III (300–50/912–61) and al-Ḥakam al-Mustanṣir billāh (350–60/961–70), wrote, at the behest of the latter in 353/964:

Khalq al-janīn wa-tadbīr al-ḥabālā wal-mawlūd Esc. ^{2}833,$_{2}$, Wüst. no. 106, Hebr. transl. Steinschn. 428.[4]

---

4 Where he persists in identifying this physician with the historian ʿArīb (p. 149), such against Dozy, *ZDMG* XX, 595ff., like Mieli § 38 n, 3, 4, cf. Dozy, *Le calendrier de Cordoue*, Leiden 1873, Steinschn., Der Kalender von Cordova, *Zeitschr. f. Math.*, 1874.

| 12. (14) Abū Jaʿfar Aḥmad b. Muḥammad b. Abi ʾl-Ashʿath, who died at an 273
advanced age in 360/970.

Uṣ. I, 245, Wüst. 107. 1. *Kitāb al-ḥayawān*, ḤKh III, 122, Bodl. I, 456$_{,6}$ (cf. II, 583), excerpt from the first chapter on man, Gotha 1$_{,31}$.—2.–4. see Suppl. (4. AS 2890$_{,3}$).—5. *Quwa ʾl-adwiya al-mufrada*, composed in 353/964, Br. Mus. Or. 11615, see Fulton, *Br. Mus. Quarterly* XI, 81.

13. (15) Abu ʾl-Ḥasan Aḥmad b. Muḥammad al-Ṭabarī, together with al-Majūsī a student of Abū Mūsā b. Sayyār, was, around 360/970, the personal physician of the Būyid Rukn al-Dawla (320–66/932–76).

Wüst. 198. *Kitāb al-muʿālaja al-Buqrāṭiyya*, the medical system in ten books, Ind. Off. 773, Bodl. I, 567, 641, 644, Munich 810 (see Suppl.).

14. (16) Abū Dāʾūd Sulaymān b. Ḥassān b. Juljul was the personal physician of the Spanish caliph Hishām II al-Muʾayyad billāh (360–99/976–1009).

Uṣ. II, 46, Wüst. 111. 1. *Kitāb al-ḥashāʾish*, supplement to the translation of Dioscorides by Stephanus and Ḥunayn, Bodl. I, 573$_{,4}$.—2. *Fī adwiyat al-tiryāq*, ibid. 5.—3. *Taʾrīkh* (*Ṭabaqāt*) *al-aṭibbāʾ wal-falāsifa* ḤKh [1]IV, 7883 (see Suppl.).

15. (17) Born in Jerusalem, Abū ʿAbdallāh Muḥammad b. Aḥmad b. Abī Saʿīd al-Tamīmī first worked for al-Ḥasan b. ʿUbaydallāh b. Ṭughuj in al-Ramla, before going, around 360/970, to Egypt, where he entered the service of the
vizier of the Fāṭimids al-Muʿizz and al-ʿAzīz, Yaʿqūb | b. Killīs (d. 380/990, b. 273
Khall. 802). He was still alive in 370/980.

Uṣ. II, 87, Wüst. 112, Leclerc I, 388. 1. *Kitāb al-murshid ilā jawāhir al-aghdhiya wa-quwa ʾl-mufradāt min al-adwiya*, Paris 2870$_{,1}$, fragm. Pet. Ros. 182$_{,4}$.—2. *Manāfiʿ* (*Khawāṣṣ*) *al-Qurʾān* see Suppl. I, 429$_{,8,2}$, II, 283$_{,1}$, 945$_{,26}$, also Bodl. I, 156, Algiers 365, AS 376/7, Sulaim. 187 (*Tabshīr khawāṣṣ asrār al-Q.*), *Mukhtaṣar* Cairo [1]V, 370.

16 (18) Also in the service of that vizier was the physician Aḥmad b. Muḥammad b. Yaḥyā al-Baladī.

Kitāb tadbīr al-ḥabālā wal-aṭfāl, diseases of pregnant women and children in their first years of life, Gotha 1875, Calcutta, p. 11, no. 1084.

17. (19) ʿAlī b. al-ʿAbbās al-Majūsī, born the son of a Zoroastrian in Ahwaz, was the personal physician of the Būyid sultan ʿAḍud al-Dawla (338–72/949–82). He died in 994.

Uṣ. I, 236, Wüst. 117, Leclerc I, 381. *Kāmil al-ṣināʿa al-ṭibbiyya*, dedicated to the aforementioned sultan, which is why it is also called *al-Kunnāsh al-malakī* or *al-Qānūn al-ʿAḍudī fī 'l-ṭibb*, complete only in Berl. 6261—5, Leid. 1315/6, Bank. IV, 12/4, individual volumes, Munich 811, Bodl. I, 523, 529, 587, 622/3, Esc. ^{2}815,$_{2}$, 818,$_{5}$, 838, Palat. 246, Paris 2871/80, Ind. Off. 774/6, Garr. 1077/8, Suppl. 1 (see Suppl.), print. Būlāq 1294, Turkish transl. Bursa Ḥu. Celebi Tip 2, *Liber totius medicinae necessaria continens quem Haly f. Abbas ed. regique inscripsit etc.* Leid. 1523, vol. I, *Maqāla* 9, chapt. 34/5, 47, vol. II, *Maq.* 8, chapt. 49, ed. de Koning in *Traité sur le calcul* (see p. 269), 124/85, Hebr. Steinschn. 426.—2. *Kitāb fī 'l-ṭibb* Gött. 96 (?).

238 | 18. (20) Abū Sahl ʿĪsā b. Yaḥyā al-Masīḥī al-Jurjānī, d. 401/1010, see Suppl.

Uṣ. I, 327, Wüst. 118, Leclerc I, 356, Barhebraeus, *Mukhtaṣar* 330. 1. *al-Kitāb (Kutub) al-miʾa fī 'l-ṣināʿa al-ṭibbiyya*, medical encyclopaedia in 100 treatises, ḤKh V, 11288, Berl. 6266, Paris 2881/2, Bodl. I, 582, Pet. Ros. 165, Upps. 353, Fez Qar. 1361 (wrongly *al-milla*), No 3557, glosses thereon by Nuʿmān b. Abi
274 'l-Riḍā al-Isrāʾīlī, Paris 2883.—| 2. *Kitāb al-ṭibb al-kullī*, on general therapy, Berl. 6207.—3. *Kitāb iẓhār ḥikmat Allāh taʿālā fī khalq al-insān*, on the purpose and use of human limbs, Gotha 1988.—4. Smaller treatises a. *Kitāb fī aṣnāf al-ʿulūm al-ḥikmiyya*.—b. *Kitāb arkān al-ʿālam*.—c. *Kitāb mabādiʾ al-mawjūdāt al-ṭabīʿiyya*.—d. *Kitāb talkhīṣ Kitāb al-samāʾ wal-ʿālam li-Ariṣṭūṭālīs* de Jong 113.

19. (21) A *faqīh* and physician at the same time was Abū ʿAbdallāh Muḥammad b. ʿAlī b. Tūmart al-Maghribī al-Andalusī al-Mālikī, d. 391/1001.

Suppl. I, 303, 424. Fragments of his *Kitāb uṣūl al-dīn al-badīʿa* and his mostly kabbalistic *Kanz al-ʿulūm wal-durr al-manẓūm fī ḥaqāʾiq ʿilm al-sharīʿa wa-daqāʾiq ʿilm al-ṭabīʿa fī 'l-ṭibb* are preserved in Gotha 17, Br. Mus. 1001,$_{1}$, Riḍā P. 3131, Tunis Zayt. *Bull. de Corr. Afr.* 1884, 11, no. 19, see *Fundgruben des Orients*, II, 293.

20. (22) Abū Jaʿfar Aḥmad b. Ibrāhīm b. Abī Khālid al-Jazzār was a student of Isḥāq b. Sulaymān (no. 10) and lived as a practising physician in Kairouan. He disdained seeking the favours of the prince but participated every summer in the maritime campaigns against the infidels, which were nothing more than

marauding piratical expeditions. He died around 395/1004, at over 80 years of age.

Uṣ. II, 37, Wüst. 120, Gesch. 158, Leclerc I, 413. 1. *Zād al-musāfir wa-qūt al-ḥāḍir*, a medical compendium, Dresd. 209, Copenhagen 109, Bodl. I, p. 135, II, 528, Paris 2884, Algiers 1746, cf. Dugat, *JA* 1853, I, 295ff., following which a listing of the chapters in A. Cherif, *Histoire de la médecine arabe en Tunisie*, Thèse de Bordeaux 1908, p. 56/61, Daremberg, *Archives des Missions, Cahier IX*. Hebr. transl. Steinschn. 449, Greek by Synesios, partly in *Synesius de febribus*, Amsterdam 1749, Latin *Viaticum peregrinantis*, attributed to himself by the translator in *Constantini Africani* (d. 1087, see Sudhoff, *Archeion* XIV, 1932, 359/69, Mieli § 52) *Opera*, Basle, 1536, 1539, also in G. de Solo, *Introductorium* 1505 and *Opera parva Abubetri*, Leid. 1510.—2. *Kitāb ṭibb al-fuqarāʾ wal-masākīn*, on cheap medicine, Gotha 2034, Esc. 852$_{,1}$, Hebr. Steinschn. 451.—3. *Kitāb iʿtimād al-adwiya al-mufrada* Algiers 1746$_{,3}$, AS 3564, Hebr. Steinschn. 448. al-Jazzār, | *Liber fiduciae de simplicibus medicinis* (*Kitāb etc.*) *in der* 275
Übersetzung von Stephanus de Saragossa, übertr. aus der Hds. München, Cod. lat. 253 v. L. Volger, Diss. Berlin–Würzburg 1941 (Texte u. Unters. zur Gesch. d. Naturw. 6).—4. *Fī siyāsat al-ṣibyān wa-tadbīrihim* Nan. II, 240.—5. *de aromatum substitutione* Esc. ^{1}891$_{,4}$.—6. *de curanda tussi, de tollendo renis et vesicae calculo et de morbo splenis sanando* Bodl. I, 579$_{,2}$.—7. *Kitāb al-khawāṣṣ*, Lat. transl. Steinschn. 452.—8. On amnesia and remedies to strengthen memory, in Hebrew and Latin, ibid.—9. 10. see Suppl.—11. *Iʿdāl al-ʿaqāqīr* Esc. ^{2}896$_{,5}$.—12. *Kitāb al-maʿida wa-amrāḍuhā wa-mudāwātuhā* ibid. 852$_{,4}$.

| 21. (23) ʿAbd al-Raḥmān b. Isḥāq b. Haytham, a physician in Cordova, was, it 239
seems, a younger contemporary of Ibn al-Jazzār, on whose *Kitāb al-iʿtimād* he wrote a critical review.

Uṣ. I, 46. *Kitāb al-iktifāʾ bil-dawāʾ min khawāṣṣ al-ashyāʾ*, Hebr. Steinschn. 454, cf. *ZDMG* 49, 251.

22. (24) Abū Manṣūr al-Ḥasan b. Nūḥ al-Qumrī was one of the teachers of Ibn Sīnā. Born in Bukhara at the beginning of the fourth/tenth century, he was the personal physican of the Sāmānid ruler al-Manṣūr. He died soon after 380/990.

Uṣ. I, 327, Wüst. 109, Leclerc I, 385. 1. *Kitāb al-ghinā wal-munā, liber vitae et mortis* Gotha 1951, 2036, Bodl. I. 642, Palat. 247, Nan. II, 218 (?), AS 3580, 3794, Aligarh 122$_{,22}$.—2. *Maqālāt fi ʾl-ṭibb* AS 3749.

23. (25) Probably in the fourth/tenth century, and certainly after Ibn al-Jazzār, an anonymous author composed a medical work in 5 books under the name of the famous physician Yaḥyā b. Māsawayh (p. 265), but which has only survived in Latin and Hebrew translations.[5]

Wüst. 125, Leclerc I, 504, Steinschneider in *Virchows Archiv*, 1860, 379ff., Hebr. transl. 465, Mieli § $23_{,10}$, Latin translation of his work Euting 1990–2002, cf.
276 J.L. Pagel, | *Die angebl. Chirurgie des Johs. Mesuë jun. nach einer Hds. der Pariser Nationalbibliothek teils herausg., teils analysiert nebst einem Nachtrag zur Chirurgie des Heinr. v. Maudeville*, Berlin 1893, F.A. Sternberg, *Das 4. Buch der angebl. Chirurgie des Joh. Mesuë, zum ersten Mal veröffentlicht*, Diss. Berlin 1893.

24. (26) Abu 'l-Qāsim Khalaf b. ʿAbbās (not ʿAyyāsh) al-Zahrāwī was a practising physician in Cordova under the caliph ʿAbd al-Raḥmān III (300–50/912–61), had social relations with a young Ibn Ḥazm (p. 399), and died soon after 400/1009.

Ibn Bashkuwāl 368, Maqq. II, 119, Uṣ. II, 52, Wüst. 147 (who fixes his death, following Casiri, around the year 500/1106), Leclerc I, 437, Rieu, Add. p. 781r, Steinschneider in *Virchows Archiv* 52, p. 482/4, E. Dognée, Abulcasis, Sa vie son œuvre, *Ėtudes arch. ling. et hist. dédiés à C. Leemans*, Leiden 1885, p. 304/5, Muḥammad Ṣubḥī Ganima, *Abu 'l-Q., ein Forscher der Medizin*, Diss. Berl. 1929, Haeser, *Lehrb. der Gesch. der Medizin*^{3}, Jena 1875, I, 578/84, Mieli § 38. 1. *Kitāb al-taṣrīf li-man ʿajiza ʿan al-taʾālīf*, medical compendium, Berl. 6254, Gotha 1989 (where further MSS are listed, see Suppl.), complete only in Vienna 1458, otherwise mostly surgery, Books 1–5 in a private library in Rabat, see Renaud, *Hespéris* XX, fragm. in Esc. ^{2}876, 4, Juzʾ 2 in Zāw., Sidi Ḥamza, *Hesp.* XXIII, $98_{,9}$, in a private library in Damascus, *RAAD* VII, 374/80, Hebr. transl. Steinschn. 476, Latin incomplete *Liber theoricae nec non practicae Alsaharavii, qui vulgo Acararius dicitur*, Augsburg 1519 (by Gerard of Cremona). From this work, individually: a. *Maqālat taqāsīm al-amrāḍ* Pet. Ros. 173.—b. *Tafsīr al-akyāl al-mawjūda fī kutub al-ṭibb bikhtilāf al-asmāʾ murattaba ʿalā ḥurūf al-muʿjam* Leid. 1338, Bodl. I, Pers. $92_{,8}$, Esc. ^{1}1, 28/9 (wrongly attributed to Ibn Bayṭār, see Wüst. 231, n. 6), Rabāt 479.—c. *al-Maqāla fī ʿamal al-yad* Paris 2953, under the title *Chyrurgia Abulcasis* in *Guy de Cauliaco (Chauliac) Chyrurgia*, Venice 1497, *Abulcasis Methodus medendi cum instrumentis ad omnes fere morbos depictis*, Basle 1541 (see Ellis I, 842), *Abulcasis de chyrurgia, ar. et lat. cura* Jo. Channing, Oxford 1778, L. Leclerc, *La*
277 *chirurgie d'Abulcasis*, Paris 1861, see H. Frölich, Abul'Kasem als Kriegschirurg, | in

5 The account by Leo Africanus concerning a putative Mesuë from Mārdīn is worthless.

Archiv f. klin. Chirurgie 1884, 364/76, P. Schleie, *Zentralbl. f. die ges. Medizin* 1884, 20 Sept.—d. *Maqāla fī aʿmār al-ʿaqāqīr al-mufrada wal-murakkaba* Br. Mus. 988,$_{1}$.—e. Essays on gynaecological disorders in Caspar Wolf, *Gynaecia*, Basle 1566, J. Spach, Argent. 1597.—f. It is doubtful if the book on the preparation of simple remedies in the translation by Simon of Genoa and Abraham Judaeus of Tortosa, *Liber servitoris sive Liber* XXVIII *Bulchasin Beneberacerin*, Venice 1471 (with the *Opera Mesuë*), belongs to these.—2. Dietetics in Latin translation, see E.M. Dognée, Un ms. inédit d'origine Cordouane, *Bol. de la Hist.* XXI, 399/401.

25. Abū Sahl Bishr b. Yaʿqūb b. Isḥāq al-Sijāzi wrote for the prince of Sijistān Abū Aḥmad Khalaf b. Aḥmad, and died in prison in 399/1008.

(Browne, *Chahār Maqāla*, transl. 39, n. 1). 1. *al-Kunnāsh* AS 3578 (Ritter). 2. *al-Rasāʾil al-ṭibbiyya* Rāmpūr I, 477,$_{88}$ (Suppl. II, 1029,$_{19}$).

26. (27) Abu 'l-Qāsim ʿAmmār b. ʿAlī al-Mawṣilī dedicated to Sultan al-Ḥākim (386–411/996–1020):

Kitāb al-muntakhab fī ʿilāj al-ʿayn Esc. ^{2}894,$_{5}$, at times mistakenly identified with the *Tractatus de oculis Canamusali* by Armeniacus, see Pansier, *Magistri David Armeniaci compilatio in libros de oculorum curationibus et diversorum philosophorum de Baldach*, Paris 1904, Noë Scalinci, *Il libro Pro sanitate oculorum di M. Davide Armenio*, Napoli 1923 (Mieli § 23, 11).

27. (28) Abu 'l-Faraj ʿAlī b. al-Ḥusayn b. Hindū studied medicine and philosophy in Nishapur and was also a distinguished poet. He died in 410/1019 or, according to others, in 420/1029.

Uṣ. I, 323, *Fawāt* II, 45. 1. *Miftāḥ al-ṭibb* ḤKh III, 252, VI, 15, Ind. Off. 1041,$_{4}$, Köpr. 981.—2.–5. see Suppl.—6. *Kitāb al-misāḥa* is cited by Ibn Isfandiyār, *Hist. of Ṭabaristān* 77.

278 | Chapter 17. Natural and Occult Sciences

E. Wiedemann, *Über die Naturwissenschaften bei den Arabern, Samml. gemeinverst. wiss. Vorträge, V, Heft* 97, Hamburg 1890.

1. On the legend of Jābir and on the person who collected the works attributed to him, al-Ḥasan b. al-Nakad al-Mawṣilī, see Suppl. I, 426/7.

Wüst., *Ärzte* 25, Berthelot, *La Chimie au moyen âge* III, *L'alchimie ar. avec la collaboration de M.O. Houdas*, Paris 1893. J. Ruska, Das Giftbuch des Jābir, *OLZ* 1928, 453ff., The History of the Jabir Problem, *Isl. Culture* XI, 303/12, *Mukhtār rasāʾil J. b. Ḥayyān biʿtināʾ al-ustādh* P. Kraus, C. 1354. *Kitāb al-sabʿīn* MS Cairo photograph *QSt.* VII, 87, VI, 14/5 (see Ruska, *Festschr. E. v. Lippmann* 40), *Sabʿīn al-usṭuqus, Jumal al-ʿishrīn* Bursa, Ḥü. Čelebi Heyet 15, Hikma 123 (Ritter).

1. *Kitāb al-riyāḍāt* Bodl. I, 522.—2. *Kitāb al-raḥma* ed. Berth.- H. 132/60, commentary *Sirr al-ḥikma* by al-Ṭughrāʾī, d. 515/1121 (p. 284), Paris 2607.—3. *Kitāb al-raḥma al-ṣaghīr* Paris 2605,$_{3}$, Berth.-H. 99/104.—4. *Kitāb al-mawāzīn al-ṣaghīr* Berth.-H. 105/31.—5. *Kitāb al-mulk* ibid. 91/8.—6. *Kitāb al-tajmīʿ* excerpts ibid. 161/79, Kraus, loc. cit., 34/91.—7. *Kitāb al-zībaq al-sharqī* ibid. 180/5.—8. *Kitāb al-zībaq al-gharbī* ibid. 187/92.—9. *Nār al-ḥajar* ibid. 193/200.—10. *Kitāb arḍ al-ḥajar* ibid. 201/5.—11. *Kitāb al-mumāthala*, completion of the *Kitāb al-muqābala* on the philosopher's stone (apocryphal), Berl. 4177.—12. *Kitāb muṣaḥḥaḥāt Aflāṭūn* Rāġib 965, Bahādur Shāh, Lahore, *JRASB* 1917, XXCVII, 115.—13. On the four elements of the philosopher's stone, Paris 1260.—14. *Kitāb al-sahl* Br. Mus. 1002,$_{3}$.—15. *Kitāb al-ṣāfī* ibid. 4.–16. *Kitāb al-shaʿar* ibid. 5.–17. Various alchemical prescriptions ibid. 7.–18. *Kitāb hatk al-asrār*, on the philosopher's stone, ibid. 13.–19. *Kitāb al-uṣūl fī jumlat kutub al-mawāzīn* ibid. 1371,$_{13}$.—20. *Kitāb sirr al-asrār* ibid. 14.–21. *Kitāb al-khawāṣṣ al-kabīr* ibid. 1373,$_{2}$ or *Maqālāt al-kubrā* Alex. Kīm. 5 from which *maqāla* 1, 2, 8, 17 ed. Kraus, loc. cit., 224/303, parts of *maqāla* 6, 10, 16, 19, 20, 21, 24, 32, 33, 38, 62 ibid. 303/32.—22. 21 smaller tracts, Paris 2606.—23.–85. see Suppl. (28. ed. Kraus, loc. cit., 1/95; 77. Kraus 533/41; 78. *Maydān al-ʿaql* Kraus, loc. cit., 206/23,
279 | see Ruska, *Tab. smaragd.* 124ff.).—86. *Kitāb al-ḥudūd* Cairo ^{1}V, 392, Kraus, loc. cit., 97/114, see *Isis* 15, 9/20.—87. *Kitāb al-ʿahd* photograph *QSt.* VII, 96, VI, 23.—88. *al-Ṭabīʿa al-khāmisa* Paris 5099, photograph *QSt.* VII, 97, VI, 34.—89. *al-Aḥjār ʿalā raʾy Bālīnūs* ibid. 3, Kraus 126/205.—90. *al-Taṣrīf* Paris 5099, Kraus 392/423.—91. *al-Mājid* Kr. 115/25.—92. *al-Qadīm* ibid. 542/7.—Later, in Latin translations and revisions, numerous additional works were falsely attributed to him (cf. e.g. *Geberi curieuse vollständige Chymische Schriften*, Frankf. 1710, Vienna 1751), see Steinscheider, *Zur pseudepigr. Literatur* 71, 84, *JA* 1854,

II, 248, *ZDMG* XIII, 649. Among these is also the *Liber claritatis totius alkimicae artis*, ed. E. Darmstaedter, *Archeion* VI, 1925, 319/30, VII, 1926, 257/66, VIII, 1927, 95/103, 214/26, IX, 1928, 63/80, 191/208, 462/484, see J. Ruska ibid. XVI, 1934, 145/67.

2. Muḥammad b. Umayl b. ʿAbdallāh b. Umayl al-Tamīmī, who flourished in the second half of the fourth century.[1]

| 1. *al-Māʾ al-waraqī wal-arḍ al-najmiyya* Fir. Ricc. 20, 1, Cairo [1]V, 393, on certain 242
winged creatures that were depicted on the ceiling and the walls of a temple in Būṣīr, which was believed to have been Joseph's prison,[2] with an alchemical commentary by the author, Paris 2610/1, Fir. Ricc. 20, 2, Pet. Rosen 198, versified in the form of a *mukhammas* by al-Jildakī (p. II, 138) Paris 2611,$_2$, with commentary Br. Mus. 1371,$_{16}$, see J. Ruska, *Isis* XXIV, 1936, 310/42.—2. *Sharḥ al-ṣuwar wal-ashkāl bil-ḥakīm* Paris 2609,$_1$.—3. *Mafātīḥ al-ḥikma fi ʾl-ṣunʿa* AS 2466, different from the *Miftāḥ al-ḥikma*, abbreviated in Artefius' *Clavis majoris sapientiae* (see Suppl.), Levi della Vida, *Speculum* XIII, 80/5.

3. Abū Bakr Muḥammad (or Aḥmad) b. ʿAlī b. Waḥshiyya al-Nabatī, who came from an Aramaic family of Iraq, flourished in the second half or toward the end of the third century and devoted himself to alchemy and other occult | sciences. In 280
his major work, *On Nabatean Agriculture*, he tried, in the spirit of the Shuʿūbiyya, to prove that the culture of the ancient Babylonians was greatly superior to that of the ruling Arabs. Yet because he had little concrete knowledge of that culture, he invented a whole literature, which he employed in addition to the few Hellenistic sources that were available to him in translation. Although he presents himself, in every way, as a good Muslim, he opposes Islamic dogma through all kinds of free thinking under the cover of the authorities that he himself invented.

Leclerc I, 307. 1. *Kitāb al-filāḥa al-Nabaṭiyya*, apparently written in 281/904 and dictated in 318/930 to Abū Ṭālib Aḥmad b. Zayyāt, whom Nöldeke, *ZDMG* XXIX, 453/5 therefore took to be the real author, Berl. 6205 (III), Leid. 1279/81, Bodl. I, 403, 506/7, Br. Mus. 997, Paris 2803, Algiers 1497, Cairo [1]V, 385.—Abstract, *Mukhtaṣar al-filāḥa wa-dhikr manāfiʿ al-mufradāt*, by ʿAlī b. Ḥasan b. Muḥammad al-Zaytūnī al-ʿAwfī, Paris 2942,$_4$ with everything pagan removed, *Khulāṣat al-ikhtiṣār fī maʿrifat al-quwā wal-khawāṣṣ* by Muḥammad b. Ibrāhīm

1 Contra Rosen, loc. cit., who placed him in the third century because Dhu ʾl-Nūn (d. 242, see p. 214) is the last authority referred to by him, already Flügel and Stapleton (see Suppl.).

2 Cf. Stricker, La prison de Joseph, *Acta Or.* XIX, 1942, 101/37.

al-Awsī b. al-Raqqām al-Mursī, d. 715/1315 (II, 266), Gotha 2119, Cambr. 342, *Khulāṣa* by ʿAlī b. Ḥusayn b. Muḥammad b. Khazʿal al-Ḥusaynī, Patna I, 263$_{,2211}$, anon. Berl. 6206, Leid. 1282, under the title *Asrār al-ṭabīʿiyyāt fī khawāṣṣ al-nabāt* Upps. 338. Cf. Chwolson, *Über die Überreste der altbabylonischen Literatur in ar. Übersetzungen, Mém. des savants étrangers publ. par l'Acad. Impér.* VIII, St. Pétersburg 1859 and against this E. Renan, *Mém. de l'Ac. des Inscr.* XXIV, 1, p. 152, A. v. Gutschmid, *ZDMG* XV, p. 1ff., Th. Nöldeke ibid. XXIX, 445ff. G.O. Darby, Ibn Waḥshiyya in Mediaeval Spanish Lit., *Isis* 33, 1941, 433/8.—2. *Kitāb Tankalūshā al-Bābilī al-Qūqānī fī ṣuwar daraj al-falak wa-mā tadullu ʿalayhi min aḥwāl al-mawlūdīn* Leid. 1047, Chwolson, loc. cit., 458/92, Gutschmid, loc. cit., on the name, Borissov, *JA* 226, 300ff. (see Suppl.).—3. *Kitāb al-sumūm wal-tiryāqāt* Leid. 1284, Br. Mus. 1357.—4. *Kitāb shawq al-mustahām fī maʿrifat rumūz*
243 *al-aqlām*, | on the various scripts and hands of different peoples and individual men, completed 241/885 (?), Munich 789, Vienna 68. *Ancient Alphabets and hieroglyphic Characters explained, with an Account of the Egyptian Priests, their*
281 *Classes, Initiation and Sacrifices* | *in the Arabic Language by A. b. Abu Bekr b. Wahshih (sic) and in English by* J. Hammer, London 1806, cf. de Sacy in Millin's *Mag. enc.* 1810, VI, 145/75.—5. *Kitāb sidrat al-muntahā*, a conversation with al-Maghribī al-Qamarī on questions of religion and natural philosophy (not alchemy, ḤKh III, 7065), Gotha 1162, cf. Hammer, loc. cit., XVI, Chwolson, *Die Ssabier* I, 823.—6. *Kitāb al-riyāsa fī ʿilm al-firāsa* Bodl. I, 479.—7. *Maṭāliʿ al-anwār fi 'l-ḥikma* ibid. 494.—8. *Kanz al-ḥikma*, on alchemy, Leid. 1267 = (?) *Kanz al-asrār* NO 3631.—9. *Kitāb uṣūl al-ḥikma* ibid. 1268 = *Kitāb al-uṣūl al-kabīr* Rāġib 963$_{,4}$.—10. *Kitāb al-shāwahid fi 'l-ḥajar al-wāḥid* Rāġib 963$_{,1}$.—11. *Kitāb al-ṭilasmāt* Bodl. I, 951.—12. *Kitāb tābqāna* Berl. Pet. 66 (Ritter).—13. *Kitāb Bālīnūs al-ḥakīm* Pet. Un. 1091, *Zap. Koll. Vost.* I, 370.

4. Abu 'l-Qāsim Maslama b. Aḥmad al-Majrīṭī, from Madrid, studied in the Orient and devoted himself, during the reign of al-Ḥakam II (350–66/961–76), to mathematics and astronomy, as well as to alchemy and magic. He died between 395/1004 and 398/1007.

Uṣ. II, 39, Wüst., *Ärzte* 122. 1. *Kitāb* (*al-taʿlīm bi*) *rutbat al-ḥakīm* or *Kanz al-faḍāʾil*, a work on alchemy falsely attributed to him (see Suppl.), Paris 2612/3, Rāġib 963$_{,5}$, NO 3923, Cairo ^{1}V, 381, Alex. Kīm. 6, Rāmpūr I, 686$_{,76}$.—2. *Ghāyat al-ḥakīm* (*wa-aḥaqq al-natījatayn bil-taqdīm*), instructions on how to make talismans, amulets etc. Vienna 1491, Leid. 1211/2, Bodl. I, 990, Esc. ^{1}941$_{,2}$, Rāġib 570, 965, AS 2443, NO 2794, Alex. Ḥurūf 15, Latin in the *Picatrix* (corrupted from Buqrātīs Hippocrates), a translation that originated in Spain, cf. Steinschneider, *Zur pseudepigr. Lit.* 37, Hebr. compendium Steinschn. 525.—3. *Kitāb al-aḥjār*, excerpts Bodl. I, 448,$_{4}$, cf. ZDMG XLIX, 251.—4. *Generatio animalium* Esc. ^{1}895.—5. Problems in spherical trigonometry, Esc. ^{1}967, ^{2}972,$_{3}$ (Renaud p. 171).—6. See Suppl. (Arīn read Uzain = Ujjaini, i.e. the meridian of Lanka, Bīrūnī *India* 93, 158 ff., transl. I, 306ff, Abu 'l-Fidā' *Geogr.* I, CCXLf., Ferrand, *Relations* 325, n. 1, 366, n. 2, Löfgren on Abū Makhrama I, 30, n. 9).—7. Improvement on the *Planisphaerium* of Ptolemy, AS 2671,$_{3}$, Latin transl. (see Suppl.) ed. Heiberg, *Ptolemaei Opera* II, 227/58, see J. Drecker, *Isis* IX, 1927, 255/78.—8.–12. see Suppl. (12. *Rawḍat al-ḥaqā'iq etc.* also Alex. Kīm. 12,$_{7}$).

| 5. In Berl. 7604, the Fāṭimid caliph al-Manṣūr al-Ḥākim bi-amrillāh, d. 411/1020, 282
is credited with an alchemical *qaṣīda* in 113 verses full of self-praise.

6. 'Uṭārid b. Muḥammad al-Ḥāsib or al-Kātib probably flourished in the third/ninth century and composed the oldest preserved work on the properties of stones, especially gemstones.

Fihrist 278. *Kitāb manāfi' al-aḥjār* Paris 2775,$_{3}$ = *Kitāb al-jawāhir wal-aḥjār* AS 3610, see Clément-Mullet, *JA* 1868 I, 11. Steinschneider, *ZDMG* XLIX, 249; excerpts in al-Majrīṭī's *Ghāyat al-ḥakīm* 106ff., see Ruska, *Griech. Planetendarstellungen*, SB Heid. 1919,$_{3}$, Ritter, *Istanbuler Mitt. Heft III*, p. 3.

| 7. Muḥammad b. Abī Yūsuf Ya'qūb b. Abī Akhī Ḥizām al-Khuttalī, ca. 251/865 244
(see Suppl.).

Kitāb al-furūsiyya wa-shiyāt al-khayl, the oldest hippological work of Arabic literature, Br. Mus. 1305, Patna I, 262,$_{2206/7}$ or *Kitāb al-khayl wal-bayṭara* (see Suppl.), Fātiḥ 3608 (Muḥammad b. Muḥammad b. 'Alī), see L. Moullé, *Hist. de la médecine véterinaire* II, 117/9 (following a Russian translation, Kazan 1896).

8. 'Īsā b. 'Alī b. Ḥassān al-Azdī, 10th cent.

Al-Jamhara fi 'l-bayzara Esc. ^{2}903, see Leclerc I, 503.

9. Abū Sa'īd (Sa'd) Naṣr b. Ya'qūb al-Dīnawarī dedicated the oldest preserved work on dream interpretation to the caliph al-Qādir billāh in 397/1006.

Kitāb al-Qādirī fi 'l-ta'bīr Paris 2745, Bodl. I, 438, 441, 447, 453, Pet. Rosen 212, Köpr. 1363, Patna I, 129,$_{1291}$; the 15th and last *maqāla*, a list of 100 famous dream interpreters, Berl. 10057 (see Suppl.).

Chapter 18. Encyclopaedias

1. The need to compose compact overviews of all or at least the greater part of
283 the sciences, which became more and more pressing as independent | production declined, only manifested itself towards the end of this period. The oldest work of this kind was dedicated by Abū ʿAbdallāh Muḥammad b. Aḥmad b. Yūsuf al-Khwārizmī[1] to Abu ʾl-Ḥasan ʿUbaydallāh b. Aḥmad al-ʿUtbī, the vizier of the Sāmānid ruler Nūḥ II (365–87/975–997).

Kitāb mafātīḥ al-ʿulūm, ed. G. van Vloten, Leid. 1895, Ğārullāh 2047. The work treats, in 2 *maqālas* of 6 and 9 *abwāb* each: I, 1. *al-fiqh*, 2. *al-kalām*, 3. *al-naḥw*, 4. *al-kitāba*, 5. *al-shiʿr wal-ʿarūḍ*, 6. *al-akhbār*;—II, 1. *al-falsafa*, 2. *al-manṭiq*, 3. *al-ṭibb*, 4. *ʿilm al-ʿadad*, 5. *al-handasa*, 6. *al-nujūm*, 7. *al-mūsīqī*, 8. *al-ḥiyal*, 9. *al-kīmiyyāʾ*. Maqrīzī, *Khiṭat* I, $258_{,4}$, says the author was Muḥammad b. Aḥmad b. Muḥammad b. Yūsuf al-Balkhī.

2. ʿAlī b. Muḥammad b. Aḥmad al-Tawḥīdī al-Ṣūfī Abū Ḥayyān, d. after 400/1009 (see Suppl.), but according to *Madīnat al-ʿulūm* (Bank. XXI, 88) his death was as early as ca. 380/990.

1. *Kitāb al-muqābasāt*, in 103 sections on questions regarding various sciences, Leid. 1443, Alex. Fun. $134_{,1}$, Bank. XXI, 2337, print. Bombay 1303 (see Suppl.).—2. *Risāla fī ʿilm al-kitāba*, on calligraphy, Krafft 11.—3. *al-Ishārāt al-ilāhiyya wal-anfās al-rūḥāniyya*, a collection of prayers and sermons (see Suppl.), Milan, estate of E. Griffini, see A. Codazzi no. 14/5, abstract with a commentary by ʿAbd al-Qādir b. Ibrāhīm b. Muḥammad b. Badr al-Maqdisī al-Shāfiʿī, ca. 934/1529, Berl. 2818.—4. *Risāla fi ʾl-ṣadāqa wal-ṣiddīq wa-risāla fī waṣf al-ʿulūm*, Istanbul 1301/2, reprint C. 1323, see Suppl., ZDMG 66, 526.—5.–13. see Suppl. (10 = 4a).—14. *Risāla fī taḥqīq anna mā yaṣduru bil-qudra wal-ikhtiyār lā bil-kurh wal-iḍṭirāb* Lāleli 3645, f. 21/2. *Madīnat al-ʿulūm* (see above) lists the following additional works: 1. *Nuzhat al-aṣḥāb*.—2. *Awsaq al-majālis*.—3. *Anīs al-muḥāḍara*.—4. *al-Rawḍ al-khaṣīb*.—5. *Naẓm al-sulūk*.—6. *Nishwān al-muḥāḍarāt*.—7. *ʿAjāʾib al-gharāʾib*.—8. *Tarwīḥ al-arwāḥ*. Individual treatises also in Lālelī 2433, 3645, 3647 (ZDMG 66, 526).

1 Whom Rieu, Cat. M. Br. 640,nc, mistakenly identified as Abū Bakr Muḥammad b. al-ʿAbbās al-Khwārizmī, d. 383/993 (see p. 92).

The Post-Classical Period of Islamic Literature from ca. 400/1000 until ca. 656/1258

With the decline of their political power and the start of a general cultural decay, the flourishing of the Arabic literature of the ʿAbbāsid period soon faded in Iraq. In poetry, which had been developed by the free spirits of the second and third centuries, the domination of a philological critique soon caused this art to petrify into the form of the *qaṣīda* once again, which increasingly encouraged the imitation of ancient patterns. It was only occasionally that various forms of popular poetry gained influence over the artistic practices of the literati. The bold flights of fancy of the men of letters, which had opened up ever larger expanses of learning, were restricted by the dictates of a cultural policy that was dominated by those with a propensity for power politics.

But this period of general decay which, as far as Asia Minor was concerned, was only rendered definitive with the onslaught of the Mongols, still saw a productive if not always impressive second blooming. At numerous small princely courts, particularly in the western areas, in those regions where Arabic was the dominant language, countless poets and masters of form spread their wings under the sponsorship of various princes. Under the Ayyūbids of Egypt, ʿUmar b. al-Fāriḍ and, especially, Bahāʾ al-Dīn Zuhayr created a type of poetry that paired classical forms with a closeness to nature and true-to-lifeness that is
inspiring even today.[1] Despite these efforts, | poor attempts at further develop- 285
ment of the old forms abound, as do the violent linguistic means by which their soulless fillings are concealed.

| However, belles lettres, too, gave up its pre-set form. The *maqāma* evolved 246
out of the rhetoric of tramps, finding its legendary master in Ḥarīrī. The rich material of the classical period, which had mostly been adopted from elsewhere, was brought together in large collective volumes and recast, time after time. The colourful and lively political scene gave historical works rich material that could be used in monographs. But from the chanceries of the state, a congested and ornate style also made its way into historiography, where

1 Typical for the pursuits of the higher classes of Iraq is the collection of *mawwāliyyāt, dūbayt* and *muwashshaḥāt* that was written for Caliph al-Mustanṣir (probably the ʿAbbāsid who reigned 623–40/1126–42).

 DOI 10.1163/9789004326262_007

rhetorical flourishing often obscures the basic facts of what is reported. The writers of universal histories consistently steer clear of such aberrations of the taste, but at the same time show little regard for the intellectual property of their predecessors.

As far as the areas of "pure" scholarship are concerned, there was still brisk activity, which from the fifth century onwards found state-promoted nurseries in the madrasas. In theology, al-Ghazzālī, the last independent thinker of Islam, brought the controversies of the foregoing era to a final close. Philosophy could still boast of some great minds, although admittedly these had more influence and recognition in the Christian West than among the Muslim peoples. In the hands of al-Bīrūnī, the exact sciences saw an excellent second blossoming in the East, both in terms of the span of their horizon and the sharpness of observation and exposition. But here, too, the activities of the commentators and writers of compendia soon became more important than individual produc-
286 tion. A new and rather unpleasant | phenomenon was that of the polyhistors and polygraphs. While they had thusfar manifested themselves only occasionally, they become ever more numerous as literature declined.

Asad Talas, *L'enseignement chez les Arabes, la Madrasa Niẓāmiyya et son histoire*, Paris 1939.

Chapter 1. Poetry

A *Poets of Baghdad, Iraq, and the Jazīra*

1. Mu'ayyad al-Dīn Abū Ismāʿīl al-Ḥusayn (Ḥusayn) b. ʿAlī b. Muḥammad al-Iṣfahānī al-Ṭughrāʾī, d. 515/1121, see Suppl. I, 439.

Recueil de textes relatifs à l'hist. des Seljoucides II, 132/3, Ibn Khall. 189, Abu 'l-Fida, *Ann. Musl.* III, 310, 46, Istanbul 1287, II, 247, *Biogr. univ.* XLVI, 196ff. 1. *Dīwān*, mostly panegyrics on al-Sulṭān al-Saʿīd Muḥammad b. Malikshāh and his son Abu 'l-Fatḥ Masʿūd, whose secretary he was, on al-Malik al-Muẓaffar, Niẓām al-Mulk, and his son Mu'ayyad al-Mulk, Berl. 7635, Br. Mus. 603, Pet. AM 283, Garr. 35, Qawala II, 194 (see Suppl.), print. Istanbul 1300.—2. *Lāmiyyat al-ʿajam*, a counterpart to the *Lāmiyyat al-ʿarab* of Shanfarā (p. 16), a dirge on the unfortunate state of affairs of his time and his own situation, ed. J. Golius, Leid. 1629, *cum vers. lat. et notis op. E. Pocockii, accedit* (*Sam. Clerici*) *tractatus de prosodia arab.* Oxford 1661, P. Vattier, *L'Élégie de Tograi*, Paris 1660. *Poema Tograi cum vers. lat. J. Golii hactenus inedita, quam e mnsto Goliano praef. et notis quibusdam auctam ed.* M. Anchersen, Utrecht 1717 (see Wahl, *Mag. f. or. Lit.* 1787, 60). J. Reiske, *Thograis sogenanntes Lamisches Gedicht*, Friedrichstad 1758. *The Traveller, an Ar. Poem, intitled Tograi, written by Abu-Ismail, transl. into lat. etc. by* E. Pocock, *now rendered into English etc. by* L.C. Chappelow, Cambridge 1758. *Poema T. cum vers. lat. J. Golii cum scholiis et notis cura* H. van der Sloot, Franeker 1769. Hirtius, *Anth. Arab.* Jena 1774, 129/74. W.F. Hezel, *Carminum ar. specimen primum*, Lemgo 1788. Gudolini *et* Bueckmann, *Lamicum carmen abi Ism. T. lat. expl. 1790.* L.G. Pareau, *Specimen academicum cont. comment. de Tograi carmine*, Utrecht | 1824, Fraehn, *Carmina arabica duo, quae Lamica dicuntur*, Kazan 1814. 287
J.D. Carlyle, *Specimens of Arabian Poetry*, Cambridge 1796, 2nd ed. London 1840, text 46/62, transl. 107/28. Printed with glosses Beirut n.d., with Turkish comm. by Labīb Efendi, Istanbul 1847.—Commentaries: a. ʿAbdallāh b. al-Ḥusayn al-ʿUkbarī, d. 616/1219 (p. 282), Berl. 7658/9, Leid. 652, Vienna 467, 1996,$_{42}$, Esc. ^{2}325,$_{3}$.—aa. Yūsuf al-Mālikī, ca. 750/1350 (II, 75), in his *al-Kanz al-madfūn etc.*, Būlāq 1288, C. 1288, 1303, 1321.—b. *al-Ghayth al-musajjam* by Ṣalāḥ al-Dīn al-Ṣafadī, d. 764/1363 (II, 31), Berl. 7660/3, Vienna 466, de Jong 95, Copenhagen 263, Paris 3119/21, Br. Mus. 604, 1363, Suppl. 1054/5, Bodl. I, 1200, '3, '6, '32, '75, '80, AS 4112/4, Patna I, 201,$_{1800}$, print. C. 1305, abstract by Muḥammad b. ʿAbbās al-Badrānī, Berl. 7670, anon. Paris 3123, 6044, | by al-Damīrī, d. 808/1405 (II, 138), 248
composed in 769/1367, autograph AS 4110 (Ritter), Berl. 7664/5, Munich 566, Leid. 654/5, Paris 3122, Esc. ^{2}321, 324, 325,$_{4}$, Algiers 1854,$_{2}$, Cambr. 616/7, from which a second abstract by Muḥammad b. al-Khalīl al-Kāzarūnī, Ind. Off. 801,$_{3}$.—c. al-Damāmīnī, d. 828/1425 (II, 26), under the title *Nuzūl al-ghayth*, composed in

794/1392, Upps. 136, Leid. 657/8, Paris 3124, Esc. ^{2}560, refutation *Taḥkīm al-ʿuqūl* by ʿAlī b. Muḥammad al-Āqbarsī, d. 862/1458, Paris 3125.—d. Muḥammad b. Aḥmad al-Maḥallī, d. 854/1400, Berl. 7666.—e. Abū Yaḥyā Zakariyyāʾ al-Anṣārī, d. 910/1504 (II, 99), Algiers 1855.—f. *Nashr al-ʿalam* by Muḥammad b. ʿUmar b. Mubārak b. Baḥraq al-Ḥaḍramī, d. 930/1524 (Suppl. II, 554), Berl. 7668/9, Gotha 2250, Leid. 656, Munich 567, Paris 2502,$_{11}$, Pet. AM 292,$_{2}$, Garr. 36, Cairo ^{1}VII, 595, Patna I, 207,$_{1849}$.—g. Jalāl b. Khiḍr al-Ḥanafī, composed in 966/1558 in Istanbul, Upps. 137.—h. Saʿīd b. Masʿūd al-Ṣanhājī Abū Jumʿa, completed in 990/1582, Berl. 7667 (Ahlw. wrongly ca. 900), Leid. 661, Pet. AM 292,$_{1}$, Algiers 1838,$_{1}$, Cairo ^{1}IV, 210, ^{2}III, 30.—i. ʿAbd al-Laṭīf b. ʿAbd al-Raḥmān al-Nuzaylī al-Yamanī, autograph from the year 1018/1609, AS 4111 (Ritter).—k. Muḥammad ʿAlī al-Minyawī, formerly professor of Arabic at al-Madrasa al-Tawfīqiyya, *Tuḥfat al-rāʾī*, Būlāq 1311, C. 1324.—l. anon. Berl. 7671.—Revisions: a. *al-Taṣdīr wal-taʿjīz*, inversion of the verses by Isḥāq b. Ibrāhīm al-Anṣārī al-Awsī, Esc. ^{2}470,$_{12}$.—b. *Taṣdīr wa-tadhyīl* by Abu ʾl-Ḥasan ʿAlī b. Muḥammad b. Farḥūn al-Yaʿmarī al-Qurṭubī, d. 746/1345 (Suppl. II, 227), ibid. 13.—c. as a counterpart to the foregoing by ʿAbdallāh b. ʿAbd al-Ḥaqq b. al-Ṣāʾim, ibid. 14.—d. *Tashṭīr* by Ibrāhīm b. Muḥammad al-Anṣārī Paris 3200,$_{5}$.—e. anon. *Tashṭīr* ibid. 6.—f. Imitation
288 under the title *Lāmiyyat al-ʿarab* by Ismāʿīl b. Abī Bakr | al-Zubadī, Br. Mus. 607,$_{3}$ see *Nufhat ool Yumun* 404; cf. Ahlw. 7673.—3. *Jāmiʿ al-asrār wa-tarākīb al-anwār*, on alchemy, ḤKh II, 500, ^{2}I, 534, Pet. Ros. 205,$_{12}$ fragm. Gotha 1298.—4. *Maṣābīḥ al-ḥikma wa-mafātīḥ al-raḥma*, on the philosopher's stone, Paris 2614.—5. *Ḥaqāʾiq al-istishhād*, a defence of alchemy against Ibn Sīnā, Landb.—Br. 486, Cairo, photograph *Qu. u. St. z. Gesch. der Nat. u. Med.* VII, 108,VI$_{,41}$.—6. Two alchemical poems, Br. Mus. 601, III, 3.—7. *al-Jawhar al-naḍīr fī ṣināʿat al-iksīr* (author?) Berl. 10361, photograph *Qu. u. St. z. Gesch. der Nat. u. Med.* VII, 104,VI$_{,40}$ (with literature).—8. *al-Maqāṭīʿ fi ʾl-ḥikma al-ilāhiyya* (alchemy) AS 469,$_{2}$ (f. 55a/98a).—9. *Sirr al-ḥikma*, see p. 278.

2. Abu ʾl-Maʿālī Saʿd b. ʿAlī b. al-Ḥaẓīrī al-Warrāq Dallāl al-kutub, from al-Ḥaẓīra, a large village north of Baghdad. He lived there as a bookseller and died in 568/1172.[1]

Ibn Khall. 245, Wüst., *Gesch.* 261. 1. *Kitāb lumaḥ al-mulaḥ*, a collection of poems, alphabetically arranged, from the year 549/1154, ḤKh no. 11164, 12869, Bodl. I, 300, 319, Esc. ^{2}465.—2. *Kitāb al-iʿjāz fi ʾl-aḥājī wal-alghāz*, a collection of riddles, alphabetically arranged, dedicated to the emir Mujāhid al-Dīn Qāymāz, guardian of the Begtigīnid Zayn al-Dīn Yūsuf, prince of Arbela (563–86/1167–90),

1 According to Ibn Khall. *Ahlw.* 7328,$_{2}$ wrongly 598/1202.

Cairo ^{1}IV, 204, ^{2}III, 16.—3. see Suppl.—4. *Ṣafwat al-maʿārif*, a poem on natural history, Berl. Brill M. 136.

3. Abū ʿAbdallāh Muḥammad b. Bakhtiyār b. ʿAbdallāh al-Ablah lived in Baghdad and died there in 579/1183, or, according to others, in 589.

Ibn Khall. 651. *Dīwān*, Munich Gl. 88, Br. Mus., see Or. Stud. Browne $145_{,58}$, individual poems in Br. Mus. $1080_{,3}$.

4. Abu ʾl-Fatḥ Muḥammad b. ʿUbaydallāh Sibṭ b. al-Taʿāwīdhī was the son of a Turkish freedman whose name was actually Ṭāshtigin, and on his mother's
side the grandson of the famous | Sufi and ascetic Ibn al-Taʿāwīdhī. He was 249
born on 10 Rajab 519/13 August 1124 in Baghdad and worked there in the *dīwān*
| *al-iqṭāʿāt*. He went blind in 579/1183 and died on 2 Shawwāl 583/5 December 289
1187, or in 584.

Ibn Khall. 652. *Dīwān*, first published before he went blind and which was later augmented, ḤKh ^{1}III, 5170, ^{2}II, 764, Berl. 7698/9, Bodl. I, 1225, 1235, Esc. ^{2}376 (see Suppl.), O. Rescher, *Beitr. zur ar. Poesie*, Stuttgart 1937, 1–116, from the *dīwān* of Ibn al-Taʿāwīdhī in the edition of Margoliouth.

5. His rival Najm al-Dīn Abu ʾl-Ghanāʾim Muḥammad b. ʿAlī b. al-Muʿallim al-Ḥurthī, d. 592/1195, see Suppl.

Ibn Khall. 653. *Dīwān* Vienna $468_{,2}$, Esc. ^{2}365.

6. In the first half of the seventh/first century Aydamur al-Muḥyawī Fakhr al-Turk, a freedman of Muḥyi ʾl-Dīn Muḥammad b. Muḥammad b. Saʿīd b. Saʿdī, flourished.[2]

Dīwān selections, copy dated 686/1287, Cairo ^{1}IV, 240, ^{2}III, 338, print. C. (Dār al-kutub) I, 1350/1931.

7. Ḥusām al-Dīn ʿĪsā b. Sanjar b. Bahrām b. Jibrīl b. Ṭāshtigin al-Ḥājirī came from a Turkish family of soldiers. When Ibn Khallikān, whose brother was a friend of his, left Irbil in 626/1229, he was imprisoned in the fortress there. After his release he donned the cloak of a Sufi and entered the service of Muẓaffar

2 Erroneously placed by Ahlw. $7878_{,8}$ around 750, see M. Hartmann *Muwashshaḥ* 13.

al-Dīn Kökbörī, whom Ṣalāḥ al-Dīn had installed as regent of Irbil in succession to his brother Zayn al-Dīn Yūsuf. After the latter's death in 630/1232 he left the city but later returned, only to be murdered there in 632/1235.

Ibn Khall. 491. I. *Dīwān* under the title *Bulbul al-gharām al-kāshif ʿan lithām al-inshijām*, collected and arranged by ʿUmar b. Muḥammad b. al-Ḥusayn in 7 chapters: 1. *ghazal*, 2. poems from prison, 3. *mukhammasāt*, 4. individual verses, 5. satirical poems, 6. *mawālī*, 7. *dūbayt*, Berl. 7742/4, Leid. 676/7, Munich
290 515, Br. Mus. $1080_{,4}$, cf. $630_{,2}$, Suppl. 1067, Calc. | 22, Garr. 56, print. n.p. 1280, C. 1305.—II. *Masāriḥ al-ghizlān al-ḥājiriyya*, collected by the same, Ind. Off. $829_{,3}$.—III. Some poems in the collection *Nuzhat al-nāẓir wa-sharḥ al-khāṭir* were written after 1008/1599, Berl. 8198.

250 | 8. (9.). Abū Zakariyyāʾ Yaḥyā b. Yūsuf al-Anṣārī al-Baghdādī al-Ṣarṣarī al-ʿIrāqī Jamāl al-Dīn, was from Ṣarṣar near Baghdad, and died in 656/1258.

1. *Dīwān*, ordered by the length of poems, ḤKh ^{1}II, $290_{,5514}$, ^{2}I, 797, Berl. 7759, Gotha 2272, NO 3887.—2. Individual poems, Berl. 7760, Bodl. II, 315.—3. *Qaṣīda* in praise of the Prophet, each verse of which contains all the letters of the alphabet, and a *qaṣīda* on mysticism, *Fi ʾl-taṣawwuf*, Esc. $^{2}363_{,1}$.—4. *Muntaqā min madāʾiḥ al-rasūl*, ibid. 460.—5. *Fī maʿrifat awāʾil shuhūr al-Rūm wa-maʿrifat ʿadadihā*, a *qaṣīda* rhyming in *lām*, Gotha $1377_{,16}$.—6. *al-Durar al-yatīma wal-maḥajja al-mustaqīma*, on Ḥanbalī law in *ṭawīl* verse, Berl. 4511.—7. 562 *ṭawīl* verses on God and His properties, the Prophet and his merits, his companions and successors, the imams, and in particular Aḥmad b. Ḥanbal and his followers, ibid. 10017.

10. Aḥmad b. Muḥammad b. Abi ʾl-Wafāʾ Sharaf al-Dīn Abu ʾl-Ṭayyib b. al-Ḥalawī al-Rabaʿī, born in 603/1206, was the court poet of the *atabeg* of Mosul, Badr al-Dīn Luʾluʾ (r. 631–57/1233–59). He died in 656/1258.

Fawāt I, 69, Hartmann, *Muwashshaḥ* 12/3. Selected poems, Gotha 2196.

11. Majd (Muḥyī) al-Dīn Muḥammad b. Abī Bakr b. Rushayd al-Wāʿiẓ al-Baghdādī al-Witrī died in 662/1264.

1. *Bustān al-ʿārifīn fī maʿrifat al-dunyā wal-dīn* or *al-Qaṣāʾid al-witriyya*, poems in praise of the Prophet, with a *takhmīs* by Muḥammad b. ʿAbd al-ʿAzīz al-Warrāq

al-Lakhmī al-Qurṭubī al-Iskandarānī, d. 680/1281,[3] under the title *al-Witriyyāt wa-maʿdin al-anwārāt*, Berl. 7767/8, Gotha 2273, Leid. 706, | Copenhagen 271, 291 Garr. 58/9, Alex. Adab 133,$_{4}$, Qawala II, 222, anon. *takhmīs* Ind. Off. 816.—2. From which especially *al-Qaṣīda al-witriyya fī madḥ khayr al-bariyya*, with *takhmīs* by the same, Berl. 7769/70, Esc. ^{2}436,$_{2}$, Alex. Adab 23, *Sharḥ wa-takhmīs al-Q. al-w.* by Muḥammad b. ʿAbd al-Wāḥid al-Naẓīfī al-Sūsī al-Marrākushī, C. 1331.—3. *al-Rawḍa al-dhahabiyya fi ʾl-ḥijja al-Makkiyya wal-zawra al-Muḥammadiyya*, a long poem about the pilgrimage in *ṭawīl* rhyming in *āḥ*, Berl. 4043 (composed in 662), Gotha 1085 (composed in 682!).

| 12. Shams al-Dīn al-Wāʿiẓ al-Kūfī, who died at almost 80 years of age in 251 675/1276, in Baghdad.

Poems, Gotha 2196,$_{9}$.

13. Majd al-Dīn Muḥammad b. Aḥmad b. Abī Shākir b. al-Ẓāhir al-Marrākushī al-Irbilī, who died in 676/1277, see Suppl., 444.

Tadhkirat al-arīb wa-tabṣirat al-adīb, a poem, Paris 3129,$_{3}$.

B *Persian Poets*

In Iran, which had been the first region to assert its independence from the central government in Baghdad, Arabic poetry continued to hold an important place under the patronage of new rulers, even though New Persian too, gained the rank of a literary language under the Sāmānids.

1. Abu ʾl-Fatḥ ʿAlī b. Muḥammad (Aḥmad) al-Bustī, who died in 401/1010 in Bukhārā, see Suppl. I, 445.

Al-Thaʿālibī, *Yatīma* IV, 204/31, Ibn Khall. 443. 1. *Dīwān* Garr. 26, a part thereof, *Nubdha*, Leid. 633.—2. His most famous poem, *Qaṣīdat al-Bustī al-nūniyya*, of edifying content, Berl. 7591/3, Vienna 475,$_{2}$, Paris 1293,$_{2}$, Ind. Off. 1038,$_{8}$, Esc. ^{2}167,$_{2}$, also under the title *ʿUnwān al-ḥilm* (wrongly *ḥukm*), Garr. 2126,$_{3}$, *Majāni ʾl-adab*, IV, 95.—Commentaries: a. ʿAbdallāh b. Muḥammad b. Aḥmad al-Nuqrakār, d. 776/1374 (Suppl. II, 21), Berl. 7594/5, Gotha 2236/7, Leipz. 519/20, Leid. 634, Copenhagen 242,$_{7}$, Garr. 27, Qaw. II, 200.—b. ʿAbd al-Raḥmān

3 Who had written a work under the same title in 661/1273, see Leid. 2801 (V, 313).

al-ʿUmarī al-Maylānī, ca. 780/1378, Berl. 7596.—c. On the first two verses by
292 ʿAbd al-Qādir b. ʿAydarūs, d. 1038/1628 (II, 418), | Berl. 7597.—3. Two poems, Gotha $26,_{1}$.—d. *al-Hidāya lil-mustafīdīn wal-dirāya lil-mustafīḍīn* by Aḥmad b. Muḥammad, Alex. Adab 141.

2. Abū Manṣūr ʿAlī b. al-Ḥasan b. ʿAlī al-Faḍl Ṣurrdurr occasionally also lived in Iraq. In Wāsiṭ he congratulated the vizier Fakhr al-Dawla Muḥammad b. Jahīr
252 upon his accession to office. | He was accidentally killed in 465/1073 when he fell into a lion's den on the way to Khurāsān.

Ibn Khall. 447, cf. 672, ḤKh III, 5263, 5513. *Dīwān* Berl. 7620, Leid. 644/5, Pet. AM 287, Calc. 22.

3. ʿAlī b. al-Ḥasan b. ʿAlī Abu ʾl-Ṭayyib al-Bākharzī Abu ʾl-Ḥasan came from Bākharz, a region with 168 communities between Nishapur and Herat. He soon turned to poetry, away from the study of Shāfiʿī law. Having occupied various offices in Baghdad, where al-Kundarī the vizier had taken him, and after living for some time in Basra, he returned to his native land where he was murdered in Dhu ʾl-Qaʿda 467/June 1075.

Ibn Khall. 448, Wüst., *Gesch.* 211. 1. *Dumyat al-qaṣr wa-ʿuṣrat ahl al-ʿaṣr*, on the poets of the fifth century up to 450, meant as a continuation of *Yatīmat al-dahr* by Thaʿālibī, Berl. 7409, Gotha 2128, Vienna 366/8, Paris 3313, 5252, 5926, Br. Mus. 573, 1126, Patna II, $319,_{2473}$, excerpt Leid. 1055.—2. A poem rhyming in *ḥāʾ*, Gotha 26, f. 146a.—3. *Ikhtiyār al-bikr min al-thayyib min shiʿr ʿA. b. al-Ḥ. b. al-Ṭayyib* by Abu ʾl-Wafāʾ Muḥammad b. Muḥammad al-Akhsīkatī, d. after 520/1126, Yāqūt, *GW* I, 162, *Dharīʿa* I, $364,_{1910}$.

4. Aḥmad b. ʿAbd al-Razzāq Muʿīn al-Dīn Abū Naṣr al-Ṭanṭarānī wrote poetry in honour of the vizier Niẓām al-Mulk (d. 485/1092) and the Saljūq sultans Alp Arslān and Malikshāh.

Al-Qaṣīda al-tarjīʿiyya, Berl. 7622/3, Vienna $461,_{2}$, ed. S. de Sacy, *Chrest, ar.*, ^{1}I, 365/70, III, 125ff., ^{2}II, 158/62, 495ff. (mistakenly attributed to Muḥammad b. Muḥammad b. ʿAbd al-Jalīl al-Rashīd al-Waṭwāṭ, d. 509/1115, see p. 275), with
293 anon. commentary | Berl. 7624, Vienna 461/2, Krafft 112, Munich 894, f. 13, Copenhagen 242, Leid. 646, Pet. Ros. 87, Paris 3116, Br. Mus. $565,_{4}$, $1617,_{4}$, Ind. Off. 805, I, Bodl. I, $1274,_{4}$, AS 4089, another ibid. 4090, $4100,_{5}$, Qawala II, 201. Commentary by Muḥammad al-Bihishtī al-Isfarāʾinī, ca. 900/1494, Berl. 7625/6, Paris $1160,_{9}$, glosses Berl. 7627, Paris $3088,_{2}$.

5. Abū Yaʿlā Muḥammad b. al-Habbāriyya al-ʿAbbāsī, d. 504/1100, see Suppl. I, 446/7.

Ibn Khall. 648. 1. *Kitāb al-ṣādiḥ wal-bāghim* (*al-munāṣiḥ wal-ḥāzim al-shāfiq wal-ʿāzim*), fables in verse, told by an Indian and a Persian, whose nightly contest over the merits of their peoples was supposedly overheard by the poet, and which was dedicated to the prince of Ḥilla, Sayf al-Dawla Abu ʾl-Ḥasan Ṣadaqa b. Dubays al-Mazyadī, d. 501/1107 (see Hammer, *Wien. Jahrb.* 90, 67/123, which contains a rather large fragment in German verse), Berl. 7630/1, Brill M. 217, Gotha 2244/5, Leipz. 596, Vienna 465, Leid. 647/8, Paris 3495/8, Br. Mus. Suppl. 1131,$_{2}$, Bodl. I, 850,$_{4}$, 1260, II, 320, Cambr. 903, Esc. ^{2}474,$_{1}$, 555, 759, Algiers 1826,$_{2}$, Garr. 725, Alex. Adab 144, Patna I, 203,$_{1813}$, print. C. 1292, 1294, 1936, Beirut 1886. | Abstract, *Tajrīd al-ṣādiḥ* by Ibn Ḥijja al-Ḥamawī, d. 837/1433 (II, 253
15), Berl. 7632.—2. *Urjūza shiʿriyya*, on chess, Berl. 5497,$_{1}$, 7632,$_{2}$, Gotha 1514, f. 137, Br. Mus. 616,$_{2}$, Bodl. II, 227,$_{4}$, Algiers 1508,$_{1}$.—3. *Falak al-maʿālī* AS 4157.—4. A satirical image of the period in al-Bundārī, *Rec. de textes rel. à l'hist. des Seldj.*, II, 64/6.

6. Abu ʾl-Muẓaffar Muḥammad b. Abi ʾl-ʿAbbās Aḥmad al-Abīwardī was a descendant of Muʿāwiya II who was born in the village of Kūfan near Abīward in Khurāsān. He distinguished himself as a poet and genealogist, and was poisoned on 20 Rabīʿ I 507/5 September 1113 in Isfahan.

Ibn Khall. 646, Abu ʾl-Fidāʾ, *Ann.*, III 380, Istanbul III, 238, Yāqūt *GW* I, 111, Wüst., *Gesch.* 223. *Dīwān* in 3 parts: 1. *al-Najdiyyāt* (only Paris 3411,$_{2}$, Br. Mus. Suppl. 1030,$_{5}$, Esc. ^{2}371,$_{2}$, 420, 1, Patna I, 197,$_{1766}$. Commentary by ʿAbd al-Muḥsin al-Qayṣarī, completed in 759/1358, Leid. 650).—2. *al-ʿIrāqiyyāt*, for the most part on the caliphs al-Muqtadī (467–87/1075–94) and al-Mustaẓhir (487–512/1094–1110) and their | viziers (only Paris 3117, Br. Mus. 602, Esc. ^{2}370, Garr. 294
34, Köpr. 1338).—3. *al-Wajdiyyāt*, Berl. 7634, Munich 518, Bodl. Uri 248, Nicoll 611; fragment, pieced together from an exemplar that only contained the first two parts, Leid. 649; print. Beirut 1327.

7. Shihāb al-Dīn Aḥmad b. Muḥammad al-Khayyāṭ was born in 450/1058 in Damascus, lived in Persia and died there in 517/1123.

Ibn. Khall. 59. 1. *Dīwān*, compiled in the year of his death, Copenhagen 264, Esc. ^{2}375.—2. Individual poems, Berl. 7675, Br. Mus. 630,$_{2}$.

8. Abū Isḥāq Ibrāhīm b. Yaḥyā b. ʿUthmān b. Muḥammad al-Kalbī al-Ashhabī al-Ghazzī was born in 441/1049 in Gaza, studied from 481/1080 onwards with

the *faqīh* Naṣr al-Maqdisī (Suppl. I, 603, 6b) in Damascus, and subsequently for another couple of years at the Niẓāmiyya in Baghdad. He later went to Khurāsān where he composed poems in praise of Sultan Malikshāh and his son Sanjar as well as other great men, in particular the vizier of Kirman, Naṣr al-Dīn Mukarram b. al-ʿAlāʾ. He died in 524/1130 somewhere between Marw and Balkh.

Ibn Khall. 170. *Dīwān*, ca. 5000 verses (according to Berl. Pet.), ḤKh ^{1}III, 242,$_{5156}$ (1000 verses), 292,$_{5595}$, ^{2}I, 763, 804, Berl. 7680, Paris 3126, Pet. AM 293, Vienna 495, Garr. 38.

9. Nāṣiḥ al-Dīn Abū Bakr Aḥmad b. Muḥammad b. al-Ḥusayn al-Qāḍī al-Arrajānī came from a family of the Anṣār and was born in 460/1068 in Shiraz. After a career as deputy *qāḍī* in Khūzistān, Tustar, and ʿAskar Mukram, he died in 544/1149 in Tustar.

254 | Ibn Khall. 62. *Dīwān*, for the most part longer, panegyric poems, collected by his son, ḤKh ^{1}III, 260,$_{5281}$, ^{2}I, 775, Berl. 7689/90, BDMG 106, Leid. 668/9 (fragm.), Garr. 39, Br. Mus. Suppl. 1062, Copenhagen 265, AS 3930, print. Beirut 1307.

10. Qāḍī Niẓām al-Dīn al-Iṣfahānī, d. 678/1278 in Isfahan, wrote:

295 | *Dīwān al-munshaʾāt* under the title *Shuraf aywān al-bayān fī sharaf bayt ṣāḥib al-dīwān*, poetical epistles, for the most part for the vizier Bahāʾ al-Dīn (Abu ʾl-F. *Ann.* V, 60) and his sons Shams al-Dīn and ʿAlāʾ al-Dīn (d. 680/1281, Abu ʾl-F., loc. cit.) over the years 631–78/1233–78, Br. Mus. 615, AS 3959, ʿĀšir, I, 978.

C *Syrian Poets*

Towards the end of the previous period, under the government of the Ḥamdānids, Syria had managed to regain the literary standing that it had lost under the first ʿAbbāsids, and produced a whole series of eminent poets.

1. In his early days, perhaps the greatest poet of the whole post-classical period, Abu ʾl-ʿAlāʾ Aḥmad b. ʿAbdallāh al-Maʿarrī al-Tanūkhī, was still under the influence of al-Mutanabbī. He was born on 27 Rabīʿ I 363/26 December 873 in the northern Syrian town of Maʿarrat al-Nuʿmān. His family counted itself as part of the Southern Arabian tribe of Tanūkh. By the age of four he had lost his sight in one of his eyes as a result of the pox, while later on he went blind in the other eye as well. This, however, did not prevent him

from devoting himself entirely to belles lettres. Having completed his studies in Aleppo in 384/994, he returned to his hometown. Driven by a desire to extend his fame, he went to Baghdad in 398/1007. His social intercourse with the director of the library ʿAbd al-Salām al-Baṣrī and his free-thinking friends steered his poetry in a philosophical direction. He was, however, unable to take a permanent foothold in the capital due to the fact that he fell out with the influential ʿAlid al-Murtaḍā, the brother of al-Sharīf al-Raḍī, when he stood up for al-Mutanabbī. News of his mother's illness possibly precipitated his return to his native land although, | when he arrived after an absence of 255
one year and seven months, he learned that his mother had already passed away. | Subsequently, he lived there as a distinguished citizen, and had a great 296
number of students. He died there on 2 (according to others, 13) Rabīʿ I 449/10 (21) May 1057. See Suppl. I, 450/2.

Ibn al-Anbārī, *Nuzhat al-alibbāʾ* 425, Ibn Khall. 46, al-Qazwīnī, *Kosm.* 172, 181, al-Suyūṭī, *al-Tabarrī min maʿarrat al-Maʿarrī* II, 262. C. Rieu, *De Abu 'l-Alae poetae arabici vita et carminibus*, Bonn 1843, A. v. Kremer, ZDMG 29, 304ff., 30, 40ff., 31, 471ff., 38, 499ff., *Culturgesch.* II, 386/94; idem, *Über die philosophischen Gedichte des Abu 'l-ʿAlāʾ Maʿarry*, SBWA 117, Vienna 1888, Goldziher, ZDMG 29, 637. ʿAbd al-Raḥīm b. Aḥmad *Notice biographique et bibliographique concernante l'illustre poète philosophe Abu 'l-ʿAlāʾ al-M., C.* 1897. Ḥusayn Futūḥ, *ʿAqīdat Abi 'l-ʿAlāʾ*, C. 1910.

1. *Sa(i)qṭ al-zand*, his adolescent poems, Berl. 7610/12, Gotha 2238, BDMG 104, Vienna 459, Wolfenbüttel 41, Leid. 638, de Jong 91, Paris 3109/10, Copenhagen 261, Br. Mus. 598, 1073, 1080, 1411, Suppl. 1051, Bodl. I, $769_{,2}$, 1195, 1256, 1277, II, 329, Esc. ^{2}273, 435, Garr. 29, Köpr. 1267, 1291/2, Patna I, $197_{,1764}$, print. Beirut 1844, C. 1304, Ind. 1319/1901. Commentaries: a. self-commentary with the title *Ḍawʾ al-saqṭ* Rieu, op. cit., 66, Paris 3111 (see de Sacy, *Chrest. ar.* III, 92), Leid. 693, Köpr. 1322, print. Beirut and India.—b. al-Tibrīzī, d. 502/1109 (p. 329), Leid. 640, Paris 3112, Copenhagen 262, Vienna 460, Br. Mus. 599, Cambr. 115.—c. al-Baṭalyawsī, d. 521/1127 (p. 309), Bodl. I, 1211, Esc. ^{2}276, 1 cf. 3, AS 4099, see de Sacy, *Chrest.* III, 92.—d. *Ḍirām al-saqṭ* by al-Qāsim b. al-Ḥusayn al-Khwārizmī, d. 617/1220, composed in 587/1191, Berl. 7614, Vienna 460, Pet. AM 284/5, NO 3986/7, Qawala II, 204.—e. anon. Berl. 7615; 5 other commentaries Ahlw., ibid.—2. *Luzūm mā lam yalzam*, thus called because of the applied rhyme of the last two letters, Leid. 642/3, Bodl. I, 1293, Pet. AM 286, Br. Mus. Suppl. 1050, 1140, print. C. 1306, 1891/2, lith. Bombay 1303, excerpts Pet. $231_{,6}$, Garr. 28.—3. *Rasāʾil* in three parts ḤKh ^{1}III, 459, ^{2}I, 901, Leid. 348 (part II) = *al-Mukātabāt* Köpr. 1396 (594 AH); of which in particular: a. *Risālat al-malāʾika*, which according ḤKh belongs to

part I, Leid. 349.—b. *al-Risāla al-ighrīḍiyya*, on the Arabic language and poetry, addressed to the vizier Abu ʾl-Qāsim al-Ḥusayn al-Maghribī (d. 418/1027, Ibn Khall. 185), Esc. $^{2}470,_{2}$, Garr. 2191.—c. *al-Risāla al-manīḥiyya*, addressed to the same, Esc. $^{2}470,_{3}$.—d. *Risālat al-ghufrān* (see Suppl.), ed. Kāmil al-Kīlānī, C. 1938, with al-Arnawṭī (Suppl. III, 390) *Firdaws al-Maʿarrī*, Beirut 1333/1915.—
297 4. *Mulqa ʾl-sabīl fi ʾl-waʿẓ* | *wal-zuhd*, in rhymed prose and verse, Br. Mus. $888,_{11}$, Esc. $^{2}276,_{2}$, $467,_{3}$, excerpts Pet. $231,_{7}$; imitation by Dhu ʾl-Wizāratayn al-Ghāfiqī, d. 540/1145 (p. 368), Br. Mus. 888, 9, Esc. $^{2}519$.—5., 6. (see Suppl.).—7. Commentary on al-Mutanabbī, see p. 88.—8. *al-Fuṣūl wal-ghāyāt fī tamjīd Allāh wal-mawāʿiẓ*, a collection of sermons glorifying God and warning against lusting for the world, free from the nonconformism of the *Luzūmiyyāt*, commenced before his journey to Baghdad and completed after his return to his homeland; it was only in light of his later works that Ibn al-Jawzī and others condemned this one too, denouncing it as an imitation of the Qurʾān; first part (up to and including *khāʾ*) ed. Maḥmūd Ḥasan Zanātī, C. 1356/1938 (cf. Goldziher, *ZDMG* 29, 640, 32, 383, *MSt.* II, 403, Thorbecke, *ZDMG* 31, 176 and A. Fischer, Der "Koran" des Abu l-ʿAlāʾ al-Maʿarrī, *B.V.S.A.W. phil.-hist. Kl.* 94, 2, 1942).—9. *ʿAbath al-walīd*, critical commentary on Buḥturī (citation ʿAbd al-Qādir, *Khiz. al-adab* III, $83,_{10}$), ed. Muḥammad ʿAlī al-Madanī, Damascus 1355/1936, see *RAAD* XIV, 5/11.

256 | 2. Abū Muḥammad ʿAbdallāh b. Saʿīd b. Sinān al-Khafājī, d. 466/1074, see Suppl. I, 454.

2a. Muḥammad b. Muḥammad al-Wāʿiẓī, d. 509/1115.

Qaṣīda mīmiyya fī makārim al-akhlāq Berl. $8088,_{5}$, Heid. *ZDMG* 91, 388.

3. Aḥmad b. Munīr b. Aḥmad Mufliḥ Muhadhdhab al-Dīn al-Ṭarābulusī al-Raffāʾ, d. 548/1135, see Suppl.

Ibn Khall. 63. *Al-Qaṣīda al-Tatariyya*, 91 verses on his servant Tatar, whom he had sent with presents to the *sharīf* al-Mūsawī, and who kept him; he explains that, to get him back, he would not be unwilling to convert from Shīʿī to Sunnī Islam, ḤKh III, 5217, Berl. 7691.

4. Abu ʾl-Fityān Muḥammad b. Sulṭān b. Ḥayyūs was born in 394/1003 in Damascus, lived as a court poet of the Banū Mirdās in Aleppo, and died in 473/1080.

Ibn Khall. 645. *Dīwān*, poems in praise of Syrian notables and princes, mostly Ḥamdānids and Mirdāsids, ḤKh ^{1}III, 245,$_{5170}$, ^{2}I, 765, Gotha 2241, cf. J.J. (Bruno) Müller, Bonn 1829, Münster 1844. Two poems Berl. 7621/2.

| 5. In the first half of the sixth/twelfth century Abū Muḥammad Maʿdān b. 298
Kathīr b. al-Ḥasan al-Bālisī, a student of the *faqīh* Abū Bakr Muḥammad b. Aḥmad al-Shāshī (see Suppl. I, 307) flourished. He glorified his master in verse.

Yāqūt, *GW* I, 479. *Dīwān*, mostly panegyrics and elegies, Gotha 2254,$_{1}$.

6. ʿAlī b. Muḥammad b. Rustam al-Dimashqī Bahāʾ al-Dīn Abu ʾl-Ḥasan b. al-Sāʿātī was born in 555/1160 in Damascus and died in Cairo in 604/1207.

Ibn Khall. 451. *Dīwān* (of which there were two, according to ḤKh III, 5188, ^{2}I, 766) AS 3872 (630 AH), ed. Anīs E. Khūrī, Beirut 1938; a *qaṣīda* Berl. 7702. ḤKh calls his second *dīwān Muqaṭṭaʿāt al-layl*.

6c. ʿAmīd al-Dīn Asʿad (Saʿd) b. Naṣr al-Anṣārī.

See Suppl. A *qaṣīda* that he dictated to his son during his imprisonment in the fortress of Ashkandān in Fārs, who then conveyed it to the father of the exegete Ṣafī al-Dīn Aḥmad b. al-Khayr Masʿūd, who was a cousin of the poet, AS 4072,$_{1}$ (Ritter).

7. Al-Malik al-Amjad Bahrāmshāh b. Farrūkhshāh, d. 627/1230, see Suppl.

Dīwān Paris 3142.

8. Yūsuf b. Ismāʿīl al-Shawwāʾ al-Ḥalabī, born 562/1166, died 635/1237.

Ibn Khall. 821. His *Dīwān* in 4 volumes is lost. A judgment on his best poems is given in Berl. 297,$_{40}$. His poem on verbs whose third radical can be wāw or yāʾ is attributed to Ibn Mālik (p. 298) in Berl. 7029/30; see al-Suyūṭī, *Muzhir*, II, 145, Naṣr al-Hūrīnī, *al-Maṭāliʿ al-Naṣriyya lil-maṭābiʿ al-Miṣriyya*, C. 1304, p. 88, M. b. Cheneb, *RAAD* VIII, 692.

| 9. ʿAbd al-Muḥsin b. Maḥmūd al-Tanūkhī al-Ḥalabī, d. 570/1174, served the 257
Mamlūk ruler ʿIzz al-Dīn Aybak, the prince of Ṣarkhad near Damascus, first as a secretary and then as vizier until the latter was murdered in 626/1229. He died in 634/1245.

299 | *Fawāt* II, 13, Wüst., *Gesch.* 328. *Miftāḥ al-afrāḥ fi 'imtidāḥ al-rāḥ*, wine- and drinking- songs in the style of Abū Nuwās, collected at the instigation of Prince ʿĪsā b. Abī Bakr b. Ayyūb, d. 624/1227, ḤKh VI, 12544/8, VII, 981, Berl. 7753, Vienna 463.

10. In 647/1249 Ṣadr al-Dīn b. ʿAlī b. Abi 'l-Faraj b. al-Ḥusayn al-Baṣrī dedicated to the prince of Aleppo, al-Malik al-Nāṣir Ṣalāḥ al-Dunyā wal-Dīn Abu 'l-Muẓaffar Yūsuf, whom Hūlāgū killed in 659/1261:

1. *al-Ḥamāsa al-Baṣriyya* ḤKh, [1]III, 116, [2]I, 693, Esc. [2]313, NO 3804.—2. *al-Manāqib al-ʿAbbāsiyya etc.* (see Suppl.), according to M. Jawad, *REI* 1938, 287 composed after 659/1260.

11. Nūr al-Dīn Muḥammad b. Rustam al-Isʿirdī, born 619/1222, was court poet of the same Ayyūbid al-Malik al-Nāṣir. He died in 652/1254.

Fawāt II 161. *Al-Nāṣiriyyāt*, poems in praise of the prince, Esc. [2]472 (cf. 399,$_1$).

12. Jalāl al-Dīn ʿAlī b. Yūsuf b. Shaybān al-Māridīnī al-Ṣaffār was born in 575/1179, served the prince of Māridīn, al-Malik al-Manṣūr, as a scribe, and was killed in a raid by the Tatars in 658/1260.

Fawāt II, 97. Poems, Gotha 2196,$_8$.

13. Tāj al-Dīn Muḥammad (Maḥmūd) b. ʿAbīd b. al-Ḥusayn al-Tamīmī al-Ṣarkhadī al-Ḥanafī was born in 598/1201 and died in 674/1275. He was a teacher of Ḥanafī law at al-Madrasa al-Nūriyya in Damascus.

1. Poems, Gotha 2196,$_8$.—2. *Maqāmat al-mufākhara bayna 'l-tūt wal-mishmish*, Esc. [2]1837,$_6$.

14. Muḥammad b. Sawwār b. Isrāʾīl Najm al-Dīn Abu 'l-Maʿālī al-Shaybānī was born in Damascus in 603/1206 and died there in 677/1278.

Fawāt II, 269. *Dīwān* Esc. [2]437, which starts with a poem in praise of his teacher Abu 'l-Ḥasan ʿAlī al-Ḥarīrī (d. 645/1247, *Fawāt* II, 55).

300 | 15. Because of his penchant for gambling, Shihāb al-Dīn Muḥammad b. Yūsuf b. Masʿūd al-Shaybānī al-Tallaʿfarī, born in 593/1197 in Mosul, lost the favour of the ruler there, al-Malik al-Ashraf, which he had previously gained through his

panegyrics. | In Aleppo and Damascus, whence he had turned after his expul- 258
sion, this passion sealed his fate as well. He found his last refuge at the court of Hama, where he died in 675/1277.

Fawāt II, 277, Hartmann, *Muwashshaḥ* 86. *Dīwān* Berl. 7780, Esc. $^{2}342_{,2}$, $369_{,2}$, Garr. 80 (see Suppl.), print. C. 1298, Beirut 1310, 1326.

16. ʿAfīf al-Dīn Sulaymān b. ʿAlī b. Yātinannā al-Tilimsānī al-Kūmī, d. 690/1291, see Suppl.

Fawāt I, 178, Ibn al-Qāḍī, *Durrat al-ḥijāl* II, 476, 1321. 1. *Dīwān*, arranged alphabetically, Berl. $7783_{,2}$, Br. Mus. 617/8, Ind, Off. 829, Bodl. II, 314, Esc. $^{2}385$, 453, Garr. 60.—2. *Risāla fī ʿilm al-ʿarūḍ*, on metrics, Berl. 7128.—3. *Risāla fī sharḥ al-asmāʾ al-ḥusnā* Patna II, $410_{,2579,17}$.

17. His son Shams al-Dīn Muḥammad b. ʿAfīf al-Dīn Sulaymān al-Tilimsānī al-Shābb al-Ẓarīf was born in 661/1263 in Cairo and died in Damascus in 680/1289.

Fawāt II, 211. 1. *Dīwān* ḤKh, ^{1}III, $247_{,5196}$, $286_{,5477}$, ^{2}I, 767, 794, Berl. 7783, Gotha 2274, Paris 3176, Br. Mus. $616_{,21}$, Esc. $^{2}383_{,2}$, 451/2, Köpr. 222, Patna II, $448_{,2624,2}$, print. Beirut 1856, lith. C. 1274, see Hartmann, *Muw.* 246.—2. *Khuṭbat taqlīd*, a comical address on the occasion of a nomination, Berl. $3853_{,2}$.—3. A lascivious sermon, ibid. 3.—4. *Maqāmāt al-ʿushshāq* Paris $3947_{,1}$, AS $3843_{,3}$ (not identical with the anonymous *M. al-ʿu.*, Top Kapu 2402, see Suppl.), of which the first *Faṣāḥat al-masbūq fī malāḥat al-maʿshūq* is preserved in Berl. $8594_{,4}$, and *al-Maqāma al-Hītiyya wal-Shīrāziyya*, of lascivious content, ibid. 5.

18. The manuscript Leid. 729 contains poems by men who, around the turn of the eighth century, lived in the Syrian fortress of ʿAjlūn (Abu ʾl-F., *Géogr.* 244), to wit:

| 1. Sharaf al-Dīn Muḥammad b. al-Ṭāʾī al-Ḥāfī, poems in praise of the *qāḍī* 301
Kamāl al-Dīn Abū Ḥafṣ ʿUmar Sharaf al-Dīn Muḥammad, and on the occasion of the death of the latter's brother Aḥmad, who drowned in Rabīʿ I 700/November 1300 in a flood in al-Bāʿūthā, a suburb of ʿAjlūn.

| 2. Yaḥyā b. Khuḍayr b. Sulaymān b. Badr al-Sulamī al-Buṣrāwī, who was 259
born in 645/1247 in Buṣrā and died in 711/1311, three poems in praise of the same Kamāl al-Dīn, when the latter was still *ḥākim* in Adhriʿāt, near Damascus, and other poems.

3. Muḥammad b. Sulaymān, in praise of the same Kamāl al-Dīn, composed in Dhu 'l-Ḥijja 715/1316 in Adhriʿāt.

4. Ẓāfir al-Māridānī, on the same.

5. Saʿd al-Dīn b. al-Mubāriz al-ʿAjlūnī, from 709/1309, on Kamāl al-Dīn and ʿAlāʾ al-Dīn b. Ghānim.

D *Arabian Poets*

While Najd, once the cradle of Arab poetry, continued to be excluded from all literary development, it did receive some attention in Mecca and Bahrain during this period, but principally in Yemen.

1. Around the year 450/1085, ʿAbd al-Raḥīm b. Aḥmad al-Burāʿī al-Yamanī flourished in South Arabia.

Dīwān, mostly of religious and mystical content, which according to J. Hell also contains some *muwashshaḥāt*, Berl. 7616/7, Gotha 2239, Paris 3113/5, 4721, Ind. Off,. 827, Esc. ^{1}338, ʿUm. 5468, Patna I, $197_{,1768}$, lith. C. 1283, 1288, print. 1280, 1297, 1310, 1319. Individual *qaṣīdas* Berl. 7618, Gotha 2201, 2205, Br. Mus. Suppl. $1215_{,7}$, Ind. Off. 827, Paris $3156_{,2}$.

2. The Sufi poet Abu 'l-Ḥasan Aḥmad b. Khumārṭāsh b. Abī Bakr b. Muḥammad b. al-Nuʿmān al-Ḥimyarī was a contemporary of ʿAlī b. Mahdī, who seized power in Zabīd in 554/1159, and who died in that very same year.[1]

Al-Khumārṭāshiyya, a Sufi poem, Patna I, $204_{,1820}$, with a commentary by
302 Muḥammad Sulaymān b. Mūsā b. al-Jawn al-Ashʿarī, | d. 652/1254 (Suyūṭī, *Bughya*, 264), composed when he was 18 years old, under the title *al-Riyāḍ fī sharḥ al-Khumārṭāshiyya*, ḤKh ^{1}III, 6708, ^{2}I, 934, Leid. 702.

3. Sometime after 622/1225 Amīn al-Dawla Abu 'l-Ghanāʾim Muslim b. Maḥmūd al-Shayzarī dedicated to al-Malik al-Masʿūd Ṣalāḥ al-Dīn Yūsuf b. al-Malik al-Kāmil, the last of the Ayyūbids in Yemen, who died in Mecca[2] in 626/1229:

Jamharat al-Islām dhāt al-nathr wal-niẓām, a poetical anthology containing only Muslim poets, arranged by subject in 16 chapters, Leid. 480, cf. Rödiger, ZDMG XIV, 481ff., Goldziher, *Abh.* I, 168.

---

1 See Johansen, *Hist. Jemenae* 143.

2 Johansen, *Hist. Jemenae* 154.

4. Muḥammad b. Ḥimyar al-Yamanī, d. 611/1214.

Qaṣīda, in admonition, Berl. 3990.

| 5. ʿAlī b. ʿAbdallāh b. al-Muqarrab b. Manṣūr al-Ibrāhīmī came from the 260
house of the ʿUyūnids, whose forebear Faḍl b. ʿAbdallāh had setted as a vassal of the ʿAbbāsids in Bahrain after the expulsion of the Qarmaṭians. The poet lived there at the court of the latter's great-grandson Muḥammad b. Aḥmad b. Muḥammad b. Faḍl and his son Masʿūd. After he fell out with the latter he left his native country, and Yāqūt met him in 617/1220 in Mosul. He later lived in Baghdad, where he died in 629/1232.

Dīwān, poems in praise of the ʿUyūnids and the caliph al-Nāṣir li-Dīn Allāh (575–622/1170–1225) and Badr al-Dīn Luʾluʾ of Mosul, Berlin 7710/1, Br. Mus. 607, Suppl. 1066, Madr. 215, Garr. 44/5, see de Goeje, *JA* s. IX, v. V, p. 1ff.

6. Al-Qāsim b. ʿAlī b. Hutaymil al-Yamanī al-Mikhlāfī al-Zabīdī, d. 656/1258.

Dīwān Rāmpūr I, 590,$_{129}$, two *qaṣīda*s Berl. 7766,$_{1}$.

| E *Egyptian Poets* 303

The government of the Fāṭimids does not seem to have looked favorably upon literary pursuits. Only from the latter part of their reign have the works of a limited number of poets come down to us. It was not until the Ayyūbids and the Mamlūks, in whose reign the material culture of Egypt reached an exceptional efflorescence, that the art of poetry saw a significant advance as well.

1. Ẓāfir b. al-Qāsim b. Manṣūr Abu ʾl-Qāsim al-Ḥaddād al-Iskandarānī al-Judhāmī lived in Alexandria and died in Muḥarram 529/November 1154 in Cairo.

Dīwān, mostly panegyrics and elegies with brief descriptions, Berl. 7683.

| 2. Naṣrallāh b. ʿAbdallāh b. Makhlūf b. Qalāqis Abu ʾl-Futūḥ al-Iskandarānī 261
was born in Alexandria in Rabīʿ II 532/December 1137. He left his homeland in 563/1168, probably in the wake of the turmoil that brought Ṣalāḥ al-Dīn into the country. He first went to Aden and then to Sicily, where he dedicated his lost work *al-Zahr al-bāsim fī awṣāf Abi ʾl-Qāsim* to the *qāʾid* Abu ʾl-Qāsim b. al-Ḥajar. In the year 565/1169 he went to Yemen where he lived for some time

in Aden with the vizier Abu 'l-Faraj Yāsir b. Abi 'l-Nadā' al-Muḥammadī. During an attempt to return to his native country he was shipwrecked off the island of Nāmūs near Dahlak, forcing him to return to Aden. During his second attempt to make the journey, he died in 567/1171 in the port of ʿAydhāb on the Egyptian Red Sea coast.

Ibn Khall. 733. *Dīwān* Vienna 468, 1, Paris 3139, Pet. AM 297; alphabetically ordered selection of ca. 1850 verses, by Ibn Nubāta, d. 768/1367 (II, 10), ḤKh [1]III, 5204, 6621, 6880, [2]I, 767, 923, Berl. 7694, individual poems, Gotha 26, I, 47a, 94,$_8$, 2211.

304 | 3. Al-Qāḍī al-Saʿīd ʿIzz al-Dīn Abu 'l-Qāsim Hibatallāh b. Jaʿfar b. al-Muʿtamad b. Sanā' al-Mulk al-Saʿdī al-Miṣrī, born 545/1150, was *qāḍī* in Cairo and died there in 608/1211.

Ibn Khall. 748, Hartmann, *Muwashshaḥ* 47/55. 1. *Dīwān*, starting with an eulogy on Ṣalāḥ al-Dīn, Bodl. I, 1225,$_2$.—2. *Dār al-ṭirāz*, consisting mostly of *muwashshaḥāt*, Leid. 286, see Hartmann, *Muw.* 95/108.—3. A poem, Berl. 7702, Br. Mus. 630,$_2$.—4. *Fuṣūṣ al-fuṣūl wa-ʿuqūd al-ʿuqūl*, an anthology, in verse and prose, of letters to himself and his father by al-Qāḍī al-Fāḍil ʿAbd al-Raḥīm al-Baysānī (p. 316 n. 1) and his son al-Qāḍī al-Ashraf, Paris 3333, Esc. [2]529.

4. Kamāl al-Dīn Abu 'l-Ḥasan ʿAlī b. Muḥammad b. Yūsuf b. al-Nabīh al-Miṣrī was court poet to several Ayyūbid rulers. It seems his last post was in Naṣībīn, as the secretary to al-Malik al-Ashraf Mūsā (607–28/1210–30), where he died in 619/1222.

262 | *Fawāt* II, 71. *Dīwān*, mostly eulogies on the caliph al-Nāṣir li-Dīn Allāh (575–622/1180–1225), from which *al-Khalīfatiyyāt*, and on the first Ayyūbids, especially al-Malik al-ʿĀdil Abū Bakr b. Ayyūb (596–615/1199–1218) from which *al-ʿĀdiliyyāt*, Berl. 7704/8, Brill M. 225 (=Daḥdāḥ 205), BDMG 107, Gotha 2261, Br. Mus. 608, Suppl. 1067,$_2$, Bodl. I, 1297, II, p. 618, Copenhagen 267, Esc. [2]344, another recension ibid. 345,$_1$, As 3877 (*riwāya* of his grandson ʿAlī), print. Beirut 1299, C. 1280, 1313; a poem with translation in Carlyle, *Specimens of Arab. Poetry*, 2nd ed. London 1810, p. 68, 139.

5. Majd al-Mulk Abu 'l-Faḍl Jaʿfar b. Shams al-Khilāfa Abū ʿAbdallāh Muḥammad b. Shams al-Khilāfa Mukhtār, born in 543/1148, had, as a client of the Egyptian vizier Amīr al-Juyūsh al-Afḍal, the *nisba* al-Afḍalī. He died in 622/1225.

Ibn Khall. 135, Wüst., *Gesch.* 307. 1. *Dīwān* ḤKh ^{1}III, $258,_{5258}$, ^{2}I, 773.—2. *Kitāb al-ādāb al-nāfiʿa bil-alfāẓ al-mukhtāra al-jāmiʿa* or *Abyāt al-ādāb* Leid. 478, Br. Mus. Suppl. 1111, Garr. 205, Alex. Adab 98.—3. Poetical | anthology, ordered by 305
subject in 11 chapters, Esc.^{2} ^{2}360, fragm. ibid. 782, Br. Mus. 1095.

6. Sharaf al-Dīn Abu ʾl-Qāsim ʿUmar b. al-Fāriḍ, born in Cairo on 2 Dhu ʾl-Qaʿda 577/12 March 1182, lived for a time in Mecca, and died in Cairo in 632/1235. His poetry, which he put entirely in the service of mysticism, eschewed all artificiality, thus invigorating worldly poetry as well. As a spiritual poet he remained an unrivalled ideal.

Nallino, *Raccolta di scritti* II, 191ff. *Dīwān*, arranged by his grandson ʿAlī around 730/1329, Berl. 7713/7, Gotha 2262/5 (where other MSS are listed), Vienna 471, Leid. 678/84, Paris 3143/56, Algiers $1838,_2$, Garr. 46/9, AS 1787/8, 4302, Fātiḥ 3766/9, NO 3861/3, Qawala II, 192, Patna I, $196,_{1761}$, print. with comm. Beirut 1887, 1891, 1895.—Commentaries: 1. His nephew, see Suppl.—1a. ʿAlawān al-Ḥamawī, d. 936/1527, see II, 333, Leipz. 535.—2. Badr al-Dīn al-Ḥasan al-Būrīnī, d. 1024/1615 (II, 292), Berl. 7718/9, Leipz. 536, Munich 521/2, Leid. 686, Paris 3157/8, 5088, 5906, Bodl. I, 1233, Garr. 50, Mosul $140,_5$, $123,_{38}$, $172,_{11}$, $229,_{26}$, Patna I, $201,_{1793}$.—3. *al-Zuhūr* (*azhār*) *al-saniyya fi ʾl-quṣud al-Fāriḍiyya* by Muḥammad b. Taqī al-Dīn al-Zuhayrī, d. 1070/1665, see Berl. 7725, Leipz. 537. anon. fragm. Cairo ^{1}IV, 268.—4. ʿAbd al-Ghanī al-Nābulusī, d. 1143/1730 (II, 345), composed in 1086/1675, with special regard for Sufism, lacking in al-Būrīnī, Berl. 7720, Brill M. 259, Paris 3159/62, Br. Mus. 611/2, 1075/6, Alex. Adab 114 (*Kashf asrār al-ghāmiḍ*), Mosul $189,_2$, together with no. 2 printed in Marseille 1853, Būlāq 1289, 1306, new recension by Rushayyid al-Daḥdāḥ (II, 769) C. 1306, 1310, 1319/20.—5. anon. Mosul $49,_{40}$, lith. C. 1313 (*Hesp.* III, $122,_{1014}$).

Individual poems with commentaries: 1. *al-Tāʾiyya al-kubrā* in 756 verses Vienna 472, Br. Mus. $888,_{12}$, AS 1994, Rāġib $1448,_2$, Köpr. 1620, Alex. Adab $122,_{10}$. *Das arabische Hohe Lied der Liebe d. i. Ibn al Fárids Táíjet in Text und Übers. hsg. v.* J. v. Hammer-Purgstall, Vienna 1854.—Commentaries: a. Ibn al-ʿArabī, d. 638/1240 (p. 441), Yeni 708.—b. *Muntaha ʾl-madārik* by Saʿīd b. ʿAbdallāh al-Farghānī, a student of al-Qūnawī (p. 449), d. ca. 700/1300, Persian original *Mashāriq al-darāri ʾl-zuhr fī kashf ḥaqāʾiq Naẓm al-durr* AS 1907/8, 4076, ʿĀšir I,
470, Ayyūb Jāmiʿ 179, Arab. transl. Gotha 2267, Br. Mus. | 861, $888,_{12}$, Ind. Off. 814, 306
Yeni 806/7, Bursa Orkhan Taş. 38, Patna I, $143,_{1385}$.—c. *Kashf al-wujūh al-ghurr li-maʿānī Naẓm al-durr* by al-Kāshī (Kāshānī), mostly understood as referring to the famous Sufi ʿAbd al-Razzāq b. Abi ʾl-Ghanāʾim, d. after 730/1330 (II, 204), as in Berl. 7727/8, Asʿad 3781, Vienna 474 (however see Flügel I, 463 n. 2) and

the printed edition C. 1310 (Macdonald, EI I, 65) and in the margin of Daḥdāḥ's commentary (see above), C. 1319/20 (see Qawala II, 210), while others point to ʿIzz al-Dīn Maḥmūd, d. 735/1334, see Leid. 694/5, Munich 523, Paris 3163.—d. Dāʾūd b. Maḥmūd al-Qayṣarī, d. 751/1350 (II, 231), Berl. 7729, Leid. 696, Upps. 141, Bodl. I, 1205, 1230, Garr. 2005$_{,5}$, Halet 304, Alex. Adab 84, Mosul 263$_{,8,\,1}$.—e. Jāmī, d. 898/1492 (II, 207), Leipz. 539.—f. *Madad al-fāʾiḍ wa-kashf al-ʿāriḍ* by ʿAlawān b. ʿAlī b. ʿAṭiyya al-Ḥamawī al-Hītī, d. 936/1529 (II, 333), Leid. 697, Bodl. I, 1242, AS 1906, Rāġib 667, Alex. Adab 157, Qawala II, 214.—g. ʿAlī b. al-Maʿarrī b. al-ʿAbbās, Berl. 7730.—h. Muḥammad b. ʿUmar al-ʿAlamī, d. 1038/1628 (II, 341), Leipz. 540.—i. ʿAllāma al-Ṭībī (II, 64?), Alex. Adab 135$_{,2}$.—k. Anon., Berl. 7731/2, Paris 3164, Cairo ^{2}III, 197, Mosul 175$_{,70}$, AS 1903.—Imitation of the *Tāʾiyya* with the same metre and rhyme by ʿĀmir b. ʿĀmir al-Baṣrī, *Dhāt al-anwār*, Berl. Brill M. 131, Vienna 481, Br. Mus. 886$_{,10}$.—2. *al-Tāʾiyya al-ṣughrā* or *Naẓm al-sulūk* Paris 3171$_{,5}$. Commentary by Shams al-Dīn al-Farghānī, Bodl. I, 126$_{,2}$, by Ḥasan b. Muḥammad al-Būrīnī, d. 1024/1615, completed in 1002/1593, Esc. ^{2}420$_{,4}$, by Muḥammad b. Taqī al-Dīn al-Zuhayrī (see 3), Leipz. 537.—3. *al-Dhāliyya*, commentary by Muḥammad b. Abī Bakr b. Muḥammad al-Zuhayrī al-Dimashqī, d. 1076/1665, Berl. 7725.—4. *al-Mīmiyya al-khamriyya* Paris 1932$_{,5}$, Br. Mus. 886$_{,1}$, Alex. Fun. 176$_{,7}$.—Commentaries: a. Dāʾūd b. Muḥammad al-Qayṣarī, d. 751/1350 (II, 231), Gotha 2266, Leipz. 110$_{,10}$, Paris 3165$_{,1}$, Leid. 638/9, Bodl. I, 1233$_{,2}$, AS 4075$_{,2}$, Alex. Adab 84.—b. Aḥmad b. Sulaymān b. Kamālpāshā, d. 940/1533 (II, 449), Berl. 7733, Krafft 179, Esc. ^{2}462$_{,2}$.—c. Muḥammad b. Muḥammad Shams al-Dīn al-Ghamrī (II, 335), completed in 959/1552, Berl. 7735/6, Leipz. 542, Paris 3165$_{,2}$.—d. ʿAbd al-Ghanī al-Nābulūsī (II, 345), Berl. 7737.—e. ʿAlāʾ al-Dīn b. Ṣadaqa, d. 975/1567, Paris 1343$_{,58}$.—f. Anon. ibid. 4, Mosul 89$_{,33,\,2}$.—g. Persian by Jāmī, d. 898/1493, Berl. 7738, Leid. 690/1, Paris 461$_{,4}$, Br. Mus. 886, AS 1904/5, Nafiz 552/3.—h. Turkish by Ismāʿīl b. Aḥmad al-Anqirāwī, d. 1042/1632 (II, 445), Vienna 475$_{,1}$, Leid. 692/3, Halet 221, 1.—i. ʿAbd al-Tawwāb al-Sukkarī al-Qūṣī al-Shāfiʿī, Garr. 53.—k.–n. see Suppl.—*Takhmīs* by ʿAbd al-Qādir b.
307 Maḥmūd al-Qādirī Gotha 39$_{,1}$.—| l. Persian by Sayyid ʿAlī al-Hamadhānī, d. 786/1484, Vienna 1491.—5. *al-Yāʾiyya*, Commentaries: a. al-Suyūṭī, d. 911/1505, Pet. Rosen 222$_{,2}$, Garr. 52.—b. Muḥammad b. Muḥammad al-Marṣafī, ca. 963/1556 (II, 335), Berl. 7721/2, Alex. Adab 135$_{,1}$.—c. Muḥammad b. ʿUmar al-ʿAlamī al-Qudsī, d. 1038/1665, Berl. 7724.—d. Muḥammad b. Abī Bakr b. Muḥammad al-Zuhayrī al-Dimashqī, d. 1076/1665, Berl. 7725.—e. Jamāl al-Dīn b. Ḥasan Layya, Esc. ^{2}462$_{,1}$.—f. *Manẓūmat al-alghāz*, a commentary by Ḥusayn al-Khabbī, Berl. 7739, by al-Nābulusī ibid. 7740.—The poet's orthodoxy was questioned by Ibrāhīm b. ʿUmar al-Biqāʿī (II, 142) in *Kitāb al-nāṭiq bil-ṣawāb al-fāriḍ li-takfīr b. al-Fāriḍ*, Leid. 2040, Bodl. I, 158$_{,2}$.

7. Yaḥyā b. ʿĪsā b. Ibrāhīm al-Miṣrī Jamāl al-Dīn Abu ʾl-Ḥusayn b. Maṭrūḥ, d. 649/1251, see Suppl.

Dīwān, collected by some unidentified friends of the poet, ḤKh ^{1}III, 5214, ^{2}I, 768, Berl. 7754/5, Br. Mus. Suppl. 1073, Köpr. 1266 (*MSOS* XIV, 12), print. Istanbul 1298 (following the *dīwān* of ʿAbbās b. al-Aḥnaf); a poem Br. Mus. 630,$_2$.

8. In the year 651/1253 an anonymous author composed for al-Malik al-Mughīth, *walī amīr al-muʾminīn* of the Ayyūbids:

Nuzhat al-ʿāshiq wa-uns al-mutayyam al-wāmiq, a poetical anthology, Esc. ^{2}391.

9. Sayf al-Dīn ʿAlī b. al-Amīr Sābiq al-Dīn ʿUmar b. Qizil al-Mushidd al-Turkumānī
al-Yārūqī, born in Cairo in 602/1205, | was employed for a time in the *dīwān* of 264
al-Malik al-Nāṣir Yūsuf (634–58/1236–60) in Damascus. He died in 656/1258.

Fawāt II, 63. *Dīwān* Esc. ^{2}342,$_3$, Br. Mus. Suppl. 1077 (which has al-Bārūqī).

10. Abu ʾl-Fatḥ Zuhayr b. Muḥammad al-Muhallabī al-ʿĀfikī Bahāʾ al-Dīn al-Kātib was a court poet of the Ayyūbids of Egypt and died in 656/1258 (see Suppl.).

| Muṣṭafā ʿAbd al-Razzāq, *al-Bahāʾ Zuhayr: Baḥth*, C. n.d., *Dīwān*, collected 308
by the poet himself, Berl. 7762/6, Gotha 2271, Br. Mus. 1669; other collections Leid. 704, Paris 3173, Bodl. I, 1272, 1278, II, 380, Ind. Off. 4633 (*JRAS* 1939, 396), Copenhagen 270, Upps. 143, Esc. ^{2}477, Algiers 1821/2, AS 3885, 3920. *The Poetical Works of B.Z. of Egypt with metrical English Translation, Notes and Introduction by* E.H. Palmer, Cambridge 1876; cf. St. Guyard, *Variantes au texte arabe, etc.* Paris 1883. *Dīwān* C. 1278, 1305, 1311, 1314, 1322, 1934.

11. Aḥmad b. Muḥammad b. Aḥmad Abu ʾl-ʿAbbās al-Andalusī al-Ishbīlī Zayn al-Dīn Katākit al-Miṣrī al-Wāʿiẓ al-Muqriʾ, whose family came from Seville, was born in 605/1208 and died in Cairo in 684/1285.

Maqqarī I, 811, poems Gotha 2196,$_5$.

12. Muḥammad b. ʿAbd al-Munʿim b. Muḥammad al-Anṣārī al-Yamanī al-Miṣrī b. al-Khiyāmī, d. 685/1286, see Suppl.

A *qaṣīda*, Berl. 7782,$_3$.

13. Ḥasan b. Sāwar b. Ṭarkhān b. al-Naqīb Nāṣir al-Dīn, who died in Cairo in 687/1288.

Fawāt I, 118 mentions a *Dīwān maqāṭīʿ*. A poem in Br. Mus. $630_{,2}$. In NO 4280 he is credited with a *Kitāb manāzil al-aḥbāb wa-manāzih al-albāb*, but see II, 55.

14. Sharaf al-Dīn Abū ʿAbdallāh (Abū ʿAlī) Muḥammad b. Saʿīd al-Dilāṣī al-Būṣīrī al-Ṣanhājī, who was born in 608/1211 and became famous for his songs in praise of the Prophet, died in 694/1294 (see Suppl.).

I. *al-Kawākib al-durriyya fī madḥ khayr al-bariyya*, a counterpart to the poem entitled *Qaṣīdat al-burda* by Kaʿb b. Zuhayr, cf. Goldziher, *RHR* XXXI, 304ff. *Carmen mysticum Borda dictum Abi Abdallah M.B.S. Busiridae Aegyptii e cod. msto Bibl. Lugd. Bat. lat. conversum, accedunt origines arabico-hebraicae, paravit et ed.* J. Uri, Leid. 1761, Utrecht 1771. *K. al-d. fī m. kh. al-b. Funkelnde Wandelsterne zum Lobe des Besten der Geschöpfe, ein arabisches, insgemein unter dem Namen*
309 Qaṣīde i Burda, *Gedicht Burda, bekanntes Gedicht von Scheich Ebu Abdallah* | *M. b. Ssaid b. Hammad Muhsin b. Abdallah b. Ssanhadsch b. Hilal is-Ssanhadschi,*
265 *genannt Busiri, übers. und durch Anmm. erläutert v.* | V. Edlem v. Rosenzweig, Vienna 1824. With a Tatar introduction and translation, Kazan 1847. *Die Burda, ein Lobgedicht auf M. von al-Busiri, neu hsg. im ar. Text mit metrischer pers.-türk. Übers. ins Deutsche übertragen und mit Anmm. versehn von* C.A. Ralfs, *bevorwortet v.* W. Behrnauer, Vienna 1860. With a French translation by J.B. Albengo, Jerusalem 1872. *The Poem of the Scarf with an Engl. Version and Notes by* Shaikh Faizullabhai Shaikh Lookmanji, Bombay 1893. *La Borda du Cheikh el Bousiri, poème en ʾl-honneur de M. trad. et commenté par* R. Basset (Bibl. or. Elzev. XXIX), Paris 1894.

Commentaries: 1. Aḥmad b. Ismāʿīl Abū Shāma, d. 665/1268 (p. 317), Munich 547, Paris $1620_{,3}$, Alex. Adab $135_{,3}$, II, 201.—2. ʿUmar. b. ʿAbd al-Raḥmān al-Fārisī, d. 745/1244, Pet. AMK 924.—3. Abū ʿUthmān Saʿīd b. Yūsuf al-Ilbīrī, ca. 751/1350 in Granada, Esc. ^{2}282/3 (which has Abū ʿAbdallāh), 318, Fez Qar. 743.—4. Abu ʾl-ʿAbbās Aḥmad b. Muḥammad b. ʿAbd al-Raḥmān al-Azdī al-Qaṣṣār al-Tūnisī, d. after 765/1364, ḤKh IV, 529, Leid. 713, Algiers 1844, Garr. 64.—5. Shihāb al-Dīn Abu ʾl-ʿAbbās Aḥmad b. Yaḥyā b. Abī Ḥajala al-Tilimsānī, d. 776/1374 (II, 12), Esc. ^{2}413.—6. *al-Raqm* by Shams al-Dīn Muḥammad b. ʿAbd al-Raḥmān al-Zumurrudhī b. al-Ṣāʾigh, d. 776/1375 (II, 25), Leipz. 548, Cairo ^{2}III, 171, on which glosses Vienna 478.—7. *Ṭīb al-ḥabīb fī sharḥ qaṣīdat al-ḥabīb* by Shams al-Dīn Muḥammad b. Marzūq al-Tilimsānī, d. 781/1379, Berl. 7788, Cambr. 57, Köpr. 1306.—8. Saʿd al-Dīn al-Taftāzānī, d. 791/1389 (II, 215), Qilič ʿA. 813.—9.

Jalāl al-Dīn al-Khujandī, d. 802/1399, Leid. 718, Paris 3189, Garr. 66.—10. *Washy al-Burda* by Zayn al-Dīn Abu 'l-Muẓaffar Ṭāhir b. Ḥasan b. ʿUmar b. Ḥabīb al-Ḥalabī, d. 808/1405, Alex. Adab 186.—11. Shihāb al-Dīn Abu 'l-ʿAbbās Aḥmad b. ʿImād al-Dīn ʿAbd al-Bāqī al-Aqfahsī, d. 808/1405 (II, 93), Cairo ^{2}III, 213, Alex. Adab 84.—11a. Aḥmad b. ʿUmar al-Dawlatābādī, d. 814/1445 (II, 220), Patna I, $201,_{1796}$.—12. *Nuzhat al-ṭālibīn wa-tuḥfat al-rāghibīn* by Aḥmad b. Muḥammad b. Abī Bakr al-Shīrāzī (author of the *Kitāb al-ṣafāʾ fī muʿāmalat ahl al-wafāʾ*, Esc. ^{2}II, 749, which has Abu 'l-ʿAbbās Aḥmad al-Shīrāzī), composed in 809/1407 (in ḤKh IV, 530, mistakenly split into two), Hamb. 92, Leid. 717, Paris 3190, Pet. AMK 924, Cairo ^{2}IV, 83 (Abū Shāma?), Mosul $99,_{10}$ (? which has Muhammad b. Aḥmad b. Muḥammad b. Abī Bakr), Mashh. XV, $43,_{126/7}$, Rāmpūr I, $600,_{219}$.—13. Yūsuf al-Bisāṭī, composed in 821/1418, Cairo ^{2}III, 214.—14. *al-Anwār* | *al-muḍīʾa* 310
by Muḥammad b. Aḥmad al-Maḥallī, d. 864/1459 (II, 114), Berl. 7790, Brill, M. 183, Paris 3191, Esc. $^{2}487,_{1}$, Vat. V. 1421, Pet. Ros. 108, Cairo ^{2}III, 20, Alex. Adab 84, $125,_{1}$, 144, Fun. $154,_{2}$, Dam. Z. 62, $186,_{1}$, Āṣaf. III, $242,_{45}$, fragm. Ambr. C. 21, iv (*RSO* VII, 51), glosses by Muḥammad ʿArafa al-Dasūqī, Cairo ^{2}IV, b, 44.—15. ʿAlī b. Muḥammad Muṣannifak al-Bisṭāmī, d. 875/1470 (II, 234), Dresd. 219, Leid. 716, Garr. 67, Pet. Amk 924, Qilič ʿA. 813, Selīm Āġā 965, Cairo ^{2}III, 214.—16. Khālid b. ʿAbdallāh al-Azharī, d. 905/1499 (II, 27), Berl. 7791, Munich 546, Paris $714,_{7}$, 3192, Br. Mus. 619/20, Suppl. 1087, i, Ind. Off. 822, Esc. $^{2}304,_{2}$, Algiers $1853,_{2}$, Vat. V, $571,_{2}$, Pet. AMBuch. 147, AS 4059, Qilič ʿA. 809, Rabat 493, *Hespéris* XII, $133,_{105b}$, Cairo ^{2}III, 203, Sbath 14b, Mosul $140,_{4}$, 229, Qawala II, 197, Alex. Adab 83, Āṣaf. II, $1714,_{9,\ 5}$, Patna I, $281,_{1797}$, II, $427,_{2601,\ 2}$, print. C. 1282, 1286, Būlāq 1297, Alexandria 1288, in the margin of al-Bājūrī's (II, 487) *Ḥāshiya*, Būlāq 1302, C. 1304, 1308, 1311.—17. *Mashāriq al-anwār al-muḍīʾa* by Aḥmad b. Muḥammad al-Qasṭallānī, d. 923/1517 (II, 73), Berl. 7792, Leid. 720, Garr. 68, Alex. Adab 160, Cairo ^{2}III, 356, IVb, 79.—18. *al-Zubda al-rāʾiqa* by Zakariyyāʾ b. Muḥammad al-Anṣārī, d. 926/1520 (II, 99), Alex. Adab 76, Cairo ^{2}III, 178.—19. Khiḍr b. Maḥmūd al-ʿAṭūfī, d. 948/1541 (*ShN* II, 110, Rescher 268, Brussali M. Ṭāhir, *ʿOthm. Müʾell.* I, 355) written in 40 days and dedicated to the sultan Süleymān, Pet. Ros. $218,_{2}$, AS 4079, Alex. Adab 82.—20. *Rāḥat al-arwāḥ* by Muḥammad b. Muṣṭafā Shaykhzāde al-Qūjawī, d. 951/1544, Berl. 7793, Copenhagen 272, Leid. 715, Paris 3198, Esc. ^{2}316, Bol. 117, $248,_{3}$, $254,_{1}$, Pet. AMK 924, Qilič ʿA. 810, Alex. Adab 83, Fun. $176,_{1}$, Cairo ^{2}III, 3 29, 156, printed in the margin of the commentary by Kharpūtī (no. 49) Istanbul 1306.—21. Muḥammad b. Muḥammad al-Ghazzī al-ʿĀmirī, d. 984/1576, Br. Mus. 621, Garr. $2002,_{10}$.—22. Ḥasan b. al-Ḥusayn al-Tālishī, d. 956/1549 in Cairo, Vienna 479.—23. Muḥammad b. Ḥasan al-Qudsī al-Baramūnī, ca. 990/1582, Berl. 7796, Paris 3193.—24. Muḥammad b. Badr al-Dīn al-Āqḥiṣārī, d. 1001/1593 (II, $439,_{5}$), completed in 998/1590 in Damascus,

Berl. 7798, Cairo ^{2}III, 214.—25. *al-Zubda* by ʿAlī b. Muḥammad al-Qāriʾ
al-Harawī, d. 1014/1605 (II, 394), Paris 2151,$_2$, Manch. 470D, Pet. AM Buch. 148,
Qilič ʿA. 804, Sulaim. 1040,$_2$, Alex. Adab 141, Cairo ^{2}III, 214.—26. Muḥammad b.
ʿAlī al-Bālī Shams al-Dīn 10, d. 1024/1615, Berl. 7799.—27. Muḥammad b. Yūsuf
b. Abi ʾl-Luṭf al-Qudsī Raḍī al-Dīn, d. 1028/1619, Berl. 7800, Qilič ʿA. 814 (? Only
311 | Raḍī al-Dīn).—28. *Shifāʾ al-qalb al-jarīḥ* by ʿAbd al-Wāḥid b. Aḥmad b. ʿĀshir
al-Anṣārī, d. 1040/1630 (Suppl. II, 699), C. 1296.—29. Abu ʾl-Baqāʾ Ayyūb b. Mūsā
al-Ḥusaynī al-Kaffawī, d. 1094/1683 (II, 454), Berl. 7801.—30. Baḥr b. Raʾīs b.
Ṣalāḥ al-Hārūnī al-Mālikī, Gotha 2292, Dam. Z. 74,$_{59}$.—31. An otherwise unidentified “al-Imām al-Ḥanbalī” excerpts Esc. ^{2}390,$_2$.—32. Muḥammad b. ʿAbd
al-Ḥaqq al-Sabtī, Munich 807, Pet. AMK 924.—33. ʿAlī b. Ibrāhīm b. Idrīs
al-Anṭākī, kabbalistic-magical, Paris 3187.—34. *al-Durra al-muḍīʾa* by
Muḥammad b. Abī Bakr b. Muḥammad b. Sulaymān al-Kurdī (Karrārī?)
al-Sahranī al-Ḥanafī, completed in 1048/1673 at the al-Azhar, Alex. Adab 42,
Cairo ^{2}III, 100.—35. *al-Durra al-farīda* by Muḥammad al-Shāfiʿī al-ʿInānī,
d. 1098/1687, Alex. Adab 42.—36.–39. see Suppl. 32–34.—39. *Zubdat al-qirā* by
ʿUthmān b. ʿAbdallāh al-Killisī al-ʿUryānī al-Ḥalabī, in Medina around 1163/1750,
Cairo ^{2}III, 178, Qawala II, 195.—40.–48. see Suppl. 36.–42.—49. *ʿAṣīdat al-
shahda* by ʿUmar b. Aḥmad al-Kharpūtī, composed in 1241/1825, Selīm Āġā 816,
Alex. Adab 100, Qawala II, 205, print. Istanbul 1289, 1292, 1298, 1317, 1320, Būlāq
1291.—50.–61. see Suppl. 44–55.—62. Muḥammad b. Saʿd al-Ālānī, MS of
1169/1750, Alex. Adab 83.—63. *al-Barz al-lamīḥ* by ʿAbd al-Ḥaqq b. al-Ḥusayn
al-Ḥajjājī, ibid. 18.—64. *al-ʿUmda*, by Ismāʿīl b. ʿUthmān b. Abī Bakr b. Yūsuf
al-Niyāzī (to be read thus, see Suppl. II, 657g), Qawala II, 206.—65. *al-Nafaḥāt
al-Shādhiliyya fī sharḥ al-burda al-Būṣīriyya* by Shaykh Ḥasan al-ʿIdwī
al-Ḥamzawī, d. 1303/1885 (II, 486), C. 1297.—67. Anon. Berl. 7789, ,95, 7802/3,
Leipz. 549, Paris 3194.—67. Persian by Yūsuf b. Muḥammad b. Shihāb al-Jāmī
Yūsuf Ahlī of Herat, who, in his preface, praises the Tīmūrid Abū Saʿīd (861–
266 73/1457–68), | Leid. 721 (autograph dated 863/1459), 722.—67a. Muḥammad
al-Anṣārī, Leipz. 549.—68. Turkish by Aḥmad b. Muṣṭafā, composed in
1001/1592, Krafft 181, Leipz. 434.—69. Turkish by Saʿdallāh al-Ḥulwānī, Qawala I,
247.—70. Turkish by Ḥasan Fehmī, Istanbul 1328.—71. *Khawāṣṣ al-Burda fī burʾ
al-dāʾ* on secret magical manipulations and sympathetic cures for which the
verses of the *Burda* can be used, by ʿAbd al-Salām b. Idrīs al-Marrākushī, d.
660/1262, Berl. 7823, Gotha 81,$_2$, in another recension ibid. 2292, Vat. V. Barb.
78,$_8$.—72. *Risāla fī khawāṣṣ al-Kawākib al-durriyya* by Muḥammad b.
Muḥammad b. ʿAbd al-Wāḥid b. ʿAbd al-Raḥīm al-Tamīmī, Qawala I, 236.—73.
Muḥammad b. Bahādur al-Zarkashī (II, 91), Patna I, 196,$_{1756}$.—74. Muḥammad
312 b. ʿAbdallāh b. Maḥmūd, Patna I, 201,$_{1795}$.—Ahlw. 7824 | mentions 31 commen-
taries—Translations: 1. Persian Berl. 7804/6.—2. Turkish paraphrases ibid.

7807/9,: in the same metre and rhyme as the original by Aḥmad Riḍwān, Krafft 182.—Adaptations: 1. *Takhmīs*: a. Muḥammad b. Abī Zayd ʿAbd al-Raḥmān al-Marrākushī, b. 739/1338, Br. Mus. 622,$_{2}$.—b. ʿAbd al-Laṭīf b. Aḥmad al-Shāfiʿī, d. 801/1398, Berl. 7812/3.—c. Saʿbān b. Muḥammad al-Āthārī, d. 828/1425 (II, 180), Leipz. 298, mistakenly attributed to al-Kitnānī by Fleischer, see *Cat. Lugd.* I, ^{2}464 and Suppl. *Ḥall al-ʿuqda fī t. al-B.*, chapter 2 of his *Miftāḥ bāb al-faraj*, Leid. 739, Cairo ^{2}III, 50.—d. Abū Bakr b. Ḥijja al-Ḥamawī, d. 837/1433 (II, 15), Paris 3248,$_{3}$, Cairo ^{2}III, 50,$_{22}$.—e. Muḥammad b. ʿAbdallāh b. Māmāyā b. al-Rūmī, d. 987/1579 (II, 271), Berl. 7817, Cairo ^{2}III, 52,$_{60}$.—f. Ṣadaqatallāh al-Qāhirī, d. 1105/1693, Berl. 7818, printed in Muḥammad b. Abī Bakr al-Baghdādī's (p. 288) *al-Qaṣīda al-witriyya*, Bombay 1884.—g. Muḥammad Khalīl b. al-Qabāqibī, d. 849/1445 (II, 113), Paris 3182, Cairo ^{2}III, 51,$_{50}$.—h. Muḥammad b. Aḥmad b. Abi ʾl-ʿĪd al-Sakhāwī, Paris 3248,$_{2}$, Cairo ^{2}III, 51,$_{48,54}$.—i. Nāṣir al-Dīn Muḥammad b. ʿAbd al-Ṣamad al-Makkī al-Fayyūmī, Berl. 7814, Gotha 2282/3, Br. Mus. 644, 1413, Garr. 2126,$_{1}$ (see Suppl.).—k. Sharīf Efendi, Br. Mus. 622,$_{3}$.—l. ʿAbd al-Raḥmān b. Aḥmad b. Yūsuf b. Maqlalish, ibid. 7.—m. Shams al-Dīn Muḥammad al-Fayyūmī, 8th cent., print. Būlāq 1287, Alex. Adab 130, C. 1308.—n. Abū Bakr b. Ramaḍān b. Mūk, Ind. Off. 1044/5.—o. Anon. Berl. 7815/67, 7819/20, Paris 3183/5, Br. Mus. 162,$_{2}$.—q.–ee. see Suppl. (q. AS 4185,$_{1}$).—ff. ʿUthmān Efendi, C. 1313.—gg. ʿUmar al-Qaṣabī al-Yaqḍī, MS dated 899/1423, Garr. 71.—hh. Muḥammad b. Ibrāhīm, d. after 984/1576, Garr. 70.—ii. ʿUshrī Ismāʿīl b. Darwīsh b. Muṣṭafā b. ʿUthmān b. ʿIwaḍ b. ʿAwīḍa al-Subkī al-Khuṣūṣī, composed in 1038/1628, Alex. Adab 28.—kk. *al-Aflāk al-dawriyya ʿala ʾl-K. al-d.* by ʿIzz al-Dīn Muḥmammad b. ʿAbdallāh al-ʿAlawī al-Yamanī, Alex. Adab 128.—ll. *Anīs al-waḥda fī takhmīs al-B.* by ʿAbbās Efendi Fawzī al-Dāghestānī, Istanbul 1300. 2. *Tasbīʿ:* a. ʿUthmān, after Gotha 2286, or Ṣalāḥ al-Dīn Aḥmad b. Muḥammad al-Sharafī al-Dimashqī, ibid. 2287, according to ḤKh IV, 532/3 and Paris 3186 by Jamāl al-Dīn Muḥammad b. al-Wafāʾ, anon. Br. Mus. 622,$_{4}$, Bodl. II, 315.—b. Muḥammad al-Miṣrī al-Niyāzī, d. 1111/1699 (Suppl. II, 662, Hammer, *Gesch. d. Osm. Dichtk.* III, 587), Gotha 2289, Vienna 1982,$_{6}$, Vat. V, 1430.—c. Anon. C. 1311.—d.—i. see Suppl. (e. Alex. Fun. 88,$_{3}$).—k. Jawīshān Wazīr Miṣr Amīr ʿUthmān Bāb al-Rūmī, Alex. Adab 25.—3. *Tatsīʿ* Anon. Berl. 7821.—4. *Tashṭīr:*[3] | a. ʿUmar b. ʿAbbās al-Qafṣī al-ʿUnnābī, composed in 313
843/1440, Berl. 7810, Br. Mus. 622,$_{5}$, on which again is *Takhmīs ṭayy al-B. wa-talkhīṣ Nashr al-warda* by Muḥammad b. Aḥmad b. Abi ʾl-ʿĪd al-Qaṣabī al-Sakhāwī al-Mālikī, Br. Mus. 622,$_{6}$, Alex. Adab 23.—b. Aḥmad al-Dalanjawī, Paris 3185,$_{2}$.—c.–p. see Suppl.—5. *Tadhyīl*: a. Aḥmad b. ʿAbdallāh al-Zawāwī

3 I.e. the introduction of two half-verses between the first and the second half of each original verse.

al-Jazāʾirī, d. 923/1517, Br Mus. 622.—b. Poetical adaptation with the title
Mufarrij al-shidda taḍmīn al-B. Berl. 7822.—*Khātima taʾrīkhiyya* by Muḥammad
b. al-ʿArabī al-Qaṣṣār, composed in 1300, Alex. Fun. 94/5.

II. *al-Qaṣīda al-hamziyya fi ʾl-madāʾiḥ al-nabawiyya* or *Umm al-qurā fī madḥ
khayr al-warā* Berl. 7826/7, Gotha 22/4, Copenhagen 49$_{,4}$, Leid. 723/4, Paris 3195,
Algiers 824, 1851, Ind. Off. 823, Bodl. I, 850$_{,3}$, 1226$_{,2}$, II, 337$_{,3}$, Garr. 74, Alex. Fun.
175$_{,2}$, print. also C. 1310.—Commentaries: 1. Aḥmad b. Muḥammad al-Ṣāghānī
al-Makkī, d. 824/1419, Berl. 7828.—2. Muḥammad b. ʿAbd al-Munʿim al-Jawjarī,
d. 889/1484 (II, 96), Berl. 7829, Paris 3198$_{,1}$ (see Suppl.).—3. *al-Minaḥ al-Makkiyya* or *Afḍal al-qirā* by Aḥmad b. Muḥammad b. Ḥajar al-Haytamī, d. 973/1565
(II, 397), Berl. 7830/1, Brill M. 185, Leid. 725, Ind. Off. 824/6, Bodl. I, 1226, Paris
3197, Esc. ^{2}315$_{,3}$, Algiers 1852$_{,2}$/3$_{,1}$, Garr. 75, AS 4096, Köpr. p. 160, no. 297, Alex.
Adab 169, Qawala II, 219/20, Tippu 77, 179, Calc. 25, Patna I, 193$_{,1740/1}$, print. C.
267 1303, 1307 (see Suppl.). | Glosses by Muḥammad b. Sālim al-Ḥifnī, d. 1181/1767,
Qawala II, 188, Alex. Adab 14, anon. Patna I, 195$_{,1755}$.—4. Shihāb al-Dīn Aḥmad
b. ʿAbd al-Ḥaqq al-Sunbāṭī, d. 990/1582, Esc. ^{2}317, Garr. 76, Alex. Adab 90.—5.
Muḥammad b. Aḥmad Bannīs, composed in 1200/1796, Cairo ^{2}III, 320, Būlāq
1296, in the margin of *OB* III, 3616.—6.–16. see Suppl. (ad 6. Makr. 32, which has
al-Suʿūdī, ad 13. Qawala II, 212$_{,15}$, Alex. Adab 90).—17. *Taqrīrāt* by Muḥammad
ʿArafa al-Dasūqī, d. 1230/1815, Alex. Adab 137.—18. *Zubdat al-qirā fī sharḥ U.
al-q.* by ʿUthmān b. ʿAlī al-Killīsī al-ʿUryānī, d. 1168/1754 (II, 321), Qawala II,
195.—*Takhmīs*: 1. ʿAbd al-Laṭīf al-Dayrabī al-Azharī b. al-Khaṭīb, ca. 932/1596,
Berl. 7852.—2. Aḥmad b. Muḥammad b. Yūsuf al-Ṣafadī, d. 1034/1624 (II, 288),
Berl. 7853 (see Suppl.).—3. Darwīsh b. ʿUthmān al-ʿUshshāqī, ca. 1125/1713, ibid.
7854.—4. ʿĪsā Abu ʾl-Surūr al-Shaʿrāwī, ca. 1150/1737, ibid. 7856, Garr. 77.—5.
ʿAbd al-Bāqī b. Sulaymān al-Yārūqī, d. 1278/1861 (Suppl. II, 702), C. 1303, 1309,
1316.—6. Anon., Leid. 726, Paris 3196.

III. *Dhukhr al-maʿād ʿalā wazn Bānat Suʿād* or *al-Kalima al-ṭayyiba wal-dīma
314 *al-ṣayyiba*, a poem in praise of the Prophet | based on the example of Kaʿb b.
Zuhayr, Berl. 7838/9, Leid. 727, Br. Mus. 884$_{,4}$, Garr. 77.

IV. *al-Qaṣīda al-khamriyya* Br. Mus. 162$_{,5}$, commentary by Dāʾūd b. Maḥmūd
b. Muḥammad al-Qayṣarī, d. 751/1350 (II, 231), Leipz. 110$_{,10}$.

V. *al-Qaṣīda al-Muḍariyya fi ʾl-ṣalāt ʿalā khayr al-bariyya* Berl. 7840/1, Munich
593, f. 48b, Heid. *ZDMG* 91, 386 AS 4082$_{,2}$, Alex. Fun. 147$_{,13}$, 175$_{,3}$, 182$_{,2}$, Qawala
II, 209.—Commentaries: 1. ʿAbd al-Ghanī al-Nābulusī, d. 1143/1730 (II, 345),
Berl. 7842, Garr. 78, Alex. Adab 141.—2. Turkish Berl. 7843.—*Takhmīs* by Ibn
al-Muqriʾ, d. 837/1433 (II, 190), Berl. 7844, Gotha 2213, by al-Ziyādī, Alex. Fun.
173$_{,6}$, others Br. Mus. 840, 956, 959/60.

VI. *al-Tawassul bil-Qurʾān*, prayer featuring all the suras after their titles, effective in the punishment or destruction of anyone at whose hands one was wronged, Berl. $3645_{,2}$.

VII. *al-Yāʾiyya* see Suppl. with a commentary by al-Ḥasan b. Muḥammad al-Būrīnī, d. 1024/1615 (II, 290), also Alex. Adab 90.

VIII.–X. see Suppl. (IX. *Takhmīs*, print. C. 1313).

15. Abū Ḥafṣ ʿUmar b. Muḥammad b. al-Ḥasan al-Warrāq al-Miṣrī al-Fāʾizī Sirāj al-Dīn, who was born in 615/1218 and died in 695/1296, was an unusually productive poet.

Fawāt II, 107, Suyūṭī, *Bughya* $363_{,15}$. From his 30-volume *dīwān*, ḤKh ^{1}III, 5457, ^{2}I, 792, he first made himself a selection in 7 hefty volumes; from this Khalīl al-Ṣafadī, d. 764/1362 (II, 31), selected the *Lumaʿ al-sirāj*, Berl. 7785. *Naẓm durrat al-ghawwāṣ*, see Suppl. I, $488_{,vi}$.

F North African and Sicilian Poets

1. Abū Isḥāq Ibrāhīm b. ʿAlī b. Tamīm al-Khuṣrī was born in Kairouan and died after 413/1022 in al-Manṣūra.

Ibn Khall. 15. 1. *Kitāb zahr al-ādāb wa-thamar al-albāb*, an anthology which, around 450/1058, he dedicated to Abu ʾl-Faḍl al-ʿAbbās b. Sulaymān, who had travelled to the East in order to buy books. This work could replace all the others, according to a report by al-Rashīd b. al-Zubayr in the biography following the preface of his *Kitāb al-Jinān*, vol. 1, | Leid. 462, Bodl. I, 386, Esc. $^{2}392_{,3}$, 315
Garr. 189, Köpr. 1281, AS 4028 (vol. 4, 596 AH), Patna I, $197_{,1783/4}$, printed in the margin of the *ʿIqd*, Būlāq 1302.—*Dhayl z. al-a. aw jamʿ al-jawāhir fī ʾl-mulaḥ wal-nawādir,* C. al-Maṭbaʿa al-Raḥmāniyya, n.d.—2. *Kitāb al-maṣūn fī sirr al-hawā wal-maknūn*, similar to the first but in only one volume, ḤKh, V, $589_{,12205}$, Leid. 463.—| 3. *Kitāb nūr al-ṭarf wa-nawr al-ẓarf*, a concise poetical anthology, Gotha 268
2129, Esc. $^{2}392_{,1}$.—4. Poem on Kairouan, Esc. $^{2}408_{,2}$.—5. *al-Muʿashsharāt*, Cairo ^{1}VII, 110.

2. Al-Muʿizz b. Bādis, of the North African Zīrid dynasty, who was born in al-Manṣūriyya in 398/1007, came to power in al-Muḥammadiyya in 406/1015. In 440/1048 he dissociated himself from his suzerains, the Fāṭimids, whom his ancestors had recognised up to that point, proclaiming the caliph al-Qāʾim bi-Amrillāh in the *khuṭba* instead. He died in 453/1061.

Ibn Khall. no. 761, Ibn Khaldūn, *Hist. des Berb.* trad. I, 30ff., II, 18ff. see Suppl.

3. Abū ʿAbdallāh Muḥammad b. Abī Saʿīd Muḥammad b. Sharaf al-Qayrawānī al-Judhāmī, d. 460/1048, see Suppl.

Fawāt II, 204, *Maqāma* on the most famous poets, Esc. $^2536_{,3}$.

4. Abū ʿAbdallāh Muḥammad b. Abī Bakr b. Yaḥyā b.[1] ʿAlī al-Shaqrāṭisī, d. 466/1073, see Suppl.

1. Poems with anon. commentary, composed in 622/1225, probably in Spain, Esc. $^2321_{,1}$.—2. *Qaṣīda lāmiyya*, in praise of the Prophet, Algiers $1735_{,2}$, Garr. 30. Commentaries: a. Abū Shāma, d. 665/1268, see Suppl. I, $530_{,4,3}$.—b. Abū ʿAbdallāh Muḥammad b. ʿAlī al-Tawzarī (2nd half 7th cent.), Br. Mus. 1406, 405b.—c. An abstract of this by Abū ʿAbdallāh Muḥammad al-Maḥjūb, Algiers $1833_{,1}$.—d. Anon., ibid. 1834.—*Takhmīs*: a. al-Tawzarī with a commentary, ibid. $1835_{,2}$.—b. Aḥmad b. Muḥammad al-Marrākushī, Br. Mus. $888_{,11}$.—c. Muḥammad b. Ibrāhīm b. Muḥammad b. ʿAbd al-Sattār al-Tamīmī, AS $4033_{,3}$. f. 164b, 180a.

316 | 5. Abu ʾl-Faḍl Yūsuf b. Muḥammad b. Yūsuf b. al-Naḥwī al-Tawzarī, who was born around 453/1041, died in 505/1113 (according to others in 513/1119).

Hartmann, *Muwashshaḥ* 22, no. 2. 1. *Waṣiyya* Berl. 3981.—2. *al-Qaṣīda al-munfarija* or *al-Faraj baʿd al-shidda*,[2] ascribed by some to al-Ghazzālī and by others to Abū ʿAbdallāh Muḥammad b. Aḥmad b. Ibrāhīm al-Andalusī al-Qurayshī, d. 590/1194, Gotha $1539_{,1}$ (where other MSS are listed, in addition:), Berl. 7636/7, Paris $743_{,14}$, $3198_{,3}$, AS 4182, Alex. Fun. $176_{,4}$, $187_{,3}$ Qawala II,
269 220.—| Commentaries: a. Abu ʾl-ʿAbbās Aḥmad b. Abī Zayd ʿAbd al-Raḥmān al-Naqāwusī al-Bijāʾī, d. 810/1403, Berl. Brill M. 226 (= Daḥdāḥ), Esc. ^{2440}, Qawala II, 188, whence the biography of the poet, Berl. 7635.—b. Abū Yaḥyā Zakariyyāʾ al-Anṣārī, d. 926/1520 (II, 99), completed in 881/1477, Berl. 7638/9, Leid. 672, Bodl. I, $1274_{,2}$, II, 617, Esc. ^{2441}, 521, Algiers 1854/5, Garr. 32/3, $2003_{,21}$, Alex. Fun. $174_{,8}$, $177_{,1}$, but $173_{,11}$, $176_{,3}$, $187_{,1}$, under the title *Mufarrij al-karab*.—c. Muḥammad b. al-Kannān, d. 1153/1740, Berl. 7647/8.—d. ʿAlī b. Yūsuf al-Buṣrawī, Paris $4118_{,2}$, Esc. $^2521_{,2}$, Rabat 90, $530_{,1}$ (al-Būṣīrī).—e. Turkish by Ismāʿīl b. Aḥmad al-Anqirawī, d. 1025/1616 (II, 445), Vienna $475_{,2}$, AS 2077, print.

1 According to ḤKh IV, $540_{,9469}$ and Br. Mus. $265_{,2}$, 405: Abū Muḥammad ʿAbdallāh b. Yaḥyā.

2 According to ḤKh IV, $551_{,9508}$ it was composed in gratitude for the fact that some potentate had restored robbed items to him following a dream; for this reason it is considered effective as a prayer.

Būlāq 1300, Turkish translation AS $2077_{,2}$.—Ahlw. 7645 mentions 6 commentaries.—*Tashṭīr*, by Abu 'l-Faḍl Muḥammad b. Aḥmad b. Ayyūb al-Dimashqī al-Shāfiʿī al-Mahdī, d. 905/1499, ḤKh IV, 553 (= Suppl. III, 1258, ad 153?) Berl. 7463.—*Takhmīs*: a. Ibn Mulayk (II, 20) d. 917/1511, Berl. 7640, Alex. Fun. $187_{,2}$.—b. Aḥmad b. ʿĀmir b. ʿAbd al-Wahhāb al-Taʿizzī, Bod. 7641.—c. Anon. Paris $3118_{,1}$.—d. 8 *takhmīs*, collected by Salām b. ʿUmar al-Mazzāḥī under the title *al-Laʾāliʾ al-mubahrija fī takhmīs al-Munfarija*, Berl. 7642.—e.–g. see Suppl.—h. ʿUmar al-Qawsī al-Qurayshī, Garr. $2003_{,9}$.—Imitations: a. Muṣṭafā b. Kamāl al-Dīn al-Ṣiddīqī al-Bakrī, d. 1162/1749, Berl. 7651/2.—b. ʿAbd al-Ghanī al-Nābulusī, d. 1143/1730 (II, 348), ibid. $7654_{,1}$.—c. Anon. ibid. $7554_{,2,3}$.

5a. The poet Abu 'l-ʿAbbās Aḥmad b. ʿAbd al-Salām al-Gharawī of Fez glorified the Almohad caliph ʿAbd al-Muʾmin and, especially, his son | Yūsuf and 317
grandson Yaʿqūb, but as a writer of *hijāʾ* poetry he made himself loathed by his compatriots. He died in Seville in 609/1212.

Ibn Khall. (not in Wüst. and Būlāq), quoted in ʿAbdallāh Gannūn, *al-Nubūgh al-Maghribī* I, 100. *Ṣafwat al-adab wa-dīwān al-ʿArab*, a collection of poems that was as famous in the Maghreb as was the *Ḥamāsa* in the East, from which a *Mukhtaṣar* Fātiḥ 4079 (*MFO* V, 505, Suppl. II, 901).

6. Abu 'l-Ḥasan Ḥāzim b. Muḥammad b. Ḥasan b. Ḥāzim al-Anṣārī al-Qartajannī, d. 684/1285, see Suppl.

1. *al-Qaṣīda al-alfiyya al-maqṣūra*, in praise of the Ḥafṣid Abū ʿAbdallāh Muḥammad al-Mustanṣir billāh of Tunis (645–75/1249–77), Esc. ^{2}382, $454_{,1}$, Algiers 1842/3, with a commentary rich in biographical information by Abū ʿAbdallāh Abu 'l-Qāsim Muḥammad b. Aḥmad al-Sharīf al-Ḥusaynī al-Gharnāṭī al-Sabtī, d. 760/1358, Copenhagen 286, Br. Mus. $366_{,21}$, 367, Paris 3175, Algiers 1840/1, Alex. Adab 73, 89.—2. Other panegyrical poems on the same prince, Esc. $^{2}382_{,2}$.—3. Another collection *Majmūʿ*, ibid. $454_{,2}$.

7. In Sicily, towards the end of the fourth/tenth century, Abu 'l-Ḥasan ʿAlī b. ʿAbd al-Raḥmān al-Ṣaqalī al-Kātib al-Ballanūbī al-Naḥwī al-Anṣārī flourished.

Poems, Esc. $^{2}467_{,1}$.

8. The most famous poet of Sicily was Abū Muḥammad ʿAbd al-Jabbār b. Abī Bakr b. Muḥammad b. Ḥamdīs al-Azdī al-Sīraqūsī al-Ṣaqalī. He was born in

447/1055 and even in his youth was famed as a poet. When the Normans conquered the island in 471/1078 he fled to Spain. It was only in Seville at the court of the ʿAbbādid al-Muʿtamid that he found a setting appropriate for developing his talents. He followed this prince into captivity when the latter was defeated by Yūsuf b. Tāshfīn in 484/1091, and was marched off to Aghmāt in Morocco. After al-Muʿtamid's death in 488/1095 he seems to have gone to al-
318 270 Mahdiyya. | | There, in 509/1115, he composed an elegy for Yaḥyā b. Bādis, and a congratulatory poem on the accession to the throne of the latter's son ʿAlī. He spent the last years of his life in Bijāya, where he died in 527/1132, having lost his vision, at around 80 years of age. According to others, though, he died on Mallorca.

Ibn Khall. 369, Ibn al-Athīr x, 357, Dozy, *Script. de Abbad.* I, 146, Wüst. *Gesch.* 234. *Il Diwan del poeta a. M. Abdalgabbar ibn Hamdis il Siciliano publ. da* C.C. Moncada, Palermo 1893. *I.H. Canzoniere, pubbl. da* C. Schiaparelli, Rome 1897.

G *Spanish Poets*

Analectes sur l'histoire et la littérature des Arabes d'Espagne par al-Makkari (II 296), *publiés par* R. Dozy, G. Dugat, L. Krehl *et* W. Wright, 2 vols. Leiden 1855/61 (hereafter Maqq.).

A. Fr. v. Schack, *Poesie und Kunst der Araber in Spanien und Sicilien*, 2 vols., Berlin 1865, 2nd ed. 1877, *Majmūʿ al-aghānī wal-alḥān min kalām al-Andalus, dīwān al-awwal. Recueil de chansons et poésies qui ont été transmises par la tradition sous le titre général de* Ghernata *et qui constituent le répertoire des anciens Maures des 8e et 9e siècles, publ. par* E. Yafil, 1904.

H. Pérès, *La Poésie andalouse en Arabe classique au XI*[e] *siècle, ses aspects généraux et sa valeur documentaire, Publications de l'Institut d'Études orientales, Faculté des Lettres d'Algiers*, Paris 1937.

Käte Axthausen, *Die Theorien über den Ursprung der provençalischen Lyrik*, Diss. Marburg 1937 (assumes a Neoplatonic origin for the common traits between Arabic poetry and that of Provence).

Menendez Pidal, Poesía árabe y poesía europea, *Bulletin hispanique* 40 (Bordeaux, Fertet Fils), 337–423, see R. Hartmann, *OLZ* 1941, 41/4, *Poesía árabe y poesía europea conotros estudios de literatura medieval,* Madrid 1941 (Coll. Austral 190), see Suppl. I, 476/8.

1. Abū ʿUmar Yūsuf b. Hārūn al-Ramādī, d. 403/1012, see Suppl.

Ibn Khall. 819, al-Ḍabbī no. 1451, p. 478/81, Hartmann, | *Muwashshaḥ* 75/8. A 319
qaṣīda composed in captivity, Berl. 7598.

2. ʿAbdallāh b. ʿAbd al-Salām al-Andalusī, who flourished around 420/1029.

Al-Durr al-manẓūm, alphabetically ordered *dīwān*, for the most part long *qaṣīda*s in praise of friends and patrons, often as a greeting for the New Year, with mention of the year and the occasion, the greater part from the period 393–426/1002–35, especially 419–20/1028/9, Berl. 7608.

3. Abu ʾl-Fatḥ b. al-Ḥaṣīna al-Sulamī flourished around the year 440/1048.

Dīwān, vol. I, Esc. ^{2}275, in which there are poems from the years 433/1041 and 445/1053.

3a. Abu ʾl-Walīd b. Ḥabīb al-Ḥimyarī was the son of the vizier of the *qāḍī* of Seville, Ibn ʿAbbād. He died in 440/1048.

Al-Badīʿ fī waṣf al-rabīʿ, an anthology of Spanish poets, written as a follow-up to the lost *Kitāb al-ḥadāʾiq* of Ibn Faraj al-Jayyānī, d. 366/976, Esc. ^{2}353 (wrongly attributed by Derenbourg to Abu ʾl-Walīd al-Gharnāṭī, vol. II, 12), see H. Pérès, *La poésie andalouse en arabe classique*, 52, 166/83, *Texte ar. publié pour la première fois par* H. Pérès, *Coll. de textes ar. publ. par l'Inst. des Hautes Études Marocaines VII*, Rabat 1940 (in the Introduction biographies from Ibn Bassām, *Dhakhīra*, al-Ḍabbī, *al-Bughya*, Ibn al-Abbār, *Takmila*).

4. Abu ʾl-Ḥasan ʿAlī b. Aḥmad b. ʿAbd al-ʿAzīz al-Mayurqī b. Ṭunayz originated from Mallorca and died in 475/1082 in Kāẓima, near Baghdad.

Yāqūt, GW IV, 722, Suyūṭī, *Bughya* 327. Poems, Esc. ^{2}467,$_2$.

5. The ʿAbbādid emir of Seville al-Muʿtamid (461–84/1068–91), who was deposed by the Almoravids and who died in captivity in Aghmāt in Morocco,
was not just a friend of poets, | but also produced first-rate poetry himself. 271

| Dozy, *Loci de Abbadidis* I, 39ff. Individual poems, Berl. 7627,$_3$, Gotha 26,$_1$, 320
Schack I, 245/97.

6. Abū ʿAbdallāh Aḥmad b. Ibrāhīm al-Numayrī flourished in the first half of the sixth/twelfth century.

A poem in praise of the Prophet, Esc. $^{2}470_{,8}$.

7. Abu ʾl-ʿAbbās Abū Jaʿfar Aḥmad b. ʿAbdallāh Hurayra al-Tuṭīlī al-Aʿmā al-Ishbīlī from Tudela died in 520/1126, when he was still very young.

Al-Rawḍ al-miʿṭār by al-Ḥimyarī, ed. Lévi-Provençal 64, Hartmann, *Muw.* 13. *Dīwān* in praise of the Almoravid ʿAlī b. Yūsuf b. Tāshfīn, e.g. on the occasion of his campaign against Alfonso of Toledo and following the conquest of Talavera in 513/1119, of his brother Abū Isḥāq Ibrāhīm and of high officials, Br. Mus. 605, Cairo ^{1}IV, 240, ^{2}III, 119.

8. Abū Muḥammad ʿAbd al-Majīd b. ʿAbdūn al-Yāburī al-Fihrī was born in Yābura (Evora). The governor there, ʿUmar al-Mutawakkil b. Afṭas, noticed his poetical talent at an early age. When the latter assumed power in Badajoz after the death of his brother Yaḥyā b. Manṣūr in 473/1080 he appointed Ibn ʿAbdūn as his secretary. After the Almoravids deposed and killed Ibn Afṭas in 485/1092, Ibn ʿAbdūn entered into the service of the commander of the Berber troops, Sīr b. Bakr, as his secretary. After Yūsuf b. Tāshfīn's death, his son and successor ʿAlī appointed him to the same office in Morocco. He died while visiting his family in Evora in 529/1134 (or, according to others, this occurred in 520/1126).

Fawāt II, 8, Ibn Bashkuwāl 831, Wüst. *Gesch.* 239. *Al-Qaṣīda al-bassāma* (*bashshāma*), a rhyming chronicle on unfortunate dynasties, from Darius to the Afṭasids, Berl. 76/7. *Prolegomena ad editionem celebratissimi I.A. poematis in luctuosum Aftasidarum interitum scr.* Marinus Hoogvliet, Leid. 1839. Commentaries: a. *Kimāmat al-zahr wa-farīdat al-dahr* by Abu ʾl-Qāsim ʿAbd al-Malik b. ʿAbdallāh al-Ḥaḍramī al-Shilbī b. Badrūn, ca. 560/1164 (MSS see Suppl., with Garr. 483, Alex. Adab 117). *Commentaire historique sur le poème*
321 | *d'Ibn ʿAbdūn par I.B. publ. par* R.P.A. Dozy, Leiden 1846.—Abstract by Aḥmad b. Muḥammad al-Ṣafadī al-Khālidī, d. 764/1362, *Ṭawq al-ḥamāma* Leid. 663.—b. by ʿImād al-Dīn Ismāʿīl b. al-Athīr, d. 699/1299 (p. 341), Paris $3134_{,1}$; a continuation by the same, a *dhayl*, on the *qaṣīda* ibid. 2.

272 | 9. Abū Isḥāq Ibrāhīm b. Abi ʾl-Fatḥ b. ʿAbdallāh b. Khafāja al-Khafājī was born in 450/1058 in Alzira on the Júcar river between Valencia and Xàtiva. He lived as a poet in his native land without making any attempt to obtain the favour of rulers, dying there in 533/1138.

Ibn Khall. 16. *Dīwān*, mostly poems in praise of Abū Isḥāq Ibrāhīm b. Yūsuf b. Tāshfīn, as well as descriptions, mostly of gardens, Berl. 7684, Copenhagen 221, Pet. AM 295, Paris 3135, Br. Mus. 1667, Esc. ^{2}378, print. C. 1286; a poem, Gotha 261.

10. Abu 'l-Ḥakam ʿUbaydallāh b. al-Muẓaffar b. ʿAbdallāh b. Muḥammad al-Bāhilī al-Marī[1] was born in 486/1093 in Almeria. Following the pilgrimages that he made in 516/1122 and 518/1124 he spent time in Damascus, Upper Egypt and Alexandria. Having worked for a time as a teacher in Baghdad he entered into the service of the Saljūq sultan Maḥmūd b. Malikshāh (511–25/1117–31) as a physician, for whom he designed a field hospital on 40 camels. Later he returned to Damascus where he died in 549/1154.

Ibn Khall. 332, Maqq. 548, 898. His *dīwān* is lost; in it satirical poems predominated, which he also collected specifically in his *Najh al-raḍāʿa li-ūli 'l-khalāʿa*. *Maʿarrat al-bayt*, a poem in the *rajaz* metre, Berl. $8157_{,3}$.

11. Abū Bakr Muḥammad b. ʿAbd al-Malik b. Quzmān, d. in 555/1160 in Cordova, see Suppl. I, 481.

| Ibn Khaldūn, *Proleg.* transl. de Slane III, 436/8. Maqq. II, 262, 431, 636, R. 273
Nykl, Biographische Fragmente über I.Q., | *Islam* XXV (1938), 101/33. *Dīwān:* 322
Iṣābat al-aghrāḍ fī dhikr al-aʿrāḍ Pet. AM 296 (from Ṣafad, second half of the seventh cent.), *Le divan d'Ibn Guzman, texte, traduction, etc. par* D. Gunzburg, *Fs. 1. Le texte d'après le Ms. unique du Musée Asiatique Imp. de St. Pétersbourg* (facs.) Berlin 1896, *I.Q. Ėdition critique partielle et provisoire* (*Ch. X, XIX, LXXIV, LXXXVII, XC*) *par* O.J. Tuulio, Helsinki 1941 (*Studia Or. ed. Soc. Or. Fennica* IX, 2).—*Takhmīs* on one of his poems, Br. Mus. 631.

12. Abū Baḥr Ṣafwān b. Idrīs al-Tujībī al-Mursī, born in 560/1165, was a student of the *qāḍī* Abu 'l-Walīd b. Rushd (p. 384) and died in 598/1202.

Yāqūt, *Irshād* IV, 269, *Fawāt* I, 193, Maqq. II, 124. 1. *Zād al-musāfir*, an anthology of Spanish poets as a supplement to the *Qalāʾid al-ʿiqyān* of Ibn Khāqān, d. 529/1134 (p. 339), ḤKh III, $527_{,6769}$, Maqq. II, 124, Esc. ^{2}355/6, ed. ʿAbd al-Qādir Maḥdād, Beirut 1358/1939.—2. Alphabetical *takhmīs* on an elegy on the death of al-Ḥusayn, Esc. $^{2}470_{,11}$.

---

1 In Cat. Berl. al-Mursī.

13. Abū Zayd ʿAbd al-Raḥmān b. Yakhlaftan b. Aḥmad al-Fazāzī served several governors of the Almohads as a secretary, but was banished from Spain by the caliph al-Ma'mūn when the latter came to power in 626/1229. Even though he succeeded in being restored to favour during a visit to Marrakesh in Shaʿbān 627/1230, he died in Dhu 'l-Qaʿda that year.

Ibn al-Khaṭīb (cod. Paris 867), f. 147r/48r. 1. Works, poetry and belles lettres, collected by one of his students, perhaps Abū Bakr b. Sayyid al-Nās, a. *Fi 'l-zuhd*, b. *al-Rasā'il al-ikhwāniyya*, c. *Fī mukhāṭabatihi ʿani 'l-umarā' wa-mā yataʿallaq bi-dhālika*, Leid. 479.—2.–6. see Suppl. 2a. *al-Qaṣā'id al-ʿishrīniyyāt* under the title *Safīnat al-saʿāda li-ahl al-ḍiʿf wal-najāda*, C. 1320.—*Dīwān al-wasā'il al-mutaqabbila*, with a *takhmīs* by Muḥammad b. al-Mahīb and explanations of individual expressions by a scholar from Timbuktu, together with *al-Ṣāfīnāt al-jiyād* by al-Nabhānī (Suppl. II, $764_{,10}$), C. 1322.

323 14. Abū Isḥāq Ibrāhīm b. Sahl al-Isrā'īlī al-Ishbīlī | had converted from Judaism
274 to Islam and was drowned in 649/1251 (or 658/1260), | together with Ibn Khallāṣ the governor of Ceuta.

Fawāt I, 23, Hartmann, *Muw.* 44. 1. *Dīwān*, mainly love songs addressed to a Jewish boy by the name of Mūsā, Esc. $^{2}379$, *Hespéris* XII, $113_{,979}$, edition by al-Ḥasan b. Muḥammad al-ʿAṭṭār, d. 1250/1834 (Suppl. II, 720), dated 1229/1814, Br. Mus. Suppl. 1074, lith. C. 1279, 1292, 1302, Beirut 1885.—2. *Muwashshaḥ* Berl. $8172_{,22}$.

15. Abu 'l-Ḥusayn ʿAlī b. ʿAbdallāh al-Shushtarī al-Numayrī al-Fāsī originated in Shushtar in the region of Wādī Āsh. He was a student of the philosopher Ibn Sabʿīn (p. 465) and died in Damietta on 17 Ṣafar 668/16 October 1269.

Maqq. I, 583, Hartmann, *Muw.* 87, Massignon, *EI* IV, 423. 1. *Dīwān*, for the most part of mystical content and in modern metres, esp. *zajal* (but not *muwashshaḥ*) and often in Spanish popular dialect, Berl. 7773/7, Munich 525, Leid. 708, Pet. 137, Br. Mus. $1527_{,3}$, Esc. $^{2}278$, Br. Mus. Or. 9254, Garr. 79, library of Shaykh Mubārak in Damascus.—2. A *muwashshaḥ*, Berl. $8072_{,1}$.—3. *Radd al-muftarī ʿan al-ṭaʿn fi 'l-Shushtarī*, commentary by al-Nābulusī, d. 1143/1730, on one of his poems, Berl. 7780, Bodl. II, p. 347, n. 47, Alex. Tawḥīd 35, Fun. $152_{,26}$.—4.–7. see Suppl.—8. *al-Maqālīd al-wujūdiyya wal-dā'ira al-qidamiyya*, kabbalistic, Taymūr, Taṣawwuf 149, p. 444/7.

16. Sharaf al-Dīn al-Ḥusayn, d. around 680/1281.

Qaṣīda mourning the grammarian Ibn Mālik, d. 672/1273 (p. 298), Berl. 7781,$_{2}$.

17. Abu 'l-Ḥakam Mālik b. ʿAbd al-Raḥmān b. al-Muraḥḥal al-Mālaqī al-Andalusī al-Sabtī was born in 604/1207 in Malaga and died in 699/1299 in Fez.

Maqq. I, 836, II, 520, Ibn al-Qāḍī, *Durrat al-ḥijāl* II, 323/7, ʿAbdallāh Gannūn, *al-Nubūgh al-maghribī* I, 158. 1. *Dūbayt* Esc. ^{2}288,$_{4,5}$.—2. *al-Wasīla al-kubrā al-marjuww nafʿuhā fi 'l-ukhrā*, poetry in praise of the Prophet, Esc. ^{2}362,$_{1}$.—| 3. *Muʿashsharāt* on the same theme, ibid. 398.—4. *Kitāb fi 'l-ʿarūḍ* Cairo ^{2}II, 324
241.—5. *Urjūza fi 'l-naḥw, Hespéris* XII, 128,$_{1037,2}$.

Chapter 2. Rhymed Prose and Stylistics

1. Abu 'l-Walīd Aḥmad b. ʿAbdallāh b. Ghālib b. Zaydūn al-Makhzūmī was born in 394/1003 in Cordova where, being from a good family, he soon gained a prominent role. He won the love of Wallāda, the witty and emancipated daughter of the Umayyad caliph al-Mustakfī billāh, who had been murdered in 416/1025.[1] This love raised the suspicions of the ruler of Cordova, Abu 'l-Ḥazm Jawhar, who had him thrown into prison. Even though he escaped to western Spain, he
275 later returned to Cordova's suburb of al-Zahrā'. | When Abu 'l-Ḥazm's son Abu 'l-Walīd came to power, he appointed him as vizier. It was during this period that he composed a famous epistle in which Abū ʿĀmir b. ʿAbdūs tries to win the heart of Wallāda, and which he named after her. But it was not long before he raised the suspicions of Abu 'l-Walīd as well, possibly because of his relations with the art-loving Ḥammūdid ruler Idrīs II of Malaga. He was banished, whereupon he went to the ʿAbbādid al-Muʿtaḍid in Seville, who appointed him as *dhu 'l-wizāratayn*, i.e. prime minister and general commander of the armed forces. He kept this post under the latter's successor al-Muʿtamid, until he died in Rajab 463/April 1070.

Ibn Khall. 56, Weijers in *Orientala* I, 384/499, *Ibn Zaiduni vitam scripsit epistolamque ejus ad Ibn Dschahvarum scriptam nunc primum ed.* R.O. Besthorn, Copenhagen 1889, al-Iskandarī, *RAAD* XI, 513/22, 577/92, 656/69, Muṣṭafā Jawād, *Mazāliq b. Z. al-lughawiyya*, *Apollo* I, 1933, 1002/7. 1. *al-Risāla*
325 *al-hazaliyya* | Letter to Ibn ʿAbdūs: *Abi 'l-Walidi b. Z. risalet seu epistolium ar. et lat. cum notulis ed.* J.J. Reiske, Leipzig 1755, ed. Hirt in *Inst. ling. ar.*, Jena 1777, cf. Behrnauer, *ZDMG* XIII, 477ff.—Commentaries: a. *Sharḥ al-ʿuyūn fī sharḥ R. b. Z.* by Muḥammad b. Muḥammad b. Nubāta, d. 768/1366 (II, 10), Gotha 2830 (where other MSS are listed), Garr. 191, Dam. ʿUm. $87_{,52}$, Qawala II, 196, print. C. 1278; its Turkish translation by Saʿīd Muḥammad Jalīl Efendīzāde, Paris Sch. Turc. 1026, and by Qara Khalīl Emīrzāde, completed in 1133/1721, Vienna 392, print. Istanbul 1257.—2. *al-Risāla al-jiddiyya*, letter to Abu 'l-Walīd b. Jahwar from captivity, in which he asks him to intercede on his behalf with his father, ed. Besthorn, loc. cit. Commentary: *Tamām al-mutūn fī sharḥ r. b. Z.* by Khalīl al-Ṣafadī, d. 764/1363 (II, 32), Berl. 8608, Ms. or. oct. 3849, Paris 3316/7, Leid. 404, Bodl. I, $1204_{,2}$, Br. Mus. 1074, Esc. $^{2}497$, 543, Garr. 190, Patna I, $195_{,1752/3}$, print. Wilāyat Sūriyya 1327 (Alex. Adab 27).—3. *al-Qaṣīda al-andalusiyya*, a call to war against the infidels and for the liberation of Spain from their rule, in

1 See Ibn Bashkuwāl, *Ṣila* 1418 (Dozy, Cat. I, 256), Maqqarī II, 563/8, al-Nawākī, *Ḥalba* $94_{,7}$.

60 verses, Gotha 2240.—4. *al-Qaṣīda al-nūniyya*, a love poem, Bodl. I, 1245, 2, II, 318.—5. Individual poems, Berl. 7619,$_{2-4}$, Gotha 261.

2. Abū Jaʿfar Aḥmad al-Kātib al-Wazīr al-Adīb, from Denia, flourished at the beginning of the sixth/twelfth century.

Risālat al-intiṣār fi ʾl-radd ʿalā ṣāḥib al-Maqāma al-Qurṭubiyya, possibly against one of *al-Maqāmāt al-Qurṭubiyya* by Abū Ṭāhir Muḥammad b. Yūsuf b. ʿAbdallāh al-Saraqusṭī b. al-Ashtarkūnī (p. 377), Esc. $^{2}488_{,2}$.

3. Abū Bakr Aḥmad (Muḥammad) b. Isḥāq b. ʿAbd al-Jalīl al-ʿUmarī (Maʿmarī) Rashīd al-Dīn al-Waṭwāṭ, who died after 578/1182 in Khwārizm, see Supppl.

| 1. Letter of apology, Berl. 8609.—2. Imitation of a *maqāma* by him, ibid. 276
8537,$_{2}$.—3. *Rasāʾil*, see Suppl. Paris 4434, see M. Jawad, REI 1938, 286, AS 4015,$_{1}$, 25 Arabic and 25 Persian letters and *qaṣīdas*, different from the *ʿUmdat al-bulaghāʾ* AS 4150 (ca. 600 A.H.).—4.–9. see Suppl.—10. *Ḥadāʾiq al-siḥr fī daqāʾiq al-shiʿr* Persian, on which an Arabic commentary, entitled *Rawḍat al-daqāʾiq*, by Maḥmūd Adham, d. after 899/1494, is in Garr. 499.

4. Rhymed prose reached its perfection in the *maqāmas* of al-Ḥarīrī. Abū Muḥammad al-Qāsim | b. ʿAlī b. Muḥammad al-Ḥarīrī was the son of a rich 326
palmgrove owner from Māshān near Basra, but he had been born in the latter town, where he could pursue his literary inclinations, even though he did hold the office of *ṣāḥib al-khabar* in his native village. He died on 6 Rajab 516/11 September 1122.

His *maqāmas* draw on the tradition of Hamadhānī (p. 93). Just like him, he recounts the adventures of a literarily gifted tramp, a certain Abū Zayd from Sarūj. But he is not so much interested in a depiction—as lively and vivid as possible—of his hero and his surroundings as he is in dressing up his stories with all kinds of syntactical and lexical trappings designed to captivate and busy the reader much more than the story itself. It represents the last flickering of the Arab national spirit,[2] but they are like fireworks; marvellous and delightful in real time but infertile and fizzling out without leaving a trace.

Ibn Khall. 508, Ibn al-Anbārī 453/8. L. Delatre, Hariri, sa vie et ses écrits, *Extr. de la Revue orientale*, Article 1, 2, Paris 1853.—I. 50 *maqāmas* which, according to an autograph seen by Ibn Khallikān, were apparently written for

2 A. v. Kremer, *Culturgesch.* II, 476.

the vizier of the caliph al-Mustarshid billāh, Jamāl al-Dīn ʿAmīd al-Dawla
Abū ʿAlī al-Ḥasan b. Abi ʾl-ʿIzz ʿAlī b. Ṣadaqa, d. 521/1127, while the adressee
of the dedication is usually identified as the vizier Sharaf al-Dīn Abū Naṣr
Anūsharwān b. Muḥammad b. Khālid b. Muḥammad al-Qāshānī (cf. Houtsma,
Préf. au Recueil de textes rel. l'hist. d. Seldj. II, p. XII). *Les Séances de H. avec
un cmt. choisi par* S. de Sacy, first ed. Paris 1822, second ed. M. Reinaud and
J. Derenbourg, 2 vols., Paris 1847/53. *H.s Assemblies, Arabic text with English
notes, grammatical critical and hist. by* F. Steingass, London 1896/7. Editions
see Suppl., Persian translation by M. Shams al-Dīn, Lucknow 1263 (*JA* s. 6, v. 3
327 p. 202ff.), Turkish translation by A. Ḥamdī, Istanbul 1290 (ibid. s. 7, v. I, | 530,
277 cf. s. 7, v. 19, p. 186, | *Bull. de l'Ac. de St. Pétersbourg* VI, 130 = *Mél. As.* I, 2), Hebrew
translation of some *maqāmas*, ed. Neubauer, *JA* s. 6, v. 12, p. 91, Fr. Rückert,
Die Verwandlungen des Abu Seid von Serug oder die Makamen des H. 1826 (collective edition of R.'s poetical works, Frankfurt a.M. vol. XI), *Makamat or
rhetorical Anecdotes, transl. with Annotations by* Th. Preston, London 1850.—Critique by Abū Muḥammad ʿAbdallāh b. Aḥmad b. al-Khashshāb al-Baghdādī,
d. 567/1171 (Suppl. I, 493), *al-Istidrākāt ʿalā maqāmāt al-Ḥ. wantiṣār b. Barrī
lil-Ḥ.*, Istanbul 1328, and after the *maqāmas* C. 1329, with Muwaffaq al-Dīn
ʿAbd al-Laṭīf b. Yūsuf al-Baghdādī, d. 629/1231 (p. 481), *al-Intiṣāf bayna Ibn
Barrī wa-Ibn al-Khashshāb fī kalāmihimā ʿala ʾl-maqāmāt*, ḤKh ^{2}417, ^{2}I, 174, VI
61[3] as *Ḥāshiya laṭīfa*, Garr. 200. Commentaries: 1. Abū ʿAbdallāh or Abū Saʿīd
Muḥammad b. Abi ʾl-Saʿāda ʿAbd al-Raḥmān b. Masʿūd al-Panjdahī, d. 584/1188
(ḤKh VI, 62), Bodl. I, 403, Manch. 686, Esc. ^{2}494, Algiers 1892, Ḥamīd. 1195
(*ZA* 27, 148), *Maghānī ʾl-muqāmāt fī maʿānī ʾl-m.*, anon. Teh. II, 302.—2. Abu
ʾl-Khayr Salāma b. ʿAbd al-Bāqī b. Salāma al-Anbārī al-Dayrī, d. 590/1194, Gotha
2770, excerpts ibid. 99, f. 11v.—3. *al-Īḍāḥ* by Abu ʾl-Fatḥ Nāṣir al-Dīn b. ʿAbd al-Sayyid al-Muṭarrizī, d. 610/1213 (p. 293), Berl. 8540/2, Ms. or oct. 3854, Munich
561, Paris 3937/8, Esc. ^{2}$269_{,1}$, 509/10, Br. Mus. 616, Alex. Adab 16, Cairo ^{1}IV, 210,
^{2}III, 378, Patna I, $202_{,1803}$.—4 ʿAbdallāh b. al-Ḥusayn al-ʿUkbarī, d. 616/1219
(p. 496), Berl. Ms. or qu. 2109, Munich 562, Upps. 85, Paris $3939_{,1}$, Garr. 198.—5. Ṣadr al-Afāḍil al-Ṭarāʾifī, d. 617/1220, Berl. 8543.—6. Abu ʾl-ʿAbbās Aḥmad
b. ʿAbd al-Muʾmin al-Qaysī al-Sharīshī, d. 619/1222, a. the great commentary,
Leid. 413/4 (where other MSS are listed), additionally: Berl. 8544, Ms. or. qu.
2056, Paris 3940/6, Algiers 1891, Patna I, $202_{,1805/6}$, print. Būlāq 1284, 1300,
C. 1306.—b. the middle commentary, Leid. 415.—7. Anon. Berl. *al-Awḍaḥ*,
perhaps by al-Taftāzānī, d. 792/1390 (II, 215), Leid. 417 (autograph).—8. al-Zabīdī, ca. 900/1494, Berl. 8545.—9. ʿAbdallāh b. Muḥammad al-Ṭaballabī,

---

3 Quoting al-Suyūṭī's *Bughya*, who does not, however, mention this work on p. 311.

d. 962/1555, up to one third of the 24th *maqāma*, completed by his student Abu 'l-Masʿūd b. Muḥammad b. ʿAlī in 960/1558, Leid. 419, Pet. AMK 943.—10. *al-Maqālāt al-jawhariyya* by Khayr al-Dīn b. Tāj al-Dīn Ilyās al-Madanī, fl. 12th cent., Cambr. 1085/7, Alex. Adab 163, Cairo ^{2}III, 367, Patna I, $206,_{1839}$.—11. Abū Ra's Muḥammad b. Aḥmad b. ʿAbd al-Qādir al-Nāṣirī, d. 1244/1828, Berl.
8546, Algiers | 1893/4.—12. Abū Jaʿfar b. Dā'ūd al-Bāghī, Leid. 416.—13. Abū 328
ʿAbdallāh Muḥammad b. Manṣūr b. Ḥamāma al-Maghrāwī al-Sijilmāsī, ḤKh ^{1}II, 534, Esc. ^{2}496.—14.–16. see Suppl.—17. *al-Maqālāt al-jawhariyya ʿala 'l-m. al-Ḥ.* by Abū Bakr b. ʿAbd al-ʿAzīz al-Zamzamī al-Shāfiʿī, ca. 993/1585, Lālelī 1850 (*MO* VII, 103), Makr. 57.—19. Anon. Leid. 418, Vienna 375, Upps. 83.—20. Maẓhar al-Dīn, Patna I, $202,_{1804}$.—21. *al-Qushāmāt* by Muḥammad Ismāʿīl Abu 'l-Mushtāq b. Muḥammad Wajīh al-Dīn, ibid. 1808.—Turkish translation by A. Ḥamdī Shirwānī (under ʿAbd al-ʿAziz), Istanbul 1290.—24 commentaries are mentioned in Ahlwardt, 8548.

II. *al-Risāla al-sīniyya* and *al-Risāla al-shīniyya*, in the first of which every word contains a *sīn*, and in the second a *shīn*, Berl. 8610, Leid. 424/5 (where other MSS are listed), print. in Arnolds, *Chr. ar.* 202/9.

III. Some *qaṣīdas*, Berl. 7674.

IV. Poem in 18 verses in the *khafīf* metre on the difference between words with a *ḍād* and a *ẓā* (see Maq. ed. de Sacy 545/7, Suyūṭī, *Muzhir* II, 149), Berl. 679.

V. *al-Farq bayna 'l-ḍād wal-ẓā'*, alphabetical, Berl. 7022.

VI. *Kitāb durrat al-ghawwāṣ fī awhām al-khawāṣṣ*, mistakes in the language of the educated, Berl. 6503/4, Ms. or. oct. 3885, Munich 689, Leid. 69 (where other MSS are listed, see Suppl.), and also AS 3866, Alex. Fun. $67,_{22}$, Patna I, $185,_{1688}$, ed. Thorbecke, Leipzig 1871, print. C. 1273. Commentary by Shihāb al-Dīn Aḥmad b. Muḥammad al-Khafājī, d. 1069/1659 (II, 285), Berl. 6505, de Jong 13, Köpr. 1312/3, Alex. Lugha 11, Qawala II, 3, Patna I, $185,_{1692}$, print. Istanbul 1299/1300.

VII. *Mulḥat al-iʿrāb*, a didactic poem on grammar with a commentary, Berl. 6507/9, BDMG 67a, Breslau Un. 213, Paris $2570,_9$, 3996/9, Leid. 157/8 (where other MSS are listed), see Suppl. Garr. 324, Qawala II, 97. *Molḥat al-iʿrāb ou les récréations grammaticales, poème grammatical, accompagné d'un cmt. par le cheikh a. M. el-Ḳ. b. ʿA. connu sous le nom de Ḥ. trad. par* L. Pinto, *avec un choix de notes explicatives et critiques ainsi les variantes tirées du cmt. intitulé Toḥfat al-adab*, 1805/9, cf. de Sacy, *Anth. gr.* 145/51. Commentaries: 1. Muḥammad b. Muḥammad b. Mālik Badr al-Dīn (p. 363), Vat. V. 320, fragm. Berl. 6510, Gotha $229,_2$.—2. ʿAlī b. Muḥammad b. ʿAlī al-Qurayshī al-Qalaṣādī (Qalaṣāwī, ḤKh
Ind. 7101), d. 891/1486, Esc. $^2121,_1$.—3. *Tuḥfat al-aḥbāb wa-ṭurfat al-aṣḥāb* | by 278

Jamāl al-Dīn Muḥammad b. ʿUmar Baḥraq al-Ḥaḍramī, d. 930/1524 (II, 403), Berl. 6511, Leid. 159, Br. Mus. Suppl. 924, Hamb. Or. Sem. 66, 72, 130, Alex. Naḥw
329 5, Patna I, | 171,$_{1684}$, print. C. 1296, 1300, 1306, 1308, 1319.—4. *Kashf al-niqāb* by ʿAbdallāh b. Aḥmad al-Fākihī, d. 972/1564 (II, 380), Hamb. Or. Sem. 59, 131, 134, Leid. 160.—5. Anon. Berl. 6512.—6.–11. see Suppl.—12. Aḥmad b. Ḥusayn b. Raslān al-Ramlī, d. 844/1440 (II, 96), BDMG 9, 83.—Abstract in verse by Muḥammad b. Aḥmad b. Jābir, d. 780/1378 (II, 13), Paris 4452,$_{4}$.

5. The Christian physician Abu ʾl-ʿAbbās Yaḥyā b. Yaḥyā b. Saʿīd al-Naṣrānī al-Baṣrī, who died in 589/1193.

Al-Maqāmāt al-masīḥiyya, an imitation of the *maqāma*s of Ḥarīrī, Vienna 384.

5a. Al-Qāḍī al-Rashīd Abu ʾl-Ḥusayn Aḥmad b. ʿAlī b. al-Zubayr al-Ghassānī al-Aswānī, who hailed from an affluent family from Upper Egypt, was appointed as an inspector (*walī al-naẓar*) in Alexandria and directed the *dīwān* of the sultan. In Yemen, where he had gone as an envoy, he became *qāḍi ʾl-quḍāt*, and even assumed power at times. But then the Egyptian government had him arrested and taken to Qūṣ. Nevertheless, he was pardoned by the emir al-Ṣāliḥ b. Ruzzīk. In spite of this, he contacted Shīrkūh when the latter invaded Egypt, but in Muḥarram 563/Oct.–Nov. 1167, even before Shīrkūh could assert himself, he was sentenced to death by the vizier of the last Fāṭimid caliph al-ʿĀḍid.

Yāqūt, *Irshād* I, ^{2}416/22, Suyūṭī, *Bughya* 146. 1. *al-Maqāma al-ḥaṣībiyya* with commentary Alex. Adab 142, 163.—2. *Jinān al-jinān wa-riyāḍ al-adhhān fī shuʿarāʾ Miṣr* as a supplement to al-Thaʿālibī's *Yatīmat al-dahr*, see Abū Makhrama, ed. Löfgren II, 4,$_{23}$, p. 267 n. 1.—3. *Shifāʾ al-ghilla fī samt al-qibla*.—4. *Munyat al-almaʿī wa-munyat al-muddaʿī*, an encyclopaedia.

5b. Rukn al-Dīn al-Wahrānī, Suppl. I, 489,$_{56}$, II, 911,$_{68}$.

5c. Muḥammad b. ʿAlī b. ʿAlī b. Ḥammūya al-Kāmilī, d. 652/1254.

330 | *Taqwīm al-naʿīm etc.* see Suppl., AS 3825 (Rescher, *WZKM* 26, no. 36).

6. Muḥammad b. ʿAbd al-Raḥmān b. Muḥammad Majd al-Dīn b. Qarnāṣ, ca. 672/1272.

Maqāma on Egypt, the Nile, and Rawḍa, Berl. 8549,$_{2}$.

7. Aḥmad b. Muḥammad b. ʿUmar b. Yūsuf al-Qurṭubī Ḍiyāʾ al-Dīn Abu ʾl-ʿAbbās, who died in 672/1272.

1. Fragment of a letter, Berl. 8613,1.—2. See Suppl.

8. Shihāb al-Dīn al-Barāʾī flourished around 674/1275.

A *maqāma* on the Nile, Berl. 8549,3.

9. Al-Qāḍī Ḥāshid, ca. 690/1291.

Beginning of a *maqāma* Berl. 8550,1.

Chapter 3. Philology

In this period Arabic linguistics saw intense activity as well. Even though in grammar no new observations were made, the material assembled by Sībawayhi and his successors was recast over and over again, thus gaining much in manageability. Furthermore, one compendium after another was produced, some of which have maintained their canonical status until this very day. Lexicography produced some smart, specialised works, which nevertheless drew on older sources. Typical of this period were studies on stylistics and poetics, which often bear testimony to a sound aesthetic judgement.
279 But this domain, too, eventually came under the sway of barren scholastics. |
331 Philology, which had originated in Iraq, now became studied in all | Islamic lands, although the Iranians still asserted their old superiority.

1 *Philology in Iraq*

1. Abū ʿAbdallāh Muḥammad ʿAbdallāh b. al-Iskāfī, who died in 421/1030.

1. *Mabādiʾ al-lugha* Yeni 1121, see Suppl.—2. ibid.—3. *Luṭf al-tadbīr* (*fī siyāsat al-mulūk* ḤKh V, 320,$_{11141}$, *fī ḥiyal al-mulūk fī umūr al-salṭana*) ʿĀšir I, 1005, Top Kapu 2633 (*RSO* IV, 725).

2. ʿĪsā b. Ibrāhīm al-Rabaʿī, from Yemen, died in 480/1087.

Niẓām al-gharīb, explanation of obsolete words in old poems, which are also quoted, Berl. 7039, Leid. 68, Br. Mus. 1010, Suppl. 918,$_{111}$, 1214,$_{1}$, Cambr. 63, AS 4335, Alex. Lugha 33, Garr. 33, Patna I, 90,$_{1719}$.

3. Abū (Bakr) Zakariyyāʾ Yaḥyā b. ʿAlī b. al-Khaṭīb al-Tabrīzī, who was born in 421/1030 in Tabrīz, studied philology with Abu ʾl-ʿAlāʾ al-Maʿarrī[1] and the science of *ḥadīth* in Ṣūr (Tyre). Having worked for a time as a teacher in Egypt he then went to Baghdad, where he held the chair of philology at the Niẓāmiyya until his death on 28 Jumādā I 502/4 January 1109.

---

1 In a library in Baghdad one could see a memento of his diligence, a copy of the *Kitāb al-tahdhīb fī ʾl-lugha* by al-Azharī (p. 134) that he, too poor to buy himself a mount, had hauled in a rucksack from Tabriz to Maʿarra to attend lectures on it there, and which was still saturated with his sweat.

Anb. 443/8, Ibn Khall. 77. 1. *al-Kāfī fī ʿilmay al-ʿarūḍ wal-qawāfī* Berl. 7110 (= Bodl. I, 1215?), Bat. 146,$_3$, versified by Shihāb al-Dīn Aḥmad b. ʿAbdallāh al-Faljī (according to ḤKh II, 413, V, 21, he was born in 829/1426, while in Freytag, *Versk.* 36, n. 10, he died in 729), maybe Gotha 376,$_2$.—2. *Kitāb al-wāfī fī ʾl-ʿarūḍ wal-qawāfī* Cairo [1]IV, 196, [2]II, 246.—3. *Kitāb al-mulakhkhaṣ fī iʿrāb al-Qurʾān* Paris 596.—4. *Sharḥ al-muʿallaqāt* see Suppl. p. 35—5. *Sharḥ al-ḥamāsa*, ed. G. Freytag, 2 vols., Bonn 1838/47, Būlāq 1286/290, C. 1322, 1341.—6. *Sharḥ dīwān Abī Tammām* see p. 85.—7. *Sharḥ saqṭ al-zand* see p. 294.—8. *Sharḥ al-qaṣāʾid al-Mufaḍḍaliyyāt* Berl. Ms. or. quart. 2047.

| 4. His most important student and his successor at the Niẓāmiyya was Abū 332
Manṣūr Mawhūb b. Aḥmad b. Muḥammad b. al-Khaḍir b. al-Jawālīqī, who was born into an old Baghdad family in 465/1073, and who passed away on 15 Muḥarram 539/19 July 1144.

Anb. 473/8, Ibn Khall. 722. 1. *Kitāb al-muʿarrab min al-kalām al-ʿAjamī ʿalā ḥurūf al-muʿjam*, explanations of foreign words, ed. E. Sachau, Leipzig 1867. Completion of a lacuna after the Cairo MS by W. Spitta, *ZDMG* 33, 208ff.; other MSS Esc. [2]124, AS 4277, Lālelī 3591, 3629.—2. *Kitāb al-takmila fī-mā yalḥanu fīhi ʾl-ʿāmma*, supplement to the *Durrat al-ghawwāṣ* of al-Ḥarīrī, see p. 326, *Le livre des locutions vicieuses*, ed. H. Derenbourg in *Morg. Forsch.* Leipzig 1875, p. 107/66, *Takmilat iṣlāḥ mā taghliṭu fīhi ʾl-ʿāmma*, ed. al-Tanūkhī in *al-Majmūʿ al-ʿilmī al-ʿArabī* no. 7, Damascus 1936 (*RAAD* XIV, 164/226).—3. *al-Mukhtaṣar fī ʾl-naḥw* Köpr. 1501.

5. ʿAbdallāh b. ʿAlī b. Isḥāq al-Ṣaymarī, who died in 541/1146.

Suyūṭī, *Bughya*, 285 (without date). *Tabṣirat al-mubtadiʾ wa-tadhkirat al-muntahī*, on grammar, ḤKh [1]II, 179, [2]I, 339, Paris 4007, Ibrāhīm b. Muḥammad b. Malkūn al-Ḥaḍramī al-Ishbīlī, d. 584/1188 (Suyūṭī, *Bughya*, 188), wrote *nukat* on this work.

6. Abū Saʿāda Hibatallāh b. ʿAlī b. Muḥammad b. Ḥamza al-ʿAlawī b. al-Shajarī, who was born in Baghdad in Ramaḍān 450/November 1058, was the *naqīb* of the ʿAlids in al-Karkh, a suburb of Baghdad, and who wrote a number of commentaries on grammatical works. He died on 26 Ramaḍān 542/9 February 1148.

Anb. 485/9, Ibn Khall. 745, *Fawāt* II, 310. 1. *Dīwān mukhtārāt al-shuʿarāʾ*, an anthology of complete *qaṣīdas*, based on the MS in the national library of Egypt, lith. C. 1306.—2.–4. see Suppl. (3. also *Br. Mus. Quart.* VIII, 15).

7. Abū Saʿīd Muḥammad b. ʿAlī b. ʿAbdallāh b. Aḥmad b. Abi ʾl-Hijāʾ b. Ḥamdān al-Ḥillī al-ʿIrāqī, d. 561/1170, see Suppl.

333 | 1. *Kitāb nuzhat al-anfus wa-rawḍat al-majlis* explains the origin of proverbs and metaphors in 29 chapters in alphabetical order (with lām-alif), Gotha 1250.—2. *Rawḍat al-ʿushshāq wa-nuzhat al-mushtāq*, anthology, Esc. ^{2}471.—3., 4. see Suppl.

8. Kāfi ʾl-Kufāt Abu ʾl-Maʿālī Muḥammad b. Abī Saʿd al-Ḥasan al-Baghdādī b.
281 Ḥamdūn was born into a noble family in Baghdad in 495/1101. 281| Having served in the army under al-Muktafī, he moved up the ranks to the position of chief warden of the palace under al-Mustanjid and, finally, to that of secretary of state. Due to the fact that in this capacity, he openly—in an official letter—criticised the damages done by the government at the time, he was evicted from his post and thrown into jail in 562/1167, where he died soon after.

Ibn Khall. 626, *Fawāt* II, 286, Wüst., *Gesch.* 255. *Kitāb al-tadhkira fi ʾl-siyāsa wal-ādāb al-malakiyya*, a philological and historical anthology in 12 volumes, Berl. 8559/60, Paris 3324, Bodl. I, 379, 389, Pet. AM 207, Esc. ^{2}508, a further part ibid. 280 (contra Derenbourg, see M. Antuña, *al-Andalus* III, 1935, 447/9), Br. Mus. Suppl. 1137/8, Istanbul Un. R. 101, ʿUm. 5363 (*ZS* III, 248), Bursa Haraccizade Edeb. 28 (vol. 5, Ritter), see A. v. Kremer, *ZDMG* VII, 215, idem, *Ideen* 469, *Beiträge zur Kenntnis der Geschichte und Sitten der Araber vor dem Islam, bearbeitet nach der Teskiret b. H., SBWA, phil.-hist. Cl.* April 1851.—abstract by Maḥmūd b. Yaḥyā b. Maḥmūd b. Sālim, composed in 618/1282, ḤKh ^{1}II, 256,$_{2780}$, ^{2}I, 383, Munich 595, anon. Gotha 2137, Paris 3325.

9. Abū Muḥammad Saʿīd b. al-Mubārak b. ʿAlī b. al-Dahhān was born on 21 Rajab 494/23 May 1101 in the Nahr Ṭābiq quarter of Baghdad, where he was regarded as one of the greatest grammarians of his time. When he was visiting the vizier Jamāl al-Dīn Iṣfahānī in Mosul, his house in Baghdad was hit by
334 a flood. He tried to restore the books that had been damaged by fumigating | them with laudanum, but ruined his eyes in the process and went blind. He died soon after, on 1 Shawwāl 569/7 May 1174.

Ibn Khall. 251. 1. *al-Fuṣūl fi ʾl-qawāfī* Gotha 358,$_{2}$ = *al-Mukhtaṣar fi ʾl-qawāfī* ḤKh V, 450,$_{11622}$ or part of the *Fuṣūl b. al-Dahhān* ibid. IV, 432,$_{9076}$?—2. A *qaṣīda* with an anonymous commentary (maybe the copyist of the MS Muḥammad b. Muḥammad al-Batanūnī al-Azharī, in the year 1162/1749) dictated by Shams al-Dīn Abu ʾl-ʿAbbās Aḥmad b. al-Ḥusayn b. al-Khabbāz, Gotha 2255.—3.–6. see Suppl.

10. Kamāl al-Dīn Abu ʾl-Barakāt ʿAbd al-Raḥmān b. Muḥammad b. ʿUbaydallāh b. Abī Saʿīd b. al-Anbārī[2] was born in Rabīʿ II 513/July 1119 in Anbār on the Euphrates. Under al-Jawālīqī and Ibn al-Shajarī he studied philology at the Niẓāmiyya in Baghdad, where he would later teach the same subject. | 282
He spent the last years of his life devoted to studying and spiritual exercises. He died on 3 Shaʿbān 577/19 December 1181.

Ibn Khall. 342, *Fawāt* I, 262, Wüst., *Gesch.* 269. 1. *Kitāb nuzhat al-alibbāʾ fī ṭabaqāt al-udabāʾ*, a history of philology from its beginnings until his own lifetime, Patna II, $318,_{2471}$, lith. C. 1294.—2. *Kitāb asrār al-ʿarabiyya*, a grammar, ed. C.F. Seybold, Leiden 1886, see E. Kautzsch, ZDMG 28 (1874) 331ff., on the MSS see Suppl. and Garr. 335.—3. *Kitāb al-inṣāf fī masāʾil al-khilāf bayna ʾl-naḥwiyyīn al-Baṣriyyīn wal-Kūfiyyīn*, composed at the request of his students at the Niẓāmiyya, Leid. 169, Esc. $^{2}119$, Yeni 1060, see Kosut, *Fünf Streitfragen der Baṣrenser und Kufenser*, Vienna 1878; ed. by G. Weil, Leiden 1913.—4. *Kitāb lumaʿ al-adilla fī uṣūl al-naḥw* Leid. 170.—5. *Kitāb lumaʿ al-ighrāb fī jadal al-iʿrāb* Paris $1013,_{3}$.—6. *Kitāb ʿumdat al-udabāʾ fī maʿrifat mā yuktab bil-alif wal-yāʾ* Leid. 171.

11. The circumstances of the life of Abū | ʿAbdallāh Muḥammad b. ʿAlī 335
b. Khālid b. al-Saqqāṭ are unknown, although he belonged to the sixth/twelfth century.

Kitāb ikhtiṣār al-ʿarūḍ or *al-Ghumūḍ min masāʾil al-ʿarūḍ* Leid. 270, Esc. $^{2}288,_{3}$, $330,_{5}$, 396, comment. by Ibn al-Barrī, d. 583/1187 (p. 365), Esc. $^{2}410,_{3}$.

12. Muḥibb al-Dīn Abu ʾl-Baqāʾ ʿAbdallāh b. al-Ḥusayn al-ʿUkbarī al-Ḥanbalī, born in 538/1143 in Baghdad, studied philology and the science of *ḥadīth* there, started his career as the mentor of Ibn al-Jawzī (p. 500), and was later regarded as the greatest philologist of his time. He died on 8 Rabīʿ II 616/24 June 1219.

---

2 Rescher, *Abriss* II, 191, n. 2 claims that, as "al-Anbārī", our author should be distinguished from the older "Ibn al-Anbārī" (p. 122); in this he can, however, only draw support from Ibn Khallikān, while the *Fawāt* and al-Ṣafadī call Abu ʾl-Barakāt also "Ibn al-Anbārī".

Ibn Khall. 322. 1. *Kitāb al-tibyān fī iʿrāb al-Qurʾān* Paris 620/1, Algiers 331, Cairo [1]I, 135, AS 73/4, Patna I, 24,$_{217}$.—2. *Kitāb al-mūjiz fī īḍāḥ al-shiʿr al-mulghiz*, a commentary on syntactically unusual phrases among ancient poets, Berl. 6581.—3. *Kitāb al-lubāb fī ʿilal al-bināʾ wal-iʿrāb*, on the causes of declension and indeclinability, Cairo [1]IV, 90, [2]II, 155.—4. *Kitāb al-talqīn fi ʾl-naḥw*, fragm. Leid. 177.—5. *Sharḥ dīwān al-Mutanabbī* see p. 88.—6. *Sharḥ maqāmāt al-Ḥarīrī* see p. 325.—7.–12. see Suppl.—13. On the basis of his *Muṣannaf*, Ibrāhīm b. Muḥammmad Kamāl al-Dīn b. Ḥamza al-Ḥusaynī al-Ḥanafī al-Dimashqī, d. 1120/1708 (Mur. II, 120), wrote *al-Bayān wal-taʿrīf fī asbāb wurūd al-ḥadīth al-sharīf*, in 2 vols., Aleppo 1329/30 (Sarkis 88).—14. *ʿAdd al-āy* Fātiḥ Waqf Ibr. 632.

13. Abū ʿAlī al-Muẓaffar b. Abī Saʿīd al-Faḍl b. Abī Jaʿfar Yaḥyā b. ʿAbdallāh al-ʿAlawī al-Ḥusaynī wrote, at the command of the vizier of the last of ʿAbbāsid caliph, Muḥammad al-ʿAlqamī, d. 655/1258:

Kitāb naḍrat al-ighrīḍ fī nuṣrat al-qarīḍ, a theory of the art of poetry, ḤKh VI, 353,$_{13841}$, Berl. 7174, Vienna 224, Paris 1303,$_{2}$, 4236,$_{3}$, 4420,$_{1}$, Br. Mus. 1055, Dāmād Ibr. 963.

14. ʿIzz al-Dīn ʿAbd al-Ḥamīd b. Hibatallāh al-Madāʾinī b. Abi ʾl-Ḥadīd, born in 586/1190 in al-Madāʾin, distinguished himself as a poet and philologist. He died in 655/1257 in Baghdad.

336 283 | | *Fawāt* I, 248. 1. *Kitāb al-falak al-dāʾir ʿala ʾl-mathal al-sāʾir*, a refutation of the errors in Ibn al-Athīr's (p. 358) *Kitāb al-mathal al-sāʾir fī adab al-kātib wal-shāʿir*, Leid. 318, Garr. 551.—2. Versification (*naẓm*) of Thaʿlab's (p. 121) *Kitāb al-faṣīḥ*, completed in 24 hours, Esc. [2]188.—3. *al-Qaṣāʾid al-sabʿ al-ʿalawiyyāt*, 1. on the conquest of Khaybar, 2. on the capture of Mecca, 3. and 4. in praise of the Prophet, 5. on the death of Ḥusayn, 6. addressed to the caliph al-Nāṣir li-Dīn Allāh (575–622/1180–1225), praise of the Prophet, Berl. 7757/8, with a commentary by an unidentified ʿAlid, Leid. 703, see ḤKh IV, 577.

15. (16.) ʿIzz al-Dīn Abu ʾl-Faḍāʾil ʿAbd al-Wahhāb b. Ibrāhīm b. ʿAbd al-Wahhāb b. Abi ʾl-Maʿālī al-Khazrajī al-Zanjānī wrote in 625/1257 in Baghdad:

Kitāb taṣrīf al-Zanjānī or *al-ʿIzzī* Gotha 194,$_{6}$ (where other MSS are listed), Berl. 6615/6, BDMG 65, b, Garr. 396/7, Qawala II, 25/6. For printed editions see Suppl. Commentaries: 1. Saʿd al-Dīn Masʿūd b. ʿUmar al-Taftāzānī, d. 792/1390

(II, 215), Berl. 6617/8, Gotha 200,$_{2}$ (where other MSS are listed), BDMG 82, Garr. 398/400, Qawala II, 34/6, print. Istanbul 1253, 1292. Glosses: a. Muḥammad b. ʿUmar al-Ḥalabī, d. 855/1451, Berl. 6619, Br. Mus. 532,$_{8}$.—b. Nāṣir al-Dīn Abū ʿAbdallāh Muḥammad al-Laqānī, autograph dated 924/1511, Esc. ^{2}103, 183, Gotha 203, Vienna 201, de Jong 17.—c. Shams al-Dīn Muḥammad b. Qāsim al-ʿIzzī (Ghazzī?) al-Shāfiʿī, 10th cent., Esc. ^{2}182.—d. Muḥammad b. ʿArab b. Ḥājjī b. ʿArab, Kazan 146.—e.–f. see Suppl.—g. Kamāl al-Dīn Qara Dede Khalīfa Jūnkī, C. 1255 (Qawala II, 28).—h.–i. see Suppl.—k. Anon. Garr. 401/2 (*al-Mufarrij*).—2. ʿAlī b. Muḥammad b. ʿAbdallāh al-Afzarī, d. 815/1412, Berl. 6620, Leid. 204.—2a. al-Jurjānī, d. 816/1413 (II, 216), Pet. AMK 926, Dam. Z. 64,$_{6}$, print. Istanbul 1280, 1292, 1301, 1318.—3. al-Qāriʾ al-Harawī, d. 1014/1605 (II, 394), Berl. 6621, Istanbul 1289.—4. Yaḥyā b. Ibrāhīm b. ʿAbd al-Salām al-Zanjānī al-Imām al-Muʿaẓẓam, around 1050/1640, Berl. 6622.—5. Yūsuf Jān b. ʿAbbās al-Pīrḥaḍrānī, around 1094/1683, ibid. 6623.—6. Ḥājjī b. Ibrāhīm ʿUkkāsha al-Jabalī, ḤKh IV, 210, Gotha 200,$_{1}$, Munich 761, Pet. 159.—7. Abu ʾl-Ḥasan ʿAlī Nūr al-Dīn b. Shihāb al-Dīn al-Kīlānī al-Shāfiʿī, Gotha 204, Ambros. 126, Esc. ^{2}86, print. C. 1305, 1307, 1312, 1344 (Alex. Adab 6).—8. Anon., Berl. 6625/6, Gotha 205,$_{2}$, Pet. 156,$_{1}$, Br. Mus. 502,$_{1}$.—9.–19. see Suppl.—20. | *Ḍiyāʾ al-Kalām* by Ibn Muḥammad Bāqir 337
Naṣrallāh al-Shīrāzī, 13th cent., Bank. XX, 2089 = Patna I, 159,$_{1507}$.—19 commentaries and glosses, 2 versifications in Ahlw. 6027.—II. *Mukhtaṣar al-hādī li-dhawi ʾl-ādāb fī ʿilm al-iʿrāb*, with comment. *al-Kāfī*, completed in 654/1256, Pet. 205.—III.–VIII. see Suppl.

17. Badr al-Dīn Abu ʾl-Maḥāsin Yūsuf b. Sayf al-Dawla b. Zammākh b. Baraka b. Thumāma al-Thaʿlabī al-Ḥamdānī al-Mihmāndār, who was born in 602/1205 and died towards the end of the seventh/thirteenth century.

Kitāb izālat al-iltibās fi ʾl-farq bayna ʾl-ishtiqāq wal-jinās, on the rhetoric of the Qurʾān, Cairo ^{1}IV, 122, ^{2}II, 175.

| 2 *Philology in Persia and Neighbouring Countries* 284

The competition for grandeur amongst the numerous royal courts of Iran led to a renewed upsurge in poetry as well as scholarship. While in poetry, New Persian had continued to gain ground ever since the era of the Sāmānids, Arabic asserted itself as the language of the sciences. However, to help with its acquisition, numerous aids were created in the national language of the Iranians.

1. Abū Manṣūr ʿAbd al-Malik b. Muḥammad b. Ismāʿīl al-Thaʿālibī was born in 350/961 in Nishapur and died in 429/1038. His great productivity in philology and belles lettres did, like that of his successors, often consist merely of compilations, whose accessible and attractive format was the only thing that counted. For instance, al-Thaʿālibī did not shrink from copying verbatim whole passages from his predecessors without mentioning his sources.[1]

Ibn Khall. 354, Wüstenfeld, GGA, 1837, p. 1103, no. 15, idem, *Gesch.* 191. 1. *Yatīmat al-dahr fī maḥāsin ahl al-ʿaṣr*, on the poets of his time and the pre-
338 vious | generation, arranged by country, with many examples of their poetry, which was of more importance to him than the details of their lives; cf. Fr. Dieterici, *De anthologia Arabica Tsaalebii Unio aetatis appellata*, Berlin 1846, idem, *Mutanabbi und Saifuddaula* 177ff. Barbier de Meynard, *JA* s. V, v. 1 p. 169 ff., vol. 3, p. 291ff., Berl. 7401/8, Ms. or. qu. 2052, Gotha 2127 (where other MSS are listed), Garr. 183/5, Köpr. 1409 (first volume), Patna II 561_{2951}, print. Damascus 1304 in 4 vols. *Dhayl yatīmat al-d.* by the author himself Berl. 7407, Vienna 365, Pet. Ros. 86, cf. ZDMG IX, 627, continuation by al-Bākharzī, see p. 292.—
285 2. *Kitāb laṭāʾif al-maʿārif* Cairo ^{2}II, 72, ed. P. de. Jong, Leid. 1867.—| 3. *Shams al-adab fī ʾstiʿmāl al-ʿArab*, a work on synonyms written in old age, in two parts: a. *Asrār al-lugha al-ʿarabiyya wa-khaṣāʾiṣuhā*, on synonyms in the narrow sense.—b. *Majārī kalām al-ʿarab bi-rusūmihā wa-mā yataʿallaq bil-naḥw wal-iʿrāb minhā wal-istishhād bil-Qurʾān ʿalā aktharihā* or *Sirr al-adab fī majārī kalām al-ʿarab*, stylistic notes mostly taken literally from the *Fiqh al-lugha* of Aḥmad b. Fāris (p. 135), ḤKh IV, 590, Berl. 7032/3, Leid. 60, Garr. 516, anon. abstract Berl. 7034, Vat. v. $1177_{,6}$.—*Kitāb fiqh al-lugha wa-sirr al-ʿarabiyya*, special edition of part 1 of no. 3, Berl. 7635/6, Ms. or. oct. $3779_{,3}$ (Fischer-Burch. 31), 3882/3, Tüb. 68, Vienna 231, Paris 4251, 4858, Br. Mus. 1648, Suppl. 853, Cambr. Preston 38/9, Palat. 515, Pet. AM 206, Algiers 244, Qawala II, 5, Dam. ʿUm. p. 70, no. 25/8, Patna I $187_{,1699/1700}$, ed. R. Daḥdāḥ, Paris 1861, C. 1284, 1325, 1341, 1345, 1357/1938 (ed. Muṣṭafā al-Saqqāʾ, Ibrāhīm al-Abyārī, ʿAbd al-Ḥāfiẓ Ṣalātī), Beirut 1885 (abbreviated, see Zayyāt, *Khazāʾin al-kutub fī Dimashq* 22ff.), cf. Fleischer, *Kl. Schr.* III, 152/66. *Procemium et specimen lexici synonymici arab. Atthalibi ed. vertit notis instr.* J. Seligmann, Uppsala 1863. Versification, *Naẓm fiqh al-l.*, by an unidentified author from the year 742/1341, Leid. 67, see Weijers, *Orient.* I, 360ff.—5. *Kitāb al-kināya wal-taʿrīḍ*, a book of rhetoric, dedicated to the Khwārizmshāh Maʾmūn b. Maʾmūn (see Barthold, *Turkestan* 275/8), Berl. 7336, Vienna $84_{,2}$, Esc. ^{2}281(?).—6. *Kitāb ajnās al-tajnīs* Esc. $^2363_{,4}$ = *Risāla fī ʾl-tajnīs* Berl. 7330?—7. *Kitāb siḥr al-balāgha wa-sirr al-barāʿa* Berl. 8339, Tüb. 67,

1 Cf. I. Goldziher, *SBWA* 73 (1873) p. 539.

Vienna 232, Paris $3314_{,1}$, 6724, Leid. 459, Esc. $^{2}504_{,8}$ Köpr. 1283, excerpts as no. 3 in *Arbaʿ rasāʾil muntakhaba min muʾallafāt al-ʿallāma Abū Manṣūr al-Thaʿālibī*, Āsitāna, Jawāʾib 1301.—8. *Ghurar al-balāgha wa-ṭuraf al-barāʿa*, a collection of aphorisms in 10 chapters, Berl. 8341, under the title *al-Laʾālīʾ wal-durar* AS 3795/6.—9. *Thimār al-qulūb fī ʾl-muḍāf wal-mansūb*, dedicated to ʿUbaydallāh | b. Aḥmad al-Mīkālī (no. 3, p. 340), an explanation of common 339
connections in the genitive, such as *sayf Allāh, qaws quzaḥ* etc., with supporting evidence, mostly in verse, Berl. 8342, Brill, M. 212, Vienna 83, Br. Mus. 725, Algiers 1442, Rāğib 1207, Yeni 939, Köpr. 1230, cf. Hammer, ZDMG V, 179ff., 289 ff., VII, 542ff. VIII, 449ff., P. de Gayangos, *Hist. of the Muh. Dynasties in Spain*, I, 330ff. Abstract, *ʿImād al-balāgha*, by ʿAbd al-Raʾūf al-Munāwī, d. 1034/1622 (II, 302), Copenhagen 206.—10. *Kitāb al-luṭf wal-laṭāʾif* in 16 chapters, Vienna $1838_{,2}$, Esc. $^{2}363_{,2}$.—11. *Kitāb nathr al-naẓm* (*wa-ḥall al-ʿiqd*), a description in prose of the verses of *Muʾnis al-udabāʾ* by an unidentified author, composed at the order of the Khwārizmshāh, Berl. 8344/5, Leid. 457, Pet. AM 775/6.—12. *Kitāb man ghāba ʿanhu ʾl-muṭrib*, a. on eloquence, b. spring and the other seasons, c. description of day and night, d. love songs, e. wine songs, f. friendship, g. varia, Berl. 8333, BDMG 103, Paris $3305_{,1}$, $3401_{,4}$, $5934_{,3}$, Br. Mus. Suppl. $1110_{,2}$ Esc. $^{2}340_{,4}$, Garr. 188, print. in *al-Tuḥfa al-bahiyya*, Istanbul 1302, p. 230/94.—13. *Kitāb bard al-akbād fī ʾl-aʿdād* Cairo ^{1}IV, 305, ^{2}III, 34, print. Istanbul 1301.—14. *Kitāb al-tawfīq lil-talfīq*, | on that which things and persons that differ have in 286
common, of serious and cheerful content, Berl. 8338.—15. *Mirʾāt al-muruwwāt wa-aʿmāl al-ḥasanāt*, on nobleness, Berl. 5409.—16. *Kitāb al-tamaththul* (*tamthīl*) *wal-muḥāḍara* Leid. 454 (where other MSS are listed), Garr. 186, as *al-Tamthīl wal-munāẓara fī ʾl-ḥikam* Patna I $195_{,754}$, *Muntakhabāt* also no. 1 in *Arbaʿ rasāʾil*, Istanbul 1301.—17. *Kitāb al-ghilmān*, a description of young men, ḤKh V, $127_{,10351}$, Berl. 8334, imitated in *Kitāb alf ghulām wa-ghulām* by ʿAlī b. Muḥammad b. al-Riḍā al-Ḥusaynī al-Mūsawī (p. 352), Esc. $^{2}461$.—18. *Tuḥfat al-wuzarāʾ*, a counterpart to his lost mirror for princes *al-Kitāb al-mulūkī* (or *Sīrat al-mulūk* ḤKh III, $643_{,7343}$), Gotha 1886.—19. *Kanz al-kuttāb*, 2500 passages from 250 poets, for use by secretaries, Vienna 242, commentary by Lāmiʿī, d. 938/1532, cf. Toderini, *Lit. Turch.* II, app. p. XXXIV.—20. *Kitāb al-farāʾid wal-qalāʾid*, a. on the excellence of science and reason, b. manual for austerity, c. control of the tongue, d. education of the soul, e. nobility of the soul, f. on the commendable lifestyle, g. good public administration, h. eloquence, Krafft 1479.—21. *Aḥsan mā samiʿtu* Köpr. 1197.—22. *Kitāb al-mubhij* (*Mubahhij*), aphorisms and anecdotes, Berl. 8332, Paris | $1176_{,35}$, $5914_{,2}$ Köpr. 1366, Garr. 187, no. 2 340
in *Arbaʿ rasāʾil*, Istanbul 1301, C. 1322/1904 (Maṭbaʿat al-Najāḥ).—23. *al-Laṭāʾif wal-ẓarāʾif fī madḥ* (*maḥāsin*) *al-ashyāʾ wa-aḍdādihā* Berl. 8334/5, Leid. 456, Esc. $^{2}531$, dedicated to the Khwārizmshāh Abu ʾl-ʿAbbās Maʾmūn, d. 407/

1016.—24. *Kitāb yawāqīt al-mawāqīt fī madḥ al-shayʾ wa-dhammihi* Berl. 8336/7, Leid. 455 (where other MSS are listed), AS 4353, Bursa Ḥü. Celebi Edeb. 16.—25. *Kitāb laṭāʾif al-ṣaḥāba wal-tābiʿīn* Leid. 452, *Selecta ex Thaalebii libro facetiarum* ed. P. Cool in the chrestomathy to Roorda's *Gramm. ar.* Leid. 1835.—26. *Aḥāsin kalim al-nabī wal-ṣaḥāba wal-tābiʿīn wa-mulūk al-jāhiliyya wa-mulūk al-islām wal-wuzarāʾ wal-kuttāb wal-bulaghāʾ wal-ḥukamāʾ wal-ʿulamāʾ*, Leid. 453, Paris 4201,$_2$ (?), from which *Talibii Syntagma dictorum brevium et acutorum*, ed. J. Ph. Valeton, Leid. 1844. Included later in the work:—27. *Kitāb ījāz al-iʿjāz* Berl. 8340/1, Paris 3305,$_2$ 5934, Bodl. I, 338, II, 347,$_3$, Br. Mus. 724, 1074, Copenhagen 207, Esc. ^{2}291 (fragm.), Köpr. 1221, Cairo ^{1}IV, 204, ^{2}III, 16, print. as no. 1 in *Majmūʿat khams rasāʾil*, Istanbul, Jawāʾib 1301, ed. Iskandar Āṣaf, C. 1897.—28. *Kitāb al-mutashābih* for Ṣāḥib al-Jaysh Abu ʾl-Muẓaffar Nāṣir, Cairo ^{1}VII, 633, Mosul 264,$_{16,3}$, also under the title of 6., Cairo ^{2}II 215.—29. Mistakenly attributed to him is *Muʾnis al-waḥīd: Der vertraute Gefährte des Einsamen in schlagfertigen Gegenreden von et-T.* ed. G. Flügel, Vienna 1829, in reality it is a part of the anthology of Rāghib al-Iṣfahānī, d. 502/1108 (see no. 9), cf. Gildemeister, *ZDMG* 34, 171.—32.–51. see Suppl. (44. Persian translation by Muḥammad al-Sāwī Fātiḥ 3716, Ritter).—52. *al-Injās al-maʿrūf wa-ʿumdat al-qulūb* Patna I 145,$_{1399}$.—53. *Nasīm al-ṣabā*, on synonyms, AS 4353,$_2$ (Ritter).—54. *al-Anwār fī āyāt al-nabī* Berl., Ms. or. qu. 2083.

2. (3.) Abu ʾl-Faḍl ʿAbd al-Raḥīm (ʿAbd al-Raḥmān) b. Aḥmad b. ʿAlī al-Mīkālī came from a noble Persian family that regarded Bahrām Gūr as their ancestor. In Khurāsān he was a poet, literary figure, and patron of the arts, dying in 436/1044.

287 | *Yatīma* IV, 247/68, *Fawāt* II, 25. 1. A collection of proverbs in alphabetical order, divided into further subsections with every letter, in each case starting with a quotation from the Qurʾān, abstract Berl. 8668.—2. *Kitāb al-maḥzūn*,
341 | stylistic examples from his letters, excerpts from *Yatīma* IV, 249/58.—cf. Suppl.

3. (4.) Abū Yūsuf Yaʿqūb b. Aḥmad al-Kurdī was an admirer and emulator of al-Thaʿālibī who died in Ramaḍān 474/February 1082.

Al-Bulgha al-mutarjama fi ʾl-lugha, divided into 40 chapters by subject, the first of which deals with man and his limbs, while the last is devoted to weights and measures, ḤKh ^{1}II, 65,$_{1917}$, ^{2}I, 253, Gotha 402.

4. (5.) Abū Bakr ʿAbd al-Qāhir b. ʿAbd al-Raḥmān al-Jurjānī, a student of Abu ʾl-Ḥusayn al-Fārisī (a nephew of Abū ʿAlī al-Fārisī) and of ʿAlī ʿAbd al-ʿAzīz al-Jurjānī, died in 471/1078 or, according to others, in 474.

Fawāt I, 297. I. *Kitāb al-ʿawāmil al-miʾa* or *Miʾat ʿāmil* Berl. 6475/6, Gotha 212/4, Munich 696/7, Vienna 147/8, Krafft 50, Upps. 511,$_2$, Copenhagen 175, 178,$_3$, Pet. 175/6, Paris 3088,$_2$, 3989/91, 4008,$_2$, 4051,$_2$, 4123,$_4$, 4130,$_2$, 4181,$_4$, Algiers 15,$_2$, 46,$_2$, 49,$_4$, 50,$_1$, 54,$_4$, Br. Mus. 486, 487,$_4$, 495, 1389, 1522, Ind. Off. 981, Esc. ^{2}92,$_3$, Garr. 391/4, 2121,$_2$, 2124,$_1$, Alex. Naḥw 34,$_2$, Fun. 142,$_5$, Qawala II, 60, 103, *Liber C. regentium*, ed. Th. Erpenius, Leiden 1617, J. Baillie, *Five Books on Arabic Grammar*, Calcutta 1803, A. Lockett, *The Miut Amil and Sharhoo M.A. two elementary treatises on Arabic Syntax transl. etc. with an Appendix, containing the original Text*, Calcutta 1814.—Commentaries: 1. Muḥammad b. Muḥammad b. Amīr al-Ḥājj al-Ḥalabī, ca. 855/1451 (II, 93), Berl. 6477.—2. Ḥājjī Bābā Ibrāhīm b. ʿAbd al-Karīm al-Ṭūsiyawī, ca. 870/1465 (II, 223), Berl. 6478, Munich 895, f. 68b, Vienna 149, Alex. Naḥw 33.—3. Yaḥyā b. Naṣūḥ b. Isrāʾīl, ca. 950/1543, Berl. 6479, Paris 3993,$_1$, Pet. 177,$_1$, Garr. 315/6, Alex. Fun. 175,$_2$.—4. al-Tūrajī, Berl. 6480/4.—5. ʿAlī b. Ḥamīd al-Shaykhānī, ibid. 6485.—6. Khalīl b. ʿĪsā b. Ibrāhīm, with a supercommentary by ʿAlī b. Rasūl al-Qaraḥiṣārī, ibid. 6486.—7. ʿAbd al-Raḥmān b. Ḥusayn b. Idrīs, ibid. 6487.—8. Muḥammad Ṣādiq b. Darwīsh Muḥammad, Ind. Off. 982,$_1$.—9. Muṣṭafā b. Bahrām, Leipzig 29, 130.—10. Anon., Gotha 217/24, Munich 762/3, Vienna 150/1, Krafft 51, Leid. 154/6 (155 = *Bibl. Ac. Scient.* ii, 6, Bat. 156,$_{12}$), Paris 3989,$_{4,5}$, 3990, 3992, 4015,$_{6,7}$, 4144,$_3$, 4149,$_2$, Pet. 174,$_2$, 176, 177,$_3$, 237, Pet. Ros. 164,$_4$, Esc. ^{2}174, 175,$_2$, Algiers 40/1, 549, Garr. 321/3.—11. Turkish by Muḥammad b. Shaʿbān, ca. 980/1572 | (probably in Gran in 342
Hungary), Leipzig 15,$_3$.—12. Turkish anon., Paris 4041,$_3$.—13.–34. see Suppl.—Turkish translation, Vienna 152.—Versifications: 1. In 35 verses in the *basīṭ* metre by Naṣrallāh b. Aḥmad al-Baghdādī al-Ḥanbalī Jalāl al-Dīn, ca. 790/1388, Berl. 6496.—2. *al-Durra al-durriyya fi ʾl-ʿawāmil al-naḥwiyya* by Muḥammad b. ʿUthmān al-Dimashqī al-Ḥamawī, d. 1090/1679, with a commentary by ʿAbd al-Raḥmān al-Arīḥawī, d. 1128/1716 (II, 286), Berl. 6497.—3. *Ḥulwat al-ṣibyān fī naẓm al-ʿawāmil* by Abū Bakr al-Qāḍī, composed in 1174/1760, Berl. 6498.—4. Ibrāhīm, ibid. 6499.—5. Anon., ibid. 6500/1.—6. Persian, Ind. Off. 983/4,$_2$.—7.–9. see Suppl.—*Hadiyyat al-ṣibyān*, grammatical analysis by Muṣṭafā b. ʿAlī al-Awralawī, Gotha 1964, Paris 4212, Garr. 317.

| II. *Kitāb al-jumal*, didactic poem on grammar, ḤKh ^{1}II, 624,$_{4196}$,^{2}I, 288
602, Calcutta 938. Commentaries: 1. Abū Muḥammad ʿAbdallāh b. Aḥmad al-Khashshāb al-Baghdādī, d. 567/1171 (Suppl. I, 493), with the title *al-Murtajal*,

Gotha 211.—2. Shams al-Dīn Muḥammad b. Abi ʾl-Fatḥ b. Abi ʾl-Faḍl al-Bālī, d. 709/1309 (II, 100), with the title *al-Fākhir*, composed in 695/1296, Esc. ^{2}27.—3. Muḥammad b. Aḥmad b. Aḥmad al-Qayṣayrī, ca. 758/1357, Esc. ^{2}173.—4. ʿĀshiq Qapū al-Iznīqī, d. 945/1538, Br. Mus. 496,$_1$.—6. Shihāb al-Dīn Aḥmad b. Sharaf al-Dīn Sharaf b. Manṣūr al-Thaʿālibī Qāḍi ʾl-quḍāt bi-Ṭarābulus al-Shām, composed in 787/1384, Esc. ^{2}28.—7. Anon., completed in 596/1199, possibly by Abu ʾl-Ḥasan ʿAlī b. Muḥammad al-Ḥaḍramī b. al-Kharūf, d. 609/1212, ḤKh II, 624, Esc. ^{2}172.

III. *Kitāb al-tatimma*, on syntax, Ind. Off. 984, Br. Mus. 472.

IV. *Asrār al-balāgha fi ʾl-maʿānī wal-bayān*, on rhetoric and poetics, one of the most brilliant works of Arabic literature, AS 4354, Köpr. 1418/9, Faiẓ. 1771.

V. *Dalāʾil al-iʿjāz wa-asrār al-balāgha* Yeni 1031.

VI. *Sharḥ kitāb al-īḍāḥ* by Abū ʿAlī b. Aḥmad b. ʿAbd al-Ghaffār, d. 377/987, p. 116.

VII. *al-Masāʾil al-mushkila*, quoted in ʿAbd al-Qādir al-Baghdādī's *Khizānat al-adab* I, 134,$_{16}$.

VIII. *Durj al-durar* see Suppl.

IX. *al-Mukhtār min dawāwīn al-Mutanabbī wal-Buḥturī wa-Abī Tammām* in *al-Ṭarāʾif al-adabiyya*, ed. ʿAbd al-ʿAzīz al-Maymanī, C. 1937, 195/305.

5. (6.) Al-Qāḍī Abu ʾl-ʿAbbās Aḥmad b. Muḥammad al-Jurjānī, d. 482/1089, see Suppl.

1. *Kitāb kināyāt al-udabāʾ wa-ishārāt al-bulaghāʾ* ḤKh V. 245, Vienna 84.—2.–4. see Suppl.

6. (7.) Abū ʿAbdallāh al-Ḥusayn b. ʿAlī b. Aḥmad al-Zawzānī, from Zawzān between Herat and Nishapur, who died in 486/1093.

343 | 1. *Kitāb al-maṣādir*, a dictionary of Arabic infinitives with explanations in Persian (see Weijers, *Orient.* I, 367ff.), Gotha 101, 399, Leipzig 1, 23, Vienna 93, Leid. 100, Upps. 12, Paris 4287/8, 6045, Br. Mus. 1685, Ind. Off. 993, Bodl. II, 231,$_3$, Pet. 227, Pet. Ros. 71/2, Köpr. p. 232, no. 697, Schefer, *Bull. hist. phil. de St. Pétersb.* VI, 256.—2. *Tarjumān al-Qurʾān*, Arabic-Persian dictionary of the Qurʾān, separately treating nouns and verbs in two sections, Gotha 401.—3. *Sharḥ al-muʿallaqāt* see Suppl. p. 35.—4. see Suppl.

7. (8.) Abū ʿAbdallāh al-Ḥusayn b. Ibrāhīm al-Naṭanzī Dhu ʾl-Bayānayn or Dhu ʾl-Lisānayn, who died in Jumādā II 499/February 1106 or, according to Ibn Jamāʿa in al-Suyūṭī and al-Qifṭī, in Muḥarram 497/October 1103.

Dustūr al-lugha, Persian explanations of difficult Arabic words in 28 books (following the number of the letters of the alphabet and of the mansions of the moon), of 12 chapters each (after the number of the months and the signs of the zodiac), with a grammatical introduction on the conjugation of transitive and intransitive verbs, the gender of the nouns etc., Leid. 102/4, Paris 4286, Upps. 10,$_{2}$.

| 8. (9.) Abu 'l-Qāsim al-Ḥusayn b. Muḥammad b. al-Mufaḍḍal[2] al-Rāghib 289
al-Iṣfahānī, d. 502/1108.

ZDMG 1851, p. 79. 1. *Kitāb muḥāḍarāt al-udabāʾ al-shuʿarāʾ wal-bulaghāʾ* or *Kitāb al-muḥāḍarāt*, a philological-historical anthology, individual parts Berl. 8346/9, BDMG 116, Vienna 369/70, Leid. 464, Br. Mus. 777, 1094, AS 4254, 4255/8, Köpr. 1371,$_{1}$, 1372, 1373/6, 1377/8, print. C. 1287.—2. *Mufradāt alfāẓ al-Qurʾān*, a dictionary of the Qurʾān, organised by the first letter in alphabetical order, with quotations of *ḥadīth* and Qurʾānic verses, very useful, ḤKh VI, 35,$_{12638}$, Berl. 675, Ms. or. qu. 2062, AS 432, Yeni 58, 159, Köpr. 1577, Cairo ^{1}I, 216, ^{2}II, 40, Qawala I, 82, Alex. Adab 27 (fragm.) Patna I, 33,$_{340}$.—3. *Tafsīr al-Qurʾān* AS 212.—4. *Ḥall mutashābihāt al-Qurʾān* Rāġib 180.—5. *Tafṣīl al-nashʾatayn wa-taḥṣīl al-saʿādatayn* ibid. AS 4027, Köpr. 1371,$_{3}$, Cairo ^{1}VII, 555.—6. *Kitāb al-akhlāq*, on ethics, Berl. 5392.—7. *al-Dharīʿa ilā makārim al-sharīʿa*, an ethical masterpiece that al-Ghazzālī supposedly carried with him at all times, Vienna 1839, Rāġib 1179, Köpr. 1371,$_{2}$, print. C. 1299, 1324, Persian translation Br. Mus. Pers. Suppl. 146.—8.–12. see Suppl.

| 9. (10.) Abu 'l-Faḍl Aḥmad b. Muḥammad b. Aḥmad b. Ibrāhīm al-Maydānī was 344
a student of al-Wāḥidī who died on 15 Ramaḍān 518/27 October 1124 in Nishapur.

Ibn al-Anb. 460, Ibn Khall. 60. 1. *Majmaʿ al-amthāl* Berl. 8670/1, Leid. 383/4 (where other MSS are listed), AS 4127, Dāmād Ibr. 95/8, Patna I 188,$_{1709/10}$, print. Būlāq 1284, C. 1310, 1320, edited by G.W. Freytag, *Arabum proverbia*, 3 vols., Bonn 1838/43. Abstract, *al-Durr al-muntakhab* by Qāsim b. Muḥammad b. ʿAlī al-Bakrajī, d. 1169/1756 (II, 287) Berl. 8672, a metrical revision by an Ottoman author from 1079/1668, ḤKh V, 393, Gotha 1250.—2. *al-Sāmī fi 'l-asāmī*, a dictionary: 1. *fiqh*, 2. living creatures, 3. heavenly creatures, 4. earthly things, Arabic terms with explanations in Persian, completed on 19 Ramaḍān 497/9 June 1104 (see Weijers, *Orient.* I, 368ff.) Berl. 7040, Leid. 105 (where other MSS are listed, and in addition:) Br. Mus. Suppl. 855, Garr. 269/70, AS 4680/1, Yeni 1128, Bursa,

2 After Berl. 675 Faḍl, after al-Suyūṭī *Bughya* 396, al-Mufaḍḍal b. Muḥammad etc.

Haraccizade Lugha 15, Cairo ^{1}IV, 173, Alex. Lugha 13. Annotations and additions to it, Leid. 106, anon. under the title *al-Ibāna* ibid. 107 (Weijers, *Orient.* I, 371ff.). Abstract following the arrangement by al-Jawharī, composed by his son Abū Saʿīd Saʿd, d. 539/1144 (Suyūṭī, *Bughya* 254), perhaps Leid. 108 (Weijers op. cit., 371ff.).—3. *Kitāb al-hādī lil-shādī,* on syntax, with Persian annotations, composed after *al-Sāmī,* Ind. Off. 1027$_{,1}$, Bodl. I, 1067$_{,2}$, AS 4441, with anonymous commentary (maybe by the author) Leid. 162 (Weijers, op. cit., I, 371 n).—4. Treatise on the formation of plurals and the *ḥurūf* Leid. 163.—5. Small grammatical treatise, Paris 4000.—6.–8. see Suppl.

10. (11.) A student of al-Maydānī, Abū Yaʿqūb Yūsuf b. Ṭāhir al-Khuwwī (Khuwayhī) wrote in 532/1137:

1. *Farāʾid al-kharāʾid,* a collection of proverbs, ḤKh IV, 3968, Paris 3968, ʿUm. 5574, Istanbul Un. R. 255 (*ZS* III, 249), abstract *ʿUqūd al-ʿuqūl* Vienna 343, with annotations in Turkish.—2. *Sharḥ saqt al-zand* Suppl. I, 453.

11. (12.) Abu ʾl-Qāsim Maḥmūd b. ʿUmar al-Zamakhsharī, born in Zamakhshar
290 in Khwārizm on 27 Rajab 467/19 March 1075, | made long study tours in his youth and, after making the pilgrimage, lived for a considerable time in Mecca (which is why he was called Jārallāh). As a theologian he declared himself
345 one of the | Muʿtazila.[3] As well as Qurʾānic exegesis he devoted himself to philological studies. Even though he explained Arabic words in Persian in his *Muqaddimat al-adab,* he was so convinced of the pre-eminence of the Arabic language that he repudiated any *shuʿūbī* tendencies in the introduction to his *Mufaṣṣal.* He died in Jurjāniyya in Khwārizm on the day of ʿArafa 538/20 June 1144.

Ibn al-Anb. 469/73, Ibn Khall. 682, Ibn Quṭlūbughā 217, Barbier de Meynard, *JA* 1875 II, 314.—1. *al-Kashshāf ʿan ḥaqāʾiq al-tanzīl wa-ʿuyūn al-aqāwīl fī wūjūh al-taʾwīl,* a Qurʾān commentary, against the study of which—in his days especially widespread in Persia—Ṭāshköprīzāde warns in *Miftāḥ al-saʿāda* II, 409/10, Berl. 769/80, Ms. or qu. 2030 (Fischer-Burch. 9), oct. 3890, Leipz. 86/93, Munich 84/7, Paris 597/603; Algiers 320/5, Br. Mus. 64/7, Ind Off. 52/6, Pet. 44, AS 242/52, Köpr. 124/37, Yeni 84/91, NO 396/414, Cairo ^{1}I, 189, Garr. 1267/70, Patna I 31$_{,306/8}$, ed. by W. Nassau Lees, Mawlawis Khadim Hosain, and ʿAbd al-Hayi, 2 vols., Calcutta 1856, print. C. 1307, 1308 (with glosses by

3 This is why he originally opened his *Kashshāf* with the words: *al-ḥamdu lillāhi alladhī khalaqa ʾl-Qurʾān,* where the chastened, orthodox *vulgata* reads *anzala* instead.

ʿAlī b. Muḥammad al-Jurgānī no. 9) C. 1354 (with *al-Intiṣāf* by Ibn al-Munayyir al-Iskandarī, *Ḥāshiyat al-Marzūqī, al-Kāfi ʾl-shāfī fī takhrīj aḥādīth al-K.* by Ibn Ḥajar al-ʿAsqalānī, II, 67). Glosses: 1. Maḥmūd b. Masʿūd al-Shīrāzī Quṭb al-Dīn al-ʿAllāma, d. 710/1310 (II, 211), Paris 604, AS 366/7.—2. *Futūḥ al-ghayb* by al-Ḥasan b. Muḥammad al-Ṭībī, d. 743/1342 (II, 64), Vienna 1639, Algiers 326, AS 368, 369/74, NO 560/1 Köpr. 195/202, Yeni 138/43, Cairo ^{1}I, 187, Patna I, $28_{,273/6}$, II, $500_{,2678}$.—3. *al-Kashf ʿan mushkilāt al-K.* by Abū Ḥafṣ ʿUmar b. ʿAbd al-Raḥmān b. ʿUmar al-Fārisī al-Qazwīnī, d. 745/1344, Berl. 790, AS 360/2, Rāġib 173, Köpr. 187/8, Yeni 154/7, NO 564/6, Cairo ^{1}I, 192.—4. Aḥmad b. al-Ḥusayn b. Ibrāhīm al-Jārabardī Fakhr al-Dīn, d. 746/1345 (II, 193), NO 554/5, Rāġib 166/7, Qawala I, 56.—5. *Sharḥ al-K.* by Muḥammad b. Muḥammad al-Taḥtānī al-Rāzī, d. 766/1364 (II, 209), Berl. 792, Leid, AS 367, Rāġib 172, Köpr. 193, Yeni 146, NO 556, Cairo ^{1}I, 168.—6. Yaḥyā b. al-Qāsim al-ʿAlawī al-Fāḍil al-Yamanī ʿImād al-Dīn, d. 750/1349 (Suyūṭī, *Bughya* 414), *Durar al-aṣdāf*, Ind. Off. | 1095, 346
NO 563, Dāmādzāde 299.—7. Muḥammad b. Muḥammad b. Maḥmūd al-Bābartī, d. 786/1384 (II, 80), Köpr. 194, Dāmādzāde 270.—8. Saʿd al-Dīn al-Taftāzānī, d. 792/1389 (II, 215), Berl. 793, Esc. ^{2}1300, 1417, NO 557, AS 364/5, Köpr. 189/91, Rāġib 168, Yeni 134, Cairo ^{1}I, 204, Qawala I, 57, Patna I, $28_{,277/8}$, on which superglosses by ʿAlāʾ al-Dīn Muḥammad al-Bukhārī al-ʿAlāʾī, first half 9th cent., Cairo ^{1}I, 168, by al-Khiṭāʾī, d. 901/1495, ibid. 204, anon. Gotha 528, Leipzig. $109_{,1}$.—9. ʿAlī b. Muḥammad al-Jurjānī, d. 816/1413, (II, 216), Berl. 794/5, Ind. Off. 60, Garr. 1271, Rāġib 171, Köpr. 192, Yeni 136/7, NO 358/9, Cairo ^{1}I, 168, Selīm. 137/8, Patna I, $28_{,279}$ = (?) *Risāla fī baʿḍ mushkilāt al-K.*, AS 410, printed in the margin of the *Kashshāf*, C. 1308 (see above), on which superglosses by Khaṭībzāde, d. 901/1495, Cairo ^{1}II, 165, 203, by Ibn Kamālpāshā, d. 940/1533, Yeni 148.—| 10. *al-Muḥākamāt ʿala ʾl-K.* by ʿAbd al-Karīm b. ʿAbd al-Jabbār, composed 291
in 825/1422, NO 562, AS 363.—11. Khiḍr al-ʿAṭūfī, d. 948/1541, Yeni 144.—12. Ismāʿīl Qara Kamāl, ca. 900/1484, NO 553.—13. ʿAbd al-Bāqī b. Mollā Khalīl, ca. 1150/1737, Berl. 797.—14. Anon., Berl. 796, Paris 605.—15. *Tanzīl al-āyāt*, commentary on the *shawāhid* of Muḥibb al-Dīn al-Muftī al-Dimashqī, d. 1016/1608 (II, 361), Leid. 1667, Būlāq 1281, C. 1300, 1307.—16.–18. see Suppl. (17. *al-Isʿāf* also Patna I, $22_{,189/201}$). Other glosses mentioned in Ahlw., 799.—Abstracts: 1. *al-Taqrīb fi ʾl-tafsīr* by Muḥammad b. Masʿūd al-Sīrāfī al-Qālī al-Shuqqār, composed in 698/1298, AS 88, Patna I, $26_{,245/6}$.—2. *Talkhīṣ al-K.* by ʿUmar b. Dāʾūd b. Sulaymān al-Fārisī al-ʿAjamī, first half of the eighth cent., Cairo ^{1}I, 154.—2a. *Taqrīb al-K.*, anon., Berl. 788 (not = 1.).—3. *Takhrīj aḥādīth al-K.* by ʿAbdallāh b. Yūsuf al-Zaylaʿī, d. 762/1360, Cairo ^{1}I, 167, Patna I, $24_{,221/2}$.—4. *al-Kāfi ʾl-shāfī fī takhrīj aḥādīth al-K.* by Ibn Ḥajar al-ʿAsqalānī, d. 852/1448 (II, 67), abstract of 3., Berl. 1348, Yeni 174, Patna I, $31_{,305}$ (see above).—6.–11. see Suppl. (6. also Patna I, $29_{,282}$, where *al-Durr al-shaffāf*, 7. *Tajrīd al-K.*, Patna I, $24_{,218/21}$).—Refutations:

1. *Kitāb al-intiṣāf min al-K.* against false teachings and some grammatical opinions, by Abū b. Muḥammad b. Manṣūr b. al-Munayyir al-Mālikī, d. 683/1284 (p. 416), Cairo ^{1}I, 127 (see above). Abstract by ʿAbdallāh b. Yūsuf b. Hishām, d. 761/1359, Berl. 791.—2. *Kitāb al-tamyīz li-bayān mā fī tafsīr al-Zamakhsharī min al-iʿtizāl fi 'l-K. al-ʿazīz*, against his Muʿtazilī views, by ʿUmar b. Muḥammad b. al-Khalīl al-Sukūnī, d. 707/1307, Cairo ^{1}I, 154, abstract *al-Muqtaḍab*, Leid. 1608, Esc. ^{2}1547, NO 475.—3. see Suppl.

347 | II. *Kitāb al-mufaṣṣal*, composed between 513/5 = 1119/21, a textbook on grammar, a classic because of the concise and clear wording of its material, ed. J.B. Broch, Oslo 1859, ed. II, ibid. 1879. Commentaries: 1. Self-commentary, Leid. 164, Vienna 154.—2. al-Qāsim b. al-Ḥusayn al-Khwārizmī, d. 617/1220, Br. Mus. Suppl. 927.—2a. *al-Muḥaṣṣal* by Abu 'l-Baqāʾ ʿAbdallāh b. Abī ʿAbdallāh Ḥusayn al-ʿUkbarī, d. 616/1219 (p. 495), Garr. 327, Cairo ^{2}II; 127. Abstract, *al-Mustarshid*, by the author himself, Patna I, 174,$_{1605}$.—3. Abu 'l-Baqāʾ b. Yaʿīsh, d. 643/1245 (p. 358), ed. by G. Jahn, Leipzig 1882, 2 vols.—4. *al-Mufaḍḍal* by ʿAlī b. Muḥammad b. ʿAbd al-Ṣamad al-Sakhāwī, d. 643/1245 (p. 410), Leid. 165, Paris 4004 (? fragm.) Esc. ^{2}61.[4]—4a. *Sifr al-saʿāda wa-safīr al-ifāda*, by the same, explanation of paradigms, ḤKh III, 599,$_{7175}$, VI, 39,$_{3}$, Berl. 7094 (wrongly identified by Ahlw.), Oct. 3582, Cairo ^{1}III, 566, ^{2}II, 17,$_{1}$, Dam. ʿUm. 86 (Z. 79,$_{14}$), A. Taymūr, *RAAD* III, 339, ibid. XII, 704, Maktabat Shaykh al-islām (*Tadhk. al-Naw.* 119).—5. *al-Īḍāḥ* by ʿUthmān b. ʿUmar b. al-Ḥājib, d. 646/1248 (p. 367), Munich 693, Alex. Naḥw 4, Patna I, 161,$_{1523}$.—6. *al-Mukammal* by Muẓhir al-Dīn al-Sharīf al-Raḍī Muḥammad completed in 659/1261, Bodl. I, 1084, Esc. ^{2}60, Algiers 43, Patna I, 174,$_{1613}$.—7. Yaḥyā b. Ḥamza b. Sayyid al-Murtaḍā, d. 749/1348, composed in 712/1312, Berl. 6521.—8. *al-Iqlīd* by Aḥmad b. Maḥmūd b. ʿUmar al-Jundī al-Andalusī, eighth cent., Esc. ^{2}62, Bodl. I, 1100, Paris 4003.—9. Anon. fragm., Br. Mus. 1031.—10. Anon., on the *shawāhid*, Leid. 166.—11.–19. see Suppl.—24 commentaries, 2 *shawāhid* commentaries, 2 abstracts, 2 versifications, and 1 rebuttal in Ahlw., 6522.

III. *Kitāb al-unmūdhaj*, a short grammar, abstract from the *Mufaṣṣal* (see de Sacy, *Anth. gramm.* 99), Leid. 167 (where other MSS are listed), autograph by J. Broch, Christiana 1867, print. C. 1289, Istanbul 1298. Commentaries: 1. Muḥammad b. ʿAbd al-Ghanī al-Ardabīlī, d. 1036/1626, Berl. 6516/7, Gotha 224/6 (where other MSS are listed), Garr. 329/31, 2121,$_{3}$, Alex. Naḥw 21, Qawala II, 89, Patna I, 167, 1560, print. Būlāq 1269.—2. Saʿd al-Dīn al-Bardaʿī, Berlin 6508, Vienna 155, Pet. 197, Ros. 129, Garr. 332/3, Alex. Naḥw 14.—3. Anon., Leid. 168, Garr 334.—4. Anon., on the *shawāhid*, Pet. 198.—5.–7. see Suppl.—8. ʿAlī b. ʿAbdallāh b. Aḥmad Zayn al-ʿArab, composed in 736/1335, Alex. Fun. 96,$_{1}$.

---

4 Contra Derenbourg, who follows Suppl. 510,$_{5a}$, see Leid., loc. cit.

IV. *al-Muḥājjāt wa-mutammim mahāmm arbāb al-ḥājāt* | *fi 'l-aḥājī wal-ughlūṭāt fi 'l-naḥw* Cairo ^{1}VII, 162, II, 157. 348

V. *al-Qusṭās fi 'l-ʿarūḍ*, on metrics, Berl. 7111, Leid. 267, Garr. 497/8, Patna I, 191,$_{1727/8}$. Commentary by Aḥmad b. al-Ḥasan b. Aḥmad al-Naḥwī al-Mawṣilī, Leid. 268, *Taṣḥīḥ al-miqyās* (attributed to ʿIzz al-Dīn ʿAbd al-Wahhāb b. Ibrāhīm al-Zanjānī al-Khazrajī [see p. 336] in ḤKh IV. 514,$_{9514}$).

VI. *Muqaddimat al-adab*, an Arabic-Persian dictionary, later with a Turkish part dedicated to Atsyz (see Suppl.) and provided with glosses in Mongolian by a later editor, Berl. 6960/2, Leid. 1090 (where other MSS are listed), Patna I, 189,$_{1718}$. *Samachscharii Lexicon Ar.-Pers.* ed. J.G. Wetzstein, 2 vols., Leipzig 1844, N.N. Poppe, *Mongolskij Slovar Muqaddimat al-Adab,* | *Čast I–III, Ak. Nauk SSSR, Trudy Inst. Vostokoved.* XIV, Moscow—Leningrad 1938. Commentaries: 1. On the last two parts, anon., Esc. ^{2}167,$_{3}$.—2. On the grammmatical introduction by Muḥammad ʿIṣmatallāh b. Maḥmūd Niʿmatallāh al-Bukhārī, composed in 645/1538, Ind. Off. 989,$_{9902}$.—3. Anonymous glosses ibid. 990,$_{1}$.—Turkish translation by Isḥāq Efendi Aḥmad b. Khayr al-Dīn al-Burūsawī, d. 1120/1708, Vienna 86. 292

VII. *al-Fāʾiq fī gharīb al-ḥadīth* Berl. 1648/9, Leid. 70, AS 4707/8, Köpr. 370/2, Yeni 1135/8, Dam ʿUm. 71,$_{36/40}$, Patna I, 187,$_{1698}$.

VIII. *Asās al-balāgha*, on eloquence, with a special emphasis on metaphors, Berl. 6958, Leid. 71/3 (where other MSS are listed), Patna I, 183,$_{1682}$, print. C. 1299, 1327. Abstract by Ibn Ḥajar al-ʿAsqalānī, d. 852/1448 (II, 67), Berl. 6959, anon. Br. Mus. Suppl. 857.

IX. *Kitāb al-amkina wal-jibāl wal-miyāh, Z. i lexicon geographicum cui titulus K. al-J. wal-a. wal-m. quod auspice T.G.J. Juynboll ed.* M. Salverda de Grave, Leiden 1856, Baghdad 1938.

X. *Masʾala fī kalimat al-shahāda* Berl. 2406.

XI. *Kitāb khaṣāʾiṣ al-ʿashara al-kirām al-barara* Berl. 9656.

XII. *Kitāb al-naṣāʾiḥ al-kibār* (also called *Maqāmāt*), sayings in which the author addresses himself at the beginning of each with the phrase "*yā Aba 'l-Qāsim*!", Vienna 348,$_{3}$, 379, Garr. 201, Mosul 144,$_{62,7}$, self-commentary Berl. 8749.

XIII. *Kitāb al-mustaqṣā fi 'l-amthāl* Leid. 394, Vienna 338, Br. Mus. 730, 1426, Suppl. 1002, Köpr. 1388/9, NO 4249.

XIV. *Nawābigh al-kalim*, a collection of sayings, Berl. 8676, Leid. 391/2 (where other MSS are listed), AS 4339, Qawala II, 211, print. C. 1287. *Anthologia sententiarum arab. cum scholiis Z., ed. vertit ill.* H.A. Schultens, Leiden 1772, | cf. Barbier de Meynard, *JA* s. 7. v. 6, p. 313ff. Commentaries: 1. ʿAlī b. Muḥammad al-Kabindī, ca. 718/1318, de Jong 52.—2. *al-Niʿam al-sawābigh* by al-Taftāzānī, d. 792/1389 (II, 215), Algiers 1445 (see Suppl.), print. Istanbul 1283, Turkish transl. by Muṣṭafā ʿIṣām al-Dīn, *Pet. Inst.* VIII, 27.—3. Abu 'l-Ḥasan b. ʿAbd al-Wahhāb 349 al-Khaywaqī, ca. 770/1368, Berl. 8675.—4. The Yemeni prince Amīr al-Muʾminīn al-Nāṣir lil-Ḥaqq al-Mubīn Ṣalāḥ al-Dīn Muḥammad, composed in 782/1380, Paris $3966_{,1}$.—5. al-Qūnawī, ca. 1000/1591, Berl. 8677.—6.–7. see Suppl.

XV. *Kitāb rabīʿ al-abrār (wa-nuṣūṣ al-akhbār)*, a collection of sayings (see Hammer, *Wien. Jahrb.* 63, Anz.-Bl. p. 231), Berl. 8351/3, Leid. 470 (where other MSS are listed), Garr. 202, AS 3985, Dāmād Ibr. 948, Patna I, $798_{,1779}$, anon. commentary entitled *Nafaḥāt azhār R. al-a.*, Patna I, $207_{,1851}$. Abstracts by: 1. The author himself, Br. Mus. 729.—2. *Rawḍ al-akhyār* by Muḥammad b. Qāsim b. Yaʿqūb, d. 940/1533 (II, 429), Berl. 8356, Gotha 2133/4, Leipz. 603, Dresd. 404, Munich 600, Paris 3501/2, Br. Mus. 513, 1125 (see Suppl.), Garr. 73, Alex. Adab 73.—3. Muḥammad b. Khalīl al-Qabāqibī, d. 849/1445, Berl. 8355.—4. Anon., Berl. 8358, Vienna 376, Alex. Fun. $107_{,9}$, with the title *Zahr al-rabīʿ*, Berl. 8356, *Anwār R. al-a.*, Patna I, $194_{,1748}$.—5. Turkish by ʿĀshiq Čelebī, d. 979/1571, Vienna 378.

XVI. *Aṭwāq al-dhahab* or *al-Naṣāʾiḥ al-ṣighār* (see de Goeje, ZDMG XXX, 569) Berl. 8678/9, Leid. 2153, Vienna $348_{,2}$, 349, Paris $3948_{,2}$, $3964_{,1}$, $3973_{,11}$, Br. Mus. Suppl. 1003, ii (see Suppl.), AS $3780_{,1}$, Patna I, $193_{,1739}$, $207_{,1850}$, *Samachscharis Goldene Halsbänder, als Neujahrsgeschenk, ar. u. deutsch b.* J. v. Hammer, Vienna 1835, *S.s. Goldene Halsbänder, von neuem übers. u. mit Anmm. begleitet v.* H.L. Fleischer, Leipzig 1835. *Gold. Halsbänder von neuem übers. v.* G. Weil, Stuttgart 1863. *Les Colliers d'or, allocutions morales de Z. Texte ar. suivi d'une trad. franç. et d'un cmt. phil. par* C. Barbier de Meynard, Paris 1876.—Imitations: a. *Aṭbāq al-dhahab* by ʿAbd al-Muʾmin b. Hibatallāh al-Maghribī al-Iṣfahānī Shufurwa, a Persian poet from around 600/1203, Berl. 8684/5, Vienna $348_{,1}$, $350_{,2}$, $3948_{,3}$, $3964_{,2}$, $3973_{,1}$, Br. Mus. 1429, Esc. $^{2}544_{,2}$, AS $3780_{,2}$, Alex. Adab $134_{,2}$, Fun. $107_{,7}$, Cairo ^{1}IV, 203, ^{2}III, 146, Patna I, $193_{,1738}$, print. Būlāq 1280, Lahore 1878, C. 1325, with glosses by Yūsuf b. Ismāʿīl al-Nabhānī (see Suppl. II, 763), Beirut 1309.—b. *Aṭwāq al-dhahab* by Aḥmad b. Muḥammad b. Maḥmūd al-Naḥwī, Brill-H. ^{1}496, $^{2}1146_{,13}$ = Garr. $2005_{,15}$ (which has al-Khuwayyī and where the
350 work | is identified with a. without any justification).—c. *Aṭbāq al-dhahab* by Abu 'l-Faraj b. al-Jawzī, d. 597/1200 (see p. 499), Garr. 204 (see Esc. ^{1}I, 221). Commentary, *Qalāʾid al-adab fī sharḥ A. al-dh.*, by Muḥammad Mīrzā Yūsuf Khān b. Iʿtiṣām al-Mulk, completed in 1319/1901, C. 1321.—d. *Akhlāq al-dhahab* by Muḥammad Amīn b. Ibrāhīm b. Yūnus b. al-Efendī, Patna I, 192, 1736.

293 | XVII. *Nuzhat al-mutaʾannis wa-nahzat al-muqtabis* AS 4331 (ZDMG 64, 508).

XVIII. *al-Qaṣīda al-baʿūḍiyya*, in praise of God and his messenger, in connection with a description of the mosquito, Berl. 7686/7.

XIX. *Qaṣīda* on the question, by al-Ghazzālī, of how God is seated on the throne and on the limitations of human knowledge, Berl. $7688_{,1}$.

XX. Other poems ibid. 2, 3.

XXI–XXV. See Suppl.
XXVI. See ibid. 965.

12. (13.) Zamakhsharī's favourite student, Ḍiyāʾ al-Dīn al-Makkī, wrote, around 550/1155:

Kifāyat al-naḥw fī ʿilm al-iʿrāb, a commentary on the *Unmūdhaj*, see Suppl. I, 510.

13. (14.) Aḥmad b. ʿAlī al-Bayhaqī Būjaʿfarak, d. 30 Ramaḍān 544/31 January 1150 (see Suppl.).

Tāj al-maṣādir, a dictionary with infinitives in Arabic and explanations in Persian, Ind. Off. 994/6, Bodl. I, 1089, AS 4664, NO 702, Yeni 1123.

14. Abū Ḥafṣ ʿUmar b. ʿUthmān al-Janzī, a teacher of Samʿānī (*Ansāb* 137b), was a poet and scholar, and died in 550/1155 in Marw.

Al-Suyūṭī, *Bughya* 362. *Al-Wāfī fi ʾl-ʿarūḍ wal-qawāfī* Ind. Off. 4618 (*JRAS* 1939, 385 with the erroneous statement that he "died in 505," caused by a misreading of the number in the facsimile edition of al-Samʿānī).

15. Abu ʾl-Fatḥ Nāṣir b. ʿAbd al-Sayyid al-Muṭarrizī was allegedly born in Khwārizm in Rajab 538/January 1144, the year in which al-Zamakhsharī passed away, for which reason this follower of the latter was called Khalīfat al-Zamakhsharī. Besides philology, he also devoted himself to the study | of 351
fiqh according to the teachings of Abū Ḥanīfa, and to Muʿtazilī dogmatics. In the year 601/1204 he lived for a time in Baghdad, and died on 21 Jumādā I 610/9 October 1213.

Ibn Khall. 729, Ibn Quṭlūbughā 241. I. *Kitāb al-miṣbāḥ fi ʾl-naḥw*, an abstract from the work of ʿAbd al-Qāhir al-Jurjānī written for his son, Berl. 6530/1, Gotha 214, Leip. 418, 887,$_5$, 894,$_2$, Munich 695/7, Vienna 159/63, Krafft 46, Leid. 172/4, Paris 1136,$_4$, 4008, 4130,$_3$, 6351, Algiers 46,$_3$, 49,$_3$, 51,$_3$, Br. Mus. 486,$_3$, 7,$_3$, 880,$_3$, 1030,$_2$, 1390, 1522,$_3$, Ind. Off. 890, Copenhagen 171,$_2$, Upps. 46, Pet. 610,$_2$, Garr. 337/9, 2105, 2121, Qawala II, 130/1, Patna I, 174,$_{1604/8}$, II, 520,$_{2796}$, print. Lucknow 1261, see de Sacy, *Anth.* 93, 224, Baillie, *Five Books*. Commentaries: 1. *al-Ḍawʾ* by Tāj al-Dīn Muḥammad b. Muḥammad b. Aḥmad al-Isfarāʾinī, d. 684/1285 (p. 356), completed in 684/1285, Berl. 6532/3, Gotha 237 (where other MSS are

listed), BDMG $81_{,1}$, Ind. Off. 4567 (*JRAS* 1939, 358), Garr. 340/5, Qawala II, 92/3, 98/9, Patna I, $171_{,1586/7}$, print. Lucknow 1850.—Glosses: a. On the Preface, by Raḍī al-Dīn al-Khwārizmī, Br. Mus. $1000_{,3}$, Esc. $^2236_{,9}$, Patna I, $166_{,1551}$.—b. Also on the Preface, by Muḥammad Rukn al-Ushwānī, Gotha 247.—c. Muḥammad b. Ḥamza al-Fanārī, d. 834/1430 (II, 233), Berl. 6536.—d. Anon., Pet. $193_{,1}$, 194, Garr. 346.—e. *Sharḥ shawāhid al-Ḍaw'* by Ismā'īl b. 'Alī, Paris $4023_{,4}$.—f. By an anonymous author, Berl. 6534/5, Gotha 246.—2. *al-Iftitāḥ* by Ḥasan Pāshā b. 'Alā' al-Dīn al-Aswad, ca. 800/1397, Berl. 6538/9, or. oct. 3866, Paris $4017_{,1}$, $4144_{,5}$, Gotha 248 (where other MSS are listed), Garr. 349/50, Alex. Naḥw 3, Qawala II, 60.—3. *al-Maqālīd* by Tāj al-Dīn Aḥmad b. Maḥmūd b. 'Umar al-Jundī, composed in 751/1350, Esc. ^{2259} (fragm.).—4. Muḥammad b. 'Alī
294 b. Barakāt Muḥammad al-Āqsarā'ī (al-Aqrānī), ca. 780/1378, Berl. 6537.—| 5. *Khulāṣat al-i'rāb* by Ḥājjī Bābā b. Ḥājj Ibrāhīm 'Abd al-Karīm al-Ṭūsiyawī, second half of the ninth century, Berl. 6541/2, Leipz. 26, Vienna 166, Pet. Ros. $139_{,1}$, Paris $4023_{,3}$, Garr. 352, Qawala II, 86.—6. Yaḥyā b. Nāṣiḥ b. Isrā'īl, ca. 950/1532 (Suppl. II, 630), Gotha 206, Pet. 177.—7. *al-Ifṣāḥ 'an anwār al-M.*, anon., Leid. 176.—8. *Mishkāt al-M.*, anon., Paris 4018.—9. Anon., Berl. 6540, '3, '4, Br. Mus. 500, Algiers 45, 47.—10. *al-Mu'rib fī sharḥ al-'awāmil*, anon., Gotha 203, 207, similar Bodl. II, 418, Munich 762/3, Krafft 51, Gotha 218/21.—10. On the *dībāja* by al-Taftāzānī, d. 791/1389 (?), Berl. 6545/6, BDMG 81a, glosses thereon: a.
352 'Alīzāde Ya'qūb, | Leipz. 27/8, Dresd. 152, 246.—b. Anon., Berl. 6545, '7, '8.—11. Tāj al-Dīn al-Isfarā'inī, d. 684/1285 (Suppl. I, 520), Berl. 6549.—12. Anon., Gotha $214_{,3}$, 229/33 (where other MSS are listed), on the *dībāja*, a supercommentary by Ya'qūb b. Sayyid 'Alī, Krafft 48 (autograph from the year 1067/1656), Paris 4023/4, Gotha 234 (where other MSS are listed), Alex. Naḥw 25.—15.–23. see Suppl.—24. *al-Iṣlāḥ fī sharḥ dībāja al-M.* by Muḥammad b. Yūsuf Qarabīrī, Alex. Naḥw 35.—25. Glosses on 19, *al-Ḥamdiyya* by Aḥmad al-'Imād al-Ḥanafī, Garr. 348, Alex. Naḥw 14.—26. Anon., Alex. Naḥw 25.—27. Anon., *I'rāb dībājat al-M.* Berl. 6545/6, Br. Mus. $406_{,11}$, Suppl. 934, Garr. 354/8.—28. Anon., *al-Ifṣāḥ* Qawala II, 61.—29. Anon., on the *Dībāja* Garr. 347, Qawala II, 90, on which glosses by Ya'qūb b. 'Alīzāde al-Burūsawī, ibid.—30. Anon., *Risāla fī abyāt al-ḍaw' wal-miṣbāḥ wal-iftitāḥ wa-mishkāt al-miṣbāḥ* Garr. 348.—8 commentaries on the *Miṣbāḥ*, 3 on the *Dībāja*, 3 on the *Ḍaw'* in Ahlw., 6550.—Versifications: a. *al-Ghurar*, anon., Esc. $^2261_{,2}$.—b. only of the *'awāmil*, by Aḥmad al-Ṣūfī, Gotha 215, Calc. 1039.

II. A grammatical treatise, different from the *Miṣbāḥ*, Paris $4254_{,2}$.

III. *Kitāb al-mughrib fī tartīb al-mu'rib*, a dictionary, arranged by the first letter, second edition of his lost *Kitāb al-mu'rib* that, written for jurisconsults, enjoys the same reputation among the Ḥanafīs as Azharī's *Gharīb al-fiqh* does among the Shāfiʿīs (see Weijers, *Orient.* I, 678ff.), Berl. 6966/7, Or. Qu. 2106, Leid. 77/8 (where other MSS are listed), Br. Mus. Suppl. 864, Garr. 1447, Alex. Lugha 32.—Commentary, *Īḍāḥ al-mushkil*, by Ibn ʿUṣfūr, d. 669/1270 (Suppl. I, 546), Ambros. 153.

IV. *al-Iqnāʿ li-mā ḥuwiya taḥta ʾl-qināʿ*, a lexicon of synonyms composed for his son, Berl. 6968, de Jong 32, Paris 4255, Esc. ^{2}608, Garr. 336.

V. *Sharḥ Maqāmāt al-Ḥarīrī* see p. 327.

16. Sirāj al-Dīn Abū Yaʿqūb b. Abī Bakr b. Muḥammad b. ʿAlī al-Sakkākī was born in Khwārizm in 555/1160 and died in Qaryat al-Kindī near Maʿlī in 626/1229.

Ibn Quṭlūbughā 250, Barthold, *Zwölf Vorlesungen*, 197. 1. *Miftāḥ al-ʿulūm* in 3 parts: 1. *ʿIlm al-ṣarf*, 2. *ʿIlm al-naḥw*, 3. *ʿIlm al-maʿānī wal-bayān*, whose third part, a treatment of rhetoric, is particularly significant, Berl. | 7184/6, 353
Leid. 294/6, Esc. ^{2}205, 232, Patna I, 182,$_{1674/6}$, print. C. 1317, Istanbul 1317; part 3 especially BDMG 93, Munich 678/9, Br. Mus. 550/1, Ind. Off. 843, Paris 3955,$_5$, 4371/2, Esc. ^{2}251/2. Commentaries on part 3: 1. ʿAlī b. Muḥammad b. Dihqān ʿAlī b. Abī Bakr b. ʿAlī al-Nasafī al-Kabindī, composed in 718/1318 in Khwārizm, Leid. 297, Algiers 197.—2. al-Taftāzānī, d. 791/1389 (II, 215), written in 748/1318 in Herat, Vienna 235,$_2$, Leid. 298, Paris 4373, de Jong 46, Ind. Off. 847/8, Cambr. 18, Esc. ^{2}26, Qawala II, 159, Patna I, 179,$_{1654/5}$.—3. ʿAbd al-Karīm al-Rashīdī, completed in 803/1400, Algiers 198, Pet. AMK 942.—4. Yaḥyā b. Aḥmad al-Kāshī, ca. 750/1349, Berl. 7240.—5. *al-Miṣbāḥ* by al-Sayyid al-Sharīf al-Jurjānī, d. 816/1413 (II, 216), Berl. 7229/30, Vienna 236, Leid. 299, Paris 4418, Esc. ^{2}63, 206/8, 210, 284,$_2$, 645, Garr. 522, Alex. Balāgha 14, Qawala II, 171/2, Patna I, 180,$_{1656/8}$, print. Istanbul 1241; glosses thereon: a. Muḥammad b. Ḥamza al-Fanārī, d. 834/1430 (II, 233), Berl. 7231.—b. ʿUthmān al-Khiṭāʾī Mawlānāzāde, around 840/1436, ibid. 7232.—c. ʿAlī b. Muḥammad al-Shāhrūdī Muṣannifak, d. 875/1470 (II, 234), Esc. ^{2}209, 701, Garr. 523, Cairo ^{2}II, 187.—d. Ibn Kamālpāshā, d. 940/1533 (II, 449), Esc. ^{2}220, Qawala II, 158, Patna I,
179,$_{1648}$.—| e. Ḥasan b. Maḥmūd al-Maqdisī al-Luddī, ca. 1080/1669, Berl. 295
7233.—f. Anon., Berl. 7234/6.—g.–k. see Suppl. (h. also Qawala II, 141). 27 glosses mentioned in Ahlw., 7237.—6. Maḥmūd b. Masʿūd al-Shīrāzī (II, 210, Suppl. 1b), Paris 4377, Br. Mus. 550, Garr. 518 (*Miftāḥ al-M.*).—7. Anon., Paris 4376.—8. *Sharḥ bayt M. al-ʿu.* by Jamāl al-Dīn ʿAlī b. Abi ʾl-Qāsim Muḥammad b. Yūsuf, Patna I, 179,$_{1652}$.—19 commentaries and glosses, as well as 3 abstracts of part 3 in Ahlw., 7247.

Abstracts of the whole *Miftāḥ:* 1. *al-Miṣbāḥ* by Badr al-Dīn b. Jamāl al-Dīn b. Mālik, d. 686/1287 (p. 363), Berl. 7249, Paris 4375, Esc. ^{2}250, Alex. Bal. 24,

Patna I, $181_{,1687}$, versified and commented on by Muḥammad b. ʿAbd al-Raḥmān al-Marrākushī al-Akmah, ninth cent., Esc. $^{2}219_{,1}$.—2. *Taghyīr al-Miftāḥ* by Ibn Kamālpāshā, d. 940/1533 (II, 449), Berl. 7238, Ind. Off. 4584 (*JRAS* 1939, 373), Alex. Bal. 4, Qawala II, 136, with comment. Paris 4374, Esc. $^{2}220_{,2}$, 234, glosses Berl. 7239.

Abstracts of part 3: 1. *Talkhīṣ al-Miftāḥ* by Jamāl al-Dīn Muḥammad b. ʿAbd al-Raḥmān al-Qazwīnī Khaṭīb Dimashq, d. 739/1338 (II, 22), Berl. 7187/8, BDMG 94, Leipz. 32, Munich $680_{,1}$, Krafft 69, Leid. 301/5, de Jong 45, Pet. 234, Paris 4378/83, Ind. Off. 849/50, Esc. $^{2}227$, $232_{,2}$, $248_{,3}$, $420_{,3}$, $636_{,3}$, $1791_{,2}$, Garr. 519,
354 Qawala II, 136/8, print. Calcutta 1813, Istanbul | 1260, 1275, 1280, Delhi 1305/1888, C. 1310, cf. Mehren, *Rhetorik* 1/46, 63/108. Commentaries: 1. *al-Īḍāḥ*, by the author himself, Berl. 7190, Ind. Off. 850; glosses *Īḍāḥ al-Īḍāḥ* by Muḥammad b. Muḥammad al-Āqsarāʾī, d. before 800/1397, Paris 4385, Patna I, $179_{,1651}$.—2. *Miftāḥ al-Miftāḥ* by Muḥammad b. Muẓaffar al-Khalkhālī, d. 745/1344, Algiers 199, Vat. V. 1024.—3. Muḥammad b. ʿUthmān b. Muḥammad al-Zawzanī Shams al-Dīn, around 750/1349, Berl. 7216.—4. al-Taftāzānī, d. 791/1389 (II, 215): A. *al-Sharḥ al-muṭawwal* Berl. 7191/2, Munich 681/2, Vienna 235, Copenhagen 200, Br. Mus. 533/4, Ind. Off. 852/60, Paris 4386/91, Algiers 200/1, BDMG 95a, 96, Garr. 524/8, Makr. 56, Qawala 172/4, Patna I, $18_{,166}$ 1_{8}, II, $520_{,2801/2}$, Istanbul 1260, 1304, Lucknow 1265. Glosses: a. al-Sayyid al-Sharīf al-Jurjānī, d. 816/1413 (II, 206), Paris 4392/4, Algiers 202, Ind. Off. 861/4, Esc. $^{2}230$, 253/5, Garr. 530/5, Alex. Bal. 9, Qawala II, 145/6, Patna I, $178_{,1631/40}$, print. Istanbul 1241, anon. superglosses Qawala II, 149.—b. Yaḥyā b. al-Sayf al-Sīrāmī, d. 833/1429, completed in 830/1426, Paris 4395, Ind. Off. 865/6, Esc. $^{2}213$, 225, Qawala II, 146.—c. Muḥammad b. ʿAlī al-Qujḥiṣārī, completed in 825/1425, Berl. 7193.—d. ʿAlī al-Bisṭāmī Muṣannifak, d. 873/1470 (II, 24), Berl. 7195, BDMG 97, Paris 4396, Esc. $^{2}226$, Qawala II, 141.—e. Abu ʾl-Layth al-Samarqandī, around 880/1475, Berl. 7194, BDMG 98, Ind. Off. 873, Pet. 209, lith. Istanbul 1307.—f. Ḥasan Čelebī al-Fanārī, d. 886/1481 (II, 229), Berl. 7203, Leid. 306, Ind. Off. 667/72, Esc. $^{2}212$, 238, Patna I, $178_{,1641}$, Alex. Bal. 9, Qawala II, 151, print. Istanbul 1271 from which a *Tajrīd* by Maḥmūd b. al-Sayyid Ayyūb, completed in 1292, print. Istanbul 1292 (Qaw. II, 135), by Aḥmad b. ʿAbd al-Awwal al-Qazwīnī, for Sultan Süleymān (926–74/1520–66), Qawala II, 182.—g. ʿAbd al-Ḥakīm al-Siyālkūtī, d. 1060/1650 (II, 417), Ind. Off. 876, Esc. $^{2}233$, Patna I, $178_{,1673/5}$, II, $521_{,2419}$, print. Istanbul 1227, 1241, 1266, 1290, 1311 (Qawala II, 147/9).—h. Aḥmad al-Abīwardī, Berl. 7196, Patna I, $178_{,1642}$.—i. Anon. Berl. 7117/7204, Buhār 404.—k.–w. see Suppl.—x. Qāḍī Quṭb al-Dīn, Patna I, $178_{,1646}$.—y. Muḥammad Farīd b. Muḥammad Sharīf b. Farīd b. Muḥammad al-Sharīf al-Ṣiddīqī al-Aḥmadābādī, ibid. 1647.—z. ʿAbdallāh al-Labīb, Patna II, $521_{,2898}$.

B. *al-Sharḥ al-Mukhtaṣar* Berl. 7206/7, Munich 863, Krafft 70, Leid. 307/8,
Pet. 207, Copenhagen 201, Br. Mus. 555/6, Ind. Off. 877/85, Paris 4386,$_2$, 4398/4405,
4415,$_2$, Esc. ^{2}211 (see F. Codera, *La Ciudad de Dios* XXXIX, 1896, 21), 231, Garr.
536/40, Qawala II, 168/71, Patna I, 181,$_{1664/6}$, print. Istanbul | 1267, 1289, 1304 (see 355
Suppl.).—Glosses: a. ʿUthmān Mollāzāde al-Khiṭāʾī, d. 901/1495, Berl. 7208/9,
Paris 4408, Ind. 886, Pet. 210, Garr. 541/4, Patna I, 177,$_{1632/6}$, print. Calcutta 1256,
superglosses by ʿAbdallāh b. al-Ḥusayn al-Yazdī, d. 1015/1606, Berl. 7210, Munich
684, Alex. Bal. 6, Patna I, 177,$_{1628}$, by Mīrzājān Ḥabīballāh al-Shīrāzī, Patna I,
177,$_{1630}$, II, 521,$_{2797}$.—b. Aḥmad b. Muḥammad b. Yaḥyā b. Muḥammad al-Harawī
Ḥafīd al-Taftāzānī, d. 916/1510 (II, 218), Berl. 7211, Leid. 309, Paris 1295, 4406/7, Esc.
^{2}227,$_2$, 256/7, Garr. 546, Makr. 97, Qawala II, 142, superglosses by Yāsīn b. Zayn
al-Dīn b. Abī Bakr al-Ḥimṣī al-ʿAlīmī, d. 1061/1651, composed in 1054/1644, Berl.
7212, Leid. 310, Paris 4412.—c. Ibrāhīm b. Muḥammad b. ʿArabshāh al-Isfarāʾinī,
d. 944/1537 (II, 410), Ind. Off. 877.—d. Aḥmad b. Qāsim al-ʿAbbādī al-Azharī, d.
994/1586 (II, 410), Gotha 2783, Paris 4409/11, Esc. ^{2}235, 239, Garr. 547, Alex. Bal.
10.—e. On the first *fann* by Ismāʿīl Ghunaym al-Jawharī, ca. 1160/1747, | Berl. 7213, 296
Gotha 2785, Algiers 210.—f. *al-Tajrīd* by Muṣṭafā b. Muḥammad al-Bannānī,
composed in 1211/1796, Makr. 8, print. Būlāq 1285, 1297, 1313, C. 1315.—g. Yūsuf b.
Sālim al-Ḥifnawī (Ḥifnī), d. 1178/1764 (II, 283), Paris 4413.—h. On the preface,
by Sīdī Aḥmad b. Muḥammad b. Yaʿqūb, Paris 4414/5.—i. Anon., Gotha 2784.—
k.–w. see Suppl. (K. Qawala II, 143/4, Makram 19, Patna I, 178,$_{1637/8}$, read correctly as *al-qawl al-jayyid etc.*, in part Patna I, 180,$_{1650/2}$).—x. Glosses by al-Jarbī,
MS from 1137/1724, Alex. Bal. 8.—y. Superglosses on the glosses by al-Khayālī by
ʿAbd al-Ḥalīm al-ʿAlāʾī, Qawala I, 149.—12 glosses, 1 commentary with glosses
and superglosses, 1 gloss on the *dībāja*, 1 commentary on the *shawāhid*, in
Ahlw. 7215.—5. *al-Aṭwal* by Ibrāhīm b. Muḥammad al-Isfarāʾinī, d. 945/1538
(II, 410), Esc. ^{2}228, 237, Qawala II, 133/4, Patna I, 176,$_{1620/1}$.—6. *Maʿāhid al-tanṣīṣ
fī sharḥ shawāhid al-Talkhīṣ* by ʿAbd al-Raḥīm b. ʿAbd al-Raḥmān al-Qāhirī
al-ʿAbbāsī, d. 963/1556 (see Suppl. II, 394), completed in 901/1496, Leid. 315,
Garr. 520, Qawala II, 175, Patna I, 162,$_{1679}$, another redaction, written in the
home of the author in Istanbul in 937/1530 by Muḥammad b. Aḥmad al-Ghazzī
al-ʿĀmirī, Berl. 7224/5, Leid. 316, Paris 4416, Copenhagen 202, Bodl. I, 1198, Köpr.
1432/3, print. Būlāq 1274, C. 1316.—7. *Sharḥ shawāhid al-T.* by Ibn al-Ṣabbān
(i.e. Muḥammad b. ʿAlī, d. 1206/1792, II, 288), Berl. 7226.—8. The same title,
anon., ibid. 7227.—9. Anon. commentary and glosses, Berl 7218/21, Paris
4397.—10–14. see Suppl.

Abstracts: 1. *al-Mulakhkhaṣ* by Zakariyyāʾ al-Anṣārī, d. 926/1520 (II, 99), Patna
I, 182,$_{1677}$, print. Būlāq 1305, on which *Sharḥ abyāt al-M.* Garr. 550.—2. *al-Masālik
fī 'l-maʿānī* | *wal-bayān* by Ḥamza b. Durghūd (Ṭurghūd) Nūr al-Dīn, composed 356
in Damascus in 862/1555 while he was on the pilgrimage, Qawala II, 171, with

the commentary *al-Hawādī* Gotha 2787, Alex. Bal. 26.—3. Anon. *Aqṣa 'l-amānī fī 'ilm al-bayān wal-badī' wal-ma'ānī* with a commentary by the author entitled *Fatḥ manzil al-mathānī*, Esc. ^{2}260$_{,1}$; another, anonymous, Qaw. II, 152.—5. *Tamḥīṣ al-T.* by Ḥasan Efendi al-Āqḥiṣārī Kāfī, d. 1025/1616 (II, 443), Paris 4418, on which glosses entitled *Khulāṣat al-ma'ānī* by Ḥasan b. 'Uthmān b. Ḥusayn b. Mazyad b. 'Abd al-Wahhāb al-Muftī, sec. half tenth cent., Qawala II, 154.—6. *al-Fawā'id al-ghiyāthiyya* see II, 219$_{,IX}$.—Versification by al-Suyūṭī, d. 911/1505, *'Uqūd al-jumān fī 'ilm al-ma'ānī wal-bayān* Berl. Ms. or oct. 3850, Br. Mus. 557, see Mehren, *Rhetorik*, 47/92, 109/40. Commentaries: a. Self-commentary *Ḥall 'Uqūd etc.* Esc. ^{2}218$_{,3}$, 247, Algiers 211, Patna I, 179$_{,1652}$.—b. 'Abd al-Raḥmān b. 'Īsā b. Murshid al-'Umarī, d. 1037/1627 (II, 380), Copenhagen 203, C. 1312.—10 glosses, 9 abstracts, and 6 versifications on the *Talkhīṣ* in Ahlw., 7228.

II. *Risāla ilā tilmīdhihi Muḥammad Sāčaqlīzāde fī 'ilm al-munāẓara wa-qawānīnihā* Munich 685.

17. Ḥamīd al-Dīn Abu 'l-Ḥasan 'Alī b. Muḥammad b. Ibrāhīm al-Ḍarīr(ī) al-Quhandizī al-Bukhārī, who died in 666/1267.

Ibn al-Jazā'irī, *Ṭab. al-qurrā'* no. 3651 (with the reading al-Quhunduzī) *Mukhtaṣar al-naḥw* Ind. Off. 956/7, 983/4, Patna I, 173$_{,1603}$, print. Lucknow 1262, anonymous commentary Patna I, 170$_{,1579}$.

18. Abu 'l-Faḍl Muḥammad b. Khālid al-Jamāl al-Qurashī (Qarshī?), born around 628/1231, wrote, in 681/1282 in Kāshghar:

Al-Ṣūra, an abstract of Jawharī's *Ṣaḥāḥ* with Persian annotations, Calcutta 1812/5, Lucknow 1289, see p. 134.

19. Tāj al-Dīn Muḥammad b. Muḥammad b. Aḥmad Sayf al-Dīn al-Fāḍil al-Isfarā'inī, who died in 684/1285.

I. (*Lubb*) *al-Lubāb* (*albāb*) *fī 'ilm al-i'rāb* Gotha 284, Vienna 183, Leid. 198, Ind. Off. 894, Ambros. 150, Algiers 134/5, AS 4576/7, Alex. Naḥw 32, Cairo ^{1}IV, 90, ^{2}II, 155.—Commentaries: 1. Quṭb al-Dīn Muḥammad b. Maḥmūd al-Sīrāfī, completed in 712/1312 in Sīrāf (according to Esc. ^{2}116 in Shīrāz ?), Leid. 199 (where other MSS are listed), Paris 4121, 4816/7, Patna I, 170$_{,1574}$.—2. Anonymous, composed in 728/1328, Esc. ^{2}169.—3. Muḥammad b. Aḥmad al-Zawzanī, composed
357 between 686–777/1287–1375, Berl. 6666, Esc. | ^{2}24.—4. 'Abdallāh b. Aḥmad, d. 776/1374, who mentions 'Abd al-Mun'im b. Muḥammad al-Abarqūhī, ḤKh
297 V, 306, as the author of the original work, Esc. ^{2}168.—| 5. *al-'Ubāb* by Jamāl

al-Dīn ʿAbdallāh b. Muḥammad al-Ḥusaynī Nuqrakār, d. 776/1374, Gotha 285, Alex. Naḥw 246, anon. Berl. 6665, 6667, Ind. Off. 898, Alex. Naḥw 24.—6 other commentaries are mentioned in Ahlw., 6688. II. *Sharḥ al-Miṣbāḥ lil-Muṭarrizī* see p. 351.

3 *Philology in Syria*

1. ʿAlī b. Ṭāhir b. Jaʿfar Abu ʾl-Ḥasan al-Sulamī al-Naḥwī was born in 431/1040. He held lectures in the mosque of Damascus and died on 21 Rabīʿ I 500/ October 1106.

Al-Suyūṭī, *Bughya*, 339 (following Ibn ʿAsākir). *Kitāb al-jihād, juzʾ* 9 Dam. Z. 30,$_{20}$, *juzʾ* 2, 8, 18 ibid. 33, 60.

1a. Ḍiyāʾ al-Dīn Fakhr al-Islām Abu ʾl-Fatḥ Naṣrallāh Muḥammad b. Muḥammad b. ʿAbd al-Karīm al-Jazarī b. al-Athīr[1] was born in Jazīrat b. ʿUmar, studied in Mosul, and entered the service of Ṣalāḥ al-Dīn in 587/1191. The following year he was made vizier under the latter's son al-Malik al-Afḍal, who inherited Syria and Damascus upon Ṣalāḥ al-Dīn's death in 589/1193, as well as formal sovereignty over all the other Ayyūbids. He is said to have alienated the ruler ever more from his affairs and to have removed him from the influence of the old emirs of his father, causing the latter to go to Egypt where they set al-Afḍal's brother al-ʿAzīz against him. Al-ʿAzīz had threatened him as early as 590 in Damascus, and in 592/1195 expelled him permanently from there by limiting his possessions to Ṣarkhad. Threatened with death by the population of Damascus, the vizier fled to Egypt. When Ṣalāḥ al-Dīn's brother al-Malik al-ʿĀdil conquered Egypt after it had been occupied for a short period of time by al-Afḍal upon the death of al-ʿAzīz in 592/1195, | Ibn al-Athīr had to remain 358
in hiding for a brief period. Once al-Afḍal had established himself in Sumaysāṭ as a vassal of the Rūm Saljūq Rukn al-Dīn II, Ibn al-Athīr went to stay with him. Nevertheless, in 607/1210 he moved into the service of the latter's brother al-Malik al-Ẓāhir. But it was not long before he left him too, to live in Mosul, Irbil, and Sinjār. In 618/1221 he once more found a job as a *munshī* with the *atabeg* of Mosul, the Zangid Nāṣir al-Dīn. He died in Jumādā I or II 637/December 1239 in Baghdad. At the end of his eventful life he still had the energy to publish a collection of sample letters and to dedicate himself to literary and aesthetic criticism.

---

1 For his brothers, the theologian Majd al-Dīn, d. 606/1209, and the historian ʿIzz al-Dīn, d. 630/1232, see Suppl. I, ad 357 and 345.

Ibn Khall. 734. 1. *Kitāb al-washy al-marqūm fī ḥall al-manẓūm* Berl. Or oct. $3847_{,1}$ (earlier Daḥdāḥ 181), Paris 4435, NO 4364, Alex. Adab 187, print. Beirut 1298, cf. D.S. Margoliouth, On the Royal Correspondence of Diya-eddin El-Jazari, in *Actes du Xe Congr. intern. des Or. Sect.* III, 7/21.—2. *Kitāb al-jāmiʿ al-kabīr fī ṣināʿat al-manẓūm min al-kalām wal-manthūr* Cairo ^{1}VII, 654, ^{2}II, 184.—3. *Kitāb al-mathal al-sāʾir fī adab al-kātib wal-shāʿir* Vienna 233, Br. Mus. $1054_{,1}$, Paris 4421, Esc. ^{2}214, 262, 507, Köpr. 1367, A 4237, Patna I, $176_{,1627}$, $205_{,1831/2}$, print. Būlāq 1282, cf. *ZDMG* XXXV, p. 148, Goldziher, *Abh.* I, 161ff. Against this work see Ibn Abi ʾl-Ḥadīd, d. 655/1257, who wrote *Kitāb al-falak al-dāʾir*, see above p. 336.—4. *Kitāb al-burhān fī ʿilm al-bayān*, on poetry, Berl. 7248.—5. *Risālat al-azhār*, a conversation with flowers, Paris $321_{,3}$.

1b. Muḥammad b. al-Ḥasan b. ʿAsākir, the youngest brother of the historian of Damascus (p. 331), was probably the author of the *Tawshīʿ al-tawāshīḥ* (MS: *tawāshīʿ*), a collection of *muwashshaḥāt*, Esc. ^{2}438, see ibid. II, XIV, Hartmann, *Muw.*, 27/30.

2. Abu ʾl-Baqāʾ Yaʿīsh b. ʿAlī b. Yaʿīsh b. al-Ṣāʾigh was born in 550/1155 in Aleppo, and studied there and in Damascus. He wanted to visit Ibn al-Anbārī in
359 Baghdad | but learned of his death while he was in Mosul on his way there, and so remained in Mosul for some time. He then returned to his hometown by way of Damascus and worked as a teacher there until his death in 643/1245.

Ibn Khall. 804. 1. *Sharḥ al-mufaṣṣal* see p. 347.—2.–4. see Suppl.

3. Tāj al-Dīn Abu ʾl-Qāsim Aḥmad b. Hibatallāh b. Saʿdallāh al-Jabrānī taught at the great mosque in Aleppo and died on 7 Rajab 668/3 March 1270.

Suyūṭī, *Bughya* 172. 1. Grammatical treatise with anonymous commentary Paris $4067_{,1}$.—2. Grammatical definitions, ibid. 2.

4. Jamāl al-Dīn Muḥammad b. ʿAbdallāh b. Muḥammad b. ʿAbdallāh b. Mālik al-Ṭāʾī al-Jayyānī was born around 600/1203 in Jaén in Spain and went to Damascus at a young age. After attending the lectures of Ibn Yaʿīsh in Baalbek he settled as a teacher in Damascus and was soon regarded as the greatest philologist of his time. He died in 672/1273.

Fawāt II, 227. I. *Tashīl al-fawāʾid wa-takmīl al-maqāṣid*, an abstract of the lost and larger *Kitāb al-fawāʾid fi ʾl-naḥw*, Berl. 6628, BDMG 77, Leid. 194, Paris $1077_{,2}$, 4117, Ind. Off. 963, Esc. ^{2}64, 140, Garr. 403, Alex. Naḥw 5, Algiers 116. Commentaries:

1. Self-commentary, Esc. ^{2}66, Cairo ^{2}II, 125.—2. Athīr al-Dīn Abu 'l-Ḥayyān Muḥammad b. Yūsuf b. ʿAlī al-Andalusī, d. 745/1344, Esc. ^{2}52/7.—3. ʿAbdallāh b. ʿAbd al-Raḥmān b. ʿAqīl, d. 769/1367, Algiers 117/8, 700$_{,3}$.—4. ʿAbd al-Qāhir b. Abi 'l-Qāsim al-ʿImādī al-Anṣārī, d. ca. 820/1417, unfinished, Esc. ^{2}13.—5. Muḥammad al-Damāmīnī, d. 827/1424 (II, 26), Ind. Off. 964$_{,3}$.—6. Ḥasan b. al-Qāsim al-Murādī, d. 749/1348 (II, 22), Esc. ^{2}58/9, Cairo ^{1}IV, 67, ^{2}II, 125.—7.–10. see Suppl. 29 commentaries, 1 abstract, and 1 versification mentioned in Ahlw., 6629.

II. *al-Alfiyya*, a didactic poem on grammar in around 1000 verses, MSS in almost every library. Printings see Suppl., C. 1936 (Dār al-kutub). *L'Alfiyya, trad. en franç. avec le texte en regard et des notes explic. dans les deux langues par* L. Pinto, Constantine 1887. A. Goguyer, *Manuel pour l'etude* | *des grammairiens ar.: L'Alfiyya d'Ibn M. suivie de la Lamiyyah du même auteur*, Beirut 1888. Commentaries: 1. *al-Durra al-muḍīʾa* by his son Abū ʿAbdallāh Muḥammad Badr al-Dīn, d. 686/1287 (no. 5), Berl. 6635$_{,1}$, 6636, Or. Qu. 2010 (*Asrār al-ʿarabiyya*), Munich 721, Vienna 180, Upps. 41, Pet. Ros. 137, Br. Mus. 509, Ind. Off. 959, Heid. A. 338 (*ZDMG* 91, 391), Garr. 406/7, Alex. Naḥw 20, Patna I, 167$_{,1558}$.—Glosses: a. Zakariyyāʾ al-Anṣārī, d. 926/1520 (II, 99), Berl. 6635$_{,2}$, Patna I, 166$_{,1552}$.—b. ʿAbd al-Qādir b. Abi 'l-Qāsim al-ʿAbbādī al-Makkī, d. 880/1475 (Suyūṭī, *Bughya* 309, Ibn al-Qāḍī, *Durrat al-ḥijāl* II, 398, no. 1121), Berl. 6637, Esc. ^{2}126, Cairo ^{2}II, 93.—c.–e. see Suppl. (e. BDMG 91, Garr. 408).—5 other glosses in Ahlw., loc. cit.—2. *al-Tawḍīḥ* by Shams al-Dīn al-Ḥasan b. al-Qāsim al-Murādī b. Umm Qāsim, d. 794/1348 (II, 22), Berl. 6638, Gotha 280, Paris 4075/6, Esc. ^{2}4, 12, 71/3 (see P. Lazcoano, *La Ciudad de Dios* XLIV 197, 600/2), 217, Algiers 77/8, on which glosses by Aḥmad b. al-Qāsim al-Qarūmī, Esc. ^{2}5.—3. *Awḍaḥ al-masālik* or *al-Tawḍīḥ* by Ibn Hishām, d. 762/1361 (II, 23), Berl. 6639/40, Leid. 195 (where other MSS are listed), Garr. 409, print. Calcutta 1832.—Glosses: a. His grandson Shihāb al-Dīn Aḥmad b. ʿAbd al-Raḥmān b. Hishām, d. 835/1431, Br. Mus. 505/6. Suppl. 964.—b. *al-Taṣrīḥ bi-maḍmūn al-T.* by Khālid b. ʿAbdallāh al-Azharī, d. 905/1499 (II, 27), | Berl. 6651/2, Or. Qu. 2095, Gotha 102 (where other MSS are listed), Paris 4078/85, Qawala II, 66, 80, Makram 10, Patna I, 163$_{,1529/31}$.—c. On the *shawāhid*, by Muḥammad b. ʿAbd al-Qādir al-Fāsī, d. 1091/1680, de Jong 18, Cairo ^{2}II, 89.—d. Nāṣir al-Dīn Muḥammad al-Laqānī, d. 958/1551, Esc. ^{2}100, 113$_{,2}$.—e.–k. see Suppl.—l. al-Maḥallī, Berl. Brill, M. 164.—16 glosses mentioned in Ahlw., 6641.—4. Muḥammad b. Aḥmad b. Jābir al-Huwārī al-Andalusī, d. 780/1378, completed in 756/1355 in Mecca, Leid. 196, Paris 4095, Esc. ^{2}74/5, Garr. 414.—5. *Manhaj al-sālik* by Abū Ḥayyān Muḥammad b. Yūsuf al-Andalusī, d. 780/1378 (II, 109), Algiers 76.—6. Ibrāhīm b. Mūsā al-Abnāsī, d. 802/1400, completed in Jerusalem in 765/1363, Esc. ^{2}68, Cairo ^{2}II, 109, Alex. Naḥw 17.—7. ʿAbdallāh b.

360

299

ʿAbd al-Raḥmān b. ʿAqīl, b. 769/1367, MSS see Suppl., Garr. 410/1, Qawala II, 89, Patna I, $167,_{1559}$. *Alfijjah, carmen didacticum grammaticum auctore I.M. et in Alf. comt. quem conscripsit I.A. ed.* Fr. Dieterici, Leipzig 1851. *I.A's Cmt. zur A. des I.M. aus dem Arab. zum ersten Mal übers. v.* Fr. Dieterici, Berlin 1852, print. Būlāq 1251, 1253, 1281, Beirut 1872, C. 1306.—Glosses: a. Muḥammad b. Aḥmad b.
361 Muḥammad Ghāzī | al-ʿUthmānī al-Miknāsī, d. 919/1513 (II, 240), on the verses Br. Mus. 512.—b. Muḥammad b. Muḥammad b. Aḥmad al-Shāfiʿī, Gotha 276.—c. Ibn al-Mayyila, ca. 1100/1688, Berl. 6644.—d. Aḥmad b. Aḥmad al-Sijāʿī, d. 1197/1783 (II, 323), completed in 1178/1764, Gotha 277, Paris 4094, Garr. 412, print. C. 1298, 1306.—e. Muḥammad al-Khiḍrī al-Dimyāṭī, d. 1288/1871, composed in 1250/1834, Garr. 412, print. C. 1305, 1322 (see Suppl.).—f. on the *shawāhid* by ʿAbd al-Munʿim al-Jirjāwī, d. ca. 1175/1781 (Suppl. II, 439), C. 1280, 1308 (in the margin of the same by Muḥammad b. Quṭṭa al-ʿAdawī, only Beirut 1872), 1325.—g. anon., Gotha 278.—h., i. see Suppl.—k. *al-Qawl al-jamīl* by Aḥmad b. ʿUmar al-Qāhirī al-Asqāṭī al-Ḥanafī, d. 1159/1746 (II, 327), Alex. Naḥw 30.—8. *Tashīl al-bunā fī taʿlīl al-binā*, on verses 15–17, by ʿUbaydallāh b. Muḥammad b. ʿAbdallāh al-Zarkashī, second half of the eighth cent., Esc. ^{2}107, 138.—9. Ibn al-Jarād, eighth cent., Esc. ^{2}114.—10. ʿAbd al-Raḥmān b. ʿAlī b. Ṣāliḥ al-Makkūdī al-Muṭarrizī, d. 801/1398 (II, 25), completed in 799/1396, Berl. 6645/6, Gotha 279 (where other MSS are listed), Garr. 415, Alex. Naḥw 21, Qawala II, 88, print. C. 1279, 1305.—Glosses: a. Sīdī Aḥmad b. ʿAbd al-Fattāḥ al-Mujīrī, d. 1181/1767 (II, 355), Paris $4097,_2$, Cairo ^{2}II, 102, in the margin of print C. 1305.—b. al-Butīwī, Algiers 91.—c. Sīdī al-Ḥājj Abū Barakāt, Krafft 35.—e.–k. see Suppl.—11. *al-Maqāṣid al-naḥwiyya fī sharḥ shawāhid al-Alfiyya* by Maḥmūd b. Aḥmad al-ʿAynī, d. 855/1451 (II, 52), on the verses in commentaries 1–3 and 7, Esc. ^{2}14 (first half), *Mukhtaṣar* ibid. $142,_2$ (see P. Lazcano in *La Ciudad de Dios* XLVII [1898], 311/2), Garr. 416, printed in the margin of the *Khizānat al-adab*, Būlāq 1299.—Abstract by the author himself, *Farāʾid al-qalāʾid*, Berl. 6647/8, Paris 1741, 2429, Br. Mus. 513, Bold. II, $610,_6$, Algiers $115,_1$, Garr. 417, Patna I, $172,_{1590}$.—12. *Manhaj al-sālik* (*al-masālik*) by ʿAlī b. Muḥammad al-Ushmūnī (-unnī), d. 872/1467 (II, 82), Munich 724, Copenhagen 186, Paris 4100/7, Algiers 92/9. Esc. ^{2}11, Alex. Naḥw 42, Qawala II, 125, Patna I, $175,_{1615}$.—Glosses: a. Muḥammad b. ʿAlī al-Ṣabbān, d. 1206/1791 (II, 288), composed in 1193/1779, Makram 21, print. C. 1305 with superglosses by Ismāʿīl al-Ḥāmidī.—b. Muḥammad b. Sālim al-Ḥifnawī, d. 1101/1689 (II, 323), Paris 4108/9, Alex. Naḥw 10.—c. *Tanwīr al-ḥālik* by Abu ʾl-Fatḥ Aḥmad b. ʿUmar al-Asqāṭī, d. 1159/1746 (II, 327), Algiers $100,_1$, Alex. Naḥw 8.—d. *Zawāhir al-kawākib* by Muḥammad b. ʿAlī b. Saʿīd al-Tūnisī al-Mālikī, d. 1199/1785, Algiers 101, print. Tunis 1298.—e., f. see Suppl.—

g. ʿUllaysh, d. 1299/1881 (II, 486), | Makram 24.—13. ʿAbd al-Raḥmān b. Abī 362
Bakr al-ʿAynī, d. 893/1487, Cairo ^{2}II, 123, Garr. 418.—14. *Tamrīn al-ṭullāb fī ṣināʿat al-iʿrāb*, on the part that deals with conjugations, by Khālid b. ʿAbdallāh al-Azharī, d. 905/1499 (II, 27), Berl. 6649/50, Or. oct. 3870, Paris 5438, 6568, Esc. ^{2}137, Algiers 108, Garr. 419, Qawala II, 69, print. C. 1305, 1308, 1310.—15. *al-Nahja* (*bahja*) *al-marḍiyya* by al-Suyūṭī, d. 911/1505, Berl. 6653/4, or. oct. 3871, Paris 4074,$_{2}$, 4110/1, Pet. 186, Esc. ^{2}69, Br. Mus. 511,$_{1}$, Ind. Off. 962, Garr. 420, Cairo ^{1}IV, 27, ^{2}II, 182, Qawala II, 63, Makram 7 (under the title *Nukat* Alex. Naḥw 44), Patna I, 162,$_{1025/6}$, print. C. 1310, glosses by Muḥammad Ṣāliḥ al-Aḥsāʾī, composed in 1073/1662, Paris 4112/3.—16. Muḥammad b. Muḥammad al-Ghazzī, d. 1061/1651 (II, 291), Algiers 109.—17. al-Juzūlī, Paris 4098.—18. ʿAbdallāh b. ʿAlī al-Damlījī, d. 1234/1819 (II, 485), Paris 4114.—19. Shams al-Dīn Muḥammad al-Fāriḍī, Esc. 28.—20. On the *shawāhid* by Muḥammad b. ʿAlī al-Kharfūshī, d. 1059/1649, Berl. 6657.—21. Anon., Berl. 6655, 6658, Gotha 280, Paris 4088, Esc. ^{2}15, Algiers 112/4.—22.–45. see Suppl.—46. Glosses by Muḥammad b. Masʿūd b. Aḥmad al-Ṭurunbulālī, composed in 1206/1791, Alex. Naḥw 90.—Anon. abstract, *Khulāṣat al-khulāṣa*, Gotha 2282, print. Lucknow n.d. (BO II, 118). Al-Suyūṭī, *al-Wafiyya fi'khtiṣār al-Alfiyya* Esc. ^{2}1792,$_{3}$. *Al-Iḥmirār fī muʿāraḍat al-A.* by al-Mukhtār b. Būn al-Shinqīṭī (see Suppl. no. 25), Rabat 262,$_{13}$, print. C. 1327.—43 commentaries and glosses and 2 abridgements mentioned in Ahlw., 6660.

| II. *Lāmiyyat al-afʿāl* or *al-Miftāḥ fī abniyat al-afʿāl* Gotha 207, Munich 718, 300
BDMG 38, Krafft 36, Paris 672,$_{4}$, Esc. ^{2}139,$_{1}$, 248,$_{10}$, Algiers 12, 68,$_{9}$, Alex. Adab 8. Commentaries: 1. His son Bahr al-Dīn, Berl. 6661, Paris 4119,$_{1}$, Esc. ^{2}16,$_{1}$, 139,$_{2}$ Algiers 14,$_{2}$, Patna I, 160,$_{1514}$. Ed. Kellgren, Helsingfors 1854, Kellgren and Volck, St. Petersburg 1864, Volck, Leipzig 1866.—2. Muḥammad b. ʿAbd al-Dāʾim al-Birmawī, d. 831/1427 (II, 95), Leid. 197, Esc. ^{2}16,$_{2}$, 144.—3. Abū ʿAbdallāh Muḥammad b. al-ʿAbbās, Esc. ^{2}16,$_{3}$, 79, 270.—4. Yaʿqūb b. Saʿīd al-Mukallātī, Esc. ^{2}16,$_{4}$, Br. Mus. ^{2}548,$_{2}$, on which glosses by al-Ḥasan b. Yūsuf al-Zayyātī, d. 1023/1614 (see Suppl.), Esc. ^{2}145.—5. Ḥamd b. Muḥammad al-Saʿīdī, Munich 719.—6. Muḥammad b. ʿUmar Baḥraq al-Yamanī al-Ḥaḍramī, d. 930/1524 (Suppl. II, 554), *al-Sharḥ al-kabīr* and *al-Sharḥ al-ṣaghīr*, Paris 4118,$_{1}$, Esc. ^{2}16,$_{7}$, 144, Cairo ^{1}VII, 104, Alex. Naḥw 7 (*al-ṣaghīr*), printed with glosses by Aḥmad al-Rafāʿī, C. 1305.—7. Muḥammad b. Muḥammad b. Saʿīd al-Ṭanjī al-Jazāʾirī,
Algiers 13.—8. | Abu 'l-ʿAbbās al-Wahrānī, Esc. ^{2}16,$_{6}$, 143,$_{1}$,—9. anon. Esc. ^{2}16,$_{7}$, 363
144.

III. *al-Kāfiya al-shāfiya*, on morphology and syntax in 2757 *rajaz* verses, Krafft 31, with a self-commentary Patna I, $170,_{1573}$.

IV. *ʿUddat al-ḥāfiẓ wa-ʿumdat al-lāfiẓ*, elements of syntax, Berl. 6641, self-commentary ibid. $6642,_{3}$, other commentaries, Ahlw., ibid.

V. *Sabk al-manẓūm wa-fakk al-makhtūm*, a grammatical treatise, Berl. 6630.

VI. *Ījāz al-taʿrīf fī ʿilm al-taṣrīf* Esc. $^{2}86,_{3}$.

VII. *Shawāhid al-tawḍīḥ wal-taṣḥīḥ li-mushkilāt al-Jāmiʿ*, a grammatical commentary on Bukhārī's *Ṣaḥīḥ*, Esc. $^{2}141$.

VIII. *Kitāb al-ʿarūḍ*, on metrics, Esc. $^{2}330,_{6}$.

IX. *Tuḥfat al-mawdūd fī 'l-maqṣūr wal-mamdūd* Cairo ^{1}IV, 166 = Gotha $207,_{2}$?

X. *Kitāb al-alfāẓ al-mukhtalifa*, on synonyms, Berl. 7041.

XI. *al-Iʿtidād fī 'l-farq bayna 'l-ẓāʾ wal-ḍād*, a *qaṣīda* with a commentary, Berl. 7023, Gotha 414.

XII. *Urjūza fī 'l-muthallathāt* Gotha 412, different from Bodl. I, $272,_{3}$ (II, 575a).

XIII. *Manẓūma fī-mā warada min al-afʿāl bil-wāw wal-yāʾ*, 39 verses in the *kāmil* metre, Berl. 7029/30; see, however, ad p. $298,_{8}$.

XIV.–XXX. see Suppl.

5. His son Badr al-Dīn Abū ʿAbdallāh Muḥammad b. Muḥammad b. ʿAbdallāh b. Mālik al-Ṭāʾī al-Jayyānī, who died in 686/1287 in Damascus (see Suppl.).

1. *Rawḍ al-adhhān fī ʿilm al-maʿānī wal-bayān* Leid. 315.—2. Abstract of al-Sakkākī's *Miftāḥ*, see p. 353.—3. Commentaries on the works of his father, see p. 360, 362.—4. *Sharḥ kāfiyat b. al-Ḥājib* see p. 367—5.,6. see Suppl.

6. Bahāʾ al-Dīn Abū ʿAbdallāh b. Ibrāhīm al-Ḥalabī b. al-Naḥḥās, who died on 9 Jumādā II 698/15 March 1299 (see Suppl.).

1. *Sharḥ Dīwān Imraʾ al-Qays al-musammā bil-Taʿlīqa* Esc. $^{2}302$, see Suppl. p. 50.—2.–4. see Suppl.

364 | 4 ***Philology in South Arabia***

1. As the owner of a castle in the Jabal Sabār region, Nashwān b. Saʿīd b. Saʿd b. Abī Ḥimyar al-Ḥimyarī belonged to the higher nobility of Yemen. He died on 24 Dhu 'l-Ḥijja 573/14 June 1178 in Ḥawt. In his role as a poet and scholar he tried to resuscitate the traditions regarding the glory of ancient South Arabia
301 as al-Ḥamdānī (p. 263) had done previously. | But unlike his predecessor, who mostly moved on the solid ground of facts, al-Ḥimyarī placed too much

confidence in a notorious Ḥimyarite pseudo-tradition that tried to whitewash a lack of learning through pompous names and empty prattle.

ʿImād al-Dīn, *Kharīdat al-qaṣr*, ed. Derenbourg, *Oumara du Yémen* II, 601/3, see ibid. XXIII, XXIV n. 1.

1. *Shams al-ʿulūm wa-dawāʾ* (*shifāʾ*) *kalām al-ʿArab min al-kulūm*, a dictionary, Berl. 6963/4, Esc. ^{2}34, 603, Cairo ^{1}IV, 173, ^{2}II, 20, Patna I, 186,$_{1815/6}$. K.V. Zetterstéen, On a proposed edition of the Sh. al-ʿU. of N. b. S. al-Ḥ. *Or. Studies publ. in commemoration of the 40th anniversary 1883–1923 of P. Haupt as Director of the Or. Sem. of the Johns Hopkins Un.*, Baltimore 1926, p. 462. Abstract by his son ʿAlī entitled *Ḍiyāʾ al-ʿulūm*, Patna I, 187,$_{1697}$. Anonymous abstract, *Lawāmiʿ al-nujūm al-mustaḍīʾa*, Ind. Off. 998 (see Suppl.), Patna I, 188,$_{1708}$.—2. *Kitāb fi ʾl-qawāfī*, on rhyme, Leid. 269.—3. *Kitāb al-ḥūr al-ʿīn wa-tanbīh al-sāmiʿīn*, in rhymed prose, pointing out the futility of the efforts of various peoples, sects, and philosophers to arrive at a sound conception of God, Berl. 8753/4.—4. *al-Qaṣīda al-Ḥimyariyya* or *al-Nashwāniyya*, with an extensive historical commentary, Berl. 9736/8, Leid. 670 (where other MSS are listed), Br. Mus. Suppl. 584/5, 1071, 1236, Garr. 585, Patna I, 281,$_{2316}$, anon. comm. *Khulāṣat al-siyar al-jāmiʿ li-ʿajāʾib akhbār mulūk al-Tabābiʿa wa-ghayrihim min mulūk al-anām*, Cambr. 348, Alex. Taʾr. 63.—*Die himyarische Qaṣīde, hsg. v.* A. v. Kremer, Leipzig 1865, W.F. Prideaux, *The Lay of the Himyarites*, Lahore 1879, Th. Nöldeke, *GGA* 1866, no. 20, D.H. Müller, *SBWA* vol. 86, p. 171, *ZDMG* XXIX, 620/8.—5. Some *qaṣīdas*, Berl. 7696.—6.–11. see Suppl.

| 5 *Philology in Egypt* 365

1. Apart from attending the classes of al-Najīramī (see Suppl.), Abu ʾl-Ṭāhir b. Aḥmad Bābāshādh also studied under al-Tabrīzī when the latter stayed in Egypt. He is believed to have given up his job in the *dīwān al-inshāʾ* in Cairo, where he edited administrative documents, trusting in God's goodness. His life came to an end in Rajab 469/February 1077, when he fell from a minaret onto the roof of the central mosque.

Ibn Khall. 285, al-Suyūṭī, *Ḥusn al-muḥ.* I, 306. 1. *al-Muqaddima* (*al-kāfiya*) *al-muḥsiba fī fann al-ʿarabiyya*, a textbook on grammar in 10 chapters, Berl. 6470/1, Leid. 147 (cf. Weijers, *Orient.* I, 333ff.), Br. Mus. Suppl. 917 Esc. ^{2}1827,$_{2}$, Alex Naḥw 41. Commentaries: 1. *al-Hādī* or *al-Jumal al-hādiya* by the author himself, see Suppl.—2. *al-Khāṣir* by ʿAlī b. Muḥammad b. Sulaymān b. Aḥmad Jamāl al-Dīn b. Huṭayl, before 800/1397, Berl. 6473/4 (where it is wrongly labelled *al-Khāṣṣ*).—3. Yaḥyā b. Ḥamza b. Rasūlallāh, d. 749/1348, Br. Mus. Suppl. 919/20, Rāmpūr I, $553_{,236}$.—2. *Sharḥ jumal al-Zajjājī* see Suppl. p. 171.

1a. Abū ʿAlī al-Ḥasan b. Jaʿfar Ḥasan b. ʿAbd al-Raḥmān b. Marwān al-Naḥwī al-Iskandarānī, ca. 517/1123.

Suyūṭī, *Bughya*, 218. *Thamarat al-ṣināʿa* Alex. Naḥw 8.

2. Abū Muḥammad ʿAbdallāh b. Barrī b. ʿAbd al-Jabbār al-Maqdisī al-Miṣrī,
302 born on 5 Rajab 499/14 March 1106, worked, like Ibn Bābāshādh, | at the
chancery as an editor of administrative documents. He died in Cairo on 27 Shawwāl 582/11 January 1187.

Ibn Khall. 326, Suyūṭī, *Ḥusn* I, 307, *Bughya*, 287. 1. *Ghalaṭ al-ḍuʿafāʾ min ahl al-fiqh* Paris $4231_{,2}$.—2. 13 verses on the different meanings of the word *al-khāl*, Berl. $7068_{,1}$.—3. Annotations on Jawharī's *Ṣaḥāḥ*, see p. 134.—4.–9. see Suppl.

3. Abu 'l-Fatḥ ʿUthmān b. ʿĪsā al-Bulayṭī (Balaṭī) was born on 27 Ramaḍān 524/3
366 September 1130 in Balaṭ on the Tigris, north of Mosul. As a young man | he
distinguished himself as a linguist and a poet in Mosul and Damascus. When Ṣalāḥ al-Dīn acceded to power in Egypt in 567/1171 he was appointed as superintendent of the old mosque in Fusṭāṭ, as a reciter of the Qurʾān, and a teacher of grammar. However, he lost the ruler's favour because of his recklessness and habitual drunkenness. He died in Ṣafar 599/November 1202.

Fawāt II, 31, Wüst., *Gesch.* 288, Hartmann, *Muw.* 94. Of his works, only the linguistic masterpiece *al-Qaṣīda al-ḥirbawiyya* is extant, whose rhyme consonants allow for different vocals depending on the construction in which they are read, Bodl. I, $1268_{,2}$, AS $4072_{,4}$ (*WZKM* XXVI, 3).

4. (5.) Sulaymān b. Banīn b. Khalaf Taqī al-Dīn Abū ʿAbd al-Ghanī al-Miṣrī al-Daqīqī al-Naḥwī, a student of Ibn Barrī, who died in 613/1216 in Cairo.

Kitāb ittifāq al-mabānī waftirāq al-maʿānī, a lexicological work, Cairo [1]IV, 162, [2]II, 1.

5. (6.) Abū Zakariyyāʾ Yaḥyā b. (ʿAbd) al-Muʿṭī b. ʿAbd al-Nūr al-Zawāwī Zayn al-Dīn had already made a name for himself as a writer and teacher in his hometown of Damascus when the Ayyūbid al-Malik al-Kāmil (615–35/1218–38)

gave him a position in Cairo. | He worked there as a teacher at the ancient 303
mosque, dying on 30 Dhu 'l-Qaʿda 628/29 September 1231.

Ibn Khall. 772, ʿAbdallāh Gannūn, *al-Nubūgh al-maghribī* 86/7. 1. *al-Durra al-alfiyya*, grammar in verse, Berl. 6552, Esc. ²195,3.—Commentaries: a. *al-Ghurra al-makhfiyya* by Aḥmad b. Ḥusayn b. Aḥmad b. al-Khabbāz al-Mawṣilī, d. 637/1239 (Suyūṭī, *Bughya* 131), by Aḥmad b. Muḥammad b. al-Isʿirdī, completed in 639/1241, Berl. 6533, Paris 6509, Esc. ²22/3, Alex. Naḥw 26.—b. Muḥammad b. Aḥmad al-Sharīshī, d. 685/1296, *al-Taʿlīqāt al-wafiyya*, Leid. 178.—c. Aḥmad b. Yūsuf Mālik al-Gharnāṭī al-Ruʿaynī, d. 779/1377, Berl. 6554, Bodl. I, 1201, 1209, II, 209, Ambr. 144.—d. see Suppl. 7 other commentaries in Ahlw., 6555.—2. *Fuṣūl khamsīn*, on grammar, Berl. 6536, Bodl. II, 247,3. Commentaries: a. *al-Maḥṣūl* by Jamāl al-Dīn Abū Muḥammad Ḥusayn b. Ayāz, d. 681/1282, Leid. 179, Bodl. I, 1079, 1097, Patna II, 173,1611.—| b. Ibn al-Khabbāz al-Mawṣilī (1a), Munich 367
703.—c. see Suppl.—3. *al-Badīʿ fī ṣināʿāt al-shiʿr*, on poetry, in verse, Leipz. 488, iii.

6. (7.) Muwaffaq al-Dīn Abu 'l-Qāsim ʿĪsā b. ʿAbd al-ʿAzīz al-Iskandarānī al-Lakhmī was born on 4 Ramaḍān 550/1 November 1155 and died in 629/1231.

Kitāb al-mithāl fi 'l-jawāb wal-suʾāl, 160 grammatical and lexical questions, abstract by Muḥammad al-Fāsī al-Ṣadafī, d. 651/1253, or al-Anṣārī, d. 662/1263 (?), Berl. 6529.

7. (8.) Son of a Kurdish chamberlain of the emir ʿIzz al-Dīn al-Ṣalāḥī, Jamāl al-Dīn Abū ʿAmr ʿUthmān b. ʿUmar b. Abī Bakr b. al-Ḥājib was born in Asnā in Upper Egypt some time after 570/1174. In Cairo he studied Qurʾān recitation and Mālikī law, but then devoted himself entirely to philology. After the completion of his studies he went to Damascus where he taught in the *zāwiya* of the Mālikīs inside the Great Mosque. When the Ayyūbid Ismāʿīl al-Ṣāliḥ relinquished Safad and Qalʿat Shaqīf to the crusaders in 639/1241 he protested against this with ʿAbd al-ʿAzīz b. ʿAbdallāh al-Sulamī (p. 430,9) by ceasing to mention the ruler's name in the *khuṭba*, something for which he was banished from Damascus. He returned to Cairo and moved later to Alexandria, where he died soon after, on 26 Shawwāl 646/12 December 1249.

Ibn Khall. 386, Suyūṭī, *Ḥusn* I, 307, *Bughya* 323, Wüst., *Ak.* 240 (following Ibn Qāḍī Shuhba).

1. *al-Kāfiya*, a short textbook on syntax, manuscripts in almost every library, print. Rome 1592, Kanpur 1888, 1891, Kazan 1889, Tashkent 1311, 1312, Istanbul

1234, 1249, 1264, 1266, 1273, 1274, 1276, 1281, 1282, 1283, 1284, 1307 (see Suppl.).—Commentaries: 1. Self-commentary, Berl. 6559/60, abstract ibid. 6561, glosses by Najm al-Dīn Saʿīd al-ʿAjamī, Ind. Off. 938.—2. Naṣīr al-Dīn al-Ṭūsī, d. 672/1273 (p. 508), Esc. ^{2}191.—3. Nāṣir al-Dīn ʿAbdallāh al-Bayḍāwī, d. 716/1316 (p. 416), on which glosses by Mawlā Ṣādiq al-Kīlānī, completed in 961/1554, Esc. ^{2}85.—4. Badr al-Dīn b. Mālik, d. 686/1287 (p. 363), Esc. ^{2}200.—5. Raḍī al-Dīn
368 Muḥammad b. Ḥasan al-Astarābādhī, | d. 686/1287, Berl. 6562/3, Munich 715, Ind. Off. 912/6, Pet. 168, Esc. ^{2}91, 318, Qawala, II, 85, Patna I, 169,$_{1569/70}$, print. Istanbul 1305, 1310, a *shawāhid* commentary entitled *Khizānat al-adab* by ʿAbd al-Qādir al-Baghdādī, d. 1093/1682 (II, 286), Berl. 6564, Köpr. 1486/7, S. 160,
304 no. 305, Qilič ʿA. 939/40, Selīm. 1132, print. Būlāq 1299, 4 vols., C. 1930ff.—| 6. ʿIzz al-Dīn ʿAbd al-ʿAzīz b. Zayd b. Jumʿa al-Mawṣilī, completed in 694/1295, Esc. ^{2}89, 90.—7. *al-Muwashshaḥ* by Muḥammad b. Abī Bakr b. Muḥammad al-Khabīṣī, d. 801/1398, Berl. 6568, Leid. 187, Gotha 257 (where other MSS are listed), Garr. 380, Alex. Naḥw 43, Patna I, 175,$_{1617}$, glosses by al-Jurjānī, d. 816/1413, Berl. 6570; *Sharḥ abyāt al-muwashshaḥ* by ʿĪsā b. Aḥmad al-Shirwānī, Garr. 381.—8. Rukn al-Dīn al-Ḥasan b. Muḥammad al-Astarābādhī, d. 715/1315 (according to others 717 or 718), composed after 672/1273: a. *al-Sharḥ al-akbar* Ind. Off. 912/6, Pet. 169, Bonn. 291, Esc. ^{2}94, print. Lucknow 1280.—b. *al-Sharḥ al-mutawassiṭ* or *al-Wāfiya fī sharḥ al-K.* Berl. 6565/6, Or. oct. 3795, Leid. 185 (where other MSS are listed), BDMG 70, Garr. 361/5, Qawala 130/1, Patna I, 175,$_{1619}$. Glosses: α. al-Jurjānī, d. 816/1413, Esc. ^{2}81,$_{1}$, 154, Alex. Naḥw 13, Patna I, 165,$_{1549}$.—β. *Kashf al-kashf* by Muḥammad b. ʿUmar al-Ḥalabī, ca. 860/1456, Berl. 6567, Paris 4040, Garr. 366/7.—γ. On the *Dībāja* by Abū Saʿīd b. Aḥmad al-Zawārī, Gotha 256 (where other MSS are listed).—δ. (ε.) *ʿAwn al-W.*, on the *shawāhid*, by Kamāl b. ʿAbd al-Raḥmān b. Isḥāq (see Suppl.), Garr. 383, Alex. Naḥw 26 (MS dated 926/1520), Qilič ʿA. 920.—c. *al-Sharḥ al-ṣaghīr* Munich 715, Cairo ^{2}II, 130.—9. Jalāl al-Dīn Aḥmad b. ʿAlī b. Maḥmūd al-Ghujduwānī, ca. 720/1320, Berl. 6571/2, Munich 714, Leid. 185 (?), Alex. Naḥw 23.—10. Aḥmad b. Muḥammad al-Qamūlī, d. 727/1327, Br. Mus. 1880/2.—11. Masʿūd b. Yaḥyā al-Kashshāfī, composed in 814/1411, Munich 709.—12. Yūsuf b. Aḥmad al-Niẓāmī (under Meḥmed b. Bāyezīd 805–24/1402–21), Paris 4041.—12a. *Sharḥ al-Hindiy(ya)* by Shihāb al-Dīn Aḥmad b. ʿUmar al-Dawwānī al-Dawlatābādī, d. 849/1445, Berl. 6584/5, Gotha 258 (where other MSS are listed), Paris 4054, Esc. ^{2}80, 151/2, Pet. 175, Garr. 370. Alex. Naḥw 23, Cairo ^{1}IV, 73, 88, Qawala II, 95, anon. abstract Ind. Off. 937, glosses *Kashf ḥujub farāʾid al-Hindī* by Shihāb al-Dīn b. ʿAlāʾ al-Dīn al-Tuqātī b. Araqiyyajī, composed in 973/1583, Esc. ^{2}184 (but see Suppl. II, 323,$_{3,23}$), glosses entitled *Ghāyat al-taḥqīq*, by Ṣafī b. Naṣr, Patna I, 171,$_{1589}$.—12b. *Awfa ʾl-wāfiya* by Ḥājjī Bābā b. Ibrāhīm b.

ʿUthmān al-Ṭūsiyawī, ca. 870/1465, Berl. 6573/4, Br. Mus. 496,$_{2,3}$, Garr. 371.—| 13. *al-Fawāʾid al-Ḍiyāʾiyya* by Mollā Jāmī, d. 898/1492 (II, 207), composed for 369
his son Ḍiyāʾ al-Dīn, Berl. 6575/6, Or. oct. 3868, Gotha 259, Leipz. 21/2, 427/8, Munich 716, Vienna 176, Krafft 39, Pet. 164/5, Ros. 133, Br. Mus. 491, 1032/4, Esc. ^{2}82, 147/8, 150 (F. Codera, *La Ciudad de Dios* 39, 1896, 81), Algiers 57/8, Garr. 372/5, Qawala II, 109/13, Patna I, 172,$_{1591/4}$, II, 520,$_{2795}$, print. Bombay 1883, Lucknow 1887, Kazan 1890.—Glosses: a. ʿAbd al-Ghafūr al-Lārī, d. 912/1506 (II 235), Berl. 6577/8, Leid. 188 (where other MSS are listed), Qawala II, 74, Patna I, 164,$_{1537}$, 165,$_{1574}$, II, 520,$_{2791}$, print. Istanbul 1253, 1272, 1282, 1306, 1309, 1312, Kazan 1889. Superglosses: α. ʿAbd al-Ḥakīm al-Siyālkūtī, d. 1067/1656 (II, 417), Ind. Off. 330/1, Qawala II, 73, Patna I, 163,$_{1532/4}$, print. Istanbul 1256, 1302, 1308.—β.–ε. see Suppl.—b. Ibrāhīm b. Muḥammad al-Maymūnī, d. 1079/1668 (II, 307,$_{12}$), Berl. 6579, Leid. 189, Paris 4187,$_2$ (autograph dated 1012/1603), on which superglosses by Maqarīmī, composed in 1080/1669, Berl. 6580, by Emīr Čelebī, ibid. 6582.—c. Shams al-Dīn Muḥammad Kūhistānī, composed in 952/1545, Ind. Off. 1040,$_{14}$.—d. *Háshiyai Ináyát Alláh Maʿrūf bi Akhund Shaikh bar Sharhi Molla Jámi*, Lucknow 1883.—e. Muḥarram Efendi, completed by ʿAbdallāh b. Ṣāliḥ, 1237/1821, Istanbul 1266, 1274, 1277, 1287, 1292, 1318, 1320 (Qawala II, 78).—f. ʿIṣām al-Dīn al-Isfarāʾinī, d. 943/1536 (II, 410), MSS see Suppl., Garr. 376/8, Qawala II, 75, 93, Patna I, 164,$_{1538/9}$, 169,$_{1572}$, II, 619,$_{2798}$, print. Istanbul 1235, 1256, 1281, 1306, 1309, 1313, 1320, Calcutta 1233, 1256, Lucknow 1265, 1282, Kazan 1307, superglosses by Muḥammad Amīn al-Uskudārī, d. 1149/1736 (II, 440), Istanbul 1310, by Ḥasan Efendi ibid. 1277, by Mūsāzāde, Garr. 379.—g. Muḥammad b. Muḥarram al-Takkānī (= e?), Copenhagen 183.—14 other glosses in Ahlw., 6583.—h.–ii. see Suppl. (and Muḥammad ʿIṣmatallāh b. Maḥmūd al-Bukhārī, Patna I, 165,$_{1540}$, print. Istanbul 1307, Qawala II, 79ff., Patna I, 165,$_{1542}$; hh. ibid. 1546; v. Patna I, 165,$_{1543}$; w. ibid. 1545).—kk. *al-ʿAqd al-nāmī* by Muḥammad Raḥmī b. al-Ḥājj Aḥmad al-Akīnī, completed 1313, Istanbul 1313 (Qaw. II, 99/100).—ll. On the *khuṭba* by Maqṣūd Efendi, Qawala II, 77.—14. Ibrāhīm b. Muḥammad b. ʿArabshāh ʿIṣām al-Dīn al-Isfarāʾinī, d. 944/1537 (II, 410), Berl. 6584/5, Esc. ^{2}17, print. Istanbul 1256, on which glosses by al-Ṣafawī, d. 955/1548, Berl. 6586.—Anon. Pet. 170.—15. Maḥmūd b. Edhem, ca. 900/1494, Berl. 6587, on which glosses by ʿIzz al-Dīn Muḥammad al-Mahdī al-Ḥaqqī, ca. 1010/1601,
Berl. 6588.—16. Turkish by Busnawī Sūdī Efendi, d. 1005/1596, | Pet. 172, Garr. 370
384.—17. al-Khālidī i.e. Aḥmad b. Muḥammad b. Yūsuf al-Khālidī al-Ṣafadī, d. 1034/1625, Berl. 6590.—18. Muḥammad Taqī b. Ḥasan, composed in 1275/1858, Berl. 6591.—19. Muḥammad b. ʿIzz al-Dīn Muftī, d. 1050/1640 (II, 407), Ind. Off. 930.—20. = 12a.—21. Muḥammad b. ʿIṣmatallāh b. Maḥmūd, Pet. 167.—22. Najm al-Dīn Saʿīd, Esc. ^{2}87.—23. Ṣafī, print. Delhi 1888.—24. Najm al-Dīn al-Riḍā, Paris 4036.—25. see 12.—26. see 12a.—27. Rukn al-Dīn ʿAlī b. al-Faḍl al-Ḥadīthī,

Paris 4056.—| 28. Muḥammad b. ʿUllaysh b. ʿAlī, d. 1299/1881 (II, 486), ibid. 305
4057.—29. Ḥusayn b. Aḥmad Zaynīzāde, composed in 1167/1754, Br. Mus. 494, Qawala II, 106/9.—30. Anon. *Tarkīb al-K.*, Ind. Off. 939/40, print. Calcutta 1261.—31. Anon., Berl. 6579, 6592, 6598, Gotha 261, Munich 714, Algiers 61/5, Garr. 382.—32.—53. see Suppl. (36. read *al-Burūd al-ḍāfiya*, re-edited as *al-Najm al-thāqib* by his son Ṣalāḥ b. ʿAlī b. al-Qāsim al-Ḥasanī, Patna I, 175$_{,1618}$).—54. *Īḍāḥ al-maʿānī al-saniyya* by ʿAlam al-Dīn Qāsim b. Yūsuf b. Muʿawwiḍa, Patna I, 162$_{,1524}$.—55. Glosses by Muḥammad b. ʿIzz al-Dīn b. Ṣalāḥ b. Ḥasan, ibid. 165$_{,1547/8}$.—56. *al-Laʾālīʾ al-ṣāfiya fī silk maʿānī alfāẓ al-K.* by ʿAbdallāh b. Yaḥyā b. Muḥammad al-Nāẓirī, Patna I, 173$_{,1600}$.—Abstract, *Lubb al-lubāb fī ʿilm al-iʿrāb*, by al-Bayḍāwī, d. 716/1316 (p. 416), Esc. ^{2}167, commentary by Muḥammad Pīr ʿAlī al-Birgilī, d. 981/1573, Paris 1293, Pet. 202, Esc. ^{2}113, on which glosses by Muṣṭafā b. Ḥanafī, Pet. 203, anon. commentary Paris 6633.—Versifications by: 1. The author himself under the title *al-Wāfiya*, Esc. ^{2}146.—Commentaries: a. Muḥammad b. ʿUmar al-Ḥalabī, Munich 713.—b. Anon., Leid. 190, Bodl. I, 1181, Algiers 66.—2. Ibrāhīm al-Naqshbandī al-Shabistarī, composed in 900/1494, Dresd. 1803, Paris 4196(?), with a commentary by Muḥammad Efendi al-ʿAjamī, Gotha 262.—3. Anonymous, composed in 752/1351, Paris 4035.—Anon. adaptation, *Hidāyat al-naḥw*, Ind. Off. 941/2, Br. Mus. 643, ed. Baillie in *Five Books on Ar. Grammar*, vol. II, Calcutta 1803.—30 Commentaries, 3 abridgements, and 3 versifications mentioned in Ahlw., 6599.

II. *al-Shāfiya*, a short textbook on morphology, Berl. 6600, Or. oct. 3837, Gotha 199 (where other MSS are listed, see Suppl. and also Qaw. II, 30/2, Patna I, 152$_{,1502/3}$), print. Calcutta 1805, Constantinople 1850, Kanpur 1885 and often elsewhere. Commentaries: 1. Raḍī al-Dīn Muḥammad b. Ḥasan al-Astarābādhī, d. 684/1285 or 686, Berl. 6601, Esc. ^{2}159, Ind. Off. 952/3, print. Lucknow 1262.—2. al-Ḥasan b. Muḥammad al-Nīshābūrī, d. ca. 710/1310 (II, 210), Berl. 6602/3, Garr. 390, Patna I, 159$_{,1508}$.—3. Rukn al-Dīn al-Astarābādhī, d. 713/1313, Berl.
371 6604, Pet. 174, Qawala II, 38.—4. Aḥmad b. al-Ḥusayn al-Jārabardī, | d. 746/1345, Berl. 6605/6, Gotha 50$_{,3}$ (where other MSS are listed), BDMG 73, Garr. 391, Alex. Adab 7, 12, Qawala II, 37, Patna I, 159$_{,1510/3}$, print. Calcutta 1262, Lahore 1304, Istanbul 1310. Glosses (see Suppl.): a. Muḥammad b. al-Qāsim al-Ghazzī al-Gharābīlī, d. 918/1512, BDMG 74, Pet. AMBuch 483.—b. ʿIzz al-Dīn Muḥammad b. Aḥmad b. Jamāʿa, d. 816/1415, Alex. Adab 12.—c. *al-Durar al-kāfiya* by Ḥusayn al-Kamālānī al-Rūmī, composed in 785/1383, Alex. Adab 12, Qawala II, 28.—5. ʿAbdallāh b. Muḥammad b. Nuqrakār, d. ca. 776/1374, Berl. 6607/8, Pet. Ros. 130/2, Algiers 19, Garr. 392/3, Qawala II, 39, Alex. Adab 12, print. also Istanbul 1319, 1320, Turkish translation Berl. 6609.—6. *al-Ṣāfiya* on the *Dībāja* by Yūsuf b. ʿAbd al-Malik b. Bakhshāyish Qara Sinān, composed in 838/1434, Berl. 6610, Qawala II, 44.—7. *al-Manāhij al-kāfiya* by Zakariyyāʾ

al-Anṣārī, d. 926/1520, Paris 4062, Garr. 394, Alex. Adab 12, Qawala II, 52.—8. *al-Manāhil al-ṣāfiya* by Luṭfallāh b. Muḥammad b. al-Ghiyāth, d. 1035/1625 (II, 400), Ind. Off, 954.—9. Abū Jum'a Sa'īd b. Mas'ūd al-Marrākushī al-Ṣanhājī, Esc. ^{2}20.—10. Abu 'l-Ḥasan 'Alī al-Kīlānī, ibid. $86,_{1}$.—11. *Sharḥ shawāhid shurūḥ al-Sh.* by 'Abd al-Qādir al-Baghdādī, d. 1093/1682 (II, 162), Leid. 193.—12.–23. see Suppl.—24. *al-Manāhil al-ṣāfiya* by Luṭfallāh b. Muḥammad b. al-Ghiyāth Ẓāfirī Ḥajjājī (Suppl. II, f. $248,_{11/19}$), Patna I, $160,_{1515}$.—Versification in *rajaz* by al-Mawāhibī, d. 1119/1707, with a commentary Berl. 6611, *al-Farā'id al-jamīla* by Ibrāhīm b. Ḥusām al-Dīn al-Garmiyānī al-Sharīfī, d. 1016/1607, Qawala II, 45.—9 commentaries and glosses, 4 versifications mentioned in Ahlw., 6612.

III. *al-Maqṣad al-jalīl fī 'ilm al-Khalīl*, on metrics (see Freytag, *Darst. d. ar. Verskunst*, 334ff.), Berl. 7126, Leid. 273, Bodl. I, $1267,_{2}$ (Hebr.), $36,_{2}$, Patna I, $191,_{1732}$. Commentaries: 1. Jamāl al-Dīn Muḥammad b. Nāṣir al-Dīn Sālim b. Wāṣil al-Ḥamawī, d. 697/1298, Paris 4451, Garr. 503.—2. Muḥammad b. Abi 'l-Maḥāsin al-Ṭībī, ca. 715/1315, Leid. 275.—3. 'Abd al-Raḥīm b. Ḥusayn al-Asnawī, d. 772/1331 (II, 90), Esc. $^{2}410,_{1}$, Patna I, $192,_{1734}$.—4. Anon., very detailed, composed between 640–65, Leid. 274, *Shifā' al-'alīl wa-siqā' al-ghalīl*, Patna I, $190,_{1724}$.—5. Other commentaries in Ahlw., 7126.

IV. *al-Amālī*, dictations, on: 1. the Qur'ān, Damascus 621/1224, 2. al-Mutanabbī and other poets, Damascus 617/21, Cairo 612/1215, 3. on general matters,
Cairo 609/10/13/14/16, Damascus 617/9, 4, | on rare and interesting questions, 306
| Cairo 613, Damascus 617/8, Jerusalem 620, 5. on *ḥadīth*, Damascus 617/20/4/5, 372
6. Controversial issues regarding "*law*", Berl. 6613, Vienna 386, Paris 4392, 6214, Cairo ^{1}IV, 24, ^{2}II, 79 (only no. 3).

V. *al-Amālī*, 1. On some passages from the Qur'ān and Zamakhsharī's *Mufaṣṣal*, in Cairo and Damascus in 610 and 624, Paris $4392,_{3,2}$, Patna II, $360,_{2052,1,2}$, 2. on the verses in the work *Ma'āni 'l-Qur'ān*, ibid. 4, cf. de Sacy, *Anth. gramm.* 454, 3. on his lost *Muqaddima fi 'l-naḥw*, ibid. 6,[1] Patna 4, *'ala 'l-masā'il al-mutafarriqa fi 'l-naḥw*, Patna 3, *'alā shi'r al-Mutanabbī wa-ghayrihi*, ibid. 5; *Ta'līqa* on this by Aḥmad b. Muḥammmad b. 'Alī al-Mālikī, ibid. 6.

VI. *al-Qaṣīda al-muwashshaḥa bil-asmā' al-mu'annatha* or *al-Q. fi 'l-mu'annathāt al-samā'iyya*, on feminine nouns without a feminine ending, Vienna $1776,_{4}$, $1805,_{1}$, Ind. Off. 982, Cairo ^{1}VI, 76, ^{2}II, 25, VII, 576.

VII. *Risāla fi 'l-'ushr*, on the forms of the words 'first' and 'last' when connected with 'tenth', Berl. 6894.

VIII. *Muntaha 'l-su'āl wal-amal fī 'ilmay al-uṣūl wal-jadal*, a handbook of Mālikī law, Berl. 4374, Leipz. 342, Paris 817, Algiers 975.—Abstract by the author himself entitled *Mukhtaṣar al-Muntahā fi 'l-uṣūl*, BDMG 42, Ind. Off. 298, As'ad $3804,_{2}$

1 His *Amālī 'alā abyāt al-Mufaṣṣal* is quoted in *Khiz.* I, 532, II, 461, 6.

(? *Uṣūl al-fiqh* 42 Bl. Kr.), Cairo [1]III, 159, Algiers 1074/6, Patna I, 74$_{,756}$, II, 354$_{,2541}$.—Commentaries: *Ghāyat al-wuṣūl* by al-Ḥasan b. Yūsuf b. ʿAlī al-Ḥillī, d. 726/1326, Br. Mus. Suppl. 262.—1a. Quṭb al-Dīn Maḥmūd b. Masʿūd al-Shīrāzī, d. 710/1312 (II, 21), Dāmādzāde 685, Fez, Qar. 1390, Patna I, 72$_{,729/30}$.—2. ʿĪsā al-Miklātī, d. 743/1342, Cairo [1]III, 168.—2a. Sulaymān b. Aḥmad b. Zakariyyāʾ al-Qurashī al-Asadī (see Suppl. I, 966, zu 537), Patna I, 72$_{,734}$.—3. *al-ʿAḍudiyya* by ʿAḍud al-Dīn ʿAbd al-Raḥmān b. Aḥmad al-Ījī, d. 756/1355 (II, 208), composed in 734/1334, Berl. 4375, Paris 801, Br. Mus. 1605, Ind. Off. 299/301, Algiers 966/7, Yeni 334/5, Löwen, Mus. L. 98, Garr. 1478/9, 1627/8, 2170$_{,1}$, Alex. Fun. Mut. 77$_{,4}$, Qawala I, 286, Bank. XIX$_{,1}$, 1545/7 = Patna I, 72$_{,731/3}$, II, 354$_{,2544,2}$.—Glosses: a. al-Taftāzānī, d. 791/1389 (II, 215), Berl. 4376, Vienna 1773, Ind. Off. 302/4, Algiers 968, Garr. 1629, Qawala I, 282, Patna I, 70$_{,710}$, print. C. 1217.—Superglosses by Aḥmad b. Sulaymān, Patna I, 69$_{,707}$.—b. *al-Sharīfiyya* by al-Jurjānī, d. 816/1413 (II, 216), Berl. 4377, Ind. Off. 305/9, 1480/5, 1873, Garr. 2170$_{,2}$, Qawala I, 282, Patna
373 I, 70$_{,711/3}$, II, 354$_{,2541,3}$, 504$_{,2710}$.—Superglosses | α–γ see Suppl.—δ Muḥammad Ḥumayd al-Kaffawī, d. 1168/1754, Qawala I, 284.—ε see Suppl.—ζ Muḥammad Yaʿqūb b. ʿAlī al-Banbānī, d. after 1081/1670, Ind. Off. 1871.—η al-Sīwāsī (Ismāʿīl b. Imām?), Alex. Fun. 99$_{,2}$.—θ Ḥasan al-Harawī, print. C. 1317.—ι Anonymous, dated 1014/1605, Gotha 1048.—κ Sayyid Mollā Ḥusayn al-Khalkhālī, Patna II, 354$_{,2541,5}$.—c. Mīrzājān Ḥabīballāh al-Shīrāzī, d. 994/1586 (II, 414), Paris 2391, Ind. Off. 310/1.—d. see Suppl., Patna II, 354$_{,2544}$.—e. Sayf al-Dīn Aḥmad al-Abharī, ca. 800/1397, Ind. Off. 1869, Bank. XIX$_{,1}$, 1549 = Patna I, 70$_{,709}$.—f. Hafīd al-Taftāzānī, d. 916/1510 (II, 218), Patna I, 70$_{,714}$(?).—4. Muḥammad b. ʿAbd al-Salām b. Yūsuf al-Khawwārī (or al-Jawādī?), ca. 700/1300, Berl. 4507, Algiers 1085.—5. Ibrāhīm b. ʿAlī b. Muḥammad Farḥūn al-Yaʿmarī, d. 799/1396 (II, 263), Br. Mus. 872$_{,9}$—6. Yaḥyā b. Mūsā b. ʿUmar al-Rahūnī, d. 774/1372 or 775 in Cairo (Ibn al-Qāḍī, *Durrat al-ḥijāl* II, 490, no. 1424), Algiers 969.—7. Anon. *al-Tawḍīḥ*, Paris 4549.—8. Anon. fragm., Algiers 1086/7.—9. Anon. biographical notes on the authorities mentioned therein, Paris 2103.—10. (12.) *Rafʿ al-ḥājib* by Tāj al-Dīn al-Subkī, d. 771/1370 (II, 89), see Suppl.—13. *al-Nuqūd* (*Nuqūl*) *walrudūd* by Shams al-Dīn Muḥammad b. Yūsuf al-Kirmānī, d. 786/1384 (Suppl. II, 211), see Suppl.—14.—20. see Suppl.—21. *Kāshif al-rumūz* by ʿAbd al-ʿAziz b. Muḥammad al-Ṭūsī, d. 706/1306 in Damascus, Alex. Uṣūl 14, Fez, Qar. 1393.—22. ʿAbd al-Qādir b. ʿAbd al-Hādī, d. 1100/1688 (*Sh.N.* II, 438), Dam. ʿUm. 57$_{,1}$.—23. Bahrām Fez, Qar. 1008/13.—24. al-Bisāṭī, ibid. 1014/7.

VIII A. *Mukhtaṣar al-Furūʿ* (*Farʿ*) or *Jāmiʿ al-ummahāt* see Suppl., and also Alex. Fiqh Māl. 7, Br. Mus. 226 (?), Commentary by Khalīl b. Isḥāq al-Jundī, d. 767/1365 (II, 83), Algiers 1077/84; glosses by Muḥammad al-Laqānī, d. 954/1551 (Suppl. II, 435), Br. Mus. 241. Along with this *Asmāʾ al-aʿlām* by Muḥammad b. ʿAbd al-Salām, Patna II, 299$_{,2381}$.

9. ʿAbd al-ʿAẓīm b. ʿAbd al-Wāḥid b. Ẓāfir b. Abi ʾl-Iṣbaʿ al-ʿAdwānī[2] al-Miṣrī, who was also known as a poet, died in 654/1256.

Fawāt I, 294 (almost exclusively samples of poetry). 1. *Kitāb taḥrīr al-taḥbīr fī ʿilm al-badīʿ*, completed in 640/1242, Cairo ¹IV, 214, ²II, 181.—2. *Badīʿ al-Qurʾān* Cairo ¹312, ²II, 178.—3. *Bayān al-burhān fī iʿjāz al-Qurʾān* Patna I, 23,212 (see Suppl.).

| | 10. Amīn al-Dīn Muḥammad b. ʿAlī b. ʿAbd al-Raḥmān b. Abī Bakr al-Anṣārī 374 307
al-Maḥallī, who died in Dhu ʾl-Qaʿda 673/May 1275.

1. *Miftāḥ al-iʿrāb* Algiers 185.—2. *Shifāʾ al-ʿalīl fī ʿilm al-Khalīl*, on metrics, Leid. 276, Köpr. 331.—3. *Urjūza fī ʾl-ʿarūḍ* Leid. 277.—4. *Kitāb al-ʿunwān fī maʿrifat al-awzān*, in verse, Cairo ¹IV, 195/6. ²II, 236.

6 *Philology in North Africa and Sicily*

1. The son of a goldsmith, Abū ʿAlī al-Ḥasan b. ʿAlī b. Rashīq al-Azdī al-Qayrawānī was born in 390/1000 (according to others in 370/980) in al-Muḥammadiyya. In 406/1016 he went to Kairouan, where his laudatory poetry won him the favour of the sovereign al-Muʿizz b. Bādis (see p. 315). When the latter rejected the dominion of the Fāṭimid caliphs of Egypt his suzerain roused the local nomadic Bedouin tribes of the Banū Hilāl to invade his country, and they ransacked the city in 443/1051.[3] Ibn Rashīq ran away from this fighting to Sicily and settled in Māzar, where he died in 456/1064 (or, according to others, in 463/1070).

Ibn Khall. 157, cod. Wetzst. II, 289, f. 107v, Wüst., *Gesch.* 210, Muḥammad al-Ḥilyawī, *Ibn Rashīq, raʾyuhu fī ʾl-shiʿr*, Apollo I, 1161/7. 1. *Kitāb al-ʿumda fī maḥāsin al-shiʿr wa-ādābihi*, on poetry, with a lengthy introduction on the art of poetry in general, hailed by Ibn Khaldūn (*Prol. Not. et Extr.* XVIII, 337) as groundbreaking in its appraisal of modern poetry, Leid. 292, Br. Mus. 600, Esc. ²285/6, Algiers 233, see de Sacy, *Anth. gramm.* 307, 442, Goldziher, *Abh.* I, 157/61. Abstract, *al-ʿUdda fī ʾkhtiṣār al-ʿUmda* by Abū ʿAmr ʿUthmān b. ʿAlī al-Anṣārī al-Khazrajī al-Ṣaqalī al-Naḥwī, Alex. Adab 98.—2. *Qurāḍat al-dhahab fī naqd ashʿār al-ʿArab* Paris 3417,7.—3. Poems, Esc. ²467.—4. *Kitāb*

2 Corrupted to al-Qayrawānī, Ahlw. 673,3.

3 Fournel, *Les Berbères* II, 169, Wüst. *Fat.* 235, A. Müller, *Islam* I, 634.

al-unmūdhaj fī shuʿarāʾ al-Qayrawān ḤKh 7901, quoted by Ibn Khall. no. 12 and elsewhere.[4]—5. *Kitāb al-gharāʾib wal-shudhūdh fi ʾl-lugha* is quoted in Damīrī II, 140, under *ʿuṣfūr*.

375 308 | | 2. Abu ʾl-Qāsim ʿAlī b. Jaʿfar b. al-Qaṭṭāʿ al-Saʿdī al-Ṣaqalī, an Aghlabid, was born in Sicily on 10 Ṣafar 433/9 October 1041. After studying in Spain he lived as a celebrated poet and philologist in his native country. When this was invaded by the Normans he went to Egypt sometime around 500/1106, where he was a tutor of the children of al-Afḍal b. Amīr al-Juyūsh Badr al-Jamālī, the vizier of the Fāṭimid caliph al-Amīr billāh Manṣūr (495–524/1101–30). He died in Fusṭāṭ in 514/1120.

Ibn Khall. 420, Wüst., *Gesch.* 228. 1. *Kitāb abniyat al-afʿāl*, an augmented edition of the work by the same name by Ibn al-Qūṭiyya (see p. 157), is probably incorrectly attributed to him, Gotha 405, Esc. [2]576, *Dībāja*, Garr. 253.—2. *Kitāb al-ʿarūḍ al-bāriʿ*, on metrics, Br. Mus., Suppl. 1214,$_{3}$, Cairo [1]IV, 194, [2]236, abstract by the author himself entitled *Kitāb al-shāfī fī ʿilm al-qawāfī*, ḤKh IV, 7384, Cairo, loc. cit., [2]II, 233, a second abstract may be in Leid. 265.

3. Abū ʿAbdallāh Muḥammad b. Aḥmad b. Hishām al-Lakhmī al-Sabtī al-Ṣūfī, ca. 557/1162.

1. *Kitāb al-madkhal ilā taqwīm al-lisān wa-taʿlīm al-bayān* or *Kitāb al-radd ʿala ʾl-Zubaydī fī Laḥn al-ʿawāmm*, written against the *Kitāb laḥn al-ʿa.* by al-Zubaydī (see p. 140) and the *Kitāb tathqīf al-lisān wa-talqīḥ al-janān* of Abū Hafṣ ʿUmar b. Makkī al-Māzarī, Esc. [2]46, 99, as well as a copy in the possession of ʿAbd al-Ḥayy al-Kattānī (Marçais, *JA* 223, 88).—2. *Sharḥ Maqṣūrat b. Durayd*, see p. 113,$_{1}$.

4. Abū Isḥāq Ibrāhīm b. Ismāʿīl b. Aḥmad b. ʿAbdallāh al-Ṭarābulusī al-Lughawī al-Maghribī al-Ifrīqī b. al-Ajdābī, who died before 600/1203.

Yāqūt, GW I, 131. *Kifāyat al-mutaḥaffiẓ wa-nihāyat al-mutalaffiẓ fi ʾl-lugha al-ʿarabiyya*, on synonyms, Berl. 7043/4, Gotha 423, Br. Mus. 1010,$_{2}$ BDMG 67a, Garr. 271, Alex. Fun. 188,$_{9}$, Patna I, 188,$_{1705}$, print. C. 1287, 1313, put into verse by Muḥammad b. Aḥmad b. ʿAbdallāh al-Ṭabarī Jamāl al-Dīn, d. 694/1294, *ʿUmdat al-mutalaffiẓ*, Vienna 88, Bursa, Haraccizade Edeb. 101.

4 Listed in the correct place in Ahlw. 7434,$_{12}$, but also as a lexicon (?) in 6981,$_{18}$.

| 5. Abū Mūsā ʿĪsā b. ʿAbd al-ʿAzīz b. Yalalbakht b. ʿĪsā b. Yūmarīlī al-Juzūlī 376
al-Yazdaktanī al-Marrākushī al-Barbarī, who died in 607/1210 in Marrakesh (see Suppl.).

Ibn Khall. 486, ʿAbdallāh Gannūn al-Ḥusaynī, *al-Nubūgh al-maghribī fi ʾl-adab al-ʿarabī,* Tetouan 1357, I, 85/6. *Al-Muqaddima al-Juzūliyya fi ʾl-naḥw*, by means of succinct, often mysterious, brief, and strange glosses, mostly of a logical character, on al-Zajjājī's *Jumal* (p. 112), following his teacher Ibn Barrī, Fez, Qar. $1457_{,1}$, commentary by ʿUmar b. Muḥammad al-Shalawbīnī, d. 645/1247 in Seville (Ibn Khall. 471), Esc. ^{2}2, 36, 190, see P. Lazcano, *La Cuidad de Dios* XLII, 1897, 341/7, which contain part of the original 10 volumes.

6. Abū Jaʿfar Aḥmad b. Yūsuf b. ʿAlī b. Yūsuf (Yaʿqūb), *al-Fihrī al-Lablī,* was born in Niebla in 623/1226 and died in Tunis in 691/1292.

Al-Suyūṭī, *Bughya* 176. 1. *Bughyat al-āmāl fī maʿrifat al-nuṭq bi-jamīʿ mustaqbalāt al-afʿāl,* on the vocals of the imperfect, Bank. XX, 2104 = Patna I, $158_{,1501}$.—2. *Sharḥ Jumal al-Zajjājī,* Suppl. I, 171.—3. *Sharḥ al-Faṣīḥ,* ibid. 181/2.

7 *Philology in Spain*

1. Abu ʾl-Ḥasan ʿAlī b. Ismāʿīl (Aḥmad) al-Mursī b. Sīda, who died in Denia on 26 Rabīʿ II 458/28 March 1066 (see Suppl.).

| Ibn Khall. 422, al-Ḍabbī 405, no. 1205. 1. *Kitāb al-mukhaṣṣaṣ fi ʾl-lugha,* a diction- 309
ary in 17 volumes, arranged by subject, Cairo ^{1}IV, 187, ^{2}II, 36, volumes 16 and 17, Esc. ^{2}575, print. C. 1316/21.—2. *Kitāb al-muḥkam wal-muḥīṭ al-aʿẓam*, likewise, Br. Mus. Suppl. 854, Cairo ^{1}VI, 84, ^{2}II, 250, 309, volume 18 Garr. 26. Abstract, *Khulāṣat al-muḥkam* by Muḥammad b. al-Ḥusayn al-Ansī, after 680/1281, Br. Mus. 471.—3. *Sharḥ mushkil dīwān al-Mutanabbī* Suppl. I, 142.—3. An *urjūza*, ed. Ḥabīb Zayyāt, *al-Mashriq* XXVI, 18/9.

2. Abu ʾl-Ḥajjāj Yūsuf b. Sulaymān (ʿĪsā) al-Aʿlam al-Shantamarī was born in 410/1019 in Santamaria, studied in Cordova from 433/1041, and died in 476/1083 in Seville.

| Ibn Khall. 812. 1. *Sharḥ al-shuʿarāʾ al-sitta*, cf. Ahlwardt, *The Divans* XVIII, Dyroff, 377
Zur Geschichte der Überlieferung des Zuhairdiwans, Munich 1892, Landberg, *Primeurs arabes*, Fasc. II.—2. *Kitāb al-ḥamāsa,* cited in Khiz. I, $563_{,6\,\text{vu}}$, III, $165_{,20}$, $330_{,24}$.—3. *Taḥṣīl ʿayn al-dhahab min maʿdin jawhar al-adab fī ʿilm majāzāt al-ʿArab* (Suppl. $160_{,5}$) ʿĀšir I, 764 (571 AH), Qawala II, 190, see Suppl.

3. Abū Bakr ʿĀṣim b. Ayyūb al-Baṭalyawsī, who died in 494/1101.

Dozy, *Ibn Badroun*, p. I, Ibn Bashkuwāl, no. 966, (ḤKh IV, 7521 mistakenly: "died in 194"), Vandenhoff, *Tarafa*, 5, Hartmann, *Muw.* 240. *Sharḥ al-shuʿarāʾ al-sitta* see Suppl. 50.

4. Abu ʾl-Ṭāhir Muḥammad b. Yūsuf b. ʿAbdallāh al-Saraqusṭī al-Ashtarkūnī al-Tamīmī, who died on 21 Jumādā I 538/2 December 1143 in Cordova.

1. *Kitāb musalsal*, on remarkable expressions in 50 chapters, each of which begins with a linguistically complicated verse, Berl. 7093, Cairo ^{1}IV, 187, ^{2}III, 38.—2. *al-Maqāmāt al-Saraqusṭiyya al-Tamīmiyya al-luzūmiyya*, 50 in number, composed in Cordova (ḤKh 12710), Berl. 8588,$_1$, Ms. or. oct. 3855.

5. Abū Bakr Muḥammad b. ʿAbd al-Malik b. al-Sarrāj al-Shantarīnī (according to Maqq. al-Shantamarī), who left Spain for Egypt and Yemen in 515/1121. Later he worked as a *muqriʾ* in the main mosque in Cairo, which is also where he died, probably in 549/1154.

310 | Maqq. I, 619. 1. *Kitāb tanbīh al-albāb fī faḍāʾil al-iʿrāb* Berl. 6523.—2. *Kitāb talqīḥ al-albāb fī ʿawāmil al-iʿrāb* ibid. 6524.—3. *Kitāb jawāhir al-ādāb wa-dhakhāʾir al-shuʿarāʾ wal-kuttāb*, an abstract of the *ʿUmda* of Ibn Rashīq (see 374), Esc. ^{2}352.—4.–6. see Suppl.

6. Abu ʾl-Qāsim Muḥammad b. Ibrāhīm b. Khayra al-Mawāʿinī al-Ishbīlī, who came from Cordova, first served as secretary to the governor of Granada, Abū Saʿīd, then under the prince of Seville, Abū Ḥafṣ ʿUmar b. al-Muʾmin, and from 558/1163 onwards under the Almohad Abū Yaʿqūb Yūsuf. He died in 564/1168 in Marrakesh.

378 | Wüst., *Gesch.* 257. *Kitāb rayḥān al-albāb wa-rayaʿān al-shabāb*, an *adab* work with historical elements in 7 *martabas*, composed in 559/1164 and dedicated to the aforementioned Almohad and his brother Abū Ḥafṣ, Leid. 471. The part dealing with the ʿAbbādids is in Dozy, *Script. ar. Loci de Abbadidis*, vol. II.

7. Abu ʾl-Ḥajjāj Yūsuf b. Muḥammad al-Balawī b. al-Shaykh was born in 526/1132 in Malaga, where he studied under al-Fakhkhār, before moving to Alexandria in 516/1166, where was taught by al-Silafī. In Malaga he was also active as a master builder and is believed to have participated in the construction of 25 mosques and 50 wells and fountains. He died in 604/1207.

Kitāb alif bā', an encyclopaedia of the knowledge of his time, composed for his son ʿAbd al-Raḥīm, Berl. 6965, Leid. 474/5, Bodl. I, 465, Algiers 8, Garr. 203, Köpr. 1215/8, print. C. (Wahbiyya) 1287.

8. Abū ʿAbdallāh b. Ḥusayn Abu 'l-Jaysh al-Andalusī al-Anṣārī al-Qisṭī, who died in 626/1229.[1]

Kitāb al-ʿarūḍ al-Andalusī, on metrics, Berl. 7141/2, Gotha 259/60 (where other MSS are listed), Garr. 500, Alex. Fun. $175_{,3}$, Qawala I, 180/1, Patna I, $191_{,1781}$, print. Istanbul 1262. Commentaries: 1. ʿAbd al-Muḥsin al-Qayṣarī, d. 761/1360, Berl. 7143/4, Ms. or. fol. $4182_{,2}$, Gotha 361, Pet. 134, Esc. $^{2}410_{,2}$, 411/2, Garr. 501/2, Alex. ʿArūḍ 2, Fun. $64_{,2}$, $69_{,5}$, $187_{,2}$, Cairo ^{1}VII, 274, ^{2}II, 238, Qawala II, 179, 182/3 (*Tarjamat Fatḥ al-nuqūd*), Patna I, $190_{,1725}$.—2., 3., 4., see Suppl.—5. Muḥammad b. al-Khalīl al-Aḥsā'ī, d. 1044/1634, Br. Mus. $1398_{,1}$.—6. Muḥammad b. al-Ṭāhir b. Abi 'l-Qāsim al-Ḥusaynī, d. 1083/1672, completed in 1076/1666, Berl. 7145.—7. Dā'ūd b. Muḥammad al-Fārisī, Vienna 223.—8. Maḥmūd b. Khalīl al-Mustarī, Pet $238_{,9}$, Cairo ^{2}II, 238.—9. Anon., Berl. 7146, Paris $3955_{,3}$, Bodl. I, $1236_{,2}$.—9 other commentaries in Ahlw., 7147.

9. Majd al-Dīn Abu 'l-Khaṭṭāb ʿUmar b. al-Ḥasan b. Diḥya al-Kalbī al-Sabtī
al-Andalusī al-Balansī Dhu 'l-Nasabayn, thus called | because on his father's side 311
he was descended from Diḥya al-Kalbī and on his mother's side from Ḥusayn
b. | ʿAlī. He was born in Valencia in 544/1149 (according to others in 546 or 379
548). Having studied *ḥadīth* and linguistics in all the major cities of the country he was twice *qāḍī* in Denia, but was eventually removed from office due to his controversial lifestyle. As a wandering man of letters he went to Morocco, Bijāya, and Tunis, where he lectured on the science of *ḥadīth* in 595/1198. While making the pilgrimage to Mecca he stayed for some time in Egypt, then travelled through Syria, Iraq, Persia, and Mazandaran, before visiting various scholars in Baghdad, Wāsiṭ, Isfahan, and Nishapur. When he arrived in Arbela on the occasion of the birthday of the Prophet in 604/1207 he offered the ruler Muẓaffar al-Dīn al-Malik al-Muʿaẓẓam a commemorative text that ended in a long *qaṣīda*, which earned him a significant fee. His enemies, however, claimed that he had stolen the *qaṣīda* from Ibn Mammātī (d. 606/1209). Upon his return to Egypt, al-Malik al-ʿĀdil made him responsible for the education of his grown-up son, who would later become Sultan al-Malik al-Kāmil. When the latter acceded to the throne in 615/1218 he held his teacher in such high regard

1 According to Freytag, *Darst. der ar. Versk.* 36, without source reference; only the margins 538/1143 and 800/1397 are known.

that in 621/1224 he had al-Kāmiliyya college constructed especially for him, which is where he went to teach *ḥadīth*. Later, however, he fell into disgrace, was ousted, and died on 14 Rabīʿ I 633/30 October 1235.

Ibn Khall. 470, al-Dhahabī, *Ḥuffāẓ* IV, 213, Ḥuff. XVIII, 16, Ibn Ḥajar, *Lisān al-mīzān* IV, 292/8, no. 829, Maqq. 525/9, Wüst., *Gesch.* 319, Goldziher, *Ẓāhir.* 175/9. 1. *Kitāb tanbīh al-baṣāʾir fī asmāʾ umm al-kabāʾir*, on the names of wine, with strong diatribes against etymologies of the names for wine that have a favourable or sympathetic basis (Goldziher, op. cit., 177), dedicated to al-Malik al-Kāmil, Leid. 79.—2. *Kitāb al-muṭrib min ashʿār ahl al-Maghrib*, an anthology, ḤKh 12247, Br. Mus. 631.—3. *Kitāb al-āyāt al-bayyināt fī khaṣāʾiṣ aʿḍāʾ rasūl Allāh*
380 ḤKh I, 498, Algiers 1679.—4. *Nihāyat al-suʾūl fī khaṣāʾiṣ al-rasūl*, | on the privileges of the Prophet, Berl. 2567, Cairo [1]I, 445, [2]I, 158.—5. Poem on the Prophet,
312 similar to the aforementioned, at the end of | *Kitāb al-tanwīr fī mawlid al-sirāj al-munīr* (ḤKh 3702)? Paris 1476, 3141,$_{2}$.—6. *Taʾrīkh khulafāʾ Ibn al-ʿAbbās* NO 3116 (read to the author in 613, Ritter).

10. Ḍiyāʾ al-Dīn Abū Muḥammad ʿAbdallāh b. ʿUthmān al-Khazrajī, who flourished around the year 650/1252 (although according to some sources he died in 626/1228).

Al-Rāmiza al-shāfiya fī ʿilm al-ʿarūḍ wal-qāfiya or *al-Qaṣīda al-Khazrajiyya*, a didactic poem on metrics, Berl. 7112/3, Paris 1077,$_{6}$, Leid. 278/9, Algiers 376,$_{12}$, Alex. ʿArūḍ 4, Fun. 64,$_{2}$, Qawala II, 189/90, ed. Ph. Guadagnoli in *Breves Ar. linguae inst.*, Rome 1642, 286ff.—Commentaries: 1. Abu ʾl-Qāsim al-Fattūḥ b. ʿĪsā b. Aḥmad al-Ṣanhājī, completed on 1 Jumādā I 816/30 July 1413, Gotha 367, Leid. 285.—2. Abu ʾl-Qāsim Muḥammad b. Aḥmad al-Ḥasanī al-Sharīf al-Andalusī al-Sabtī al-Gharnāṭī, d. 760/1359, Berl. 7114/5, Gotha 363, Leid. 280, Paris 446,$_{1}$, Algiers 87,$_{2}$, 235, Alex. ʿArūḍ 1, Fun. 68,$_{1}$, Cairo [1]VII, 284, [2]II, 235.—3. *al-ʿUyūn al-fākhira* by Muḥammad b. Abī Bakr al-Damāmīnī, d. 828/1424, Berl. 7116/7, Leid. 282/4, Br. Mus. 1398,$_{2}$, Esc. [2]186,$_{2}$, 410,$_{4}$, Algiers 1236, AS 4093, 4176, Alex. ʿArūḍ 2, Qawala II, 182.—4. Muḥammad b. ʿIzz al-Dīn Khalīl b. Muḥammad al-Buṣrawī Muḥibb al-Dīn, ca. 881/1476, Berl. 7119/20, Bodl. I, 1236,$_{4}$, Garr. 505, Alex. ʿArūḍ 4 (which has al-Baṣrī).—5. By the same, a larger commentary, Berl. 7121.—6. Aḥmad b. Muḥammad al-Dimashqī al-Ṣāliḥī b. Shukūr, d. 893/1488, Berl. 7118.—8. *Fatḥ rabb al-bariyya* by Zakariyyāʾ al-Anṣārī, d. 926/1520 (II, 99), Berl. 7122/3, Gotha 364/5, Algiers 237, Alex. ʿArūḍ 2, Fun. 65,$_{5}$, 131,$_{13}$, Patna II, 368,$_{2551,\,1}$.—9. Abu ʾl-Baqāʾ Muḥammad b. ʿAlī b. Khalaf al-Aḥmadī, composed in 904/1499, Paris 447.—10. Badr al-Dīn b. ʿUmar Khūj b. ʿAbdallāh al-Fattanī, second half of the twelfth cent. (Suppl. II, 511), ibid. 4450, with glosses by ʿAbd al-Raḥmān b. Muṣṭafā.—11. Aḥmad b. ʿUmar b. Muḥammad al-Naqāwusī, Br. Mus. $511_{,3}$.—12. *Rafʿ ḥājib al-ʿuyūn al-ghāmiza* by Muḥammad b. Muḥammad al-Dalajī, d. 950/1544 (II, 319), Bodl. I, $1236_{,5}$, Alex. ʿArūḍ 413, *Taqyīd al-abyāt al-mushār ilayhā fī Q. al-Kh.* (only scansion of verses) by Abu ʾl-ʿAbbās Aḥmad b. ʿAlī al-Manjūrī, d. 955/1587 (Suppl. II, 697), Leid. 281.—14. Anon., Berl. 7124, Paris $3955_{,4}$, Esc. ^{2}334, 416.—15.–27. see Suppl.—28. Mollā Ghulām Naqshbandī b. ʿAṭāʾallāh al-Laknawī, Patna I, $190_{,1723}$, II, $368_{,2551,\ 2}$.—II. *Mukhtaṣar fī ʿilal al-aʿārīḍ wa-ḍurūb khāṣṣa* Alex. ʿArūḍ 4.

| 11. Sharaf al-Dīn Abū ʿAbdallāh Muḥammad b. ʿAbdallāh al-Mursī al-Sulamī, 381
who died on 15 Rabīʿ I/3 April 1257 (see Suppl.).

Al-Ḍawābiṭ al-kulliyya fī-mā tamassu al-ḥāja ilayhi min al-ʿarabiyya ḤKh IV, 7858 (imprecise), Berl. 6614, a didactic letter on grammar to various students, ibid. $150_{,2}$.[2]

12. Abu ʾl-Muṭarrif Aḥmad b. ʿAbdallāh al-Makhzūmī, who was born in 580/1184 in Valencia. He initially studied *fiqh* but felt more attracted to philology. He later emigrated to Morocco, where the caliph al-Rashīd (630–40/1232–42) first appointed him as his secretary and then as *qāḍī* in Salé and subsequently in various other towns, the last of which was Ceuta. When this town was conquered by the Marīnids he lost all his possessions, so emigrated to Tunis. | 313
Having worked for a considerable period of time as a *qāḍī* in Urbus and Gabès, the Ḥafṣid al-Mustanṣir billāh I (647–75/1249–77) appointed him to his court where he wielded great influence on the government. He died on 20th[3] Dhu ʾl-Ḥijja 658/26 November 1261.

Maqq. I, 200ff. *Kitāb al-tanbīhat ʿalā mā fi ʾl-Tibyān min al-tamwīhāt*, a rebuttal of a work by ʿAbd al-Wāḥid b. ʿAbd al-Karīm al-Zamlakānī (p. $415_{,2}$), Esc. ^{2}115.—Derenbourg wrongly takes him to be the same author as Abu ʾl-Muṭarrif who is criticised in Esc. ^{2}296 (*Kitāb al-tanbīh ʿalā ghalaṭ al-adīb*), in which an equally unidentified Abū Ḥātim confronts the former with his inaccuracies in his explanations of the poems of Imraʾ al-Qays and Nābigha al-Ḍubyānī; see Melchor M. Antuña, *al-Andalus* VI, 271/6.

---

2 Listed once more as *al-Ḍawābiṭ al-naḥwiyya fī ʿilm al-ʿarabiyya* in Ahlw., 6844/5.

3 Such according to Maqq., but in fact the 19th, given that it was a Friday.

12a. Abu ’l-Ḥasan ʿAlī b. Muʾmin b. Muḥammad b. ʿUṣfūr, d. 669/1270 (see Suppl.).

4 *Kitāb al-muqarrib fi ’l-naḥw* additionally Taymūr, *RAAD* III, 341, Patna I, 174,1612.

382 | 13. (14.) Abu ’l-Ḥusayn ʿUbaydallāh b. Aḥmad b. Abi ’l-Rabīʿ al-Qurashī, who died in 688/1289 in Seville (see Suppl.).

Chapter 4. Historiography

1 *Individual Biographies*[1]

Just as the beginnings of Arabic historiography had been inspired by chronicles written in Middle Persian, it was again the literary taste of the Iranians that had a decisive influence on one of its most important offshoots. In the chancelleries of the states that arose upon the remains of the crumbling caliphate secretaries developed a pompous administrative style of writing that took its example from Iranian rhetoric and that was embellished by rhymed endings and dazzling, obscure expressions. This style they now applied to the biographies that were written to glorify their sovereigns and which, though they must be used with caution, grant us an insight | into the inner workings of these 314
states far sharper than the one provided by general histories.

1. The first book of this kind originated on Iranian soil itself, namely the biography of the Turkish sultan Maḥmūd of Ghazna. Its composer, Abū Naṣr Muḥammad b. ʿAbd al-Jabbār al-ʿUtbī, who hailed from a distinguished Arab family, served under Sebüktigin and his son Maḥmūd in the administration, finally becoming postmaster in Ganj Rustāq, before dying in 427/1036.

Wüst., *Gesch.* 174. *Al-Kitāb al-Yamīnī*, a history of Yamīn al-Dawla Maḥmūd al-Ghaznawī, d. 421/1030, but which ends in the year 409/1018 with a eulogy on the brother of the sultan, Naṣr, who died that year; in an appendix he complains about having been pushed out of office by a certain | Abu ʾl-Ḥasan 383
al-Baghawī, and it seems as if the book was a means of warning the sultan of conspiracies; Berl. 9807/9, Munich 423, Vienna 947, Leid. 1006/7, Br. Mus. 311, 1214, Suppl. 548, Or. 5615 (DL 36), Ind. Off. 701, Paris 1894/5, Pet. AM 157, Rosen 34, Yeni 830, Qawala II, 250, Patna I, 289,$_{2338}$, ed. Maulawi Mamluk al-Aliy and A. Sprenger (lith.), Delhi 1847, Ḥamīd al-Dīn, Lahore 1883; cf. Th. Nöldeke, Über das Kitab Jamini, *SBWA* 23, 1857, p. 15ff., Elliot-Dowson, *History of India* II, 14 ff.—Commentaries: 1. *Basātīn al-fuḍalāʾ* by Abū ʿAbdallāh Maḥmūd b. ʿUmar al-Najātī al-Nīshābūrī, ca. 720/1320 (Suppl. II, 257), NO 3357, Yeni 859/60.—2. *al-Fatḥ al-wahbī ʿalā taʾrīkh Abī Naṣr al-ʿUtbī* by Aḥmad b. ʿUmar al-Dimashqī al-Manīnī, composed in 1144–7/1731–4, Vienna 948, Pet. Ros. 35, Qawala II, 242, print. C. 1286.—3. ʿAlī b. Muṣliḥ al-Samʿānī al-Kirmānī, abstract Br. Mus. Suppl. 549.—Persian translations: 1. Abu ʾl-Sharaf Nāṣiḥ b. Ẓafar al-Jarbādhakānī, composed in 582/1186, Vienna 949/50, Br. Mus. Pers. I, 157, Paris Sch. pers. 1564,

1 With the exception of biographies of the Prophet which will be treated separately in the chapter on Tradition.

cf. de Sacy, *Not. et extr.* IV, 325.—2. more literal by Muḥammad Karāmat ʿAlī, Berl. 441, Br. Mus. Pers. III, 900, *JAS Bengal* XXIII, 1855, 239, no. 68.—Engl. transl. by J. Reynolds, London 1858.

1a. The long list of Shīʿī martyrologies begins with Abū Isḥāq Ibrāhīm al-Isfarāʾinī, who died on ʿĀshūrā 418/21 February 1027.

Nūr al-ʿayn fī mashhad al-Ḥusayn, Cat. Browne 13, C5 (different from Berl. 6129), print. C. 1271, 1298 (together with *Qurrat al-ʿayn fī akhdh thaʾr al-Ḥusayn* by Abū ʿAbdallāh b. Muḥammad, Alex. Taʾr. 113), Bombay 1302.

2. In the Near East the strong personality of Ṣalāḥ al-Dīn provided much material for biographical representations, such as the one written by his contemporary Muḥammad b. Muḥammad b. Ḥāmid b. ʿAbdallāh b. ʿAlī b. Maḥmūd b. Hibatallāh b. Āluh ʿImād al-Dīn al-Kātib al-Iṣfahānī. Born in 519/1125 in Isfahan, he studied at the Niẓāmiyya in Baghdad before the vizier Yaḥyā b. Hubayra ʿAwn al-Dīn conferred administrative posts on him, first in Basra, and then in
384 Wāsiṭ. When ʿAwn al-Dīn died in 560/1165 | al-Iṣfahānī not only lost his job, but
315 was also thrown into prison. | Even though he was soon released, he could not regain his previous positions in Iraq and so two years later left for Damascus. There, the *qāḍī* Kamāl al-Dīn b. al-Shahrazūrī introduced him to the Kurdish emir Najm al-Dīn b. Ayyūb, while he also gained the favours of the latter's son Ṣalāḥ al-Dīn. The *atabeg* Nūr al-Dīn Maḥmūd b. Zangī made him his secretary and entrusted him with a mission to the caliph al-Mustanjid in Baghdad. Once he had completed this mission with success, Nūr al-Dīn conferred upon him a professorship in the newly constructed al-ʿImādiyya academy in 569/1173, an academy that was named in al-Iṣfahānī's honour. A year later Nūr al-Dīn made him president of the council of state. However, the latter's son and successor al-Malik al-Ṣāliḥ Ismāʿīl, who acceded to the throne in 569/1171 at the age of eleven, relieved him of all his duties and banished him from the court. On his way to Baghdad al-Iṣfahānī fell ill in Mosul, where he learned that Ṣalāḥ al-Dīn had seized power in Egypt and was already marching on Syria. He went to see him in Homs, gained his favour, and accompanied him on all his future campaigns. After Ṣalāḥ al-Dīn passed away in 589/1193 he had to retire from public life, devoting the rest of his days to literary pursuits, until he himself died on 13 Ramaḍān 597/20 June 1201.

Ibn Khall. 676, al-Suyūṭī, *Ḥusn al-muḥ.* I, 325, Wüst., *Gesch.* 284, *JA* s. IX, v. 3, p. 489. 1. *Kitāb al-fatḥ al-Qussī fi 'l-fatḥ al-Qudsī*[2] (MSS Suppl. ʿĀšir I, 656/7

2 On the title see Landberg, *ZDMG* 48, 166.

and Garr. 587), *Conquête de la Syrie et de la Palestine par Ṣalāḥaddīn, publ. par C. de Landberg, vol. I, texte ar.*, Leiden 1888.—2. *Kitāb al-barq al-Shāmī*, a history of his time in 7 volumes, ḤKh ^{1}1778, ^{2}I, 229, vol. V on the years 578–80/1182–4, Bodl. I, 761, selection of poems and stylistic examples Leid. 966.—| 3. *Nuṣrat* 385
al-fitra wa-ʿuṣrat al-faṭra, a history of the Saljūqs and their viziers, being a condensed translation of the copious Persian work by Sharaf al-Dīn Anūsharwān, d. 532/1137, in a bombastic *munshiʾ* style, Bodl. I, 662, Paris 2145; abstract by al-Bundārī, see $2,_{2}$.—4. *Kharīdat al-qaṣr wa-jarīdat ahl al-ʿaṣr*, on the poets of the sixth century, as a complement to the *Yatīmat al-dahr* of al-Thaʿālibī (p. 337) and the *Zīnat al-dahr* of Abu ʾl-Maʿālī Saʿd b. ʿAlī al-Ḥaẓīrī (p. 248), Paris 3326/32, Br. Mus. 574, 1096, Leid. 1125, Vol. I Munich 505, NO 3774 (*MSOS* XV, 11), abstract *ʿAwd al-shabāb* by ʿAlī b. Muḥammad al-Riḍāʾī al-Qusṭanṭīnī al-Rūmī, d. 1039/1629, Berl. 7412/3, Cairo ^{2}III, 259.—3. a poem, Gotha 26, f. 136b.[3]

| 2. Abu ʾl-Maḥāsin Yūsuf b. Rāfiʿ b. Shaddād Bahāʾ al-Dīn al-Ḥalabī was born in 386
Mosul on 10 Ramaḍān 539/6 March 1145. He studied in his hometown before becoming a lecturer at the Niẓāmiyya in Baghdad, until he was appointed as a professor at the academy in his hometown in 569/1173 (?). When, on his

3 Here al-Qāḍī al-Fāḍil ʿAbd al-Raḥīm b. ʿAlī b. Muḥammad al-Lakhmī al-ʿAsqalānī al-Baysānī, a friend of ʿImād al-Dīn, should also be mentioned. Despite the fact that he did not present himself as a historian, his literary legacy interests us most of all as a record of the history of his time. Son of the *qāḍī* of Ashkelon and born on 15 Jumādā I 529/3 April 1135, he started his career in the *dīwān al-inshāʾ* in Cairo and then became a secretary to the *qāḍī* of Alexandria. He was called back from there by al-ʿĀdil Ruzzik to join the *dīwān al-jaysh* in Cairo, where he asserted himself in office during the turmoil marking the end of the Fāṭimid reign, until Ṣalāḥ al-Dīn—then vizier—appointed him as the chairman of the *dīwān al-inshāʾ*. When the latter seized power himself the following year it was al-Baysānī who led the reforms in the military and finances, accompanying the sultan on his campaigns until his death in 589/1193. When war broke out between Ṣalāḥ al-Dīn's sons al-Malik al-Afḍal in Damascus and al-Malik al-ʿAzīz in Egypt he sided with al-ʿAzīz and brokered a peace between the brothers in 591/1195. He then retired from public life and died on 6 or 7 Rabīʿ II 596/26 or 27 January 1200.—Ibn Khall. 384, 857, Wüst., *Gesch.* 283, Maqr. *Khiṭaṭ* II, 366, Suyūṭī, *Ḥusn al-muḥ.* I, 325, *Hist. d. Crois.* I, Introd. LVI, *JA* s. 9, v. 3, p. 303. A description of his life was given by Qāḍī Muḥyi ʾl-Dīn ʿAbdallāh b. ʿAbd al-Ẓāhir (no. 8) under the title *al-Durr al-naẓīm fī awṣāf al-Qāḍī ʿAbd al-Raḥīm*.—A selection of stylistic examples taken from his private correspondence with ʿImād al-Dīn is preserved in Munich 402, Br. Mus. 778/9, letters to the caliph in Baghdad as volume 1 in a collection of 8 volumes Paris 6024, individual pieces Berl. 8621. A selection from his correspondence with ʿAbdallāh b. ʿAlī b. Muḥammad al-Jaʿfarī, Br. Mus. 1540, another collection ibid. 1541, his correspondence with Usāma b. Munqidh (see no. 9) on the occasion of his book *Kitāb al-ʿAṣā* from the *Kharida* by ʿImād al-Dīn in Derenbourg, *Nouv. Mél. or.* 147/52, *Vie d'Ousama* transl. 383/92. His diary (*al-Mutajaddidāt*) is cited in Maqr., *Khiṭaṭ* I, 269, 10, 19, 281, 8, 11, 164, 6 (see Suppl.).

way back from the pilgrimage, he visited Damascus in 584/1188, Ṣalāḥ al-Dīn appointed him both as *qāḍi 'l-ʿaskar* and as a *qāḍī* in Jerusalem. After the latter's death, he joined his son al-Malik al-Ẓāhir in Aleppo and served him and
317 his son al-Malik al-ʿAzīz as a judge. | His income allowed him to found two academies there. When al-ʿAzīz relinquished power in 629/1231 he retired from public life, dying in 632/1234.

Ibn Khall. 813, Abu 'l-F. *Ann.* IV, 408, Wüst., *Gesch.* 318. 1. *Kitāb al-nawādir al-sulṭāniyya wal-maḥāsin al-Yūsufiyya* Berl. 9811, Leid. 967, Br. Mus. 1630, Bodl. I, 588, II, 135 (p. 368). *Vita et res gestae Saladini auctore Bohadino f. Sjeddadī ed.* A. Schultens, Leiden 1732, 1755, cf. de Slane, *Hist. d. crois.* Introd. 45, C.R. Conder, *The Life of Saladin by Beha ad Din compared with the original Arabic and annotated, with a Preface by* Ch. Wilson, London, Palestine Pilgrims Texts Soc. 1897.—2. *Sīrat al-Malik al-Ẓāhir Baybars*, vol. II, Adrianopolis, Selīm. 1507, Turkish translation *Baipars Tarihi, al-Malik al-Zahir (Baypars) hakkindaki tarihin ikinci cildi, türkçeye çeviren* M. Şerefüddin Yaltkaya, Istanbul 1941 (Türk Tarih Kurumu yayinlarindan II, Seri, no. 3).—3. *Taʾrīkh Ḥalab*, Pet. AM 203.—4. *Dalāʾil al-aḥkām*, the foundations of jurisprudence with specification of relevant traditions, Paris 736.—5. *Maljaʾ al-ḥukkām ʿinda 'ltibās al-aḥkām*, Cairo ^{1}III, 277/8.—6. Lectures on *ḥadīth*, held by him in Cairo when he was staying there as an envoy in 629/1231, Bodl. I, $117_{,3}$, cf. II, 569.—7. *Kitāb al-ʿaṣā* (Moses and Pharaoh) Patna II, $516_{,2772}$.

4. Shihāb al-Dīn Abu 'l-Qāsim ʿAbd al-Raḥmān b. Ismāʿīl Abu 'l-Samāʾ[4] was born
387 in Damascus on 23 Rabīʿ II 599/10 January 1203. | There and in Alexandria he studied philology and jurisprudence. When he returned to his hometown he became a professor at the Rukniyya madrasa and in 662/1264 head of the Dār al-ḥadīth al-Ashrafiyya. When his obsession with slander finally turned itself against him, he was murdered by a rabble on 19 Ramaḍān 665/13 June 1268.

Fawāt I, 252, *Ḥuff.* XIX, 10, Maqr., *Khiṭ.* I, 46, *Orientalia* II, 253, Wüst., *Gesch.* 349. 1. *Kitāb al-rawḍatayn fī akhbār al-dawlatayn*, a history of the reigns of sultans Nūr al-Dīn and Ṣalāḥ al-Dīn, Berl. 9812, Munich 404, Vienna 898, Leid. 968, Br. Mus. 313, 1228, Bodl. I, 745, II, 138, Paris 1700/1, 5882, Patna I, $283_{,2323}$, print.

4 The man with the birthmark (over the left eyebrow).

C. 1287/8, 1292, 2 vols., cf. Fleischer, SB SGW 1859,$_{11}$, p. 14ff., *Arab. Quellenbeiträge zur Gesch. der Kreuzzüge, übers. u. hsg. v.* E.P. Goergens *und* R. Röhricht, vol. I, *Zur Gesch. Ṣalāḥaddīns*, Berlin 1879. Abstract of *ʿUyūn al-R.* by Khalīl b. Kaikäldī al-ʿAlāʾī, d. 767/1360 (II, 64), autograph Br. Mus. Suppl. 554.—2. *Dhayl al-Rawḍatayn* on the years 591–665/1195–1266, Berl. 9813/4, Copenhagen 156, Paris 5852, Br. Mus. Suppl. 555/6, cf. Wahl, *Neue arab. Anthologie*, p. 208.—3. *Sharḥ sabʿ qaṣāʾid al-Sakhāwī fī madḥ al-nabī*, composed in 642/1244, Paris 3142.—4. *Sharḥ al-burda* (p. 309) Munich 547, Paris 1620,$_{3}$.—5. *Qaṣīda* in 40 verses, in which he complains about depression, his violent temper, and feelings of resentment, asking his teacher ʿAlam al-Dīn al-Sakhāwī, d. 643/1245, for advice, Berl. 103 = 7772.—6. *Ibrāz al-maʿānī fī sharḥ Ḥirz al-amānī* (i.e. the *Shāṭibiyya*) see p. 409.—7.–13. cf. Suppl. (10. also Alex. Mawāʿiẓ 7, Patna I, 40,$_{408}$).

| 5. Abu ʾl-Maḥāsin Muḥammad b. Naṣrallāh (al-Dīn) b. Naṣr b. Ḥusayn Sharaf 318
al-Dīn al-Anṣārī b. ʿUnayn was born in Damascus on 9 Shaʿbān 549/20 October
1154. He distinguished himself as a poet at an early age, but was banished by
Ṣalāḥ al-Dīn on account of his caustic wit. After a long journey through Persia
and India he arrived in Yemen, which was ruled by Ṣalāḥ al-Dīn's brother al-
Malik al-ʿAzīz. He stayed there for some time, before going to Cairo by way
of the Hijaz. | When Ṣalāḥ al-Dīn died, he returned to Damascus. The latter's 388
successor al-Malik al-Afḍal appointed him as vizier and entrusted him with diplomatic missions several times. He died in his hometown on 22 Rabīʿ I 630/7 January 1233.

Ibn Khall. 656, Wüst., *Gesch.* 317. 1. *al-Taʾrīkh al-ʿAzīzī*, a biography of al-Malik al-ʿAzīz, ḤKh ^{1}2257, ^{2}298.—2. Elegy on al-Malik al-Muʿaẓẓam, d. 624/1227, Berl. 7712.

6. Sharaf al-Dīn Yaḥyā b. Abi ʾl-Qāsim b. Yaḥyā al-Ḥamzī, who studied around the year 666/1267 under Aḥmad b. Abi ʾl-Khayr al-ʿUmarī al-Madhḥijī and died in 677/1278 in Yemen.

Sīrat mawlānā wa-malikina ʾl-imām al-Mahdī li-dīn allāh amīr al-muʾminīn Aḥmad b. al-Ḥusayn b. al-Qāsim b. Rasūlallāh, who was born in 612/1216 and died in battle in 656/1258. It was begun in Rabīʿ I 646/1248, Berl. 9741, Ambr. NF 434, C 178.

7. A biography of al-Malik al-Nāṣir Dā'ūd b. ʿĪsā b. Abī Bakr[5] was written by one of his sons with the title:

Al-Fawā'id al-jaliyya fi 'l-farā'id al-Nāṣiriyya, with a selection of his poems and prose writings, Br. Mus. Suppl. 557, AS 4823 (photograph Cairo ^{2}III, 277).

8. Muḥyi 'l-Dīn Abu 'l-Faḍl ʿAbdallāh b. ʿAbd al-Ẓāhir al-Saʿdī al-Judhāmī al-Rawḥī was born in Cairo on 9 Muḥarram 620/12 February 1223. He served in the chancery of Baybars and died at the age of 72 in 692/1293.

Fawāt I, 271, *Orient.* II, 285, Wüst., 366 (contra Björkman, *Beitr.* 82ff., see E. Strausz, *WZKM* 45, 191/202). 1. *Sīrat al-sulṭān al-Malik al-Ẓāhir Baybars* (r. 658–76/1260–77), in verse, vol. I, Br. Mus. 1229, rendered as an abstract into prose
389 by Shāfiʿ al-Asqalānī (II, 28), ḤKh 7341, Paris 1717.—| 2. *al-Alṭāf al-khafiyya min al-sīra al-sharīfa al-sulṭāniyya al-Malikiyya al-Ashrafiyya*, a history of the
319 reign of the Egyptian sultan al-Malik al-Ashraf (689–93/1290–3), | vol. III, on the last three months of the year 690 until Rabīʿ I 691, Munich 405 (autograph), cf. J. Marcel, *Hist. de l'Égypte*, p. XIV. 3. Selected poems, Leid. 710.—4. *Maqāma* about Egypt, the Nile, and the Rawḍa, Berl. $8550,_2$.—5. A biography of al-Qāḍī al-Fāḍil, p. 385.—6. *al-Rawḍa al-bahiyya al-ẓāhira fī khiṭaṭ al-Muʿizziyya al-Qāhira*, an important source for Maqrīzī's *Khiṭaṭ*, see ibid. I, 5, 20, II, 365 etc.—7. *Tamā'im al-ḥamā'im*, on the pedigrees of pigeons, ḤKh II, 420, 3582, ^{2}I, 483 (which seems to transfer him to the era of the Fāṭimids), see R. Hartmann, *ZDMG* 70, 500, n. 5.

9. An unknown author wrote:

Al-Faḍl al-ma'thūr min sīrat al-sulṭān al-Malik al-Manṣūr Sayf al-Dīn Abu 'l-Fatḥ Qalāwūn al-Ṣāliḥī (678–89/1279–90) Bodl. I, 766.[6]

---

5 Born in 603/1206, son of Muʿaẓẓam ʿĪsā and grandson of Sayf al-Dīn al-ʿĀdil, he assumed power in Damascus in 624/1227, but two years later was bought off with Karak, conquered Jerusalem in 637/1239, was expelled from Karak by the Egyptian sultan al-Malik al-Ṣāliḥ in 647/1249, spent some years after that wandering, and then died in Damascus on 26 Jumādā I 656/1 June 1258, see Abu 'l-Fidā', *Ann.* IV, 336, 350, 448, 500, ʿAbd al-Qādir b. Abi 'l-Wafā', *Jawāhir* I, 237.

6 ḤKh III, 641, 7342 attributes this work to Qāḍī al-Fāḍil al-Baysānī, d. 596 (p. 385), which involves a glaring anachronism. This is why Wüstenfeld posits another author by the same name and whose death he fixes in 695, which is not very likely to be correct either.

10. In Persia, where the biography genre originated, al-ʿUtbī found just one successor in the person of Muḥammad b. Aḥmad b. ʿAlī b. Muḥammad al-Nasawī (see Suppl.).

Sīrat al-sulṭān Jalāl al-Dīn Mankubirtī, composed in 639/1241, ed. O. Houdas, text and translation, 2 vols., Paris 1891, 1895 (*Publ. de l'École des lang. or. viv.* IIIe s., vol. IX, X); cf. Abu 'l-F. IV, 278, d'Ohsson, *Hist. d. Mongols*, 1834, I, p. XVIff., Wüst., *Gesch.* 324.

11. A new kind of literature,[7] the autobiography, was introduced by Abu 'l-Muẓaffar Usāma b. Murshid Majd al-Dīn Mu'ayyad al-Dawla b. Munqidh. He was born on 27 Jumādā II 488/25 June 1095 in Shayzar, where his family possessed a small princedom. In | the year 532/1138 he was banished by his uncle 390
ʿIzz al-Dīn, for whom his bravery and ambition were on the point of becoming a threat. | He then went to Damascus where he received a friendly recep- 320
tion from the *atabeg* Shihāb al-Dīn Maḥmūd b. Tāj al-Mulk Būrī. Here, he was also able to enter into friendly relations with the Templars because relations between the Būrids and the Kingdom of Jerusalem were governed by a treaty. Driven out of Damascus by conspiracies, he left for Egypt in 538/1144 where he initially lived a reclusive life devoted exclusively to hunting. In 544/1150 and 548/1153 he took part in the battles against the crusaders at Ashkelon. Loathing his life in Egypt, he returned to Damascus in 549/1154. Meanwhile, Zangī's son Nūr al-Dīn, in whose army he had already served in Mosul in the years 1129–38, had come to power there. After completing the pilgrimage in 555/1160 he took part in Nūr al-Dīn's campaign against the Franks that ended with the capture of Ḥārim in 560/1164. The same year he migrated to Diyarbakr where he was welcomed by the Artuqid Qara Arslān in Ḥīṣn Kayfā. He lived there for ten years, devoting himself mainly to his literary work. In 570/1174, Ṣalāḥ al-Dīn, whose favours his son Murhaf had already won before him, called him to his court in Damascus. However, after some time he fell into disgrace, and was forced to stay there when the sultan moved his residence to Cairo. He died in Damascus on 13 Ramaḍān 584/6 November 1188.

H. Derenbourg, *Opuscules d'un arabisant*, Paris 1905, 313/36, Ph. Hitti, *RAAD* X (1930), 513/25, 592/603. 1. *Kitāb al-Iʿtibār*, an autobiography with colourful descriptions of the life of that period,[8] ed. H. Derenbourg, *Ousama b.*

---

7 If we disregard the essentially different autobiography of ʿUmāra (p. 407).

8 The much briefer autobiography of his contemporary and polymath Ibn al-Jawzī (see p. 502) essentially only describes his studies.

391 *Mounkidh* | II, Paris 1886 (*Publ. de l'École d. lang. or. viv.* II, s. vol. XII), ed. Ph. Hitti, Princeton 1930 (with a better text after the Escorial MS), translation see Suppl., also Russian by M. Sallier, Petrograd 1922 (with a preface, notes and a bibliography by I. Kračkovsky).—2. *Kitāb al-badīʿ fi 'l-badīʿ*, on the good and the bad in poetical style, Berl. 7277, Leningrad, Kračkovsky, *Zap. Koll. Vost.* I, 3/4, Alex. Adab 17 (*fī naqd al-shiʿr*), Cairo ^{1}IV, 124. Abstract, *Mukhtaṣar muqaddimat al-shiʿr*, Leid. 293, see Derenbourg, *Ousama* I, 691/722.—3. *Kitāb al-ʿaṣā* Leid. 472, see Derenbourg, *Mél. or.* 1886, p. 116, *Ousama* I, 449/543.—4. Selected poems, Gotha 2196,$_{2}$, see Derenbourg, *Nouv. mél. or.* p. 115, Ousama I, 543–51.—5.–8. see Suppl.

321 | 2 ***Histories of Dynasties***

1. Jamāl al-Dīn Abu 'l-Ḥasan ʿAlī b. Ẓāfir al-Azdī al-Khazrajī, d. 613/1216 in Cairo (see Suppl.).

Fawāt II, 51, Wüst., *Gesch.* 309. 1. *Kitāb al-duwal al-munqaṭiʿa*, in 4 volumes (ḤKh 5142), the last one of which covers the history of the Ḥamdānids, Sājids, Ṭūlūnids, Ikhshīdids, Fāṭimids, and ʿAbbāsids up to the year 622/1225, Gotha 1555, Br. Mus. Suppl. 461; the history of the Sājids was edited by Freytag in *Lokmani Fabulae*, Bonn 1823; for the Ḥamdānids see *ZDMG* X, 439; for the Egyptian dynasties Wüst., *Statthalter von Ägypten und Geschichte der Fāṭimiden.*—2. *al-Manāqib al-nūriyya*, on poetical metaphors, completed in 587/1191 and dedicated to Ṣalāḥ al-Dīn, Esc. ^{2}425.—3. *Badāʾiʿ al-badāʾih*, literary improvisations in an artificial style, often interlaced with reminiscenses from his personal life, which he dedicated—after having worked for 25 years on them—to al-Malik al-Ashraf in 603/1206, on the advice of al-Qāḍī al-Fāḍil, Paris 3514 (where he is designated a Sicilian due to confusion with Ibn Ẓafar, p. 431), Copenhagen 209, abstract by Zayn al-Dīn al-Ḥalabī, Esc. ^{2}420,$_{2}$.—4.–5. see Suppl.

2. Abū Ibrāhīm Fakhr al-Dīn al-Fatḥ b. Muḥammad b. al-Fatḥ Qiwām al-Dīn al-Bundārī al-Iṣbahānī wrote, in 623/1226:

1. *Zubdat al-nuṣra wa-nukhbat al-ʿuṣra*, an abstract of ʿImād al-Dīn's history of
392 the Saljūqs (p. 385) in a more accessible | style: *Histoire des Seldjoucides de l'Iraq publ. p.* M. Th. Houtsma, *Recueil de textes rel. à l'hist. des Seldj.* vol. 2, Leiden 1889.—2. Arabic translation of Firdawsī's *Shāhnāme*, dedicated to Sultan al-Malik al-Muʿaẓẓam ʿĪsā b. ʿĀdil of Damascus, d. 624/1257, Berl. 8440, Esc. ^{2}1660, Bodl. I, 845, II, 769, Tunis, *Bull. de Corr. Afr.* 1884, p. 27, no. 93; cf. Nöldeke, *Das*

Iranische Nationalepos,[2] p. 85, § 62; ed. by Dr. ʿAbd al-Wahhāb al-Aʿẓam, 2 vols., C. 1350.—Wüst., *Gesch.* 312.

3. During the caliphate of al-Nāṣir li-Dīn Allāh (575–622/1180–1225), Ṣadr al-Dīn Abu ʾl-Ḥasan ʿAlī b. al-Sayyid al-Imām al-Shāhid Abu ʾl-Fawāris Nāṣir b. ʿAlī al-Ḥusaynī wrote:

| *Zubdat al-tawārīkh*, for the older period a summary of the history of the 322
Saljūqs by ʿImād al-Dīn (385) up to the death of Sultan Ṭughril, d. 590/1194, then it follows the history of the *atabegs* to 620/1223, Br. Mus. Suppl. 550, cf. v. Rosen, *Zapiski* I, 243/52, Houtsma, *Recueil* I, ix, II, p. xxvi.

4. Abū ʿAbdallāh Muḥammad b. ʿAlī b. Ḥammād wrote, around the year 617/1220:

A history of the North African dynasty of the ʿUbaydids up to 617/1220, Paris 1888, 4614/5, 4625,$_2$, Algiers 1588,$_2$, cf. Cherbonneau, *JA* 1852, v. II, p. 470, 1853, p. 575, 1855, v. I, p. 159.

5. Abū Muḥammad ʿAbd al-Waḥīd b. ʿAlī Muḥyi ʾl-Dīn al-Tamīmī al-Marrākushī, who was born in Marrakesh on 8 Rabīʿ II 581/10 July 1185. He studied there under Ibn Zuhr (p. 489), then in Fez and Spain, where he stayed in the period 605–10, and again in 611–13. In 613/1216 he went to Egypt which, apart from a pilgrimage to Mecca in 620/1223, he does not appear to have left again.

Wüst., *Gesch.* 306, ʿAbdallāh Gannūn, *al-Nubūgh al-Maghribī fi ʾl-adab al-ʿarabī*, Tetouan 1357, I, 87. *Kitāb al-muʿjib fī akhbār ahl al-maghrib*, composed in 621/1224, Leid. 997, *The History of the Almohades, preceded by a Sketch of the History of Spain from the Times of the Conquest till the Reign of* | *Yusuf Ibn-Tāshfīn* 393
and of the History of the Almoravides by Abd-al-wáhid al-Marrékoshi, ed. by R.A. Dozy, Leiden 1847, 2nd ed. 1881. E. Fagnan, L'Histoire des Almohades d'après Abd el Wahid Marrakechi, *Rev. Afr.* XXXVI, 205, p. 166/208, 206, 262/88, 207, 347/88, XXXVII, 208, p. 22/51, 209/10, p. 181/246, offprint, Algiers: Jourdan, 1893.

5a. Muḥammad b. al-Ḥusayn al-Ḥasanī al-Miṣrī wrote, in 659/1260:

Al-Tuḥfa, an introduction to a lengthy work on the genealogy of the Arab tribes, dedicated to the Ḥafṣid Abū ʿAbdallāh Muḥammad b. Abī Zakariyyāʾ Yaḥyā (647–75/1249–76) as propaganda against the ʿAbbāsids in Cairo, see M. Jawad, *REI* 1938, 286.

6. Jamāl al-Dīn Muḥammad b. Sālim b. Wāṣil Abū ʿAbdallāh al-Ḥamawī was born in 604/1207. He taught Shāfiʿī fiqh, philosophy, mathematics, and astronomy in Hama. In 659/1261 he was summoned to Cairo, whence Sultan Baybars sent him as an envoy to the court of King Manfred—the son of Frederick II—in Sicily, where he stayed for a considerable period of time. After his return he became the chief *qāḍī* and professor at the academy of Hama, dying on 28 Shawwāl 697/9 August 1298.

323 | Abu ʾl-F. V, 144, *Orient.* II, 295, Wüst., *Gesch.* 371. 1. *Kitāb mufarrij al-kurūb fī akhbār Banī Ayyūb*, 3 vols., ḤKh 12620 (cites al-Ṣafadī, *al-Wāfī* I, $52_{,3}$), vol. 2. (the years 595–635), Molla Celebi 119 (Ritter), fragments Paris $1702/3_{,1}$, Cambr. 241, a continuation until the year 695/1296 by ʿAlī b. ʿAbd al-Raḥīm b. Aḥmad, secretary and client of al-Malik al-Muẓaffar, the predecessor of Abu ʾl-Fidāʾ as ruler of Ḥamā, ibid. $1703_{,2}$, excerpts in Reinaud, *Extraits d'hist. ar.* Paris 1822, p. 548, Quatremère, *Mamlouks* I, 252. An abstract, different from the MSS in Paris, by Qarṭāy al-ʿIzzī al-Khazandārī, for the years 626–89/1128–90, Gotha 1655, see v. Tiesenhausen, *Goldene Horde* I, 70/5.–2. *Sharḥ al-maqṣad al-jalīl li-Ibn Ḥājib* p. 371.—3. *al-Impirūriyya*, a précis of logic, composed for Emperor Manfred and published after his return to the Orient as *Nukhabāt al-fikar fi ʾl-manṭiq*, ḤKh VI, $317_{,13635}$.—4., 5. see Suppl.

394 | 7. Badr al-Dīn Muḥammad b. Ḥātim al-Yamanī al-Hamdānī wrote, around the year 694/1295:

Kitāb al-simṭ al-ghāli ʾl-thaman fī akhbār al-mulūk min al-Ghuzz bil-Yaman, a history of the Ayyūbids and Rasūlids covering the years 569–694/1173–1295, which ended at the year of death of al-Malik al-Muẓaffar Yūsuf, in whose army he held the rank of *amīr*, Br. Mus. 1584, Leid. 491, Cairo ^{2}V, 220.

8. Al-Ḥasan b. Muḥammad al-Ḥasanī wrote, in 700/1300 in Cairo:

Kitāb al-taqrīb fī-mā yataʿallaq bil-sayyid al-naqīb, a history of the sharifs of Mecca, Esc. ^{2}1694, Wüst. *Gesch.* 374.

3 *Histories of Individuals and Genealogy*

Following the example of the books of classes of men used in the science of *ḥadīth*, collections of biographical data on important men from other professions, notably poets and philologists, made their first appearance in the previous period. In the post-classical era, too, this type of literature was eagerly pursued. All the relevant works are mentioned here, with the exception of those dealing with traditionists, which will be discussed in the section on *ḥadīth*. Furthermore, local histories, though often consisting solely of accounts of the great men of a city or state, can nevertheless not be separated from works that also take political history into account.

1. Abu 'l-Ḥusayn b. al-Muḥassin b. Ibrāhīm (Suppl. p. 153) b. Hilāl b. Zahrūn (Chwolson, *Die Ssabier* I, 517) al-Ṣābi', a nephew of Ibn Sinān (Suppl. I, p. 386), was born in Shawwāl 359/August 969 and converted to Islam while he was a *kātib* in the service of the state. He died on 17 Ramaḍān 448/29 November 1056.

| Ibn Khall. 756, Wüst., *Gesch.* 198, Chwolson, *Die Ssabier* I, 604, 606. 1. *Kitāb* 324
al-amāthil wal-aʿyān or *Akhbār al-wuzarāʾ* ḤKh [1]I, 192, [2]I, 30, or *Tuḥfat*
al-umarāʾ fī taʾrīkh al-wuzarāʾ | Paris 5901; from the life of three viziers of the 395
caliph al-Muqtadir billāh (r. 295–320/908–32), Gotha 1756, cf. A. v. Kremer, Das Einnahmebudget des Abbasidenreiches v. J. 306, *Denkschr. der ph. hist. Cl. der Vienna. Ak.* 36, p. 283–362.—2. *Taʾrīkh*, a continuation of the history of Thābit b. Sinān, d. 365/975, from 290 until his own time (447/1055), ḤKh I, 123,$_{2191}$, [2]I, 290, vol. 8 is on the years 390–2/1000–2, Br. Mus. 930; an edition of the *Akhbār al-qarāmiṭa* is in preparation by B. Lewis (*Or.* VIII, 285).

2. His son Ghars al-Niʿma Abu 'l-Ḥusayn (Ḥusayn) b. Hilāl al-Ṣābiʾ wrote:

1. *Rusūm dār al-khilāfa*, MS in al-Azhar, see al-ʿAzzāwī in *Belleten* IV, 17, n. (245, n. 1).—2. *al-Hafawāt* (*al-bādira min al-muʿaqqalīn al-malḥūẓīn wal-saqaṭāt al-bārida al-mughaffalīn al-malfūẓīn*) ḤKh VI, 503,$_{14419}$ (which has al-Ṣābūnī), Top Kapu 2631,$_2$ (*RSO* IV, 725).—3. *ʿUyūn al-tawārīkh*, following Ṭabarī up to the year 479, cited in Maqrīzī, ed. Bunz, 15, 18, Ibn Taghribirdī, year 776,$_3$.

1b. Aḥmad b. ʿAlī al-Najāsī, *Kitāb al-rijāl* Patna II, 309,$_{2496}$.

2a. (see Suppl.) *Ṭabaqāt al-Ḥanābila* Patna II, 307,$_{2465}$.

3. Qiwām al-Dīn Ismāʿīl b. Muḥammad al-Faḍl al-Taymī al-Ḥāfiẓ al-Iṣbahānī Abu 'l-Qāsim, d. 538/1140.

Kitāb siyar al-salaf, biographies of the companions of Muḥammad, the *tābiʿūn*, and a number of saints, Paris 2012.—4 commentaries on the Qurʾān are mentioned in Ahlw., 939,$_{23}$.

4. Ẓāhir al-Dīn Abu ʾl-Ḥasan ʿAlī b. Abi ʾl-Qāsim Zayd al-Bayhaqī, d. 565/1169 (see Suppl.).

1. *Taʾrīkh ḥukamāʾ al-Islām*, a supplement to the *Ṣiwān al-ḥikma* of Muḥammad b. Ṭāhir b. Bahrām al-Sijazī (Suppl. I, 378), Berl. 10052, see al-Maghribī, *RAAD* II, 193/7, Mīrzā Muḥammad Qazwīnī, *Bīst Maqāla*, Tehran 1313, p. 78ff.—2. Persian history of Bayhaq, completed 5 Shawwāl 563/14 July 1168 in Shastamad, Berl. pers. 535, Br. Mus. Pers. Suppl. 89 (cf. Ibn Khall. transl. de Slane II, 323, ḤKh III, 238, VI, 443, 510).—3., 4. see Suppl.—5. *Azhār al-riyāḍ al-marīʿa wa-tafāsīr alfāẓ al-muḥāwara wal-sharīʿa*, A. Taymūr, *RAAD* III, 339.

396 | 5. Abu ʾl-Ḥasan Aḥmad b. Muḥammad b. Ibrāhīm al-Ashʿarī al-Yamanī al-Nassāba Shihāb al-Dīn, d. 500/1106, or, according to others, 600/1203 (see Suppl. I, 558).

ḤKh V, 298,$_1$. 1. *al-Taʿrīf bil-ansāb*, an abstract of al-Samʿānī's *Kitāb al-ansāb* (p. 401).—3. *Lubb al-lubāb al-majmūʿ min kulli kitāb*, 100 tales, Vienna 414, with the title *L. al-l. fī laṭāʾif al-ḥikāyāt wa-maḥāsin dhawi ʾl-albāb*, composed in 600/1203, fragm. Esc. ^{2}1702, 1, *L. al-l. wa-nuzhat al-aḥbāb* Garr. 242.

6. (7.) After the death of his father in 587/1191 Abu ʾl-Maʿālī al-Malik al-Manṣūr Muḥammad b. ʿUmar b. Shāhanshāh b. Ayyūb took over as the governor of Hama, Maʿarra, Salamiyya, and their hinterlands. Even though he lived in a perpetual state of warfare with the crusaders the sciences were very important at his court. He died in his castle in Hama in Dhu ʾl-Qaʿda 617/January 1221.

Abu ʾl-F. IV, 114, 288, Wüst., *Gesch.* 303. 1. *Akhbār al-mulūk wa-nuzhat al-malik wal-mamlūk fī ṭabaqāt al-shuʿarāʾ al-mutaqaddimīn min al-jāhiliyya wal-muḥaḍramīn etc.*, ḤKh 7901, vol. IX, composed in 602/1205, Leid. 884, cf. Weijers, *Spec. crit.* 13, *Orient.* I, 490/9.—2. *Durar al-ādāb wa-maḥāsin dhawi ʾl-albāb*, composed in 600/1203, frgm. Leipz. 606.

325 | 7. Abu ʾl-Ḥasan ʿAlī b. Yūsuf b. Ibrāhīm al-Shaybānī al-Qifṭī Jamāl al-Dīn, d. 646/1248 (see Suppl.).

Fawāt II, 96, Yāqūt, *GW* IV, 152, al-Ṣafadī, ed. Flügel in *Abulfeda, Hist. anteisl.*, ed. Fleischer, p. 233/5, al-Suyūṭī, *Ḥusn al-muḥ.* I, 319, Wüst., *Gesch.* 331, Steinschneider, *Polem. u. apolog. Literatur* (AKM 1877), p. 129, no. 111, Leclerc II, 193/8. 1. *Ikhbār al-ʿulamāʾ bi-akhbār al-ḥukamāʾ* = *Rawḍat al-ʿulamāʾ* Yeni 854, abstract entitled *al-Muntakhabāt al-multaqaṭāt min k. Ṭ. al-ḥ.* or *Ṭabaqāt*

al-ḥukamāʾ or *Taʾrīkh al-ḥ.*, by Muḥammad b. ʿAlī b. Muḥammad al-Zawzanī, composed in 647/1249, Berl. 10053/4, Vienna 1161/2, Strassb. 30, Munich 440, Leid. 1059/60, Paris 2112, Br. Mus. 1583, Esc. ^{2}1778, Rāġib 988, cf. Wenrich p. IV–IX, A. Müller, Verzeichnis der aristotelischen Schriften, in *Morg. Forsch.*, Leipzig 1875, 1–32, idem, Über das sogen. *Taʾrīkh al-ḥ.* des Ibn al-Qifṭī, | in *Actes du 8ème* 397
congr. intern. d. or. sect. I, fsc. 1, Leiden 1891, p. 15/36, J. Lippert, Ibn al-Qifṭī über den Ursprung der Apaturien, ZDMG 48, p. 486/9.—2. *Kitāb akhbār al-naḥwiyyīn*, abstract by al-Dhahabī, d. 748/1347 (II, 46), Leid. 1048 (autograph).—3. *Kitāb al-Muḥammadīn min al-shuʿarāʾ wa-ashʿāruhum*, on poets named Muḥammad, arranged alphabetically by their fathers' names, an opus posthumum, Paris 3335, Cairo ^{2}III, 336 (photograph).

8. Abū Naṣr Sahl b. ʿAbdallāh al-Bukhārī al-Nassāba wrote, during the reign of the caliph al-Nāṣir billāh (575–622/1180–1225):

Ansāb āl Abī Ṭālib, MS in the library of al-Ḥasan Ṣadr al-Dīn, *Dharīʿa* II, 337$_{,1517}$.

9. Ḥusām al-Dīn Abī ʿAbdallāh Ḥamīd (Ḥumayd) b. Aḥmad al-Muḥallī al-Hamdānī al-Shahīd, who was killed in 652/1254 in Yemen by a sharif of the Banū Ḥamza.

1. *Kitāb al-ḥadāʾiq al-wardiyya fī dhikr aʾimmat al-Zaydiyya* Landberg—Brill 261 (see Suppl.); a continuation by Muḥammad b. ʿAlī b. Yūsuf b. ʿAlī al-Raḥīf b. Fand al-Ṣaʿdī, composed in 916/1510 with the title *Maʾāthir al-abrār etc.*, MS. Or. Qu. 2038 (Burch. Fischer 37), Garr. 1622; another continuation *al-Laʾāliʾ al-muḍīʾa* by Aḥmad b. Muḥammad b. Ṣalāḥ al-Sharafī, d. 1045/1645, see Suppl. II, 550.—3. *Maḥāsin al-azhār fī manāqib al-ʿitra al-aṭhār*, a commentary on a *qaṣīda* in praise of ʿAlī and his offspring, additionally Hamb. Or. Sem. 382.

9a. Abu 'l-Barakāt al-Mubārak b. Abī Bakr b. Shiʿār (?) al-Mawṣilī, d. 654/1256.

ḤKh II, 236$_{,8220}$, *ʿUqūd al-jumān fī farāʾid shuʿarāʾ hādha 'l-zamān* (*al-mudhayyal ʿalā k. Muʿjam al-shuʿarāʾ li-Muḥammad b. ʿImrān al-Marzubānī* Suppl. I, 191, vol. I (Hamza) Asʿad 2323 (he refers in his preface to his *Tuḥfat al-wuzarāʾ*, Ritter).

10. Muwaffaq al-Dīn Abu 'l-ʿAbbās Aḥmad b. al-Qāsim b. Abī Uṣaybiʿa al-Saʿdī al-Khazrajī, who was born in 590/1194 in Damascus, where his father was an ophthalmologist. He studied medicine in his hometown and then at the
Nāṣiriyya hospital in Cairo. | He was particularly motivated by the famous 326

398 physician and botanist Ibn al-Bayṭār | (p. 492). In 631/1233 Ṣalāḥ al-Dīn gave
him a position in a newly founded hospital in Cairo, but as soon as 632 he went
to the Bīmāristān al-Nūrī in Damascus and in 634 became the personal physician of the emir ʿIzz al-Dīn Aydamur b. ʿAbdallāh in Safad. He died there in
Jumādā I 668/January 1270.

Wüst., *Gesch.* 350, Leclerc II, 187/93. *ʿUyūn al-anbāʾ fī ṭabaqāt al-aṭibbāʾ* (additionally Patna II, 317,$_{2469}$), in two recensions, one from the year 640/1242 and a later one with many additions, ed. A. Müller, Königsberg (Cairo) 1884, cf. idem, ZDMG 34, 471, *Travaux du VIe congr. intern. d. or. à Leyde II*, 218ff., *SBBA, phil.-hist. Cl.* 1884, p. 857ff.

11 (13). Shams al-Dīn Abu ʾl-ʿAbbās Aḥmad b. Muḥammad b. Ibrāhīm b. Abī
Bakr b. Khallikān al-Barmakī al-Irbilī al-Shāfiʿī was born on Thursday[1] 11
Rabīʿ II 698/23 September 1211 in Arbela, the son of a professor at al-Madrasa
al-Muẓaffariyya who traced his lineage back to the Barmakids. Having initially completed his studies in his homeland, in 626/1229 he went to Mosul
and Aleppo, where he heard the lectures of—among others—the grammarian
Abu ʾl-Baqāʾ b. Yaʿīsh (p. 358) at the academy that had been founded by Ibn
327 Shaddād (p. 386). | After the death of Ibn Shaddād he went to Damascus, and
in the following years he lived alternately there and in Aleppo. In 636/1238 he
went to Alexandria and Cairo, and shortly after replaced the chief *qāḍī* Yūsuf b.
al-Ḥasan al-Sinjārī, marrying in 650/1252. After some years of literary activity,
he received the profitable post of chief *qāḍī* of Syria, which had its main office
399 in Damascus. However, in 664/1266 the sultan appointed | independent chief
*qāḍī*s for the other three *madhhab*s as well, which had thus far come under
his jurisdiction. Then, on 13 Shawwāl 669/26 May 1271, he lost his office altogether, although its influence had, by that time, been diminished by the others. Following a temporary professorship at al-Madrasa al-Fakhriyya in Cairo
and having completed his historical work, he was reinstated in his office on
17 Muḥarram 676/11 June 1278. At the beginning of the year 679/1280, he fell
under suspicion of favouring a revolt by the governor of Damascus and spent
some weeks in jail, but was then restored to his office. However, in Muḥarram
680/May 1281 he was deposed once more. He died as a professor at al-Madrasa
al-Amīniyya, on 16 Rajab 681/21 October 1282.

Al-Suyūṭī, *Ḥusn al-muḥ.* I, 320, Wüst., *Gesch.* 358, de Slane, *Biogr. Dict.*, Introd., Quatremère, *Mamlouks* I, 2, p. 1801, II, 21, *JA* s. IX, v. 3, p. 467. *Kitāb wafayāt*[2]

1 As stated by himself in no. 205; according to Wüst. is was a Tuesday.

2 Called thus because it only contains those persons whose year of death has been ascertained.

al-aʿyān wa-anbāʾ abnāʾ al-zamān, started in Cairo in 654/1256 and completed there on 12 Jumādā II 672/4 January 1274, after the work had been suspended by his move to Damascus. Excluded from his scheme were the contemporaries of the Prophet, as well as the first four caliphs and the *tābiʿūn*. In this period he wanted to modify and enlarge the work once more, but he seems to have given up on this idea when he picked up where he had left off. This is why the biographies from no. 817 (Wüst.) until the end are much more elaborate than the earlier ones. It is sigificant that his autograph (Br. Mus. 1505, Suppl. 607, cf. Cureton, *JRAS* VI, 1841, p. 225, Wüstenfeld, *GGA* 1841, 286) shows many additions. MSS in Gotha 1725/31 and Suppl. (with Berl. Ms. Or. Qu. 2080, Garr. 678/80, AS 3530/6, Patna II, 300,$_{2387/8}$), | *Ibn Challikani Vitae* 328
illustrium virorum nunc primum ar. ed. F. Wüstenfeld, Göttingen 1835/43. *Vies des hommes illustres de l'Islamisme en Arabe par I. Kh.*, ed. M.G. de Slane, Paris 1838/42 (only up to no. 678), print. Būlāq 1275, 1299.[3] Cod. Amsterd. 106 contains 24 biographies that are missing in the other | MSS, 13 of which are 400
in J. Pijnappel, *Vitae ex lex biogr. Ibn Challicanis quae non extant nisi in cod. Amstelod.*, Amsterdam 1845.—Persian translation by: 1. Yūsuf b. Aḥmad b. Muḥammad b. ʿUthmān, completed in 895/1490, Br. Mus. Pers. I, 334.—2. Kabīr b. Uways b. Muḥammad al-Laṭīfī, composed under Sultan Selīm I (918–26/1512–19), Ouseley, no. 376, Kings Coll. 110, Cambr. Suppl. 1359, Bodl. Pers. 361.—Abstracts: 1. by his son Mūsā (who was born on 2 Ṣafar 651/13 April 1253 in Cairo, Wüst., *Gesch.* 376), completed in 752/1351, Ind. Off. 705.—2. *Mukhtaṣar al-anbāʾ* by ʿAlī b. Yaʿqūb al-Bārizī, completed in 751/1350, Paris 2060.—3. on poets and *udabāʾ* by al-Ḥasan b. ʿUmar b. Ḥabīb al-Ḥalabī, d. 779/1377 (II, 36), Berl. 9860.—4. Others, Br. Mus. 353,$_{3}$, Bodl. I, 299,$_{4}$, II, 120, Munich 436, Pet. AM 204 (biographies of older Arab poets,[4] making use of the *Qalāʾid al-ʿiqyān*, p. 414, among other works), cf. Strandmann, *De cod. msto vitas veterum poetarum Arabum sub nomine Ibn Challikani exhibente* (Helsinki, 1866), Calcutta p. 30, no. 250, Constantine, *JA* 1854, p. 435, no. 12.—5.–10. see Suppl. (7. Patna II, 299,$_{2383}$).—Continuations: 1. *Tālī Kitāb wafayāt al-aʿyān* by al-Muwaffaq Faḍlallāh b. Abī Muḥammad Fakhr al-Ṣaqāʿī (Wüst., *Gesch.* 391), on those who died in Egypt and Syria in the years 660–715 and 717–25/1261–1325, Paris 2061.—2. *Fawāt al-wafayāt* by Muḥammad b. Aḥmad al-Kutubī, d. 764/1362 (II, 40), 2 vols., Būlāq 1283, 1299.—3.–4. see Suppl.—II. Poems, which are rated as mediocre, Berl. 7781,$_{3,4}$, Gotha 2196,$_{5}$, *Fawāt* I, 55ff., Subkī, *Ṭab.* V, 15.

3 For a concordance of the printing cited here with the edition by Wüstenfeld, see p. 3.

4 Cited by Wüstenfeld as an independent work.

12. (14.) His brother, Bahāʾ al-Dīn Muḥammad b. Muḥammad b. Khallikān, who died in 683/1284 as the *qāḍī* of Baalbek, probably wrote:

Kitāb al-taʾrīkh al-akbar fī ṭabaqāt al-ʿulamāʾ wa-akhbārihim Bodl. I, 747, Wüst., *Gesch.* 359.

4 *Local history*

329 | A Baghdad

1. Abū Bakr Aḥmad b. ʿAlī b. Thābit al-Khaṭīb al-Baghdādī, d. 7 Dhu ʾl-Ḥijja 463/5 September 1071 (see Suppl.).

401 | Ibn Khall. 33, *Ḥuff.* XIV, 14, Yāqūt, *GW* II, 567, Wüst., *Gesch.* 208, *Schaf.* 423. 1. *Taʾrīkh Baghdād*, mostly a history of scholars, in 14 vols., ḤKh [1]II, 2179, [2]I, 288, individual volumes Berl. 9449, 9757, Br. Mus. 1281/3, 1625, Suppl. 655/6, Paris 2128/9, Algiers 1006/7, Cairo [1]V, 26, [2]V 109, print. C. 1349/1931 (a gap in the section on Muḥammad is appended in vol. V, 231/477), see G. Le Strange, A Greek embassy to Baghdad in 917, transl. from the Ar. Ms. of al-Khatib in the Br. Mus. Libr., *JRAS* 1897, 35/45, A. Riḍā in *RAAD* III, 129/36, 161/8, 260/7.—Abstracts: a. Masʿūd b. Muḥammad b. Ḥamīd al-Bukhārī, d. 461/1068 (ḤKh, loc. cit., Wüst., *Gesch.* 209), Berl. 9850, Buhār 243, Bank. XII, 799 = Patna II, 320,$_{2479}$, from which a further abstract by Abū ʿAlī Yaḥyā b. ʿĪsā b. Jazla, d. 493/1100 (p. 485), Br. Mus. 1625.—b. Anon., autograph from the 14th cent., Paris 2132.—2. *Kitāb al-kifāya fī maʿrifat uṣūl ʿilm al-riwāya* Berl. 1034 (2nd half), Leid. 1737, AS 1364, Qara Muṣṭafā p. 144, Cairo [1]I, 244, Bank, V, 498 = Patna I, 36,$_{363}$, a detailed exposition of the requirements for a specialist of *ḥadīth*, a monument to his zeal in the cleansing of *ḥadīth*, Goldziher, *MSt.* II, 183.—3. *Kitāb taqyīd al-ʿilm*, which proves that it is certainly admissible to write down *ḥadīth*s, Berl. 1035, cf. Goldziher, op. cit., II, 198ff.—4. *Sharaf aṣḥāb al-ḥadīth* Berl. 9920/1.—5. *al-Muʾtanaf fī takmilat al-Muʾtalaf wal-mukhtalaf*, on the proper spelling and pronunciation of names, surnames, and sobriquets, with biographical information, meant as a supplement to the *Kitāb al-muʾtalaf wal-m.* of Dāraquṭnī, d. 385/995 (p. 173), Berl. 10157.—6. *Talkhīṣ al-mutashābih fi ʾl-rasm wa-ḥimāyat mā ashkala minhu ʿan nawādir al-taṣḥīf wal-wahm* Cairo [1]I, 232, Dam. Z. 35, 95, ʿUm. 26,$_{390}$.—abstract by ʿAlī b. ʿUthmān al-Turkumānī, d. 750/1349 (II, 64), Leid. 134.—7. *Kitāb al-bukhalāʾ* Br. Mus. Suppl. 1132.—8.—22. see Suppl. (14. *Muntakhab min al-zuhd wal-raqāʾiq*, in 10 volumes, MS from 500 AH, Alex. Muṣt. Ḥad. 8.—15. read: *wa-ādāb al-sāmiʿ*).—23. *Kitāb al-riḥla fī ṭalab al-ḥadīth* ḤKh 10131, Goldziher, *MSt.* II, 175ff.

2. Abū Saʿd (Saʿīd) ʿAbd al-Karīm b. Muḥammad b. Manṣūr al-Tamīmī al-Samʿānī was born on 21 Shaʿbān 506/11 February 1113 into a family of scholars from Marw. He made lengthy journeys[1] to study *ḥadīth,* | during | which he 330 402 also stayed in then-Christian Jerusalem and Damascus. He returned to Marw in 538/1143, where he taught at al-Madrasa al-Aḥmadiyya, dying on 10 Rabīʿ I 562/5 January 1167.

Ibn Khall. 368, *Ḥuff.* XVI, 12, Abulf. III, 605, Wüst. in *Lüddes Zeitschr. f. Geogr.* I, 43, no. 73, *Gesch.* 234, al-Kattānī, *Fihris* II, 373. 1. *Dhayl taʾrīkh Baghdād,* a continuation of the history of Baghdad by al-Khaṭīb in 15 vols., ḤKh 2179. Abstract Leid. 1023 (see Suppl.).—2. *Kitāb al-ansāb,* which was begun in 550/1155 at the behest of ʿUmar b. ʿAlī al-Bisṭāmī, whom he had met in Transoxania, and which explains *nisba*s. The information on Iranian and Transoxanian names offers particularly important data, with brief biographies of the most famous bearers of the names, in 8 vols., ḤKh ^{1}I, 1350, ^{2}I, 179, complete Köpr. 1010, Br. Mus. 1286, Patna I, 304,$_{2410}$, individual parts Br. Mus. 345, Lee 91, Pet. AM 196, AS 2976 (just individual leaves, remainder Ibn Khall.), 2980, Yeni II, 244, Bešīr Āġā 445.—Abstract *al-Lubāb* in 3 vols., which almost completely superseded the original work, by ʿIzz al-Dīn b. al-Athīr, d. 630/1232 (p. 345), Gotha 481 (*Alif-Khāʾ*), Lee 91 (*sīn-ʿayn*), Cairo ^{1}VI, 21, ^{2}V, 314, Garr. 293/4, print. C. 1358, cf. *Specimen al-Lobabi s. Genealogiarum Arabum, quas conscriptas ab Abū Saʿd Samʿanensi abbrev. emend. Ibn el-Athir,* ed. F. Wüstenfeld, Göttingen 1835. Abstract *Lubb al-lubāb fī taḥrīr al-ansāb* by al-Suyūṭī, d. 911/1505 (see Suppl., Patna II, 308,$_{2421}$), ed. P.J. Veth, Leiden 1830/2.–3.—12. see Suppl.—13. His work on Tradition, *Afānīn (al-basātīn),* ḤKh ^{1}I, 307,$_{1001}$, ^{2}I, 131, is cited in Yāqūt, GW III, 135,$_{15}$.—14. *al-Muntakhab,* a *muʿjam* of his shaykhs, Topqapū Sarayi 2234 (photograph Berlin).

3. Abū ʿAbdallāh Muḥammad b. Abi ʾl-Maʿālī Saʿīd b. Abī Ṭālib Yaḥyā b. al-Dubaythī al-Wāsiṭī al-Shāfiʿī, whose ancestors had migrated from Ganja in Arrān to Dubaytha near Wāsiṭ, was born in Wāsiṭ on 26 Rajab 558/1 July 1163. A specialist of Tradition, he lived most of his life in Baghdad, where he died on 8 Rabīʿ II 637/8 October 1239.

Ibn Khall. 633, *Ḥuff.* XVIII, 14, Wüst., *Gesch.* 323. 1. *Dhayl taʾrīkh Baghdād,* a follow-up to al-Samʿānī (ḤKh 2179), a first redaction, Br. Mus. Add. 2524 (*ʿayn*),

---

1 Which were ungenerously called into question by the Ḥanbalī Ibn al-Jawzī (p. 500), see Ibn al-Athīr XI, 134, Goldziher, *M.St.* II, 185.

403 a second redaction, | 10 years later, Paris 2133, Cambr. 169 (according to Muṣṭafā Jawād). Abstract by al-Dhahabī, d. 748/1374 (II, 46), Cairo ^{1}V, 145, ^{2}V, 335.—2. see Suppl.

B Damascus

1. Abu 'l-Ḥasan ʿAlī b. Muḥammad b. Shujāʿ al-Rabaʿī al-Mālikī, who died in 435/1043.

331 | *Kitāb al-iʿlām fī faḍāʾil al-Shām wa-Dimashq wa-dhikr mā fīhimā min al-āthār wal-biqāʿ al-sharīfa*, a historical topography of Damascus, ḤKh IV, 9126, on which a didactic letter by Muḥammad b. Ṭūlūn, d. 952/1546 (II, 367), Berl. $173_{,1}$, an abstract by Burhān al-Dīn Ibrāhīm b. ʿAbd al-Raḥmān al-Fazārī, d. 729/1329 (II, 130), ḤKh ^{1}I, 952, ^{2}I, 127, Berl. 6074, Gotha $54_{,1}$, Tüb. Wetzst. $26_{,2}$ (not in Weisw.).

2. Abu 'l-Qāsim ʿAlī b. al-Ḥasan b. Hibatallāh Thiqat al-Dīn b. ʿAsākir al-Shāfiʿī, born on 1 Rajab 499/9 March 1106, studied, from the year 520/1126, *ḥadīth* at the Niẓāmiyya in Baghdad and the most important towns of Persia. After his return to Syria he became a professor at al-Madrasa al-Nūriyya in Damascus, where he died on 11 Rajab 571/26 January 1176.

Ibn Khall. 414, *Ḥuff.* XIV, 16, Wüst., *Gesch.* 267, see *Orientalia* II, 161. 1. *Taʾrīkh madīnat Dimashq*, biographies of famous Damascenes and of scholars who had resided there for some time, following the example of the *Taʾrīkh Baghdād*, which he worked on from early adolescence, in 80 volumes, ḤKh II, 2101, 2218, ^{2}I, 294, complete (?) in 7 volumes in Istanbul (see Suppl.), individual parts Berl. 9781, Gotha 1775 (where other MSS are listed, in addition 2 volumes that formerly belonged to Landberg, Br. Mus. Suppl. 658, see Suppl. and Paris 2087, after M. Jawad, *REI* 1938, 285, Patna II, $320_{,2480/1}$).—Abstracts by: a. Abū Shāma, d. 665/1266 (p. 387), a part Berl. 9782, Paris 2137 (M. Jawad, *REI* 1938, 285).—b. Muḥammad b. al-Mukarram al-Kātib al-Anṣārī, d. 711/1311 (II, 21), part II, Gotha 1776 (autograph), Köpr. 1148/51.—c. Ibn Qāḍī Shuhba, d. 851/1447 (II, 51), Berl. 9783.—d. Anon., Gotha 1777 (beginning), see *ZDPV* IV, 83, Goldziher, *WZKM* IX, 359/71.—e.,–f. see Suppl.—g. Abu 'l-Fatḥ al-Khaṭīb, Garr. 584.—2. *Tabyīn*
404 *kadhib* | *al-muftarī fī-mā nusiba ilā Abu 'l-Ḥasan al-Ashʿarī* (see p. 307), Leipz. 113, Leid. 1097, Bodl. I, 181, Esc. ^{2}1801, Patna II, $295_{,2368}$: Abstract with the addition of the *ṭabaqāt* under the title *Ashraf al-mafākhir al-ʿaliyya fī manāqib al-aʾimma al-ashʿariyya* by ʿAbdallāh b. Asʿad al-Yamanī, Leid. 1098, cf. Spitta, *Zur Gesch. des A. 'l-Ḥ. al-A.*, p. 10ff.—3. *Kitāb al-ishrāf ʿalā maʿrifat al-aṭrāf*, indices to the

4 works on *ḥadīth* (excluding Bukhārī and Muslim), AS 455/6, Cairo [1]I, 268, [2]I, 89.—4. *Kitāb al-arbaʿīn al-buldāniyya*, 40 traditions, ḤKh I, 397, [2]I, 54/5, maybe Berl. 1466.—5. *Tabyīn al-imtinān bil-amr bil-ikhtitān* Cairo [1]I, 278, [2]I, 94.—6.–8. see Suppl.

3. An anonymous author wrote a chronicle of Syria covering the years 490–593/1097–1197.

Bustān al-jāmiʿ, une chronique syriaque du VIe/VIIe siècle (Bodl. Hunt. 142, Istanbul, Sarāi 2959) publié par Cl. Cahen, *Bull. d'Études or. de l'Institut franç. de Damas*, VII/VIII, 1937/8, p. 113/58.

C Jerusalem

1. Al-Qāsim b. ʿAsākir, son of the aforementioned person, d. 600/1203 (see Suppl.).

Al-Jāmiʿ al-mustaqṣā fī faḍāʾil al-Masjid al-Aqṣā, revised by an anonymous editor with excerpts from the *Faḍāʾil al-Quds wal-Shām* by Abu ʾl-Maʿālī al-Musharraf b. al-Murajjā b. Ibrāhīm al-Maqdisī (see Suppl. I, 567,$_{1}^{a}$, 876,$_{2a}$), and which forms the basis of the *Bāʿith al-nufūs ilā ziyārat al-Quds al-maḥrūs* by Ibn al-Firkāḥ II, 130.

| 2. Abū Saʿd ʿAbdallāh b. al-Ḥasan Niẓām al-Dīn b. ʿAsākir was born in 600/1203 332
in Damascus and died in 645/1247.

Wüst., *Gesch.* 330. *Faḍāʾil al-maqdis*, ḤKh 9149, has not been preserved.

D Aleppo

Kamāl al-Dīn Abu ʾl-Qāsim ʿUmar b. Aḥmad Hibatallāh b. ʿAbd al-ʿAzīz b. Abī Jarāda b. al-ʿAdīm al-ʿUqaylī al-Ḥalabī was born in Dhu ʾl-Ḥijja 588/Jan. 1193 in Aleppo, where his ancestors had held the office of | the Ḥanafī *qāḍī* for five 405
generations. He studied in his hometown and then in Baghdad, Damascus, Jerusalem, the Hijaz, and Iraq. After his return to Aleppo he first became a secretary, then a *qāḍī*, and served several petty kings as vizier. When the Tatars captured and destroyed Aleppo on 8 Ṣafar 658/26 January 1260 he fled with al-Malik al-Nāṣir to Egypt. Appointed chief *qāḍī* of Syria by Hulāgū, he returned there for a brief spell but died on 26 Jumādā I 660/21 April 1262 in Cairo.

Fawāt II, 101, Abu'l-F. IV, 634, Ibn Quṭlūbughā, *Ṭab. al-Ḥan.* 143, *Orient.* II, 248, Wüst., *Gesch.* 345. 1. *Kitāb bughyat al-ṭalab fī ta'rīkh Ḥalab*, an alphabetically ordered history of learned men in 10 volumes, dispersed as a result of the Mongol onslaught, which is why from an early date there was hardly a complete copy to be found, ḤKh ^{1}II, 1877, 2205, ^{2}I, 249, 291, individual parts Paris 2138, Br. Mus. 1290, in Istanbul (see Cahen, *REI* 1936, no. IV), Sarāi A. III, 2925, 8 vols., (vol. III, Paris 2138), Faiẓ. 1404, see Hamdani, *JRAS* 1938, 562.—Continuations: a. *Nuzhat al-nawāẓir* by Muḥammad b. Muḥammad b. al-Shiḥna, d. 890/1485 (II, 43), exordium Leid. 951, anon. abstract by one of his descendants with additions up to the year 936, MSS see Suppl.—b. using a., *al-Durr al-muntakhab fī (takmilat) Ta'rīkh Ḥalab* by ʿAlī b. Muḥammad b. Khaṭīb al-Nāṣiriyya al-Jibrīnī, who died in 843/1439 (II, 34), see Suppl.—2. *Zubdat al-ḥalab fī ta'rīkh Ḥalab*, an alphabetically ordered abstract of the previous work up to the year 641/1243, which he could not turn into a clean copy before he died, Paris 1666, Pet. AM 160. *Selecta ex historia Halebi*, ed. G.W. Freytag, Paris 1819, *Regnum Saahd-Aldaulae in oppido Halebo*, ed. G.W. Freytag, Bonn 1820, E. Blochet, L'histoire d'Alep de Kamaladdin, vers. franç. d'après le texte ar., *Revue de l'or. lat.* 1896, p. 509/65, 1897, p. 146/235, 1898, p. 37/107.—3. *Kitāb al-darārī fī dhikr al-dharārī*, which was presented to al-Malik al-Ẓāhir Ghāzī on the birth of his son al-Malik al-ʿAzīz in the year 610/1213, NO 3790, printed as no. 2 in *Majmūʿa*, Istanbul 1298.—4. *al-Wasīla (wuṣla) ila 'l-ḥabīb fī waṣf al-ṭayyibāt wal-ṭīb*, on the preparation of delicacies and perfumes, ḤKh VI, 14273 (without author), Berl. 5464 (see Suppl.), Patna,
406 I, 259_{2193}.—5. 54 verses in praise of ʿĀ'isha, Berl. 7760_{2}.—6. Elegy | on the fall
of Aleppo, fragment in Abu 'l-F., loc. cit.—7. *Tadhkirat b. al-ʿAdīm*, an anthology, Cairo ^{2}III, 58, IV, b, 42.—8. *Bulūgh al-āmāl mimmā ḥawa 'l-kamāl*, an alphabetically ordered collection of *qaṣīda*s and *muwashshaḥāt*, *Mukhtaṣar*, Alex. Adab 123.—9. *al-Inṣāf wal-taḥarrī fī dafʿ al-ẓulm wal-tajarrī ʿan Abi 'l-ʿAlā' al-Maʿarrī*, as *Dafʿ al-ẓulm wal-t.* in ḤKh ^{1}III, 231_{5098}, ^{2}I, 757, as *Dafʿ al-tajarrī* in Ṭāsköprīzāde, *Miftāḥ al-saʿāda* Ind. I, 192, MSS Aḥmad Taymūr and ʿĪsā Iskandar al-Maʿlūf, see *RAAD* II, 236/44.

333 | E Dunaysir

The physician Abū Ḥafṣ ʿUmar b. Abi 'l-ʿAbbās al-Khiḍr b. Ilälämiš b. Ildüzmiš al-Turkī wrote, around 610/1233:

Kitāb ḥilyat al-sariyyīn min khawāṣṣ al-Dunaysariyyīn, on scholars in various fields who lived or resided temporarily in Dunaysir, with an abstract, the *Muntakhab*, by the author himself, Berl. 9851.

F South Arabia

1. Abu 'l-ʿAbbās Aḥmad b. ʿAbdallāh b. Muḥammad al-Rāzī from Ṣanʿāʾ was alive in 460/1068.

Taʾrīkh al-Rāzī, part III, a description of Ṣanʿāʾ and its surroundings, with information on legends and traditions, together with biographical notes on the companions of the Prophet and other important people who resided there, Paris 1643, 5824, Br. Mus. Suppl. 583.

2. Abū Muḥammad ʿUmāra b. ʿAlī b. Zaydān Najm al-Dīn al-Yamanī al-Ḥakamī was born around 515/1121 in Murṭān in the Wādī Wasāʿ region of the Tihāma in Yemen. He studied in Zabīd from 531/1137 onwards and went on the pilgrimage to Mecca in 549/1154. The emir of the city sent him as an emissary to Cairo, where he gained the favour of al-Fāʾiz and his vizier. In Shawwāl 550/December 1155 he returned to Mecca and in Ṣafar 551/March 1156 to Zabīd. When he again went | as a pilgrim to Mecca that same year he was once more entrusted with a 407
mission to Cairo. He arrived there in Shaʿbān 552/September 1157 and took up permanent residence. Even though he remained a Sunnī, he nevertheless recognized the Fāṭimids' claim to the infallible Imamate. When Ṣalāḥ al-Dīn conquered the country he initially tried to win his favour through laudatory poems while remaining true to the Fāṭimids. However, because of some poems in their praise, or, according to others, because he was implicated in a conspiracy to raise the son of the last of the Fāṭimids to the throne with the aid of the Franks, Ṣalāḥ al-Dīn had him executed by strangulation on 2 Ramaḍān 569/6 April 1175.

| Ibn Khall. 462, Wüst., *Gesch.* 263. H. Derenbourg, *ʿOumāra du Yemen, sa vie et* 334
son œuvre (*XII*^{e} *s.*), vol. 1 *Autobiographie et récits sur les vizirs d'Égypte et choix de poésies, Texte ar. Publ. de École d. lang. or. viv.* s. IV, v. X, Paris 1898. 1. *Taʾrīkh al-Yaman*, dedicated to al-Qāḍī al-Fāḍil (p. 385, n. 1). *Yaman its early mediaeval history by Najm al-din Omarah al-Hakami, etc., the orig. texts with translation and notes by* H. Cassels Kay, London 1892; cf. W. Robertson Smith, *JRAS* 1893, p. 181/207, Kay, ibid., 218/36.—2. *Kitāb al-nukat al-ʿaṣriyya fī akhbār al-wuzarāʾ al-miṣriyya*, an autobiography with an account of his poetic relations with the viziers al-Ṣalāḥ Ṭalāʾiʿ b. Ruzzīk, Shāwar, al-Kāmil, and the son of the latter, with poems and poetic letters, Gotha 2256, Paris 2147,$_{1}$, Bodl. I, 835, ed. Derenbourg, see above.—3. *Dīwān* Copenhagen 266, Pet. AM 298, Cairo ^{2}III, 140, *Mukhtārāt* ibid. 341.—4. *Qaṣīda* on the Nile, Egypt, and the downfall of the Fāṭimids, Berl. 7696,$_{1}$.—5. Poems on the pyramids, *Fundgr. d. Or.* IV, 238.—6. *Qaṣīda* on Ṣalāḥ al-Dīn, see al-Qalqashandī, *Geogr. und Verwaltung v. Ägypten*, transl. by Wüst., p. 222, Maqrīzī, *Khiṭaṭ* I, 495.

G Jurjān

Abu ’l-Qāsim Ḥamza b. Yūsuf b. Ibrāhīm b. Mūsā al-Qurashī al-Sahmī al-Jurjānī, a well-travelled *ḥadīth* specialist who died in 427/1036.

408 | *Ḥuff.* XIII, 60, Wüst., *Gesch.* 186. 1. *Taʾrīkh Jurjān* ḤKh ^{1}II, 219, ^{2}I, 290 (where it is incorrectly stated that he died in 670) = *Notitiae doctorum virorum Gurganae*, Bodl. I, 746.—2. *Taʾrīkh Astarābādh*, ḤKh II, 2135, ^{2}I, 281 (with the incorrect year 670).—3. *Arbaʿīn fī faḍāʾil al-ʿAbbās*, ḤKh ^{1}I, 397, 422, VI, 13040, ^{2}I, 55, 57 (lacking date).

H Egypt

1. Al-Amīr al-Mukhtār ʿIzz al-Mulk Muḥammad b. Abi ’l-Qāsim ʿUbaydallāh b. Aḥmad b. Ismāʿīl b. ʿAbd al-ʿAzīz al-Musabbiḥī was born on 10 Rajab 366/4 March 977 in Fusṭāṭ. In 398/1007 he entered the service of the Fāṭimid caliph al-Ḥākim as a secretary and gained his total trust. Having governed the districts of al-Qays and al-Bahnasāʾ in Upper Egypt for a time he became head of the pay office, before dying in Rabīʿ II 420/April 1029.

Ibn Khall. 625, al-Suyūṭī, *Ḥusn al-muḥ.* I, 254, Wüst., *Gesch.* 81. *Kitāb akhbār Miṣr wa-faḍāʾilihā wa-ʿajāʾibihā wa-ṭarāʾifihā wa-gharāʾibihā wa-mā bihā min al-biqāʿ wal-āthār wa-siyar man ḥallahā wa-ḥalla ghayrahā min al-wulāt wal-umarāʾ wal-aʾimma al-khulafāʾ ābāʾ amīr al-muʾminīn*, vol. 40 (sic), on the years 514–5/1023–4, Esc. $^2543_{,2}$. Continuation by Muḥammad b. ʿAlī b. al-Muyassar, see Suppl. 574.

335 | 2. Abu ’l-Makārim Asʿad b. al-Khaṭīr b. Abi ’l-Malīḥ b. Mammātī, d. 606/1209, see Suppl.

Ibn Khall. 88, Maqrīzī, *Khiṭaṭ* II, $160_{,if}$, al-Suyūṭī, *Ḥusn al-muḥ.* I, 325, Wüst., *Gesch.* 295. 1. *Kitāb qawānīn al-dawāwīn*, administrative measures regarding the *dīwāns* of Egypt at the time of Ṣalāḥ al-Dīn and the sultan al-ʿAzīz (see Suppl.), Gotha 47, 1892, Br. Mus. Suppl. 553, AS 3360, Esad 2352, cf. Hammer, *SBWA* XV, 5ff., Wüst., *Calcaschandi*, 35, 148, *Heerwesen der Mus.* 1.—2. *Kitāb al-fāshūsh fī aḥkām Qaraqūsh*, a satirical account of the poor administration of Qāsim, a minister of Ṣalāḥ al-Dīn (Ibn Khall. 516), ḤKh 8655, Paris 3552, Qawala II, 236 (*Risāla fī-mā warada fī Q.*), wrongly attributed to al-Suyūṭī, cf. de Sacy, *Abd-Allatif* p. 206.—Abstract Cairo ^{1}VI, 95, ^{2}V, 280, 328. P. Casanova, *Qarakouch, sa légende et son histoire*, Communication faite à l’Institut Égyptien, Cairo 1892,

idem, Karakouch, *Mém. publ. par les membres de la* | *Mission archéologique* 409
franç. au Caire, v. VII, Paris 1893, G. Jacob, *Ramaḍān, Mitt. der Geogr. Ges. zu Greifswald*, special issue, 25.—3.–4. see Suppl.—5. *Aʿlām al-naṣr*, see Kračkovsky, CR Ac. Leningrad 1928, 1/6.

3. ʿUthmān b. Ibrāhīm al-Nābulusī al-Ṣafadī Fakhr al-Dīn wrote, during the reign of Najm al-Dīn Ayyūb (637–48/1240–9):

1. *Kitāb lumaʿ al-qawānīn al-muḍīʾa fī dawānīn al-diyār al-miṣriyya*, on the administration of Egypt, using his many years of experience as the basis, Gotha 1891 (with the wrong date), Cairo ^{1}VI, 22, ^{2}V, 319.—2.–3. see Suppl.

4. Jamāl al-Dīn Abu ʾl-Ḥasan Yaḥyā b. ʿAbd al-ʿAẓīm b. Yaḥyā al-Jazzār al-Anṣārī, d. 669/1270, see Suppl.

Orient. II, 267, Wüst., *Gesch.* 357. 1. *al-ʿUqūd al-durriyya fī ʾl-umarāʾ al-miṣriyya*, a chronicle in verse of the Egyptian sovereigns up to al-Malik al-Ẓāhir Baybars, d. 676/1277, or al-Malik al-Saʿīd, deposed in 678/1279, with a continuation up to the reign of al-Malik al-Ẓāhir Jaqmaq, d. 857/1453, Berl. $9814_{,2}$, $9824_{,1}$, ii, Leid. 969, Esc. $^{2}470_{,10}$ anon. until 872/1467, Gotha, 1667/8, Pet. $139_{,2}$, by al-Suyūṭī, d. 911/1505, Paris 1608.—2.–3. see Suppl. (2. AS $4296_{,2}$).

5. Ibrāhīm b. Waṣīf Shāh al-Miṣrī wrote, before 606/1209, which is the date on MS Pet. AM 204 (Dorn):

| *Kitāb jawāhir al-buḥūr wa-waqāʾiʿ al-umūr wa-ʿajāʾib al-duhūr wa-akhbār* 336
al-diyār al-Miṣriyya, a history of Egypt from its earliest, legendary times until 606, often used in al-Maqrīzī's *Khiṭaṭ*, ḤKh ^{1}II, 4272, ^{2}I, 613 (where 599 is given as the year of death). An abstract with a simple list of the names of the sultans up to Qānṣūh al-Ghūrī in 923/1517, which is further continued in Gotha 1644 (where other MSS are listed, with Br. Mus. Suppl. 687, Bursa Ḥü. Čelebi Heyet 18). From this: F. Wüstenfeld, Die älteste ägyptische Geschichte nach den Zauber- und Wundererzählungen der Araber, *Orient u. Occident* 1861, I, 326ff., Chwolson, *ZDMG* VI, 408, Wüst., *Gesch.* 373a.

I The Maghreb

ʿAbdallāh Gannūn al-Ḥasanī, *al-Nubūgh al-Maghribī fī ʾl-adab al-ʿArabī*, 2 vols., Tetouan 1357.

410 | 1. Abū Zakariyyā' Yaḥyā b. Abī Bakr al-Warjalānī was born in Warjalān in the Algerian Sahara, studied in Wād Rirʿ under the famous Ibāḍī shaykh Abū Rabīʿa Sulaymān b. Ikhlaf al-Mazatī, and died in 471/1078.

Kitāb al-sīra wa-akhbār al-a'imma, a history of the Ibāḍī imams of the Mzab: *Chronique d'Abou Zakarya*, ed. Masqueray, Paris-Algiers 1878, cf. *Bull. de Corr. Afr.* 1885, p. 36/8, 242, no. 2.

2. Abu 'l-ʿAbbās Aḥmad b. Saʿīd b. Sulaymān b. ʿAlī b. Ikhlaf al-Darjīnī wrote, soon after 626/1229:

Kitāb ṭabaqāt al-mashāyikh, biographies of the companions of the Prophet, the *tābiʿūn*, the Rustamid imams, and the major teachers of the Ibāḍis up to the seventh century AH. See *Bull. de Corr. Afr.* 1885, 38/43, Motylinski, *Bibliographie du Mzab*.

3. Abu 'l-Ḥasan ʿAlī b. Mūsā b. Muḥammad b. Saʿīd al-Maghribī Nūr al-Dīn was born on 22 Ramaḍān 610/5 February 1214 in the castle of Yaḥṣub (Alcala la Real) near Granada, and studied in Seville. Having left on the pilgrimage with his father in 638/1240, the latter passed away six months after their arrival in Alexandria on 8 Shawwāl 640/2 March 1243. Ibn Saʿīd remained in Cairo and Fusṭāṭ until 648/1250. Then he went to Baghdad, accompanied Ibn al-ʿAdīm (p. 404) to Aleppo, and travelled by way of Damascus, Baghdad, and Basra to Arrajān. After finally visiting Mecca as well he returned to the Maghreb, and in the year 652/1254 entered the service of the emir Abū ʿAbdallāh al-Mustanṣir in Tunis. In 666/1267 he travelled to the Orient again. Having learned of Hūlāgū's
337 feats in Alexandria, | he went to see him in Armenia. After staying as his guest for a period of time he returned to north Africa and died in Tunis in 685/1286,[1] or as early as 673/1274 in Damascus.[2]

411 | *Fawāt* II, 112, al-Suyūṭī, *Ḥusn al-muḥ.* I, 320, Maqq. I, 534/7, 634/707, Wüst., *Gesch.* 353. 1. *Falak al-arab al-muḥīṭ bi-ḥulā lisān al-ʿarab al-muḥtawī ʿalā kitābay al-Mushriq fī ḥula 'l-mashriq wal-Mughrib fī ḥulā* (*maḥāsin ahl*) *al-maghrib* (see Suppl.), of which only the second part, *al-Mughrib*, has been preserved, ḤKh V, 12079. Fragmente aus dem *Mughrib* des b. S. ed. by K. Vollers in *Semit. Stud.*, ed. by C. Bezold, part I, Weimar 1895 (for an account of the MSS and of the life of Aḥmad Ibn Ṭūlūn, see de Goeje, *ZDMG* 49, 706ff.).—

1 According to al-Suyūṭī and Maqq.

2 According to Ibn Taghribirdī and ḤKh.

2. *Nashwat al-ṭarab fī taʾrīkh jāhiliyyat al-ʿarab*, autograph Tüb. 1, see Suppl.—3. *Kitāb basṭ al-arḍ fī ṭūlihā wal-ʿarḍ*, an abstract based on his *Kitāb al-jughrāfiyya* or *Jughrāfiyya fi 'l-aqālīm al-sabʿa*, based on Ptolemy, often used by Abu 'l-Fidāʾ, whose personal copy is preserved in Paris 2234,$_{1}$, also Br. Mus. Suppl. 696, Ğārullāh 1581,$_{1}$, an abstract with a determination of the degrees by Ibn Fāṭima, Bodl. I, 1015, II, 266,$_{6}$, Pet. AM 233.—4. *Kitāb al-badʾ*, a general geographical work (Griffini, *Cent. Amari* I, 416, n. 3), Bodl. I, 984, II, 263, excerpts in Amari, *Bibl. Ar. Sic.* 136ff., *Boll. ital. degli studi or.*, N.S. Sept. 1881, 388/92.—5. *ʿUnwān al-murqiṣāt wal-muṭribāt*, an anthology of Western poets in 2 parts (I. Spain: a. western Spain, b. eastern Spain, c. central Spain, d. the Balearic islands, with an appendix on poets of unknown origin, II. al-Maghrib: a. Morocco, b. Algeria, c. Tunisia, d. Sicily) as an introduction to the larger work *Jāmiʿ al-murqiṣāt wal-muṭribāṭ*, which contains samples of around 150 contemporary poets classified on the basis of five aesthetical considerations: 1. *murqiṣ*, delightful, 2. *muṭrib*, delectable, 3. *maqbūl*, pleasing, 4. *masmūʿ*, bearable, 5. *matrūk*, boring, Berl. 7175, Copenhagen 212, print. C. 1286.—6. *Kitāb al-qidḥ al-muʿallā fi 'l-taʾrīkh al-muḥallā*, on the poets of Spain of the first half of the seventh century, following the example of the *Qalāʾid* of Ibn Khāqān, in a very artificial style, abstract by Muḥammad b. ʿAbdallāh b. Jalīl, dedicated to Prince Abū Zakariyyāʾ, the son of the Ḥafṣid caliph al-Mustanṣir billāh (I, 647–75/1249–77), Paris 3340, Patna I, 204,$_{1818}$, probably = *al-Muḥallā bil-ashʿār*, Maqr. II, 181,$_{37}$, Maqq. I, 653 in Vollers, op. cit., no. V, who does not mention the Paris MS.—8.–9. see Suppl.

4. Ibn al-ʿIdhārī[3] al-Marrākushī wrote, towards the end of the seventh century:

| *Histoire de l'Afrique et de l'Espagne, intitulée* al-Bayano l-moghrib *par Ibn* 412
al-Adhari (*de Maroc*) *publ.* (*Leid. 995*), *par* R.P.A. Dozy, Leiden 1848/51, Wüst., *Gesch.* 373.

5. Two anonymous authors offer material for the history of the Almohads in the years 1170–1263:

L'Anónimo de Copenhague y Anónimo de Madrid, ed. Huici 1917.

J Spain

| 1. Abu 'l-Walīd ʿAbdallāh b. Muḥammad b. Yūsuf b. Naṣr al-Azdī b. al-Faraḍī, 338
who was born on 21 Dhu 'l-Qaʿda 351/22 December 962 in Cordova. He made the pilgrimage in 382/992 and on the way studied in Egypt and Kairouan. In

3 Thus according to *Lubb* 177, cf. Gildemeister, *Cat. Bonn* 13.

400/1009 he became a *qāḍī* in Valencia. When the Berbers captured Cordova in 403/1012 he was killed during the plundering of the city, on 7 Shawwāl/ 22 April.

Wüst., *Gesch.* 165. *Taʾrīkh ʿulamāʾ al-Andalus*, ed. Fr. Codera, *Bibl. Ar.-Hisp.* vols. 7 and 8, Madrid 1891/2.

2. Abū Marwān Ḥayyān b. Khalaf b. Ḥasan b. Ḥayyān was born in Cordova in 377/987 and was one of the foremost historians of Spain. He died on 28 Rabīʿ I 469/31 October 1076 (or, according to others, on 28 Rabīʿ I 460/6 February 1068).[1]

Ibn Khall. 199, al-Ḍabbī, p. 260, no. 679, Ibn Bashkuwāl 342, Maqq. II, 119, 122, Wüst., *Gesch.* 212, Pons Boigues, no. 114. 1. *Kitāb al-matīn* (or *al-mubīn*, according to ḤKh 2166, 10460, 11345), a history of Spain in 60 volumes, which is said to have formerly been kept in the great mosque of Tunis (*ZDMG* IX, 626), but is now lost.—2. *Kitāb al-muqtabis fī taʾrīkh al-Andalus* in 10 volumes (about which ḤKh 12730 only has confused information, see Wüst.), of which only remain, of vol. 3, the history of the seventh Marwānid caliph ʿAbdallāh b. Muḥammad (275–308/881–912) in Bodl. II, 137 and the history of al-Ḥakam II (359–66/961–976), in fragments for the years 360/2, in Constantine in the library of the estate of Sīdī Ḥammūda (see F. Codera, *Bol. R. Ac. Hist.* v. XIII, 53ff.). The chronicle of the years in power, which mostly follows ʿĪsā al-Rāzī
413 (p. 156), | is preceded by information on his officials, the rebels that he fought, and the poets who sang his praise, with brief facts about the circumstances of their lives. *Ibn Ḥ. al-M. Tome troisième, chronique du règne du calife Umaiyade Abdallah à Cordoue, texte ar. publié pour la première fois d'après le ms. de la Bodl. avec une introduction par le P.* Melchior M. Antuña *O.S.S.* (*Textes rel. à l'histoire de l'occident musulman*, vol. III), Paris 1937, see Brockelmann, *OLZ* 1941, 168/71.—3.–5. see Suppl.

3. Abū ʿAbdallāh Muḥammad b. Abī Naṣr Futūḥ b. ʿAbdallāh al-Ḥumaydī al-Mayurqī, whose father hailed from Ruṣāfa, a suburb of Cordova, but who had settled in Mallorca, was born there in 420/1029. After studying under the Ẓāhirī Ibn Ḥazm (p. 400) he made the pilgrimage in 448/1056, after which he settled in Baghdad, where he died on 17 Dhu 'l-Ḥijja 488/19 December 1095.

Ibn Khall. 588, *Ḥuff.* XV, 9, Abu 'l-F. III, 306, Ibn Bashk. no. 1114, al-Ḍabbī, p. 113, no. 257, Wüst., *Gesch.* 219, Goldziher, *Ẓāhiriten*, 172. 1. *Kitāb jadhwat al-muqtabis*

1 Antuña, *al-Muqtabis* VIII: Oct. 1070, Palencia, 136: 1070.

fī dhikr wulāt al-Andalus wa-asmāʾ ruwāt al-ḥadīth wa-ahl al-fiqh wal-adab wa-dhawi ʾl-nabāha wal-shiʿr, drawn up chronologically at the request of his acquaintances in Baghdad and then ordered alphabetically following the advice of his friend Ibn Mākūlā (p. 435), ḤKh ^{1}II, 4000, ^{2}II, 783; according to ḤKh 12730 an abstract of Ibn Ḥayyān's *Muqtabis*.—2.–5. see Suppl. (3. Patna I, $47,_{474}$, commentary *al-Ifṣāḥ*, also Qawala I, 423).

3a. The last Zīrid of Granada, ʿAbdallāh (460–83/1073–90), wrote an account of his deeds as the ending of a lost history of his dynasty:

Lévi Provençal, *Les Mémoires de ʿAbd Allah dernier Ziride de Grenade, texte ar. et trad. Andalus* III, 2 (1935), 233/344, IV (1936), 29/145.

| 4. Abū Naṣr al-Fatḥ b. Muḥammad b. ʿUbaydallāh b. Khāqān al-Qaysī, from 339
Ṣakhrat al-Walad, a village in the district of Qalʿat Yaḥṣub near Granada, lived
the life of a literary vagrant and a freeloader until | he found a job as a secretary 414
with Tāshfīn b. ʿAlī, the ruler of Granada. He then went to Morocco where he was strangled in a tavern on 22 Muḥarram 529/13 November 1134 (or, according to others, in 535/1140), possibly at the instigation of ʿAlī b. Yūsuf b. Tāshfīn, whose enmity he had incurred by an extravagant poem in praise of his brother Ibrāhīm.

Ibn Khall. 498, Lisān al-Dīn, *al-Iḥāṭa* in Dozy, *Abbad.* I, 4ff., Wüst., *Gesch.* 238. 1. *Qalāʾid al-ʿiqyān wa* (*fī*) *maḥāsin al-aʿyān*, dedicated to the aforementioned prince Ibrāhīm, in 4 parts: a. sovereigns, b. viziers, c. *qāḍī*s and scholars, d. aesthetes and poets. It was particularly appreciated because of its stylistic form, as it was in rhymed prose, Gotha 2130/2 (where other MSS are listed), Br. Mus. 366, $530,_{2}$, Suppl. 604, Paris 3318/20, Algiers 1727/8, NO 4144, Qawala II, 209, Patna II, $321,_{2484}$, ed. S. al-Ḥarāʾirī in the magazine *al-Birjīs*, offprint, Paris 1277, Beirut 1283.—2. *Maṭmaḥ al-anfus wa-masraḥ al-taʾannus fī mulaḥ ahl al-Andalus* in a smaller edition, Leipz. 546, Pet. AM 776, a medium one, Br. Mus. 367, and a large edition, which is probably identical with no. 1 and developed gradually out of the smaller, cf. Dozy, *Script. ar. loci de Abbadidis* I, 10; print. Istanbul, Jawāʾib 1302.—3. A biography of his teacher ʿAbdallāh b. Muḥammad b. al-Sīd al-Baṭalyawsī, d. 521/1127 (see p. 427), with a selection from his poems, Esc. $^{2}488,_{1}$. 4. *Maqāma* on the same, ibid. $538,_{7}$.

5. Abu ʾl-Ḥasan ʿAlī b. Bassām al-Shantarīnī, from Santarém, was born in 477/1084 in Lisbon and in 494/1101 went to Cordova. He secured a living with his literary work since many dilettantes purchased the honour of being mentioned by him for a fee. He is said to have died in 542/1147.

Wüst., *Gesch.* 244a. *Kitāb al-dhakhīra fī maḥāsin ahl al-Jazīra*, a Spanish history and literary history of the fifth century, Paris 3321/3, Algiers $1615_{,2}$, 1616, part I, Mohl 1755, part II Bodl. I, 749, II, 594, part III Gotha 2136, Copenhagen 162, vols. I–III, see Lévi Provençal, *Hespéris* XVII (1934), p. 19ff., vol. IV in Moroccco, see Allouche, ibid. XXV, 92, cf. de Slane, *JA* s. 5, v. 17, p. 261ff., 415 Dozy, *Recherches* ^{2}II, 7ff., | Wright, *JRAS* XVI, 353. Abstract *Laṭāʾif al-dhakhīra wa-ẓarāʾif* (Gómez mistakenly *ṭarāʾiq*) *al-Jazīra* by Asʿad b. Mammātī (p. 408), Welīeddīn 2636 (*MFO* V, 527), photograph in possession of A. Zeki P.S., see S.E.G. Gómez, *al-Andalus* II, 329/36, Leningrad, see Kračkovsky, ibid. III, 89/96.

340 | 6. (7.) Abū Marwān Abu ʾl-Qāsim ʿAbd al-Malik b. ʿAbdallāh b. Badrūn al-Shilbī al-Ḥaḍramī was from Silves. He probably lived in Seville, wrote during the reign of Yūsuf b. ʿAbd al-Muʾmin al-Muwaḥḥidī (558–80/1163–84), and died in 608/1211.

Sharḥ Qaṣīdat b. ʿAbdūn (p. 320) *Commentaire historique sur le poème d'Ibn A. publié par* R. Dozy, Leiden 1846, Wüst., *Gesch.* 271.

7. (8.) Abu ʾl-Qāsim Khalaf ʿAbd al-Malik b. Masʿūd b. Bashkuwāl al-Qurṭubī, born on 3 Dhu ʾl-Ḥijja 494/30 September 1101, was for a time the deputy *qāḍī* of Seville. He died in Cordova on 8 Ramaḍān 578/5 January 1183.

Ibn Khall. 204, *Ḥuff.* XVII, 1, Wüst., *Gesch.* 270. 1. *Kitāb al-ṣila fī akhbār aʾimmat al-Andalus*, a continuation of the history of learned men by Ibn al-Faraḍī (no. 1), completed on 3 Jumādā I 534/27 December 1139, ed. F. Codera in *Bibl. Ar.-Hisp.* I, II, Madrid 1883.—Continuations: a. *Ṣilat al-ṣila* by Aḥmad b. Ibrāhīm b. Aḥmad b. al-Zubayr al-Gharnāṭī, d. 708/1308, Pons Boigues, no. 268 (Suppl. I, $733_{,10a}$), ed. E. Lévi Provençal, Paris 1938.—b. *Kitāb al-dhayl wal-takmila li-kitābay al-Ṣila wal-Mawṣūl* by Muḥammad b. Muḥammad b. ʿAbd al-Malik al-Awsī al-Anṣārī al-Marrākushī, a contemporary of al-ʿAbdarī (p. 482) who died after 688/1289 (Pons Boigues, 414), Paris 2156 (see Suppl.).—2. *Kitāb al-ghawāmiḍ wal-mubhamāt min al-asmāʾ*, on persons inadequately identified in *ḥadīth*, Berl. 1673; abstract by the author himself entitled *Ghawāmiḍ al-asmāʾ al-mubhama al-wāqiʿa fī mutūn al-aḥādīth al-musnada*, ibid. 1674.—3.–5. see Suppl. (4. Garr. 1893).

8. (9.) Abū Jaʿfar Aḥmad b. Yahyā b. Aḥmad b. ʿAmīra al-Ḍabbī al-Qurṭubī was born in Vélez, lived in Murcia and Cordoba, and died in 599/1202 (?).

| Maqq. 714, Wüst., *Gesch.* 282. *Kitāb bughyat al-multamis fī taʾrīkh rijāl ahl al-Andalus*, a history of the conquest of Spain and of the Umayyad caliphs and their successors up to 592/1196, including the biographies of famous men and women, ed. Fr. Codera and J. Ribera, *Bibl. Ar.-Hisp.* III, Madrid 1885. 416

9. (10.) Abū ʿAbdallāh Muḥammad b. ʿAbdallāh b. Abī Bakr b. al-Abbār al-Quḍāʿī was born in 595/1199 in Valencia. He became the secretary of the local governor Muḥammad b. Abī Ḥafṣ and his son Abū Zayd and, when the latter converted to Christianity for the king of Aragon, he joined Zayyān b. Mardānish. When the Christian prince of Barcelona laid siege to Valencia he left on a mission to Africa to beg for help. A *qaṣīda* that he recited on that occasion soon became legendary (Ibn Khaldūn, *Hist. d. Berbères* I, 392, Maqq. II, 755/9). The armada that he had summoned was, however, unable to prevent the capture of his hometown in 636/1238. He next went to Bijāya and then to Tunis, where he was employed in the *dīwān*. Under al-Mustanṣir he was promoted to the rank of vizier, | but was then suspected of having participated in a conspiracy, and 341 consequently was murdered in his own house on the order of the ruler on 15 Muḥarram 658/2 January 1260.

Maqq. I, 827, Wüst., *Gesch.* 344, al-Kattānī, *Fihris* I, 99. 1. *Kitāb al-ḥulla al-siyarāʾ*, biographies of princes and notables who were active as poets in North Africa and Spain, Esc. ^{2}1654$_{,1}$, cf. M.J. Müller, *Beiträge zur Gesch. der westl. Araber* p. 161, Dozy, *Notices sur quelques mss. arabes*, Leiden 1847/51, p. 29 ff.—2. *Tuḥfat al-qādim*, an imitation of the *Zād al-musāfir* of Abū Baḥr Ṣafwān b. Idrīs (p. 322), ḤKh ^{1}II, 2642, III, 6769, ^{2}I, 372, *Muntakhab* Esc. ^{2}356$_{,2}$.—3. *Kitāb takmilat al-ṣila*, a continuation of the history of learned men by Ibn Bashkuwāl (no. 8), ed. Fr. Codera, *Bibl. Ar.-Hisp.* V. VI, Madrid 1887/9.—4. *Iʿtāb al-kuttāb*, on secretaries who had fallen into disgrace and were then pardoned, which he used to regain the favour of the prince of Tunis after he had incurred the latter's wrath (Maqq. II, 755$_{,17}$), Esc. ^{2}1731.—5.–6. see Suppl.

| 11. Abu ʾl-Fidāʾ Ismāʿīl b. Abī Saʿīd b. Muḥammad ʿImād al-Dīn b. al-Athīr was 417 born in 652/1254 in Cairo and succeeded to his father's position at the chancellery when the latter passed away on 19 Shawwāl 691/4 October 1292. He was supposed to accompany Sultan al-Malik al-Ashraf to Damascus in Jumādā I 692/April 1292, but he refused to issue a death sentence in Karak, whereupon he returned to Cairo to join the governor Baydarā, who had stayed behind. When the latter had the sultan murdered in Muḥarram 693/December 1293

but subsequently failed to assert himself in power, it seems that Ibn al-Athīr lost his position. In 699/1299 he took part in the campaign against the Tatar Qāzān, but after the defeat of the Egyptian army on 28 Rabīʿ I/29 December, there is no further trace of him.

Orient. II, 299, Wüst., *Gesch.* 372. 1. *Kitāb ʿibrat uli ʾl-abṣār fī mulūk al-amṣār*, a commentary on a poem by Ibn ʿAbdūn (p. 320), taken almost literally from Ibn Badrūn (no. 6), with a continuation in 55 verses up to the year 697/1297, with a commentary, ḤKh 8037, 9444, Paris 3134, Br. Mus. 2, 74, Gayangos, *Praef.* XXII.—2. *Sharḥ kitāb ʿUmdat al-aḥkām min kalām sayyid al-anām* of al-Jammāʿīlī, cf. S. 437.—3.–4. see Suppl.

5 *Histories of the Caliphs and World History*

342 | 1. Abū Manṣūr al-Ḥusayn b. Muḥammad al-Marghanī (from Marghan, in Ghūr in Afghanistan) al-Thaʿālibī dedicated to Abu ʾl-Muẓaffar Naṣr, the brother of Maḥmūd of Ghazna who died in 412/1021:

Kitāb al-ghurar fī siyar al-mulūk wa-akhbārihim (see Suppl.); volumes 3 and 4, which have been lost, related the history of the caliphs, with particular emphasis on Abū Muslim and the Barmakids, as well as the Ṭāhirids, Sāmānids, Ḥamdānids, Būyids, Sebuktegīn, and Maḥmūd.

2. Abū ʿAlī Aḥmad b. Muḥammad b. Yaʿqūb b. Miskawayh, d. 421/1030, see Suppl.

418 | *Abulf. hist. anteisl.* ed. Fleischer, p. 203. Wüst. *Ärzte*, no. 126, *Gesch.* 182, Leclerc I, 482. 1. *Kitāb tajārib al-umam wa-taʿāqib al-himam*, a general history up to the death of his patron, the Būyid ʿAḍud al-Dawla, in 372/982, ḤKh [1]II, 2430, [2]I, 344.—2. *Kitāb ādāb al-ʿarab wal-furs*, a book of practical philosophy in 6 parts: a. a portion of the *Jawīdān khirad*, AS 4304, which, according to al-Jāḥiẓ, had been translated from Pahlavi into Arabic by Ḥasan b. Sahl, the brother of the vizier al-Faḍl b. Sahl,[1] under the title *Istiṭālat al-fahm*, see al-Rājkūtī, *RAAD* IX, 131/9, 139/202. *Muntakhab J. kh. fi ʾl-naṣāʾiḥ*, AS 4304, b. Persians, c. Indians, d. Arabs, e. Greeks, f. modern philosophers, Leid. 381, Bodl. I, 292, Paris 3957, see de Sacy, *Not. et Extr.* X 95n, *Mém. de l'Ac. des Inscr.* IX, 1ff. From the part on the Greeks: *Tabula Cebetis, Graece, Arabice, Latine. Item aurea carmina Pythagorae cum paraphrasi Arab. auctore* Joh. Elichmann, 343 | *cum praef.*

---

1 According to Éthé, *Cat. of the Pers. Mss. in the Bodl. Libr.* no. 1417, the Persian work *Qānūn al-ḥikma wa-dastūr* discussed there is the basis for this book (?), see also *Nawāʾī* in Quatremère, *Chrest. Turc. or.* I, Paris 1841, 41_{9}.

S. Salmasii, Leiden 1640; cf. Wenrich 86.—Persian translations by: a. Muḥammad b. Aḥmad al-Arrajānī al-Tusturī (during the reign of Akbar), Br. Mus. Pers. II, 441a.—b. Muḥammad Ḥusayn Ḥakīm, Ind. Off. 173.—3. *Tahdhīb al-akhlāq wa-taḥrīr al-aʿrāq*, on ethics, Br. Mus. Suppl. $721_{,ii}$, print. C. 1298, 1299 (in the margin *OB* II, 6081). Abstract Br. Mus. $1349_{,22}$.—4. *Kitāb al-fawz al-aṣghar*, on theology, Esc. $^{2}609_{,2}$, Patna II, $373_{,2558,14}$.—5. Proof that death is not to be feared, Br. Mus. $980_{,22}$.

3. Abū ʿAbdallāh Muḥammad b. Salāma (Sālim) b. Jaʿfar b. ʿAlī b. Ḥakmūn al-Quḍāʿī studied *ḥadīth* and Shāfiʿī law in Baghdad, became a *qāḍī* in Egypt, and was entrusted on one occasion with a mission from there to Byzantium. When the Fāṭimid caliph al-Ẓāhir appointed Abu ʾl-Qāsim ʿAlī al-Jarjarāʾī—both of whose hands his father al-Ḥākim had had cut off—in 418/1027 as vizier, al-Quḍāʿī was ordered to sign the decrees on his behalf. In 445/1053, while on pilgrimage, he met Abū Bakr al-Khaṭīb al-Baghdādī (p. 400) and studied *ḥadīth* under him. He died in Dhu ʾl-Qaʿda 454/November 1062[2] in Fusṭāṭ.

| Ibn Khall. 565, Abulf. III, 189, al-Suyūṭī, *Ḥusn al-muḥ.* I, 227, Wüst., *Gesch.* 199. 419
1. *Kitāb al-inbāʾ ʿalā (bi-anbāʾ) al-anbiyāʾ wa-tawārīkh al-khulafāʾ* or *ʿUyūn al-maʿārif wa-funūn akhbār al-khalāʾif*, a survey of world history from the Creation until the year 417/1026 or 422/1031, Berl. 9433, Bodl. I, 713 (see II, 592), 865, Paris $1490_{,1}$, 1491, Dāmādzāde 1410 (see Cahen, *REI* 1936/8, SA 4), anon. continuation until 926/1520, Paris $1490_{,2}$.—2. (4). *Kitāb al-shubuhāt fi ʾl-mawāʿiẓ wal-ādāb min ḥadīth rasūl Allāh ṣlʿm* or *Shihāb al-akhbār fi ʾl-ḥikam wal-amthāl wal-ādāb min al-aḥādīth al-marwiyya ʿan al-rasūl al-mukhtār* Berl. 1271, Paris 1952, Leid. 372 (where other MSS are listed), Garr. 240, Cairo ^{1}I, 367, 408, VII, 57, Alex. Ḥad. 34, 49, with the title *Risāla tashtamil ʿalā alf kalima min al-ḥikam al-nabawiyya wa-kathīr min al-waṣāyā wal-mawāʿiẓ*, Alex. Adab $134_{,1}$, with the title *Jawāhir al-kalim al-saniyya wa-badāʾiʿ al-ḥikam al-nabawiyya*, see Suppl. Garr. 1370, Persian adaptation *Tark al-iṭnāb fī sharḥ al-Sh.* by Najm al-quḍāt Abu ʾl-Ḥasan, AS 602 (Ritter).—3. (5). *Musnad al-Shihāb*, an index of transmitters for the previous work, Esc. ^{2}752, 1529, Cairo ^{1}I, 419, ^{2}I, 147.—4. (6). *Kitāb al-mukhtār fī dhikr al-khiṭaṭ wal-akhbār*, which is mentioned by Maqrīzī, *Khiṭaṭ* I, $5_{,1}$, $36_{,10}$, among his sources, and as *Khiṭaṭ Miṣr* in Yāqūt, *Irshād* VI, $393_{,14}$.—5,6 (7, 8). see Suppl.

2 According to Maqr., *Khiṭaṭ* I, $5_{,2}$, in 457/1065.

4. Abu 'l-Qāsim Ṣā'id b. Aḥmad b. 'Abd al-Raḥmān b. Muḥammad b. Ṣā'id al-Qurṭubī, who was born in 420/1029 in Almería, was a *qāḍī* in Toledo, and died on 4 Shawwāl 462/6 July 1070.

344 | Wüst., *Gesch.* 206. 1. *Kitāb al-ta'rīf bi-ṭabaqāt al-umam*, a history of the sciences among different peoples, composed in 460/1068 (Maqq. I, 905), Br. Mus. 1622, extracts ibid. 281, $1503_{,2}$, Leid. 754, cf. Steinschneider, *al-Farabi* p. 141/6; the chapter on India was translated by G. Ferrand in Les grands rois du monde, BSOS 1931, 329ff.—2. See Suppl.

5. Abū Shujā' Shīrawayh b. Shahridār b. Fannā Khusraw al-Hamadhānī al-Daylamī, who was born in 445/1053, was a Shāfi'ī *faqīh* and traditionist, and a lecturer at the madrasa of Hamadan. He died on 9 Rajab 509/29 November 1115.

Ḥuff. XV, 31, Wüst., *Gesch.* 225. 1. *Kitāb riyāḍ al-uns li-'uqalā' al-ins*, a history of prophets and caliphs up to al-Mustaẓhir billāh (487–512/1094–1118), Cairo V,
420 64, | ^{2}V, 209.—2. *Ta'rīkh Hamadhān* ḤKh ^{1}II, 2339, ^{2}I, 310, which was used by Yāqūt in GW, see F.J. Heer, *Die hist. u. geogr. Quellen J.'s* GW, Strasbourg 1898, p. 35/6.—3. *Kitāb Firdaws al-akhbār*, a collection of 10,000 short traditions from the *Kitāb shihāb al-akhbār* by al-Quḍā'ī, alphabetically ordered, without *isnād* but containing information on the *rāwī*, Berl. 1278, Cairo ^{1}I, 382, Bursa Ulu Cami Hadis 188, Patna I, $57_{,575}$.—Abstracts: *Nuzūl al-sā'irīn ila 'llāh rabb al-'ālamīn* by Maḥmūd b. Muḥammad al-Darkazīnī, d. 743/1342 (Ibn Ḥajar, DK IV, 338) Berl. 1279, Gotha 595.—b. by Ibn al-Shihāb al-Hamadhānī, d. 786/1384, Br. Mus. $890_{,4}$.—c. *al-Bustān al-mustakhraj min al-Firdaws*, 1140 traditions by 'Alī b. Abi 'l-Qāsim b. 'Alī, Algiers 496.—4. *Nuzhat al-aḥdāq fī makārim al-akhlāq*, a small collection of traditions, Algiers $497_{,1}$.

5a. Abū 'Abdallāh Muḥammad b. Aḥmad al-'Aẓīmī al-Tanūkhī al-Ḥalabī was born in 483/1090, lived as a teacher and court poet in Aleppo, and died sometime after 556/1161.

1. *Ta'rīkh*, starting with the history of the Bible, ordered by year from the Hijra onwards, and ending with the year 538/1143, Qara Muṣṭafā 398, see Horovitz, MSOS X, 6, Mükrimin Yinanç: *XII asir tarihçileri ve müverrihi Azimi*, Istanbul 1937, Ikinci Türk Tarik Kongresi neşriyati, the years 455–538 are reproduced in Cl. Cahen, La chronique abrégée d'al-'A., JA CCXXX, 353/448.—2. *Ta'rīkh Ḥalab* ḤKh ^{1}II, $127_{,2}$, $138_{,1}$, ^{2}I, 291.—3. *Kitāb al-muwaṣṣal 'ala 'l-aṣl al-mawṣil* (?), biographies of famous Muslims, cited Kamāl al-Dīn, in Cahen, op. cit., 354.

5b. Aḥmad b. ʿAlī Abu ʾl-ʿAbbās b. Bābā wrote, during the reign of al-Muqtafī billāh (530–55/1136–60):

Raʾs māl al-nadīm, a collection of historical notes up to his own time, see al-Ṣafadī, preface to the *Nakth al-himyān*, ḤKh [1]III, 342, [2]I, 830, autograph Yeni 234 (see Hamdani, *JRAS* 1938, S. 562), NO 3296, Bank. XV, 1044 = Patna I, 270,$_{2247}$.

5c. During the reign of al-Mustanjid billāh (555–66/1160–70) an anonymous author wrote *Taʾrīkh al-dawla al-ʿAbbāsiyya*, Veliyeddīn 2360 (Ritter).

6. Abū Qāsim ʿAbd al-Raḥmān b. Muḥammad ʿAbdallāh b. Yūsuf b. Ḥubaysh (Ḥabīsh) al-Anṣārī, born in Almería in 504/1110, was | released from prison on 421
20 Jumādā I 542/24 October 1147 because Alfonso VII—who had conquered Almería—was impressed by his knowledge of genealogy. He then went to Murcia, became a *qāḍī* there, and died on 14 Ṣafar 584/14 April 1188.

Ḥuff. XVII, 2, Maqq. II, 761, Wüst., *Gesch.* 277. D.M. Dunlop, *JRAS* 1941, 359ff.—*Kitāb al-ghazawāt al-ḍāmina al-kāfila wal-futūḥ al-jāmiʿa al-ḥāfila* or shorter *Kitāb al-maghāzī*, a history of the first three caliphs and the Muslim conquests, mostly following Wāqidī and Ṭabarī, composed on the order of the Almohad Yūsuf[3] (558–80/1163–84), completed in 583/1187, Berl. 9689, Leid. 885, cf. de Goeje, *Mém. d'hist. et de géographie or.* Leiden 1864, p. 3ff., App. IVff.

7. In the fifth or sixth century, an unidentified supporter of the Fāṭimids wrote:

Kitāb al-ʿuyūn wal-ḥadāʾiq fi ʾl-ḥaqāʾiq, a history of the caliphs from al-Walīd b. ʿAbd al-Malik up to al-Muʿtaṣim, valuable because of its extensive and unbiased history of the Umayyads; III, ed. M.J. de Goeje and P. de Jong, *Fragm. Hist. Ar.* I, Leiden 1869.

| 8. Abū Marwān ʿAbd al-Malik b. al-Kardabūs al-Tawzarī wrote, probably 345
towards the end of the sixth century:

Al-Iktifāʾ fī akhbār al-khulafāʾ, up to the Almohad Yūsuf, ḤKh [1]II, 129,$_{4}$, [2]I, 293,$_{26}$, MS of ¾ of the text formerly in the possession of Gayangos, now Madr. 139, extracts in his *Hist. of the Moh. Dynasties in Spain*, vol. I, App. D, vol. II, App. C,

---

3 Of course not Caliph al-Nāṣir li-Dīn Allāh of Baghdad (575–622), as Ahlwardt inferred from the *laqab* without taking the *kunya* Abū Yaʿqūb into consideration, cf. Ibn Khall. no. 815.

Dozy, *Script. ar loci de Abbad.* vol. II, 11, *Recherches*, 2nd ed. v. II, XXI, cf. 45, 3rd ed. II, XVIII, cf. p. 41; other MSS Tlemcen 27 and Tunis, *Bull. de Corr. Afr.* 1884, p. 18, no. 55.—Wüst., *Gesch.* 298.

9. Badr al-Dīn Badal b. Abi 'l-Maʿmar Ismāʿīl al-Tabrīzī, who flourished around 601/1204.

422 | Wüst., 293. 1. *Tuḥfat al-awliyāʾ al-atqiyāʾ fī dhikr ḥāl sabīl al-anbiyāʾ wa-maʿrifat al-khulafāʾ*, a history of Muḥammad, his companions, and the caliphs, up to the coming to power of al-Mustaḍīʾ in the year 566/1170, ḤKh [1]II, 223,$_{2555}$, [2]I, 363, Gotha 45 (see Suppl.).—2. *Arbaʿūn*, dictated in 601/1204, ḤKh I, 232, 396, [2]I, 54.

10. Abu 'l-Ḥasan ʿAlī b. Abi 'l-Karam Athīr al-Dīn Muḥammad b. Muḥammad b. ʿAbd al-Karīm ʿIzz al-Dīn Muḥammad b. al-Athīr al-Shaybānī[4] was born on 4 Jumādā I 555/13 May 1160 in Jazīrat b. ʿUmar in Mesopotamia. When his father was removed from his position as a prefect in 576/1180 Ibn al-Athīr moved with his family to Mosul, where he completed his studies. In 584/1188 he took part in the battles against the crusaders in Syria. He increased his knowledge of *ḥadīth* and history, both in Baghdad—which he had visited as part of the pilgrimage but also as an envoy of the ruler of Mosul—as well as in Syria and Jerusalem, which he appears to have visited in 603/1206 (Kāmil I, 232,$_{16}$) for this specific purpose. Later he lived as a private individual in Mosul where he devoted himself entirely to scholarship. In the year 626/1229 Ibn Khallikān (p. 398) met him as a guest of Shihāb al-Dīn Tughril, the *atabeg* of al-Malik al-ʿAzīz in Aleppo. In 627/1230 he travelled first to Damascus, returned to Aleppo the following year, whence he went, after a brief stay, again to Mosul. He died there in Shaʿbān or Ramaḍān 630/May or June 1233.

Ibn Khall. 433, Abu 'l-F. IV, 389, *Ḥuff.* XVII, 4, de Slane, *Hist. des Crois.*, p. 752, Wüst., *Gesch.* 315. 1. *Kitāb al-kāmil fi 'l-taʾrīkh*, a world history up to the year 628/1231. The first part, running to the year 310, is, with the exception of the
346 section on the battles of the Arabs, | an abridgement of Ṭabarī (see p. 148), augmented with elements from other sources. *Ibn-el-Athiri Chronicon, quod perfectissimum inscribitur*, ed. C.J. Tornberg, 12 vols, Leiden. 1851/76.
423 | *Ibn-el-Athirs Chrönika, Elfte delen ifrån Arabiskan öfversatt af* C.J. Tornberg, Hälftet I, Lund 1851. C. Brockelmann, *Das Verhältnis von Ibn al-Athīrs Kāmil*

4 For his brothers Ḍiyāʾ al-Dīn, see above p 357, and Majd al-Dīn, see below p. 436.

fi-l-taʾrīkh zu Ṭabarīs Akhbār al-rusul wal-mulūk, Diss. Strasbourg 1890, E. Mittwoch, *Proelia Arabum paganorum*, Berlin 1899, p. 30 ff.—Continuation by Ibn Fahd al-Ḥalabī, d. 725/1325, see II, 44.—2. *Historia Dynastiae Atabegidarum Mosulae principum*, composed in 608/1211, Paris 1898, an abstract in de Guignes, *Not. et Extr.* I, 542, print. in *Recueil des historiens arabes des croisades* II, 1869.—3. *Kitāb usd al-ghāba fī maʿrifat al-ṣaḥāba*, AS 3379 (vol. 3.), Patna II, 300,$_{2396/8}$, accounts of more than 7,500 contemporaries of Muḥammad, 5 vols., C. 1285/7.—3. *Kitāb al-lubāb Mukhtaṣar al-ansāb lil-Samʿānī*, see p. 402.

11. Abū Isḥāq Ibrāhīm b. ʿAbdallāh b. ʿAbd al-Munʿim Shihāb al-Dīn b. Abi ʾl-Dam al-Hamdānī al-Ḥamawī was born in Hama on 21 Jumādā II 583/29 September 1187. He studied in Baghdad, taught in Aleppo and Cairo, and then became a Shāfiʿī *qāḍī* in his hometown. When al-Malik al-Muẓaffar Ghāzī, the ruler of Mayyafāriqīn, died in 642/1244, the ruler of Hama, al-Malik al-Manṣūr, sent him to Baghdad as the head of a diplomatic delegation to obtain the enfeoffment of the vacant territory. On the way he fell ill, which obliged him to return from Maʿarrat al-Nuʿmān to Hama, where he died in the same year, on 15 Jumādā II/19 November 1244.

Abu ʾl-F. IV, 480, Wüst., *Gesch.* 326. 1. *Taʾrīkh*, a history of prophets and caliphs until the year 628/1231, ḤKh II, 99,$_{268}$, ^{2}I, 276, Bodl. I, 728, Patna II, 533,$_{2868/9}$.—2. *al-Taʾrīkh al-Muẓaffarī*, a detailed history of the Islamic peoples in 6 volumes up to 627, dedicated to al-Malik al-Muẓaffar Taqī al-Dīn Maḥmūd of Hama, (626/42) (Zambaur 98), ḤKh ^{1}II, 150,$_{2313}$, ^{2}I, 305, Alex. Taʾrīkh 40. Passages with references to Sicily in an Italian translation in Aug. Inveges, *Annali di Palermo*, 1650, Part II, 659, *lat. excerpta ab historia cui Titulus Almodferi composita in 6 voll. ab Alkadi Scichabadin filio Abiddami Amaniensi, conservata in Bibl. Esc. lat. reddita à Marco Dobelio et relata in secundo Tomo Annal. ab Aug. Inveges, in Bibl. hist. regni Siciliae op. et studio Jo. Bapt. Carusii*, Palermo 1723, V. I, 19/23 | reprinted in Muratori, *Rerum Ital. Scr.* V. I, P. 2, p. 251. *Al-Kadi Sheaboddini his-* 424
toria Siciliae supplementis aucta et innumeris mendis expurgata, quibus antea scatebat in ed. Carusii in Rerum Arab. quae ad hist. Siculam spectant ampla collectio op. et st. Rosarii Gregorio, Palermo 1790, p. 53/68.—3. *Kitāb tadqīq al-ʿināya fī taḥqīq al-riwāya* Algiers 544.—4. *Kitāb adab al-qaḍāʾ* Paris 996.—5. *al-Firaq al-islāmiyya* ḤKh IV, 414,$_{9024}$, see Suppl.

12. Jamāl al-Dīn Abu ʾl-Ḥajjāj Yūsuf b. Muḥammad b. Ibrāhīm al-Anṣārī al-Bayyāsī, from Baeza in Spain, moved to Tunis and died there in 653/1255.

Ibn Khall. 822, Maqq. II, 213, Wüst., *Gesch.* 338. 1. *Kitāb al-iʿlām bil-ḥurūb*
347 *al-wāqiʿa fī ṣadr al-islām*, from the assasination of ʿUmar to the uprising | of Walīd b. Ṭarīf against Hārūn al-Rashīd in Mesopotamia, 2 vols., presented to the emir Abū Zakariyyāʾ Yaḥyā al-Ḥafṣī in Tunis, ḤKh ^{1}II, 362,$_{950}$, ^{2}I, 126, Cairo ^{1}V, II, ^{2}V, 22.—2. *Kitāb al-ḥamāsa al-maghribiyya*, composed in Tunis in Shawwāl 646/Dec.–Jan. 1248–9, ḤKh ^{1}III, 116, ^{2}I, 692, abstract Gotha 13.

13. Shams al-Dīn Abu ʾl-Muẓaffar Yūsuf b. Qizoghlū b. ʿAbdallāh Sibṭ b. al-Jawzī was born in 582/1185 in Baghdad. His father had been a Turkish slave of the vizier Ibn Hubayra (d. 560/1165), who set him free and had him educated. His father married a daughter of the famous Ḥanbalī preacher and polymath Ibn al-Jawzī, d. 597/1200 (p. 500), and seems to have died shortly after the birth of Yūsuf, who was brought up by his maternal grandfather. From him the grandson inherited a talent for uplifting sermons and an inclination for historiography. After the completion of his studies in Baghdad he went travelling, eventually settling in Damascus where he was a preacher and a teacher of Ḥanafī *fiqh*. By the year 606/1209 he had recruited, with great success, people for the struggle against the crusaders, and even led a victorious army to Nablus. He died in Damascus on 21 Dhu ʾl-Ḥijja 654/10 January 1257.

425 | Ibn Khall. 378, 817, Maqq. I, 64, Ibn Quṭlūbughā, *Ṭab. al-ḥan.* 236, Wüst., *Gesch.* 340, al-Kattānī, *Fihris* II, 451. *Kitāb mirʾāt al-zamān fī taʾrīkh al-aʿyān*, a general history from the Creation until the year 654/1256, see Suppl., Patna I, 267,$_{2228}$; cf. *Recueil d. Hist. d. Croisades* II, *Hist. or.* V. I, Introd. 60, III (1872), Introd. Abstracts by: a. Anon., on the year 134/645, Br. Mus. 279.—b. Muḥammad b. al-Sinjābī, from part I, Bodl. I, 294,$_{2}$.—c. Mūsā b. Muḥammad b. Aḥmad al-Yūnīnī al-Baʿlabakkī, d. 726/1326, part I, Berl. 9442, the years 56/74, 75/96, 577/654, Br. Mus. 1225/7.[5] A continuation (*dhayl*) by the same, in 4 vols., of which the first, on Egypt and Syria in the years 658/74, is preserved in Bodl. I, 700, anon., on the years 655–7, 671–86, Cairo ^{1}V, 58, ^{2}V 192.—d. see Suppl. and II, 35.—2. *Tadhkirat khawāṣṣ al-umma bi-dhikr khaṣāʾiṣ al-aʾimma*, a history of ʿAlī, his family, and the 12 imams, Leid. 906, Patna I, 276,$_{2193}$.—3. *Kitāb*
348 *al-jalīs al-ṣāliḥ wal-anīs al-nāṣiḥ*, partly in praise of, | and partly lecturing, the Ayyūbid ruler Abu ʾl-Muẓaffar Mūsā b. Abī Bakr b. Ayyūb (d. 635/1237), the governor of Damascus; a. his birth and education, b. the necessity of admonishment, c. what the sovereign should make use of, d. the rank and dignity of the

5 The abstract by Ibn Majd al-Dīn al-Jawzī of Paris 772, mentioned by Wüstenfeld, loc. cit., is instead based on the *Kitāb al-muntaẓam* by Ibn al-Jawzī; see de Slane 1550.

governor, e. the virtue of justice and of the encouragement of the righteous, f. on censuring injustice, g. the struggle for the faith, h. a selection of royal biographies, i. selected tales of pious and abstinent men, their speeches, who made it to kingship, and who did not, k. admonishments of sovereigns by the ancients, especially regarding who among them accepted money and who did not, Gotha 1881.—4. *Kanz al-mulūk fī kayfiyyat al-sulūk*, a collection of anecdotes, Paris 3515, AS 2021.—5. An edifying work, whose title and author remain uncertain, Berl. 8781.—6. *Sharḥ al-Ḥamāsa* Istanbul Un. R. 3180 (*ZS* III, 252).—7. *al-Aḥādīth al-Mustaʿṣimiyyāt al-thamāniyyāt*, cf. al-Kattānī, *Fihris*, I, 145.

14. Jirjīs (ʿAbdallāh) b. Abi ʾl-Yasīr b. Abi ʾl-Makārim al-Makīn b. al-ʿAmīd was born in 602/1205 in Cairo, the son of a Christian official in the ministry of war, and, as a young man, he held a | similar post. When his father's patron, the 426 proconsul of Syria ʿAlāʾ al-Dīn Ṭaybars, fell into disgrace with the sultan, all the officials of his war office, among them Abu ʾl-Yasir and his son, were summoned to Egypt and incarcerated there. The father died in 636/1238. The son, however, was soon released and restored to his post in Syria. But after a jealous colleague raised suspicions about him there, leading to him spending some more time in jail, he retired from public life to Damascus, where he died in 672/1273.

Jourdain, *Biogr. univ.* XIII, 42, Rödiger in *Ersch. u. Grubers Enc.* XXIII, 426, A. Bonneau, *Biogr. génér.* XV, 901, Wüst., *Gesch.* 351. *Kitāb al-majmūʿ al-mubārak*, a general world history, part I from Creation until Muḥammad, Gotha 1557 (where other manuscripts are listed), excerpts in *Hottingers Smnegma or.*, part II from Muḥammad until 658/1260 Berl. 9443, Bodl. II, 47. *Historia Saracenica qua res gestae Muslimorum inde a Muhammede, Primo Imperii et Religionis Muslimicae auctore, usque ad initium imperii Atabacaei, Per XLIX imperatorum successionem fidelissime explicantur, insertis etiam passim Christianorum rebus in Orientis potissimum ecclesiis eodem tempore gestis, arabice olim exarata a Georgio Elmacino fil. Abuljaferi Elamidi Abulmacaremi Abultibi, et lat. reddita op. et st. Thomae Erpenii*, Leiden 1625, English translation by S. Purchas, London 1626, French: *L'histoire Mahommétane ou les quarante-neuf Chalifes du Macine, etc. par* Pierre Vattier, Paris 1657. Continuation *al-Nahj al-sadīd wal-durr al-farīd fī-mā baʿd taʾrīkh b. al-ʿAmīd* by the Egyptian Christian al-Mufaḍḍal b. Abi ʾl-Faḍāʾil, a history of the Mamlūk sultans from al-Malik al-Ẓāhir Baybars 658/1260 until al-Malik al-Nāṣir b. Qalāwūn 741/1340, and specific events up to 749/1348, including a history of the patriarchs of Alexandria, the Muslims of Yemen and India, and the Tatars, Paris 4525.

349 | 15. Abū Bakr Buṭrus b. al-Rāhib Abū Karam b. Muhadhdhib was, in 669/1270, a deacon at the Muʿallaqa, i.e. the Church of Mary in al-Fusṭāṭ, and is known to have still been alive in 681/1282.

427 | Wüst., 360. *Chronicon orientale*, from the creation of the world until the year 657/1259, Assemani, *BO* I, 574, with the exception of the history of the 7 ecumenical councils figuring at the end translated in: *Chron. or. nunc primum latinitate donatum ab Abr. Ecchelensi*, Paris 1651, in *Scrip. hist. Byzant. nova ed.*, Paris 1685; again, in the new edition of *Script. hist. Byz.: Chron. or. Petri Rahebi Ägyptii primum ex Ar. lat. redditum ab Abr. Ecch. nunc nova interpretat. donatum a.* J.S. Assemani, Venice 1729, see *Revue de l'Or. chrét.* XXVIII, 390/405.

16. ʿAbd al-Raḥīm b. Ibrāhīm al-Bārizī al-Ḥamawī al-Juhanī Najm al-Dīn, born in 608/1211, was a *qāḍī* in Hama and died in Dhu 'l-Qaʿda 683/Jan.–Febr. 1284 on the pilgrimage, being buried in Medina.

Orient. II, 273; on his father (see p. 92) Abu 'l-F. IV, 538. 1. *Mudāwalat al-ayyām wa-mumāthalat al-aḥkām*, a historical poem in *rajaz*: a. the life of Muḥammad and the history of Islamic dynasties in Asia, Africa, and Spain; b. geographical overview of the regions brought under Islam; c. non-Islamic dynasties and dynasties from before the time of Islam, Vienna 808.—2. 41 verses on the Prophet in *ṭawīl*, Berl. 7782,$_{1}$.

17. Yuḥannā Abu 'l-Faraj b. al-ʿIbrī, Barhebreus, al-Malaṭī was born in 623/1226 in Malaṭiyya as the son of the physician Ahron, a baptized Jew. After the invasion of the Mongols in 643/1243 his father moved with him to Antioch, where he became a monk. Soon after he went to Tripoli to study dialectics and medicine with a Nestorian. On 12 September 1246 he was appointed the bishop of Gubos near Malaṭiyya, and in that capacity he adopted the name Gregorius. In 1252 he was elevated to the position of bishop of Aleppo by the new Jacobite patriarch, whose election he had actively promoted. On 20 January 1264 he was elected Mafriyān or Head of the Eastern Jacobites in Sīs, in Cilicia. In this capacity he had his seat in Mosul, but often resided in Tabriz and Marāgha to
428 | keep in contact with the Mongol rulers. He died in Marāgha on the night of 29–30 July 1286.

Wüst., *Ärzte* 214, *Gesch.* 363, Leclerc II, 147, Nöldeke, *Or. Skizzen* 253/73, L. Cheikho in *al-Mashriq*, I, 1898, 289/295, 365/70, 413/8, 449/53, 505/10, 555/61, 605/12, A. Baumstark, *Gesch. der syr. Lit.* 312/20. 1. *Kitāb mukhtaṣar al-duwal*, an abbreviated translation of his Syriac chronicle, augmented with additions, in particular on the medical and | mathematical history of the Arabs, prepared shortly before his death at the request of some highbred Muslims. *Historia or. autore Gregorio Abul-Pharagio*, ed. E. Pococke, Oxford 1663, Suppl. 1672, ed. A. Ṣālḥānī, Beirut 1890. *Ebülfereb Ibnülicri Tarihi Muhtasar üddüvel türkceye çeviren* Şerefeddin Yaltkaya, Istanbul 1941.—2. see Suppl.—3. *Mukhtaṣar fī ʿilm al-nafs al-insāniyya*, C. 1928, partly different from the *Maqāla mukhtaṣara fi ʾl-nafs al-bashariyya, al-Mashriq* I, 745f., 838f., 934f., 1084f. 1113, in *Douze Traités phil.*, Beirut 1918, 76/102. 350

18. Muḥammad b. ʿAlī b. ʿAbd al-ʿAzīz b. ʿAlī b. Barakāt al-Ḥamawī wrote, in the second half of the seventh century:

1. *Mukhtaṣar siyar al-awāʾil wal-mulūk wa-wasīlat al-ʿabd al-mamlūk*, a compendium of pre-Islamic history and the history of Islam up to the caliph al-Muhtadī 255/869, dedicated to the Isfahsālār Sayf al-Dīn ʿAlī b. Hasan, Paris 1507.—2. *al-Taʾrīkh al-Manṣūrī talkhīṣ al-Kashf wal-bayān fī ḥawādith al-zamān*, composed in 631/1233, Pet. AM 159. see Suppl.

19. ʿAlī b. Muḥammad b. Maḥmūd al-Kāzarūnī al-Baghdādī was born in 610/1213. He was an estate executor, poet, and historian, and died around 700/1300.

Al-Subkī, *Ṭab. al-kubrā* (not in print), Ibn Qāḍī Shuhba, *Ṭab.*, al-Adfuwī, *al-Badr al-sāfir. Mukhtaṣar al-taʾrīkh min awwal al-zamān ilā muntahā dawlat Ibn al-ʿAbbās*, autograph Carullah 1625, from a lost work in 27 volumes. Lost: *al-Nibrās al-muḍīʾ fi ʾl-fiqh; Kanz al-ḥussāb; al-Milāḥa fi ʾl-filāḥa;* and others.

6 *Histories of Prophets*

1. Abū Bakr (Abu ʾl-Ḥasan Abū ʿAbdallāh) Muḥammad b. ʿAbdallāh (ʿAbd al-Malik) or Ḥasan b. Muḥammad al-Kisāʾī, who wrote at the beginning of the fifth century.

| Brockelmann, *EI* II, 1114. 1. *Kitāb badʾ* (*khalq*) *al-dunyā wa-qiṣaṣ al-anbiyāʾ* Berl. 1021, Bonn 7, Munich 444/5, Leipz. 106, Leid. 2042, Paris 1909/17, Br. Mus. 351, 811/2, 1274/5, 1500, Suppl. 497/8, Ind. Off. 715, Bodl. I, 127,3, 756, 833, II, 123, Garr. 728, 765, see J.H. Hottinger, *Promptuarium s. Bibliotheca or.,* Heidelberg 1658, p. 209, M. Lidzbarski, *De propheticis quae dicuntur leg. Ar.* Diss., Leipzig 1893, 20/5. 2. *Kitāb ʿajāʾib al-malakūt*, a history of Creation, Berl. 6160, Landb.—Br. 281, Cairo ¹VII, 328.[1] 429

1 Of course not to be identified with Muḥammad Masīḥ al-Kisāʾī, author of a *khuṭba* in a Cairene *majmūʿa*, as surmised in *Qu. St. z. Gesch. d. Nat. u. Med.* VII, 124.

2. Abū Isḥāq Aḥmad b. Muḥammad b. Ibrāhīm al-Thaʿlabī al-Nīshābūrī al-Shāfiʿī, who died in Muḥarram 427/November 1035.

Ibn Khall. 30, Wüst., *Gesch.* 185. 1. *Kitāb ʿarāʾis al-majālis fī qiṣaṣ al-anbiyāʾ* Berl. 1019/20, Bodl. II, 47, Br. Mus. 901 Suppl. 494/6, abstract Gotha 99,$_6$ (where other MSS are listed), print. C. 1297, 1306, 1308, 1310, Bombay 1306, with the title *Nafāʾis al-ʿarāʾis* (see Suppl.) Patna I, 34,$_{346}$.—Anon. *Qiṣaṣ al-anbiyāʾ*, from al-Kisāʾī and al-Thaʿlabī combined, Paris 1923.—2. A different work, on the pre-Islamic prophets, Algiers 848,$_2$.—3. *Kitāb al-kashf wal-bayān ʿan tafsīr al-Qurʾān* Berl. 737/43, Landb.-Br. 489, Br. Mus. 821, Garr. 1255, AS 289, 296, Cairo ^{1}I, 198, ^{2}I, 58, cf. Nöldeke, *Gesch. des Qor.*, ^{1}76,$_4$, ^{2}II, 173; along with the criticism of *Mabāḥith al-tafsīr* by Aḥmad b. Muḥammad al-Mukhtār al-Rāzī, ca. 631/1233, Cairo ^{1}I, 198; abstract by Ibn Abī Randaqa, d. 521/1126, Cairo ^{1}I, 209.—4. *Kitāb mubārak yudhkar fīhi qaṭla ʾl-Qurʾān al-ʿaẓīm alladhīna samiʿu ʾl-Qurʾān wa-mātū bi-samāʿihi*
351 Leid. 1988, AS 65,$_3$, f. 128a/130a.—| 5. *Kitāb al-durra al-fākhira fi ʾl-amthāl al-sāʾira* Rāġib 1079 (perhaps composed by al-Thaʿālibī, p. 337?).

Chapter 5. Belles Lettres in Prose

1. Abū Saʿīd (Saʿd) Manṣūr b. al-Ḥusayn al-Ābī, the vizier of the Būyid Majd al-Dawla, the ruler of Rayy, Hamadan, and Isfahan (387–420/997–1029), who died in 421/1030.

Yāqūt, GW I, 57. *Kitāb nathr al-durar (wa-nafāʾis al-jawhar) fi ʾl-muḥāḍarāt*, an anthology in verse and prose, in brief | pieces arranged by subject, with a wide 430
range of interest, Berl. 8329/31, Leid. 450 (parts I and II), Bodl. I, 301 (?), 374, Pet. AM Dorn p. 19, Cairo ^{1}IV, 336, ^{2}III, 403.—Abstract by ʿAbdallāh b. Naṣr b. ʿAbd al-ʿAzīz al-Zaydī, Paris 3490.

1a. Abu ʾl-Ḥusayn Yaḥyā b. Najāḥ b. al-Fallās al-Qurṭubī, d. 422/1031 (see Suppl.).

1. *Jāmiʿ subul al-khayrāt fi ʾl-dhikr wal-daʿawāt* also Fez, Qar. 1520.—2. *al-Gharīb al-muntaqā min akhbār ahl al-tuqā* ibid. 1517.

1b. Abū ʿAbdallāh Ṭāhir b. Muḥammad b. Naṣr al-Ḥaddādī al-Marwazī al-Bukhārī, d. 406/1015.

ʿUyūn al-majālis wa-surūr al-dāris, an *adab* work, ḤKh ^{1}IV, $291,_{8477}$, Garr. 182.

1d. Abu ʾl-ʿAlāʾ Muḥammad b. ʿAlī b. Ḥassūl Ṣafī al-Ḥaḍratayn, who came from Hamadan, grew up in Rayy, and was in charge of the *dīwān al-rasāʾil* there. Later he worked in a similar position with Masʿūd of Ghazna, and died in that town in 450/1058.

Al-Thaʿālibī, *Tatimmat al-Yatīma* I, 407, al-Bākharzī, *Dumyat al-qaṣr*, 90. *Kitāb tafḍīl al-Atrāk ʿalā sāʾir al-ajnād wa-manāqib al-ḥaḍra al-sulṭāniyya*, a polemic against the glorification of the Būyids in Hilāl al-Ṣābiʾ ʾs *Kitāb al-tājī*, ed. ʿAbbās al-ʿAzzāwī in *Belleten* IV, 14/5, Ankara 1940, p. 1/50 with Turkish translation Şerefettin Yaltkaya ibid 235/66.

2. Abū Yūsuf Yaʿqūb b. Sulaymān al-Isfarāʾinī, d. 488/1095.

Maḥāsin al-adab waijtināb al-riyab ḤKh V. $411,_{11489}$, 8 chapters on morals and the intercourse between men, Paris $3401,_{5}$ (see Suppl.).

3. In the second half of the fifth century Abu ʾl-ʿAbbās Muḥammad b. Isḥāq b. Ibrāhīm al-Jurjānī al-Thaqafī wrote:

Al-Muntakhab min kināyāt al-udabāʾ wa-ishārāt al-bulaghāʾ Cairo [1]IV, 332, print. C. 1308, together with al-Thaʿālibī, *al-Nihāya fī ʾl-taʿrīḍ*.

431 | 4. Abū Muḥammad Jaʿfar b. Aḥmad b. al-Ḥusayn al-Sarrāj al-Qāriʾ al-Baghdādī, who died in 500/1106 in Baghdad (see Suppl.).

Ibn Khall. I, 311. *Kitāb maṣāriʿ al-ʿushshāq*, tales and poems on lovers and love, Br. Mus. 1419, Suppl. 1133, print. Istanbul 1302; Abstract, *Kitāb aswāq al-ashwāq min M. al-ʿu*, by Abu ʾl-Ḥasan Ibrāhīm b. ʿUmar b. Ḥusayn al-Biqāʿī, d. 885/1480 (II, 142), Paris 3065 (see Kosegarten, *Chrest.* X, 3), Esc. [2]468 (vol. II).—Selection *Tazyīn al-aswāq bi-tafṣīl tartīb ashwāq al-ʿushshāq* by Dāʾūd al-Anṭākī, d. 1005/1596 (II, 364), Berl. 8421, Gotha 2700/1, Vienna 410, Br. Mus. 774, Suppl. 1120/2, Copenhagen 287, print. C. 1279, Būlāq 1281, 1299, see Kosegarten, *Chrest.* 22, A. v. Kremer, *Ideen* 408, Goldziher, *SBWA, ph.-hist. Cl.* 78, p. 513, no. VII.—2. *Urjūza fī naẓāʾir al-Qurʾān* Alex. Fun. 200,$_{2}$.

5. Abū ʿAbdallāh (Abū Hāshim) Muḥammad b. ʿAbdallāh Abū Muḥammad b. Muḥammad b. Ẓafar al-Ṣaqalī Ḥujjat al-Dīn, d. 565/1169 (see Suppl.).

352 | 1. *Kitāb sulwān al-muṭāʿ fī ʿudwān al-atbāʿ*, a mirror for princes (outline by Flügel in *Intelligenzbl. der Leipz. Litztg.* 1829, p. 312). 1st version from the year 545/1150, Br. Mus. 1530,$_{1}$, 2nd version from the year 554/1159, dedicated to Abū ʿAbdallāh Muḥammad b. Abi ʾl-Qāsim ʿAlī al-Qurashī, the *qāʾid* of Sicily, Berl. 8750/1, Leid. 537/40 (where other MSS are listed), Br. Mus. Suppl. 1160 (uncertain AS 4043,$_{1}$, Alex. Adab 152, Patna I, 200,$_{1788}$), print. C. 1278, Tunis 1279, Beirut 1300, M. Amari, *Conforti politici di Ibn Zafar*, Florence 1851, *Solwan or waiters comfort by M.A. rendered into Engl. by the translator of "the Sicilian Vespers"*, London 1851, 2 vols.—Turkish translation by Qara Khalīl Efendīzāde, d. 1168/1754, Berl. 8752, Vienna 382, see Hammer, *Gesch. des Osm. Reiches* VIII, 251/3, *JA* 1869, II, p. 86,$_{23}$.—2. *Kitāb anbāʾ nujabāʾ al-abnāʾ*, characters and anecdotes of: a. 10 *ṣaḥāba*, b. the descendants of the *ṣaḥāba*, c. of pious men, d. of the princes of the pagan Arabs and of Persian kings, Paris 212/3, Garr. 675/6, shortened, revised edition *Durar al-ghurar fī An. al-ab.* (already cited *Sulwān*, Tunis 4,$_{2}$), Berl. 9506/7, Gotha 1780, Br. Mus. Suppl. 1139.—3. *Kitāb khayr al-bishar bi-khayr al-bashar*, prophecies on the Prophet, a. in Holy Scripture , b. by Jewish *aḥbār*,
432 c. by the | Arab *kuhhān*, d. by the *jinn*, Paris 1959, Cairo [1]VII, 520, lith. C. 1863, see Amari, *Storia dei Musulmani di Sicilia* [1]III, 728, Steinschneider, *Pol. u. apolog. Lit.* 396.—4. *Kitāb yanbūʿ al-ḥayāt*, Qurʾān commentary vol. 2, Paris 608, vol. 6, ibid. 6607, vols. 2. 3, 5, Cairo [1]I, 223.

6. Ṣafī al-Dīn Abu 'l-Fatḥ 'Īsā b al-Buḥturī al-Ḥalabī wrote, in the second half of the sixth century:

Kitāb uns al-masjūn wa-rāḥat al-maḥzūn, poems and tales that he had collected to comfort himself while in captivity, Br. Mus. 1097.

7. Abū Yaḥyā Zakariyyā' b. 'Abdallāh b. Zakariyyā' al-Marāghī wrote, in the second half of the sixth century:

Kitāb al-'adad al-ma'dūd fi 'l-muḥāḍarāt, in 5 chapters, Cairo [1]IV, 281, [2]III, 248, Selīm Āġā 750, Patna I, $203_{,1815/6}$.

8. In 632/1234, Abū Isḥāq Ibrāhīm b. Abi 'l-Ḥasan 'Alī al-Fihrī wrote:

Kitāb kanz al-kuttāb wa-muntakhab al-ādāb, a florilegium of the best prose writers and poets of Spain of the fifth and sixth centuries, Krafft 147.

8c. *Sharḥ al-risāla al-qawsiyya* by Rafī' al-Dīn Maḥmūd b. Muḥammad al-Abharī, 'Āšir I, 1000.

8l. *Nuzhat al-albāb al-jāmi'a li-funūn al-ādāb* (Suppl. I, 897) Patna I, $202_{,1836}$.

9. Al-Amīr 'Alī b. Muḥammad b. al-Riḍā al-Ḥusaynī al-Mūsawī al-Ṭūsī b. al-Sharīf Defterkhān al-'Ādilī wrote, around 654/1256:

Kitāb alf jāriya wa-jāriya, as a side piece to his *Kitāb alf ghulām wa-ghulām*, an imitation of the *Kitāb al-ghilmān* by al-Tha'ālībī (p. 339), in 8 chapters, in which he dedicates an epigram of 3 or 4 distiches to each girl at a time, Vienna 387.

| 10. Jamāl al-Dīn Abu 'l-Durr Yāqūt al-Musta'ṣimī al-Baghdādī, who was famous 353
as a calligrapher. He died in 698/1298 in Baghdad (see Suppl.).

Orient. II, 291, Quatremère, *Hist. des sultans mamlouks* II, 140. 1. *Kitāb akhbār wa-ash'ār wa-mulaḥ wa-fiqar wa-ḥikam wa-waṣāyā muntakhaba*, written in 662/1264, an anthology, Br. Mus. 1428.—2. *Asrār al-ḥukamā'*, a collection of
aphorisms, | Köpr. 1205, print. Istanbul 1300.—3. *Fiqar ultuqiṭat etc.*, see Suppl., 433
also Fātiḥ 4011 (Ritter). A *risāla* by him, Patna I, $198_{,1780}$.

11.–18. See Suppl.

19. ʿAbdallāh b. Aḥmad al-ʿIrāqī wrote, before 714/1314:

Uns al-waḥīd, an anthology of poets, AS 1667,$_2$, 3786 (wrongly attributed to Nūr al-Dīn al-Wāsiṭī by Rescher in *WZKM* 26, 80, afterwards Suppl. II, 913,$_{84}$, Ritter).

Chapter 6. *Ḥadīth*

When the widespread movement that resulted in the shaping and collecting of *ḥadīths* had come to a standstill as a consequence of the completion of the canonical collections, any possibility of further creative production in this area ceased. But the *ʿilm al-ḥadīth* continued to keep writers busy. From the large collections, smaller collections were put together by disregarding the *isnād* and putting the emphasis on content and edifying effect. Following a saying of the Prophet, collections of 40 traditions summarising the quintessence of the creed were particularly popular. While these works addressed a wide audience, other books, directed at a small circle of specialists, would either summarise whatever was known about the circumstances of the lives of the traditionists, thus serving as a measure of their trustworthiness, or critically engage with individual traditions. But it is also true that this criticism did no more than apply the principles of *ʿilm al-rijāl* which had long-since been fixed, which is why no new or seminal insights were produced. In general there was no area of literature that came to be dominated by | the custom of excerpting and compil- 434
ing—so characteristic of utter decay—as early as did *ḥadīth* studies.

1 *Iraq, the Jazīra, Syria, and Arabia*

1. Abu ʾl-Qāsim al-Ḥusayn b. ʿAlī b. Muḥammad b. Yūsuf b. Baḥr b. Bahrām al-Wazīr al-Maghribī, who died in 418/1027 or 428/1037 (see Suppl.).

| Ibn Khall. 185, cf. 72. 1. *Sīrat al-nabī*, following Ibn Hishām, vol. II Landb.-Br. 354
243.—2. *Kitāb al-īnās bi-ʿilm al-ansāb*, names of Arab tribes that are alike, in alphabetical order, with quotations from poetry, accompanied by occasional biographical and historical notes, Br. Mus. Suppl. 594.—3. *Kitāb fi ʾl-siyāsa* Cairo [1]VII 565.—4.–7. cf. Suppl.

2. Abu ʾl-Fatḥ Muḥammad b. ʿAlī al-Karājakī al-Shīʿī was born in Egypt around 425/1034 and died in 449/1057.

1. *Kitāb maʿdin al-jawāhir wa-riyāḍat al-khawāṭir*, sayings by Muḥammad, including, among others, those in which the numbers 1–10 occur, in the sense that they are associated with some property or their occurrence in association with people or things is discussed, Berl. 8704, Rāmpūr II, $366,_{312}$.—2. *Kanz al-fawāʾid*, in individual *rasāʾil*, Mashh. I, $70,_{226}$.—3. *al-Istinṣār fi ʾl-naṣṣ ʿala ʾl-aʾimma al-aṭhār*, Tabriz, cf. *Lughat al-ʿArab* VII, 159, print. Najaf 1346, cf. *Dharīʿa* II, $16,_{14}$, $34,_{132a}$ (which has *al-Istibṣār*).

2a. Abū Manṣūr Muḥammad b. ʿAbd al-Jabbār b. Aḥmad b. Muḥammad b. Jaʿfar b. ʿAbd al-Jabbār al-Samʿānī al-Tamīmī al-Qāḍī, who died in 450/1058.

Al-Samʿānī, *Ansāb* 307v, ʿAbd al-Qādir, *al-Jawāhīr al-muḍīʾa* II, 73, *al-Fawāʾid al-bahiyya* 70. *Majmūʿ arghāʾib al-aḥādīth*, Köpr. 396 (Ritter).

2b. Abū Ḥafṣ ʿUmar b. ʿAlī b. Aḥmad al-Zanjānī al-Dāraquṭnī al-Baghdādī studied in Damascus and then settled in Baghdad, where he died in Jumādā I 459/March–April 1064.

Subkī, *Ṭab.* IV, 8. *Al-Muʿtamad min al-manqūl fī-mā ūḥiya ila ʾl-rasūl* ḤKh V, $623_{,12303}$, Alex. Ḥad. 61 (however, see Suppl. II, $212_{,3a}$).

435 | 3. ʿAbd al-Wahhāb b. Muḥammad b. Isḥāq b. Manda, who died in 473/1082.

Ṣaḥīfat Hammām b. Manda (d. 151/748), traditions by Abū Hurayra, d. 58/678, ḤKh IV, 7731, Berl. 1348.

4. Al-Amīr Abū Naṣr ʿAlī b. Hibatallāh b. ʿAlī b. Mākūlāʾ al-ʿIjlī was born into a highbred Persian family in ʿUkbarā near Baghdad on 5 Shaʿbān 422/29 July 1031.
355 | When his father became the vizier of the caliph al-Qāʾim (422–67/1031–75) he went to the capital and studied there. On one of his lengthy study tours he was robbed and murdered by his Turkish slave. Information regarding his place of death varies between Khurāsān, al-Ahwāz, and Jurjān, and its date between 475, 479, 486, and 487/1094.

Ibn Khall. 420, *Fawāt* II, 93, *Ḥuff.* XV, 1, Wüst., *Gesch.* 215. 1. *Kitāb al-ikmāl fi ʾl-Mukhtalaf wal-muʾtalaf min asmāʾ al-Baghdādī* (p. 400), supplemented by the books of al-Dāraquṭnī (Suppl. I, 275) and al-Azdī (ibid. 281), written in 464–7/1071–4, Berl. 10158/60, Br. Mus. Suppl. 621, Esc. ^{2}1647/9, Cairo ^{1}I, 228. Supplements of this are *Kitāb takmilat al-Ikmāl* and *Kitāb mushtabih al-nisba* by Muḥammad b. ʿAbd al-Ghanī b. Abī Bakr b. Nuqṭa al-Baghdādī, d. 629/1231 (p. 439), vol. I, Gotha 1759, vols. II, III, Br. Mus. Suppl. 622, vol. III, Garr. 1448, with a *Dhayl* by Wajīh al-Dīn Manṣūr b. Salīm al-Hamadhānī Muḥtasib al-Iskandariyya, d. 673/1274 (Suppl. I, 573), Cairo ^{1}I, 239, ^{2}V, 192.

5. Al-Qāsim b. al-Faḍl al-Thaqafī, d. 489/1096.

Arbaʿūn, 40 traditions, Paris $722_{,4}$.

6. Muḥammad b. ʿAlī b. ʿAbdallāh al-Mawṣilī b. Wadʿān Abū Naṣr, d. 494/1101.

Kitāb (*al-Khuṭab*) *al-arbaʿīn al-Wadʿāniyya*, edited with a commentary by his student Aḥmad b. Muḥammad al-Silafī, d. 576/1180 (p. 449), ḤKh III, $159_{,4728}$, VI, $433_{,14201}$, Berl. 1458/60, Paris $722_{,7}$, Cambr. 591, Cairo ^{1}I, 409, Alex. Ḥad. 5, Garr. $2168_{,1}$, with a commentary by ʿAbd al-ʿAzīz b. Aḥmad al-Bārjīlaghī (ḤKh III, 4728), eighth cent., Berl. 1461, Selīm Āġā 193, Alex. Ḥad. 30 (which has al-Daylamī).

| 7. Ibrāhīm b. Muḥammad b. Khalaf b. Ḥamdān, fifth cent. 436

Kitāb muʿjizāt al-anbiyāʾ, miracles by the prophets, ḤKh V, $152_{,10504}$, Berl. 2553.

8. Abu ʾl-Faḍl Muḥammad b. Ṭāhir b. ʿAlī al-Maqdisī b. al-Qayrasānī al-Ẓāhirī was born in Jerusalem on 6 Shawwāl 448/18 December 1058 and started studying in 468/1074 in Baghdad. After a study tour that lasted many years, and during which he endured many hardships, he took up residence in his home town. Returning from the pilgrimage, he died in Baghdad in Rabīʿ I or II 507/August or September 1113.

Ibn Khall. 59, *Ḥuff.* XV, 21, Yāqūt, *GW* IV, 601, Wüst., *Gesch.* 224. 1. *Kitāb al-ansāb al-muttafiqa fi ʾl-khaṭṭ al-mutamāthila fi ʾl-naqṭ wal-ḍabṭ* Berl. 10162, Leid. 132, with an appendix by | Abū Mūsā Muḥammad b. Abī Bakr al-Iṣfahānī, d. 581/1185 356 (p. 450): *Homonyma inter nomina relativa*, ed. P. de Jong, Leiden 1865.—2. *Kitāb fi ʾl-aḥādīth allatī rawatha ʾl-kadhaba wal-mudallisūn*, ca. 1400 bogus traditions, Berl. 1628, Alex. Fun. $95_{,9}$ (see Suppl.).—3. *Aṭrāf al-gharāʾib wal-afrād* Cairo ^{1}I, 269.—4.–11. see Suppl. (5. Patna II, $371_{,2557,\,2}$, 9. also Alex. Ḥad. 10).—12. *Dhakhīrat al-ḥuffāẓ ʿala ʾl-ḥurūf wal-alfāẓ*, a reworking of the *Kitāb al-kāmil* of Abū Aḥmad ʿAbdallāh b. ʿAdī al-Jurjānī, d. 375/985 (al-Samʿānī, *Ansāb*, 126v) Köpr. 290 (Ritter).

9. Abū ʿAbdallāh Muḥammad b. al-Faḍl al-Farāwī, d. 530/1137 (see Suppl.)

Arbaʿūn, composed in 528/1134, Paris $722_{,4}$.

9a. Saʿd al-Dīn al-Ḥusayn b. Muḥammad b. Abī Tammām al-Takrītī.

Sīrat al-nabī, which his son had read to him in 546/1151, ʿUmūm. 748 (Ritter).

10. Abu ʾl-Futūḥ Muḥammad b. Muḥammad b. ʿAlī al-Ṭāʾī al-Hamadhānī, d. 555/1160.

Kitāb al-arbaʿīn al-Ṭāʾiyya ilā irshād al-sāʾirīn ilā manāzil al-yaqīn ḤKh [1]I, 414, [2]I, 56 (following al-Samʿānī) following 40 shaykhs, each one from among the *ṣaḥāba*, with biographical data and an explanation of the edifying elements
437 within each *ḥadīth*, | Berl. 1464/5, Landb.—Br. 173, Cairo [1]I, 263, Wargla (?) Bull. de Corr. *Afr.* 1885, p. 244, no. 30.

11. Abū Muḥammad ʿAbd al-Raḥmān b. Marwān b. al-Munajjim al-Maʿarrī was a court chaplain of the ʿAbbāsids who died in 557/1162.

Kitāb al-ʿaqāʾiq, sermons on the life of the Prophet, Leipz. 165, Br. Mus. 352, 1440, cf. add. p. 771.—2. See Suppl.

12. Muḥammad b. ʿAbd al-Raḥmān b. Masʿūd al-Fanjdahī (al-Banjdahī or al-Bandahī), who died in 584/1188 (see Suppl.).

Ibn Khall. 631. *Muntakhab min Kitāb al-zuhd*, an abstract of the work of Ibn Ḥanbal (p. 193) following Abū Hurayra, ḤKh V, 91_{10162}, Berl. 1385.

13. Abū Bakr Muḥammad b. Mūsā b. ʿUthmān b. Ḥāzim Zayn al-Dīn al-Ḥāzimī al-Hamadhānī al-Shāfiʿī was born in Hamadan in 548/1153 and studied in Baghdad, where he settled after an extended study tour. He died on 18 Jumādā I 584/16 July 1188.

Ibn Khall. 597, *Ḥuff.* XVII, 10, Wüst., *Gesch.* 278. 1. *Kitāb al-iʿtibār fi ʾl-nāsikh wal-mansūkh min al-ḥadīth* Berl. 1627, Cairo [1]I, 269, [2]I, 90, Garr. 1337, Patna I, $39_{,399/400}$.—2. *Kitāb ʿujālat al-mubtadiʾ wa-fuḍālat al-muntahī, nisbas* of *ḥadīth*-scholars in alphabetical order, Berl. 9378.—3.–4. See Suppl.

14. Taqī al-Dīn ʿAbd al-Ghanī b. ʿAbd al-Wāḥid b. Surūr al-Jammāʿīlī al-Maqdisī al-Ḥanbalī, who died in 600/1203 in Cairo.

Ḥuff. XVIII, 16. 1. *Kitāb al-aḥkām al-kubrā* Landb.—Br. 43.—2. Abstract of which *Kitāb ʿumdat al-aḥkām ʿan sayyid al-anām* (*min aḥādīth al-nabī ʿam.*) or *fī maʿālim al-ḥalāl wal-ḥarām ʿan khayr al-anām*, traditions on the principles of law shared by Bukhārī and Muslim, ḤKh IV, $254_{,8300}$, Berl. 1304/8, Hamb. Or. Sem. 58, Paris 726/7, Garr. 1377/9, Cairo [1]I, 371, Qawala I, 137, 424, Alex.
357 Ḥad. 35.—Commentaries: a. *Iḥkām al-aḥkām* by | Ismāʿīl b. Aḥmad b. al-Athīr

al-Ḥalabī, d. 699/1299 (p. 417), in the rendering of Ibn Daqīq al-ʿĪd, d. 702/1302 (II, 63), Berl. 1309, Landb.—Br. 42, Paris 2088, Garr. 1390, Cairo ^{1}I, 260.—b. *ʿUmdat al-afhām*, | composed between 600 and 703, Berl. 1310.—c. ʿAlī b. Thābit, 438
excerpt Br. Mus. $548_{,ii}$.—d. Muḥammad b. Farḥūn al-Yaʿmarī, d. 769/1367, Alex. Ḥad. 4, Cairo ^{1}I, 368.—e. Muḥammad b. Aḥmad b. Marzūq al-Tilimsānī, d. 781/1379 (II, 239), AS 1331, Cairo ^{1}I, 292.—f. Ibn al-Mulaqqin, d. 804/1401 (II, 92), Cairo ^{1}I, 269, ^{2}I, 90.—g. (Patna I, $50_{,495}$).—h. see Suppl.—i. Abū ʿAbdallāh ʿAlī b. Ibrāhīm b. Dāʾūd b. al-ʿAṭṭār al-Shāfiʿī, d. 724/1324 (II, 85), Garr. 1391.—k.–o. see Suppl.—3. *Kitāb al-kamāl fī maʿrifat (asmāʾ) al-rijāl*, based on the authoritative opinions of the 6 canonical books, Berl. 9924/5, Br. Mus. Suppl. 625/6 Cairo ^{1}I, 244, Patna II, $307_{,2426}$, cf. Yāqūt, GW II, $113_{,17}$, Goldziher, *MSt.* II, 263 (see Suppl. *Tahdhīb al-kamāl*, Patna II, $305_{,2416}$, *Taqrīb al-tahdhīb*, ibid. 2415, *al-Kāshif fī asmāʾ al-rijāl* also Alex. Taʾr. 101, Muṣṭ. Ḥad. 13).—4. *Kitāb al-durra al-muḍīʾa fi ʾl-sīra al-nabawiyya*, Paris 1966.—5. *ʿAqīda*, Creed, Berl. 1985.—6. *Kitāb miḥnat al-imām Aḥmad b. Ḥanbal al-Shaybānī*, the afflictions and punishments that Aḥmad b. Ḥanbal (p. 193) endured as a result of his stance on the question of whether or not the Qurʾān is created, Berl. 10016.[1]—7. *al-Naṣīḥa fi ʾl-adʿiya al-ṣaḥīḥa* Cairo ^{1}I, 410, 444.

14a. Abū Muḥammad ʿAbd al-Jalīl b. Mūsā al-Anṣārī, before 605/1208 (see Suppl.).

2. *Mukhtaṣar shuʿab al-īmān*, also Alex. Ḥad. 33, Dam. Z. $49_{,15}$ (which has al-Qaṣrī).

15. Majd al-Dīn Abu ʾl-Saʿādāt al-Mubārak b. Muḥammad b. Muḥammad b. ʿAbd al-Karīm b. ʿAbd al-Wāḥid b. al-Athīr al-Shaybānī al-Jazarī,[2] who died on 30 Dhu ʾl-Ḥijja 606/26 June 1210 (see Suppl.)

Ibn Khall. 524. 1. *Kitāb jāmiʿ al-uṣūl li-aḥādīth al-rasūl*, a. Introduction, b. Arrangement of the traditions by subject in alphabetically ordered sections, c. Biographies of the Prophet and his contemporaries, Berl. 1311/6, Paris 728/9, Br. Mus. Suppl. 483, Garr. 1381/3, Yeni 183/93, Faiẓ. 300, Alex. Ḥad. 13, Cairo ^{1}I, 294, Patna I, $43_{,436/7}$.—Commentary entitled *al-Fuṣūl* by ʿAlī b. Ḥusām al-Dīn al-Muttaqī (II, 384), Patna I, $56_{,559}$.—Abstracts: 1. *Tajrīd al-uṣūl* by Hibatallāh b. ʿAbd
| al-Raḥīm al-Ḥamawī b. al-Bārizī, d. 738/1337 (II, 116), Munich 129, Cairo ^{1}I, 278, 439
Patna I, $40_{,411/2}$, probably also Berl. 1317 (anon.).—2. *Taysīr al-wuṣūl* by ʿAbd al-Raḥmān b. ʿAlī b. Muḥammad b. al-Daybaʿ al-Zabīdī, d. 944/1537 (II, 400),

1 Not used by W.M. Patton, *A. b. Ḥanbal and the Miḥna*, Leiden 1897.

2 For his brothers ʿIzz al-Dīn and Ḍiyāʾ al-Dīn, see p. 357, 422.

in alphabetical order with several alterations, Paris 730, Algiers 498, Rāġib 251, Cairo [1]I, 291, *Dībāja*, Gotha 2,$_{109}$, with a commentary by Muḥammad ʿAbbād al-Mawzaʿī, ca. 1215/1800, Berl. 1318.—3. ʿAbdallāh al-Madanī, completed in Mecca in 971/1563, Berl. 1319.—4. *Jamʿ al-fawāʾid min Jāmiʿ al-uṣūl wa-Majmaʿ al-zawāʾid* (by ʿAlī b. Ḥajar al-Haythamī, d. 807/1405, [II, 76], with special consideration of Ibn Māja) by Muḥammad b. Sulaymān al-Maghribī, d. 1094/1683 (see Suppl.), Berl. 1320, Garr. 1414, Alex. Ḥad. 16, Qawala I, 112.—5. Anon. Cairo [1]I, 411.—6. see Suppl.—II. *Kitāb al-nihāya fī gharīb al-ḥadīth wal-athar*, a dictionary of *ḥādīth*, Berl. 1650/8, Ind. Off. 999, Br Mus. 1386, 1686, Bodl. I, 1061, II, 607, AS 4781/2, Rāġib 359/62, Cairo [1]I, 445, Patna I, 190,$_{1720/1}$, II, 523,$_{2809}$, print. Tehran 1269, C. 1308, 1311, 1322.—Abstract (*talkhīṣ*), *al-Durr al-nathīr* by al-Suyūṭī, d. 911/1505, Bodl. I, 208, Br. Mus. 1687, Ind. Off. 1000, Garr. 1384, Patna I, 185,$_{1689}$, printed in the margin of *OB* V, 2414, 5137, in *Majmūʿa* C. 1322 (Qawala I, 102), excerpt Gotha 98,$_{12}$.—Versification *al-Kifāya fī naẓm al-N.* by Ismāʿīl b. Muḥammad b. Bardis al-Baʿlī, d. 786/1384 (II, 34,$_{6}$), Berl. 1659.—Supplement *al-Tadhyīl wal-tadhnīb ʿalā N. al-gh.* by al-Suyūṭī, Berl. 1660, anon. abstract ibid. 1661.—III. *Kitāb al-muraṣṣaʿ*, a *kunya* dictionary Berl. Ms. or. oct. 3884, NO 4115, print. Istanbul 1304 (*OB* II, 4331), not used in the edition by C.F. Seybold, in *Semit. Stud.* (*Ergänzungshefte zur ZA*), 10, 11, Weimar 1896.—IV. *Kitāb al-mukhtār fī manāqib al-akhyār* (*abrār*), biographies of famous Muslims, vol. I, Leid. 1090.—V.–VII. see Suppl. The cosmography *al-Durra al-muḍīʾa etc.* is attributed to ʿIzz al-Dīn al-Jazarī in Top Kapu Serāi 2963.

16. Abū Bakr Muḥammad b. ʿAbd al-Ghanī b. Abī Bakr Muʿīn al-Dīn al-Ḥanbalī al-Baghdādī b. Nuqṭa, who was born soon after 550/1155, lived, following extensive study tours, as a teacher of *ḥādīth* in Baghdad where he died on 22 Ṣafar 629/20 December 1231.

Ibn Khall. 632, *Ḥuff.* XVIII, 13, Wüst., *Gesch.* 313. 1. *Kitāb al-taqyīd li-maʿrifat al-ruwāt wal-sunan wal-masānīd* Br. Mus. 1629.—2. *Takmilat al-Ikmāl*, p. 435.

440 | 17. ʿUmar b. Badr b. Saʿīd al-Ḥanafī al-Mawṣilī was born in 557/1162 in Damascus and died in 622/1225, or, according to others, in 619/1222.

Ibn Quṭlūbughā, *Ṭab. al-Ḥan* no. 138. *Kitāb al-mughnī ʿan al-ḥifẓ wal-kitāb fī-mā lam yaṣiḥḥi min al-aḥādīth* ḤKh V, 653,$_{12488}$, Berl. 1629.

18. Al-Muʿāfā b. Ismāʿīl b. al-Ḥasan b. al-Ḥusayn b. Abi ʾl-Fatḥ b. Muḥammad b. Ḥaddūs al-Nahrawānī Abu ʾl-Sinān al-Mawṣilī was born in 551/1156 and died in Ramaḍān or Shaʿbān 630/May or June 1233.

Ibn Qāḍī Shuhba in Wüst., *Ak. d. Ar.*, no. 180. 1. *Kitāb ins* (*anīs*) *al-munqaṭiʿīn wa-riyāḍ al-sālikīn*, 300 traditions mixed with as many tales, Berl. 8777/8, Gotha 612, Breslau St. I, 14,$_{1}$, Br. Suppl. 144, Esc. ^{2}747, Algiers 518/20, 763, AS 1671/2, Nafiz 142, Halis I, 14, Riza P. 667, Alex. Ḥad. 7, Mawāʿiẓ 6, Cairo ^{1}I, 273, 400, ^{2}I, Patna I, 40,$_{406}$; cf. J. Cohn, *al-Muafae b. Ism. Mausiliensis K. Anīs al-M. pars I*, Diss. Wroclaw 1875.—2. *Nihāyat al-bayān fī tafsīr al-Qurʾān* Br. Mus. Suppl. 112, Cairo ^{1}I, 220.—3. *Kitāb al-bayān fī tafsīr al-Qurʾān* Köpr. 65.

19. Taqī al-Dīn Abū ʿAmr ʿUthmān b. Ṣalāḥ al-Dīn Abu ʾl-Qāsim ʿAbd al-Raḥmān b. ʿUthmān b. Mūsā b. Abi ʾl-Naṣr b. al-Ṣalāḥ al-Shahrazūrī, who was of Kurdish descent, was born in 577/1181 in | Sharakhān between Arbela and Hamadan. 359
Having started his studies in Mosul, he continued them in the most important cities of Islam, after which he came to Jerusalem where he taught at the al-Madrasa al-Ṣāliḥiyya. In 616/1209 he received the Shāfiʿī professorship at the Rawāḥiyya in Damascus, the head professorship at the Shaʾmiyya Juwāniyya—the madrasa that had newly been founded by Sitt al-Shaʾm Zumurrud, the sister of Sultan Ṣalāḥ al-Dīn—as well as a senior teaching position at the al-Ashrafiyya school of *ḥādīth*. He died there on 25 Rabīʿ II 643/ 20 September 1243.

Ibn Khall. 384, Abulf. IV, 466, 482, *Ḥuff.* XVIII, 21, Wüst. *Gesch.* 325. 1. *Kitāb aqṣa ʾl-amal wal-shawq fī ʿulūm ḥadīth al-rasūl* | Br. Mus. 1597/8, Suppl. 1237, Pet. 120, 441
Algiers 545,$_{3}$, Yeni 164, Patna I, 36,$_{370/1}$ = *Kitāb maʿrifat anwāʿ al-ʿulūm* Cairo ^{1}I, 253, Alex. Ḥad. 63, see Goldziher, *MSt.* II, 187 n. 5, printed as *Muqaddima fī ʿulūm al-ḥadīth*, Bombay 1938.—Commentary by ʿAbd al-Raḥīm al-ʿIrāqī, d. 806/1403 (II, 65), Berl. Br. M. 255, Br. Mus. 1598, Cairo ^{1}I, 232, Patna I, 35,$_{350}$, glosses thereon *Iṣlāḥ b. al-Ṣalāḥ* by Mughlaṭāʾī, d. 762/1360 (II, 48), Cairo ^{1}I, 232.—Abstracts: a. *Irshād al-ḥadīth* or *Irshād ṭullāb al-ḥaqāʾiq ilā maʿrifat sunan khayr al-khalāʾiq* (or *li-maʿrifat ḥadīth khayr al-ʿibād*) by al-Nawawī, d. 676/1277 (p. 394), Berl. 1038/40, Br. Mus. Suppl. 164, AS 433, Alex. Fun. 63, commentary by ʿUmar b. Aḥmad al-Dūmānī, AS 439.—Second abstract, *al-Taqrīb wal-taysīr li-maʿrifat sunan al-bashīr al-nadhīr*, Berl. 1041/3, Leipz. 851, ii, Garr. 1453, Rāğib 235, Alex. Ḥad. 52, Cairo ^{1}I, 231.—Commentaries: *α. Tadrīb al-rāwī*, together with the original work, by al-Suyūṭī, d. 911/1505, Berl. 1044/5, Alex. Muṣṭ. Ḥad. 6, Cairo ^{1}I, 229, Qawala I, 89, print. C. 1307.—*β.* see Suppl.—b. Badr al-Dīn Muḥammad b. Jamāʿa, d. 733/1332 (II, 74), Br. Mus. 191, ii.—c. *Mukhtaṣar ʿulūm al-dīn* by Ismāʿīl b. ʿUmar b. Kathīr, d. 774/1372 (II, 74), Garr. 1451/2, print. C. 1937.—d. *Maḥāsin al-iṣṭilāḥ wa-taḍmīn kitāb Ibn al-Ṣalāḥ*, with additions, by ʿUmar b. Raslān al-Bulqīnī, d. 805/1402 (II, 93), Berl. 1048.—e. *Nukhabat al-fikar fī muṣṭalaḥ al-athar* by Aḥmad b. Ḥajar al-ʿAsqalānī, d. 852/1448

(II, 67), with the self-commentary *al-Tawḍīḥ* or *Nuzhat al-naẓar*, Berl. 1088/1107, Ind. Off. 199, $1036_{,3}$, Paris $760/1_{,1}$, $4257_{,2}$, 5049, Esc. $^2853_{,3}$, Algiers $193_{,3}$, $724_{,8}$, Alex. Muṣṭ. al-Ḥad. 14/6, Fun. $103_{,2}$, $110_{,2}$, Cairo ^{1}I, 246, VII, 254, Qawala I, 95/6, Garr. 1452, 1467, Patna I, $36_{,372}$, ed. Nassau Lees, Calcutta 1862, print. C. 1308, 1323.—Commentaries and glosses: α. Qāsim b. Quṭlūbughā, d. 879/1474 (II, 82), Tunis Zayt. II, 134, Alex. Muṣṭ. Ḥad. 15.—αα. a. Kamāl al-Dīn Muḥammad b. Maḥmūd, b. Abu 'l-Sharīf al-Majdī, d. 906/1500, Berl. 1108.—β. al-Qāriʾ al-Harawī, d. 1014/1605 (II, 394), Berl. 1109/10, Ind. Off. 200/1, Alex. Muṣṭ. 16, Cairo ^{1}I, 251, Qawala I, 94, Patna I, $35_{,360/1}$.—γ. ʿAbd al-Raʾūf al-Munāwī, d. 1031/1622 (II, 306), Cairo ^{1}I, 255, Garr. 1468.—δ. *Qaḍāʾ al-waṭar* by Ibrāhīm al-Laqānī, d. 1041/1631 (II, 310), composed in 1023/1614, Paris $761_{,2}$, Cairo ^{1}I, 242, Patna I, $35_{,362}$.—ε. Athīr al-Dīn, composed in 1053/1633, Cairo ^{1}I, 243, ^{2}I, 72.—ζ. Ibrāhīm al-Kurdī, d. 1142/1729, Berl. 1111.—η. the same, amalgamated with the
442 glosses of Ibn al-Ṣāʾigh, d. 1060/1655, Berl. 1112.—ϑ.–Φ. see Suppl.—| ϰ. Mollā Taqī b. Shāh Muḥammad Lāhūrī, Patna I, $35_{,359}$.—ψ. *Muṣṭalaḥāt ahl al-athar* by ʿAbdallāh b. Ḥusayn Khāṭir al-ʿAdawī al-Mālikī, completed in 1309/1891, C. 1323. Other commentaries in Ahlw., 1115.—Versifications: a. *Aqṣa 'l-amal wal-sūl fī ʿulūm ḥadīth al-rasūl* by Muḥammad b. Aḥmad b. al-Khalīl al-Khuwayyī, d. 693/1294, Berl. 1046, Alex. Muṣṭ. Ḥad. 18.—b. *Tabṣirat al-mubtadiʾ wa-tadhkirat al-muntahī* or *al-Maqāṣid al-muhmala* or *Alfiyyat al-ʿIrāqī* by ʿAbd al-Raḥīm al-ʿIrāqī, d. 806/1463 (II, 65), composed in 768/1366 in Medina, Berl. 1071/5, Gotha 579, Paris 754/5, Ind. Off. 197, NO 409/10, Cairo ^{1}I, 228, Garr. 1459/60, Patna I, 35.—Commentaries: α. Self-commentary *Fatḥ al-ghayth* (*mughīth*), Berl. 1076/7, Yeni 1608, NO 414, Cairo ^{1}I, 241, Patna I, $35_{,353/6}$, print. Bombay n.d.—β. *Fatḥ al-bāqī* by Zakariyyāʾ al-Anṣārī, d. 926/1520 (II, 99), Berl. 1078/83, Ms. or. oct. 3975, Gotha 580, Algiers $193_{,4}$, 547/8, Alex. Fun. $64_{,3}$, Muṣṭ. Ḥad. 72, glosses Cairo ^{1}I, 325, by Sulṭān al-Mazzāḥī al-Shāfiʿī, d. 1075/1665 (Suppl. II, $452_{,7a}$), Garr. $2114_{,1}$.—γ.–ε. see Suppl.—c. (versified) *Silk al-durar fī muṣṭalaḥ ahl al-athar* by Raḍī al-Dīn Muḥammad b. Muḥammad b. Aḥmad al-Ghazzī, d. 936/1528 (II, 284), Berl. 1113, Leipz, 330II.—d. anon. Berl. 1114.—f., g. see Suppl.—h. *al-Shadha 'l-fayyāḥ min ʿulūm Ibn al-Ṣalāḥ* by Burhān Ibrāhīm b. Mūsā al-Abnāsī, d. 802/1400, ḤKh IV, $16_{,7429}$, Alex. Muṣṭ. Ḥad. 10.

II. *Kitāb al-aḥādīth fī faḍl al-Iskandariyya wa-ʿAsqalān*, Berl. 1389.

III. *Liber oderatus odorum terrae sanctae*, a fantastical life of Muḥammad, Flor. 121.

IV. *Kitāb adab al-muftī wal-mustaftī* ḤKh ^{1}I, $204_{,341}$, ^{2}I, 48, Flor. 121.

V. *Fatāwī b. al-Ṣalāḥ fi 'l-tafsīr wal-ḥadīth wal-uṣūl* Sulaim. 650, Cairo ^{1}III, 248, ^{2}I, 527, print. C. 1348.

VI. *Ṣilat al-nāsik fī ṣifat al-manāsik* Cairo [1]VII, 691, [2]I, 524.
VII–XI. see Suppl.

20. Abū ʿAbdallāh Muḥammad b. Maḥmūd b. al-Ḥasan b. al-Najjār Muḥibb al-Dīn al-Baghdādī al-Shāfiʿī, born in Dhu ʾl-Qaʿda 578/February 1183, was a student of Ibn al-Jawzī (p. 500). Having travelled for 27 years, he finally settled down in Baghdad as a teacher and writer. He died there on 5 Shaʿbān 643/27 December 1245.

| *Fawāt* II, 264, *Ḥuff.* XVIII, 20, Wüst., *Gesch.* 327. 1. *Kitāb al-nuzha* (*durra*) *al-thamīna fī akhbār al-Madīna*, composed in 593/1196 in Medina, Gotha 1713, Paris 1630, adapted in *Taḥqīq al-nuṣra fī talkhīṣ maʿālim Dār al-Hijra* by Zayn al-Dīn al-Marāghī, d. 816/1413 (II, 172), Lee 112 (autograph), Bodl. I, 769, 852, cf. II. 595.—2. *Dhayl* (*al-Mustadrak*) *ʿalā Taʾrīkh Baghdād*, p. 401, abstract by Aḥmad b. Aybak b. al-Dimyāṭī, d. 749/1348, Cairo [1]V 150, *al-Mukhtār al-mudhayyal bihi ʿalā Taʾrīkh b. al-Najjār* by Abu ʾl-Maʿālī Muḥammad b. Rāfiʿa al-Sallānī, d. 774/1372 (II, 33), from which *Muntakhab al-Mukhtār* by Taqī al-Dīn al-Fāsī, ed. ʿAbbās al-ʿAzzāwī, Baghdad 1357/1938. 443

21. Raḍī al-Dīn Abu ʾl-Faḍāʾil al-Ḥasan b. Muḥammad al-Ṣaghānī (Ṣāghānī) b. Ḥaydar b. ʿAlī b. Ismāʿīl al-ʿUmarī al-ʿAdawī al-Hindī al-Ḥanafī, who died in 650/1252 in Baghdad (see Suppl.).

Ibn Quṭlūbughā, *Ṭab. al-Ḥan.* no. 61, Wüst., *Gesch.* 336. 1. *Mashāriq al-anwār al-nabawiyya min ṣiḥāḥ al-akhbār al-Muṣṭafawiyya*, collections of *ḥādīth* from | Bukhārī and Muslim, together with the genuine traditions from the 361 *Kitāb al-shihāb* of al-Quḍāʿī, d. 454/1062 (p. 418), and the *Kitāb al-najm* of al-Uqlīsī, d. 550/1155 (p. 370), Berl. 1322, Upps. 394, Br. Mus. p. 713a, Suppl. 145, Paris 737, 5788, Algiers 476, Yeni 280/4, Istanbul Un. ZS III, 83, Alex. Ḥad. 60, Cairo [1]I, 420, [2]I, 147, Qawala I, 151, Garr. 1385/8, cf. V. Zetterstéen, *Om el-Ḥ. b. M. b. el-Ḥ. al-Ṣarānī och hans arbeite* M. el a. enn. min ṣ. a. al-M., Leipzig 1896.—Commentaries: a. *Ḥadāʾiq al-azhār* by ʿAbd al-Raḥmān b. Muḥammad al-Arzanjānī, d. 643/1245, Alex. Ḥad. 19, Cairo [1]I, 335, [2]I, 110.—b. *Tuḥfat al-abrār* by Muḥammad b. Maḥmūd al-Bābartī al-Ḥanafī, d. 786/1384 (II, 80), Br. Mus. 1575/6, Alex. Ḥad. 9, Cairo [1]I, 280, [2]I, 94, 127.—c. *Mabāriq al-azhār* by ʿAbd al-Laṭīf b. ʿAbd al-ʿAzīz al-Kirmānī b. Malikshāh b. Fereshte, ca. 800/1397 (II, 213), Berl. 1323/4, Vienna 1651, Copenhagen 56, Paris 738/9, Alex. Ḥad. 45, Cairo [1]I, 395, [2]I, 142, Qawala I, 147/8, Patna I, 59_{593}, print. Istanbul 1311, 1315,

1328; rearranged under the title *al-Muḥawwal* by ʿAlī b. Ḥasan, completed in 936/1529, ḤKh v, 551, Garr. 1396/7.—d. Muḥammad b. ʿAṭāʾallāh al-Rāzī al-Harawī, d. 829/1426 (al-Sakhāwī, *Ḍawʾ* VIII, 51/5, al-Shawkānī II, 201/8), Berl. 1325, glosses thereon by Shaykhzāde, d. 950/1453, ibid. 1326, Qilič ʿA. 252.—e. Anon., Algiers 477, Patna I, $53_{,539/40}$.—g.–i. see Suppl.—a.–d. Abstracts: see
444 Suppl. (b. *Bāwariq al-anwār* Patna II, $501_{,2682}$).—| e. Muḥammad b. Muṣṭafā b. Faḍlallāh al-Ḥamawī, ca. 1148/1738, Garr. $2071_{,3}$.—f. Anon., Vienna 1650.—2. *Risālat al-aḥādīth al-mawḍūʿāt* (see Suppl.) Cairo ^{1}VII, $123_{,1}$, Qawala I, 156, Alex. Fun. $162_{,6}$, $174_{,6}$, different from *al-Durr al-multaqaṭ fī tabyīn al-ghalaṭ*, proof of spurious traditions in *al-Shihāb* and *Kitāb al-najm*, Algiers $1359_{,4}$, Alex. Fun. $95_{,10}$, $174_{,7}$.—2a. *Risāla fī ʾl-ḥadīth al-mawḍūʿ fī faḍāʾil al-qirāʾa sūra sūra al-marwiyya ʿan Abī Umāma* Alex. Fun. $95_{,11}$.—3. *Kitāb dār (darr) al-ṣaḥāb fī bayān mawāḍiʿ wafayāt al-ṣaḥāba* Berl. 9652, Cairo ^{1}V, 52, ^{2}V, 175.—4. *Kitāb al-ʿubāb al-zākhir wal-lubāb al-fākhir*, a dictionary in 20 volumes, AS 4702/4, Köpr. 1551/3, Cairo ^{1}IV, 175, ^{2}II, 20.—5. *Majmaʿ al-baḥrayn fī ʾl-lugha* Köpr. 1570.—6. *Kitāb al-takmila wal-dhayl wal-ṣila*, see Suppl. I, 197.—7. *Kitāb al-aḍdād* Berl. 7092.—8. *Mukhtaṣar fī ʾl-ʿarūḍ* Berl. 7127, Dāmādzāde 1789g.—9. *Taʿzīz baytay al-Ḥarīrī*, a poem in honour of two verses in the 41st *maqāma* of al-Ḥarīrī, Berl. 7756, Dāmādzāde 1789d.—10.–20. see Suppl. (11. see *RAAD* V, 524/5).—21. *Risāla fī ʾl-aḥādīth al-wārida fī ṣadr al-tafāsīr fī faḍāʾil al-Qurʾān wa-ghayrihā* Qawala I, 118 (= 2a?).

21a. ʿIzz al-Dīn Abū Muḥammad ʿAbd al-ʿAzīz b. Riḍwān b. ʿAbd al-Ḥaqq al-Ḥanbalī wrote, probably in the seventh century:

Maṭlaʿ al-nayyirayn al-mukhtaṣar min al-Ṣaḥīḥayn, MS dated 706/1306, Garr. 1425, dated 902, Rāmpūr I, $196_{,304}$.

22. Ṣadr al-Dīn Kāmil al-Mukhtār, d. 674/1278.

Kitāb jāmiʿ al-ṣaghīr maʿa ziyādāt, Yeni 395.

23. Muḥibb al-Dīn Abu ʾl-ʿAbbās (Abū Muḥammad Abū Jaʿfar) Aḥmad b. ʿAbdallāh al-Ṭabarī al-Makkī al-Shāfiʿī, who died in Jumādā II 684/March 1295 (see Suppl.).

Ḥuff. XX, 4, *Orient.* II, 290, Wüst., *Gesch.* 367. 1. *Kitāb al-riyāḍ al-naḍira fī faḍāʾil (manāqib) al-ʿashara*, on the 10 companions of Muḥammad distinguished by the promise of Paradise, ḤKh ^{1}III, 6735, IV, 9135, ^{2}I, 937, Berl. 9657, Leid.

1748, Landb.-Br 232, Cairo ^{1}v, 65, ^{2}v, 210, Patna II, $306_{,2418}$, abstract Berl. 9658,
Tatimma, supplement by al-Ḥurayfīsh, d. 801/1398 (II, 177), Berl. 9759.—2. *Kitāb*
dhakhāʾir al-ʿuqbā fī manāqib dhawi ʾl-qurbā, on the relatives of the Prophet,
ḤKh ^{1}III, 5770, ^{2}I, 821, Goth. 1834, ed. Ḥusām al-Dīn al-Qudsī, C. 1356/1937,
attributed to Muḥammad Bāqir b. Muḥammad Taqī (II, 411), just like Berl.
9684 | and Patna II, $534_{,2875}$.—3. *Aḥādīth mushkila* Landb.—Br. 51.—4. *Ṣafwat* 445
al-qirā fī ṣifat ḥijjat al-Muṣṭafā wa-ṭawāfihi bi-umm al-qurā, ibid., Cairo ^{2}v, 239,
an abstract of *al-Qirā li-qāṣid umm al-qurā*, Cairo ^{1}III, 260, ^{2}I, 137.—5. *Ghāyat*
al-iḥkām fi ʾl-aḥādīth wal-aḥkām Paris 793, vol. II, Garr. 1802.—6. *Khulāṣat siyar*
sayyid al-bashar, | the life of Muḥammad in 24 chapters, Paris 1546, Alex. Taʾr. 362
7, from which *Nuqāyat al-athar* by Abū Bakr Muḥammad b. Aḥmad b. al-Ḥasan
(see Suppl.) additionally Patna II, $535_{,2880}$.—7. A Sufi *qaṣīda*, Berl. 3435.—8.
see Suppl. (Khālidiyya Jerusalem).

24. Al-Wāʿiẓ Abu ʾl-Ḥasan Abū b. ʿAbdallāh b. Muḥammad al-Bakrī al-Baṣrī (see Suppl.).

14. *Ghazāt sabʿ ḥuṣūn* AS 3307.—15. *Islām al-Ṭufayl b. ʿĀmir al-Dawsī* C. 1322 (Alex. Qiṣaṣ 7).

2 *Persia*

1. Abū Nuʿaym Aḥmad b. ʿAbdallāh b. Isḥāq al-Iṣfahānī, who died on 20 Muḥarram 430/23 October 1038 (see Suppl.).

Ibn Khall. 32, *Ḥuff.* XIII, 62, Wüst., *Gesch.* 187, *Schaf.* 346. 1. *Kitāb ḥilyat al-awliyāʾ wa-ṭabaqāt al-aṣfiyāʾ* or *Ḥilyat al-abrār*, a history of pious and holy men, Berl. 8512, 8669, 9973/4, Leid. 1071, Paris 2028/9, Garr. 669/72, Rāġib 1004/5, vols. I–VIII, C. 1932/8.—Abstract, supplemented from other sources, *Ṣafwat* (*ṣifat*) *al-ṣafwa* in 5 volumes by Ibn al-Jawzī, d. 597/1200 (p. 500), starts with Muḥammad and the pious men of Mecca and Medina, then moves to Baghdad, subsequently treats those of the lands to its east and its west, and ends with the pious among the *jinn*, Berl. 8069, 9975/8, Paris 2030/1, Br. Mus. 962/3, Suppl. 638, Köpr. 1100, Cairo ^{1}v, 75, ^{2}v, 239; whence, in turn, abstracts: a. *Aḥāsin al-maḥāsin* by Ibrāhīm b. Aḥmad al-Raqqī, d. 703/1303 (II, 31), Berl. 9979, Ms. Or. Qu. 2130, Leipz. 242, Gött. 84, Bursa, Haraccizade Tarih 10, Alex. Mawāʿiẓ 3.—b. *Majmaʿ al-aḥbāb wa-tadhkirat uli ʾl-albāb* by Muḥammad b. Ḥasan b. ʿAbdallāh al-Ḥusaynī, d. 776/1374, Paris 2032.—c. see Suppl. Additionally a. *Naẓm rijāl Ḥ. al-a.* by Muḥammad b. Jābir, composed in 793/1391, Cairo ^{1}VII, 32, ^{2}v, 393.—b. *Taqrīb al-bughya fī tartīb aḥādīth al-Ḥ.* by ʿAlī b. Abī Bakr

al-Haythamī, d. 807/1104 (II, 76), Cairo [1]I, 286, [2]I, 97.—2. *Ṭibb al-nabī*, tradi-
446 tions related to | medicine, Esc. [2]1619, Yeni 273b, cf. Leclerc I, 484; abstract, omitting the *isnād*s and with additions from other works, by ʿAbd al-Wahhāb b. Aḥmad b. Maḥmūd al-Rūmī, Pet. Ros. 224$_{,2}$.—3. Two booklets with traditions, Berl. 1567/8.—4. *Dhikr akhbār Iṣbahān* ḤKh [1]II, 2142, [2]I, 282, Leid. 1020, ed. S. Dedering I, Leiden 1931, II, 1934.—5. *al-Musnad al-mustakhraj ʿalā Muslim* Br. Mus. Suppl. 137, Bursa Ulu Cami Hadis 187.—6. *Dalāʾil al-nubuwwa* Br. Mus. Suppl. 510, Cairo [1]I, 341, [2]I, 116, Patna I, 270$_{,2246}$.—7. *Musnad* Cairo [1]I, 418.

2. Abū Yaʿlā al-Khalīl b. ʿAbdallāh b. Aḥmad al-Khalīlī al-Qazwīnī was a *qāḍī* in Qazvin and died in 446/1054.

1. *Kitāb al-irshād fī maʿrifat ʿulamāʾ al-bilād*, short statements on ancient, trustworthy traditionists, arranged by their place of residence, abstract by Aḥmad b. Muḥammad al-Silafī, d. 576/1180 (p. 449), Berl. 99$_{,9}$ (see Suppl.).

3. Abū ʿUthmān Ismāʿīl b. ʿAbd al-Raḥmān b. Aḥmad al-Ṣābūnī, the son of a preacher, was born in 373/983 in Nishapur (acccording to Yāqūt in Būshanj). After studies at home and abroad he succeeded his father, whom he had lost to
363 violence. | A highly respected authority, he died of the plague on 4 Muḥarram 449/13 March 1057.

Wüst., *Schaf.* 393. *Kitāb al-miʾatayn*, 100 choice traditions and 100 tales, Landb.—Br. 102.—2., 3. see Suppl.

4. Abū Bakr Aḥmad b. al-Ḥusayn b. ʿAlī b. Mūsā al-Bayhaqī al-Khusrawjirdī was born in Shaʿbān 384/September 994 in Khusrawjird in the district of Bayhaq, 20 parasangs from Nishapur. During long travels he had devoted himself to the study of *ḥadīth*, but after his return to his homeland he was persecuted by the vizier ʿAmīd al-Mulk because of his Ashʿarī leanings, forcing him to flee to Mecca with al-Qushayrī (p. 432) and Imām al-Ḥaramayn (p. 388). However, in
447 441/1049 he was called to Nishapur where | he taught Shāfiʿī law, using his own collection of al-Shāfiʿī's legal propositions (no. 9). He died there on 10 Jumādā I 458/9 April 1066.

Ibn Khall. 27, *Ḥuff.* XIV, 13, Yāqūt, *GW* I, 804 (where it is stated that he died in 454), Wüst., *Gesch.* 203, *Schaf.* 407. 1. *Kitāb al-sunan wal-āthār* or *Kitāb al-sunan al-kabīr*, a collection of traditions in 10 volumes, Löwen L 97, Garr. 1371, Yeni 204/6, Cairo [1]I, 452/4 (among which there is an autograph); thereto *Fawāʾid al-muntaqī li-zawāʾid al-B.* by Aḥmad b. Abī Bakr al-Būṣīrī, d. 840/1436 (II, 67),

Cairo [1]I, 383, [2]I, 136, *Dībāja*, Gotha 2,$_{122}$; against this work ʿAbū b.ʿUthmān b. al-Turkumānī, d. 747/1346 (II, 64), wrote *Kitāb jawhar al-naqī fi ʾl-radd ʿala ʾl-B.*, Paris 753, Copenhagen 54, Cairo [1]I, 328, [2]I, App. 13, V, 110.—2. *Kitāb al-sunan al-ṣughrā* Cairo [1]I, 351, [2]I, 124.—3. *Kitāb dalāʾil al-nubuwwa* Br. Mus. Suppl. 511, Cairo [1]I, 341, [2]I, 116, cf. K. Nylander, *Die Upsalaer Hds. der D. al-N.* Upsala 1891.[1]—4. *Kitāb al-baʿth wal-nushūr*, on the Last Judgement, Pet. AMK 924, Mosul 228,$_{17}$, a part of it in, Berl. 2734.—5. *al-Jāmiʿ al-muṣannaf fī shuʿab al-īmān* Alex. Ḥad. 16, Cairo [1]I, 324, abstract by Abū Ḥafṣ ʿUmar al-Qazwīnī, Patna I, 59,$_{598}$, II, 513,$_{2757}$, Persian translation Muḥammad b. ʿAbdallāh b. Muḥammad al-Ījī, AS 1738.—6. *Kitāb al-adab* Cairo [1]I, 257 abstract *al-Adab fī taʿrīb al-arīb* by Zakariyyāʾ al-Anṣārī, d. 926/1520 (II, 99), Paris 4593.—7. *Kitāb takhrīj aḥādīth al-Umm* (see Suppl. I, 180,$_{3}$) vol. 2, Cairo [1]III, 206.—8. *Kitāb faḍāʾil al-awqāt*, a prayer book, Vienna 1675.—9. *Kitāb nuṣūṣ al-imām al-Shāfiʿī* (see above), in 10 volumes, ḤKh VI, 11330, 13823, Bodl. I, 828.—10. *Kitāb fī ḥayāt al-anbiyāʾ fī qubūrihim* Landb.—Br. 108.—11.–22. see Suppl. (11. Patna I, 113,$_{1134}$).

5. Abu ʾl-Qāsim ʿAbdallāh b. Aḥmad b. Maḥmūd al-Balkhī died in Balkh in Jumādā II 488/June 1095.

1. *Kitāb qabūl al-akhbār wa-maʿrifat al-rijāl* Cairo [1]I, 242, [2]I, 77.—2. see Suppl. (no. 3 to be excised, see Suppl. I, 343).

6. Abū Muḥammad al-Ḥusayn b. Masʿūd al-Farrāʾ al-Baghawī, who died in Shawwāl 516/December 1122 or, according to others, in Shawwāl 510/February 1117 (see Suppl.).

| Ibn Khall. 177, *Ḥuff.* XV, 31. Suyūṭī, *De Interpr.* ed. Meursinge, p. 12, no. 35. 1. 448
Kitāb maṣābīḥ (*al-dujā*) *al-sunna* (*sunan*), a collection of traditions compiled from | seven foundational works, divided into *ṣaḥīḥ* from Bukhārī and Muslim, 364
ḥasan from the *Sunan*, *gharīb* and *ḍaʿīf* for the very uncertain ones, Berl. 1280/8, Paris 719, 5497, 6606, Copenhagen 55, Br. Mus. 1190, Suppl. 138/9, Ind. Off. 149/50, 4580 (JRAS 1939, 370), Yeni 281/91, Cairo [2]I, 422, [2]I, 148, Qawala I, 94, Garr. 1372/5, 152, Patna I, 62,$_{630/3}$, a *Madkhal* by the author himself, Qawala I, 94.—Commentaries: a. ʿAbd al-Laṭīf b. ʿAbd al-ʿAzīz b. Malak (Fereshte), ca. 850/1446, Rāġib 322/4, Sulaim. 282/3, NO 1102/4, Cairo [1]I, 362, [2]I, 128.—b. ʿAbdallāh b. ʿUmar al-Bayḍāwī, d. 716/1316 (p. 416), Cairo [1]I 326.—c. Zayn al-ʿArab

1 On which C. Landberg, *Dr. K. Nylanders Specimenschrift kritisch beleuchtet*, Leiden 1892, K.N., Dr. C.A. Graf *L. als Kritiker beleuchtet*, Uppsala 1892.

ʿAlī b. ʿUbaydallāh b. Aḥmad, Berl. 1289, Leipz. 185, Br. Mus. 1573, Alex. Ḥad. 32, Cairo ^{1}I, 363, ^{2}I, 128.—d. *al-Mafātīḥ* by al-Ḥusayn b. Maḥmūd b. al-Ḥasan al-Zaydānī Muẓhir al-Dīn, composed in 720/1320, Berl. 1290, Rāġib 325, Alex. Ḥad. 63, Cairo ^{1}I, 427, ^{2}I, 128, Qawala I, 153, Patna I, 63$_{,642}$.—e. Abū ʿAbdallāh Ismāʿīl b. Muḥammad b. Ismāʿīl b. ʿAbd al-Malik b. ʿUmar al-Fuqqāʿī al-Ashraf, d. Jum. I 715/Aug. 1315 (Ibn Ḥajar, *DK*, I, 377), Alex. Ḥad. 32.—f. Aḥmad al-Rūmī al-Āqḥiṣārī, d. 1041/1631 (ḤKh, I, 250, 1043 ibid. III, 392, see II, 445), in 100 *majālis*, Vienna 1652/4, Munich 125.—g. Anon., Berl. 1291, Ind. Off. 151, Cairo ^{1}I, 363.—h. ʿUthmān b. Muḥammad al-Harawī, Alex. Ḥad. 32 (MS dated 858), Selīm Āġā 216.—i.–q. see Suppl.—r. *Asmāʾ al-ṣaḥāba wal-tābiʿīn mimmā dhakarahu ʾl-M.* by Abū Muḥammad Muḥammad b. Muḥammad b. Ḥusayn al-Fuḍālī al-Fargharī (gh?) al-Sakādārī, from the year 777 AH, AS 39, f. 83b/90b (Ritter).—An abstract, *Kashf al-manāhij wal-tanqīḥ fī takhrīj aḥādīth al-Maṣābīḥ*, by Muḥammad b. Ibrāhīm al-Munāwī, d. 803/1400 (see Suppl.), Cairo ^{1}I, 389.—A revised edition, *Mishkāt al-Maṣābīḥ* by Muḥammad b. ʿAbdallāh al-Khaṭīb al-Tabrīzī (II, 195), composed in 737/1336, is, due to its richness and practical usefulness, still widely in circulation; for the Muslim, in particular scholars, it replaces all other collections, avoids all the complicated, ostentatious business of *isnād*s, and is not so much geared towards pedantry as it is towards edification (Goldziher, *MSt.* II, 270/1), Gotha 597 (where other MSS are listed), Yeni 285, Faiẓ. 257, Cairo ^{1}I, 420, ^{2}I, 148, Patna I, 61$_{,634/7}$, II, 503$_{,2705}$, printed several times in India (see Suppl.), lith. St. Petersburg 1898/9 in 2 vols.; to this *Asmāʾ al-rijāl* Patna II, 302$_{,2399}$.—Commentaries: a. Aḥmad b. Muḥammad al-Ṭībī, d. 743/1342, *al-Kāshif ʿan ḥaqāʾiq al-sunan* Berl. 1293, Gotha 597, Paris 751/2, Br. Mus. 1569, Ind. Off. 157,
449 Rāġib | 321, Yeni 245, 259, Qawala I, 144, Patna I, 56$_{,568/9}$, *Muqaddima*, Alex. Fun. 100, 2, idem, *Asmāʾ rijāl al-Mishkāt* NO 656.—b. al-Jurjānī, d. 816/1413 (II, 216), BDMG 13, Cairo ^{1}I, 332, Patna I, 49$_{,488}$.—c. Ibn Ḥajar al-Haytamī, d. 974/1566 (II, 387), Cairo ^{1}I, 374.—d. *Mirqāt al-mafātīḥ* by al-Qāriʾ al-Harawī, d. 1014/1605 (II, 394), Ind. Off. 158/60, Br. Mus. Suppl. 140, Algiers 510/6, Rāġib 319/20, Yeni 246/54, Cairo ^{1}I, 416, Qawala I, 149, Patna I, 59$_{,601/4}$, print. C. 1309, 5 vols.—e. *Nujūm al-M.* by al-Ṣiddīq b. al-Sharīf, Patna I 64$_{,672}$.—Persian translation with commentary, Tippu 20/1, Berl. Spr. 526/9, Persian commentary *Lamaʿāt al-Tanqīḥ* by ʿAbd al-Ḥaqq Miskīn al-Dihlawī, d. 1052/1642, Br. Mus. Suppl. 141, Patna I, 58$_{,59}$, print. Calcutta and Chinsura 1251/9, anon. abstract Ind. Off. 16.—2. *Kitāb sharḥ al-sunna*, an extensive collection of traditions, Berl. 1295/6, Yeni 235, Cairo ^{1}I, 357, Patna I, 52$_{,521}$ (no. 14 attributed).—3. *Kitāb al-tahdhīb fi ʾl-furūʿ*, a juridical handbook, Cairo ^{1}III, 212, ^{2}I, 507.—4. *Kitāb maʿālim al-tanzīl*, Qurʾān commentary, an abstract from Thaʿlabī's *al-Kashf wal-bayān*, Gotha 524/7 (where other MSS are listed), BDMG 8/9, Br. Mus. 62/3, 1544/8, Suppl. 101/3, Esc. ^{2}1279, Algiers 317/8, AS 269, 295, 277, 279, 272/3, 283, 271, 270, 275/6, 274 (ordered by

date, Ritter), Rāġib 230, Yeni 95, Garr. 1262/4, Cairo [1]I, 211, [2]I, 62, Qawala I, 80, Patna I, 32,$_{325/6}$.—Abstracts by: a. Aḥmad b. Muḥammad b. ʿAlī al-Fayyūmī, d. 770/1368 (II, 25), Esc. [2]1327.—b. *Nafāʾis al-marjān fī jamʿ qiṣaṣ al-Qurʾān* by ʿAbd al-Wahhāb b. Muḥammad al-Ḥusaynī, d. 875/1470 (II, 132), Algiers 319.—c., d. see Suppl.—5.–8. see Suppl.

7. Abu ʾl-Ḥasan ʿAbd al-Ghāfir b. Ismāʿīl b. ʿAbd al-Ghāfir al-Fārisī was born in Rabīʿ II 451/May 1059 in Nishapur. He studied in his hometown at al-Madrasa al-Niẓāmiyya and then travelled through Khwārizm and, by way of Ghazna, all the way to India. After his return he became a preacher in Nishapur, where he died in 529/1134.

| Ibn Khall. 375, *Ḥuff.* XV, 41, Wüst., *Gesch.* 236. 1. *Kitāb al-arbaʿīn*, a collection of 365
40 traditions, Berl. 1463, Cairo [2]I, 87.—2. *Kitāb majmaʿ al-gharāʾib wa-manbaʿ al-raghāʾib*, a collection of traditions, completed in 527/1133, Bodl. I, 1154, Cairo [1]I, 400, [2]I, 144.—3. (4.) see Suppl.

8. Zāhir b. Ṭāhir b. Muḥammad al-Shaḥḥāmī al-Nīsābūrī Abu ʾl-Qāsim, who died in 533/1138.

| *Kitāb al-aḥādīth al-ilāhiyya*, traditions with precise *isnād*s in 19 books, with two 450
*nawʿ*s from the work of Ibn Ḥibbān, d. 354/965 (p. 172), as book 10, Berl. 1297.

8a. Abu ʾl-Ḥusayn Saʿīd b. Hibatallāh (Saʿdallāh b. ʿAbdallāh) b. Abi ʾl-Ḥasan (Ḥusayn) Quṭb al-Dīn al-Rāwandī was a Shīʿī *faqīh* who died in 573/1177.

Al-Ḥurr al-ʿĀmilī, *Amal al-āmil*, 476. *Al-Kharāʾij wal-jarāʾiḥ fi ʾl-muʿjizāt*, on the miracles of the Prophet and the 12 imams (Kentūrī 1046), Berl. 2619, Oct. 3164, Mashh. IV, 35,$_{110/1}$.

9. Abu ʾl-Ṭāhir Aḥmad b. Muḥammad b. Aḥmad al-Silafī (b. Silafa) al-Iṣbahānī al-Jarwānī, who died in 576/1180 or 578 (see Suppl.).

Ibn Khall. 43, *Ḥuff.* XVI, 4, Wüst., *Gesch.* 268, al-Kattānī, *Fihris* II, 339/42, 1. *Kitāb al-abḥāth*, a collection of traditions, vols. 5 and 9 Landb.-Br. 75/6.—2. *al-Mashyakha al-Baghdādiyya*, in more than 100 quires, completed in 574/1178, Esc. [2]1783 (MS from Alexandria dated 594/1198), see al-Kattānī II, 61, selection in *Muntaqāt min al-Safīna al-Baghdādiyya* by Aḥmad b. Khalīl al-Lubūdī (Suppl. II, 85, 23), Landb.-Br. 117.—3. *Kitāb al-arbaʿīn al-mustaghnā bi-taʿyīn mā fīhi min al-muʿīn*, usually called *al-Buldāniyya* because each tradition was collected in another town (cf. Ibn Khall.), Paris 722$_{,1}$, Algiers 763$_{,4}$.—4. An explanation of remarkable expressions in the Qur'ān, incorporated by Muḥammad b. ʿAlī b. ʿArrāq, d. 933/1526 (II, 332), into his work *Jawharat al-ghawwāṣ*, Berl. 427, cf. 698.—5. a *qaṣīda*, Berl. 7697$_{,1}$.—6.–10. see Suppl.—11. *Arbaʿīn ḥadīth fī ḥaqq al-fuqarā'*, collected by his student ʿĪsā b. Ḥasan al-Silafī, Alex. Ḥad. 48.—12. Correspondence with al-Zamakhsharī, Garr. 2066$_{,3}$.

9a. Aḥmad b. Maḥmūd b. Saʿīd al-Ghaznawī, d. 593/1197.

Rawḍat al-shihāb fī bayān maʿāni 'l-alfāẓ al-nabawiyya wal-ādāb al-sharʿiyya Alex. Ḥad. 64.

10. Abu 'l-Karam ʿAbd al-Salām b. Muḥammad b. al-Ḥasan b. ʿAlī al-Ḥijjī[2] al-Firdawsī al-Andarasfānī, who flourished in the second half of the sixth century in Khwārizm.

451 | 1. *Kitāb al-mustaqṣā*, an expansion of his earlier work *al-Mujtabā*, a history of Muḥammad according to Bukhārī, Muslim and the *al-Muwaṭṭa'* of Mālik, of the conquests, of the first 4 caliphs and of Ḥasan, translated into Persian by Kamāl al-Dīn Ḥusayn al-Khwārizmī, d. ca. 840/1436, Br. Mus. Pers. I, 144.—2. *al-Jāmiʿ al-bahī li-daʿawāt al-nabī*, composed in 564/1169, Garr. 1945, Mosul 36, 49.

11. Muḥyi 'l-Sunna Abū Mūsā Muḥammad b. Abī Bakr ʿUmar b. Abī ʿĪsā Aḥmad b. ʿUmar b. Muḥammad b. Abī ʿĪsā al-Iṣbahānī was born in Dhu 'l-Qaʿda 501/June 1108 in Isfahan where he died on 8 Jumādā I 581/8 August 1185.

366 | 1. *al-Laṭā'if min daqā'iq al-maʿārif fī ʿulūm al-ḥuffāẓ al-aʿārif* Cairo ^{1}I, 394, ^{2}I, 142, app. 16.—2. *Kitāb taqdhiyat mā yuqdhi 'l-ʿayn min hafawāt Kitāb al-gharībayn* by Abū ʿUbayd al-Harawī (p. 137), Bodl. II, 381$_{,4}$.—3. see Suppl.

12. (13). Ḍiyā' al-Dīn Abū Bakr ʿĀtiq b. ʿAlī b. Muḥammad b. ʿUmar al-Harawī dictated to a student in 637/1239:

Arbaʿūn, 40 traditions, each of which was taken from another work, Paris 722$_{,2}$.

13. (14). Fakhr al-Dīn Abu 'l-Ḥasan ʿAlī b. Aḥmad b. al-Bukhārī al-Ḥanbalī, who died in 690/1291 (see Suppl.).

2 According to al-Samʿānī, *Ansāb* 157b, the common form of al-Ḥājj in Khwārizm.

Al-Kattānī, *Fihris* II, 58. *Kitāb al-Mashyakha al-Fakhriyya* or *Asna 'l-maqāṣid wa-aʿdhab al-mawārid*, a collection of traditions, arranged by his 62 male and 6 female teachers, Paris 750, Bank. V, 2, 322 = Patna I, 62,$_{269}$.

13a. *Jamʿ masānīd imām Abī Ḥanīfa* Patna I, 47,$_{481}$.

14. (15). Abū ʿAbdallāh Muḥammad b. ʿUmar al-Baghawī, seventh cent., see Suppl.

1. *Kitāb fi 'l-ḥadīth* also Patna I, 57,$_{576}$.—2. *al-Jawāhir* Alex. Mawāʿiẓ 14.—3. *Sharḥ al-sunna* Patna I, 52,$_{521}$ (but see no. 7,$_{11}$).

3 *Egypt and North Africa*

1. Abū ʿAlī Muḥammad b. Asʿad b. ʿAlī al-Jawwānī al-Ḥusaynī al-Mālikī al-Qāḍi 'l-Ajall Dhu 'l-Ḥasabayn Nassābat Amīr al-Mu'minīn, who was born on 1 Jumādā II 525/1 May 1131 and died in 588/1192 in Egypt.

| 1. *Kitāb shajarat rasūl Allāh*, a genealogy of the Prophet and his family, with a 452
brief mention of historical ties, dedicated to Ṣalāḥ al-Dīn, Berl. 9511.—2.–6. see Suppl. (3. also Paris 2101).

2. Abu 'l-ʿAbbās Muḥammad b. Aḥmad al-Lakhmī al-Sabtī b. al-ʿAzafī wrote, in 633/1256:

Kitāb al-durr al-munaẓẓam fī mawlid al-nabī al-muʿaẓẓam, completed by his son Abu 'l-Qāsim, Br. Mus. 919 (where Ibn ʿAbdallāh), Esc. ^{2}1741, Yeni 851.

3. Sharaf al-Dīn Abu 'l-Ḥasan ʿAlī b. al-Qāḍī Abu 'l-Makārim al-Mufaḍḍal b. ʿAlī b. al-Mufarrij al-Maqdisī, who was born in 544/1149 in a place near the Syrian-Egyptian border. He was for a time the acting *qāḍī* in Alexandria and then a professor at the madrasa of Ibn Shukr in Cairo, where he died in Shaʿbān 611/December 1214.

Ibn Khall. 404, *Ḥuff.* XVII, 23, al-Suyūṭī, *Ḥusn al-muḥ.* I, 200. *Kitāb al-arbaʿīn al-murattaba ʿalā ṭabaqāt al-arbaʿīn* or *Arbaʿūna ḥadīthan ʿan arbaʿīna shaykhan*, with precise information on the lifetime of each teacher and complete *isnād*s, Berl. 1467, Br. Mus. 1628, Suppl. 158.—2. see Suppl.

| 4. Abū Muḥammad ʿAbd al-ʿAẓīm b. ʿAbd al-Qawī Zakī al-Dīn al-Mundhirī 367
was born in Egypt on 1 Shaʿbān 581/28 October 1185, studied in Mecca,

Damascus, Ḥarrān, Edessa and Alexandria, before becoming a teacher at al-Ẓāfirī mosque in Cairo. He then held the Shāfiʿī professorship for the science of *ḥadīth* at al-Kāmiliyya mosque for twenty years, dying on 4 Dhu ʾl-Qaʿda 656/ 3 November 1258.

Ḥuff. XVIII, 24, al-Suyūṭī, *Ḥusn al-muḥ.* I, 201, Wüst., *Gesch.* 342. 1. *Kitāb al-targhīb wal-tarhīb*, *ḥadīth*s, ordered by subject, encouraging the good and the just and discouraging the bad and unjust, ḤKh ^{1}II, 2937, ^{2}I, 400, Berl. 1328/31, Ms. Or. Qu. 2067, Paris 740/1, Garr. 1309, Yeni 175/6, *Bull. de Corr. Afr.* 1884, p. 369,
453 no. 20, Cairo ^{1}I, 284, ^{2}I, 96, Qawala I, 105, Patna I, $41,_{4203}$.—Commentaries: | a.
ʿUjālat al-imlāʾ, mainly to correct flippancies, slips of the pen, and omissions, by Ibrāhīm b. Muḥammad b. Maḥmūd al-Nājī, d. 900/1495 (II, 98), Berl. 1332/3, Br. Mus. Suppl. 1269.—b. Ḥasan b. ʿAlī al-Fayyūmī, ninth cent., Br. Mus Suppl. 146.—Abstracts: *al-Taysīr wal-taqrīb* by Muḥammad b. ʿAmmār al-Mālikī, d. 844/1440, Paris 742.—b. *al-Taqrīb al-muntazaʿ* by Sālim al-Murtaḍā al-Wāsiṭī al-Ḥuburī al-Saʿdī (see Suppl.), Br. Mus. 1594.—c. *Itḥāf al-muslim bi-aḥādīth al-T. wal-t.*, only from Bukhārī and Muslim, by Yūsuf b. Ismāʿīl al-Nabhānī, d. after 1345/1926 (Suppl. II, 764), C. 1329.—2. *Arbaʿūn (fī ʾiṣṭināʿ al-maʿrūf lil-muslimīn)*, from Bukhārī and Muslim, Berl. 1470.—3. *Majālis fī ṣawm yawm ʿĀshūrā* Landb.-Br. 103.—4. *al-Takmila li-wafayāt al-naqala*, biographies of *ḥadīth* scholars from 625/1228 until 642/1244, Br. Mus. Suppl. 629, Alex. Taʾr. 52.—5. *Kifāyat al-mutaʿabbid wa-tuḥfat al-mutazahhid* Cairo ^{1}VII, 66, ^{2}I, 139.—7. see Suppl.

4 *Spain*

1. Abū ʿUmar Yūsuf b. ʿAbdallāh b. Muḥammad b. ʿAbd al-Barr al-Namarī al-Qurṭubī, who was born on 24 Rabīʿ II 368/30 November 978, studied in Cordova and became the greatest *ḥadīth* specialist in the Maghreb in his lifetime. While having been a Ẓāhirī in his younger years, he later professed
368 Mālikism, | although he was also very much inclined towards the teachings
of al-Shāfiʿī. Having wandered around western Spain for some time, he finally settled in Denia, but also often stayed in Valencia and Játiva. During the reign of the Afṭasid al-Muẓaffar he was appointed *qāḍī* of Lisbon and Santarem. He died in Játiva on 29 Rabīʿ II 463/3 February 1071.

Ibn Khall. 808, *Ḥuff.* XIV, 12, Ibn Bashkuwāl no. 1386, Wüst., *Gesch.* 207, Goldziher, *Ẓāhir.* 171/2. 1. *Kitāb al-istīʿāb fī maʿrifat al-aṣḥāb*, in alphabetical order, Berl. Ms. Or. Qu. 2107, Br. Mus. 1623/4, Suppl. 623, *Cat. Ital.* 288, no. 67, Madr. 511, 527,

Garr. 673, AS 4353/4, Cairo ^{1}I, 225, ^{2}I, 78, Patna II, $301,_{2391/5}$.—Abstract: a. *Iʿlām*
al-iṣāba bi-aʿlām al-ṣaḥāba by Muḥammad b. Yaʿqūb b. Muḥammad b. Aḥmad
al-Khalīlī, eighth cent., Cairo ^{1}I, 227, ^{2}I, 69, Beirut 109.—b.–e. see Suppl.—
2.| *Kitāb al-durar fī 'khtiṣār al-maghāzī wal-siyar* Cairo ^{1}V, 53, ^{2}V, 180.—3. *Kitāb* 454
jāmiʿ bayān al-ʿilm wa-faḍlihi wa-mā yanbaghī fī riwāyatihi wa-ḥamlihi Cairo
^{1}II, 77, ^{2}I, 283, Dam. Z. $79,_{13}$.—4. *Kitāb al-intiqāʾ fī faḍāʾil al-thalātha al-fuqahāʾ*,
i.e. Mālik, Abū Ḥanīfa, and al-Shāfiʿī, Esc. ^{2}1807.—5. *al-Istidhkār fī sharḥ*
madhāhib ʿulamāʾ al-amṣār etc., see Suppl. I, 297.—6. *Kitāb al-inbāh fī dhikr*
uṣūl al-qabāʾil wal-ruwāt ʿan rasūl Allāh Esc. ^{2}1699.—7. *Kitāb bahjat al-majālis*
wa-uns al-mujālis, an anthology of proverbs, verses of poetry, aphorisms, and
tales, dedicated to the prince al-Muẓaffar, Br. Mus. 333, Bodl. II, 106, Algiers 1868,
Tunis, Zaytūna IV, 676 (*Bull. de Corr. Afr.* 1884, p. 9, no. 10), AS 3812, Cairo ^{1}IV,
213, ^{2}III, 39, printed together with Ibn al-Muqaffaʿ's *al-Adab al-kabīr* with the
title *Jawāhir al-ḥukamāʾ*, C. 1907.—Abstract Algiers 1869.—8. Another anthology in verse and in prose, in 70 chapters, ordered by subject, Br. Mus. 726.—
9.–15. see Suppl.—16. *al-Taqaṣṣī fī 'l-ḥadīth al-nabawī* Cairo ^{2}I, 98.

2. (3). Abū ʿAlī al-Ḥusayn b. Muḥammad b. Aḥmad al-Ghassānī al-Jayyānī, professor of *ḥadīth* at the mosque of Cordova, died on 12 Shaʿbān 498/30 April 1105.

Ibn Khall. 187, Ibn Bashkuwāl 326, al-Kattānī, *Fihris* II, 254. 1. *Taqyīd al-muhmal wa-tamyīz al-mushkil fī rijāl al-Ṣaḥīḥayn*, alphabetically listed, in 2 volumes, Berl. 10161, Patna II, $538,_{2896}$.—2. *Kitāb al-kunā wal-alqāb* Garr. 1449.—3. see Suppl.

4. Abū ʿAbdallāh Muḥammad b. Masʿūd b. Khalṣa b. Abi 'l-Khiṣāl al-Ghāfiqī was
born in 465/1072 in Burghalīṭ (Farghalīṭ, i.e. Gorgolitas?) in the Shaqūra dis-
trict in the province of Jayyān. | He was a multifaceted scholar and poet, lived 369
in Cordova and Granada, and held a high military and government post with
the title Dhu 'l-wizāratayn. When the Almoravids stormed Cordova, he died
in Pharaoh's Street, not far from ʿAbd al-Jabbār gate, on 12 Dhu 'l-Ḥijja 540/
27 May 1146.

Maqq. II, 124. Wüst., *Gesch.* 242. 1. *Kitāb ẓill al-saḥāb*, on Muḥammad's
wives and relatives, Br. Mus. $888,_5$, with the title *Ẓill al-ghamāma wa-ṭawq*
al-ḥamāma, Esc. ^{2}1787, versified ibid. $1745,_3$.—2. *Minhāj al-manāqib wa-miʿrāj*
al-ḥasab al-thāqib, | a poem in praise of the Prophet and his companions, 455
Br. Mus. $888,_6$, Esc. $^2404,_1$.—3. *Manāqib al-ʿashara wa-ʿammay rasūl Allāh* Esc.
$^2 1745,_2$.—4. Imitation of *Mulqa 'l-sabīl* by Abu 'l-ʿAlāʾ al-Maʿarrī (p. 296), ordered

by the letters of the alphabet, with, for each person, an aphorism and a verse, Br. Mus. $888_{,11}$.—4. Letters, *maqāmas* and an imitation of the *Mulqa 'l-sabīl*, Esc. ^{2}519.—5. Letters on religion to ʿAbd b. Ḥabīb, Esc. $^{2}306_{,2}$.—6.–9. see Suppl.

5. Abu 'l-Faḍl ʿIyād b. Mūsā b. ʿIyād al-Yaḥṣibī (Yaḥṣubī) al-Sabtī al-Mālikī, who was born in the middle of Shaʿbān 476/December 1083 in Ceuta, studied in Cordova and became a *qāḍī* in his hometown. In 532/1137 he assumed the same office in Cordova, but soon after went to Marrakesh. He died there on 7 Jumādā II 544/13 October 1149, or, according to others, in Ramaḍān.

Al-Ḍabbī no. 1269, Maqq. I, 388, Ibn Khall. 484, *Ḥuff.* XVI, 5, Wüst., *Gesch.* 246, al-Kattānī, *Fihris* II, 183/9, ʿAbdallāh Gannūn, *al-Nubūgh al-Maghribī* I, 79/81, *Kitāb azhār al-riyāḍ fī akhbār ʿIyāḍ* by Aḥmad b. Muḥammad al-Maqqarī, d. 1041/1631 (II, 297), Paris 2106 (see Suppl.), O. Houdas and R. Basset, *Mission scientifique en Tunisie*, Algiers 1884, p. 46, no. 6, Basset, *Gion. d. Soc. As. Ital.* X, 56, n. 2. 1. *Kitāb al-shifāʾ fī taʿrīf ḥuqūq al-Muṣṭafā*, on the duties of Muslims towards the Prophet, Berl. 2559/63, Ms. or. oct. 3910, Paris 1953/6, Br. Mus. Suppl. 159, Gotha 719 (where other MSS are listed), Garr. 634/5, Cairo ^{1}I, 363/6, ^{2}I, 128, Patna I, $271_{,2358/61}$, lith. C. 1276, print. ibid. 1312 and later (see Suppl.).—Commentaries: a. *al-Iktifāʾ* by ʿAbd al-Bāqī b. ʿAbd al-Majīd al-Qurashī al-Yamanī, d. 743/1342 (II, 171), Esc. ^{2}1795, anon. abstract, ca. 900/1494, Berl. 2566.—b. Ibrāhīm b. Muḥammad b. al-ʿAjamī, d. 841/1437 (II, 67), composed in 797/1394, Cairo^{1} I, 428, ^{2}I, 151.—c. Shams al-Dīn al-Ḥijāzī, ca. 850/1446, Berl. 2564.—d. *Muzīl al-khafāʾ ʿan alfāẓ al-Sh.* by Aḥmad b. Muḥammad al-Qāhirī al-Shumunnī, d. 872/1467 (II, 82), Berl. 2565, Leid. 2102, Paris $1957_{,2}$, 4626, Br. Mus. $872_{,7}$, Algiers $1075_{,2}$, Yeni 237, Cairo ^{1}I, 417, Makram 55.—e. *al-Manhal al-aṣfā* by Muḥammad b. Abi 'l-Sharīf al-Ḥasanī al-Tilimsānī, completed in 917/1511, Algiers 1678.—f. *Rafʿ al-khafāʾ ʿan dhāt al-Sh.* by al-Qāriʾ al-Harawī, d. 1014/1605 (II, 394), Paris 1958, Cairo ^{1}I, 359, ^{2}I, 126, Qawala I, 128/9,
456 | Patna I, $271_{,2250/1}$, print. Istanbul 1264, 1290, 1316, Būlāq 1257, C. 1264, 1325/7 (together with i.).—g. ʿAbd al-Raʾūf al-Munāwī, d. 1031/1622 (II, 306), Paris 1957.—h. *Manhaj al-wafāʾ* by Aḥmad b. Khalīl al-Subkī, d. 1037/1627, Gotha 720.—i. *Nasīm al-riyāḍ* by Aḥmad b. Muḥammad al-Khafājī, d. 1069/1659 (II, 285), Algiers 824/9, 1673/6, Yeni 238/40, Cairo ^{1}I, 443, Qawala I, 157, Patna I, $274_{,2277/80}$, printed in 4 vols. Istanbul, 1267, 1314, 1317, C. 1315/7.—k. Shihāb al-Dīn Aḥmad b. Raslān al-Ramlī, d. 844/1440 (II, 96), Algiers $1677_{,1}$.—l.–w. see Suppl.—Abstracts of the *ḥadīths*: a. *Manāhil al-ṣafāʾ* by al-Suyūṭī, d. 911/1505, Berl. 1434, Esc. ^{2}1796, Cairo ^{1}I, 428, Alex. Ḥad. 54, lith. C. 1276.—b.–c. see Suppl.
370 (c. Garr. 1441).—| Juridical adaptation *al-Hidāya wal-iʿlām fī-mā yatarattab ʿalā qabīḥ al-qawl min al-aḥkām* by Ibrāhīm b. Muḥammad al-Saʿdī al-Mālikī,

d. 778/1375, Cairo [1]I, 448.—2. *Kitāb al-ilmāʿ ilā maʿrifat uṣūl al-riwāya wa (taqyīd) al-samāʿ* (ḤKh [1]I, 1158, [2]I, 158, *al-Ilmāʿ fī ḍabṭ al-riwāya etc.*), on the theory of *ḥadīth*, published by one of his students, Esc. [2]1572, AS 433.—3. *Kitāb mashāriq al-anwār ʿalā ṣaḥīḥ (ṣaḥāʾiḥ, ṣiḥāḥ) al-āthār fī tafsīr gharīb al-ḥadīth*, on genuine traditions, Algiers 540, Cairo [1]I, 420, [2]I, 147, Qawala I, 150, Patna I, 61,$_{622}$, print. Fez 1328/9 (at the end of vol. 2: 1333), revision by Muḥammad b. Muṣṭafā b. Fatḥallāh al-Ḥamawī ca. 1148/1735, Garr. 2071,$_{3}$.—4. *Bughyat al-rāʾid fī-mā fī ḥadīth Umm Zarʿ min al-fawāʾid* Berl. 1567/8.—5. *Tartīb al-madārik wa-taqrīb al-masālik li-maʿrifat aʿlām madhhab Mālik*, *Br. Mus. Quart.* X, 134, Zaouiyah d'El Hamel, *Giorn. d. Soc. As. It.* X, 56, Codera and Zaidin, *Missión histórica en la Argelica y Tunez*, Madrid 1892, 174/5.—6. *Kitāb al-iʿlām bi-ḥudūd qawāʿid al-Islām* Esc. [2]1487,$_{1}$, Vat. V, 416,$_{12}$, *al-I. fī ḥudūd al-aḥkām*, a commentary by Abu 'l-ʿAbbās Aḥmad b. al-Qāsim al-Judhāmī al-Qabbāb, d. 779/1377 (Suppl. II, 347), Algiers 570, probably = the *ʿaqīda* with an anonymous commentary Cairo VII, 295.—7. *Qaṣīda* on sura 65,$_{7}$, Berl. 7691.—8.–13. see Suppl.

6. Abu 'l-ʿAbbās (Abū Jaʿfar) Aḥmad b. Maʿadd b. ʿĪsā b. Wakīl al-Tujībī al-Uqlīshī was born in Denia, and studied there and in Valencia. In 542/1147 he made the pilgrimage and then stayed for a number of years in Mecca. He untertook the return journey only in 547/1152, but died on the way in Qūṣ in Upper Egypt on 4 Ramaḍān 549/13 November 1154.

| Maqq. I, 872, cf. 809,$_{15}$. 1. *Kitāb al-kawkab al-durrī al-mustakhraj min kalām (kalim) al-nabī*, alphabetical abstract based on the 10 canonical collections, Berl. 1298, Leid. 373, Alex. Fun. 143,$_{1}$, Cairo [1]I, 392, [2]I, 141.—2. *Anwār al-āthār*, 40 traditions on the blessing of the Prophet, Br. Mus. Suppl. 157,$_{1}$.—3. *Kitāb al-najm min kalām sayyid al-ʿarab wal-ʿajam* Cairo [2]I, 442, [2]I, 157, [1]VII, 270, print. C. 1302 (see above p. 444).—4. *al-Durr al-munaẓẓam fī-mā yuzīl al-humūm wal-ghumūm* Cairo [1]VII, 467, [2]I, 294.—5.–6. see Suppl. 457

7. As a young man Abū ʿAbdallāh (Abū Bakr) Muḥammad b. ʿAlī b. Yasīr al-Anṣārī al-Jayyānī travelled to the East where he lived for a time in Damascus. In 520/1126 he went from there with Ibn ʿAsākir (p. 403) to Baghdad, then to Khurāsān and, by way of Mosul, back to Ḥalabiyya, where he died in 563/1167.

Maqq. I, 564. *Kitāb al-arbaʿīn min riwāyat al-Muḥammadīn*, composed in 557/1162, Paris 722,$_{3}$, Cairo [2]I, 88.

8. Abū Isḥāq Ibrāhīm b. Yūsuf b. Ibrāhīm b. ʿAbdallāh b. Bādīs al-Qāʾid al-Ḥamzī b. Qurqūl was born in Almería in 505/1111 and died in Fez in 569/1173.

371 | Ibn Khall. no. 18. *Kitāb maṭāliʿ al-anwār ʿalā ṣiḥāḥ al-āthār* (*fī gharīb al-ḥadīth*), following the example of Ibn ʿIyāḍ's *Kitāb mashāriq al-anwār* (see Suppl.). Abstracts: a. see Suppl.—b. *Tahdhīb al-maṭāliʿ* by Ibn Khaṭīb al-Dahsha, d. 834/1430 (II, 66), Cairo [1]I, 291, [2]I, 99, *Khātima*, Alex. Ḥad. 22, used by al-Suyūṭī, d. 911/1505, in his *Kitāb tuḥfat dhawi 'l-adab* (II, 149,$_{97}$).—c. see Suppl.—d. *Mushkil al-Ṣaḥīḥayn* (from the *Maṭāliʿ* and the *Mashāriq*) by ʿAbd al-ʿAzīz al-ʿAṣṣārī, Köpr. 334 (758 AH, Ritter).

9. Abū Ḥafṣ ʿUmar b. ʿAbd al-Majīd b. ʿUmar al-Qurashī al-Mayyānishī al-Mahdawī, who was born in Mayyānish, a village near al-Mahdiyya in Ifrīqiya, and died in Mecca, wrote, in 579/1183:

1. *Kitāb maʿrifat ma lā yasaʿu 'l-muḥaddithīn jahluhu* ḤKh V, 354, Leid. 1743.—2.–3. see Suppl.

10. Abū Muḥammad ʿAbd al-Ḥaqq b. ʿAbd al-Raḥmān b. ʿAbdallāh al-Azdī
458 al-Ishbīlī b. al-Kharrāṭ was born in Rabīʿ I 510/July | 1116, moved from Spain to Bijāya where he became an imam and a preacher, and died in Rabīʿ II 581/July 1185 after Abū Yūsuf Yaʿqūb had threatened to kill him because he refused to mention his name in the *khuṭba*.

Nawawī 375, *Fawāt* I, 248, *Ḥuff.* XVII, 4, Maqq. I, 807, II, 47, Wüst., *Gesch.* 274. 1. *Kitāb al-jamʿ bayna 'l-Ṣaḥīḥayn*, put together from Bukhārī and Muslim, Br. Mus. 1563, Cairo [1]I, 325, [2]I, 109, Patna I, 47,$_{473}$, see Goldziher, *MSt.* II, 270.—2. *Kitāb al-aḥkām*: a. *al-kubrā* Br. Mus. 1574, Garr. 376, Alex. Ḥad. 4, Cairo, [1]260, [2]84, Patna I, 37,$_{375}$.—b. *al-wusṭā* Cairo [1]I, 261.—c. *al-ṣughrā* Br. Mus. 1593, Cairo [1]I, 261. Criticism: *Kitāb al-wahm wal-īhām al-wāqiʿayn fī Kitāb al-aḥkām* by Ibn al-Qaṭṭān al-Fāsī, d. 628/1230 (whose *Masāʾil al-muṭāraḥāt* are preserved in Ind. Off. 1777), Cairo [1]I, 450, [2]I, 161.—3. *Kitāb al-ʿāqiba fī 'l-baʿth* (*fī aḥwāl al-ākhira*), reflections on death, traditions, passages from the Qurʾān, aphorisms, pious verses etc., Berl. 2652/4, Leid. 2008, Yeni 725.—4.–5. see Suppl.

11. (12). As a preacher and *qāḍī*, Abu 'l-Rabīʿ Sulaymān b. Mūsā b. Sālim al-Kalāʿī, born in Murcia on 3 Ramaḍān 565/22 May 1172, actively participated in the struggle against the Christians and died in battle against James I the Conquerer on 20 Dhu 'l-Ḥijja 634/16 August 1237, near Ānisha (Inja), not far from Valencia.

Ḥuff. XVIII, 15, Maqq. II, 768, Wüst., *Gesch.* 320, al-Kattānī, *Fihris* I, 367. *Kitāb al-iktifāʾ bi-mā taḍammanahu min maghāzī rasūl Allāh ṣlʿm wa-maghāzi 'l-thalātha al-khulafā'* Berl. 9575, Paris 1568/9, Br. Mus. 918, 1277, Algiers 1577/84, Garr. 639, Alex. Ta'r. 4.

| 12. (14). Abu 'l-Makārim b. Abī Aḥmad b. Musdī al-Azdī al-Andalusī al-Gharnāṭī, 372
who was born in 599/1202 in Wādī Āsh and died in Mecca on 10 Shawwāl 663/27 July 1267.

Al-Arbaʿūn al-mukhtāra fī faḍl al-ḥajj wal-ziyāra Cairo ^{1}I, 264 (attributed by others to Jamāl al-Dīn Abū Bakr Muḥammad b. Yūsuf b. al-Mughīra).

13. (15). ʿAbdallāh b. Saʿd (Saʿīd) b. Abi 'l-ʿAbbās Aḥmad b. Abī Jamra (Ḥamza?) al-Azdī al-Andalusī, who died in Cairo in 699/1300 (or, according to others, in 675/1276 or 695).

| 1. *Kitāb jamʿ al-nihāya*, see p. 166 (Suppl. I, 263).—2. *Kitāb al-marā'ī* 459
(*al-ḥisān*), a collection of dreams proving the excellence of his commentary on no. 1, the *Bahjat al-nufūs*, Br. Mus. 1468,$_{4}$, Cairo ^{1}I, 416, Patna I, 59,$_{600}$.—3. see Suppl.

14. (16). Shihāb al-Dīn Abu 'l-ʿAbbās (Abu 'l-Qāsim) Aḥmad b. Muḥammad b. Faraḥ al-Lakhmī al-Ishbīlī was born in 625/1227, taken prisoner by the Franks in 646/1248, and after his release in the fifties of that century, went to Cairo, where he died in Jumādā II 699/March 1300.

Maqq. I, 819. 1. *Qaṣīda (manẓūma) ghazaliyya fī alqāb al-ḥadīth*, in which the technical vocabulary from the science of *ḥadīth* is used for puns, Berl. 1049/50, Leid. 83, Algiers 377,$_{3}$, 701,$_{4}$, Alex. Muṣṭ. Ḥad. 15, Fun. 198,$_{8}$.—Commentaries: 1. *Zawāl al-taraḥ* by ʿIzz al-Dīn Muḥammad b. Abī Bakr b. Jamāʿa, d. 816/1413 (II, 94), Berl. 1051/4 Paris 746,$_{2}$, Garr. 1454/5, Alex. Muṣṭ. Ḥad. 15, Fun. 123,$_{5}$, 145,$_{2}$, edited with explanations by F. Risch, Leiden 1885.—2. *al-Bahja al-saniyya* by Muḥammad b. Ibrāhīm b. Khalīl al-Tatā'ī, d. 937/1540 (II, 316), Cairo ^{2}I, 250.—3. Yaḥyā b. ʿAbd al-Raḥmān al-Iṣfahānī al-Qarāfī al-Zabīdī, composed in 962/1555, Berl. 1056/8, Paris 4257,$_{1}$, Algiers 546, 995,$_{2}$, Cairo ^{1}I, 249, Alex. Muṣṭ. Ḥad. 14, Fun. 123,$_{4}$.—4. Muḥammad b. Muḥammad b. al-Amīr al-Kabīr, d. 1232/1816 (II, 328), Berl. 1059, Alex. Muṣṭ. Ḥad. 11.—5. Anon., Berl. 1055 (after 894/1488), 1060/1 (dated 887/1482), 1062, Gotha 578.—6.–14. see Suppl.

Chapter 7. *Fiqh*

1 *The Ḥanafīs*

1. Aḥmad b. Muḥammad b. ʿUmar al-Nāṭifī, who died in Rayy in 444/1054.

Ibn Quṭlūbughā 16. 1. *Kitāb al-aḥkām fi ʾl-fiqh al-Ḥanafī* Cairo ^{1}III, 111. = *Jumal al-aḥkām* Br. Mus. Suppl. 275 ii, Garr. 2129, Alex. Fiqh Ḥan. 4.—2. *al-Rawḍa fi ʾl-furūʿ* ḤKh ^{1}III, 509$_{,6668}$, ^{2}I, 931, Alex. Fiqh Ḥan. 29.

2. Abū Muḥammad ʿAbdallāh b. al-Ḥusayn al-Nāṣihī, a *qāḍī* in Bukhārā who died in 447/1055 (see Suppl.).

460 | Ibn Quṭl. 90. *Jamʿ* (*Mukhtaṣar*) *Waqfay al-Hilāl wal-Khaṣṣāf* (p. 181) Yeni 351.—2. see Suppl.

2a. Abu ʾl-Ḥasan (Ḥusayn) ʿAlī b. al-Ḥusayn b. Muḥammad al-Ṣughdī, the Shaykh al-Islām in Bukhārā, died in 461/1069.

Cf. Suppl. *Nutaf al-fatāwī* additionally Alex. Fiqh Ḥan. 69.

3. Abū ʿAbdallāh Muḥammad b. ʿAlī b. Muḥammad b. al-Hasan (Ḥusayn) al-Dāmaghānī, *qāḍi ʾl-quḍāt*, was born in Dāmaghān in Rabīʿ II 398/December 1007 and died on 24 Rajab 478/16 November 1085 (see Suppl.).

1. *Kitāb masāʾil al-ḥīṭān wal-ṭuruq*, legal claims involving ownership of walls, corridors, water courses etc., Berl. 4982.—2. *al-Zawāʾid wal-naẓāʾir wa-fawāʾid al-baṣāʾir* (*fī gharīb al-Qurʾān*) ḤKh III, 543$_{,6871}$, Cairo ^{1}I, 176 (anon.).

4. Abu ʾl-Ḥasan ʿAlī b. Muḥammad al-Pazdawī Fakhr al-Islām, who was born around 400/1009 and died in 482/1089 in Samarqand.

Ibn Quṭl. 122, Flügel, *Classen* 275, 307. 1. *Kanz al-wuṣūl ilā maʿrifat al-uṣūl* Berl. 4369/70, Paris 836, 4541, Br. Mus. Suppl. 258, Ind. Off. 1423/5, Pet. Rosen 16, Garr. 1677, Rāġib 364/5, Yeni 305/7, Cairo ^{1}II, 236, Qawala I, 273, Patna I, 66$_{,682/3}$.—Commentaries: a. Sulaymān b. Aḥmad al-Sindī, Cairo ^{1}II, 248, ^{2}I, 389 (MS dated 689/1298).—b. al-Ḥusayn b. ʿAlī al-Samʿānī, d. 704/1304, Yeni 324.—c. *Kashf al-asrār* by ʿAbd al-ʿAzīz b. Aḥmad al-Bukhārī, d. 730/1329 (II, 198), Yeni 325/30, Qawala I, 293, Patna I, 74$_{,751/3}$, print. Istanbul 1307.—d. *al-Taqrīr* by Muḥammad b. Maḥmūd al-Bābartī, d. 786/1384 (II, 80), Yeni 323, Cairo ^{1}II, 241, Qawala I, 275.—e. Anon. Berl. 4371, Ind. Off. 1426/7.—f.–i. see

Suppl., 8 commentaries and glosses mentioned in Ahlw.—2. *Risāla fī qirāʾat al-muṣallī wa-mā yataʿallaq bihā* Cairo ^{1}III, 114.—3.–6. see Suppl.—7. *Zallat al-qāriʾ* Köpr. III, 3, 1.

5. Shams al-Aʾimma Abū Bakr Muḥammad b. Abī Sahl Aḥmad al-Sarakhsī, who died in 483/1090 (see Suppl.).

Ibn Quṭl. 157, 477, Flügel, *Cl.* p. 303. 1. *Kitāb al-uṣūl* Gotha 997, Cairo ^{1}II, 237, ^{2}I, 378.—2. *Kitāb al-mabsūṭ fi ʾl-furūʿ* (see Suppl.), in 15 vols., ḤKh ^{1}V, 11323, Br. Mus. Suppl. 276/7, Ind. Off. 204, 1523, Ibr. Pāshā 648/51, Yeni | 542/4, Cairo 461
^{1}III, 109, Calcutta 349, As. Soc. p. 18, Buhār 151, printed in 30 *juzʾ*, C. 1324/31.—3. *Kitāb ashrāṭ al-sāʿa*, on the signs of the Day of Judgement, Paris 2800,$_{24}$.—4.–6. see Suppl.

5a. His student Muḥammad b. Ibrāhīm b. Anūsh al-Ḥaṣīrī, who died in 500/1106.

Al-Ḥāwī fi ʾl-fiqh (*furūʿ*), which contains legal opinions of many *fuqahāʾ* and which is regarded as one of the foundational works of the Ḥanafīs, ḤKh ^{1}III, 5,$_{4378}$, ^{2}I, 624, Berl. Qu. 1661 (in Suppl. 653 mistakenly attributed to no. 36), Garr. 1686 (with the wrong name, following no. 36), Alex. Fiqh Ḥan. 22, possibly also Qilič ʿA. 484, see ʿAbd al-Qādir, *al-Jawāhir al-muḍīʾa* II, 2.

6. Abu ʾl-Qāsim ʿAlī b. Muḥammad b. Aḥmad al-Simanānī, who died in 493/1100 (see Suppl.).

1. *Kitāb rawḍat al-quḍāt wa-ṭarīq al-najāt* or *Adab al-qāḍī*, completed in 478/1085, details everything a *qāḍī* should know, ḤKh ^{1}II, 510,$_{6676}$, ^{2}I, 931 (attributed to Fakhr al-Dīn al-Zaylaʿī, d. 743/1342, II, 78), Cairo ^{1}III, 62.—2. see Suppl.

7. Abū Yaʿqūb Yūsuf b. ʿAlī b. Muḥammad al-Jurjānī wrote, in 522/1128:

Kitāb khizānat al-akmal fi ʾl-furūʿ Yeni 413/5, ^{1}III, 43 (see Suppl.), Patna I, 86,$_{874}$.

8. Aḥmad b. Muḥammad b. Abī Bakr al-Ḥanafī, who died in 522/1128.

1. *Khizānat al-fatāwā fi ʾl-furūʿ* Yeni 606/7, Alex. Fiqh Ḥan. 23 (anon. abstract of 2.)—2. *Majmaʿ al-fatāwī* Sulaim. 684, Alex. Fiqh Ḥan. 51.—3. see Suppl.

9. Abū Muḥammad ʿAbd al-ʿAzīz b. ʿUthmān al-Faḍlī al-Qāḍī al-Nasafī was a *qāḍī* and *muftī* in Khurāsān who died in Rabīʿ I 533/November 1138.

Ibn Quṭl. 105. *Kitāb kifāyat al-fuḥūl fī ʿilm al-uṣūl* ḤKh v. 10785, mistakenly identified with Gotha 643 by Pertsch.

10. Ḥusām al-Dīn ʿUmar b. ʿAbd al-ʿAzīz b. Māza al-Ṣadr al-Shahīd al-Bukhārī, who was born in 483/1090 and died on 5 Ṣafar 536/10 September 1141 (see Suppl.).

462 | Ibn Quṭl. 139. 1. *Kitāb uṣūl al-fiqh* Ind. Off. 1429 (? Berl. 4372 is rather *al-Ḥusāmī*, p. 381, see Ind. Off. 1438).—2. *al-Wāqiʿāt al-Ḥusāmiyya fī madhhab al-Ḥanafiyya*, legal cases and decisions, organised by the usual chapters of the *furūʿ*, Gotha 1144, Yeni 689/90.—3. *Kitāb ʿumdat al-fatāwā* Berl. 4812, Brill, M. 290 = *ʿUmdat al-muftī* (*wal-mustaftī*) Br. Mus. Suppl. 278, Cairo ^{1}III, 81 = Gotha 1041?.—4. *Kitāb al-fatāwa ʾl-kubrā* Yeni 639/40, Patna I, $99_{,1008}$.—5. *al-Fatāwa ʾl-ṣughrā* ibid. 657/9, Garr. 1687, Patna I, $98_{,991}$.—6. *al-Fatāwi ʾl-Khāṣṣiyya*, ed. Yūsuf al-Khāṣṣī, ca. 620/1223, Cairo ^{1}III, 89[1], see below p. $380_{,31}$.—7. *Kitāb masāʾil daʿwa ʾl-ḥīṭān wal-ṭuruq wa-masīl al-māʾ*, a sequel to the work by al-Dāmaghānī (no. 3), Berl. 4983.—8. *Kitāb masāʾil ṭabkh al-ʿaṣīr* Leid. 1789.—9. Revised edition of *al-Jāmiʿ al-ṣaghīr* by al-Shaybānī, see p. 179, Qawala I, 316.—10., 11. see Suppl.

11. ʿAlāʾ al-Dīn al-Manṣūr Muḥammad b. Aḥmad al-Samarqandī Abū Bakr, who died in 538/1144.

1. *Kitāb tuḥfat al-fuqahāʾ* Yeni 374, Patna I, 81_{818}, commentary *Badāʾiʿ al-ṣanāʾiʿ fī tartīb al-sharāʾiʿ* by Abū Bakr Masʿūd b. Aḥmad al-Kāshānī, d. 587/1191 (no. 22), Berl. 447/9, Yeni 370/3, Cairo ^{1}II, 12, abstract *Zād al-ghāʾib al-ḍāʾiʿ min B. al-sh.* by Muḥammad al-Bardīnī al-Ḥusaynī al-Ḥanafī, with a *taqrīẓ* of the ʿAbbāsid caliph al-Mutawakkil from the year 925/1519, *RAAD* IX, 308.—2., 3. see Suppl.—4. *Mīzān al-uṣūl fī natāʾij al-ʿuqūl* Garr. 1626.

12. Ṭāhir b. Aḥmad b. ʿAbd al-Rashīd al-Bukhārī Iftikhār al-Dīn, who died in 542/1147 in Bukhārā.

1. *Kitāb khizānat al-fatāwā* Cairo ^{1} III, 44.—2. *Kitāb khulāṣat al-fatāwā* Paris 840, Landb.-Br. 654, Ind. Off. 205, Yeni 610/2, Garr. 1688/90, Alex. Fiqh Ḥan. 24, Cairo ^{1}III, (see Suppl.), Patna I, $87_{,881}$ = Bank. XX, 1616.

---

1 Where he is confused with Muwaffaq b. Muḥammmad al-Khāṣṣī, d. 634/1237 (Ibn Quṭl. no. 238).

13. Rukn al-Dīn Abu 'l-Faḍl ʿAbd al-Raḥmān b. Muḥammad al-Kirmānī, who was born in Kirmān in Shawwāl 457/1063, studied in Marw and died there on 20 Dhu 'l-Qaʿda 543/2 April 1149.

| Ibn Quṭl. 96. 1. *Kitāb al-īḍāḥ fi 'l-furūʿ*, commentary thereon Yeni 369.— 463
2. *Fatāwā Abi 'l-Faḍl* ibid. 626.—3. see Suppl.

13a. His student Rukn al-Dīn Abū Bakr Muḥammad b. Abi 'l-Mafākhir ʿAbd al-Rashīd b. Naṣr b. Muḥammad b. Ibrāhīm b. Isḥāq Abū Bakr Rukn al-Dīn al-Kirmānī wrote, in 577/1181:

Jawāhir al-fatāwī, in which he mainly collected the fatwas of his teacher and of al-Muṭahhar b. al-Ḥusayn al-Yazdī, d. 591/1195 (see Suppl. I, 296,$_{5}$), ḤKh II, 644,$_{6490}$, ^{2}I, 615, Br. Mus. Or. 6906 (DL 23), Qawala I, 318, Rāmpur I, 184,$_{133/4}$.

14. Raḍī al-Dīn Muḥammad b. Muḥammad al-Sarakhsī, a student of Ḥuṣām al-Dīn (no. 10), had teaching positions at two academies in Aleppo but was fired by Nūr al-Dīn after being accused of plagiarising his teacher in his magnus opus *al-Muḥīṭ al-Raḍawī*. He then went to Damascus, | where he taught at 375
the Khātūniyya, dying there in 544/1149.

Flügel p. 317. 1. *Kitāb al-muḥīṭ al-Raḍawī* in 2 vols., Ind. Off. 206/7, Garr. 1691, Alex. Fiqh Ḥan. 61, Yeni 561/3, Patna I, 103,$_{1047}$. Abstract, *al-Wajīz al-muḥīṭ*, Bank. XIX, 1619 = Patna I, 118,$_{1018}$, with the title *Wasīṭ al-muḥīṭ* Bank. XIX, 1718.—2. *al-Ṭarīqa al-Raḍawiyya* Munich 330, Cairo ^{1}III, 79, 125, 444, 460.—3. *al-Wajīz* Leipz. 199, Mosul 64,$_{225}$, Alex. Fiqh Ḥan. 72 (attributed to Burhān al-Dīn Maḥmūd b. Aḥmad al-Bukhārī, d. 616/1119).

15. Aḥmad b. Mūsā b. ʿĪsā al-Kashshī wrote, around 550/1155:

Kitāb majmaʿ al-nawāzil wal-ḥawādith wal-wāqiʿāt Yeni 547/8.

16. Abu 'l-Fatḥ ʿAlā' al-Dīn Muḥammad b. ʿAbd al-Ḥamīd b. al-Ḥasan al-Usmandī al-Samarqandī, who died in 552/1157 (see Suppl.).

Mukhtalif al-riwāya Patna I, 105,$_{1103}$, with the title *Ṭarīqat al-khilāf bayna 'l-a'imma* Qawala I, 368.

17. His student Asʿad b. Muḥammad al-Karābīsī al-Nīsābūrī Jamāl al-Dīn Abu 'l-Muẓaffar, who died in 570/1174.

464 | *Kitāb al-furūq fi 'l-furūʿ* Cairo ^{1}III, 96, ^{2}I 451.

18. Burhān al-Dīn (al-Islām) Maḥmūd b. Aḥmad b. al-Ṣadr al-Shahīd (no. 10) al-Bukhārī b. Māza, who was born in Marghinān in 551/1156 and died in 616/1219.[2]

1. *Kitāb al-muḥīṭ al-Burhānī fi 'l-fiqh al-Nuʿmānī* Yeni 549/60, Alex. Fiqh Ḥan 60, Cairo ^{1}III, 125, ^{2}I, 460.—2. *Kitāb al-dhakhīra al-Burhāniyya*, according to ḤKh an abstract of 1., Yeni 613/8, Cairo ^{1}III, 51, ^{2}I, 421, Patna I, $88_{,891/3}$.—3. *Tatimmat al-fatāwī* Yeni 597.

19. Rukn al-Islām Sadīd al-Dīn Muḥammad b. Abī Bakr al-Bukhārī Imāmzāde al-Sharghī, who was born in Rabīʿ I 491/February 1098 and died in Bukhārā in 573/1177.

I. *Kitāb sharīʿat (shirʿat) al-islām ilā dār al-salām* Berl. 1730/3, Krafft 429, Bodl. II, 82, Pet. 44, AM 109, *Cat. Ital.* p. 213, no. 35, Ind. Off. 1524, Garr. 1693/5, Mosul $63_{,193}$, $156_{,86}$, $175_{,74/5}$, $232_{,88}$, Alex. Taṣ. 22, Qawala I, 248.—Commentaries: 1. *Mafātīḥ al-jinān wa-maṣābīḥ al-janān* by Yaʿqūb b. ʿAlī al-Rūmī al-Burūsawī, d. 931/1524, Berl. 1734/5, Paris 1248/9, Br. Mus. Suppl. 178/9, Ind. Off. 209, 1526, Pet. 80, Algiers 575/6, Yeni 711, Garr. 1696, Alex. Mawāʿiẓ 44, Taṣ. 45, Qawala I, 264, Patna I, $106_{,1072}$, print. Istanbul 1306, 1326, with the title *Asrār al-aḥkām*, Patna II, $515_{,2767}$.—2. *Murshid al-anām ilā dār al-salām* by Muḥammad b. ʿUmar Qurd Efendi, d. 996/1588, Berl. 736, Leipz. 214.—3. Yaḥyā b. Yaʿīsh, Paris 1250.—4. *Asrār al-aḥkām* by Muḥammad Yaʿqūb al-Banbānī, completed in 1081/1670, Ind. Off. 1525.—4a., 5. see Suppl.—6. Anon. Mosul $127_{,90}$.—II, III see Suppl.

20. Nūr al-Dīn Aḥmad b. Maḥmūd b. Abī Bakr al-Ṣābūnī al-Bukhārī, who died in Bukhārā on 16 Ṣafar 580/30 May 1184.

Ibn Quṭl. 20. *Kitāb al-kifāya fi 'l-hidāya*, abstract of *al-Bidāya min al-kifāya*, Berl. 1737, Garr. 862/3 (see Suppl.), anon. *Ḥāshiya*, Ind. Off. 1714.

465 | 21. Zayn al-Dīn Abū Naṣr (Abū ʿUmar) Aḥmad b. Muḥammad b. ʿUmar al-ʿAttābī al-Bukhārī, who died in Bukhārā in 586/1190.

---

2 According to Ahlw. $4436_{,2}$, $4851_{,4}$ ca. 570/1174. *Faw. al-bah.* 85, ḤKh V, 431 without date, Cat. Yeni: d. 536. Because of a confusion with his father, the catalogues of Cairo and Alexandria give the above dates without source reference; what supports the above date is the fact that he made the pilgrimage as late as the year 603/1206.

Kitāb jāmiʿ al-fiqh or *al-Fatāwi ʾl-ʿAttābiyya* Cairo [1]III, 111, [2]I, 414.

22. Abū Bakr Masʿūd b. Aḥmad al-Kāsānī was a student and the son-in-law of ʿAlāʾ al-Dīn al-Samarqandī (no. 11). At the court of the Saljūq ruler Masʿūd I in Qonya he had made himself impossible as a result of his obsessive arguing. As such, he was sent, on the advice of the vizier, as an envoy to Nūr al-Dīn in Aleppo (after 541/1146). There he was received with all honours and appointed as professor of Ḥanafī *fiqh* in the newly founded (543/1148) Madrasa Ḥalawiyya, replacing al-Sarakhsī (no. 14), who was not up to the task because of a speech defect. He died on 10 Rajab 587/3 August 1191.

| Ibn Quṭl. no. 262, Heffening, EI *Erg.* 115/6. 1. *Kitāb badāʾiʿ al-ṣanāʾiʿ fī tartīb* 376
al-sharāʾiʿ, supposedly a commentary on the *Tuḥfa* of his teacher that served him as a dowry when he married his daughter, but in truth a more independent work of a rigidly systematic structure, ḤKh II, 235, print. C. 1327/8, 7 vols.—2. *Kitāb al-taʾwīlāt*, a Qurʾān commentary, Rāġib 32/4.

23. Fakhr al-Dīn al-Ḥasan b. Manṣūr al-Ūzjandī al-Farghānī Qāḍīkhān, who died on 15 Ramaḍān 592/13 August 1196.

Ibn Quṭl. 16, 56, Flügel p. 314. 1. *Fatāwā Qāḍīkhān*, vol. I, Gotha 999 (where other MSS are listed), vol. IV, Berl. 4813, Ind. Off. 1643/8, Alex. Fiqh Ḥan. 67, Qawala I, 378, Bank. XIX, 1623/6 = Patna I, 98,$_{1004/7}$.—Abstracts: a. *Maḥkama* by Ashraf b. Yūsuf Īnāl al-Ṭirāzī, d. 761/1360, Cairo [1]III, 124, [2]I, 460.—b. Anon. *Muntakhab*, Alex. Fiqh Ḥan. 67.—c. *Munyat al-dalāʾil etc.* see Suppl.—2. *Kitāb masāʾil al-ghurūr*, on fraud in business deals, Berl. 4984.—3.–4. see Suppl.[3]

| 24. ʿAlī b. Abī Bakr b. ʿAbd al-Jalīl al-Farghānī al-Marghīnānī al-Rishtānī 466
Burhān al-Dīn, who died in 593/1197.

Ibn Quṭl. 124, Flügel 316, Krafft, *Wiener Jahrb.* 110, *Anz. Bl.* p. 27; anon. biography *al-ʿIqd al-thamīn* Garr. 2102$_2$. I. *Bidāyat al-mubtadiʾ*, a compendium of the *furūʿ*, mainly based on al-Shaybānī's *al-Jāmiʿ al-ṣaghīr* (S. 179) and al-Qudūrī's *Mukhtaṣar* (p. 183), Berl. 4487, Leid. 1799, Ind. Off. 1538/48, Garr. 1697 Cairo [1]III, 16, Qawala I, 406/7, Mosul 159,$_{144}$.—Commentaries: 1. Self-commentary, *al-Hidāya*, Berl. 4488/9, Vienna 1779, Munich 268/73, Leid. 1800, Paris 842/4, Br.

3 The works attributed to him in Derenbourg, Esc. [2]405, 4, 5, 7 are by an author of the tenth century at the earliest; one would think of al-Muttaqī al-Hindī (II, 384) were it not for the fact that he is named al-Ḥasan in 405, 4.

Mus. 196/8, Ind. Off. 211/7, Algiers 985/6, Garr. 1698/1700, Cairo ^{1}III, 149, Patna I, 109,$_{1100/4}$, print. Calcutta 1234, 2 vols., Kazan 1888 (cf. Suppl.), see Reinaud, *JA* 1833, I, 71. *Hedayah or Guide, a commentary on the moossoolman Laws*, transl. by Ch. Hamilton, London 1791 (based on the Persian translation by Ghulām Yaḥyā, made in 1190/1776, print. Calcutta 1807, see Rieu, *Pers. Cat.* 23/4), 2nd ed. with Pref. by S.G. Grady, London 1870.—Super-commentaries: 1. Ḥamīd al-Dīn ʿAlī b. Muḥammad al-Ḍarīr al-Bukhārī, born in 666/1268 (Ibn Quṭl. 136), Ind. Off. 1549.—1a. ʿUmar b. Muḥammad al-Khabbāzī, d. 691/1292 (p. 476), according to ḤKh VI, 482, 14366, completed by Muḥammad b. Aḥmad al-Qūnawī, d. 764/1362, with the title *Takmilat al-fawāʾid*, Berl. 4491, Yeni 406.—2. *Nihāyat al-kifāya li-dirāyat al-Hidāya* by Tāj al-Sharīʿa ʿUmar b. Ṣadr al-Sharīʿa al-Awwal (p. 473), composed in 694/1295,[4] Cairo ^{1}III, 146.—3. (4.) *al-Nihāya* by Ḥusayn b. ʿAlī al-Sighnāqī, d. 710/1310 (II, 116), completed in 700/1300, Ind. Off. 218, Alex. Fiqh Ḥan. 70, Cairo ^{1}III, 148, Patna I, 94,$_{5920}$, on which *Khulāṣat al-N.* by Maḥmūd b. Aḥmad al-Qūnawī, see II, 81.—4. (5.) *al-Kifāya* by Maḥmūd b. ʿUbaydallāh b. Tāj al-Sharīʿa al-Maḥbūbī, d. 745/1344, Yeni 509, 517 Patna I, 103,$_{1036}$.[5]—5. (6.) *Miʿrāj al-dirāya* by Muḥammad b. Muḥammad al-Sinjārī al-Kākī, d. 749/1348, Paris 845, 5444/6, Cairo ^{1}III, 132.—6. (7.) *Ghāyat al-bayān* by Amīr Kātib b. Amīr ʿUmar b. Amīr Ghāzī al-Itqānī, d. 758/1357 (II, 79), commenced in 721/1321 in Cairo, continued in Arrān and Baghdad, and completed in 747/1346 in Damascus (ḤKh VI, 483), Berl. 4492, Yeni 490/502, Cairo ^{1}III, 83, Patna I, 96,$_{970/4}$.—7. (8.) *al-ʿInāya* by Akmal al-Dīn Muḥammad b. Maḥmūd al-Bābartī, d. 786/1384 (II, 80), Berl. 4493, Ind. Off. 219, Garr. 1746/8, Yeni 487/9, 511,
467 Cairo ^{1}III, 81, | Qawala I, 371, Alex. Fiqh Ḥan. 38, Patna I, 95,$_{915/6}$, ed. Moonshee Ramdhan Len, Calcutta 1831, 1837, 1840. Glosses thereon: a. Saʿdallāh ʿĪsā Saʿdī, d. 945/1538, completed by his student ʿAbd al-Raḥmān, Berl. 4494, Br. Mus. Suppl. 279, Cairo ^{1}III, 37, Qawala I, 321.—b. Abu ʾl-Suʿūd Muḥammad b. Ibrāhīm al-Durūrī, d. 1066/1655, Yeni 405.—8. (9.) *al-Nihāya* by Maḥmūd b. Aḥmad al-ʿAynī, d. 855/1451 (II, 52), Algiers 987/8, Yeni 512/4.—9. (10.) *Fatḥ al-qadīr lil-ʿājiz al-faqīr* by Muḥammad b. ʿAbd al-Wāḥid b. al-Humām, d. 861/1457 (II, 82), commenced in 829/1424, Berl. Ms. Or. Qu. 2068, Paris 850, Ind. Off. 1650, Yeni 503/8, Qawala I, 380, Bank. XIX 1643/9 = Patna I, 99,$_{1011/6}$, *As. Soc. Beng.* 1904, p. 17, on which a *Dhayl* by Shams A. Qāḍīzāde, d. 988/1580, Yeni 377, Tunis, Zayt. IV 260,$_{2429}$, Qawala I, 403.—10. (11.) *Nihāyat al-Nihāya* by Muḥammad b. Muḥammad b. al-Shiḥna, d. 890/1485 (II, 42), Yeni 510.—
377 11. (12.) on particular passages by Sulaymān b. Kamālpāshā, | d. 940/1553, Berl. 4497, Leid. 1808, *Kitāb al-ḥajj*, Alex. Fiqh Ḥan. 33.—12. (13.) ʿArabzāde,

---

4 According ḤKh VI, 482, 2 it was completed in 673/1274 in Kirman.

5 *Tashīl al-hidāya etc.*, Suppl. I, 644, ab penultimo, see p. 485.

d. 950/1543, Yeni 405.—13. (14.) Sinān Efendi, d. 980/1572, Gotha 1000, on the *Kitāb al-karāhiya* and the *Kitāb al-waṣāyā*, Alex. Fiqh Ḥan. 21 (where it is stated that he died in 965).—14. (15.) *Taʿlīqāt* by Abu 'l-Suʿūd al-ʿImādī, d. 982/1574 (II, 438), Yeni 372.—15. (16.) Muḥammad b. Muṣṭafā Shaykhzāde, d. 951/1544 (II, 438), ḤKh VI, 490, Berl. 4498 (mistakenly ca. 1000/1591).—16. (17.) Zakariyyāʾ b. Bayrām, d. 1001/1592, Berl. 4499, on the *Bāb al-wakāla*, Bank. XIX, 1, 1649.—17. (18) ʿAbd al-Ḥalīm Akhīzāde, d. 1013/1604, Berl. 4495.—18. (19.) Ismāʿīl b. al-Yāzijī, d. 1121/1709, Berl. 4496.—19. (20.) ʿAbd al-Ghanī al-Nābulusī, d. 1143/1730 (II, 345), Berl. 4500.—20. (21.) Sayyid Efendi, Leid. 1807.—21. (22.) *al-Kifāya* by Jalāl al-Dīn b. Shams al-Dīn al-Karlānī al-Khwārizmī, Berl. Brill M. 300, Cairo ^{1}III, 104 (MS dated 748/1347), print. Bombay 1280, 4 vols., 1288.—22. (23.) Anon., Berl. 4501/2, Garr. 1702.—23.–42. see Suppl. (30. 1. al-Ḥamawī, 33. Garr. 1701).—43. *Risāla fi 'l-ghaṣb min Kitāb al-Hidāya* by Ḥinnālīzāde, d. 979/1572 (II, 433), Qawala I, 348.—44. *Risāla fī tafsīr baʿḍ masāʾil al-H. min k. al-rahn* by Walī b. Yūsuf al-ʿImādī, composed in 988/1580, ibid. I, 342.—Abstracts covering traditions: a. *Naṣb al-rāya* (Suppl. 42, Patna I, $188_{,1094}$), abstract *al-Dirāya fī takhrīj aḥādīth al-H.* by Ibn Ḥajar al-ʿAsqalānī, d. 852/1448 (II, 67), Pet. $81_{,4}$ Cairo ^{1}I, 239, cf. V, 132, Patna I, $87_{,883}$, print. Delhi 1882.—b. *Takhrīj aḥ. al-H.* by Muḥammad b. Abi 'l-Wafāʾ, d. 775/1373, Yeni 261, Cairo ^{1}I, 283.—c. the same by ʿAbdallāh b. Muḥammad al-Zaylaʿī, d. 762/1362 (Suppl. II, 232), Cairo ^{1}I, 283.—| 28 commentaries, 18 glosses, 4 abstracts, 3 abstracts of the *ḥadīth*s are mentioned in Ahlw. 4503.— 468

Abstracts: 1. *Wiqāyat al-riwāya fī masāʾil al-Hidāya* (sometimes mistakenly referred to as a commentary) by Burhān al-Dīn (al-Sharīʿa) Ṣadr al-Sharīʿa al-Awwal ʿUbaydallāh b. Maḥmūd b. Muḥammad al-Maḥbūbī, seventh cent., Berl. 4491, Ind. Off. 1559/61, Garr. 1680/2, Br. Mus. Suppl. 285, Qawala I, 408, Patna I, $109_{,1099}$.—Commentaries: a. His grandson ʿUbaydallāh b. Masʿūd Ṣadr al-Sharīʿa al-Thānī al-Maḥbūbī, d. 747/1346 (II, 214), Berl. 4548/9, Ms. Or. Qu. 2071/2, BDMG 356, Gotha 1024 (where other MSS are listed), Br. Mus. Suppl. 287, Ind. Off. 1577/91, Garr. 1744/5, Qawala I, 362/3, Bank. XIX, 1654/7, Rāmpūr 304/9, print. Lucknow 1883 (see Suppl.).—Glosses: α *Dhakhīrat al-ʿuqbā* by Akhī Čelebī Yūsuf b. Junayd Tūqātī, d. 905/1499 (II, 227), Berl. 4552/3, Ind. Off. 231/2, 1592/3, Yeni 401/2, Alex. Fiqh Ḥan. 20, 26, Qawala I, 335, Tunis Zayt. IV, $120_{,2052/4}$, Mosul $62_{,178}$, $96_{,70}$, Calc. Madr. 306, Patna I, $85_{,859/60}$, II, $506_{,2722}$, print. Calcutta 1245, Lucknow 1304.—αα Muḥammad Khaṭībzāde al-Rūmī, d. 901/1495 (II, 229), Esc. $^{2}236_{,10}$.—β Ibrāhīm b. Muḥammad ʿIṣām al-Dīn al-Isfarāʾinī, d. 944/1537 (II, 410), Ind. Off. 1594, Alex. Fiqh Ḥan. 20, Qawala I, 324, Āṣaf. 1082.—γ Qara Ḥasan al-Ḥamīdī, composed in 959/1552, Leid. 1804, Yeni 403.—γγ al-Taftāzānī (see Suppl.), Patna I, $85_{,861}$.—δ Yaʿqūb Pāshā b. Khiḍr Bek, d. 891/1480, | Berl. 4550, Paris 914/6, Algiers 1015, Alex. Fiqh 378

Ḥan. 21.—ε Zakariyyā' b. Bayrām al-Muftī, d. 1001/1592, Gotha 1025.—ζ Dede Efendi, Paris 922.—η Sinān Efendi, d. 986/1578, Berl. 4554.—ϑ Ṭūrsūn b. Murād, d. 966/1588, ibid. 4557.—ι Anon. ibid. 4555/6.—κ–ββ see Suppl. (κ Garr. 1684).—γγ Sayyid Mahdī al-Ḥanafī, Patna I, 85_{862}.—b. ʿIzz al-Dīn Muḥammad b. ʿAbd al-Laṭīf b. ʿAbd al-ʿAzīz b. al-Malak, d. 854/1450 (Suppl. II, 315), Alex. Fiqh Ḥan. 36, Qawala I, 367 (see Suppl. I).—c. *Īḍāḥ al-iṣlāḥ* by Aḥmad b. Sulaymān b. Kamālpāshā, d. 940/1533 (II, 449), Berl. 4559, Paris 917/20, Algiers 1016, Br. Mus. 212, Ind. Off. 1595/6, Garr. 1749, Yeni 365, Alex. Fiqh Ḥan. 8, Qawala I, 306/7, perhaps also Upps. 438 (anon.).—d. ʿAlī b. ʿUmar al-Aswad, Cairo ^{1}III, 81.—e. *Sharhi Wikaya maʿ Hashiyahi Umdat al-Riʿayah, commentary by Maulavi M. Abdulhaqq on the W. etc.* Lucknow 1883, 2nd ed. 1884.—f. M. Abdur Rahim, *Sharhi Ilyās*, (i.e. Mollā Ilyās Efendi Alex. Fiqh Ḥan 36) *a commentary on the W.*, Delhi 1883.—g. M. Qamaruddīn, *Sharhi W.*, Delhi 1889.—h. Turkish translation and annotations by Muṣṭafā b. Nūḥ al-Rūmī, Berl. 4560.—i.–t. see Suppl. (r. also Alex. Fiqh
469 | Ḥan. 15, MS dated 926, Qawala I, 315, where *tawfīq*).—u. *Kitāb fī baʿḍ mabāḥith al-ṭalāq min k. al-W.* by Khwājazāde, composed in 1045/1635, Qawala I, 339.—v. *Risāla fī sharḥ baʿḍ al-mawāḍiʿ min al-W.* by ʿAlā' al-Dīn al-Isbījābī, ibid. 346.—w. *al-Fawā'id al-ʿĀrifiyya* by Mahdī al-Ḥanafī, Patna I, 101_{1028}.—Abstract of the *Wiqāya* entitled *al-Nuqāya* by Ṣadr al-Sharīʿa al-Thānī (see above), Berl. 4562, Munich 280, Leid. 1805, Ind. Off. 234/5, 1561/8, Garr. 1683, Cairo ^{1}III, 143, ^{2}I, 470, Qawala I, 405 Patna I, $105_{1061/2}$, ed. Mirza Kazem Beg, Kazan 1260, Lucknow 1873, 1884, Delhi 1885, Lahore n.d. (see Suppl.).—Commentaries: a. ʿAbd al-Wāḥid b. Muḥammad, composed in 806/1403, Munich 281, Yeni 481.—b. *Kamāl al-dirāya* by Aḥmad b. Muḥammad al-Shumunnī, d. 872/1467 (II, 82), Munich 282, Yeni 403, Alex. Fiqh Ḥan. 35, Cairo ^{1}III, 305, Qawala I, 366.—c. Ibn Quṭlūbughā, d. 879/1474 (II, 82), Yeni 480.—d. Abu 'l-Makārim b. ʿAbdallāh b. Muḥammad, composed in 907/1501 (his *al-Ajwiba al-rāḍiya al-murḍiya ʿani 'l-as'ila al-Rāziyya al-muzriya*, Qawala I, 159), Munich 283, Ind. Off. 236, 1573, Bank. XIX, 1668/70 = Patna I, $93_{942/4}$.—e. ʿAbd al-ʿAlī b. Muḥammad al-Barjandī, d. 932/1525 (II, 413), Ind. Off. 1569/71, Yeni 482, Alex. Fiqh Ḥan. 35, Bank. XIX, 1671 = Patna I, 93_{945}, print. Lucknow 1301, 1314.—f. *Jāmiʿ al-rumūz* by Shams al-Dīn Muḥammad al-Kūhistānī, d. ca. 950/1534 (see Suppl.), Munich 284, Leid. 808, Ind. Off. 237, 1552/3, Algiers 1017, Yeni 382/5, Alex. Fiqh Ḥan. 16, Bank. XIX, 1672 = Patna I, 83_{841}, ed. W. Nassau Lees, Calcutta 1858, Istanbul 1289, Kazan 1890.—g. Anon. Ind Off. 1576.—h.–m. see Suppl. (i. additionally Ind. Off. 1572, k. ibid. 1574, Delhi 1314/5, m. Taqī al-Dīn Abu 'l-ʿAbbās ʿAbdallāh b. Muḥammad al-Yamanī, Patna I, 93_{341}).—Versification *al-Fawā'id al-saniyya* by Muḥammad b. Ḥasan al-Kawākibī, d. 1096/1685 (II, 315), with the commentary *al-Fawā'id al-samiyya*, composed in 1067/1656, Munich 285, Alex. Fiqh Ḥan. 45.—2. *Mukhtārāt al-hidāya* by ʿAlī b. Aḥmad al-Jamālī, d. 931/1525 (II, 431),

Paris 851, Yeni 564.—Versification of the *Hidāya: al-Naẓm al-manthūr* or *Durr al-muhtadī wa-dhukhr al-muqtadī* by Abū Bakr b. ʿAlī al-Hāmilī, d. 769/1367 II, 185), completed in 760/1359, Paris 927, Bodl. I, 254, cf. II, 575.

II. *Mukhtār al-nawāzil* (*Mukhtaṣar al-nuzūl*), Yeni 565/6, Alex. Fiqh Ḥan. 61, Qawala I, 391 (anon.), Patna I, 103,$_{1048}$.

III. *al-Tajnīs wal-mazīd fi ʾl-fatāwā* Yeni 533, Alex. Fiqh Ḥan. 11, Cairo ^{2}III, 17.

| 25. Jamāl al-Dīn Aḥmad b. Muḥammad b. Saʿīd al-Ghaznawī was a tutor for 470
al-Kāsānī (no. 22) in Aleppo, and died there in 593/1197.

Flügel 318. 1. *Muqaddimat al-Ghaznawī*, on the *ʿibādāt* or religious duties, Gotha 1003/6, Leipz. 110,$_{4}$ Paris 852, Algiers 577/8, Garr. 1894, Alex. Fiqh Ḥan. 66, Cairo ^{1}III, 135, Mosul 160,$_{182}$.—Commentaries: a. *al-Ḍiyāʾ al-maʿnawī* by Abu ʾl-Baqāʾ Muḥammad b. al-Ḍiyāʾ al-Qurashī, d. 852/1448, Paris 606,$_{5}$, 4804, Yeni 470, Alex. Fiqh Ḥan. 37, Cairo ^{1}III, 78, Patna I, 94,$_{963}$. Abstract by Muṣliḥ al-Dīn Ḥamza b. Ibrāhīm al-Rūmī, Paris 853 (autograph, from the year 1007/1598).—b., c. see Suppl. (c. also Alex. Fiqh Ḥan. 71).—2. *Kitāb al-ḥāwi ʾl-Qudsī fi ʾl-furūʿ* Berl. Qu. 1600, Yeni 408/9, Alex. Fiqh Ḥan. 22, Cairo ^{1}III, 40, Patna I, 86,$_{864}$.—3. *ʿAqāʾid*, creed, Cairo ^{1}II, 50.

26. Sirāj al-Dīn Abū Ṭāhir Muḥammad b. Muḥammad b. ʿAbd al-Rashīd al-Sajāwandī, who flourished towards the end of the sixth century.

Ibn Qutl. 42, 116, Flügel 318, Basset, *Giorn. d. Soc. As. Ital.* X, 58 ff. I. *Kitāb al-farāʾiḍ al-Sirājiyya*, law of inheritance, Gotha 1099 (where other MSS are listed), Heid. *ZDMG* 91, 384, Ind. Off. 1741/7, Alex. Fun. 174,$_{10}$, Qawala I, 429, Patna I, 110,$_{1112/6}$, II, 362,$_{2545,\ 2}$ 363,$_{2546,\ 2}$, cf. W. Jones, *Works*, vol. III, London 1799, print. Calcutta 1260, Ind. n.d. 1284 (Euting 2688), Persian translation by Maulawi M. Rashīd, Calcutta 1811, Turkish translation in verse, with a commentary, by Ṭūrsūnzāde Efendi, Paris 861,$_{6}$.—*The Serajiyyah, or the Muhammedan Law of Inheritance*, transl. by Prasauna Kumár Sen, Serampore 1885. A.
Rumsey, *Al Sirajiyyah, or* | *the Muhammedan Law of Inheritance, reprinted* 379
from the Translation of J.W. Jones, with Notes and Appendix, London 1869, 2nd ed. 1890.—Commentaries: 1. Ḥasan b. Aḥmad Majd al-Dīn b. Amīn al-Dawla, d. 658/1260, Leid. 1810.—2. *Ḍawʾ al-Sirāj*, by Maḥmūd b. Abī Bakr al-Kalābādhī al-Bukhārī, d. 700/1300, completed in 676/1277, Paris 865,$_{2}$, Ind. Off. 245, Bodl. I, 82, Alex. Far. 11, Qawala I, 431, Patna I, 111,$_{1121}$, *al-Minhāj al-muntakhab min Ḍawʾ al-S.*, Alex. Far. 17.—3. *al-Fawāʾid al-Khurāsāniyya* by Abu ʾl-ʿAlāʾ Aḥmad b. Muḥammad al-Bihishtī al-Isfarāʾinī Fakhr al-Dīn al-Khurāsānī, eighth cent., Ind. Off. 246/8.—4. Shihāb al-Dīn Aḥmad b. Maḥmūd al-Sīwāsī, d. 803/1400

(see Suppl. II, 973,$_{16}$), Berl. 4703, on which glosses ibid. 4704, Pet. AMK 937.—
471 5. *al-Farāʾiḍ al-Sharīfiyya* by al-Jurjānī, | d. 816/1413 (II, 217), Berl. 4705, Gotha 1102 (where other MSS are listed), Br. Mus. Suppl. 435, Ind. Off. 1748/54, Garr. 1872/3, Alex. Far. 10, 15, Qawala I, 429/30, Patna I, 111,$_{119, 21}$, II, 362,$_{2015, 5}$, print. Kazan 1889, 1894, on which glosses: a. Muḥyi ʾl-Dīn Muḥammad b. ʿAlī al-ʿAjamī, from the time of Bāyezīd II (886–918/1481–1512), Esc. ^{2}547,$_3$, Garr. 2073,$_1$.—b. Muḥyi ʾl-Dīn Muḥammad b. Khaṭīb Qāsim b. Yaʿqūb, completed in 922/1516, ibid. 2.—c. see Suppl.—d. Badr al-Dīn, Mosul 81,$_{28}$.—e. Muḥammad b. Muṣṭafā al-Kūrānī al-Wānī, composed in 992/1584, Alex. Far. 6, 15.—f. Aḥmad b. ʿAbd al-Awwal al-ʿAbdī al-Saʿīdī al-Qazwīnī, d. 966/1559 (II, 438), Alex. Far. 16.—5a. Muḥammad b. Ḥamza al-Fanārī, d. 834/1430 (II, 233), Paris 864.—6. ʿAbd al-Laṭīf b. al-Ḥājj Aḥmad al-Jānī, composed in 872/1467, Munich 328.—7. Aḥmad b. Sulaymān b. Kamālpāshā, d. 940/1533 (II, 449), Algiers 1314/5, Alex. Far. 10, 15, Qawala I, 430.—8. *Sharḥ taṣḥīḥ Mukhtaṣar al-S.*, by the same, Alex. Far. 8.—9. Badīʿ al-Dīn, before 956/1549, Dresd. 257, Pet. Ros. 23,$_5$.—10. Ibrāhīm b. Khiḍr, composed in 961/1554, Vienna 1797,$_1$.—11. Ḥaydar b. Muḥammad b. Ibrāhīm al-Ḥalabī al-Harawī (d. 830/1427?), Alex. Far. 10.—12.–24. see Suppl. (22. also Garr. 1874, 2112,$_4$ Alex Far. 7, MS dated 1133. 24. with the title *Jāmiʿ al-durar, Alex.* Far. 5).—25. *Iẓhār al-Sirājiyya* by Muḥammad b. ʿAbd al-Qādir b. Muḥammad b. ʿAlī b. Muḥammad, Suppl. I, 970, Patna I, 110,$_{1108}$.—26. *Taṣwīr al-farāʾiḍ* (Suppl. I, 970) Patna II, 362,$_{2546, 1}$.—27. Anon. *al-Jadalī*, Alex. Far. 13, others Berl. 4706/7, Gotha 1100,$_1$, 1101, Paris 861,$_2$, 866/72.—Versification by ʿAbd al-Muḥsin al-Qayṣarī, d. 755/1354 (ḤKh. II, 408,$_{8997}$), Munich 313,$_2$, 322,$_2$, Paris 1266,$_7$, with a commentary, Paris 867,$_4$.—b. *Khulāṣat al-farāʾiḍ*, with a commentary by ʿAbd al-Malik al-Fattanī al-Makkī al-Madanī (Indian, ca. 1900 in Cairo) print. C. 1292/3, 1305.—19 commentaries, numerous glosses, and an abstract are mentioned in Ahlw. 4708.—II. *Kitāb al-tajnīs fi ʾl-ḥisāb* Paris 2330,$_{12}$, perhaps a part of I.—III. *al-Fatāwā al-Sirājiyya* is wrongly attributed to him in Algiers 1034,$_3$ and elsewhere, see p. 430.

27. Ẓahīr al-Dīn al-Ḥasan b. ʿAlī al-Marghīnānī Abu ʾl-Maḥāsin, who flourished around 600/1203.

Ibn Quṭl. no. 59, p. 153, no. 474, *al-Fatāwā al-Ẓahīriyya*, ḤKh IV, 368, part II on the *shurūṭ*, Br. Mus. Suppl. 280. Beginning of the *furūʿ* Ind. Off. 1671, Rāmpūr 371/2, Bank. XIX, 1, 1678/80.

27a. Ẓahīr al-Dīn Aḥmad b. Ismāʿīl al-Timurtāshī, the *muftī* of Khwārizm in Gurganj, who died around 600/1203.

| ʿAq., *Jaw.* I, 61, *al-Faw. al-bah.* 12, al-Laknawī, *Ṭab. al-Ḥan.* 15, Ibn Quṭl. 90, no. 89. *Kitāb al-farāʾiḍ* Vat. V. 1477,$_{5}$, Tunis, Zayt. IV, 406,$_{2861}$. 472

28. ʿImād al-Dīn Abu ʾl-Qāsim Maḥmūd b. Aḥmad b. Abi ʾl-Ḥasan al-Fārābī (Faryābī) Abu ʾl-Maḥāmil, who died on 20 Jumādā I 607/10 November 1210.

Ibn Quṭl. 207. *Kitāb khāliṣat al-ḥaqāʾiq li-mā fīhi min al-asālīb al-daqāʾiq*, compiled from around 70 works and completed in 597/1200, Berl. 8771/3, Ind. Off. 623/4, Pet. AM 87, Garr. 2076,$_{3}$, Alex. Taṣ. 16, Mosul 72,$_{20}$.—Abstracts: 1. by the author himself, *Khāliṣat al-ḥaqāʾiq wa-niṣāb ghāʾiṣat al-daqāʾiq*, Berl. 8774.—2. *Akhlaṣ al-Kh.* or *Khulāṣat al-Kh.* by ʿAlī b. Maḥmūd b. Muḥammad al-Rāʾiḍ al-Badakhshānī, composed in 854/1450, Berl. 8775/6, Gotha 1216, Vienna 1844, Garr. 925, 2028,$_{1}$, ed. Gottwaldt, Kazan 1850, cf. Flügel, *ZDMG* VI, 436/8.—3. Anon., Cairo ^{1}VII, 114, Calcutta p. 58, no. 410.

29. Badīʿ al-Dīn ʿAlī al-Sūbākhī wrote, in 615/1218:

Mawāhib al-niẓām Yeni 581 (where al-Sūkhī, see ʿAq. *Jaw.* I, 319, corrupted to al-Suwaykhī, ibid. I, 382, see al-Samʿānī, *Ansāb* 316 b).

30. Ẓahīr al-Dīn Abū Bakr Muḥammad b. Aḥmad b. ʿUmar al-Bukhārī, who was *muḥtasib* of Bukhārā and who died in 619/1222.

Al-Fawāʾid al-Ẓahīriyya, a collection of fatwas, Paris 856/7, Yeni 643/4 (see Suppl.), as *Fatāwī Ẓ.* Qawala I, 377, Patna I, 98,$_{992/4}$.

| 31. Yūsuf b. Aḥmad b. Abī Bakr al-Khwārizmī al-Khāṣṣī Najm al-Dīn, ca. 620/1223. 380

Kitāb al-fatāwā al-ṣughrā, a sequel to the work by al-Ṣadr al-Shahīd (no. 10), Berl. 4814 = Yeni 680?

32. Aḥmad b. Abī Bakr b. ʿAbd al-Wahhāb al-Qazwīnī Badīʿ al-Dīn wrote, around 620/1223:

Kitāb jamʿ alfāẓ al-kufr, expressions common among ordinary people, but whose use actually characterises them as infidels, Berl. 3102.

33. ʿĪsā b. Abī Bakr b. Ayyūb al-Sulṭān al-Malik al-Muʿaẓẓam Sharaf al-Dīn Abu
473 ʾl-Ghanāʾim, born in 576/1180, | came to power in Damascus in 615/1218 and
died on 30 Dhu ʾl-Qaʿda 624/11 November 1227.

Ibn Quṭl. no. 146. 1. *Sharḥ al-Jāmiʿ al-kabīr* (p. 178) Cairo ^{1}V, 70.—2. see Suppl.

34. Aḥmad b. ʿUbaydallāh b. Ibrāhīm al-Maḥbūbī Ṣadr al-Sharīʿa al-Awwal al-Akbar, ca. 630/1232.

Kitāb talqīḥ al-ʿuqūl fi ʾl-furūq bayna ahl al-nuqūl, in which particular cases are used to show and explain different legal opinions, Berl. 4505, Paris 923.

35. Muḥammad b. Maḥmūd al-Ustrūshanī Majd al-Dīn, who died in 632/1234.

1. *Kitāb al-aḥkām al-ṣaghāʾir fi ʾl-furūʿ or Jāmiʿ al-ṣighār* Garr. 1704, Algiers 991, Yeni 348, Alex. Fiqh Ḥan. 16, Cairo ^{1}III, 31, 124, Qawala I, 315.—2. *Kitāb al-fuṣūl fi ʾl-muʿādālāt (muʿāmalāt)* Yeni 527/9, Mosul $97_{,83}$, Ind. Off. 1649, Patna I, $101_{,1027}$.—3., 4. see Suppl.

36. Jamāl al-Dīn Abu ʾl-Maḥāmid Maḥmūd b. Aḥmad al-Ḥaṣīrī was born in Jumādā I 546/August-September 1151 in Bukhārā, studied in his hometown, Nishapur and Aleppo, became a professor at al-Nūriyya in Damascus, and died on 8 Ṣafar 636/21 September 1238.

Ibn Quṭl. 208. 1. *Kitāb khayr al-maṭlūb fi ʾl-ʿilm al-marghūb* Cairo ^{1}III, 43.—2. *Kitāb al-ṭarīqa al-Ḥaṣīriyya fī ʿilm al-khilāf bayna ʾl-Shāfiʿiyya wal-Ḥanafiyya,* Cairo ^{1}III, 243 (ad Suppl. 3 and 5, see no. 5a).

37. Yūsuf b. Abī Saʿīd Aḥmad al-Sijistāni wrote, in 639/1240 in Sīwās:

Kitāb munyat al-muftī in 40 books, Gotha 1140, Paris 858, Yeni 684/7, Alex. Fiqh Ḥan. 68, Cairo ^{1}III, 115, 140.

381 | 38. Abū Naṣr Masʿūd b. Abī Bakr b. al-Ḥusayn al-Farāhī, ca. 640/1242.

ʿAbd al-Qādir b. Abi ʾl-Wafāʾ, *Jaw.* II, 172. *Dhāt al-ʿiqdayn,* a poem about the
474 legal | opinions of Abū Ḥanīfa, with due regard to al-Shāfiʿī and Mālik, ḤKh ^{1}III,
$324_{,5761}$, ^{2}I, 821 (only the title) Berl. 4506.

39. Shams al-Dīn Abu ʾl-Wajh Muḥammad b. Muḥammad b. ʿAbd al-Sattār al-ʿImādī al-Kardarī al-Barānīqī, who died in 642/1244 in Bukhārā (see Suppl.).

Kitāb al-radd wal-intiṣār li-Abī Ḥanīfa imām fuqahāʾ al-amṣār or *al-Fawāʾid al-munīfa fi ʾl-dhabb ʿan Abī Ḥanīfa* Cairo ^{1}V, 59, 127, ^{2}V, 94, 361.

40. Muḥammad b. Muḥammad b. ʿUmar al-Akhsīkatī Ḥusām al-Dīn, who died on 23 Dhu ʾl-Qaʿda 644/2 April 1247.

Ibn Quṭl. 167, Flügel 277. *Kitāb al-muntakhab fī uṣūl al-madhhab*, usually called *al-Ḥusāmī*, ḤKh VI, 163, 335, Berl. 4372 (wrongly attributed to Ibn Māza), Br. Mus. 118, Ind. Off. 293/7, 1430/3, Garr. 1705, Yeni 304, Alex. Fun. 103,$_{3}$ Cairo ^{1}II, 260, 266, ^{2}I, 395, Patna I, 75,$_{767/8}$, II, 505,$_{272/3}$.—Commentaries: 1. *al-Wāfī* by Ḥusayn b. ʿAlī al-Sighnāqī, d. 710/1310 (II, 116), Paris 880, 6452, Cairo ^{1}II, 269,$_{31}$, 347.—2. *Ghāyat al-taḥqīq* by ʿAbd al-ʿAzīz b. Aḥmad b. Muḥammad al-Bukhārī, d. 730/1330 (Suppl. II, 268), Leid. 1816, Br. Mus. 1578, Suppl. 261, Ind. Off. 1434/6, Esc. ^{1}1163, Cairo ^{1}II, 239, ^{2}I, 380, Patna I, 67,$_{689}$.—3. *al-Tabyīn* by Amīr Kātib b. Amīr ʿUmar al-Itqānī, d. 758/1357 (II, 79), composed in 716/1316 in Tustar while he was on his way to the Hijaz, Berl. 4858, Paris 802, Br. Mus. 207, Alex. Uṣūl 5, Cairo ^{1}II, 239, ^{2}I, 372, Yeni 339/41.—4.–8. see Suppl.—9. *Ḥāshiyat al-Sāmī* by Muḥammad Yaʿqūb al-Banbānī, d. after 1081/1670, composed in Kabul, also Ind. Off. 1437.—10., 11. see Suppl.—12. Anon., Ind. Off. 1438.

41. ʿAlāʾ al-Dīn Muḥammad b. Maḥmūd al-Tarjumānī al-Makkī al-Khwārizmī, who died in 645/1257 in al-Jurjāniyya in Khwārizm.

Yatīmat al-dahr fī fatāwā ahl al-ʿaṣr Vienna 1807, Yeni 593/4, Cairo ^{1}III, 151.

41a. Muḥammad b. Muḥammad b. Ismāʿīl al-Khaṭīb al-Ushfūrqānī fled in 616/1219 ahead of the Mongols from Khurāsān to India and wrote, in 642/1244, probably in Delhi:

| *Ṣinwān al-qaḍāʾ wa-ʿunwān al-iftāʾ* Bank. XIX, 1682/3, Āṣaf. I, 33. 475

42. Muḥammad b. ʿAbbād b. Malakdādh b. al-Ḥasan b. Dāʾūd Abū ʿAbdallāh Ṣadr al-Dīn (Kamāl al-Dīn) al-Khilāṭī, who died in Rajab 652/August–September 1254.

Ibn Quṭl. 187. 1. *Talkhīṣ al-Jāmiʿ al-kabīr* (p. 178) Yeni 378.—Commentaries: a. Self-commentary, vol. 3, Landb.-Br. 655.—b. *Tuḥfat al-ḥarīṣ* by ʿAlāʾ al-Dīn Muḥammad b. Balabān b. ʿAbdallāh al-Fārisī, d. 739/1338 in Cairo, Alex. Fiqh Ḥan. 11.—c. *al-Īḍāḥ* see Suppl.—2. see ibid.

42a. Najm al-Dīn Abu ʾl-Faḍāʾil Abu ʾl-Shujāʿ Bakbars (Mängübars) b. Yaltaqqilič al-Turkī, d. 652/1254 (see Suppl.).

Al-Mukhtaṣar al-ḥāwī li-Bayān al-shāfī, additionally Garr. 1706.

43. Nāṣir al-Dīn Abu ʾl-Qāsim Muḥammad b. Yūsuf (according to others, Yūsuf b. Muḥammad) al-Samarqandī al-Madanī, who died in 656/1258.

1. *Kitāb al-fiqh al-nāfiʿ*, composed in 655/1257, Berl. 4480, Munich 286/7, Leipz. 477, Garr. 1692, Yeni 530, Cairo ^{1}III, 97.—Commentaries: a. *al-Mustaṣfā* by ʿAbdallāh b. Aḥmad al-Nasafī, d. 710/1310 (II, 196), Berl. Ms. or. oct. 3728, Ind. Off. 208, Cairo ^{1}III, 130, $_{2}$I, 462.—b., c. see Suppl.—2. *Kitāb al-multaqaṭ fi ʾl-fatāwa ʾl-Ḥanafiyya* Yeni 575, on which *Tajnīs* (*Tartīb*) by Maḥmūd b. Ḥusayn al-Ustrūshanī (son of no. 35?), Garr. $2125_{,1}$, Alex. Fiqh Ḥan. 13.

382 | 44. Najm al-Dīn Abu ʾl-Rajāʾ Mukhtār b. Maḥmūd b. Muḥammad al-Zāhidī al-Ghazmīnī, from Khwārizm, who died in 658/1260.

1. *Kitāb qunyat al-munya li-tatmīm al-Ghunya*, an abstract of the *Munyat al-fuqahāʾ* by his teacher Fakhr al-Dīn Badīʿ b. Abī Manṣūr al-ʿArabī al-Qubaznī, Munich 288/9, Br. Mus. 199, Suppl. 281, Ind. Off. 1651, Yeni 531, Alex. Fiqh Ḥan. 41, Cairo ^{1}III, 99, ^{2}I, 454.—2. *Jawāhir al-fiqh* Leipz. 295.—3. *al-Ḥāwī fī masāʾil al-Wāqiʿāt wal-Munya* (see 10, 2) Yeni 407, Alex. Fiqh Ḥan. 22, Qawala I, 337.—4. *Qunyat al-fatāwā* (= 1.?) Yeni 670/2.—5. *Faḍāʾil Ramaḍān* Berl. 3827.

476 45. Abu ʾl-Fatḥ Zayn al-Dīn ʿAbd al-Raḥīm b. Abī Bakr | ʿImād al-Dīn b. ʿAlī (no. 24) Burhān al-Dīn b. Abī Bakr b. ʿAbd al-Jalīl al-Farghānī al-Marghīnānī al-Rishtānī, ca. 670/1271.

Kitāb fuṣūl al-Iḥkām fī uṣūl al-aḥkām (mistakenly believed by some to be the *Fuṣūl al-ʿImādī* of Jamāl al-Dīn b. ʿImād al-Dīn, ḤKh, IV. $440_{,9094}$), on legal procedures in civil cases, started by his father and which he completed in Samarqand in 651/1253, Berl. 4788, Br. Mus. 1606, Ind. Off. 1652/3, Garr. 1707/8 Mosul $219_{,138}$, Patna I, $100_{,1024/5}$, II, $508_{,2734}$.

46. Abu ʾl-Rabīʿ Ṣadr al-Dīn Sulaymān b. Abi ʾl-ʿIzz Wuhayb al-Adhraʿī, who was a professor at the Ṣāliḥiyya and *qāḍi ʾl-ʿaskar* in Cairo, then *qāḍī* in Syria, and who died in 677/1278.

Al-Suyūṭī, Ḥusn al-muḥ. I, 260. *Kitāb al-wajīz al-jāmiʿ li-masāʾil al-Jāmiʿ* (see Suppl. p. 290), commentary by al-Māridīnī, d. 731/1331, Cairo ^{1}III, 75, 148.

47. Abu ʾl-Faḍl Majd al-Dīn ʿAbdallāh b. Maḥmūd b. Mawdūd al-Mawṣilī al-Buldajī was born in Mosul in 599/1202 (according to others in 609), was a *qāḍī* in Kufa before being removed from that position, after which he lectured in Baghdad, where he died in 683/1284.

Ibn Quṭl. no. 88, Flügel p. 326. 1. *Kitāb al-mukhtār lil-fatwā* Berl. 4565/6, Gotha 1009/11, Munich 290/4, Leid. 1814, Br. Mus. Suppl. 282/3, Ind. Off. 1527, Paris 875/7, 891,$_{2}$, Nan. 31, Algiers 993, Garr. 709/12, Qilič ʿA. 393, Alex. Fiqh Ḥan. 5, 61, Cairo ^{1}III, 119, Bank. XIX, 1, 1684a = Patna I, 103,$_{1049}$.—Commentaries: a. Self-commentary, *al-Ikhtiyār*, Paris 878/9, Ind. Off. 238, Garr. 1713, Yeni 595/6, Cairo ^{1}III, 3.—b. see Suppl.—c. Anon., Garr. 1714.—7 commentaries, abstracts and versifications in Ahlw.—2. *Kitāb al-fawāʾid* Yeni 534.

48. Jalāl al-Dīn ʿUmar b. Muḥammad b. ʿUmar al-Khabbāzī al-Bakhtiyārī al-Khujandī, a professor at the Khātūniyya in Damascus who died in 691/1292.

Ibn Quṭl. 141, Flügel 329, Ibn al-ʿImād, *Shadharāt al-dhahab* V, 419. 1. *Kitāb al-mughnī fī uṣūl al-fiqh* Leipz. 475, Leid. | 1825, Garr. 1715, Alex. Uṣūl 20, Cairo 477
^{1}II, 265.—Commentaries: a. Abū Muḥammad Manṣūr b. Aḥmad al-Qāʾānī al-Khwārizmī, d. 705/1305, Garr. 1716, Qawala I, 286, Patna I, 72,$_{737}$ (see Suppl.).—c. ʿUmar b. Isḥāq al-Ghaznawī al-Dawlatābādī, d. 773/1371 (II, 80), completed in 746/1345, Berl. 4384, Alex. Uṣūl 11.—b. see Suppl.—8 other commentaries and 1 gloss in Ahlw.—2. *Sharḥ al-Hidāya*, p. 466.

49. Muẓaffar al-Dīn Aḥmad b. ʿAlī b. Thaʿlab b. al-Sāʿātī al-Baghdādī, who died in 696/1296 (or, according to others, in 694) (see Suppl.).

| 1. *Kitāb majmaʿ al-baḥrayn wa-multaqa ʾl-nayyirayn*, compiled from the 383
Mukhtaṣar of Qudūrī (p. 183) and the *Manẓūma* of al-Nasafī, d. 537/1142 (p. 427), completed in 690/1291, Berl. 4569/70, Gotha 1012 (where other MSS are listed), Paris 881/4, 6189, Garr. 1678/9, Qawala I, 390, Mosul 97,$_{89}$, 167,$_{45}$, Patna I, 102,$_{1042/3}$.—Commentaries: a. Self-commentary, Berl. 4571, Ms. or. qu. 2073,

Yeni 454, Alex. Fiqh Ḥan. 34, Cairo ^{1}III, 65, ^{2}I, 438, 460, on which glosses by Muḥammad b. Muḥammad al-Āqsarāʾī, eighth cent. (Suppl. II, 328), Paris 885.—b. Aḥmad b. Ibrāhīm al-ʿAntabī, d. 767/1365, Cairo ^{1}III, 137.—c. ʿAbd al-Laṭīf b. ʿAbd al-ʿAzīz b. Malakshāh (Firishte), ca. 850/1447 (II, 213), Berl. 4572, Copenhagen 64, Munich 2, 6/7, Leid. 1828, Paris 886/9, 970,$_2$, Ind. Off. 4579 (*JRAS* 1939, 370, dated 28 Muḥarram 842/21 July 1438), Yeni 456, Alex. Fiqh Ḥan. 34, Qawala I, 354.—d. Muḥammad b. Aḥmad al-Qurashī al-ʿUmarī, d. 854/1450, Cairo ^{1}III, 67.—e. *al-Mustajmaʿ* by Maḥmūd b. Aḥmad al-ʿAynī, d. 855/1451 (II, 52), Bodl. I, 244, Cairo ^{1}III, 130, ^{2}I, 463, versified Paris 4543/4, Br. Mus. 202, cf. Add. p. 767.—f. Aḥmad b. Muḥammad b. Saʿbān al-Ṭarābulusī, d. 967/1559, Yeni 455.—g. Muṣṭafā b. ʿUmar, composed in 1066/1655, Cairo ^{1}III, 137.—h. Anon., Leid. 1829, Pet. AMBuch. 918.—Anon. metrical reworking, Br. Mus. 202. Calcutta p. 57, no. 852.—10 other commentaries, 1 abstract, and 1 versification in Ahlw. 4573.—2. *Kitāb badīʿ al-niẓām fī uṣūl al-fiqh*, which unites the *Uṣūl* of al-Pazdawī (see no. 4) with the *Aḥkām* of al-Āmidī (Ibn Quṭl. no. 10), Leid. 1826.—Commentaries: a. Sirāj al-Dīn al-Hindī, d. 773/1371 (II, 80), Leid. 1827, Paris 1260, Cairo ^{1}II, 256.—b. *Bayān mushkil* (*maʿānī*) *al-Badīʿ* by Maḥmūd b. ʿAbd al-Raḥmān al-Iṣfahānī, d. 749/1348 (II, 110), Ind. Off. 1460, Cairo ^{1}I, 379.—c., d.—3., 4. see Suppl.

478 | 50. Zayn (Tāj) al-Dīn Muḥammad b. Abī Bakr b. ʿAbd al-Muḥsin b. ʿAbd al-Qādir al-Rāzī, fl. around the end of the seventh century.

1. *Tuḥfat al-mulūk* (also attributed to Muḥammad b. Tāj al-Dīn Ibrāhīm al-Tūqātī in ḤKh ^{1}II, 2673, ^{2}I, 375), Berl. 4517/8, Gotha 1007/8 (where other MSS are listed), Paris 873, Garr. 1717, Alex. Fiqh Ḥan. 12, Qawala I, 311.—Commentaries: a. Muḥammad b. ʿAbd al-Laṭīf al-Kirmānī b. Malikshāh, ca. 850/1446 (II, 213), Berl. 4519, Paris 874.—b. Maḥmūd b. Aḥmad al-ʿAynī, d. 855/1451 (II, 52), Berl. 4520/1, Algiers 992.—c. *Hadiyyat al-sulūk* by Abu ʾl-Layth al-Muḥarram b. Muḥammad al-Zīlī (Zaylaʿī), tenth cent. (II, 439), written in Sīwās, Upps. 435.—d. see Suppl.—e. Anon., Garr. 1713.—2.–9. see Suppl. (2. Berl. Oct. 3889, AS 87/8, 6. Garr. 1904, Bursa, Ulu Cami Tas. 101).—10. *Muʿāni ʾl-maʿānī*, literary criticism, Alex. Adab 101.—11. *al-Mukhtār min Kitāb al-taḥbīr* by al-Qushayrī, p. 432,$_3$.

51. Sadīd al-Dīn al-Kāshgharī, seventh century.

Kitāb munyat al-muṣallī wa-ghunyat al-mubtadiʾ, on the theory of prayer, Leid. 1812 (where other MSS are listed), Hamb. Or. Sem. 22, Ind. Off. 1654/66, Garr. 1750/1, Qawala I, 402, Mosul 97,$_9$, 114,$_{209/10}$, 133,$_{196,1}$, 146,$_{106}$, Patna X, 107,$_{1085}$, print. Kazan 1889 (see Suppl.).—Commentaries: 1. *Ḥilyat al-mujallī* (*muḥallī*) by Muḥammad b. Muḥammad al-Ḥalabī, d. 879/1474, Paris 1147/8, Ind. Off. 1668, Qawala I, 327, Bank. XIX, 1. 1690.—2. Ibrāhīm b. Muḥammad al-Ḥalabī, d. 956/1549 (II, 432): a. the larger one, *Ghunyat al-mutamallī* (*mustamlī*), Gotha 766 (where other MSS are listed), Ind. Off. 1667, Garr. 1752, Alex Fiqh Ḥan. 55, Qawala I, 373, Patna I, 86,$_{873}$.—b. the smaller one, *Mukhtaṣar Gh. al-m.*, Munich 166/9, Dresd. 185, 225, Leid. 1813, Ind. Off. 359, Paris 1149/51, Algiers 778/86, Garr. 1753, Alex. Fiqh Ḥan. 34, 62, Cairo ^{1}III, 69, Qawala I, 356/7, Mosul 181,$_{21}$, Patna I, 104,$_{1051/2}$, print. Istanbul 1242, 1268, 1286, 1289, 1275, 1312, 1316, 1317, lith. Lahore 1889.—Glosses: *Ḥilyat al-nājī* by Sayyid Muṣṭafā b. Muḥammad Güzelḥiṣārī, completed in 1241/1825 (Qawala I, 328), print. Istanbul 1251, 1308, 1322 (see Suppl.).—c. *Tamniyat al-mutamallī* Paris 1152.—3. see Suppl.

52. Abu 'l-Ḥasan ʿAlī b. Zakariyyāʾ (Zikrī) b. Masʿūd al-Anṣārī al-Manīḥī (?) al-Ḥanafī, whose son Muḥammad became a professor at the Muʿaẓẓamiyya in Jerusalem in 711/1311, wrote:

Al-Lubāb fī 'l-jamʿ bayna 'l-sunna wal-Kitāb Yeni 536 (where al-Masīḥī), photograph Cairo ^{2}I, App. 16, Alex. Fiqh Ḥan. 49 | (attributed to Yūsuf b. Abī Saʿīd 479
Aḥmad al-Sijistānī, p. 473), Rāmpūr I, 106,$_{314}$ (which has al-Manbijī), see ʿAq., *Jaw.* I, 362, II, 93, ḤKh V, 301,$_{11054}$ (which has Musabbiḥī, without date).

2 *The Mālikīs*

1. Abu 'l-Ḥasan ʿAlī b. ʿAbdallāh b. Ibrāhīm b. Muḥammad b. ʿAbdallāh al-Lakhmī, who died in 478/1085 or, according to others, 498/1104 (see Suppl.).

1. *Kitāb al-tabṣira*, on Malikī law, Paris 1071.—2. *Kitāb al-nihāya wal-tamām fī maʿrifat al-wathāʾiq wal-aḥkām*, Algiers 1072, abstract ibid. 1073.

1a. Aḥmad b. Mughīth Abū Jaʿfar, who was born in 406/1015, was the greatest *faqīh* of Toledo of his time. He died in 459/1067.

Ibn Farḥūn, C. 40, S. Vila, Abenmoguit, Formulario notarial in *Anuario de Historia del Derecho Español* VII, 1, 1931,$_{6ff}$.

2. Abu 'l-Aṣbagh ʿĪsā b. Sahl b. ʿAbdallāh al-Asadī, who died in 486/1093 (see Suppl.).

E. Lévi-Provençal, *L'Espagne musulmane au X. siècle*, p. 80, n. 2. *Kitāb al-iʿlām bi-nawāzil al-aḥkām*, | legal rulings by eminent Mālikīs, Algiers 1332, abstract 384
ibid. 1298,$_4$.

3. Abu 'l-Walīd Hishām b. Aḥmad al-Waqashī al-Kinānī al-Ṭulaytilī, who died in Denia on 28 Jumādā II 489/24 June 1096 (see Suppl.).

Maqq. II, 256. *Mukhtaṣar fī 'l-fiqh* Br. Mus. 251,$_6$, commentary by Muḥammad b. ʿAlī al-Fakhkhār Abū Bakr al-Arkushī al-Judhāmī, d. 723/1323 in Malaga, Br. Mus. 228,$_2$ (cf. Add. 768).

4. Abu 'l-Walīd Muḥammad b. Aḥmad b. Rushd,[1] born in 450/1058, was *qāḍī* and imam of the great mosque in Cordova, and died in 520/1126.

Al-Ḍabbī, p. 40, no. 24. 1. *Compendium juris canonici* Br. Mus. 251,$_4$.—2. *al-Muqaddamāt al-mumahhadāt li-bayān mā iqtaḍathu rusūm al-*
480 *Mudawwana* (p. 186) *min al-aḥkām* | *al-sharʿiyyāt wal-taḥṣīlāt al-muḥkamāt li-ummahāt masāʾiliha 'l-mushkilāt* Cairo ^{1}III, 184.—3. Treatise on forbidden meat, Paris 1057,$_3$.—4. *al-Fatāwā*, compiled by al-Warrāq, Paris 1072.—5. *Risāla fī ḥukm amwāl al-ẓalama al-wulāt al-muʿtadīn wa-man kāna fī maʿnāhum* Cairo ^{1}VII, 690.—6. *Sharḥ mukhtaṣar maʿāni 'l-āthār lil-Ṭaḥāwī* (p. 181), from the year 503/1109, Cairo ^{1}I, 414, ^{2}I, 493.—7.–11. see Suppl.

5. Aḥmad b. Muḥammad b. Khalaf al-Ḥawfī, from Seville, died in 588/1192 (see Suppl.)

Kitāb al-farāʾiḍ, on laws of inheritance, Paris 213, Algiers 1311.—Commentaries: 1. Muḥammad b. Muḥammad b. ʿArafa al-Warghamī, d. 803/1400 (II, 247), Algiers 1311,$_2$.—2. Muḥammad b. Abī Bakr b. ʿAjāna al-ʿAdnānī, Paris 1075, Algiers 1312.—3. Abū ʿAbdallāh Muḥammad al-Sanūsī, Algiers 1450, see *JA* 1854,$_1$, p. 175.—4. Saʿīd b. Muḥammad al-ʿUqbānī, see Suppl. I, 664, II, 251, 1018.

6. Abu 'l-Walīd Hishām b. ʿAbdallāh b. Hishām al-Azdī, who died in 606/1309.

Kitāb al-mufīd lil-ḥukkām (al-mulham) fī-mā yaʿriḍu lahum min nawāzil al-aḥkām, a handbook for judges to help settle difficult legal cases, Paris 1074, Br. Mus. 225, Algiers 1364/5, *Bull. de Corr. Afr.* 1885, p. 472, no. 16.

6b. Abū ʿAbdallāh Muḥammad b. Najm b. Shās al-Jalāl al-Judhāmī, d. 610/1213 (see Suppl.).

ʿIqd al-jawāhir etc. also Fez Qar. 812/5, 857.

---

1 Grandfather of the philosopher of the same name.

6c. Abū ʿAbdallāh Muḥammad b. ʿĪsā b. Muḥammad b. Aṣbagh al-Azdī al-Qurṭubī al-Mālikī b. al-Munāṣif was born in Rajab 563/April 1168 in Tunis (or, according to others, in al-Mahdiyya), where his father had fled after the downfall of the Almoravids of Cordova. He studied there and in Tlemcen before returning to Spain. He became a *qāḍī* in Valencia and from 608/1211 onwards in Murcia, but was deposed because of his excessive harshness. In 614/1217 he was in Cordova, but then he went to Marrakesh, where he died in Rabīʿ II 620/May 1223.

Ibn al-Abbār, *Takmila* (Bibl. Ar.-Hisp. V), 326, no. 963, Aḥmad Bābā, *Nayl*, $229_{,3}$. 1. *Tanbīh al-ḥukkām fi 'l-aḥkām* Tunis Zayt. IV, $283_{,2441}$.—2. *Kitāb al-mudhhaba fī naẓm al-ṣifāt* | *min al-ḥulā wal-shiyāt*, ca. 1000 *rajaz* verses on Arabic lexicology, 481
Berl. 5370 (mistakenly identified by Ahlwardt as being about physiognomy, thus it was listed as such in Suppl. I, 910 in chapter 17), Esc. $^{2}581_{,1}$, Bank. XX, 1989 = Patna I, $187_{,1704}$, see J.M. Peñuela, *Die "Goldene" des b. al-M., ein Betrag zur mediz. ar. Lexikographie etc.*, Rome 1941.—3. *al-Muʿaqqiba*, supplement thereto, Esc. $^{2}581_{,2}$.

7. Abu 'l-ʿAbbās Aḥmad b. ʿUmar al-Anṣārī al-Qurṭubī died in Alexandria on 14 Dhu 'l-Qaʿda 656/12 November 1258.

Al-Suyūṭī, *Ḥusn al-muḥ.* I, 260. 1. *Kashf al-qināʿ ʿan ḥukm al-wajh wal-samāʿ* Cairo ^{1}VII, 546.—2. see Suppl.

8. Shams al-Dīn Abū ʿAbdallāh Muḥammad b. Mūsā b. al-Nuʿmān al-Fāsī al-Marrākushī al-Muzālī al-Ishbīlī al-Hintātī, fl. seventh cent.

| 1. *Kitāb al-nūr al-wāḍiḥ ilā maḥajjat al-munkir ʿala 'l-ṣārikh fī wajdihi 'l-ṣāʾiḥ*, a 385
detailed answer to the question of whether it is right or wrong to express one's feelings loudly in case of excitement or grief, Berl. $3350_{,14}$, 5410.—2. *Miṣbāḥ al-ẓalām fi 'l-mustaghīthīn bi-khayr al-anām fi 'l-yaqaẓa wal-manām*, composed during the pilgrimage in 639/1241, demonstrates the effectiveness of the invocation of Muḥammad in various kinds of hardship by means of examples, Berl. 3914, Garr. 1902, Cairo ^{1}VII, 94, ^{2}I, 359.—3. *Iʿlām al-ajnād wal-ʿibād ahl al-ijtihād bi-faḍl al-ribāṭ wal-jihād* Berl. 4089.

9. Shihāb al-Dīn Abu 'l-ʿAbbās Aḥmad b. Idrīs b. ʿAlī b. ʿAbdallāh b. Yallīn al-Qarāfī al-Ṣanhājī al-Bahnasī, who died in Jumādā II 684/August 1285 (see Suppl.).

1. *Kitāb anwāʾ (anwār) al-burūq fī anwār (anwāʾ) al-furūq fī uṣūl al-fiqh*, Algiers 1355/6, Alex. Fiqh Māl. Cairo ^{1}III, 154, *Dībāja*, Gotha 2,$_{28}$.—Comment.: a. *Idrār al-shurūq* by al-Ishbīlī, d. 725/1325 (II, 264), see Suppl.—b. al-Qalqashandī, d. 1035/1625, mentioned in Ahlw. 4380.—*Mukhtaṣar al-qawāʿid*, abridged and completed by Muḥammad b. Ibrāhīm al-Baqqūrī al-Ṣūfī al-Sabtī, d. 707/1307, Berl. 4380.—2. *Kitāb al-dhakhīra fi ʾl-furūʿ* Cairo ^{1}III, 165, ^{2}I, 482.—3. *Kitāb al-istighnāʾ fī aḥkām al-istithnāʾ*, on legal exceptions, Esc. ^{2}620.—4. *Kitāb al-istibṣār fī-mā tudrikuhu ʾl-abṣār* Esc. ^{2}707,$_{9}$, Cairo ^{1}VI, 88.—
482 5. *Kitāb al-qawāʿid al-saniyya* | *fī asrār al-ʿArabiyya* Paris 1013,$_{5}$.—6. *Kitāb al-ajwiba al-fākhira ʿan (fi ʾl-radd ʿala) al-asʾila al-fājira*, a rebuttal of objections against the truth of Islam raised by Jews and Christians, Gotha 858, Leid. 2105 (where other MSS are listed), Cairo ^{1}III, 153, cf. Steinschneider, *Polem. u. apolog. Lit.* 8, 17.—7.–11. see Suppl.—12. *al-Munjiyāt wal-mūbiqāt fi ʾl-adʿiya*, Alex. Fiqh Māl. 16.

10. Abū Isḥāq (ʿAbdallāh) Ibrāhīm b. Abī Bakr b. ʿAbdallāh b. Mūsā al-Tilimsānī al-Anṣārī al-Burrī al-Washqī, who was born in Tlemcen in 609/1212 and died in Ceuta in 690/1291.

1. See Suppl.—2. *al-Urjūza (al-Manẓūma al-Tilimsāniyya) fi ʾl-farāʾiḍ*, a didactic poem on the law of inheritance composed in 635/1237, Algiers 149,$_{0}$, 1317. Commentaries see Suppl. (d. Alex. Far. 8., Patna I, 111,$_{1117}$).

10a. Abū Yaḥyā b. Jamāʿa al-Tūnisī, seventh cent.

Masāʾil fi ʾl-buyūʿ, with a commentary by Abu ʾl-ʿAbbās Aḥmad b. Qāsim al-Judhāmī al-Fāsī al-Qabbāb, d. 778/1376, see Suppl. II, 346, Leid. 1824, Rabat 503,$_{3}$.

3 *The Shāfiʿīs*

1. Abū Manṣūr ʿAbd al-Qāhir b. Ṭāhir b. Muḥammad al-Baghdādī, who died in 429/1037 in Isfarāʾīn (see Suppl.).

Ibn Khall. 365, Wüst., *Schaf.* 345. 1. *Kitāb al-nāsikh wal-mansūkh* Berl. 478/9.—2. *Kitāb al-farq bayna ʾl-firaq*, on sects in Islam, ibid. 2800.—3.–9. see Suppl.

2. Abū Muḥammad ʿAbdallāh b. Yūsuf al-Juwaynī studied with his father in Juwayn, on the caravan route between Bisṭām and Nishapur, then in Nishapur
386 and Marw, | returned to Nishapur in 407/1016, and died there in Dhu ʾl-Qaʿda 438/May 1047.

Ibn Khall. 308, Yāqūt, *GW* II, 165/6 (where it is said that he died in 434), Wüst., *Schaf.* 365a. 1. *Kitāb al-jamʿ wal-farq*, on legal questions, Berl. 4811, Cairo ^{1}III, 215, ^{2}I, 508.—2. *al-Wasāʾil fī furūq al-masāʾil* Garr. 1653.—3. *Mawqif al-imām wal-maʾmūm* Alex. Fiqh Shāf. 38,$_{2}$.

3. Abū Ḥātim Maḥmūd b. al-Ḥasan b. Muḥammad al-Qazwīnī | began his stud- 483
ies in Āmul, continued them in Baghdad, and died in 440/1048 or, according to others, in 460/1068.

Wüst., *Schaf.* 371. *Kitāb al-ḥiyal*, on legal tricks, Berl. 4974.

4. Abu ʾl-Ḥasan ʿAlī b. Muḥammad b. Ḥabīb al-Māwardī studied in Basra and Baghdad, then lectured in both cities, was for a time chief *qāḍī* in Ustuwā near Nishapur, and finally settled permanently in Baghdad. It is said that he published nothing during his lifetime, and that it was not until after his death that his works were published by one of his students. He died at the age of 86 on 30 Rabīʿ I 450/27 May 1058.

Ibn Khall. 401, Wüst., *Schaf.* 395, R. Enger, *de vita et scriptis M.*, Bonn 1851. 1. *Kitāb al-aḥkām al-sulṭāniyya*, a purely abstract representation of Islamic constitutional law without any regard for reality, *Constitutiones politicae*, ed. R. Enger, Bonn 1853, C. 1298, 1324, 1327, revised by Ṭoghan Shaykh 875/1470 for Qāʾit Bāy, AS 2905, see H.A.R. Gibb, Al-M's Theory of the Khiláfat, *Isl. Cult.* XI, 291/302.—2. *Kitāb naṣīḥat al-mulūk* Paris 2447,$_{3}$.—3. *Kitāb qawānīn al-wizāra* Krafft 475.—4. *Kitāb tashīl al-naẓar wa-taʿjīl al-ẓafar*, on politics and the art of government, Gotha 1872.—5. *Kitāb al-ḥāwi ʾl-kabīr fi ʾl-furūʿ* Garr. 1778, Cairo ^{2}III, 215, ^{2}I, 512, Patna I, 85,$_{865/7}$.—6. *Kitāb aʿlām al-nubuwwa*, on the signs of prophethood, Berl. 2527, Cairo ^{1}I, 270, ^{2}I, 90, cf. Fr. Diez, *Denkwürdigkeiten von Asien*, II, 382, M. Schreiner in *Kohuts Sem. Studies*, 502/13.—7. *Kitāb al-amthāl wal-ḥikam*, 300 traditions, 300 aphorisms, and 300 verses in 10 *fuṣūl* of 30 each, Leid. 382.—8. *Kitāb al-bughya al-ʿulyā fī adab al-dīn wal-dunyā*, on ethics, Berl. 5393/4, Br. Mus. 1512, Bodl. I, 299, 307, 322, Qawala I, 217, Patna I, 192,$_{1737}$, print. Constantinople 1299, C. 1309, 1310, in the margin *OB* I, 4500.—9. *Kitāb maʿrifat al-faḍāʾil* Esc. ^{2}224.—10. *Kitāb al-ḥisba*, an independent work, Jer., Khāl. 49, 17,$_{2}$ *al-Rutba fī ṭalab al-ḥisba*, Fātiḥ 3495, see Suppl. III, 1223/4.—11. see Suppl.—12. *Kitāb al-nukat wal-ʿuyūn*, a Qurʾān commentary, additionally Garr. 1258, library of Yāsīn Bāshaʿyān al-ʿAbbāsī in Basra (letter to Ritter).

| 5. Abū ʿĀmir Muḥammad b. Aḥmad b. Muḥammad b. ʿAbbād al-ʿAbbādī 484
al-Harawī was born in Herat in 375/985, and studied there and in Nishapur.

After much travelling he became a *qāḍī* in Herat where he died in Shawwāl 458/September 1066.

Ibn Khall. 558, Wüst., *Gesch.* 204. *Ṭabaqāt al-Shāfiʿiyyīn* ḤKh IV, $139_{,7900}$, Berl. 1033, Br. Mus. Suppl. $1203_{,5}$, AS 3302, Alex. Fun. $170_{,4}$, see Suppl.

387 | 6. Abu 'l-Qāsim ʿAbd al-Raḥmān b. Muḥammad b. Aḥmad b. Muḥammad al-Fūrānī al-Marwazī was the head of the Shāfiʿīs in Marw and died at the age of 73 in Ramaḍān 461/June 1069.

Ibn Khall. 337, Wüst., *Schaf.* 417. *Kitāb al-ibāna fi 'l-fiqh*, on which a *Tatimma* by al-Mutawallī ʿAbd al-Raḥmān b. Maʾmūn al-Nīsābūrī, d. 478/1085, Cairo ^{1}III, 200.

7. Abū ʿAlī al-Ḥusayn b. Muḥammad b. Aḥmad al-Marwarrūdhī al-Qāḍī was regarded as the greatest *faqīh* of his time in Khurāsān, and died on 23 Muḥarram 462/1 November 1069.

Ibn Khall. 337, Wüst., *Schaf.* 418. *Fatāwā* Paris 983, see Suppl.

8. Abu 'l-Muẓaffar ʿImād al-Dīn Shahfūr Ṭāhir b. Muḥammad al-Isfarāʾinī, who died in 471/1078.

Kitāb al-tabṣīr fi 'l-dīn wa-tamyīz al-firqa al-nājiya ʿan firaq al-hālikīn Berl. 2801, Paris 1452 (see Suppl.).

9. Abū Isḥāq Ibrāhīm b. ʿAlī b. Yūsuf al-Fīrūzābādī al-Shīrāzī, born in 393/1003 in Fīrūzābād, went to Shiraz in 410/1019, then to Basra, and in 415/1024 to Baghdad. When Niẓām al-Mulk founded the Madrasa that was named after him in 459/1066 he appointed him as its head on the first of Dhū 'l-Ḥijja, despite earlier doubts. In Dhu 'l-Ḥijja 475/April 1083 he went as an envoy to the caliph al-Muqtadī in Nishapur. This trip was something of a homecoming parade, as people everywhere paid homage to this famous scholar. He died soon after his return, on 21 Jumādā II 476/6 November 1083.

485 | Ibn Khall. 5, Wüst., *Schaf.* 452. 1. *Kitāb al-muhadhdhab fi 'l-madhhab* Berl. 4456/8, Gotha 939 (fragment), Pet. Ros. 18, Ind. Off. 1775, Cairo ^{1}III, 280, ^{2}I, 542.—Commentaries: a. al-Nawawī, d. 676/1277 (p. 496), Berl. 4459, Garr. 1780/1, Cairo ^{1}III, 241.—b. *Kitāb al-suʾāl ʿammā fī kitāb al-M. min al-ishkāl* by

Abu ʾl-Ḥasan Yaḥyā b. Abi ʾl-Khayr b. Sālim al-ʿImrānī al-Yamanī, d. 558/1163 (Subkī, *Ṭab.* IV, 324, Ibn al-ʿImād, *Shadh. al-dhahab* IV, 185), Leid. 1783.—c. *Iḥtirāzāt al-M.* by Ibn al-Haytham ʿUbaydallāh b. Yaḥyā al-Ṣanʿī, d. 550/1158 (ḤKh VI, 275), Ind. Off. 1776.—d. *Maʿānī alfāẓ al-M.* by Abu ʾl-Qāsim ʿUmar b. Muḥammad b. ʿIkrima al-Jazarī, AS $457_{,4}$, f. 94a/163b).—e. Anon. *Tafsīr alfāẓ al-mushkilāt fi ʾl-M.* AS $457_{,3}$ (f. 55a/93a).—10 other commentaries, 3 abstracts, and 3 books with traditions in Ahlw, loc. cit.—II. *Kitāb al-tanbīh fi ʾl fiqh*, composed in 452–3/1061–2, one of the five most famous works on Shāfiʿī law, Berl. 4460, Leid. 1782, Bodl. I, 200, Cairo [1]III, 210, [2]I, 506, H. Keizer, *Handboek voor het Mohammedaansch regt*, Leid. 1853, ed. Th. W. Juynboll, Leiden 1879, see R. Grasshof, *Die allgemeinen Lehren des Obligationenrechts usw. Ein Abschnitt aus dem* K. al-buyūʿ *des A.Y. al-Sh.*, Diss. Göttingen 1895.—Commentaries: 1. *Ghunyat al-muftī* by Aḥmad b. Muḥammad b. Yūnus al-Irbilī al-Mawṣilī, d. 622/1225, Bodl. I, 212, 238, Cairo [1]III, 236, 248, [2]I, 527.—2. ʿAbd al-ʿAzīz b. ʿAbd al-Karīm al-Jīlī, completed in 629/1231, Cairo [1]III, 282, [2]I, 543.—3. *Taṣḥīḥ al-T.* by al-Nawawī, d. 676/1277 (p. 496), Br. Mus. 254, Cairo [1]III, 111, 202 (glosses see Suppl. in Fir. Ricc. 7).—4. *al-Iqlīd li-darʾ al-taqlīd* by ʿAbd al-Raḥmān b. Ibrāhīm b. al-Firkāḥ, d. 690/1291 (p. 497), Berl. 4461, Patna I, $78_{,788}$.—5. *Kifāyat al-nabīh* by Aḥmad b. Muḥammad al-Bukhārī b. al-Rafʿa, d. 710/1310 (II, 133), Cairo [1]III, 266/7, [2]I, 536, Patna I, $103_{,1035}$. Abstract, *Tashīl al-hidāya*, by Aḥmad b. Luʾluʾ al-Miṣrī b. al-Naqīb, d. 769/1367 (II, 104), Berl. 4465, Garr. 1782.—6. (see Suppl.) Abū Bakr b. | Ibrāhīm al-Zankalūnī (Sankalūnī), d 740/1339, Berl. 4462/3, Paris 388
1023 (?), Bodl. I, 210.—7. *Nukat al-nabīh* by Kamāl al-Dīn al-Nashāʾī, d. 757/1356, Cairo [1]III, 287.—8. Badr al-Dīn al Zarkashī, d. 794/1392 (II, 91), vol. I Berl. 4466, Patna I, $91_{,927}$.—9. ʿUmar b. ʿAlī b. al-Mulaqqin, d. 804/1401 (II, 92), Cairo [1]III, 236.—10. *al-Wāḍiḥ al-nabīh* by Muḥammad b. Ibrāhīm al-Sulamī, eighth cent., Cairo [1]III, 289, [2]I, 546.—11., 12. see Suppl.—13. Abu ʾl-ʿAbbās Aḥmad al-Zuhrī, composed in 784/1382, Alex. Fiqh Shāf. 25.—Abstracts: 1. *al-Mughnī fiʾkhtiṣār al-T.* by Hibatallāh b. ʿAbd al-Raḥīm al-Ḥamawī b. al-Bārizī, d. 738/1337 (II, 86), Berl. 4467, commentary by Ibrāhīm b. Mūsā al-Abnāsī, d. 802/1399, Cairo
| [1]III, 211.—2. *Taṣḥīḥ al-nabīh fiʾkhtiṣār al-T.* by Aḥmad b. Ṣāliḥ al-Dimashqī 486
al-Biqāʿī, d. 795/1393, Berl. 4468.—29 commentaries, 2 abstracts, and 1 versification are mentioned in Ahlw., 4469.—III. *Talkhīṣ ʿilal al-fiqh*, on all kinds of legal questions, Berl. 4980.—IV. *Kitāb al-maʿūna fi ʾl-jadal*, on the art of disputation, Gotha 1183, possibly identical with *Maʿūnat al-mubtadiʾīn wa-tadhkirat al-muntahīn*, Garr. 867.—V. *ʿAqīda*, creed, Berl. 1946.—VI. *Ṭabaqāt al-fuqahāʾ* Berl. 9991, Leipz. 704, Esc. [1]1848, printed together with *Ṭabaqāt al-Shāfiʿiyya* by Ibn Hidāyatallāh al-Ḥusaynī, d. 1014/1605, Baghdad 1356.—VII. *al-Ishāra ilā madhhab al-ḥaqq* Alex. Tawḥīd $30_{,2}$.—VIII., IX. see Suppl.

10. Abū Ḥākim ʿAbdallāh b. Ibrāhīm b. ʿAbdallāh al-Khabrī came from Khabr near Shiraz. A student of Abū Isḥāq, he lived as a teacher in Baghdad and died in Dhu ʾl-Ḥijja 476/April–May 1083.

Wüst., *Schaf.* 453. *Kitāb al-talkhīṣ fī ʿilm al-farāʾiḍ*, on the law of inheritance, Berl. 4687, BDMG 43.

11. Abū Naṣr ʿAbd al-Sayyid b. Muḥammad b. al-Ṣabbāgh was born in Baghdad in 400/1009. When, at the opening of the Niẓāmiyya, Abū Isḥāq was reluctant to assume the position as its head, Abū Naṣr was given this task, but just three weeks into the job, had to step aside to make way for Abū Isḥāq. After the latter's death Abū Naṣr first became his successor, but after going blind he was no longer up to the task and had to cede his position to Abū Saʿd al-Mutawallī, d. 478/1086 (Ibn Khall. 338, Abū Bakr b. Hidāyatallāh, *Ṭab. al-shāf.* 62, see no. 6). Niẓam al-Mulk, whom he visited in Isfahan, promised him his own school in Baghdad, but he died died within three days of his return, on 14 Jumādā I 477/19 September 1083.

Ibn Khall. 372, Wüst., *Schaf.* 457. *Kitāb al-shāmil fi ʾl-furūʿ* Cairo [1]III, 234, [2]520, *Muntakhab* by Ismāʿīl b. Muḥammad b. Maymūn al-Ḥaḍramī, d. 776/1374, ibid. III, 273, [2]I, 537.

12. Abu ʾl-Maʿālī ʿAbd al-Malik b. Abī Muḥammad ʿAbdallāh (no. 2) b. Yūsuf
487 al-Juwaynī Imām al-Ḥaramayn, was born | on 18 Muḥarram 419/12 February 1028 in Bushtaniqān,[1] a village near Nishapur. When he was not even twenty years old he assumed his father's teaching position after the latter had died.
389 However, | when Sultan Ṭughril Beg persecuted the Muʿtazilīs at the instigation of his vizier Manṣūr al-Kundarī he had to flee to the Hijaz, in 445/1053. There he taught for four years in Mecca and Medina, which is how he got his *laqab*. After he returned to his homeland Niẓām al-Mulk founded a Niẓāmiyya for him in Nishapur, where he continued to work until the end of his life. He died in his village of origin, where he had gone in hopes of being healed from an illness, on 25 Rabīʿ II 478/20 August 1085.

Ibn Khall. 351. Wüst., *Akad.* no. 38, Schaf. 365c, M. Schreiner in *Graetz' Monatsschr.* XXV, 314ff. 1. *Kitāb al-waraqāt*, on the *uṣūl al-fiqh*, Berl. 4358/9, Hamb. Or. Sem. 128, Paris 672,$_5$ (?), Br. Mus. 252,$_3$, 557,$_3$, Algiers 213,$_3$, 959/62.—Commentaries: 1. *al-Darakāt* by ʿAbd al-Raḥmān b. Ibrāhīm b. al-Firkāḥ,

1 Corrupted to Nashiqān in Ibn ʿAsākir, *Tabyīn kadhib al-muftarī* 284,$_{14}$.

d. 680/1291 (p. 497), Berl. 4360, Gotha 922, Tüb. 108, Paris 1266,$_2$, Br. Mus. 548,$_3$, Suppl. 256.—2. Jalāl al-Dīn b. Muḥammad b. Aḥmad al-Maḥallī, d. 864/1460 (II, 114), Berl. 4361/2, Gotha 923, Tüb. 107,$_2$, Br. Mus. Suppl. 257, Bodl. I, 152, (cf. II, 570b), Esc. ^{2}102,$_1$, 521,$_6$, Garr. 1794, *Bull. de Corr. Afr.* 1884, p. 371, no. 34, Alex. Fun. 170,$_1$, Cairo ^{1}II, 262, 254, 258, Makr. 45.—Glosses: a. *Qurrat al-ʿayn* by Muḥammad b. Muḥammad al-Ḥaṭṭāb al-Mālikī (II, 387), completed in 953/1546, Gotha 924, Esc. ^{2}102,$_5$, 521,$_6$, Paris 813, Algiers 963, Alex. Uṣūl 17.—b. Aḥmad b. Muḥammad al-Dimyāṭī al-Shāfiʿī, print. C. 1303.—3. Muḥammad b. Muḥammad b. ʿAbd al-Raḥmān b. Imām al-Kāmiliyya, d. 874/1469 (II, 77), Berl. 4368, Paris 624,$_2$, Alex. Uṣūl 12, 18, Fun. 176,$_2$, Cairo ^{1}II, 261.—4. At the same time glosses to 2, by Aḥmad b. Muḥammad b. Qāsim al-ʿUbādī al-Qāhirī, d. 994/1586 (II, 320), a. *al-Kabīra* Berl. 4363/4, Patna II, 45,$_{2628,1}$.—b. *al-Ṣaghīra* Berl. 4365, Alex. Uṣūl 12.—Glosses by Aḥmad b. Aḥmad al-Sunbāṭī, d. 995/1587 (II, 368), Berl. 4366, Algiers 218,$_2$, by Aḥmad b. Salāma al-Qalyūbī, d. 1069/1658 (II, 364), Berl. 4367, Alex. Uṣūl 9, 18.—5.–10. see Suppl. (6. also Alex. Fun. 114).—11. *Zubdat al-mukhtaṣarāt* | by Sharaf al-Dīn Yūnus al-ʿAythāwī, d. 978/1570 (II, 320), Alex. 488
Fun. 174,$_{14}$.—5 commentaries and 4 versifications are mentioned in Ahlw., 4368.—II (III). *Nihāyat al-maṭlab fī dirāyat al-madhhab* Alex. Fiqh Shāf. 44, Cairo ^{1}III, 288, ^{2}I, 546.—Abstract, *Ghāya fī ikhtiṣār al-N.*, by ʿAbd al-ʿAzīz b. ʿAbd al-Salām al-Sulamī, d. 660/1262 (p. 430), Gotha 949 (autograph dated 645/1247), Cairo ^{2}III, 245, abstract *Ṣafwat al-madhhab*, see Suppl. I, 971,$_{672}$, with Patna I, 104,$_{1066}$ (autograph). Versification *al-Kifāya fī naẓm bayt al-Gh.* by Muḥammad Najal Fatā al-Ẓahīr, Garr. 1783.—III (IV). *Mughīth al-khalq fī bayān al-ḥaqq*, a demonstration of the fact that the legal opinons of al-Shāfiʿī are superior to those of the other orthodox imams, Berl. 4853 (only the preamble), Paris 984, Br. Mus. Suppl. 1221,$_1$, Alex. Uṣūl 20, Cairo ^{1}II, 265, VII, 700, ^{2}I, 395.—IV (V). *Kitāb al-irshād (ilā qawāṭiʿ al-adilla) fī uṣūl al-iʿtiqād (ilā sawāʾ al-iʿtiqād)* Leid. 1983, Br. Mus. 1628,$_2$, Algiers 616, ed. and transl. J. Luciani, Paris 1938.—Commentaries: 1. Ibrāhīm b. Yūsuf b. Muḥammad b. al-Marʾa, d. after 616/1219, Cairo ^{1}II, 58, ^{2}I, 188.—2. *al-Muqtaraḥ* by Abu ʾl-ʿIzz b. al-Muẓaffar b. ʿAlī al-Shāfiʿī, Algiers 617, abstract by the same, ibid. 618.—Abbreviation *al-ʿAqīda al-Silālajiyya* by Abū ʿAmr ʿUthmān b. ʿAbdallāh al-Silālajī (Suppl. I, 676), ḤKh IV, 243, Garr. 1559.—V (VI). *Kitāb lumaʿ al-adilla fī qawāʿid ʿaqāʾid ahl al-sunna* Berl. 2073, BDMG 16.—Commentary by ʿAbdallāh b. Muḥammad al-Fihrī al-Tilimsānī, d. 658/1260 (Subkī, *Ṭab.* V, 60), Berl. 2074, Cairo ^{1}II, 30.—VI (VII). *Risāla fī ithbāt al-istiwāʾ wal-fawqiyya*, on sura 20,4, Landb.—Br. 591.—VII (VIII). A sermon, Berl. 3953.—VIII (IX). A *qaṣīda* for his son as an injunction to piety (usually attributed to Ismāʿīl b. Abī Bakr b. al-Muqriʾ, d. 837/1433, II, 190) Berl. 7621,$_3$.—IX. *Ghiyāth al-umam fī ʾltiyāth al-ẓulam* Alex. Taʾr. 92.—X.–XVII. see Suppl. (XI. expressly attributed to Imām al-Ḥaramayn in AS 2246,$_3$ Ritter; XII.

cited as *al-Risāla al-Niẓāmiyya* by Ibn Taymiyya, *Majm. ras. al-kubrā* I, $464_{,9}$; XVII. also Patna II, $543_{,2916}$).—XVIII. *Risāla fi 'l-fiqh* Mosul $101_{,387}$ (corrupted, see Suppl. II, $973_{,8}$).

390 | 13. (14). ʿAbd al-Wāḥid b. Ismāʿīl al-Rūyānī Abu 'l-Maḥāsin, d. 502/1108 (see Suppl.).

Ibn Khall. 363. 1. *Kitāb baḥr al-madhhab,* the most detailed account of Shāfiʿī *fiqh,* Cairo ^{1}III, 197, ^{2}I, 500.—2. See Suppl.

489 | 15. ʿAlī b. Muḥammad b. ʿAlī al-Kiyāʾ al-Harāsī al-Ṭabaristānī, who was born on 5 Dhu 'l-Qaʿda 450/25 December 1058, studied together with al-Ghazzāli in Nishapur under Imām al-Ḥaramayn then taught for a time in Bayhaq, before becoming a professor at the Niẓāmiyya in Baghdad. Under the Saljūq Barkyārūq b. Malikshāh (487–98/1094–1104), with whom he stood in high regard, he occasionally acted as a *qāḍī.* He died on 1 Muḥarram 504/20 July 1110.

Ibn Khall. 403, al-Damīrī, *Ḥayāt al-ḥay.* II, 196. 1. *Kitāb uṣūl al-dīn* Cairo ^{1}II, 4, ^{2}I, 164.—2. *Aḥkām al-Qurʾān* ibid. ^{1}I, 122, ^{2}I, 31.—e. see Suppl.

16. Abu 'l-Faḍl ʿAbd al-ʿAzīz b. ʿAlī b. ʿAbd al-ʿAzīz al-Ushnuhī, who came from Ushnuh[2] in Azerbaijan, flourished around 505/1111.

Al-Ushnuhiyya fi 'l-farāʾiḍ, on the laws of inheritance, ḤKh IV, 8973, Berl. 4689, Gotha 1098, Garr. $2109_{,2}$.—Commentaries: 1. Badr al-Dīn b. Qāḍī Shuhba, d. 874/1469 (II, 30), composed in 832/1428, Munich 367, Bodl. I, $277_{,3}$.—2. Muḥammad b. Muḥammad al-Shaʿbī (ḤKh IV, 397), Tüb. 127, Paris 1037, Alex. Far. 3.—3.–5. see Suppl.—6. Anon. *al-Mawāhib al-saniyya,* Alex. Far. 17.

17. Abū Bakr Muḥammad b. Aḥmad b. al-Ḥusayn b. ʿUmar al-Shāshī[3] al-Qaffāl Fakhr al-Islām al-Mustaẓhirī, d. 507/1113 (see Suppl.).

---

2 I.e. the capital of what is now the Kurdish district of Ushnūya, on the southern tip of Lake Urmiya; see M. Bittner, *SBWA, phil.-hist. Cl.* 133, 1895, III.

3 Whose family came from Shāsh (following Kāshgharī, *Dīwān lughāt al-Turk* I, $369_{,5}$ also Täshkân = Täshkänd, misprint Tärken) on the right bank of the Syr Daryā, al-Samʿānī $325_{,r9}$, Bartold, *Turkestan* 169ff.

| Ibn Khall. 561. *Kitāb ḥilyat al-ʿulamāʾ fī madhāhib al-fuqahāʾ*, an account of 391
Shāfiʿī doctrine with a rejection of the other *madhhabs*, named *al-Mustaẓhirī* because it was dedicated to the caliph al-Mustaẓhir billāh, vol. I, Gotha 1149, Cairo ^{1}III, 224, ^{2}I, 512.—Abstract *Tuḥfat al-nubahāʾ fi ʾkhtilāf al-fuqahāʾ* by Muḥammad b. Muḥammad b. Bahrām al-Dimashqī, d. 705/1305, Berl. 4860.—2. *Kitāb al-ʿumda fī furūʿ al-Shāfiʿiyya* ḤKh IV, 8339, Mosul 170,$_{26}$. Commentaries: a. Ibn al-ʿAṭṭār, *Dībāja*, Gotha | 2, 79.—b. Muḥammad b. ʿAbd al-Dāʾim 490
al-Birmāwī, d. 831/1427 (II, 95), *Dībāja*, ibid. 80.—3. *Talkhīṣ al-qawl fi ʾl-masʾala al-mansūba li-Abi ʾl-ʿAbbās b. Surayj* (d. 306/918, p. 191) *fi ʾl-ṭalāq* Br. Mus. Suppl. 1203,$_{2}$.—4. *Kitāb al-uṣūl* or *Kitāb al-khamsīn fī u. al-Ḥanafiyya* ḤKh V, 81,$_{10091}$, Ind. Off. 1439/40, Bank. XIX, 1, 1501, Āṣaf. 88, Rāmpūr 2, Calc. Madr. 17, print. Lucknow 1210, 1279, Delhi 1303.—Commentaries: a. Ilāhdād al-Jawnpūrī (? d. 923/1517 or 932/1525, see Suppl. II, 267/8), Ind. Off. 1441/3, Bank. XIX, 1, 1494, Calc. Madr. 18, print. Delhi 1293, 1302.—b. *Maʿdin al-uṣūl* by Ṣafī Allāh b. Nuṣayr, Ind. Off. 1444.

18. Abu ʾl-Maʿālī ʿAyn al-quḍāt ʿAbdallāh b. Muḥammad b. ʿAlī al-Miyānajī al-Hamadhānī, who died in 525/1131 (see Suppl.).

Ibn Khall. 561. 1. *Kitāb zubdat al-ḥaqāʾiq*, on the foundations of religion, Berl. 1727, AS 1839/40, Šehīd ʿAlī Pāšā 1209 (Meier, *Isl.* XXIV, 6), Zanjān, *Lughat al-ʿArab* VI, 1928, 94.—2. *Kitāb shakwa ʾl-gharīb ʿani ʾl-awṭān ilā ʿulamāʾ al-buldān*, a defence against accusations of heresy and pretention to prophethood, for which he was jailed in Baghdad and then crucified in Hamadan, Berl. 2076.

19. Abu ʾl-Khayr Yaḥyā b. Saʿd b. Yaḥyā al-ʿImrānī, who died in 558/1163 (see Suppl.)

Ibn Hidāyatallāh, *Ṭab. al-Shāf.* 79. *Kitāb al-bayān fi ʾl-furūʿ* Brit. Mus. Suppl. 308/9, Cairo ^{1}III, 199.

19a. Quṭb al-Dīn Abu ʾl-Maʿālī Masʿūd b. Muḥammad al-Nīsābūrī, who taught in Damascus and died in 578/1182.

Kitāb al-hādī fi ʾl-furūʿ ḤKh VI, 470,$_{14331}$, Alex. Fiqh Shāf. 45 (al-Subkī, *Ṭab.* IV, 317 who only mentions his brother Mawdūd, d. 554/1159).

20. Abū ʿAbdallāh Muḥammad b. ʿAlī b. Muḥammad b. al-Ḥusayn al-Raḥbī Muwaffaq al-Dīn b. al-Muttaqīna, who died in 579/1183.

Bughyat (*Ghunyat*) *al-bāḥith ʿan jumal al-mawārīth* (*fī ʿilm al-wārith wal-farāʾiḍ*), usually *al-Urjūza al-Raḥbiyya*, 180 *rajaz* verses on the law of inheritance (wrongly attributed to a certain Ṣalāḥ al-Dīn Yūsuf b. ʿAbd al-Laṭīf
491 al-Ḥamawī | in ḤKh IV, 8636), Berl. 4691/2, Gotha 111/2 (where other MSS are listed), Alex. Fun. 92,$_{1}$, 146,$_{5}$, 149,$_{6}$, print. C. 1310, cf. *Jones' Works*, quarto ed. III, 467ff.—Commentaries: 1. Ibrāhīm b. ʿAlī al-Zamzamī, d. 864/1460, Berl. 4693.—2. Muḥammad b. Ibrāhīm al-Salāmī, d. 879/1474, Berl. 4676, 4696, Alex. Far. 9.—3. Muḥammad b. Muḥammad Sibṭ al-Māridīnī, d. 934/1527 (II, 357), Berl. 4694/5, Gotha 1113/4 (where other MSS are listed), Heid. *ZDMG* 91, 394, Garr. 2111,$_{1}$, Alex. Far. 9, 15.—Glosses, see Suppl.—4. *al-Fawāʾid al-Shinshawriyya*, by ʿAbdallāh b. Muḥammad al-Shinshawrī, d. 999/1590, (II, 320), Berl. 4697, Garr. 1870, 2111,$_{2}$.—Glosses: a. Muḥammad b. ʿAlī al-Adfīnī al-Buḥayrī, completed in 1018/1609, Berl. 4698.—b. Yūsuf al-Zayyāt, ibid. 4699.—c. Muḥammad al-Ḥifnāwī (see Suppl.), also Alex. Far. 6.—d. see Suppl.—e. Muḥammad al-Khiḍrī al-Dimyāṭī al-Shāfiʿī, Būlāq 1293.—5. Anon., Berl. 4700, Gotha 1114, *Taʿlīq*, Ind. Off. 1740.—6. *Fatḥ aqfāl al-mabāḥith* by ʿAbdallāh al-Sirmīnī al-Shafiʿī or by Yūsuf al-Ḥalabī, Alex. Far 12, Mosul 36,$_{173}$.—7.–15. see Suppl. (11. Alex. Fun. 82,$_{3}$, 14. Ibid. Far. 7).—16. al-Ushmūnī, Berl. Brill M. 161,$_{4}$.—17. al-Jawjarī, ibid. 5.—II. *Nuzhat al-mushtāq fī ʿulamāʾ al-firāq*, Medina, *ZDMG* 90, 119 (where Abu 'l-Barakāt?).

21. ʿUmar b. ʿAlī b. Samura b. al-Ḥusayn al-Jaʿdī, who died in 586/1190.

Ṭabaqāt fuqahāʾ jibāl al-Yaman wa-ʿuyūn (*sādāt, ruʾasāʾ*) *al-Yaman*, on the Shāfiʿīs in Yemen, Berl. 10034, ʿA. Emīrī 2401, Alex. Taʾr. 85.

392 | 22. Abū Shujāʿ Muḥammad b. ʿAlī b. Muḥammad b. Shuʿayb b. al-Dahhān Fakhr al-Dīn al-Baghdādī received a very diverse education in law, philology, mathematics, and astronomy in Baghdad. In Mosul he joined the vizier Jamāl al-Dīn al-Iṣfahānī, then went to Ṣalāḥ al-Dīn, who sent him to Mayyafāriqīn to take up an administrative post. But because he did not get along with his principal there he left for Damascus, and in 586/1190 went to Egypt, hoping to find a better job there, but soon returned to Damascus. In 589/1193 he made the
492 pilgrimage but, on | the way back, in Ṣafar of the following year/February 1194, he was killed by the fall of his camel near Ḥilla.

Ibn Khall. 655, Wüst., *Gesch.* 281. *Taqwīm al-naẓar fi 'l-masāʾil al-khilāfiyya*, tables over several columns: 1. a question, 2. the Shāfiʿī position, 3. the Ḥanafīs, 4–7. the foundations of these views, 8. the Mālikī view, 9. the Ḥanbalī view, 10. general remarks. The questions are divided into four classes: 1. *al-ʿibādāt*,

2. *muʿāmala* 3. *nikāḥ*, 4. *jināyāt*. In the introduction there is a summary of the elements of logic and grammar. It was composed in 563/1167, Paris 788/9, Cairo ^{1}III, 209.

23. Abū Shujāʿ Aḥmad b. al-Ḥasan b. Aḥmad al-Iṣfahānī al-ʿAbbādānī Taqī al-Dīn, allegedly born in 434/1042 in Basra, taught there for more than 40 years and died after 500/1106.[4]

Yāqūt, GW III, 598. *Kitāb al-taqrīb fi 'l-fiqh* or *Mukhtaṣar fi 'l-fiqh ʿalā madhhab al-imām al-Shāfiʿī* or *Ghāyat al-ikhtiṣār*, a compendium of the *furūʿ*, Berl. 4481, Gotha 942 (where other MSS are listed), Br. Mus. Suppl. 307, 1234,$_{2}$, Patna I, 96,$_{969}$, II, 418,$_{2587,4}$; *Précis de jurisprudence musulmane selon le rite châféite par A. Ch. publiée par* S. Keijzer, Leiden 1859, cf. E. Sachau, *Muhammedanisches Recht nach shāfiʿtischem Ritus*, Berlin 1897 (*Lehrb. des Or. Sem.* XVII)—Commentaries: 1. *Tuḥfat al-labīb* by Muḥammad b. ʿAlī b. Daqīq al-ʿĪd, d. 702/1302 (II, 66), Berl. 4482.—2. *Kifāyat al-akhyār* by Taqī al-Dīn Abū Bakr b. Muḥammad al-Ḥiṣnī, d. 829/1426 (II, 95), Berl. 4483, Ms. or. qu. 2042, Gotha 946 (where other MSS are listed), Hamb. Or. Sem. 62,$_{4}$, Garr. 1785, Patna I, 10,$_{1083}$.—3. *Fatḥ al-qarīb al-mujīb* or *al-Qawl al-mukhtār fi sharḥ Gh. al-i.* by Muḥammad b. al-Qāsim al-Ghazzī, d. 918/1512 (II, 320), Patna I, 99,$_{1017}$. *La révélation de l'omniprésent, publ. et trad. par* L.W.C. van den Berg, Leiden 1895 (cf. Goldziher, ZDMG L, 313), lith. C. 1279, print. C. 1285, 1289 (see Suppl.).—Glosses: a. Ibrāhīm al-Bājūrī, d. 1277/1861 (II, 487), print. Būlāq 1272, 1285, 1289 and others (used by Sachau as the basis for his account).—b.–e. see Suppl. | (c. Garr. 493
1786)—f. Ibrāhīm b. ʿAbd al-Raḥmān al-Bilbaysī, completed in 1179/1765, Alex. Fiqh Shāf. 16 (but going by the title rather to 4.).—g. Ibrāhīm b. Muḥammad b. Shihāb al-Dīn b. Khālid al-Anṣārī, Patna I, 85,$_{858}$.—4. *al-Iqnāʿ* by Muḥammad b. Muḥammad al-Khaṭīb al-Shirbīnī, d. 977/1569 (II, 320), Berl. 4494, Munich 364, Leid. 1791, Garr. 1787, Makr. 5, Patna I, 78,$_{789}$, print. C. 1306, 1307.—Glosses: a.–d. see Suppl.—e. Ibrāhīm b. ʿAṭāʾ al-Marḥūmī al-Azharī, completed in 1073/1662, Gotha 944, Haupt 115, Alex. Fiqh Shāf. 20.—f. *Taqrīb al-jumal* by Sulaymān al-Jamal, d. 1202/1790 (II, 353), Alex. Fiqh Shāf. 2.—g. al-Qalyūbī, ibid. 19. | — 393
7 glosses in Ahlw., 4484.—5.–11. see Suppl.—12. *Tuḥfat al-abrār fī ḥall alfāẓ Gh. al-i.* by Abu 'l-ʿAbbās Aḥmad al-Bulqīnī al-Shāfiʿī, Alex. Fiqh Shāf. 9.—13. Anon. on the preamble, Garr. 1788, anon. *al-Bidāya* Patna I, 79,$_{802}$.

23a. ʿAlī b. Ḥusayn Jamāl al-Dīn al-Amīr, sixth cent.

4 The information 'd. 593' taken from Sarkis 318 in the Supplement is not authenticated.

Durar al-farāʾiḍ, with the commentary *Taʿlīqa* from the seventh century, Berl. 1746, Bank. XX,$_{2}$, 1941 = Patna I, 110,$_{1109}$.

24. Muẓaffar b. Muḥammad b. Ismāʿīl al-Tabrīzī, who was born in 558/1163 and died in 621/1224.

Al-Mukhtaṣar fi ʾl-furūʿ, commentaries: 1. Majd al-Dīn al-Sankalūnī, d. 740/1339, Cairo ^{1}III, 235.—2. ʿUmar b. ʿAlī b. al-Mulaqqin, d. 804/1401 (II, 96), ibid. 236.—3. Anon., Leid. 1808.—4. others in Ahlw., 4663,$_{7}$.

25. Abu ʾl-Qāsim ʿAbd al-Karīm b. Muḥammad b. ʿAbd al-Karīm al-Rāfiʿī al-Qazwīnī lectured in the great mosque of Qazvin and died at the age of around 66 in Dhu ʾl-Qaʿda 623/November 1226.

Naw. 753, *Fawāt* II, 3, Suyūṭī, *de Interpr.*, ed. Meursinge 63, Ibn Hidāyatallāh, *Ṭab. al-Shāf.* 83. 1. *Kitāb al-muḥarrar* Br. Mus. Suppl. 310, Ind. Off. 278, Cairo ^{1}III, 272, Patna I, 103,$_{1046}$. Commentaries: a.–e. see Suppl. (e. Garr. 1790).—f. Abu Bakr al-Shahrazūrī, Br. Mus. Suppl. 311.—Abstracts: a. *Minhāj al-ṭālibīn* by al-Nawāwī, no. 29.—b. *al-Ījāz fī mukhtaṣar al-M.* by Taqī al-Dīn Maḥmūd b. Muḥammad al-Kirmānī al-Shāṭibī, d. 807/1404, Alex. Fiqh Shāf. 7, anon. commentary on the *farāʾiḍ* Garr. 2060,$_{3}$.—c. Anon., Br. Mus. Suppl.
494 312.—2. *Kitāb al-tadwīn fī dhikr ahl al-ʿilm bi-Qazwīn* Br. Mus. | 959, Alex. Taʾr. 47.—3. *al-Amāli ʾl-shāriḥa li-mufradāt al-Fātiḥa,* in 30 *majlis*, Cairo ^{1}I, 272, ^{2}I, 91.—4. *Sharḥ al-wajīz* see p. 543.—5., 6. see Suppl.

26. Sayf al-Dīn Abu ʾl-Ḥasan ʿAlī b. Abī ʿAlī b. Muḥammad al-Thaʿlabī al-Āmidī, who was born in 551/1156 in Āmid, was originally a Ḥanbalī, but moved to Shāfiʿism in Baghdad. Having studied philosophy in Syria, he became a teacher at the Madrasat al-Qarāfa al-Ṣughrā, and in 592/1196 became a professor at the Ẓāfirī mosque in Cairo. Because he had an interest in philosophy he was accused of heresy, causing him to flee to Hama. Even though he once more received an appointment, at the al-Madrasa al-ʿAzīziyya in Damascus, he was soon dismissed because, behind al-Malik al-Kāmil's back, he was negotiating a post as a judge with the prince of Āmid, who had been deposed by the former in 631/1233. He died in 631/1233.

Ibn Khall. 405, I. A. Uṣ. II, 174. 1. *Kitāb abkār al-afkār*, on philosophical dogmatics, composed in 612/1215, Berl. 1741, AS 2163/8.—2. *Kitāb iḥkām al-ḥukkām fī uṣūl al-aḥkām*, dedicated to al-Malik al-Muʿaẓẓam of Damascus (615–24/1218–27), Paris 791, Yeni 303, Cairo ^{1}II, 235, ^{2}I, 377.—3.–6. see Suppl. (4. Garr. 828).

27. (29). Najm al-Dīn ʿAbd al-Ghaffār b. ʿAbd al-Karīm (no. 25) al-Qazwīnī, who was famous as a Sufi and a miracle worker, died in Muḥarram 665/October 1266 in Qazvin.

1. *al-Ḥāwi ʾl-ṣaghīr fi ʾl-fatāwī* Leipz. 374, Paris 997, Br. Mus. 252, Bodl. I, 188, II, 94, Ambros. 64, Esc. ^{1}1047, Garr. 1801, Patna I, $85_{,863}$.—Commentaries: 1. ʿAbd al-ʿAzīz b. Muḥammad al-Ṭūsī, d. 707/1307, Cairo ^{1}III, 275.—2. ʿAlī b. Ismāʿīl al-Qūnawī, d. 727/1326 (II 86), Berl. 4512, Ind. Off. 1767, Cairo ^{1}III, 236, Patna I, $91_{,9239/31}$.—3. *Iẓhār* (*Taysīr*) *al-fatāwī min asrār al-Ḥ.* by Hibatallāh b. ʿAbd al-Raḥīm al-Bārizī, d. 738/1337 (II, 86), Ind. Off. 1768, Alex. Fiqh Shāf. 17, Yeni 437.—4. Aḥmad b. Ḥasan al-Jārabardī, d. 746/1345 (II, 193), Yeni 438.—5. *Khulāṣat al-fatāwī* by ʿUmar b. ʿAlī b. al-Mulaqqin, d. 804/1401 (II, 92), Cairo ^{1}III, 225, ^{2}I, 513.—6. Anon., eighth cent., Br. Mus. Suppl. 315.—
| 7. Muḥammad b. Zankī al-Shuʿaybī al-ʿIrāqī, d. 747/1346, Berl. 4515.— 495
8. Anon., Paris 998 (dated 710/1310), Cairo ^{1}III, 237, 264.—9.–11. cf. Suppl. (9. Ind. Off. 1769, anon.).—12. *Bayān al-fatāwī* by ʿUthmān b. Aḥmad al-Kūhī al-Kīlūnī, Ind. Off. 1770.—Abstract *Irshād al-ghāwī ilā masālik al-Ḥ.* by Sharaf al-Dīn Ismāʿīl b. Abī Bakr al-Muqriʾ al-Yamanī, d. 837/1433 (II, 190), Berl. 4513, Gotha 951, Bodl. I, 236, Hamb. Or. Sem. 54, Alex. Fiqh Shāf. 3.—Commentaries: 1. Self-commentary, *Ikhlāṣ al-nāwī*, Br. Mus. Supp. 316(?), Bodl. I, 186 (cf. II, 571), Cairo ^{1}III, 190.—2. Muḥammad b. ʿAbd al-Munʿim al-Jawjarī, d. 889/1484 (II, 97), Berl. 4514, Bodl. I, 198/201.—3. *Fatḥ al-jawād fī sharḥ al-I.* by Ibn Ḥajar al-Haytamī, d. 973/1565 (II, 387), 2 vols., C. 1305/6.—4. see Suppl.—5. Anon., *al-Tamshiya*, Dam. ʿUm. 51, 403/4, Alex. Fiqh Shāf. 13, on which *al-Masāʾil al-mufīda al-ṣarīḥa fī ʿibārāt al-I. al-ṣaḥīḥa* by Taqī al-Dīn ʿUmar al-Fatā b. Muʿaybid al-ʿAbdalī al-Zabīdī, d. 781/1379, Alex. Fiqh Shāf. 40.—16 commentaries and 4 abstracts mentioned in Ahlw., 4516.—Versifications: 1. *Kitāb al-bahja al-Wardiyya* by Abū Ḥafṣ ʿUmar b. Muẓaffar b. al-Wardī, d. 749/1348 (II, 140), Garr. 83, Cairo ^{1}III, 199, ^{2}I, 501, lith. C. 1311.—Commentaries: a. *al-Bahja al-marḍiyya* by Aḥmad b. ʿAbd al-Raḥīm al-ʿIrāqī, d. 826/1423 (II, 66), Gotha 952/3, Paris 999, Br. Mus. 897. Bodl. I, 208, II, 572, Garr. 1805/6, on which glosses by Zakariyyāʾ al-Anṣārī, d. 926/1520 (II, 99), Garr. 1807.—b. Anon., Gotha 954.—c. *al-Ghurar al-bahiyya* by Zakariyyāʾ al-Anṣārī, Paris 1000, Cairo ^{1}III, 247.—d. see Suppl.—2. *Naẓm al-Ḥāwī* by Ibrāhīm al-Fazārī, d. 729/1329 (II, 130), Cairo ^{1}III, 286.—3. see Suppl.—Anon. revision entitled *Tashīl al-fatāwī fī khulāṣat asrār al-Ḥāwī*, Paris 1001.—II. *al-Lubāb fī uṣūl al-fiqh* ḤKh V, 302, self-commentary, *al-ʿUjāb*, Ind. Off. 285.

28. ʿAbd al-Raḥīm b. Muḥammad b. Muḥammad b. Yūnus b. Rabīʿa al-Mawṣilī was born in Mosul in 598/1201, left his native land upon the invasion of the

Tatars and acceded to judicial office in the western part of Baghdad, where he died in 671/1272.

Al-Subkī, *Ṭab.* v, 72, Ibn Hidāyatallāh 86. *Al-Taʿjīz*, abstract of al-Ghazzālī's *al-Wajīz* (p. 543) with a commentary, *al-Taṭrīz*, Alex. Fiqh Shāf. 12. At the request of the Ḥanafīs he also composed an abstract of al-Qudūrī that was still available to al-Subkī.

496 | 29. (30). Abū Zakariyyāʾ Yaḥyā b. Sharaf b. Murī b. Ḥasan b. Ḥusayn b. Jumʿa b. Ḥizām al-Ḥizāmī al-Ḥawrānī Muḥyi 'l-Dīn al-Nawawī (Nawāwī) was born in Muḥarram 631/October 1233 in Nawā, south of Damascus in the Jawlān.[5] He studied theology at the Rawāḥiyya in Damascus from 649/1251 onwards. After making the pilgrimage in 651/1253 he became a private teacher in Damascus until he took over Abū Shāma's (p. 387) professorship at the Ashrafiyya school of *ḥadīth* following the latter's death in 665/1262. He was the only *faqīh* in Damascus to have the courage to refuse to consent to Sultan Baybars' levying of extraordinary war taxes, which is why he was banished. In his native Nawā, where he had hoped to recuperate from the side effects of an ascetic life and intense labour, he passed away on 24 Rajab 676/22 December 1278.

F. Wüstenfeld, *Über das Leben und die Schriften Scheich Abu Z.J. el N.* in *Abh.*, GGW 4, 1849, *Gesch.* 355, Heffening, *Isl.* XXII, 165/90, XXIV, 131/50.

I. *Minhāj al-ṭālibīn*, an abstract of *al-Muḥarrar* by Rāfiʿī (no. 25), completed in 669/1270, Berl. 4522/3, Gotha 955/7 (where other MSS are listed), BDMG 44, Mosul 160,$_{184}$, 182,$_{118}$, 200,$_{211}$, Patna I, 107,$_{1082}$. *Le guide des zélés croyants, manuel de jurisprudence musulmane selon le rite de Châfiʿī, texte ar. publié par ordre du gouvernement avec traduction et annotation par* L.W.C. van den Berg, 3 vols., Batavia 1882/4, print. C. 1305, 1308, 1314, cf. Sachau, *Muh. Recht* XXII.—Commentaries: 1. *al-Nukat ʿalā baʿḍ alfāẓ al-M.* by Ibrāhīm b. ʿAbd al-Raḥmān b. al-Firkāḥ, d. 729/1339 (II, 130), Cairo ^{1}III, 286.—2. al-Zankalūnī, d. 740/1339, Cairo ^{1}III, 240.—3. *al-Ib(ti)hāj fī sharḥ al-M.* by Taqī al-Dīn al-Subkī, d. 756/1355 (II, 66), see Suppl., Alex. Fiqh Shāf. 3.—4. *al-Nukat* or *al-Sirāj fī nukat al-M.* by Ibn al-Naqīb, d. 764/1362, Berl. 4524, Garr. 2128, (fragm.), Cairo ^{1}III, 240.—5. *al-Furūq* by Jamāl al-Dīn ʿAbd al-Raḥīm b. al-Ḥasan al-Asnawī, d. 772/1370
497 (II, 90), Gotha 964/5, Bodl. I, 245, Alex. | Fiqh Shāf. 32/3.—6. Aḥmad b. Ḥamdān al-Adhraʿī, d. 783/1381 (II, 90): a. *Qūt al-muḥtāj* Berl. 4526/7, Gotha 964,$_{3}$, Paris 1005, Cairo ^{1}III, 261, Patna I, 101,$_{1030}$.—b. *Ghunyat al-muḥtāj* Berl. 4528.—c. *Tuḥfat al-nabīh* by al-Zankalūni (see Suppl.), Patna I, 81,$_{824}$.—7. *Tawḍīḥ al-M.*

5 See al-Qalqashandī, *Ṣubḥ al-aʿshā* IV, 105,$_{3}$.

by Badr al-Din Muḥammad al-Zarkashī, d. 794/1392 (II, 91), Berl. 4525, Paris 1007/8.—8. *Tuḥfat al-muḥtāj* by ʿĪsā b. ʿUthmān al-Ghazzī, d. 799/1396 (III, 92), Berl. 4530 (?).—9. *Taṣḥīḥ al-muḥtāj* by ʿUmar al-Bulqīnī, d. 805/1402 (II, 93), Cairo [1]III, 207.—10. ʿUmar b. ʿAlī b. al-Mulaqqin, d. 804/1401 (II, 93): a. *ʿUmdat al-muḥtāj* Berl. 4536/7, Paris 1009, Alex. Fiqh Shāf. 28.—b. *al-Ishārāt ʿalā mā waqaʿa fi ʾl-M. min al-asmāʾ wal-amākin*, completed in 774/1374, Berl. 4531/5, Gotha 960, Br. Mus. 255, Alex. Fiqh Shāf. 5.—c. *Tuḥfat al-muḥtāj fī adillat al-M.*, AS 463, Cairo [1], 95, Patna I, 81,$_{819}$.—d. *ʿUjālat al-muḥtāj*, see Suppl., Garr. 1790, Alex. Fiqh Shāf. 21.—11. *al-Najm al-wahhāj* by Muḥammad b. Mūsā al-Damīrī, d. 808/1405 (II, 138), Hamb. Or. Sem. 52, Ind. Off. 279.—12. Abu ʾl-Barakāt Muḥammad b. Muḥammad b. al-ʿIrāqī, d. 842/1438, Berl. 4529. 13. Aḥmad b. al-Ḥusayn b. Raslān al-Ramlī, d. 844/1440 (II, 96), Gotha 968, on which glosses: a. *Ghāyat al-muḥtāj* by Muḥammad b. Aḥmad b. Ḥamza al-Ramlī, d. 1004/1596 (II, 321), Paris 1017/20.—b. ʿAlī al-Shabrāmallisī, d. 1087/1676 (II, 322), Gotha 969, Paris 1021/2.—14. *Ghawāmiḍ al-fikar fī tartīb masāʾil al-M. al-mukhtaṣar* by ʿAlī b. ʿUthmān b. ʿUmar b. Ṣāliḥ al-Ṣayrafī, d. 844/1440 (Suppl. II, 114), Garr. 1798.—14a. Abu ʾl-Fatḥ al-Marāghī, d. 859/1455, Leid. 1820.—15. Jalāl al-Dīn Muḥammad b. Aḥmad al-Maḥallī, d. 864/1460, Berl. 4538, Gotha 958/62 (where other MSS are listed), Garr. 1792, Patna I, 94,$_{952}$.—Glosses: a. al-Bakrī al-Ṣiddīqī, Paris 1012.—b. al-Qalyūbī and Shihābaddīn b. ʿAmīra al-Burullusī (ca. 950/1543), printed in 4 vols., C. 1306, 1318.—16. Muḥammad b. Abī Bakr b. Qāḍī Shuhba, d. 874/1469 (II, 30), see Suppl.—17. *Durr al-tāj fī iʿrāb mushkil al-M.* by al-Suyūṭī, d. 911/1505, Gotha 967, Paris 2677,$_{18}$.—18. *Fatḥ al-wahhāb* by Zakariyyāʾ al-Anṣārī, d. 926/1530 (II, 99), see Suppl. (delete Princ. 262 = Garr. 1792, p. 15), glosses by ʿAlī al-Ḥalabī, d. 1044/1634 (II, 307), Paris 1015/6.—19. *Tuḥfat al-muḥtāj* by Aḥmad b. Muḥammad b. Ḥajar al-Haythamī, d. 973/1565 (II, 387), Ind. Off. 218, Alex. Fiqh Shāf. 11, Patna I, 81,$_{820/3}$, C. 1282, 1290, see Suppl. Glosses: a. Aḥmad b. al-Qāsim al-ʿIbādī, d. 994/1586 (II, 320), additionally Alex. Fiqh Shāf. 18.—20. *Ghāyat* | *Nihāyat al-muḥtāj* by Zayn al-Dīn 498
Muḥammad b. Aḥmad b. Ḥamza al-Ramlī, d. 1004/1595 (II, 321), composed in 973/1565, Paris 1017/20, 6453, Alex. Fiqh Shāf. 44 (see Suppl.).—Glosses by ʿAlī al-Shabrāmallisī, d. 1087/1676 (II, 322), Paris 1021/2.—21. *Mughni ʾl-muḥtāj* by Muḥammad b. al-Khaṭīb al-Shirbīnī, d. 977/1569 (II, 330), print. C. 1308, 1329, 4 vols.—22. Shams al-Dīn b. al-Qāyātī, Paris 1013,$_{1}$.—23. Muḥammad b. Fakhr al-Dīn al-Abbār al-Māridīnī, composed in 865–70/1460–5 in Aleppo, Bodl. I, 219.—24. Anon., Gotha 960, 970/2, Garr. 1793/7.—25.–31. see Suppl. (30. read: *Khatm al-M.*).—32. *Surūr al-rāghibīn* by Muḥammad b. Aḥmad al-Dayrūṭī, ca. 950/1543, Bank. XIX, 1843 = Patna I, 90,$_{918}$.—33. See Suppl. I, 972 and 682, Patna I, 88,$_{896}$.—34. Anon., Garr. 1793/7.—Abbreviations: 1. *Minhāj al-rāghibīn* by Muḥammad al-Qūnawī, d. 788/1386, Paris 1006.—2. *Manhaj al-ṭullāb* by

396 Zakariyyā' al-Anṣārī, | d. 926/1520 (II, 99), Berl. 4539.—Commentaries: a. Self-commentary, *Fatḥ al-wahhāb*, Berl. 4540/1, Gotha 973/5 (where other MSS are listed), Br. Mus. Suppl. 314, Patna I, 100,$_{1001/23}$. Glosses: *α* ʿAlī b. Ibrāhīm al-Ḥalabī, d. 1044/1624 (II, 307), Alex. Fiqh Shāf. 16.—*β* see Suppl.—*γ* Sulaymān b. ʿUmar al-Jamal, d. 1204/1789 (II, 353), print. C. 1305.—*δ* Sulaymān al-Bajīramī, d. 1221/1806, Alex. Fiqh Shāf. 15, Būlāq 1296, 1309.—*ε*, *ζ* see Suppl.—*η* Shams al-Dīn al-Shawbarī, d. 1069/1158 (II, 330), part III (?) Marseille 1632.—*ϑ* ʿAbd al-Barr b. ʿAbdallāh al-Ujhūrī, after 1080/1669, Alex. Fiqh Shāf. 15.—*ι* ʿAlī b. Yaḥyā al-Ziyādī al-Miṣrī, d. 1024/1615, ibid. 17.—b.–d. see Suppl. (c. Garr. 1799).—supplement *Iʿlām al-nabīh bi-mā zāda ʿala 'l-M. al-Ḥāwī wal-Bahja* (no. 29) *wal-Tanbīh* (no. 9) by Shaykh al-Islām b. Qāḍī ʿAjlūn, d. 928/1522 (Suppl. II, 119), Gotha 977.—31 commentaries, 2 abstracts, 3 versifications are mentioned in Ahlw., 4544, abstracts with reference to traditions, ibid. 1833,$_{54/5}$.

II. *Kitāb al-daqā'iq*, glosses on his *Minhāj* and the *Muḥarrar* of Rāfiʿī (no. 25), see Suppl., Alex. Fiqh Shāf. 38,$_2$, Mosul 36,$_{187}$; on which *al-Rawḍ al-fā'iq fi 'l-Minhāj wal-D.* by Ibrāhīm b. Yaḥyā al-Nawāwī, autograph dated 871/1466, Gotha 876.—III. *Kitāb* (*al-ma'thūrāt wa*) *ʿuyūn al-masā'il al-muhimmāt*, legal opinions collected and published by his student ʿAlī b. Ibrāhīm b. al-ʿAṭṭār, d. 724/1324, Berl. 4816, Gotha 1136, Ind. Off. 288 ii, Yeni 656 (?), Cairo VII, 180 = (?) *Ru'ūs al-masā'il* Alex. Fiqh Shāf. 39,$_1$ = (?) *Fatāwī*, Patna II, 446,$_{2642/10}$.—IV. *Kitāb taṣḥīḥ al-Tanbīh* (see no. 9), completed in 671/1272, Cairo ^{1}III, 207.—
499 V. *Kitāb al-taḥrīr fī sharḥ alfāẓ al-Tanbīh*, dictionary to the same, Berl. | 6969/70 (see Suppl.).—VI. *Kitāb al-qawāʿid wal-ḍawābiṭ fī uṣūl al-fiqh* Berl. 4379, with the title *Ḍawābiṭ al-fuṣūl* Ind. Off. 1171 (?), extract Br. Mus. Suppl. 1203,$_6$.—VII. *Rawḍat al-ṭālibīn wa-ʿumdat al-muftīn*, see p. 424,$_{30c}$.—VIII. *Khulāṣat al-aḥkām min muhimmāt al-sunan wa-qawāʿid al-islām* Cairo ^{1}I, 338, ^{2}I, 114.—IX. *Kitāb al-arbaʿīn* 40 traditions, Berl. 1476/87, Leipz. 325, Munich 127, Leid. 1746/7, Paris 744, Br. Mus. 878, 1488,$_4$, Garr. 1430/1, Alex. Fun. 175,$_1$, Cairo ^{1}I, 264, ^{2}I, 87, Qawala I, 99.—Commentaries: 1. Self-commentary, Alex. Ḥad. 29, Cairo ^{1}I, 403, ^{2}I, 125, Patna I 37,$_{379/80}$, 52,$_{519}$.—2. Aḥmad b. Faraḥ al-Ishbīlī, d. 699/1299 (p. 459), Berl. 1488/9.—3. Aḥmad b. ʿAbd al-Wahhāb al-Miṣrī, ca. 730/1329, Berl. 1490/1.—4. *al-Manhaj al-mubīn* by Ibn ʿUmar b. ʿAlī b. al-Fākihānī, d. 731/1331 (II, 22), Berlin, Brill M. 219, Cairo ^{1}I, 432, ^{2}I, 153, Garr. 1432/3.—4a. Najm al-Dīn Sulaymān b. ʿAbd al-Qawī al-Ṭawfī al-Ḥanbalī, d. 716/1316 (II, 108), Alex. Ḥad. 29.—5. Muḥammad b. Aḥmad al-Masʿūdī, composed in 788/1386, Cairo ^{1}I, 340.—6. *Jāmiʿ al-ʿulūm wal-ḥikam* by ʿAbd al-Raḥmān b. Aḥmad b. Rajab al-Baghdādī, d. 795/1393 (II, 107), completed up to 50 traditions, Berl. 1492, Cairo ^{1}I, 321, Rāmpūr I, 76,$_{99}$, Patna I, 46,$_{471}$.—7. Asʿad b. Masʿūd Ẓāhir al-ʿUmarī, composed in 812/1409, Cairo ^{1}I, 355.—8. ʿIzz al-Dīn b. Jamāʿa, d. 819/1416 (II, 94), Cairo ^{1}I, 410, ^{2}I, 94.—8a. *Īḍāḥ al-kalimāt al-nūrāniyya* by Ibrāhīm

b. Aḥmad al-Ḥanafī, d. 851/1447, Alex. Ḥad. 30.—9. Zakariyyāʾ al-Anṣārī, d. 926/1520 (1196), Gotha 617/8.—10. Muḥammad b. Muḥammad al-Dalajī al-ʿUthmānī, d. 947/1540 (II, 319), Gotha 614.—11. *al-Fatḥ al-mubīn* by Aḥmad b. Ḥajar al-Haythamī, d. 973/1565 (II, 387), composed in 951/1544, Berl. 1493/6, Paris 748$_{,1}$, Ind. Off. 169/70, Garr. 1434, Alex. Fun. 117$_{,3}$, Cairo ^{1}I, 379, 400, Qawala I, 140, Makr. 49, Mosul 232$_{,10}$, Patna I, 55$_{,5537}$, C. 1317.—Glosses: a. Aḥmad al-Madābighī, d. 1170/1756, Cairo ^{1}I, 334, Makr. 25.—b. *Taʿlīqāt* by Muḥammad b. Aḥmad al-Khaṭīb al-Shawbarī, d. 1069/1658 (II, 330), Cairo ^{1}I, 286, Garr. 2003$_{,7}$.—12. *al-Majālis al-saniyya etc.* by Aḥmad b. Ḥijāzī al-Fashnī (II, 305), completed in 978/1570, Berl. Ms. or. oct. 3895, Qawala I, 148/9, print. C. 1278, 1299, 1303, 1305, 1310, 1323 (*Fihr.* ^{1}I, 397).—13. *al-Jawāhir al-bahiyya* by Walāʾ al-Dīn Abu ʾl-Faḍl Muḥammad al-Shabshīrī, tenth cent., ḤKh I, 241, Garr. 1436, Cairo ^{1}I, 327, ^{2}I, 110, on which glosses Gotha 616.—14. *al-Mubīn al-muʿīn* by al-Qāriʾ al-Harawī, d. 1014/1605 (II, 394), Berl. 1497, Garr. 1435, Cairo ^{1}I, 396, Patna I, 59$_{,594}$.—15. ʿAbd al-Raʾūf al-Munāwī, d. 1031/1622 (II, 306), Berl. | 1500, Garr. 1435.— 500
16. *al-Futūḥāt al-wahbiyya* (*ilāhiyya*) by Ibrāhīm b. Marʿī al-Sabrakhītī, d. 1106/1694, Berl. 1501/2, Paris 749, Cairo ^{1}I, 381, ^{2}I, 135, Qawala I, 141, Patna I, 55$_{,558}$, print. C. 1304, 1307, 1318.—17. ʿAbdallāh al-Nabrāwī, composed in 1255/1839, C. 1291 (Fihr. ^{1}I, 369).—18. Muḥammad b. Aḥmad al-Ḥanafī, Paris 746.—19. Abu ʾl-ʿAbbās Aḥmad al-Lakhmī, Paris 1746.—19a. *Tuḥfat al-muḥibbīn* by Muḥammad Ḥayāt al-Sindī al-Madanī, d. after 1158/1745 (Suppl. II, 522), Algiers 1532, Patna I, 41$_{,418}$, 360$_{,2540}$.—20. *Zād al-muttaqīn*, to the first two traditions, Gotha 615 (= ḤKh ^{1}III, 6788, by Muḥammad b. Abī Ḥafṣ al-Bukhārī ?). |— 397
21. Anon., Berl. 1503, Paris 745, Br. Mus. Suppl. 1231 i, Mosul 102$_{,56,11}$, 6.—22.–35. see Suppl. (25. Alex. Ḥad. 44).—36. Muʿīn b. Ṣafī, Garr. 1437.—37. Muḥammad b. al-ʿAbbās al-Masʿūdī al-Ḥanafī, Patna I, 52$_{,516}$.—38. ʿAlī b. ʿAbd al-Hādī al-ʿAsqalānī, ibid. 518.—39. Saʿīd b. Muḥammad al-Muttaqī, ibid. 519.—40. Turkish translation, *Qyrq ḥadīth*, Istanbul 1341/3.—Other commentaries Ahlw., 1504.

X. *Riyāḍ al-ṣāliḥīn*, traditions leading to a blissful life, in 256 chapters, Berl. 1334/41, Munich 128, Br. Mus. Suppl. 1202, Ind. Off. 167/8, Algiers 879, Garr. 1898, Alex. Mawāʿiẓ 20, Cairo ^{1}I, 345, ^{2}I, 121, Mosul 165$_{,7}$, Patna I, 133$_{,1321}$, II, 514$_{,2763}$, *Dībāja*, Gotha 2$_{,97}$.—Commentaries: 1. Muḥammad ʿAlī b. Muḥammad ʿAllān al-Bakrī al-Ṣiddīqī, d. 1057/1647 (II, 390), Berl. 1342, Garr. 1899/1900, Cairo ^{1}I, 343, ^{2}I, 116.—2. Anon., *Dībāja*, Gotha 2$_{,98}$—absract Paris 743.

XI. *Sharḥ Ṣaḥīḥ Muslim* see p. 167.—XII. *Irshād al-ḥadīth* see p. 441.

XIII. *al-Īḍāḥ fī ʾl-manāsik*, on the pilgrimage, Berl. 4045, Ind. Off. 1038$_{,11}$, Cairo ^{1}III, 195, *ḥāshiya* by Ibn Ḥajar al-Haythamī (II, 387), Ind. Off. 1772 (cf. Suppl.), Patna I, 84$_{,849}$, anon. comm. Alex. Fiqh Shāf. 25, anon. gloss completed in 938/1531, ibid. 17.

XIV. *Tahdhīb al-asmāʾ wal-lughāt* (see Suppl.) Berl. Brill M 200, Alex. Lugha 10, Qawala II, 231, Patna II, $295_{,2369}$, part I = *Biographical dictionary of illustrious men, chiefly at the beginning of Islamism*, ed. F. Wüstenfeld, 2 vols., Göttingen 1843/8.—Abstracts, see Suppl. c. Garr. 715, with the title *Talkhīṣ laṭīf*, ibid. 716, d. by Ibrāhīm al-Dharaʿī, Patna II, $299_{,2384}$.

XV. *Kitāb al-ishārāt ilā bayān al-asmāʾ al-mubhamāt*, a medium-large abstract of the work by al-Khaṭīb al-Baghdādī (p. 401), enlarged with additions, Berl. 1675.

501 XVI. *Ṭabaqāt al-fuqahāʾ al-Shāfiʿiyya*, abstract of | the work of Ibn al-Ṣalāḥ (p. 441), Cairo ^{1}V, 79, ^{2}, 249, excerpts Gotha $99_{,7}$.

XVII. *Kitāb al-tibyān fī ādāb ḥamalat al-Qurʾān*, composed in 666/1267, on the merits of studying the Qurʾān, the requirements made of reciters and teachers, and how they should conduct themselves, Berl. 6104/2, Leid. 1636, Br. Mus. Suppl. $1206_{,2}$, Paris $592_{,5}$, Esc. ^{2}1425, Garr. 1209, AS 33, Alex. Fun. $63_{,1}$, $87_{,1}$, $167_{,11}$, Cairo ^{1}VI, 180, 536 (abstract ibid. 181), ^{2}I, 275, Mosul $100_{,28,12}$, Patna I, $24_{,216}$.

XVIII. *Kitāb bustān al-ʿārifīn*, unfinished, Berl. 3018, Cairo ^{1}VII, 542, ^{2}I, 272, Patna I, $129_{,1286}$, *Dībāja*, Gotha $2_{,34}$.

XIX. *Kitāb ḥilyat* (*nuzhat*) *al-abrār wa-shiʿār* (*shaʿāʾir*) *al-akhyār*, regulations for religious worship in accordance with the sunna, also called *Adhkār al-N.*, completed in Muḥarram 667/September 1268, Berl. 3694/5, Gotha 806 (where other MSS are listed), Leipz. 194/5, Paris $1177_{,1}$, 1130, 5117, Brit. Mus. Suppl. 248, 1206, Ind. Off. 340, Garr. 1949/50, Yeni 170/2, Alex. Ḥad. 21, Cairo ^{1}I, 337, 406, ^{2}I, 113, Mosul $72_{,16,17}$, print. C. 1306.—Commentaries: a. *Tuḥfat al-abrār bi-nukat al-adhkār* by al-Suyūṭī, Garr. 1951.—b. *al-Futūḥāt al-rabbāniyya* by Muḥammad ʿAlī b. Muḥammad ʿAllān al-Bakrī al-Ṣiddiqī (II, 390), Rāmpūr I, $354_{,237}$.—c. al-Mollāwī, book I, Paris 1131.—Abstracts: 1. *Adhkār al-Adhkār* by al-Suyūṭī, Paris 1178, Cairo ^{1}VII, 11, 465.—2. Anon., Garr. $2168_{,2}$, Yeni 276, Mosul $106_{,30,10}$.

XX. *Kitāb al-qiyām li-ahl al-takrīm wal-iḥtirām*, completed in 665/1266, Paris $4577_{,2}$, Cairo VII, 320, 563, ^{2}I, 135.—Abstract by Muḥammad b. Sālim al-Ḥifnī, d. 1181/1767 (II, 323), Garr. $2036_{,6}$.

XXI. *al-Adʿiya al-muʿadda ʿinda ʾl-karab wal-shidda* Paris $744_{,2}$.

XXII. *Ḥizb*, ejaculatory prayer, Berl. 3882, Gotha 821, 864, Leid. $2200_{,6}$, Bodl. II, $73_{,3,2}$, Mosul $128_{,169,8}$, Patna II, $374_{,2561/3}$, $444_{,2620/2}$.—Commentaries: 1. *al-Maṭlaʿ al-tāmm al-sawī* by Muṣṭafā b. Kamāl al-Dīn al-Bakrī al-Ṣiddīqī, d. 1162/1749 (II, 348), Berl. 3883, Garr. $1948_{,1}$.—2. Aḥmad al-Sijāʿī, d. 1190/1777 (II, 323), Berl. 3884, Garr. $1948_{,3}$.—3.–7. see Suppl.

XXIII. *Tadhkirat al-tawwābīn*, a paraenesis (author?), Berl. 8788, Nafiz 373 (attributed to Ibn ʿArabī).

XXIV.–XXXIII. See Suppl. (XXVI. = III. also Garr. 1803, Mosul $38_{,219,3}$, XXVII. Mosul $200_{,20,9}$).

31. Tāj al-Dīn Abū Muḥammad ʿAbd al-Raḥmān b. Ibrāhīm al-Fazārī | al-Badrī 502
al-Miṣrī b. al-Firkāḥ, born in Rabīʿ I 624/February 1227, studied in Damascus under Ibn al-Ṣalāḥ (p. 440). In 650/1252 he became a lecturer at the newly founded Madrasa Nāṣiriyya. In 676/1277 he became senior professor at the Bādharāʾiyya, the Supreme Head of the Shāfiʿis, and *muftī* of Syria. He died in Jumādā II 690/June 1291.

Fawāt I, 250, *Orient.* II, 282, Wüst., *Gesch.* 365. 1. *Kitāb al-ishkālāt*, legal questions, Berl. 4957.—2. *Sharḥ Waraqāt* by al-Juwaynī, p. 487.—3. See Suppl.

| 4 *The Ḥanbalīs* 398

1. Abū Yaʿlā Muḥammad b. al-Ḥusayn b. Muḥammad b. al-Farrāʾ al-Baghdādī, who died in 458/1066 (see Suppl.).

1. *Kitāb al-kifāya fī uṣūl al-fiqh* Cairo ^{1}III, 268.—2. *Kitāb al-ʿidad fi ʾl-uṣūl*, completed in 428/1036, ibid. II, 254.—3. *al-Aḥkām al-sulṭāniyya* Asʿad 543 (mistakenly Suppl. I, 557, 2a).—4.–7. see Suppl.—8. *Ibṭāl al-taʾwīl* is quoted in Ibn al-Taymiyya, *Majm. ras. al-kubrā* I, 445$_{,1}$.

1b. Abu ʾl-Khaṭṭāb Maḥfūẓ b. Aḥmad al-Kalwadhānī, d. 510/1116 (see Suppl.).

Al-Samʿānī, *Ansāb* 486v. 6. *al-Tahdhīb fi ʾl-farāʾiḍ*, Munich 338.

2. Abu ʾl-Wafāʾ ʿAlī b. ʿAqīl b. Muḥammad b. ʿAqīl, who died in 513/1119 (see Suppl.).

1. *Kitāb al-fuṣūl* Cairo ^{1}III, 295, ^{2}I, 550.—2. *al-Wāḍiḥ fi ʾl-uṣūl* Garr. 1842.—3. See Suppl.—4. *Kitāb al-funūn*, vol. 70 Paris 787, Muṣṭafā Jawād after Massignon, *REI* 1938, 285.

2b. ʿAwn al-Dīn Abu ʾl-Muẓaffar Yaḥyā b. Muḥammad al-Shaybānī b. Hubayra al-Ḥanbalī, d. 560/1165 (see Suppl.).

2. *Kitāb al-ishrāf ʿalā madhāhib al-ashrāf*, also Alex. Fiqh Shāf. 5, Patna I, 78,$_{786}$.

3. Muwaffaq al-Dīn Abū Muḥammad ʿAbdallāh b. Aḥmad b. Muḥammad b. Qudāma al-Maqdisī, d. 620/1223 (see Suppl.).

| *Fawāt* I, 203, Wüst., *Gesch.* 305. 1. *Kitāb al-Muqniʿ*, on Ḥanbalī law, Tüb. 503
114.—Commentaries: a.–g. see Suppl.—h. Anon., de Jong 152.—Abstracts: a. *al-Iqnāʿ li-ṭālib al-intifāʿ* or *Zād al-mustaqniʿ* by Abu ʾl-Najāʾ Mūsā b. Aḥmad

al-Muqaddasī al-Khūjawī al-Ṣāliḥī, d. 968/1560 (II, 325), Berl. 4504, Garr. 1845 Patna I, $104_{,1057}$.—Commentaries: a, b. see Suppl. (a. Patna I, $91_{,925}$, II, $501_{,2729}$, $507_{,2725/9}$, supercommentary *al-Rawḍ al-murbiʿ*, also Alex. Fiqh Ḥanb. 4, Indian printing 1305.—b. *al-Tanqīḥ al-mushbiʿ fī taḥrīr aḥkām al-M.* by Aḥmad b. Sulaymān al-Mardāwī, d. 885/1480 (Suppl. II, 130), Cairo ^{2}I, 548 (anon. comm. ibid.), Garr. 1844. Abstract *al-Iqnāʿ* (see Suppl.), Patna II, $305_{,2714}$.—Imitation a. *al-Muṭliʿ ʿalā abwāb al-M.* by Muḥammad al-Baʿlī, d. 709/1309 (II, 102), Gotha 596.—b. al-Najjār al-Futūḥī, *Muntaha 'l-irādāt* (see Suppl.), also Alex. Fiqh Ḥanb. 7, Patna I, $93_{,951}$, commentary by Manṣūr b. Yūnus al-Bahūtī (II, 447), *Irshād uli 'l-nuhā li-daqāʾiq al-M.* ibid. 3.—2. *Kitāb al-mīzān fī uṣūl al-fiqh*, Berl. 4373.—3. *al-Kāfī fi 'l-furūʿ* Paris 1104, Garr. 1843.—4. *Kitāb al-rawḍa fi 'l-uṣūl* Esc. ^{1}1233.—Abstracts: a. Muḥammad b. Abi 'l-Fatḥ al-Baʿlī, d. 709/1309 (II, 102), Br. Mus. Suppl. 260.—b. Sulaymān b. ʿAbd al-Qawī al-Ṭawfī, d. 716/1316 (II, 108), Alex. Uṣūl 19.—5. *Kitāb al-mughnī Sharḥ Mukhtaṣar al-Khiraqī*, d. 333/944 (I, 194), Cairo ^{1}III, 298.—6. *Juzʾ fī dhamm al-waswās wa-ahlihi*, on combatting the influence of Satan, Berl. 2518/9, with the title *Risāla fi 'l-waswās wal-muwaswis* Alex. Tawḥīd $43_{,16}$.—7. *Kitāb al-tawwābīn* Paris 1384/5, Leid. 1074, Alex. Mawāʿiẓ 31, Patna I, $149_{,1429}$.—8. Treatise in 6 *faṣl* on the conditions of purity, ritual cleansing, and prayer, Algiers $1349_{,2}$.—9. *Risāla fi 'ʿtiqād ahl al-sunna wal-jamāʿa* Ind. Off. 467 = *Lumʿa fi 'ʿtiqād al-hādī ilā sabīl al-rashād*, Berl. 1986?—10. *Kitāb al-riqqa fī akhbār al-ṣāliḥīn* Cairo ^{1}V 60 ^{2}V, 203.—11. *Kitāb minhāj al-qāṣidīn fī fadl al-khulafāʾ al-rāshidīn* Leipz. 650 (see Suppl.).—12. *Kitāb ghāyat al-kamāl fī sāʾir al-amthāl wa-anāb al-ʿArab al-jāhiliyya wal-tabyīn fī ansāb al-ṣaḥāba al-Qurashiyyīn*, the geneological part Munich 453, Algiers 656, ʿĀšir I, 593, ʿAlī Emīrī ʿArabī 2413, the proverbs Leid. 396 (where the name of the author is mistaken).[1]—13. *Kitāb al-mutaḥābbīn fi 'llāhi taʿālā* Cairo ^{1}VII, 189, ^{2}I, 138.—14.–24. see Suppl.—25. *Kitāb ʿumdat al-aḥkām*
504 ḤKh IV, $254_{,8299}$, | on which a commentary, *al-Mudda*, by Bahāʾ al-Dīn al-Maqdīsī, Alex. Fiqh Ḥanb. 4.—26. *Risāla fi 'l-taṣawwuf* Patna I, $132_{,1311}$.

4. Shams al-Dīn Muḥammad b. Ibrāhīm b. ʿAbd al-Wāḥid b. ʿAlī b. Abi 'l-Surūr al-Maqdisī wrote, around 630/1232:

1. *Kitāb al-jadal*, on the art of disputation, Berl. 5319.—2. See Suppl.

5. Ḍiyāʾ al-Dīn Muḥammad b. ʿAbd al-Wāḥid al-Maqdisī was born in Dayr
399 al-Mubārak in 569/1173, commenced his studies in Egypt in 595/1197, | then

1 Rödiger, *ZDMG* XIII, 229. Anm. and Aumer, loc. cit., disagree, without sufficient reason, against Dozy's identification.

continued them in Baghdad, where he studied under Ibn al-Jawzī (d. 597/1200), and after that in Hamadan. In 600/1203 he went to Damascus, but undertook a second study tour which he extended all the way to Marw, and then made the pilgrimage. He died in 643/1245.

Fawāt II, 238. 1. *Kitāb al-ṭibb al-nabawī* Paris 2562,$_{18}$.—2. *Kitāb faḍāʾil al-aʿmāl*, in particular on the merits of *dhikr*, Berl. 3692, Cairo [1]VI, 161, abstract Berl. 3693.—3. *Aḥkām al-ṣibā* Cairo [1]I, 260, [2]I, 184.—4.–14. see Suppl.

6. Majd al-Dīn Abu ʾl-Barakāt ʿAbd al-Salām b. ʿAbdallāh b. Taymiyya al-Ḥarrānī, the grandfather of Taqī al-Dīn (II, 100), was born in 590/1194, studied in Baghdad and Ḥarrān, and died in 652/1254.

Fawāt I, 254. 1. *Kitāb uṣūl al-fiqh*, with addenda by his son ʿAbd al-Ḥalīm, d. 682/1283, and by his famous grandson Aḥmad, Cairo [1]II, 257, [2]I, 392.—2. *Kitāb al-muḥarrar* Cairo [1]III, 297, commentary by Ṣafī al-Dīn ʿAbd al-Muʾmin, before 766/1365, Garr. 1846.—3. *Kitāb al-muntaqā fi ʾl-aḥkām al-sharʿiyya min kalām khayr al-bariyya*, a collection of *ḥadīth*, an abstract from his *al-Aḥkām al-kubrā*, Br. Mus. 1192, Alex. Ḥad. 65, Cairo [1]I, 429, [2]I, 551, Patna I, 64,$_{660}$.—4. *Kitāb fi ʾl-aḥādīth al-mawḍūʿa allatī yarwīha ʾl-ʿāmma wal-quṣṣāṣ ʿala ʾl-ṭuruqāt* Cairo [1]VIII, 664.—5., 6. See Suppl.

7. Shams al-Dīn Abu ʾl-Faraj ʿAbd al-Raḥmān b. Abī ʿUmar Muḥammad b. Aḥmad b. Qudāma al-Maqdisī, who was born in Muḥarram 597/October | 1200[2] in Damascus, studied under his uncle Muwaffaq al-Dīn (no. 3), among 505 others, on whose *Mughnī* he wrote a commentary of ten volumes, which is lost. He then became a preacher and professor at the Dār al-Ḥadīth. When, in 664/1265, separate chief judgeships for each of the four *madhhab*s were established in Damascus, he received the Ḥanbalī post. He was regarded as the greatest Ḥanbalī of his time and his named lived on in a madrasa endowed by him. He died in 683/1283.

Cod. Wetzst. II, 289, fol. 32r, *JA* s. IX. v. 3, p. 295, Quatremère, *Mamlouks* II, 68. 1. *Tashīl al-maṭlab fī taḥṣīl al-madhhab* Cairo [1]III, 293, [2]I, 548.—2.–5. see Suppl.

---

2 The statement according to which Ibn al-Jawzī, who died in this very same year, gave him an *ijāza* is not credible, despite the abomination discussed in Goldziher, *MSt* II, 191.

5 *The Ẓāhirīs and Almohads*

1. The most important representative of Ẓāhirī doctrine and the only one
400 whose literary work is known to us in some detail | was Abū Muḥammad ʿAlī b. Aḥmad b. Saʿīd b. Ḥazm, who died in 456/1064 (see Suppl.).

C. van Arendonk, *EI*, add. 93, ad A. I, *Ṭawq al-ḥamāma*, Ožerelie golubki, Russian translation by M.A. Salie, with an introduction by I. Kračkovsky, Moscow and Leningrad 1933. *Halsband der Taube über die Liebe und die Liebenden von a. M. ʿA. b. Ḥazm al-Andalusī, aus dem Arab. übers. v.* M. Weisweiler, Leiden 1941 (see Brockelmann, *ZDMG* 96, 552/7, J.H. Kramers, *Act. Or.* 19, 459/64). E. García Gómez, El Ṭawq de J.Ḥ. y el Dīwān al-sabāba (II, 13), *al-Andalus* VI, 65/72.—3. The *Naqṭ al-ʿarūs* as contained in the Munich MS, edited by Seybold (also ʿUm. 5215), is only an abstract of a more complete text that was used by al-Nuwayrī in the *Nihāya*; appendix *Taʾnīf al-nufūs fī ikmāl N. al-ʿa.* by Ismāʿīl b. Yūsuf b. Aḥmar (II, 241), see G. Marçais, Ibn al-Aḥmar, *Hist. des B. Merin* IX; L. Seco de Lucina Paredes, *al-Andalus* VI, 357/75.—A. 4. *Jamharat al-nasab*,
506 Patna I, 282$_{2317/8}$.—17. *Marātib* | *al-ijmāʿ*, additionally Patna I, 105$_{1064}$, with a critique, *naqd*, by Ibn Taymiyya, printed at the end of the *Maḥāsin al-islām wa-asrār al-islām* by Abū ʿAbdallāh al-Bukhārī, C. 1357.

2. While still a young man, Muḥammad b. ʿAbdallāh b. Tūmart[1] had acquired a reputation for extraordinary piety amongst the late-fifth century Berbers of the
401 Maṣmūda tribe | in the Deren Mountains (Western Atlas), in the province of Sus, in the south-west of present-day Morocco. In 501/1107 he went to Cordova and, after making the pilgrimage, to Baghdad, where he immersed himself at the Niẓāmiyya in the study of Ashʿarī dogma. On the way back to his country of origin, in Tripoli, he lectured on their teachings, which he called *tawḥīd*, but which he associated with the Shīʿī dogma of the infallibility of the Imam of the house of ʿAlī. Chased from Tripoli and, in 512/1118, from Bijāya because of the unrest that he had created there, he retired to his tribe the Maṣmūda, among whom he soon gained many devoted supporters. In 515/1121 he openly declared himself the Mahdi and started his war against the Almoravids. He died in 524/1130, four months after a failed assault on Marrakesh. However, his successors did subject North Africa and Spain to his teachings.

Ibn Khall. 699, Ibn Khaldūn, *Hist. des Berbères*, transl. de Slane II, 161, Goldziher, *ZDMG* XLI, 30ff., A. Müller, *der Islam* II, 640ff., Brockelmann,

---

1 This is the Berber form of the name ʿUmar.

Gesch. der isl. Völker 190. All in Paris 1451. 1. *Aʿazzu mā yuṭlabu fī uṣūl al-fiqh*,
dictated in the *ribāṭ* of the Hergha, a Berber tribe in the south of Morocco,
in 515/1121.—2. *al-Kalām fi ʾl-ṣalāt.*—3. *al-Dalīl ʿalā anna ʾl-sharīʿa lā tath-
butu bil-ʿaql min wujūh.*—4. *al-Kalām fi ʾl-ʿumūm wal-khuṣūs wal-muṭlaq wal-
muqayyad wal-mujmal wal-mufassar wal-nāsikh wal-mansūkh wal-ḥaqīqa
wal-majāz wa fāʾidatihā wal-kināya wal-taʿrīḍ wal-taṣrīḥ wal-asmāʾ al-lughawiyya
allatī ghalaba ʿalayha ʾl-ʿurf wa-khaṣṣaṣahā wal-asmāʾ al-manqūla min al-lugha
ilā ʿurf al-sharʿ.*—| 5. *al-Kalām ʿala ʾl-ʿilm.*—6. *al-Maʿlūmāt* (*fi ʾl-maʿlūm wal-* 507
mawjūd).—7. *al-Muḥaddath*, print. Algiers 1325.—8. *al-ʿIbādāt.*—9. *al-ʿAqīda*,
printed in *Majmūʿat al-rasāʾil*, C. 1328.—10. On the oneness of the Creator and
the Imamate.—11. On the principles of the religious sciences.—12. Against the
Murābiṭūn and the Mulaththamūn, printed in *Majm.*—13. Islam and the duties
of the believers.—14. *al-Tawḥīd.*—15. Traditions on dogma.—16. Traditions on
Muḥammad.—17. Against *ghulūl*, the embezzlement of booty.—18. Against
wine drinking.—19. *al-Jihād.*—20. See Suppl.

| 6 *The Shīʿa* 402

A The Zaydīs

1. Al-Imām al-Nāṭiq bil-Ḥaqq Abū Ṭālib Yaḥyā b. al-Ḥusayn b. Hārūn al-Baṭḥānī, born in 340/951, was recognized as the caliph by the Zaydīs in Daylam, and died in 424/1033.

1. *Kitāb al-taḥrīr fi ʾl-fiqh* Berl. or. Oct. 3777 (Fischer-Burch. 28), Br. Mus. Suppl. 340, augmented edition ibid. 342, with the title *al-Lumʿa* by ʿAlī b. al-Ḥusayn b. al-Hādī, beginning of the sixth cent., ibid. 342, a gloss thereon ibid. 343.—Commentaries, see Suppl.—2. *Kitāb al-ifāda fī taʾrīkh al-aʾimma al-sāda*, a history of the Zaydī imams up to al-Mahdī li-Dīn Allāh, d. 360/971, with a continuation, *Tatimma*, by ʿImād al-Dīn Yaḥyā b. ʿAlī al-Ḥasanī al-Qāsimī up to al-Mutawakkil ʿala ʾllāh Ismāʿīl, d. 1087/1676, Berl. 9665/6.—3.–5. see Suppl. (3. read: Ambr. B. 49, *RSO* IV, 106).

1d. Abu ʾl-Qāsim Zayd b. ʿAbdallāh b. Masʿūd al-Hāshimī, fl. fifth century.

See Suppl. I, 699. *Al-Arbaʿūn al-Saylaqiyya*, additionally Ambr. A, 29, 472, B. 12, 4, commentary by Yaḥyā b. Ḥamza, *al-Anwār al-muḍīʾa*, ibid. D 454, anon. B 74 xxxi, 123 iii, Patna I, 40,$_{407}$.

2. Taqī al-Dīn ʿAbdallāh b. Muḥammad b. Ḥamza b. Abi ʾl-Najm wrote, around 560/1165:

Durar al-aḥādīth al-nabawiyya bil-asānīd al-Yaḥyawiyya after Yaḥyā b. al-Ḥusayn b. al-Qāsim, who himself did not find time to collect *ḥadīth* as he was entirely taken up with religious war, Berl. 1299.

508 | 2a. Aḥmad b. Sulaymān al-Hādī ila 'l-Ḥaqq al-Mutawakkil billāh, d. 566/1070 (see Suppl.).

1. *Uṣūl al-aḥkām fi 'l-ḥalāl wal-ḥarām*, revised by Abu 'l-Ḥasan ʿAlī b. al-Ḥasan b. Aḥmad b. Abī Ḥurayṣa, Hamb. Or. Sem. 18 (copy dated 1136 AH).

3. Ḥamza b. Sulaymān b. Ḥamza, who died in 613/1216.

Al-Durar al-yatīma fī tabyīn al-sibāʿ wal-ghanīma, a Zaydī polemical pamphlet that makes use of the *Kitāb al-ʿumda fi 'l-radd ʿala 'l-Muṭarrifiyya al-murtadda* of Aḥmad b. Sulaymān b. al-Hādī, d. 566/1170 (2a), Berl. 2077.

4. Zayd b. Aḥmad al-ʿAnsī, ca. 600/1203.

Kitāb al-sirāj al-wahhāj al-mumayyiz bayna 'l-istiqāma wal-iʿwijāj, on the nature of God, Berl. 10284.

5. His son ʿAbdallāh b. Zayd b. Aḥmad al-ʿAnsī, fl. ca. 630/1233.

1. *al-Fatāwi 'l-nabawiyya al-mufṣiḥa ʿan aḥkām al-Muṭarrifiyya*, a demonstration that the Muṭarrifīs are heretics, Berl. 10286.—2. *Manāhij al-bayān li-rijāl*
403 *Sinḥān*, a warning against heresy, | with special regard to the Muṭarrifīs, directed at the inhabitants of the Sinḥān district in Yemen, ibid. 10287.—3. *al-Risāla al-ḥākima bi-taḥrīm munākaḥat al-firqa al-Muṭarrifiyya* ibid. 10288.—4. *al-Risāla al-nāṭiqa bi-ḍalāl al-Muṭarrifiyya al-zanādiqa* ibid. 10289.—5. *al-Risāla al-nāʿiya ʿalā muṣāramat al-kuffār min al-Muṭarrifiyya al-kafara al-ashrār* ibid. 10290.—6. *Risālat al-tawqīf ʿalā tawbat ahl al-taṭrīf* ibid. 10291.—7. *Kitāb al-irshād ilā (ṭarīq al)-najāt al-ʿibād*, composed in 632/1234, Berl. 3134, Or. Qu. 2039 (= Fischer-Burch. 38).—8., 9. see Suppl.

5a. Al-Qāḍī Shams al-Dīn Jaʿfar b. Aḥmad b. ʿAbd al-Salām b. Abī Yaḥyā, who died in 573/1177 (see Suppl.).

RSO II, 166. 5. *Masāʾil al-ijmāʿ* Ambr. C. 56, iv (*RSO* VII, 69).—6. *al-Naqḍ ʿalā ṣāḥib Majmūʿ al-muḥīṭ fī-mā khālafa fīhi 'l-Zaydiyya min bāb al-imāma* Alex. Fun. 132,1.

6. Ḥusām al-Dīn Abū Muḥammad al-Ḥasan b. Muḥammad b. al-Ḥasan b. Abī Bakr al-Raṣṣāṣ, who died in 584/1188 (see Suppl.).

1. *Kitāb al-tafṣīl li-jumal al-taḥṣīl*, on God's mercy, in particular with regard to Muḥammad and the imams, revised by Sulaymān b. ʿAbdallāh al-Kharrāshī, Berl. 10279, part 3.—2. *Kashf al-aḥkām* | *wal-ṣifāt ʿan khaṣāʾiṣ al-muʾaththarāt* 509
wal-muqtaḍabāt, metaphysical investigations, Berl. 5126.—3.–5. see Suppl.

7. His son Shihāb al-Dīn Zayn al-Muwaḥḥidīn Aḥmad b. al-Ḥasan b. Muḥammad b. al-Ḥasan al-Raṣṣāṣ, who died on 22 Muḥarram 621/17 February 1224.

See Suppl. Versification, *Durrat al-ghawwāṣ etc.*, additionally Alex. Adab $129_{,16}$.—2. *al-Shihāb al-thāqib fī manāqib ʿAlī b. Abī Ṭālib* Patna II, $353_{,2539,\ 13}$.

8. His grandson Shams (Bahāʾ) al-Dīn Abu 'l-Ḥasan Aḥmad b. Muḥammad b. al-Ḥasan al-Raṣṣāṣ al-Hafīd, who died on 19 Ramaḍān 656/19 September 1258.

1. *Miṣbāḥ al-ʿulūm etc.*, see Suppl. Commentaries: b. *al-Īḍāḥ* by Aḥmad b. Yaḥyā b. Aḥmad Ḥābis (II, 359), also Hamb. Or. Sem. 20.—c. ibid. 76.—2. Epistle to the two emirs Yaḥyā and Muḥammad, sons of al-Ḥasan, written in 635/1237, an admonition to return from unbelief, Berl. 2175, 6.—3., 4. see Suppl.

9. Al-Imām al-Manṣūr billāh ʿAbdallāh b. Ḥamza b. Sulaymān, who was born in Rabīʿ I 561/January 1166, became the Imam in 594/1198 and died in 614/1217 (or, according to others, in 613) in Kawkabān.

Biography from Abū Makhrama, *Cat. Leid.* ^{2}I, 417ff. 1. *Dīwān* Berl. 7703, Leid. 675, Brit. Mus. 1668, Suppl. 1065.—2. *Rajaz* on horses with commentary, Berl. 6181, Brit. Mus. Suppl. 814.—3. *Kitāb al-bayān wal-thabāt ilā kāffat al-banīn wal-banāt*, on mutual care between parents and children, Berl. 5598.—4. *al-Risāla al-kāfiya li-ahl al-ʿuqūl al-wāfiya*, a call to true belief and the party of the Zaydīs, Berl. $1275_{,4}$.—5. *Risāla ilā bilād ins walhān*, a letter of consolation, ibid. 5.—6. *Kitāb al-shāfī*, on the principles of religion, in refutation of *al-Khāriqa*, a treatise in which Zaydī teachings had been vehemently attacked, completed in 609/1212, Berl. 12080.—7. Answers to questions about the first three caliphs, Br. Mus. Suppl. 157v.—8. *al-ʿIqd al-thamīn fī tabyīn aḥkām al-aʾimma al-hādīn*, ibid. 210, i.—9. Polemic against the Muṭarrifiyya, ibid. ii. |— 404
10. *al-Durra al-yatīma fī tabyīn aḥkām al-sibāʿ wal-ghanīma*, ibid. iii, 1230, iv.—11. *al-Jawhara al-shawwāfa rāthiyat al-ṭawwāfa* ibid. v.—12. *al-ʿAqīda al-nabawiyya* ibid. 211. i.—13. *al-Risāla al-nāṣiḥa* ibid. ii.—14. Answers to various

questions, ibid. 210$_{,4,\ 9}$, 211$_{,4,\ 16}$.—15.–21. See Suppl. Other works in Ahlw., 4950 xi.

510 | 10. In 614/1217, after the death of al-Manṣūr, Yaḥyā b. al-Muḥsin b. Maḥfūẓ al-Muʿtaḍid billāh arrogated the imamate to himself, which was, however, disputed by his son. He died in 636/1238.

Al-Muqniʿ fī uṣūl al-fiqh, with a continuation by al-Muqtadir billāh, seventh cent., Br. Mus. Suppl. 266.

11. Al-Faḍl b. Abī al-Saʿd al-Uṣayfirī, who flourished around 600/1203.

1. *Miftāḥ al-fāʾiḍ fī ʿilm al-farāʾiḍ* Hamb. Or. Sem. 122, Br. Mus. Suppl. 439 iii. Commentaries: a. *Īḍāḥ al-ghāmiḍ* by Aḥmad b. Muḥammad al-Khālidī, composed in 867/1462, B. Mus. Suppl. 440/1. Ambr. D. 445.—b.—see Suppl. (c. also Hamb. Or. Sem. 19, 19B, 74, 129).—2. See Suppl.

12. Al-Mahdī li-Dīn Allāh Aḥmad b. al-Ḥusayn b. Aḥmad, who died in 656/1258 (see Suppl.).

1. *Risālat Khalīfat al-Qurʾān fī nukat min aḥkām ahl al-zamān*, which defends Zaydī claims with some passages from the Qurʾān, Berl. 275$_{,2}$.—2. An epistle calling for people to be pious and to join the Zaydīs, ibid. 10282.—3. See Suppl.

13. ʿAlī b. Yaḥyā b. Muḥammad al-Bannāʾ who flourished around 680/1281.

Al-Manhaj al-qawīm fī tafsīr al-Qurʾān al-karīm Br. Mus. Suppl. 115.

14. Al-Mutawakkil ʿala ʾllāh al-Muṭahhar b. Yaḥyā b. al-Hādī, who died in 697/1298.

Al-Khazrajī, *al-ʿUqūd al-luʾluʾiyya*, 310. 1. *al-Risāla al-muzalzila li-aʿḍāʾ al-Muʿtazila* Patna II, 352$_{,2539,\ 6}$.—2. *al-Masāʾil al-nājiya* ibid. 7.—3. *al-Kawākib al-durriyya* ibid. 353$_{,2539,\ 14}$.

B The Imāmīs

Dwight M. Donaldson, *The Shiite Religion, an History of Islam in Persia and Irak*, London 1933.

1. Dhu ʾl-Majdayn ʿAlam al-Hudā al-Sharīf al-Murtaḍā Abu ʾl-Qāsim ʿAlī b. al-Ṭāhir Dhi ʾl-Manāqib Abū Aḥmad al-Ḥusayn b. Mūsā b. Muḥammad b. Mūsā b. Ibrāhīm b. Mūsā al-Kāẓim b. Jaʿfar al-Ṣādiq b. Muḥammad al-Bāqir b. ʿAlī Zayn | al-ʿĀbidīn b. al-Ḥusayn b. ʿAlī b. Abī Ṭālib, who was born in Rajab 355/ 511
July 967, was the *naqīb* of the ʿAlids in Baghdad and died in 436/1044.

Ibn Khall. 416. List of his writings, Berl. 16, see 16 f. *Ijāza* regarding his works for Abu ʾl-Hasan Muḥammad b. Muḥammad al-Buṣrāwī, dated 417, at the beginning of a *majmūʿa* of his *Rasāʾil* and *Masāʾil* in Mashhad, *Dharīʿa* I, $216,_{1132}$. 1. *Kitāb al-ghurar wal-durar* or *Ghurar al-fawāʾid wa-durar al-qalāʾid bil-muḥāḍarāt*, in 82 *majālis* (see Suppl.), part II also Berl. Or. Qu. 2059, 2064, Mosul $36,_{186}$, $66,_{261}$ (which has *Majālis al-Sharīf al-Mūsawī*) appendix, *Mulḥaqāt*, Berl. 8743, probably = *al-Majlis fī kashf āyāt al-Qurʾān* NO 594. | — 405
2. Answers to dogmatic, juridical, and philosophical questions, Berl. 4977/8.—3. *Kitāb al-shihāb fi ʾl-shayb wal-shabāb* print. Constantinople (Jawāʾib) 1302.—4. A *qaṣīda*, Berl. $7609,_{6}$.—5. *Nahj al-balāgha*, composed in 400/1009 according to AS 4344 (Ritter), see Suppl., Massignon, Salman Pāk, *Publ. de la soc. ét. ir.* no. 7 (1933), p. 49, also Garr. 238, AS 4342/4, 4346, Patna I, $208,_{1853/4}$, see Hibat al-Dīn al-Shahrastānī (Suppl. II, 807), *Mā huwa Nahj al-balāgha*, Sidon (ʿIrfān) 1352.—Commentary by ʿIzz al-Dīn ʿAbd al-Ḥamīd al-Madāʾinī (see 335), also Garr. 239, Patna $202,_{1809/10}$.—b. Mītham b. ʿAlī al-Baḥrānī, Patna I, $203,_{1811/2}$, dedicated to the Ata Malik, Juwaynī *Taʾr. Jahāngushā* I, 41, abstract *Anwār al-faṣāḥa wa-asrār al-balāgha* by Niẓām al-Dīn ʿAlī b. al-Hasan b. Niẓāmaddīn al-Jīlānī, MSS *Dharīʿa* II, $436,_{1701}$.—f. Fatḥallāh al-Kāshānī, who died, according to the chronogram in the *Rawḍat al-j*, in 988 (Heffening).—i. *Minhāj al-barāʿa* by Ḥabīballāh al-Mujtahid al-ʿAlawī al-Mūsawī, lith. in 6 vols., Tehran 1350/1. (Suppl. wrongly under no. 18).—6.–20. see Suppl. (7. see *Lughat al-ʿArab* VI, 512, 4; 8. *Dharīʿa* II, $260,_{1455}$; 10. i.e. questions asked from Abū ʿAlī Muḥammad b. ʿAbd al-Malik al-Tabbān, d. 27 Dhu ʾl-Qaʿda 419/18 December 1028, *Dharīʿa* II, $78,_{310}$).—21. *Aḥkām ahl al-ākhira*, printed in *Kalimāt al-muḥaqqiqīn*, see *Dharīʿa* I, $295,_{1542}$.—22. *al-Asʾila al-Sallāriyya* by Yaḥyā b. Ḥamza Sallār b. ʿAbd al-ʿAzīz al-Daylamī, d. 463/1070 in Mashhad, *Dharīʿa*, II, $83,_{331}$.—23. *al-Asʾīla al-rassiyya al-ūlā wal-thāniya*, asked by Abu ʾl-Ḥusayn al-Muḥsin b. Muḥammad b. al-Naṣr al-Ḥusaynī al-Rassī and answered in 429/1037, MS in possession of Muḥammad Muḥsin, ibid. II, 82_{3278}.—24. *Risāla fī jawāb masāʾil kathīra*, see *Lughat al-ʿArab* VI, $514,_{18}$.—25. *Masāʾil al-Ramliyya, al-Ṭarābulusiyyāt al-thāniya, al-thālitha, al-Radd ʿala ʾl-munajjimīn*, | and *Ajwibat al-masāʾil al-wārida ʿalayhi* 512
min al-Rayy are preserved in Birjand, *Lughat al-ʿArab* VI, $515,_{317}$.

1a. ʿAbd al-Wāḥid b. Muḥammad b. ʿAbd al-Wāḥid al-Tamīmī al-Āmidī, who died in 436/1144.

Rawḍat al-jannāt 464. 1. *Ghurar al-ḥikam* see Suppl. I, 75.—2. *Jawāhir al-kalām fi ʾl-ḥikam wal-aḥkām min kalām* (ḤKh *qiṣṣat*) *sayyid al-anām* is wrongly attributed to him in ḤKh ^{1}II, $646_{,4294}$, ^{2}I, 616; since, according to the preface, the author had studied in 510/1116 in Āmid under his father Qāḍī Muḥammad and Aḥmad al-Ghazzālī, he can surely only be a grandson of ʿAbd al-Wāḥid; Abstract *Nafāʾis al-jawāhir* by Qudratallāh al-Murtaḍā al-Ādharī, composed in 937/1530, Alex. Fun. $68_{,8}$.

1b. Abu ʾl-Ḥasan Muḥammad b. Muḥammad al-Baṣrī, who was a student of ʿAlam al-Hudā.

Risāla fī taʾlīfāt al-sayyid al-Murtaḍā Mashh. V, $66_{,216}$.

2. Abū Jaʿfar Muḥammad b. al-Ḥasan b. ʿAlī al-Ṭūsī Shaykh al-Ṭāʾifa, who was born in 385/995 and died in Najaf in 458/1066 (or, according to others in, 459 or 460).

Shahrāshūb § 742. *Kitāb al-fuṣūl fi ʾl-uṣūl* with anon. commentary, Ind. Off. $471_{,13}$.—2. *Kitāb tahdhīb al-aḥkām* Bodl. II, $87_{,1}$, Ind. Off. 1782, Garr. 1610, Birjand, *Lughat al-ʿArab* VI, 512 Patna, I, 42, $_{430/2}$, II, $501_{,4684}$.—Abstract *Kitāb al-istibṣār fī-ma ʾkhtulifa fīhi min al-akhbār* Berl. 1272/6, Pet. AM 56, Birjand loc. cit., cf. Goldziher, *M.St.* II, 148, n. 4: on harmony with respect to legislating traditions. On the commentaries and glosses see *Dharīʿa* II, $14/6_{,43}$.—*Miṣbāḥ al-mutahajjid*, regulations regarding acts of worship recurring in the course of the year, including selected prayers for each of these, Berl. 3513, Patna I, $157_{,1494}$. *M. al-m. al-ṣaghīr* Patna II, $518_{,2784}$. An abbreviation in verse, Berl. 3514, abstract *Minhāj al-ṣalāh* by Muḥammad b. Yūsuf b. al-Muṭahhar al-Ḥillī, d. 726/1326 (II, 164), Ind. Off. 342.—4. *Kitāb al-ḥall wal-ʿaqd fi ʾl-ʿibādāt*, a prayer book, Ind. Off. 336.—5. *Kitāb al-mabsūṭ fi ʾl-fiqh* Br. Mus. Suppl. 331, Patna I, $102_{,1041}$.—6. *Kitāb asmāʾ al-rijāl*, with industrious detailing of book titles, Berl. 10044.—7. *Fihrist kutub al-shīʿa, List of Shyah Books* ed. A. Sprenger and Mawlawy
513 Abdal Haqq, Bibl. Ind. | no. 60, 71, 91, 107, Calcutta 1853/5, ed. M. Ṣādiq Āl Baḥr al-ʿUlūm, Najaf 1356/1937. Completion by Muḥammad b. Aḥmad b. Shahrāshūb al-Māzandarānī, d. 588/1192 (Suppl. I, 710), Berl. 1004.—7. *Maʿālim al-ʿulamāʾ*, ed. ʿAbbās Eghbal, Tehran 1934. Continuation by ʿAlī b. ʿUbaydallāh b. Bābūya, d. 580/1184 (Suppl. I, 710), Berl. 10048 printed in the last volume of the *Biḥār al-anwār* by al-Majlisī.—8. *al-Amālī fi ʾl-ḥadīth* Mashh. IV, 5, 16,

in edition Tehran 1313 mistakenly attributed to his son Abū ʿAlī al-Ḥasan, see *Dharīʿa* II, 309,$_{1236}$. Vol. II divided into *Majālis*, ibid. 313,$_{1248}$.—8.–13. see Suppl. (9 = 1a; 10. Mashh. VI, 62,$_{188}$; 11. Ind. Off. 1781, Garr. 1779).—14. *al-Tibyān* Garr. 1259.—15. *Thalāthūna masʾala ʿalā madhhab al-Shīʿa* Taymūr *ʿAqāʾid* 237.—16. *al-Iqtiṣād al-hādī ilā ṭarīq al-rashād*, MSS in Najaf and Yazd, *Dharīʿa* II, 269, 1089.—17. *Iṣṭilāḥāt al-mutakallimīn*, with a commentary by Muḥammad Saʿīd b. Muḥammad Mufīd al-Qummī, ca. 1099/1688, in the library of Rājā Muḥammad Mahdī in Fayḍābād, *Dharīʿa* II, 123,$_{495}$.—18. *al-Ījāz fi ʾl-farāʾiḍ*, MSS in Najaf, *Dharīʿa* II, 486,$_{1905}$.—19. *Tamhīd fi ʾl-uṣūl* Mashh. I, 23,$_{54}$.

2b. Muḥammad b. Aḥmad b. ʿAlī al-Fattāl.

The *Rawḍat al-wāʿiẓīn wa-tabṣirat al-muttaʿiẓīn* is attributed in Mashh. IV, 40,$_{124}$ to a certain Abū ʿAbdallāh Muḥammad b. al-Ḥasan b. ʿAlī al-Ḥāfiẓ al-Wāʿiẓ al-Nīsābūrī al-Fārisī Fattāl.

3. Raḍī al-Dīn Abū ʿAlī al-Faḍl b. al-Ḥasan Amīn al-Dīn al-Ṭabarsī, who died in 518/1153 (see Suppl.).

1. *Kitāb majmaʿ al-bayān li-ʿulūm al-Qurʾān*, a large Qurʾān commentary completed in 536/1141, Berl. 802/4, Ind. Off. 61/3, Br. Mus. 1473, Bodl. I, 50, Garr. 1272, Patna I, 32,$_{316/8}$, print. Tehran 1275 and others (wrongly attributed to al-Ṭūsī, d. 561/1166, in ḤKh V II, 437).—2. *Kitāb jāmiʿ al-jawāmiʿ fī tafsīr al-Qurʾān* interconnects the content of the *Majmaʿ* and *al-Kāfi ʾl-shāfī*, which he had written after his completion of the *Majmaʿ* and after reading Zamakhsharī's *Kashshāf*. This work was composed in 542/1147 at the request of his son Abū Naṣr al-Ḥasan, Ind. Off. 64, Mosul 94, 27 (where the *nisba* is corrupted to al-Ṭurṭūshī, as it is in ḤKh [1]II, 638,$_{4248}$ [2]I, 611 to al-Ṭarasūsī).—3. *Kitāb al-iḥtijāj*, a defence of the Shīʿī doctrine of the twelve imams, Ind. Off. 166, Patna I, 122,$_{130}$ (attributed to 3a), as *al-Iḥtijāj ʿalā ahl al-lijāj*, attributed to Ibn Shahrāshūb (Suppl. I, 710, 3 f.), printed in Persia 1268, 1300, Najaf 1354 (*Dharīʿa* I, 283,$_{1472}$).—4. *Kitāb* | *al-ījāz al-* 514
muttasim bi-simat al-iʿjāz, a grammar book with an anonymous commentary, Esc. [2]180.—5. *Makārim al-akhlāq*, according to *Dharīʿa* I, 18/9,$_{89}$, abstracted by his son from his *al-Ādāb al-dīniyya lil-khizāna al-Muʿīniyya*, and preserved in the library of Ḥasan Ṣadr al-Dīn.—6.–8. See Suppl. (ad 7. see 2, 19).

3b. Abu ʾl-Ḥusayn Warrām al-Ashtarī see Suppl.

2. *Majmūʿa* Rāmpūr I, 109,$_{337}$, see Kantūrī 3261.

3d. ʿUbaydallāh b. Muḥammad b. al-Ḥasan b. Bābūyā al-Qummī, d. 585/1178 (see Suppl.).

1. *Arbaʿūna ḥadīthan*, written as the counterpart to the *Arb. ḥad. fī faḍāʾil amīr al-muʾminīn* by Abū Saʿīd Muḥammad b. Aḥmad b. Ḥusayn al-Khuzāʿī Ṣāḥib *Rawḍat al-zahrāʾ* (Suppl. I, 708, 2a), numerous MSS in Iraq, *Dharīʿa* I, 432/3,$_{2210/2}$.

3ea. His nephew Muḥyi ʾl-Dīn Abū Ḥāmid Muḥammad b. ʿAbdallāh b. ʿAlī b. Zuhra al-Ḥusaynī, who died in 655/1257.

Arbaʿūna ḥadīthan, MSS in different private libraries, *Dharīʿa* I, 426,$_{2181}$.

3eb. His student Sadīd al-Dīn Abu ʾl-Faḍl Shādhān b. Jabrāʾīl b. Ismāʿīl b. Abī Ṭālib al-Qummī Nazīl al-Madīna.

Amal al-āmil 474,$_{13}$, 476. 1. *al-Faḍāʾil wal-manāqib*, print. Tabriz 1304.—2. *Izāḥat al-ʿilla fī maʿrifat al-qibla min sāʾir al-aqālīm*, composed in 558/1163, included by al-Majlisī in his *Biḥār al-anwār*, vol. *Ṣalāt, Bāb al-qibla*, and wrongly attributed to al-Faḍl b. Shādhān (Suppl. II, 1201 zu 319) by al-Ḥurr al-ʿĀmilī, *Dharīʿa* I, I, 517,$_{2572}$.

3g. Muḥammad b. Idrīs al-ʿIjlī, who died in 598/1202 (see Suppl.).

Sarāʾir al-ḥāwī fī taḥrīr al-fatāwī, additionally Alex. Firaq 11, Patna I, 90,$_{917}$.

4. Najm al-Dīn Jaʿfar b. Muḥammad b. Saʿīd al-Ḥillī Abu ʾl-Qāsim al-Muḥaqqiq al-Awwal was born in Ḥilla in 602/1205 and died in Baghdad in 676/1277 (or, according to others, in 726).

1. *Kitāb sharāʾiʿ al-islām*, the account of *fiqh* that is the most celebrated among the Shīʿīs, Leid. 1792, Br. Mus. 1607, Ind. Off. 1783/5, Alex. Firaq 7, Patna I, 91,$_{920/3}$, print. Calcutta 1839 and others, with a Russian translation by Kazembeg, fs. I,
515 St. Petersburg | 1862 (see *JA*, 1865, 295).—Commentaries: a. *Masālik al-afhām ilā tanqīḥ Sh. al-i.* by Zayn al-Dīn b. ʿAlī b. Aḥmad al-Shāmī al-ʿĀmilī al-Shahīd al-Thānī (II, 325), composed in 964/1557, Leid. 1793, BDMG 45, Patna I, 84,$_{847}$, 105,$_{1065, 7}$, a *Ḥāshiya* thereon by his grandson Muḥammad b. Ḥasan b. Zayn al-Dīn al-ʿĀmilī, eleventh/seventeenth cent., Ind. Off. 1789, by his son ʿAlī, d. 1103/1691 (*Rawḍāt al-jannāt* 44), ibid. 1788, Āṣaf. 1180, according to Bank. XIX, p. 134, by ʿAlī b. ʿAbd al-ʿĀlī al-Karakī, d. 940/1533 (II, 411).—b.–o. see Suppl.

(b. al-Aʿsam *Dharīʿa* II, $497_{,1951}$, where other MSS).—Abstract *al-Nāfiʿ fī mukhtaṣar al-Sh.* by the author himself, Leid. 1794/5, Br. Mus. Suppl. 332, Ind. Off. 1786/7, Alex. Firaq 17, Patna I, $104_{,1058/9}$ lith. Delhi, *BO* II, 92.—Commentaries and glosses: a.—i. see Suppl. (c. Patna I, $83_{,836/7}$).—k. ʿAlī b. ʿAbd al-ʿĀlī, Leid. 1796.—2.–6. see Suppl.—7. *Irshād al-adhān* Br. Mus. Or. 8335/6 (Quart. VIII, 286).

4a. Asʿad b. Ibrāhīm b. Ḥasan b. ʿAlī al-Ḥillī wrote, in 610/1213:

Arbaʿūna ḥadīthan, MSS in private libraries in Tehran and Najaf, *Dharīʿa* I, $410_{,2131}$.

5.–2. See Suppl.

10, 1 *Kashf al-ghumma etc.*, Patna I, $277_{,2302}$.—2. *Risālat al-ṭayf*, an autobiographical tale resembling a *maqāma*, in which the author relates an encounter with a beautiful girl on a spring meadow, and with whom he has a literary conversation; in the end it all turns out to be a dream (Ritter), additionally AS 3850, 4137, Sarāi 2393 (*RSO* IV, 707).

Chapter 8. Sciences of the Qurʾān

1 *The Art of Reading the Qurʾān*

1. Abū Muḥammad Makkī[1] b. Abī Ṭālib Ḥammūsh al-Qaysī was born in Kairouan on 23 Shaʿbān 354/25 August 975 and travelled to Egypt at the age of 13 in order to study philology and arithmetic. Upon returning to his homeland he turned to the study of the readings of the Qurʾān,
516 | which he completed in 374/984. After making the pilgrimage in 377/987 he again studied in Egypt and then returned to Kairouan. In 382/992 he went to Egypt for a third time and remained there until 383. In 387/997 he went to Mecca, where he remained for four years. By way of Egypt and Kairouan, where he stayed for about another year, he arrived in Spain in Rajab 393/May 1003. After lecturing at various mosques in Cordova, he was appointed as preacher and imam of the main mosque by al-Ḥasan b. Jawhar. Despite not being quite up to the task, he kept these posts until his death on 2 Muḥarram 437/21 July 1045.

Ibn Khall. 708, Ibn al-Anbārī 421. 1. *Kitāb al-riʿāya fī tajwīd al-qirāʾa wa-taḥqīq lafẓ al-tilāwa* Bodl. II, 244, Qawala I, 19, q 15.—2. *al-Tabṣira*, an enlargement of his compendium *al-Mūjiz*, on the art of reciting/reading the Qurʾān (composed in 385/995, but which he did not publish because of several shortcomings), composed in 392/1002, with 14 *riwāyāt* based on the 7 well-known readers, following the lectures of—notably—Ibn Ghalbūn, d. 389/999, Berl. 577; in this work he announced a further work, *al-Kashf ʿan wujūh al-qirāʾāt*, which he completed in 424/1033, ibid. 578.—3. *Iʿrāb mushkilāt al-Qurʾān wa-dhikr ʿilalihi*
407 *wa-ṣaʿbihi* | *wa-nādirihi* (*mushkil iʿrāb al-Qurʾān*), grammatical explanations, Berl. 703, Garr. 1257, Cairo [1]I, 211, [2]I, 62.—4. *Kitāb sarḥ kallā wa-balā wa-naʿam wal-waqf ʿalā kulli wāḥida minhunna wa-dhikr maʿānīhā wa-ʿilalihā*, Gotha 548 (ḤKh V, 10614 only has *kallā*, Ibn Khall., loc. cit., has *kallā* and *balā*), as the *Risāla fī ḥukm kallā wa-balā wa-naʿam wal-waqf ʿalayhā wal-ibtidāʾ* in Fātiḥ Waqf Ibr. 28,$_2$, Fātiḥ 68,$_8$, Qawala I, 17, q 23.—5.–7. see Suppl.

2. Abū ʿAmr ʿUthmān b. Saʿīd al-Dānī al-Qurṭubī b. al-Ṣayrafī al-Umawī al-Munīrī, who was born in 371/981, spent four months in Kairouan and one year in Cairo when he went on pilgrimage in 397/1006. In 399/1008 he settled in Cordova, moved to Denia in 409/1018 and, in the same year, to Mallorca, then
517 returned in | 417/1026 to Denia where he died in the middle of Shawwāl 444/February 1053 or, according to others, in 441.

---

1 Thus not Makī (Nöldeke, *Gesch. des Qorans* 336, n. 1), as is shown by the diminutive *mukayk* (Yāqūt, *Irshād* VII, 177,$_8$, Ibn Khall. II, 160,$_7$), see my *Ar. Gramm.* § 73, Anm. 1.

Maqq. I, 550, *Ḥuff.* XIV, 5, Yāqūt, GW II, 540, Wüst., *Gesch.* 197. *Kitāb al-taysīr fi 'l-qirā'āt al-sab'*, which contains the fourteen readings that all go back to seven but, out of the fourteen different *riwāyāt*, it considers only one in each case (Nöldeke, *Gesch. d. Qor.* ^{1}337), Berl. 379/89, Gotha 550 (where other MSS are listed), Br. Mus. Suppl. 84, Garr. 1 191, 2067$_{,4}$, Fātiḥ 72$_{,3}$, Waqf Ibr. 39, Köpr. 14, Carullah 17$_{,8}$, Patna I, 12$_{,104/7}$. Commentary *al-Durr al-nathīr wal-'adhb al-namīr*, by Abū Muḥammad 'Abd al-Wāḥid b. Muḥammad b. 'Alī b. Abi 'l-Saddād al-Umawī al-Mālaqī (Jazarī, *Ṭab.* 1985, Suppl. II, 370$_{,1b)}$, Fātiḥ Waqf Ibr. 10.—Versification *Ḥirz al-amānī*, by al-Shāṭibī, d. 590/1194, see no. 12.—The three recensions (out of ten) that are missing here are supplemented by Muḥammad b. Muḥammad al-Jazarī, d. 833/1429 (II, 201), in *al-Durra al-muḍī'a fī qirā'at al-a' imma al-thalātha al-marḍiyya*, Gotha 558 (where other MSS are listed), lith. C. 1285, and in *Taḥbīr al-Taysīr*, Berl. 590, Garr. 1192, NO 60, Fātiḥ Waqf Ibr. 54, 70 Cairo ^{1}I, 92, Patna I, 12$_{,10}$, II, 367$_{,2549/4}$.—2. *Jāmi' al-bayān fi 'l-qirā'āt al-sab' al-mashhūra* Cairo ^{1}I, 94, ^{2}I, 18 Patna I, 13$_{,110}$.—3. *Kitāb al-muqni' fī ma'rifat rasm (khaṭṭ) maṣāḥif al-amṣār*, on the compilation of the Qur'ān and the determination of the orthography, Berl. 419, Vienna 1624, Paris 593, Br. Mus. Suppl. 83, Qawala I, 33/4, Patna I, 20$_{,174/5}$, a fragment (?) in Leid. 1635, see de Sacy, *Not. et Extr.* VIII, 290/332, Nöldeke, *Gesch. d. Qor.* ^{1}243. Abstract AS 48$_{,14}$ (Suppl. I, 158$_{,2}$ to be deleted, Ritter).—Versification *al-'Aqīla*, by al-Shāṭibī, see no. 12.—4. *Kitāb al-tahdhīb fi 'l-qirā'a* AS 39, Patna I, 12$_{,103}$.—5. *Kitāb al-ījāz wal-bayān*, the foundation of the system of Nāfi', Paris 592$_{,3}$.—6. *Kitāb al-ta'rīf (fi 'l-qirā'āt al-shawādhdh)* Algiers 367$_{,2}$ 374$_{,1}$.—7. *Mufradāt al-qurrā' al-sab'a* Cairo ^{1}I, 114.—8. *Kitāb al-muktafā fi 'l-waqf wal-mubtada'* Paris 592, as *al-Waqf al-tāmm wal-kāfī wal-ḥasan* in Qawala I, 28/9.—9. *Kitāb al-iḍḍighām* Br. Mus. Suppl. 92 i.—10.–21. see Suppl. (16. also Fātiḥ Waqf Ibr. 14$_{,3}$, Qawala I, 8 q 48).—22. *al-Tarjama* Qawala I, 27.—23. *Zawā'id*, 26 verses on the spelling of the Qur'ān, Paris 610$_{,3}$, *rajaz* on the pronunciation of the letters, ibid. 4, see de Sacy, *Not. et Extr.* VIII, 352.

3. Abū 'Alī al-Ḥasan b. 'Alī b. Ibrāhīm b. Yazdād b. Shāhūh (Shāhwayh?) b.
Hurmuz al-Ahwāzī, who was born in 362/972, | declared himself a Sālimī and 518
settled in Damascus in Dhu 'l-Ḥijja 391/October 1001, dying there in Dhu 'l-Ḥijja
446/March 1055.

See Suppl. 3., additionally Istanbul Un. R 259 (*ZS* III, 249). Bergsträsser-Pretzl, *Gesch. d. Qor.* III, 229 mistakenly called him al-Hudhalī al-Miṣrī; the *Kitāb al-iqnā'* mentioned there is identical with the one mentioned in note 8 following ḤKh ^{1}I, 385$_{,1078}$, ^{2}I, 140 (Spitaler).

4. Abu 'l-Ṭāhir Ismā'īl b. Khalaf b. Sa'īd b. 'Imrān al-Ṣaqalī al-Saraqusṭī al-Miṣrī, who died in Egypt on 1 Muḥarram 455/4 Janury 1063.

Ibn Khall. 94, al-Suyūṭī, *Ḥusn al-muḥ.* I, 283. 1. *Kitāb al-iktifāʾ fi ʾl-qirāʾāt* NO 53,$_{2}$, abstract *al-ʿUnwān fi ʾl-qirāʾāt al-sabʿ* Berl. 591/2, AS 58, Patna I, 17,$_{51}$ (wrongly *al-ʿUyūn*), commentary by Rashīd al-Dīn Abū Muḥammad b. al-Ẓāhir b. Abi ʾl-Makārim Nashwān al-Rūḥī, d. 649/1251, AS 55.—2., 3. see Suppl.

408 | 5. Abū Maʿshar ʿAbd al-Karīm b. ʿAbd al-Ṣamad b. Muḥammad b. ʿAlī b. Muḥammad al-Qaṭṭān al-Ṭabarī al-Shāfiʿī, who died in 478/1085 in Mecca, was a teacher of Qurʾān recitation.

1. *Kitāb sūq al-ʿarūs*, which lists the most important reciters of the Qurʾān, with their students and their students' students, ḤKh ^{1}III, 7289, Berl. 593, Makram 30, abstract *Kitāb fahm al-Qurʾān*, Alex. Fun. 144,$_{3}$.—2. *Kitāb al-talkhīṣ fi ʾl-qirāʾāt al-thamānī*, on the 8 readers and their principal *rāwīs*, each of whom is again represented by two main branches of his tradition, Berl. 653.—3. *ʿUyūn al-masāʾil* (*fi ʾl-tafsīr*) Cairo ^{1}I, 183, ^{2}I, 55.

5a. Aḥmad b. ʿAlī b. ʿAbdallāh al-Ṣūfī al-Baghdādī was born in 392/1002 and died in 486/1093.

Ibn al-Jazarī, *Ṭab.* no. 368. A *qaṣīda* on the number of Qurʾān verses, AS 4914,$_{2}$.

6. Abu ʾl-Qāsim ʿAbd al-Raḥmān b. ʿAtīq b. Khalaf b. Abī Bakr b. Abī Saʿīd b. al-Faḥḥām al-Ṣaqalī, who died in Alexandria in 516/1122.

1. *Kitāb al-tajrīd li-bughyat al-murīd* Berl. Ms. or. oct. 3813 (652,$_{h}$), Garr. 2094,$_{1}$, Makram 8 (Pretzl, *Islca* VI, 31).—2. *Kitāb mufradāt Yaʿqūb* NO 95 (ibid. 46).

519 | 7. Abu ʾl-ʿIzz Muḥammad b. al-Ḥusayn (b. ʿAlī) b. Bundār al-Wāsiṭī al-Qalānisī was born in 435/1044 in Wāsiṭ and died in 521/1127.

1. *Kitāb irshād al-mubtadiʾ wa-tadhkirat al-muntahī* assembles the readings of the 10, following their many students and students' students, Berl. 654/5, Br. Mus. Suppl. 86, NO 88, see Nöldeke, *Gesch.* ^{1}339.—2. *Risāla fi ʾl-qirāʾāt al-thalāth*, on the readings of the Qurʾān in the Hijaz, Syria, and Iraq, Vienna 1627.—3. See Suppl.

8. Abu ʾl-Karam al-Mubārak b. al-Ḥasan b. Aḥmad b. ʿAlī al-Shahrazūrī was born on 17 Rabīʿ II 462/3 February 1070 and died in Baghdad on 22 Dhu ʾl-Ḥijja 550/17 February 1156.

Kitāb al-miṣbāḥ al-zāhir fi 'l-qirā'āt al-ʿashr Bodl. I, 35 (*Rend-Linc.* 1938, 86, n. 1).

9. Aḥmad b. Jaʿfar al-Ghāfiqī Abu 'l-Qāsim b. al-Abzārī was born in 500/1106 and died in Alexandria in 569/1173.

Treatise on the Qur'ān reading of Abū ʿAmr b. al-ʿAlā' (p. 97) in the *riwāya* of al-Yazīdī, d. 202/817, and Abū Nuʿaym, ca. 200, Berl. 634, see Nöldeke, p. 343.

10. Muḥammad (Aḥmad) b. Ṭayfūr al-Ghaznawī al-Sajāwandī, who died around 560/1165.

Suyūṭī, ed. Meursinge, 98. 1. *Kitāb al-waqf wal-ibtidā'*, which names 7 kinds of pause, each of which is marked by a separate letter, a system which, despite its artificiality, was soon universally adopted, Munich 100, Vienna 1625, Ind. Off. 46/7, Garr. 1193, AS 42/3, Fātiḥ 64, 66, Waqf Ibr. 7, Qawala I, 29 (*Kitāb al-wuqūf*), Patna I, 21,$_{187/8}$. See Nöldeke 352.—Commentary by Niẓām al-Dīn al-Nīsābūrī (II, 200,) Br. Mus. 85, Garr. 1194.—2. *Kitāb al-mūjiz*, from which a passage on the fivefold pause, Berl. 565 (= 1? Ritter).—3. *ʿAyn al-maʿānī fī tafsīr al-sabʿ al-mathānī* Cairo [1]I, 182, [2]I, 55.—4. Précis on syntax and etymology, Ind. Off. 889, anon. commentary, *al-Durar*, ibid. 981,$_3$.—5., 6. See Suppl.

11. Abū Isḥāq Ibrāhīm b. Muḥammad b. ʿAlī al-Qawwāsī al-Marandī, a second-generation student of | Abu 'l-ʿAlā' al-Hamadhānī who died in 569/1173 (Ibn 520
al-Jazārī I, 945, Suppl. I, 724, 11d).

Qurrat ʿayn al-qurrā' fi 'l-qirā'āt Esc. [1]1337 (Pretzl, *Gesch. des Qorantextes* 229).

11a. Abū Isḥāq b. Ibrāhīm b. Muḥammad b. Wāthiq al-Umawī al-Ishbīlī al-Andalusī, who was born in 567/1171 and died on 4 Rabīʿ II 651/2 June 1256.

Ibn al-Jazarī, *Ṭab.* I, 24, no. 101, *ShDh* V, 2641. *Fī tajwīd al-qirā'a wa-makhārij al-ḥurūf* AS 39,$_7$, Pretzl, *Iscla* VI, 233.

12. Abu 'l-Qāsim (Abū Muḥammad) al-Qāsim b. Firruh[2] b. Abi 'l-Qāsim Khalaf b. Aḥmad al-Ruʿaynī al-Shāṭibī, born in 539/1143 in Játiva, went to Cairo in

2 Probably *ferro* (Old Spanish for *hierro* 'iron'), Nöldeke, *Gesch. des Qor.* 337, n. 5.

572/1176 where he became a teacher in the reading of the Qurʾān at the al-Madrasa al-Fāḍiliyya, and died on 18 or 28 Jumādā II 590/11 or 21 June 1194.

Ibn Khall. 510, al-Suyūṭī, *Ḥusn al-muḥ.* I, 284; Aḥmad b. Muḥammad al-Qasṭallānī, d. 923/1517 (II, 73), *al-Fatḥ al-wahhāb fī tarjamat (sīrat) al-imām (Abu 'l-Qāsim) al-Shāṭibī* Berl. 10123, Br. Mus. 88$_{,2}$, whence *Minḥa min minaḥ Fatḥ al-Mawāhibī tunbiʾ ʿan lamḥa min sīrat Abi 'l-Qāsim al-Shāṭibī*, Garr. 707. I. *Ḥirz al-amānī wa-wajh al-tahānī al-Shāṭibiyya*, versification of the *Taysīr* (p. 517) "which incorporates the content of the *Taysīr* in a barbaric language, which is unintelligible if one does not know the meaning of the characters that are jotted down in many colours. The reputation of this work is founded only on its brevity, made possible by an idiosyncratic arrangement facilitating the memorization of its verses. Other than that, it is a vacuous work, which really shows the obscurity of this science", Nöldeke, *Gesch. d. Qor.*, [1]338. Berl. 594/603, Gotha 501/3 (where other MSS are listed), Br. Mus. Suppl. 87i, 88$_{,1}$, Garr. 1196/9, 2094$_{,2}$., Makr. 26, Teh. II, 30, Patna I, 144$_{,116/9}$, lith. C. 1286, Persian translation by Muḥammad b. ʿAbdallāh b. Maḥmūd, *Kashf al-amānī fī sabʿ al-mathānī*, AS 57$_{,1}$.—Commentaries: 1. *Fatḥ al-waṣīd* by ʿAlī b. Muḥammad al-Sakhāwī (no. 14), Munich 102, Paris 611, Cairo [1]I, 103, [2]I, 25, Patna I, 16$_{,141}$.—1a. *al-Mabsūṭ*
521 by Muḥammad b. Maḥmūd | al-Samarqandī, ca. 600/1203 (see Suppl.), Garr. 1204, 2094$_{,3}$.—2. Muḥammad b. Aḥmad Suʿla al-Mawṣilī, d. 656/1258, Berl. 604, BDMG 10, AS 46, Fātiḥ 51, Cairo [1]I, 104.—3. *al-Laʾālīʾ al-farīda* by Muḥammad b. al-Ḥasan al-Fāsī, d. 656/1258 (no. 16), Fāṭih 48, AS 49, 50, Cairo [1]I, 104.—3a. *Kanz al-Maʿānī* by the same (see Suppl.), lith. Peshawar 1279.—4. Anon., maybe by ʿAlam al-Dīn Qāsim b. Aḥmad al-Lūrqī, d. 661/1263 (whose *Qaṣīda fī riḥlatihi fī ṭalab al-Qurʾān wa-qiraʾātihi maʿa riwāyatihi*, Dam. Z. 34, 82$_{,1}$), Garr. 1200 or by Abu 'l-ʿAbbās Aḥmad b. ʿAlī al-Andalusī, d. ca. 660/1262, Berl. 605.—5. *Ibrāz al-maʿānī* by Abū Shāma, d. 665/1266 (p. 386), Berl. 606/7, Br. Mus. 1558, Garr. 1200, Fātiḥ 46, 56, Patna I, 11$_{,87}$.—6. *Ḥall al-rumūz* by Yaʿqūb b. Badrān al-Jarāʾidī, d. 688/1289, in 199 *ṭawīl* verses, Vienna 1629.—7. ʿUmar b. ʿUthmān, composed in 723/1323, Cairo [1]I, 100.—8. *Kanz al-maʿānī* by Ibrāhīm b. ʿUmar al-Jaʿbarī, d. 732/1331 (Suppl. II, 134), Berl. 611, (see 612), Gotha 554, Munich 103, Algiers 371, *Hespéris* XII, 1931, 119$_{,1007}$, Garr. 1201/3, AS 47, Köpr. 25, Fātiḥ 52, Waqf Ibr. 7, Cairo [1]I, 100, Patna I, 18$_{,160/4}$.—9. On the *Bāb waqf Hamza wa-Hishām ʿala 'l-hamz* by Ibn Umm Qāsim, d. 749/1348 (II, 22), Cairo [1]I, 99.—10. Aḥmad b. Yūsuf al-Samīn, d. 756/1355, Cairo [1]I, 102, [2]I, 24.—11. *Sirāj al-qāriʾ al-mubtadiʾ wa-tadhkīr al-muqriʾ al muntahī* by ʿAlī b. ʿUthmān b. al-Qāṣiḥ, d. 801/1398 (II, 165), completed in 759/1358, Berl. 609, Paris 612$_{,1}$, 5127, 5430, Algiers 372, Fātiḥ Waqf Ibr. 8, Qawala I, 19. q. 61, Patna I, 15$_{,130/1}$, print. C. 1293, 1304, 1317.—

12. *al-Farīda al-bāriziyya* by Abū Bakr al-Maghribī, Cambr. p. 19, Suppl. 399
(Abū ʿAbdallāh).—13. al-Suyūṭī, d. 911/1505, Cairo ^{1}I, 100. |—14. Aḥmad b. 410
Aḥmad al-Sunbāṭī, d. 990/1582 (II, 368), ibid. 101.—15. Muḥammad b. ʿAbdallāh
b. Maḥmūd, AS 57.—16. Anon., Berl. 608, 610, Leipz. 100,$_2$, Paris 4530, Br. Mus.
1559/60.—17.–30. see Suppl. (22. also Patna I, 17,$_{147}$; 23., also Qawala I, 21, q 32.
27. al-Dabbāʿ, *Isl.* XXI, 133).—31. Muḥammad b. Muṣṭafā al-Qūṣī (i.e. al-Qūjawī)
Shaykhzāde, d. 950/1543 (Suppl. II, 650), Qawala 23 q 7.—32. Abū ʿAbdallāh
Muḥammad b. Ḥasan al-Fārisī, Patna I, 16,$_{130/40}$.—33. *Jāmiʿ al-fawāʾid fī sharḥ
asna 'l-qaṣāʾid* by al-Zahidī (Suppl. I, 656,3), Fātiḥ 471 (Ritter).

II. *ʿAqīlat atrāb al-qaṣāʾid fī asna 'l-maqāṣid*, a versification of al-Dānī's
Muqniʿ on *rāʾ*, Berl. 487/94, Gotha 555,$_2$/6 (where other MSS are listed), Br. Mus.
87 ii, 88 ii, Garr. 1205, 1253,$_2$, AS 37,$_2$, 38, 60,$_3$, Fātiḥ Waqf Ibr. 61,$_3$, Qawala | I, 522
23/4, lith. C. 1282, see de Sacy, *Mém. de l'Ac. des Inscr.* L. 419, 329ff., *Not. et Extr.*
VIII, 1, 1787, 342ff.—Commentaries: 1. *al-Wasīla ilā kashf al-ʿAqīla* by al-Sakhāwī
(no. 14), Berl. 495/6, Vienna 1634, Paris 610,$_1$, Br. Mus. Suppl. 89, Cairo ^{1}I, 119, ^{2}I,
30, Qawala I, 36, Patna I, 21,$_{186}$.—2.–7. see Suppl. (2. Waqf Ibr. 40, Qawala I, 9, q
56. 7. Fātiḥ Waqf Ibr. 45, Fātiḥ 40$_3$, 45, Köpr III, 14).—8. Anon. *Sharḥ al-Rāʾiyya*,
Garr. 1206, *Taysīr al-ʿAqīla* Qawala I, 10 q 18.—6 commentaries are mentioned
by Ahlw., loc. cit.—III. *Tafsīr al-Qurʾān* Copenhagen 47.—IV. *al-Risāla al-qudsiyya* AS 37.—V. *Nāẓimat al-zahr fī aʿdād āyāt al-Qurʾān etc.*, Fātiḥ, Waqf
Ibr. 41, Garr. 1195; commentaries: a. Riḍwān b. Muḥammad al-Mukhallilātī,
see Spitaler, *Verszählung* 6, b. ʿAbdallāh Ṣāliḥ al-Ayyūbī, d. 1252/1836 (II, 505),
Lawāmiʿ al-badr fī N. al-z., Fātiḥ Waqf Ibr. 27.—VI.–X. see Suppl.

12a. See Suppl. I, 727, II, 982,$_{36}$. 4. Book without title on *wuqūf*, the arrangement and number of verses of the Qurʾān, Fātiḥ, Waqf Ibr. 15 (Ritter).

13. ʿAbd al-Raḥmān b. ʿAbd al-Majīd al-Ṣafrāwī, d. 636/1238.

Kitāb al-taqrīb wal-bayān fī maʿrifat shawādhdh al-Qurʾān, supplement to his *al-Iʿlān fi 'l-qirāʾāt al-sabʿ* (*bil-mukhtār min riwāyāt al-Q. fi 'l-q. al-sabʿ*), Garr. 1207, assembles readings that are transmitted only sporadically and go against linguistic usage and analogy, Berl. 613.

14. ʿAlam al-Dīn Abu 'l-Ḥasan ʿAlī b. Muḥammad b. ʿAbd al-Ṣamad al-Sakhāwī al-Hamadhānī, who died in 634/1243 (see Suppl.).

Ibn Khall. 429, al-Suyūṭī, *de Interpret.* 78. 1. *Hidāyat al-murtāb wa-ghāyat al-ḥuffāẓ wal-ṭullāb*, 427 *rajaz* verses about identical and similar expressions

and passages in the Qur'ān, Berl. 710/4, Br. Mus. Suppl. 95v, Garr. 1208, Cairo ^{1}I, 129, ^{2}I, 30, 65, Patna I, $20_{,172}$.—2. *ʿUmdat al-mufīd wa-ʿuddat al-mujīd*, 64 *kāmil* verses on *tajwīd*, Ber. 497, Algiers $561_{,6}$, with the title *ʿUmdat al-mujīd fi 'l-naẓm wal-tajrīd* in Garr. $1263_{,6}$.—Commentary, see Suppl. anon. Patna I, $16_{,144/5}$.—3. Poem on the reading of the Qur'ān, ending in *ān*, Paris $651_{,4}$.—3a. Abstract of his book on the pausa, Br. Mus. 1406.—4. *Jamāl al-qurrā' wa-kamāl al-iqrā'*, Cairo ^{1}I, 94, ^{2}I, 18.—5. *Sharḥ ḥirz al-amānī*, see no. 12, I.—6. *Sharḥ al-ʿaqīla*, ibid. II.—7. *Urjūza fī sīrat al-nabī*, 770 verses in 20 chapters, Berl. 9576.—8. *al-Kawkab al-waqqād fi 'l-iʿtiqād, fī uṣūl ad-dīn*, a commentary thereon by
523 al-Suyūṭī, Munich $883_{,2}$, Alex. Fun. | $134_{,7}$, $190_{,1}$.—9. *Tuḥfat al-furrāḍ wa-ṭurfat al-muhadhdhib al-murtāḍ*, 330 *rajaz* verses on the law of inheritance, Berl. 4709, a didactic letter on the same dated 640/1242, Berl. $150_{,1}$.—10. Lexical poem containing homonyms, 225 verses with commentary, Berl. 7062.—11. *al-Qaṣā'id al-sabʿ*, religious poems in praise of the Prophet, collected by one of his contemporaries, Berl. 7752, commentary by Shihāb al-Dīn ʿAbd al-Raḥmān b. Ismāʿīl b. al-Maqdisī al-Ḥanafī Abū Shāma, d. 665/1268 (p. 387), composed in 642/1244, Paris $3141_{,1}$.—12. A poetical correspondence with Kamāl al-Dīn al-Sharīshī (the commentator of al-Ḥarīrī, d. 619/1222 ?), Gotha $104_{,2}$.—13. *Sifr al-saʿāda wa-safīr al-ifāda fi 'l-lugha*, a commentary on Zamakhsharī's
411 | *Mufaṣṣal*, see p. 347.—14. *al-Mufaḍḍal* ibid.—14a.–16. See Suppl.—17. *Manẓūma fī aḥzāb al-Qur'ān* Bursa, Ulu Cami Lugha I, ff. 121b/23a (Ritter).

15. Abu 'l-Faḍl Ismāʿīl b. ʿAlī b. Saʿd al-Wāsiṭī, d. ca. 690/1291.

Kitāb durr al-afkār fī qirā'āt al-ʿashara a'immat al-amṣār, in *rajaz* verse, ḤKh III, $186_{,4850}$, ^{2}I, 730, with an anon. comm. Esc. $^2244_{,1}$, used in Berl. 608.

16.–18. See Suppl.

19. Aḥmad b. ʿAbdallāh b. al-Zubayr al-Khābūrī, who died in 690/1291 in Aleppo.

Ibn al-Jazarī, *Ṭab.* no. 322. *Al-durr al-naḍīd fi 'l-tajwīd* Fātiḥ $52_{,2}$ (Ritter).

2 *Qur'ānic Exegesis*

1. ʿAlī b. Ibrāhīm (Faḍḍāl) b. Saʿīd al-Ḥawfī Abu 'l-Ḥasan hailed from the village of Shubrā near Bilbīs (vulg. Bilbays) in north-eastern Egypt and died on 1 Dhu 'l-Ḥijja 430/24 August 1039.

Ibn Khall. 409, al-Suyūṭī, *de Interpr.*, 76. 1. *Kitāb al-burhān fī tafsīr (ʿulūm) al-Qur'ān* vols. 2, 3, 4, 6, 8, 9, 12, 15, 20, 24/8, Cairo ^{1}I, 132, ^{2}34, vol. 3 Garr. 1256, vol. 4 Landb.-Br. 217, vol. 13 Leid. 1656, vol. 15, Berl. 744.—Abstract *Iʿrāb al-Q.* by Ismāʿīl b. Khalaf al-Ṣaqalī, d. 455/1063 (p. 518), vol. 4, Berl. 745.

2. Abu 'l-ʿAbbās Aḥmad b. ʿAmmār al-Mahdawī al-Tamīmī, who died after 430/1038.

| Al-Suyūṭī, *Interpr.* 9 (d. 403/1012?). *Al-Taḥṣīl li-fawāʾid Kitāb al-tafṣīl al-jāmiʿ* 524
li-ʿulūm al-tanzīl Cairo ^{1}I, 136.—2.–4. see Suppl.

3. Abu 'l-Ḥasan ʿAlī b. Aḥmad b. Muḥammad b. ʿAlī b. Mattūya[1] al-Wāḥidī al-Nīsābūrī was a student of al-Thaʿālibī (p. 429) and died in 468/1075 (see Suppl.).

Ibn Khall. 411, al-Suyūṭī, *Int.*, 70. 1. *Kitāb asbāb al-nuzūl*, which explains when the various suras and verses were revealed, Berl. 464, Leid. 1660, Landb.-Br. 216, AS 65, Rāġib 19, Yeni 11, Cairo ^{1}I, 124, ^{2}I, 32, Makr. 4, omitting the authorities Berl. 463.—2. *al-Tafsīr al-basīṭ*, a lengthy commentary, vol. 17, Cairo ^{1}I, 133, ^{2}I, 35, Patna I, 242.—3. *Tafsīr al-Qurʾān al-wajīz* Berl. 740/9, Leid. 1661, Algiers 315, AS 290/1, Yeni 99, Cairo ^{1}I, 221, ^{2}I, 66, Patna I, 26_{243}.—4. *al-Wasīṭ bayna 'l-maqbūḍ wal-basīṭ*, | extensive commentary, Berl. 750/2, Br. Mus. Suppl. 991, 412
Esc. ^{2}1267/8, Algiers 316, Cairo ^{1}I, 221, ^{2}I, 66, Garr. 1260. Thereon *ʿUmdat al-qawī wal-ḍaʿīf al-kāshif li-mā waqaʿa fī Wasīṭ al-W. min al-tabdīl wal-taḥrīf* by Ismāʿīl b. Muḥammad al-Ḥaḍramī, d. 678/1279 (Ibn al-ʿImād, *ShDh* V, 361), Cairo ^{1}I, 181.—5. *Sharḥ dīwān al-Mutanabbī* p. 88.—6.–8. See Suppl.

4. Abu 'l-Muẓaffar Manṣūr b. Muḥammad b. ʿAbd al-Jabbār al-Marwazī al-Samʿānī al-Tamīmī al-Shāfiʿī, d. 489/1096 (see Suppl.).

Tafsīr, Br. Mus. Suppl. 1291, Cairo ^{1}I, 147, ^{2}I, 39.

5. Abū Saʿīd al-Muḥsin b. Muḥammad b. Karāma al-Jushamī al-Bayhaqī died in 494/1101 or, (according to others, in 545/1150, see Suppl.).

1. *Kitāb al-tahdhīb fī tafsīr al-Qurʾān* Leid. 1662, Landb.-Br. 214/5, Patna II, 499$_{2670/6}$.—2. *Sharḥ ʿuyūn al-masāʾil fī ʿilm al-uṣūl* Landb. -Br. 215.—3.–5. See Suppl.

---

1 From Mattai (Nöldeke, *Pers. St.* 1, 407) and therefore originally from a Christian, Aramaic, or Persian family.

6. Burhān al-Dīn Tāj al-Qurrāʾ Maḥmūd b. Ḥamza b. Naṣr al-Kirmānī, who died soon after 500/1106.

1. *Lubāb al-tafāsīr*, which ḤKh V, 299 criticises for its arbitrary interpretations,
525 | vol. 1 Br. Mus. Suppl. 100.—2. *al-Burhān fī (tawjīh) mutashābih al-Qurʾān* Cairo [1]I, 133, VII, 397, [2]I, 34, Qawala I, 43, Patna I, 23$_{,211}$.

7. Abū Saʿīd al-Dihistānī, d. 503/1109.

Commentary on sura 1, Berl. 949$_{,2}$.

8. ʿAbd al-Ḥaqq b. Abī Bakr Ghālib b. ʿAbd al-Malik al-Muḥāribī al-Gharnāṭī b. ʿAṭiyya, born in 481/1088, was a *qāḍī* in Almería and died in Lorqa in 546/1151.

Ibn Farḥūn, *Dībāj* C. 1329, 174/5, Suyūṭī, *Interpr.*, 49. *Kitāb al-jāmiʿ al-muḥarrar al-ṣaḥīḥ al-wajīz fī tafsīr al-Qurʾān al-ʿazīz* Berl. 800, Algiers 327/9, AS 119/21 Cairo [1]I, 208.—2. See Suppl.

9. Abū Bakr Muḥammad b. ʿAbdallāh al-Ishbīlī al-Maʿāfirī b. al-ʿArabī, who was born in Seville in 469/1076, travelled to the Orient with his father in 485/1092, going to Damascus, Baghdad, and the Hijaz. After making the pilgrimage in 489/1096 he studied in Baghdad under al-Ghazzālī and then returned to Spain by way of Alexandria and Cairo, arriving in 493/1100. After that he taught in Seville, where he died in 546/1151.

413 | Ibn Khall. 598, Suyūṭī, *Interpr.*, 103. 1. *Qānūn al-taʾwīl fi ʾl-tafsīr* Cairo [1]I, 188, [2]I, 57.—2. *Kitāb aḥkām al-Qurʾān* Berl. 801 (suras 1–4), Brit. Mus. 142, Cairo [1]I, 121, Makram 2.—3. *Farāʾiḍ al-nikāḥ wa-sunanuhu wa-ādābuhu* Cairo [1]VII, 128.—4.–9. see Suppl.

9a. Maḥmūd b. Abi ʾl-Ḥasan al-Nīsābūrī, see Suppl. 733, 10b.

Ījāz al-bayān fī maʿāni ʾl-Qurʾān also in *Majmūʿa* Köpr. 1589 (Ritter).

10. Muḥammad b. Yūsuf Nāṣir al-Dīn Abu ʾl-Qāsim al-Ḥusaynī al-Samarqandī, who died in 556/1161 (see Suppl.).

Kitāb al-iḥqāq, on the rhetorical subtleties of the Qurʾān, with an appendix, Berl. 728.

11. Abu 'l-Qāsim (Abū Zayd) ʿAbd al-Raḥmān b. ʿAbdallāh b. Abi 'l-Ḥasan Aḥmad al-Suhaylī al-Khathʿamī, who was born in 508/1114 in Suhayl, a | village near 526
Malaga. He studied philology in Granada, then resided for a time in Seville, before finally settling in Malaga. When his fame in learning reached Morocco the Almohad ruler Yaʿqūb al-Manṣūr summoned him there, where he died on 25 Shaʿbān 581/22 November 1285.

Ibn Khall. 344, Wüst., *Gesch.* no. 272. 1. *Kitāb al-taʿrīf wal-iʿlām li (fī) mā ubhima min al-Qur'ān min al-asmā' wal-aʿlām*, which explains, for each sura, the passages where nouns, especially proper nouns, are not specifically mentioned but are instead implied, Berl. 720/1 (under the title *al-Īḍāḥ wal-tabyīn li-mā ubhima min tafsīr al-Kitāb al-mubīn*), Landb.-Br. 504, Br. Mus. Suppl. 110, Bodl. II, 19, Garr. 2067,$_{2}$, Cairo ^{1}I, 138, ^{2}I, 36. His student's student Muḥammad b. ʿAlī b. Khiḍr b. Hārūn al-Ghassānī b. ʿAskar, d. 636/1238, wrote thereon *al-Takmīl wal-itmām* Cairo ^{1}I, 153, ^{2}I, 42.—2. *al-Rawḍ al-unuf wal-mashraʿ al-riwā fī tafsīr mā yashtamil ʿalayhi ḥadīth al-sīra waḥtawā*, a commentary on Ibn Hishām (see p. 141); see P. Brönnle, *Die Commentatoren des Ibn Isḥāq* VIII ff., with Garr. 636, 638, Yeni 852/3, Bursa Ḥü. Celebī Ta'r. 4, Alex. Ta'r. 8.—3. *al-Qaṣīda al-ʿayniyya* ḤKh IV, 541,$_{9479}$ or *al-Istighātha* Berl. 3938,$_{1}$, with a *takhmīs* by ʿAbd al-Ḥalīm b. Taymiyya, d. 682/1283, composed in 668/1269, Leid. 671, by al-Fayyūmī, Gotha 94,$_{7}$, several others Berl. 6797,$_{2}$.—4. A Sufi *qaṣīda* Berl. 3436.—5. Answers to grammatical questions asked by his teacher, the *faqīh* Abū Isḥāq b. Qurqūl (see p. 457), Esc. ^{2}189.—6. *Fī ʿilm al-farā'iḍ* Br. Mus. 420,$_{6}$.

12. Nāṣir al-Dīn ʿAlī b. Ibrāhīm b. Ismāʿīl al-Ghaznawī al-Ḥanafī, d. 582/1186.

Al-Taqshīr fi 'l-tafsīr ḤKh ^{1}II, 391, ^{2}I, 466, Mashh. III, 15,$_{42}$.

13. Ibrāhīm b. Muḥammad b. Abi 'l-Rajā' al-Jankānī wrote, around the year 600/1204:

Kitāb al-īḍāḥ, a Qur'ān commentary abridged from *al-Jāmiʿ fi 'l-tafsīr*, Berl. 806, different from ḤKh ^{1}I, 511,$_{1562}$, ^{2}I, 211.

| 14. Ṣadr al-Dīn Abū Muḥammad Rūzbihān b. Abi 'l-Naṣr al-Fasawī al-Shīrāzī 414
al-Baqlī al-Kāzarūnī al-Ṣūfī, d. 606/1209 (see Suppl.).

| 1. *Kitāb ʿarā'is al-bayān fī ḥaqā'iq al-Qur'ān* Berl. 807, Ns. or. oct. 3983, Br. Mus. 527
1587, Rāġib 197, Yeni 150, Cairo ^{1}I, 180, ^{2}I, 155, print. Calcutta 1883 (can therefore

not have been composed in refutation of al-Kāshānī's *Tafsīr*, as assumed in Suppl. II, 280).—2.–6. See Suppl.

14a. Abu 'l-Qāsim Muḥammad b. ʿAbd al-Wāḥid b. Ibrāhīm al-Ghāfiqī al-Mallāḥī, who was born in al-Mallāḥa near Granada in 549/1154 and died in 619/1222.

Ibn al-Abbār, *Takmila* (*Bibl. Ar.-Hisp.* V), 323/5, no. 960. *Lamaḥāt al-anwār wa-nafaḥāt al-asrār fī thawāb qāriʾ al-Qurʾān* (ḤKh V, 11165 *fī faḍāʾil al-Qurʾān al-ʿaẓīm*) Fez, Qar. 263 (see al-Kattānī, *Fihris* II, 252), Āṣaf. I, 302$_{,40}$ (*fī 'l-tajwīd*, with the wrong name, see Suppl. II, 981$_{,27}$). Not preserved is his *Shajara fī ansāb al-umam al-ʿArab wal-ʿAjam*.

15. Fakhr al-Dīn Abū ʿAbdallāh ʿAlī b. Aḥmad b. al-Ḥasan b. Aḥmad al-Ḥirālī (Ḥarālī)[2] was born in Morocco, travelled to the Orient, settled in Hama, and died there in 637/1239.

Suyūṭī, *Interpr.*, 68. 1. *Miftāḥ al-bāb* (*lubb*) *al-muqaffal li-fahm al-Qurʾān al-munazzal* Paris 1398$_{,1}$, an appendix to it, entitled *ʿUrwat al-miftāḥ*, ibid. 6, Cairo ^{1}I, 180 (where the author is not mentioned).—2. *Kitāb al-lamḥa*, on the mystical meaning of letters, Paris 1398$_{,2}$ = Br. Mus. 984$_{,6}$?—3. *Tafhīm maʿāni 'l-ḥurūf allatī hiya mawādd al-kalim fī alsinat jamīʿ al-umam* Paris 1398$_{,3}$.—4. *Kitāb al-tawshiya wal-tawfiya*, a mystical treatise on the Qurʾān, ibid. 5.—5. *Kitāb al-īmān al-tāmm bi-Muḥammad ʿalayhi al-salām* Berl. 1743.—6.,7. See Suppl.

16. Abu 'l-Faḍāʾil Aḥmad b. Muḥammad b. Muẓaffar b. al-Mukhtār al-Rāzī wrote, around 631/1233:[3]

1. *Adhkār al-Qurʾān*.—2. *Faḍāʾil al-Qurʾān*.—3. *Laṭāʾif al-Qurʾān*.—4. *al-Istidrākāt*, on traditions whose literal meanings contradict the teachings of al-Shāfiʿī, Cairo ^{1}VII, 470, ^{2}I, 89.—5. *Ḥujaj al-Qurʾān* Cairo ^{1}I, 170, print.
528 C. | 1320.—6. *Mabāḥith al-tafsīr*, against al-Thaʿlabī, see p. 429.—7. *Kitāb fī maʿrifat khuṭūṭ al-kaff* Patna II, 551$_{,2924,1}$.—8. *Kitāb al-ḥurūf* Lālelī 3739.—9. *Dhakhīrat al-mulūk fī ʿilm al-sulūk* ibid.—10. *Dhikr al-āyāt allatī nazalat fī amīr al-muʾminīn ʿAlī* ibid.—11. *Sirr al-asrār w* (?) *al-astār* ibid. (Ritter).

---

2 In Ḥrāla near Murcia.

3 From this year dates an *ijāza* in the author's own hand from the Madrasa al-Muẓaffariyya in Āqsarā in the Cairo MSS.

17. Abu 'l-ʿAbbās Aḥmad b. Muḥammad b. Abī Khalīl al-ʿAshshāb al-Ifrīqī, who died in 637/1239 in Seville.

Tafsīr Cairo ^{1}I, 148, ^{2}I, 40.

18. Al-Muntakhab b. Abi 'l-ʿIzz b. Rashīd b. Abī Yūsuf al-Hamdānī al-Muqriʾ al-Shāfiʿī, who died in Damascus in Rabīʿ I 643/August 1245.

Al-Farīd fī iʿrāb al-Qurʾān al-majīd Cairo ^{1}I, 188, ^{2}I, 37.

| 19. Kamāl al-Dīn Abū Muḥammad ʿAbd al-Wāḥid b. ʿAbd al-Karīm b. Khalaf 415
al-Anṣārī al-Zamlakānī, who died in Damascus in 651/1253 (see Suppl.).

1. *Kitāb al-tibyān fī ʿilm al-bayān al-muṭṭaliʿ ʿalā iʿjāz al-Qurʾān*, composed in 637/1239, Esc. ^{2}223, 263, on which *Kitāb al-tanbīhāt ʿalā mā fi 'l-Tibyān min al-tamwīhāt* by Aḥmad b. ʿAbdallāh b. Muḥammad al-Makhzūmī, d. 658/1260, ibid. 115.—1a., 2.–4. see Suppl.

20. ʿAbd al-Razzāq b. Rizqallāh b. Abi 'l-Hayjāʾ al-Raʾs ʿAynī al-Ḥanbalī ʿIzz al-Dīn, who was born in Raʾs al-ʿAyn in 589/1193 and died in 661/1263.

1. *Kitāb rumūz al-kunūz*, a Qurʾān commentary (= *Maṭāliʿ anwār al-tanzīl wa-mafātīḥ asrār al-taʾwīl*), completed in 659/1261, ḤKh, ^{1}II, 369,$_{3330}$, V, 594,$_{12231}$, ^{2}I, 452, vol. 2. Paris 622, vol. 4. Berl. 809.—2. *Durrat al-qāriʾ*, on words with a *ẓāʾ* occurring the Qurʾān, brought together in 31 *basīṭ* verses, Berl. 679a/81, Garr. 1253/4,$_{3}$.—3. On ethics, Berl. 5395.

21. Aḥmad (ḤKh Muḥammad) b. Asʿad al-ʿIrāqī was born in 580/1184 and died in 667/1268.

Kitāb asbāb nuzūl al-Qurʾān bil-āyāt al-qurʾāniyya wal-qiṣaṣ al-furqāniyya explains when a certain verse was revealed, linking it to the story of the prophets mentioned therein, Berl. 465.

| 22. Shams al-Dīn Muḥammad b. Aḥmad b. Abī Bakr b. Farḥ al-Anṣārī 529
al-Qurṭubī died on 9 Shawwāl 671/31 March 1273 (according to ḤKh ^{1}II, 255, ^{2}I, 383, in 668/1269) in Munyat Banī Khaṣīb in Upper Egypt.

Suyūṭī, *Interpr.*, 88. *Kitāb jāmiʿ aḥkām al-Qurʾān*, very extensive, vol. 1 Berl. 810, vol. 3 ibid. 812 (see 813), vol. 4 ibid. 811, vol. 6 Landb.-Br. 213, several parts Leid.

1674, Garr. 1274, Cairo ^{1}I, 159, Patna I, 26,$_{252}$.—2. *Kitāb al-tadhkira bi-aḥwāl al-mawtā wa-aḥwāl al-ākhira*, on eschatology, Berl. 2744/5, Gotha 749/51 (see 753), Br. Mus. 173, Algiers 848/92, Bursa Ula Cami Taş 104, Alex. Mawāʿiẓ 10, Qawala I, 224, Patna I, 145,$_{1403}$, abstract by Muḥammad b. ʿUthmān b. Ayyūb b. Dāʾūd al-Kutubī al-Luʾluʾī (eighth or beginning of the ninth cent.), *al-Nujūm al-muzhira bikhtiṣār al-Tadhkira* Berl. 2746.—3. *Qamʿ al-ḥirṣ bil-zuhd wal-qanāʿa*
416 | *wa-dhill al-suʾāl bil-kaff wal-shafāʿa*, on the reprehensibility of the pursuit of wealth and begging as opposed to abstention and trust in God's goodness, Berl. 8787.—6.–9. See Suppl. (6. Fātiḥ Waqf Ibr. 42, *Br. Mus. Quart.* x, 34; 8. Garr. 265, Patna I, 24,$_{223}$).

23. Aḥmad b. Yūsuf b. al-Ḥasan al-Kawāshī al-Mawṣilī al-Shaybānī was born in 951/1195 in al-Kawāsha, which was previously known as Ardmusht, in the mountains east of Mosul, and died in Mosul in Jumādā II 680/September–October 1281.

1. *Tabṣirat al-mutadhakkir wa-tadhkirat al-mutadabbir*, sometimes shortened to *al-Tabṣira fi ʾl-tafsīr*, ḤKh, ^{1}II, 181,$_{2385}$, 377,$_{3390}$, ^{2}I, 339, 457, vol. 2 Berl. 814, vol. 4 Cairo ^{1}I, 135, ^{2}I, 35; abbreviation *al-Talkhīṣ fi ʾl-tafsīr* Berl. 815/6, Leid. 1675, Basle M. II, 5, AS 90/3, Yeni 92/3, Cairo ^{1}I, 154, ^{2}I, 42.—Anon. excerpt on pausas from the original work: *Rawḍat al-nāẓir wa-jannat al-manāẓir* Berl. 563.—2. *Kitāb mutashābih al-Qurʾān*, a compilation of phrases that occur just once in the Qurʾān, and then of those that are repeated in two or more places, Berl. 715.—3. *Kitāb ʿadad aḥzāb al-Qurʾān*, the division of the Qurʾān into 120 *aḥzāb*, 28 *ajzāʾ* and ninths, Berl. 432.—4 . *al-Maṭāliʿ fi ʾl-mabādīʾ wal-maqāṭiʿ*, on pausas, Cairo ^{1}I, 203, ^{2}I, 62.

24. Nāṣir al-Dīn Abu ʾl-ʿAbbās Aḥmad b. Muḥammad b. Manṣūr b. Abī Bakr
530 Manṣūr b. Abi ʾl-Qāsim b. Mukhtār b. Abī Bakr ʿAlī b. | al-Munayyir al-Iskandarānī al-Mālikī, who was born in 620/1223 and died in 683/1284.

1. *al-Baḥr al-kabīr fī baḥth al-tafsīr* Cairo ^{1}I, 130, ^{2}I, 34.—2. *Kitāb al-intiṣāf min al-Kashshaf* see p. 346.

25. Abū Saʿīd (Saʿd) ʿAbdallāh b. ʿUmar b. Muḥammad b. ʿAlī Abu ʾl-Khayr Nāṣir al-Dīn al-Bayḍāwī was the son of the chief judge of Fārs under the *atabeg* Abū Bakr b. Saʿd, worked as *qāḍi ʾl-quḍāt* in Shiraz and died there (or in Tabriz), probably in 685/1286.

Al-Ṣafadī mentions this year in Suyūṭī, *Bughya*, 286; in Ḥamdallāh Mustawfī, *Ta'rīkhi Guzīda*, p. 811 it is corrupted to 605 (transl. 222). According to al-Suyūṭī, al-Subkī supposedly said 691; in the printed edition V, 59 the date is lacking. In Ibn al-Qāḍī, *Durrat al-ḥijāl* II, 348, no. 969, who mentions the same sources, both numbers are corrupted to 785 and 791. Al-Yāfiʿī, *Mir'āt al-janān* IV, 220 (cit. *Ḥabīb al-siyar* III, 177) gives 692. The date 685 also tallies with the statement of ʿAlī b. ʿAbdallāh al-Ardabīlī (see Suppl. I, 535, no. 46)—who was born in the seventies of the seventh century and who died in 747/1346—that even though he had lived to see al-Bayḍāwī, he did not study under him (Ibn Ḥajar, *al-Durar al-kāmina* III, 73,$_3$, cod. Vienna II, 267r). See also Cod. Wetzst. II, 289, f. 152, Elliot, *Hist. of India* II, 252ff., Rieu, *Pers. Cat.* II, 823. | 417

1. *Anwār al-tanzīl wa-asrār al-ta'wīl*, a Qur'ān commentary using al-Zamakhsharī's *Kashshāf*, which he corrected and supplemented with the help of other sources. "Among the Sunnis he is today regarded as the best and almost as a saint. Having said this, he stands out by incorporating a lot of material in a succinct and lucid manner, though he is imprecise and for none of the fields that he considers—historical interpretation, lexicography, grammar, dialectics, readings—anywhere near complete", Nöldeke, *Gesch. d. Qor.* [1]XXIX. Ed. H.O. Fleischer, 2 vols., Leipzig 1846/8, indices by W. Fell, ibid. 1878. Print. Būlāq 1282/3, Istanbul 1285 and others (see Suppl.). D.S. Margoliouth, *Chrestomathia Bayḍāwiana* (sura III with translation), London 1894.—Glosses: 1. Amīr Pādishāh al-Ḥusaynī al-Bukhārī, end tenth cent. (II, 412), Ind. Off. 81, Yeni 129, Rāġib 155.—2. Ḥājjī Bābā al-Ṭūsiyawī, d. 871/1466 (? II, 223), Yeni 123/4, | print. Istanbul 1287, 7 vols.—3. Muṣṭafā b. Ibrāhīm b. al-Tamjīd 531
ca. 880/1475, Cairo [1]I, 202, [2]I, 44.—4. Mollā Khusraw b. Farāmurz, d. 885/1480 (II, 226), Garr. 1283, AS 307/8, Yeni 130/2, Rāġib 138, Cairo [1]I, 202, [2]I, 47, Qawala I, 62.—5. *Nawāhid al-abkār wa-shawārid al-afkār* by al-Suyūṭī, d. 911/1505, Berl. 834, Ind. Off. 82, AS 305, Cairo [1]I, 220.—6. *Fatḥ al-jalīl* by Zakariyyā' al-Anṣārī, d. 926/1520 (II, 99), Algiers 340, Rāġib 137, Cairo [1]I, 185, [2]I, 156, Makram 47.—7. Muḥammad b. Muṣṭafā b. al-Ḥājj Ḥasanzāde, Berl. 835.—8. Muḥammad al-Qurayshī al-Ṣiddīqī al-Khaṭīb al-Kāzarūnī, d. 940/1533, Ind. Off. 83, AS 355/6, Yeni 127, Rāġib 159/60, Cairo [1]I, 169, [2]I, 72.—9. Kamālpāshāzāde, d. 940/1533 (II, 449), Rāġib 145, Cairo [1]I, 163, [2]I, 44.—10. Ibrāhīm b. Muḥammad b. ʿArabshāh al-Isfarā'inī, d. 944/1537 (II, 410), Berl. 836/7, Br. Mus. Suppl. 117, Ind. Off. 84, AS 324/34, Garr. 1284, Patna I, 27,$_{264/5}$, superglosses by al-Kawākibī AS 358.—11. *al-Fawā'id al-bahiyya* by Saʿdallāh ʿIsā Saʿdī Efendi, d. 945/1538, Berl. 638/42, de Jong 125, Ind. Off. 85, Pet. 46, Garr. 1285, AS 312/20, Yeni 102/4, Rāġib 124/7, Alex. Fun. 95,$_1$, Qawala I, 57.—Superglosses by Muḥammad al-Kawākibī, d. 1096/1685

(II, 315), Garr. 1288, AS 358, larger 316.—12. Muḥammad b. Muṣṭafā al-Qūjawī
Shaykhzāde, d. 950/1543, Berl. 843/5, Rāġib 111/6, Yeni 114/23, AS 335/8, Cairo ^{1}I,
169, ^{2}I, 47, Qawala I, 59/60, Garr. 1286.—13. Shams (ʿIṣām) al-Dīn al-Isfarāʾinī, d.
951/1544, Cairo ^{1}I, 167, Qawala I, 60.—14. On the *Fātiḥa* by al-Sayyid al-Ṣafawī,
d. 953/1546, Cairo ^{1}I, 201.—15. Muṣṭafā b. Shaʿbān al-Surūrī, d. 969/1561
(II, 438), Munich 93, Rāġib 128/31.—15a. *Wāridāt* by Muḥammad b. Muḥammad
b. Bilāl (II, 334,$_8$, Suppl. II, 993,$_{37}$), AS 406.—16. Faḍl Rawshanīzāde, d. 969/1561,
Cairo ^{1}I, 165, ^{2}I, 45.—17. Maḥmūd b. Ḥusayn al-Ṣādiqī al-Jīlānī, d. ca. 970/1562,
Algiers 377.—18. Muṣliḥ al-Dīn Bustān, d. 977/1567, Cairo ^{1}I, 170, Patna I,
28,$_{270/2}$ (Muḥammad b. Shaykh Muṣliḥ al-Dīn).—18a. Muḥammad b. Aḥmad
b. Ḥasan al-Bukhārī Ṣāmisūnīzāde, d. 978/1570 (ʿAṭāʾī, *Dhayl al-Shaqāʾiq*
145), AS 322,$_{186}$.—18b. Ibrāhīm b. Sulaymān b. Ibrāhīm al-Kurdī al-Ḥalabī, d.
984/1576 (Sič. Osm. I, 95), AS 303.—19. Sinān Efendi Yūsuf b. Ḥusām al-Dīn
al-Amāsī, d. 986/1578, Berl. 846/52, Leipz. 107, Munich 94, AS 319/21, 440ff.,
Rāġib 147/8, Yeni 105/7, Cairo ^{1}I, 165, ^{2}I, 45, Qawala I, 58.—20. ʿAbd al-Qādir b.
Aḥmad al-Fākihī, d. 982/1574 (II, 339), composed in 963/1555, Esc. ^{2}237,$_{15}$.—
532 21. On sura 7 by Zakariyyāʾ b. Bayrām al-Anqirawī, | d. 1001/1592, Cairo ^{1}I, 19.—
22. On the *Fātiḥa* of Ḥusayn al-Khalkhālī, d. 1014/1605 (II, 413), NO 486,
AS 303, Cairo ^{1}I, 201, ^{2}I, 45 (fragm.).—22a. On the same by Ḥasan al-Būrīnī,
completed in 1039/1629 (II, 290), Cairo^1, I, 201, Berl. Oct. 1334 (?).—22b. see
Suppl. also Patna I, 28,$_{268}$.—23. Muḥammad Bahāʾ al-Dīn al-ʿĀmilī, d. 1030/1621
(II, 414), Gotha 531, Br. Mus. 77, Patna I, 28,$_{266/7}$.—24. Muḥammad b. Jamāl
al-Dīn al-Shirwānī, d. 1063/1653, Copenhagen 46, Ind. Off. 86/9, AS 354/5, Yeni
122, Rāġib 144, Cairo ^{1}I, 167, Patna I, 29,$_{261/2}$.—25. Muḥammad b. ʿAbd al-Ḥaqq,
d. 1033/1623, Berl. 862.—26. Ghanīzāde Nādirī, d. 1036/1626, Cairo ^{1}I, 168.—
27. Muḥammad b. Mūsā al-Busnawī, d. 1046/1636, Cairo ^{1}I, 164, 201.—
28. ʿAbdallāh b. Ibrāhīm al-Kūrānī, dedicated to Sultan Murād, d. 1049/1639,
Berl. 853.—29. ʿAbd al-Ḥakīm al-Siyālkūtī, d. 1067/1656 (II, 417), Ind. Off.
90/1, 1122, Garr. 1287, AS 302, Rāġib 140/1, Cairo ^{1}I, 166, Qawala I, 58, Patna II,
500,$_{2677}$.—30. *ʿInāyat al-qāḍī wa-kifāyat al-rāḍī* by Aḥmad b. Muḥammad
al-Khafājī, d. 1069/1658 (II, 285), Algiers 338/9 (author only al-Shihāb), *Bull.
de Corr. Afr.* 1884, p. 373, no. 45, Yeni 108/17, Rāġib 103/10, AS 339, 341/53,
418 Qawala I, 72, Cairo ^{1}I, 181, print. Būlāq 1283, 8 vols., Istanbul 1854, | used in
Berl. 864.—31. ʿAbd al-Qādir b. Muṣṭafā al-Ṣaffūrī, d. 1081/1670, on sura 19,$_{33}$,
Berl. 865.—32. Muḥammad al-Kawākibī, d. 1096/1685 (II, 315), Yeni 128, AS
358.—33. Muḥammad al-Marʿashī Sājaqlīzāde, d. 1150/1737 (II, 370), Berl.
861.—34. Muḥammad b. Muḥammad al-Bulaydī al-Ashʿarī al-Andalusī,
d. 1176/1762 (II, 331), Cairo ^{1}I, 164, ^{2}I, 45.—35. Ismāʿīl b. Muḥammad al-Qūnawī,
d. 1195/1781, Cairo ^{1}I, 168, Qawala I, 62.—36. ʿAbdallāh b. Muḥammad, *qāḍī*
of Medina, twelfth cent., ibid. 163.—37. Anon., Berl. 854/60, 863, Leid.

1680/3.—39.–83. see Suppl. (62. Garr. 1389; 67. Ibid. 1290).—84. Abu 'l-Faḍl al-Qurashī al-Ṣiddīqī al-Kāzarūni, Patna I, 27,$_{263}$.—85. ʿAbdallāh Mestjīzāde, d. 1148/1735 (*Osm. Müʾell.* II, 27), AS 304.—86. ʿAbd al-Raḥīm b. Muḥammad Ghurābzāde, AS 323.—Anon. abstract *al-ʿImādī*, Philadelphia, no. 23—Anon. supplement *Taḥqīq al-tafsīr wa-takthīr al-tanwīr*, Qawala I, 44.—Critiques: 1. *al-Itḥāf bi-tamyīz mā tabiʿa fīhi 'l-Bayḍāwī ṣāḥib al-Kashshāf* by Muḥammad b. ʿAlī al-Dāʾūdī, d. 945/1538 (II, 289), following up on the glosses of his teacher al-Suyūṭī, Garr. 1298, Cairo ^{1}I, 120, ^{2}I, 31, Alex. Fun. 95,$_3$ (where the author is Muḥammad b. Yūsuf al-Shāmī?).—2. *Kashf al-aqwāl al-mubtadhala fī sabq qalam al-Bayḍāwī li-madhhab al-Muʿtazila* by Aḥmad al-Nūbī | (II, 385), auto- 533
graph from al-Ṭāʾif dated 1027/1617, identification of places where al-Bayḍāwī seems to approach Muʿtazilī phraseology out of negligence, Gotha 532.

II. *Minhāj al-wuṣūl ilā ʿilm al-uṣūl* Berl. 4381/2, Paris 727,$_2$, Algiers 949, Alex. Uṣūl 21.—Commentaries: 1. ʿAbdallāh b. Muḥammad al-Farghānī, d. 743/1342 (II, 198), Yeni 242, Patna I, 73,$_{742}$.—2. Shams al-Dīn Maḥmūd b. ʿAbd al-Raḥmān al-Iṣfahānī, d. 749/1348, composed in 734/1333, Paris, 799, Ind. Off. 1477, Bank. XIX, 1. 1562 = Patna I, 73,$_{741}$, Āṣaf. p. 98 (?)—3. *Nihāyat al-suʾūl* by ʿAbd al-Raḥīm b. Ḥasan al-Asnawī, d. 772/1370, Algiers 950, Bodl. II, 88 Alex. Uṣūl 22, Qawala I, 301.—4. Aḥmad b. Ḥusayn al-Ramlī b. Raslān, d. 844/1440 (II, 92), Berl. 4383, Paris 800.—5.–19. see Suppl.—20. Anon. *Manāhij al-ʿuqūl* Patna I, 75,$_{766}$.

III. *al-Ghāya al-quṣwā* on Shāfiʿī law, an abstract of al-Ghazzālī's *al-Wasīṭ* (p. 543), Cairo ^{1}III 246.—Commentary by Muḥammad b. ʿAbdallāh al-Farghānī (see II, 1)?, Paris 1024.

IV. *Lubb al-albāb fī ʿilm al-iʿrāb* Qawala (II, 119. Cmt) a. see Suppl.—b. *Imtiḥān al-adhkiyāʾ* by al-Birgili (Birkawī), d. 981/1573 (II, 441, 17), Paris 4120, Cairo ^{1}IV, 25, ^{2}II, 79.

V. *Miṣbāḥ al-arwāḥ*, a handbook of theology, Ambros. 319, Esc. ^{2}650, 6, anon. comm. Leid. 1545, Br. Mus. 171.

VI. *Ṭawāliʿ al-anwār min maṭāliʿ al-anẓār*, on metaphysics, Berl. 1772/4, Gotha 645 (where other MSS are listed), BDMG 87, Garr. 1487, Qawala I, 204.—Commentaries: 1. ʿAbdallāh b. Muḥammad al-Farghānī, d. 743/1342, Berl. 1775/6, Gotha 646, Bodl. I, 146, II, 570, Esc. ^{1}1161, Alex. Tawḥīd 21, Qawala I, 195, Patna I, 121,$_{1217}$.—2. *Maṭāliʿ al-anẓār* by Abu 'l-Thanāʾ Maḥmūd b. ʿAbd al-Raḥmān al-Iṣfahānī, d. 749/1348, Berl. 1777/85, Gotha 645 (where other MSS are listed), Br. Mus. Suppl. 186, Garr. 1489/91, Alex. Tawḥīd 44/5, Qawala I, 210/1, Makram 56, Patna I, 126,$_{1259/60}$.—Glosses thereon: a. al-Jurjānī (II, 216), d. 816/1413, Berl. 786/9, Vienna 1534, Paris 2390, Ind. Off. 595, Esc^{2}664,$_2$, 666.—Superglosses γ *Sharḥ awāʾil al-Ṭawāliʿ min al-ḥikma* by Jalāl al-Dīn al-Dawwānī (II, 217), Rāġib 1457,$_{13}$, print. C. 1323.—b. Ḥamīd al-Dīn b. Afḍal al-Dīn al-Ḥusaynī, d. 909/1503, Leid. 2014, Esc. ^{2}664,$_1$, 678,^{2}, Alex. Tawḥīd 14.—3. Humām Gulnārī, Ind. Off.

432.—4. *Nashr Ṭawāliʿ al-anwār* by Sājaqlīzāde, d. 1150/1737 (II, 370), Berl. 1790.—5.–11. see Suppl.—12. Muḥammad b. ʿUmar al-Khalafī, Qawala I, 168.—13. Anon. *Nihāyat al-afkār* ibid. I, 212.—14. Muʿīn al-Dīn Ḥasan b. Muḥammad al-Tūnī, Patna I, 119$_{,1200/1}$.

534 | VII. *Risāla fī mawḍūʿāt al-ʿulūm wa-taʿrīfihā* Cairo ^{1}VII, 482.

VIII. *Niẓām al-tawārīkh*, a universal history in Persian from Adam until 674/1275, Br. Mus. Pers. II, 823 (where other MSS are listed), see de Sacy, *Not. et Extr.* IV, 672/95.

IX. *Mukhtaṣar al-Kāfiya li-Ibn al-Ḥājib* see p. 370.—X.–XIII. see Suppl.—XIV. *Taʿrīfāt al-ʿulūm* Alex. Fun. 79$_{,7}$ (= VII?).

Chapter 9. Dogmatics[1]

1 (2). Abu 'l-Walīd Sulaymān b. Khalaf al-Bājī, who was born in Badajoz in 403/1012, travelled to the East in 426/1034 where he stayed for 13 years, 3 of which were in Mecca, 3 in Baghdad, and one in Mosul. After his return to his native land he strove to promote Ashʿarī dogma. The Mālikī Muḥammad b. Saʿīd invited him to Mallorca, where Ibn Ḥazm was in those days highly regarded by the island's governor (see Suppl. I, 694), to assist him in his struggle against him. Having pushed through Ibn Ḥazm's expulsion, he then tried—as a *qāḍī* in various towns—to incite the smaller potentates in his homeland to take up arms together against the Christian enemy, but without any success. He died in Almeria in 474/1081.

Al-Ḍabbī, p. 289, no. 777, Ibn Khall. 261, Maqqarī I, 504/11, Ibn Farḥūn, *Dībāj* 123, Asín Palacios, *Abenházam* I, 200/10, J. López Ortiz, *al-Andalus* VI, 79.

1. *Sunan al-ṣāliḥīn*, ethical traditions, Leid. 1738.—2. *Sharḥ fuṣūl al-aḥkām wa-bayān mā maḍā bihi 'l-ʿamal ʿinda 'l-fuqahāʾ wal-ḥukkām* Cairo ^{1}II, 181, Fez Qar. 1392 (title corrupted).—3. Answer to the apology of Christianity in a letter from the monk from 'Ifransa' for al-Muqtadir billāh, ruler of Zaragoza (438–741, 1046–81), Esc. $^{2}538_{,11,12}$.—5.–7. see Suppl.—8. *Sharḥ al-Sawād al-aʿẓam* 183.

| 2. Abū Saʿīd b. Abī Saʿīd al-Mutawallī, al-Shāfiʿī, d. 478/1085. 535

Al-Mughnī fī uṣūl al-dīn ʿalā ṭarīqat Abi 'l-Ḥasan al-Ashʿarī Alex. Tawḥīd 30.

3 (4). Abū Shukūr Muḥammad b. ʿAbd al-Sayyid b. Shuʿayb al-Kashshī (Kashshānī) al-Ḥanafī al-Sālimī, who flourished in the second half of the fifth century.

Kitāb al-tamhīd fī bayān al-tawḥīd wa-hidāya li-kull mustarshid wa-rashīd, dogmatics following the ideas of Abū Ḥanīfa with particular attention to the Muʿtazila and the philosophers, ḤKh ^{1}II, 423, ^{2}I, 484, Ind. Off. 384, $1033_{,2}$ (see Suppl.), Patna I, $115_{,1152/3}$, II, 511_{2743}.

---

1 This chapter includes some authors of works on religious practices who should actually have been classed among the *fuqahāʾ* and not among the *mutakallimūn*, but whose allegiance to one of the Schools of *fiqh* could not be ascertained.

3a. Saʿīd b. Dādhurmuz wrote before 471/1078 (the date of the MS):

1. *Kitāb fī faḍl al-ākhira ʿala ʾl-dunyā*, against the claim that the pursuit of the sciences only serves the purpose of making money.—2. *Risāla fī ʾl-rūḥ wal-badan*, a continuation of the same.—3. *Risāla fī ʾl-tawḥīd* Bursa Ulu Cami Taṣ 11, f. 1–74b (Ritter).

4 (5). Abū Ḥāmid Muḥammad b. Muḥammad al-Ghazzālī[2] was born in
420 451/1059 and spent his youth in Ṭūs in Khurāsān. | He received his theological training in Nishapur under Imām al-Ḥaramayn, during whose lifetime he began writing. After the former's death in 478/1085 he joined the vizier Niẓām al-Mulk, who assigned him a professorship at the al-Niẓāmiyya academy that he had founded in Baghdad. While he was still in his youth he rejected *taqlīd*. He tried to live up to the obligations of his office by an intensive study of all the *madhāhib* and philosophical schools while also composing various works
536 on *fiqh* | and polemic pamphlets against the Bāṭiniyya, who had murdered Niẓām al-Mulk in 485/1092. But none of these systems could satisfy him. In the end he did not only feel his faith falter, but despaired even of the possiblity of achieving any knowledge whatsoever. An intense struggle for the salvation of his soul, which he saw threatened in the hereafter, shook him from Rajab until Dhu ʾl-Qaʿda 488/July–November 1095. As a result of this he relinquished his professorship in favour of his brother Aḥmad and, as a wandering dervish, regained his inward peace through asceticism and mystical contemplation. Perhaps the conflict between the Sultan Barqyārūq and the latter's uncle Tutush had also precipitated his decision to step down from his post. He was a close ally of the caliph who had declared himself in favour of Tutush and who, after the elimination of the latter, had to fear Barqyārūq's revenge. He first went to Damascus, and in 490/1097 made the pilgrimage to Mecca. He then lived for nine years in silent reclusion in various places, rarely interrupted by visits to his kin. His spiritual crisis was resolved in a mystical experience of beatific vision, after which he not only rejected the sciences of the *fuqahāʾ* but also those of the *mutakallimūn* as being of no value. The only thing he would recommend as a means to purify the soul was asceticism, by which one acquired the power to depart from the earth, with all its impurities, towards the pure, uncontaminated sphere of the godhead. This turn towards Platonism

---

2 I.e. "the spinner" (see Suppl., *JRAS* 1902, 18/22, *OM* XV, 58). This is apparently also what is alluded to by a verse, quoted without source reference by al-Rayḥānī, *Rayḥāniyyāt* III, 110,$_{13/4}$: *ghazaltu lahum ghazlan daqīqan fa-lam ajid li-ghazlī nassājan fa-kassartu mighzalī.*

was for him connected to an ethics akin to the one of Christianity, and, vanquishing the sanctity of the praxis of Islamic deontology, he had released it from its impending ossification. This new way of thinking he developed in his *Iḥyāʾ*, from which, even during his years of seclusion, he occasionally recited in Damascus and Baghdad.

| After the death of Baryārūq, the latter's brother Muḥammad assumed power 537
in 498/1104. It was to him that al-Ghazzālī dedicated his mirror for princes *al-Tibr al-masbūk*, which he had originally written in Persian. He believed there was reason to regard Muḥammad as the prince who could make his religious ideals come true. His homeland of Khurāsān was governed by the latter's brother Sanjar, and his vizier was Fakhr al-Mulk, the son of Niẓām al-Mulk. The latter succeded in motivating al-Ghazzālī to resume his teaching at the Niẓāmiyya of Nishapur. But he did not live a life in the public sphere for very long, and he soon retired to his hometown of Ṭūs. In the Ṭabarān quarter there he worked at a madrasa with a small circle of students, and also at a *khānqāh* that he had founded, until he died on 14 Jumādā II 505/19 December 1111.

While al-Ashʿarī had used Greek dialectic to deliver Islamic dogmatics from the naïve subtleties of the old *mutakallimūn*, al-Ghazzālī secured for Islam the vigour of its religious life. He did this by bringing about the recognition of a mysticism that had been purged of its excesses and which he had philosophically underpinned. That he was very much aware of his calling as a renewer of religion, who, according to *ḥadīth*, was expected at the turn of every century, is evident from the title of his magnum opus, *al-Iḥyāʾ*.

Ibn al-Jawzī, *Muntaẓam*, n.d., 520., Ibn Khall. 566, Jāmī, *Nafaḥāt* 422, *Rawḍāt al-jannāt* 75, Ibn Ḥajar, *Lisān al-mīzān* I, 293, Ṭāshköprīzāde, *Miftāḥ al-saʿāda* II, 191/210.—R. Gosche, Über Ghazzālīs Leben und Werke, *Phil.-hist. Abh. der Berl. Ak. für 1858* (Berlin 1859), p. 239/311 (outdated). See Suppl. M. Umaruddin, An Exposition of al-Ghazzali's View on the Problem of the Freedom of the Will, *Muslim Univ. Journal* III, 1, 1936, 31/51, A.J. Wensinck, *La pensée de Ghazzālī*, Paris 1940, idem, Ghazālīs Bekeering in *Semietische Studien*, Leiden 1941, 154/77.

| I. Theology. 1. *Jawāhir al-Qurʾān*, a systematic theology, in spirit often in 538
agreement with the *Iḥyāʾ*, Leid. 1986/7, Br. Mus. 143, Hayn. 59, Pet. 55, AS 338, Esʿad Efendi Medr. 182, Ğārullāh 1261,$_{20}$, Amuča Ḥü. 451, Hüdāʾī Ṭas. 155, 246, Fātiḥ 5375,$_{4}$, Šehīd A. 2795, 1254, 1362, Nafiz 354, Alex. Fun. 152,$_{29}$, Cairo ^{1}VII, 198, Qawala I, 55, Mosul 156,$_{16}$, Patna I, 130,$_{1296}$, II, 448,$_{2623/4}$, thereof especially the third main division *Kitāb al-arbaʿīn fī uṣūl al-dīn* Berl. 1715/8, Patna I, 128,$_{1278}$.—1a. *Anwār al-asrār wa-hiya Risāla fī tafsīr qawlihi taʿālā* sura 2, 21 *wa-mā fī maʿnahā fi 'l-ḥadīth* Alex. Fun. 126,$_{5}$.—2. *Faḍāʾil al-Qurʾān* Cairo ^{1}VII, 544, ^{2}I,

135.—3. *ʿAqīda*, Creed, Berl. 1947, Bodl. II, 68, Tippu 140, no. 21, Alex. Fun. $164_{,4}$,
Cavalla Ef. Cat. no. 1973, see P. Kraus, *Abstracta Isl.* V, *REI* 1936, ed. Pococke
in *Spec. Hist. Ar.* ed. II, p. 269ff.—Commentaries: a. Aḥmad b. Aḥmad Zarrūq
al-Burnusī, d. 899/1493 (II, 253), Br. Mus. $126_{,9}$.—b. see Suppl.—4. *al-ʿAqīda
al-qudsiyya*, on God's names and properties, Berl. 1948, Gotha 95, $661_{,4}$, 666,
Ṣāḥib Mollā 511.—5. *Kitāb al-maqṣad al-asnā fī asmāʾ Allāh al-ḥusnā*, on the 99
most beautiful names of God, Berl. 2210/20, Gotha 716, Ind. Off. 337, Esc. $^{2}631_{,4}$,
$1130_{,2}$, Garr. 1891, Alex. Ṭas. $35_{,9}$, abstract Gotha $99_{,3}$ by Ibn al-ʿArabī, d. 638/1240
(p. 441), Berl. 2226/7.—6. *al-Durra al-fākhira fī kashf ʿulūm al-ākhira*, eschatology (MSS see Suppl. Alex. Mawāʿiẓ $40_{,2}$, Fun. $75_{,2}$, Mosul $263_{,8}$), *La perle précieuse
de Gh.* ed. L. Gauthier, Geneva 1878, print. C. 1308.—6a. *al-Jawāhir al-ghawālī
lil-imām al-Gh.* C. 1924 (*Jāmiʿ al-taṣānīf al-ḥadītha* no. 766).—7. *al-Budūr fī
akhbār al-baʿth wal-nushūr* Cairo ^{1}VII, 592.—8. *al-Risāla al-qudsiyya*, on God's
nature, his properties, and the acts and truthfulness of the Prophet, abstract
al-Musāyara by Muḥammad b. Humāmaddīn, d. 861/1456 (Suppl. II, 91), Berl.
1720, 1826, Gotha $652_{,3}$, Cairo ^{1}VII, 78, 555, 576.—9. *Kitāb al-iqtiṣād fī ʾl-iʿtiqād*,
the way to religious understanding, Berl. 1719, Esc. ^{1}I, 517, ^{2}1273, Qawala I, 160.—
10. *Kitāb al-mawāʿiẓ fī ʾl-aḥādīth al-qudsiyya*, of doubtful authenticity, Gotha
$3_{,13}$.—11. *Kitāb iljām al-ʿawāmm ʿan ʿilm al-kalām* print. Madras 1306, C. 1309
and others (see Suppl.), fragm. Leid. 1492, excerpt Gotha $99_{,4}$, with the title
Risāla fī madhāhib ahl al-salaf Berl. 2801, AS $2200_{,2}$,—12. Creed in the form of
a letter to Abu ʾl-Fatḥ Aḥmad b. Salāma al-Damīmī, published by al-Hakkārī,
539 d. 558/1163 (p. 434), Berl. 1950/1, under the title *Mawāʿiẓ* Garr. 1544.—13. | *Kitāb
al-tafriqa bayna ʾl-īmān wal-zandaqa*, against the accusation of heresy, Berl.
2075, Garr. $2005_{,12}$ = *Fayṣal al-tafriqa bayna ʾl-islām wal-zandaqa* AS 2200, 4792
f. 733a/44b, ʿA. Emiri Fārisī 19 f. 17b/21b, Welieddīn 1819, Cairo ^{1}VII, 554, Mosul
$75_{,1}$, translated by H.J. Runge, Kiel 1938, paraphrased by Asín Palacios, *El justo
medio en la creenzia*, Madrid 1926, App. V, p. 499/540.—14. *Risāla fī ʾl-mawt*
Alex. Fun. $65_{,1}$.—15. Small treatise on the *Futūḥ al-Qurʾān*, i.e. a compilation
of verses in which there is question of an opening by God, Berl. 2302.—16. See.
Suppl. with Garr. $2167_{,2}$.—17. *Risāla fī bayān maʿrifat Allāh* Leid. 1491 = *Risāla fī
ʾl-maʿrifa* Berl. 3208.—18. *Sharḥ ʿalā qawl ḥujjat al-islām Abī Ḥāmid Muḥammad
b. Muḥammad al-Ghazzālī laysa fī ʾl-imkān abdaʿ min ṣūrat hādha ʾl-ʿālam etc.*
422 by Muḥammad al-Nashshārī, Qawala I, 200. |—19. *Risāla fī uṣūl al-dīn* Munich
$885_{,4}$.—20. *Nuzhat al-sālikīn* = *al-Bayān fī masālik al-īmān*, on God's nature,
the Last Judgment, Paradise and Hell, accounting for one's deeds, and the 10
ways to escape serious punishment, apocryphal, Berl. 3209.—21. *al-Qānūn
al-kullī fī ʾl-taʾwīl* Cairo ^{1}VII, 231, see Suppl. ed. A.J. Casas y Manrique, Uppsala
1937.—22., 23. See Suppl.

II. Ethics and sufism. 24. *Kitāb jāmiʿ al-ḥaqāʾiq bi-tajrīd al-ʿalāʾiq*, an exposition on ethics in 15 chapters wrongly attributed to him and in fact identical with the *Tuḥfat al-safara* of Ibn ʿArabī (p. 444, no. 26), Upps. 402.—25. *Iḥyāʾ ʿulūm al-dīn*, his magnus opus (see above), Berl. 1675/1706, Vienna 1656, Leid. 2146, Br. Mus. 854/8, 1432, Suppl. 173/4, Ind. Off. 602/10, Bodl. I, 287, 295, 297, Algiers 554/8, Yeni 693/5, Garr. 1877/81, Patna I, 127$_{,12717}$, II, 513$_{,2760}$, print. Būlāq 1289, C. 1306, 1334, Istanbul 1321 (see Suppl.); see Carra de Vaux, *CR Congr. scient. intern. des catholiques* 1891, 2e sect. p. 209; on the history of the book under the Almoravids in Spain see Dozy, *Hist. d. mus. d'Espagne* [1]IV, 253ff., translations etc. see Suppl. and also H. Wehr, *Al-Gs. Buch vom Gottvertrauen, Das 35. Buch des I. ʿu. al-d.* Halle 1940 (Isl. Ethik 4), H.H. Dingemans, *Al-Gh.s Boek der Liefde*, Leiden 1938. Commentaries: a. *Itḥāf al-sāda al-muttaqīn* by Muḥammad b. Muḥammad b. al-Ḥusayn al-Murtaḍā, d. 1205/1791 (II, 287), Munich 150, print. Fez 1301/4, 13 vols. (see Vollers, ZDMG 47, 538), C. 1311, 10 vols.—b. Anon., Ind. Off. 611.—Justification of the *Iḥyāʾ* by the author himself *al-Imlāʾ ʿalā mushkil al-I.* or *al-Ajwiba al-musakkina* (*muskita?*) *ʿan al-asʾila al-mubhama* or *al-Intiṣār li-mā fi ʾl-I. min al-asrār* Berl. 1714, Ms. or. fol. 4249$_{,1}$.—Abstracts: 1. *Lubāb I. ʿu. al-d.* | by 540
his brother Aḥmad (no. 5), according to others by the author himself, Berl. 1708/9, Bodl. I, 324 (see II, 578a), Garr. 1482, Esc. [2]731.—2. *Minhāj al-qāṣidīn*, omitting all weak traditions and unfounded Sufi teachings, by Ibn al-Jawzī, d. 597/1200 (see 500), Paris 1295, Fātiḥ 2872, from which *Kitāb ādāb al-nikāḥ* Garr. 2136, second abstract *al-Mulakhkhaṣ* by Aḥmad b. Muḥammad b. Qudāma al-Maqdisī, d. 742/1341, Berl. 1711/2, Cairo [1]II, 132, [2]I, 356, Alex. Taṣ. 43, Mawāʿiẓ 49.—3. *Rūḥ al-Iḥyāʾ*, by Aḥmad b. Mūsā b. Yūnus, Bodl. I, 121$_{,2}$.—4. ʿAlī b. Muḥammad b. al-Rāzī, AS 2097.—5. Muḥyi ʾl-Dīn Abū Zakariyyāʾ Yaḥyā b. Muḥammad b. Mūsā al-Yamanī, Patna I, 142$_{,1378}$.—6. Muḥammad b. ʿAbdallāh al-Khwārizmī al-Shāfiʿī, d. 679/1280, Br. Mus. 740, Cairo [1]VII 297.—7. Anon., Cairo [1]II, 132, under the title *Khulāṣat al-taṣānīf fi ʾl-taṣawwuf* C. 1327 (see Suppl.), *Isʿād al-umma fī-mā jāʾa bi-hi ʾl-Qurʾān wal-sunna* Tunis 1342.—8.–20. see Suppl. (17. *ʿAyn al-ʿilm* also Patna I, 138$_{,353}$, commentary by al-Qāriʾ al-Harawī ibid. 135$_{,335}$, 18. = 10. read: al-Bilālī).—21. *Mawʿiẓat al-muʾminīn min I. ʿu. al-d.* by Muḥammad Jamāl al-Dīn al-Qāsimī al-Dimashqī, d. 1332/1914 (Suppl. II, 777), C. 1331.—Introductory remarks with a biography of the author *Taʿrīf al-aḥyāʾ bi-faḍāʾil al-Iḥyāʾ* by ʿAbd al-Qādir b. Shaykh ʿAbdallāh b. ʿAydarūs, d. 1038/1628 (II, 419), Berl. 1713.—26. *Kitāb bidāyat al-hidāya*, composed after the *Iḥyāʾ*, Berl. 3263/4, Gotha 882, Munich 614, Paris 1293$_{,1}$, Br. Mus. 739, 126$_{,2}$, Bodl. I, 569, Algiers 876/7, Pet. Rosen 219$_{,2}$, Garr. 921, Alex. Mawāʿiz 40$_{,1}$, Patna II, 411$_{,2582,\ 2}$, print. Būlāq 1287, 1291, C. 1277, (in *Majmūʿa*) 1303; on which glosses by Muḥammad al-Nawāwī al-Jāwī (II, 501), C. 1308, Būlāq 1309, and others see Suppl. Abstract by

Muḥammad b. Yaḥyā al-Baṣrī, Br. Mus. 1594$_{,2}$.—27. *Kitāb mīzān al-ʿamal* Esc. ^{2}875$_{,2}$ (fragm.), Cairo ^{1}VII, 376 = *Mōzenē ṣedeq, Compendium doctrinae ethicae auctore al-Gazali Tusensi de arabico hebraice conversum ab Abrahamo Bar Chasdai Barcinonensi*, ed. J. Goldenthal, Leipzig-Paris 1839.—28. *Kitāb al-qusṭās al-mustaqīm*, a polemical dialogue with an Ismaili, one of his last works (see Suppl.), Berl. 1724, Esc. ^{2}631$_{,3}$, Cairo ^{1}VII, 700[3], anon. comm. *al-Mīzān al-qawīm* Bat. 122$_{,7}$, commentary by Muḥammad Qāḍī Patna I, 122$_{,1227}$.—29. *Kīmiyyāʾ
423 al-saʿāda*, popular representation | of ethics with special regard to mysticism,
541 Berl. 3132, according to ḤKh V, 10918 originally | written in Persian, this Persian text is preserved in Berl. pers. 288/90, Dresd. 255, fragm. ibid. 4, 87, Paris 13/6, Br. Mus. I, 37, Bodl. Pers. 1429/30, print. Calcutta n.d., Lucknow 1279, 1282, Bombay 1883, Turkish transl. Dresd. 15, Upps. 460, print. Istanbul 1260; after the Turkish transl. H.A. Homes, *The Alchemy of Happiness by M. al-Gh. the Mohammedan Philosopher*, Albany, NY 1873, Urdu transl. Lucknow 1313.—On this is based the Persian treatise *Chahār ʿunwān* by Bābā Afḍal al-Dīn Kāshī, d. 710/1310, Br. Mus. Pers. II, 829b.—20. *al-Tibr al-masbūk fī naṣīḥat al-mulūk*, originally in Persian under the title *Naṣīḥat al-mulūk*, composed for Muḥammad b. Malikshāh (see above), in several MSS in Istanbul in Horn, *ZDMG* 54, 314, no. 384, and F. Meier, ibid. 93, 398, ed. Jalālī Humāʾī, Tehran, Majlis 1315/7, Arabic transl. by ʿAlī b. Mubārak b. Mawhūb for the *atabeg* Alp Qutlugh of Mosul, d. 595/1199, Gotha 1874/7, where other MSS are listed, with Basle M. III, 4, *Bull. de Corr. Afr.* 1884, p. 37, no. 149, in Tunis, Alex. Mawāʿiẓ 48, Qawala I, 223, Patna I, 146$_{,1404}$ and MSS in Istanbul in Meier, op. cit., 399/402 (see Suppl.), print. C. 1277, and in the margin of *Sirāj al-mulūk* by al-Ṭurṭūshī, ibid. 1306, 1319, see Goldziher, *ZDMG* 50, 100, n. 2. The separately transmitted Persian introduction in Arabic transl. AS 2911; 5 Turkish translations in Meier, op. cit., 404/5.—31. *Sirr al-ʿālamayn wa-kashf mā fi ʾl-dārayn* see Suppl. also Alex. Mawāʿiẓ 23.—32. *Kitāb ayyuha ʾl-walad* Berl. 3975/6 Gotha 1165 (where other MSS are listed), see Suppl. with Alex. Mawāʿiẓ 35, Fun. 194$_{,8}$, Qawala I, 234. *O Kind! Die berühmte ethische Abh. Ghazalis ar. u. deutsch v.* Hammer Purgstall, Vienna 1838.—Commentaries: a. Ḥasan b. ʿAbdallāh, composed in 756/1355, Vienna 1842, Munich 174, fol. 110b.—b. *Ayyuha ʾl-etc.* by ʿAbd al-Raḥmān b. Aḥmad al-Ṣabrī, composed in 1117/1705, Cairo ^{1}VII, 623, ^{2}I, 271.—c. see Suppl.—d. Abū Saʿīd Muḥammad b. Muḥammad b. Muṣṭafā al-Khādimī, d. 1160/1747, Berl. 3977, Vienna 1843, Qawala I, 245.—e. ʿAbd al-Raḥmān b. Aḥmad ʿUmar Baṣīrī,

3 Not—as assumed in Gosche, no. 14—the original of the *Mōzenē hāʿiyyūnīm*, the Hebrew translation of a lost treatise that is probably falsely attributed to al-Ghazzālī, see Steinschneider, *hebr. Übers.* § 194.

Qawala I, 245.—f. *Minḥat al-ṣamad* by Muḥammad b. Yūsuf al-Ḥalabī al-Sāqizī,
Garr. 784.—g. Turkish paraphrase Coburg III, b.—33. See Suppl., also Fātiḥ 2856.—
34a–c. *Mịshkāt al-anwār* see Suppl. (ad a., which still relies on a literal translation of Plotinus *Enneads* IV, see p. 222, see A.J. Wensinck, *Semietische Studien*,
Leiden 1941, 192/212, and also Garr. 1892, Alex. Fun. 152$_{,30}$, Qawala, I, 262, Mosul
176$_{,8}$, Patna II, 412$_{,2580,8}$).—35. *Nūr al-shamʿa fī bayān ẓuhr al-jumʿa* Leid. 483.—
36. *Madkhal al-sūlūk ilā manāzil al-mulūk*, on Sufi life, the science of *ḥadīth*, | 542
the Arabic language, and the history of the ancient Arabs, Br. Mus. Suppl. 1089$_{,2}$,
Esc. ^{2}732$_{,1}$, 763$_{,1}$.—37. *Kitāb al-zuhd al-fātiḥ*, an admonishment, Br. Mus. 741.—
38. *Minhāj al-ʿābidīn ilā jannat rabb al-ʿālamīn* (see Suppl.) Berl. 3265/6, BDMG
19, Leid. 2147, Paris 1248$_{,3}$, 1292, Br. Mus. 165$_{,6}$, Suppl. 229, Algiers 876$_{,2}$, Garr.
2068, Qawala I, 267, Mosul 124$_{,52}$, 155$_{,66}$, 192$_{,33}$, Patna I, 143$_{,1386}$, print. C. 1305 (in
the margin of the *Bidāya*), see Suppl. 1351 (with the *Bidāya* in the margin).—
Abstracts by: a. al-Balaṭunisī, ca. 850/1446 (but see II, 320), Berl. 3267 and
al-Shaʿrānī (II, 335), on which a commentary by Muṣṭafā al-Bakrī(?) ibid.
3268.—b.–e. see Suppl. (b. Patna I, 142$_{,138}$), f. Anon., Berl. 3269.—Turkish translation by Nisānī (Nishānī, Nhānī, Nhālī) Gotha türk. 77, Vienna 168, Krafft
504.—39. *Fī ʾl-ʿibādāt*, on religious duties, Berl. 3815, Garr. 2175$_{,2}$.—40. *Fī bayān
ʿilm al-ladunī*, on the deeper mystical knowledge of God, Berl. 3210 = *al-Risāla
al-laduniyya* Ind. Off. 312, transl. by Margaret Smith, *JRAS* 1938, 177/200,
353/74.—41. *Maqāmāt al-ʿulamāʾ bayna yaday al-khulafāʾ wal-umarāʾ* Berl.
8537$_{,1}$.—42. *al-Kashf wal-tabyīn fī ghurūr al-khalq ajmaʿīn*, | sets out the various 424
cases in which God's commands were neglected, discussing the unbelievers
first, and then the believers, in four classes, Berl. 8744, Cairo ^{1}VII, 79, 376, 418, ^{2}I,
348, Qawala I, 259, Patna II, 411$_{,2580,7}$.—43. *al-Ḥikma fī ʾl-makhlūqāt*, on the miracle of Creation, Berl. 8747, Paris 2310, partly from the *Kitāb al-dalāʾil wal-iʿtibār*
attributed to al-Jāḥiẓ (Suppl. I, 247, no. 5), see Baneth, *Magnus Anniversary Vol.*
Jerusalem 1938, p. 23ff.—44. A prayer, Berl. 3644$_{,1}$.—45. On the submission to
God's will and on resisting it, Berl. 2632.—46. *Maghālīṭ al-maghrūrīn*, of decep-
tions to which believers and unbelievers are exposed and their causes, Berl.
3167.—47. *Risālat al-ṭayr*, an allegory similar to the one by al-Maqdisī (p. 450/1),
Leid. 2145, Alex. Taṣ. 35$_{,8}$.—47. a.—ff. see Suppl. (w. *al-Ḥiṣn al-ḥaṣīn fī khawāṣṣ
lā ilāha illa ʾllāh* Patna II, 447$_{,2663,5}$.—x. also Alex. Fun. 90$_{,20}$.—z. under the title
Risāla fī taḥqīq bayān maʿna ʾl-rūḥ Patna I, 132$_{,1309}$).—gg. *Aṣnāf al-maghrūrīn*
Taymūr, Akhlāq 164.—hh. *al-Jawāhir al-fākhira* Heid. 337, *ZDMG* 91$_{,399}$—ii.
Wiqāyat al-sālik min al-āfāt wal-mahālik Patna I, 144$_{,392}$.—kk. *al-ʿIlq al-nafīs*
ibid. II, 411$_{,2500,4}$.—

III. Fiqh. 48. *Kitāb al-basīṭ fī ʾl-furūʿ*, based on the *Nihāyat al-maṭlab* of
his teacher Imām al-Ḥaramayn, Ind. Off. 1766, Esc.^{1} 1125, Cairo ^{1}III, 197.—
49. *Kitāb al-Wasīṭ al-muḥīṭ bi-āthār al-Basīṭ*, abstract of the above, | Munich 359 543

(?), Bodl. I, 233, II, 82, part IV, Ambr. RSO III, 277.—Commentaries: a. *Sharḥ mushkil al-W.* by ʿUthmān b. ʿAbd al-Raḥmān b. al-Ṣalāḥ, d. 643/1245 (p. 440), Cairo [1]III, 242, 275, [2]I, 539.—b. *Muntaqa ʾl-ghāyāt fī mushkilāt al-W.* by Ḥamza b. Yūsuf al-Ḥamawī al-Tanūkhī, d. 670/1271, Cairo [1]III, 278, [2]I, 540.—c. Aḥmad b. Muḥammad al-Rafʿa, d. 710/1310 (II, 133), Cairo [1]III, 276.—d. *al-Baḥr al-muḥīṭ* by Aḥmad b. Muḥammad al-Qamūlī, d. 727/1327 (II, 86), part IV, Paris 1026. Abstract by the author, *Jawāhir al-baḥr*, Cairo [1]III, 215, [1]I, 508, Patna I, 79,$_{801}$.—e., f. see Suppl.—g. Anon., Cairo [1]III, 242.—Abstracts: a. *al-Ghāya al-quṣwā* by al-Bayḍāwī (p. 530), Berl. 4597/8, Garr. 1789.—b. al-Masʿūdī, Cairo [1]III, 278.—50. *Kitāb al-Wajīz*, abstract of the above, Paris 985, Cairo [1]III, 289.—Commentaries: a. *Sharḥ ibhām al-Wajīz wal-Wasīṭ* by Asʿad b. Maḥmūd al-ʿIjlī, d. 600/1203 (Subkī, *Ṭab.* V, 50), Cairo [1]III, 235.—b. *Fatḥ al-ʿazīz* by ʿAbd al-Karīm al-Rāfiʿī al-Qazwīnī, d. 623/1226 (p. 493), Berl. 4470/1, Br. Mus. Suppl. 305, Cairo [1]III, 238, 251, [2]I, 528, 546, Gotha 940 (where other MSS are listed).—a smaller commentary by the same, Berl. 4472/3, Patna I, 104,$_{1053}$.—Abstract by Abū Bakr b. Bahrām al-Anṣārī, ca. 890/1485, Paris 1032.—Abstract of the traditions in the larger commentary by ʿUmar b. ʿAlī b. al-Mulaqqin, d. 814/1401 (II, 92), Berl. 1345, Cairo [2]I, 114, *al-Talkhīṣ al-kabīr etc.* (see Suppl.) by Ibn Ḥajar al-ʿAsqalānī, d. 852/1449 (II, 68), Berl. 1346, Alex. Ḥad. 11, Cairo [1]I, 282, [2]I, 98 Patna I, 82,$_{814}$.—c. *al-Rawḍa* or *Rawḍat al-ṭālibīn* by al-Nawawī, d. 676/1177 (p. 496), abstract of the great commentary by al-Rāfiʿī, Berl. 4474, Paris 990, 6451, Br. Mus. Suppl. 306, Garr. 1804, Patna I, 90,$_{913}$.—Glosses: *α al-Muhimmāt* by Jamāl al-Dīn al-Asnawī, d. 772/1370 (II, 90), completed in 769/1367, Cairo [1]III, 280, [2]I, 542, *al-Kalimāt al-muhimma, Br. Mus. Quart.* X, 134; on which again glosses *αα al-Mubhamāt ʿala ʾl-Muhimmāt* by Zayn al-Dīn al-ʿIrāqī, d. 806/1403, thereto anonymous *Zawāʾid*, from which an abstract by Abū Yazīd al-Dawwānī, Paris 992.—*ββ al-Taʿaqqubāt* by Aḥmad b. ʿImād b. Yūsuf al-Aqfahsī, d. 808/1405 (II, 93), Berl. 4476, Cairo [1]III, 208, 280, Dam. ʿUm. 51, 394/3.—Rebuttal *al-Mulimmāt ʿala ʾl-Muhimmāt* by ʿUmar b. Raslān al-Bulqīnī, d. 805/1403 (II, 93), Pet. AM 125, Cairo [1]III, 278, [2]I, 540.—*β. Khādim al-Rāfiʿī wal-Rawḍa* by Muḥammad al-Zarkashī, d. 794/1391, Paris 991.—*γ.* See Suppl., Patna I, 83,$_{838/40}$.—*δ.* Jalāl al-Dīn Muḥammad b.
544 ʿAlī Abū Bakr al-Ṣiddīqī, *qāḍī* | of Alexandria, d. 891/1648 (al-Sakhāwī, *al-Ḍawʾ al-lāmiʿ* VII, 284), Alex. Fiqh Shāf. 17.—Abstract of the *Rawḍa* by Ismāʿīl b. Abī Bakr b. al-Muqriʾ al-Yamanī, d. 837/1433 (II, 254), Gotha 941, on which a commentary by Zakariyyāʾ al-Anṣārī, d. 926/1520 (II, 99), Paris 993/5, Alex. Fiqh Shāf. 4.—d., e. see Suppl., f. Anon. Alex. Fiqh Shāf. 26.—Abstract *al-Taʿjīz* by ʿAbd al-Raḥīm b. Muḥammad al-Mawṣilī, d. 671/1272 (p. 495,$_{28}$).—Versification of b. and c.: *Rumūz al-kunūz* by ʿAbd al-ʿAzīz b. Aḥmad al-Dīrīnī, d. 697/1297 (p. 451), Bank. XIX, 183,$_{8}$ = Patna I, 89,$_{96}$.—51. *Kitāb al-mustaṣfā min ʿilm al-uṣūl*

Gotha 925,[4] Cairo ^{1}III, 275, Mosul 64$_{,216}$, see M. Schreiner, *Actes du 8e congr. intern. des or.* II, 97. |—52. *Kitāb al-manḥūl fi 'l-uṣūl* (see Suppl.) Cairo ^{1}III, 425
267, Patna I, 75$_{,69}$.—53. (*Bayān*) *Ghāyat al-ghawr fī masā'il* (*dirāyat*) *al-dawr*, on marital law, Br. Mus. Suppl. 1203, i, Rāġib 569.—53a.–g. see Suppl. (ad 53a p. 180).—53h. *Risāla mā lā budd minhu* Patna II, 439$_{,2616,3}$.

IV. Philosophy and encyclopaedias. 54. *Kitāb al-ma'ārif al-'aliyya wa* (*lubāb*) *al-ḥikma* (*ḥikam*) *al-ilāhiyya*, on logic, metaphysics, speech, writing, and decision-making, Paris 1331, Bodl. I, 133.—55. *Kitāb tahāfut al-falāsifa*, composed immediately after 56 (see Suppl. MS Pet. As. Mus., *Kračkovskij Dokl. Ak. Nauk*. 1925, 47/9) with the rebuttals of Ibn Rushd (p. 462) and Muṣṭafā b. Yūsuf Khājazāde (II, 230) printed together C. 1302/3, 1319, 1320, alone lith. Bombay 1304. S.T. de Boer, *Die Widersprüche der Philosophie nach al-Ghazzālī und ihr Ausgleich durch Ibn Roshd*, Strassburg 1894. Cf. Steinschneider, *Hebr. Übers.* § 184.—56. *Maqāṣid al-falāsifa*, which attempts to give an account of the system of logic, natural philosophy, and metaphysics which the *Tahāfut* exposes in its inner contradictions, as an introduction to the same, composed in 488/1095, Berl. 5059, *M. al-F. Teil I, die Logik, Cap. 1 u. 2 nach der Berliner und der Oxforder Hds. zum ersten Mal hsg. und mit Vorrede und Anmm. versehn v.* G. Beer, Leiden 1888.—Latin by Dom. Gundisalvi, *Logica et philosophia*, Venice 1506.—Cf. Steinschneider, *Hebr. Übers.* § 164.—57. *al-Munqidh min al-ḍalāl*, which he composed after resuming his teaching in Nishapur, gives an account of all his philosophical transformations, Berl. 1725, Leid. 1490, Paris 1331$_{,2}$, Esc. ^{2}694,
1130, Garr. 1572, Alex. Tawḥīd 45, Cairo ^{1}II, 57, VII, 146; ed. | Schmölders, *Essai* 545
sur les écoles philosophiques chez les Arabes, Paris 1842, p. 1/64, print. Istanbul 1870, 1287, 1289, 1293, from which transl. by Barbier de Meynard, *JA* s. III, v. 9, 1877, I, p. 1/93.—58. *Kitāb al-maḍnūn bi-hi 'an ghayr ahlihi*, dedicated to his brother Aḥmad, on knowledge of God and the angels, the nature of miracles, and the Afterlife, Berl. 1721, Leid. 1894/5, Paris 1331$_{,3}$, Pet. 247$_{,3}$, AS 2000$_{,3}$, Cairo ^{1}VI, 115, Taymūr, Majm. I, 12, Alex. Fun. 87$_{,1}$, 151$_{,9}$ (with the title *al-'Ilq al-m. etc.*), print. in *Majmū'a*, C. 1309; with the same title but completely different Berl. 1722/3.[5]—59. *Fatḥiyyāt al-'ulūm*, on the excellence, usefulness, and disadvantages of knowledge, reports of the lives of previous scholars, and the

---

4 The MS Paris 408 = de Slane 790 mentioned there is not an abstract of it, but rather the *Kitāb al-maḥṣūl* by Fakhr al-Dīn al-Rāzī, p. 531.

5 Printed in the collective volume mentioned in *OB* V, 5134, with the subtitle *al-Ajwiba* (*al-Ghazzāliyya fi 'l-masā'il al-ukhrawiyya*), Serāi A III, 1419$_{,63b/68a}$, Hebrew transl. Steinschneider § 192; in reality it is a work—published in his name—by the poet Abu 'l-Ḥasan 'Alī b. al-Musaffir al-Sabtī, ca. 600/1203, see Suppl. I, 751, no. 38.

hallmarks of the worldly and the pious scholar, Berl. 102, Paris 2311, Med. 190, Alex. Fun. $64_{,1}$.—60. *Risāla fī ḥaqāʾiq al-ʿulūm li-ahl al-fuhūm* Paris $1337_{,12}$.—61. *Mukāshafat al-qulūb al-muqarriba ilā ʿilm al-ghuyūb* Berl. 8836, print. C. 1323, 1327, anon. abstract Qawala I, 265, print. Būlāq 1300.—62. *Miʿyār al-ʿilm* Rāġib 912.—63. A metaphysical work without title in 7 *maqālāt* Br. Mus. Suppl. 724.—64. *Die Abh. des a. Ḥ. al-Gh. Antworten auf Fragen, die an ihn gerichtet wurden, in hebr. Übers. hsg. von* H. Malter, Frankfurt a. M. 1896, which in many
426 places touches on the *Maqāṣid al-falāsifa.* |—64a. *Maʿārij al-quds fī madārij maʿrifat al-nafs* C. 1927.—64aa.—f. see Suppl. (e. AS 2200, $2446_{,4}$).—64g. *Maʿārij al-quds*, on the soul, Welīddīn $1814_{,10}$, Baghdad, *Lughat al-ʿArab* II, 107, 112, see Suppl. I, 973,

V. Occult sciences. 65. *Kanz al-qawm wa-sirr al-maktūm*, on the secrets of letters, Berl. 4123.—66. *Maqālat al-fawz*, on alchemy, Berl. 4179, Rāġib 963 (*Islca* IV, 548).—67. *Kitāb al-khātam*, a poem on the fabrication of talismans, Leid. 1214, Ambros. 254, Berl. 4110 (see Suppl.), under the title *al-Sirr al-maṣūn wa-l-durr al-maknūn*, Alex. Faw. $24_{,1}$. Commentary, *Mustawjibat al-maḥāmid* by Muḥammad b. ʿUthmān al-Anṣārī, Paris 2570/1.—67a.—f. see Suppl.

546 VI. Poems. 68. *Ghāya wa-nihāya*, three Sufi *qaṣidas* | in praise of the Prophet, Berl. 7633.—69. *Qaṣīda*, supposedly written in consolation for and admonition of his students shortly before his death (see Suppl.), Berl. 3978/9, Gotha $28_{,2}$, Br. Mus. $754_{,2}$, Steinschneider, *Hebr. Übers.* § 197, cf. M. Schreiner, *ZDMG* 48, p. 43.

VII. Letters collected under the title *Faḍāʾil al-anām*, AS $4821_{,43a/46b}$, 4301, $4792_{,692b/726b}$, from which *Risāla arsalahā ila ʾl-sulṭān Muḥammad b. Malikshāh*, C. 1325, a Persian letter to the son of Niẓām al-Mulk, Ḍiyāʾ al-Mulk, ed. by Dhabīḥullāhi Ṣafā in the Tehrani Magazine *Mihr* VI, no. 5, p. 363/7 (Meier, *ZDMG* 93, 406), a letter to al-Hakkārī (p. 560) ʿUm. 3750 (cf. 12, Suppl. 47d).

6. His brother Shihāb al-Dīn (Majd al-Dīn) Aḥmad b. Muḥammad al-Ghazzālī succeeded him when he gave up his teaching position in Baghdad. He shared Abū Ḥāmid's penchant for mysticism but tried to work more practically as a preacher. He died in 520/1126 in Qazvin or, according to others, in 517/1123.

Ibn Khall. 37, Jāmī, *Nafaḥāt* 426, Ibn al-Jawzī, *Muntaẓam* a 520, *Lisān al-mīzān* I, 293 (Ritter). 1. *Kitāb al-tajrīd fī kalimat al-tawḥīd* Berl. 2396/2405, Ind. Off. $694_{,3}$, Ambr. B. 75_{ix} (*RSO* IV, 1030), Garr. $2003_{,19}$, Alex. Tawḥīd 6, Fun. $160_{,1}$, Cairo ^{1}II, 8, VII, 5, 47, 229, 359, 373, 518, 531, Qawala I, 162, Un. Egypt 11900, 15008, anon. comm. Cairo ^{1}II, 5.—2. *Manhaj al-albāb*, Sufi instructions, Berl. 2832.—3. *Risāla fī faḍl al-faqr wal-fuqarāʾ*, on the fact that during the Miʿrāj the Prophet was clad in the garments of the poor, which then gradually devolved upon Ibn Junayd (p. 214), and that this is the reason why the donning of this attire is

regarded as foundational in Sufism, Berl. 3344.—4. *Bawāriq al-ilmāʿ fī 'l-radd ʿalā man yuḥarrimu 'l-samāʿ*, on the permissibility of music, Berl. 5505, Paris 4580, Cairo ^{1}VI, 118, VII, 228, ^{2}I, 274, *Nashr.* 6, ed. J. Robson, together with Ibn Abi 'l-Dunyā's *Dhamm al-malāhī* in *Tracts on Listening to Music* (Or. Transl. Fund NS, 5), London 1938.—5. On the merits of *Lā ilāha illa 'llāh* Paris 1248, 2.—6. *Kitāb al-dhakhīra li-ahl al-baṣīra*, an overview of the system of his brother, Berl. 1726, Taymūr ʿAqāʾid 252, Fez, Qar. 1452,$_{1}$.—7. Abstract of the *Iḥyāʾ*, see p. 539.—8.–16. see Suppl. (13. ʿA. Emīrī Fārisī 199,$_{4}$).—16. *Sawāniḥ, Aphorismen über die Liebe, hsg.* | *von* H. Ritter, *Bibl. Isl.* 15, 1942 (see *Isl.* XXI, 94). 6b. Suppl. 547
see ibid. 769,$_{25}$.

7. Abū Muʿīn Maymūn b. Muḥammad al-Nasafī al-Makḥūlī, who died in 508/1114.

Ibn Quṭl. 283. 1. *Kitāb baḥr al-kalām* (*afkār*) Berl. 1941/3,[6] Gotha 100,$_{3}$, Heid. ZDMG 91, 402,$_{6}$, Munich 892, f. 72b, Vienna 1523,$_{1}$, Paris 1232/3, 4599,$_{4}$, Br. Mus. Suppl. 175, NO 2095, Alex. Tawḥīd 5, Fun. 80,$_{2}$, 86,$_{3}$ Cairo ^{1}II, 6, 42, 46, 50/1, VII, 537, ^{2}I, 167, Patna I, 113,$_{1138}$, under the title *Mubāḥathat ahl al-sunna wal-jamāʿa maʿa ahl al-firaq al-ḍālla wal-mubtadiʿa* Leid. 1989/90, Bodl. I, 114, see A. v. Kremer, *Ideen* 470.—2. *Kitāb tabṣirat al-adilla*, a scholastic polemic, Algiers 619, Yeni 755, NO 2097, Cairo ^{1}II, 8, ^{2}I, 167, Alex. Tawḥīd 6.—3. *Kitāb al-tamhīd li-qawāʿid al-tawḥīd* Cairo ^{1}II, 51, ^{2}I, 170, Baghdad, Makt. al-awqāf 2746 (see al-ʿAzzāwī, *Taʾrīkh al-yazīdiyya* 20, n.).—6., 7. See Suppl.

| 8. Abū Muḥammad ʿAbdallāh b. Muḥammad b. al-Sīd al-Baṭalyawsī, who died 427
in Valencia in 521/1127 (see Suppl.).

Ibn Khall. 320, Ibn Bashkuwāl 639, Ibn Farḥūn, *Dībāj* 140/1, al-Kattānī, *Fihris* II, 382. 1. *Kitāb al-ḥadāʾiq* in 7 chapters, theologico-philosophical questions, especially about thought, imagination, the nature and properties of God, and the survival of the soul after death, Berl. 2303, Land.-Brill 566 under the title *Sharḥ al-khams al-maqālāt min kalām al-falāsifa* Garr. 796, see M. Asín Palacios, Ibn al-Sid de Badayoz y su libro de los circos, *al-Andalus* IV, 45/54.—2. *Sharḥ adab al-kātib li-Ibn Qutayba* see p. 126.—4.–11. see Suppl. (4. Patna I, 66,$_{686}$ 7 see Asín Palacios, *al-Andalus* III, 345/89, text of a *masʾala* 380/3, = ? *Risāla fī ruʾūs masāʾil al-falsafa*, AS 2415, 2, Krause).

6 In Garr. 1545 a work with the title *Muʿtaqad fī uṣūl al-dīn* is identified with this, but from the incomplete description it is not clear whether we are perhaps not dealing with the *ʿAqāʾid al-Nasafī* (no. 11), as Brill-H. ^{2}982,$_{5}$ would leave us reason to suspect.

9. Muḥammad b. Faḍl al-Kārizyātī al-Farawī al-Nīsabūrī, d. 530/1135.

Kitāb najāt al-murīdīn, an overview of religious duties with the force of law, Berl. 1728 (fragm.).

548 | 10. Abū Isḥāq Ibrāhīm b. Isḥāq[7] al-Ṣaffār al-Bukhārī, who died in 534/1139.

1. *Kitāb talkhīṣ al-adilla li-qawāʿid al-tawḥīd*, a defence of Sunnī teachings against heretics, Br. Mus. 1577, Esc. ^{2}1472.—2. Answers to questions of dogma, Cairo ^{1}VII, 314, ^{2}I, 162.

11. Najm al-Dīn Abū Ḥafṣ ʿUmar b. Muḥammad b. Aḥmad al-Nasafī al-Māturīdī, who was born in 460/1068 in Nasaf, a large city between the Oxus and Samarqand, was one of the greatest Ḥanafī *fuqahāʾ* of his time. He died in Samarqand on 12 Jumādā I 537/4 December 1142.

Ibn Quṭl. 140, Suyūṭī, *Interpr.* 27, de Sacy, *Biogr. univ.* XXXII, 7, Flügel, *Classen* p. 310, Wüst., *Gesch.* 241.

I. *al-ʿAqāʾid*, creed, Berl. 1953/4, Gotha $55_{,1}$, Tüb. $138_{,5}$ (where other MSS are listed), Garr. 1545, $2100_{,1}$, Alex. Tawḥīd 31, Qawala I, 204/5. *Pillar of the Creed of the Sunnites by Hafidh uldín abu l-Barakát Abdullah al-Nasafi (d. 710/1310) to which is subjoined a shorter treatise of a similar nature by Najmuldin Abu Hafs Umar al-Nasafi*, ed. by W. Cureton, London 1843; transl. by Muradjea d'Ohsson, *Tableau de l'empire ottoman*, vol. I. *Türkischer Catechismus der Religion, nach dem arab. Original übers. und erklärt von* C.H. Ziegler, Hamburg and Leipzig 1792.—Commentaries: 1. Saʿd al-Dīn al-Taftāzānī, d. 791/1389 (II, 215), Berl. 1855/65, Gotha 671/3 (where other MSS are listed), Heid. A. $359_{,1}$ (*ZDMG* 91, 391), Br. Mus. Suppl. 176, Garr. 1546/9, $2147_{,2}$, $2155_{,2}$, $2179_{,1}$, Alex. Tawḥīd $22_{,1}$, $31_{,2}$, Patna I, $112_{,1220/1}$, print. Calcutta 1224, 1244, Istanbul 1260.—Glosses: a. Qara Aḥmad, d. 854/1450, Garr. 1550, Alex. Tawḥīd II, Qawala I, 169, 172, Makram 18. *The Commentary of Maulavi A. on the Commentary on Akáidi Nasafi and the Second Commentary of Mulla Kasim on the Last Portion of the Commentary on Akáidi Nasafi*, Lucknow 1883, 1894.—aa. *Ḥall al-maʿāqid fī sharḥ al-ʿAqāʾid* by Shams al-Dīn Manlāzāde al-Harawī al-Ḥaraziyānī, completed before 845/1441 (date of the MS, ad ḤKh IV, 227, see Houtsma ad Br. 980), Garr. 1554.—b. Aḥmad b. Mūsā al-Khayālī, d. after 862/1458 (Suppl. II, 318), Berl. 1966/70, Gotha $673_{,2}$ (where other MSS are listed), Garr. 1550, Alex.

7 See Br. Mus. Cairo Ism.

Tawḥīd 11, | Qawala I, 169/72, Makram 18, Patna I, $119_{,1126/8}$, II, $511_{,2746}$, print. 549
C. 1297, 1335.—Superglosses: *α*. Qara Kamāl Ismāʿīl Qaramānī, ca. 900/1494,
Berl. 1972, Paris $1243_{,1}$, Ind. Off. 396, Garr. 1551, Qawala I, 179, on which super-
glosses by Muḥammad Ṣāliḥ al-Ghazzī b. al-Gharābīlī, d. 918/1512 (II, 320),
Garr. 1582, $2179_{,2}$, designated as a straight gloss on Taftazānī by ḤKh IV, 120
and Esc. ^{2}1583/4, 1586.—*β*. ʿAbd al-Ḥakīm al-Siyālkūtī, d. 1067/1656 (II, 417),
Gotha 675, Paris 1242, Qawala I, 173, Patna I, $117_{,1174/8}$, print. Istanbul 1820, 1841,
1304, lith. Delhi 1870, 1880; superglosses by Muḥammad b. al-Ḥājj al-Manlā
Rasūl b. Ḥasan b. Muḥammad b. al-Rasūl, d. 1264/1848, Istanbul 1303.—*γ*. Qul
Aḥmad, Ind. Off. 399, Qawala I, 179, print. Istanbul 1227.—*δ*. Ḥilmī, Pet. 49.—*ε*.
Anon., Paris 1241.—*ϑ–Ψ*. See Suppl. (*μ*. Patna I, $116_{,1160}$, II, $511_{,2744}$).—*ω*. Aḥmad
Rushdī b. ʿUthmān Efendi Bakjajīzāde, Qawala I, 165.—*αα*. ʿAlī b. Ṣāliḥ b. Ismāʿīl
al-Ayyūbī, Istanbul 1306.—*ββ*. Shujāʿ al-Dīn, Qawala I, 176.—*γγ*. ʿAbdallāh b.
Ḥasan al-Uskudārī al-Anṣāri al-Kānqarī, thirteenth cent., Būlāq 1244 (Qawala I,
179).—c. Muṣliḥ al-Dīn al-Qasṭallānī, d. 907/1495, Berl. 1973, Leid. 1998, Esc.
^{2}1582, Garr. 1553, | on which glosses by Jaʿfarshāh al-Kistālī al-Rūmī, Leid. 428
1999.—d. Zakariyyāʾ al-Anṣārī, d. 926/1520 (II, 99), Berl 1974/5.—e. al-Qāriʾ
al-Harawī, d. 1014/1605 (II, 394), Berl. 1436, Munich 866.—f. Aḥmad Jundī, Ind.
Off. $399_{,1}$.—g. Mollā ʿAlāʾ al-Dīn, Ind. Off. 400.—h. Kamāl al-Dīn Muḥammad
b. Abi ʾl-Sharīf al-Maqdisī, d. 907/1500 (II, 98), ibid. 401, Alex. Tawḥīd 26,
Makram 49.—i. Niẓām al-Dīn Aḥmad b. ʿAlī Arīkān al-Qāḍī al-Badakhshī, Ind.
Off. 402, Paris 1244.—k. Muḥammad al-Shiḥna, Paris 1240.—l. *Kanz al-farāʾid*
by Ramaḍān b. Muḥammad al-Ḥanafī, Leid. 1997, Algiers 568, print. Istanbul
1292/3, 1316.—m. al-Qarabāghī, Qawala I, 178 (= suppl. I, 760, Φ ?).—n. Aḥmad
al-Fursī, Yeni 743.—o. Anon., Leid. 1996, Ind. Off. 403, Paris 1245.—p. al-Bājūrī,
Alex. Tawḥīd 9.—q.—ff. see Suppl. (y. print. Istanbul 1276, 1304, 1317, Qawala
I, 177),—Abstract of the traditions by al-Suyūṭī, d. 911/1505, Cairo ^{1}VII, 51, by
al-Qāriʾ al-Harawī, d. 1014/1605, Cairo^{1}, VII, 123.—2. Glosses on an anonymous
commentary, by al-Sīnābī, Pet. $49_{,2}$.—4.–9. see Suppl.—Versifications: a.
Ṣiyānat al-ʿaqāʾid by Manṣūr al-Ṭablāwī, d. 1014/1605 (II, 321), Berl. 1977/8, Gotha
$866_{,2}$, 688, Cairo ^{2}I, 195, 211, Bat. Suppl. 196.—b. see Suppl.—c. *Naẓm al-ʿAqāʾid
al-N.* by Muḥammad b. Aḥmad al-Jawharī, d. 1215/1800 (II, 488), Cairo | ^{2}I, 550
211.—d. *Iḍāʾat al-dujunna fī ʿaqāʾid ahl al-sunna* by Aḥmad al-Maqqari,
d. 1041/1632 (II, 296), Alex. Tawḥīd 38. 5 commentaries, 17 glosses, 3 versifications in Ahlw. 1979.

II. *al-Manẓūma al-Nasafiyya fi ʾl-khilāfiyyāt*, 2700 *rajaz* verses on the different views of the major Imāms, Berl, 4854/5, Gotha 1150 (where other MSS are listed), Br. Mus. Suppl. 320, Ind. Off. 1779, Garr. 1623/4, Alex. Fiqh Ḥan. 67, Bank. XIX, 1, 1609 = Patna I, $107_{,1081}$.—Commentaries: 1. *Ḥaṣr al-masāʾil wa-qaṣr al-dalāʾil* by ʿAlāʾ al-Dīn b. Muḥammad al-Samarqandī, d. 552/1157, Br. Mus. 229,

Yeni 410, Alex. Fiqh Ḥan. 22.—2. *Ḥuṣūl al-maʾmūl* by Maḥmūd b. Dāʾūd al-Luluʾī al-Bukhārī al-Afshanjī, d. 671/1272 (?), Paris 4570, Cairo ^{1}III, 41, Alex. Fiqh Ḥan. 22, Patna I, 86$_{,872}$.—3. Ibrāhīm b. Aḥmad al-Mawṣilī, d. 652/1254, Paris 4569.—4. *al-Mustaṣfā* by Ḥāfiẓ al-Dīn al-Nasafī, d. 710/1310 (II, 196), Yeni 473, abstract *al-Muṣaffā*, completed in 670, Berl. 4856, Leid. 1787, Paris 4571, Alex. Fiqh Ḥan. 64, Cairo ^{1}III, 131, 275.—5. Muḥammad b. Maḥmūd al-Sadīdī, Yeni 474.—7.–12. see Suppl.—13. *Multaqa ʾl-biḥār* (see Suppl. II, 270$_{,6,3}$), Patna I, 106$_{,1076/7}$ (only here qualified as a commentary).—Supplement: *Khilāfiyyāt al-imām Aḥmad b. Ḥanbal*, 580 *rajaz* verses by ʿAbd al-Raḥmān b. Muḥmammad al-Lakhmī al-Ḥanafī, d. 643/1243 in Cairo (ʿAbd al-Qādir b. Abi ʾl-Wafāʾ, *Jaw.* I, 305), Berl. 4851.

III. *Kitāb al-taysīr fi ʾl-tafsīr*, Qurʾān commentary, Berl. 767/8, AS 94/7, Fātiḥ 236$_{,19}$, Halis 169, 325, 335, 338, Cairo I, 1155, ^{2}42/3.

IV. *al-Akmal wal-aṭwal* (*fī tafsīr al-Qurʾān*) Cairo ^{1}I, 126.

V. *Kitāb zallat al-qāriʾ* Berl. or. oct. 3808, Paris 592$_{,4}$ = *Risāla fī bayān anwāʿ khaṭaʾ al-qāriʾ fi ʾl-ṣalāh*, mistakes that one can make while reading the Qurʾān, Cairo^{1} III, 114.

VI. *Ṭalibat al-ṭalaba* (*fi ʾl-lugha ʿalā alfāẓ kutub fiqh al-Ḥanafiyya*) Br. Mus. Suppl. 275$_{,i}$, Garr. 1625, Yeni 1146, Alex. Lugha 14, = *Sharḥ al-gharīb* Algiers 964.—

VII.–XII. See Suppl (VIII, Alex. Fun. 179$_{,9}$, XI Patna I, 189$_{,1106}$).

XIII. *Taṭwīl al-asfār li-taḥṣīl al-akhbār* see al-Kattānī, *Fihris al-fahāris* I, 215.

XIV. *Risāla fi ʾl-firaq al-islāmiyya*, and an anonymous commentary on it, entitled *Jāmiʿ ikhtilāf al-madhāhib fī kashf al-maqāṣid wal-maʿārib* Qawala I, 165.

551 12. Abu ʾl-Fatḥ Muḥammad b. ʿAbd al-Karīm al-Shahrastānī | was born in Shahrastān in Khurāsān in 469/1077 (or, according to others, in 479) and studied in al-Jurjāniyya and Nishapur, where he spent most of his time studying Ashʿarī dogmatics. In the year 510/1116 he made the pilgrimage to Mecca, after which he stayed for three years in Baghdad. Having returned to his homeland he died at the end of Shaʿbān 548/November 1153.

Ibn Khall. 583, Yāqūt, GW III, 343, Wüst., *Gesch.* 247 1. *Kitāb al-milal wal-niḥal*, composed in 521/1127, MSS see Suppl., Garr. 1605, Alex. Fun. 95$_{,8}$, Patna I, 268$_{,2230/1}$, *Book of religious and philosophical Sects*, ed. W. Cureton, 2 vols. London 1846, print. Būlāq 1261 and others, *Religionspartheien und Philosophenschulen*, transl. Th. Haarbrücker, 2 vols., Halle 1850/1, Turkish transl. by Nūḥ b. Muṣṭafā, d. 1070/1659, Berl. 2804/5, Gotha 82/3, Vienna 976, Upps. 311, cf. *Wiener Jahrb.*
429 LXXI, Anz.-Bl. p. 50; | Persian transl. by Afḍal al-Dīn, made in 843/1439 in

Isfahan, Ind. Off. 1323, by Muṣṭafā Khāliqdād al-Hāshimī, made in 1021/1612 in Lahore, Br. Mus. Pers. I, 139, a Persian commentary in Eton College, cf. Bland, *JRAS* 1844, 104.—2. *Taʾrīkh al-ḥukamāʾ* (*al-falāsifa* ḤKh, [1]II, 2204, [2]I, 291), 2 vols., in the possession of Bland, Persian translation in the possession of Fraser, purchased from the Prince of Oud and taken to India, see Cureton II, p. 11 n. 4.—3. *Kitāb nihāyat al-iqdām fī ʿilm al-kalām*, a lengthy exposition on dogmatics, Berl. 1729, Paris 1246, Bodl. I, 444, Yeni 758, *The Summa Philosophiae of Al-Sh.*, ed. A. Guillaume, Oxford, 1934, see P. Kraus, ZDMG 89, 131/6.—4. *Muṣāraʿat al-falāsifa*, a discussion of 7 metaphysical questions, against Ibn Sīnā, dedicated to Majd al-Dīn Abu ʾl-Qāsim ʿAlī b. Jaʿfar al-Mūsawī, Gotha 1163.—5. See Suppl.

13. Abū Bakr Yaḥyā b. ʿUmar b. Saʿdūn b. Tammām b. Muḥammad al-Azdī al-Qurṭubī, who died in Mosul in 567/1171 (see Suppl.).

Ibn Khall. 767. *Urjūzat al-wildān* or *al-Muqaddima al-qurṭubiyya*, on the 5 pillars of Islam, Br. Mus. 126,$_3$, 862, 1463, 1617, Fez Qar. 1103. Commentaries: a. Aḥmad b. ʿAbdallāh b. Zarrūq al-Fāsī, d. 899/1493 (II, 253), Berl. 1871, Br. Mus. 126,$_3$, 862, Algiers 573.—b. *al-Durra al-bahiyya fī ḥall alfāẓ al-qurṭubiyya* by Muḥammad b. Ibrāhīm b. Khalīl al-Tatāʾī, d. 942/1535 (II, 316), Makram 27.

| 14. Muḥammad b. Abī Bakr Kh(w)āharzāde wrote, around 560/1165: 552

Kitāb al-jawāhir wa-ʿuqūd al-ʿaqāʾid fī funūn al-fawāʾid, in verse, Cairo [2]II, 12, [2]I, 171.

15. Sirāj al-Dīn ʿAlī b. ʿUthmān al-Ūshī al-Farghānī Imām al-Ḥaramayn, fl. ca. 569/1173.

ZDMG 16, 685. I. *al-Qaṣīda al-lāmiyya fi ʾl-tawḥīd*, also called *Badʾ al-amālī* or, from the words with which it begins, *Qaṣīdat yaqūlu ʾl-ʿabd*, creed, MSS see Suppl., AS 4059,$_2$, Alex. Tawḥīd 40, Fun. 195,$_1$, Qawala I, 161, Patna II, 379,$_{2564}$, with a Persian transl. Halet, Ilave 174,$_1$, *Carmen arab. Amali dictum*, ed. P. v. Bohlen, Königsberg 1825.—Commentaries: 1. *al-Hidāya min al-iʿtiqād li-kathrat nafʿ bayna ʾl-ʿibād* by Muḥammad b. Abī Bakr al-Rāzī, d. 660/1262, Berl. 2409/10, Br. Mus. Suppl. 177, Garr. 2003,$_{21}$, 2127,$_3$, Alex. Tawḥīd 47, Cairo [1]II, 60.—2. *Nafīs al-riyāḍ* by Khalīl b. al-ʿAlāʾ al-Bukhārī Gharth al-Dīn, ca. 750/1349, Berl. 2411, Leipz. 872$_{11}$, Alex. Tawḥīd 46, Qawala I, 212.—3. *Daraj al-maʿālī* by Muḥammad b. Jamāʿa, d. 819/1416 (II, 94), Berl. 2412, Gotha 667, Bodl. I, 498,$_2$, Alex. Tawḥīd 16.—4. Muḥammad b. ʿAbd al-Luṭf al-Ṣafawī, d. 928/1522,

Berl. 2413/4.—5. al-Qarabāghī, d. 942/1535, on which glosses by Muṣṭafā b. Yūsuf, Pet. 57.—6. *Ḍaw' al-amālī* by al-Qārī' al-Harawī, d. 1014/1605 (II, 394), composed in 1010/1601 in Mecca, Berl. 2415/8, Paris $1251_{,1}$, $4051_{,4}$, $4282_{,1}$, $6084_{,1}$, Garr. 1555/7, $2100_{,2}$, Alex. Tawḥīd 24, Fun. $86_{,1}$, $102_{,2}$, $109_{,5}$, Qawala I, 202/3, Patna I, $122_{,1228}$, on which anon. glosses *Tuḥfat al-a'ālī* C. 1309.—7. Muḥammad b. Aḥmad al-Nīkūsārī, Berl. 2420.—8. Muṣṭafā b. al-Ḥājj Muḥammad al-Naẓīf, Berl. 2421.—9. Abu 'l-Faḍā'il Wālastī Iftikhār, twelfth cent., Berl. 2422.—10. Sharaf al-Dīn Qāsim al-Ḥanafī, Berl. 7695, Munich 147.—11. *'Iqd al-la'ālī'* by Raḍī al-Dīn Abu 'l-Qāsim b. al-Ḥusayn al-Bakrī, Gotha 668/9, Leid. 2004.—12. Abū Bakr b. Muḥammad b. Aḥmad al-Bustī (? MS al-Istī), Leid. 2005.—13. Muḥammad b. Muḥammad al-Miṣrī, d. 1105/1663 (see Suppl.), Br. Mus. $160_{,2}$.—14. Ibrāhīm al-Tūnisī, ibid. $166_{,1}$.—15. Ibn Kamālpāshā, d. 940/1533 (II, 449), Alex. Tawḥīd 23.—15a. Anon. Berl. 2419, 2423, Leipz. $878_{,1}$, Leid. 2006/7, Algiers $574_{,2}$, Mosul $36_{,175,8}$, $224_{,32,2}$.—16. Turkish by Faḍlallāh, Vienna 469, Pet. 28, Copenhagen, 142,
430 | Upps. 91, Br. Mus. 96, 105.—17. Anon. Turkish, Vienna $1661_{,1}$.—18.–29. See Suppl. (18. Patna I, $15_{,1158}$, 23. Muḥammad b. Muḥammad al-Rafī', Patna II, $512_{,2752}$).—
553 | 30. *al-Nihāya* by Raḍī al-Dīn b. Abi 'l-Qāsim b. Ḥasan al-Bakrī, Patna I, $127_{,1267}$.—31. 'Abd al-Ghanī b. Mawlā Rājī Muḥammad al-'Abbāsī, Patna II, $494_{,2653,7}$.

II. *Kitāb ghurar al-akhbār wa-durar al-ash'ār*, abstract *Niṣāb al-akhbār wa-tadhkirat al-akhyār*, 1000 short traditions in 100 chapters, Berl. 1300/1, Munich 126, Cairo ^{1}I, 444, ^{2}I, 158.

III. See Suppl.

IV. *al-Fatāwi 'l-Sirājiyya*, completed in 569/1173, ḤKh IV, $338_{,8787}$, Ind. Off. $1640_{,2}$, Algiers $1034_{,3}$, Pet. Buch. 689, Buhār II, 168, Bank. XIX, 1, 1674.[8]

16. Shihāb al-Dīn Abu 'l-Ḥasan b. Ibrāhīm al-Ash'arī al-Shāfi'ī, who died around 600/1203.

1. *Ṭurfat al-majālis wa-tuḥfat al-mujālis*, a collection of tales, Br. Mus. 1531, Pet. Rosen 106 (without title).—2. *Kitāb shajarat al-yaqīn wa-taḥlīq nūr sayyid al-mursalīn wa-bayān ḥāl al-khalā'iq yawm al-dīn* Br. Mus. $146_{,16}$ (attributed to Abu 'l-Ḥasan al-Ash'arī in Rieu, Add. 765), falsely attributed to him, is a later concoction, see Suppl. 346.—3., 4. See Suppl.

17. Abu 'l-Baqā' Ṣāliḥ b. al-Ḥusayn al-Ja'farī wrote, in 618/1221:

8 Not to be confused with the work of the same title by al-Shiblī (II, 80).

1. *Kitāb al-bayān al-wāḍiḥ al-mashhūd min faḍāʾiḥ al-Naṣārā wal-Yahūd*, an abstract of his *Takhjīl man ḥarrafa ʾl-Tawriya wal-Injīl*, ḤKh ^{1}II, 249,$_{2636}$, ^{2}I, 379, a refutation of Christianity and Judaism on the occasion of an open letter from the Greek emperor to the Egyptian sultan al-Malik al-Kāmil (615–35/1218–37), de Jong 133, Br. Mus. 864, Bodl. I, 131, 167, II, 569, abstract by Abu ʾl-Fidāʾ al-Suʿūdī, written in 942/1535, Br. Mus. Suppl. 190, cf. Steinschneider, *Polem. u. apolog. Lit.* 36, Spitta, ZDMG 30, 313. *Liber decem quaestionum contra Christianos, auctore Ṣaliḥo ibn al-Ḥusain*, ed. F. Triebs, Diss. Bonn 1897.

17a. Ḥaydar b. Muḥammad b. Zayd b. Muḥammad b. Muḥammad b. ʿUbaydallāh al-Ḥusaynī (Zaydī) wrote, in 631/1233:

Hidāyat al-ghabī al-mutaḥayyir min ḍalālat al-jabrī al-mughawwir autograph Qara Muṣṭafā P. 364 (photograph Ritter).

18. Abu ʾl-ʿAbbās Aḥmad b. Fahd al-ʿAlfī, d. 627/1229.

| *Kitāb al-ʿudda*, on the 99 names of God, Berl. 1527. 554

19. ʿAbd al-ʿAzīz (b. ʿAbdallāh) b. ʿAbd al-Salām b. Abi ʾl-Qāsim Nāṣir al-Ḥaqq Mufti ʾl-Shām wal-Miṣr ʿIzz al-Dīn Abū Muḥammad al-Sulamī Sulṭān al-ʿUlamāʾ, d. 660/1262 (see Suppl., Qalʿat Shaqīf).

Anon., *Manāqib al-shaykh ʿIzz al-Dīn al-Sulamī* Garr. 2083,$_3$, Suyūṭī, *Ḥusn al-muḥ.* I, 141. 1. *Qawāʿid al-sharīʿa al-kubrā* Gotha 948 (?), abstract Leid. 1817.—2. *al-Qawāʿid al-ṣughrā* Gotha 947, Br. Mus. Suppl. 234.—2b. *Qawāʿid al-aḥkām fī maṣāliḥ al-anām* Alex. Fiqh Shāf. 33, Cairo ^{2}I, 533.—3. *Kitāb al-ghāya fi ʾkhtiṣār al-Nihāya*, on the Shāfiʿī *furūʿ*, an abbreviation of the *Nihāyat al-maṭlab* of Imām al-Ḥaramayn, p. 488.—4. *Farāʾid al-fawāʾid wa-taʿāruḍ al-qawlayn li-mujtahid wāḥid*, on the contradictions for which al-Shāfiʿī is criticised, Berl. 4359.—5. *Fatāwī* Berl. 4815, Cairo ^{1}VII, 31, ^{2}I, 527.—6. *Majāz al-Qurʾān* Br. Mus. 834.—| 7. *al-Majāz ilā ḥaqāʾiq al-iʿjāz* Landb. Br. 503.—8. *Kitāb* 431
al-fawāʾid fi ʾkhtiṣār al-maqāṣid, what one has to do and to abstain from in order to obtain one's future reward, Berl. 3013.—9. *Maqāṣid al-ṣalāh*, composed when he was still in Damascus, Paris 1178,$_2$, Esc. ^{2}679,$_4$, 1536,$_4$, Cairo ^{1}VII, 3, ^{2}I, 539, with the title *Risāla fī anna ʾl-maqṣūd bil-ʿibādāt kulliha ʾl-taqarrub ila ʾllāh taʿālā* Kairouan, *Bull. de Corr. Afr.* 1884, p. 184, n. 33.—10. *Kitāb aḥkām al-jihād wa-faḍāʾiluhā*, on religious war, Berl. 4088.—11. *Mulḥat al-iʿtiqād*, an exposition of Ashʿarī dogma and polemic against the Ḥashwiyya sect and other

innovators, Berl. 2080.—12. *Kitāb shajarat al-maʿārif wa-adillat al-aḥkām*, guidance towards a true understanding of God and the duties respecting Him, one's
neighbours, and oneself, Berl. 2304.—13. *Kitāb al-anwāʿ* insights into individual aspects of God's nature, with a commentary, Berl. 2426.—14. *Kitāb bidāyat
al-suʾūl fī tafḍīl al-rasūl* Berl. 2568, Cairo ^{1}I, 400, VII, 3, 41, 685, ^{2}I, 92.—15. *Qiṣṣat
wafāt al-nabī* Berl. 9614.—16. *Kitāb bayān al-aḥkām al-mutaʿalliqa lil-malāʾika
wal-mursalīn*, rules applying to angels, God's messengers, and all believers in
general, Berl. 4787.—17. Answers to 90 legal questions asked of him by ʿAbd
al-Raḥmān b. al-Ṭūsī Shams al-Dīn of Mosul, and dated Cairo 654/1256, Berl.
4986.—18. *Kitāb targhīb ahl al-islām fī sukna ʾl-Shām* Copenhagen 296.—19. 33
555 *wāfir* verses in praise of the Kaʿba, Berl. 6068.—20. *al-Amālī*, | dictations from
various scientific fields, mostly theology, Berl. 294, a fragment of which is, so
it seems, *Fi ʾl-maṣāliḥ wal-mafāsid* ibid. 2634 (but see Suppl. 2).—21. *Masāʾil
al-ṭarīqa fī ʿilm al-ḥaqīqa al-mushtahira bil-sittīn masʾala*, print. C. 1322 together
with Aḥmad al-Dardīr, *Tuḥfat al-ikhwān fī uṣūl wa-ādāb ṭarīq al-qawm*.—22.
Kitāb fi ʾl-farq bayna ʾl-īmān wal-islām Kairouan, *Bull. de Corr. Afr.* 1884, p. 184.—
23. *Fawāʾid fī tafsīr al-Qurʾān* Cairo ^{1}I, 188.—24. *al-Ishāra ila ʾl-iʿjāz fī baʿḍ anwāʿ
majāz al-Qurʾān* Selīm Āġā 1016, print. Istanbul 1311, 1313.—26.–35. see Suppl.
(35. printed in *Jarīdat al-Islām* 1317/1899, p. 86, Sarkis 165).

19a. His son ʿAbd wrote:

Muntaha ʾl-suʾūl fī tafḍīl al-rasūl Pet. AMK 944.

20. Faḍlallāh al-Ḥasan al-Tūrapushtī died in 661/1263. He wrote:

Kitāb maṭlab al-nāsik fī ʿilm al-manāsik, anon. abstract Leid. 1818.

21. ʿIzz al-Dawla Saʿd b. Manṣūr b. Abī Saʿd b. Ḥasan b. Hibatallāh b. Kammūna al-Isrāʾīlī, d. 683/1284, see Suppl.

Collection of his writings from the year 670/9: *al-Lumaʿ al-Juwainiyya fi ʾl-ḥikma al-ʿilmiyya wal-ʿamaliyya* for Ṣāḥib Shams al-Dīn Muḥammad b. al-Ṣāḥib Bahāʾ al-Dīn Muḥammad al-Juwaynī, together with excerpts from al-Bīrūnī's *al-Āthār al-bāqiya*, the *Shamsiyya* by al-Kātibī, *al-Qānūn al-Masʿūdī* and *Kitāb al-hayʾa* by Muʾayyad al-Dīn al-ʿArūḍī in *al-Khizāna al-Gharawiyya*, see *Dharīʿa* II, 296$_{,1157/60}$, excerpts from *al-Iʿtirāḍāt* (Suppl. I, 817$_{,20,c}$) ibid. 1161.—1. excise: Berl. 101.—6. *Risāla fī abadiyyat al-nafs* Rāġib 1482.—8. *al-ʿAqliyyāt*, a *risāla* to the vizier Shams al-Dīn Juwaynī, also Fātiḥ 3141 f. 263a/285b.—9. Correspondence with Najm al-Dawla, also Rāġib 1482.—10. A dogmatic treatise without title, Fātiḥ 3141, 696h, f. 1–262.—11. Answer to the question about the reason for his conversion, ibid. f. 263a/264b.

22. Bahāʾ al-Dīn Abu ʾl-Faḍl Yūsuf b. Yaḥyā b. Muḥammad b. ʿAlī al-Maqdisī al-Dimashqī al-Sulamī, d. 685/1286.

Kitāb ʿiqd al-durar fī akhbār al-imām al-muntaẓar, on the manifestation of the Mahdī, composed in 658/1260 in Damascus on | the occasion of the 556
civil disturbances at the time, Berl. 2723, Gotha 854, Alex. Firaq 8, cf. Wüst. *Gesch.* 346.

| 23. Badr al-Dīn Muḥammad b. Asʿad al-Yamanī al-Tustarī wrote, around 432
700/1300:

(ḤKh v, 597) a brief theological treatise, with the beginning of a commentary, Ind. Off. 433.

Chapter 10. Mysticism

1. Abu 'l-Qāsim ʿAbd al-Karīm b. Hawāzin b. ʿAbd al-Malik b. Ṭalḥa b. Muḥammad al-Qushayrī, d. 465/1072 (see Suppl.).

Ibn Khall. 367, Jāmī, *Nafaḥāt* 354, Flügel, *Wiener Jahrb.* 47, Anz. Bl. p. 3. 1. *Risālat al-Qushayrī*, written in 438/1045, an exposition of the foundations of mysticism, with an introduction describing the lives of famous Sufis and an explanation of their terminology, addressed to Sufis in general, with the aim of giving a boost to mysticism, which had fallen into neglect at the time, Berl. 2822/3, Munich 136, Heid. ZDMG 91, $383_{,7}$, Vienna 1890, Paris 1330, Br. Mus. Suppl. 227, Ind. Off. 598, Bodl. I, 325, Dāmād Ibr. 739 (488h), Köpr. 724 (608h), Murād Mollā 1244 (610h), ʿĀšir I, 460, ʿĀṭif 1403, Esʿad 1435/6, Nafiz 403/4, Hūdāi Taṣ. 661, Sarāi 1385, 1387/90, 1445, Lālelī 1366, Alex. Fun. $96_{,4}$, Qawala I, 240, Patna I, $133_{,1318/20}$, print. Būlāq 1284, see *Not. et Extr.* XII, 321, Allioli, *Denkschr. d. Kgl. Bayr. Ak. d. Wiss. phil. hist. Cl.* 1835, I, 55ff., Merx, *Mystik* 29, Goldziher, *Vorl.* 175.—Abstract by Nuʿmān Pāshā Köprülüzāde, d. 1132/1720, Köpr. II, 121, Persian transl. Br. Mus. Pers. Suppl. no. 16.—Commentaries: a. *Iḥkām al-dalāla ʿalā taḥrīr al-R.* by Zakariyyāʾ al-Anṣārī, d. 926/1520 (II, 99), completed in 893/1488, Berl. 2824, Leid. 1659, Basel M II, 4, Yeni 709/10, AS 1818/20, Halet 224, Šehīd ʿAlī 1237, NO 4, 2429, Sarāi 1386, print. C. 1304, abstract Berl. 2825.—b, c. see Suppl.—*Mukhtaṣar al-R.* by Muḥyi 'l-Dīn b. Muḥammad al-Ḥalabī, composed in 954/1547, Fātiḥ 2823.—Persian transl. AS $2077_{,3}$, Turkish transl. AS 1712.—2. *Kitāb tartīb al-sulūk fī ṭarīq Allāh*, for the beginner in mysticism, Berl. 3262, Bursa Ulu Cami 15, Nafiz 745.—3. *Kitāb al-taḥbīr fī ʿilm al-tadhkīr*, on God's names and their use in prayer, Berl. 3753, Algiers 746, AS 1703, Köpr. 711, Alex. Mawāʿiẓ $40_{,1}$, Cairo ^{1}VII, 243, ^{2}I, 275, extract (*mukhtār*) by Muḥammad
557 b. Abī Bakr | al-Rāzī (p. $478_{,50}$), Paris 1383, Tūnis, Zayt. III, 36, 353, Bursa Ulu Cami Taṣ. 14, anon. *Mukhtaṣar* Alex. Faw. 21 (where *al-takhyīr*).—4. *Istifādāt al-murādāt fī asmāʾ Allāh taʿālā ʿalā wajh al-khāṣṣ* AS 1793.—5. *ʿIqd al-jawāhir wa-nūr al-baṣāʾir fī faḍīlat dhikr al-dhākir* Munich 161 (not in ḤKh, by another al-Qāsim?).—6. *Arbaʿūna ḥadīthan* Berl. 1457?, Garr. 1419.—7. *Laṭāʾif al-ishārāt bi-tafsīr al-Qurʾān*, composed before 410/1019, Yeni 101, Ğārullāh 119, Fātiḥ 640, Faiz. 224, Patna I, $323_{,3210}$.—8. A dogmatic *qaṣīda* Berl. $7619_{,5}$ = *Manthūr al-khiṭāb fī mashhūr al-abwāb* Garr. $2217_{,2}$, AS $4128_{,3}$, Bursa, Ulu Cami, Taṣ. 163f. 151a/b, Alex. Taṣ. 21, with the title *Sharḥ asmāʾ Allāh al-ḥusnā* Kairouan, *Bull. de Corr. Afr.* 1884, p. 190, no. 74.—11. *Bulghat al-maqāṣid* Cairo ^{1}VII, 556.—12. *Kanz al-yawāqīt*, *Br. Mus. Quart.* VI, 97.—13. *al-Fuṣūl fī 'l-uṣūl* Cairo ^{1}VII, 551,

^{2}I, 200.—14.–18. see Suppl. (15. Garr. 1261$_{,16}$, Patna I, 273$_{,2269}$).—19. *al-Uṣūl fī naḥw arbāb al-qulūb al-mustanbaṭ min naḥw arbāb al-ghuyūb* Alex. Taṣ. 6 = *Naḥw al-qulūb* ḤKh 1314, Berl. Ms. or. oct. 3805.—20. *al-Maqāmāt al-thalātha* ʿUm. 3551 (Ritter).

1a. His son ʿAbd al-Raḥīm, d. 514/1120 (see Suppl.).

1. *al-Maqāmāt wal-ādāb* Alex. Taṣ. 46.—2. *al-Shawāhid wal-amthāl*, Sufi sayings that were collected by his father, AS 4128$_{,1}$ (Ritter).

1b. Abu ʾl-Qāsim al-Ḥusayn b. Jaʿfar b. Muḥammad al-Wāʿiẓ al-Maʿrūf bil-Wazzān, who wrote before 484/1091:

Kitāb al-adab, on mystical ethics, AS 2021$_{,2}$.

2. Abū Ismāʿīl ʿAbdallāh b. Muḥammad b. ʿAlī al-Anṣārī al-Harawī, who was born in 396/1005 in Quhandiz and died in Herat in 481/1005 (see Suppl.).

Ibn Rajab, *Ṭab. al-Ḥanābila* (ʿĀšir I, 669) f. 17a (Ritter). Jāmī, *Nafaḥāt* 316, Rieu, *Pers. Cat.* I, 35, de Sacy, *Not. et Extr.* XII, 352, *Grundr. der Ir. Phil.* II, 282, Browne, *Lit. Hist.* II, 269/70. I. *Manāzil al-sāʾirīn*, an overview of Sufism and its developmental stages, to be learned by heart, Berl. 2826/7, Vienna 1891$_{,112,1}$, Br. Mus. 753$_{,1}$, Ind. Off. 599, Cairo ^{1}VII, 556, Garr. 2117$_{,3}$, Patna I, 142$_{,383/4}$.—Commentaries: | 1. ʿAbd al-Razzāq al-Kāshānī, d. 735/1335 (II, 204), completed 558
in 731/1331, Paris 1346, Ind. Off. 600, Bodl. II, 81, Bat. 116$_{,2}$; abstract by ʿAlawī b. ʿAbdallāh, Ind. Off. 601.—2. Explanation of three verses at the end concerning the profession of the unity of God by Yūsuf b. ʿAbdallāh al-Kūrānī, d. 768/1366 (II, 205), Berl. 2831.—3. Supposedly by ʿAfīf al-Dīn Sulaymān b. ʿAlī al-Tilimsānī, d. 690/1291 (p. 300), ibid. 2828, (see ḤKh, VI, 131, 1).—4. Muḥammad b. Ibrāhīm al-Ḥanbalī, d. 971/1563, ibid. 2830 (fragm.).—5. Anonymous, ibid. 2829.—6.–13. see Suppl. 1. (6. Qawala I, 261).—5 other commentaries mentioned in Ahlw. 2831.

II. *Kitāb dhamm (ʿilm) al-kalām*, on metaphysics, Br. Mus. 1571, Dam. ʿUm. 24, 587.

III. *Ṭabaqāt al-ṣūfiyya*, an enlargement of the work by al-Sulamī (p. 218), lies at the basis of the Persian *Nafaḥāt al-uns* by Jāmī, d. 898/1492 (II, 207), ed. Lees, Calcutta 1859, see Rieu, *Pers. Cat.* p. 349.—IV–VIII see Suppl. IX. *Anwār al-taḥqīq fi ʾl-muntakhab min kalimāt Khwāja Harawī*, selected by ʿAlī b. Ṭayfūr al-Bisṭāmī, library of ʿImād al-Fihrisī al-Ṭihrānī in Mashhad, *Dharīʿa* II, 421$_{,1664}$.

3. Abu ʾl-Maʿālī ʿAzīzī b. ʿAbd al-Malik b. Manṣūr al-Jīlī Saydhala, a *faqīh* and *wāʿiẓ* who died in Baghdad on 17 Ṣafar 494/23 December 1100.

Ibn Khall. 391. *Kitāb lawāmiʿ anwār al-qulūb fī jamʿ asrār al-maḥbūb*, on the different levels of mystical love for God, Berl. $3084_{,3}$, Cairo ^{1}IV, 298, see Pines, *Or.* VII, 1938, p. 336ff.

3a. Abu ʾl-Khalīl Aḥmad b. Muḥammad b. ʿAbd al-Malik al-Ashʿarī al-Tabrīzī (see Suppl.).

Sirāj al-qulūb Berl. 3314, Gotha $915_{,3}$, Vienna $1916_{,17}$, Pet. AMK 934, Ğārullāh $1084_{,97a/104b}$, $206_{,135a/6b}$, Cairo ^{2}I, 317, Alex. Fun. $98_{,2}$, Bank. XIII, 959,IV = Patna II, $447_{,2623,4}$.

4. Abū Muḥammad ʿAbdallāh b. al-Qāsim b. al-Muẓaffar b. ʿAlī al-Shahrazūrī al-Murtaḍā was born in Shaʿbān 468/April 1073, studied in Baghdad, became a *qāḍī* in Mosul, and died in Rabīʿ I 511/July 1117.[1]

559 | Ibn Khall. 310. 44 *khafīf* verses of mystical content, Berl. 3404 (mistakenly attributed by Ahlw. to his father al-Qāsim, d. 489/1096, Ibn Khall. 509), in Ibn Khall., loc. cit., and following him in Ulughkhānī, *Hist. of Gujarat*, ed. Ross I, 12/4.

434 | 5. ʿAbd al-Salām b. ʿAbd al-Raḥmān b. Muḥammad al-Ishbīlī al-Lakhmī b. Barrajān, d. 536/1141 in Morocco.

Sharḥ maʿānī asmāʾ Allāh al-ḥusnā Br. Mus. 1612, whence the *Mulakhkhaṣ* of ʿAbd al-Qāhir b. Ibrāhīm b. Muḥammad b. Badr al-Maqdisī, composed in 934/1527, Berl. 2221.—2. *Kitāb tanbīh al-afhām ilā tadabbur al-Kitāb wa-taʿarruf al-āyāt wal-nabaʾ al-ʿaẓīm*, a Sufi Qurʾān commentary, part II, Munich 83.—3. *Tarjumān lisān al-ḥaqq al-mabthūth fi ʾl-amr wal-khulq*, on kabbalah and divination, Paris 2642.

6. Abu ʾl-ʿAbbās Aḥmad b. Muḥammad Mūsā al-Ṣanhājī al-Marī al-Andalusī b. al-ʿIrrīf,[2] who died in 536/1143 in Morocco.

---

1 According to al-Samʿānī in the *Kharīda* of al-Kātib al-Iṣfahānī (384); in Ibn Khall. only after 520/1126.

2 Like this, with a *tashdīd* on the *rāʾ*, Welieddīn 1821 (Ritter).

Ibn Khall. 67, Jāmī, *Nafaḥāt* 615. 1. *Kitāb maḥāsin al-majālis*, an overview of the qualities that are required in a Sufi, Berl. 2834/5, Alex. Fun. 173$_{,7}$, Patna I, 508$_{,2579,4}$, under the title *Majālis al-mujālis* Alex. Mawāʿiẓ 37$_{,3}$, see Horten *Islca* = *AKM* XXIII, 1/17, commentary by Isḥāq b. Daḥḥān, Patna I, 409$_{,2579,5}$.—2. A Sufi poem, Berl. 7685$_{,2}$.

6a. Abu 'l-Qāsim Aḥmad b. Qasī (read thus), see Suppl.

Ibn Ḥajar, *Lisān al-mīzān* I, 247, no. 775 (Ritter).

6b. Here belongs, perhaps, Muḥammad b. ʿAbd al-Raḥmān al-Hamadhānī, see II, 412,3, Suppl. II, 583.

7. Tāj al-Islām Majd al-Dīn al-Ḥusayn b. Naṣr b. Muḥammad al-Kaʿbī b. Khamīs al-Mawṣilī al-Juhanī was born on 20 Muḥarram 460/1 December 1067 in Juhayna, a village in the vicinity and to the south of Mosul, on the same bank of the Tigris. He studied Shāfiʿī law in Baghdad under al-Ghazzālī, became a *qāḍī* in Raḥbat Malik b. Ṭawq on the Euphrates between Raqqa and Baghdad, and subsequently moved to Mosul, dying there in Rabīʿ II 552/May 1157.

| Ibn Khall. 180, Wüst., *Gesch.* 249. *Kitāb manāqib al-abrār wa-maḥāsin al-akhyār*, 560
an imitation of Qushayrī's *Risāla* with a history of the Sufis, Berl. 9980, Bodl. I, 816, Br. Mus. 1285, 1627, Bursa, Haraccizade Ta'r. 20, Cairo ^{1}VII, 672, ^{2}V, 360, Garr. 674, with the title *Ṭabaqāt al-awliyāʾ* Alex. Ta'r. 84 (with the incorrect year of 762).

7a. Sulaymān b. Dā'ūd al-Saqsīnī, see Suppl. I, 776, II, 1010$_{,137}$.

Zahrāt al-riyāḍ also AS 4329, Sarāi 1420, Bursa, Haraccizade Muḥāḍarāt 43 (part II, Ritter).

8. ʿAdī b. Musāfir b. Ismāʿīl al-Umawī al-Shāmī al-Hakkārī was born in Bayt Fār near Baalbek, and the house in which he was born was still a place of pilgrimage at the time of Ibn Khallikān. After extensive travels, during which he befriended some of the most distinguished Sufis of his time, he founded a monastery on the mountain of Hakkār[3] near Mosul where, as a descendant of the Umayyads, he assembled the last representatives of the ultra-Umayyad Yazīdī sect, who lived in those mountainous regions. He died there in 558/1163

3 Cf. *Rachideldin, Histoire des Mongols par* Quatremère I, 328, n. 125.

or 557. The Sufi order of the ʿAdawiyya, which he founded with some of his followers, was still flourishing under the leadership of one of his descendants at the time of Ibn Khallikān.

Ibn Khall. 338, Jāmī, *Nafaḥāt* 617, *Akhbār ʿAlī b. Musāfir b. Marwān al-Umawī* from the *Kitāb al-ḥabashī fī tarājim al-ṣūfiyya wa-akhbārihim wa-ḥikāyātihim wa-manāqibihim* (II, 189) Makram 2, 51, M. Guidi, RSO XIII, 408/14. R. Lescot, *Enquête sur les Yezidis de Syrie et du Djebel Sindjār*, Beirut 1938.—1. *Iʿtiqād ahl*
435 *al-sunna wal-jamāʿa*, a creed, Berl. 1980/1.—| 2. *Waṣāyā*, admonitions to the caliphs, Berl. 3982, to his students ibid. ʾ3.—3. Two Sufi *qaṣīda*s Berl. 3405.—A letter to him by al-Ghazzālī, ʿUm. 3750 (Ritter).

9. Muḥyi ʾl-Dīn ʿAbd al-Qādir b. Abī Ṣāliḥ b. ʿAbdallāh b. Mūsā b. Jandikūst al-Jīlī
561 al-Ḥanbalī al-Zāhidī, | allegedly of ʿAlid stock, was born in Gilan in 471/1078 and studied, from 488/1095 onward, Ḥanbalī *fiqh* in Baghdad. In 521/1127 he started to organise Sufi gatherings and was soon regarded as the greatest Sufi of his time. He was just as certain himself of his own holiness as were the masses whom he succeeded in convincing of it through the miracles (*karāmāt*) he performed. He died on 8 or 9 Ramaḍān 561/9 or 10 July 1167. His teachings live on in the dervish Qādiriyya order, which he founded.

Biographies: 1. *Bahjat al-asrār* by ʿAlī b. Yūsuf b. Jaḥẓam al-Hamdānī al-Shaṭṭanawfī, d. 713/1313 (II, 118), Leipz. 225, Paris 2016,$_{2}$, 2038/9, Ind. Off. 702, Garr. 683/4, ʿĀšir I, 443, Serāi 1379, Patna II, 362, 2442, print. C. 1304.—2. *al-Janī al-dānī fī dhikr nabdha min manāqib ʿAbd al-Qādir al-J.* by Jaʿfar b. Ḥasan al-Barzanjī, d. 1179/1765 (II, 384), Berl. 10064,$_{3}$ Leipz. 268.—3. Anon. AS 2105 (723 h).—4.–20. see Suppl. (6. Patna II, 312,$_{2444}$; 7. Garr. 703, Halet 278, Patna II, 312,$_{2445}$; 8. Fātiḥ 5328,$_{24}$).—21. *ʿIqd al-jawāhir fī manāqib al-shaykh ʿAbd al-Qādir al-J.* by Aḥmad b. ʿAbd al-Qādir, twelfth cent. (Suppl. II, 999,$_{30}$), Alex. Taṣ. 42,$_{2}$, 43.—*Fawāt* II, 2, Jāmī, *Nafaḥāt* 586.—M.ʿA. ʿAynī, *Abd al-Qādir Guilani, Un grand saint de l'islam en collaboration avec* F.J. Simore-Munir, Paris 1938 (*Les grandes figures de l'orient*, VII).

1. *Kitāb al-ghunya li-ṭālibī ṭarīq al-ḥaqq*, a detailed exposition and rationale of the religious and legal prescripts that aim at knowledge of God, Berl. 2836, Leid. 1940, Ind. Off. 617/8, Stewart 141, Yeni 718/9, Wehbī 734, Köpr. 752/3, Garr. 1484, Patna I, 138,$_{1354}$.—2. *Kitāb futūḥ al-ghayb*, rules of conduct for believers, with a Persian paraphrase, probably by the author's son, Berl. 2837/9 (Pers. Cat. 233, print. Lucknow 1880), Leipz. 22, Leid. 2154, Ind. Off. 616, ʿĀšir, 485, III, 134,

Fātiḥ 5388$_{,8}$, 5339, Lālelī 1473, Wehbi 697$_{,1}$, Qaṣīdajī S. Sirrī 321, Hālis 1869, Yildiz 804, 820, 831, 837, ʿUm. 3444, Ḥusāmaddīn 228, Köpr. 761, Cairo ¹VII 37, 181, print. C. 1289, 1304, in the margin of *OB* I, 905.—3. *Kitāb asmāʾ* | *maqāmāt sulūk* 562
al-ṭarīq ila ʾllāh taʿālā Berl. 3690.—4. *Khawāṣṣ al-fātiḥa al-sharīfa* Cairo ¹VII, 523.—5. A collection of short Sufi treatises, Ind. Off. 692.—6. *Jalāʾ al-khāṭir*, a collection of sermons from the years 545/1150 and 546/1151, some given in the madrasa and some in the *ribāṭ* of the Sufis in Baghdad and collected after his death, Ind. Off. 619/21, a part of which Berl. 3986.—7. Collection of 15 sermons (*khuṭab*), Berl. 3401, a continuation *al-Fatḥ al-rabbānī wal-fayḍ al-raḥmānī*, 62 *majālis* from the years 454/6, ibid. ʾ2, Esʿad 1676, Wehbī 702, Hālis 3369, Yildiz 336/7, ʿUm. 3813, 3716, print. Būlāq 1289, C. 1302; *Malfūẓāt al-Qādiriyya* (see Suppl.) Patna I, 142$_{,1382}$ II, 555$_{,2929,4}$.—8. *Waṣiyya, Nuzhat al-khāṭir* to his son and students, Berl. 3984/5, Fātiḥ 5388$_{,8}$.—9. *Ḥikam al-mawāʿiẓ*, translated from the Persian by ʿAlī b. Ḥusām al-Dīn al-Muttaqī, d. 977/1569 (II, 384), Berl. 8680.—10. *al-Asmāʾ al-ʿaẓīma lil-ṭarīqa ila ʾllāh taʿālā*, a Sufi explanation of the 130 chief names of God, of which 7 are understood as *uṣūl* and 6 as *furūʿ*, Berl. 2222, Gotha 96$_{,4}$.—11. *Duʿāʾ fatḥ al-baṣāʾir* Gotha 808, Br. Mus. 125$_{,3}$, Calcutta 697.—12. *Ḥizb al-kabīr al-aʿẓam* Gotha, 808$_{,4}$, 822, another prayer with the same title, Br. Mus. 136$_{,6}$, 844$_{,3}$.—13. *al-Ḥizb al-sharīf wal-wird al-munīf* Vienna 1844$_{,2}$.—14. *Ḥizb bashāʾir al-khayrāt*, | print. Alexandria 1304 (*OB* I, 436
302).—15. *Ḥizb*, a quick prayer, Berl. 3867.—16. A prayer, ibid. 3653.—17. *Awrād*, a pericope prayer, Berl. 3771.—18. *Munājāt*, a prayer, ibid. 3901.—19. Prayers, Copenhagen 52.—20. Five Sufi *qaṣīdas*, Berl. 3406, *al-Qaṣīda al-ghawthiyya* Patna II, 345, 2531$_{,8}$.—21. Edifying poems, partly with *takhmīs*, Berl. 7692/3.—22. *Farīdat asna ʾl-dhakhāʾir wa-lahjat al-nāẓir*, a *muwashshaḥ* on his ascent to the highest sphere, Br. Mus. 887$_{,1}$ (not in Hartmann).—23. *Qaṣīda* on unification with God, ibid. ʾ2.—24. *al-Wasīla*, a short poem, ibid. 98.—25. *al-Risāla al-ghawthiyya*, Alex. Taṣ. 45$_{,5}$.—26.–52. see Suppl. (35. *Kawkab al-mabānī* also Alex. Faw. 16; 37. print. Tunis 1325 in *Majmūʿa* with *Taʿālīq al-tisʿ ṣalawāt*, Patna I, 204$_{,1821}$, with a commentary by Muḥyi ʾl-Dīn Abu ʾl-Faraj Muḥammad Fāḍil ibid. 201$_{,1799}$; 46. *Nuzhat al-khāṭir* Garr. 40, which has Muḥammad Ṣadaqa b. ʿUmar b. Muḥammad b. Muḥammad).—53. *Ḥizb al-wasīla* with the commentary *al-Mawāhib al-jalīla* by Muḥammad al-Amīn al-Kattānī, completed in 1272/1855, in *Majmūʿa*, Tūnis 1325, no. 3.—54. *Qaṣīda min kalām al-Quṭb al-Jīlānī maʿa qaṣāʾid wa-amdāḥ qīlat fīhi min baʿḍ murīdīhi* ibid. 4, Patna II, 555$_{,2929,7}$.—55. *Wird al-bāz al-ashhab* Alex. Faw. 247.—56. *al-Waṣāyā* Patna II,
| 426$_{,2599,25}$.—57. Letters, ibid. 555$_{,2929,2}$ (see 43), 15 letters translated from 563
Arabic into Persian with explanations in Turkish by ʿAlī Ḥusām al-Dīn

al-Muttaqī, Istanbul 1276 (Maṭb. ʿĀmire).—58. Persian *dīwān*, Gr. ir. Phil. $22_{,282}$, ʿAlī Emīrī Fārisī 397, Kanpur 1308/1882.

10 (11). ʿAbd al-Qāhir b. ʿAbdallāh b. Muḥammad b. ʿAbdallāh b. Saʿd al-Suhrawardī Ḍiyāʾ al-Dīn Abu ʾl-Najīb b. ʿAmmūya was a descendant of the caliph Abū Bakr. He was born in Ṣafar 490/January–February 1097, studied Shāfiʿī *fiqh* at the Niẓāmiyya in Baghdad, and worked there from 15 Muḥarram 545/14 May 1150 onwards as Vice-Chancellor. He then turned to Sufism and, after living for a long time in seclusion, built a convent on the western side of Baghdad. Because of the crusaders he was unable to carry out a planned pilgrimage to Jerusalem, but was received with all honours by Nūr al-Dīn Maḥmūd in Damascus. Having returned to Baghdad, he died in Jumādā II 563/March 1168.

Ibn Khall. 366, Jāmī, *Nafaḥāt* 478, 872, Ritter, *Isl.* XXV, 31ff. 1. *Kitāb ādāb al-murīdīn fi ʾl-taṣawwuf* Berl. 3084/5, Paris 1337, 6, Algiers 908, AS 1643, Köpr. 702, Alex. Fun. $87_{,3}$, Patna I, $127_{,1269}$, II, $513_{,2859}$, commentary by al-Qāriʾ al-Harawī (II, 394), d. 1014/1605, Berl. 3086.—2. *Sharḥ al-asmāʾ al-ḥusnā* Vienna $1661_{,11}$, probably pseudepigraphic, see Suppl. p. 783, n.—3. See Suppl.

11. Muḥammad b. Muḥammad al-Burrī, d. 576/1180.

Sirāj al-ʿuqūl ilā minhāj al-wuṣūl AS 1848.

12. ʿAbd al-Raḥmān b. Yūsuf b. ʿAbd al-Raḥmān al-Bijāʾī Abu ʾl-Qāsim Jamāl al-Dīn wrote, in 577/1181:

1. *Quṭb al-ʿārifīn wa-maqāmāt al-abrār wal-aṣfiyāʾ wal-ṣiddīqīn*, a Sufi understanding of God's nature, of the means by which it is possible to get nearer to God by immersion in Him, and to gain paradise through self-improve-
564 ment, Berl. 2840/1, Rabāṭ $519_{,1}$, Alex. Taṣ. $36_{,2}$.—2. *Maḥajjat al-saʿāda* | Alex. Taṣ. $36_{,3}$.—3. *ʿAyn al-ḥaqīqa* ibid. 4.—4. *al-Bustān al-maʿrūf bi-shams al-qulūb* ibid. $36_{,1}$.

12a. Aḥmad b. Abi ʾl-Ḥasan ʿAlī b. Aḥmad b. Yaḥyā b. Rafāʿa al-Rifāʿ, d. 578/1182. (see Suppl.)

Kitāb al-barāhīn Alex. Taṣ. 26.

| 13. Shihāb al-Dīn Yaḥyā b. Ḥabash b. Amīrak[4] al-Suhrawardī studied *fiqh* in Marāgha, and then wandered as a Sufi through Anatolia in the Saljūq empire. There, at the court of Qilič Arslan II, he was able to propagate his doctrine of enlightenment (*Ḥikmat al-ishrāq*) among the young, a doctrine that would continue to have influence well into eighteenth-century Persia amongst the dervish orders of the Ishrāqiyyūn and the Nūrbakhshiyya. Following Ibn Sīnā, he had begun with Aristotle, but then soon turned to Neoplatonic ideas, which he amalgamated with hermetic, gnostic, and Neopythagorean elements. At the centre of his doctrine was his appreciation of light, which was not regarded, as it was by Ibn Sīnā and other philosophers, as the symbol of emanation, but rather as the nature of all existence, and from which he even deduced his proof of the existence of God. With these gnostic teachings he connected the Shīʿī dogma of the hidden Imām. Passing through Baghdad, he arrived at Aleppo in 579/1183 where he was initially well received by the local ruler Bahāʾ al-Dīn, the son of Ṣalāḥ al-Dīn. However, it was not long before his teachings raised the suspicions of the orthodox, who denounced him to Ṣalāḥ al-Dīn, accusing him of propagating Qarmaṭian sentiments. At the latter's order, Bahāʾ al-Dīn had him executed in 587/1191. Through his still-extant tomb, his memory as *al-Shaykh al-maqtūl* lives on, even to the present day. 437

| Ibn Abī Uṣ. II, 167/71$_{,b}$, Khall. 784, al-Qazwīnī, *Kosmol.* 383, Jāmī, *Nafaḥāt* 683, A. v. Kremer, *Gesch. der herrsch. Ideen* 89ff., S. van den Bergh, *EI* IV, 547/8, H. Corbin, *S. d'Alep (± 1191) fondateur de la doctrine illuminative (Ishrāqī)*, Publ. de la Soc d'Études Iran. no. 16, Paris 1939. 1. *Ḥikmat al-ishrāq*, completed in 582/1186, Vienna 1521, Leid. 1498, Br. Mus. 427, Bodl. I, 461, Taymūr Ḥikma 94.—Commentaries: a. Maḥmūd b. Masʿūd al-Shīrāzī, d. 710/1310 (II, 211), Leid. 1499/1501, Paris 2349, Köpr. 881, Alex. Fun. 131$_{,9}$, Patna I, 212$_{,1895/6}$, glosses by Ṣadr al-Dīn Muḥammad b. Ibrāhīm al-Shīrāzī (II, 413), Patna I, 209$_{,1863}$.—b. Muḥammad b. Maḥmūd al-Shahrazūrī, Yeni 767.—c. Persian by Muḥammad Sharīf b. Niẓām al-Dīn Aḥmad al-Harawī, Berl. 5062.—2. *Kitāb al-talwīḥāt*, on logic, physics, metaphysics, from his early, peripatetic period, Berl. 5062, Taymūr Ḥikma 119/20, 130 (only physics and metaphysics), Zanjān, *Lughat al-ʿArab* VI, 93, Patna II, 456$_{,263,4}$.—Commentaries: a. Self-commentary Yeni 765.—b. Saʿd b. Manṣūr b. Kammūna al-Isrāʾīlī (p. 555), completed in 667/1268, 565

4 Ibn Abī ʿUṣaybiʿa calls him, loc. cit., Abū Ḥafṣ ʿUmar … (the name of the father was already missing in the copy used by Ibn Khallikān), apparently because of a confusion with the younger Shihāb al-Dīn al-Suhrawardī (no. 22). In catalogues, too, the two are not always clearly separated, which is why the above inventories of their writings may not be entirely without mistakes either.

Vienna 1531, Leid. 1496, Yeni 766, Br. Mus. Or. 7728 (DL. 12), Taymūr Ḥikma 92 (only part 2), Patna I, $212_{,1812/4}$.—3. *Kitāb al-mashāriʿ wal-muṭāraḥāt*, propa-
438 deutics to the foregoing, | Cambr. p. 84, Leid. 1502, Yeni 775/6, Cairo ^{1}VI, 105 ^{2}I, 257, Zanjān loc. cit.—4. *Kitāb al-lamaḥāt fi 'l-ḥaqā'iq*, on logic, physics, and metaphysics, Leid. 1503, Alex. Ḥikma 20.—5. *Kitāb hayākil al-nūr*, on mysticism, commentaries: a. *Shawākil al-ḥūr* by Muḥammad al-Dawwānī, d. 907/1501 (II, 217), Gotha, $87_{,10}$, Vienna 1895, Leid. 1504/5, Ind. Off. $485_{,1032}$, Pet. $86_{,1}$, Esc. ^{2}706, Alex. Fals. 15, Cairo ^{1}VI, 99, ^{2}I, 253, Ṭalʿat (Dār al-kutub al-miṣriyya) Ḥikma 359, Taymūr Ḥikma 15/6, Calcutta 832, Patna I, $213_{,1901/3}$ II, $410_{,2579,19}$, glosses by Mīr Zāhid b. Qāḍī Aslam al-Harawī (Suppl. II, $621_{,20}$), Patna I, $211_{,1877}$.—b. *Ibrāq H. al-n. li-kashf ẓulumāt shawākil al-ḥūr* by Ghiyāth al-Dīn Manṣūr al-Ḥusaynī, d. 949/1542 (II, 414), Leid. 1506, Rāġib $1478_{,2,3}$, under the title *Ishrāq H. al-n ʿan ẓulumāt shawākil al-ghurūr*, MS in the possession of the author of the *Dharīʿa* II, $103_{,404}$.—6. *al-Alwāḥ al-ʿimādiyya*, a work he wrote when he was still quite young, composed on the order of ʿImād al-Dīn Qara Arslān Dā'ūd b. Artuq, on the limits of finitude, the absolute, the properties of God and the nature of the soul, Berl. 1738, Leipz. $261_{,2}$, Upps. $393_{,10}$.—7. *Maqāmāt al-Ṣūfiyya wa-maʿānī muṣṭalaḥātihim* Br. Mus. $1349_{,23}$.—8. *Kitāb al-munājāt* Cairo VII, 624, ^{2}I, 207, commentary by Muḥammad al-Isfarā'inī, Cairo ^{1}VII, 625.—9. *al-Arbaʿūn ism al-Idrīsiyya*, the effects of God's names,
566 Berl. 4143, | Cairo ^{1}VII, 299, with a commentary Gotha 717 (attributed to the younger al-Suhrawardī), Paris 2644, Br. Mus. $105_{,8}$, $175_{,4}$, Jakarta $28_{,2}$.—10. A mystical poem, Br. Mus. $886_{,1}$.—11. Samples of poetry, Berl. $7699_{,2}$.—14.–34. see Suppl. (14. Taymūr, Ḥikma 189; 17. *Le Familier des amants, trad. fr. avec introd. par* H. Corbin, *Recherches phil. II*, 1932/3, 371/423; 21. Three treatises ed. and transl. by O. Spies and S.K. Khattas, Stuttgart 1935, trad. fr. Deux épîtres mystiques de S. d'A. par H. Corbin, Ėpître de la modulation de Simourgh et Épître de la langue des fourmis, in *Revue Hermes III*, 1939; 25 = 30, original title 25; 28. Gotha $914_{,5}$ see ḤKh V, $209_{,1720}$.—29. See Gunzbourg, *Les mss. ar. de l'inst. d. I. or. St. Pétersbourg* 1891, no. 230, Corbin p. 46).

13a. Muḥammad b. Ibrāhīm b. Aḥmad al-Bustī wrote, before 589/1193 (the date of the MS):

Al-Riʿāya bi-waṣiyyat al-murīdīn fī makārim al-akhlāq Bursa Haraccizade Taṣ. 17 (Ritter).

14. Abu 'l-Qāsim ʿAbd al-Raḥmān b. Abi 'l-Ḥajjāj al-Naḥḥās completed, in 599/1202:

Shams al-qulūb Alex. Taṣ. 22.

14a. *Wasīlat al-muta'abbidīn* Patna I, 274,$_{2281/6}$.

15. al-Ghawth Abū Madyan Shu'ayb b. al-Ḥasan al-Maghribī al-Andalusī al-Tilimsānī, d. 598/1193 (see Suppl.).

Jāmī, *Nafaḥāt* 612. 1. *'Aqīda* Berl. 1892/4.—Commentaries: a. Shams al-Dīn Muḥammad b. Abi 'l-Luṭf, composed in 957/1550, Cairo ¹VII, 618.—b. *al-Qawl al-abyan* by 'Abd al-Ghanī al-Nābulusī (II, 345) also Heid., ZDMG 91, 382, Alex. Fun. 90,$_{15}$.—2. *Ḥikam*, aphorisms, a part of which Berl. 8682 (different from *Ḥikam mufīda* Cairo ¹VII, 228 ?).—Commentaries: a. Aḥmad b. Ibrāhīm b. 'Allān al-Naqshbandī, d. 1033/1624, Berl. 8681.—b. *al-Asrār al-khafiyya al-muwaṣṣila ila 'l-ḥaḍra al-'aliyya* by 'Alī b. Ḥijāzī al-Bayyūmī, d. 1183/1769 (II, 351), Gotha 1228.—3. Shihāb al-Dīn Aḥmad b. 'Abd al-Qādir, *al-Bayān wal-mazīd*, a commentary on the mystical tradition of the A.M., C. 1306.—4. *al-Istighfāra*, a *qaṣīda*, each verse of which starts with *astaghfiru*, Berl. 3940,$_{1}$, Gotha 2254,$_{2}$, 2258, Bodl. I, 9,$_{4,5}$, II, 566,$_{6}$.—5. *Takhmīs* thereon and various *qaṣīdas*, Berl. 7700.—6. | Four *basīṭ* verses, an admonition to patience and faith, Berl. 3987.— 567
7. *Bidāyat al-murīdīn*, on the spiritual life, recorded by one of his students, Algiers 938.—8. *Uns al-waḥīd*[5] *wa-nuzhat al-murīd*, a moral piece, Paris 2405,$_{8}$.—10.–17. See Suppl. (10. Alex. Taṣ. 41,$_{3}$, 13. ibid. 145,$_{1}$).

16. Ḍiyā' al-Dīn Abū 'Umar (Abū Yāsir) 'Ammār b. Muḥammad b. 'Ammār al-Bidlīsī wrote, around 590/1194:

| 1. *Kitāb bahjat al-ṭā'ifa*, a Sufi work, Berl. 2842.—2. *Kitāb ṣawm al-qulūb*, on the 439
purification of the heart, ibid. 3133.

16a. Abū 'Abdallāh al-Qurayshī al-Hāshimī al-Andalusī, d. 599/1203.

Ahlw. 8471 f. 148b. *Al-Ishārāt*, selection Welīeddīn 1821, whence *Lisān al-qawm* Rāmpūr I, 328,$_{34}$, (Suppl. II, 906,$_{9}$).

17. Abu 'l-Faḍl 'Abd al-Mun'im b. 'Umar b. 'Abdallāh b. Ḥassān al-Ghassānī al-Andalusī al-Jilyānī, who was born in 531/1136 in Jilyāna, near Guadix and Granada, settled as a pharmacist in Damascus, dying there in 602/1205.

5 In Ahlw. 2478,$_{5}$ *Uss al-tawḥīd*, which is why it ended up in the wrong category.

Ibn Abī Uṣ. II, 157, *Fawāt* II, 16, Hartmann, *Muw.* 20. 1. *Kitāb adab al-sulūk*, a manual on mysticism, composed in 562–80/1167–84, Berl. 3360/1, selections in Gotha 883.—2. *Manādiḥ al-mamādiḥ wa-rawḍat al-maʾāthir wal-mafākhir min* (*fī*) *khaṣāʾiṣ al-Malik al-Nāṣir*, dedicated to Ṣalāḥ al-Dīn, in verse and rhymed prose, Gotha 2259, ca. 569/1173 = *Manār al-mamādiḥ*, composed in 583/1187 on the occasion of the festivities surounding the capture of Jerusalem, ḤKh VI, 12912?—3. *Dīwān al-dībāj*, a collection of poems in the form of trees, intersecting circles, chessboards, pillars etc., in praise of Ṣalāḥ al-Dīn, when he resided in Jerusalem in 588/1192, Paris 3140, Upps. 142.—4. *Dīwān al-ḥikam wa-maydān al-kalim* Br. Mus. 606.

18. Sharaf b. Muʾayyad b. Abi ʾl-Fatḥ al-Baghdādī Majd al-Dīn Abū Saʿīd al-Ḥanafī, who was the son of a physician who had been sent by the caliph of Baghdad
568 to the Khwārizmshāh.[6] When he started preaching in Khwārizm | he gained the favour of the mother of Sultan Muḥammad. His enemies denigrated him to the sultan, saying that he had married her, so the former had him drowned in 606/1209 (according to others this happened in 616/1219).[7] His wife had him buried Nishapur, from where his relics were transferred to Isfaraʾīn in 833/1429.

Jāmī, *Nafaḥāt* 487, Khwānsārī, *Rawḍāt al-j.* 630/19. *Kitāb* (*Tuḥfat*) *al-barara fī ajwibat al-masāʾil al-ʿashara* ḤKh II, 224,$_{2561}$, ^{2}I, 364, answers to 10 Sufi questions posed by his student Aḥmad b. ʿAlī al-Khuwārī, Berl. 3088 (wrongly: composed around 650/1252), AS 1697; chapter 6 preserved in Vienna 1892,$_3$.

19. Rukn al-Dīn Abū Ḥāmid Muḥammad b. Muḥammad b. al-ʿAmīdī al-Samarqandī, who died in Bukhārā in 615/1218.

440 | Ibn Khall. 575, Ibn Quṭl. 171. 1. *Ḥawḍ* (*Mirʾāt*) *al-ḥayāt* (*ḥayāt al-maʿānī fī idrāk al-ʿālam al-insānī*), on the microcosm's dependence on the macrocosm and the parallels between the two, an Arabic adaptation of the Indian Amṛtakuṇda by Bahučara (?) Brahman Yogi, cf. de Guignes, *Mém. de l'Ac. des Inscr.* XXVI, 791, Gildemeister, *Script. ar. de rebus Ind.* p. 115, W. Pertsch in *Festgruss an Roth* p. 209/12, Paris 773,$_2$, NO 2548,$_2$, Alex. Fun. 151,$_{10}$, revision by Ibn al-ʿArabī, see no. 23.—2. *Kitāb al-ṭarīqa al-ʿAmīdiyya fi ʾl-khilāf wal-jadal* Cairo ^{1}IV, 79.—3. *Kitāb al-irshād*, a handbook on the art of disputation, Esc. ^{2},650,$_2$.

6 According to others his *nisba* came from Baghdādān, a village in Kwārizm.

7 Surely not in the Tigris, as stated by Jāmī.

20. Najm al-Dīn Abu ʾl-Jamāl Abu ʾl-Jannāb Aḥmad b. ʿUmar b. Muḥammad al-Kubrā al-Khiwaqī, the founder of the Kubrawiyya order, who died in 618/1221 (see Suppl.).

Abulghazi Shajaraʾi Türkī, ed. Romanzoff, Kazan, 1825, $58_{,8}$ (on his relation with Khwārizmshāh Muḥammad $65_{,3}$ ff. Čingizkhān's sons offer to rescue him from Bukhārā)—1. *Fawātiḥ al-jamāl wa-fawāʾiḥ al-jalāl*, a Sufi work, Vienna 1897.—2. *Risālat al-khāʾif al-hāʾim min lawmat al-lāʾim*, on the 10 ways in which one achieves corporeal and spiritual purity so that one may approach God, Berl. 3087, Paris $1343_{,2}$.—3. *Risāla fi ʾl-ṭuruq*, on the ways to God, Berl. 3272/3, under the title *Aqrab al-ṭuruq* Alex Fun. | $193_{,9}$, Patna II, $447_{,2623,3}$.—4. *Risāla fī ʿilm* 569
al-sulūk, an explanation of the technical terminology of the Sufis, Berl. 3456, Alex. Fun. $86_{,4}$, $151_{,10}$ (*fi ʾl-ṭarīq ila ʾllāh*).—5. A digest of the lives of the Sufis, Br. Mus. $886_{,1}$.

20a. Fakhr al-Dīn Abū ʿAbdallāh Muḥammad b. Ibrāhīm b. Ṭāhir al-Fīrūzābādī (al-Khabarī?), d. 622/1225 (see Suppl.).

Ibn Ḥajar, *Lisān al-mīzān* V, 29, no. 107. 6. *Dalālat al-mustanhij ilā maʿālim al-maʿārif wa-risālat al-mustabhij ilā ʿawālim al-ʿawārif* AS 1785, Sarāi 1544 (composed in 590 AH, Ritter).

21. Abū Muḥammad ʿAbd al-Salām b. Mashīsh (Bashīsh) b. Abī Bakr b. Aḥmad b. Khurma al-Ḥasanī al-Idrīsī al-Kāmilī, who died in 625/1228 and was buried in the Jabal al-ʿAlam near Wazzān (see Suppl.).

ʿAbdallāh Gannūn, *al-Nubūgh al-maghribī fi ʾl-adab al-ʿarabī* I, 83/5. *Iʿānat al-rāghibīn wal-salām ʿalā afḍal al-mursalīn*, a prayer for the Prophet, Qawala I, 249, as *Risāla fi ʾl-ṣalāt ʿalā ʾl-nabī* Patna II, $443_{,2620,3}$.—Commentaries: 1. Muḥammad b. ʿAlī al-Kharrūbī al-Ṭarābulusī, d. 963/1556 (Suppl. II, 701), Berl. 3912, Alex. Fun. 19.—2. *al-Lamaḥāt al-rāfiʿāt lil-tadhīsh ʿan maʿānī ṣalāt b. M.* by Muṣṭafā b. Kamāl al-Dīn al-Bakrī, d. 1162/1749, Berl. 3913.—2a.–12. see Suppl. (4. *al-Nafaḥāt al-qudsiyya* Alex. Faw. 29; 6. ibid. 4).

22. Shihāb al-Dīn Abū ʿAbdallāh Abū Ḥafṣ ʿUmar b. Muḥammad b. ʿAbdallāh b. ʿAmmūya al-Suhrawardī, who died in Baghdad in 632/1234 (see Suppl.).

Ibn Khall. 468, Jāmī, *Nafaḥāt* 544, H. Ritter, *Isl.* XXIV, 36ff. 1. *Kitāb ʿawārif al-maʿārif*, on mysticism, Berl. 2845/7, Vienna 1896, Paris 1332, 4799, Ind. Off. 625/7 Algiers 909, Garr. 1573, Yeni 716/7, Bursa Orkhan Taş. 35, Ulu Cami $64_{,2}$,

Qawala I, 254, Patna I, $137_{,1350/3}$, printed in the margin of al-Ghazzālī's *Iḥyāʾ*, Būlāq 1289, anon. comm. *Dhawārif al-laṭāʾif* Patna I, $132_{,1307}$.—Abstracts by Muḥammad b. ʿAbdallāh al-Ṭabarī, d. 694/1295, Br. Mus. $884_{,1}$, and by Aḥmad al-Ḥārithī al-Zubaydī, d. 945/1538, Cairo ^{1}II, 138.—Persian transl. Berl. Pers. 38, 251/2, cf. de Sacy, *Not. et Extr.* XII, 322/52, 377ff; Persian comm. Cambr. (Browne) XXVIII.—2. *Kashf al-faḍāʾiḥ al-yūnāniyya wa-rashf al-naṣāʾiḥ al-īmāniyya*, a polemical tract defending Islam against the study of Greek philosophy, ded-
570 icated to the caliph | al-Nāṣir, whom he repeatedly cites as an authority on *ḥadīth*, Berl. 2078, Vienna 1667, Gotha 857, Bursa Ulu Cami Taṣ $95_{,1}$ (a piece from *Sunūḥ al-futūḥ* see no. 37), cf. Hammer, *Wiener Jahrb.* LXXX, *Anz. Bl.* p. 46, no. 267 (who mistakenly attributes the work to the older Suhrawardī, no. 14), A. v. Kremer, *Ideen* 99; Persian transl. Br. Mus. Pers. II, 853a.—3. *Kitāb*
441 *iʿlām al-hudā wa-ʿaqīdat arbāb al-tuqā*, | composed in Mecca, Berl. 1742, Cairo ^{1}VII, 554, ^{2}I, 164, 267, Patna I, $113_{,1136}$.—4. *Nughbat al-bayān fī tafsīr al-Qurʾān* Cairo ^{1}I, 219, ^{2}I, 65.—5. *Risāla fi ʾl-faqr*, on poverty and abnegation, decrees regarding what the Sufi should beware of, Berl. 3141/2.—6. *Fī ghurar al-khalq wa-istidrājihim*, on misconceptions people have about themselves and their relationship with God, Berl. 3168.—7. Fragment of a treatise on how to become a Sufi, for which guidance by an experienced master over many years is said to be needed, and a polemic against the superficial conception of this relationship by his contemporaries, Berl. 3178.—8. *Kitāb al-raḥīq al-makhtūm li-dhawi ʾl-ʿuqūl wal-fuhūm*, on the various states through which the soul must pass in order to achieve a proper understanding of God, Berl. 3302/3.—9. Sufi contemplations of Muḥammad's use of the expression 'moves', Berl. 3304 = *Risālat al-sayr wal-ṭayr* Cairo ^{1}VII, 370, Bursa Ulu Cami Taṣ. $65_{,5}$.—10. *Maqāmāt al-ʿārifīn*, the stations of the Sufis on their approach to God, Berl. 3305, with the title *al-Bāriqāt al-ilāhiyya* Patna II, $460_{,6335}$.—11. Answers to 18 Sufi questions by an imām from Khurāsān, Berl. 3476, Bursa Ulu Cami Taṣ. $65_{,6}$.—12. On *dhikr* as a means to godliness, ibid. 3691.—13. *Kitāb al-awrād*, a Persian prayer book, with the commentary *Kanz al-ʿibād* by ʿAlī b. Aḥmad al-Ghūrī, Ind. Off. 363/4, Patna I, $156_{,1487/8}$.—14. A treatise on asceticism, ibid. $1038_{,6}$.—15. *Risāla fī iʿtiqād al-ḥukamāʾ* Paris $1247_{,3}$ (by the older al-S.?).—16. *Risāla fī lubs al-khirqa* Pet. AM 147.—17. *Waṣiyya*, to his son ʿImād al-Dīn, warning against the Sufis, Munich 895, fol. 65, Leid. 2161, Br. Mus. $644_{,4}$, Suppl. $237_{,4}$, Ind. Off. 1038_{xiv}, Esc. $^2707_{,16}$.—18. *Waṣiyya*, to a Sufi, Berl. 3991/2 Patna $444_{,2621,2}$, with anon. comm. according to ḤKh I, 482 (cf. VII, 582) by Asad b. Aḥmad al-Burūsāwī, Berl. 3993.—19. Two admonitions, ibid. 3994.—22.–34. see Suppl. (26. Comm. also Alex. Taṣ. 16, Qawala I, 229.—24. Read: Jurayrī [Ritter].—31. *Īḍālat etc.* Bursa Ulu Cami Taṣ $65_{,4}$.—32. *Irshād al-murīdīn wa-injād al-ṭālibīn* also Patna II, $514_{,2761}$).—35. *Risāla fi ʾl-taṣawwuf* Patna I, $244_{,2529,3}$.—36. *al-Rawḍa*

ibid. | $391_{,2569,19}$.—37. *Sunūḥ al-futūḥ bi-dhikr al-rūḥ* (see no. 2) ibid. $417_{,2586,5}$.— 571
38. *Shams asrār anwār al-ilāhiyya* ibid. 7.—39. *al-Qawl al-mukhtaṣar fī akhbār al-Mahdī al-muntaẓar* ibid. 8.—40. *Nisbat ṣuḥbatihi*, listing his shaykhs, Bursa Ulu Cami Taş. 65, 9.

23. Muḥyi ʾl-Dīn Abū ʿAbdallāh Muḥammad b. ʿAlī b. Muḥammad b. (al-) ʿArabī al-Ḥātimī al-Ṭāʾī al-Shaykh al-Akbar was born in Murcia on 17 Ramaḍān 560/28 July 1165, started his studies in 568/1172 in Seville, and continued them in Ceuta. In these locations he learnt *ḥadīth* and *fiqh* according to the Ẓāhirī school. After a stay in Tunis, he went to the Hijaz in 598/1201, and then, by way of Baghdad and Mosul, to Asia Minor. In the field of mysticism he had already explored the teachings of Ibn Masarra in his homeland; later he surrendered himself completely to the teachings of the Qarmaṭians that had been spread there by Ibn Barrajān and Ibn al-ʿIrrīf, leading to victory the pantheistic strand of mysticism that they had started, through his numerous writings. He died in Damascus on 26 Rabīʿ II 638/16 November 1240.

Maqqarī I, 567/82, *Fawāt* II, 241, Jāmī, *Nafaḥāt* 428, 633f, *al-Durr al-thamīn etc.* (see Suppl.) also Patna II, 411, $2580_{,5}$, $539_{,2903}$. ʿAbd al-Ḥayy al-Kattānī, *Fihris* I, 233/5, Muḥammad Rajab Ḥilmī (supposedly one of his descendants) *al-Burhān al-azhar fī manāqib al-shaykh al-akbar*, C. 1326. Haneberg, *Munich Gel. Anz.* XXXVIII, 361, A. v. Kremer, *Ideen* 102ff., Goldziher, *Ẓāhir*. 185, | general descrip- 442
tion Ahlw. 2848. A.E. ʿAfīfī, *The mystical Philosophy of M. b. al-A.* Cambridge 1939.—Inventory of his writings, by himself, Cairo ^{1}VII, 378 = 379 and? 45 treatises Nafiz 685. 1. *Ijāza lil-Malik al-Muẓaffar Bahāʾ al-Dīn Ghāzī al-Malik al-ʿĀdil fī jamīʿ mā rawā ʿan ashyākhihi wa-mā lahu min nathr wa-naẓm*, issued in Damascus in 632/1234, with the titles of 298 treatises, Berl. 147/8.—2. Didactic letter to his students, ibid. 149.—3. (*Kitāb al-Tafsīr*, in reality by al-Kāshānī, d. 730/1330?, II, 204, see Suppl. but here I, 527, Berl. 808).—4. *Kitāb al-ʿaẓama*, commentary on sura 1, Berl. 2911/2, Ind. Off. 693 ii, Ğārullāh 1080, Cairo ^{1}VII 14, 369, abstract Ind. Off. 658.—5. (6.) *Kitāb mishkāt al-anwār fī mā ruwiya ʿani ʾllāh subḥānahu min al-akhbār*, 40 = 21 traditions, collected | in Mecca in 599/1202, 572
Berl. 1469, Ind. Off. $658_{,6}$, Br. Mus. $918_{,14}$, Upps. $393_{,1}$.—6. (7.) Enlargement of the previous work to 101 traditions, *al-Aḥādīth al-qudsiyya*, Gotha $3_{,5}$, $64_{,2}$, $564_{,2}$, from which were taken *al-Arbaʿūna, ṣaḥīfa min al-aḥādīth al-qudsiyya* Cairo ^{1}I, 262 = II, $232_{,6}$?—7. (8.) *Tadhkirat al-khawāṣṣ wa-ʿaqīdat ahl al-ikhtiṣāṣ* Berl. 2899, Vienna $1993_{,24}$, Paris $1338_{,2}$, Gotha 670, Persian ibid. 51.—8. (9.) *Risālat al-ʿulūm min ʿaqāʾid ʿulamāʾ al-rusūm*, abstract, Esc. $^2417_{,4}$.—9. (10.) *Ṣayḥat al-būm bi-ḥawādith al-Rūm*, 143 *basīṭ* verses on the Last Judgement, Berl. 2743, Paris $2669_{,11}$, see Suppl. 146b.—10. (11.) *al-Futūḥāt al-Makkiyya fī maʿrifat*

al-asrār al-malakiyya, begun during his sojourn in Mecca in 598/1201 and completed in Ṣafar 629/end 1231 (see Suppl.), Berl. 2856/73, Gotha 884 (where other MSS are listed), Br. Mus. Suppl. 231. Qawala I, 255, Patna I, 139$_{,1356/60}$.—Commentaries: a. ʿAbd al-Karīm al-Kīlānī, d. 838/1428 (II, 208), Berl. 2874, Ind. Off. 693 (to chapter 559), Halet 271, Patna II, 409$_{,579,10}$.—b. Discussion of the question whether the beginning of the *Futūḥāt* is heretical or not, by ʿAlī b. Aḥmad al-Ashʿarī, d. 1084/1673, ibid. 2875.—abstract *Lawāqiḥ al-anwār al-qudsiyya fī bayān qawāʿid al-ṣūfiyya* by ʿAbd al-Wahhāb al-Shaʿrānī, d. 973/1565 (II, 336), Berl. 3046, Leipz. 229, cf. Gotha 885.—11. (12.) *Fuṣūṣ al-ḥikam*, the nature and significance of the 27 major prophets, composed in 627/1230 in Damascus after an appearance by the Prophet, Berl. 2876/7, Gotha 888, Vienna 1898, Krafft 494, Paris 1340/1, Ind. Off. 645/6, Bodl. I, 170, Algiers 910/1, Qawala I, 255, Patna I, 139$_{,1305,5}$ printed with Turkish commentary by ʿĀrifallāh, Būlāq 1252, Istanbul 1897.—Commentaries: a. Self-commentary *Miftāḥ F. al-ḥ.* Alex. Adab 132$_{,2}$.—b. *Fukūk al-F.* by his student al-Qūnawī (no. 32), Berl. 2878/9, Halet 259, Cairo [1]VII, 382, Patna I, 135$_{,1336}$.—bb. ʿAfīf al-Dīn Sulaymān b. ʿAlī al-Tilimsānī, d. 690/1291 (p. 300), Patna II, 410$_{,2579,22}$.—c. Muʾayyad al-Dīn b. Maḥmūd al-Janadī, a student of al-Qūnawī (no. 38), Berl. 2880, Halet 261, Nāfiz 238, Yaḥyā 2231.—d. ʿAbd al-Razzāq b. Abi ʾl-Faḍāʾil Muḥammad al-Qāshānī, d. 730/1330 (II, 204), composed in 730/1330, Paris 1342, Algiers 912, Nāfiz 539/40, Halet ʿIlāve 52, NO 2457, Patna I, 126$_{,1338}$, lith. C. 1309.—e. *Muṭṭalaʿ khuṣūṣ al-kalim* by Dāʾūd b. Maḥmūd al-Qayṣarī, d. 751/1350 (II, 213), Berl. 2881/2, or. oct. 3737 (autograph dated 752 AH), Vienna 1899, Pet. 52, Algiers 913, Yeni 714, Cairo [1]II, 110, VII, 16/7, Patna I, 136$_{,1339}$, II, 514$_{,2764}$.—f. Arabic and Persian by ʿAlī b.
573 Shihāb al-Dīn al-Ḥusaynī al-Hamadhānī, d. 786/1384 (Khwandamīr, | *Ḥabīb, al-siyar* III, 3, 87), Br. Mus. 890$_{,5}$, Suppl. 233, Pers. II, 836b.—g. ʿAbd al-Karīm al-Jīlī, ca. 820/1417, Halet 257, NO 2456.—h. *Naqd al-nuṣūṣ* by ʿAbd al-Raḥmān b. Aḥmad al-Jāmī, d. 898/1492 (II, 207), Berl. 2883, Ind. Off. 647/8, Nāfiz 536, ʿĀšir II, 163, Patna I, 136$_{,1341/2}$, II, 489$_{,2630,8}$.—i. Bālī Khalīfa al-Ṣūfiyawī, d. 960/1553, Berl. 2884, in Qawala I, 247 Muṣṭafā b. Sulaymān Bālīzāde (II 435).—j. ʿAlī b. Muḥammad al-Qasṭamūnī, composed in 1080/1670 in Skutari, Berl. 2885, Vienna 1901.—k. *Jawāhir al-nuṣūṣ* by ʿAbd al-Ghanī al-Nābulusī, d. 1143/1730 (II, 345), Berl. 2886, Vienna 1902, BDMG 22, Garr. 1596, NO 2461/2, Halet 264, Nafiz 589, Patna I, 131$_{,1297}$, print. C. 1304 and others (see Suppl.).—l. On 2 passages by Ibn Kamālpāshā, d. 940/1533 (II, 449), Berl. 2887.—m. Anon., Munich 137, Vienna 1900, Ind. Off. 649/52, Pet. 58$_{,2}$, Algiers 914.—n.–dd. see Suppl. (p. also Halet 260, NO 2460, Nāfiz 536.—r. Maḥmūd b. Ṣāʿid b. Muḥammad b. Maḥmūd al-Najdī al-Khānjī, Sütlüče Mewlewī Tekke 486, Patna I, 136$_{,1337}$.—y. [see II, 231] additionally Nāfiz 541, Halet 265, Yaḥyā 2223.—dd. Attributed to Muḥammad Ṣāliḥ (II, 321) NO 2466).—ee. *Majmaʿ al-baḥrayn* by al-Sharīt

Nāṣir al-Ḥusaynī al-Jīlānī al-Ḥakīm, completed in 940/1533, Alex. Taṣ. 31.—ff. Aḥmad b. Aḥmad b. Rumḥ al-Zabīdī, completed in 992/1584, ibid. 21.—Abstract by the author, *Naqsh al-fuṣūṣ*, Berl. 2888, Paris 6640, Patna I, 143$_{,1390}$.—Commentaries: a. Jāmī, d. 898/1492, Persian, Berl. 2888 (pers. 232$_{,1}$), Ind. Off. 653/4, Halet 263, NO 2477, print. *OB* VI, 4929, Arabic completed in 891/1486, Berl. 2889/90.—b. *Anfas al-khawāṣṣ* by Maḥbūb al-Ḥaqq Muḥibballāh Allāhābādī, Patna I, 129$_{,1284}$.—Refutations: a. *Fāḍiḥat al-mulḥidīn* by ʿAlāʾ al-Dīn Muḥammad al-Bukhārī, d. 841/1437 (ḤKh IV, 345$_{,8687}$), Garr. 1580.—b. *Niʿmat al-dharīʿa* by Ibrāhīm b. Muḥammad al-Ḥalabī, d. 956/1540 (II, 432), Fātiḥ 2880, AS 1745/6, ʿĀšir II, 155, Nailī Mīrzāzāde Khalīl 363.—c. *al-Radd wal-tashnīʿ* by Saʿd al-Dīn al-Taftāzānī, d. 791/1389 (II, 215), Garr. 2005$_{,8}$, against which *Kitāb al-ḥaqq al-mubīn* by Abū Bakr b. Aḥmad al-Naqshbandī, Berl. 2892.—d. al-Qāriʾ al-Harawī, d. 1014/1605 (II, 394), Berl. 2893.—12. (13.) *Shajarat al-wujūd wal-baḥr al-mawrūd* Cairo ^{1}VII 529 = *Shajarat al-kawn* ibid. 14, print. Būlāq 1292.—13. (14.) *ʿAnqāʾ mughrib fī maʿrifat khatm al-awliyāʾ wa-shams al-maghrib*, on the relationship of man as a microcosm to the macrocosm, as a supplement to no. 17, in rhymed prose, Berl. 2894/7, Vienna 1906, ʿĀšir I, 483, Cairo ^{1}VII, 46, Patna I, 137$_{,1349}$, | extract Paris 1339.—Commentaries: a. Qāsim b. 574
Abi ʾl-Faḍl al-Saʿdī al-Jūkhī al-Shāfiʿī, d. 982/1574, completed in 954/1547, Alex. Taṣ. 51, Cairo ^{1}II, 144, ^{2}I, 376, under the title *al-Wiʿāʾ al-makhtūm*, under the title *al-Barq al-lāmiʿ al-mughrib* Berl. 2898, or. oct. 4047, ʿĀšir I, 483, Cairo ^{2}I, 324, Āṣaf. I, 360$_{,149}$.—b. See Suppl.—c. Anon., Pet. 501, under the title *al-Aghrab min al-ʿujāb etc.* Alex. Taṣ. 35$_{,7}$.—14. (15.) *Risālat kunhi mā lā budda lil-mustarshid (murīd) ʿanhu*, on what the Sufi must absolutely believe and do, Berl. 2900, Gotha 914$_{,1}$, Ind. Off. 660, Cairo ^{1}VII, 16, 374$_{,2}$, Alex. Taṣ. 41$_{,2}$, Patna I, 141$_{,1375}$, II, 410$_{,2579/16}$, 412$_{,2580,11}$.—15. (16.) *al-Isrāʾ ila ʾl-maqām al-asrā* Berl. 2901/2, Vienna 1908, under the title *al-Asrār wakhtiṣār tartīb al-riḥla min al-ʿālam al-kawnī ila ʾl-mawqif al-aʿlā* Leipz. 231$_{,1}$.—Commentaries: a. On 14. (15.) and 15. (16). by Ismāʿīl b. Sawdakīn al-Nūrī, d. 646/1248 (no. 26), Berl. 2903/4.—b. On 15. (16.) alone by Sitt al-ʿAjam bint al-Nafīs of Baghdad,[8] Berl. 2905, Algiers 915.—c. Zayn al-ʿĀbidīn b. ʿAbd al-Raʾūf al-Munāwī, d. 1022/1613, Ahlw., loc. cit.—16. (17.) *Mashāhid al-asrār al-qudsiyya wa-maṭāliʿ al-anwār al-ilāhiyya* (see Suppl.) Gotha 888$_{,2}$, cf. *JA* 1860, I, 437.—17. (18.) *al-Tadbīrāt al-ilāhiyya fī iṣlāḥ al-mamlaka al-insāniyya*, divine guidance for various layers of human society in completion of the profession of unity, Berl. 2906/7, Upps. 393$_{,5}$, Ind. Off. 658$_{,7}$, *Br. Mus. Quart.* VI, 55, Bodl. II, 252$_{,1}$, Algiers 911, Fātīḥ 2630$_{,8}$, 5376$_{,14}$, Halet

8 She claims to have been completely uneducated and to have come out of her ignorance in linguistic and other matters requiring an interpreter and to have reached the necessary insight and understanding by illumination in a single night.

ʿIlāwe 3, Alex. Taṣ. 11, Cairo ^{1}VII, 13, 16, 32, ^{2}I, 278, Patna I, 129$_{,1289}$, II, 489$_{,2650,3}$.—
18. (19.) *Mawāqiʿ al-nujūm wa-maṭāliʿ ahillat al-asrār wal-ʿulūm*, composed in
595/1199 after he moved from Murcia to Almería, Berl. 2908, Gotha 887, Vienna
1907, Paris 1338$_{,3}$, Algiers 911$_{,2}$, Constantine, *JA* 1860, I, 437, Šehīd ʿA. 1277$_{,2}$, 1431,
Fātiḥ 2630$_{,2}$, 5376$_{,2}$, Nāfiz 470, Patna II, 488$_{,2650,1}$; a commentary by al-Qāshānī,
d. 730/1330 (II, 204), Berl. 2909.—19. (20.) *Maqām al-qurba* (*wa-fakk al-kurba*),
on the state of mind that is required for closeness to God, Berl. 2910, Br. Mus.
886$_{,19}$, Cairo ^{1}VII, 15, 45, Patna II, 343$_{,2528,3}$.—20. (21.) *al-Anwār fī-mā yuftaḥ ʿalā*
(*yumnaḥ*) *ṣāḥib al-khalwa min al-asrār*, written in 606/1209 in Qonya, Berl.
575 2913/4, Leipz. 230, Paris 1337$_{,3}$, 2405$_{,7}$, Br. Mus. 886$_{,26}$, Garr. 1574$_{,2}$. Alex. | Taṣ. 78,
Cairo ^{1}VII, 16, 38, 47, 230, 383.—21. (22.) *Kitāb al-khalwa*, on solitude, Berl.
2916/7, Br. Mus. 886$_{,25}$, Ind. Off. 657$_{,2}$, Alex. Taṣ. 37, Cairo ^{1}VII, 15, 383, as *Asrār
al-khalwa* Patna I, 128$_{,1282}$, 408$_{,2579,1}$, commentary by ʿAbd al-Karīm al-Jīlī (II,
200), see Suppl. also Patna I, 134$_{,1327}$, II, 48$_{,2650,5}$.—22. (23.) *Inshāʾ al-dawāʾir
al-iḥāṭiyya ʿala ʾl-daqāʾiq ʿalā muḍāhāt al-insān lil-khāliq wal-khāʾlāʾiq*, on the
elevated station of man in Creation and the beginning of times, Berl. 2918/9,
Upps. 393$_{,9}$, Ind Off. 658$_{,3}$, Fātiḥ 2630$_{,7}$, Ğārullāh 2061$_{,2}$, ʿUm. 3750.—23. (24.)
Kitāb al-ḥaqq, on God's true nature, Berl. 2920/2, Br. Mus. 886$_{,16}$, Paris 6640,
f. 104v, Cairo ^{1}VII, 16.—24. (25.) *ʿUqlat al-mustawfiz*, on creations of the higher
444 and | the lower worlds, spirits, reason, the divine throne, the heavens, earth,
and the beginning of mankind, Berl. 2923/4, Br. Mus. 886$_{,24}$, ʿUm. 3780, Fātiḥ
2630$_{,4}$ 5376$_{,1}$, Alex. Taṣ. 34$_{,4}$, Fun. 151$_{,20}$, Cairo ^{1}VII, 15, 380, Patna I, 137$_{,1348}$.—
25. (26.) *Tuḥfat al-safara ilā ḥaḍrat al-barara*, the developmental stages of the
Sufi in gaining a greater understanding of God, Berl. 2925/6, Cairo ^{1}VII, 374, 384,
print. Istanbul 1300, see Asín, *Psicologia* 79, *Islam crist.* 271/99 (according to
ḤKh II, 228$_{,2592}$, ^{2}I, 367, by Jalāl al-Dīn Aḥmad al-Bisṭāmī, but in reality it was
by Qiwām al-Dīn Muḥammad al-Bisṭāmī, a student of Aṣīl al-Dīn ʿAbdallāh
al-Balyānī, Suppl. II, 286, see A.J. Casas y Manrique, *Jāmiʿ al-ḥaqāʾiq bi-tajrīd
al-ʿalāʾiq*, Uppsala 1937, Foreword, see Alex. Fun. 68$_{,3}$, which has Ibn ʿAbd
al-Ḥamīd, and Tunis, Zayt. III, 164$_{,1581}$ which has Ibn Ḥāmid).—
26. (27.) *al-Ḥujub*, on levels of love for God which, like curtains, hinder admit-
tance, Berl. 2927/8, Ind. Off. 693 ii, Alex. Taṣ. 33$_{,6}$, Cairo ^{1}VII, 16, 215.—27. (28.)
Waṣf tajalli ʾl-dhāt Berl. 2929/30 (not in ḤKh, probably a forgery).—28. (29.)
Ḥilyat al-abdāl wa-mā yaẓharu fīhā min al-maʿārif wal-aḥwāl, the path to salvation, composed as his fifth work at the request of two of his friends during a
visit to al-Ṭāʾif on pilgrimage in 599/1202, Berl. 1469 (?), 2931/2, Paris 1338, 6614,
f. 114a, Ind. Off. 694$_{,2}$, Upps. 393$_{,16}$, Welīeddīn 1520, Fātiḥ 2630$_{,7}$, 5378, Nafiz 384,
Cairo ^{1}VII, 16, 47, 57, 371, 374, 556, Patna II, 412$_{,2559,3}$.—29. (30.) *Shujūn
al-mashjūn wa-futūn al-maftūn* Berl. 2933.—30. (31.) *al-Shawāhid*, proofs of the

nature of God, reposing in the heart, Berl. 2934, Welīeddīn 1832,$_2$, Fātiḥ 5376, Es'ad 1323, Cairo ^{1}VII, 369.—31. (32.) *al-Ittiḥād al-kawnī fī ḥaḍrat* | *al-ishhād* 576 *al-ʿaynī*, on humanity in general, primeval reason, the cause of matter, and the body in general, in rhymed prose mixed with poems, Berl. 2935 (ʿUm. 3750 *Ījād al-kawn*).—32. (33.) *Kīmiyyāʾ al-saʿāda*, on the most excellent properties of the *tawḥīd* formula, Berl. 2936, Paris 1343,$_1$, Cairo ^{1}VII, 16, 208.—33. (35.) *al-Ifāḍa li-man arāda 'l-istifāḍa*, on the three basic sciences, one of which treats God exclusive of His relation to the two worlds, another the world as grasped by reason, and the third the world as perceived by the senses, with a statement on the number of sciences into which each of these is divided, Berl. 2937.—34. (36.) *al-Fahwāniyya manzil al-manāzil*, on the stations that man has to pass through in order to gain understanding of God, Berlin 2938.—35. (37.) *al-Muwāzana*, a comparison between the two worlds from the standpoint of the Sufi, Berl. 2939.—36. (38.) *Fī naʿt al-arwāḥ*, on how the soul is created by God and through which stations it must pass in order to attain knowledge of Him, Berl. 2940 = (?) *Kitāb fī 'l-rūḥ* Br. Mus. 886,$_{14}$.—37. (39.) *Tartīb al-sulūk ilā malik al-mulūk* Berl. 2941, Vienna 1910,$_5$ (?), Ind. Off. 657 (?).—38. (40.) *al-Amr al-muḥkam al-marbūṭ fī-mā yalzam ahl ṭarīq Allāh min al-shurūṭ*, on the most essential duties of the Sufi, Berl. 2942 (fragm.), Gotha 914,$_3$, Vienna 1909, Upps. 393,$_{13}$, Paris 1337,$_{14}$, 6614,$_3$, Garr. 1574.—Commentary by Aḥmad b. ʿAbd al-Qādir al-Dawʿanī, d. 1052/1642, Berl. 2942, Patna II, 409,$_{2579,13}$, 412,$_{2580,12}$, Ind. Off. 698,$_2$.—39. (41.) *al-Iʿlām fī-mā buniya ʿalayhi 'l-Islām* Berl. 2943.—40. (42.) *al-Iʿlām bi-ishārāt ahl al-ilhām* Berl. 2944, Ind. Off. 695,$_1$ = *al-Ḥikma al-ilhāmiyya fī 'l-radd ʿala 'l-falsafa* Leid. 1514/5?), Taymūr, Ḥikma 85 (anon.).—41. (43.) *al-Fanāʾ fī 'l-mushāhada*, on knowledge of God's nature, Berl. 2945, Vienna 1910,$_7$, Br. Mus. 886,$_{17}$.—42. (44.) *Marātib ʿulūm al-wahb*, on the stages of inspiration, Berl. 2946, Br. Mus. 886,$_{18}$, Cairo ^{1}VII, 371, Patna I, 1343,$_{2528,4}$.—43. (45.) *Fi 'l-azal*, on eternity, Berl. 2947, Ğārullāh 1080,$_4$.—44. (46.) *Shaqq al-jayb wa-rafʿ ḥijāb al-rayb ʿan* | *iẓhār asrār al-ghayb* Cairo ^{1}VII, 46.—45. (47.) *Tafsīr* 445 *āyat al-kursī*, on sura 2, 256, Berl. 2948.—46. (48.) *Ishārāt al-Qurʾān fī ʿālam al-insān* Berl. 2949.—47. (49.) *Kitāb al-sabʿa wa-huwa Kitāb al-shaʾn*, on the meaning of the week and its days, Berl. 2950, = Ind. Off. 657,$_4$, Ğārullāh 1880,$_2$, ʿUm. 3750, from which *Kitāb al-shaʾn*, abstract explaining the Qurʾānic verse *fī kulli yawmin huwa fī shaʾnayn* | (sura 55,$_{29}$), Paris 2502,$_3$.—48. (50.) *Tanazzul(āt)* 577 *al-imlāk lil-amlāk fī ḥarakāt al-aflāk*, on divine missions, of humans, station and duties of the emissary, Berl. 2951, Šehīd ʿA, 1155, Alex. Taṣ 12.—49. (51.) *Tawḥīd al-tawḥīd*, on the fact that truth consists in the recognition of the eternal, and that nearness to God increases with surrendering the heart to God and ignoring the emotions and passions of the soul, wherein is found the way to

salvation, Berl. 2952.—50. (52.) *al-Tadqīq fī baʿth al-taḥqīq*, guidance towards
attainment of God, Berl. 2953.—51. (53.) *al-Qasam al-ilāhī bism al-rabbānī*,
several verses in which God swears by Himself, Berl. 2954.—52. (54.)
al-Muḍādda fī ʿilm al-ẓāhir wal-bāṭin, on opposites in nature etc., from which
God Himself is not free, Berl. 2955.—53. (55.) *al-Ghāyāt fī-mā warada min al-
ghayb fī tafsīr baʿḍ al-āyāt* Berl. 2956.—54. (56.) *Tāj al-rasāʾil wa-minhāj
al-wasāʾil*, a letter to a friend in Mecca, Berl. 2957.—55. (57.) *al-Risāla al-mūqiẓa*
Cairo ^{1}VII, 378.—56. (58.) *al-Durra al-fākhira fī dhikr ma ʾntafaʿat bihim fī
ʾl-ākhira wa-risālat rūḥ al-quds*, a letter written in the year 600/1203 from Mecca
to a friend in Tunis and in which he tells him about the mood of his soul and
his wrestling for relief, Berl. 2958 = *Risālat al-quds fī munāṣaḥat al-nafs* Bodl. I,
320, Ind. Off. 659$_{,2}$.—57. (59.) *al-Jalāla*, on the secret meaning and strength of
this word, Berl. 2959, Paris 1339$_{,2}$, 6640, f. 62v, Br. Mus. 886$_{,20}$, Ğārullāh 1080,
Fātiḥ 5378, Cairo ^{1}VII, 371, 380.—58. (60.) *Jawāb ʿan masʾalat al-sabḥa al-sawdāʾ
wa-hiya ʾl-hayūlā*, on matter, Berl. 2960, Cairo ^{1}VI, 90.—59. (61.) *Risālat
al-nashʾatayn*, on the relation and connection between the two creations, i.e.
the spiritual and the corporeal, Berl. 2961.—60. (62.) *Mafātīḥ al-ghayb*, on the
secrets of God's nature, Berl. 2962, Br. Mus. 886$_{,22}$, Patna II, 343$_{,2528,\ 2}$.—
61. (64.) *Tahdhīb al-akhlāq* Cairo ^{1}VII, 528.—62. (65.) *al-Mudkhal ilā maʿrifat
maʾkhadh al-naẓar fī ʾl-asmāʾ wal-kināyāt al-ilāhiyya*, on God's names in the
Qurʾān, as an introduction to his *Kitāb al-maqṣad al-asnā*, Berl. 2963, Br. Mus.
627$_{,18}$, Ind. Off. 658, Upps. 393$_{,3}$.—60. (66.) (*al-Quṭb wa*) *al-Nuqabāʾ*, on the
spiritual heads of the Sufis, Berl. 2964, Vienna 1910$_{,5}$ (cf. ZDMG VII, 22), Cairo
^{1}VII, 16.—64. (67.) *Wasāʾil al-masāʾil*, definitions of Sufi concepts, Berl. 2965
(questions by his student Ibn Sawdakīn, no. 26, different from Vienna 1911$_{,1}$)
578 Vienna 1910$_{,3}$, Esc. ^{2}417$_{,5}$.—65. (68.) (*Tāj*) *al-Tarājim*, | by the same, Berl. 2966,
Gotha 888$_{,2}$, Ind. Off. 657$_{,6}$, Cairo ^{1}VII, 369.—66. (69.) *Tarjumān al-alfāẓ
al-Muḥammadiyya* Berl. 2967/9.—67. (70.) *al-Iṣṭilāḥāt al-ṣūfiyya*, Leid. 80
(where other MSS are listed), Cairo ^{1}VII, 15, ed. G. Flügel together with
al-Jurjānī's *Taʿrīfāt, Definitiones viri meritissimi Sejjid Sherif ʿA. b. M. Dsch.*
Leipzig 1845, AS 2048$_{,2}$, Nafiz 384, 632, ʿUm. 3750, Patna II, 412$_{,2580,\ 10}$.—69. (71.)
Sharḥ al-alfāẓ allatī tadāwalatha ʾl-Ṣūfiyya Ind. Off. 657$_{,7}$, different from the
anonymous Vat. V. 296$_{,1}$.—69. (72.) *al-Muqtanaʿ fī īḍāḥ al-sahl al-mumtanaʿ*, on
the secret meanings of letters, Berl. 2969.—70. (73.) *al-Ḥurūf al-thalātha allati
ʾnʿaṭafat awākhiruhā ʿalā awāʾilihā*, i.e. nūn, wāw, mīm, Berl. 2970.—71. (74.) *al-
Alif wa-huwa Kitāb al-aḥadiyya* Berl. 2971, Upps. 393$_{,8}$, Ind. Off. 658$_{,4}$, Br. Mus.
836$_{,21}$, Cairo ^{1}VII, 45 = Krafft 496 (?).—72. (75.) *al-Bāʾ wa-huwa miftāḥ dār
446 *al-ḥaqīqa* Berl. 2972, Paris 1339$_{,4}$. |—73. (76.) *Kitāb al-yāʾ wa-huwa Kitāb al-
huwa* Berl. 2973, Cairo ^{1}VII, 384, Ğārullāh 1080$_{,6}$.—74. (77). *Miftāḥ*

al-jafr al-jāmiʿ, on the relation between letters and the nature of things, Berl. 4213 = Paris 2669,14 (?), Br. Mus. Or. 10887 = *al-Jafr al-jāmiʿ* Alex. Ḥurūf, 9.—75. (78.) *Jafr al-imām ʿAlī b. Abī Ṭālib* Leipz. 833,1.—76. (79.) *Asrār al-ḥurūf*, Br. Mus. 754,4.—77. (80.) *Jafr al-nihāya wa-mubīn khabāyā asrār kunūz al-bidāya wal-ghāya* Algiers 1522.—78. (81.) *Fāʾida*, on magical games with letters, Gotha 1278.—79. (82.) Commentary on a work by him in which he demonstrates that, and why, a student must have a master to guide and instruct him in all stages in order to arrive at a true understanding of God and obedience to His commands and prohibitions, Berl. 2980.—80. (83.) *Miʾat ḥadīth wa-wāḥid Qudsiyya* Cairo ^{1}VII, 221.—81. (84.) *Nisbat al-khirqa*, on investiture and admission among the Sufis, Berl. 2981/2, Ind. Off. 657,3, Bursa Haraccizade Ṭaṣ. 53,2.—82. (85.) An account of his admission into the circle of Sufis, first in Mecca in 599/1202, then in Mosul and Seville, Berl. 2984.—83. (86.) *al-Tajalliyāt al-ilāhiyya* Gotha 886, Br. Mus. 886,27, Fātiḥ 5378,6, Alex. Ṭaṣ. 10. Cairo ^{1}VII, 46, 529, ^{2}I, 275; commentary by Ismāʿīl b. Sawdakīn al-Nūrī, d. 646/1248, Vienna 1911.—84. (87.) *ʿIẓat al-albāb wa-dhakhīrat al-iktisāb*, an abstract of *Tatimmat al-durra al-yatīma* by Ibn al-Muqaffaʿ (p. 158), Gotha 3, 16, Paris 1344.—85. (88.) *Inshāʾ al-jusūm al-insāniyya* Esc. ^{2}530,3.—86. (89.) *Natījat al-ḥaqq* Cairo ^{1}VII, 371, 373, 375.—87. (90.) *ʿUyūn al-masāʾil* Cairo ^{1}VII, 16.—| 88. (91.) *al-Tawqīʿāt* ibid.— 579
89. (92.) *Asrār al-wuḍūʾ* ibid. 358.—90. (93.) *Sirr al-maḥabba* ibid.—91. (94). *Bulghat al-ghawwāṣ fi ʾl-akwān ilā maʿdin al-ikhlāṣ fī maʿrifat al-insān* Paris 2405,6, Esc. ^{2}417,3, Welīeddīn 1832,3.—92. (95.) *Qabs al-anwār wa-bahjat al-asrār* Leid. 1220.—93. (96.) *al-Firaq al-sitt al-bāṭila wa-dhikr aʿdādihā* Ind. Off. 657,5.—94. (97.) *al-Ajwiba al-lāʾiqa ʿan al-asʾila al-fāʾiqa* Vienna 1910,6, Ind. Off. 659.—96. (99.) *al-Ṭarīqa* Krafft 495, *fī ʾl-ṭarīq* Alex. Fun. 149, 15. *Shams al-ṭarīqa fī bayān al-sharīʿa wal-ḥaqīqa* Cairo ^{1}VII, 528 (?).—97. (100.) *Mirʾāt (ḥayāt) al-maʿānī li-idrāk al-ʿālam al-insānī*, a revision of the translation of the *Amṛtakuṇḍa* by al-Samarqandī (no. 19), which he undertook on the basis of the original text with the help of a yogi, Gotha 1265/6 Leid. 1205, Paris 1699,3, Esc. ^{2}707,2, Cairo ^{1}VI, 93, Turkish translation *Ḥawḍ al-ḥayāt* Cairo ^{1}VII, 561, see Pertsch, loc. cit.—98. (101.) *Tawāb qaḍāʾ ḥawāʾij al-ikhwān wa-ighāthat al-lahfān* Paris 1699,14.—98a. see Suppl. with Welīeddīn 1820/1.—99. (103.) *al-Imām al-mubīn alladhī lā yadkhuluhu rayb wa-lā takhmīn*, man as a microcosm, Br. Mus. 1371,1.—100. (104.) *al-Tanazzulāt al-Mawṣiliyya*, original Shaykh Murād 187, Murād Mollā 1236 (read in the presence of the author), Cairo ^{1}VII, 380.—101. (105.) *Jadwal ʿaẓīm listikhrāj al-faʾl min al-Qūrʾān al-ʿaẓīm* Cairo VII, 76.—102. (106.) *Isfār fī sifr Nūḥ* Gotha pers. 5, 2.—103. (107.) *Risālat al-ʿIbād* ibid. 3.—103a. *Sharḥ Kitāb khalʿ al-naʿlayn fi ʾl-wuṣūl ilā ḥaḍrat al-jamʿayn* by Abu ʾl-Qāsim b. Qaṣī, Vienna 1929,3, Fātiḥ 2599,5, Nāfiz 503 (attributed to ʿAbdī

Busnawī).—104. (108.) *Risāla fī 'l-Aḥadiyya* Gotha pers. 5, 4, Krafft 496, Alex. Taṣ. $151_{,17}$, Patna II, $492_{,2652,\ 10}$.—105. (109.) *Risālat al-anwār* Gotha Pers 5, 5, Paris $2405_{,7}$.—106. (110.) Answers to questions by Ḥakīm Tirmidhī, Persian, Br. Mus. Pers. II, 852, f.—107. (111.) *Risāla arsalahā li-aṣḥāb al-Shaykh ʿAbd al-ʿAzīz b. Muḥammad al-Mahdawī*, composed in 590/1194 on his return from Tunis, Vienna 1910, 4, Fātiḥ 2031.—108. (112.) *al-Risāla al-Ghawthiyya*, a dialogue between God and the mystic al-Ghawth al-Aʿẓam, Gotha Pers. $5_{,7}$, Br. Mus. $754_{,5}$, Esc. [2]$417_{,2}$, Alex. Taṣ $34_{,3}$ (?), with anon. comm. Ind. Off. $653_{,2}$, 655/6.—109. (113.) Letter to Fakhr al-Dīn al-Rāzī, d. 606/1209 (p. 506), Gotha $914_{,7}$, Fātiḥ $5375_{,7}$, Alex. Fun. $151_{,14}$, Cairo [1]VII, 46.—110. (114.) *Risāla fī taṣwīr Ādam ʿalā ṣūrat al-kamāl* Cairo [1]VII, 279.—111. (115.) Four Sufi *Rasāʾil*, ibid.—112. (116.) *Nuskhat al-ḥaqq* Br. Mus. $886_{,15}$, Patna II, $343_{,2528,\ 5}$.—113. (117.) *Lughat al-arwāḥ*,
580 | ibid. 23.—114. (118.) *al-Dawr al-aʿlā* (*wal-durr al-aghlā*), prayer pericopes, Berl. 2974/5, Pet. 64, Br. Mus. 103, Cairo [1]VII, 351, Qawala I, 204, (*al-Durr al-aʿlā*); commentary by Muḥammad b. Muḥammad al-Tāfilātī, d. 1191/1777, Berl. 2976/7.—115. (119.) *al-Ṣalāt al-Akbariyya*, a prayer, Berl. $3644_{,2}$, commentary by Muṣṭafā b. Kamāl al-Dīn al-Bakrī, d. 1162/1749 (II, 348), ibid. 3, 4.—116. (120.) *Awrād al-ayyām wal-layālī* Br. Mus. 103 = Paris 1199 (?), Cairo [1]VII, 45.—117. (121.) *Awrād al-usbūʿ*, prayers for individual weekdays, in rhymed prose, Berl. 3773/5, Ind. Off. 393, Bodl. I, 120, II, $50_{,3}$.—118. (122.) *Ḥizb*, an ejaculatory prayer, Berl. $3687_{,2}$.—119. *al-Ṣalāt al-Fayḍiyya* Qawala I, 249.—120. (123.) *Waṣiyya* Berl. 3995.—121. (123a.) like the previous one from the year 624/1227, ibid. 3996.—122. (124.) *al-Ḥikam al-ilāhiyya* Alex. Taṣ. 15, $42_{,2}$. Fun. $151_{,4}$, Cairo [1]VII, 379.—123. (125.) *al-Ṣuḥuf al-nāmūsiyya wal-sujuf al-nāwūsiyya* Cairo [1]VII, 104.—124. (126.) *al-Shajara al-Nuʿmāniyya fī 'l-dawla al-ʿUthmāniyya*, prophecies, especially concerning the future of Egypt, Alex. Ḥurūf 5.—Commentaries: a. *al-Lumʿa al-nūrāniyya fī ḥall mushkilāt al-Sh. al-N.* by Ṣadr al-Dīn al-Qūnawī (no. 32), Berl. 4214/5, Garr. $2103_{,2}$, Alex. Ḥurūf 8, Cairo [1]VII, 552.—b. Ibn Khalīl al-Ṣafadī, d. 764/1363 (II, 11), Paris $2678/80_{,1}$, Garr. $2103_{,3}$, Alex. Ḥurūf 5, Cairo [1]VII, 155.—c. Anon., Berl. 4216/8, Garr. $2103_{,1}$.—d.,e. see Suppl. c., d.—f. Anon. *Zuhūr al-bustān* Alex. Ḥurūf 4.—g. *al-Dāʾira al-kubrā* by Muṣṭafā Efendi b. Suhrāb, Alex. Ḥurūf 12.—125. (127.) *Ḥikam*, in rhymed prose in two versions, Berl. 8687.—126. (128.) *Kitāb al-ʿAbādila*, a compilation of men with the name ʿAbdallāh and Sufi statements by them, Berl. 2979, Patna II, $411_{,2513,\ 20}$.—126a. See Suppl. Garr. 942 with a commentary by Aḥmad b. Sulaymān al-Sālimī, see Suppl. II, $1039_{,19,\ 1}$.—127. (129.) *al-Lumaʿ al-ufqiyya*, an anthology of his sayings, Gotha $914_{,2}$.—128. (130.) *Muḥāḍarāt al-abrār wa-musāmarāt al-akhyār* (or *Mus. al-ab. wa-muḥ. al-akh.*) Berl. 8365/8, Br. Mus. Suppl. 1142, Leid. 482/4 (where other MSS are listed), AS 4252, Dāmād Ibr. 959, lith. C. 1282, print.

C. 1305.—129. (131.) *Tarjumān al-ashwāq*, a collection of Sufi poems, published for the first time in 598/1201 in Mecca, Gotha 2268, Leid. 698, ʿĀšir II, 2821, Patna II, $448_{,2624,\ 4}$ then with a commentary by the poet *al-Dhakhāʾir wal-aghlāq* dated 611/1214, and which, according to Bodl. I, 1276, he composed to defend himself against the accusation that he did not act so much from heavenly as from earthly motives, Berl. 7750/1, or. oct. 3930, Gotha 2269 (where other MSS are listed), BDMG 109, ʿUm. 5766, Halet ʿIlāwe 132, 138, Halet 686, Bursa, Haraccizade Taș. $53_{,1}$.—| 130. (132.) *Dīwān* with one poem from the year 581
630/1232, incomplete Leid. 700 = Būlāq 1271, Cairo ^{1}IV, 234, with the title *al-Dīwān al-akbar*, Bombay n.d.—131. (133.) *Dīwān ishrāq al-bahāʾ al-amjad ʿalā tartīb ḥurūf al-abjad* Berl. 7747.—132. (134.) *Dīwān al-murtajalāt*, improvisations, composed around 599/1203, Berl. 7746.—133. (135.) *Kitāb al-muʿashsharāt* or *al-Dīwān al-aṣghar* Paris $3171_{,3}$, Br. Mus. $1527_{,2}$, Esc. $^2417_{,1}$, Cairo ^{1}VII, 384.—134. (136.) A collection of Sufi poems, Br. Mus. 614.—135. (137.) *Tanazzul al-arwāḥ bil-rūḥ etc.* or *Dīwān al-maʿārif al-ilāhiyya wal-laṭāʾif al-rūḥawiyya*, a collection of mystical poems, Paris $2348_{,2}$.—136. (138.) *al-Qaṣīda al-tāʾiyya* with an extensive commentary by ʿAbdallāh Efendi al-Busnawī, d. 1054/1644, Leid. 701.—137. (139.) *Minhāj al-ʿārif wal-muttaqī wa-miʿrāj al-sālik al-murtajī* in 1007 *ṭawīl* verses on attaining God, Berl. 2984/5.—138. (140.) *al-Muʿāsharāt al-maymūna*, Sufi poems, Berl. 2986.—139. (141.) An alchemical poem, Br. Mus. 601, iv, 1.—140. ʿAlawān b. ʿAlī b. ʿAṭiyya al-Ḥamawī, d. 936/1530 (II, 333), *Kashf al-kāʾināt fī qawl Muḥyi ʾl-Dīn* "kunnā ḥurūfan ʿāliyāt," regarding verses by Muḥammad al-Sīlīnī al-Maghribī, Makram 52.—141. Commentary on 2 verses by al-Dawwānī, d. 908/1502 (II, 217), Berl. 2987.—142. Anon. commentary on 2 other verses, ibid. 2988.—143. Commentary on 2 verses by Aḥmad b. Sulaymān al-Khālidī, 1270/1853 (II, 485), Berl. 2989.—144. The same by Muḥammad al-Ṣūrānī, ibid. 2990.—145. Commentary on 2 verses by ʿAbd al-Ghanī al-Nābulusī, d. 1143/1730 (II, 345), ibid.—146. *Qaṣīda fī manāsik al-ḥajj* Algiers 612.—146a. *Manẓūmat kashf al-rān*, commentary on a verse therefrom by Aḥmad b. Muḥammad al-Ghamrī (Suppl. II, 173), Garr. 942.—147. *al-Jamāl wal-jalāl*, perhaps by al-Qūnawī, Berl. 2994/5.—148. *al-ʿUjāla fi ʾl-tawajjuh al-atamm* ibid. 2946.—149. (150.) *al-Jawāb al-mustaqīm*, answers to questions that al-Tirmidhī, d. 320/932 (p. 199), had raised in his *Khatm al-awliyāʾ*, perhaps by Ibn ʿArabī, Berl. 2998, ʿUm. $3750_{,1}$, Alex. Taș. $34_{,7}$, Patna II, $410_{,2579,\ 14}$.—151.–217. See Suppl. (152. Leipz. 251, mistakenly Suppl. II, 284, Patna II, $343_{,2528,\ 6}$.—156. = 39a. AS $2087_{,1}$, composed in Qonya in 602/1205.—157. Patna I, $140_{,1372}$.—189. ʿUm. 3750.—194. Nafiz 495, Bursa, Haraccizade $52_{,3}$.—160. Garr 934.—216. Köpr. II, $163_{,1}$).—218. *Risāla fi ʾl-taṣawwuf* Alex. Taș. 17.—219. *al-Zahr al-fāʾiḥ fī satr al-ʿuyūb wal-qabāʾiḥ* Alex. Mawāʿiẓ 21.—220. *al-Dhakhāʾir*

wal-iʿlān Fez Qar. 1446,$_{1}$.—221. *Muzhirāt ʿarāʾis al-mukhabbaʾāt bil-lisān*
582 *al-ʿarabī,* commentary by al-Jawharī al-Khālidī, d. 1187/1773 | (II, 331), Garr. 947.—222. *Risāla fī taḥqīq wujūb al-wājib li-dhātihi* ibid. Fun. 149,$_{6}$.—223. *Fī sirr al-ḥurūf* ibid. 16.—224. *Naghamāt al-aflāk* or *al-Sirr al-maktūm* Alex. Ḥurūf 19.—225. *Mawlid al-nabī* ibid. Tar. 16, Patna II, 407,$_{2576,\ 2}$.—226. *al-Durar* Alex. Taṣ. 39.—227. *Risāla fi ʾsmihi taʿāla ʾl-ḥasīb* ibid. 34,$_{5}$ (?).—228. *Mishkāt al-anwār* Patna I, 61,$_{623}$ (but see Suppl. I, 751,$_{34c}$).—229. *al-Ghinā fi ʾl-mushāhadāt* ibid. II, 343,$_{2528,\ 1}$.—230. *Mirʾāt al-ʿārifīn fī-mā yatamayyaz bayna ʾl-ʿābidīn* ibid. II, 410,$_{2579,\ 16}$ (= Suppl. 179 ?).—232. *Risāla fī maʿrifat Allāh taʿālā* ibid. 427,$_{2600,\ 6}$.—233. *al-Risāla al-barzakhiyya* ibid. 489,$_{2650,\ 4}$.—234. *al-Ifāḍa fī ʿilm al-riyāḍa* AS 2160,$_{4}$ (Ritter).—235. *Tadhkirat al-tawwābīn* (p. 377, xxi, attributed to al-Nawawī) Nāfiz 373.—236. *Risālat al-tawḥīd* Fātiḥ 2630,$_{5}$.—237. *ʿUlūm al-wahb* ʿUm. 3750.—238. *al-Muʿawwil ʿala ʾl-muʿawwal ʿalayhi* ʿUm. 3750.—239. *Kawn Allāh sabaq qabla an fataq wa-rataq* Welīeddīn 1820, f. 43b/59a (Ritter).—Refutation: *Tanbīh al-ghabī ʿalā takfīr b. al-ʿArabi* by Ibrāhīm b. ʿUmar b. ʿAlī al-Biqāʿī, d. 885/1480 (II, 142), Leid. 2039, Bodl. I, 158,$_{1}$. Against this al-Suyūṭī, d. 911/1505, wrote *Tanzīh al-ghabī fī tanzīh b. al-ʿArabī,* Berl. 2850, Cairo ^{1}VII, 234, Patna II, 395,$_{2570,\ 25}$, and ʿAlī b. Maymūn al-Idrīsī, d. 917/1511 (II, 123), *Kitāb al-radd fī munkiri ʾl-shaykh al-akbar,* composed in 909/1503, Berl. 2851; ʿAlī b. ʿAṭiyya ʿAlawān, d. 936/1530 (II, 333), defended this treatise against the accusation of heresy, ibid. 2852, also al-Fīrūzābādī, d. 817/1415 (II, 183), *Fatwā fī ḥaqq al-shaykh b. ʿA.* Fātiḥ 5376,$_{3}$ and Ibrāhīm al-Madanī *al-Radd al-matīn ʿan al-shaykh Muḥyi ʾl-Dīn,* composed in 1093/1682, Alex. Taṣ. 42,$_{4}$ (see Suppl.). Mawlānā Qirimī (between 841/936, 1437/1529), *Nāṣiḥat al-hāʾimīn wa-fāḍiḥat al-ḥātimīn,* a defence of Ibn al-ʿArabī and Saʿd al-Dīn al-Qūniyawī against Ibn Abi ʾl-Ḥajala (d. 776/1374 Suppl. II, 5) and, especially, ʿAlāʾ al-Dīn al-Bukhārī (d. 841/1437 Suppl. I, 794), whose work *Fāḍiḥat al-mulḥidīn wa-nāṣiḥat al-muwaḥḥidīn* (Suppl. I, 794) must have occasioned the choice of our title, MS dates from around 936 AH, Basel M III, 25.

24. His student Ismāʿīl al-Tūnisī wrote:

Tuḥfat al-tadbīr li-ahl al-tabṣīr Alex. Kīm. 10.

25. His student Abu ʾl-Qāsim b. Muḥammad b. Ibrāhīm wrote:

A mystical poem, Esc. ^{2}626,$_{13}$.

26. Al-Shaykh al-Zāhid Abū Ṭāhir Ismāʿīl b. Sawdakīn | b. ʿAbdallāh al-Nūrī was 583
born in Cairo in 588/1192, was a friend of Ibn ʿArabī, and died in Aleppo in 646/1248.

Poems, Gotha 2196$_{,17}$, cf. 23$_{,17,8}$.

26a. Muḥammad b. Ḥusayn b. Aḥmad b. Yazdyār Abū Jaʿfar al-Anbārī wrote, before 651/1253:

Rawḍat al-murīdīn ḤKh ^{1}III, 511$_{,6686}$, ^{2}I, 932, Berl. Oct. 3542$_{,4}$, Paris 1369, Köpr. 739 (archetype 651 AH), Sul. 1028, f. 173b/214a, Fātiḥ 2692.

27. Muḥammad b. Muḥammad b. ʿAlī Saʿd al-Dīn b. al-ʿArabī, the son of the famous Sufi, was born in Malaṭiyya in Ramaḍān 618/October–November 1221 and died in Damascus in 659/1258.

Dīwān, for the most part *maqṭūʿāt*, often about pederasty, Garr. 554/5, Auswahl, Berl. 7761 (see Suppl.).

28. ʿAbdallāh b. Muḥammad b. Shahwār al-Rāzī Najm al-Dīn Dāya was a student of Najm al-Dīn al-Kubrā (no. 20) who fled to Asia Minor following the invasion of Khwārizm by Čingiz Khān, where he became friends with the poet Jalāl al-Dīn Rūmī. He died in Baghdad in 654/1256.

Jāmī, *Nafaḥāt* 499. 1. *Mirṣād al-ʿibād min al-mabdaʾ ila ʾl-maʿād*, a Persian introduction to mysticism, written in Qayṣariyya, Bodl. Pers. 1248, Br. Mus. Pers. Suppl. no. 17, translated into Arabic by an unknown author and cast into the form of an abstract under the title *Muntakhab al-Mirṣād* Berl. 3006, AS 2065/9; from which selected aphorisms Berl. 8688.—2. *Manārāt al-sāʾirīn ilā ḥaḍrat Allāh wa-maqāmāt al-ṭāʾirīn billāh*, a shorter work on the same subject, written 32 years later, around 650/1252, Berl. 3007/8.—3. *Baḥr al-ḥaqāʾiq wal-maʿānī*, commentary on the *Fātiḥa*, Ind. Off. 68/9 (erroneously: d. 618), Patna I, 23$_{,208}$.—4.–9. see Suppl.

| 29. Nūr al-Dīn Abu ʾl-Ḥasan ʿAlī b. ʿAbdallāh b. ʿAbd al-Jabbār al-Ḥasanī al-Idrīsī 449
al-Miʿmārī al-Shadhalī was born in Shādhilla, at the foot of Jabal Zaghwān in Tunisia, and died in 656/1258 (see Suppl.).

Jāmī, *Nafaḥāt* 659, Suyūṭī, *Ḥusn al-muḥ.* I, 298, Maqqarī I, 587. Biographies by: a. his grandson Taqī al-Dīn Abū ʿAbdallāh Muḥammad b. Aḥmad, *Shifāʾ al-ghalīl wa-ʿāfiyat al-ʿalīl fī ajwiba lil-sāʾil*, Esc. ^{2}487$_{,2}$.—b. Muḥammad b. Abi ʾl-Qāsim b. al-Ṣabbāgh al-Ḥimyarī, *Durrat al-asrār etc.* (see Suppl.), also
584 Garr. 719.—c. Muḥammad | b. Ẓāfir al-Madanī, *al-Anwār al-qudsiyya etc.* (Suppl. II, 1009).—d. cf. Suppl.—Cf. Haneberg, ZDMG VII, 13ff.

1. *al-Muntaqā*, abstract of a Sufi work, Berl. 3089, Vat. V, 573$_{,11}$.—1a. *al-Muqaddima al-ʿizziyya etc.* See Suppl. Galtier, *Bull. de l'Inst. franç. d'archéologie or.* V, 134ff. defends his authorship of this work.—2. *Kitāb al-ikhwa* Br. Mus. 1436$_{,2}$.—3. Sermons, ibid. 3$_{,4}$.—4. *Ḥizb al-baḥr*, a prayer that he claims to have received from Muḥammad himself (cf. Ibn Baṭṭūṭa I, 40), Berl. 3868/9, Copenhagen 302, f. 490, Paris 2637$_{,3}$, Br. Mus. 98$_{,4}$, 110$_{,3}$, 120$_{,3}$, 520$_{,4}$ Ind. Off. 373$_{,2}$, Cairo ^{1}VII, 229, ^{2}I, 287, Patna II, 444$_{,2620,13}$.—Commentaries: a. Aḥmad b. Aḥmad Zarrūq, d. 899/1493 (II, 253), Br. Mus. 125$_{,1}$, 126, Alex. Fun. 172$_{,3}$.—b. ʿAbdallāh b. Murād, ca.1046/1636, Berl. 3870.—c. Muṣṭafā al-ʿAdanī, ibid. 3872.—d. Anon., ibid. 3871$_{,3}$.—e.–p. see Suppl. (h. with the title *Kawkab al-fajr* Garr. 1946).—6 other commentaries in Ahlw. 3874.—5. *al-Ḥizb al-kabīr* Berl. 3875, Leid. 2191, Br. Mus. 1254, Copenhagen 301, f. 21, cf. ZDMG VII, 25.—Commentaries: a. ʿAbd al-Raḥmān b. Muḥammad al-Fāsī, d. 1036/1626, Berl. 3876, Paris 1204$_{,3}$.—b. Muṣṭafā al-ʿAdanī, Berl. 3877.—c. Muḥammad b. ʿAbd al-Salām al-Bannānī, d. 1163/1750 (Suppl. II, 686), Alex. Faw. 20 (see Suppl.).—d. *al-Fatḥ al-qadīr bi-sharḥ al-Ḥ. al-k.* by al-Ḥasan b. ʿAlī al-Manṭāwī al-Madābighī, d. 1170/1757 (II, 328), Heid. ZDMG 91, 387 (anon.), Garr. 2058, Alex. Faw. 13.—e.–i. see Suppl.—6. *Ḥizb al-ṭams ʿalā ʿuyūn al-aʿdā*, Berl. 3878, Br. Mus. 125, ii, 2.—7. *Ḥizb al-naṣr* Berl. 3879$_{,1}$, Br. Mus. 125, ii, 3, Qawala I, 229.—8. *Ḥizb al-luṭf* Berl. 3879$_{,2}$, Br. Mus. 136$_{,7}$.—9. *Ḥizb al-faṭh wa-yusammā Ḥizb al-anwār* Br. Mus. 125 ii, 6.—10. *Ṣalāt al-fatḥ wal-maghrib*, comm., Algiers 824.—11. Several prayers, Berl. 3654, Algiers 827/32.—12. An admonition, Berl. 3997$_{,1}$.—13. *Duʿāʾ* Ind. Off. 4576 (*JRAS* 1939, 307).—14.–28. see Suppl. (26. Garr. 57; ad 27. see II, 215).—29. *al-Risāla al-ḥawḍiyya*, with a commentary by ʿAbdallāh b. Ḥusayn al-Ḥasanī al-Sharīf, Alex. Tawḥīd 28.—30. *al-Tasallī wal-tabaṣṣur ʿalā mā qaḍāhu ʾllāh min aḥkām ahl al-tajabbur wal-takabbur* Alex. Mawāʿiẓ 38$_{,1}$.—31. *Ḥizb al-ikhfāʾ* Patna I, 152$_{,1451}$.—32. *al-Ḥizb al-awwal, al-thānī* ibid. II, 376$_{,2561,1,2}$.

30. (31.) Abu ʾl-Ḥasan Ṣafī (Zayn) al-Dīn Aḥmad b. ʿAṭṭāf b. ʿAlawān al-Yafrusī, the son of the *Kātib al-inshāʾ* of the last Ayyūbids of Yemen, was born in ʿUqāqa, grew up in Dhu ʾl-Jinān, and died in Yafrus in Yemen in 665/1266.

| Biography in al-Khazrajī, ed. M. ʿAsal I, 160/2. 1. *Dīwān* Cairo ^{2}III 169 = *Kitāb al-futūḥ li-kulli qalb majrūḥ* Gotha 99,$_{5}$, a lengthier MS in Kračkovsky's possession.—2., 3. see Suppl.—4. Poems, letters, etc. Leid. 2248, Vat. V. 1184,$_{1}$.—5. *Kitāb al-tawḥīd* Garr. 1897, *al-T. al-aʿẓam* Alex. Fawāʾid 15, Patna II, 423,$_{2593,7}$. 585

31. Aḥmad b. ʿAbd al-Raḥīm b. ʿUthmān b. Ḥasan al-Ḥusaynī al-Ṣayyādī al-Rifāʿī, who died in 670/1271 at the age of 96.

Al-Maʿārif al-Muḥammadiyya fi 'l-waẓāʾif al-Aḥmadiyya C. 1305, *Fihris* II, 135.

32. Ṣadr al-Dīn Abu 'l-Maʿālī Muḥammad b. Isḥāq b. Muḥammad al-Qūnawī was educated by Ibn al-ʿArabī in his native town of Qonya when the latter resided there in 607/1210. He died in 672/1263.

Al-Subkī, *Ṭab.* V, 19, Jāmī, *Nafaḥāt* 645, Khwandamīr, *Ḥabīb al-siyar* III, 66. M. Amīn Dede *Raghāʾib al-manāqib*, composed in 1006/1597, Ist. Un. 842. 1. *Iʿjāz al-bayān fī kashf baʿḍ asrār (fī tafsīr) Umm al-Qurʾān*, on the *Fātiḥa*, AS 402, 4806,$_{1}$, Rāġib 79, Yeni 62/3, Köpr. 41 (with *ijāza* 671 A.H.), Alex. Taṣ. 33,$_{5}$, Cairo ^{1}I, 125, ^{2}I, 32, Qawala I, 38, Patna I, 22,$_{202/3}$, glosses by Shams al-Dīn Muḥammad b. Ḥamza al-Anṣārī Patna II, 412,$_{2581,1}$.—2. *Sharḥ al-aḥādīth al-arbaʿīniyya* Berl. 1471/5, Leid. 1745, Pet. AM 187,$_{2}$, Garr. 1429.—3. *Ḥaqāʾiq al-asmāʾ fī sharḥ asmāʾ Allāh al-ḥusnā* Berl. 2228/32.—4. *al-Risāla al-hādiya*, against misconceptions over the nature of God, the essential properties of things and their origin, contained in Nāṣir al-Dīn's (cf. 16) | answer to his treatise *al-Risāla* 450 *al-mufṣiḥa* (no. 10), Berl. 2305.—5. *al-Nuṣūṣ fī taḥqīq al-ṭawr al-makhṣūṣ* or *al-Nuṣūṣ fī baḥr al-taḥqīq wa-jawāhir al-fuṣūṣ*, on the main tenets of Sufism, Berl. 3015, Leid. 1521/2, Ind. Off. 1032,$_{2}$, Cairo ^{1}VII, 46, 176, 382.—Commentaries: a. *al-Khuṣūṣ* by ʿAlī b. Aḥmad al-Mahāʾimī, d. 835/1432 (II, 221), completed in 815/1412, Berl. 3016, Patna I, 131,$_{1305}$.—b. Muḥammad b. Quṭb al-Dīn al-Khūyī, completed in 856/1452, Paris 1386,$_{3}$.—6. *al-Nafaḥāt al-ilāhiyya al-qudsiyya* Berl. 3017, Qawala I, 268, Patna I, 143,$_{1389}$, Bursa Ulu Cami Taṣ. 135.—7. *Marātib al-taqwā* Berl. 3152.—8. *Shuʿab al-īmān*, on the branches of belief, of inner uplifting and self-ennoblement, Berl. 3211, attributed to him by his student Saʿīd al-Farghānī, d. 699/1299 (ḤKh IV, 7572, Suppl. I, 463, 812,$_{49}$, b).—
| 9. *Miftāḥ al-ghayb*, scientific guidance towards knowledge of the divine 586
essence and its secrets, Berl. 3212/3, Vienna 1914, AS 1655, 2088,$_{1}$, 2090, Bursa, Ulu Cami Taṣ. 137, Alex. Taṣ. 46, Cairo ^{1}VII, 382, 518, ^{2}I, 361.—Commentary by Muḥammad b. Ḥamza al-Rūmī al-Fanārī, d. 834/1430 (II, 233), Berl. 3214/5, abstract by Abu 'l-Ṭayyib b. Badr al-Dīn al-Ghazzī, ca. 1020/1611, Berl. 3216, Pers.

transl. AS 1657, 2089.—d. *Miftāḥ al-qalb* by Atpāzārī Shaykh ʿUthmān, autograph from 1097, ʿĀšir I, $511_{,1}$.—10. *al-Risāla al-mufṣiḥa ʿan muntaha ʾl-afkār wa-sabab ikhtilāf al-umam*, on knowledge of God and the proofs for His existence, the nature of the human soul, and the possibility of understanding and attaining God, Berl. 3274.—11. *al-Risāla al-murshidiyya fī aḥkām al-ṣifāt al-ilāhiyya*, on the way to reach God, Berl. 3275.—12. *Laṭāʾif al-iʿlām fī ishārāt ahl al-ilhām*, an explanation of Sufi terminology, Berl. 3457/8.—13. *Nafthat al-maṣdūr wa-tuḥfat al-shakūr* Leid. 2192.—14. *al-Nafaḥāt* (*al-raḥmāniyya wa-thamarāt al-tajalliyāt al-ikhtiṣāṣiyya*) *al-rabbāniyya*, completed by his grandson Muḥammad b. Aḥmad b. Muḥammad in 739/1338, Vienna 1913, Paris 1354.—15. *Tabṣirat al-mubtadiʾ wa-tadhkirat al-muntahī* AS 2286.—16. Correspondence with al-Ṭūsī, Leid. 1523.—17. *Duʿāʾ al-tawḥīd* Berl. 3654.—18.–28. see Suppl. (18. Garr. $2005_{,7}$; 23. under the title *Kashf asrār jawāhir al-aḥkām al-mustakhraja al-mūratha min jawāmiʿ al-kalim* Qawala I, 144).—29. *Risāla jafriyya* Alex. Ḥurūf 10.—30. *Sharḥ al-arbaʿīn* Patna II, $413_{,2581,3}$.—31. *Tafsīr al-basmala* ibid. $417_{,2581,4}$.—32. *Barzakh al-barāzikh* Bursa Ulu Cami Taş. 1319 (Ritter).

33. Abu ʾl-Fityān Abu ʾl-ʿAbbās Aḥmad b. ʿAlī b. Ibrāhīm al-Badawī was born in Fez in 596/1199, made the pilgrimage to Mecca with his father in 603/1206, and settled in 634/1236 in Tanta in Lower Egypt, where he died on 12 Rabīʿ I 675/25 August 1276. His tomb has remained a much-visited shrine to this very day.

Suyūṭi, *Ḥusn al-muḥ*, I, 299. Lane, *Manners and Customs* I, 308. Biography by Ibn Ḥajar al-ʿAsqalānī, d. 852/1448 (II, 67), Berl. 10101, by Zayn al-Dīn ʿAbd al-Ṣamad around 900/1494, ibid. 10102/3, anon. *Manāqib* Br. Mus. Suppl. 639.—1. *Ḥizb*, a quick prayer, Berl. 3881.—2. *Ṣalawāt*, commentary by ʿAbd al-Raḥmān
587 | b. Muṣṭafā al-ʿAydarūsī, d. 1192/1778 (II, 352), Cairo ^{1}VII, 88.—(3. *Bayān aḥkām al-farāʾiḍ fī ʿilm al-mīrāth* Garr. 1871? only Aḥmad al-Badawī).

34. ʿIzz al-Dīn ʿAbd al-Salām b. Aḥmad b. Ghānim al-Maqdisī al-Wāʿiẓ, who died in 678/1279 (?).

1. *Kashf al-asrār ʿan* (*al*)-*ḥikam* (*al-mūdaʿa fi*)*ʾl-ṭuyūr wal-azhār*, reflections on animate and inanimate creatures, especially flowers and birds, whose properties demonstrate the wisdom of the Creator, Berl. 8783/4, Gotha 2693/4,
451 Leid. 427 | (where other MSS are listed), in Kračkowsky's possession, AS $2011_{,5}$, 4205, Alex. Adab 114, Mawāʿiẓ 32, Cairo ^{1}VII, 86, 685, ^{2}III, 301, Tunis Zayt., *Bull. de Corr. Afr.* 1884, p. 15, no. 34, Pers. transl. Welīeddin 1630. *Les oiseaux et les fleurs*, ed. Garcin de Tassy, Paris 1821, print. C. 1280 and others (see Suppl.), translated by C.R.R. Peiper, *Stimmen aus dem Morgenlande*, Hirschberg 1850,

p. 165/265.[9]—2. *Ḥall al-rumūz wa-kashf mafātīḥ al-kunūz* Berl. 3010/1, Bodl. II, 80, 321, Esc. ^{2}530,$_2$, 1546, Algiers 939, *Bull. de Corr. Afr.* 1884, p. 372, no. 40, Cairo ^{1}II, 80, 172, VII, 13, 138, 372, AS 1773, Patna I, 131,$_{1304}$.—3. (*al-Qawl al-nafīs fī*) *Taflīs Iblīs li-yakshifa lil-nāẓir fīhi talbīs Iblīs fa-yumayyiza bayna 'l-khaṣīṣ wal-nafīs*, the devil exposed, based on the example of *Talbīs Iblīs* by Ibn al-Jawzī (p. 504,$_{38}$), against the claim of those who believe that God has no part in the evil of this world but rather allows it to happen on purpose, Berl. 2520/1, Gotha 748 (where other MSS are listed), Bursa Ulu Cami Taş. 134,$_4$, Cairo ^{1}II, 76, VII, 286, 687, print. C. 1291 and others (see Suppl.).—4. *al-Futūḥāt al-ghaybiyya fī 'l-asrār al-qalbiyya* Berl. 3012.—5. *al-Rawḍ al-anīq fī 'l-waʿẓ al-rashīq*, an edifying work, Berl. 8782, Esc. ^{2}762,$_5$.—6. *Kashf al-asrār wa-manāqib al-abrār wa-maḥāsin al-akhyār*, on the major companions of the Prophet and pious men of exception, Berl. 8785 (fragment).—7. *Fī sharḥ ḥāl al-ṣaḥāba wal-awliyāʾ*, on the ecstatic states of the companions, and friends of the Prophet, Munich 887, f. 163, Bodl. I, 850, II, 597.—8. Edifying contemplations, Berl. 8786.—9. Two long Sufi poems, Berl. 7766,$_3$.—10.–14. see Suppl.—15. *Manāzil* Bursa Ulu Cami Taş. 134,$_1$.

| 35. Zakī al-Dīn Abu 'l-ʿAbbās Aḥmad al-Hamdānī, a student of al-Qūnawī 588
(no. 31).

Al-Risāla al-qudsiyya fī asrār al-nuqla al-khāṣṣiyya, on the mystical meaning of the dotting of letters, Berl. 3444, AS 4807,$_4$.

36. Abū Bakr Quṭb al-Dīn Muḥammad b. Aḥmad b. ʿAlī al-Qasṭallānī al-Tawzarī al-Shāfiʿī, d. 686/1287 (see Suppl.).

1. *Al-Adwiya al-shāfiya fī 'l-adʿiya al-kāfiya*, a prayer manual, Berl. 3518.—2.–6. see Suppl.

37. (38.) Muʾayyad b. Maḥmūd b. Ṣāʿid al-Ṣūfī al-Ḥātimī al-Janadī, a student of al-Qūnawī, fl. ca. 690/1291.

1. *al-Qaṣīda al-ghaybiyya* (*al-dāliyya*), Sufi poem in 142 verses, with many rhetorical fireworks, at the beginning of his commentary on the *Kitāb al-fuṣūṣ* by Ibn al-ʿArabī (no. 23, 12b), Berl. 3408, Bank. XIII, 874.—2. *Dīwān* Beirut 1872.—3. *Lāmiyya* ḤKh (Ist.) II, 350, composed in 671, with a Persian commentary by the poet himself AS 4184.

---

9 *Al-Asad wal-ghawwāṣ* (see Suppl. ʿĀshir 1002,$_1$ 783 AH, Patna I, 204,$_{1825}$), is a mirror for princes in the form of an animal fable and has nothing to do with the *Kashf al-asrār* (Ritter).

38. (39.) ʿIzz al-Dīn Abū Muḥammad ʿAbd al-ʿAzīz b. Aḥmad b. Saʿīd al-Dīrīnī al-Damīrī al-Dahrī was born in 612/1215 or 613 in Dīrīn in Egypt, where his birthday is still celebrated every year. He travelled as a wandering dervish, and died in 697/1297.

452 | Wüst., *Gesch.* 368. 1. *Ṭahārat al-qalb wal-khuḍūʿ li-ʿallām al-ghuyūb*, a discussion of verses from the Qurʾān, edifying anecdotes, counsels, prayers etc., Berl. 8789/90, Gotha 648/9 (where other MSS are listed), Paris 1313, Br. Mus. Suppl. 235, Ind. Off. 1731, Patna I, 148,$_{422}$.—2. *Qilādat al-durr al-manshūr fī dhikr al-baʿth wal-nushūr*, poem about the Last Judgement, Berl. 2748/9, Gotha 1514, f. 136b, as an appendix to Ibn al-Wardī's *Kharīdat al-ʿajāʾib*, C. 1288, p. 300, S. Freund, *de rebus die resurrectionis eventuris*, Breslau 1853, V, XXXV.—3. 33 *rajaz* verses on the suras of the Qurʾān and the way in which they were revealed, Berl. 466/7.—4. Explanation of the *Fātiḥa*, Berl. 942.—5. *al-Taysīr fī ʿilm* (*ʿulūm*) *al-tafsīr*, over 3,200 *rajaz* verses, composed in Dhu 'l-Qaʿda and Dhu 'l-Ḥijja of the year 673/May—June 1275, Yeni 39/41, print. C. 1310 (*Fihris* I, 156, 205).—6. *al-Anwār al-wāḍiḥa fī tafsīr al-Fātiḥa*, composed before no. 4, Berl. 3450.—
589 7. *Arkān al-islām fi 'l-tawḥīd* | *wal-aḥkām* Berl. 1792/3.—8. *al-Maqṣad al-asnā fī sharḥ al-asmāʾ al-ḥusnā* Berl. 2234, Alex. Faw. 28.—9. Two *qaṣīdas* on Sufism, a confession of faith, and the education that is necessary for a Sufi, Berl. 3409.—10. *Irshād al-ḥayārā fi 'l-radd ʿala 'l-Naṣārā* Paris 1457, 3204, Bursa, Ulu Cami Taṣ. 134.—11. *Fi 'l-farq bayna 'l-tāʾ wal-thāʾ*, a list of words with a *thāʾ*, Berl. 7026.—12. *Fi 'l-farq bayna 'l-dāl wal-dhāl*, a list of words with a *dāl*, ibid. 2.—13. *Jawāhir al-iqtibās fī ʿilm al-jinās*, on puns, Berl. 7331/2, Vienna 234.—14. A *qaṣīda* Berl. 7784,$_{2}$.—15. A long *urjūza* on man as a microcosm, ibid. 8158,$_{1}$, Munich 819,$_{3}$.—16. *al-Durar al-multaqaṭa fi 'l-masāʾil al-mukhtalaṭa* Cairo ^{1}III, 225.—17.–26. see Suppl. (17. Garr. 1575. 20. read: *al-Shajara fī dhikr nasab al-nabī* AS 4348,$_{1}$).—27.—*Muthallathāt lughawiyya* Berl. 7081/2, Garr. 272, Alex. Lugha 25.—28. *Majlis fi 'stiqbāl shahr Ramaḍān* Alex. Fun. 147,$_{14}$.—29. *al-Wasāʾil al-ilāhiyya wal-rasāʾil al-Muḥammadiyya* AS 4348,$_{1}$ (Ritter).

39. (40.) Raslān b. Yaʿqūb b. ʿAbd al-Raḥmān al-Jaʿbarī al-Dimashqī, who died around 695/1296.

I. *Risālat al-tawḥīd*, Sufi, Gotha Pers. 5,$_{10}$, Br. Mus. 884,$_{3}$,—Commentaries: 1. *Fatḥ al-raḥmān* by Zakariyyāʾ al-Anṣārī, d. 926/1526 (II, 99), Berl. 2427/8, Br. Mus. 884,$_{4}$, Suppl. 245, i, Cairo ^{1}VII, 103, 300, 522, ^{2}I, 335.—2. ʿAlī b. ʿAṭiyya al-Ḥamawī ʿAlawān, d. 936/1530 (II, 333), Berl. 2429/31, Leipz. 874, v.—3. Abū b. Badr al-Dīn al-Ṭayyibī, d. ca. 961/1554, Berl. 2432/3.—4. *Khamrat al-khān etc.* by ʿAbd al-Ghanī al-Nābulusī, d. 1143/1730 (II, 345), Berl. 2334, Alex. Fun. $90_{,14}$, $151_{,12}$.—5. al-Ḥasan b. Mūsā al-Kurdī al-Jīlānī al-Bānī, d. 1148/1735 (II, 345), Leipz. 240.—6. Ibn Ṣadaqa, Br. Mus. $884_{,3}$.—7. Abu ʾl-Wafāʾ al-ʿIrāqī al-Ḥusaynī, Cairo ^{1}VII, 93.—II. *Risāla fi ʾl-taṣawwuf* Alex. Fun. $150_{,8}$.

40. Ṣadr al-Milla wal-Dīn Abu ʾl-Maʿālī al-Muẓaffar b. Muẓaffar al-Baghawī al-Shīrāzī.

Al-Marmūzāt al-ʿishrūn, MS dated 714/1314, by the grandson of the author ʿAlī b. Masʿūd, Alex. Mawāʿiẓ 43.

Chapter 11. Philosophy and Politics

1. Abū ʿAlī al-Ḥusayn (Ḥasan) b. ʿAlī b. Sīnā (Avicenna) al-Qānūnī was born
590 in Ṣafar 370/August 980 | in Afshana, near Bukhārā, the son of the governor
453 of Ḥarmaythān. | Having studied philosophy under Abū ʿAbdallāh al-Nātilī and medicine under the Christian physician ʿĪsā b. Yaḥyā, by the age of 17 he gained the favour of Nūḥ b. Manṣūr of Bukhārā after succesfully curing him. At the age of 22 he lost his father and an unsteady life of wandering began, taking him first to the Khwārizmshāh ʿAlī b. Manṣūr, and then to Nasā, Abīward, Ṭūs, and Dahistān. In Jurjān he lived for a long time as a teacher, and it was there that he composed his major work on medicine, the Qānūn. By way of Rayy and Qazvin he then arrived in Hamadan, where he became the vizier of the Būyid Shams al-Dawla Abū Ṭāhir, but soon after he had to relinquish his post because the military rejected his authority. When Shams al-Dawla died in 412/1021, his son Tāj al-Dawla accused Ibn Sīnā of high treason and had him transferred to a fortress. However, he succeeded in escaping to Isfahan, to ʿAlāʾ al-Dawla Abū Jaʿfar Muḥammad b. Dushmanziyār (Dushmanzār) b. Kākūya, who, in 398/1007, had made himself independent from his cousin, the Būyid Majd al-Dawla. It was for him that he wrote the Persian encyclopaedia the *Dānishnāme-yi ʿAlāʾī*, whose section on mathematics was completed after his death by his student al-Jūzajānī (Br. Mus. Pers. Cat. II, 433). Excessive work and intemperance had exhausted his body so much that after a military campaign against Hamadan in 428/1037 he died after a brief illness. His huge corpus of works encompass, besides philosophy and medicine, the entire body of profane learning of his time, admittedly without any further research by himself, but still in an elegant and easily comprehensible style. It is for this reason that they had a lasting influence on scholarly studies, not only in the Orient, but in Europe as well.

591 | Autobiography, continued by his favorite student al-Jūzajānī, Ibn Abī Uṣ. II, 2–9, see ibid. 2/20, Ibn Khall. 182, *Khiz.* IV, 466ff., Wüst., *Ärzte* no. 128, Leclerc I, 466, Munk, *Mélanges* 352ff., A. Müller, *Der Islam* II, 67ff. Collected works AS 4829, 4849/53. *Majmūʿ rasāʾil al-Shaykh al-raʾīs*, Hyderabad 1354/1935 (*Risāla fī sirr al-qadr, Risāla fi ʾl-saʿāda, fī dhikr asbāb al-raʿd, al-Risāla al-ʿarshiyya fi ʾl-tawḥīd, Risāla fi ʾl-ḥathth ʿala ʾl-dhikr, Risāla fi ʾl-mūsīqī*).

I. Theology and philosophy. Exposition of his philosophical system, al-Shahrastānī 348/429. F. Mehren, Les rapports de la philosophie d'Avicenna avec l'Islam, *Muséon* 1883.—1. *Risāla fī tafsīr sūrat al-Ikhlāṣ* (112) Berl. 972, Patna I, 419$_{,3590,\ 2}$.—2. *Risāla fī tafsīr al-Muʿawwidhatayn* (p. 113/4) ibid. 977, Gotha

543 | (where other MSS are listed).—3. *Tafsīr sūrat al-Falaq* (113) Gotha 754$_{,3}$, 1158$_{,3}$, Br. Mus. 978$_{,39}$, Mosul 75$_{,83,\ 7}$, Patna, loc. cit., 3.—4. *Tafsīr sūrat al-Nās* (114) Gotha 543$_{,1}$, 1158$_{,4}$, Br. Mus. 978$_{,40}$, Bodl. Uri 980$_{,5}$, Patna, loc. cit., 4.—5. *Tafsīr sūrat al-Tawḥīd* Br. Mus. 978$_{,38,\ 41}$, together with 3., 4., Mashh. I, 31, 104.—6. *Kitāb al-ʿarūs*, on the nature of God as the creator of the universe and finite things, Berl. 2295$_{,16}$, Br. Mus. 1349$_{,17}$, Esc. ^{2}703$_{,6}$.—7. On God's transcendence and man's dependence on Him, in answer to a letter by al-Ḥusayn b. Muḥammad b. ʿUmar Abū Manṣūr Zayla, Berl. 2297.—8. *al-Kalima al-ilāhiyya*, on God's nature and properties, Berl. 2298.—9. *Masʾala fi 'l-wasaʿa*, on the same subject, ibid. 2299.—10. *Fī taṣdīq (ithbāt) al-nubuwwa* Gotha 1158$_{,5}$, Leid. 1464$_{,7}$, Br. Mus. 1349$_{,10}$, *Pet. Bull. de l'Ac.* 1860, 518, n. 40.—11. *al-Risāla al-aḍḥawiyya*, on the Last Judgement, Berl. 2734, Leid. 1465, Br. Mus. 978$_{,4}$, Cairo ^{1}II, 48, Persian transl. Bodl. Pers. 1422v.—12. Explanation of Sufi expressions and terms, Berl. 3454.—13. *Risāla fī (bayān māhiyyat) al-ṣalāt* Berl. 3512, Gotha 1158$_{,7}$, Leid. 2141, Br. Mus. 978$_{,43}$, 1349$_{,16}$, Bodl. I, 980$_{,4}$, Najaf and Tehran, *Dharīʿa* II, 48, 195, Patna I, 88$_{,898}$.—14. Answer to a question concerning prayer and visiting tombs, Berl. 3568, Esc. ^{2}703$_{,5}$.—15. *Risāla fī ziyārat al-qubūr* Berl. 408$_{,3}$, Taymūr, Ḥikma 102.—16. *al-Fayḍ al-ilāhī*, on revelation and gifts of grace, miracles and dreams, witchcraft and talismans, Berl. 4094, Br. Mus. 978$_{,17}$.—17. *al-Risāla al-nayrūziyya fī ḥurūf al-abjad*, on the letters that stand at the beginning of various suras, dedicated to Emir al-Sayyid Abī Bakr Muḥammad b. ʿAbdallāh on the occasion of the festivities of Nawrūz, | Gotha 1158$_{,6}$ (where 592 other MSS are listed), Taymūr, Ḥikma 121, Patna II, 456$_{,2631,\ 5,\ 8}$, print. Istanbul 1298.—18. *Kitāb al-shifāʾ*, a. logic, b. physics, c. mathematics and astronomy, d. theology, Berl. 5044, Br. Mus. Suppl. 711, Ind. Off. 475/6, Bodl. II, 435/7, 452, 467/8, 471/3, 475/7, 481/2, 485/7, 483, 490, 495, 893, II, 581ff., Upps. 344, Yeni 770/5, Mosul 189$_{,16}$, Patna I, 213, 904/6, d. ibid. II, 525$_{,2822}$. *Fann-i samāʿ-i ṭabīʿī az Kitāb al-shifāʾ*, transl. by M.ʿA. Furūghī, Tehran 1316/1937.—b. Garr. 861.—d. *Ilāhiyyāt al-Sh.* Patna II, 525$_{,2822}$, on which a *ḥāshiya* by Mullā Ṣadrā (II, 412), ibid. I, 271$_{,1878/9}$; *Minhāj al-Sh. fi 'l-ilāhiyyāt* by Aḥmad b. Zayn al-ʿĀbidīn al-ʿAlawī, ibid. I, 215$_{,1923}$.—*Mukhtaṣar Uqlīdis* Fātiḥ 3211, *Kitāb al-arithmāṭīqī* Emir 2850, an independent part of the *Shifāʾ*, Erg. 165/6, cf. Steinschneider, *Hebr. Übers.* § 150.—Abstract, *Kitāb al-najāt*, Br. Mus. 978$_{,5}$, 979, Bodl. I, 456$_{,2}$, Cairo ^{1}VI, 105, Yeni 777, print. Rome 1593, C. 1331, ed. Muḥyi 'l-Dīn Ṣabrī al-Kurdī, C. 1939.—19. *Risāla ilā ʿUbaydallāh al-Jūzajānī*, a defence against the accusation that in the *Shifāʾ* he went against the teachings of the Qurʾān, Berl. 2072, Br. Mus. 978$_{,2}$.—20. *Kitāb al-ishārāt wal-tanbīhāt*, a handbook on logic, Berl. 5046/7, Leid. 1449/51, Pet. 87/8, Esc. ^{2}656/7, Yeni 762, Sarāi A. III, 3248$_{,1}$ (Ritter, *Isl.* XXIV, 276, n. 1.), Cairo ^{1}VI, 93, Qawala II, 380, Patna I, 209$_{,1858}$. Pers. transl. of 454

the first and the second part, Br. Mus. Pers. II, 438. *Le Livre des theorèmes et des avertissements, publ. par* J. Forget, Leiden 1892. *Fann-i samāʿ-i ṭabīʿī* from Avicenna's philos. treatise Isharat, transl. into Persian by M.A. Furūghī, Tehran 1939.—Commentaries: a. Saʿd b. Kammūna, d. 676/1277 (Suppl. I, 768), Ind. Off. 484.—b. *Lubāb al-ishārāt,* with critical attacks by Fakhr al-Dīn al-Rāzī, d. 606/1209 (p. 506), Br. Mus. Suppl. 723, Bodl. I, 480, Yeni 764, Patna I, $212_{,1889/90}$; from which *Sharḥ al-Ishārāt fi 'l-ṭabīʿiyyāt,* Lucknow 1293.—Against this, ʿAlī al-Āmidī, d. 641/1243, wrote the *Kashf al-tamwīhāt,* Berl. 5048, and Naṣīr al-Dīn al-Ṭūsī, d. 672/1273 (p. 508), wrote the *Ḥall mushkilāt al-Ishārāt,* Berl. 5049/50 (second half), Or. qu. 2044, Paris 2366, Leid. 1452, Pet. $89_{,2}$, Esc. ^{1}655, Ambros. 311, Yeni 763, Cairo ^{1}VI, 93, Garr. 806, Patna I, $212_{,1891}$, II, $561_{,2944}$, print. Lucknow 1293.—The differences between the two commentaries are discussed by Muḥammad b. Saʿīd al-Yamanī al-Tustarī (ca. 707/1306) in *al-Muḥākama bayna Naṣīr al-Dīn wal-Rāzī,* Berl. 5052, print. Tehran 1886, and by Quṭb al-Dīn
593 Muḥammad b. Muḥammad | al-Rāzī al-Taḥtānī, d. 766/1364 (II, 209), in his *Kitāb al-muḥākama bayna 'l-imām wal-Naṣīr,* composed in 755/1355, Berl. 5053, Ind. Off. 482, Br. Mus. 1350., Ambros. 311, Esc. ^{2}613, Dāmādzāde 1407, Cairo ^{1}VI,
455 104, Patna I, $215_{,1919/21}$. | Glosses by (see Suppl.): γ Ibn Kamālpāshā, d. 940/1533 (II, 449), Esc. ^{2}623.—δ Mīrzājān Ḥabīballāh al-Shīrāzī al-Bāghandī, d. 994/1585 (II, 414), Berl. 5054, Leid. 1457, Ind. Off. 483, Patna I, $211_{,1884/6}$.—c.–l. see Suppl. (c = h? under the title *Zubdat al-naqd wa-lubāb al-Kashf,* completed in 679/1280, in al-Khizāna al-Gharawiyya, *Dharīʿa* II, $97_{,382}$).—m. *Sharḥ masāʾil ʿawīṣa fi 'l-Ishārāt* by Zayn al-Dīn Ṣadaqa, Carullah 1573.—n. Comments on the ninth chapter on Sufism by Shaykhzāde al-Hindī, d. 959/1552, Br. Mus. 757.—o. Anon. glosses, Leid. 1454/5, Bodl. I, $462_{,1}$ Esc. ^{2}618/21.—p. Syriac transl. by Barhebraeus, Wright, *Syr. Lit.* 271, n. 1, Baumstark, 317, n. 3.—21. *al-Taʿlīqāt,* on logic and metaphysics, Br. Mus. 978, Zanjān, *Lughat al-ʿArab* II, 194.[1]—21a. *Taʿliqāt ʿalā Uthūlūjiyya,* Taymūr, Ḥikma 102.—23. *ʿUyūn al-ḥikma*: a. logic, b. physics, c. theology, Leid. 1446; cf. Haneberg, *Abh. der Bayer. Ak.* XI, 256/67. Commentary by Fakhr al-Dīn al-Rāzī, d. 606/1209, Berl. 5043, Vienna 1522, Leid. 1446, Ambros. 321, Esc. ^{2}628, Ind. Off. 478, Landb. Br. 558.—23a. *al-Mūjiz fi 'l-manṭiq* AS $4849_{,19}$.—23b.–f. see Suppl.—24. *Taqāsīm al-ḥikma* Leid. 1478 = *Fī aqsām al-ʿulūm al-ḥikmiyya* Gotha $1158_{,29}$, cf. 1160, Bodl. I, $980_{,10}$, Br. Mus. $430_{,3}$, $978_{,13}$, $980_{,7}$, $981_{,10}$, print. in *Tisʿ rasāʾil,* Istanbul 1298 (see *JA* 1881, II, 531) p. 171/80, Alex. Fun. $100_{,8}$.—24a. *Mukhtaṣar al-ḥudūd* Patna II, $471_{,2638,\ 1}$.—25. *al-Mubāḥathāt* Bodl. I, 456, *Lughat al-ʿarab* VI, 94.—26. *Risālat Ḥayy b.*

---

1 Against the *Ilāhiyyāt* of nos. 18–21 al-Shahrastānī, d. 548/1153 (p. 428), wrote *al-Muṣāraʿa* Berl. 5055.

Yaqẓān Leid. 1464,$_{9}$, Bodl. I, 456,$_{3}$, Esc. ^{2}703,$_{3}$ (in Cairo ^{1}VI, 95 lumped together with the work by Ibn Ṭufayl with the same title), with a commentary by his student al-Ḥusayn b. Ṭāhir b. Zayla al-Iṣfahānī, d. 440/1048, Br. Mus. 978,$_{3}$, cf. Mehren, *Muséon* 1886, 41ff., idem, Avicenne, *Traités mystiques*, Leiden 1889.—27. *al-Risāla al-Ṭabariyya*, which he addressed as a prisoner in Fardajūn near Hamadan to Tāj al-Dawla, Br. Mus. 978,$_{2}$.—27a. *Qiṣṣat Salamān wa Absāl*, see Suppl. print. in *Tis' rasā'il*, C. 1326, p. 158ff.—28. Philosophical questions and answers, expositions on the nature of existence, possibility and necessity
| Berl. 5124.—29. *Risāla (Maqāla) fi 'l-nafs* Paris 2322,$_{9}$, Leid. 1467, 1470, Br. Mus. 594
426,$_{22}$, Ambros. 320c, Esc. ^{2}656, 663(?), see S. Landauer, die Psychologie des I.S. *ZDMG* XXIX, 355ff., Siebeck, *Archiv f. Gesch. der Philosophie* I, 4, 525ff., II, 22ff.—30. *Risāla fī quwa 'l-nafs* Berl. 5341, Br. Mus. 978,$_{81}$, *fī quwā rūḥ al-insān* Patna II, 476,$_{2640,\ 15}$.—31. *Risāla fī bayān al-nafs al-nāṭiqa wa-aḥwālihā*, Berl. 5342, Leid. 1468.—32. *Fī aḥwāl al-nafs*, Berl. 5343.—32a.–d. see Suppl. (c. Faiḍ. 2144,$_{1}$).—33. Answers to objections by his friend Bahmanyār on whether the soul, upon awakening, has consciousness of itself or not, Berl. 5344.—34. Whether or not the imaginations of reason are extinguished after death when *phantasia* ceases its activity, Berl. 5345.—35. *al-Qaṣīda al-'ayniyya* or *al-nafsiyya*, 21 verses on the relationship between the soul and the body and their separation, Berl. 5346/7, Gotha 1,$_{3}$ (where other MSS are listed), see Hammer, *Wiener Ztschr. f. Kunst u. Lit.* 1837. Commentaries: a. 'Abd al-Wājid b. Muḥammad Mudarris Kutāhya (see Suppl.), Berl. 5348 (wrongly), Munich, 676,$_{2}$, Vienna 461,$_{2}$.—b. 'Afīf al-Dīn al-Tilimsānī, d. 690/1291 (p. 258), Cairo ^{1}VII, 12, 468.—c. Sulaymān al-Maḥūzī al-Baḥrānī, Br. Mus. 886,$_{18}$.—d. Dā'ūd al-Anṭākī (II, 364), Paris 2944, Cairo ^{1}VI, 101.—e. Sa'īd al-Samnānī, Landb.—Br. 578, al-Sam'ānī, Leid. 1473.—f. Anon., Paris 5349/52, Gotha 1167, Munich 676,$_{3}$, Leid. 1473/4, Bodl. I, 1230,$_{2}$, 1258.—h. (Wehbi 1340)—p. see Suppl.—q. Shams al-Dīn al-Samarqandī, Heid. *ZDMG* 91, 389 = Berl. 5353 (which has Abu 'l-Baqā' al-Aḥmadī).—35a. *Risāla mukhtaṣara fī ma'rifat tarkīb al-rūḥ wal-nafs wal-jasad* Patna I, 341,$_{2586,\ 3}$. |—36. *Risāla fī 'ilm al-nafs* Gotha 52,$_{6}$, Leid. 456
1466, Bodl. I, 1012,$_{2}$, ed. Landauer, loc. cit.—37. *Risāla fī ḥudūd al-ashyā' wa-rusūmihā*, definitions of philosophical terms, Berl. 5375, Leid. 1460/3, Ind. Off. 771, Br. Mus. 978,$_{23}$, Bodl. II, 290,$_{1}$, Esc. ^{2}703,$_{9}$, 844, print. Istanbul 1298, p. 150/69, Latin transl. by Andreas Alpago Bellunensis, Venice 1586.—38. *Risāla fi 'l-akhlāq*, on ethics, Berl. 5391, Leid. 1464,$_{6}$, 2143, Br. Mus. 978,$_{24}$.—39. *Risāla fi 'l-'ishq* Leid. 1480, Bodl. I, 980,$_{12}$, II, 290,$_{3}$, Br. Mus. 978,$_{1}$; ed. Mehren, *Traités myst.* Leid. 1894.—40. *Risāla fi 'l-siyāsa* Leid. 1464,$_{5}$.—41. *al-Khuṭba al-gharrā'* Leid. 1464,$_{1}$, 2139, Br. Mus. 978,$_{16}$, Esc. ^{2}700,$_{10}$, ed. Golius, Leiden 1629, with comm. Gotha 1158,$_{17}$, Esc. ^{2}703,$_{11}$, Persian comm. Bodl. Pers. 1422iii.—42. *Risālat al-mabda' wal-ma'ād* Leid. 1464,$_{2}$, Gotha 1158,$_{8}$, (fragm.), Br. Mus. 978,$_{33}$,

595 (Pers. ibid. 22), Ambros. 320,$_{6}$, Esc. ^{2}703,$_{10}$, Patna | II, 420,$_{5390}$, Persian transl. by the author himself, Bodl. Pers. 1422,$_{11}$.—42a. *Risāla fī maʿād al-nafs* Taymūr, Ḥikma 5, Zanjān, *Lughat al-ʿArab* VI, 93, Patna II, 419,$_{2590,\ 1}$ 2590,$_{5}$.—43. *al-Anmāṭ al-thalāth* Leid. 1564,$_{7}$ = *Ishārāt* II, 8/10.—44. *Risālat al-ṭayr*, a mystical parable about a captured bird, Leid. 1564,$_{10}$, 2144, ed. Mehren, *Traités myst.* fs. III, Leiden 1891, idem *Muséon* VI, 383/93; Persian comm. by ʿUmar b. Sahlān al-Sāwajī, ca. 540/1145, Br. Mus. Pers. II, 439b, Bodl. Pers. 1422,$_{1}$.—45. *Risālat al-qaḍāʾ wal-qadar* Leid. 1464,$_{11}$, Br. Mus. 978,$_{25}$, AS 4849,$_{25}$, Mehren, *Muséon* 1885, 35/50.—46. *Risāla fī anna lil-māḍī mabdaʾan zamāniyyan* Leid. 1464,$_{12}$, Br. Mus. 426,$_{14}$, 978,$_{37}$ 1349,$_{14}$.—47. *Risāla fi ʾl-radd ʿala ʾl-munajjimīn* = *Ibṭāl aḥkām al-nujūm* Leid. 1464,$_{13}$, Br. Mus. 1349,$_{6}$, Mehren, *Muséon* 1884, 383ff.—48. *Ajwibat al-masāʾil al-ʿashara* Patna II, 420, 5290,$_{7}$.—49. On the meaning of the Sufi saying: *Man aʿrafa sirr al-qadar fa-qad alḥada*, Br. Mus. 978,$_{16}$.—50. *Risāla fi ʾl-farq bayna ʾl-ḥarāra al-gharīza wal-gharība* ibid. 29.—1. *Risāla fī bayān al-ṣūra al-manqūla al-mukhālifa lil-ḥaqq* ibid. 30.—52. *Risālat al-firdaws fī māhiyyat al-insān* ibid. 34, 1349,$_{7}$, Patna II, 420,$_{5290,\ 6}$.—53. *al-Risāla al-manāmiyya* Br. Mus. 978,$_{44}$.—54. *Risāla fī ḥudūth al-ḥurūf* Leid. 1479, Br. Mus. 978,$_{45}$, Patna II, 456,$_{2531,\ 51}$.—55. *Risāla tashtamil ʿalā īḍāḥ barāhīn mustanīṭa min masāʾil ʿawīṣa* Br. Mus. 978,$_{48}$, 980,$_{9}$.—56. *Risāla fī taḥqīq jawhar al-ajsām al-thamāniya* Patna II, 420, 5290,$_{8}$ = 71/2?—57. *Risāla fi ʾl-ʿilm wal-nuṭq* Br. Mus. 1349,$_{5}$.—58. *Risāla fi ʾl-afʿāl wal-infiʿālāt* ibid. 9, Taymūr, Ḥikma 37, Mashh. II, 31,$_{105}$, *Dharīʿa* II, 260,$_{1056}$.—59. *Fi ʾl-muʿjiza wal-siḥr wal-nayranjiyyāt*, on the existence of the Creator, Br. Mus. 1349,$_{15}$.—60. *Sharḥ asmāʾ Allāh* ibid. 18.—61. Demonstration of the existence of the Universal Intellect, ibid. 20.—62. The 7 principles of Aristotle concerning the soul, ibid. 21.—63. *Risāla fī dafʿ al-ghamm (al-khawf) min al-mawt* Leid. 2140,$_{2}$, Persian Br. Mus. 978,$_{9}$, Mehren, *Traités myst.* Leiden 1894, see *al-Mashriq* XI, 839.—64. *al-Ḥikma al-ʿarūḍiyya* Upps. 364,$_{1}$.—65. *Jumlat maʿānī Kitāb Sufisṭīqī fī ibānat al-mawāḍiʿ al-mughliṭa lil-bāḥith* ibid. 2.—66. *Fī maʿānī Kitāb Rīṭūrīqī ay al-balāgha fi ʾl-ḥukūma wal-khaṭāba* ibid. 3.—67. *Maʿānī Kitāb Fūyīṭīqī wa-huwa Kitāb ʾnṭūrīqī* (sic) *fi ʾl-shiʿriyyāt* ibid. 4; cf. Margoliouth, *Analecta orientalia* 8ff.—68. *al-Rajaz al-manṭiqī*, in 290 verses, Leid. 1458/9, Br. Mus. 978,$_{7}$, ed. Schmölders, *Documenta philosophiae Arabum*, Bonn 1836. Commentary by
596 Abū Bakr Bundūd, sixth cent., cf. Renan Averroes ^{2}39, Esc. ^{2}627.—68a–yyy | see Suppl. (c. *Risālat al-ʿarsh*, also Taymūr, Ḥikma 102.—g = *Risāla fī khaṭaʾ man qāla inna shayʾan wāḥidan jawhar wa-ʿarḍ maʿan*, Zanjān, *Lughat al-ʿArab* VI, 93.—p. Patna II, 417,$_{2586,\ 6}$.—y. in *Majmūʿa*, Hyderabad 1354, no. 6.—nn. Mosul 180,$_{159,\ 2}$).—zzz. *Ithbāt al-nubuwwa wa-taʾwīl mā fī kalimāt al-anbiyāʾ min al-rumūz* in a *majmūʿa*, in the library of Hādī Āl Kāshif al-Ghiṭāʾ, *Dharīʿa* I,

100,$_{492}$.—aaaa. *Risāla fī 'l-khuṭab wal-jumaʿāt*, Zanjān, *Lughat al-ʿArab* VI, 93.—bbbb. *Risāla fī īḍāḥ barāhīn thalāth masāʾil* ibid. (= 55 ?).—cccc. *Sharḥ-i miʿrāj*, a rational explanation of the Prophet's ascension to heaven, in Persian, Bodl. Pers. 1422ii.

| II. Astronomy and science. 69. *Mukhtaṣar fī ʿilm al-hayʾa* Br. Mus. 977,$_{27}$, 457
Algiers 1452.—70. *Mukhtaṣar al-Mijisṭī* Paris 2484, Bodl. I. 1012.—71. *Risālat al-ajsām al-samāwiyya* Esc. ^{2}703,$_{1}$.—72. *Risālat al-fawāʾid fī 'l-raʾy al-muḥaṣṣal min al-aqdamīn fī jawhar al-ajrām al-samāwiyya wa-bayān madhāhibihim* Br. Mus. 978,$_{36}$.—73. *Risāla fī qiyām al-arḍ wasṭ al-samāʾ*, composed in Jurjāniyya for Aḥmad b. Muḥammad al-Sahlī, Br. Mus. 981,$_{11}$, 1349,$_{8}$, Bodl. I, 980,$_{1}$.—74. Letter to al-Bīrūnī (p. 626) on Aristotle's *περὶ οὐρανοῦ* and on physics in general, Leid. 1476, Bodl. I, 980,$_{2}$, Br. Mus. 978,$_{50}$, 980,$_{15}$, Ambros. 320e, AS 2737, 4853,$_{4}$, printed in *Jāmiʿ al-badāʾiʿ*, C. 1335, 119/51.—75. *Risāla* on two questions of physics, Leid. 1477.—76. *Maqāla fī 'l-ṭarīq alladhī aththarahu ʿalā sāʾir al-ṭuruq fī 'ttikhādh al-ālāt al-raṣadiyya*, perhaps from the lost *Kitāb lawāḥiq ʿilm al-mijisṭī*, Leid. 1061.—77. *Risālat dhikr asbāb al-raʿd wal-barq* Br. Mus. 978,$_{15}$.—78. *Risāla fī ḥudūth al-ajsām Esc.* ^{2}703,$_{2}$.—79. *Risāla fī 'l-ʿilm al-ṭabīʿī* Upps. 364,$_{5}$.—79a.–q. see Suppl. (a. 1. *li-faḍl* see Nallino, Esc. ^{2}II, XXIV.—i = k; m. Patna II, 341,$_{2526,\ 2}$, *Epistula ad regem Hasan de re recta*, see Ruska, *Isis* XXI, 1934, 14. no. 51).—79r. *Risāla fī taḥqīq al-zāwiya* Patna II, 456,$_{2631,\ 6}$.

III. Medicine. 80. *Rajaz* on the 25 signs of the fatal ending of diseases according to Hippocrates, Berl. 6229, Br. Mus. 893,$_{6}$, Mosul 273,$_{63,\ 1}$.—81. *Manẓūma fī 'l-ṭibb*, 1316 *rajaz* verses, Berl. 6268, 6295/9, Dresd. 139, Gött. 97, Basle M. III, 5 Br. Mus. Suppl. 801, Leningrad, As. Mus., Esc. ^{2}788,$_{12}$, 853,$_{2}$, 863, 8,$_{1}$, Garr. 1093, lith. Lucknow 1261, see K. Opitz, Avicenna, Das Lehrgedicht über die Heilkunde, aus dem Arab. übers. *Qu. u. St. z. Gesch. der Nat. u. Med.* VII (1940) 150/220.—Commentaries: a. Ibn Rushd (Averroes), d. 595/1199 (no. 15), Gotha 2027,$_{2}$ (where other MSS are listed), | Esc. ^{2}788,$_{2}$, 803,$_{2}$, 831,$_{2}$, 851,$_{2}$, 853,$_{2}$, 597
863,$_{1}$, Garr. 1094.—b.–f. see Suppl. (c. *al-Jawhar al-nafīs*, also Alex. Ṭibb 15, Patna I, 246,$_{2096}$, by Mūsā b. Ibrāhīm b. Mūsā al-Baghdādī, d. 876/1471, author of *al-Nukat al-wafiyyāt fī aḥkām al-ḥummayāt*, Garr. 1115?).—g. Muḥammad b. Ismāʿīl b. Muḥammad, composed in 988/1580, Paris 2943.—another *urjūza*, Gotha 2027,$_{4}$, Beirut 289.—82. *al-Qānūn fī 'l-ṭibb*, Berl. 6269/71, Gotha 1911/5 (where other MSS are listed), Br. Mus. Suppl. 787/90, Esc. ^{2}822/7, 862, Garr. 1079/83, Mashh. XVI, 30, 86/90, Patna I, 253,$_{2154/60}$, see *BO* 1140ff., Choulant, *Bücherkunde der älteren Medizin*, Leipzig 1841, 361ff., Steinschneider, *Hebr. Übers.* § 431, M. Meyerhof and D. Joannides, *La Gynécologie et l'obstétrique chez Avicenne et leurs rapports avec celles des Grecs*, Cairo 1938.—Commentaries: a. Fakhr al-Dīn al-Rāzī, d. 606/1209 (p. 506), Bodl. I, 525, 708, fragm. Gotha

1916, glosses Paris 2936.—b. ʿAlī b. al-Nafīs al-Qarshī, d. 687/1288 (p. 493), on anatomy in Book 1 and 3, Berl. 6272/3, Paris 2939, Bodl. II, 178, Esc. ^{2}828 (*Sharḥ abḥāth al-Q.*), 885/6 (Book VI), Mosul 217,$_{99}$, Patna I, 249,$_{2120/1}$.—c. Quṭb al-Dīn al-Shīrāzī, d. 710/1310 (II, 211): aa. On the complete work, Gotha 1917 (fragm.), vol. I, Paris 2940, Bodl. II, 160 Esc. ^{1}291, Patna I, 249,$_{2122/3}$, 250,$_{2131}$.—bb. *al-Tuḥfa al-Saʿdiyya*, on the *Kulliyyāt*, dedicated to Saʿd al-Dīn, vizier of Sultan Khudābende, Ind. Off. 779 (frgm.), Book I, Bodl. II, 177, Nan. 102, Esc. ^{2}864/5.—d. Muḥammad b. Maḥmūd al-Āmulī, d. 753/1352, abbreviated from the commentary by al-Shīrāzī, Br. Mus. 1449,$_{2}$, Suppl. 891, Ind. Off. 780, dam. *RAAD* XII, 320 (*Sharḥ Muqaddimat al-Q.*), Patna I, 249,$_{2124}$, on which glosses by ʿAlī al-Jīlānī, d. 1018/1609, see Suppl., also Patna I, 249,$_{2127/30}$.—e. Muḥammad b. ʿAbdallāh al-Āqsarāʾī, ca. 800/1397, Leid. 1322, Bodl. I, 581, 606, 629, 635, Palat. 254, Esc. ^{1}831.—f.–n. see Suppl. (f. Patna 249,$_{2118}$.—g. ibid. 2125/6.—l. ibid. 250,$_{2139}$.—m. ibid. 2132).—Abstracts: a. *Ikhtiṣār Kitāb al-q.* from the *Kulliyyāt* or from *al-Fuṣūl al-Īlāqiyya* by Muḥammad b. Yūsuf al-Īlāqī, d. 485/1092, Paris 2917, 5105, Pet. Ros. 167/8, Bank. IV, 42, Āṣaf. II, 928,$_{278, 429}$, with the title *al-Asbāb wal-ʿalāmāt* Beirut 309,$_{1}$, Alex. Ṭibb 4. *Muʿālajāt al-Ī.* Rampūr I, 497,$_{232/3}$.—Commentaries: α Muḥammad b. ʿAlī al-Nīsābūrī, completed in 683/1284, Gotha 1931, Leipz. 756.—β Muḥammad b. Maḥmūd al-Āmulī, Selīm Āġā 871.—γ Sadīd
598 al-Dīn Muḥammad al-Samnānī, Paris 2907,$_{2}$.—δ *al-Īmāqī* by | Kamāl al-Dīn ʿAbd al-Raḥmān b. Muḥammad b. Ibrāhīm b. Muḥammad b. Yūsuf b. al-ʿAtāʾiqī al-Ḥillī, composed in 754/5, al-Khizāna al-Gharawiyya, *Dharīʿa* II, 509,$_{2000}$.—ε Maḥmūd Tāj al-Rāzī, ca. 730/1330, Berl. 6284.—b. *al-Mūjiz* by ʿAlī b. al-Nafīs al-Qarshī, d. 687/1288, (p. 493), therein the first representation of the pulmonary circulation, see O.S. Hadded, *Münch. Med. Wochenschr.* 1941, 1088, Berl. 6275/6, Gotha 1925/7 (where other MSS are listed), Br. Mus. Suppl. 805, Esc. ^{2}826,$_{2}$, Garr. 1084/6, Mosul 192,$_{22}$, 237,$_{178}$, Alex. Ṭibb 49, Qawala II, 290, Patna I, 250,$_{2172/3}$, print. Calcutta 1261.—Commentaries: aa. *al-Mughnī* by Sadīd al-Dīn al-Kāzarūnī al-Sadīdī, ca. 745/1344 (II, 195), Berl. 6277/8, Gotha 1925/7 (where other MSS are listed), Br. Mus. Suppl. 806, Garr. 1087, Alex. Ṭibb. 46, Patna I, 254,$_{2168}$, II, 322,$_{2866}$, print. Calcutta 1832.—bb. Abu ʾl-Mubārak Muḥammad, ca. 925/1519, Berl. 6279.—cc. Nafīs b. ʿIwaḍ al-Kirmānī, d. 853/1449 (II, 213), completed in 841/1437, Ind. Off. 785, Bodl. II, 686, Esc. ^{2}829, 866, Garr. 1089/90, Mosul 270,$_{24}$, Patna I, 256,$_{2178/9}$.—Glosses: α Ḥakīm Aʿājib b. Muʿālij Khān Bank. IV, 46/7.—β Ḥakīm Aḥmad Sharīf Khān b. Ḥādhiq al-Mulk Makmal Khān b. al-Wakīl Khān, d. 1231/1799 in Delhi, Bank. IV, 48.—γ see Suppl.—δ Aḥmad al-Adranawī, Paris 2932.—dd. *Ḥall al-mūjiz* by Jamāl (Shams) al-Dīn Muḥammad b. Muḥammad al-Āqsarāʾī, d. 779/1378, Bodl. I, 629, Garr. 1088, Esc. ^{2}836, 867,$_{2}$, Alex. Ṭibb 15.—ff.—oo. see Suppl. (gg. al-Amshāṭī, d. 902/1496, II, 169; oo. also Patna I, 250,$_{2125/6}$).—c. *al-Qānūnja fi ʾl-ṭibb* by Maḥmūd b. ʿUmar al-Jaghmīnī, d. 745/1344 (II, 213), Berl. 6293, Gotha 1928/9 (where other

MSS are listed), Esc. ^{2}868, Alex. Ṭibb 34, Patna I, 251,$_{2140}$.—Commentaries: aa. al-Fāḍil al-Baghdādī, after 710/1310, Berl. 6294.—bb. Ḥusayn b. Muḥammad al-Astarābādī, composed in 831/1427, Ind. Off. 1041,$_{3}$.—cc. Muḥammad b. Muḥammad al-Ṭabīb al-Miṣrī, dedicated to Sultan Bāyezīd II (886–918/1481–1512), Gotha 1930.—dd. Ḥasan al-Ḥalabī, Leid. 1324. |—ee.—pp. see Suppl. (gg. 458
also Patna I, 250,$_{2133}$).—d. *Mukhtaṣar al-kulliyyāt* by Najm al-Dīn Aḥmad b. Muḥammad al-Lubūdī, seventh cent. p. 651, Paris 2918 (autograph).—e. Nidā' b. ʿĪsā b. al-Ḥājj Nidā' b. ʿImrān, Paris 2933 (autograph dated 990/1582), see Suppl.—f. *al-Maknūn fī tanqīḥ al-Qānūn* by Hibatallāh b. Jumayʿ, d. 594/1198 (p. 489), Bodl. I, 596, Garr. 1092, whence *al-Talwīḥ ilā asrār al-Tanqīḥ* or *Tanqīḥ al-maknūn* by Fakhr al-Dīn al-Khujandī (II, 213), Paris 2941, Patna I, 252,$_{2147}$.—g.—m. see Suppl.—83. *Risāla fi 'l-hindubā'*, on the use of unwashed chicory, Gotha 1158,$_{26}$, 1930,$_{5}$, *Risāla fī khawāṣṣ al-kūshānī* Mashh. XII, 19,$_{58}$ (Krause), | *Hindibā* 599
risālesī, Buharali b. S. L'article d'Avicenne sur la chicorée par A. Süheyl, Univers. Istanbul, Tip Tarihi Enstitüsü no. 7, 1937.—84. *Urjūza fi 'l-tashrīḥ*, on anatomy, Gotha 13.—85. *Risāla fi 'l-ṭibb* Leid. 2140.—86. *Fī aḥkām al-adwiya al-qalbiyya*, on diseases of the heart, Berl. 6359, Gotha 1995, Leid. 1330/1, Esc. ^{2}860,$_{2}$, 875,$_{3}$, Qawala II, 290, MSS in private possesion *Dharīʿa* I, 403,$_{2099}$, beginning printed in *al-ʿIrfān*, Sidon 1345, Rabīʿ I, abstract Esc. ^{2}844/5.—87. Medical *waṣiyya* in *kāmil* verse, Berl. 3974, Esc. ^{2}883.—88. *Urjūzat tadbīr al-fuḥūl fi 'l-fuṣūl*, 81 or 121 *rajaz* verses on dietetics acccording to the seasons of the year, Berl. 6395, 6397/9, Vienna 1457, Cairo ^{1}VII, 525, library of Niʿma al-Ṭarīḥī, *Dharīʿa* I, 495,$_{2438}$.—89. *Urjūza fi 'l-mujarrabāt min al-aḥkām al-nujūmiyya wal-qawānīn al-ṭibbiyya*, tested medicines, composed in 428/1037, Vienna 1457,$_{2}$, Paris 2661,$_{4}$, 2942,$_{2}$, Br. Mus. 893,$_{5}$, Esc. ^{2}863,$_{2}$.—90. *Risāla fī tadbīr al-musāfirīn* Br. Mus. 1349,$_{11}$.—91. *Risāla fi 'l-bāh* ibid. 13.—92. *Maqādīr al-sharābāt*, on liquid substances in unadulterated form with information on their harmful effects, Berl. 6412.—93. *Risāla fi 'l-ashriba wal-ajwiba* Patna I, 375,$_{2550,21}$.—94. *al-Risāla al-mawsūma bil-Fuṣūl* ibid. 22 (= 88?) or Suppl. 959? c. l. AS 4854,$_{10}$, in Erg. 75.—95. Letter of Abū Saʿīd b. Abi 'l-Khayr to Ibn Sīnā, Alex. Fun. 126,$_{11}$.—95a.–gg. see Suppl. (a. Patna II, 374,$_{2559,10}$, k. ibid. 11).

IV. Poetry.—96. *al-Jumāna al-ilāhiyya fi 'l-tawḥīd, qaṣīda nūniyya* Cairo ^{1}VII, 625.—97. *Qaṣīda* on the impending, disastrous events of the year 657/8, Berl. 7609,$_{1}$ (falsely attributed?).—98. *Qaṣīda* on change and the perishability of everything material, ibid. 2.—99. Letter of invitation to a friend in rhymed prose, ibid. 8604.—100.–102. see Suppl.

V. Occult sciences. 103. *Khulāṣat al-taʿbīr* Garr. 930.—104.–107. see Suppl.

2. His student Abū ʿAbdallāh Muḥammad b. Aḥmad al-Maʿṣūmī wrote, around 430/1038:

Demonstration of the four absolute manifestations, Berl. 5058.

3. His student Abu 'l-Ḥasan Bahmanyār b. Marzubān, ca. 430/1038.

1. *Risāla fī marātib al-mawjūdāt* Leid. 1482/3.—2. *Risāla fī mawḍūʿ al-ʿilm al-maʿrūf bi-mā baʿd al-ṭabīʿa*, the object of metaphysics, ibid. 1484, no. 1 and 2
600 edited by S. Poper, | *B. ben El-M. der persische Aristoteliker aus Avicennas Schule, zwei metaphysische Abbh. von ihm, ar. u. deutsch mit Anm.*, Leipzig 1851.—3. Excerpts from his correspondence with his teacher Ibn Sīnā, Leid. 1485, Bodl. I, 456, Ambros. 320a.—4. *al-Taḥṣīlāt*, see Suppl., also Patna I, 209,$_{1062}$.

4. His student Abū Manṣūr al-Ḥusayn b. Muḥammad b. Ṭāhir b. ʿUmar b. Zaylā, who died in 440/1048.

Ibn Abī Uṣ. II, 19. *Al-Kāfī fi 'l-mūsīqī* Br. Mus. Suppl. 823ii, Or. 2361, f. 220/36, see Farmer, *Sources* 42, Rāmpūr I, 417,$_{57b}$.

459 | 5. Abu 'l-Ḥusayn Muḥammad b. ʿAlī al-Ṭabīb al-Baṣrī, who died in 436/1044 in Baghdad.

Ibn Khall. 581. *Sharḥ al-samāʿ al-ṭabīʿī*, commentary on Aristotle's *περὶ Φυσικης ἀκροάσεως*, Book VIII in the translation of Isḥāq b. Ḥunayn, Leid. 1433.

6. Abu 'l-Wafāʾ al-Mubashshir b. Fātik al-Qāʾid, an Egyptian emir, wrote, in 445/1053:

(Ibn Abū Uṣ. II, 98/9, Suyūṭī, *Ḥusn al-muḥ.* I, 311, without date of death). *Mukhtār al-ḥikam wa-maḥāsin al-kalim*, sayings of wise men: 1. Seth, 2. Hermes-Idris-Enoch, 3. Ṣāb, the ancestor of the Ṣābians, 4. Asclepius, 5. Homer, 6. Solon, 7. Zenon, 8. Hippocrates, 9. Pythagoras, 10. Plato, 11. Aristotle, 12. Alexander, 13. Ptolemy, author of the *Almagest*, 14. Luqmān, 15. Mahādar Jīsh, 16. Basilios, 17. Gregorios, 18. Galen, 19. varia, 20. anonyma, Leid. 1487, Lee 40 = *Ādāb al-ḥukamāʾ* Berl. 7859; cf. Steinschneider, *Centralbl. f. Bibl. Beiheft* V, 289, Meissner, ZDMG 49, 583ff. (*Akhbār al-Iskandar*). J. Lippert, *Studien auf dem Gebiete der griech.-ar. Übersetzungsliteratur* p. 1ff. (biography of Plato). Spanish transl. *Bocados de oro*, ed. Knust, *Mitteilungen aus dem Eskurial* p. 80ff., Latin Liber philosophorum moralium, ed. Salvatore de Renzi in *Collectio Salernitana* III, 68/150, cf. J. Gildemeister, *Jahrb. f. rom. u. engl. Lit.* XII, 236ff.

7. Abū Bakr Muḥammad b. al-Walīd b. Muḥammad b. Khalaf al-Ṭurṭūshī al-Fihrī b. Abī Randaqa, d. 520/1126 or 525/1131, see Suppl.

| Ibn Khall. 377, al-Ḍabbī p. 123, no. 295, Maqq. I, 517, Yāqūt, *GW* III, 529, Suyūṭī, 601
Ḥusn al-muḥ. I, 257, Wüst., *Gesch.* 229. 1. *Sirāj al-mulūk*, a mirror for princes, completed on 14 Rajab 516/19 September 1122 in Fusṭāṭ and dedicated to the vizier al-Ma'mūn Abū 'Abdallāh Muḥammad al-Umawī b. al-Bāṭa'iḥī, Gotha 1878/9 (where other MSS are listed), 'Um. 5105, Br. Mus. Suppl. 742/3, Cairo ^{1}V, 67, ^{2}I, App. 43, print. Būlāq 1289.—Abstracts by: a. 'Abd al-Ṣamad b. 'Abdallāh al-Muqri' al-Lakhmī, de Jong 155.—b. 'Abd al-Raḥmān b. Muḥammad al-Azharī, twelfth cent., Leid. 469, Persian transl. *Pet. Bull. scient.* III, 63, *Bull. hist. phil.* III, 221, IV, 238, cf. Dozy, *Recherches* 3rd ed. vol. 2, p. 234.—2. *Taḥrīm al-istimnā'*, proof that onanism is forbidden, Berl. 4981.—3. Abstract of the Qur'ān commentary of al-Tha'ālibī, d. 427/1036, see p. 350.

7a. See Suppl. = 594, 1,$_{c}$.

| 8. Abū Bakr Muḥammad b. Yaḥyā b. al-Ṣā'igh b. Bājja (Avempace) was born 460
in Zaragoza and lived in 512/1118 in Seville and Granada. Later he went to the court of the Almoravid 'Alī b. Yūsuf in Fez, where he was poisoned on the order of the physician Abu 'l-'Alā' b. Zuhr in 533/1138. Besides philosophy, he was also active in the theory and practice of music.

Ibn Khāqān, *Qalā'id* 298ff., Ibn Khall. 642, Ibn Abī Uṣ. II, 62/4, Maqq. II, 423, S. Munk, *Mélanges* 383ff., Leclerc II, 75, Hartmann, *Muw.* 30, M. Asín Palacios, il filosofo Zaragozano Avempace, *Rev. de Aragon*, 1901, 242 f., Avenpace botánico, *al-Andalus* VII (in which a treatise from Berl. 5060, Bodl. I, 499). 1. Collection of 24 smaller tracts on philosophy, medicine, and physics, Berl. 5060, Bodl. I, 499 (on the *Kitāb al-nafs* see Farmer, *Sources*, 44).—2. *Risālat al-widā'*, a farewell letter to Ibn al-Imām, the publisher of his works (Ibn Abī Uṣ. II, 62), Asín, La carta de Adiós de Avempace (Berl. 5067, f. 97/204, Bodl. Poc. 206, f. 217/220), *al-Andalus* VIII, 1/87, see Steinschneider, *Hebr. Übers.* § 206.—3. *Fī tadbīr al-mutawaḥḥid* ibid. 2, *Die Abh. des a. B. b. as-S. vom Verhalten des Einsiedlers, K. t. al-m. nach Mose Narb.'s Auszug hsg. v.* D. Herzog, Berl. 1896, *Beitr. z. Phil. des MA*, Heft I, see E. Rosen, Staatspolitische Gedanken bei I.B., *MWJ* 1937, 168/86.

| 9. Awḥad al-Zamān Hibatallāh 'Alī b. Malkā Abu 'l-Barakāt al-Baghdādī 602
al-Baladī, d. after 560/1165, see Suppl.

Ibn Abī Uṣ. I, 278/80.—1. *Risāla fī sabab ẓuhūr al-kawākib laylan wa-khafāʾihā nahāran* Berl. 5671.—2. *al-Muʿtabar fi ʾl-ḥikma* Hyderabad 1357 (in Berl. 5061 he is mistakenly credited with a work by al-Fārābī, p. 210, *ʿUyūn al-masāʾil*). S. Pines, Études sur Awḥad al-Zamān Abu ʾl-Barakāt al-Baghdādī, *REJuiv.* N.S. IV (CLIV), 1938, 1ff.—3.–5. see Suppl. (3. Hyderabad 1357).—6. *Barshaʿthā al-mujarrab*, on an Indian cure, AS 3555, f. 41a/164b (Ritter).

10. Abū Manṣūr Muḥammad al-Barawī, born in 517/1123 in Ṭūs, arrived in Baghdad in 527/1132 and became a teacher at al-Bahāʾiyya Madrasa. He died in 567/1172.

Ibn Khall. 564. *Al-Muqtaraḥ fi ʾl-muṣṭalaḥ*, on the terminology of dialectic, with a commentary by Taqī al-Dīn Muẓaffar b. Abi ʾl-ʿIzz al-Miṣrī, 6th cent., Esc. [2]693, Fez, Qar. 1409.

10a. Abu ʾl-ʿAbbās al-Faḍl b. Muḥammad al-Lawkarī was a contemporary of ʿUmar al-Khayyām, d. 517/1123 (p. 620), who, like him, was also active as a poet.

Tatimmat ṣiwān al-ḥikma 120, 204. 1. *Bayān al-ḥaqq wa-ḍamān al-ṣidq*, on natural philosophy in 5 chapters, based on the smaller *Physics* of Aristotle and Ibn Sīnā's commentaries, Paris 5900.

11. Abū Bakr Muḥammad b. ʿAbd al-Malik b. Ṭufayl al-Qaysī was born in Guadix near Granada. He served the governor of Granada as a secretary and then became the personal physician and vizier of the Almohad Abū Yaʿqūb Yūsuf. He died at the latter's court in Marrakesh in 581/1185.

Wüst., *Ärzte* 194, *Gesch.* 273, Leclerc II, 113, Munk, *Mélanges* 410ff. *Risālat Ḥayy b. Yaqẓān*, a philosophical novel which depicts the gradual awakening of the intellect of a child born on a deserted island, Bodl. I, 133,$_{2}$, Br. Mus. 978,$_{10}$, under the title *Kitāb asrār al-ḥikma al-mashriqiyya* Esc. [2]699,$_{3}$, print. Būlāq 1299, Landb. Br. 533, 573, Cairo [1]VI, 88, Taymūr, Ḥikma 19, wrongly attributed to Ibn Sabʿīn
603 (p. 611) with the title *Mirqāt al-zulfā wal-mashrab* | *al-aṣfā*, Taymūr, Taṣawwuf 149. *Philosophus autodidactus*, ed. E. Pococke, Oxford 1671, cf. A. Merx, *Eine maliche Kritik der Offenbarung, Protest. Kirchenzeitung* 1885, 667/73, 688/93, 708/14, 730/7, Massignon, *Textes* 125 (on Garcia Gómez, see Suppl., Kračkovsky, *Literis* IV, 1927, 28/33).

461 | 12. Burhān al-Dīn Abu ʾl-Rashīd Mubashshir b. Aḥmad al-Rāzī, d. 583/1187, see Suppl.

ḤKh IV, 396. 1. *al-Risāla al-Amīniyya fi 'l-tanbīh 'ala 'l-sa'āda al-ḥaqīqiyya* Leid. 1495.—2. A manual of arithmetic, Bursa Haraccizade Heyet ve Hikmet 171.—3. Answers to questions, written on 16 Jumādā II 596, ibid.

13. 'Abd al-Raḥmān b. Naṣr (Allāh) b. 'Abdallāh al-Shayzarī wrote for Ṣalāḥ al-Dīn, who died in 589/1193:

1. *al-Nahj al-maslūk fī siyāsat al-mulūk*, a mirror for princes, Munich 611, Leid. 473, Paris 2438, Garr. 781, 2115,2, Istanbul H. 4196 (ZS III, 253), print. Būlāq 1256, C. 1326, see Babinger, *Gesch.* 329, no. 15.—2. *Nihāyat al-rutba fī ṭalab al-ḥisba*, see Suppl. also Br. Mus. 9221, 9588, Top Kapu 2479, *RSO* IV, 727 (which has al-Ḥarrānī), see Gaudefroy Demombynes, *JA* 230, p. 453.—3.–5. see Suppl. (3. also Alex. Ṭibb 7, 41,1).

14. Muḥammad b. Aḥmad b. Ibrāhīm al-Qurashī al-Hāshimī, d. 590/1194.

1. *al-Fuṣūl*, statements on behaviour, customs, and self-knowledge, collected by his student Aḥmad b. 'Alī b. al-Ḥasan al-Qasṭallānī, d. 636/1238, Berl. 8683, Fātiḥ 5375, 72a/89a, Cairo [2]I, 338.—2. See Suppl.

14a. Al-Khiḍr b. Abī Bakr b. Aḥmad wrote, for al-Malik al-Mu'izz, i.e. Fatḥ al-Dīn Abu 'l-Fidā' Ismā'īl, the son of Sayf al-Islām and nephew of Ṣalāḥ al-Dīn, prince of Yemen (Ibn Khall., *Biogr. Dict.* I, 656, Abu 'l-Fidā' in *Hist. d. crois.* I, 83):

Kitāb al-waẓā'if al-ma'rūfa lil-manāqib al-mawṣūfa, abstract *al-I'āna lil-ḥaqq li-man waliya shay'an min umūr al-khalq* Esc. [2]775.

| 15. Abu 'l-Walīd Muḥammad b. Aḥmad b. Muḥammad b. Rushd (Averroes), 604
grandson of the jurisconsult (p. 384), was born in Cordova in 520/1126 and studied law in his hometown. In Marrakesh in 548/1153 he was introduced by Ibn Ṭufayl to the then-crown prince Abū Ya'qūb Yūsuf, who suggested that he write a commentary on the works of Aristotle. In 565/1169 he became *qāḍī* in Seville, and two years after that in Cordova. This is where his main works were written, despite the heavy load of his administrative duties. In 578/1182 Yūsuf appointed him as replacement to an ageing Ibn Ṭufayl as his personal physician in Marrakesh, but soon let him go to become chief *qāḍī* in his home town. Because he could not do without the support of the Spanish *fuqahā'* in his struggle against Alfonso VIII of Castile, Yūsuf's successor Ya'qūb al-Manṣūr was compelled to give in to their complaints about Ibn Rushd's doctrines, and after he had all of his books burned, exiled him to Alyusāna (Lucena) near Cordova.

But after his return to Marrakesh the former reconvened him there, where Ibn Rushd died on 9 Ṣafar 595/10 December 1198.

Ibn Abī Uṣ. II, 75/8, al-Marrakechi, *Hist. des Almohades*, trad. Fagnan, Leclerc II, 97, Munk, *Mélanges* 418ff., E. Renan, *Averroes et l'Averroisme*, 2nd ed. Paris 1861. Lasinio, Studii sopra Averroe, *Annuario della società ital. per gli studii or.* I/II, 1872/3. A.F. Mehren, Études sur la philosophie d'Averrhoes concernant ses rapports avec celle d'Avicenne et Ghazzālī, *Muséon* VII, 613/27, VIII, 1/20, Siebeck, Zur Psychologie der Scholastik, 8. Averroes, *Arch. f. Gesch. der Philos.* II, 517/25, G. Gabrieli, *Arch. d. storia delle scienze* V, 1924, 156/62, L. Strauss, *Philosophie und Gesetz*, Berlin 1935, p. 69ff. Goffredo Quadri, *La filosofia degli Arabi nel suo fiore*, II, *Il pensiero filosofico di Averroe*, Florence 1939. List of his works, Esc. $^{2}884_{,10}$.

1. *Kitāb faṣl al-maqāl fī-mā bayna 'l-sharīʿa wal-ḥikma min al-ittiṣāl* Esc. $^{2}632$, Madr. 132 (Gg. 151), see Esc. ^{2}I, XIX, see M.J. Müller, *Philosophie u. Theologie des*
605 *Av.*, Munich | 1859, p. 3/21 *aus dem Ar. übers.* Munich 1875, cf. Steinschneider, *Hebr. Übers* § $149_{,1}$.—2. Supplement of which Esc. $^{2}632_{,2}$, ed. Müller, op. cit.,
462 p. 120/31. |—3. *Kitāb al-kashf ʿan manāhij al-adilla fī ʿaqāʾid al-milla wa-taʿrīf mā waqaʿa fī-hā bi-ḥasb al-taʾwīl min al-shubah al-muzayyifa wal-bidaʿ al-muḍilla*, composed in 575/1179, ed. Müller, op. cit., 27/127, Taymūr, Ḥikma 129, cf. Steinschneider § $149_{,2}$.—4. *al-Masāʾil*, mostly on logic, Esc. $^{2}632_{,4}$, Madr. $102_{,2}$, cf. Steinschneider, *al-Fārābī*, 22, 38, 50/1.—5. *Tahāfut al-tahāfut*, a refutation of al-Ghazzālī's *Tahāfut al-falāsifa* (p. 544), print. C. 1303.—6. *Kulliyyāt*, on therapeutics, composed in 557/1162, Pet. 124, Latin transl. Euting 2217/31, Steinschneider, *Hebr. Übers.* § 429.—7. His adaptations of Aristotle in a Hebrew translation in Steinschneider § 21ff.—8. *Il commento medio di Averroe alla poetica di Aristotele, pubbl. in Arabico e in Hebr. e recato in ital. da* F. Lasinio, Pisa 1873 (Annali della Università Toscana XIV).—9. Averrois paraphrasis in librum poeticae Aristotelis Jacobo Mantino Hispano interprete, ed. F. Heidenhain, *Jahbr. f. class. Phill. Suppl.* XVII, 2, p. 351/82, see F. Gabrieli, Estetica e poesia araba nell' interpretazione della Poetica Aristotelica presso Avicenna e Averroe, RSO 1930, 305.—10. E. Rosenthal, Averroes' Middle Cmt. on Aristotle's *Analytica Priora et Posteriora, Bull. John Rylands Libr. Manchester* XXI (1937) 479/83 (ad Mingana 374).—11. *Mā baʿd al-ṭabīʿa min talkhīṣ b. R.*, Taymūr, Ḥikma $117_{,3}$, *Tafsīr ma baʿd al-ṭabīʿa* ed. M. Bouyges, *Bibl. Ar. Schol.* V, 1. 2, Beirut 1938.—12. Die durch Averroes erhaltenen Fragmente Alexanders zur *Metaphysik* des Aristoteles, unters. u. übers. v. J. Freudenthal, mit Beiträgen zur Erläuterung des arab. Textes von S. Fraenkel, *AbhAWB* a. d. J. 1884, Berlin 1885, I, 1/34.—13. *Drei Abhh. über die Conjunction des separaten Intellekts mit dem*

Menschen von A. aus dem Arab. übers. v. Samuel b. Tibbōn, hsg. übers. u. erl. v. J. Hercz, Berlin 1869, L. Hannes, *Des A. Abh. „Über die Möglichkeit der Conjunction" oder „Über den materiellen Intellekt", in hebr. Übers. hsg. u. erl.*, Halle 1892.—14. *Talkhīṣ kutub Arisṭū al-arbaʿa Kitāb al-Māʿqūlāt wa-Kitāb al-Qaḍāyā wa-Kitāb al-Qiyās wa-Kitāb al-Burhān* Cairo ^{1}VI, 52, 90.—17.–20. cf. Suppl. (18. MS Paris $2458_{,8}$ is dated 539, and cannot therefore be by Ibn Rushd, P. Kraus).—21. *al-Kashf ʿan manāhij al-adilla*, Taymūr, Ḥikma 129.—22. A treatise on theriac (Bouyges, Inv. nr. 64), Esc. $^{2}873_{,3}$ $884_{,6}$.—23. *Talkhīṣ* of 3 treatises by Galen: a) *de dementia*, b) *de* | *temperamentis*, c) *de facultatibus naturalibus*, Esc. ^{2}881, 606
$884_{,2}$.—24. *Talkhīṣ Kitāb al-ḥummayāt*, Galen, *De differentiis febrium*, ibid. $884_{,1}$.—25. *Kalām fi 'khtiṣār al-ʿilal wal-aʿrāḍ li-Jālīnūs de morborum et symptomatum differentiis et causis*, ibid. $884_{,3}$.—26. *Maqāla fī aṣnāf al-mizāj* ibid. 4.—27. *Maqāla fī ḥummayāt al-ʿafan* ibid. 5.—28. *Fī ḥifẓ al-ṣiḥḥa* ibid. 7.

15a. His son Abū Muḥammad ʿAbdallāh (Leclerc II, 109) wrote:

1. Abstracts of Galen's *Methodi medendi* l. XIV and other works.—2. A *maqāla* on the intellect (Bouyges p. 31, n. 54), Esc. $^{2}884_{,8,9}$.

16. Taqī al-Dīn al-Najrānī wrote, between 505/1111 and 675/1276:

Al-Kāmil fi 'l-istiqṣāʾ fī-mā balaghanā min kalām al-qudamāʾ, on the main points of philosophical dogmatics according to the ancients, Leid. 1516.

17. Burhān al-Dīn al-Zarnūjī wrote, around 600/1203:

Taʿlīm al-mutaʿallim li-taʿallum ṭarīq al-ʿilm, Berl. 111/28 and in almost every library. *Enchiridion studiosii*, ed. H. Relandus, Utrecht 1709. *Enchiridion studiosi*, ed. C. Caspari, Leipzig 1838.—Commentaries: 1. Nawʿī (II, $443_{,6}$), Munich 662, f. 33ff., Algiers $887_{,2}$, 1384/6.—2. Ibrāhīm b. Ismāʿīl, composed in 996/1588, Leipz. $186_{,3}$, Krafft 4, Garr. 786, Cairo ^{1}VII, 175, Qawala I, 241/2, print. Istanbul 1273, 1289, 1306, 1319.—3.–7. see Suppl. (7. Ḥasan b. ʿAbdallāh al-Faqī, according to Qawala I, 244).

| 18. Abu 'l-Qāsim b. Riḍwān wrote, after 600/1203, during the reign of a Mārinid 463
prince:

Al-Shuhub al-lāmiʿa fi 'l-siyāsa al-nāfiʿa, on politics, Leid. 1943, Bodl. I, 296.

19. Abu 'l-Ḥajjāj Yūsuf b. Muḥammad b. Tumlūs was born in Alcira (or, according to others, in Valencia) and died in 620/1223.

1. Commentary on Aristotle's *ἀναλυτικά πρότερα καὶ ὕστερα* and *περὶ ἑρμηνείας*, Esc. ^{2}649$_{,1}$.—2. *Quaesitum de mistione propositionis de inesse et necessariae*, Steinschneider, *Hebr. Übers.* § 44, XXIII.—3., 4. see Suppl.

607 | 20. During the reign of al-Nāṣir li-Dīn Allāh, d. 622/1225, Aḥmad b. Ja'far b. Shādhān wrote:

Kitāb adab al-wuzarā' Leid. 1942.

21. Afḍal al-Dīn Abu 'l-Faḍā'il Abū 'Abdallāh Muḥammad b. Nāmwar b. 'Abd al-Malik al-Khūnajī, of Persian stock, was born in 590/1194 and became a *qāḍī* in Cairo in 641, where he died on 5 Ramaḍān 646/23 December 1249.

Ibn Abī Uṣ. II, 120, Suyūṭī, *Ḥusn al-muḥ.* I, 131, 312. I. *al-Jumal* or *al-Mukhtaṣar*, a handbook of logic, composed in Mecca in 624/1227, Br. Mus. 156 iii, 542, Cairo ^{1}II, 84.—Commentaries: 1. Muḥammad b. Sālim b. Naṣrallāh b. Wāṣil al-Ḥamawī, d. 697/1297 (the teacher of Abu 'l-Fidā', see his *Ann.* V, 144ff.), Esc. ^{2}615, 647, Algiers 1387.—2. Muḥammad b. Aḥmad b. Marzūq al-Sharīf al-Tilimsānī, d. 770/1368, Algiers 1388.—3. Muḥammad b. Abi 'l-'Abbās Aḥmad al-Ḥusaynī, ca. 800/1397, Br. Mus. 542$_{,2}$.—4. Muḥammad b. Marzūq al-'Ajīsī al-Tilimsānī, d. 842/1438 (Suppl. II, 342), completed in 804/1400 in Tlemcen, Esc. ^{2}614, 654.—5. Anon., completed in 754/1353, ibid. 617.—6. The same, completed in 793/1371, ibid. 616.—Versification, *Naẓm al-Jumal* by Muḥammad b. 'Abd al-Jabbār (?), *Hesp.* XVIII, 94, 16d, anon. comm. ibid. e.—On *al-Mūjaz* differing therefrom, see Suppl.—II. *Kashf al-asrār 'an ghawāmiḍ al-afkār fi 'l-manṭiq* Esc. ^{2}667, Cairo ^{2}VII, 646.—III, IV. see Suppl.

22. Kamāl al-Dīn Abū Sālim Muḥammad b. Ṭalḥa b. Muḥammad b. al-Ḥasan al-Qurashī al-'Adawī, d. 652/1254, see Suppl.

Wüst., *Gesch.* 337. 1. *al-'Iqd al-farīd lil-Malik al-Sa'īd*, a mirror for princes, Gotha 1882/3, Paris 2440, Br. Mus. 1435, Ind. Off. 661, Bodl. I, 291, II, 576a, Esc. ^{2}720, AS 4147/8, Garr. 782/3, print. C. 1283, 1306, 1311.—Extracts Bodl. I, 272, maybe Leid.
464 1950, *Jawāhir* by Ṣāliḥ b. al-Ṣiddīq al-Namāzī (II, 405), Garr. 178 (mistaken). |—2. *Taḥṣīl al-marām fī tafḍīl al-ṣalāt 'ala 'l-maṣām*, a demonstration that prayer

is more praiseworthy than fasting, Berl. 3569.—3. *Nafāʾis al-ʿanāṣir li-majālis al-Malik al-Nāṣir*, an edifying work, Berl. 8779/90, Br. Mus. 1530.—4. *al-Durr al-munaẓẓam fi ʾl-sirr al-aʿẓam*, a kabbalistic work, Berl. 4142, Gotha $1258_{,1}$, Paris 2663/9, $4606_{,1}$, Bodl. I, 1036, Lee 60, with the title *Miftāḥ al-jafr al-jāmiʿ wa-miṣbāḥ al-nūr al-lāmiʿ*, also Patna I, $243_{,2083}$.—explanations of the final part of the 10th *ṭarīq* by Aḥmad b. ʿAbd al-Karīm b. Khallāl | al-Ḥimṣī, Berl. 4219, 608
Gotha 1259, Paris 266, with the title *al-Jawāb*, composed in 662/1264, Gotha 9, $1258_{,2}$, Paris 6598, f. 108v.—7., 8. see Suppl. (7. read: *manāqib āl al-rasūl*).

23. Athīr al-Dīn Mufaḍḍal b. ʿUmar al-Abharī, who died in 663/1264, see Suppl.

Barhebraeus, *Hist. Dyn.* 485 (gives 1262 as the year of death).

1. *Hidāyat al-ḥikma*: a. *fi ʾl-manṭiq* b. *fi ʾl-ṭabīʿiyyāt*, c. *fi ʾl-ilāhiyyāt*, Gotha 1217, Paris $2330_{,5}$, Pet. 230, AM 18, Bodl. I, $455_{,2}$, 516, $981_{,2}$, Esc. ^{2}631, $636_{,4}$, 704, Cairo ^{1}VI, 106, Qawala II, 388.—Commentaries: 1. On b. and c., Muḥammad b. Sharīf al-Ḥusaynī, ca. 825/1422, Berl. 5070, Algiers 1390, Garr. 834/5, Patna II, $424_{,2596,1}$.—2. al-Sharīf al-Ḥusayn al-Shānawī, Berl. 5071.—3. Mīrak Shams al-Dīn Muḥammad b. Mubārakshāh al-Bukhārī (II, 212), Ind. Off. 493, $584_{,2}$, $592_{,2}$, Garr. 830, Patna I, $212_{,1897}$, on which glosses by Muḥammad Hāshim al-Ḥasanī al-Ṭabīb, Patna II, $526_{,2825}$.—4. Mawlānāzāde Aḥmad b. Maḥmūd al-Harawī, Gotha $1217_{,2}$, Leid. 1517/8, Br. Mus. 1353, Ind. Off. 494/5, Paris 2360/1, Esc. $^2635_{,1}$, Garr. 831/2, Yeni 768, Alex. Fals. 15, Qawala II, 387, Cairo ^{1}VI, 99, Patna I, $213_{,1900}$, glosses by Qāḍīzāde al-Rūmī (II, 212), on the last two parts Garr. 833, other glosses Esc. $^2635_{,3}$, Paris $2362_{,1}$.—(4a. see Suppl. also Makram 44).—5. On b. and c., Mīr Ḥusayn b. Muʿīn al-Dīn al-Maybudī (II, 210), composed in 880/1475, Berl. 5065, Paris 2363, Br. Mus. 1352, *Pet. AM Bull.* X, 77, Kazan 82, $99_{,5}$, Esc. $^2236_{,1}$, Algiers 1389, Ambr. B, 77i, 82 (*RSO* IV, 103), Garr. 829, $2155_{,1}$, Yeni 769, Cairo ^{1}VI, 98, Patna I, $213_{,1898/9}$, II, $416_{,2886,1}$, $527_{,2834}$ (printed editions see Suppl.)—Glosses: a. Fakhr al-Dīn Muḥammad b. Ḥusayn al-Sammākī al-Astarābādī (II, 414), ca. 1040/1630, Ind. Off. 492, Esc. ^{2}673, Alex. Fals. 7, Patna I, $210_{,1873}$, II, $526_{,2829}$.—b. Naṣrallāh Muḥammad al-Khalkhālī al-Bukhārī, Cairo ^{1}VI, 92.—c. Muḥammad Muṣliḥ al-Dīn al-Lārī, d. 971/1569 (II, 120), Berl. 5067/9, Gotha 1218, Paris 2364, Lee 42, Algiers $1389_{,2}$ Garr. 2130/1, Qawala II, 383/4, with superglosses by Muḥammad b. Ḥumayd al-Kaffawī, Qawala II, 382/3 and al-Kalanbawī, Cairo ^{1}VI, 92, Qawala II, 383.—d.–l. see Suppl. (f. *Ghāyat al-nihāya* by Muḥammad b. Ḥasan al-ʿAlamī, ca. 960/1553, Patna I, $210_{,1875}$; l. ibid. $211_{,1876}$).—m. Muḥammad Iṣmatallāh, Patna I, $210_{,1874}$.—6. Muḥammad b. Ibrāhīm al-Shīrāzī Ṣadr al-Dīn, d. 1051/1640 (II, 413), Berl. 5072, Ind. Off. 496,

Stewart 417, Alex. Fals. 15, Patna I, $214_{,1911/2}$.—Glosses see Suppl. (*β* Patna I,
609 $210_{,1867}$, *γ* ibid. | 1868, *δ* ibid. 1869, *ζ* ibid. 1864/6, *ϑ* ibid. 1871/2, *ι* ibid. 1870.)—
7. Anon., Berl. 5073/4, Paris $2500_{,7}$, Esc. ²634.—16 commentaries and glosses in
Ahlw. 5075.

II. *Kitāb al-īsāghūjī*, an adaptation of the *ἰσαγωγή* of Porphyry, Berl. 5228/9,
Gotha 1171/4, Vienna 1524/5, Krafft 391, Leipz. $34_{,2}$, Hamb. Or. Sem. $105_{,1}$, Paris
$253_{,2}$, $'4_{,2}$, $'6_{,2}$, $2500_{,10}$, Br. Mus. 531, $532_{,7}$, Suppl. 729, *Hesp.* XVIII, 1934, $90_{,82}$,
Alex. Manṭiq $23_{,2}$, Fun. $120_{,4}$, $129_{,5}$, $142_{,3}$, Qawala II, 317/21, Patna II, $528_{,2837/8}$.—
Commentaries: 1. Ḥusām al-Dīn al-Ḥasan al-Kātī, d. 760/1359, Berl. 5230/1, Gotha
$1171_{,3}$ (where other MSS are listed), Ambr. A 88 (*RSO* III, 591), Garr. 807, $2081_{,3}$,
$2141_{,1}$, $2152_{,1}$, $2156_{,1}$, Alex. Manṭiq 15, 22/3, $25_{,4}$, $28_{,4}$, Fun. $172_{,2}$, $187_{,4}$, Qawala II,
360.—Glosses: a. Muḥammad b. Muḥammad al-Bardaʿī, d. 927/1521, Berl. 5232,
Gotha $1171_{,3}$ (where other MSS are listed), Garr. 808, Alex. Manṭiq 7, $29_{,2}$, Qawala II,
330.—b. Madhkūr b. Sulaymān al-Kurdī, Gotha 1076.—c. al-Qarabāghī,
465 d. 942/1535, Berl. 5233, Garr. $2081_{,2}$.—d. Muḥyi 'l-Dīn al-Tālijī (Tālishī), | Berl.
5234/5, Munich 671/2, Haupt. 207, Copenhagen $183_{,3}$, Krafft 398, Paris $1243_{,2}$,
$2356_{,1}$, Leid. 1520, Pet. 96, Qawala II, $330_{,1}$, Alex. Manṭiq 11, $28_{,3}$, Garr. $2081_{,4}$,
$2152_{,2}$.—e. Anon., Berl. 5236, Gotha 1177, Paris $1267_{,2}$, $2359_{,1}$, Munich. 669/70,
Br. Mus. Suppl. $729_{,2}$.—f. al-Shirwānī (?), Alex. Manṭiq 11.—g.–r. see Suppl.
(g. Alex. Manṭiq 15, superglosses by Muḥammad b. Ghulām Muḥammad,
Patna I, $223_{,1956}$; p. Alex. Manṭiq 11).—s. Yaḥyā al-Ruhawī al-Ḥanafī, Alex.
Manṭiq 11, Fun. $96_{,1}$.—2. *al-Fawāʾid al-Fanāriyya* by Shams al-Dīn Muḥammad
b. Ḥamza al-Fanārī, d. 834/1431 (II, 233), Berl. 5237/8, Leipz. 887, vii, Gotha 1178
(where other MSS are listed), Garr. 809/10, $2130_{,2}$, Alex. Manṭiq 18, 24, 28/9, Fun.
$177_{,2}$, Qawala 369/73, Istanbul 1236—Glosses: a. Qul Aḥmad b. Muḥammad b.
Khiḍr, ca. 950/1543, Berl. 5240/1, Esc. $^2633_{,2}$, Garr. $810/2_{,2}$, 2156, Alex. Manṭiq
11, $24_{,2}$ $28_{,2}$, 31, Qawala II, 344/8.—Superglosses: *α* Maḥmūd Efendi, eleventh
cent., Berl. 5242.—*β*, *γ* see Suppl. (*β*. by al-Tīrawī, twelfth cent., also Istanbul
1242, 1275, 1307; *γ* al-Ḥāfiẓ b. ʿAlī al-ʿImādī, Garr. $2079_{,1}$, Qawala II, 342).—*δ*
on the beginning by Maḥmūd Efendi. Amīr Shahrī, Qawala II, 349.—b. ʿAbd
al-Raḥīm, Pet. 1054.—c. al-Patkarī, ibid. 5.—d. Burhān al-Dīn b. Kamāl al-Dīn
b. Ḥamīd al-Bulghārī, Br. Mus. Suppl. $723_{,3}$, Garr. 813, Alex. Manṭiq $24_{,1}$, $31_{,2}$,
Istanbul 1276, Qawala II, 369.—e., f. see Suppl.—g. Aḥmad b. ʿAbdallāh
Shawqī, completed in 1193/1779, Qawala II, 338, print. Istanbul 1302.—h. Abū
610 Muḥammad ʿAbdallāh b. Ḥasan al-Kanqārī al-Anṣārī al-Uskudārī, | thirteenth
cent., Istanbul 1279 (Qaw. II, 348).—i. Muḥammad al-Fawzī al-Yārānkamawī,
Khulāṣat al-mīzān, al-Āsitāna 1288, 1301.—3. Khayr al-Dīn al-Ghazāwī al-Bitlīsī,
composed in 855/1451, Berl. 5244, Paris $1013_{,10}$.—4. Sulaymān b. ʿAbd al-Raḥmān
al-Jarbī ʿAlam al-Dīn, ca. 915/1509, based on the lectures held in 913/1507 by ʿAlī b.
Ibrāhīm al-Kīlānī in Būlāq, Berl. 5245, Garr. 814/6.—5. *al-Muṭṭalaʿ* by Zakariyyāʾ

al-Anṣārī, d. 926/1520 (II, 99), Berl. 5246/7, Brill M. 161$_{,6}$, Gotha 1179/80 (where other MSS are listed), Hamb. Or. Sem. 105$_{,2}$, 119, *Hespéris* XVIII, 92, 11, b, Alex. Manṭiq 20$_{,5}$, 22$_{,2}$, 25$_{,1,5}$, 32$_{,5}$, Fun. 87$_{,2}$, Garr. 817.—Glosses: a. Aḥmad al-Fayyūmī, composed in 1096/1685, Berl. 5248.—b. Muḥammad b. ʿAbdallāh al-Kharashī, d. 1100/1688, Berl. 5249, Alex. Manṭiq 8.—c. Aḥmad b. ʿAlī al-Miṣrī, ca. 1151/1738, Berl. 5250.—d. Yūsuf b. Sālim al-Ḥafnāwī, d. 1178/1764 (II, 283), Berl. 5251, Alex. Manṭiq 8, print. C. 1283, 1297, 1302, 1305, 1306, 1310.—e. Shihāb al-Dīn al-Qalyūbī, d. 1029/1620 (II, 364), Garr. 818.—f. *Kashf al-lithām*, by Muḥammad al-Bahūtī, Alex. Manṭiq 19.—g. Aḥmad b. Muḥammad b. ʿAlī al-Ghunaymī al-Anṣārī, d. 1044/1634, Qawala II, 343.—h. Muḥammad b. Ibrāhīm al-Dalajī, Alex. Manṭiq 8, 22$_{,1}$, Makram 19.—i. ʿAlī b. Khiḍr b. Aḥmad al-ʿUmrūsī al-Mālikī, Makram 24.—6. ʿAbd al-Raḥmān b. Ramaḍān al-Izmīrī, Algiers 1407$_{,2}$.—7. Anon., Munich. 669/70, Esc. ^{2}673$_{,1}$, Algiers 1437$_{,2}$.—8. ʿAbdallāh b. ʿAlī b. Ṣalāḥ al-Ṭabarī, ca. 1070/1660, Berl. 5252.—10.–31. see Suppl. (11. *Mughni ʾl-ṭullāb* by Maḥmūd b. Ḥasan al-Maghnīsī, Garr. 825/6, Qawala II, 376/7.—Glosses: a. *Sayf al-ghallāb* by Muḥammad al-Fawzī b. al-Ḥājj A. al-Yārānkamawī al-Adranawī, Qawala II, 359.—b. ʿUthmān b. Nuʿmān al-Anjustāwī, ca. 1279/1862, Qawala II, 329.—16. *Durr al-nājī*, Qawala II, 355/7, glosses on the *Dībāja* by Ibrāhīm b. al-Yalwajī, Qawala II, 352/3.—24. ʿAlī b. Zākhir, completed in Suwayr by Yuwāqīm, Berl. Ms. or. oct. 3427).—28. *Tuḥfat al-Rushdī*, additionally Istanbul 1279, (Qawala II, 326).—32. Nūr al-Dīn ʿAlī al-Ujhūrī, d. 1066/1656 (II, 317), Alex. Manṭiq 15.—33. *Dharīʿat al-imtiḥān* by Aḥmad al-Ṣidqī b. ʿAlī Burūsawī, Istanbul 1300 (Qaw. II. 357).—34. Ismāʿīl b. Muṣṭafā b. Maḥmūd al-Kalanbawī Shaykhzāde (Suppl. II, 302 n. 1), Qawala II, 360.—35. ʿAlī b. Ḥusayn al-Ḥanafī, Istanbul 1310 (Qaw. I, 361).—37. *Mīr īsāghūjī* by Muḥammad Faḍl al-Ḥaqq al-Rāmghūrī, Indian printing 1309, C. Muʾayyad 1321 (mistakenly attributed to al-Jurjānī).—revised edition, augmented with examples by Abu ʾl-Ḥasan ʿAlī b. ʿUmar al-Shāfiʿī al-Biqāʿī, d. 885/1480 (II, 142), with a commentary by Muḥammad b. Yūsuf al-Sanūsī, d. 892/1486 (II, 142), Algiers | 1307$_{,2}$, 1382$_{,1}$.—18 611
commentaries and glosses and 4 versifications are mentioned in Ahlw. 5255.

III–XIII. see Suppl. (III. Paris 2515, V. Cairo ^{1}VII, 647, VI. Heid. TA 385$_{,2}$, *ZDMG* 91, 395).

24. Muḥyi ʾl-Dīn Abū Muḥammad ʿAbd al-Ḥaqq b. Ibrāhīm b. Muḥammad al-Ishbīlī b. Sabʿīn b. Dāra was born in Murcia, studied under Ibn al-Marʾa b. Dahhāq of Malaga (see Suppl. I, 776, 61, 1), lived for a time in Bijāya, and founded the mystical-philosophical sect named after him. When he was living in Ceuta he answered, at the behest of the Almohad ʿAbd al-Wāḥid (630–40/1232–42), some philosophical questions that the emperor Frederick II of Hohenstaufen had asked the men of learning there. Seeking to attain

unification with God, he killed himself by slashing his wrists in Mecca in 669/1270.

Fawāt I, 247. L. Massignon, *Eranosjahrb.* 1937, 76. 1. *Budd al-ʿārif wa-ʿaqīdat al-muḥaqqiq al-muqarrab al-kāshif wa-ṭarīq al-sālik al-mutabattil al-ʿākif*, an introduction to metaphysics, Berl. 1774.—2. *al-Maqālīd al-wujūdiyya* Alex. Ḥikma 27.—3. *al-Ajwiba ʿani ʾl-asʾila al-Ṣaqaliyya* Bodl. I, 456,$_{5}$ cf. M. Amari, *JA* s. V, 240ff. A.F. Mehren, Correspondence du philosophe-soufi I.S.A. avec
466 l'empereur Fréderic de Hohenstaufen, ibid., 14, 341ff. |—4. *Duʿāʾ ḥarf al-qāf*, prayers whose words start with a *qāf*, Berl. 3654.—5. *Kitāb al-daraj* Cairo ^{1}VII, 682 = (?) *Risāla fī asrār al-kawākib wal-daraj wal-burūj wa-khawāṣṣihā* Alex. Ḥurūf 12,$_{1}$.—6., 7. see Suppl.—8. *Adwār al-mansūb*, Taymūr, see Farmer, *Sources* 47.—9. *ʿAwāṣim al-qawāṣim*, Taymūr, Taṣ. 318.—10. 20 tracts, mostly without a title, among which are the *Kitāb al-ʿiqd, al-Naṣīḥa wa-hiya al-Risāla al-Nūriyya* and others, ibid. 149, 321 (Kraus, *Or.* VIII, 286).—The *Kitāb asrār al-ḥikma al-mashriqiyya* of Ibn Ṭufayl (p. 460) is sometimes wrongly attributed to him.

25. Abu ʾl-Ḥasan b. Abī Dharr wrote, following Barhebreus:

Kitāb al-saʿāda wal-isʿād, on Greek philosophy, see M. Kurd ʿAlī, *RAAD* IX, 563/73.

612 | 26. Najm al-Dīn ʿAlī b. ʿUmar al-Qazwīnī al-Kātibī (Dabīrān), a student of Naṣīr al-Dīn Ṭūsī (p. 508), who died in 675/1276 or in 693/1294.

1. *al-Risāla al-Shamsiyya fī ʾl-qawāʿid al-manṭiqiyya*, a work on logic, composed at the request of Shams al-Dīn Muḥammad b. Bahāʾ al-Dīn Muḥammad al-Juwaynī, d. 683/1284, Berl. 5256/7, Alex. Fun. 142,$_{4}$, Qawala II, 367/8, ed. A. Sprenger, App. I to *Dictionary of the Technical Terms*, Calcutta 1854.—Commentaries: 1. *Taḥrīr al-qawāʿid al-manṭiqiyya* or *al-Quṭbī* on Part I, *al-Taṣawwurāt*, by Muḥammad b. Quṭb al-Dīn Muḥammad al-Rāzī al-Taḥtānī, d. 766/1364 (II, 209), Berl. 5258/9, Br. Mus. Suppl. 99, iii, 730, Garr. 836/7, 2157,$_{2}$, Alex. Fun. 148,$_{2}$, Qawala II, 365, Makram 9, Patna I, 227,$_{1997/8}$, II, 499,$_{2651,5}$, 529,$_{2849}$, print. Calcutta 1815, n.p. (Lucknow?) 1263, Istanbul 1264, 1266, 1272, 1279, 1288, 1304, 1319, 1325, C. 1307, 1311 (Qawala II, 323/4).—Glosses: a. *al-Kūchak* by al-Sayyid al-Jurjānī, d. 816/1413, Berl. 5260/1, Ind. Off. 584, Garr. 840/3, 2157,$_{1}$, Alex. Manṭiq 29,$_{3}$, Fun. 120,$_{1}$, Qawala II, 335, Patna I, 224,$_{1969/72}$, print. Calcutta 1261, Lucknow 1883.—Superglosses: α Qara Dāʾūd al-Qūčawī, d. 948/1541, Berl. 5262, Gotha 1192, Ind. Off. 516/7, Cambr. *JRAS* III, 126, Esc.

^{2}638, Pet. 92, Algiers 1398/9, Alex. Manṭiq 10, Qawala II, 343/4, Calcutta 1230.—β ʿAbd al-Ḥakīm al-Sālikūtī, d. 1067/1657 (II, 417), Berl. 5264, Ind. Off. 518/9, Qawala II, 334/5, Patna I, 222$_{,1955}$, print. Istanbul 1238, 1259, 1268, 1276, 1288, 1289, 1307, 1309.—γ Sulṭānshāh, composed in 929/1523, Esc. ^{2}637.—δ *Qara Ḥāshiya* by ʿImād al-Dīn b. Yaḥyā al-Fārisī, d. ca. 900/1494, Ind. Off. 513/5, Esc. ^{2}630 (?), Garr. 485, Qawala II, 341/2, Patna I, 222$_{,1904}$.—ε al-Dawwānī, d. 907/1501 (II, 217), Leid. 1534, Esc. ^{2}677$_{,3}$, Garr. 846, Rāġib 1478$_{,11}$, Qawala II, 333, Patna I, 224$_{,1973}$, print. Istanbul 1309.—ζ Ṣadr al-Dīn Abū Naṣr Muḥammad b. Ibrāhīm al-Shīrāzī, d. 903/1497, Esc. ^{2}677$_{,4}$.—η Shāʿirzāde (Shāʿiroghlū), Vienna 1537$_{,1}$, Pet. 92$_{,3}$.—ϑ Maḥmūd b. Niʿmatallāh al-Bukhārī (Suppl. II, 587), Br. Mus. Suppl. 731.—ι Anon. Munich 192$_{,2}$, Ind. Off. 520$_{,1}$.—κ see Suppl. ϑ.—π–υ see Suppl. (ν by ʿIṣām al-Dīn al-Isfarāʾinī, Qāwala II, 339, Patna I, 225$_{,1975}$, on the *Qism al-taṣawwurāt*, Istanbul 1307, superglosses by Muḥammad b. Ḥasan Kharpūtī Dallālzāde, print. Istanbul 1275, Qaw. II, 332.—υ Patna I, 225$_{,1977,8}$).—b. Muḥammad b. Ḥusayn b. Muḥammad Ṭursūn al-Andijānī, d. 966/1558(?), Esc. ^{2}405.—c. Aḥmad al-Janadī, | ibid. 671.—d. Anon., on the Preface, ibid. 613
673$_{,2}$.—e. The same, by Aḥmad b. ʿAbd al-Fattāḥ al-Mollawī, d. 1181/1767, Berl. 5265, Paris 2377$_{,1}$.—f. Burhān al-Dīn b. Kamāl al-Dīn b. Ḥamīd, Pet. 90, 106$_{,9}$, Garr. 847.—g. On the *Qism al-taṣdīqāt* by Khalīl b. Muḥammad al-Riḍawī, completed in 759/1358 in al-Madrasa al-Sulṭāniyya, print. Istanbul 1309.—h.–m. see Suppl. (i. by Mīr Zāhid also Patna I, 225$_{,1976}$. Superglosses by Ghulām Yaḥyā b. Najm al-Dīn al-Bihārī, Patna II, 338$_{,2521,5}$, by Ḥaydar b. ʿAlī, ibid. II, 338$_{,2521,7}$, by ʿAẓīmallāh b. Kifāyatallāh Gūpamānī Fārūqī, ibid. I, 221$_{,1945/6}$, by Ḥasan b. Qāḍī Ghulām Muṣṭafā al-Laknawī, ibid. 1947, by Turāb ʿAlī b. Shajāʿat ʿAlī al-Laknawī, ibid. 220$_{,1937}$, II, 528$_{,2339}$, by Aḥmad b. ʿAlī Sayyid Fatḥ Muḥammad al-Sandīlī, ibid. I, 222, by ʿAbd al-ʿĀlī b. Niẓām al-Dīn Baḥr al-ʿUlūm, ibid. I, 950$_{,1948/9}$, by Ẓuhūrallāh b. Muḥammad Walī b. Muftī Ghulām Muṣṭafā al-Laknawī, ibid. 1951, by ʿImād al-Dīn al-ʿUthmānī al-Labkanī, ibid. 1952).—n. *Taqrīr ʿalā dībājat T. al-q.* by Shukrī b. Ṭāhir al-Brštawī, Istanbul 1310 (Qawala II, 327).—2. Jamāl al-Dīn Ḥasan b. Yūsuf b. al-Muṭahhar al-Ḥillī, d. 726/1325 (II, 164), Leid. 1530.—3. Saʿd al-Dīn al-Taftāzānī, d. 791/1389 (II, 215), Berl. 5266/8, Esc. ^{2}660, 699$_{,2}$, 670, Cairo ^{1}VI, 63, Garr. 838, Qawala II, 365, glosses on the Preface by Walī al-Dīn al-Qaramānī (?), Ind. Off. 522, Esc. ^{2}699, anon. Br. Mus. Suppl. 732$_{,1}$.—4. Ḥusayn b. Muʿīn al-Dīn al-Maybudī, ca. 890/1485, Berl. 5269, Leid. 1533, Garr. 844, Qawala II, 365.—5. Muḥammad b. Mūsā al-Busnawī, d. 1045/1635, Algiers 1397.—6. ʿAbdallāh b. al-Ḥaddād al-ʿUthmānī, Br. Mus. 982$_{,2}$.—7. Anon., Berl. 5270, Leid. 1531/2, 1535, Paris 2379/83.—8.–24. see Suppl.—25. Muḥammad Nūrī al-Ṣūfiyawī, completed 17 Ṣafar 1295/21 February 1878, in the margin of the printed edition of Istanbul 1301.—26. Muṣṭafā b. Yūsuf al-Fāshilī al-Mūstārī,

completed on 17 Jumādā II 1101/29 March 1690, Qawala II, 365.—27. *Mīzān al-intiẓām* by Aḥmad al-Ṣidqī al-Burūsawī, Istanbul 1303, 1327.—19 commentaries and glosses mentioned in Ahlw. 5271.

II. *Kitāb ḥikmat al-ʿayn*, on metaphysics and physics, Berl. 5080, Br. Mus. 428, $1200_{,8}$, Esc. $^{2}668_{,2}$, Un. Eg. 11654, 117, 88, Taymūr, Ḥikma 97, Patna I, $211_{,1887}$.—Commentaries: 1. Self-commentary (see Suppl.) also Qawala II, 386.—1a. Mīrak Shams al-Dīn Muḥammad b. Mubārakshāh al-Bukhārī,
467 eighth cent., Berl. 5081/2, Pet. 99, Paris 2384/5, Br. Mus. 1351, | Suppl. 726, Ind. Off. 498/500, Cairo ^{1}VI, 97, Garr. $2065_{,2}$, 2137, Patna I, $212_{,1897}$, II, $526_{,2829}$.—Glosses: a. al-Jurjānī, d. 816/1413 (II, 216), Leid. 1527, Esc. $^{2}629$, 662/3, Cairo ^{1}VI,
614 91, print. Calcutta | 1845.—b. Ḥabīballāh Mīrzājān al-Bāghandī al-Muḥaqqiq, d. 994/1586 (II, 414), Landb.-Br. 583, Paris $2385_{,2}$, Br. Mus. Suppl. 727, Yeni 762, Cairo ^{1}VI, 92.—c. Mollā Ḥaydar (see Suppl.), Paris $2385_{,4}$.—d. Muḥammad b. Hishām al-Ḥasanī, Ind. Off. 501.—e. Anon., Berl. 5083/6, Paris $2385_{,3,5,6}$.—f.–o. see Suppl. (o. 4 *Rasāʾil* by Shamsā Gīlānī, Patna II, 432/$3_{,2609}$).—p. Mīrzājān, d. 994/1586, Garr. $2065_{,1}$, $2137_{,2}$.—2. Muḥammad b. Mūsā al-Tālishī, composed in 884/1479, Cairo ^{1}VII, 97.—3. *Īḍāḥ al-maqāṣid min Ḥikmat al-ʿayn al-qawāʿid* by Āyatallāh al-ʿAllāma al-Ḥillī (II, $208_{,29}$), Ist. Ḥālet, Baghdad al-Maktaba al-Marjāniyya, *Dharīʿa* II, 501, 1961.—4. Anon., *al-Fawāʾid* (*fī sharḥ Ḥ. al-ʿA. al-qawāʿid*), Berl. Ms. or. oct. 3809.

III. *ʿAyn al-qawāʿid fī ʾl-manṭiq wal-ḥikma* Leid. 1525, Esc. $^{2}668$, Mosul $184_{,250}$. Self-commentary, *Baḥr al-fawāʾid*, Leid. 1526, Esc. $^{2}665$, *Br. Mus. Quart.* X, 133.

IV. *al-Mufaṣṣal sharḥ al-Muḥaṣṣal*, see p. 507.

V. *al-Munaṣṣas*, see ibid. 24.

VI. *Jāmiʿ al-daqāʾiq fī kashf al-ḥaqāʾiq*, on logic, physics, and metaphysics, Paris 2370, Cairo ^{1}VII, 647, ^{2}I, 225.

VII. Correspondence with al-Ṭūsī, d. 672/1273 (p. 508), on the demonstration of the existence of the necessary existent, Br. Mus. $429_{,1-3}$, Esc. $^{2}703_{,8}$.

VIII, IX. see Suppl.

27. Sirāj al-Dīn Abu ʾl-Thanāʾ Maḥmūd b. Abī Bakr al-Urmawī, who died in Qonya in 682/1283.

I. *Maṭāliʿ al-anwār fī ʾl-manṭiq*, on logic, Paris 2386/7, 5318, Esc. $^{2}641$, 686, Algiers 1402.—Commentaries: 1. Self-commentary, *Lawāmiʿ al-maṭāliʿ*, Cairo ^{1}VI, 70, on which glosses by al-Jurjānī, d. 816/1413 (II, 216), Qilič ʿA. 653, with superglosses by al-Luṭfī, d. 900/1495, Cairo ^{1}VI, 92.—2. *Lawāmiʿ al-asrār* by Quṭb al-Dīn Muḥammad b. Muḥammad al-Taḥtānī al-Rāzī, d. 766/1364, Berl. 5087/8, Bodl. I, 455, II, 364, Kazan 80, *JAOS* I, p. XXIII, no. XIV, Garr. 848, Alex. Manṭiq $23_{,2}$, Qawala II, 373/5, Patna I, $227_{,2002}$.—Glosses: a. al-Jurjānī, d. 816/1413 (II, 216), Gotha 1184/5 (where other MSS are listed), *Br. Mus. Suppl.*

733/4, Garr. 849, Alex. Manṭiq 8, Qawala II, 338, Patna I, 225$_{,1980}$.—Superglosses:
α Dā'ūd al-Shirwānī, ca. 850/1446, Berl. 5090, Esc. ^{2}643, Alex. Manṭiq 23,
Qawala II, 350.—β *Tanwīr al-maṭāliʿ wa-tabṣīr al-muṭāliʿ* or *al-Ḥāshiya al-jadīda*
by al-Dawwānī, d. 908/1502 (II, 217), Berl. 5091, Paris 2398, Esc. ^{2}687$_{,7}$, Qawala II,
327, Rāġib 1478$_{,9}$, Patna I, 219$_{,1933}$.—γ 'Alā' al-Dīn | 'Alī al-Ṭūsī, d. 887/1482, 615
Leid. 1542/3.—δ Mīrzājān Ḥabīballāh al-Bāghandī al-Shīrāzī, d. 994/1586, Ind.
Off. 529 Qawala II, 352, Patna I, 219$_{,1934}$.—ε Sayyid 'Alī al-'Ajamī, d. 860/1456,
Ind. Off. 528, Esc. ^{2}683.—ζ, η Anon., Ind. Off. 530, Leid. 1540.—ϑ–ν see Suppl.
(ϑ Garr. 850, ϰ, ν also Patna I, 220$_{,935,\ 946}$).—ο On the *Baḥth al-fayyāḍ*, from
which *Risālat al-fayyāḍ* by Qāḍīzāde al-Rūmī, d. 815/1412 (II, 212), Qawala II, 343,
358.—π 'Alī al-Astarabādī, Qawala II, 329.—ρ Ḥusayn al-Muḥtasib, ibid. 351.—
b. Jalāl al-Dīn Khiḍr b. 'Alī b. al-Khaṭṭāb Ḥājjī Pāshā Āydīnī, d. after 816/1413
(II, 233), Paris 2388, Esc. ^{2}680, Mashh. II, 18$_{,20}$.—c. Mīrzājān, d. 994/1586, Ind.
Off. 531.—3. Ḥusayn al-Ardabīlī al-Abharī, d. 950/1543, Esc. ^{2}681.—4. Glosses
on an unnamed commentary, by Abū Naṣr Muḥammad b. Ibrāhīm al-Shīrāzī,
d. 903/1497, Esc. ^{2}684, 687$_{,1}$.—5. Anon., also Teh. II, 116.

II. *al-Taḥṣīl min al-maḥṣūl fī 'l-uṣūl* see p. 506.

III. *Laṭā'if al-ḥikma* Mashh. I, 71$_{,230}$.

IV, V. see Suppl.

28. Burhān al-Dīn Muḥammad b. Muḥammad al-Nasafī, who was born around 606/1209, taught in Baghdad, and died in 687/1288.

Ibn Quṭl. 170. 1. *al-Fuṣūl fī 'ilm al-jadal*, on the art of disputation, a commentary by Nuʿmān al-Khwārizmī, Berl. 5167.—2. *al-Muqaddima al-Burhāniyya fī
'l-khilāf* Berl. 5168, Esc. ^{2}788$_{,22}$, anon. comm. with glosses, Pet. Coll. sc. VI, 234.—
3. *Mansha' al-naẓar fī 'ilm al-khilāf* Berl. 5170, anon. comm. Paris 2500$_{,2,3}$.—
4. *al-Qawāḍiḥ al-jadaliyya*, logical discussions, Berl. 5169. |—5. *Dafʿ al-nuṣūṣ* 468
wal-nuqūḍ ibid. 5170.—6. *al-Tarājīʿ* ibid. 5171.—7. *Taʿāruḍāt* ibid. 5173.—
8. *Sharḥ al-asmā' al-ḥusnā* by al-Ghazzālī and al-Rāzī, ibid. 2233.

29. Shams al-Dīn Muḥammad b. Ashraf al-Ḥusaynī al-Samarqandī, who flourished around the year 690/1291.

1. *Risāla fī ādāb al-baḥth*, on the art of disputation, Berl. 5272/3, Munich 664,
668$_{,4}$, Leipz. 351/3, Landb.-Br. 446, 851, 990, Paris 2350, Bodl. I, 511$_{,3}$, 521, II, 255,
Br. Mus. 421$_{,8}$, Ind. Off. 486, Garr. 868, 2118$_{,2}$ Alex. Fun. 120$_{,5}$.—Commentaries:
1. Quṭb al-Dīn al-Kīlānī, ca. 830/1427, Berl. 5274, Munich. 664$_{,4}$, Alex. Ādāb al-b. 5,
print. Tashkent 1894 (*OB* VIII, 5441).—2. *al-Masʿūdī* by Kamāl al-Dīn Masʿūd b.
Ḥusayn al-Shirwānī al-Rūmī, d. 905/1499, Berl. 5275/6, Gotha 2809/10, Leipz.
|403, Munich 664, Paris 1262$_{,2}$, 2351$_{,2}$, Heid. *ZDMG* 91, 385$_{,319}$, Alex. Ādāb al-b. 616

$7_{,3}$, $8_{,3}$, $10_{,1}$, Qawala II, 306/7, Garr. 869, $2118_{,3}$.—Glosses: a. Mīr Abu 'l-Fatḥ Muḥammad b. Amīn Tāj al-Saʿīdī, dedicated to Ulugh Beg, d. 854/1450, Berl. 5277/8, Heid. ZDMG 91, $385_{,319,\ 2}$, Garr. 870, Patna II, $530_{,2852}$.—Superglosses: α (also on f.) Luṭfallāh b. Shujāʿ al-Dīn Kharḍama, Berl. 5281, Gotha $2809_{,2}$, Munich 664, ii, Garr. $2139_{,1}$, Qawala II, 296.—β Ramaḍān al-Bihishtī, d. 979/1571, Berl. 5282.—b. Aḥmad Dunqūz Shams al-Dīn al-Rūmī, ca. 870/1465, Berl. 5283, Leipz, 36. Esc. $^{2}678_{,5}$, Qawala II, 297.—c. Muḥammad b. Asʿad al-Dawwānī, d. 907/1501 (II, 217), Munich $664_{,3}$, Garr. $2139_{,2}$, Qawala II, 297.—d. Muḥammad b. Idrīs al-Nakhjuwānī, ca. 950/1543, Berl. 5284.—e. Aḥmad b. ʿUmar al-Janadī, ibid. 5285.—f. *Qara Ḥāshiya* by ʿImād al-Dīn Yaḥyā b. Aḥmad al-Kāshī, ca. 750/1350 (II, 211), Gotha $2809_{,2}$ (where other MSS are listed), Esc. $^{2}678_{,1}$, Alex. Ādāb al-b. $7_{,2}$, 8, $9_{,2}$.—Superglosses, see Suppl. (α also Alex. Ādāb al-b. $6_{,1}$, Fun. $148_{,1}$).—g. Anon., Berl. 5286, Ind. Off. 590, Pet. 241.—h. see Suppl.—i. Muḥammad b. al-Ḥājj Ḥamīd al-Kaffawī, Qawala II, 300.—k. Ḥamīd b. Burhān al-Dīn b. Abī Dharr al-Ghifārī, Qawala II, 296.—3. Ḥamīd al-Dīn al-Shāshī, ca. 850/1446, Berl. 5287.—4. Ulugh Beg Muḥammad b. Shāh Rukh b. Tīmūr, d. 853/1449 (II, 213), Alex. Ādāb al-b. 9.—5. Ḥusayn b. Muʿīn al-Dīn al-Maybudī, d. ca 890/1485, Garr. $2147_{,1}$.—6. Muḥammad b. Aḥmad al-Isfarāʾinī, ca. 900/1494, Berl. 5288, Leid. 1509, Pet. $101_{,2}$, Qawala II, 314.—7. Sinān al-Dīn Yūsuf al-Rūmī, ca. 900/1494, Berl. 5289, Paris $2351_{,1}$.—8. *Fatḥ al-wahhāb* by Zakariyyāʾ al-Anṣārī, d. 926/1520 (II, 99), Berl. Brill M. $314_{,2}$, Garr. 871, Alex. Ādāb al-b. $6_{,1,81}$, Āṣaf. II, $1320_{,135}$, on which glosses by Aḥmad b. Yūnus al-Khalīfī al-Shāfiʿī, d. 1209/1794, Alex. Ādāb al-b. 3.—9. see Suppl.—10. Anon., Berl. 5290/1, Paris $1262_{,2}$, $2350_{,1}$, Algiers $561_{,8}$, $1468_{,7}$.—11. Commentaries and glosses in Ahlw. 5292.

II. (*Mīzān*) *al-qusṭās*, on logic, with a commentary, Berl. 5166, Alex. Manṭiq 16, Patna I, $227_{,1999,\ 2001}$.

III. *Ashkāl al-taʾsīs* (*al-Risāla al-riyāḍiyya*), a compendium of geometry based on Euclid, Gotha 1496/7, Br. Mus. 388, 1332/3, Fātiḥ $3385_{,2}$, 5330, Rāġib $919_{,4}$, Asʿad $3797_{,3}$, Yeni $1176_{,17}$, *Hesp.* XVIII, $91_{,9}$.—Commentaries: a. Mūsā b. Muḥammad al-Rūmī Qāḍīzāde, d. 815/1412, Berl. 5943/4, Gotha 1498/9 (where other MSS are listed), Garr. 1058/9, Alex. Ḥisāb 30, Fun. $106_{,3}$, *Hesp.* XVIII, $91_{,9}$,
617 $93_{,13a}$, cf. Steinschneider, ZDMG 50, 169. | Glosses see Suppl. (γ also Garr. 1060, Cairo ^{1}V, 195), δ by Muḥammad al-ʿAṭṭār (II, $127_{,9}$), Patna II, $556_{,2930,2}$.

IV. *al-Ṣaḥāʾif al-ilāhiyya*, dogmatics with the commentary *al-Maʿārif*, Paris $1247_{,2}$, Br. Mus. Suppl. 181, Garr. 1485, Alex. Fals. 16 (*al-Ṣaḥāʾif fi 'l-kalām*).

V. *ʿAyn al-naẓar fi 'l-manṭiq* Br. Mus. Suppl. 1124, v, 1227.

VI. *Bayān madhhab ahl al-sunna* Garr. 1558 = (?) *Risāla fī kalimat al-tawḥīd* Alex. Fun. $88_{,3}$.

VII. *al-Tadhkira fi 'l-hayʾa* Berl. Oct. $3586_{,1}$.

30. Shams al-Dīn Muḥammad b. Maḥmūd al-Shahrazūrī al-Ishrāqī, who flourished in the 7th century.

Chwolson, *Ssabier* I, 228, Sachau, *Alberuni, Chron.* Lff. Rieu, *Cat.* 827. 1. *Rawḍat al-afrāḥ wa-nuzhat al-arwāḥ*, a history of the philosophers | from Adam to 469
Galen, Berl. 10056, Leid. 1488, Br. Mus. 601, 688, Lee 40, Ind. Off. 4613 (*JRAS* 1939, 383), Yeni 908, As'ad 3804,$_5$ (dated 665 AH Krause), Beveridge *JRAS* 1900, 550/1, a somewhat different recension Berl. 10055, *Mukhtaṣar* 'Um. 5573 (*ZS* III, 243), Persian transl. by Maqṣūd 'Alī Tabrīzī, started in 1011/1602, Br. Mus. Pers. Suppl. 100.—2. *al-Rumūz wal-amthāl al-ilāhūtiyya fi 'l-anwār al-mujarrada al-malakūtiyya* Vat. V. 299, Esc. ^{2}696.—3. *al-Shajara al-ilāhiyya fī 'ulūm al-ḥaqā'iq al-rabbāniyya*, on logic, ethics, physics, and metaphysics, Berl. 5063, Leid. 1489, Cairo ^{1}VI, 95.

Chapter 12. Mathematics

1. While he was still an official in his hometown of Basra Abū ʿAlī al-Ḥasan (Muḥammad) b. al-Ḥasan (al-Ḥusayn b. Ḥusayn) b. al-Haytham al-Baṣrī al-Miṣrī (the Latin Alhazen) had made a name for himself by his knowledge of applied methematics. Since he had volunteered to regulate the floodings of the Nile the caliph al-Ḥākim brought him to Egypt. Cruising the Nile, he supposedly saw the impossibility of his undertaking when he got to Aswan. In order to escape any arbitrary action on the part of al-Ḥākim, he allegedly feigned madness until the latter's death in 411/1020. He was then given back his confiscated property and, until his death in 430/1038, he lived exclusively through his work as a writer.

618 | Ibn Abī Uṣ. II, 90/8, Wüst., *Ärzte* 130, Leclerc I, 512/25, Cantor, *Vorl.* 677ff., M. Narducci in *Boncompagnis Boll. di bibl. e di storia delle scienze math. e fis.* IV (Roma 1871) 1/48, 137, A. Mieli, *La Science Arabe* 105/8. 1. *Fi 'l-ashkāl al-hilāliyya* Ind. Off. $734_{,12}$, Pet. Ros. $192_{,2}$.—2. *Fī misāḥat al-kura* Berl. $2970_{,13}$, Pet. Ros. $192_{,4}$.—3. *Fī qismat al-miqdārayn al-mukhtalifayn al-madhkūrayn fi 'l-shakl al-awwal min al-maqāla al-ʿāshira min kitāb Uqlīdis* ibid. 5.—4. *Fī masāʾil al-talāqī* ibid. 7.—5. *Fi 'l-masʾala al-handasiyya* ibid. 8, Bodl. I, $877_{,5}$, Cairo ^{1}V, 205, photograph *Qu. u. St.* VII, 1, 7, I, 3, transl. C. Schoy, *Isis* VIII, 254/9.—6. *Fī barkār al-dawāʾir al-ʿiẓām* Pet. Ros. $192_{,11}$, Leid. 1064, Ind. Off. $34_{,10}$.—7. *Fī ḥall shukūk kitāb Uqlīdis fi 'l-uṣūl wa-sharḥ maʿānīhi* Leid. 1129 (fragm.), Alex. Ḥisāb 42, Bursa, Haraccizade, Heyet $20_{,2}$, different from Algiers $1446_{,1}$, anon. abstract Berl. 5921.—8. *Sharḥ al-muṣādarāt*, on the introductions to all the treatises by Euclid, Bodl. I, 908, Bursa, Haraccizade, Heyet 20, Steinschneider, *Hebr. Übers.* § $314_{,2}$.—9. *Fī tarbīʿ al-dāʾira*, on the squaring of the circle, Berl., 5941, Patna II, $554_{,2928,9}$.—10. *Fī qismat al-khaṭṭ alladhi 'staʿmala Arshīmīdīs fi 'l-kura wal-usṭuwāna* Leid. 1009, Ind. Off. $734_{,18}$, photograph *Qu. u. St.* VII, 10, I, 11 = Algiers $1446_{,8}$ (?), cf. Woepcke, *l'Algèbre d'Omar* 91ff.—11. *Maqāla fi 'l-maʿlūmāt* Paris 2488, M. Sédillot, Notice du traité des connues géometriques de H. al-H. *JA* s. II, v. 14, 435ff.—12. *Qawl fi 'l-makān* Ind. Off. $734_{,7}$.—13. *Fī shakl B. Mūsā*, on a passage in Mūsā b. Shākir's (p. 241) preface to Apollonius' *Conics*, Br. Mus. $975_{,1}$,
470 Ind. Off. $734_{,8}$. |—14. *Fī misāḥat al-mujassam al-mukāfī'* Ind. Off. $734_{,11}$.—15. *Fī masʾala ʿadadiyya mujassama* ibid. 17, photograph *Qu. u. St.* VII, 11, I, 12.—16. *Fi 'stikhrāj masʾala ʿadadiyya* ibid. 20.—17. *Faṣl fī Muqaddimat ḍilʿ al-musabbaʿ*, with consideration of Archimedes' *Tasbīʿ al-dāʾira* (Fihr. 266, Steinschneider, *ZDMG* 50, 175), ibid. 21 (photograph *Qu. u. St.* VII, 11, I, 13), Bodl. I, $940_{,8}$ (photograph ibid. VII, 8, I, 5).—18. *Fi 'stikhrāj aʿmidat al-jibāl* Leid. 1008, Bodl. I,

$877_{,10}$.—19. *Fī ḥall shukūk ḥarakat al-iltifāf* Berl. $2970_{,1}$, Pet. Ros. $192_{,1}$.—20. *Fī
ṣūrat al-kusūf* Pet Ros. 192, Ind. Off. $734_{,18}$, $767_{,2}$ Bodl. I, $877_{,2}$.—21. *Fī ḥarakat
al-qamar* Pet. Ros, $192_{,6}$, Bodl. I, $877_{,3}$.—22. *Fi 'stikhrāj samt al-qibla* Pet. Ros.
$192_{,9}$, Bodl. I, $877_{,4}$, Berl. Oct. $2970_{,1}$ (photograph *Qu. u. St.* VII, 35, II, 2, see
C. Schoy, ZDMG 75, 1921, 242/3).—23. *Fi 'khtilāf manẓar al-qamar* Pet. Ros.
$192_{,10}$, Ind. Off. | $734_{,19}$ (photograph *Qu. u. St.* VII, 32, II, 27).—24. *Fī aḍwāʾ* 619
al-kawākib, a demonstration that the stars, with the exception of the moon,
have their own light, Berl. 5668, Oct. $2970_{,16}$, Ind. Off. $734_{,3}$, Bodl. I, $877_{,7}$, cf.
E. Wiedemann, *Wochensch. f. Astr. Meteor. u. Geogr.* 1890, p. 17.—25. *Maqāla
fi 'stikhrāj al-quṭb ʿalā ghāyat al-taḥqīq* Berl. Oct. $2970_{,6}$, Leid. 1063 (photograph
Qu. u. St. VII, 34, I, 24), Br. Mus. 404, Bodl. I, $877_{,6}$, transl. by C. Schoy, Abh. des
al-H. über eine Methode, die Polhöhe mit grösster Genauigkeit zu bestimmen,
De Zee 1920, 10, p. 586/601.—26. *Jawāb ʿan suʾāl al-sāʾil ʿani 'l-majarra hal hiya fi
'l-hawāʾ am fī jism al-samāʾ*, on the Milky Way, Leid. 1065.—27. *Maqāla fī ḍawʾ
al-qamar* Ind. Off. $734_{,9}$ (photograph *Qu. u. St.* VII, 35, ii, 27).—28. *Fī hayʾat
al-ʿālam* Ind. Off. $734_{,15}$, Steinschneider, *Extr. du Bull* XIV, 1881, p. 721ff. (Rome
1883), App. 1884, *Hebr. Übers.* § 347.—29. *Fī taṣḥīḥ al-aʿmāl al-nujūmiyya*,
Bodl. I, $877_{,8}$.—30. *al-Shukūk ʿalā Baṭlūmiyyūs*, ibid. 9, Berl. Oct. 3548.—31.
Maqāla fī kayfiyyat al-aẓlāl, Berl. 6019.—32. *Maqāla fi 'l-ḍawʾ*, Berl. 6018. Ind.
Off. $734_{,4}$. *I. al-H. 's Abh. über das Licht, ar. u. deutsch v.* J. Baarmann, Halle 1882,
cf. ZDMG 36, 195ff.—33. *Fi 'l-marāyā 'l-muḥriqa bil-quṭūʿ*, on convex burning
mirrors, Berl. Oct. $2970_{,7}$, Leid. 1010, Ind. Off. $734_{,6}$.—34. *Taḥrīr al-munāẓara*,
Paris 2460, a small abstract of the *Kitāb (ikhtilāf) al-Manāẓir*, see Suppl. *Tanqīḥ
al-manāẓir* (II, 211), Rāmpūr I, $412_{,20}$, Patna I, $235_{,2045}$, II, $561_{,2945}$. *Opticae the-
saurus Alhazeni Arabis libri VII, nunc primum ed. ejusdem liber de crepusculis
et nubium ascensionibus, etc. a. Fr. Rösnero*, Basle 1572. Commentary by Kamāl
al-Dīn Abu 'l-Ḥasan al-Fārisī, ca. 700/1300, Leid. 1011. Cf. E. Wiedemann, *Ann. f.
Physik* N.F. VII (1879), p. 679, XXI (1884), 541/4, Hirschfeld, *Die ar. Lehrbücher
der Augenheilk.* 111.—25.—50. see Suppl. (37. *Māhiyyat al-ithr alladhī fī
wajh al-qamar* Alex. Ḥisāb 42, photograph, *Qu. u. St.* VII, 36, I, 29.—39. Berl.
Oct. $2970_{,17}$.—41. ibid. 10.—44. ibid. 9.—45. ibid. 5.—46. ibid. 4).—51. *Maqāla
fī kayfiyyat al-raṣad* Alex. Ḥisāb 42.—52. *Maqāla fi 'l-tanbīh ʿalā mawāḍiʿ
al-ghalaṭ fī kayfiyyat al-raṣad* ibid. 61.

2. Abu 'l-Jūd Muḥammad b. al-Layth wrote, around the year 400/1009:

1. Answers to questions by al-Bīrūnī (p. 626), Leid. 1013.—2. The same on a
geometrical question by Abū Jaʿfar al-Khāzin, ibid. 1014.—3. On a geometrical
problem formulated by | Abū Saʿīd al-Sijazī and solved in part by Abū Sahl 620

al-Kūhī (p. 254), ibid. 1015.—4. On the properties of rectangular triangles that are not isosceles, ibid. 1016.—5. *Risāla ilā Abī Muḥammad ʿAbdallāh al-Ḥāsib fī ṭarīqay Abī Sahl al-Qūhī wa-shaykhihi Abī Ḥāmid al-Ṣaʿānī* (sic) *fī anna ʾl-musabbaʿ al-musāwiya al-aḍlāʿ fi ʾl-dāʾira* Bodl. I, 940,$_{8}$ (photograph *Qu. u. St.* VII, 9, I, 6).—6. *Kitāb fī ʿamal al-musabbaʿ fi ʾl-dāʾira* Cairo ^{1}V, 204 (photograph *Qu. u. St.* VII, 13, I, 19).—7. *Maqāla*, Drei planimetrische Aufgaben des Mathematikers a. l-J.M. b. al-Lith (sic), übers. v. C. Schoy, *Isis* 1925, 5/8.

3. Isḥāq b. Yūsuf b. Yaʿqūb al-Ṣardafī al-Yamanī, d. 500/1106.

1. *Mukhtaṣar al-Hindī*, on arithmetic, Berl. 5960/1.–2. *al-Kāfī fi ʾl-farāʾiḍ*, on the division of estates, ibid. 4688 (see Suppl.).

471 | 4. Together with Abu ʾl-Muẓaffar al-Asfizārī and Maymūn b. Najīb al-Wāsiṭī, Abu ʾl-Fatḥ ʿUmar b. Ibrāhīm al-Khayyām (Khayyāmī), who came from Nishapur or its vicinity, was ordered by Malikshāh to work on the reform of the Persian calendar. Called the "Age of Jalāl al-Dīn" (i.e. Malikshāh), it was meant to establish the solar year with accuracy, but apparently never gained any practical significance. However, his theory of cubic equations elevated his algebra to a degree of universal acceptance that did not see its equal before the seventeenth century. In philosophy he was regarded as a follower of Ibn Sīnā. His fame as a poet is based on the Persian quatrains circulating in his name, although it is likely that none are his. He died, in all likelihood, in 526/1132.

Sarton, *Introduction to the Hist. of Science* I, 759/61. Mieli, *La Science Arabe* 113, Cantor, *Vorl.* 666ff., V. Minorski, *EI* III, 1064/8, W.E. Story, *Omar as Mathematician*, Boston 1918. 1. *Maqāla fi ʾl-jabr wal-muqābala* Leid. 1020, Paris 2458,$_{7}$, 2461, Ind. Off. 734,$_{10}$, Woepcke, *L'Algèbre d'Omar al-Khayyami*, Paris 1851, Ghulām Ḥusayn Muṣāḥib, *Jabr wa-muqābala-i Kh.* Tehran 1317/1938.—2. *Risāla fī sharḥ*
621 *mā ashkala min muṣādarāt kitāb Uqlīdis* Leid. 967, anon. Paris | 4946,$_{4}$.—3. *Fi ʾl-iḥtiyāl li-maʿrifat miqdāray al-dhahab wal-fiḍḍa fī jism murakkab minhumā* Gotha 1158,$_{11}$, see E. Wiedemann, Über Bestimmung der spezifischen Gewichte, *SBPMS Erlangen* XXXVIII, 1906, 170/3.—4.–8. see Suppl. (8 = 4, also in Sayyid S. Nadwī, *Khayyām ōr uske Sawāniḥ wataṣānīf pur naqidana naẓar*, Azamgaḍh 1933, together with *Risālat al-kawn wal-taklīf, Risālat al-wujūd* or *al-Awṣāf lil-mawṣūfāt, Risāla fī kulliyyāt-i wujūd*, Persian and *Mizān al-ḥikam*).

4a.–h. see Suppl.

4c. Two geometrical problems, Leid. 1006.—4d., with the title *Kitāb al-ḥisāb fi ʾl-jabr wal-muqābala*, Garr. 1045.

5. Abu ʾl-Ḥasan Aḥmad b. Ibrāhīm, d. 552/1157.

Al-Fuṣūl fi ʾl-ḥisāb Yeni 802.

6. Muḥammad b. al-Ḥusayn b. Muḥammad b. Ḥusayn wrote for Ṣalāḥ al-Dīn, around the year 580/1184:

Risāla fi ʾl-barkār al-tāmm wa-kayfiyyat al-takhṭīṭ bihi Leid. 1076, Paris 2468,$_4$, Algiers 1446,$_5$, ed. with a French transl. by F. Woepcke, *Not. et Extr.* XXIII, 1. P.

7. Abū Muḥammad ʿAbdallāh b. Muḥammad al-Ḥajjāj al-Adrīnī b. al-Yāsamīnī, d. 601/1204 (see Suppl.).

ʿAbdallāh Gannūn, *al-Nubūgh al-maghribī fi ʾl-adab al-ʿarabī* I, 89. I. *al-Urjūza al-Yāsamīniyya*, 57 verses on algebra, Paris 4151,$_6$, Algiers 376,$_8$.—Commentaries: 1. Ibn al-Hāʾim, d. 815/1412 (II, 125), Bodl. I, 966,$_6$, 1238.—2. al-ʿIrāqī, d. 826/1423, perhaps Berl. 5693/4, cf. ʿ5—3. Ibn al-Jamāʿa, Franck 453.—4. Muḥammad Sibṭ al-Māridīnī, d. 912/1506 (II, 167), a. *al-Lumʿa* Berl. 5966/7, Gotha 1475, Fort William 1203, Garr. 1050, Alex. Ḥisāb 24, Fun. 128,$_2$ (photograph *Qu. u. St.* VII, 5, I, 1), glosses entitled *Farāʾid ʿawāʾid jabriyya* by Muḥammad al-Ḥifnī, d. 1181/1707 (Suppl. II, 423,$_{27a}$), Garr. 1052, 2120,$_2$, Alex. Ḥisāb 23, Makram 17.—b. shorter *al-Tuḥfa*, Berl. 5968, Gotha 1476, on which glosses by Muḥammad b. Aḥmad al-Jannābī, Berl. 5969.—5. ʿAlī b. Muḥammad al-Qurashī al-Qalaṣādī, d. 891/1486 (II, 266), Ind. Off. 770,$_2$.—6.–9. see Suppl. (9. also Alex. Ḥisāb 22).—II. see Suppl.—III. *Tanqīḥ al-afkār fi ʾl-ʿilm bi-rusūm al-ghubār* Alex. Ḥisāb 6.

| 8. Jamāl al-Dīn Abū Ḥafṣ ʿUmar b. Ḥassān b. ʿIyāḍ b. al-Mīlī wrote, around the 622
year 600/1203:

Munqidh al-hālik wa-ʿumdat al-sālik, a detailed explanation of arithmetic and geometry based on Euclid, Nichomachus, and al-Karajī (p. 247), Leid. 1028.

8a. Abū Ḥāmid Aḥmad b. Muḥammad b. Abī Ṭālib al-Malaṭī al-Khāṭirī wrote, before 609/1212:

Bayān al-ḥikma, a book of geometry, based on Euclid, Ptolemy, and Archimedes, Garr. 1057.

472 | 9. Sharaf al-Dīn al-Muẓaffar b. Muḥammad al-Ṭūsī wrote, around the year 606/1209:

1. *al-Jabr wal-muqābala*, with *muʿādalāt* by an anonymous author, Ind. Off. 767,$_{3}$.—2. Answer to a question by Amīr al-Umarāʾ Shams al-Dīn, Leid. 1027.—3.–5. see Suppl.

9a–e. See Suppl.

9f. Abu ʾl-Majd b. ʿAṭiyya b. al-Majd al-Kātib wrote, before 639/1241 (the date of the MS):

On multiplication, division etc., Br. Mus. 426,$_{21}$ (Suter 498).

10. Ismāʿīl b. Ibrāhīm b. Ghāzī b. ʿAlī b. Muḥammad al-Numayrī al-Ḥanafī Shams al-Dīn Abu ʾl-Ṭāhir al-Māridīnī b. Fallūs, who was born in 590/1194 and died around 650/1252.

1. *Iʿdād al-asrār fī asrār al-aʿdād*, arithmetic in the manner of the letter by Nicomachus to Pythagoras, composed during the pilgrimage, Berl. 5970, AS 2761,$_{7}$.—2. *Irshād al-ḥussāb fi ʾl-maftūḥ min ʿilm al-ḥisāb*, composed in Mecca, ibid. 5971.—3. *Niṣāb al-ḥabr fī ḥisāb al-jabr*, on equations, composed in Mecca, ibid. 5972.—4. see Suppl.—5. *al-Tuffāḥa fī iʿmāl al-misāḥa* Rabat 507,$_{23}$, print. in *Majmūʿa* C. 1310 (Qawala II, 266).

11.–14. See Suppl.

15. Shams al-Dīn Muḥammad b. Rabīʿ al-Zarkashī al-Muhandis issued an *ijāza* in 684/1285 for his work:

Kulliyyāt al-ḥisāb, MS dated 677, Alex. Ḥisāb 4.

| Chapter 13. Astronomy 623

1. Aṣbagh b. Muḥammad al-Gharnāṭī b. al-Samḥ was a mathematician, physician, and astronomer in Granada, who died on 18 Rajab 426/30 May 1035.

Ibn Abī Uṣ. II, 391. 1. *Kitāb fī 'l-ʿamal bil-asṭurlāb* Br. Mus. $405_{,2}$.—2, 3. see Suppl.—Cf. Steinschneider, *Zur pseudepigr. Lit.* p. 74.

2. Abū Naṣr Manṣūr b. ʿAlī b. ʿIrāq, who died before 427/1036 (see Suppl.).

Sachau, *Alberunis Chron.* XXXIII, Steinschneider, ZDMG L, 168. 1. *Kitāb fī ṣanʿat al-asṭurlāb bil-ṭarīq al-ṣināʿī* Berl. 5797.—2. *Risāla fī ḥall shubha ʿaraḍat lahu fi 'l-maqāla al-thālita ʿashara min Kitāb al-uṣūl*, addressed to al-Bīrūnī, on a dubious passage from the 13th *maqāla* of Euclid, Berl. 5925, Bank. $2519_{,14}$ = Patna II, $332_{,2519,20}$, where *thālitha.*—3. *Iṣlāḥ kitāb Menelaos fī 'l-kuriyyāt* Leid. 989/90, Bodl. I, 960, Patna II, $332_{,2519,9}$, cf. Steinschneider, op. cit., 197.—4. *Istikhrāj buʿd mā bayna 'l-markazayn min al-Mijisṭī al-Shāhī* Ind. Off. $734_{,2}$, cf. Ṭūsī in Steinschneider, op. cit., 207.—5.–7. see Suppl. (5–6 = Patna II, $332_{,2519,7-21}$).

3. Abū Isḥāq Ibrāhīm b. Yaḥyā al-Naqqāsh b. al-Zarqāla al-Qurṭubī, d. 493/1100 (see Suppl.).

Steinschneider, in Boncompagni's *Bull. di bibl. e di storia delle sc. math. e fisiche* XX, 1/36, 575/602, *Archeion, Archivo di storia della scienzia* XIV, 1932, 392/412, on the name see Renaud, *Hesp.* 1937, 1, n. 6. 1. *Kitāb al-ʿamal bil-ṣafīḥa al-zījiyya*, written for the prince of Seville al-Muʿtamid b. ʿAbbād, d. 488/1095, Leid. 1070/1, Br. Mus. $426_{,12}$, Inst. Reg. Belg. 50 d, cf. Steinschneider, *Hebr. Übers.* § $369_{,1}$, Don Profeit Tibbon, *Tractat de l'Assafea d'Azarquiel*, Bibl. hebr. catalana IV, Barcelona 1933. | —2. *Risālat b. al-Zarqāla* Esc. ^{1}957, de Jong 111.—3. *al-Qānūn* 473
(*li-Eumathion*?), astron. tables, Munich 853.—4. *Kitāb al-tadbīr*, on astrology, Vienna 1421, Br. Mus. $977_{,18}$.—5. On the movement of fixed stars (author?), Steinschneider, op. cit., $371_{,2}$.—6. see Suppl.

3a. Abū Naṣr Yaḥyā b. Jarīr al-Takrītī, see Suppl.

Graf, *Christl. ar. Lit.* 51/2, *Theol. Quartalschr.* 95, 1913, | 183, Cheikho, *Cat.* 624
Beyrouth 75/6, 267/8 (also on his brother Abū Saʿd al-Faḍl b. Jarīr).

4. Bahā' al-Dīn Abū Muḥammad 'Abd al-Jabbār b. 'Abd al-Jabbār b. Muḥammad al-Kharaqī al-Thābitī, who died in 527/1132 in his birthplace of Kharaq, near Marw.

1. *Muntaha 'l-idrāk fī taqāsīm al-aflāk*, a completion of the astronomy of Ibn al-Haytham (p. 618), Berl. 5669, Paris 2499.—2. *Kitāb al-tabṣira fī 'ilm al-hay'a*, abstract of the previous, Berl. 5670, Gotha 1384 (where other MSS are listed), see Lasinio, *ZDMG* XXVI, 806, ad Med. 293.

4a.–h. See Suppl.

4b. 2 also AS 2602/3.—c. read: Ibn al-Kammād.—e. *Aḥkām al-Dāmaghānī* Garr. 970.

5. Maḥmūd b. Muḥammad b. 'Umar al-Jaghmīnī al-Khwārizmī, who died after 618/1221.

Al-Mulakhkhaṣ fi 'l-hay'a, Kompendium der Astronomie, translation by Rudloff and Hochheim, *ZDMG* 47, 213ff. where the MSS are listed, with Garr. 974, 2104$_{,3}$, Patna I, 237$_{,2059}$, cf. Nallino, ibid. 48, 120. Commentaries: 1. Mūsā b. Muḥammad b. Maḥmūd al-Rūmī Qāḍīzāde, d. 815/1412 (II, 212), Berl. 5675/6, Dresd. 131, Munich 854, Paris 2503/4, 4386, 6384, Copenhagen 84, Br. Mus. 401/2, 1341, Suppl. 760/1, Ind. Off. 751/3, Bodl. I, 967, 1027, II, 276, 291$_{,4}$, Leid. 1086/8, Pet. 126$_{,2}$, Garr. 975/7, 'Āšir Ḥafīd 2031, Alex. Ḥisāb 39/41, Patna I, 237$_{,2056}$, lith. Persia 1286.—Glosses by: a. Faṣīḥ (al-Dīn) 'Abd al-Karīm al-Niẓāmī (ca. 850/1446), Leid. 1089, Qawala II, 270.—b. 'Abd al-'Alī al-Birjandī, ca. 930/1524 (II, 413), Berl. 5677, Br. Mus. Suppl. 762, Ind. Off. 754, Garr. 988/9, Qawala II, 261, Patna I, 236$_{,2046/7}$.—c. Anon., Berl. 5678.—d.–f. see Suppl.—g. Sinān Pāshā b. Yūsuf b. Khiḍr, d. 891/1486 (Suppl. II, 327), Qawala II, 270.—h. see Suppl. II, 857$_{,5}$.—2. al-Jurjānī, d. 816/1413 (II, 216), Gotha 1388 (where other MSS are listed), Paris 2505, Garr. 2104$_{,2}$, Ğārullāh 1496, Alex. Ḥisāb 39, Qawala II, 272.—3. Ṣafī al-Dīn al-Nahrīrī (?), Esc. ^{1}952.—4. Persian by Ḥusayn b. al-Ḥusayn, Bodl. I, 73$_{,3}$.—5. Anon., Cambr. 51/2, Pet. 27, 131.—6.–9. see Suppl.—10. Jalāl al-Dīn al-'Ubaydī, Faiḍ. 1330$_{,2}$ (copied in 751, during the lifetime of the
625 author).—II. *Risāla fī ḥisāb al-tis'* Garr. 502.—III, IV. | see Suppl.—V. *al-Farā'id*, astronomy, on which an anonymous commentary, Paris 2865$_{,11}$.

6. Riḍwān b. Muḥammad b. 'Alī al-Khurāsānī wrote, around 600/1203, in Damascus:

Risāla fī ʿamal al-sāʿāt wastiʿmālihā, on astronomical clocks, with numerous illustrations, Gotha 1348,$_{1}$.

6a.–c. see Suppl. (b. al-Biṭrawjī, Suyūṭī, *Lubb*, Bitrawshī).

6d. Al-Muẓaffar b. ʿAlī b. al-Muẓaffar wrote, before 639/1241 (the date of the MS):

Al-Mukhtaṣar fī ʾl-qirānāt Br. Mus. 426,$_{9}$.

7. Abū ʿAlī al-Ḥusayn b. ʿUmar al-Marrākushī, who died around 660/1262.

1. *Jāmiʿ al-mabādiʾ wal-ghāyāt fī ʿilm al-mīqāt*, composed in 627/1230, Leid. 1098/9, Paris 2507/98, cf. *Traité des instruments astronomiques des Arabes par*
Abu ʾl-Ḥasan ʿAlī (sic) de Maroc, trad. par | J.S. Sédillot *et publié par* L.A. Sédillot, 474
Paris 1835, Carra de Vaux, *JA* s. IX, t, 5, p. 464/516.

8. Muḥammad b. Abī Bakr al-Fārisī al-Kawwās Badr al-Dīn, d. 677/1278 (see Suppl.).

1. *Nihāyat al-idrāk fī asrār ʿulūm al-aflāk*, on astrology, Berl. 5888, Garr. 971.—2.–6. see Suppl. (3. also Alex. Ḥisāb 61).—7. *Taysīr al-maṭālib fī tasyīr al-kawākib* Alex. Ḥisāb 47.

9. ʿAlam al-Dīn Qayṣar b. Abi ʾl-Qāsim b. ʿAbd al-Ghanī b. Musāfir Taʿāsīf, d. 649/1251 (see Suppl.).

Correspondence with Naṣīr al-Dīn al-Ṭūsī (p. 508) on Euclid's postulates, Berl. 5942, MSS in Istanbul in Krause, p. 496,$_{10}$.

10. Abū Saʿīd ʿAbd al-Raḥmān b. Abī Ḥafṣ ʿUmar b. Muḥammad al-Abharī, d. 673/1274.

Suter 153, no. 369. *Lawāmiʿ al-wasāʾil fī maṭāliʿ al-rasāʾil*, on the maintenance of astronomical instruments, Gotha 1414, Esc. ^{1}960 (photograph *Qu. u. St.* VII, 30, I, 17) cf. L.A. Sédillot in *Mém. présentés par divers savants à l'Ac. des Inscr.* s. I, v. 1, p. 219b.

626 | 11. Muḥyi ʾl-Milla wal-Dīn Yaḥyā b. Muḥammad b. Abī Shukr al-Maghribī al-Andalusī, who died between 680–90/1281–91 (see Suppl.).

Khwandamīr, *Ḥabīb al-siyar* III, 1, 62, Steinschneider, *Bibl. Math.* 1892, $39_{,1}$. 1. *Kitāb al-mudkhal*, on astrology, Gotha $65_{,1}$.—2. *Taṣṭīḥ al-aṣṭurlāb* Berl. 5816, Patna I, $234_{,2040}$.—3. *Arbaʿ maqālāt fi ʾl-nujūm*, library of al-Muḥaddith al-ʿImād al-Fihrisī in Mashhad, *Dharīʿa* I, $408_{,2124}$.—4. *Kitāb al-nujūm*, on astrology, Munich 873, Br. Mus. $431_{,4}$. Ind. Off. 769, 1, Bodl. I, 982 = *Kayfiyyat al-ḥukm ʿalā taḥwīl sini ʾl-ʿālam* Paris $2593_{,11}$, different from Paris 2594 (= *al-Jāmiʿ al-ṣaghīr?* ḤKh V, 560) = (?) *al-Durr al-thamīn fi ʾl-ḥukm ʿalā taḥāwīl al-sinīn* Alex. Ḥurūf 14.—5. *al-Ḥukm ʿalā qirānāt al-kawākib fi ʾl-burūj al-ithnay ʿashar* Br. Mus. $414_{,2}$, Ind. Off. $769_{,2}$.—6. *Risālat al-khiṭāʾ wal-īghūr*, calendars of the Chinese and the Uyghurs, Bodl. I, $971_{,9}$.—7. Edition of Euclid, Steinschneider, ZDMG L, 169.—8. *Kitāb al-makhrūṭāt*, edition of the *Conics* of Apollonius of Perga with a brief preface, Br. Mus. $975_{,4}$, Manch. 358, Patna II, $554_{,2928,11}$.—9. *al-Shakl al-qaṭṭāʿ* Berl. 5957.—10. *Iṣlāḥ kitāb Menelaos fi ʾl-ashkāl al-kuriyya*, edition of the *Sphaerica* of Menelaus, Ind. Off. 741, see Steinschneider, ZDMG L, 197.—11. *Khulāṣat al-Mijisṭī*, appendix to Ptolemy, Leid. 1101, Steinschneider, op. cit., 207.—12. *Tahdhīb maqālat Theodosios fi ʾl-ukar*, edition of the *Sphaerica* of Theodosius, Leid. 985, Paris $2468_{,4}$, Mashh. XVII, 3, 5, Teh. II, $200_{,2}$, see Steinschneider, op. cit., 34.—13.–20. see Suppl.—15.–22.

12. Jamāl al-Dīn Abu ʾl-ʿAbbās Aḥmad b. ʿUmar b. Ismāʿīl al-Ṣūfī al-Maqdisī wrote, around 700/1300:

Astronomical tables, Gotha 1402 (see Suppl.).

475 | 14. Abū ʿAlī al-Ḥusayn b. Aḥmad b. Yūsuf b. Bāṣ al-Salamī, ca. 693/1294 (see Suppl.).

H.J.P. Renaud, Les Ibn Bāṣo, *Hespéris* 1937, 1/12.

Chapter 14. Travelogues and Geographies

1. Abū Rayḥān Muḥammad b. Aḥmad al-Bīrūnī, d. 440/1048, see Suppl.

Taeschner ZDMG 77, 31ff. M. Krause, Alb. ein iranischer Forscher im MA,
Islam XXVI, 1/15. M. Yaḥyā al-Hāshimī, | Naẓariyyat al-iqtiṣād ʿinda ʾl-B., RAAD 627
XV, 456/65. 1. *al-Āthār al-bāqiya etc.* also Patna I, $265_{,2218}$.—2. *Taʾrīkh al-Hind*, according to Sachau, *India*, Introd., completed between 30 April and
30 September 1030.—3. *al-Tafhīm li-awāʾil ṣināʿat al-tanjīm*, see RAAD V, 247, ed.
Jalal Humar, Tehran 1940.—4. *al-Qānūn al-Masʿūdī*, fragm. Br. Mus. Or. 1997,
9551, | photograph *Qu. u. St.* VII, 35, II, 26, ibid. 8230, photograph ibid. 58, Berl. 476
616, photograph ibid. 57. Part of chapter 14 translated by C. Schoy, *Die trigonometrischen Lehren des pers. Astronomen a. R.M. b. A. al-B.*, Hannover 1927, p.
66.—7. *Istikhrāj al-awtār etc.*, see Patna II, $336_{,2519,40}$.—8. *Fī rashīkāt al-Hind*,
photograph *Qu. u. St.* VII, 16, I, 25 see K. Käfer, Der Kettensatz, ein Beitrag
zur Gesch. u. Theorie u. Methodik des Kaufmännischen Rechnens, *Mitt. d. handelswiss. Sem. Zürich.*—11. *Kitāb al-jamāhir fī maʿrifat al-jawāhir* Esc ²905,
photograph *Qu. u. St.* VII, 69, V, 2/5, fragm. Taymūr, Ṭab. 953, print. Hyderabad
1355; *Die Einleitung zu al-B. ʾs Steinbuch mit Erläuterungen übers. v. Taqīaddīn al-Hilālī*, Leipzig 1941 (Sammlg. or. Arb. VII).—12. *Maqāla fī ʾl-nisab etc.*, see *al-Mashriq* IX, $1906_{,19}$.—13. *Risāla fī tasṭīḥ al-ṣuwar etc.* photograph *Qu. u. St.* VII,
34, II, 25.—15. *Taḥdīd nihāyāt al-amākin li-taṣḥīḥ masāfāt al-masākin*, see Zeki
Velidi Togan, B.'s Picture of the World in *Mem. Ant. Soc. of India* 43, p. 56.—19.
Tamhīd al-mustaqarr = Patna II, $335_{,2519,36}$.—27. *Kitāb al-ṣaydhala, Birunlu Eba Rayhan Kitabussaydele fittibb mukaddimesi türkçeye çeviren Yaltkaya Ṣerefeddin* Istanbul 1937 (*Ist. Un. Tib Tar. Enst* IX).—28. *Ifrād al-maqāl fī amr al-ẓilāl* Patna II, $335_{,2519,34}$.—29. *Risāla fī ashkāl al-handasa* ibid. 35.

2. Abū ʿUbayd ʿAbdallāh b. ʿAbd al-ʿAzīz b. Muḥammad b. Ayyūb al-Bakrī, d. 487/1094, see Suppl.

Ibn Abī Uṣ. II, 52, Leclerc I, 553. 1. *Muʿjam ma ʾstaʿjama, Das geographische Wörterbuch (der bei altar. Dichtern vorkommenden Ortsnamen mit einer Einleitung über die Sitze der ar. Stämme) des. al-B. nach den Hdss. in Leiden, Cambridge, London u. Mailand hsg. v.* F. Wüstenfeld, Göttingen-Paris 1877.—
2. *al-Masālik wal-mamālik*, a comprehensive handbook on geography, Paris
2218 (frgm.), 5905, Algiers 1548, Morocco (V. Minorsky, BSOS IX, 149, n. 1), Pet.
AM 101. From this *Description de l'Afrique septentrionale par Abou Obaid al-B., texte ar. par le Baron de Slane*, Algiers 1857, 2nd ed. 1910, A. Kunik i, V. | Rosen, 628

Izvestiya al-B. i drugich avtorov o Rusi i Slavjanach I, St. Petersburg 1878, II, 1903. Cf. Quatremére, *Not. et Extr.* XII, 437, Cherbonneau, *JA* s. V, v. 1, p. 437, Defrémery ibid. s. IV, v. 13, p. 460ff. Anon. abstract from the sixth cent., Krafft 319.—3. *Sharḥ al-amālī lil-qālī* see p. 139.—4. *Sharḥ al-amthāl li-Abī ʿUbayd al-Qāsim b. Sallām* p. 106.

477 | 3. Muḥammad b. Abī Bakr al-Zuhrī, who lived in Granada in 532/1137.

Kitāb al-jaghrāfiya, see Suppl., Paris 2220, Tunis, Kairouan, Algiers; from which Description du Sous el aqṣā, *Bull. de Corr. Afr.* 1884, 192/8; cf. Amari, *Bibl. Ar.-Sic.* 158.

4. Abū ʿAbdallāh Muḥammad b. Muḥammad b. ʿAbdallāh b. Idrīs al-Sharīf al-Idrīsī, who was born into an ʿAlid family in Ceuta in 493/1099, studied in Cordova and, after lengthy travels, arrived at the court of the Norman king Roger II of Sicily, for whom he wrote his famous geographical work in 548/1154.

ʿAbdallāh Gannūn, *Nubūgh* I, 88/9. 1. *Nuzhat al-mushtāq fī ʾkhtirāq al-āfāq* (named succinctly *Kitāb Rujīr*, Ibn Khald., Prol. I, $75_{,11}$, $81_{,13}$) Paris 2221/2, Bodl. I, 884/7, II, $131_{,3}$, $262_{,4}$, Leningrad, Öff. Bibl., Shumen in Bulgaria, *Petermanns Mitt.* 1933, no. 11/2, 304, see Suppl. Th. Nöldeke, *Ein Abschnitt aus dem ar. Geographen Idrisi* (on the Baltic countries), *Verh. d. Gel. Esthn. Ges. zu Dorpat* VII, 3, 1875, E. Saavedra, La geografia de España del Edrisi, *Boletin de la sociedad geogr. de Madrid* 1885, vol. 18, p. 225/42, W. Tomaschek, Zur Kunde der Haemus-Halbinsel, II. Die Handelswege im 12. Jahrh. nach den Erkundigungen des Arabers Idrisi, *SBWA, phil-hist. Cl. Bd.* 113 (1887), 285/373. R.A. Brandel, *Om och ur den arabiske geografen Idrisi*, Uppsala 1894 (with the description of Syria and Palestine in Arabic and Swedish). W. Hoenerbach, Deutschland u. seine Nachbarländer nach der Geographie des Idrīsī, *Bonner Or. Stud.* XXI, 1938.—Abstract *Nuzhat al-mushtāq fī dhikr al-amṣār wal-aqṭār wal-buldān wal-juzur wal-madāʾin wal-āfāq* Gotha 1524, Paris 2223, Algiers 1550, de Jong 99, Br. Mus. Suppl. 685, Cambr. 1174.—2., 3. see Suppl.

5. Abū Ḥāmid Abū ʿAbdallāh Muḥammad b. ʿAbd al-Raḥīm (ʿAbd al-Raḥmān) b. Sulaymān al-Māzinī al-Qaysī al-Andalusī, d. 565/1169, see Suppl.

629 | Maqq. I, 617, Wüst. in *Lüdde's Zeitschr.* I, 43, Reinaud, *Aboulf.* transl. CXI/II, Mehren, *Ann. f. nord.* Oldk. 1857, 29. 1. *Nukhbat al-adhhān fī ʿajāʾib al-buldān*
478 or *al-Mughrib ʿan baʿḍ ʿajāʾib al-buldān*, | a description of a trip through Spain,

Africa, Alexandria, Cairo, Ashkelon, Damascus, Ardabil, the Caspian Sea, Darband, and the land of the Khazars, often of fabled content, composed for the vizier Yaḥyā b. Muḥammad b. Hubayra after 516/1122, Gotha 1539 (see Derenbourg, *Rev. Cr.* 1882, I, 210, n. 3), cf. *Bolletino ital. degli stud. or.* NS 315.—2. *Tuḥfat al-albāb wa-nukhbat al-aʿjāb*, composed in 557/1162, Berl. 6038/9, Gotha 1501/2 (where other MSS are listed), Algiers 1549$_{,1}$, 1870$_{,3}$, Br. Mus. Suppl. 686, Garr. 766, cf. B. Dorn, *Bull. de l'Ac. de St. Pétersbourg* XVIII, 150, 299, 321 = *Mél. As.* VI, 675, 685, 777, A. v. Kremer, *SBWA* CIX, 209, 137, de Goeje, *Mededeeling betr. den zwaardcultus, Ac. Amsterd.* V, G. Jacob, *Studien in ar. Geographen*, Part III, Berlin 1892.—3. *ʿAjāʾib al-makhlūqāt* ḤKh IV, 189, Bodl. I, 965, II, 259, see Suppl.—4.–6. see ibid.

6. Muḥammad b. ʿAlī b. Muḥammad al-Anṣārī al-Mawṣilī wrote, in 592/1196 in Suyūṭ:

ʿUyūn al-akhbār, an account of his travels in Syria, Palestine, and Egypt in 537–85/1142–89, and of the scholars whom he met on the way, Berl. 6131.

6a. Murtaḍā b. ʿAfīf (?) wrote after the traditionist ʿAlī b. Muḥammad al-Silafī, d. 576/1180 (p. 450), whom he quotes:

L'Égypte de Murtada fils de Gaphiphe etc. see Suppl. II, 1026$_{,7}$, see Galtier, *Bull. de l'Inst. franç. d'arch. or.* V, 133/4.

7. Abu 'l-Ḥusayn Muḥammad b. Aḥmad b. Jubayr al-Kinānī, who died in Alexandria in 614/1217 (see Suppl.).

Riḥlat al-Kinānī (Leid. 793). *The Travels of Ibn Jubair* ed. by W. Wright, Leiden 1852, 2nd ed. by M.J. de Goeje, Gibb Mem. V, Leiden 1907. Extrait d'un voyage en orient de M. b. Djobair, texte ar. accompagné d'une trad. franç. et des notes par M. Amari, *JA* s. IV, vol. 6, p. 507, v. 7, p. 73, 201, cf. M. al-Tantawi, ibid. v. 9, p. 351, G. Crolla, La Sicile au XIIe s. récit du voyage de I.J. en l'an 581 de l'h. (1187) trad. de l'ar., *Muséon* VI, 123/32.

8. Abu 'l-Ḥasan ʿAlī b. Abī Bakr b. ʿAlī al-Shaykh al-Harawī, d. 611/1214 (see Suppl.).

| 1. *Ishārāt ilā maʿrifat al-ziyārāt*, a description of popular shrines in Aleppo, 630
in Syria with its coastal regions and the possessions of the Franks, Palestine, Jerusalem, Egypt, the countries around the Mediterranean, its islands,

Diyarbakr, Iraq, India, Mecca, Medina, Yemen, and Persia, Berl. 6120/3, Cairo [1]V, 58, [2]VI, 32.—2. *al-Khuṭab al-Harawiyya*, pious aphorisms that he had affixed to all sides and doors of a building erected next to a tomb for pious Sufis which he had built during his lifetime, Berl. 8656.—3. See Suppl. Turkish transl. by Muḥammad ʿĀrif Ḥilmī, made in 1253/1837, Fātiḥ 3469.

9. Jamāl al-Dīn Muḥammad b. ʿAbd al-ʿAzīz al-Idrīsī Abū Jaʿfar wrote for the Egyptian sultan al-Malik al-ʿĀdil (635–7/1238–40):

479 | *Anwār ʿuluww al-aḥrām fi ʾl-kashf ʿan asrār al-ahrām*, revised by ʿAbd al-Qādir al-Baghdādī, d. 1093/1682 (II, 286), Munich 417, Paris 2274/7. Wyse, *Operations at the Pyramids* II, 344ff., gives an "Extract from Schereef Djemaleddyn Aboo Djafar M. Edrysys History of the Pyramids" and considers the date of composition of 623 as mistaken because he confuses this Idrīsī with the famous geographer (no. 4). In the MS in Paris mention is made of a Sultan Abū Bakr Khalīl b. al-Malik al-Afḍal Najm al-Dīn, but since there was never anyone like this, de Slane took the work to be a pseudepigraph, which supposedly only came into being around 1232 AH, the date of the four MSS in Paris; but the MS in Munich dates from 1072/1661. While de Slane assumed that before the conquest of Egypt by the Ottomans no sultan had carried the title of *amīr al-muʾminīn*, Casanova *JA* s. IX, vol. 7, p. 129ff. confirms this title on the basis of an inscription of al-Malik al-ʿĀdil.

10. Yāqūt[1] b. ʿAbdallāh al-Rūmī, born the son of Greek parents in Byzantine territory in 574 or 575/1179, was captured as a boy. Being the slave of a merchant from Hama, he received the *nisba* al-Ḥamawī. His master had him educated
631 with care and sent him out on business trips from a young age onward. | When he returned in 590/1194 from his third trip to Kish in the Persian Gulf he had an argument with his owner. After his liberty had been restored to him, he made a living as a copyist and studied among other things under the grammarian al-ʿUkbarī. In 596/1199 he went once more on behalf of his former master to Kish. But when he returned the following year, the latter was no longer alive. He now set up his own business as a bookseller, and in this capacity he travelled to Syria in 607/1210 (*Irshād* VI, 147). The following years he became also productive as a writer. In 610/1213 he left on a trip again, first to Tabriz, then by way of Mosul to Syria and Egypt, where he stayed in 612 (*Irshād* I, 161,
480 17). From there he returned, by way of Damascus, to the east. | In Nishapur he

1 This slave name he later changed to the nobler Yaʿqūb, which never caught on.

bought a Turkish slavegirl in 613, but soon had to sell her again because he was short of money. The rich treasures of the libraries of Marw consoled him for this loss; it was there, in 615/1218, that he drew up the plan for his geographical dictionary. After a stay of about two years he continued on to Khwārizm. On the news that the Tatars had conquered Bukhārā and Samarqand, he fled from Balkh to Khurāsān, leaving all his goods behind. By way of Irbil he arrived in Mosul in 617/1220, where he made a living as a copyist. The vizier Jamāl al-Dīn ʿAlī b. Yūsuf al-Shaybānī al-Qifṭī (p. 396), to whom he had poured out his troubles, enabled him to travel to Aleppo in 619/1222, but he soon returned to Mosul where he started working on the draft of his geographical dictionary, which he completed on 20 Ṣafar 621/13 March 1224. In 624/1227 he travelled once more to Alexandria and, upon his return to Aleppo, he started, on 21 Muḥarram 625/1 January 1228, to prepare the clean copy of his work. In the middle of this task,
death overtook him | in a tavern on the outskirts of the city, on 20 Ramaḍān 632
626/20 August 1229.

Ibn Khall. 761, Wüst., *ZDMG* 1864, 397ff., *NGGW* 1865, 333ff., *Gesch.* 310, Mehren, *Ann. f. nord. Oldk.* 1857, 38, no. 20. 1. *Muʿjam al-buldān, Jacuts geographisches Wörterbuch, hsg. v.* F. Wüstenfeld, 6 vols., Leipzig 1866/73.[2]—Abstracts: a. *Marāṣid al-iṭṭilāʿ ʿalā asmāʾ al-amkina wal-biqāʿ*, ed. T.G. Juynboll, Leiden 1850/64, also Patna II, $325_{,2497}$, $540_{,2906}$, lith. Tehran 1315.—b. See Suppl.—2. *al-Mushtarik waḍʿan wal-mukhtalif ṣaqʿan*, composed in 623/1226, revised edition in 626/1229 with *al-muftariq* instead of *al-mukhtalif*, ed. F. Wüstenfeld, Göttingen 1846.—3. *Muʿjam al-udabāʾ al-musammā bi-Irshād al-arīb ilā
maʿrifat al-adīb* | Köpr. 1103, abstract part 3 Berl. 9852, see Suppl. new impres- 481
sion, vocalised in part, by A. Farīd Rifāʿī in 20 vols., C. 1936/8; on the sources see also Bergsträsser, *ZDMG* 65, 797ff.—4. *al-Muqtaḍab min kitāb Jamharat al-nasab* (by Ibn al-Kalbī, see *ZDMG* 43, 117), Cairo ^{1}V, 156, ^{2}V, 355.—5.–9. see Suppl.

11. Muwaffaq al-Dīn ʿAbd al-Laṭīf b. Yūsuf al-Baghdādī, a physician and natural scientist, d. 629/1231 (see Suppl.).

2 Cf. Barbier de Meynard, *Dictionnaire géographique, historique et littéraire de la Perse et des contrées adjacentes, extrait du Moʾdjem elbouldan de Jaqout et complété à l'aide de documents arabes et persans pour la plupart inédits*, Paris 1871; F.J. Heer, *Die historischen und geographischen Quellen in Jaquts Geographischem Wörterbuch*, Strasburg 1898; H. Derenbourg, Les croisades d'après le dict. géogr. de Jaqout in *Le vol. du centenaire de l'École des langues or. viv.* p. 71/92.

Ibn Abī Uṣ. II, 201/13 (*Abdollatiphi Bagdadensis vita auct. Ibn abi Oseibia*, ed. Joh. Mousley, Oxford 1808), *Fawāt* II, 7, Suyūṭī, *Ḥusn al-muḥ.* I, 312, Wüst., *Ärzte* 220, *Gesch.* 314, Leclerc II, 182. 1. *Kitāb al-ifāda wal-iʿtibār fi ʾl-umūr al-mushāhada wal-ḥawādith al-muʿāyana bi-arḍ Miṣr, Abdollatiphi Compendium memorabilium gypti*, ed. J. White, Oxford 1788, *praefatus est* H.E.G. Paulus, Tübingen 1789. *A.'s Denkwürdigkeiten Ägyptens, übers. von* S.F.G. Wahl, Halle 1790. *Historiae Aegypti compendium ar. et lat. partim ipse vertit, partim a Brookio versum edendum curavit* J. White, Oxford 1800. *Relation de l'Égypte par A. trad. par*
633 | S. de Sacy, Paris 1810. New impression, C. 1286.—2. *al-Tajrīd min alfāẓ rasūl Allāh wal-ṣaḥāba wal-tābiʿīn* Bodl. I, 1149.—3. *Mulakhkhaṣ min kitāb Maqālat al-tāj fī ṣifāt al-nabī* Cairo ^{1}VII, 95.—Inventory of his logical works in Steinschneider, *Alfārābī* 29.—5.–16. see Suppl. (11. also Patna I, $249,_{2115}$).—17. *Fī ʿilm mā baʿd al-ṭabīʿa*, Taymūr, Ḥikma $116,_{2}$.—18. *Maqāla fi ʾl-ḥawāss wa-maqāla thāniya fi ʾl-ḥiss wa-masāʾil ṭabīʿiyya* Esc. $^{2}889,_{1}$.

12. Zakariyyāʾ b. Muḥammad b. Maḥmūd al-Qazwīnī, a descendant of Anas b. Mālik, was born in Qazvin around 600/1203. For unknown reasons he was forced to leave his hometown, staying in Damascus in 630/1232, where he made the acquaintance of Ibn al-ʿArabī (p. 571). Under the last caliph al-Muʿtaṣim he was a *qāḍī* in Wāsiṭ and al-Ḥilla, and he died in 682/1283.

S. de Sacy, *Chrest.* ^{2}III, 443ff., Wüst. *GGA*, 1848, 1, 345ff. Reinaud, *Aboulf.* I, CXLIII, Mehren, *Ann. f. nord. Oldk.* 1857, 80, Leclerc II, 135. *ʿAjāʾib al-makhlūqāt wa-āthār al-bilād*, a cosmography (see Suppl., additional MSS Esc. ^{2}899 fragm., Patna II, $324,_{2496}$, photograph of Munich 464, Paris 2775, *Qu. u. St.* VII, 75, V, 7/8), *Āthār al-bilād*, Bursa Hü. Celebi Heyet 14.—Persian transl. Fātiḥ 4171/3, 4174, supposedly from 659 AH, 4179, Sarāi 2962, 2989. The third edition by Wüstenfeld, Göttingen 1848, printed in the margin of Damīrī, C. 1309, lith. Tehran 1310. *Das Steinbuch aus der Kosmographie des Z. b. M. b. M. al-K. übers. u. mit Anm. versehn v.* J. Ruska, *Beilage zum Jahresber. der prov. Oberrealschule zu Heidelberg*, Kirchhain N/L, 1896. *Ein ar. Berichterstatter aus d. 10. Jahrh. über Fulda, Schleswig, Soest, Paderborn u. a. Städte des Abendlandes, Artikel aus Q. 's Āthār albilād aus dem Ar. übertr. mit Cmt. u. einer Einl. versehn v.* G. Jacob, 3. verm. u. verb. Aufl., Berlin 1896 (cf. Karabacek, *WZKM* VII, 364ff.)—Abstracts: a. *Talkhīṣ al-āthār wa-ʿajāʾib al-malik al-qahhār*, with the addition of longitudes and latitudes, by ʿAbd al-Rashīd b. Ṣāliḥ al-Bākuwī, ca. 806/1403, Munich 889, f. 211ff. following Paris 2246/7, cf. de Guignes. *Not. et Extr.* II, 386ff., Mehren, *Ann. a. a. O.* 70. Extraits de lá géogr. de ʿA. al-B. in J.J. Marcel, *Mélanges de litt. or.*,
634 Paris 1800.—b. Anon., Paris 2181/3, $2419,_{3}$ (photograph | Cairo ^{2}V, 334), Br. Mus. 386. Persian transl. Vienna 1438/9, Leid. 798, Cambr. Suppl. $851,_{3}$, lith. Lucknow
482 1283, Tehran 1264. |—Turkish transl. see Suppl., Čagatai Chanykow 108.

13. Abū ʿAbdallāh Muḥammad b. Ibrāhīm b. ʿAlī (Leid. ʿAlī b. Ibrāhīm) b. Shaddād ʿIzz al-Dīn al-Anṣārī al-Kātib al-Ḥalabī, who died at the age of 74 in the year 684/1285 in Egypt.

Orient. II, 274, Wüst., *Gesch.* 362. 1. *al-Aʿlāq al-ḥaẓīra (khaṭīra) fī dhikr umarāʾ al-Shām wal-Jazīra*, a historical geography of Syria and Mesopotamia, DMG 58, Br. Mus. 282,$_{3}$, 1323/4, Bodl. Marsh 33 (anon. see Amedroz, *JRAS* 1902, 80), Pet. AM 162, best MS Topkapi Sarai Revan Köşk 1564 (Bursa), cf. *Cent. Amari* II, 152ff., Ledit, *al-Mashriq* XXXIII (1935), 161/223, Cl. Cahen, La Djezira au milieu du XIIIe s. d'après ʿIzz al-Dīn b. Shaddād, *REI* I, 109/28.—2. *al-Qurʿa al-Shaddādiyya al-Ḥimyariyya* or *Tuḥfat al-zaman fī ṭuraf ahl al-Yaman* Patna I, 190,$_{1720}$.

14. Abū Muḥammad al-ʿAbdarī of Valencia started a trip through North Africa in 688/1289.

Al-Riḥla al-maghribiyya, a description of African towns and the customs of their inhabitants, with reports on the scholars there, Leid. 801, Paris 2283, Esc. ^{2}1738, Tunis, *Bull. de Corr. Afr.* 1884, p. 35, no. 140, note on Tripoli Paris 1889,$_{2}$, see Vincent, *JA* s. IV, vol. 5, p. 405, Dozy, ibid., vol. 3, 394, Cherbonneau. see V, vol. 4, p. 144ff., W. Hoenerbach, Das Nordafrikanische Itinerar des A. v. J. 688/1289, *AKM*, XXV (1940), 4.

15. Najm (Jamāl) al-Dīn Abu ʾl-Fatḥ Yūsuf b. Yaʿqūb al-Shaybānī al-Dimashqī b. al-Mujāwir, who died in 690/1291.

Taʾrīkh al-mustabṣir (often corrupted to *al-mustanṣir*, see G. Ferrand, *JA*, s. XI, vol. 13 1919, 469ff.), a description of Mecca and Yemen, Br. Mus. 1511 (see Suppl. Paris 6021, contains, however, a work by Ibn Muḥammad b. Masʿūd b. ʿAlī b. Aḥmad b. al-Mujāwir al-Baghdādī al-Nīsābūrī, composed around 626/1229, see M. Jawad, *REI*, 1938, 286).

16. Al-Faḍl b. Yaḥyā b. ʿAlī al-Ṭībī wrote in Ḥilla, in 699/1299:

| Account of the trip of Zayn al-Dīn ʿAlī b. Fāḍil al-Māzandārānī to Egypt, Spain, 635
the land of the Berbers, the island of the Rāfiḍites (i.e. Djerba) and to the Green Island in the White Sea, where he was entertained by the Qurʾān scholar Shams al-Dīn Muḥammad al-ʿĀlim, but which he had to leave after just eight days, Berl. 6132.

Chapter 15. Medicine

1. Abu 'l-Faraj ʿAbdallāh b. al-Ṭayyib al-ʿIrāqī was the secretary to the Catholicos Elias I, and a doctor and teacher at the ʿAḍudī hospital in Baghdad. He died in 435/1043.

Ibn Abī Uṣ. I, 241, Wüst., *Ärzte* 132, Leclerc I, 486, Cat. Beyrouth 22/3. 1. *al-Nukat wal-thimār al-ṭibbiyya wal-falsafiyya*, abstracts from Hippocrates' *de octimestri partu; de plantis secundum Aristotelem* (see Bouyges, MUSJ IX, 2, 1924); *de odoribus et variis aromatum generibus; de capillis et calvitie; al-Farq bayna 'l-rūḥ wal-nafs, de siti ejusque causis; de clysteribus eorumque usu. Kalām Jālīnūs fi 'l-ḥaqn*, on the golden verses of Pythagoras and the commentary by Hierocles,
483 *de urinis, de pulsibus* Esc. ^{2}888$_{,1-9}$. |—2. *Tafsīr kitāb Jālīnūs li-ḥīlat al-bur'*, a paraphrase of *περὶ μεθόδον θεραπευτικῆς*, Leid. 1298.—3. *Kitāb tadbīr al-aṣiḥḥā'*, a paraphrase of Galen's *ὑγιεινῶν*, ibid. 1299, Paris 2858, Med. 226, 235, 250, 263.—4. *Tafsīr* Maqūlāt *Arisṭāṭālīs* Cairo ^{1}VI, 89.—5.–11. see Suppl. (10. Garr. 1096).—12. *Maqāla fi 'l-ḥurūf wa-mā yatarakkab minhā* Esc. ^{2}888$_{,13}$.—13. A commentary on the *Tabula Cebetis* in the translation of Ibn Miskawayh (p. 418), ibid. 14.—14. *Thimār Maqālat Arisṭūtālīs fī tadbīr al-manzil*, apocryphal, perhaps translated by him, ibid. 11.—See G. Graf, *Die christl.-ar. Lit. bis zur fränk. Zeit*, Freiburg, 1905, 55/8.

1a. Sharaf al-Dīn ʿAlī b. ʿĪsā al-Kaḥḥāl, d. after 400/1010 (see Suppl.).

Tadhkirat al-kaḥḥālīn also Leningrad, see Kračkovsky, *RAAD* IV, 285, 318, Patna I, 244$_{,2091}$.

1b. Abū Bakr Ḥāmid b. Samḥūn worked as a physician in Cordova during the reign of Ḥājib al-Manṣūr (d. 392/1002).

636 | Ibn Abī Uṣ., II, 51/2. *Kitāb al-adwiya al-mufrada* Br. Mus. Or. 11614, see Fulton, *Br. Mus. Qu.* XI, 81.

2. Abu 'l-Ṭayyib's student Abu 'l-Ḥasan al-Mukhtār b. ʿAbdūn b. Saʿdūn b. Buṭlān was a Christian like him and worked as a physician in Baghdad. In order to get to know his literary opponent Ibn Riḍwān (no. 4), he went to Egypt in 439/1047. Sensing that he was no match for him, he went to Antioch, by way of Constantinople, where he entered a monastery. He died there after 460/1068.

Ibn Abī Uṣ. I, 241, Wüst. 133, Leclerc I, 489. V. Rosen, *Auszüge aus Yaḥyā al-Anṭākī,* 038/52 (on his theology of the Eucharist see G. Graf, *Or. Chr.* II, 13, 1938, 44/70). 1. *Taqwīm*[1] *al-ṣiḥḥa,* 40 tables of macrobiotics, Munich. 821, Paris 2945, 2947,$_{3}$, Br. Mus. 441, Suppl. 792/3, Bodl. I, 554, II, 180, Naples, Cat. Ital. 237, no. 96, 2. *Tacuini* (*so*) *sanitatis,* Strasburg 1531. *Schachtafeln der Gesundheit, übers. durch* Mich. Herr, Strasbourg 1532. On this is based the *Hygiene,* which in Latin translation is attributed to Abulhasen de Bagdad f. Habde, ed. E. Dogne in *Boletin de la R. Ac. de Hist.* 1892, XVI, see Renaud, *La prétendue* Hygiène *d'Abulcasis et sa véritable origine, Petrus Nonnus* III, Lisbon 1941, fs. 3/4.—2. *Daʿwat al-aṭibbāʾ,* a dialogue between the author and a 70-year old physician in Mayyāfāriqīn on medicine and its disciplines in general, composed in 450/1058 (Uṣ.), Berl. 6282/3, Gotha 1909.—2. *Tadbīr al-amrāḍ al-ʿāriḍa ʿala ʾl-akthar bil-aghdhiya al-maʾlūfa wal-adwiya al-mawjūda yantafiʿu bihā ruhbān al-adyira wa-man baʿuda min al-madīna* Gotha 1952,$_{2}$, Gött. 98, Paris 2918,$_{2}$.—3. *Risāla fī shirāʾ al-raqīq wa-taqlīb al-ʿabīd,* instructions on how to spot physical defects when buying slaves, Berl. 4979.—5. *al-Maqāla fī anna ʾl-farrūj aḥarru min al-farkh,* also with the title *al-Shaʿbadha al-ʿaqliyya,* proof that a chicklet is warmer than any other young bird, Bodl. I, 1264,$_{3}$.—6.–8. see Suppl.

3. Abū Saʿīd (Saʿd) ʿUbaydallāh b. Jibrīl b. Bukhtyishūʿ, a member of the famous
Christian family of physicians | (Ibn Abī Uṣ. I, 125ff.) and a friend of Ibn Buṭlān, 637
lived in Mayyāfāriqīn and died in the fifties of the fifth century.

Ibn Abī Uṣ. I, 148, Wüst., 35. 1. *Kitāb al-ʿishq maraḍan* Leid. 1332.—2. *Kitāb al-khawāṣṣ mujarrab al-manāfiʿ* Garr. 1065, AS 2943, from which *Manāfiʿ al-ḥayawān* Paris 2782, Br. Mus. Suppl. 778.—3. *Tadhkirat al-ḥāḍir wa-zād al-musāfir,* abstract of *al-Rawḍa al-ṭibbiyya,* Paris 3028,$_{2}$, Esc. ^{2}889,$_{2}$.—4. see Suppl.

| 4. Abu ʾl-Ḥasan ʿAlī b. Riḍwān b. ʿAlī b. Jaʿfar al-Miṣrī was born in Giza and 484
studied in Cairo where he had originally made a living as a street astrologer. He amassed great wealth as the personal physician of the caliph al-Ḥākim, but lost it all because of a wayward adopted child. He died in 460/1068.

1 See Thorndike and Sarton, *Isis* X, 489/93.

Fragment of an autobiography, Gotha 2035$_{,10}$, Genua, *Bol. ital. degli studii or.* 410, *ZDMG* XXXI, 761 (or an excerpt from Ibn Abī Uṣ.? see Steinschneider, *Hebr. Übers.* § 203), Ibn Abī Uṣ. II, 99/105, Wüst, 138, Leclerc I, 525, de Sacy, *'Abdallaṭīf* 103, Steinschneider in Baldi, *Vite di matematici arabi*, Rome 1874, 45/55. G. Gabrieli, *Isis* 1924, 500/6. 1. *Kifāyat al-ṭabīb fī-mā ṣaḥḥa ladayya min al-tajārīb*, reviews the various diseases without any introduction and ends with a tract on the pulse and other methods of diagnosis, focussed particularly on urine, Gotha 1952$_{,1}$.—2. *Kitāb al-uṣūl fi 'l-ṭibb*, before in Esc. see Morata, *al-Andalus* II, 273, A. Taymūr, *RAAD* III, 361, Hebrew transl. Steinschneider § 471.—3. Answers to various medical questions, Gotha 2015$_{,1,\ 2,\ 9}$.—4. *Fī-mā yajibu 'ala 'l-ra'īs al-fāḍil min maṣāliḥ badanihi wa-ādāb labībihī wa-qahramānihi* ibid. 3.—5. Demonstration of the truth of Galen's statement about milk, ibid. 5.—6. That every member is fed by its corresponding humour, ibid. 7.—7. On barley, from a medical point of view, ibid. 8.—8. On sugar, ibid. 11.—9. On the number of fevers, ibid. 12.—10. On the periods of fevers, ibid. 13.—11. On beverages, Bodl. I, 941$_{,8}$.—12. Commentary on Galen's *De arte medendi ad Glauconem*, Esc. ^{2}887$_{,3}$ (fragm.) from which notes by Abū Ja'far b. Ḥasdāy, ibid. 803$_{,1}$.—13. Commentary on Galen on the three schools of medicine, ibid. 852$_{,1}$ (fragm.).—14. *Sharḥ al-ṣinā'a al-ṣaghīra li-Jālīnūs*, a commentary on Galen's *Ars parva*, ibid. ^{2}883, Bursa Haraccizade Tip 43 (Ritter), Latin *Haly Ebn Rodan* see *Rodoham*
638 *Aegyptius, Liber Tegni Galeni* etc. Venice 1496; | Hebrew Steinschneider § 471$_{,2}$.—15. Commentary on Galen on the elements, Hebr. ibid. 3.—16. Commentary on Ptolemy's Quadripartitum *Sharḥ maqālat al-arba' fi 'l-qaḍāyā bil-nujūm li-B.*, Bodl. I, 992, Esc. ^{1}908, Patna I, 338$_{,2066}$, Latin in the *Q.* Venice 1413, 1484, 1493.—17. Aphorisms, fragm. Esc. ^{1}888$_{,10}$ now Madrid, Robles DCI.—18. Open letter to the physicians of Egypt on his conflict with Ibn Buṭlān (no. 2), Leid. 1334.—19. Small *maqālāt* on logic, Esc. ^{2}649$_{,2}$, 1925$_{,1}$.—20. *Dalīl mūjaz 'alā ḥadath al-'ālam* Br. Mus. 426$_{,20}$.—21.–27. see Suppl. (21. Cairo ^{1}VI, 15).

5. Abu 'l-Qāsim 'Abd al-Raḥmān b. Abī Ṣādiq al-Nīsābūrī al-Buqrāṭ al-Thānī, a student of Ibn Sīnā, who died after 460/1068.

Ibn Abī Uṣ. II, 32, Wüst., 139. 1. Commentary on Hippocrates' *Aphorisms*, with special consideration of Galen, Berl. 6223, Leid. 1294, Paris 2838/40, Bodl. I, 533, Cambr. 91, Esc. ^{2}877, Algiers 1743, Garr. 1096, Alex. Ṭibb 22, augmented by an anonymous author 1744.—2. Commentary on the medical questions of Ḥunayn b. Isḥāq (p. 225), Leid. 1303, Bodl. I, 608, Paris 2861/2, Palat. 228, Garr. 1097.—3., 4. see Suppl.

485 | 6. Muḥammad b. 'Alī al-Īlāqī, likewise a student of Ibn Sīnā, who died in 536/1141, see Suppl.

Ibn Abī Uṣ. II, 20, Wüst., 137. 1. *Kitāb al-asbāb wal-ʿalāmāt* Munich 820.—2. *Mukhtaṣar fi 'l-ṭibb* see Suppl. I, 825aa.—3., 4. see Suppl.

7. Abu 'l-Muṭarrif ʿAbd al-Raḥmān b. Muḥammad b. ʿAbd al-Karīm b. Yaḥyā b. Wāfid (Abenguefit) al-Lakhmī, born in 389/999, was one of the most important physicians of Spain of his time. He held the office of vizier in Toledo for a time and died sometime after 460/1068.

Ibn Abī Uṣ. II, 49, Wüst., 141, Leclerc I, 545. 1. *al-Adwiya al-mufrada*, abstract Gotha $72,_{5}$; Latin transl. in Choulant, *Bücherkunde* 370, Hebr. Steinschneider § 475.—2. *al-Tadhkira* in Groningen, see Dozy Suppl. I, p. XXIII.—3. *De balneis sermo* in *De balneis quae exstant apud graecos, latinos et arabes*, Venice 1553 (Mieli, $183,_{7}$).—3. *Kitāb al-wisād*, a collection of recipes, Esc. $^{2}833,_{1}$ (see Simonet, *Glosario* CXLV).

| 8. Abū ʿAlī Yaḥyā b. ʿĪsā b. Jazla, from a Christian background, converted to 639
Islam in 466/1074 and became secretary to the Ḥanafī *qāḍī* of Baghdad. In his spare time he practised medicine and worked as a doctor, asking no fee. He died in Shaʿbān 493/June 1100.

Ibn Khall. 783, Ibn Abī Uṣ. I, 254, Wüst., 145, Leclerc I, 493. 1. *Taqwīm al-abdān fī tadbīr al-insān* or *Minhāj al-bayān fī taqwīm al-abdān*, disease tables based on the example of stellar tables, Berl. 6415, Paris 2947/52, Upps. 346/7, Br. Mus. Suppl. $792,_{2}$, Bodl I, 549, Pet. Ros. $183,_{1}$, Med. 214, Garr. 1099, 1100, Cairo ^{1}VI, 10, 36, Patna I, $245,_{2094}$, II, $341,_{2525}$, 3. *Tacuini aegritudinum Buhahylyha Byngezla auctore*, Strasburg 1582. Persian transl. by Muʿīn b. Maḥmūd al-Mutaṭabbib al-Kirmānī for Meḥmed II, written in 863/1458, AS 3587.—2. *Minhāj al-bayān fī-mā yastaʿmiluhu al-insān*, an alphabetical register of simple and compound medicines, Berl. 614/5, Munich 823/4, Leid. 1355/7, Paris 2948/52, Br. Mus. 452, Ind. Off. 786, Bodl. I, 541, 545, 556, 576, Copenhagen 112/3, Pet. AM 670, Ros. $182,_{2}$, Šehīd A. 2107, Cairo ^{1}VI, 44, Qawala II, 290, Patna I, $259,_{2197}$, Mashh. XVI, $36,_{110/1}$, anon. comm. Esc. $^{2}875,_{5}$.—3. see Suppl.—His lost *Risāla fī 'l-radd ʿala 'l-Naṣārā* in Steinschneider, *Polem. u. apol. Lit.* 57.

8a. Al-Ḥusayn b. Abī Thaʿlab b. al-Mubārak al-Ṭabīb composed around 484/1091, for al-Mufaḍḍal b. Abi 'l-Barakāt, the minister of Sayyida Ḥurra who played the leading role in Ṣanʿāʾ after the death of the Ṣulayḥid al-Mukram Aḥmad (473–84/1080–91):

Al-Munqidh min al-halaka etc. (see Suppl. II, $169,_{1b}$) Garr. 1098.

9. Abu ʾl-Ḥasan Saʿīd b. Hibatallāh b. al-Ḥasan, born in 436/1044, was the personal physician of the caliph al-Muqtadir, and died in 495/1101.

Ibn Abī Uṣ. I, 254, Wüst., 143, Leclerc I, 492. 1. *al-Mughnī fī tadbīr al-amrāḍ*
486 *wa-maʿrifat al-ʿilal wal-aʿrāḍ* Goth. 1953, Munich $833_{,1}$, Paris 2957/8, | Bodl. I,
599, 611, II, 181, Br. Mus. Suppl. 794/5, Pet. AM 372, Ros. 172, Garr. 1101, Bursa
640 Haraccizade Tip 420, Alex. Tibb 46.—2. *Kitāb khalq* | *al-insān* Bodl. I, 609, de
Rossi, *Cod. ar.* 31.—3. *Maqālat al-ḥudūd wal-furūq* Br. Mus. $984_{,8}$, Alex. Fals. 8
(MS from the time of the author).—5., 6. see Suppl.—7. *al-Mujadwal fi ʾl-ṭibb*
Mosul 259.—8. *al-Talkhīṣ al-niẓāmī* Bursa, Hü. Celebi Tip 20 (Ritter).

10. Ṭāhir b. Ibrāhīm (b. Muḥammad b. Ṭāhir) al-Shajarī wrote, around 500/1106:

(Ibn Abī Uṣ. II, 23, Wüst., 146). 1. *Īḍāḥ maḥajjat al-ʿilāj*, Berl. 6338 (which has al-Sanjārī), Paris 2946, Patna II, $338_{,2522,\ 1}$ (*Qarabādhīn al-fattāḥ fī m. al-ʿi.*), see Suppl.

11. ʿAbd al-Wāḥid b. ʿAbd al-Razzāq al-Khaṭīb al-Nasawī wrote, around 500/1106:

Al-Tāj fī kayfiyyat al-ʿilāj, in 28 chapters, the third and last of which are in Persian, Paris $2947_{,4}$, cf. Leclerc II, 47.

12. Yūsuf b. Isḥāq b. Baklārash al-Isrāʾīlī, a Jewish physician, wrote, around 500/1106:

Kitāb al-mustaʿīnī, on simple medicines in tabular form, dedicated to the prince of Zaragoza al-Mustaʿīn billāh Aḥmad b. Hūd (478–503/1085–1109), Leid. 1339, Naples, *Cat. It.* 237, no. 96; cf. Ibn Abī Uṣ. II, 52.

13. Abu ʾl-ʿAlāʾ Zuhr b. ʿAbd al-Malik b. Muḥammad b. Marwān b. Zuhr al-Ishbīlī al-Iyādī came from a distinguished family of Spanish scholars and studied in Seville. Through his renown as a physician he rose to the rank of vizier under the Almoravids. He died in Cordova in 525/1131.

Ibn Abī Uṣ. II, 64, Maqq. I, 623, Wüst., 1581. Leclerc II, 83f. 1. *Mujarrabāt al-khawāṣṣ*, tried specifica, Vienna 1460, Bodl. I, 626, Pet. 122, Esc. $^{2}844_{,3}$. Abstracts: a. *Fawāʾid al-muntakhab* Leid. 1340, Paris $2954_{,1}$, Esc. $^{2}844_{,3}$, Cairo ^{1}VI, 26.—b. *Khawāṣṣ al-ḥayawān*, on the secret powers of animals, Berl. 6166.—

2. *al-Tadhkira*, medical advice to his son (no. 17), Paris $2960_{,2}$, Esc. $^{2}844_{,4}$.—3.–5. see Suppl.

| 14. Abu 'l-Ṣalt Umayya b. Abi 'l-Ṣalt 'Abd al-'Azīz al-Andalusī, who was born 641
in 460/1068 in Denia, went to Alexandria in 489/1096 and later to Cairo, where he gained the favour of the vizier Shāhanshāh b. Badr. However, he blew it all through a failed attempt to raise a sunken ship, and was even incarcerated, only being released in 505/1111. He was then received with honours in al-Mahdiyya in Tunisia, and died on 10 Muḥarram 529/30 October 1134.

Ibn Abī Uṣ. II, 52/62, Ibn Khall. 101, Suyūṭī, *Ḥuṣn al-muḥ.* I, 311, Maqq. I, 530/2, Wüst., *Ärzte* 162, *Gesch.* 237, Leclerc II, 74, Steinschneider in *Virchows Arch.* XCIV, 28/65, Suter, 272. 1. *al-Adwiya al-mufrada*, according to the categories of
members | that suffer from similar ailments, Bodl. I, $578_{,2}$, II, 587.—2. *Risāla* 487
fi 'l-'amal bil-asṭurlāb Berl. 5798, Leid. 1072, Bodl. I, $967_{,10}$, Ambr. 179, Palat. $128_{,2}$, Mosul $259_{,1}$.—3. 6 astronomical problems, with figures, Esc. $^{2}646_{,2}$.—4. *Taqwīm al-dhihn*, on logic, Esc. $^{2}646_{,1}$.—5. A *qaṣīda*, Berl. 7682.—6. On the different meanings of the word *nuqṭa*, Leid. 1024.—7. *al-Risāla al-Miṣriyya* is cited by al-Maqrīzī, *Khiṭaṭ* I, $15_{,29}$, $118_{,11}$.—8., 9. see Suppl.

15. Zayn al-Dīn Abu 'l-Faḍā'il Ismā'īl b. al-Ḥusayn al-Jurjānī died in 531/1136 or 535.

Bayhaqī, *Tatimmat ṣiwān al-ḥikma* I, 11, Wüst. 165. 1. *al-Tadhkira al-ashrafiyya fi 'l-ṣinā'a al-ṭibbiyya*, translated from the Persian *Mukhtaṣar-i 'Alā'ī* (AS $3730_{,1}$?), which was written for 'Alā' al-Dīn Alp Arslān, Paris 2955; abstract *al-Aghrād al-ṭibbiyya wal-mabāḥith al-'Alā'iyya* (= Suppl. 7?) for the vizier of Khwārizmshāh, 'Alā' al-Dīn Tukush Majd al-Dīn al-Bukhārī, Meshhed XVI, 1, 2, al-Kāẓimiyya, *Dharī'a* II, $251_{,1009}$.—2. *Dhakhīrat Khwārizmshāh*, a handbook of medicine, Arabic according to ḤKh ^{1}III, $330_{,5794}$, ^{2}I, 824, Persian in 12 volumes Yeni 915/6, see ḤKh ^{1}I, $368_{,987}$, ^{2}I, 130.—3. *Fi 'l-qiyās* Esc. $^{2}612_{,9}$.—4. *Fi 'l-taḥlīl* ibid. 10.—5. *al-Munabbih*, on the vanity of carnal desire and the duty of abstention, Berl. 8748.—6., 7. see Suppl.

16. Abū Naṣr 'Adnān b. Naṣr al-'Aynzarbī | was the personal physician of the 642
Fāṭimid caliph al-Ẓāfir bi-Amrillāh Ismā'īl (r. 544–9/1149–54) in Cairo. He died in 548/1153.

Ibn Abī Uṣ. II, 107, Wüst., 167, Leclerc II, 51, Suter, 288. 1. *al-Kāfī fī ʿilm (ṣināʿat) al-ṭibb* Munich 825, Paris 2956, Br. Mus. 453, Bodl. I, 586, Cairo ^{2}VI, 28.—2. *Fī-mā yaḥtāj al-ṭabīb min ʿilm al-falak*, on the application of astrology in medicine, Berl. 6247.—3. see Suppl.

17. Abū Marwān ʿAbd al-Malik b. Abī Bakr b. Muḥammad b. Marwān b. Zuhr (Avenzoar) worked, like his father (no. 13), for the Almoravids. After their downfall he was sent to Marrakesh by the Almohad ʿAbd al-Muʾmin, the ruler of Seville, dying in 557/1162.

Ibn Abī Uṣ. II, 66, Wüst., 159, Leclerc II, 86, Mieli 204. 1. *al-Taysīr fī ʾl-mudāwāt wal-tadbīr* Paris 2960$_{,1}$, Bodl. I, 628, Med. 216, Br. Mus. Or. 9128, Hebr. Steinschneider 477$_{,1}$.—2. *al-Jāmiʿ fī ʾl-ashriba wal-maʿjūnāt*, appendix to 1, Gotha 72, Bodl. I, 628$_{,2}$.—3. *Kitāb al-aghdhiya* Paris 2960$_{,1}$, Landb.-Br. 168 (wrongly attributed to the younger Ibn Zuhr, no. 24), see *Virchows Archiv* 57, 115.—4. *al-Iqtiṣād fī iṣlāḥ al-anfus wal-ajsād*, dedicated to the Almoravid Ibrāhīm b. Yūsuf b. Tāshfīn, Paris 2959, Esc. ^{2}834 = *de regimine sanitatis*, Basle 1618 (?), see Steinschneider § 477$_{,5}$, see H.P.J. Renaud, Trois études II, *Hespéris* 1931, 91.—5. see Suppl.

18. Amīn al-Dawla (al-Dīn) Abu ʾl-Ḥusayn Hibatallāh b. Ṣāʿid b. al-Tilmīdh b. Salāma, the Christian personal physician of the caliph al-Muqtafī, died, at almost 100 years of age, on 28 Rabīʿ I 560/11 February 1165.

Ibn Abī Uṣ. I, 259, Ibn Khall. 750, biography Gotha 94$_{,14}$, Wüst. 174, Leclerc II, 24. 1. *al-Maqāla al-amīniyya fī ʾl-faṣd*, on bloodletting, Br. Mus. 984$_{,7}$, Bodl. I,
488 632$_{,4}$.—2. *Aqrābādhīn*, antidotarium, | Gotha 1996/7, Br. Mus. Or. 8293 (dated 525 AH), Cairo ^{1}VI, 35, abstract by Ṣafī al-Dawla Maḥmūd, Bodl. I, Turc. 49$_{,2}$, see Steinschneider, ZDMG VIII, 378.—3. *al-Mujarrabāt*, a pharmacological abstract of 2, Gotha 1996$_{,2}$.—4. *Kitāb al-iqnāʿ* Cairo ^{1}VI, 5 (where the name is corrupted).—5. *Quwa ʾl-adwiya* Br. Mus. Or. 8294.—6. A poem in Carlyle, *Spec. of ar. Poetry*, no. 58.

643 | 19. Abū Jaʿfar Aḥmad b. Muḥammad al-Ghāfiqī, a Spanish physician, who died in 560/1165.

Ibn Abī Uṣ. II, 52, Wüst., 176, Leclerc II, 79. 1. *al-Jāmiʿ fī ʾl-ṭibb fī ʾl-adwiya al-mufrada*, first half Bibl. Osleriana (McGill Un. Canada) Oxford 1929, no. 7508 (Meyerhof in *Mieli* 206), abbreviated from Barhebraeus between 1264/86,

Gotha 1998, ed. Meyerhof and Sobhy, Cairo 1932/40, abstract by Aḥmad b. ʿAlī al-Jumhūrī Bodl. I, 632,$_{1}$, Latin transl. by Magister G. fil. magistri Johannis in Lerida 1258 (Steinschneider, loc. cit.).—2. On fevers and swellings, Bodl. I, 632,$_{2}$.—3. *Fī dafʿ al-maḍārr al-kulliyya lil-abdān al-insāniyya* ibid. 3.

20. Abū Naṣr al-Samaw'al b. Yaḥyā Abu 'l-Maghribī al-Isrāʾīlī went from the Maghreb to Azerbaijan with his father. On 9 Dhu 'l-Ḥijja 558/8 November 1163 he converted from Judaism to Islam and settled as a physician in Marāgha. He died in 570/1174 (although, according to others, his death was as late as 576 or even 598).

Ibn Abī Uṣ. II, 20, Wüst., 180, Leclerc II, 12. 1. *Nuzhat al-aṣḥāb fī muʿāsharat al-aḥbāb*, on coitus, dedicated to the Artuqid Muḥammad b. Qara Arslān of Ḥiṣn Kayfā (r. 570–81/1174–85), Gotha 2045, Berl. 6381, Paris 3054, Esc. [1]830, AS 2121.—2. *al-Tabṣira fī ʿilm al-ḥisāb*, an arithmetic manual, Berl. 5962.—3. *Fī kashf ʿawār al-munajjimīn wa-ghalaṭihim fī akthar al-aʿmāl wal-aghlāṭ* Leid. 1074, Bodl. I, 964, II, 603.—4. *Ifḥām al-Yahūd* Teh. I, 184, II, 593, Cairo [1]VI, 113, cf. Steinschneider, *Polem. u. apol. Lit.* 26, M. Schreiner, *Monatsschr.* GWJ, N.S. VI, 123/33, 170/80, 214/23, 407/18.—5.–10. see Suppl.

21. Abu 'l-Makārim Hibatallāh b. Jumayʿ al-Isrāʾīlī, who was born in al-Fusṭāṭ, was the personal physician of Ṣalāḥ al-Dīn (567–89/1171–93). He died in 594/1198.

Ibn Abī Uṣ. II, 112, Wüst. 183, Leclerc II, 53. 1. *Kitāb al-irshād li-maṣāliḥ al-anfus wal-ajsād*, a medical compendium dedicated to ʿAbd al-Raḥmān b. ʿAlī al-Baysānī, the vizier of Ṣalāḥ al-Dīn, which was completed by his son Abū Ṭāhir Ismāʿīl, Berl. 6287, Gotha 1934/6, Paris 2963, 6564, Br. Mus. 1360, Suppl. 797, Bodl. I, 547, 589, 601, 604, Vat. 155, Patna I, 251,$_{2141}$.—2. *al-Maknūn fī tanqīḥ al-Qānūn* see p. 598,$_{5}$.

| 22. Badr al-Dīn Muḥammad b. Bahrām al-Qalānisī wrote, in 590/1194: 644

Aqrābādhīn Paris 2946,$_{3}$, 669, Br. Mus. Suppl. 796,$_{1}$, Patna I, 260,$_{2200/1}$.

23. Abū Bakr Muḥammad b. ʿAbd al-Malik b. Zuhr al-Ishbīlī was born in 507/1113 in Seville, the son of physician no. 17. He followed the Almohad ruler Yaʿqūb b. Yūsuf al-Manṣūr to Marrakesh as his personal physician, where he died in 595/1199.

Ibn Abī Uṣ. II, 67/74, Ibn Khall. 644, Wüst. 160, Hartmann, *Muw.* no. 84. Of his writings, of which his *muwashshaḥāt* was particularly famous, nothing survives; Ahlw. 6455$_{,8}$ wrongly attributes his grandfather's *Kitāb mujarrabāt fi 'l-ṭibb* to him.

23a. Abu 'l-Mu'ayyad Muḥammad al-Jazarī al-Anṣārī, a physician in Iraq, fl. twelfth cent.

Treatise on weights and measures in medicine, from his book of recipes, Esc. ^{2}844$_{,2}$, Leclerc II, 32.

23b. Yaʿqūb b. Isḥāq al-Isrāʾīlī studied Dioscorides in 583/1187 under Abū Muḥammad ʿAbdallāh b. Ṣāliḥ al-Kattānī al-Ḥarīrī and moved to Damascus in 598/1201.

A collection of his writings is preserved in NO 3589: 1. *Maqāla* 2–4 of his book on the *ustuquṣṣāt.*—2. A defence of this work from attacks.—3. Answer to a question by Ṣadaqa b. Mīkhā b. Ṣadaqa al-Sāmirī al-Isrāʾīlī.—4. Another defence of 1.—5. On the difference in climate between Damascus and Cairo.—6. On foodstuffs.—7. Comments by his teacher al-Ḥarīrī (Ritter).

24. Abū ʿImrān Mūsā b. ʿUbaydallāh b. Maymūn al-Qurṭubī, who was born in Cordova in 534/1139, studied Jewish theology as well as medicine and philosophy under Ibn Ṭufayl and Ibn Rushd. When ʿAbd al-Mu'min (524–58/1130–63), the first Almohad, gave the Jews and the Christians of his empire the choice to either embrace Islam or emigrate, he behaved for a while as a Muslim so
645 as to take his time to put his affairs in order. | He then emigrated to Egypt and founded a Talmudic school in al-Fusṭāṭ. Although initially reluctant to practice as a physician he nevertheless gained the confidence to Ṣalāḥ al-Dīn's family, and served as the personal physician to Ṣalāḥ al-Dīn's son al-Malik al-ʿAzīz. He died on 19 Rabīʿ II 601/13 December 1204.

Ibn Abī Uṣ. II, 117, Wüst. 198, Leclerc II, 47, Carmoly, *Médecins juifs*, 49, G. Gabrieli, *Arch. d. storia delle scienze* V, 1924, 12/5. 1. *Maqāla fī tadbīr al-siḥḥa al-Afḍaliyya*, dedicated to al-Malik al-Afḍal of Damascus (Uṣ.) = (?) *al-Waṣāya 'l-nāfiʿa ʿala 'l-ʿumūm wal-khuṣūṣ lil-aṣiḥḥāʾ wal-marḍā fī kulli makān wa-kulli zamān* Bodl. I, 555, 608$_{,3}$, cf. Steinschneider, *Hebr. Üb.* 482$_{,7}$.—2. *al-Fuṣūl fi 'l-ṭibb*, whose last *maqāla* was added by his nephew Abu 'l-Maʿānī Yūsuf b.

ʿAbdallāh,[2] | who helped him in a number of ways to finish his writings, Gotha 490
1937, Leid. 1344, Esc. ^{2}863$_{,1}$ 869, Rāmpūr I, 493$_{,200}$, Steinschneider § 481$_{,4}$.—3. *Mukhtaṣarāt* from the writings of Galen, Berl. 6231 (part 5) Esc. ^{2}802$_{,4}$ (*Talkhīṣ k. ḥīlat al-burʾ*).—4. Commentary on the *Aphorisms* of Hippocrates, Bodl. I, 608, Paris hebr. 1202, Steinschneider § 481$_{,6}$.—5. *Fi ʾl-bawāsīr*, on hemorrhoids, Bodl. I, H. 78 (II, 561), A. 608$_{,2}$, Paris hebr. 1202$_{,4,6}$, Steinschn. § 481$_{,1}$.—6. *al-Risāla al-fāḍiliyya fī ʿilāj al-sumūm wa-dhikr al-adwiya al-nāfiʿa minhā wa-min al-nuhūsh*, on the poisons of reptiles and their effects, composed in 575/1179 for al-Qāḍī al-Fāḍil (p. 385), Gotha 1986, Paris 2962$_{,1}$, Bodl. I, 578$_{,2}$, 608$_{,5}$ (*Maq. fī dhikr al-sumūm wa-mudāwāt al-malsūʿīn wal-masmūmīn*), Hebr. 78$_{,7}$, Med. 253, Esc. ^{2}889$_{,3}$, Steinschn. § 481$_{,3}$ = (?) *Maqāla fī dafʿ al-sumūm* Mosul 237$_{,157,10}$, *Maq. fi ʾl-sumūm wal-taḥarruz min al-adwiya al-qattāla* (Uṣ.).—7. *Maqāla fī bayān al-aʿrāḍ*, written for the prince of Raqqa (al-Malik al-Afḍal?), Bodl. I, 608, Hebr. 78, Paris hebr. 1211, Steinschn. § 482, supposedly first written in Hebrew and then translated into Arabic by Sulaymān b. Ḥubaysh al-Maqdisī, Bodl. I, 594, Paris hebr. 411.—8. *Kitāb al-asbāb wal-ʿalāmāt*, translated from Hebrew by Ibn Ḥubaysh, Bodl. I, 594.—9. *Canones de medicina practica* Esc. ^{2}888$_{,9}$. = 10. *Maqāla fi ʾl-rabu* = *Kitāb qawānīn al-juzʾ al-ʿamalī min ṣināʿat al-ṭibb* Madr. 601$_{,9}$ (Derenbourg, notes 46), in Hebrew letters, Paris 1211, Steinschn.
§ 482, *Die* | *ar. Lit. der Juden*, 215, no. 18.—11. *Risāla fi ʾl-jimāʿ*, on coitus, 646
Munich 877, in a shorter version, Granada, del Sacro Monte 112, see Steinschn. § 481$_{,2}$.—12., 13. see Suppl. (13. Garr. 1070). For his theological writings in Arabic see Steinschn., *Ar. Lit. der Juden*, 200ff.

25. ʿAlāʾ al-Dīn Abū Muḥammad b. Muḥammad b. Aḥmad (Abū Muḥammad Aḥmad) al-Ilbīrī wrote, before 612/1215 (the date of the MS in Paris):

Al-Natāʾij al-ʿaqliyya fi ʾl-wuṣūl ila ʾl-manāhij al-falsafiyya wal-qawānīn al-ṭibbiyya Paris 2961, Dam. Z. 88$_{,32,2}$, copy Beirut 335.

26. Abu ʾl-Ḥasan ʿAlī b. Aḥmad b. ʿAlī b. Hubal Muhadhdhab al-Dīn al-Baghdādī, d. 610/1213, see Suppl.

Ibn Abī Uṣ. I, 304, Wüst. 202, Leclerc II, 141. 1. *al-Mukhtār fi ʾl-ṭibb* Leid. 1345, Br. Mus. Suppl. 796$_{,2}$, Cairo ^{1}VI, 38 Patna I, 254$_{,2165/6}$; whence two sections on the kidneys and gallstones in *Traité sur le calcul*, ed. P. de Koning (p. 270), 186/228.—2. *al-Ārāʾ wal-mushāwarāt*, on some matters of logic, Paris 2348$_{,1}$.

---

2 D. Kaufmann, *REJ*, 1883, 152.

27. ʿAlī al-Ṭarābulusī wrote, in 616/1219:

Ornamentum medici, tractatus chymicomedicus Med. 237.

491 28. Abū Ḥāmid Muḥammad b. ʿAlī b. ʿUmar Najīb al-Dīn al-Samarqandī, | who died during the capture of Herat by the Mongols in 619/1222.

Ibn Abī Uṣ. II, 31, Wüst. 207, Leclerc II, 127. 1. *al-Asbāb wal-ʿalāmāt* Berl. 6289/90, Gotha 1954/7 (where other MSS are listed), Esc. ^{2}890, Köpr. 964, Cairo ^{1}VI, 3, Mosul 237$_{,164}$, Patna I, 248$_{,2111/4}$.—Commentary by Nafīs b. ʿIwaḍ al-Kirmānī, d. 853/1449 (II, 213), completed in 827/1424, Berl. 6291/2, Gotha 1955 (where other MSS are listed), Garr. 1103, Madr. Fāḍiliyya, *Dharīʿa* II, 12, 36, print. Calcutta 1836.—Glosses: a.–e. see Suppl. (a., b. also Patna I, 246$_{,2097/8}$).—2. *Ghāyat al-gharaḍ fī muʿālajat al-amrāḍ*, Arabic translation of the Persian *al-Manhaj*, by Manṣūr al-Ḥasanī, Berl. 6288.—3. *Uṣūl tarkīb al-adwiya*, on compound medicines, Berl. 6416, Gotha 1999$_{,1}$, 2030$_{,2}$, fragm. 2000, Leid. 1352, Cairo ^{1}VI, 33, Madr. Fāḍil Khān in Mashhad, *Dharīʿa* II, 179, 658, Patna I, 260$_{,2198}$, *Mukhtaṣar* Gotha 2086, AS 3555 (f. 36/40).—4. *al-Adwiya al-mufrada* Leid. 1354, Cairo ^{1}VI, 34.—5. *Kitāb al-qarābādhīn ʿalā tartīb al-ʿilal* Gotha
647 1999$_{,2}$, Berl. 6417, Leid. 1353, | Bodl. I, 630$_{,2}$, AS 3555$_{,3}$, Patna II, 339$_{,2522,\ 3}$.—6. *Aghdhiyat al-marḍā* Gotha 1999$_{,3}$, Leid. 1350/1, Cairo ^{1}VI, 33, Madr. Fāḍil Khān, *Dharīʿa* II, 217$_{,848}$, under the title *Aṭʿimat al-marḍā* Patna I, 256$_{,2176,\ 1}$.—7. *Kitāb al-aghdhiya wal-ashriba wa-mā yattaṣil bi-hā* Gotha 1999$_{,4}$, Leid. 1349, Mosul 237$_{,175,\ 2}$. = *Kitāb al-aghdhiya wal-ashriba lil-aṣiḥḥāʾ* Cairo ^{1}VI, 4, 34.—8. Tractatus de medicamentis repertu facilibus, Bodl. I, 630$_{,3}$.—9. *Risāla fī mudāwāt wajaʿ al-mafāṣil* Cairo ^{1}VI, 18.—10.–12. see Suppl.—13. *Kitāb fi ʾl-ṭibb* Mosul 33$_{,148}$ (dated 594 AH).—14. *Maqāla fī kayfiyyat tarkīb ṭabaqāt al-ʿayn* ibid. 260$_{,14,\ 10}$.

29. Muhadhdhab al-Dīn ʿAbd al-Raḥīm b. ʿAlī al-Dimashqī al-Dakhwār was born in 565/1169 and died on 15 Ṣafar 628/24 December 1230 in Damascus, having lost his voice (see Suppl.).

Ibn Abī Uṣ. II, 239/46, *Fawāt* I, 271, *JA* s. IX, v. 4, 497. *Sharḥ taqdimat al-maʿrifa* (*Hippocratis Prognostica*), collected by his student Badr al-Dīn al-Muẓaffar b. Qāḍī Baʿlabakk, Bodl. I, 533,2, II, 191, Alex. Ṭibb 22.

30. Abu ʾl-Faḍl Dāʾūd b. Abi ʾl-Bayān al-Isrāʾīlī, born in 556/1161, was the secretary of Ibn Jumayʿ (no. 22) and then the personal physician of Sultan al-Malik al-ʿĀdil and a teacher of medicine at the Nāṣirī hospital in Cairo, where Ibn Abī Uṣaybiʿa (p. 397) was one of his students.

Ibn Abī Uṣ. II, 181. 1. *al-Dustūr al-bīmāristānī* (*fi 'l-adwiya al-murakkaba*) Munich 832, Bodl. I, $941_{,9}$.—2. *Risālat al-mujarrabāt* Bodl. I, $608_{,6}$.

31. Abū Jaʿfar Aḥmad b. Muḥammad al-Ḥashshā' wrote, during the reign of the first Ḥafṣid in Tunis, Abū Zakariyyā' Yaḥyā, d. 647/1249:

| *Mufīd al-ʿulūm wa-mubīd al-humūm* or *Tafsīr al-alfāẓ al-ṭibbiyya wal-lughawiyya al-wāqiʿa fi 'l-kitāb al-Manṣūrī* (p. 269) Leid. 1356. 492

32. After a botanical study tour through Egypt, Asia Minor, and Greece, Abū Muḥammad ʿAbdallāh b. Aḥmad Ḍiyā' al-Dīn al-Mālaqī b. al-Bayṭār, who was born in Malaga, became the first botanist in the service of al-Malik al-Kāmil in Damascus. After the latter's death in 635/1237 | he went to Cairo, where he was 648 honorably received by al-Malik al-Ṣāliḥ, but soon returned to Damascus. He died there in Shaʿbān 646/November 1248.

Ibn Abī Uṣ. II, 133, *Fawāt* I, 204, Suyūṭī, *Ḥusn al-muḥ.* I, 313, Wüst. 231, Leclerc II, 225, *JA* 1862, I, 433ff. 1. *al-Mughnī fi 'l-adwiya al-mufrada*, dedicated either to al-Malik al-ʿĀdil or his brother and successor al-Malik al-Ṣāliḥ, Gotha 21, $49_{,2}$, $99_{,15}$, Leid. 1356, Paris 2990/1, Br. Mus. Suppl. 798/800, Bodl. I, 588, 624, Med. 224, 244. Abstract Gotha $99_{,15}$, $2026_{,2}$.—2. *Jāmiʿ mufradāt al-adwiya wal-aghdhiya* or *al-Jāmiʿ fi 'l-ṭibb* Berl. 6418/20, Gotha 2001/2, where other MSS are listed, Esc. ²839, Mosul $58_{,42}$, Patna I, $258_{,2184,\,7}$ print. Būlāq 1291. *Grosse Zusammenstellung über die Kräfte der bekannten einfachen Heil-u. Nahrungsmittel von… Ebn Baithar, übers. v.* J. v. Sontheimer, 2 vols., Stuttgart 1870/2, cf. Dozy, *ZDMG* 23, 183ff. *Traité des simples par I. al-B. trad. par* L. Leclerc, *Not. et Extr.* 23, 25/6, Paris, 1877/83, E. Sickenberger, Les plantes égyptiennes d. I. el B., *Bull. de l'Inst. Egypt.*, 2 s. no. 10, 2nd part, Cairo 1890.—Abstracts by: a. al-Baghdādī, Berl. 6422.—b. Ibn al-Quṭbī, Bodl. I, 563.—c. Anon., Berl. 6421, Gotha 2003 (perhaps by Jamāl al-Dīn Muḥammad b. Manẓūr al-Anṣārī, d. 711/1311, II, 21, ḤKh VI, $34_{,12623}$, A. Taymūr, *RAAD* III, 361). Turkish transl. Istanbul Un. T. 1204, made at the order of ʿUmar Beg of Āydīn, 741–9/1340–8, Abdülhak Adnan-Adivar, *Ilim*, Ist. 1943, p. 3.—3. *Mīzān al-ṭibb* Upps. 351.—4. *Risāla fī tadāwi 'l-sumūm* Qawala II, 288.

33. Abu 'l-Munā (Munayyir)[3] b. Abī Naṣr b. Ḥaffāẓ al-Kōhēn b. al-ʿAṭṭār al-Isrā'īlī al-Hārūnī wrote, in 658/1260 in Cairo:

Minhāj al-dukkān, a handbook of pharmacy in 25 chapters, Gotha 2005/7, Munich 833, Leid. 1360, Paris $2695_{,2}$, 2993/6, Br. Mus. Suppl. 8 Ol. 2 ²/2, Bodl.

3 See Steinschneider, *ZDMG* XXX, 146.

II, 171, Pet. Dorn 232$_{,2}$, Ros. 182$_{,3}$ (fragm.), Algiers 1757, Patna I, 260$_{,2203}$, II, 341$_{,2525,\ 2}$, print. Būlāq 1287, C. 1305.—2. See Suppl.

34b. Abū Saʿd b. Abī Surūr al-Sāwī al-Isrāʾīlī, see Suppl.

Al-Lamḥa al-ʿafīfa fi ʾl-ṭibb = (?) *al-Lamḥa al-ʿafīfa fi ʾl-asbāb wal-ʿalāmat* Mosul 193$_{,153,\ 5}$ (anon.), commentary by al-ʿAynṭābī, see II, 82$_{,22}$.

649 | 34d. *Jāmiʿ al-iftirāq etc.* Garr. 1104.

35. Al-Mufaḍḍal b. Mājid (ḤKh: Mājid b. al-Muf.) b. al-Bishr al-Isrāʾīlī wrote, in 667/1268:

Urjūza fi ʾl-ṭibb, under the title *Naqʿ al-ghalal wa-nafʿ al-ʿilal* Paris 2997 (autograph), ʾ8, Cairo ^{1}VI, 48.

36. Abu ʾl-Faraj (b.) Yaʿqūb b. Isḥāq al-Masīḥī (Naṣrānī) b. al-Quff Amīn al-Dawla al-Karakī, born in Karak on 13 Dhu ʾl-Qaʿda 630/22 August 1233, was a student of Ibn Abī Uṣaybiʿa (p. 397), practised first in ʿAjlūn, and died in Damascus in 685/1286.

Ibn Abī Uṣ. II, 273, Suyūṭī, *Ḥusn al-muḥ.* I, 313, Wüst. 241, Leclerc II, 203. 1. *al-ʿUmda fī ṣināʿat al-jirāḥa*, on general surgery, Berl. 6255, Gotha 1990, Br. Mus. 755/7, 1361, Paris 3000, Algiers 1755, Cairo ^{1}VI, 24, Patna I, 257$_{,2181}$, a fragment Gotha 2029$_{,2}$.—2. *Jāmiʿ al-gharaḍ fī ḥifẓ al-ṣiḥḥa wa-dafʿ al-amrāḍ* Br. Mus. Suppl. 803.—3. *al-Uṣūl fī sharḥ al-fuṣūl*, a commentary on the *Aphorisms* of Hippocrates (mistakenly attributed to Barhebreus by Wüstenfeld), Gotha 1894/5, Br. Mus. Suppl. 804, Algiers 1745 (vol. 2), Alex. Ṭibb 6.—4. *Risāla fī manāfiʿ al-aʿḍāʾ al-insāniyya wa-mawāḍiʿihā* Cairo ^{1}VII, 257.—5., 6. see Suppl.

37. ʿAlāʾ al-Dīn Abu ʾl-Ḥasan ʿAlī b. al-Ḥazm al-Qurashī b. al-Nafīs, d. 687/1288, see Suppl.

Wüst. 244, Leclerc II, 207. 1. *al-Mukhtār min al-aghdhiya*, on nutrition, Berl. 6400.—2. *Mūjiz al-Qānūn* see p. 598.—3. *Tafāsīr al-ʿilal wa-asbāb al-amrāḍ* (author?) Munich 830.—4. *Sharḥ Fuṣūl Ibbuqrāṭ* Berl. 62, 24, Gotha 1897/8, Paris 2843, Bodl. I, 544, Esc. ^{1}799, Patna I, 249$_{,2116/7}$.—5. *Sharḥ Taqdimat al-maʿrifa li-Ibbuqrāt* Berl. 6224, Gotha 1899, Leid. 1296(?), Bodl. I, 639.—6. *Sharḥ al-Masāʾil al-ṭibbiyya li-Ḥunayn* Leid. 1304.—7. Commentary on the anatomy of the *Qānūn* p. 598.—8. *al-Wurayqāt*, on logic, with a commentary, Bodl. I, 464.—9. *al-Mukhtaṣar fī ʿilm uṣūl al-ḥadīth*, Cairo ^{1}VII, 257.—10. *al-Risāla al-kāmiliyya fī ʾl-sīra al-nabawiyya*, an orthodox counterpiece to Ibn Sīnā's *Ḥayy b. Yaqẓān*, in which Fāḍil b. Nāṭiq plays the role of the storyteller, ʿĀšir I, 461, Cairo ^{2}VII, 201.—11.–15. see Suppl.—16. A medical work in four *fanns*, ʿĀšir I, 732.

| 38. ʿIzz al-Dīn Abū Isḥāq Ibrāhīm b. Muḥammad b. Tarkhān b. al-Suwaydī 650
al-Anṣārī, a physician and philosopher from Damascus, who died in 690/1292.

Ibn Abī Uṣ. II, 266, Wüst. 245, Leclerc II, 199, Meyerhof, *Qu. u. St. z. Gesch. der Med. u. Nat.* IV, 47. 1. *al-Tadhkira al-hādiya* (*mufrada*), a text book on medicine, Paris 3001/2, Patna I, 257,$_{2183}$.—Abstracts: a. ʿAbd al-Wahhāb al-Shaʿrānī, d. 973/1565 (II, 335), Gotha 1958/60, 1970,$_{2}$, Upps. 342/3, Alex. Fun. 89,$_{2}$, print. C. 1271, 1310.—b. al-Qawsūnī (?), Gotha 2026.—c. Anon., dated 953/1546, Paris 3003, another Garr. 1120.—2. *al-Bāhir fī ʾl-jawāhir* (*fī khawāṣṣ al-aḥjār min al-yawāqīt wal-jawāhir*) Berl. 6215 (see Ritter, *Ist. Mitt.* III, 8, 8), Bodl. I, 510, II, 883, Cairo ^{1}VII, 184.—3. *al-Simāt fī asmāʾ al-nabāt* Paris 3004 (autograph).

38a. Fakhr al-Dīn Abū Isḥāq Ibrāhīm b. Muḥammad Ghadanfar al-Tabrīzī was born around 630/1232 and lived in Qonya, where he supposedly treated Jalāl al-Dīn Rūmī, dying around 692/1292.

Risāle-yi Sipehsālār, Bombay 1319, p. 58, M. Meyerhof, *Qu. u. St.* III, 3 (1932), 12/3. 1. *Ḥāṣil al-maḥṣūl* (Suppl. I, 367,$_{2b}$) AS 35, 55, 149b/156a.—2. Bibliography of Bīrūnī (Suppl. I, 872).—3. *Mukhtaṣar Ṣiwān al-ḥikma.*

| 39. The third sultan from the house of the Rasūlids in Yemen, al-Malik al- 494
Ashraf ʿUmar b. Yūsuf (r. 694–6/1295–7), also dabbled in medicine, astronomy, and genealogy.

1. *al-Muʿtamad fī mufradāt al-ṭibb* (*al-adwiya al-mufrada*), in alphabetical order, Berl. 6426, Br. Mus. Suppl. 1, 807, Bodl. I, 558 (cf. II, 586), Cairo ^{1}VI, 41.[4]—2. *al-Tabṣira fī ʿilm al-nujūm* Bodl. I, 905.—3.–5. see Suppl.

40/1. See Suppl.

4 ḤKh V, 622,$_{12356}$, followed by Ahlw., mentions his father Yūsuf b. ʿUmar as the author. Wüst. 246 attributes the work to a student of Maimonides, Abu ʾl-Ḥajjāj Yūsuf (Uṣ. II, 213), and has it dedicated to al-Malik al-Ashraf of Syria and Egypt.

42. Muḥammad b. Khalīfa Yaʿqūb al-ʿArabī wrote, together with Saʿd al-Dīn b. al-Ẓāhir al-ʿAjamī:

651 | *Qarābādhīn al-khayl*, which the king of Armenia (Cilicia) had brought over from Baghdad and translated into Armenian during the reign of al-Ẓāhir Baybars 658–76/1260–79. After Manṣūr Sayf al-Dīn Qalāwūn's victory over the Rubenid Leo in 1285, the emir Ḥusām al-Dīn reportedly obtained the book as war booty and had it translated back into Arabic, Patna I, 261,$_{2204}$.

43. Najm al-Dīn Abū Zakariyyāʾ Yaḥyā b. Muḥammad b. al-Lubūdī, a Syrian physician of the seventh century.

Leclerc I, 414, II, 160/1. 1. *Taḥqīq al-mabāḥith al-ṭibbiyya fī tadqīq al-masāʾil al-khilāfiyya* Esc. ^{2}892.—2. *Mukhtaṣar al-Kulliyyāt* p. 598,$_{d}$.

Chapter 16.

A *Natural Sciences and Technology*

1a.–c. See Suppl.

1d. Muḥammad b. al-Ḥasan b. Ibrāhīm al-Khāzin Abū Bakr wrote, in 421/1030 in Ghazna:

Kitāb al-ṭīb Garr. 2154$_{,1}$.

2. Badīʿ al-Zamān Abū Bakr al-Muʿizz b. Ismāʿīl b. al-Razzāz al-Jazarī, see Suppl.

Ad Serāi 3472, see Holter, *Jahrb. des kunsthist. Inst. Vienna* N.S. 11, 1937, p. 37.

2a. Ṭāhir al-Marwazī, see Suppl.

See Minorsky, *CR Ac. Inscr.* 1937, 317/24.

2b. In the eleventh or twelfth century an anonymous author wrote in Seville:

ʿUmdat al-ṭabīb fī maʿrifat al-nabāt li-kulli labīb, a dictionary of the names of plants, often used by al-Ghāfiqī but unknown to Ibn al-Bayṭār, with its own botanical system of classification, see G. Colin, *Actes du XXe Congr. int. des or. Bruxelles* 1938 (1941), p. 323.

3. Abū Zakariyyāʾ Yaḥyā b. Muḥammad b. al-ʿAwwām wrote, in the first half of the sixth century:

Kitāb al-filāḥa, on agriculture, based on Greek sources and personal experience, Leid. 1285, Paris 2804, Br. Mus. 998, Esc. [1]901 (see Suppl.). *Libro de agricultura, su autor el doctor excellente a. Z.J. b. M.b. el Awam Sevillanno traducido al castellano y anotado por* Don J.A. Banqueri, | Madrid 1802, 2 vols. 495
(with Arabic text); cf. C. | Moncada, *Actes du 8e congr. intern. des or. Sect.* I, 652
p. 217/57, C.E. Dubler, *al-Andalus* VI, 136, 142ff. Shakīb Arslān, *RAAD* XI, 436/40.—Turkish transl. by Muḥammad b. Muṣṭafā b. Luṭfallāh, made in 998/1590, autograph Welīeddīn 2534, Bursa Asari atika Müzesi E 32 (Ritter).

4. Shihāb al-Dīn Abu 'l-ʿAbbās Aḥmad b. Yūsuf al-Tifāshī, d. 651/1253.

1. *Azhār al-afkār fī jawāhir al-aḥjār*, composed in 621/4, Berl. Ms. or. oct. 3944/5, Gotha 2210/4, Leid. 1287, 2688, Upps. 339 (copy of a Flor. codex by Celsius dated 1697), Paris $2770_{,3}$, 2773/7, Algiers 1502/3, Br. Mus. 435/6, 999, Suppl. 781, Pet. AM 208, Garr. 1073, MSS in Istanbul in Ritter, *Ist. Mitt.* III, 4, no. 6, photograph of an MS in Cairo in *QSt* VII, 73, V, 6, Alex. Kīm. 3, Patna I, $264_{,2212}$, Turkish transl. Leipz. 264. Cf. S.F. Ravius, *Specimen arabicum continens descriptionem et excerpta libri A.T. de gemmis et lapidibus pretiosis, quod praeside patre S. Ravio defendet*, Utrecht 1784; Clément Mullet, *JA* 1868, I, 1ff., Steinschneider, *ZDMG* 49, 254ff.—2. *Maṭāliʿ al-budūr fī manāzil al-surūr*, on minerals, Paris $1176_{,16}$.—3. *Nuzhat al-albāb fī-ma lā yūjad fī kitāb*, anecdotes and verses on coitus, Berl. 6382, Paris 3055, 5954.—4. *Rujūʿ al-shaykh ilā ṣibāh fī ʾl-quwwa ʿala ʾl-bāh* Gotha 2055, Franck 558, Alex. Ṭibb $41_{,3}$, Cairo ^{1}VI, 16, cf. Vollers, *ZDMG* 46, 386, Persian transl. Br. Mus. Pers. II, 471.—5. *Risāla fī-mā yaḥtāj ilayhi ʾl-rijāl wal-nisāʾ fi ʾstiʿmāl al-bāh mim-mā yaḍurr wa-yanfaʿ* Cairo ^{1}VI, 18.—6. See Suppl.

5. Baylaq b. ʿAbdallāh al-Qubčāqī wrote, for al-Muẓaffar II of Hama (626–42/1229–44):

Kanz al-tijār fī maʿrifat al-aḥjār, on the distinguishing marks of gemstones, closely following al-Tīfāshī, Paris 2779 (autograph dated 681/1282), see Steinschneider, *ZDMG* 49, 256.

6. See Suppl. 904, 9.

Wuṣlat al-ḥabīb (sic), Bursa Ḥü. Čelebi Tip 23 (Ritter), Patna I, 259, (where the author is identified as Kamāl al-Dīn Abu ʾl-Qāsim ʿAbd al-Dāʾim al-ʿUqaylī al-Ḥabīb).

B *Games, Sports, and War*

1. a. Read: Lālā Ism. 560, 1. An anonymous chess manual, also Berlin Or. 2890 (dated 591 AH).

653 | 2. Marḍī b. ʿAlī b. Marḍī al-Ṭarasūsī wrote, around 570/1174 for Ṣalāḥ al-Dīn:

Al-Tabṣira fi ʾl-ḥurūb, on the art of war, Bodl. I, 371.

3. Ḥusayn b. ʿAbd al-Raḥmān b. Muḥammad b. ʿAbdallāh al-Yūnīnī, ca. 676/1277 (see Suppl.).

2. *Urjūza*, on archery, also Dam. Z. 86,$_{22}$.

4.–7. See Suppl.

8. Towards the end of the seventh century, Ibn Muḥammad b. Aḥmad b. Khālid wrote:

Khazāʾin al-silāḥ Qara Muṣṭafā 41 (Ritter).

C Music

H.G. Farmer, *The Sources of Arabic Music*, Edinburgh 1940.

1. Al-Ḥasan b. Aḥmad b. ʿAlī al-Kātib wrote, before 625/1228 (the date of the MS):

Kamāl ādāb al-ghināʾ Top Kapu 1729, photograph Cairo, *Nashara* 23, Farmer 46.

2. Ṣafī al-Dīn Abu ʾl-Mafākhir ʿAbd al-Muʾmin b. Yūsuf b. Fākhir al-Urmawī al-Baghdādī, d. 693/1294, see Suppl.

Juwaynī, *Taʾr. Jahāngushā* I, LI, Farmer 48. 1. *Kitāb al-adwār wal-īqāʿ* Berl. 5533 (see Farmer *JRAS* 1926, 94), NO 3653/4, Rāġib 919,$_3$, 134b/171a, photograph Cairo Nash. 2, anon. commentary Br. Mus. Or. 2361, 68/123, transl. by d'Erlanger, *La Musique arabe* III, Paris 1938, in Farmer, p. 56, attributed to al-Jurjānī.—2. *al-Risāla al-Sharafiyya fī ʾl-nisab al-taʾlīfiyya* additionally Garr. 2107,$_3$ (part 2), Cairo, *Nash.* 11.—3., 4. see Suppl.—5. *Dāʾirat al-buḥūr wal-awzān* Cairo Nash. 10.—6. *Sharḥ dāʾirat al-aṣl al-awwal* (*al-rāst*) ibid. 17.

3. Muḥammad b. Sālim b. Wāṣil Jamāl al-Dīn al-Ḥamawī, the teacher of Abu ʾl-Fidāʾ, fl. around 697/1297.

Abulf., *Ann.* V, 144ff. *Tajrīd al-aghānī min al-mathālith wal-mathānī* Br. Mus. 571, AS 1400, Farmer, p. 49.

Chapter 17. Occult Sciences

1. Abu 'l-Faḍl Muḥammad b. Aḥmad al-Ṭabasī, d. 482/1089.

654 *Kitāb al-shāmil min al-baḥr al-kāmil fi 'l-dawr al-ʿāmil,* | on magic, amulets, and astrology, adapted from *Nuzhat al-āfāqi yawm al-ijtimāʿ wal-talāqī,* a work that he had written for a distinguished patron but which had attracted little interest, for Abu 'l-Barakāt Muḥammad b. al-Faḍl al-Nīsābūrī, d. 530/1135, Berl. 5885, Turkish transl. Qilič ʿA. 685.

2. Burhān (Shams) al-Dīn Abu 'l-Ḥasan ʿAlī b. Mūsā b. Arfaʿ ra'sahu al-Anṣārī al-Jayyānī al-Shudhūrī al-Gharnāṭī, who died as a preacher in Fez in 593/1197.

Fawāt II, 91, Maqq. II, 410, Cod. Goth. 1289, folios 1r, 60r, where his death is placed in 500/1106, Hartmann, *Muwashshaḥ* 26. 1. *Dīwān shudhūr al-dhahab fī fann al-salāmāt,* alphabetically ordered collection of poems on the philosopher's stone, Gotha 1289/90 (where other MSS are listed), Garr. 931, Alex. Kīm. 7, Cairo ^{1}VII, 571, Ṭab. 731, Taymūr, Ṭab. 70/1, 110; individual verses of the *qaṣīda* ending in *fā'*, Berl. 4180, Gotha $85_{,12}$.—Commentaries: a. Self-commentary *Ḥall al-mushkilāt al-Shudhūriyyāt,* in the form of a dialogue with his student Abu 'l-Qāsim Muḥammad b. ʿAbdallāh al-Anṣārī, Berl. 4181/2, Pet. Ros. 201, Garr. 932.—b. *Ghāyat al-surūr* by ʿAlī b. Aydamur al-Jildakī, d. 743/1342 (II, 138), Berl. 4183, Gotha 1291, Leid, 1273, Esc. ^{2}652, excerpts Br. Mus. $601_{,3}$, $1002_{,14,\ 19}$, $1371_{,5}$.—c. ʿAbdallāh al-Umawī, Alex. Kīm. 7.—d. Abū ʿAbdallāh al-Sīmāwī, Taymūr, Ṭab. 72.—d. see Suppl.—e. Anon., Br. Mus. $100_{,1}$.—*Tashmīs al-budūr fī takhmīs al-Shudhūr* by Ḥasan b. ʿAlī b. al-Iṣfahānī Jalāl-al-Dīn al-Naqqāsh, composed in 810/1408 in Mashhad ʿAlī, BDMG 65.—2. *al-Ṭibb al-rūḥānī bil-Qur'ān al-raḥmānī* Paris 2643.—3. *al-Jihāt fī ʿilm al-tawajjuhāt fī sharḥ qaṣīdat Thābit b. S.* Garr. 41.—4. Alchemy, untitled, Taymūr, Ṭab. 152.

3. Abu 'l-Qāsim Muḥammad b. Aḥmad (Aḥmad b. Muḥammad) al-ʿIrāqī al-Sīmāwī, fl. sixth century.[1]

1. *Kitāb al-muktasab fī zirāʿat al-dhahab* Alex. Kīm. 13, Cairo ^{1}V, 390, Ṭab. 435/6,
655 commentary *Nihāyat al-ṭalab* by al-Jildakī, | d. 743/1342, II, 139, Berl. 4184,

1 ḤKh V, $47_{,18979}$, VI, $304_{,13599}$, gives no date. According to Nicoll the Mamlūk sultan Jaqmaq, r. 842–57/1438–53, is mentioned in the preface (which is why in Br. Mus. Suppl. 784i the date is fixed around 860); but because al-Jildakī (II, 138), who lived 100 years earlier, had commented one of his works, that can only be an interpolation.

Vienna 1495, Leid. 1272, Bodl. I, 459, 640, Patna II, 326,$_{2830/2}$, abstract Gotha 1289,$_{4}$.—2. *al-Kanz al-afkhar wal-sirr al-aʿẓam fī taṣrīf al-ḥajar al-mukarram* Cairo ^{1}V, 387.—3. *ʿUyūn al-ḥaqāʾiq wa-īḍāḥ al-ṭarāʾiq* Gotha 1274, Bodl. I, 1019, II, 378, Br. Mus. 1337,$_{2}$, Suppl. 784, Pet. Ros. 210, photo *QSt.* VII, 120, abstract Gotha 2026,$_{3}$, Garr. 936/7, Cairo Ṭab. 419, 426, Patna I, 242,$_{2080}$.—4. *al-Aqālīm al-sabʿa fī ʾl-ʿilm al-mawsūm bil-ṣunʿa*, an Arabic “Höllenzwang”, Gotha 1261,$_{1}$, Cairo ^{1}V, 276.—5. *Ṣifāt al-ʿamal bil-ramal* Alex. Ḥurūf 6.

3a. Shams al-Dīn Abu ʾl-ʿAbbās Muḥammad b. Masʿūd al-Khazrajī al-Sabtī, d. 698/1298 (? see Suppl.).

Sharḥ al-Zāʾiraja al-Sabtiyya, anon., Alex. Ḥurūf 5.

4. Zayn al-Dīn ʿAbd al-Raḥmān b. ʿUmar al-Dimashqī al-Jawbarī was, in 613/1216, in Ḥarrān, and in 616/1219 in Qonya, and he wrote for the Artuqid ruler al-Malik al-Mawdūd of Ḥiṣn Kayfā (r. 619–29/1222–31):

Al-Mukhtār fī kashf al-asrār wa-hatk al-astār, a disclosure of delusions and shams, Berl. 5563, Gotha 1374/6, Dresd. 413, Vienna 1434, Paris 4640, Br. Mus. 1002,$_{15}$, 1373,$_{1}$, Lee 61,$_{5}$, MSS in Istanbul in Rescher, *ZS* III, 247/8, anon. abstracts Berl. 5564/6, cf. Steinschneider, *ZDMG* XIX, 562, *Pol. u. apol. Lit.* 189, de Goeje, *ZDMG* XX, 485 (on which Fleischer, ibid. XXI, 274).

5. Muḥyi ʾl-Dīn Abu ʾl-ʿAbbās Aḥmad b. ʿAlī al-Būnī al-Qurashī, d. 622/1225.

1. *Risāla fī faḍāʾil* (*fawāʾid*) *al-basmala*, on the use of the *basmala* for magical purposes, Berl. 4156, Gotha 55,$_{3}$, Br. Mus. 886,$_{6}$, Garr. 2173,$_{1}$, Patna II, 419,$_{2589, 3}$.—2. *Qabs al-iqtidāʾ ilā ufq* (*waqf, falak*) *al-saʿāda wa-najm al-ihtidāʾ ilā sharaf al-sāda* (*siyāda*), on the secret properties of the names of God and the way to use them as talismans, Berl. Ms. or oct. 3928,$_{2}$, Gotha 1256,$_{2}$, Vienna 1499,$_{2}$, Alex. Taṣ. 34,$_{2}$, Ḥurūf 17,$_{10}$ (where the author is Sulaymān b. ʿAbdallāh b. ʿAbd al-Raḥmān al-ʿAbbāsī Abu ʾl-Rabīʿ).—3. *Shams al-maʿārif wa-laṭāʾif al-ʿawārif*, on occult sciences, especially the names of God and the secrets of letters, Berl. 4125, Gotha 1262 (where other MSS are listed), Br. Mus. Suppl. 824,$_{ii}$, AS 2798/2802, 2804/6, | Alex. Ḥurūf 5, 15, Patna I, 136,$_{1344}$, a small edition lith. 656
Bombay 1267, 1298 a larger one ibid. 1296.—4. From the beginning of his Qurʾān commentary Ibn ʿArrāq, d. 933/1526, incorporated a list of 100 expressions from the Qurʾān, with Sufi explanations, into his own *Jawharat al-ghawwāṣ*, Berl. 427.—5. *ʿIlm al-hudā wa-asrār* (*qabs*) *al-ihtidāʾ fī sharḥ al-asmāʾ al-ḥusnā* (mistakenly attributed in ḤKh, IV, 248,$_{8287}$, to Shihāb al-Dīn al-Suhrawardī

p. 569), Berl. 2224.—6. *Mawāqif al-ghāyāt fī sulūk (asrār) al-riyāḍāt*, a description of the three grades of Sufis and the progress needed for each of these, Berl. 2843/4, cf. 3301, abstract Garr. $2023_{,2}$, AS $2160_{,2}$.—7. *al-Lumʿa al-nūrāniyya fī kushūfāt (awrād) al-rabbāniyya*, prayers for different hours of the day, Berl. 3798, Ms. or. oct. $3928_{,4}$, Vienna $1494_{,3}$, Paris 1225/6, Bodl. II, 55, AS 2810, ʿĀšir
498 II, 169, Patna I, $157_{,1491}$, II, $518_{,2781}$.—8. *Fī faḍl (khawāṣṣ) āyat al-kursī* p. 2, 256, | as resistance against all kinds of bewitchments, Berl. $3894_{,2}$, Cairo [1]VII, 46.—9. *Laṭāʾif al-ishārāt fī asrār al-falak wal-ḥurūf al-maʿnawiyyāt (ʿulwiyyāt)* Berl. 4127.—10. 25 *ṭawīl* verses on the powers of the letters of the great names of God, Berl. 4146.—11. *Khawāṣṣ al-asmāʾ al-ḥusnā* Vienna $1661_{,9}$, Ind. Off. 338.—12. See Suppl.—13. *Asrār al-ḥurūf wal-kalimāt* Vienna $1494_{,4}$.—14. *Sirr al-ḥikam wa-jawāmiʿ al-kalim*, on Kaballah and divination, Paris $2595_{,6}$.—14a. *al-Durr al-munaẓẓam fi ʾl-sirr al-aʿẓam*, on the secret properties of letters and of the names of God, Paris 2646.—15. *al-Uṣūl wal-ḍawābiṭ*, on occult sciences, Paris 2656, Cairo [1]VII, 570, Alex. Ḥurūf 8, Rabāṭ 468.—16. An edifying work in prose and verse, without title, Br. Mus. Suppl. 230.—17. *Risāla fī taṣrīf khalkhalat al-hawā wa-fatq al-jawā wal-naẓar ila ʾl-rūḥāniyya al-ʿulyā* Cairo [1]VII, 682.—18.–33. See Suppl. (23. AS 2160, Veliyeddīn $1821_{,7}$—24. Alex. Taṣ. $34_{,1}$).—34. *Sharḥ taṣarrufāt al-wafq (wa-huwa ism Allāh al-aʿẓam al-muntakhab min al-āyāt al-qurʾāniyya)* Qawala I, 243.—35. *al-Rafīʿ al-asnā fī sharḥ asmāʾ allāh al-ḥusnā* Berl. Ms. or oct. $3928_{,1}$ = *al-Mashhad al-asnā fī sharḥ a. Allāh al-ḥ.* ḤKh V, 561 (?).—36. *Lawḥ al-dhahab min kitāb al-ḥurūf* ibid. 3.—37. *Risāla fi ʾl-ism al-aʿẓam* ibid. 4.—38. *Silk al-jawāhir wal-maʿānī wal-muqtabas min al-sabʿ al-mathānī* Alex. Mawāʿiẓ 23.—39. *al-Ṣarf fī ʿilm al-ḥarf* AS $2160_{,3}$.

657 6. Raḍī al-Dīn Abu ʾl-Qāsim ʿAlī b. Mūsā b. Jaʿfar b. | Muḥammad b. Muḥammad b. Ṭāʾūs al-Ṭāʾūsī al-ʿAlawī al-Fāṭimī, d. 664/1266, see Suppl.

1. *Kitāb al-amān min akhṭār al-asfār wal-azmān*, a manual for prayers and ceremonies while travelling, cures, etc. Ind. Off. 341, *Br. Mus. Quart.* VI, 55, MSS in Iraq in *Dharīʿa* II, $343_{,1365}$.—2. *Muhaj al-daʿawāt wa-manhaj al-ghāyāt*, prayers, incantations, amulets, etc. Paris 1173, Patna I, $158_{,1499}$.—3.–17. See Suppl. (6. also Patna II, $348_{,2533/4}$. 7. See *Dharīʿa* II, $264_{,1078,\ 9}$. 9. Ibid. II, $418_{,1656}$).—19. *Asrār al-ṣalāt wa-anwār al-daʿawāt* or *Mukhtār al-daʿawāt wa-asrār al-ṣalāt*, fragment in a *majmūʿa* in the possession of Ḥasan Ṣadr al-Dīn al-Kāẓimī, *Dharīʿa* II, $49_{,199}$.

7. Muḥammad b. Aḥmad b. Suhayl al-Jawzī b. al-Khashshāb, ca. 650/1252.

Kitāb al-durr al-naẓīm fī faḍāʾil al-Qurʾān al-ʿaẓīm, see Suppl., also Patna I, 29,285.

8. Abu ʾl-Ṭāhir (Abū Isḥāq) Ibrāhīm b. Yaḥyā b. Ghannām al-Ḥarrānī al-Numayrī al-Ḥanbalī al-Maqdisī, who died in 674/1275 or, according to others, 693/1294.

1. *ʿArūs al-bustān fi ʾl-nisāʾ wal-aʿḍāʾ wal-insān*, a *rajaz* on the interpretation of dreams, Berl. 4263.—2. *Durrat al-aḥlām wa-ghāyat al-marām*, last part ibid. 4264.—3. *al-Nāmaj fī taʿbīr al-ruʾyā*, Köpr. 1227, Qawala II, 254, Garr. 935.—4., 5. see Suppl. (4. 1. *al-Muʿlam*).

9. Al-Maqrīzī, who was 70 years old in 687/1288, wrote in Egypt:

Ḥall al-rumūz wal-ṭilasmāt wal-khabāyā wal-kunūz wal-khafiyyāt Bodl. II, 375.

Chapter 18. Encyclopaedias and Polyhistors

The decline in Arabic literature that followed original works no longer being
written led to the appearance of a whole succession of polymaths and poly-
graphs, who pretended to singlehandedly sum up the totality of knowledge
of their time in encyclopaedias or to process it in monographs. Some of these
658 499 authors | we have already come across, | namely those who excelled to such a
degree in a particular area of knowledge that they simply had to be included
there. The following contains a listing of scholars who could not lay claim to
such inclusion, neither by the quality nor the quantity of their production.

1. Jamāl al-Dīn Abū ʿAbdallāh Muḥammad b. Aḥmad al-Qazwīnī wrote, in 551/1156:

Mufīd al-ʿulūm wa-mubīd al-humūm, a popular encyclopaedia of religious, moral, political, natural historical, geographical, and historical content, Gotha 173, Paris 2334/7, Br. Mus. Suppl. 712, 3, vol. II, AS 4281, Cairo [1]VII, 701, [2]VI, 212 (in Garr. 181 and Cambr. 1081 wrongly attributed to the Shīʿī Abū Bakr al-Khwārizmī).

2. Abū ʿĀmir Muḥammad b. Aḥmad b. ʿĀmir al-Ṭarasūsī (Ṭarṭūshī) al-Balawī al-Sālimī, who died in Seville in 559/1164.

Dozy, *Notices* 174/6, Wüst. *Gesch.* 253.—1. *Unmūdhaj al-ʿulūm*, on 24 sciences each divided into *muqaddima, masāʾil, jawāb, fāʾida*, and *khātima*, Vienna 3, Garr. 1129a.—2. see Suppl.

3. Abū Bakr Muḥammad b. Khayr b. ʿUmar b. Khalīfa al-Ishbīlī was born in Seville in 502/1108 and studied there and in almost all of the larger cities of Spain. He became imam of the great mosque of Cordova at the age of 70, and died there on 4 Rabīʿ I 575/10 August 1179.

Ibn al-Abbār 780, al-Ḍabbī 112. *Fihrist mā rawāhu ʿan shuyūkhihī min al-dawāwīn al-muṣannafa fī ḍurūb al-ʿilm wa-anwāʿ al-maʿārif*, an inventory of more than 1400 book titles from all the sciences, with complete *isnāds*, ed. Fr. Codera et J. Ribera Tarrago, *Bibl. Ar.-Hisp.* IX, X, 1894/5.

4. Muḥammad b. ʿAlī b. Muḥammad al-Wādīʾāshī al-Barrāq, d. 596/1199.

| Wüst. *Gesch.* 285. *Jāmiʿ al-funūn wa-qāmiʿ al-ẓunūn*, part IX, on astronomy, 659
Berl. 5672.

| 5. Abu ʾl-Faḍāʾil Jamāl al-Dīn Abu ʾl-Faraj ʿAbd al-Raḥmān b. Abi ʾl-Ḥasan ʿAlī 500
b. Muḥammad b. ʿUmar b. al-Jawzī[1] hailed from a family that regarded itself as being descended from the caliph Abū Bakr. He was born in Baghdad around 508, or, according to others, in 510/1116 (Ibn al-Athīr XII, 112). He tells us about his life in his *Liftat al-kabid fī naṣīḥat al-walad*, which is an admonition to his son Abu ʾl-Qāsim[2] to devote himself to the sciences, just as he had done (Berl. 3988, Esc. ^{2}1432,$_{5}$, Fātiḥ 5295,$_{3}$, Cairo ^{1}VII, 177, ed. M. Ḥāmid al-Faqqī in *Min dafāʾin al-kutub*, C. 1349, no. 4). His father had given him a thorough education at great cost and left him two houses upon his death. Of these, he lived in one and rented out the other. But he then sold them both in order to invest the money thus made in books, as he had done earlier with all his cash. Even though he disdained wandering around like the other preachers did to curry favour with princes,[3] God's mercy never let him starve.

By the age of seven he started studying *ḥadīth* with the *Musnad* of Ibn Ḥanbal; in the year 554/1159 he attended the lectures of Maʿmar b. ʿAbd al-Waḥīd, which took place on hallowed ground in Medina, between the pulpit and the Prophet's
tomb. | Because of his fervour against the falsification of *ḥadīth*s he brought 660
many a literary feud upon himself.[4] In fact, he did not even spare al-Ghazzālī's
Iḥyāʾ ʿulūm al-dīn his criticism.[5] | He simply represented Ḥanbalī fanaticism 501
in its most extreme form, something for which he was justly upbraided by Ibn al-Athīr.[6] His productivity as a writer was only later surpassed by al-Suyūṭī,

1 According to Ibn Khallikān, it is the *nisba* of al-Jawz, "a well-known port" (= Nahr al-Jawz on the Euphrates, between Aleppo and al-Bīra; Yāqūt, GW II, 151, 8?), according to Ḥuff., it is the nisba of *al-jawz*, the nut, figuring on the dirhams current in Wāsit.

2 Another son, Muḥyi ʾl-Dīn Abu ʾl-Muẓaffar Yūsuf, born in 580/1184, was *ustāddār* (majordomo) of the caliph al-Mustaʿṣim and was killed in 656/1258 at the order of Hūlāgū, *JA* s. 9, v. 4. p. 465–6. 125, 482. For his grandson Sibṭ b. al-Jawzī see p. 424.

3 ʿImād al-Dīn in Jenisch, ad Mirchond, *Hist. pr. reg. Pers.* 146, claims however that he accompanied Ṣalāḥ al-Dīn on his campaigns.

4 see Goldziher, *M. St.* II, 272.

5 Ibid. 154, see above p. 540.

6 Goldziher 186. Until the eleventh cent. AH he remained the archetype of the severe critic of *ḥadīth*, such as opposed to the more casual opinions of someone like Suyūṭī. Cf. the marginal note in MS Wetzst. II, 289, fol. 236 r.

and extended across all fields of learning, with the exception of grammar, dogmatics, and the exact sciences. Even though his writings were mostly compilations, which Yāqūt, *Irshād* VI, 204 calls untrustworthy, in paraenesis he seems to have struck out on his own.

Ibn al-Jawzī's life was not only dedicated to learning, but also to practical religious virtue. In Mecca and Baghdad especially, he did not preach in the mosque, but rather in conventicles at home or in the street. The Spanish voyager Ibn Jubayr tells us about two sermons that were held in Ṣafar 581/May 1185 in front of his house near Bāb al-Baṣaliyya[7] and on the morning of the eleventh in the court of the caliphal palace behind the Bāb Badr[8] for the caliph and his harem. His reputation as a preacher was so great that, when Sunnīs and Shīʿīs were arguing once more over the precedence of Abū Bakr or ʿAlī, they called upon him to render a verdict, which he avoided by giving an ambigu-
661 ous answer. | At the end of his *Kitāb al-quṣṣāṣ* (*Cat. Lugd.* IV, 318 ff.) and in the
502 work addressed to his son he boasts of the achievements of his preaching: | he
supposedly converted more than a 100,000 men to a pious lifestyle and brought 10,000 youngsters to taking the inward turn.[9]

He died in 597/1200.

Ibn Khall. 343, *Ḥuff.* III, 45, no. 2, al-Suyūṭī, *Interpr.* 17, no. 5, al-Kattānī, *Fihris* I, 226/8, anon. *Sīrat b. al-Jawzī*, Garr. 2198, Wüst. *Gesch.* 287. He gives a short inventory of his writings at the end of the *Kitāb al-quṣṣāṣ*, as well as in the *Liftat al-kabid*; a more detailed one from *al-Muntakhab* is occasionally cited in ḤKh. An inventory, very rich in detail, was added by whoever continued the *Talqīḥ* under the year of his death, see also the *Mirʾāt al-zamān* by his grandson, Br. Mus. Suppl. 722. There remains (collective volume of his writings in Fātiḥ 5295):

I. Linguistics. 1. *Taqwīm al-lugha*, on errors among the *ʿāmma* in alphabetical order, Bodl. II, 383$_{,2}$.[10]—1. a. *Nuzhat al-aʿyun wal-nawāẓir fī ʿilm al-wujūh wal-naẓāʾir*, ʿUm. 498/9.

II. History: a. World history: 2. *Kitāb al-muntaẓam wa-multaqaṭ al-multazam*, cf. Suppl. (ad Dam. ʿUm. 842, see *RADD* XI, 119).—Abstracts: a. the author

7 see G. Le Strange, *Baghdad during the Abbasid Caliphate*, 290 ff.

8 Ibid. 270, Ibn al-Jubayr, ed. de Goeje, 220 ff.

9 Compare the thousands and tens of thousands of Jews and heretics converted by Rabbūlā, *Ephraemi Syri Rabbulae etc. opera sel.* ed. J.J. Overbeck, Oxford 1865, 193$_{,10}$.

10 Quoted by al-ʿĀmilī in Goldziher, *ZDMG* 35, 147, whose doubts concerning Ibn al-Jawzī's authorship are disproven by its being mentioned in the *Talqīḥ*.

himself, up to the year 569/1173, Cairo [1]v, 145, [2]v, 337.—b. ʿAlī b. Muḥammad Muṣannifak, d. 875/1470 (II, 234), Paris 1550, ʿUm. 5139, vol. II, Cairo [1]v, 160, [2]v, 337.—c. Anon., de Jong 102.—3. *al-Dhahab al-masbūk fī siyāsat al-mulūk*, ḤKh III, 337, [2]I, 829 (according to a quotation in *al-Kharīda*), a fragment from which is in Berl. 9437.—Abstracts by: a. Ibn al-Wardī, ca. 850/1446 (II, 131) in the appendix to *Kharīdat al-ʿajāʾib*, see S. Freund, *De rebus die resurrectionsis eventuris*, Wroclaw 1853, n. 1.—b. A student of Ibn al-Sāʿī, d. 674/1275 (Suppl. I, 590), Sanbāṭ al-Irbilī, Beirut 75 (ZDMG 43, 313).—c. Anon., Kazan 11, 2.—4. *Shudhūr al-ʿuqūd fī taʾrīkh al-ʿuhūd*, an abstract of 2, Leid. 833 (vol. I only about prophets and angels), de Jong 102.—5. *ʿAjāʾib al-badāʾiʿ*, historical | anec- 662
dotes and stories, part 1, a short chronicle until the year 520/1126, Paris 1567.—6. *Talqīḥ fuhūm al-āthār fī mukhtaṣar al-siyar wal-akhbār*, see C. Brockelmann, *Ibn al-Jawzī's T. nach der Berliner Hds. untersucht*, Breslau 1893, also library of Yāsīn b. Bāshaʿyān al-ʿAbbāsī in Basra (Ritter).

| b. Biographies:[11] aa. Collective works. 7. *Ṣafwat (Ṣifat) al-ṣafwa*, an abstract 503
of the *Ḥilyat al-awliyāʾ* of Abū Nuʿaym, p. 445.—8. *Kitāb fī akhbār al-adhkiyāʾ alladhīna qawiyat fiṭanuhum wa-tanaqqada dhakāʾuhum bi-quwwat jawhariyyat ʿuqūlihim*, Bodl. I, 370, 385, 395, Köpr. 1198, Cairo [1]IV, 293, [2]III, 296, print. C. 1304, 1306, extract Berl. 8363, Bodl. I, 294,$_{5}$.—9. *Kitāb al-ḥamqā wal-mughaffalīn*, a counterpart to the previous one, Paris 3543,$_{2}$, 3547, abstract Berl. 8363, possibly also Algiers 1870,$_{2}$ (according to Fagnan from the *ʿUyūn al-ḥikāyāt*, ḤKh. IV, 990?).—10. *al-Quṣṣāṣ wal-mudhakkirīn*, Leid. 2156, used by Goldziher, *M.St.* II.—10a—g. see Suppl.—10. h. *Irshād al-murīdīn fī ḥikāyāt al-ṣāliḥīn*, ḤKh [1]I, 252, [2]I, 67, Garr. 677.

bb. Biographies of individuals: 11. *Kitāb al-wafāʾ fī faḍāʾil al-Muṣṭafā*, Berl. 9573/4, Leid. 865, cf. Brockelmann, BASS II, 1/59.—12. *ʿUyun al-ḥikāyāt fī sīrat sayyid al-bariyyāt*, Leipz. 19.—13. *Mawlid al-nabī*, Berl. 9517/8, Cairo [1]I, 408; a commentary by Muḥammad ʿUmar al-Nawawī (II, 501), composed in 1294/1877, Cairo [1]I, 276.—14. *Manāqib ʿUmar b. al-Khaṭṭāb*, Cairo [1]V, 159, [2]V, 336, 368, ʿUm. 5299, Ist. ʿUn. A 956, Alex. Taʾr. 133.—15. *Maṭlaʿ al-nayyirayn fī sīrat al-ʿUmarayn*, Berl. 9763, 9769, Köpr. 1081.—16. *al-Radd ʿala ʾl-mutaʿaṣṣib al-māniʿ min dhamm Yazīd*, Berl. 9708, Leid. 909,$_{1}$.—17. see Suppl.—18. *Manāqib Aḥmad b. Ḥanbal*, Cairo [1]V, 158, [2]V, 336, abstract by Zakī al-Dīn ʿAbdallāh b. Muḥammad al-Khazrajī, ca. 650/1252 (p. 380), Br. Mus. Suppl. 640.—19. *Faḍāʾil Bishr al-Ḥāfī* (Suppl. I, 35).

---

11 In the *Muntaẓam* too, as in his other historical works, biographies receive special consideration, which is why he is praised by Sibṭ Abū Shāma, ḤKh III, 347,$_{5875}$.

III. *Ḥadīth.* 20. *Jāmiʿ al-masānīd wal-alqāb*, in 5 vols. only, from Aḥmad b. Ḥanbal, Bukhārī, Muslim, and al-Tirmidhī (Goldziher, *MSt.* II, 263). Edited by al-Muḥibb Aḥmad b. ʿAbdallāh al-Ṭabarī, d. 694/1293 (p. 444), ḤKh ^{1}II, 574, ^{2}I, 573, Cairo ^{1}I, 323 (Br. H. ^{2}776 = Suppl. 27d?).—21. *Sharḥ* (*kashf*) *mushkil al-Ṣaḥīḥayn*, Garr. 1450, Cairo ^{1}I, 362, ^{2}128, Rampūr II, 224, 563, Patna I, $54_{,541}$.—22. *al-Manṭiq*
663 (*Nuṭq*) *al-mafhūm min ahl al-ṣamt* | *al-maʿlūm*, traditions on animals and lifeless things that, by a miracle of the Prophet, became endowed with speech, Berl. 8761, Gotha 624/5, Br. Mus. Suppl. 1143, *Bibl. Ital.* XLIX, 21, Pet. Ros. 26, Garr. 2192, Algiers $1688_{,2}$, As 4333, Faiẓ. 1280, Cairo ^{1}II, 202.—Abstracts: a. Only a little shortened by Aḥmad b. Ṭughrilbek, Gotha 626, print. C. 1281, 1308.—b. Anon., Berl. 8762.—23. *Ikhbār ahl al-rusūkh fi ʾl-fiqh wal-taḥdīth bi-miqdār al-nāsikh wal-mansūkh min al-ḥadīth*, Br. Mus. 1594, $_{4}$.—24. *ʿUmdat al-dalāʾil fī mashḥūr al-masāʾil*, ḤKh IV, 267, maybe Gotha 574 which has the clearly not original title *Masāʾil bi-ʿilm al-ḥadīth.*—25. *Kitāb al-ḍuʿafāʾ* (*wal-matrūkīn*), Br. Mus. Suppl. 624.—26. *Kitāb al-mawḍūʿāt* (*min al-aḥādīth al-marfūʿāt*), Fātiḥ 1212, Cairo ^{1}I, 436, ^{2}I, 154, a critique of it, entitled *al-Nukat al-badīʿāt*, by al-Suyūṭī, d. 911/1521, Cairo ^{1}I, 445.—27. On surnames of traditionists, Berl. 1016, 2.—27a.–h. see Suppl.

504 | IV. *Fiqh.* 28. *al-Taḥqīq fī aḥādīth al-khilāf*, ḤKh ^{1}II, 247, ^{2}I, 379, Cairo ^{1}III, 293, ^{2}I, 548, under the title *Aḥādīth al-taʿlīq* (Talq.), Bodl. II, 40, Landb. Br. 38.—29. *al-Bāziʾ al-ashhab al-munqaḍḍ ʿalā mukhālifi ʾl-madhhab*, a defence of Ḥanbalī doctrine aganst the Mujassimūn, ḤKh ^{1}II, 5, ^{1}I, 218, Gotha 716 (lost save for its title), Āṣaf. II, $1294_{,225}$.—29a.–c. see Suppl. (29a. in Patna I, $82_{,832}$ attributed to Ibn Rajab, d. 795/1393, II, 107).

V. *Qurʾān.* 30. *Kitāb fī ʿajāʾib ʿulūm al-Qurʾān*, a general introduction, similar to al-Suyūṭī's *al-Itqān*, Gotha 544 (fragm.), cf. Nöldeke, *Gesch. d. Qorans*, ^{1}257, n. 1.—31. *Mukhtaṣar funūn al-afnān fī ʿulūm al-Qurʾān*, Cairo ^{1}VII, 530, I, 61.—32. *al-Mujtabā fī ʿulūm al-Qurʾān*, Cairo ^{1}VII, 530, ^{2}V, 325.—33. *Zād al-masīr* (Berl. wrongly *al-musāfirīn*) *fī ʿilm al-tafsīr* in 4 vols., for daily use by preachers, Berl. 805, Gotha 530, Garr. 1273, Esc. ^{2}1274/5, Rāġib 194, Ist. Ün. A. 668 (596 AH), Cairo ^{1}I, 176, ^{2}I, 53, Zaouiyah d'El Hamel, *Giorn. d. Soc. As. It.* X, 55.—34. *al-Arīb fī tafsīr al-gharīb*, ḤKh ^{1}I, 260, IV, 331, ^{2}I, 71, with the title *Tafsīr gharīb al-Qurʾān*, Bodl. I, 62.—34a.– see Suppl.

VI. Ethics and mysticism. 36. *Minhāj al-qāṣidīn wa-mufīd al-ṣādiqīn*, an abstract of al-Ghazzālī's *Iḥyāʾ*, p. 540.

VII. Homiletics and paraenesis. 36. *Bustān al-wāʿiẓīn wa-riyāḍ al-sāmiʿīn*, Berl. 8756, Cairo ^{1}II, 147, ^{2}I, 272.—37. *Tabṣirat al-mubtadiʾ*, Br. Mus. I, 338, Yeni 696, abstract Leid. 2189, Ist. Ün. A. 6243, Patna I, $149_{,1428}$.—38. (*an-Nāmūs fī*)
664 *Talbīs Iblīs*, ḤKh ^{1}II, 239, ^{2}I, 471, see Suppl., | Patna I, $144_{,1150}$, as *Kashf T.I.* Heid., ZDMG 91, 382, as *Kashf nāmūs T.I.* Alex. Mawāʿiẓ 32, see W. Braune,

Publ. Inst. Un. de Napoli, Annali I, 1940, 305/13; imitation of *Taflīs Iblīs* by
ʿIzz al-Dīn al-Maqdisī, d. 678/1279, see p. 587.—39. *al-Thabāt ʿinda ʾl-mamāt*,
ḤKh [1]II, 490, [2]I, 521, abstract by Fakhr al-Dīn al-Baʿlabakkī, ca. 729/1329
(II, 74), Leid. 2158.—40. *al-Ḥadāʾiq*, traditions from Bukhārī and Muslim, as well
as edifying stories on Muḥammad, his wives, and companions, Berl. 1303, fragment Cairo [1]I, 335, which is probably different from *al-Ḥadāʾiq li-ahl al-ḥaqāʾiq*,
Bāyazīd 1761, which, according to ḤKh [1]III, 22, [2]I, 634, are divided into 100 *majālis*,
while the MS Berl. is broken up in *bābs*; cf. also al-Diyārbakrī, *al-Khamīs* I, 2.—
41. *Ḥusn al-sulūk ilā mawāʿiẓ al-mulūk*, ḤKh [1]III, 262, [2]I, 66, may be the same
as the nameless mirror for princes of Gotha 1880, which Pertsch, because it
lacks an introduction, takes to be a part of a larger work; but cf. also *Mawāʿiẓ
al-mulūk wal-salāṭīn*, Dāmīrī, I, 68, line 6 from below and Br. Mus. Suppl.
744.—42. *Ṣabā Najd*,[12] with many verses ḤKh [1]IV, 90, Esc. [2]389,1, Bāyezīd
1761.—43. *al-Muntakhab fī ʾl-nuwab*, a collection of Qurʾān verses suitable for
reading at the occurrence of a *nawba*, with a list of his works at the end, ḤKh
VI, 165, *Br. Mus. Quart.* XIII, 3. 90, Cairo [1]II, 177.—44. Abstract of *Muntakhab
al-muntakhab*, Landb.-Br. 159 or *Nukhbat al-M.*, Berl. 9437, as *Mukhtaṣar al-M.*
Ambr. A. 105 xiii (*RSO* III, 905).—45. *al-Rubʿ al-ʿāmir*, edifying anecdotes, Br.
Mus. 1141,1.—46. *al-Manshūr fī majālis al-ṣudūr*, ibid. I, 338, | possibly cited 505
as *Fi ʾl-nashr, al-Ḥalabī, Sīra* I, 421.—47. *Yāqūtat al-mawāʿiẓ wal-mawʿiẓa*,
ḤKh VI, 508, *Talq.*, Fātiḥ 5295/7 = *al-Yāqūtiyyāt*, an appendix to ʿUthmān
b. Yaḥyā b. ʿAbd al-Wahhāb, *Mukhtaṣar rawnaq al-majālis* (Suppl. II, 285),
C. Maymaniyya 1309.—48. *Salwat al-aḥzān bi-mā ruwiya ʿan dhawi ʾl-ʿirfān*,
Bodl. I, 289, Cairo [1]II, 88 = *Salwat al-ḥazīn*, Berl. 8765?.—49. *Ṣayd al-khāṭir*,
Fātiḥ 4004, Cairo [1]II, 93/4.—50. *al-Jalīs al-ṣāliḥ wal-anīs al-nāṣiḥ*, Cairo [1]II, 153
probably = *Anīs al-jalīs*, Garr. 1895, also attributed to his grandson, see Suppl. I,
589,13, 3.—51. *Muntakhab al-zīr ʿan ruʾūs al-qawārīr fī ʾl-mawāʿiẓ wal-tadhkīr*,
| Berl. 8767.—52. *al-Mawrid al-ʿadhb fī ʾl-mawāʿiẓ wal-khuṭab*, 70 sermons 665
pronounced in the main mosque in Mecca, Br. Mus. 145, Esc. [2]717.—
53. *al-Muwāfiq lil-murāfiq*, Br. Mus. 744, Or. 9249, Esc. [2]389,2.—54. *al-Murtajal*,
an improvised manual for beginner preachers in 10 *majālis*, Copenhagen
70,2.—55. *Tanbīh al-nāʾim al-ghumr ʿalā mawāsim al-ʿumr*, printed as no. 6 of
al-Tuḥfa al-bahiyya, Constantinople 1302, 55/65.—56. *Luṭf al-mawāʿiẓ*, Alex.
Mawāʿiz 34, 39,2.—57. *al-Maqāmāt al-Jawziyya fī ʾl-maʿāni ʾl-waʿẓiyya*, with
a lexicon; a commentary, written in 34 days in the Bāb al-Āzaj quarter in
Baghdad, Leid. 426, Cambr. 1098, MSS in Istanbul *ZS* III, 248, Bursa Ulu Cami

12 The title may allude to the name of his wife, Nasīm al-ṣabā, with whom he had an unhappy marriage, despite his love for her, al-Nawājī, *Ḥalbat al-kumayt*, C. 1299, 321, 12 ff., Cod. Goth. 215, f. 1184 v, al-Juzūlī, *Maṭāliʿ al-budūr*, I, 53, 7 ff.

Taṣ. 57.—58. *Risāla fī birr al-wālidayn*, Cairo [1]VII, 553.—59. *Hādi ʾl-nufūs ila ʾl-malik al-quddūs*, Berl. 8770, Landb.-Br. 245.—60. *Dhamm al-hawā*, on love, Berl. 8362.—61. *al-Majālis al-Yūsufiyya*, edifying stories about Yūsuf, Br. Mus. 1488,$_2$.—62. *Widāʿ shahr Ramaḍān*, Esc. [2]436,$_2$.—63. *Rawḍat al-majālis wa-nuzhat al-mustaʾnis*, an entertaining work, Berl. 8361.—64. *Qalāʾid al-nuhūr*, pious reflections and admonitions, in verse and prose, ordered alphabetically, Berl. 8757.—65. *Sūq al-ʿarūs*, sayings by Muḥammad and pious men, anecdotes, edifying verses, etc. in 14 sessions, Berl. 8759.—66. *al-Laṭāʾif al-kubrā*, solemn expostulations, Pet. AM 85, Köpr. 717,$_2$, Alex. Mawāʿiẓ 34, Cairo, *ZDMG* XXX, 313, abstract Berl. 8760.—67. *al-Zahr al-fāʾiḥ fī-man tanazzaha ʿani ʾl-dhunūb wal-qabāʾiḥ*, Berl. 8768/9, Paris 1324, 2033, Alex. Mawāʿiẓ 39,$_1$, another recension Paris 2034.—68. *Baḥr al-dumūʿ*, 32 sermons, Paris 1297, Alex. Mawāʿiẓ 7.—69. *al-Majālis fi ʾl-waʿẓ*, Leipz. 166, *Nukat al-majālis fi ʾl-waʿẓ*, ibid. 167.—70. *Inshād al-wāʿiẓ ilā ashraf al-mawāʿiẓ*, Br. Mus. 743.—71. *Dawā dhawi ʾl-ghafalāt*, AS 1786.—72. *Kitāb al-maʿshūq*, abstract by Fakhr al-Dīn al-Baʿlabakkī, Leid. 2157.—73. *Rawḥ al-arwāḥ*, Alex. Mawāʿiẓ 18, print. C. 1309, anon. abstract Alex. Maw. 37,$_1$.—74. *Narjis al-qulūb wa-dāll al-ḥarīq al-maḥbūb*, Berl. 8766, fragm. Leid. 1309.—75. *Tanwīr al-jabaṣ fī faḍl al-sūdān al-Ḥabash*, Gotha 1692, Esc. [2]1835, Alex. Mawāʿiẓ 35, *Mukhtaṣar* Ğārullāh 2108,$_2$, cf. Flügel, *ZDMG* XVI, 697.—75 a–q. see Suppl. (75c. Bursa Haraccizade Taş. 59), h. an abstract entitled *Tadhkirat al-ayqāẓ* by Shams al-Dīn Muḥammad al-Luʾluʾī al-Shāfiʿī al-Muḥaddith al-Makkī, Fātiḥ 2830 (964 AH).—75 r. *Dīwān khuṭab*, Alex.
666 Mawāʿiẓ 37,$_3$.—75 s. *al-Nūr fī faḍāʾil al-yawm wal-shuhūr*, ibid. 49.—| 75 t. *Risāla fī kayd al-shayṭān li-nafsihi qabla kaydihi Ādam maʿa sharḥ al-firaq al-muḍilla*, ibid. Fun. 136,$_{11}$.—75 u. *Īqāẓ al-wasnān*, Fātiḥ 5295,2.—75 v. *Bustān al-ṣādiqīn*, Köpr. 701,1.—75 w. *Tuḥfat al-wāʿiẓ wa-nuzhat al-mulāḥiẓ*, Fātiḥ 5295,10.—75 x. *Jawāhir al-mawāʿiẓ*, ʿUm. 1437.—75 y. *ʿAjab al-khuṭab*, Fātiḥ 5295,$_4$.—75 z. *al-Laʾāliʾ*, Fātiḥ 5295,$_5$.—75 aa. *al-Mughliq*, ibid. 9.—75 bb. *al-Manthūr*, ibid. 8.—75 cc. *Mawāʿiẓ al-mulūk*, AS 4825,$_1$.—75 dd. *Nasīm al-saḥar*, Fātiḥ 5295,$_1$.—75 ee. *al-Yawāqīt*, Fātiḥ 5295,$_6$.—75 ff. *Lughat al-jumān*, paraenetical poems, among which is *Kān mā kān, Fātiḥ 4861 (Ritter)*.—75 gg. *Muntahā mushtahā*, revised *Māʾ al-ḥayāt* by al-Qāsim Aḥmad al-Qaffāl, Fātiḥ 2805.

VIII. Medicine. 76. *Luqaṭ al-amān fi ʾl-ṭibb*, a history of medicine, on temperaments, foodstuffs and cures, sleep, waking, coitus, and diseases, Leipz. 766,$_1$, Bodl. I, 593 (which is different from ibid. 529, despite the identical title), Garr. 1102, ʿUm. 4206, abstract Leid. 1342/3.—77. *al-Ṭibb al-rūḥānī*, on dietetics of the soul, Gotha 1238.

506 | IX. Geography. 78. *Taʾrīkh al-khamīs al-musammā bi-Muthīr ʿazm al-sākin ilā ashraf al-amākin* (on the title see Bodl. II, 571), Berl. 4042, Bodl. II, 129, Fātiḥ 4470 (*Muthīr al-gharām*), excerpts in Gagnier, *La Vie de Mahomet*, Amsterdam

1732, II, 231, see J. de Somogyi, *JRAS* 1938, 541/6.—79. *Faḍāʾil al-Quds*, Garr. 586, used in Berl. 6098.—80. *Tabṣirat al-akhyār fī dhikr Nīl Miṣr wa-akhawātihi min al-anhār*, Algiers 1551.

X. Encyclopaedias. 81. *Kitāb al-mudhish* treats, in 15 chapters, the sciences of the Qurʾān, linguistics, *ḥadīth*, and history, as well as of paraenesis, completed on 14 Jumādā II 591/27 May 1195, Bodl. I, 279 (cf. II, 511) II, 48, Copenhagen 60, Cairo ^{1}I, 176, ^{2}VI, 189, library of ʿAbd al-Ḥamīd in Istanbul (Jenisch, on Mirchond, *Hist. reg. pr. Pers.* 145/6). Abstract Gotha 842, Br. Mus. Suppl. 1247$_{,ii}$, Leid. 2155 (probably only chapter 5 with a new *dībāja* and in a new arrangement), ʿUm. 5567, Fātiḥ 4081, 4114.

6. Fakhr al-Dīn Abū ʿAbdallāh Muḥammad b. ʿUmar b. al-Ḥusayn (Ḥasan) b. al-Khaṭīb al-Rāzī, d. 606/1209 (see Suppl.).

Ibn Abī Uṣ. II, 23/30, Ibn al-Qifṭī 190/2, Khwandamīr, *Ḥabīb al-siyar* III, 1, 60 ff. Ibn Quṭlūbughā 93, Wüst. *Ärzte* 200, *Gesch.* 249, Leclerc II, 20, G. Gabrieli, *Isis* 1925, 91/3, P. Kraus, Les controverses de F. ar.-R., *Bull. de l'Inst. Ég.* XIX, 1939, 187/214.

I. History. 1. *Manāqib al-imām al-Shāfiʿī*, Berl. | 10008/9, Paris 3497$_{,2}$, Br. Mus. 667
Suppl. 641, Cairo ^{1}V, 158, ^{2}V, 364, Alex. Taʾr. 95.—2. *Qalāʾid ʿuqūd al-ʿiqyān fī manāqib Abī Nuʿmān*, Āṣaf. II, 1322$_{,65}$.

II. *Fiqh*. 3. *al-Maḥṣūl fī uṣūl al-fiqh*, Paris 790, Ind. Off. 1445, Cairo ^{1}II, 263, Patna I, 74$_{,755}$.—Abbreviations: a. *al-Ḥāṣil*, see Suppl.—b. *al-Taḥṣīl* by Sirāj al-Dīn Abu 'l-Thanāʾ Maḥmūd b. Abī Bakr al-Urmawī, d. 682/1283 (p. 614), Gotha 934, Br. Mus. Suppl. 259, Ind. Off. 293, Bodl. I, 267$_{,1}$, Landb.-Br. 604, Asʿad 3804$_{,1}$.—c. *Tanqīḥ al-fuṣūl*, by Shihāb al-Dīn Aḥmad b. Idrīs al-Qarāfī, d. 684/1285 (p. 481), with comm., Gotha 935.—4. *Mushtamil al-aḥkām*, legal rulings, Upps. 439, Selīm Āġā 398.—5. *al-Maʿālim fī uṣūl al-dīn* (*kalām*), see Suppl., Patna II, 513$_{,2758}$.—Commentaries: a.–d. see Suppl. (c. by ʿAlāʾ al-Dīn Ḥusayn b. Mīrzā Rafīʿ al-Dīn Muḥammad b. Amīr Shujāʿ al-Dīn Maḥmūd al-Ḥusaynī al-Āmulī al-Iṣfahānī, d. 1064/1654, Teh. Sip. I, 567/9).—e. Mollā Mīrzā Shirwānī Muḥammad b. Ḥasan, d. 1098/1687, Teh. Sip. I, 574/6.—f. Āqā Bihbihānī, d. 1208/1794, ibid. 564.—g. *Hidāyat al-mustarshidīn* by Muḥammad Taqī b. ʿAbd al-Raḥīm, d. 1248/1832 (*Rawḍāt al-jannāt* I, 131), ibid. 570/2.—h. Muḥammad b. Ibrāhīm al-Ḥusaynī al-Ḥasanī, Alex. Uṣūl 8.—i. *Aṣl al-uṣūl* by Rafīʿ b. Rafīʿ al-Jīlānī, the author of *al-Madārik*, ca. 1233/1818, print. 1268 with *Muqaddimaʾi Kashf al-madārik* in the margin, *Dharīʿa* II, 168$_{,261}$.

III. Qurʾān. 6. *Mafātīḥ al-ghayb* or *al-Tafsīr al-kabīr*, Paris 613, 6526$_{i}$, Bodl. I, 26, Br. Mus. Suppl. 111, Ind. Off. 65/6, Yeni 64/70, AS 232/41, Rāġib 85/9, Algiers 330, Cairo ^{1}I, 213, Qawala I, 81, Patna I, 33$_{,329/39}$, print. Būlāq 1278, 1289, Cairo ^{1}307/9,

Istanbul 1294, 1307; cf. M. Schreiner, ZDMG 52, 506ff.—Abstracts: a. *al-Tanwīr fī 'l-tafsīr* by Muḥammad b. Abi 'l-Qāsim b. ʿAbd al-Salām al-Rājī al-Tūnisī, d. 715/1315, completed in 707/1307, Paris 614/9.—b. *Gharāʾib al-Qurʾān*, by his student al-Niẓām al-Aʿraj al-Nisābūrī (II, 201), Cairo ^{1}I, 183.—7. *Risālat* (*al-tanbīh ʿalā baʿḍ*) *asrār* (*al-mūdaʿa fī*) *baʿḍ suwar al-Qurʾān*, Berl. 704/5, Gotha $543_{,2}$.—8. *Durrat al-tanzīl wa-ghurrat al-taʾwīl*, on the *mushtabih* in the Qurʾān, Cairo ^{1}I, 173, ^{2}I, 48, *Dībāja* Gotha 2, 48 (see Suppl. I, 491, 16, 2).

507 | IV. Dogmatics. 9. *al-Mabāḥith al-arbaʿūn fī uṣūl al-dīn*, Qawala I, 160, Ind. Off. 404, Bodl. II, 86, Garr. 1486, print. Hyderabad 1353/1934, anon. comm. thereon Esc. $^2676_{,1}$, Cairo ^{1}II, 2, Mashh. I, $21_{,41}$.—10. *Asrār al-tanzīl wa-anwār*
668 *al-taʾwīl*, on the three foundations of religion and | law, Berl. 1739, Rāġib 20/1, Cairo ^{1}II, 3, Patna I, $22_{,197}$.—11. *al-Maṭālib al-ʿaliyya*, on demonstrations of God's existence, his nature and workings, the soul, matter, and eternity, Yeni 755, Cairo ^{1}II, 54, ^{2}I, 170, anon. abstract Berl. 1740.—12. *al-Lawāmiʿ al-bayyināt fī sharḥ asmāʾ allāh al-ḥusnā wal-ṣifāt*, Berl. 2223, Yeni 703/4, Rāġib 614, Cairo ^{1}VII, 70.—13. *Risāla fī tafsīr lā ilāha illa 'llāh*, Berl. 2425.—14. *ʿIṣmat al-anbiyāʾ*, proof that prophets are blameless and free of sin, Berl. 2528, Alex. Fun. 43, $67_{,11}$, print. C. 1355.—15. *Waṣiyya*, Berl. 3989.—16. *Nihāyat al-ʿuqūl fī dirāyat al-uṣūl*, Yeni 759.—17. *Mukhtār al-Taḥbīr*, a commentary on the 99 names of God, perhaps an abstract of *al-Taḥbīr fī ʿilm al-tadhkīr* by al-Qushayrī (p. 556), Paris 1383.—18. *al-Āyāt al-bayyināt*, theology, Esc. $^2650_{,4}$, Landb.-Br. 557, comm. *Ghāyat al-āyāt* by Maḥmūd al-Urmawī, d. 672/1273 (p. 614), Alex. Manṭiq 17, anon. comm. Cairo ^{1}VI, 60.—19. *Asās al-taqdīs*, composed for Sultan Abū Bakr b. Ayyūb (Sayf al-Dīn 596–615/1199–1218), Cairo ^{1}VII, 199.—20. *al-Masāʾil al-khamsūn fī uṣūl al-kalām*, Paris 1253, Cairo ^{1}VII, 252.—20a—d. see Suppl. (20b. also Patna II, $431_{,2607,\,5}$).—20e. *Wird*, Qawala I, 269.—20f. *Aghāz-i anjām*, eschatology in Persian, library of al-Taqawī in Tehran, *Dharīʿa* I, $36_{,173}$.

V. Philosophy. 21. *al-Mabāḥith al-mashriqiyya*, on fundamental notions in physics and metaphysics, Berl. 5064, Leid. 1513, Br. Mus. Or. 9004, Esc. ^{2675}, 692, Yeni 774, Patna I, $215_{,1917/8}$, anon. abstract Alex. Ḥikma 26.—22. *Muḥaṣṣal afkār al-mutaqaddimīn wal-mutaʾakhkhirīn* or *al-Muḥassal min nihāyat al-ʿuqūl fī ʿilm al-uṣūl* (also an abstract of no. 16?), a handbook of metaphysics, Esc. $^2650_{,5}$, Cairo ^{1}VI, 105, Taymūr ʿAq. 268, cf. Schmölders, *Essai sur les écoles phil. chez les Arabes*, p. 140ff., Schreiner, ZDMG 52, 505, with comm. *al-Mufaṣṣal* by al-Qazwīnī (p. 612), Leid. 1572, Landb.-Br. 565, Paris 1254 (anon.), Ibr. Pasha 821, Patna I, $126_{,1262}$.—Critical revision by al-Ṭūsī (no. 7), composed in 669/1270, entitled *Talkhīṣ al-Muḥaṣṣal*, Gotha 644, Br. Mus. Suppl. 180, on which selected comments by Ibn Kammūna (Suppl. I, 768), Br. Mus. $429_{,6}$.—23. *al-Manṭiq al-kabīr* with a commentary, a part of which Berl. 5165.—24. *al-Mulakhkhas*

fī 'l-ḥikma wal-manṭiq, completed in 579/1183, Leid. 1510, Br. Mus. Suppl. 725, Bodl. I, 501.—Commentary *al-Munaṣṣaṣ* by al-Qazwīnī, d. 675/1276, Leid. 1511, Yeni 747, Patna II, $527_{,2836}$.—25. *I'tiqādāt al-muslimīn wal-mushrikīn*, Landb.-Br. 585, Taymūr 'Aq. 178, ed. al-Nashshār, | C. 1938.—26. *Uns al-ḥāḍir wa-zād al-musāfir*, 669
Leipz. 227.—27. *Dhamm ladhdhat al-dunyā*, composed in 604/1207 in Herat and Khwārizm, Berl. 5426.—27a.–k. see Suppl. (27b. *Munāẓarat al-'allām F. al-R. fī hijratihi ilā Samarqand thumma jihat al-Hind*, see P. Kraus, *Isl. Culture* XII, 1938, 131/53, Les Controverses de F. al-R. *Bull. de l'Inst. Egypt.* 1939, 187/234).—27l. *Risāla fī 'l-nafs*, Alex. Fun. $155_{,5}$.

VI. Astrology. 28. On the basic notions of astronomy, Leid 1078.—29. *al-Sirr al-maktūm fī mukhāṭabat al-nujūm*, detailed astrology (according to ḤKh III, 7155, by 'Alī b. 'Alī al-Ḥirālī, p. 527, but because of a self-quotation in *al-Mulakhkhaṣ, bāb* 5, confirmed as a work by al-Rāzī, see M. Sherefeddīn in Ritter, *Isl.* XXIV, 285, n. 2), Berl. 5886, Leid. 1080/1, Paris 2645, Bodl. I, 917, 950, 981, II, 282, 2389, Br. Mus. Or. 9147, Dāmād Ibr. 845, NO 2784, Aleppo Aḥmadiyya 1341, Garr. 933, Patna I, $238_{,2062/3}$, II, $487_{,2648,\ 6}$—Abstract by Muḥammad b. Muḥammad al-Fullānī al-Kishnawī (II, 366), composed in 1141/1728 in Medina, Gotha 1267, Cairo ^{1}V, 337.—30. *al-Ikhtiyārāt al-ilāhiyya fī 'l-ikhtiyārāt al-samāwiyya*, astrology, originally composed in Persian for the Khwārizmshāh 'Alā' al-Dīn, d. 596/1199 (see Suppl.) | and translated into Arabic by an unknown 508
individual, Paris $1360_{,2}$, $2521_{,5}$ = *al-Aḥkām al-'Alā'iyya fī 'l-aḥkām al-samāwiyya* by the author himself, Berl. Oct. 2488, Paris 2592.—(30b. *Bīst Bāb*, a treatise in Persian on the astrolabe, Br. Mus. Suppl. 155_{ii}, Pers. 38).—30c. *Risāla fī nafy al-ḥayyiz wal-jiha*, Mashh. II, $31_{,110}$.—30d. *Risālat dar ḥaqīqat-i marg va aḥvāl-i rūḥ*, ibid. II, $31_{,109}$).

VII. Chiromancy. *Risāla fī ma'rifat khuṭūṭ al-kaff etc.*, Cairo ^{1}VI, 32 (see Suppl.).

VIII. Rhetoric. *Nihāyat al-ījāz fī dirāyat al-i'jāz*, Alex. Bal. 26, Cairo ^{1}VII, 198, ^{2}II, 227, Qawala II, 178.

IX. Encyclopaedias. 33. *Jāmi' al-'ulūm*, NO 3760 (see Farmer, *Sources* 45), AS 3832 (33a. a Persian encyclopaedia, Berl. Pers. 92, Bodl. Pers. 1481/2, Br. Mus. Pers. Suppl. 142).

X. Medicine. see Suppl.

XI. Physiognomy. 35. *Risāla fī 'ilm al-firāsa*, see Suppl., Br. Mus. Or. 9510, Y. Mourad, *La Physiognomie arabe et le k. al-Firasa de F. ar R.*, Paris 1939.

XII. Alchemy. see Suppl.

XIII. Mineralogy (37. Persian *Tansūqnāma* Br. Mus. Pers. Suppl. 157).

7. His student Shams al-Dīn Aḥmad b. Khalīl b. Sa'āda al-Khuwayyī, who was the *qāḍī al-quḍāt* in Damascus, died at a young age on 7 Sha'bān 637/5 March 1240.

670 | 1. *Yanābīʿ al-ʿulūm* or *Aqālīm al-taʿālīm fi 'l-funūn al-sabʿa*, composed in 630/1232, on the seven sciences of *tafsīr, ḥadīth, fiqh, adab*, medicine, geometry, arithmetic, teaches in each of them 7 smart and 7 funny jokes, Vienna 6, Leid. 4, 1939, Paris 2321, abstract Paris 2322$_{,1}$.—2. see Suppl.

8. Abū Jaʿfar Naṣīr al-Dīn Muḥammad b. Muḥammad b. al-Ḥasan al-Ṭūsī al-Shīʿī, who died in 672/1274, see Suppl.

Fawāt II, 149, Khwandamīr, *Ḥabīb al-siyar* II, 480, III, 1, 54, *Rawḍat al-ṣafā'*, Bombay V, 70 (cit. Rieu, *Pers. Cat.* II, 442a), Leclerc II, 137, Cantor, *Vorl.* I, 669, Wurm in *Zachs Monatl. Correspondenz zur Beförderung der Erd-und*
509 *Himmelskunde*, 1811, XXIII, 64/78, 341/61, | Jourdain, *Magazin enc.* 1809, VI, *Biogr. univ.* XXX, 58, A. v. Braunmühl, *Nassīr Eddīn Ṭūsī und Regiomontan*, Abh. d. K. Leop. Car. Ak. der Nat. 71, no. 2, Halle 1897, Mieli 153. He preferred to revise older works, but has the merit of having been the first to deal with trigonometry as an independent subject.

I. *Fiqh.* 1. *Jawāhir al-farā'iḍ al-Naṣīriyya*, Berl. 4710, Br. Mus. 881$_{,3}$. Glosses by al-Jurjānī, d. 816/1413, ibid. 4.—Commentaries: a. ʿAlī b. Ḥusayn al-Karakī, d. 940/1533 (II, 574 Suppl.), library of Rājā Muḥammad Mahdī Ṣāḥib in Fayḍābād, *Dharīʿa* I, 446$_{,2243}$.—b. Abu 'l-Ḥasan b. Aḥmad al-Sharīf al-Qā'īnī, written during the reign of Ṭahmāsp (930–84/1524–76), in various libraries in Tehran, ibid. I, 439$_{,2214}$.—c. With a Persian translation by the same, library of Muḥammad ʿAlī Khwānsārī, ibid. 2213.

II. Dogmatics. 2. *Tajrīd al-ʿaqā'id* (*al-kalām*),[13] Berl. 1745/7, Leipz. 109$_{,21}$, Pet. 242, Bodl. I, 129, 172, 520, Esc. ²615, 641$_{,2}$, 645, 648, 685/7, Bīrjand, *Lughat al-ʿArab* VI, 513, Patna I, 113$_{,1143}$ (where *Taḥrīr al-k.*).—Commentaries: a. His student Ḥasan b. Yūsuf b. al-Muṭahhar al-Ḥillī, d. 726/1326 (II, 164), Ind. Off. 471$_{,14}$, Patna I, 120$_{,1215/6}$.—b. *al-Sharḥ al-qadīm* by Maḥmūd b. ʿAbd al-Raḥmān al-Iṣfahānī, d. 749/1348 (II, 110), Leid. 2009, Br. Mus. Suppl. 182, Ind. Off. 406, Bīrjand, *Lughat al-ʿArab* VI, 514$_{,5}$, Patna I, 114$_{,114/6}$.—Glosses: α al-Jurjānī,
671 d. 816/1413 (II, 216), Berl. 1748/50, | Leipz. 388, Br. Mus. Suppl. 183, Ind. Off. 407/8, Paris 269, Esc. ²618, 689, 690, Garr. 865/6, 2148$_{,1}$, Alex. Tawḥīd 10, Patna I, 116$_{,1164}$, completed by Muḥammad b. Ibrāhīm Khaṭībzāde, d. 901/1495 (II, 229), thereof the *Talkhīṣ* by Ṭāsköprīzāde, d. 962/1555 (II, 425), Esc. ²644$_{,1}$, superglosses on Jurjānī and Khaṭībzāde by Ibn Muʿīd al-Rūmī, Esc. ²644$_{,2}$, on Jurjānī by Muḥammad al-Amāsī, d. 904/1499, Berl. 1752/3, by Mīr Ṣadr al-Dīn Muḥammad

---

13 Which was also famous among the Sunnīs and studied by someone like Ibn Zarrūq al-Burnusī, d. 899/1493, in his youth in Morocco, A. Bābā *Nayl* (in the margin of Ibn Farḥūn), 85$_{,1}$.

al-Shīrāzī, d. 903/1497 (II, 204), Münch. 656, by Muḥammad al-Khafārī Br. Mus. 170$_{,3}$, anon. Berl. 1755/6, Br. Mus. 170$_{,1}$.—*β–δ* see Suppl.—c. *al-Sharḥ al-jadīd* by ʿAlī b. Muḥammad al-Qūshjī, d. 879/1474 (II, 234), Vienna 1535, Pet. 229, 303, Ros. 195, Ind. Off. 409/16, Bīrjand, *Lughat al-ʿArab* VI, 514$_{,8}$, Patna I, 121$_{,1211/4}$, lith. Persia n.p. 1274, Tabriz 1301.—Glosses: *α* in three series by al-Dawwānī, d. 907/1501 (II, 217), Berl. 1757/9, Esc. ^{2}661$_{,2}$, 688, Br. Mus. Suppl. 184, Ind. Off. 417/20, *al-qadīma*, Patna I, 118$_{,1187}$, *al-jadīda*, ibid. 1186, II, 511$_{,2745}$; against the first two Ṣadr al-Dīn b. Ghiyāth al-Dīn al-Shīrāzī, d. 903/1497 (II, 204), wrote *al-Ḥāshiya al-jadīda al-Ṣadriyya*, Münch. 656, Ind. Off. 424/5, al-Dawwānī answered this in *al-Ḥāshiya al-jadīda* (see Suppl.) under the title *al-Ṭabaqāt al-Jalāliyya*, Qawala II, 368, rebutted by Ghiyāth al-Dīn b. Ṣadr al-Dīn al-Shīrāzī, d. 949/1542 (II, 414), in *al-Mawāʿid al-ʿurqūbiyya bil-nuqūd al-Yaʿqūbiyya*, Esc. ^{2}651.—Superglosses by Mīrzājān Ḥabīballāh al-Bāghandī, d. 994/1586 (II, 414), Berl. 1761, Br. Mus. 387, 859, Ind. Off. 421/2, thereon again superglosses by Āghā Ḥusayn Khafārī, ibid. 423.—*β* Muḥammad b. Muḥammad al-Laqānī Nāṣir al-Dīn al-Mālikī, d. 958/1551 (Rieu, *Cat.* 768), Esc. ^{2}661$_{,1}$, 688$_{,2}$,—*γ* Ṭāsköprīzāde, d. 968/1560(?), Berl. 1760.—*δ Taʿlīqāt* by Muḥammad b. Aḥmad al-Khiḍrī (Khafārī), written during the reign of Shāh Ismāʿīl (907–30/1502–24), Berl. 1762, Br. Mus. 170$_{,3}$, Ind. Off. 416$_{,2}$, Esc. ^{2}661$_{,3}$, Alex. Tawḥīd 32. *Superglosses*: *αα–κκ*, see Suppl. (*εε* Alex. Tawḥīd 33$_{,3}$, *ηη* ibid. 24, Patna I, 123$_{,1234}$).—*ϑ* Mīrzā Fatḥallāh Shirwānī, Patna I, 118$_{,1185}$.—*ζ* Nūrallāh al-Ḥusaynī al-Shushtarī (Suppl. II, 607), Ind. Off. 417$_{,15}$.—d. *al-Tajwīd* by Ibn Kamālpāshā, d. 940/1533 (II, 449), Paris 4374$_{,2}$.—e. Anon. Berl. 1763/5, glosses ibid. 1766.—28 commentaries, glosses, and superglosses in Ahlw. 1767.—3. *Qawāʿid al-ʿaqāʾid*, on the nature and properties of God, the meaning and the role of prophecy, the imamate, and resurrection, in 5 chapters, Berl. 1768, Ind. Off. 4589$_{,1}$ (*JRAS* 1936, 375). Commentary by Maḥmūd b. | ʿAlī al-Ḥimṣī Tāj al-Rāzī, ca. 750/1349, ibid.—3a.–e. see Suppl. (3d. is a work 672
by Shaykh al-Ṭāʾifa, p. 512).—3f. *ʿAqāʾid mā yajibu ʾl-iʿtiqād bihi* in various copies in Karbala, *Dharīʿa* I, 226$_{,888}$, 274$_{,1108b}$.—3g. *Muqaddima fi ʾl-kalām*, Br. Mus. Or. 1096, 8.

III. Philosophy. 4. *al-Fuṣūl*, translated from the Persian into Arabic by ʿAllāma al-Ḥillī al-Jurjānī, a student of Rukn al-Dīn Muḥammad ʿAlī al-Ḥillī al-Gharawī, Br. Mus. Suppl. 185, Pet. 54.—Commentaries: a. *al-Anwār al-Jalāliyya* by al-Miqdād b. ʿAbdallāh b. Ḥusayn al-Suyūrī al-Ḥillī, d. 826/1432 (II, 199), Pet. 54$_{,2}$, AM Buch. 746, Najaf *Dharīʿa* II, 423, 1670.—b, c. see Suppl.—d. Anonymous, composed on the order of Sultan ʿAbd al-Muṭṭalib al-Mūsawī, Berl. 1770.—5. Three questions on metaphysics with their answers, Berl. 1771.—6. Answers to questions raised by al-Qūnawī (p. 585) who had answered them in his *al-Risāla al-mufṣiḥa*, Berl. 3477, Patna II, 417$_{,2586,\ 2}$.—7. *Sharḥ al-muḥaqqiq*, notes to a treatise on the absolute existence of God by the

philosopher al-Kātibī, d. 675/1276 (p. 612), Berl. 2307.—8. *Fī ḍarūrat al-mawt,*
ibid. 2655.—9. *Awṣāf al-ashrāf fi 'l-siyar wal-sulūk,* a Persian treatise on Sufism,
ḤKh, ^{1}I, 494,$_{1487}$, ^{2}I, 202 (see Suppl.), Arabic transl. by Muḥammad ʿAlī al-Jurjānī,
510 ca. 730/1329, Berl. 3014. |—10. *Aqsām al-ḥikma,* a brief overview of the classi-
fication of philosophy, Berl. 5076, Rāġib, *Dharīʿa* II, 272,$_{1098}$.—11. Answers to
20 philosophical questions by al-Ḥasan b. Muḥammad al-Astarābādī, d. 718/
1318, ibid. 5077, Rāġib see *Dharīʿa* II, 83,$_{329}$.—12. Various assertions from the
works of al-Fārābī that regard the education of the soul as a way to personal
happiness and true wisdom, Berl. 5079.—13. A discussion of philosophical
dicta on the universal and the particular, compiled by Najm al-Dīn al-Kātibī, d.
675/1276, ibid. 5078.—14. Answer to al-Kātibī on Ibn Sīnā's doctrine of the influence of heat and cold on the colours of dry and wet bodies, Br. Mus. 980,$_{17}$.—
15. Treatise on the nature of the Good and the Bad and their relation to each other,
Berl. 5127,$_1$.—16. On the inseparability of cause and effect, ibid. 2.—17. *Risāla
fī baqāʾ al-nafs al-insāniyya,* Berl. 5355, Rāġib 1482, Fātiḥ 5380,$_3$, Najaf *Dharīʿa* I,
86,$_{407}$, with a commentary by Abū ʿAbdallāh al-Zanjānī, print. 1341 (*Jāmiʿ al-taṣ.
al-j.* 909).—18. *Risāla fī ithbāt al-jawhar al mufāriq* (*al-ʿaql al-kullī*), on rea-
673 son and its limits, Berl. 5356/7, | Br. Mus. 980,$_{21}$, commentary by al-Dawwānī,
d. 907/1501, Berl. 5358/9, Br. Mus. 980,$_2$, Ind. Off. 581,$_8$, Gotha 11, 58,$_{31}$, Garr.
797, by Shams al-Dīn al-Kashshī, Berl. 5360, anon. glosses ibid. 5361, anon.
comm. Asʿad 3748,$_4$.—19. On the philosophical doctrine of emanation, composed in 666/1267 at the request of the chief judge of Herat, Br. Mus. 980,$_{18}$.—
20. Answer to Najm al-Dīn al-Ḥillī, d. 679/1280 (p. 514), on the origin of taste
Br. Mus. 985,$_2$.—21. *Talkhīṣ al-muḥaṣṣal,* p. 668.—22. *al-Tajrīd fī ʿilm al-manṭiq,*
with a commentary by his student al-Ḥasan b. al-Muṭahhar (II, 164), Br.
Mus. 980, Patna I, 218,$_{1932}$.—22a. *Risāla fī taḥqīq al-ʿilm,* Br. Mus. 980,$_{16}$.—
22a.–q. see Suppl. (22e. Fātiḥ 5380, 22m. Mashh. I, 86,$_{267}$).—22r. *al-Risāla
al-hādiya,* Patna II, 417,$_{2586,\ 3}$.—22s. *Ithbāt al-wājib,* abstract in Persian by
Muḥammad ʿAlī al-Khwānsārī, Istanbul M. Pāshā, *Dharīʿa* I, 108,$_{525}$.—22t. *Asās
al-iqtibās fi 'l-manṭiq,* Persian, Mashh. II, 1, 2, Teh. II, 295, *Dharīʿa* II, 5,$_9$.—
22u. *Risālat nafs al-amr, Dharīʿa* II, 83,$_{329}$.—22v. *Risālat al-nufūs al-ʿaraḍiyya,*
AS 2623,$_4$, Asʿad 3748,$_5$.—22w. *Adab al-mutaʿallimīn,* Patna II, 349,$_{2526,\ 1}$.—
(22x. Persian *Akhlāq-i Nāṣirī,* see Suppl., *Dharīʿa* I, 380,$_{1973}$).

IV. Mathematics. 23. *Taḥrīr uṣūl al-handasa li-Uqlīdīs,* a short version with
additions from the manuscripts of al-Ḥajjāj and Thābit, with various colours
and figures as a special feature, completed in 646/1248, Berl. 5918/9, Paris
2465/6, Br. Mus. 1334/5, Garr. 1054, Mashh. XVII, 12,$_{33/4}$, Patna I, 232,$_{2027/8}$.
Euclidis elementa geometricae ex traditione Nasireddini Tusi arab., Rome 1594.
Abstract Münch. 848, print. Istanbul 1216/1801. Six *maqālāt,* printed for the
School Book Society of Calcutta in 1824; cf. H. Suter, Einiges aus Nassīr ed

Dīns Euklidausgabe, *Bibl. Math.* N.F. VI, 3/6, *Zeitschr. f. Math.* 1893, lit. hist.
Abt. 195, see Steinschneider, ZDMG L, 170. Persian transl. by Khayrallāh Khān
b. Luṭfallāh Khān, completed in 1144/1731, Ind. Off. Pers. 2260, Zanjān, *Lughat
al-ʿArab* VI, 95. |—Commentaries: a. Abū Isḥāq, Br. Mus. Suppl. 751.—b. Mīr 511
Muḥammad Hāshim al-ʿAlawī (see Suppl.), Patna I, 232,$_{2032/3}$.—c. Mawlawī
Muḥammad Barakāt (ibid.), ibid. 2031.—23a. *Taḥrīr uṣūl al-handasa wal-
ḥisāb*, Alex. Ḥisāb 28.—24. *Uṣūl Menelaos fī ʾl-ashkāl al-kuriyya* based on
Manṣūr b. ʿIrāq, d. 430/1038 (p. 623), Berl. 5930/1, Paris 2467,1, Garr. 1055.—
25. Edition of Archimedes' *On the Sphere and the Cylinder* following Thābit b.
Qurra (p. 241), with the use of the commentary by Eutocius of Ashkelon in the
translation of Isḥāq b. Ḥunayn, with an appendix on the measurement of the
circle (*Taḥrīr al-maqāla fī* | *taksīr al-dāʾira li-A.* Rāmpūr I, 411), Berl. 5934, Ind. Off. 674
743,$_6$, Paris 2467,$_8$, Teh. II, 207,$_1$, Mashh. XVII, 13,$_{35}$.—26. *Kitāb al-maʾkhūdhāt
li-Arshīmīdīs* based on Thābit b. Qurra, with a commentary by Abu ʾl-Ḥasan
ʿAlī b. Aḥmad al-Nasawī (Suppl. I. 390), Berl. 5936.—27. *al-Risāla al-shāfiya ʿani
ʾl-shakk fī ʾl-khuṭūṭ al-mutasāwiya*, Berl. 5942.—28. *Taḥrīr al-mafrūḍāt li-Thābit
b. Qurra* (p. 241), Leid. 1029.—29. *Kitāb al-muʿṭayāt li-Uqlīdis*, Ind. Off. 743,$_1$,
Mashh. XVII, 11,$_{30}$.—30. Exposition on Euclid's postulates, Paris 2467,$_5$, in a
letter to ʿAlam al-Dīn Qayṣar (see Suppl.), also Mashh. XVII, 27,$_{82}$.—31. *Kitāb
al-mutawassiṭāt*, Bodl. I, 875, 895.—32. *Kitāb al-shakl al-qaṭṭāʿ*, also Zanjān
Lughat al-ʿArab VI, 96, *Traité du quadrilatère, texte ar. d'aprés un ms. tiré de la
bibl. de S.A. Edhem Pacha, trad. par.* Al. Pacha Caratheodory, Constantinople
1891; cf. Carra de Vaux, *JA* 1892 II, 176/81, *Bibl. Math.* IX (1892) 94, Suter ibid.
N.F. VII (1894) 1/8.—33. *Apollonii Pergaei Conica*, Bodl. I, 943, Ind. Off. 748.—34.
al-Kura al-mutaḥarrika, περὶ τῆς κινουμένης σΦαίρας by Autolycus after Thābit
b. Qurra, Ind. Off. 744,$_1$, Paris 2467,$_{20}$, Mashh. XVII, 11,$_{32}$.—35. *Jāmiʿ al-ḥisāb
(bil-takht wal-turāb)*, arithmetic, end with an appendix, Berl. 5973.—36. *Risāla
fī annahu lā yumkinu an yajtamiʿa min ʿadadayn murabbaʿayn fardayn ʿadad
murabbaʿ*, Paris 2467,$_1$ (anon.), Ind. Off. 1043,$_4$.—36a—g. see Suppl. (d. also
Teh. II, 155, 205, 207,$_2$, 208,$_4$, 209,$_8$.—f. = 25 Anh.).—36h. *Risāla fī iʿmāl al-ʿaṣā*,
Patna II, 554,$_{2928, 7}$.

V. Physics. 37. *Kitāb al-manāẓir*, Euclid's *Optics*, Berl. 6016/7, cf. Steinschneider ZDMG L, 171.—38. *Risāla fī nʿikās al-shuʿāʿāt*, on the refraction of rays, Berl. 1091, library of al-Qāsim al-Khwānsārī al-Mūsawī, *Dharīʿa* II, 399,$_{1601}$.—(38a. Suppl. = 55c. also Fātiḥ 5380,$_{10}$, Asʿad 3748,$_9$).

VI. Astronomy. 39. *Taḥrīr al-Mijisṭī*, edition of the Almagest, Berl. 5685, Paris 2485, Br. Mus. 391, 1338, 1657, Ind. Off. 741, Pet. AM, Dorn, p. 208, Ros. 188, Rāġib 913/4, Patna I, 234,$_{2036/8}$.—Commentaries: a. Self-commentary, Yeni 799.—b. Shams al-Dīn al-Samarqandī (?), Berl. 5686.—c. Niẓām al-Dīn al-Ḥasan b. Muḥammad al-Nīsābūrī, completed in Shaʿbān 704/March 1305, Br. Mus.

392, Alex. Ḥisāb 37, Qawala II, 269, glosses by Qāḍīzāde al-Rūmī (II, 212),
Berl. 5657.—d. ʿAbd al-ʿAlī b. Muḥammad al-Barjandī (II, 413), completed in
921/1515, Ind. Off. 742.—e., f., g. see Suppl.—40. *al-Tadhkira al-Nāṣiriyya*, a pré-
675 cis on astronomy, originally in Persian *R.-i Muʿīniyya*, also Mashh. XVII, | 31, 93,
Arabic transl. Leipz. 262, Leid. 1092, Bodl. I, 1229, II, 292, Br. Mus. 1339, Paris
2509, Pet. Ros. 187, Rāġib 919.—Commentaries: a. Muḥammad b. ʿAlī b. Ḥusayn
al-Ḥimādī, his contemporary, with glosses by Maḥmūd b. Masʿūd al-Shīrāzī,
d. 710/1310, Br. Mus. 397.—b. *Tawḍīḥ al-T.* by Niẓām al-Dīn Ḥasan b. Muḥammad
al-Nīsābūrī (II, 211), composed in 711/1311, Berl. Ms. or. fol. $4182_{,1}$, Paris 2510, Br.
Mus. 396, $1342_{,3}$, Yeni 792, Garr. $2106_{,1}$, Patna I, $236_{,2051}$; glosses by Faṣīḥ al-Dīn,
Leid. 1097.—c. al-Jurjānī (II, 216), d. 816/1413, Berl. 5681, Leid. 1094/5, Ind.
Off. 746, Garr. 978/9, Alex. Ḥisāb 39, Makram 33, Patna I, $236_{,2052}$, II, $531_{,2856}$,
$561_{,2146}$.—d. *al-Takmila* by Muḥammad b. Aḥmad al-Khiḍrī (II, 204), (Khafarī,
ḤKh [1]II, 269, [2]I, 392) Ind. Off. 747, Bodl. I, 1018, Yeni 791, Patna I, $235_{,2044}$.—
e. Mūsā Qāḍīzāde, d. 815/1412, Palat. 313.—f., g. see Suppl.—41. *al-Tashīl fī
ʾl-nujūm*, Bodl. I, 901.—42. *Kitāb al-bāriʿ fī ʿulūm al-taqwīm wa-ḥarakāt al-aflāk
wa-aḥkām al-nujūm wa-dalāʾilihā wakhtilāf al-maṭāliʿ wal-buldān*, Bodl. I,
882.—43. *Sī faṣl*, see Suppl. 47 (Commentaries: b. Anon., also Paris 2512, Bodl.
II, 301, Br. Mus. 1889, Patna I, $238_{,2065}$.—c. Ḥasan b. Muḥammad al-Nīsābūrī,
Leid. 1176, AS 2664.—d. Muḥammad b. Muḥammad al-Kāshgharī Zanjān,
Lughat al-ʿArab VI, 95 = (?) *Istikhrāj al-taqwīm*, Ḥamīd, *Dharīʿa* II, $20_{,65}$.—44.
Zubdat al-idrāk fī hayʾat al-aflāk, on aspects of astronomy, Paris 2511.—45.
Nihāyat al-idrāk, based on the *Tadhkira*, Patna I, $2237_{,2060,\ 9}$ (MS of Maḥmūd
b. Masʿūd al-Shīrāzī).—46. *al-Zīj al-Īlkhānī*, composed in 670/1271 for Hūlāgū,
Persian, Br. Mus. Pers. II, 454b, Bodl. Pers. 1513, Med. Laur. 269, Arabic *Ḥall al-zīj*
by ʿAlī b. al-Rifāʿī al-Ḥusaynī, completed in 934/1527, Gotha 1404, Bodl. I, p.
195; augmented version entitled *Tawḍīḥ* by al-Ḥasan b. al-Ḥusayn al-Simnānī,
ca. 795/1394, Br. Mus. Pers. II, 455a; commentary by Maḥmūd Shāh Khukjī,
512 whose introduction was edited by | J. Greaves, *Astronomica quaedam ex tradi-
tione Shah Cholgii Persae*, London 1652.—47. Mathematico-astronomical treatise on Mercury, Berl. 5680.—48. *Bīst Bāb*, Persian, on the astrolabe, Br. mus.
Pers. II, 453a, Bodl. I, 287, Copenhagen 199, Pet. 128, I, 1308, Persian commentary by ʿAbd al-ʿAlī b. Muḥammad al-Barjandī, ca. 930/1523, Br. Mus. Pers. II,
433b, Zanjān *Lughat al-ʿArab* VI, 95 (b–e. see Suppl., c. to be deleted; d. Mashh.
XVII, $38_{,16}$).—49. *Taḥrīr Ẓāhirāt al-falak* (Euclid's *Phainomena*), Berl. 5645/6,
see. Steinschneider, ZDMG L, 170.—50. Autolycus' *Fī ʾl-ṭulūʿ wal-ghurūb*, based
676 on Thābit b. Qurra, Ind. Off. 743/4.—51. *Kitāb al-maṭāliʿ*, Hypsicles' *περὶ | τῆς
τῶν ζῳδίων ἀναφορᾶς* based on Qusṭā b. Lūqā and al-Kindī, Ind. Off. $743_{,5}$.—
52. *Taḥrīr Kitāb al-Masākin*, Theodosius' *περὶ οἰκήσεων* after Qusṭā b. Lūqā,
Berl. 5649/50, Ind. Off. $744_{,2}$.—53. *Risālat al-ayyām wal-layālī*, Theodosius'

περὶ ἡμερῶν καὶ νύκτων, completed in 658/1260, Berl. 5648, Ind. Off. 744,3.—54. Aristarchus' *Fī jurmay al-nayyirayn wa-buʿdayhimā*, Berl. 5651, Ind. Off. 744,4.—54a.–f. see Suppl. (d. Mashh. XVII, 8_{23}).

VII. Medicine. 55. *Albāb al-bāhiyya fi 'l-tarākīb al-sulṭāniyya*, a medical guidebook for the ailing son of the sultan of Kazan, with the last third focussed on coitus and aphrodisiacs, Berl. 6383, Turkish transl. Gotha 124.

VIII. Superstition. 56. *Risāla (al-wāfī) fī ʿilm al-raml*, Münch 880.

IX. Mineralogy. 57. *Tansūqnāme'i Īlkhānī*, see Suppl. also Berl. Oct. 3071 (supposedly composed in 995 AH), see *Istanbuler Mitt.* III, 1935, p. 4, no. 7.—58. *Jawāhirnāme*, Berl. Oct. 1384.

X. Music. 59. *Risāla fī ʿilm al-mūsīqī*, on intervals only, Paris 2466, perhaps from an Arabic translation of the *Akhlāq-i Nāṣirī*, and not a translation of the Persian *Kanz al-tuḥaf* as was conjectured by Sarton, *Introd.* II, ii, 1009; see Farmer, *Sources* 47.